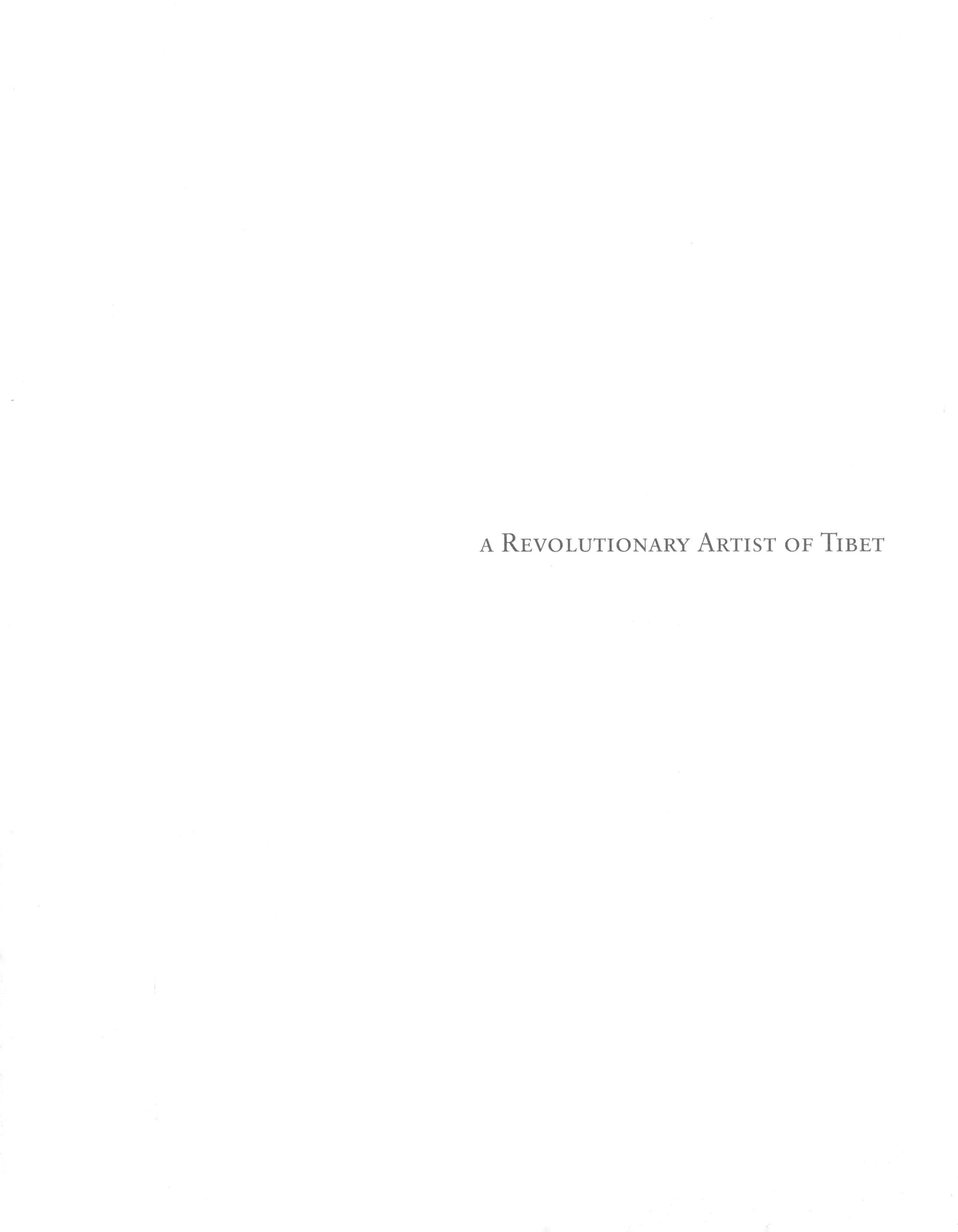

A Revolutionary Artist of Tibet

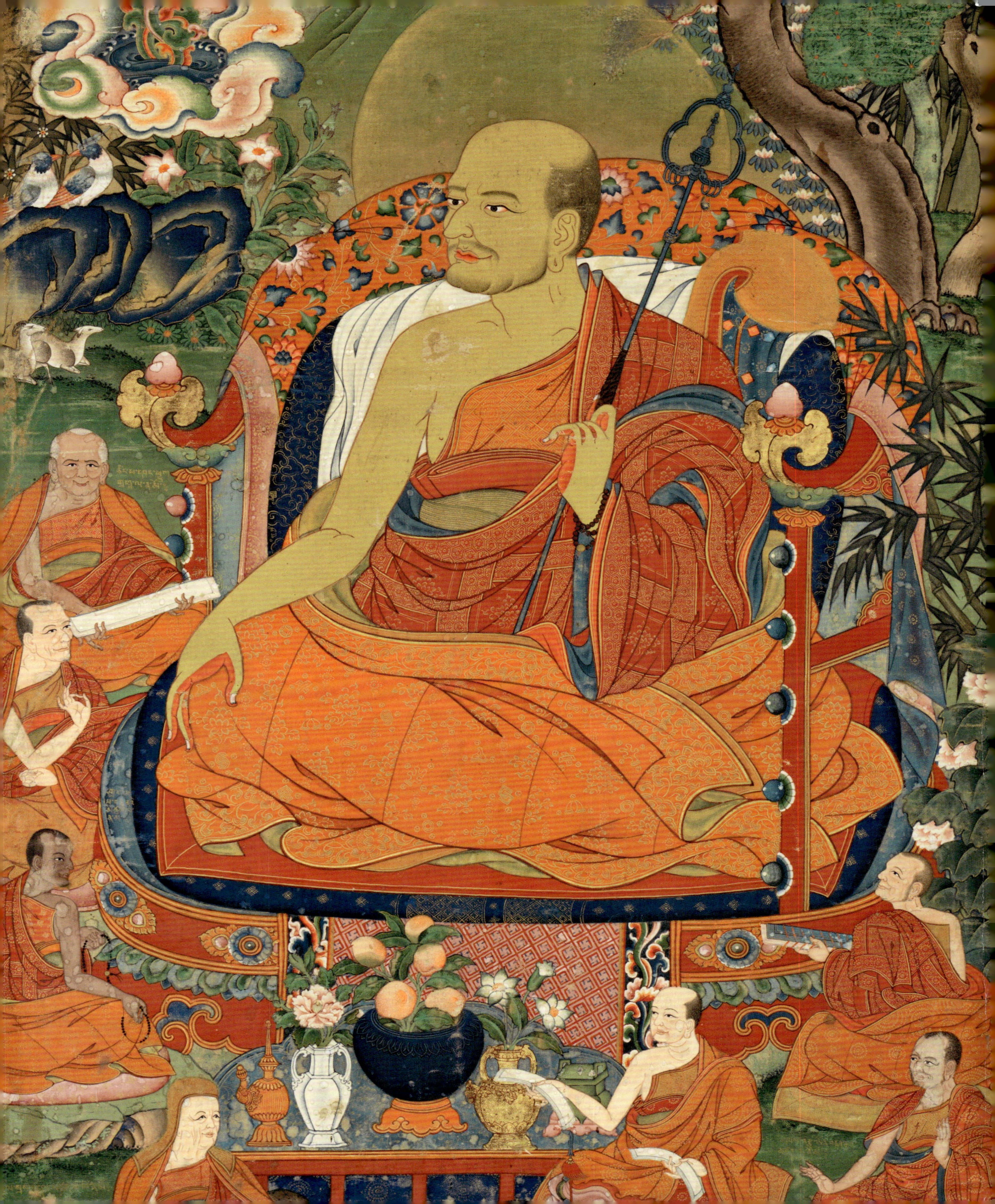

A REVOLUTIONARY ARTIST OF TIBET

Khyentse Chenmo of Gongkar

DAVID P. JACKSON

WITH CONTRIBUTIONS BY MATHIAS FERMER

From the Masterworks of Tibetan Painting Series

RUBIN MUSEUM OF ART
NEW YORK

This catalog is published by the Rubin Museum of Art, New York, and written by David P. Jackson, with a contribution from Mathias Fermer. *A Revolutionary Artist of Tibet: Khyentse Chenmo of Gongkar* is the sixth volume in the series *Masterworks of Tibetan Painting* by David P. Jackson, published by the Rubin Museum of Art, New York, and distributed by the University of Washington Press, Seattle and London.

ISBN-13: 978-0-9912241-1-1 (hardcover)
ISBN-13: 978-0-9845190-9-5 (paperback)

Project Director, Helen Abbott
Project Assistant, Jessica Baker
Designed by Phil Kovacevich
Edited by Deanna Lee
Photography research by Helen Chen and Annie Sicherman
Printed and bound in Italy

Front cover: detail of Fig. 9.9a
Back cover: Fig. 1.25
Frontispiece: detail of Fig. 1.19
p. viii: detail of Fig. 2.12

Library of Congress Cataloging-in-Publication Data
Names: Jackson, David Paul, author.
Title: A revolutionary artist of Tibet : Khyentse Chenmo of Gongkar / by
  David Jackson.
Description: New York, NY : Rubin Museum of Art, 2016. | Series: [Masterworks
  of Tibetan painting ; sixth volume]
Identifiers: LCCN 2016020954 | ISBN 9780991224111 (hardcover)
Subjects: LCSH: Mkhyen-brtse, Chen-mo, active 1450-1490--Criticism and
  interpretation. | Painting, Tibetan. | Buddhist painting--Tibet Region.
Classification: LCC ND1049.M67 J33 2016 | DDC 759.951/5--dc23
LC record available at https://lccn.loc.gov/2016020954

A NOTE OF SPECIAL THANKS

THE RUBIN MUSEUM OF ART OFFERS ITS MOST SINCERE GRATITUDE TO
HELEN ABBOTT, WHO HAS OVERSEEN THE PUBLISHING PROGRAM OF THE
MUSEUM FOR OVER A DECADE. HER TIRELESS EFFORT HAS RESULTED IN MORE
THAN TWENTY BOOKS OF SIGNIFICANT BREADTH, LASTING CONSEQUENCE,
AND GREAT BEAUTY.

Contents

PATRICK SEARS, EXECUTIVE DIRECTOR
RUBIN MUSEUM OF ART

WITH EXTRAORDINARY FORESIGHT and courage, in 2004, Shelley and Donald Rubin founded a new museum, with the support of a key group of trustees. It was centered on an art collection of world importance from Tibet and surrounding regions. But from the outset the Rubin Museum was intended as a place where visitors—mostly unfamiliar with Tibetan art and culture—might also engage in discovery of and conversation about the ideas, philosophies, and concepts that underlie much of the art. It was intentionally a wide platform, one in which art would intersect with ideas. These expressions continue to take many forms—exhibitions, lectures, conversations, performances, festivals, and publications—designed for the full spectrum of participants, from newcomers to experts.

In the expert realm, some of the world's best-known and most widely respected scholars and writers in the field were engaged, prominent among them David P. Jackson. Through the Museum's auspices, he has written a six-volume series of books on Tibetan painting styles. This endeavor has taken him more than a decade of full-time attention and bolstered the efforts of the Rubin Museum to contribute to the research of the arts of the Himalayas. The current volume focuses on the master artist Khyentse of Gongkar who, with his exceptional abilities, in many ways revolutionized painting in fifteenth-century Tibet. Surprisingly—given the fact that Khyentse gave rise to an artistic tradition that was among the three main ones in later Tibetan painting—little is known about him and his art. David P. Jackson in his detailed account of this outstanding artist, the milieu in which he flourished, and the influence he had on later traditions bridges many gaps in our knowledge about painting from this period and well beyond.

While David Jackson must certainly be acknowledged for his remarkable scholarship, he should also be praised for inviting other scholars to enrich this series and broaden our understanding of the art and contexts that are examined. They include Karl Debreczeny, Rob Linrothe, Christian Luczanits, Kristen Muldowney Roberts, and—in the present volume—Mathias Fermer. Supporting this group of scholars is the full force of the Rubin Museum, including the curatorial and development staffs, with editors, designers, and skilled printers all contributing with utmost professionalism. A few people who worked on the entire series must be named: Helen Abbott, Publisher and the series manager; Michelle Bennett, Head of Collections Management and her team; and Phil Kovacevich, graphic designer. Deanna Lee, Neil Liebman, and Lorna Price served as editors on various volumes; and new photography came from Gavin Ashworth, David De Armas, and Bruce M. White. We at the Rubin Museum, and many others around the world, are grateful for their collective work, which has resulted in this magisterial series, one that was conceived and supported from the outset by The Shelley and Donald Rubin Foundation and, for most of these volumes, by the Henry Luce Foundation as well. Therefore, we express our enduring thanks for the many creative talents and supporting efforts that result in these volumes.

This publication and others in this series have been generously supported by the Henry Luce Foundation. The work of David Jackson, lead scholar and general editor of this series, was underwritten by The Shelley and Donald Rubin Foundation. Additional support for this volume was provided by John and Fausta Eskenazi.

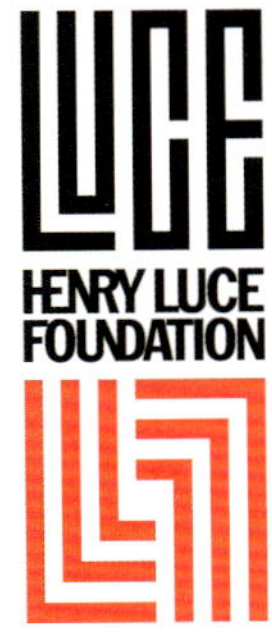

THE SHELLEY AND DONALD RUBIN FOUNDATION

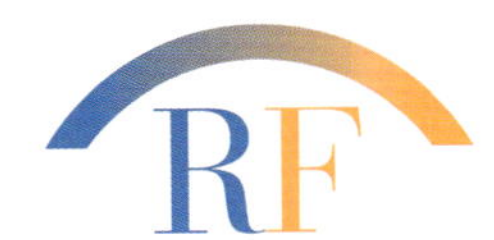

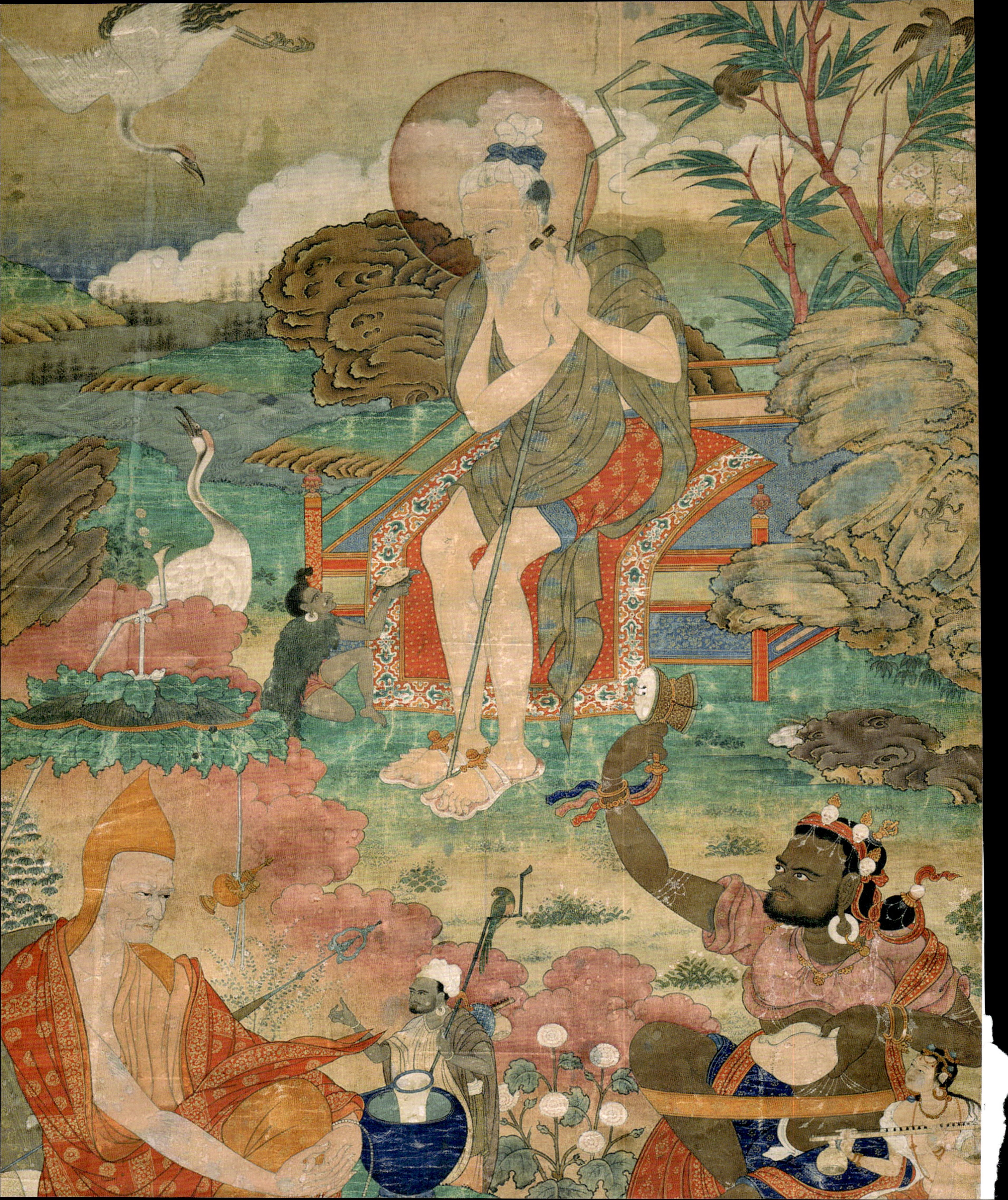

THIS CATALOG presents the art of Khyentse Chenmo, an artistic genius of Tibet who flourished from the 1450s to the 1490s. His painting style, the Khyenri or Khyenluk, is a sort of missing link in the history of Tibetan painting. Among the three major styles of Tibetan painting, the Khyenri is the least known among Western scholars. Works in this style have often been overlooked or misidentified as very early examples of the Karma Gardri style, the subject of the first catalog in this series published by the Rubin Museum of Art, *Patron and Painter*.

However, the general place of Khyentse Chenmo within the stylistic progression of Tibetan painting is quite clear. In the 1450s and 1460s, he led the establishment of a revolutionary new style. Rejecting the prevailing classical Indic Beri style, with its formal red backgrounds arranged in strict registers and columns—presented in the second catalog in this series, *The Nepalese Legacy*—he enthusiastically adopted more open and naturalistic Chinese landscapes with their intense greens and blues, and he also explored many other ways of depicting backgrounds that had never been tried before. This volume explores a new and almost modern Tibetan style that Khyentse Chenmo established through his cutting-edge art of the mid-to-late fifteenth century.

Khyentse was famed for his fine details and unusually realistic depictions, and equally talented as painter and sculptor. His work is frustrating for anyone looking for a simple system, for he detested repetition. He loved variation almost as much as he loved creating the illusion of lifelike representation.

Nowadays the most important in-situ murals by Khyentse Chenmo survive in the monastery of Gongkar Chöde in southern Ü province of Tibet, south of Lhasa. In that monastery some of his murals continue to exist, some having been painted over with whitewash in the 1960s and thus escaping complete destruction during the chaos of the Cultural Revolution. Based on photos of those murals, I have identified several major sets of Khyentse's paintings in museums outside Tibet—including Boston, Paris, and London—where they have lain unrecognized for decades. I was recently highly gratified to discover that one of Khyentse Chenmo's major set of statues still survives in another monastery of Lhokha, not far from Gongkar.

This publication has benefited from the kind assistance of my colleagues. Rob Linrothe improved the book immensely by commenting on the manuscript and sharing a number of beautiful photographs. Tsechang Penba Wangdu, a young art-history expert and practicing artist from Tibet, allowed me to feature his recent contributions on Khyentse Chenmo and his art (see chapter 3). Mathias Fermer made two illuminating contributions, one on a major mural of Khyentse Chenmo at Gongkar (in chapter 4b) and the other on the later artist of Gongkar Yeshe Tendzin (in chapter 12).

Helen Abbott as editor has patiently and very skillfully guided this complicated publication through to its happy conclusion. She was ably assisted by Deanna Lee, who copyedited the manuscript. Phil Kovacevich as book designer has again worked his inimitable magic, transforming the book's raw materials into a true feast for the eyes.

In writing this catalog, I have had the great pleasure to recover, art historically, some lost treasures of Khyentse Chenmo's art. When I first visited Gongkar in the summer of 1986, with the main aim of photographing the murals, my brand-new flash unit exploded with the first shot; that disappointment certainly made me appreciate every mural photograph I have seen since then. Thus I am particularly pleased that I am able to present high-quality photographs, very kindly provided by a number of colleagues. Penba Wangdu shared many photographs featured in this book, especially in chapter 3. The book is also enriched by the photographs of Roberto Fortuna, made available by Knud Larsen. I am very much indebted to Kazuo Kano for letting me use his many photographs of Gongkar in 2007, both inside and out; his thorough documentation made it possible for me to clarify many points. Mathias Fermer shared with me dozens of photographss, including some recently taken at Drathang. Lionel Fournier also shared many essential photographs from his collection. Moke Mokotoff has been an invaluable source of information on many topics, including woven thangkas and their silk mountings. Cyrus Stearns shared some important information and images of his own and provided the photographs of A. Lustgarten.

This survey of Khyentse Chenmo and his art is the sixth and final catalog of my series, *Masterpieces of Tibetan Painting*. I hope that future volumes devoted to the early Menri style—including the murals of Tashilhunpo and the painting traditions of Amdo, such as the Jonang school—may be considered. I also hope that readers will be inspired by the art of Khyentse Chenmo and the art presented in my previous catalogs and will be able to clarify in the future any points that I omitted, mistook, or left unclear.

D. Jackson
October 2015

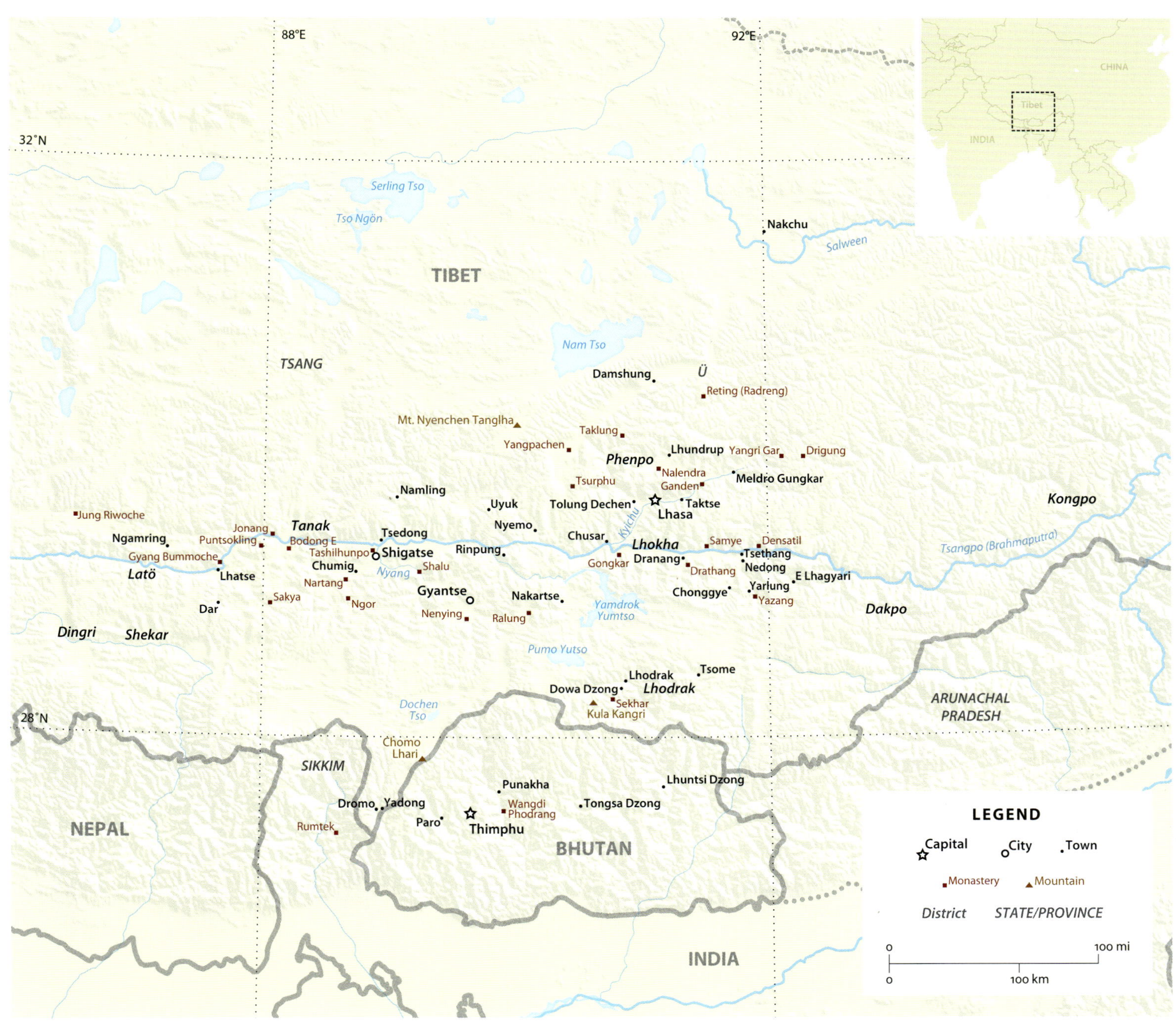

88°E
92°E
32°N
28°N
CHINA
INDIA
Tibet
TIBET
TSANG
Serling Tso
Tso Ngön
Nam Tso
Damshung
Ü
Reting (Radreng)
Nakchu
Salween
Mt. Nyenchen Tanglha
Taklung
Yangpachen
Lhundrup
Yangri Gar
Drigung
Phenpo
Nalendra
Ganden
Meldro Gungkar
Tsurphu
Namling
Uyuk
Tolung Dechen
Taktse
Jung Riwoche
Nyemo
Lhasa
Kongpo
Ngamring
Jonang
Tanak
Tsedong
Chusar
Lhokha
Samye
Densatil
Puntsokling
Bodong E
Kyichu
Tsangpo (Brahmaputra)
Gyang Bummoche
Tashilhunpo
Shigatse
Rinpung
Dranang
Tsethang
Chumig
Shalu
Gongkar
Nedong
Lató
Lhatse
Nartang
Nyang
Drathang
E Lhagyari
Dar
Sakya
Ngor
Gyantse
Nakartse
Chonggye
Yarlung
Dakpo
Nenying
Ralung
Yamdrok
Yumtso
Yazang
Dingri
Shekar
Pumo Yutso
Lhodrak
Tsome
Dochen
Tso
Dowa Dzong
Lhodrak
ARUNACHAL
PRADESH
Sekhar
Kula Kangri
Chomo
Lhari
SIKKIM
Punakha
Lhuntsi Dzong
Dromo
Yadong
Wangdi
Phodrang
Tongsa Dzong
NEPAL
Rumtek
Paro
Thimphu
BHUTAN
INDIA
LEGEND
Capital
City
Town
Monastery
Mountain
District
STATE/PROVINCE
0
100 mi
0
100 km

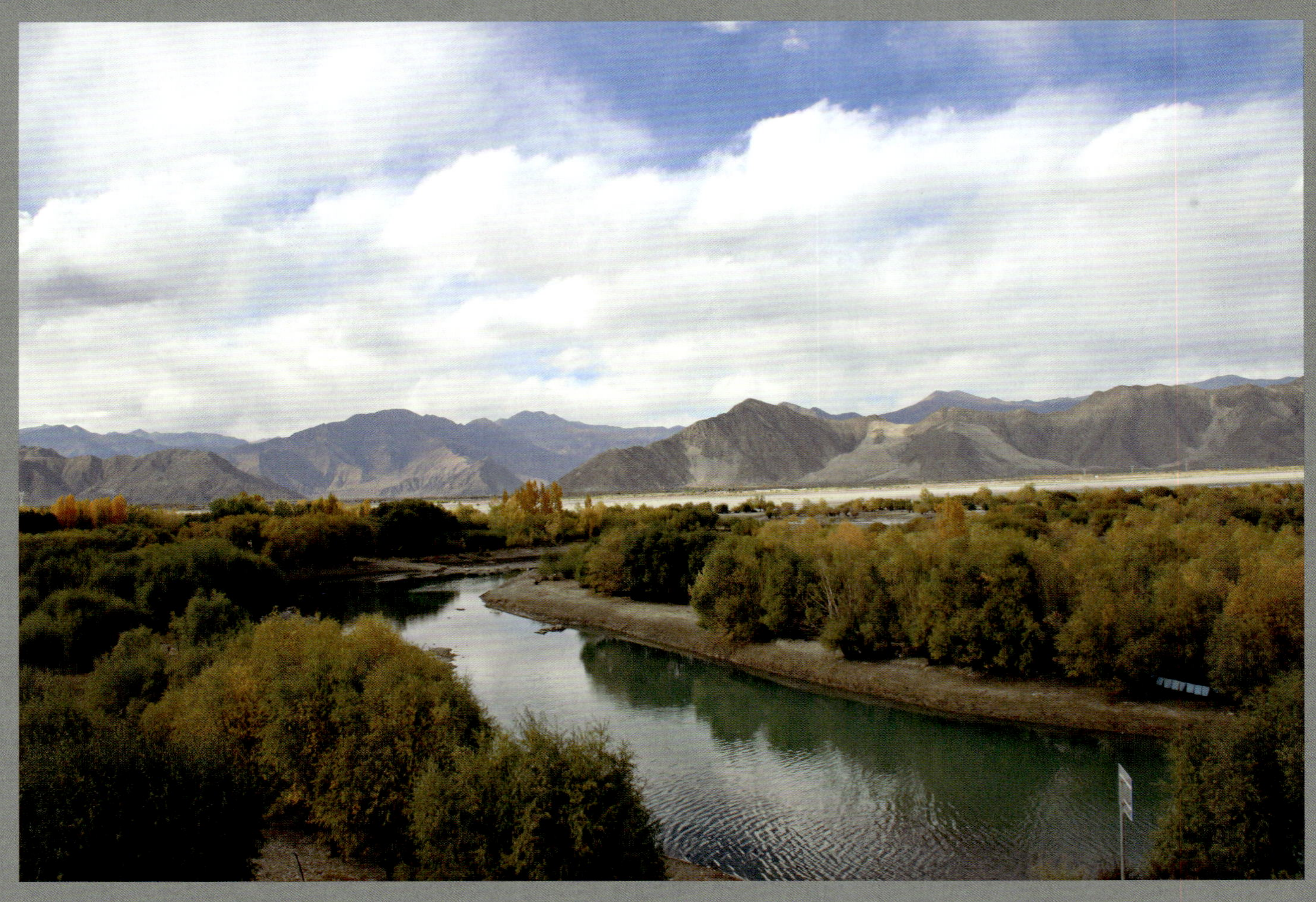

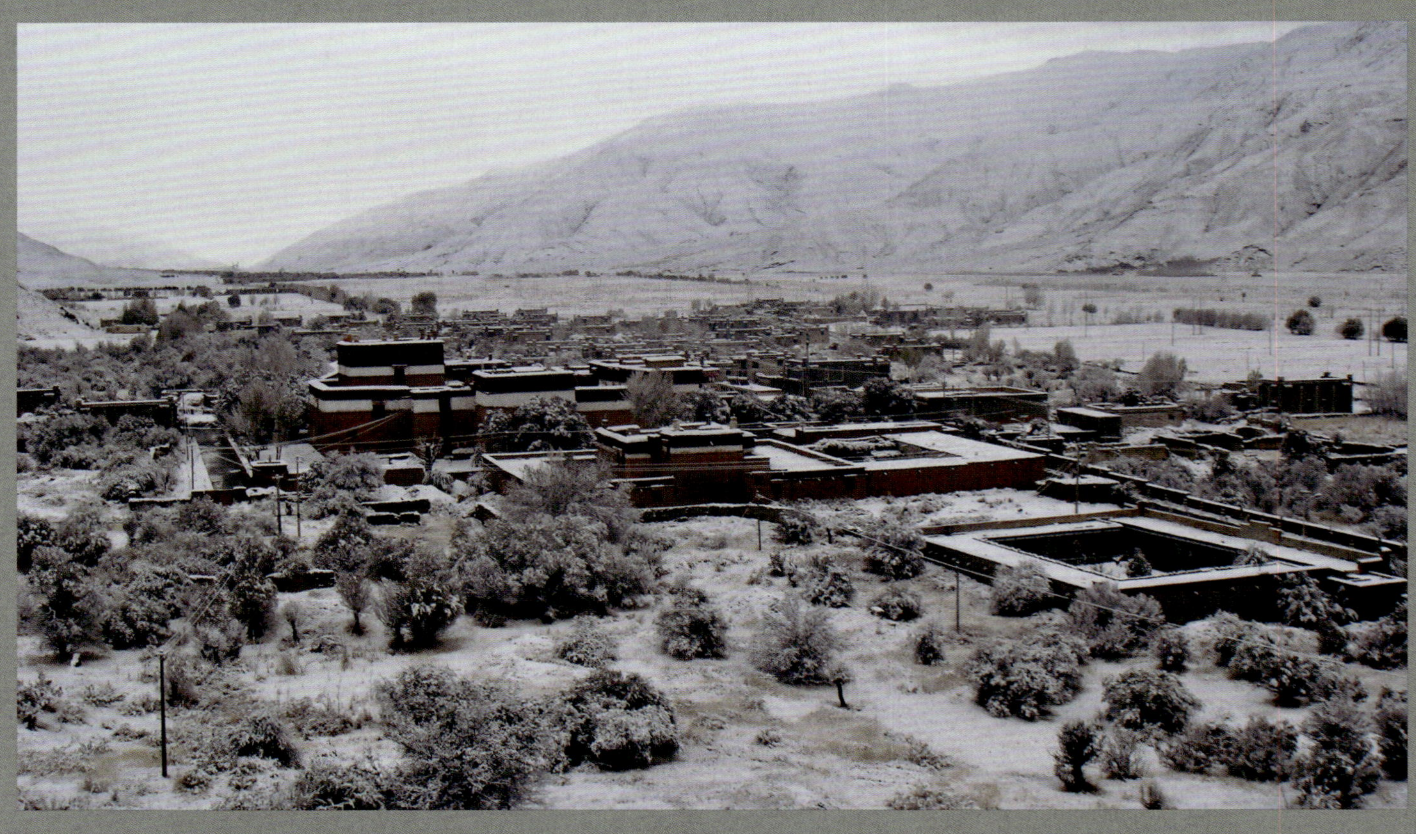

Introduction

PART 1: *Khyentse Chenmo: His Life and Art*

THE MASTER ARTIST Khyentse Chenmo of Gongkar was a phenomenally gifted artist of fifteenth-century Tibet. Though equally skilled as a painter and sculptor, he helped launch a stylistic revolution within Tibetan painting. All traditional historical summaries of Tibetan art agree that he founded a school of painting that became one of the three main later traditions in Tibet. Yet until now, little could be ascertained about him or his art.

In this chapter I will begin to rectify that, summarizing what I could learn about his life and career. In addition to discussing his place and time of birth, in the following pages I will also try to trace what is known about his apprenticeship under an outstanding artist of Tsang, establishing the concrete context from which he emerged. Tracing his main known patrons and projects, I will also mention his chief disciple and the principal murals that survive in the Khyenri style.

FIG. 1.0A
View of special lake of Putra near Gongkar, looking toward Sinpori in the north
Photo: Jampel Shedrup, 2014

FIG. 1.0B
Gongkar Monastery with nearby village in winter
Photo: Jampel Shedrup, 2014

A. THE LIFE OF KHYENTSE CHENMO OF GONGKAR

1. Birthplace

Khyentse Chenmo was born in the Lhokha district of Ü province, south of Lhasa. He was born at Gangtö (sGang stod), a place in Gongkar just outside of what became in the 1460s, a few decades after his birth, the precincts of Gongkar Dorjeden Monastery.

Though Khyentse Chenmo's exact year of birth is not known, he probably was born in the 1420s. After studying art in the 1430s or early 1440s, he likely achieved his original style by the late 1440s or early 1450s and went on to lead major projects by the early 1460s, at the latest. He painted his most famous murals at Gongkar between 1464 and 1476, some of which survive. He remained a very prominent artist in the 1470s and 1480s; in those decades, he painted murals at the great stupa of Champaling, none of which survive. In Drathang, he also produced a set of outstanding gilt-copper sculptures, which still exist. His career continued to flourish in the 1490s, and in 1503 he was invited to work on a major artistic project, the murals of Yangpachen (Yangs pa can) Monastery, though by then he must have been quite old. The last time his name appears in historical records is in association with the Yangpachen project;

he presumably died at some point during the following twenty years.

2. His Titles and Names

Khyentse Chenmo's full title was "Master-artist Khyentse of Gongkar" (*Gong dkar mKhyen brtse chen mo*). He was also commonly called just "Khyentse of Gongkar" (Gong dkar mKhyen brtse) in some sources, or simply "he of Khyentse" (Khyentsewa, mKhyen brtse ba).[1] I am not sure what "Khyentse" refers to; it is not a known place or family name. In the following pages, I will generally call him Khyentse Chenmo, *chen mo* being part of his title, indicating his role as a master artist and overseer of large projects, something like *uchenmo* (*dbu chen mo*) or *pönmoche* (dPon mo che).

Khyentse Chenmo's personal ordained name and status as a Buddhist lay adherent is revealed by one source: Kunga Namgyal's biography by Gyatön Changchup Wangyal. That source, in a long section that enumerates Gongkar Dorjedenpa's disciples, calls him "Khyentsewa Genyen Nampar Gyalwa." *Genyen* (*dge bsnyen*) was his vow status as a Buddhist lay-adherent (Skt. Upāsaka), and his personal given name was Nampar Gyalwa ("Victorious One," rNam par rgyal ba).[2]

It is wrong to call him "Khyentse Wangchuk," as many previous Western sources have.[3] We should also not confuse him with Jamyang Khyentse

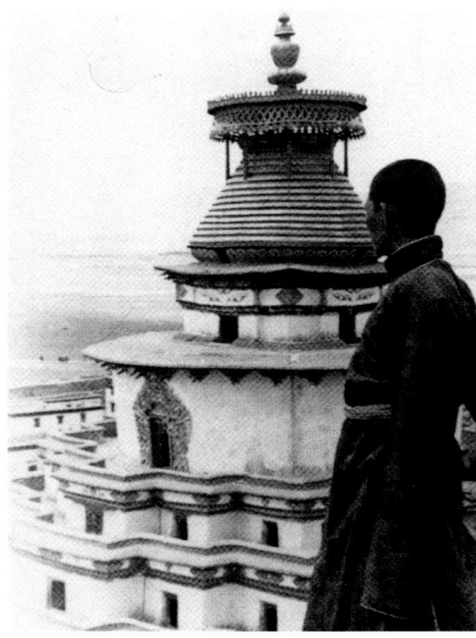

The Gyantse Monastic Compound
After: P. F. Mele, *Tibet* (Calcutta, 1975)
Literature: Jackson 1996, fig. 37

Wangchuk (mKhyen brtse dbang phyug, 1524–1568), the disciple of Tsharchen (Tshar chen Blo gsal rgya mtsho, 1502–1566/67), who lived about a century later than Khyentse Chenmo.[4]

3. Training as an Apprentice Artist

Khyentse of Gongkar studied art professionally in the 1430s or early 1440s, leaving Ü province and apprenticing himself under a master painter in Tsang. He belonged to the same generation of artists as the famous Menthangpa Menla Döndrup of Lhodrak, the founder of the Menri style who likewise emerged as a major artist leading large projects by the late 1450s. Both Khyentse and Menthangpa were born in southern Ü province. They came separately to southeastern Tsang to study as apprentices under the same outstanding artist. In the 1430s, the Gyantse principality in the upper Nyang valley of Tsang was an unrivaled center of art and artistic patronage, so it is hardly surprising that both young men gravitated there from their respective homes. (See Fig. 1.1.)

An important traditional summary of art history, found in the writings of Desi Sanggye Gyatsho (sDe Srid Sangs rgyas rgya mtsho, 1653–1705), asserts that Khyentse's fellow student Menthangpa studied painting in Tsang "at such places as Sakya."[5] Yet we know that Menthangpa learned art mainly in the upper Nyang valley. That same later historical tradition—embodied by the Desi and the sources following him— also asserts that both Khyentse and Menthangpa studied under a painting master named Dopa Tregyal (rDo pa bKras rgyal). Yet we know from one of Menthangpa's writings that the real name of Menthangpa's main teacher was different and that he came from Nenying. In one of his minor writings, Menthangpa humbly mentioned two prominent artists from Nenying Monastery, praising them as the highest experts; they must have been his teachers. Menthangpa had another historical link to Nenying: there, he was aesthetically inspired and transformed when he viewed a famous Chinese painting.

Keeping in mind the close links of Menthangpa with Nenying (and not Sakya), we can assume that the young Khyentse—who is said to have been his co-student in Tsang—also trained in Gyantse under the same eminent artists of Nenying. Concerning Menthangpa's actual teachers: at the beginning of his smaller artist manual, he pays respects to his two main painting masters, who were named Paljor Rinchen and Sönam Paljor, describing them as the most learned and expert artists then living in Tibet.[6] There, Menthangpa says:

> Homage to the highest experts, Paljor Rinchen and Sönam Paljor, a rosary of stars, who possess correct proportions for the bodily forms of the buddhas here [in Tibet] amidst the glacier peaks regarding precisely the highest field of knowledge, [the art] of [the divine artist]

Viśvakarma, the emanation of the buddhas. Having followed all of them . . . [7]

The two master artists whom Menthangpa mentions also occur prominently among the painters who worked on the murals of both the multistoried stupa and the main temple of Palkhor (dPal 'khor) of Gyantse in the 1420s and 1430s. There, they are called Paljor Rinchen of Nenying, a monk artist, and Geshe (*dGe bshes*) Sönam Paljor, also of Nenying.[8]

It has been recorded that Paljor Rinchen of Nenying, the first artist Menthangpa mentioned, directed a group of thirty-seven artisans at Gyantse in 1418 for the making of a great cloth image whose main figure was Buddha Śākyamuni.[9] (See Fig. 1.2.)

The master artist (*dpon mo che*) Paljor Rinchen of Nenying was furthermore responsible for the exquisite murals in the Lamdre Lhakhang of the Palkhor monastic center, painted in 1425.[10] (See Figs. 1.3 and 1.4.) The inscription recorded in Lo Bue and Ricca states: "These were painted in as fine a manner as possible by the expert painter of Nenying, the master artist Paljorwa (*dPal 'byor ba*) together with his students."[11] One of the patrons of the murals was a Nenying Pöntsün (dPon btsun), Paljor Rinchen, presumably the same artist; *dPon btsun* usually means "noble monk," but here it may mean "monk artist" since *dpon* is also a term for "artist" in Tsang and Ngari, and in Gyantse it was current in the title *pönmoche*.[12]

Figure 1.5 depicts a section of another mural panel in the Lamdre Lhakhang. It illustrates how Paljorwa (Paljor Rinchen) treated a landscape ringed with snowy mountains. It is different from how such a subject was depicted before and after in Tibetan painting. The artist attempts to create a unified background, but is still working

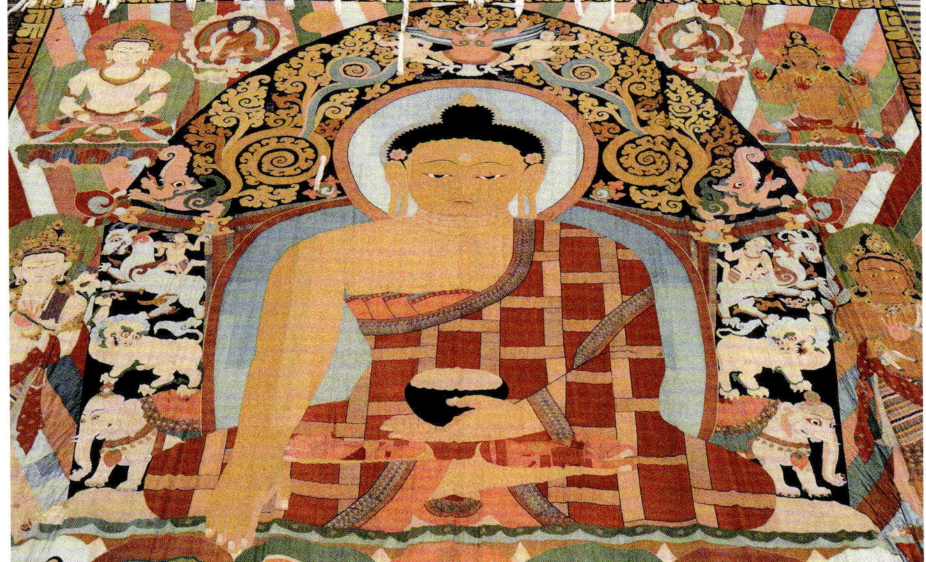

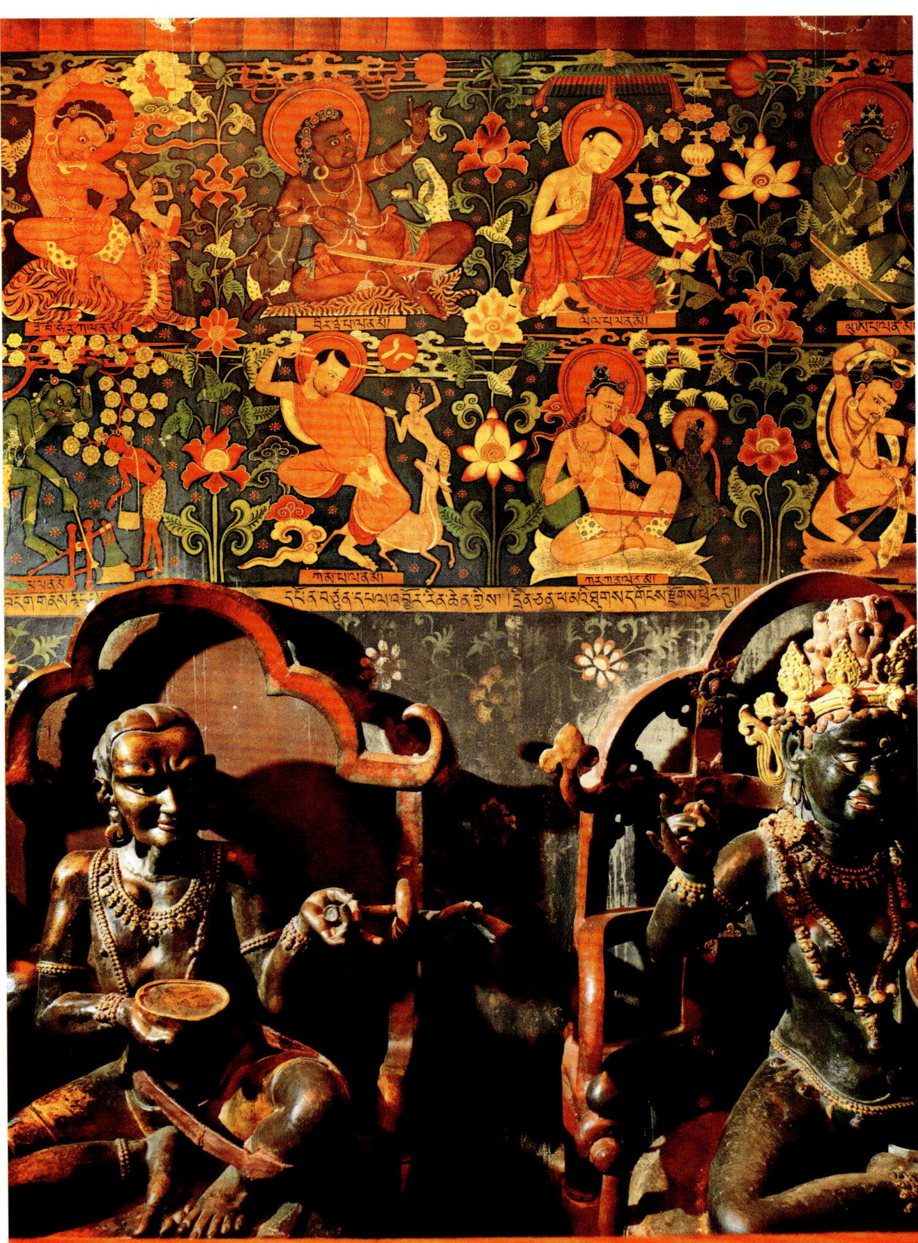

out how to do that, with repetitive hills and clouds, though still breaking up the previous divisions. Phakpa is the second of two main figures in the panel. The main figure is his uncle Sakya Paṇḍita, debating a group of non-Buddhist Indians at Kyirong (see Fig. 6.17).

Both master painters mentioned by Menthangpa worked together on the same chapel of the Gyantse Kumbum (II.l5; on the second floor, south side, chapel b'), namely the so-called Maseng Lhakhang (sMra seng Lha khang).[13] The main sculpture in this chapel depicted Vādisiṃha Mañjughoṣa ('Jam dbyangs sMra ba'i seng ge). (See Figs. 1.6 and 1.7.) In one inscription, the two artists who painted it are called "the kings of painters, the one from Glorious Nenying Monastery, master artist Paljor Rinchen, and Geshe Sönam Paljor."[14] They are also painters 23 and 25 in a list of Gyantse artists.[15]

Geshe Sönam Paljor from Nenying is also mentioned as the only artist who painted a temple on the west side of the fifth level (5W), a later temple devoted to Śākyasiṃha (Śākya seng ge), the so-called Western Chapel (Nub phyogs kyi gZhal yas khang). Lo Bue and Ricca recorded the relevant inscription there, which I translate as: "the one from Glorious Nenying Monastery, master

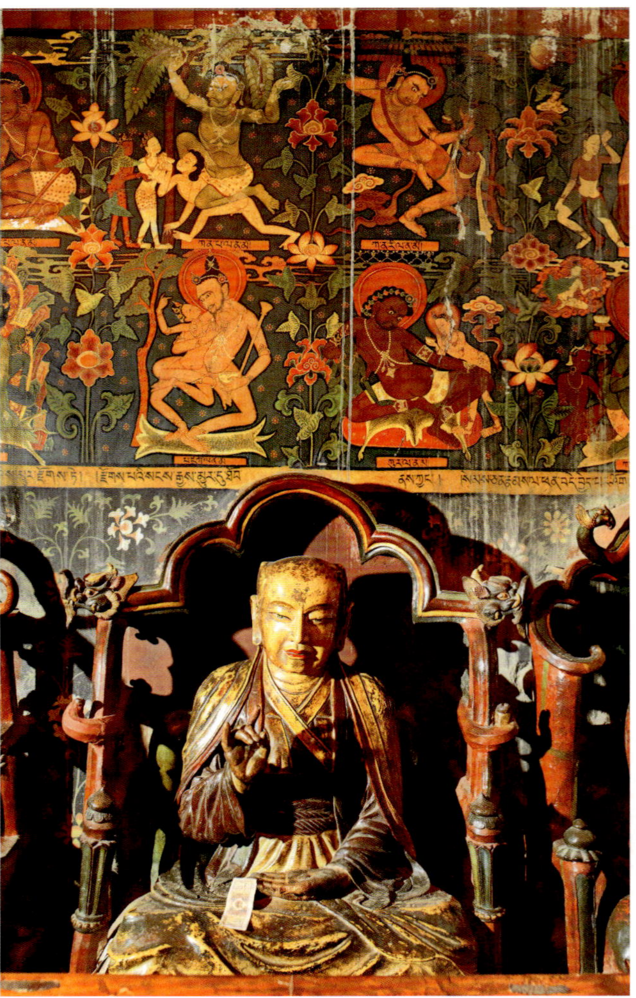

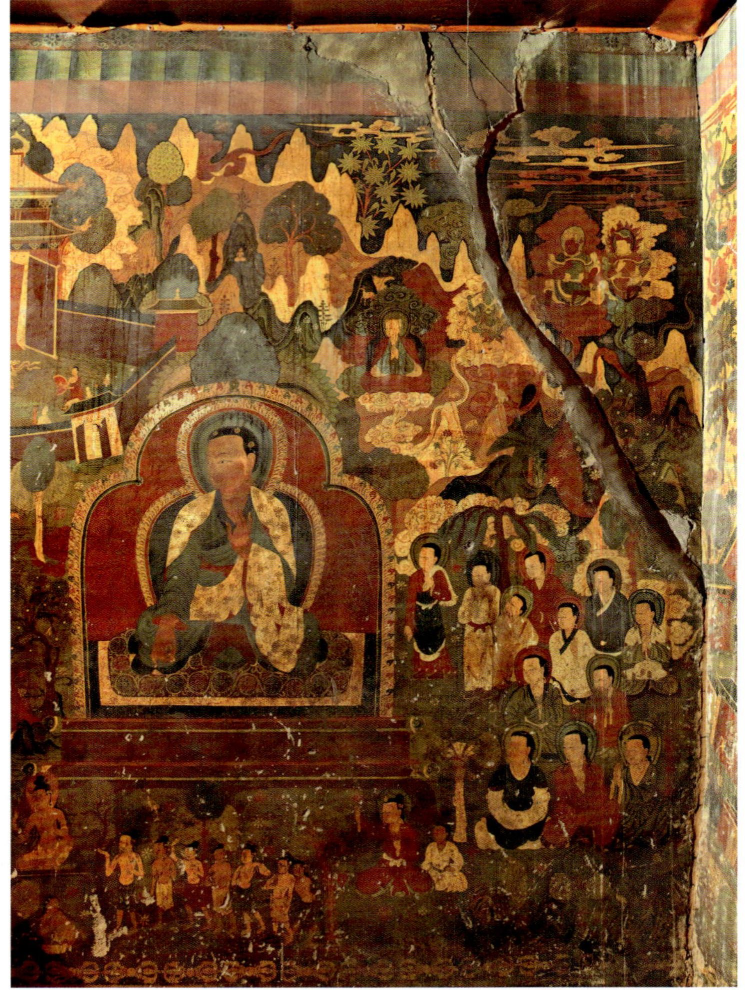

artist Sönam Paljorwa."[16] Here, Paljor Rinchen is no longer present, and Sönam Paljor is called the head artist *(dpon mo che)* of glorious Nenying, which he evidently became by the 1440s.

A similarly named artist, Rinchen Paljor, also of Nenying, worked in chapel 2 on the fourth floor, south side of the great stupa, painting the chapel whose main sculpture depicted Butön Rinchen Drup (Bu ston Rin chen Grub), the so-called Khyenrab Lhakhang (mKhyen rab Lha khang). One of the sculptures depicted Jamyang Rinchen Gyaltshen of Nenying. Tucci assumed that Rinchen Paljor and Paljor Rinchen were the same person, since both came from Nenying, and he thought that the elements of their names had been transposed by mistake. But that requires reconsideration.

Tucci also notes the "remarkable artistic value" of the chapel 4–1 on the south side of the fourth level ('Jam dbyangs sMra seng Lha khang, 4S2), which he says was painted by Rinchen Paljor of Nenying and his son.[17] But this individual seems to be a different person than Paljor Rinchen.[18]

Thus in the 1430s, the same two artists from Nenying mentioned by Menthangpa—Paljor Rinchen and Sönam Paljor—were known to have been leading artists who directed major projects. The life of the Gyantse prince Rabten Kunzang Phak mentions Paljor Rinchen as "he of Nenying, who has perfected his skills as an artist" (*rig byed mkhas pa mthar phyin pa gnas snying pa*). Pönmoche (dPon mo che) Paljor, father and son, are mentioned at the head of the list of the greatest artists who participated in the painting of the Gyantse stūpa, consecrated in 1436.[19] Mentioned after them are the two great sculptors Namkha Zangpo (Nam mkha' bzang po) and Lhe

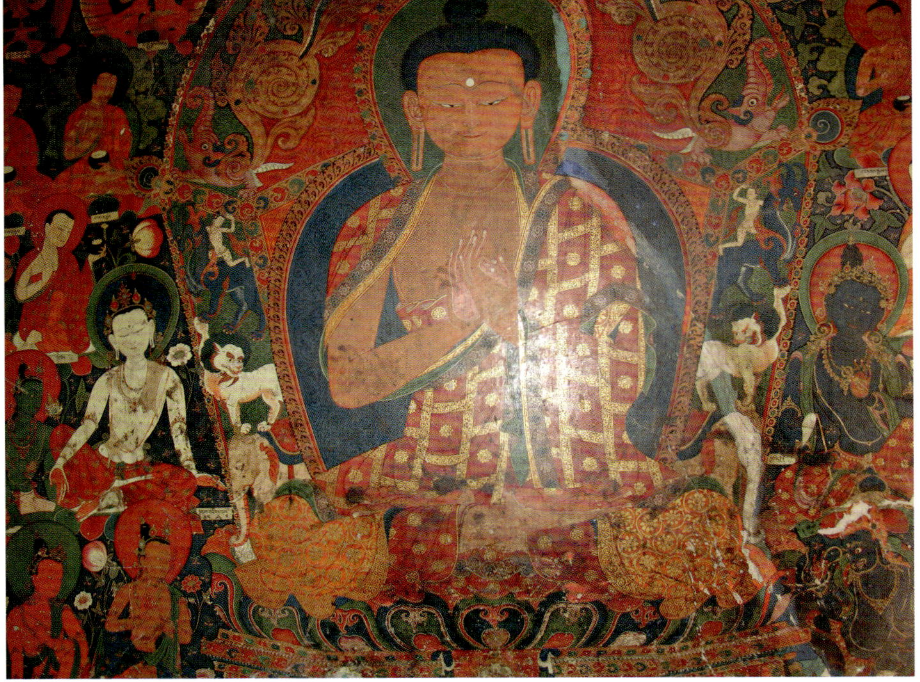

Gyaltshen (Lha'i rgyal mtshan). About
1437, the master artist Pönmoche (dPon
mo che) Mathewa (Ma the ba) Sönam
Paljor executed the sketch for the great
cloth image of Maitreya that was completed in 1439.[20] But his teacher Paljor
Rinchen is in this case not mentioned.

Thus I estimate that Khyentse
and Menthangpa were apprentices at
Gyantse and Nenying in the 1430s.
We do not know the personal circumstances of Khyentse, but his co-student
Menthangpa is said to have run away
from an unhappy marriage in Lhodrak.
It is not surprising that the young
Menthangpa would have been drawn in
the course of his wanderings from his
home in southern Ü to the then-thriving
Gyantse principality or to one of its
main religious centers, the ancient monastery of Nenying. Gyantse was at that
time experiencing the peak of its glory,
during the thirty-year reign of the prince
Rabten Kunzang Phak (Rab brtan kun
bzang 'phags, r. 1412–1442), the great
patron of the Palkhor complex.[21] Under
this man's leadership, Gyantse could
vie politically and culturally even with
the Tibetan central government of the
Phakmotrupa rulers, whose seat was at
Nedong in southern Ü.

The ancient monastery of Nenying in the upper Nyang valley was an

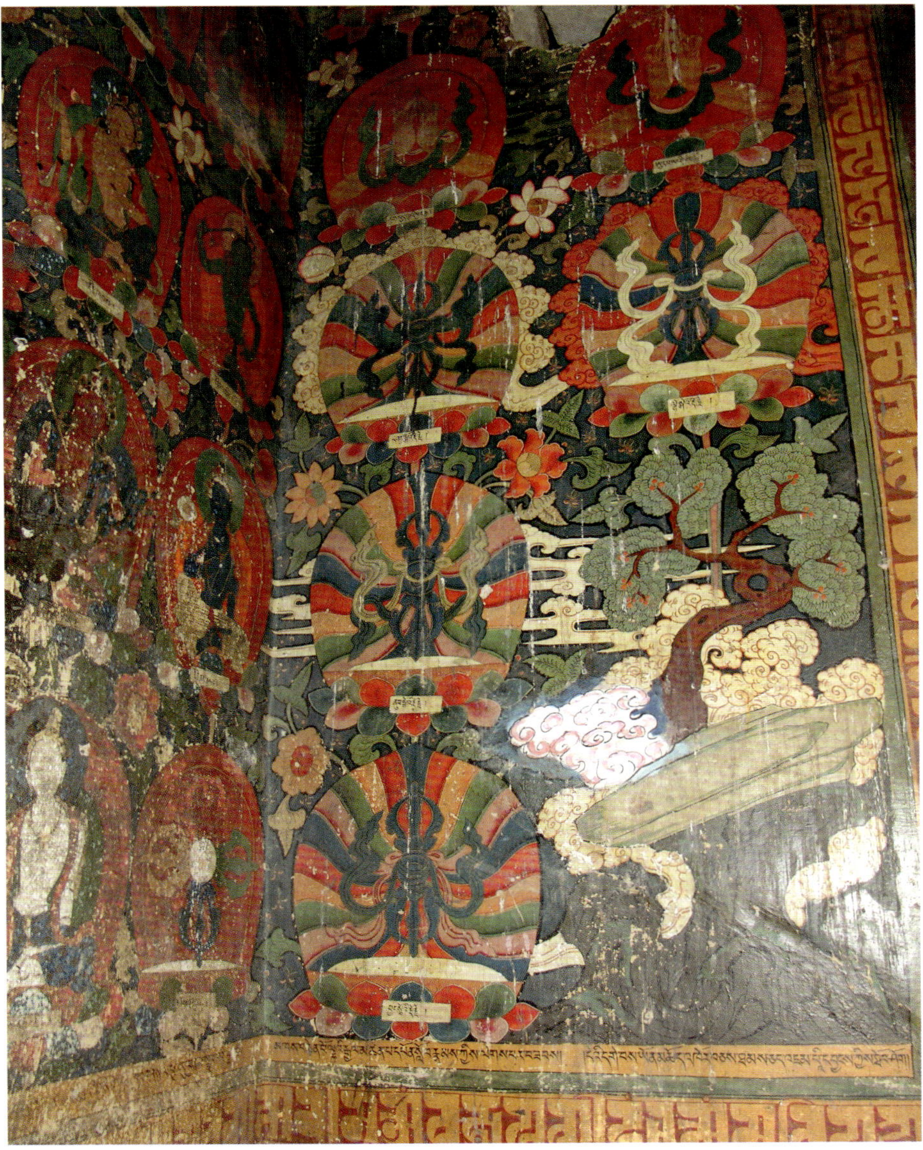

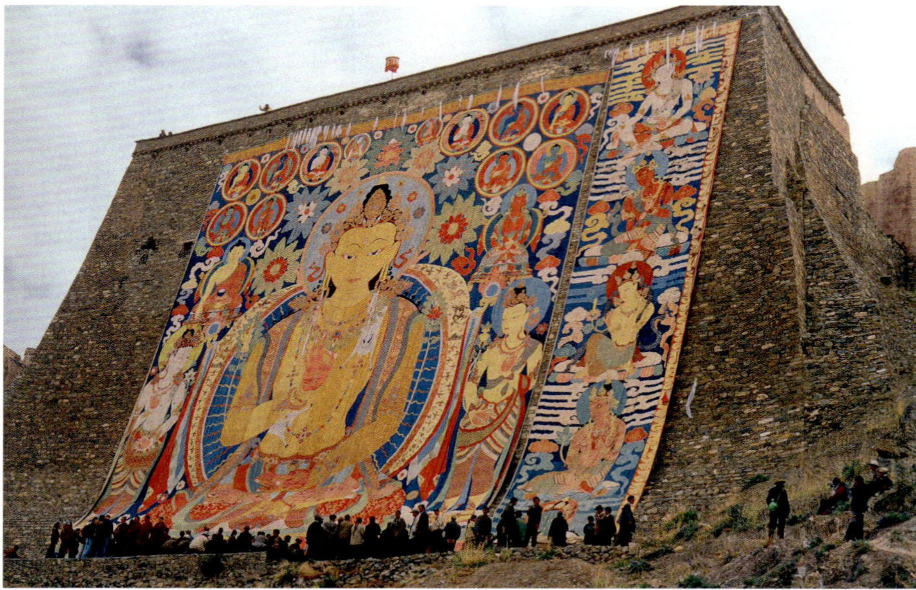

important center of religious art in its own right. About one generation before Khyentse Chenmo and Menthangpa, it was the seat of the illustrious and powerful master Khenchen Jamyang Rinchen Gyaltshen ('Jam dbyangs Rinchen rgyal mtshan, 1364–1422), until his death in 1422, as well as home to a flourishing group of painters, who included some of the best in all of Tsang.[22] This great abbot had a highly developed knowledge of arts and crafts (*bzo rig*), and he was the chief patron and overseer of numerous projects, including a great brocade appliqué thangka (*gos sku chen mo*).[23] For this project, he gathered a number of master artists, chief among whom were Mathewa Paljor Rinchen and Pön Tashi Gön (dPon bKra shis mgon).[24] After the thangka's completion, the abbot was invited to China by the Chinese emperor (probably the Yongle Emperor, temple name Chengzu, r. 1403–1424).[25] In his place, the Nenying abbot sent Chenpo Ngödrup Rinchen (Chen po dNgos grub Rin chen), who went to Jongdo (Cong rdo)[26] and received—in the name of the abbot and his abbatial successors—a crystal seal, a patent confirming rank and certain jurisdictions, inner and outer robes and other gifts.[27] The famous *si thang* silk Chinese scroll painting of Nenying, which mesmerized the young

Menthangpa when he saw it in the 1430s, may have been sent from China to Nenying during this period. I have found no other similar mentions in the Nenying history of close contacts with China on the part of earlier or later abbots. Another important Ming-period painting dating to 1412 still survives at Nenying, though it depicts a standing Buddha without any landscape in the background (see Figs. 1.10a and 1.10b).[28]

Oddly enough, no contemporaneous records from Gyantse mention the presence of an artist named Dopa Tashi Gyalpo, who is widely believed to have been Menthangpa and Khyentse's teacher in Tsang. Some mistake in the transmitting of his name may have occurred. The earliest source to mention a Dopa Tragyal (rDo pa bKra rgyal) in this role was Desi Sanggye Gyatsho's sketch of art history, found in his treatise *Vaiḍūrya g.Ya' sel*. I believe the Desi repeated there a story his teachers or informants had heard about events that had transpired two centuries earlier.[29] Though no Tashi Gyalpo can be found at Gyantse in the 1430s, one prominent Nenying artist with "Tashi" in his name was one of Paljor Rinchen's prominent fellow artists. Named Tashi Gön (bKra shis mgon), he was a fairly eminent painter, almost the equal of the two other Nenying artists whom Menthangpa mentioned as his teachers.[30] Among the Palkhor stupa painters who came from Nenying, one artist had "rGyal"—but not "Gyalpo"—in his name: number 11, Gyaltshenpa of Nenying.[31]

The large thangka illustrated by Figure 1.11 gives an idea of how a painting by Paljor Rinchen might have looked. This Tsang painting style of the 1430s would have been very close to the style Khyentse Chenmo learned from his teachers. It was his and Menthangpa's stylistic point of departure. Note the Chinese-style, ring-shape robe fastener depicted over the proper-left shoulder.

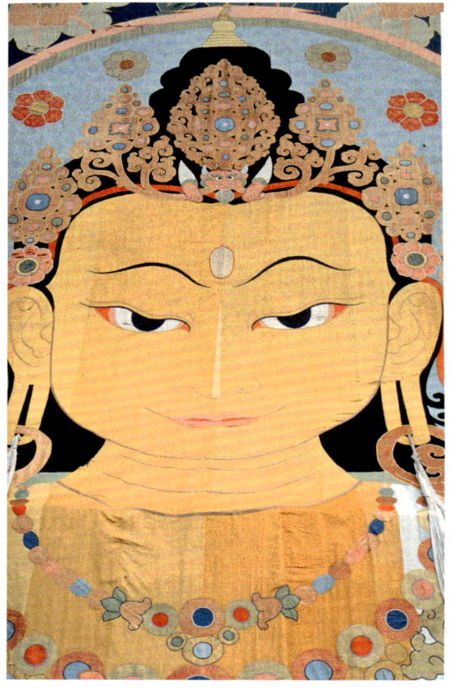

Fig. 1.8
Great Cloth Image of Maitreya
Embroidered and painted cloth, designed by Sönam Paljor
Palkhor Chöde, Gyantse; 1437–1439
Photo: M. Henss, 2000
After: Henss 2014, fig. 727

Fig. 1.9
Great Cloth Image of Maitreya (detail)
Embroidered and painted cloth, designed by Sönam Paljor
Palkhor Chöde, Gyantse; 1437–1439
Photo: M. Henss, 2000
After: Henss 2014, fig. 730

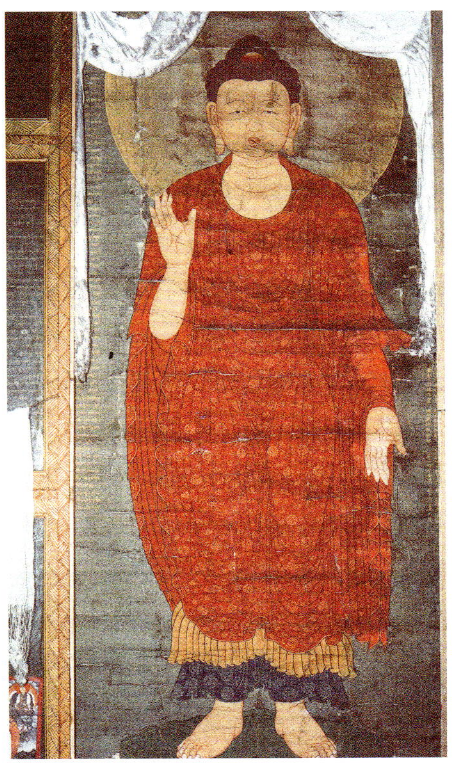

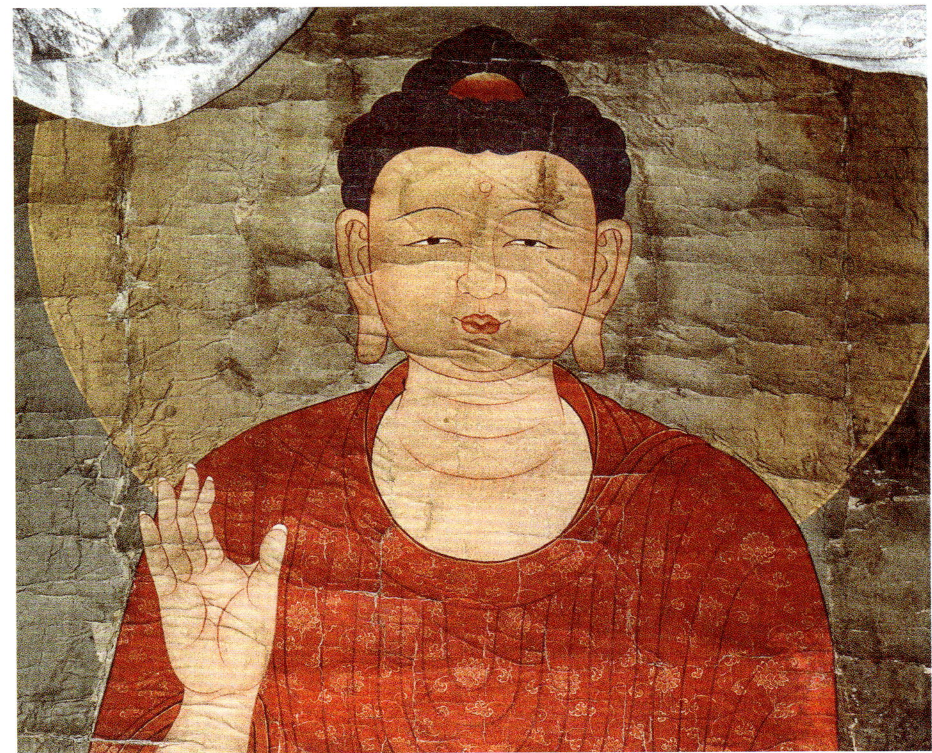

Fig. 1.10a
Standing Buddha of Nenying
Painted scroll, dated 1412
98 3/5 x 51 ⅛ in. (250 x 130 cm)
Now in assembly hall, Nenying
Photo from 1994
After: Henss 2014, fig. 797

Fig. 1.10b
Head of Standing Buddha of Nenying
(detail)
Painted scroll, dated 1412
Now in assembly hall, Nenying
After: Henss 2014, fig. 797a

Fig. 1.11
Buddha in a Stupa
1420s–1450s
59 ⅞ x 43 ¾ in. (152 x 111 cm)
Michael Henss Collection, Zurich
Literature: Pal 2003, no. 154; and Jackson
2010, fig. 7.16

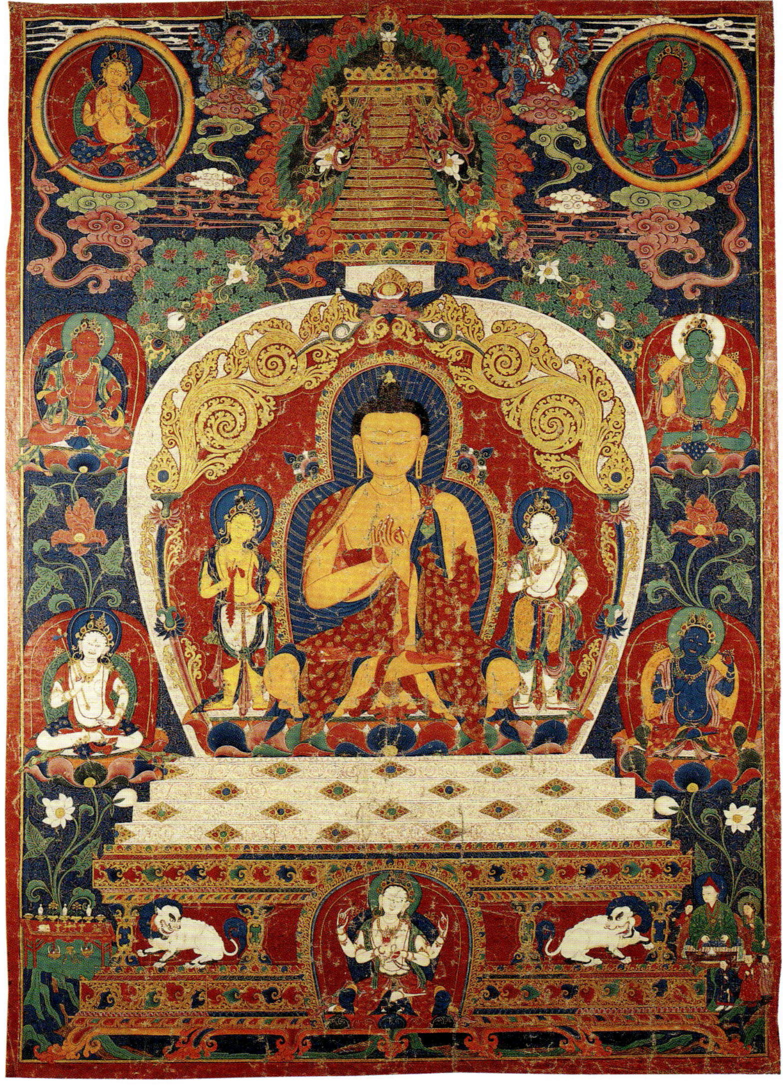

FIG. 1.12
Śākyamuni surrounded by scenes of Tuṣita
Mural detail, Champa Lhakhang, second
floor, east side, Palkhor Chöde, Gyantse
Great Stupa
Photo: Tsechang Penba Wangdu, 2005
Literature: Ricca and Lo Bue 1993, 241,
no. 4

FIG. 1.13
Buddha
Mural detail, Dīpaṃkara Lhakhang,
second floor, north side, Palkhor Chöde,
Gyantse Great Stupa
Photo: Tsechang Penba Wangdu, 2005
Literature: Ricca and Lo Bue 1993, 236,
nos. 5 and 6

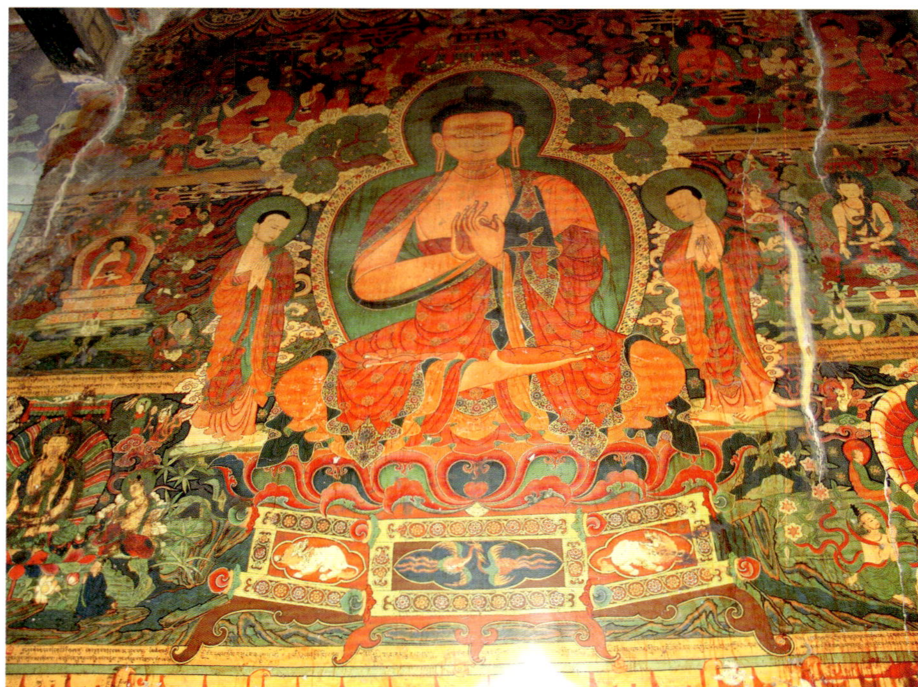

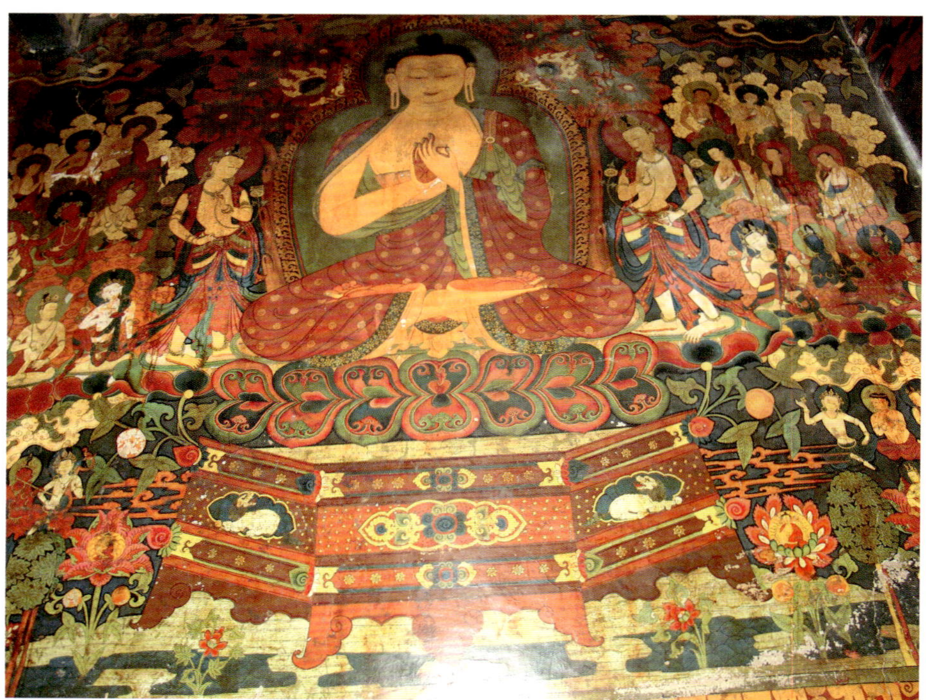

Note also the strip of blue-green rocks along the bottom of the painting, visible even between the legs of the throne base.

Figure 1.12 is a detail of a mural from the Maitreya chapel (Champa Lhakhang) in the Gyantse stupa. The names of the painters of this chapel, on the eastern side of the first floor of the stupa, are not known. Note the elaborate device used to fasten the Buddha's robe at his shoulder, which includes a piece of red silk with golden embroidery.

Figure 1.13 is a detail of a mural from the Dīpaṃkara chapel (Marmedze Lhakhang) in the Gyantse stupa. The name of the painter of this chapel, also on the eastern side of the first floor of the stupa, is not known. Note the small white ring used to fasten the Buddha's robe at his shoulder with a cord. (Though common in Chinese paintings and sculptures of all sorts, such ring fasteners were taken up by Khyentse fairly commonly in buddha robes, unlike the Menri tradition, and in sculptures or paintings such rings in Tibetan lama robes become a definitive marker of his style.)

Artists from the Mathewa family, led by Paljor Rinchen and Sönam Rinchen, formed the outstanding artistic clan of the upper Nyang valley of Tsang during Khyentse's youth. The succeeding generations continued to flourish

at Nenying, long after Khyentse and Menthangpa left Gyantse and founded their own schools of art elsewhere, with the help of relatives or other disciples. Mathe (Ma the) may have been the name of the artists' paternal line or of a small locale in the upper Nyang valley. The *gNas rnying chos 'byung* mentions other great artists from the family. About 1472, for instance, Mathewa Pön Paljor and also Lekpa Changchup (Legs pa Byang

chub) painted murals.[32] In the same period, the same Mathewa Pön Paljor was in charge of sketching the basic drawing for a large brocade appliqué image of Maitreya with fifteen deities.[33] About 1496, the painter (Ri mo ba) and head artist (Pönmoche) Mathewa, an uncle, and the painter (Lha ris pa) Lekpa (Legs pa), a nephew, created murals.[34] In 1504, the head artist (Pönmoche) Mathewa Lekpa Changchup planned and sketched a great Amitābha brocade appliqué thangka that depicted seven deities.[35] It would be interesting to know to what extent these later painters were affected by the great stylistic revolution that Khyentse and Menthangpa set loose.

4. Early Major Projects as a Master Artist

I believe that Khyentse Chenmo completed his apprenticeship and developed his strikingly Chinese style by the late 1440s. Both he and Menthangpa probably learned as much as they could from the great Nenying artists, but they also assiduously studied and copied the best available works of Chinese art.

The brief traditional sources all stress that the pair of co-disciples, Menthang Chenmo and Khyentse Chenmo, both finally excelled their teacher in artistic expertise, which would justify their establishing new styles. After finishing their apprenticeships, the talented Khyentse and Menthangpa probably left Gyantse and pursued careers elsewhere in Tibet as highly competent masters, who were quickly becoming famous in their own right, in the 1450s. In the late 1440s and 1450s, the aesthetic revolution that Khyentse and Menthangpa were championing, each in his own way, would have been shocking for many conservative-minded patrons. Their work must have been stylistically too innovative for such people, who would have preferred to support the established Beri style. Tibetan aesthetic taste was at the cusp of change.

But by the 1450s and 1460s, Khyentse and Menthangpa apparently found some acceptance among a few highly placed and influential patrons who patronized the striking new styles of painting. Menthangpa stayed in Tsang. Khyentse left the artistically sophisticated Gyantse area of Tsang and returned to his home district of Lhokha in Ü and worked for local patrons. When he did so, he was returning to the seat of the Tibetan national capital, another highly cultured area.

Khyentse and Menthangpa led an aesthetic revolution that was inspired by Chinese art of the Ming dynasty. In the mid-fifteenth century, Tibetan aesthetic taste—at least in Ü and Tsang provinces—began to turn away from the classic style that featured more Indic decorative elements in the backgrounds of paintings and began to adopt more Chinese styles for depicting everything in the paintings except the divine figures. (But it remained Tibetan art and would never be confused for Chinese painting.)

The motivation for Khyentse's and Menthangpa's stylistic change in the 1450s is not to be found, as some proposed, in the insights or activities of any Tibetan religious master, including Tsongkhapa, about fifty years earlier.[36] Rather, the aesthetic development should be considered a delayed reaction to the generosity and taste of the Ming imperial court under the Yongle Emperor.[37]

Reigning from 1403 to 1424, the Yongle Emperor sowed the seeds for the coming revolution in Tibetan aesthetic taste by commissioning exquisite works of Buddhist art and offering them to the leading lamas of Tibet—including the three great dharma-kings whom he personally invited and hosted at his court: the Fifth Karmapa, the Sakya hierarch Thekchen Chöje (1349–1425), and one of Tsongkhapa's most eminent disciples, Chamchen Chöje.[38] For it was Buddhist Ming-period masterpieces that Khyentse and Menthangpa took, in the 1440s, as their main sources of inspiration.

The penetration of Chinese landscapes into the backgrounds of Tibetan paintings began in the mid-fifteenth century; it took about a century and a half for this approach to completely replace the Indic Beri style in central Tibet. Chinese landscapes reached universal acceptance as settings for deities only in the late sixteenth century.[39]

A Painting with an Indic theme: Vanaratna with Lineage

I do not think that Khyentse Chenmo felt limited by or forced to use the Chinese elements that he had adopted. He also could incorporate, when appropriate, stylistic elements that expressed a more Indian atmosphere. Figure 1.14 may exemplify this. Khyentse Chenmo made it in the 1470s, as instructed by Lochen Sönam Gyatsho.

The structure of the painting is shown in Diagram [A]. About this painting, in an earlier catalog (*Mirror of the Buddha*), I wrongly asserted, "The main figure, Vanaratna (13b), occurs a second time in the painting as a small lineal guru (13a)."[40] Actually the main figure is 14b, so the text should read "the main figure, Vanaratna (14b), occurs a second time in the painting as a small lineal guru (14a)." The patron of this painting did not come from Tsang, as some have suggested, but rather from Ü province. However, I wrongly said that the patron belonged to the Phagmotrupa government; for the teaching lineage depicted in this painting, Vanaratna's disciple and patron came from the Phagmotrupa royal family.

One of the great lamas supported by the Yargyap (g.Yar rgyab) noble family may be seen in the lower left as the painting's patron (P in the diagram) or as one of the two nameless lamas above (17 or 18).[41] On his third visit to Tibet, in 1454, Vanaratna visited Champaling in Dranang and met for a second time Lochen Sönam Nampar Gyalwa, who had previously seen Vanaratna at Rinpung earlier on that trip. While at Champaling, Vanaratna gave teachings to Sönam Nampar Gyalwa and his disciples.[42] Another eminent lama in the vicinity, Panchen Champalingpa (d. 1475), is known to have worn a yellow pandit hat with tucked in ear-flaps, just like that of Vanaratna. Khyentse Chenmo was evidently asked by one of the great

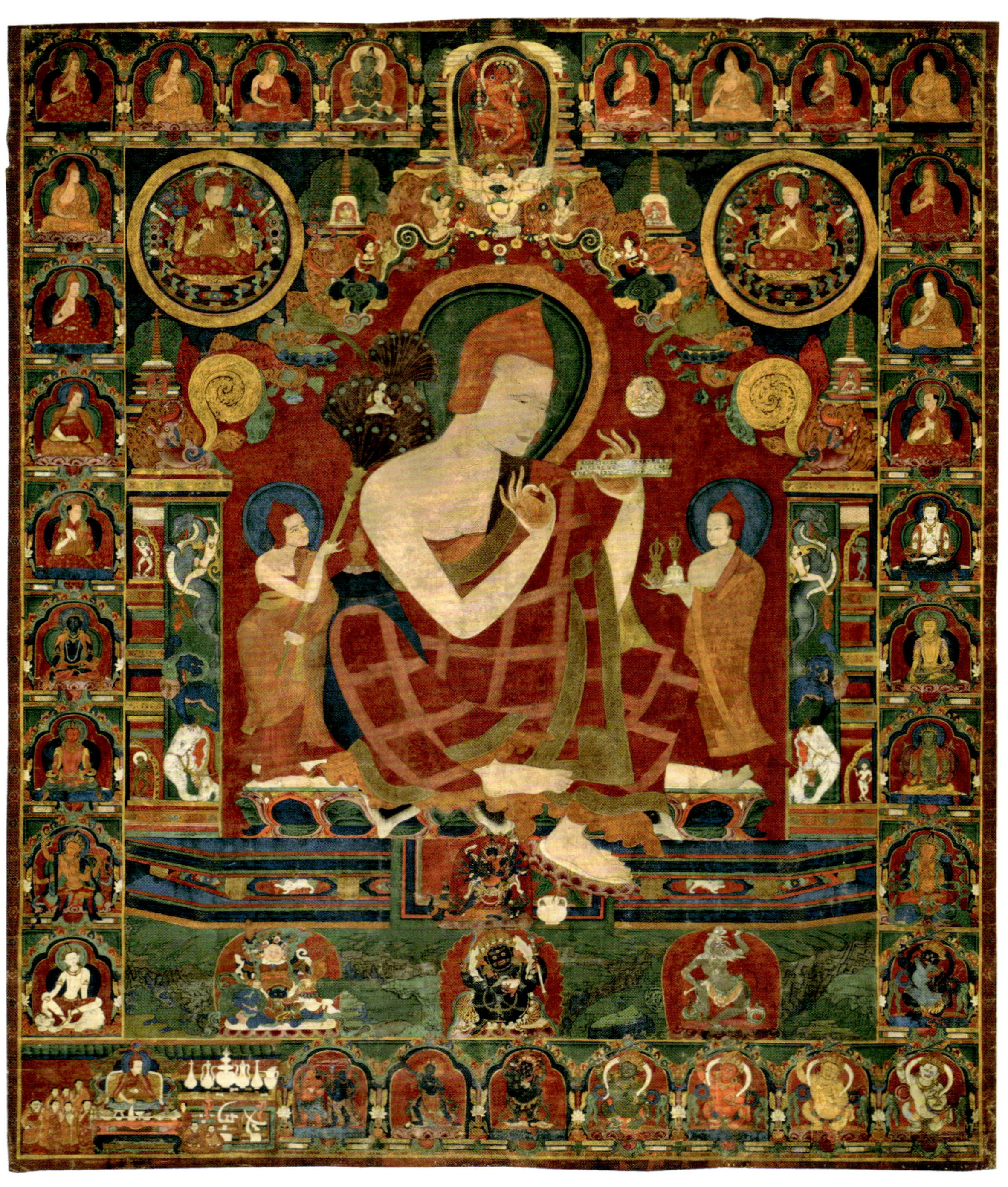

Fig. 1.14
The Indian Pandit Vanaratna with Lineage
Late 1470s
40 ¼ x 34 ½ in. (102.2 x 87.6 cm)
Kronos Collections
Literature: Kossak and Singer 1998, fig. 55;
Stoddard 2003, fig. 14; Ehrhard 2004, 265;
and Jackson 2011, fig. 3.20

8	6	4	1	2	3	5	7	9
10	17?						18?	11
12								13
14a								15
16				14b				d1
d2								d3
d4								d5
d6								d7
d8		d8		d10		d11		d12
P		d13	d14	d15	d16	d17	d18	d19

lamas of Lhokha, such as Trimkhang Lotsāwa Sönam Gyatsho, to commemorate the Indian pandit in a painting, in the decade after his death in 1468.

This painting is mentioned in Franz-Karl Ehrhard's book *Life and Travels of Lo-chen bSod-nams rgya-mtsho*, which records that Vanaratna appeared in dreams to Lochen; in one dream, he held his right hand in a gesture of teaching and held in his left a volume of scriptures. The dreams occurred in 1477, two years after Champalingpa had passed away, a time when Lochen Sönam Gyatsho was staying in the Yargyap region and the local lord Shidzom Rinchen Tönyö (bZhi' 'dzoms Rin chen don yod) and his family were his main donors. As Ehrhard wrote:

> On the ninth month of the year 1477 found bSod-nams rgya-mtsho at bSam-gdan-gling, a "site for spiritual practice" which he had established in the Yar-rgyab area and which served as his main retreat place in the final years of his life. After three days Vanaratna appeared to him in a dream dressed in the robe of a paṇḍita, his right hand in the "gesture of teaching the doctrine"… and his left holding a manuscript of the *Mañjuśrīnāmasaṃgītī*. He addressed his disciple in words from the Sanskrit language that moved bSod-nams rGya-mtsho to tears when he awakened from his dream.[43]

Not long afterward, he had a second dream. Ehrhard adds, "These dreams were later interpreted as further 'encouragement' from the Chittagong yogin, while it is mentioned that they were also depicted in a painting of fine quality." In a footnote, Ehrhard suggests that this painting (Fig. 1.14) might be the one referred to in Lochen's biography.[44]

As seen in Figure 1.14, Khyentse Chenmo carefully worked a great amount of detail into the faces, hats, and robes of the main and minor figures. In his proper left hand, the pandit holds a white manuscript leaf with tiny Nagari characters that are almost legible in the photo; we now know the volume was the *Mañjuśrīnāmasaṃgītī*. The painting also shows two standing attendants with uncommon postures; the one to the left holds a complicated fan made of peacock feathers.

This painting is not in any usual style of Khyentse Chenmo but is rather more Indic. Yet the striking, bright-green Chinese landscape that he has artfully limited to one area of the painting—directly beneath the base of Vanaratna's throne—can hardly be overlooked, a hallmark of the artist that now commands the viewer's attention. Note that he uses a kind of perspectival depiction in the receding sides of the throne base.

Khyentse Chenmo sometimes inserted little features in the central painting in a thangka set, such as asymmetric little boys (*bu chung*) riding the griffins in the throne back. To the right and left of Vanaratna's head nimbus, the inclusion of the two green parrots or parakeets with long tails is a mystery; they stand with different lifelike postures on lotus seats.[45] Only an artist like Khyentse Chenmo could have produced such a distinctive iconography.[46] (Though rare in Tibetan art, parrots were considered auspicious in China and were an established motif of Chinese art, as will be explained below.)[47]

Also of art-historical interest in connection with Vanaratna are two paintings from Nepal dating to 1469, the year after his death, that depict Vanaratna having a vision of White Tārā. They survive in the collections of the Bharat Kala Bhavan, Benares Hindu University, in Varanasi, India, and of the Los Angeles County Museum of Art.[48]

Somewhat like the dream-inspired painting of Vanaratna that he was asked to make for Lochen Sönam Gyatsho, once at or near Gongkar, Khyentse Chenmo was requested to execute an extraordinary visionary painting for his patron Gongkar Dorjedenpa. Once late at night while meditating, that lama saw a vision of the protective deity Mahākāla Pañjaranātha (Gur gyi mgon po) and immediately afterward made a small sketch of the deity as it had appeared before him.[49] The following morning he gave Khyentse Chenmo the sketch, and the great artist (*rig byed*) then completed it with colors. This painting became treasured later as a very sacred object. Gongkar Dorjedenpa used this image for giving an initiation when his student and "chief attendant" (*nye gnas chen mo*), that is, his devoted business manager Gyajinpa (brGya sbyin pa) became ill. For some time, that disciple kept it to ward off harm, and it remained for many years as the main sacred image in the shrine at Namgyal Rabten (rNam rgyal rab brtan), a private estate.[50]

5. Main Places of Patronage and Patrons

By the 1460s, Khyentse Chenmo led major artistic projects of his own, heading teams of artist assistants and decorating whole monasteries. His first major project known from written sources was Gongkar Chöde, where he painted and sculpted for twelve years, beginning in 1464. There his main patron was Gongkar Dorjedenpa (Gong dkar rDo rje gdan pa) Kunga Namgyal. Building and decorating the temple and its sacred contents took more than a decade. Regarding the building and furnishing of the monastery, Gyatön Changchup Wangyal wrote in his biography of Kunga Namgyal:

> In just one cycle of [twelve] years the entire temple together with its sacred contents [including many sculptures] was completed. Moreover, because of the differences of the seasons of summer and

winter, the time actually available to the workers was just half of that. Hence if we consider regarding even a fairly negligible project that we try to achieve now, if we think of the difficulties and efforts involved and how long it takes, then the completion of [the large and ornate] Gongkar monastery was nothing less than the magical deed of an emanated [divine] being, and it cannot be fathomed by ordinary people. [51]

Dungkar Losang Trinle's Tibetan-Tibetan dictionary defines the expression *lo skor bcu gnyis* as twelve years; *lo skor gcig* cannot mean one year. Thus Dungkar's understanding is probably right, and the monastery took twelve years to complete.[52]

Khyentse's fellow student Menthangpa stayed in Tsang, where he became very famous and successful.[53] Khyentse, for his part, was known to have painted only in Ü, and there he remained a prominent master in the 1470s and 1480s. As his works are better documented, it should be possible to find several paintings that depict his layman patrons. Figure 1.15, for example, is a detail of a thangka from his circles of Sakya patronage in Lhokha, from the 1460s to the 1490s. In this work, which might be the central painting of a Lamdre lineage, two lay-noblemen brothers are shown as chief donors. Sitting to the left is a single noblewoman, prominently holding a cluster of jewels on a tray, which unmistakably marks her as a generous donor. She might be Dorje Dema (d. ca. 1490), Gongkarwa's mother, a legendary patroness of Buddhism in Lhokha; for example, she was the main patron of the Champaling stupa. I suspect that she was directly or indirectly the chief supporter of much sacred art produced by Khyentse Chenmo from the 1460s to the 1480s.

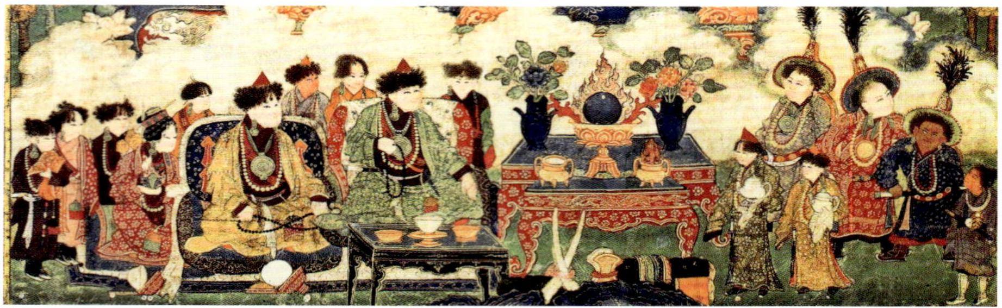

Prominent Non-Sakya Patrons

For many years, I expected that a special connection existed between the Khyenri painting style and the Gongkarwa Sakya tradition based at Gongkar Dorjeden. Such a link would not be completely far-fetched, given that Khyentse's birthplace was in Gongkar and that he was a devoted disciple of the great master of Sakyapa tantric traditions, Gongkar Dorjedenpa.[54] The greatest Khyenri paintings that have survived down to recent generations were, in fact, the murals of Gongkar Dorjeden Monastery.

Nevertheless, though Khyentse did possess close personal links with Gongkar Dorjedena and its founder, his art was not exclusively associated with either the Sakyapa religious school or its special iconographic subjects. He painted many thangkas for patrons from the other known major and minor religious traditions. Later exponents of the Khyenri painting style likewise produced paintings of various subjects for a wide variety of patrons from various religious backgrounds.

Besides his period as an apprentice in Tsang, Khyentse is known to have lived and worked only in Ü province. Khyentse Chenmo's patrons in Lhokha included such eminent noble lamas as Gongkarwa and Champalingpa. I believe they also included the highest noble lords and rulers of his day in southern Ü, such as the lords of Yargyap (the relatives of the noble lamas) and even the kings of Tibet, the Phagmotrupa rulers. Hints to that effect are given by Kathok Situ, who mentioned a set of twenty-three extremely fine

Fig. 1.15 (detail of Fig. 2.3)
Detail of lay patrons beneath central Vajradhara
After: Tucci 1949, pl. O

Khyenri thangkas depicting the sixteen arhats, with green borders, which was then preserved at Nedong Bentsang (sNe gdong Ban gtsang). These paintings are specified by Kathok Situ to have formerly been the sacred possessions of the Nedong (Phagmotrupa) ruler.[55] This implies that the set was commissioned through royal patronage.

Khyentse Chenmo or his early successors were also esteemed and patronized by prominent lamas of the Drukpa Kagyu, Drigung Kagyu, and Nyingma traditions. Regarding the Drigung Kagyu, I have published a number of important Khyenri paintings of that religious tradition, though none seem likely to have been painted by Khyentse.[56] A branch of the Khyenri style continued at Drigung Monastery from the early or mid-eighteenth century, as spread by the students of the religious master Könchok Trinle Zangpo (dKon mchog phrin las bzang po, 1656–1719), the twenty-fourth abbot of Drigung, who had been an exceptionally skilled painter.[57]

Regarding thangkas painted for Drukpa Kagyu patrons in Lhokha, Kathok Situ in his pilgrimage record mentioned at Dra Dingpoche (Grwa lDing po che) three very large thangkas depicting Drukpa Kagyu lineage masters, attributing them to Khyentse Chenmo personally: "Three thangka paintings whose excellent material, color [and] layout, [luminous] like the arising of a rainbow, reaching the

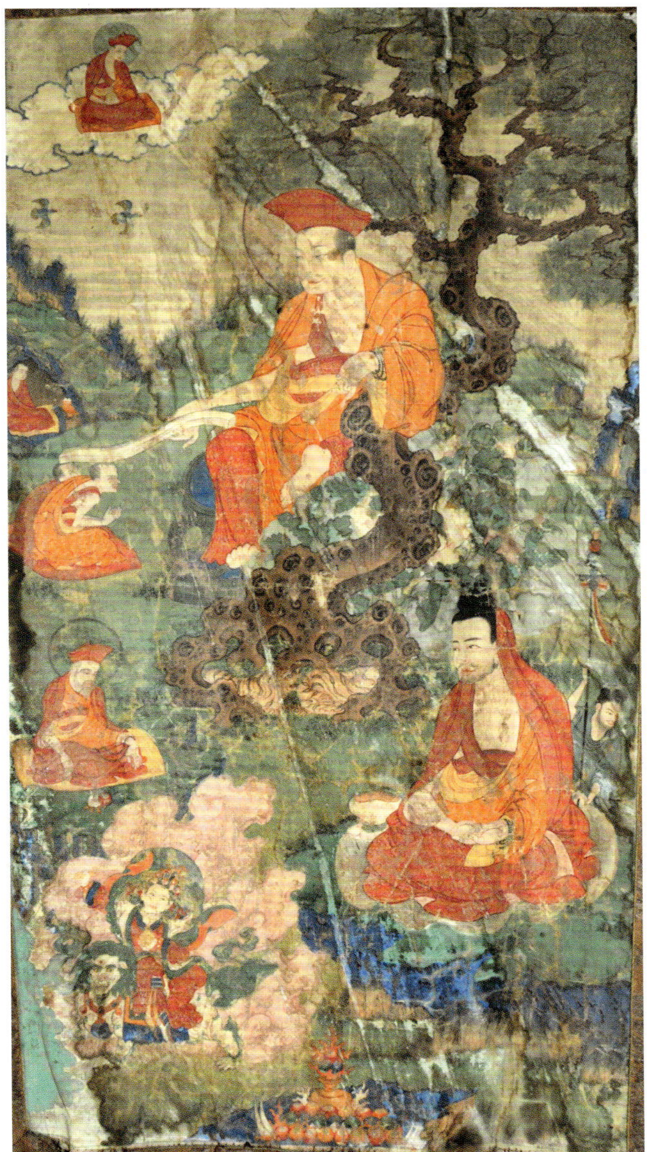

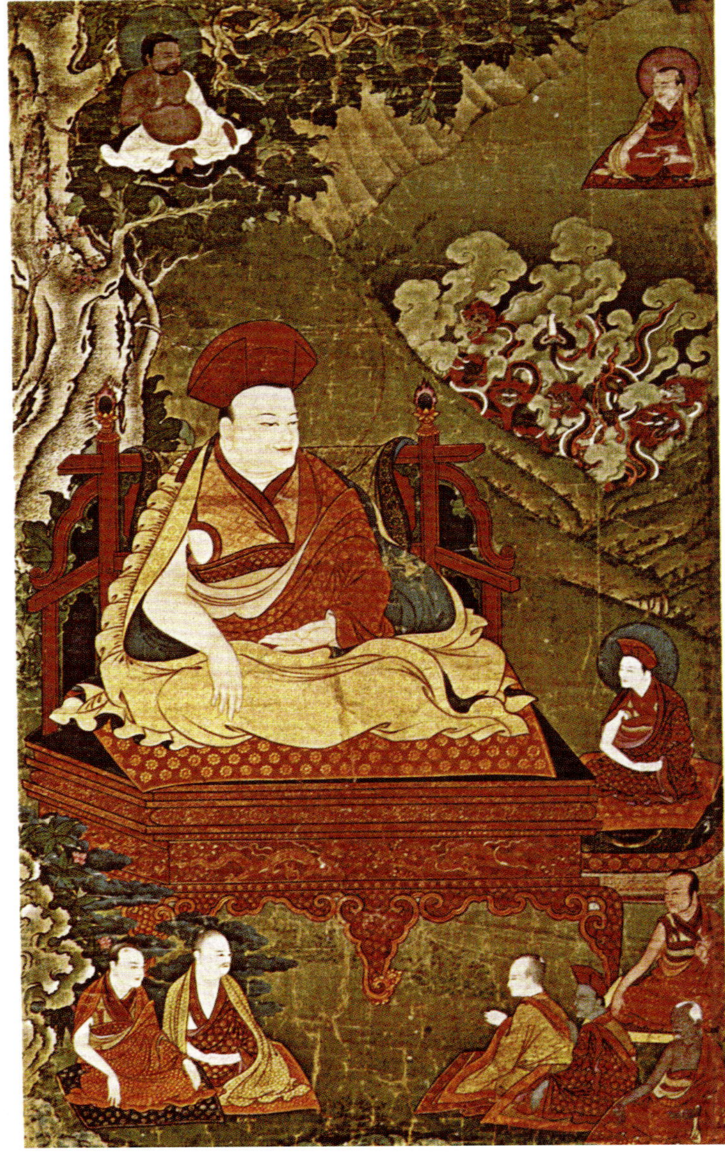

ceiling [in size], were capable of transforming one's ordinary perceptions [into
a divine realm]."[58] I think the phrase
"reaching the ceiling" (*thog sleb ma*)
could be used for works with a painting
height about 47 or 55 inches (120 or
140 centimeters); with brocade, the total
height of the thangka would be almost
one story high.

Figure 1.16 is a remarkable painting of two Drukpa Kagyu lineal lamas. It
was located by the scholar Rob Linrothe
in Tetsa Shrine, in the Markha valley in
Ladakh, a cliff shrine tended by a single
monk deputed by Hemis Monastery, a
Drukpa Kagyu monastery in Ladakh.
It is remarkable for its naturalism and
sensitive artistry; Linrothe convincingly
explains this in his detailed description.[59]
Note the details of the minor figures and
the presence of a pair of birds flying
across the sky. But rather than taking it
as an example of an early phase of the
Karma Gardri, it might more plausibly
represent the work of Khyentse Chenmo
for a Kagyu, or possibly Drukpa, patron.
The complicated seat of the upper main
figure, leaning against a contorted tree
trunk, is something that recurs in Khyentse's paintings of arhats. Though
such elements are normal in a Chinese
depiction of arhats, Khyentse Chenmo
was the first to use them when depicting
Tibetan masters.

In 2009, I attributed Figure 1.17
as possibly the work of another great

FIG. 1.16
Two Kagyu Lineage Masters
second half of the fifteenth century
30 x 17 in (76.2 x 43.2 cm)
Now in Tetsa Shrine, Markha valley,
Ladakh
Literature: Linrothe 2012, fig. 9.5

FIG. 1.17
Tsangpa Gyare
second half of the fifteenth century
35 ½ x 22 ½ in (90.2 x 52.1 cm)
Literature: Chogyam Trungpa 1975, no. 29;
and Jackson 2009, fig. 1.7

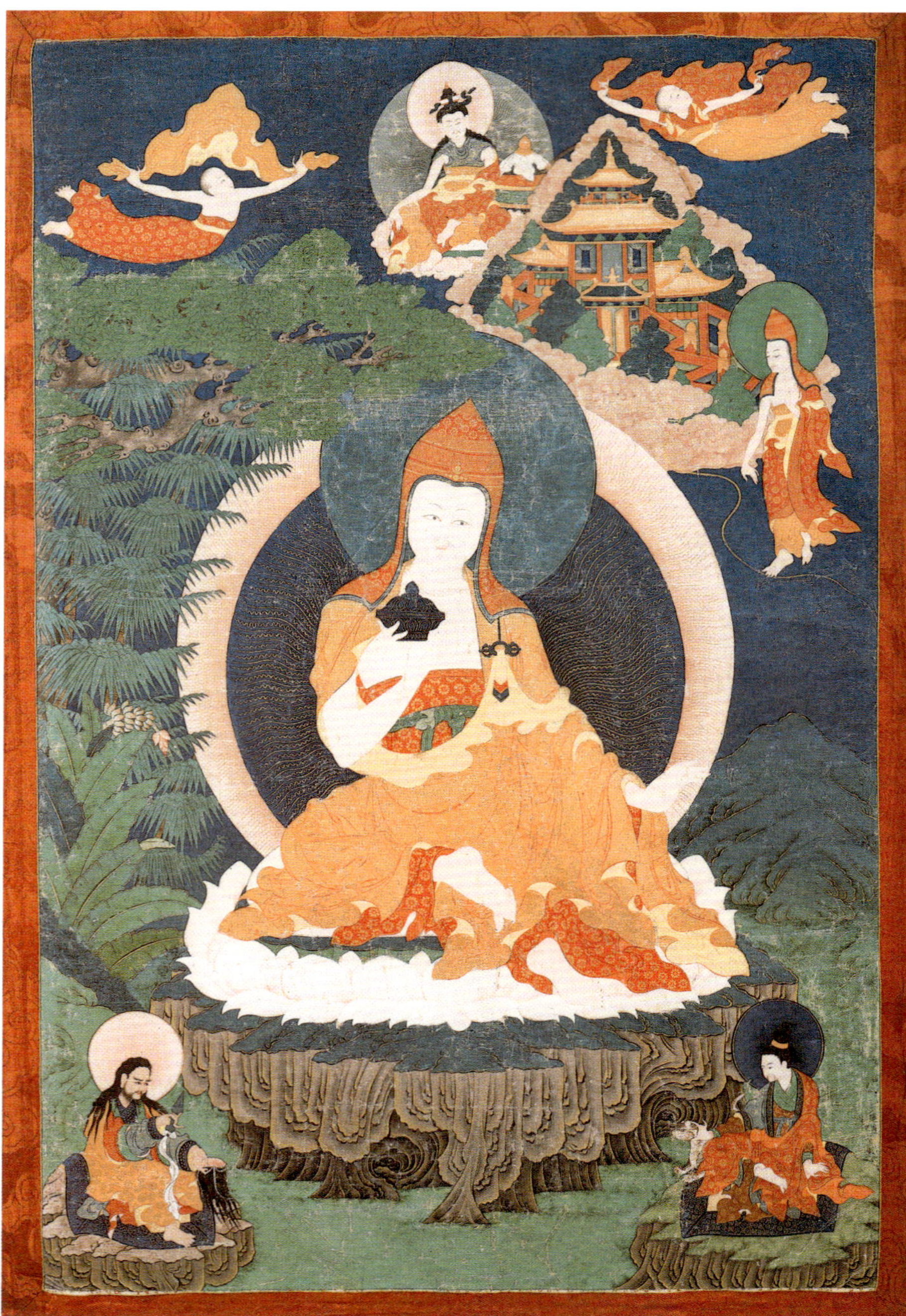

said by Kathok Situ to have depicted the lineage gurus of the Dzogchen (rDzogs chen) teachings following the artistic tradition of Khyentse Chenmo.[60] He listed twelve paintings in the set; see Appendix A for a more detailed list of this set's contents.

Figure 1.18 exemplifies a similar Nyingma subject painted in an early Khyenri style. Its main figure's robe fastener is highly distinctive, the sort of fancy Chinese fastener that Khyentse Chenmo often depicted. (They are particularly telling when used for the robes not of arhats but of Tibetan lamas.) This painting most closely resembles painting number 8 in the Dzogchen guru lineage, namely with Śrīsiṃha as the main figure and Vimalamitra, Jñānasūtra, and Chöku Kunzang Öbar as minor ones. (See Appendix A.) Rhie and Thurman 1999 speculated that one of the lamas flying in the sky could be Namkhe Nyingpo, one of Padmasambhava's early disciples, who was famed for riding on sunlight (Tib. *nyi ma'i 'od zer la chibs*).[61] But this one is not the one Rhie discusses; here, one lama is walking on a sunbeam.

Identifying Figure 1.19 as the Khyenri style offers a convincing solution to a long-standing stylistic puzzle. This classification would also show that Khyentse Chenmo was supported by non-Sakya patrons in Lhokha. The painting depicts the abbots of Gendungang, one of the four monk communities of Śākyaśrībhadra. The details of the landscape are distinctively Khyentse. Two pairs of birds are depicted: at the top center of the painting, one bird flies with a flowering branch in its beak toward its mate in the tree; to the left of the main figure, one pair is perched together atop blue craggy rocks. Beneath the perched birds, a pair of deer—too small to be in the same part of the landscape as the birds—rests peacefully, one calmly kneeling and the other with a single hoof planted before it. Note also the great variety of poses of the minor figures seated around

artist, Chö Tashi of the Karma Gardri style. But it more likely falls within the scope of paintings that Khyentse Chenmo or his early followers might have painted for Drukpa Kagyu patrons. Note the variety of poses of the minor figures, including full profile. Also of note is the swarming nest of seven dragons to the right of the main figure, wreathed by a cluster of elegant stylized nimbus clouds.

Regarding Nyingma patronage, an exceptional series of thangkas at Mindröling (sMin grol gling) Monastery is the main figure and at the base. Though such elements were perfectly normal in arhat paintings inspired by Chinese models, they are special when transferred into the backgrounds of depictions of Tibetan saints.

6. *The Last Known Project: The Murals of Yangpachen (1503)*

Khyentse Chenmo's last known major artistic project was in 1503. In that year, he was invited by the Fourth Shamar Rinpoche to paint the murals of Yangpachen (Yangs pa can) Monastery, northwest of Lhasa. According to the history of the Karma Kagyu by Pawo Tsuklak Trengwa, both Menthang Chenmo and Khyentse Chenmo came to Yangpachen and painted the murals there. Menthangpa came with his son, and no doubt both he and Khyentse led large teams of assistants, including Khyentse's nephew. Both of the master artists must have been quite old.

According to Pawo, "Above and below, the special layout of the mural paintings [at Yangpachen] was painted by Menthangpa Menla Döndrup, father and son, and Khyentse"; he added that because the inner and outer parts of the monastery were completed simultaneously, people commented that they had never seen such speed, good arrangement, or such a wide upper covering as this monastery had when it was built; what people used to say about Yangpachen, when Pawo was young, one could see that it was true.[62] The account of Yangpachen's murals by Be Lotsāwa

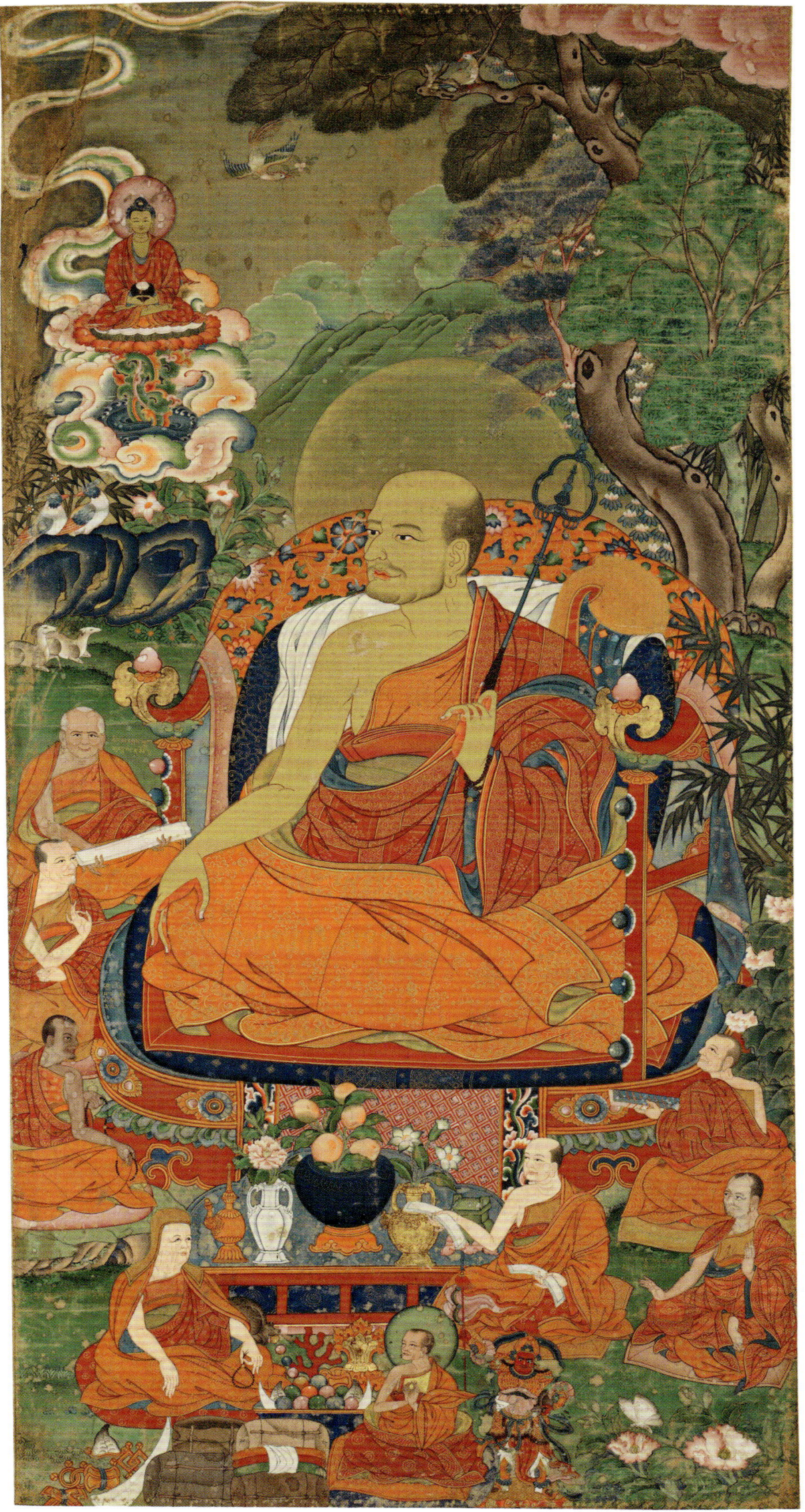

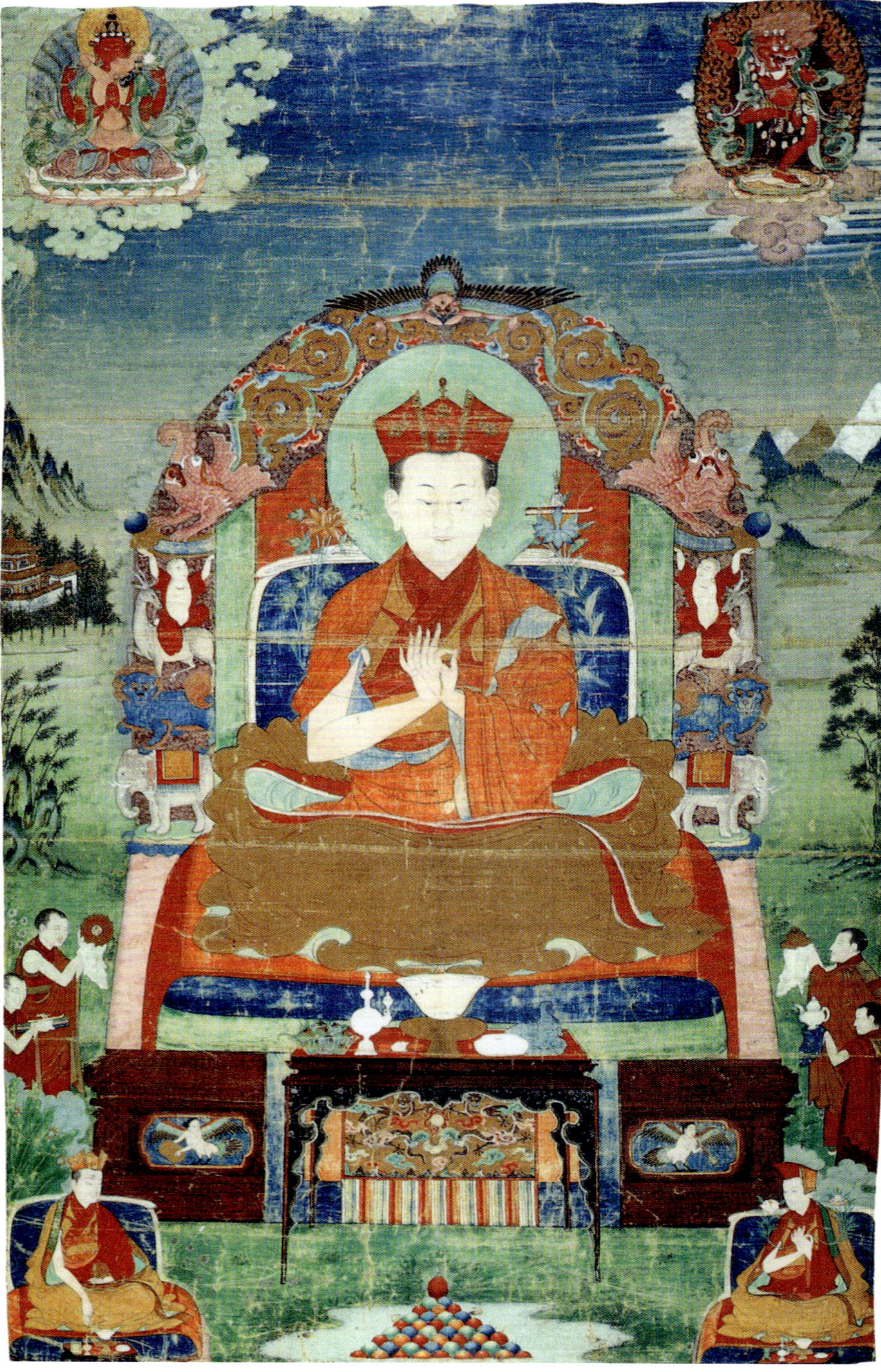

Figure 1.20 portrays a previously unidentified Shamar Trulku. I suspect that he is the Fourth Shamar, Chödrak Yeshe, as painted by Khyentse Chenmo. I once considered this painting as an example of early Karma Gardri, dating it to the first half of the seventeenth century.[64] Now, having seen many more of Khyentse Chenmo's paintings, I believe that this elegant portrait falls within the range of his style and possible workmanship.

One piece of strong iconographic evidence that this painting depicts the *Fourth* Shamar (and not the fifth) is that one of the attendant monks, standing to the left, offers him the golden wheel of political rule. The artist employs hues of pastel green and pink and fine details everywhere, including two fanciful bird-men, in the decorative panels in the base of the Shamar's throne, that each plays a different instrument. The depictions of the four standing attendants are highly naturalistic, and the artist has allowed a bit of asymmetry in the treatment of the two sea monsters (*makara*) in the formal backrest, to the right and left of the main figure's head nimbus. (If the painting is pre-Yangpachen, then the wooded monastery in the upper landscape to the left of the main figure's shoulder might be Ganden Mamo Monastery, the Shamar Trulku's monastery in Kongpo.) Though inscriptional evidence is lacking, we can speculate that if its subject is the Fourth Shamar, then the painting would date to Khyentse's time, since he did not belong to the main Karma Kagyu transmission lineages and hence does not appear in the lineage thangka sets as main figure. It would have been a virtually royal commission, and that might account for the extreme fineness of workmanship. (I discussed a biographical painting of the Fourth Shamar and his historical place in my *Patron and Painter* catalog.)[65]

In addition to the Fourth Shamar, whom the histories name as one of Khyentse's main patrons, it would be

['Be Lo tsā ba] in his Karma Kagyu history is the same.[63]

Thus we know that Khyentse Chenmo painted murals for the very prominent Shamar Trulku Chödrak Yeshe (1453–1524), who was both a high Karma Kagyu lama and an influential political dignitary. At Yangpachen, Khyentse must have painted many Karma Kagyu iconographic themes, three generations before the establishment of the Karma Gardri style.

reasonable to assume the contemporary
Black-hat Karmapa (the Seventh Karmapa Chödrak Gyatsho, 1454–1506)
or other lamas in his rich and powerful
Karmapa entourage would also have
commissioned artworks from Khyentse
or from eminent Khyenri painters of
the sixteenth century. It is likely that
Khyentse Chenmo made complete sets
of paintings of the Karma Kagyu lineal
gurus, just as he did for patrons from
other traditions. (See Figs. 2.17–2.20.)

Figure 1.21 is an excellent example of the early Khyenri style, and it
may even be a stray example of one of
Khyentse's Karma Kagyu paintings.
Its style and contents are certainly distinctive. Depicting the Fourth Karmapa
Rolpe Dorje (1340–1383) as the main
subject, it includes impressive details
from his life, such as his visits to the
Yuan court during its waning days. His
face reminds one of another image of
the Fourth Karmapa (see Fig. 2.19).
His main patron was Togön Temür, at
whose palace, Tai-ya Tu, he stayed for
three years. Togön Temür asked him to
remain in China, so they could collabo-
rate "like Qubilai and Phakpa."[66] Khyentse paid much attention to replicating
the details of the Chinese materials,
including the elaborate drapes and canopies in a Yuan palace.

Khyentse worked for the highest
lamas of the Karma Kagyu, carefully
painting portraits of their lamas both
living and dead. Khyentse's art was not
only greatly admired by the leading
Karma Kagyu lamas of his time—
including the influential Fifth Shamar—
but also highly esteemed by some of
the most discriminating lamas from that
school in later generations. For instance,
about two-and-a-half centuries after
Khyentse's time, the highly discerning
painter and patron Situ Panchen (1700–
1774)—the subject of my *Patron and
Painter* catalog in this series—visited
Gongkar Dorjeden and described his
experience in an autobiography. He was

extremely impressed with Khyentse
Chenmo's paintings and sculptures,
saying they were "suitable for being
copied" (*dper 'os pa*), one of the highest
praises a patron and artist like Situ could
give. After briefly describing some
of the main things to see at Gongkar
Dorjeden, Situ Panchen summed up his
impressions of its sacred art:

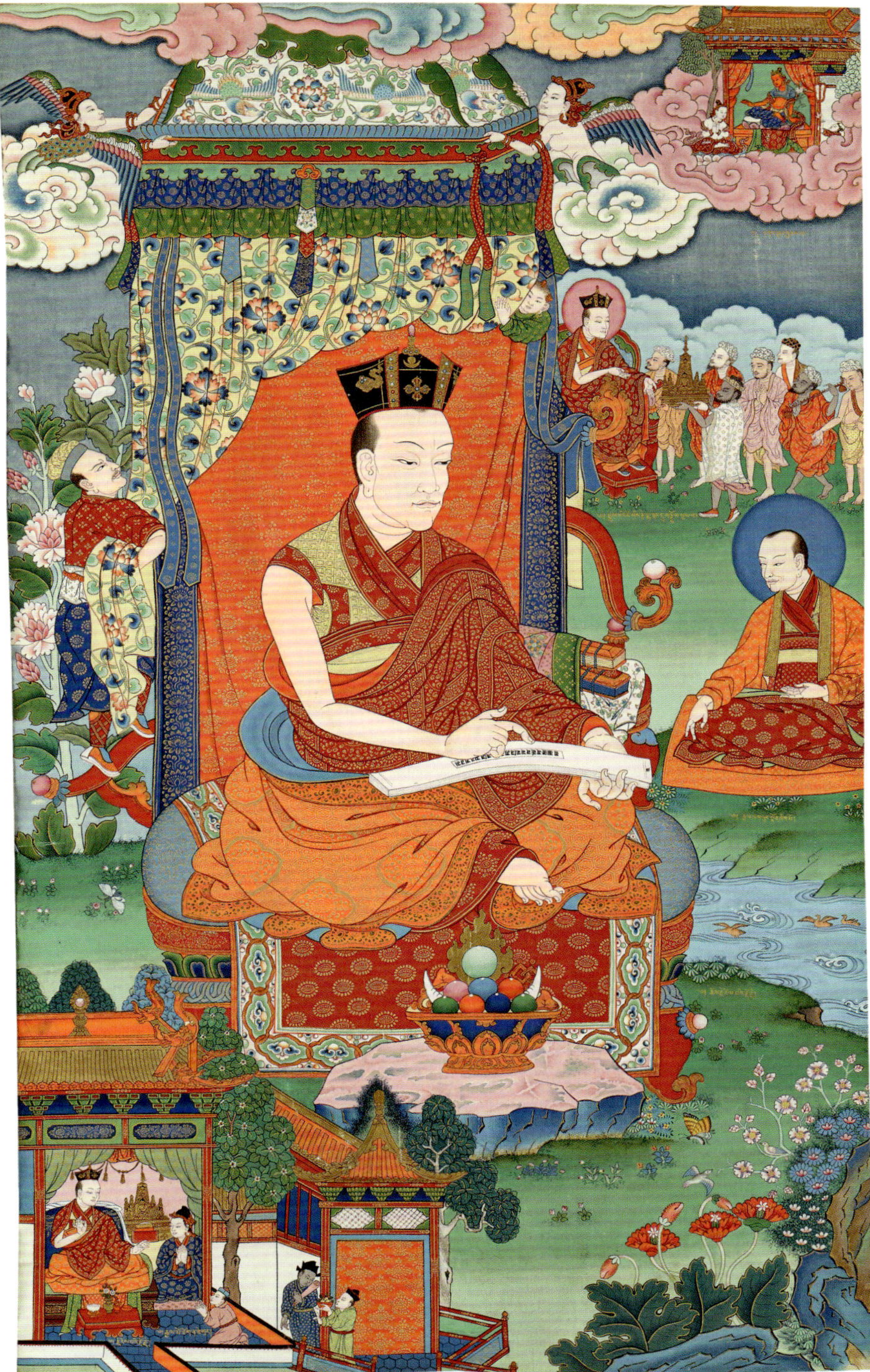

In brief, there were many sacred objects to see and they were well arranged. And since all the paintings and sculptures were works of Khyentsewa himself, their outstanding features of art were worthy of being taken as objects for copying. When I first visited Gongkar they looked down on me as a Khampa beggar (*a jo ba*) and they abused me very impolitely, not allowing me to see anything . . . [7]

What saved Situ from being turned away at Gongkar was his lucky meeting of an acquaintance, a certain Sokpö Chöje (Sog po'i Chos rje) Dale Huthukthu (Da las kho thug tu), who was then going to serve as abbot of Champa Ling Monastery. [68]

7. Special Features of Khyentse's Painting Style

I previously believed that Khyentse Chenmo's painting style incorporated Chinese influences to a lesser extent than the Menri (sMan ris) had.[69] Following the opinion expressed in minor writings of the Thirteenth Karmapa, I wrongly deduced from those statements that the Khyenri was more conservative, that is, less Chinese influenced, than the Menri.[70]

Khyentse was obviously enthused and captivated by Chinese landscape paintings and became completely fluent in Chinese styles. As a young artist, he must have avidly studied and copied the best Chinese examples he could find, and later in his career, after internalizing many features, he must have reproduced many of the brilliant new effects in thangkas and murals. In some respects he became a more radical stylistic rebel than Menthangpa.

One of the defining features of the painting style developed by Khyentse was its use of strongly Chinese elements, not only in its depictions of the background landscapes but also in certain other details, such as the treatment of head nimbuses. Giuseppe Tucci, the first and only Western scholar to visit Gongkar in the 1950s, described murals by Khyentse:

I saw the assembly hall, where statues of the Buddhas of the Three Times were surrounded by the eight Bodhisattvas; and the circumambulation corridor with good frescoes of the Lord Buddha's life showing a marked Chinese influence. On the walls right and left of the cell were painted the Lamas of the Sakyapa sect and the main events of their lives: dignified but spirited and lively pictures, free from the hieratic stiffness that too often burdens Tibetan art.[71]

Another striking feature was the naturalism of the paintings and sculptures. Though Tucci did not directly remark on this, he may be alluding to it when he speaks of the murals as "dignified but spirited and lively." Regarding Khyentse's sculptures, he said they were extremely expressive. After seeing Khyentse's sculptures at Gongkar in the 1940s, he remarked: "A statue of Dorje Jiche in the Gönkhang, the most expressive I ever saw in Tibet, came close to frightening me out of my wits."[72]

Khyentse had reached such a level of technical virtuosity as both a sculptor and painter that virtually anything was possible. His naturalistic depiction of birds and animals that he copied from Chinese arhat paintings was distinctive in Tibetan art. He often showed birds in pairs, as positioned together or as one flying toward the other. He often showed the mythical animals typically seen on the Buddha's throne back in unusually naturalistic ways. The other great Tibetan artist known for his careful depiction of birds and animals in arhat landscapes was the Tenth Karmapa (1604-1674).[73] He, too, followed Chinese models, yet he never depicted Khyentse's favorite bird, parrots.

Minor human and divine figures in the landscape were often depicted in lifelike postures and from various angles. He adopted minor human figures from the landscapes of arhat paintings, including certain favorite ones that he showed in profile, wearing white turbans. He often placed decorative silk canopies floating in the sky above the head of the main buddha or saint.

One way that he made a strongly Chinese stylistic statement was to depict a lama's head nimbus as a simple, thin ring of gold, with a faint haze of pink coloring the field within, or to not paint any nimbus at all. He seemed to love pastel colors, using them more often than his predecessors did, such as in clouds and nimbuses. But he would avoid any element if it became boring and repetitive.

By introducing his strikingly beautiful Chinese landscape models, he was the main forerunner of the Karma Gardri style in certain important respects. For art historians, he had been a proto-Gardri artist; for years, his paintings were considered Sino-Tibetan or Eastern Tibetan. Now we know they were Khyentse Chenmo breaking new ground.

8. Murals that Khyentse Chenmo Painted

The mural paintings for which Khyentse Chenmo was best known were painted from 1464 to 1476 and survive at Gongkar Dorjeden Monastery, near his birthplace; they will be described in more detail in chapter 4. The other murals he is known to have painted in Ü province, none of which survives, include the above-mentioned Yangpachen Monastery. Nearby in Lhokha, east of Gongkar, was the capital of Tibet, a likely source of highly discerning patronage. He painted murals from 1473 to 1474 in the great stūpa of Dra Champa Ling (Grwa Byams

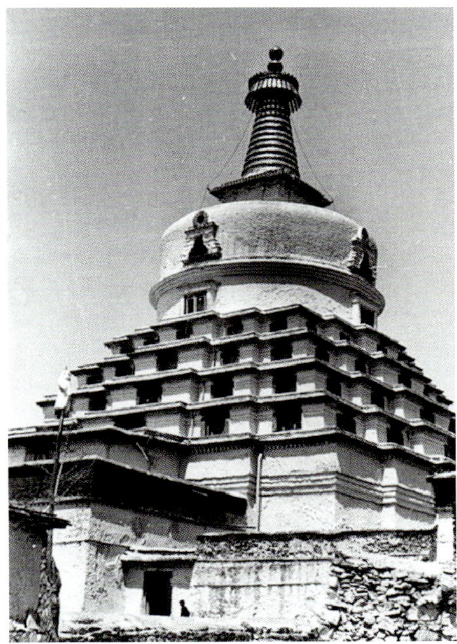

The Great Stupa of Champaling
Photo by Ernst Krause, Schäfer Tibet
Expedition, 1938/39.
Literature: Henss 2014, fig. 538

pa Gling), in a nearby valley to the south
of the Brahmaputra (gTsang po) River.
Some murals of that huge structure,
which was begun in 1472 by Champa
Lingpa Sönam Namgyal (Byams pa gling
pa bSod nams rnam rgyal, 1400–1475)
and finished by Lotsāwa Sönam Gyatsho (Lo tsā ba bSod nams rgya mtsho,
1424–1482), were attributed to Khyentse Chenmo.[74] In the summer of 1474,
Lotsāwa Sönam Gyatsho supervised the
completion of the murals, "covering them
with a protective liquid."[75] The stupa was
ruined in the 1960s. (See Figure 1.22,
which shows the exterior of the Champaling stupa.)

Figure 1.23 depicts Gongkarwa's
clearly labeled guru Champalingpa, to
the left, wearing a golden pandit hat with
tucked-in earflaps. It is a detail of Figure
7.39, which depicts Gongkar Dorjedenpa
as the central figure, probably as a lineage guru of the Lamdre instructions.
Gongkarwa's other main guru, Drakthok
Chöje, is shown to the right.

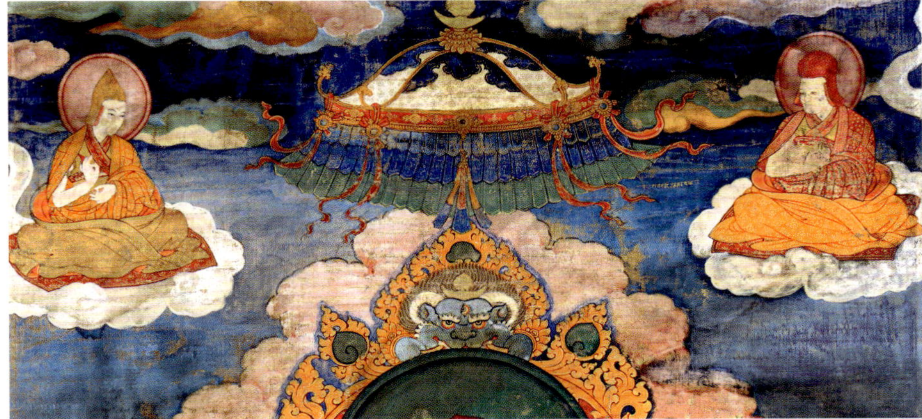

9. Main Disciples and Early Followers of Khyenri Style

Khyentse's principal disciple was his
nephew and main assistant, whose
personal name has not been transmitted in any source. Gyatön Changchup
Wangyal referred to him in the passage
that mentions "Khyentse, uncle and
nephew."[76] One of Khyentse's most
prominent followers in the next few generations was a great-nephew, who was
mentioned in the writings of Drukchen
Pema Karpo ('Brug chen Padma dkar
po, 1527–1592). That lama, according to
the colophon to his treatise on the classification of sacred images, stated that
he composed the work at the request of
the Khyentse Önpo Tshewang Kunkhyen
(mKhyen brtse dBon po Tshe dbang
Kun mkhyen), among others.[77] Perhaps
the same nephew of Khyentse (*mkhyen
brtse'i dbon po*) from Gongkar Dorjeden
was the one mentioned in Pema Karpo's
autobiography, who came to him to clarify his doubts about certain tantric passages; Pema Karpo fulfilled his wishes
by resolving those doubts.[78]

About 1576, Ngakchang Kunga
Rinchen (1517–1584), the twenty-fourth
throne-holder of Sakya, invited Gongkar
Trulku Jinpa Namgyal (Gong dkar sPrul
sku sByin pa rNam rgyal) to be the main
artist when commissioning an image of
Mahākāla at Sakya. He followed in Khyentse's tradition and was an exceptional
artist (*sprul sku*) of Gongkar, but it is
unknown if he was related to Khyentse.[79]

Panchen Champalingpa (detail)
ca. eighteenth century
26 x 17 ½ in. (66.0 x 44. 5 cm)
Rubin Museum of Art
C2002.14.1 (HAR 65097)

One of the writings of Kongtrül
seems to assert that Gongkar Khyentse
also wrote a manual on religious art
or iconometry; such a work is otherwise unknown.[80] Perhaps later tradition
ascribed to Khyentse a treatise composed
by a subsequent follower of the Khyenri
tradition. For instance, one such manual
is attributed to a later artist from Gongkar,
named Shenyen Namgyal (bShes gnyen
rnam rgyal), who no doubt followed
Khyentse's artistic tradition in Gongkar.
This work was an incomplete treatise on
iconometry (*tshad yig thor bu*).[81]

10. Main Surviving Sites of Later Khyenri-Style Murals

In chapter 3 of this book, Pemba
Wangdu lists several sites of Khyenri
murals, furnishing photos of three of
them. (See Figs. 3.17–3.23.) To list nine
sites:

1. Yamdrok Taklung (circa sixteenth
   century)[82]
2. Jonang Takten Phüntshokling (first
   half of the seventeenth century)
   (See Figs. 3.17–3.18.)

3. Drepung Tshokchen (second half
of the seventeenth century) (See
Figs. 3.19–3.21.)
4. Gongkar Kunzang Tse College
(early twentieth century) (See, for
instance, Figs. 5.16–5.17 and
5.19–5.24.)
6. Drathang Monastery (early
twentieth century) (See Figs.
5.25–5.26.)
7. Gyantse (19th century) (See Figs.
3.22–3.23.)
8. Sakya
9. Mindröling

Khyenri Painters Outside Central Tibet

The Khyenri style is not known to have spread outside of Ü province. Still, it is certain that sets of Khyenri paintings circulated more broadly. Some reached Ngari in Drikung and Drukpa monasteries.[83] I suspect some important thangka sets may also have been brought to Drukpa Kagyu monasteries in Kham. Some major Khyenri sets must have gone to Bhutan and Ngari (Ladakh).

In 2003, however, I was surprised when a Tibetan colleague—the central Tibetan Menri (E pa) painting authority, Tenpa Rabten (bsTan pa rab brtan) of Lhasa University, who is now retired—suggested that Amdo traditions of painting might derive from both the Menri (sMan ris) and Khyenri. He believed the Khyenri style might have come to Amdo during the life of Jamyang Shepa ('Jam dbyangs bzhad pa), who—when returning in the 1720s to his home province of Amdo and founding his monastic seat, Labrang Tashi Khyil (Bla brang bKra shis 'khyil)—brought with him a master painter from central Tibet, an artist from Dechen Sangngak Khar (bDe chen gSang sngags mKhar). This master is presumed to have worked in a later Khyenri style, just as some of the Fifth Dalai Lama's main painters from Sangngak Khar in Gongkar a few generations

earlier painted in that style. Another recent source asserts that Nyentok Monastery in Rebgong (or Rebkong) town of Amdo province preserves a temple containing late-seventeenth-century murals in a mixed Menri and Khyenri style.[84] Except for these references, no other evidence exists that Khyenri traditions reached Kham or Amdo in the form of painters who went there to work. But it is certain that some compositions by Khyentse Chenmo reached Kham and were copied by painters there. (See Fig. 2.15.)

Gyatön's Description of Khyentse

One of the main original sources on Khyentse Chenmo's life and career was Gongkarwa's biography. Tsechang Penba Wangdu noticed this telling passage about Khyentse in Kunga Namgyal's biography by Gyatön Changchup Wangyal:

> Moreover, in order that the noble venerable one [i.e., Dorjedenpa] could achieve a vast wave of service to the Buddha's Doctrine, thanks to a part of the lord's own wisdom appearing in the form of an artist (*rig byed*), [there was] the miraculously emanated great being Khyentsewa, whose fingers could produce all the Buddha's mandalas in their entirety as if they were actually present. Called lay follower Nampar Gyalwa, uncle and nephew, the uncle wrote a eulogy of Gongkarwa entitled "Wonderful Vine" (*Ngo mtshar 'khri shing*). [85]

Thus Gyatön Changchup Wangyal in his mention of Khyentse "uncle and nephew," adds that the former, that is, Khyentse Chenmo, had written a eulogy of Gongkarwa. There still exists a work with the same abbreviated title, *rJe btsun rdo rje gdan pa'i rnam thar mdor bsdus ngo mtshar gyi khri shing*, which

is enumerated in the Drepung Catalog (*'Bras spungs dkar chag*).[86] Though that work was at first noted as a brief biography of Gongkarwa of unknown authorship, it is evidently *not* the eulogy written by Khyentse Chenmo.

Tsechang Penba Wangdu quotes another passage from Gongkarwa's life by Gyatön that refers to Khyentse's knowing and mastering four national artistic styles of sculpture: Indian, Chinese, Nepalese, and Tibetan.[87] The passage refers to a group of sculptures depicting eight bodhisattvas that originally stood near the main buddha of the inner sanctum, beginning with Maitreya, Avalokiteśvara, and Vajrapāṇi. As he described Khyentse Chenmo's work:

> The bodily forms of the Eight Great Bodhisattvas agreed in their posture, dress, ornaments, and rosaries with the separate traditions of the expert artists of India, China, Nepal, and Tibet, leaving each style distinct and without mixing them up.[88]

In this section I introduce Gongkar Dorjeden Monastery and its Thekchen Chöje traditions of religion and art. After sketching the life of its founder, Gongkarwa Kunga Namgyal, I shall describe the place of his Buddhist tradition within the Dzongpa sub-school of the Sakya. I shall also explore the Lamdre silk thangkas of the Thekchen tradition that once existed at Serdokjen Monastery. After sketching the career of Thekchen Chöje, I shall investigate his surviving portraits and also related silk thangka paintings connected with Khyentse Chenmo.

GONGKAR DORJEDEN MONASTERY

The main site of Khyentse Chenmo's surviving mural paintings in Tibet is Gongkar Monastery. Called Gongkar Chöde (Gong dkar Chos sde) or Gongkar Dorjeden (Gong dkar rDo rje gDan) in Tibetan, the monastery stands in the Gongkar district of central Tibet, south of Lhasa, not far from Lhasa Gongkar Airport.

Gongkar Monastery was founded by the eminent Sakya master Dorjedenpa Kunga Namgyal (1432–1496), who performed the site-blessing rituals for this monastery in 1464. It took him, as the main patron, twelve years to build the structure and complete the sacred art in its interior, including sculptures and murals. The monastery became the main seat of a subsect of the Sakya school that

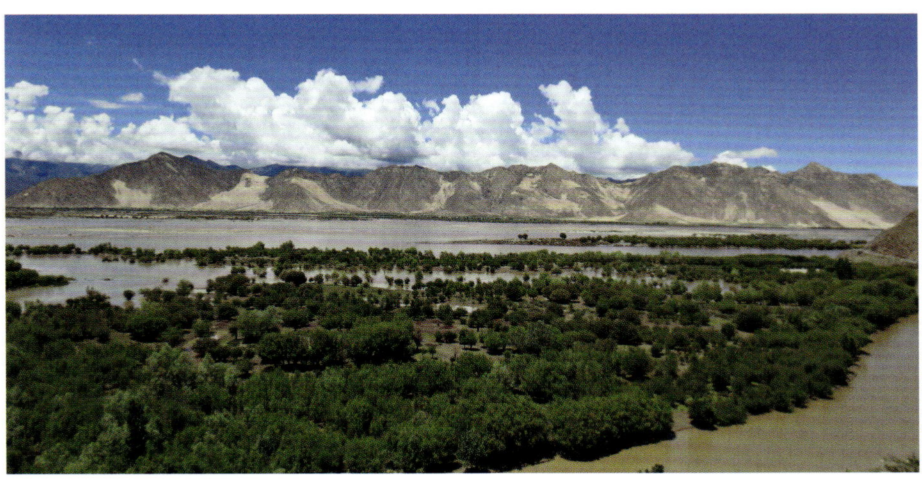

Fig. 1.24
Brahmaputra River near Gongkar
Photo: Jampel Shedrub, 2014

Fig. 1.25
Gongkar Monastery in winter
Photo: Jampel Shedrub, March 2014

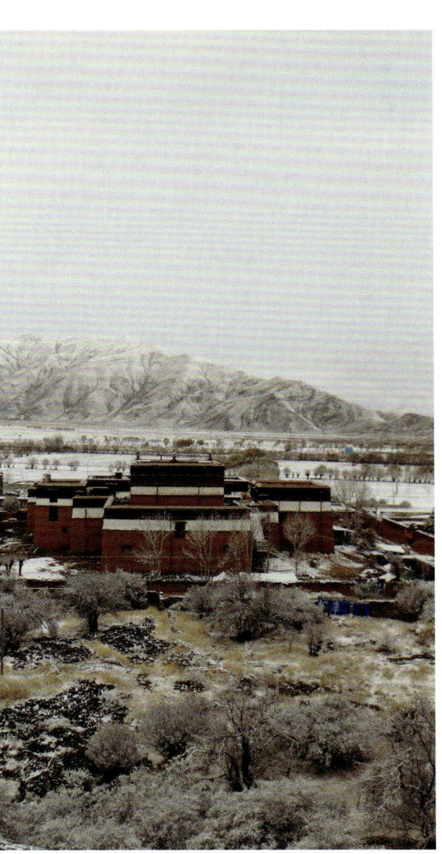

he founded, which was famed for its tantric ritual practice and for its distinctive tradition of Lamdre practice and art. In it, many glorious paintings and sculptures by the artist Khyentse Chenmo once existed. This monastery is still the best location to see what survives of his art.

THE LIFE OF GONGKARWA

Gongkar Dorjedenpa Kunga Namgyal (or Gongkarwa) was an important Buddhist master of the Sakya school and

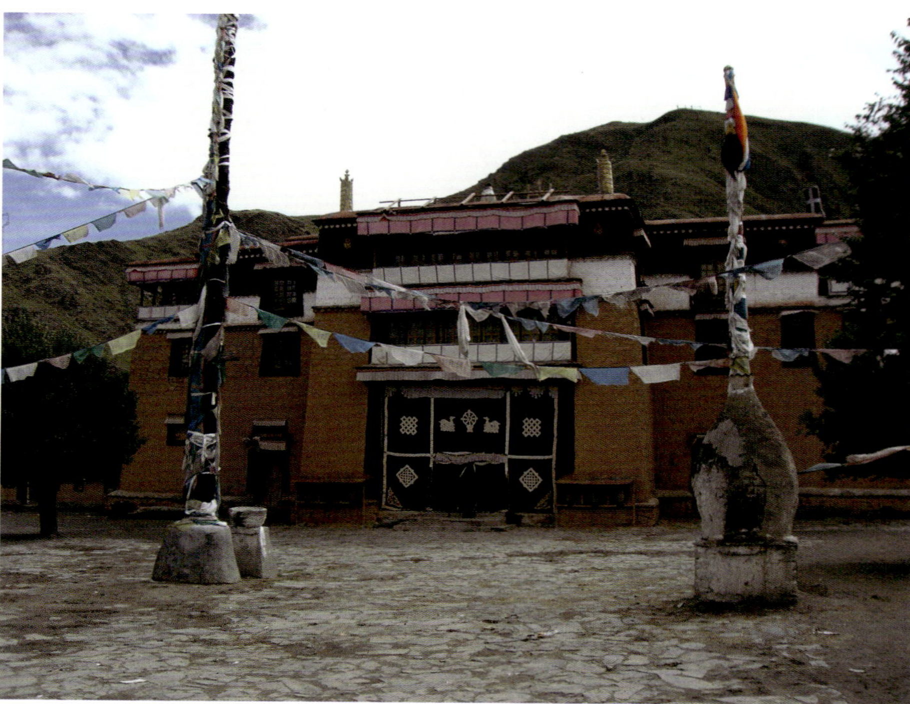

was about one generation younger than Khyentse Chenmo.[89] He was the son of Gyalwa Sherab (rGyal ba shes rab) of the Yargyap noble family. His grandfather, Gongkar Shidzom (Gong dkar bZhi 'dzom) or Inak Shidzom (I nag bZhi 'dzom), had been a minister to the Phagmotrupa ruler Trakpa Gyaltshen (1388–1440), and was one of the most powerful men of central Tibet in the 1420s. His mother, Palden Dorje Dema (dPal ldan rdo rje bde ma, d. ca. 1490), was also a very influential person.

Gongkarwa was born in 1432 at Gyalchenling (rGyal chen gling) in Yoru Dra (g.Yo ru Grwa). Since lamas recited the *Pañcarakṣā Dhāraṇī* (*gZungs grwa lnga*) scripture as a supportive religious ceremony immediately following his birth, he was given the unusual name Dranga Gyalpo ("King of *Pañcarakṣā*," Grwa lnga rGyal po). He was not only born into high nobility but also considered by his family to be the main heir to its political position, and his mother was determined that he become a great ruler

in the secular sphere. However, already as a teenager he felt inclined toward a more spiritual life. He was taught to read and write and educated by several treatises of politics and aphorisms of worldly wisdom, but he also secretly read Buddhist scriptures.

It seems that his father died fairly young, which must have put more pressure upon Gongkarwa to quickly assume high political positions. At the age of twelve, he was taken by his mother to the Phagmotrupa court, where the ruler Trakpa Jungne appointed him ruler (Pönchen) of Yargyap. At age fourteen (1446), he was appointed lord of the Gongkar fortress and district governor (Gongkar dzongpön). At his mother's insistence, he married as a teenager and fathered heirs, but he still felt the call of the religious life. At that time, he lived as a tantric practitioner and was known by the name Jigme Pawo. At age nineteen, he greatly desired to take monastic vows from the Sakya master Drakthok Chöje Sönam Sangpo, but his mother objected.

Finally in 1458, at the age of twenty-six, he was allowed to take novice ordination from Champalingpa Sönam Nampar Gyalwa (1401–1475), a lama with whom his family had both

religious and familial links. It was only then that he received the name Kunga Namgyal. Gongkarwa's three main religious teachers were: Drakthok Chöje, from whom he received the Lamdre and other important transmissions; Champalingpa, from whom he received not just ordination but also tantric teachings, such as on the Kālacakra, and instruction on the traditional fields of knowledge; and Sharchen Yeshe Gyatsho (1404–1473), a lama of Shalu Monastery, from whom he received the Yogatantra teachings in the tradition of Butön. Gongkarwa did not receive full monastic ordination until he was forty-two (1474), that is, ten years after beginning to build his monastery and two years before he finished it.

Coming to the monkhood late and through his particular route, Kunga Namgyal might have been a less doctrinaire and more flexible patron of religious art than many more conservative monks. He had only been a monk for four years when he began his monastery. I estimate that he was ten or fifteen years younger than Khyentse, so he would have been amazed by Khyentse's abilities as a master artist in his forties. The willingness of his mother and brother to sponsor many works of art would have been another important factor in the patronage of the monastery. That Khyentse found such generous patrons as Kunga Namgyal and his family was a great boon to him.

Dzongpa and Gongkarwa Lineages

Gongkar Dorjeden Monastery was the seat of a subsect of the Sakya school called the Gongkarwa. With only twenty-seven branch monasteries and temples, it was the smallest subsect of the Sakya tradition, evidently too small to be mentioned in the usual list of three subschools.[90] As the historian Cyrus Stearns wrote about the Sakya tradition in the *Encyclopedia of Buddhism*:

> Several important subdivisions
> later developed within the Sa skya
> tradition. Two of these are most
> significant: the Ngor pa (Ngorpa)
> sub-sect established by Ngor chen
> Kun dga' bzang po (Ngorchen
> Kunga Zangpo, 1382–1456) and
> the Tsharpa (Tshar pa) sub-sect fol-
> lowing the teachings of Tshar chen
> Blo gsal rgya mtsho (Tsarchen
> Losel Gyatso, 1502–1566). It is
> customary to refer to the Sa skya,
> Ngor pa, and Tshar pa traditions
> when discussing the entire range of
> the Sa skya school.[91]

However, the Gongkarwa or Later
Dzongpa should be added as a fourth
sub-school. In southern central Tibet, it
was a significant presence, and numerous important pre-1959 sources do mention the Gongkarwa school as a distinct
tradition.[92] The common recent division
of the Sakya school into the triad of
Sakya, Ngorpa, and Tsharpa may reflect
the fact that the Gongkarwa tradition
was not prominently represented until
recently, in Indian exile.

Thus Gongkar Monastery represented a small and rare tradition
within the Sakya school. Near Gongkar
in Lhokha, some Sakya monasteries
belonged to the Nalendrapa tradition,
the largest subschool of the Tsharpa, and
some belonged to another Tsharpa subsect. In general, in Ü province, branches
of the Ngorpa tradition were rare, and the
only branch of the Sakya mother monastery that I know of nearby was Samye
Monastery, where Sakya appointed its
tratshang abbot and two other monastic
officials for indefinite tenures.[93]

Main Colleges

Gongkar Monastery originally had four
colleges (*grwa tshang*) as its main internal divisions, each with its own head

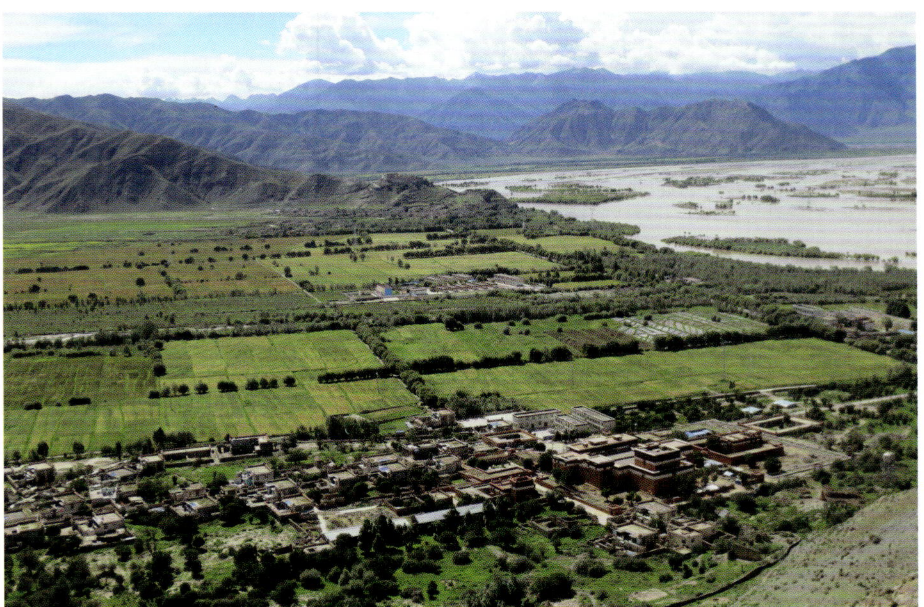

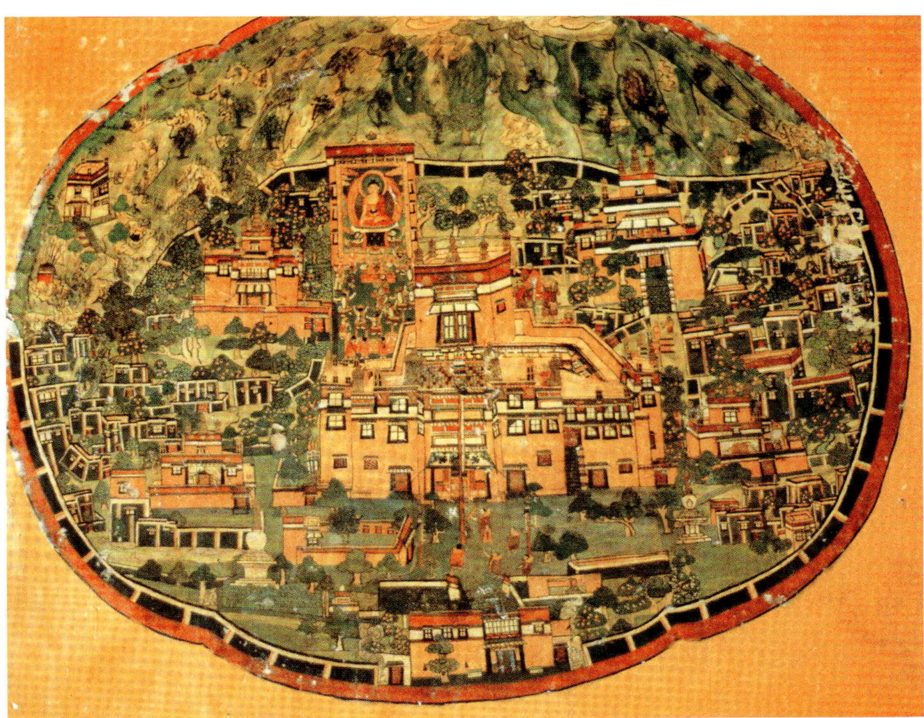

lama. I was told in 1986 that the colleges
were named: Kunzang Tse (Kun bzang
rtse), Rinchen Gang (Rin chen sgang),
Kunthang (Kun thang), and Drepung
('Bras spungs).[94] The buildings of Kunthang and Rinchen Gang were leveled
during the Cultural Revolution in the
1960s and never rebuilt. The buildings
of the colleges Drepung (to the south)
and Kunzang Tse (to the north) survived
until the 1980s with very damaged
interiors, but some pre-1959 murals survived in both.

Fig. 1.27a
Gongkar Monastic Complex in summer,
with fertile fields nearby
Photo: Jampel Shedrup, 2014

Fig. 1.27b
Gongkar Monastic Complex
Mural by Yeshe Tendzin, Gongkar
Monastery, 1930s
Photo: D. Jackson, 1986

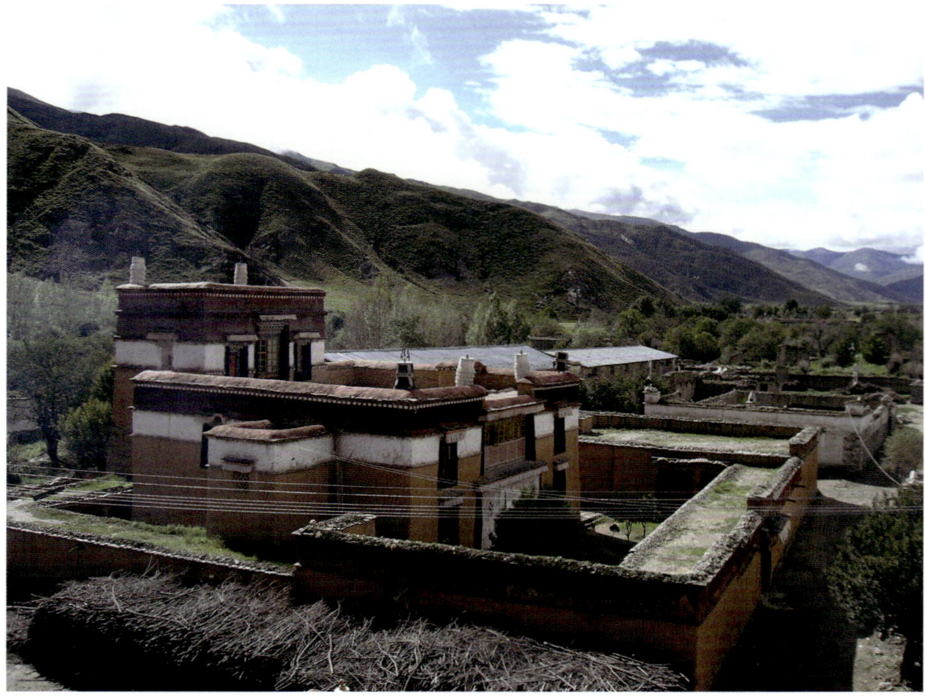

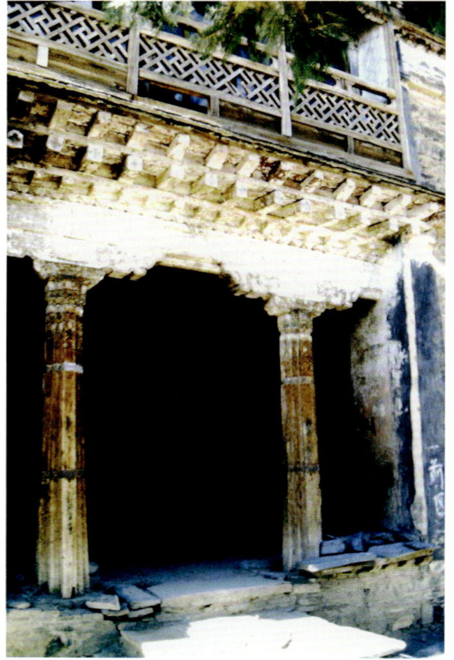

The Gongkarwa Lamdre Lineage of Thekchen Chöje

The Gongkarwa or Later Dzongpa school possessed a distinctive Thekchen tradition (*theg chen lugs*) of the Lamdre ("Path with the Result" or "Path with the Fruit") instructions. Its founder, Gongkar Dorjedenpa, had received that tradition from Drakthok Chöje, a direct disciple of Thekchen Chökyi Gyalpo. According to Kunga Namgyal's record of teachings received, he was number 23 in the main lineage, and his lineal guru Thekchen Chöje (1349–1425) was number 21, two lineage generations earlier:[95]

1. Vajradhara (rGyal ba Khyab bdag rDo rje 'chang)
2. Nairātmyā (dPal ye shes kyi mkha' gro bDag med ma)
3. Virūpa (mThu stobs kyi dbang phyug mGon po Shri Bi ru pa)
4. Kṛṣṇapāda (Shar phyogs Nag po pa)
5. Ḍamarupa
6. Awadhutipa
7. Paṇchen Gayadhara
8. Drokmi Lotsāwa (sGra sgyur Bla chen 'Brog)
9. Setön Kunrik (Se ston Kun rig)
10. Shang Gönpawa (Zhang dGon pa ba)
11. Sachen (Sa skya pa Chen po)
12. Sönam Tsemo (rJe btsun rTse mo)
13. Drakpa Gyaltshen (Grags pa rgyal mtshan)
14. Sakya Paṇḍita (gNas lnga yongs su rdzogs pa'i Paṇ chen)
15. Chögyal Phakpa ('Gro mgon Chos kyi rgyal po)
16. Shang Könchok Pal (Zhang dKon mchog dpal)
17. Namsa Drakphukpa (Nam bza' Brag phug pa)
18. Lama Dampa Sönam Gyaltshen (dPal ldan Bla ma Dam pa bSod nams rgyal mtshan)

Fig. 1.28
Drepung College, seen from the main monastic building
Photo: J. Heimbel, 2007

Fig. 1.29
Still-damaged entrance to Kunzang Tse College
Photo: D. Jackson, 1986

Fig. 1.30
Gongkar monastic courtyard with numerous lay pilgrims
Photo: Lionel Fournier, 2008

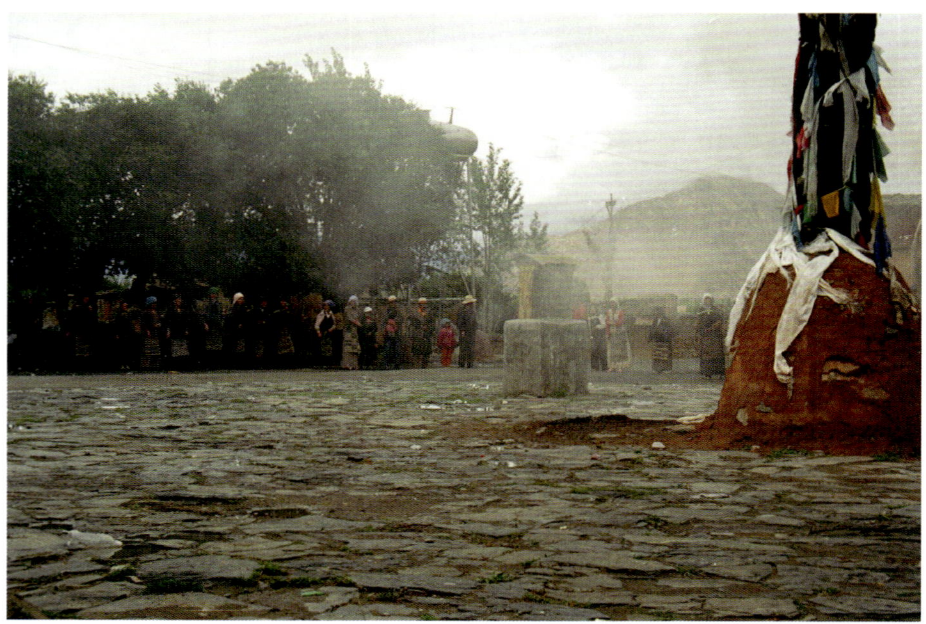

19. Mati Panchen (Ma ti Paṇ chen)
20. Sakya Butön Wangchuk Dar (Sa skya Bu ston dBang phyug dar) [He was also a disciple of 18.]
21. [from both 19 and 20] Thekchen Chökyi Gyalpo (Theg chen Chos kyi rgyal po)
22. Drakthokpa Chöje Sönam Sangpo (Brag thog Chos rje bSod nams bzang po)
23. [Kunga Namgyal]

This lineage only diverges from the common (Ngorpa and Tsharpa) tradition after number 17, Drakphukpa. Beginning with Lama Dampa, the last six generations of teachers represent the special transmission of number 21, Thekchen Chöje, and his disciples. Figure 1.31 depicts in artistic form the crucial lineal gurus of Drakphukpa and Lama Dampa; it depicts as minor figures the important Lamdre transmitter Sakya Butön Wangchuk Dar, below to the left, and Thekchen Chöje, below to the right.

A Dzongpa Tradition of Ü Province

Nowadays, Kunga Namgyal and his Gongkarwa tradition are also commonly included in the Dzongpa tradition. The classical differentiation of the Dzongpa from the Ngorpa traditions of the Lamdre is a treatise by the Sakya historian Ameshab.[96] Dzongpa is a fairly old term for Kunga Namgyal's Gongkarwa tradition. According to the 2005 edition of Dorjedenpa's record of teachings received, Kunga Namgyal belonged to the Later Dzongpa (*rdzong pa phyi rabs pa*) or Thekchen Chöje tradition (*theg chen lugs*).

Another important authority, the Fifth Dalai Lama, clearly discriminates, in places, the Dzong tradition (*rdzong lugs*) from the Gongkarwa (*gong dkar ba*). What he normally calls the Dzong tradition (*rdzong lugs*) is yet another lineage that goes from Lama Dampa and Zungkyi Palwa (gZungs kyi dPal ba) and passes down through Tsang Müsepa (rTsang Mus srad pa Byams pa rdo rje rgyal mtshan). That lineage was connected with the Dzongpa Labrang of Sakya and can be considered the original or true Dzong tradition of Tsang province that had no connection to Thekchen Chöje or Gongkar Dorjedenpa in Ü province.[97]

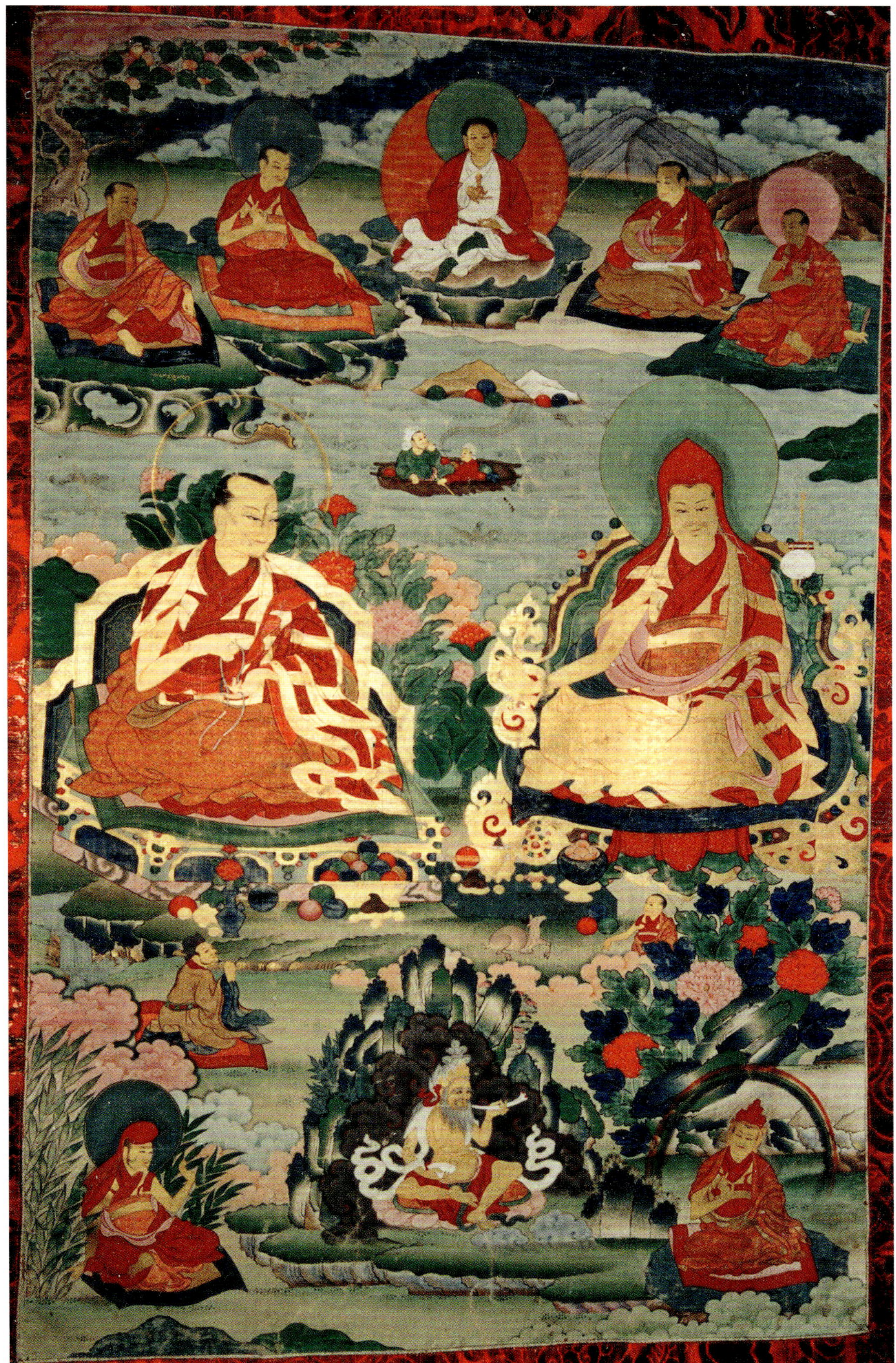

Fig. 1.31
Drakphukpa and Lama Dampa as Lamdre Gurus
34 ½ x 22 ½ in. (87.7 x 57.2 cm)
seventeenth century, originating from Lhokha
Collection of Cyrus Stearns
Photo: Tania Stearns

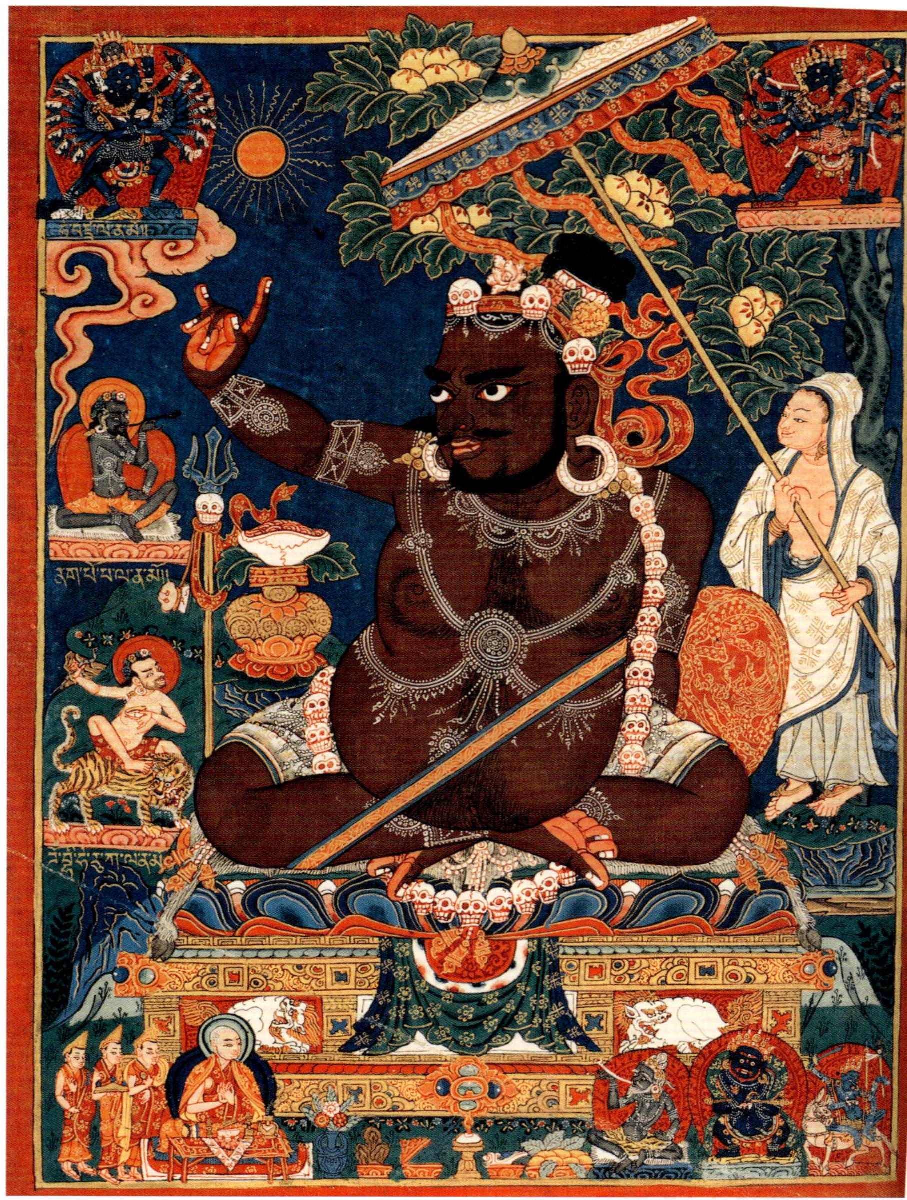

In his record of teachings received (*gsan yig*), the Fifth Dalai Lama quotes or compares Dorjedenpa's *gsan yig* many times. At one point he knowingly includes Gongkarwa's lineage even though, down to Lama Dampa in that lineage, he had actually received the Ngorpa lineage for the teaching in question.[98] The Fifth Dalai Lama calls the Gongkarwa tradition (*Gong dkar ba lugs*) the corresponding lineage of Gongkar Kunga Namgyal, whom he usually calls "Omniscient Dorjedenpa." For one teaching, he documented three lamas who passed it from Lama Dampa to Thekchen Chöje: namely, Kangtröpa (Gangs khrod pa), Mati Panchen, and Sakya Butön.[99]

A Painting from the Other Dzongpa Lineage

A small set of thangkas that may depict a Lamdre lineage of the other, Tsang-based, Dzongpa lineage has been identified. The Virūpa from this set (Fig. 1.32) has been published by Pratapaditya Pal

in *Himalayas: An Aesthetic Adventure*.[100] Elsewhere in that catalog, Amy Heller asserted that the final two masters of the set were Ngorchen and Müchen, the second abbot of Ngor.[101] However, according to Cyrus Stearns, who has seen photographs of several of the paintings, the actual lineage is that of the Tsang-based Dzongpa tradition, not the Gongkar- or Gyama-based Thekchen tradition of Ü province. The exact contents of this set of paintings remains to be clarified through future research. But art historically, the thangka represents the earlier Indic style, the Beri, and is not relevant stylistically to the present study.

Lamdre Silk Thangkas of the Thekchen Tradition at Serdokjen

One of the Tibetan historians who mentioned the existence of Lamdre lineal paintings in an intriguing way was the Mustang-born scholar-adept Jonang Kunga Drölchok (1507–1566), who often discerned fine details of physical culture, including art. In one passage of his biography of Serdok Paṇchen Shākya Chokden (gSer mdog Paṇ chen Shākya mchog ldan, 1428–1507), he briefly refers in passing to a Lamdre *si thang* (*lam 'bras bsi thang*), that is, to a series of paintings depicting the "Path with the Result" lineal masters in the style of Chinese silk paintings (*si thang*).[102] These paintings were given to Shākya Chokden in Ü province by his disciples from Gyama (rGya ma), about thirty miles (fifty kilometers) east of Lhasa and six miles (ten kilometers) south of Metro Gungkar (Mal gro Gung dkar). They depicted a non-Ngorpa lineage, namely that of Thekchen Chöje Kunga Tashi (Theg chen Chos rje Kun dga' bkra shis) of Sakya. In 1506, upon completing a set of sculptures depicting the Lamdre masters of his main Ngor lineage, Shākya Chokden also wanted to have murals of the same lineage masters painted by the outstanding artist Men-thangpa Lhündruppa (Lhun grub pa), but that could not be managed in time. So he had the Chinese-style thangkas hung on the walls behind the sculptures, remarking, "It is good to have both lineages."[103]

Shākya Chokden as a young monk had received the Lamdre instructions in two lineages: the Ngor tradition from Ngorchen and a variety of the so-called Dzongpa tradition. He received, more precisely, the Thekchen tradition from his master, Janglung Rinpoche Shönnu Lotrö (sPyang lung Rin po che gZhon nu blo gros, 1371–1475).[104] That master was a direct disciple of Thekchen Chöje who highly prized his connection, through his teacher, with the five founders of Sakya; for instance, he traced his lineage for Amitāyus from the five founders to Daknyi Chenpo Zangpo Pal (bDag nyid Chen po bZang po dpal), to Chöje Lama Dampa, to Thekchen Chöje, and then to Janglungpa.[105] Janglung Rinpoche often repeated that Daknyi Chenpo Zangpo Pal (the progenitor of the later Sakya Khön) as a youth of eighteen years had received teachings from Phakpa, such as initiations for Hevajra and Mahākāla.[106] (That must have occurred in the year 1280, shortly before Phakpa's death at Sakya.)

From among the two Lamdre instruction lineages he had received, Shākya Chokden as a mature teacher mainly taught the Ngorpa. In his monastic constitution of Serdokjen, he prescribed following the tradition of Rongtön [Rong ston] for sutra—non-tantric, scholastic—studies and the tradition of Ngorchen for tantric studies.[107] He was a direct disciple of Ngorchen, Müchen (Mus chen), and several other great masters who had been active at Ngor in the 1450s.[108] Though Shākya Chokden at the time of his studies under Ngorchen was still only in his early or mid-twenties, Ngorchen urged him to go to Sakya and perform a public scholastic examination (*grwa skor*) there.[109] After its

conclusion, Ngorchen was very pleased with what Shākya Chokden had accomplished and honored him greatly.[110]

Nevertheless, later in Shākya Chokden's life there were occasions when he could not refuse to give the comparatively rare transmission of the Thekchen tradition of the Lamdre instructions, especially when in central Tibet, to successors of his old guru Janglugpa. In 1490, for instance, after participating in the new establishment of the Gyama monastic community (*grwa tshang*), he gave the instructions in the Ngor tradition to an assembly of about three hundred at Langthang (Glang thang) Monastery, in Phenpo, near Nalendra.[111] Simultaneously, to a highly restricted group, including nobles from Gyama and Janglungpa Shönnu Chödrup (gZhon nu chos grub)—called the "Chöding nephew" (Chos sdings dbon po), presumably the nephew or great-nephew of his late guru at Chöding—Shākya Chokden bestowed the full teachings of the Thekchen Chöje tradition. Janglungpa Shönnu Chödrup was later a teacher of Jonang Kunga Drölchok.

In 1496 at Serdokjen Monastery, Shākya Chokden gave the Lamdre instructions in the Ngorpa tradition to the assembly. After completing those teachings, he was requested by Chöje Trangpowa ('Phrang po ba) to give the Thekchen tradition. He first refused, citing the existing rules of the monastic constitution. But since Trangpowa had come all the way from Ü especially for this teaching, and because Chöje Ram-dowa (Rab mdo ba) also insistently petitioned for it, Shākya Chokden relented and secretly gave an abridged and hurried transmission of just the teachings connected with the basic text.[112] The next year, however, in the summer of 1497, Shākya Chokden was in Ü and then gave the Lamdre instructions in the Thekchen tradition to the full assembly at Gyama.[113] This was the year following

Gongkar Kunga Namgyal's death. It may have been on this occasion that he was presented with the Chinese-style paintings of the Lamdre lineage masters (*lam 'bras si thang*) that he hung at Serdokjen Monastery in 1506, shortly before his death.

THE LIFE OF THEKCHEN CHÖJE

Thekchen Chöje Kunga Tashi, according to the *Chronology of Buddhism (bsTan rtsis)* by Mangthö Ludrup (Mang thos Klu sgrub, 1523–1596) was born at Sakya in 1349, thirty-seven years after the birth of his uncle Lama Dampa (Fig. 1.33).[114] He was the grandson of Tishri Kungyal (Ti shri Kun rgyal) of the Lhakhang Labrang (Lha khang Bla brang) and son of Tawen Chögyen (Ta dben Chos rgyan). He took initial ordination from Sazang Mati Panchen and full monastic orders from his uncle Lama Dampa. His other early teachers included Gangtröpa Trakpa Pal (Gangs khrod pa Grags pa dpal) and Jonang Chokle Namgyal (Phyogs las rNam rgyal).

Some Tibetan historians of the Lamdre discussed precisely which lineage Thekchen Chöje had received and whether he had received it in Lama Dampa's lineage. Mangthö Ludrup, for instance, explained:

> His first teacher for the Path with the Result instructions was Sazang Mati Panchen, but since the latter did not possess the unbroken daily practice of the Hevajra *sādhana*, he later received the teachings again from Sakya Butön Wangchuk Dar at Sakya Surkhang (Zur khang). Some said that, in that case, Lama Dampa was not in his lineage.[115]

Mangthö Ludrup then stated the opinion of his teacher Jonang Kunga Drölchok, who was a well-informed historian, that he had received the Lamdre instructions a third time, from Lama Dampa's

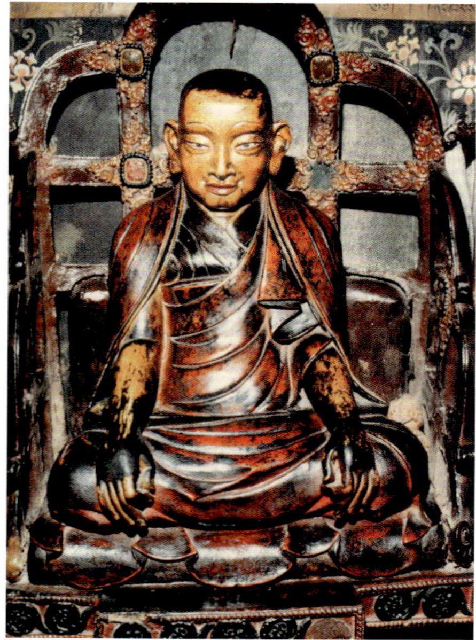

direct student Khenchen Changseng (mKhan chen Byang chub seng ge). But Mangthö Ludrup's great master, Tsharchen Losal Gyatsho (1502–1566), stated that though Thekchen Chöje had received many other profound teachings from Khenchen Changseng, he only received the Lamdre instructions from the first two masters, Sazang Mati and Sakya Butön. According to Cyrus Stearns, Khenchen Kunkhyen Changchup Sengge was the ninth abbot of Jonang, installed in 1381, and was a known disciple of Lama Dampa.

Thus Thekchen Chöje's main lineage for the Lamdre instructions, according to Tsharchen's tradition, was said to be:[116]

> Drakphukpa (Brag phug pa)
> Drakphuk Könchok Gyaltshen
> (Brag phug dKon mchog rgyal mtshan)
> Sakya Butön Wangchuk Dar

(Sakya Bu ston dBang phyug dar)
Thekchen Chöje

By 1410, Thekchen Chöje was the highest-ranking Sakya Khön master of his generation, and he was also highly esteemed by the Chinese Ming court. According to Mangthö Ludrup's account, after receiving an official invitation, he set out from Sakya for China in 1412 (at age sixty-three), and he met the Ming emperor in 1413 in a golden pavilion, bestowing initiations on the emperor and his retinue. It is said that the emperor favored him with the gift of (the whole of) Tibet, like the imperial preceptor Phakpa had been favored; then they went to the Tsa'i-tu capital. The emperor showered him with costly presents, including sculptures of the Buddha surrounded by the eight bodhisattvas of gold and silver, with an ornate Indian Buddhist temple (*gaṇḍola*) roof over them. He was also given two costly sculptures—a figure of Red Yamāri made of red coral and an image of Yamāntaka made of a different expensive material[117]—two thangkas of woven silk brocade (*gse'u thags kyi thang ka*), and two *thogs* (possibly rolls) of *za 'og* golden brocade.[118] In 1414 he departed from the royal court and reached Sakya in 1415.[119]

Figure 1.34 shows the kind of thangka, of woven silk brocade (*se'u thags*), that the Yongle Emperor offered to Thekchen Chöje. There are similar words for two different types of Chinese silk thangkas: *si thang* is painted, and *se'u thang* is made of woven brocade. The word *se'u* is defined in the *Bod rgya tshig mdzod chen mo* as a Chinese loan word meaning "the name of one type of brocade" (*gos chen gyi rigs shig gi ming*). Silk thangkas in general are called *gos thang*.[120] According to Dagyab Rinpoche, the term for a hand-embroidered thangka is *tshem drub ma*, and that for a silk hand-woven thangka is *'thag drub ma*.[121] I explained the term

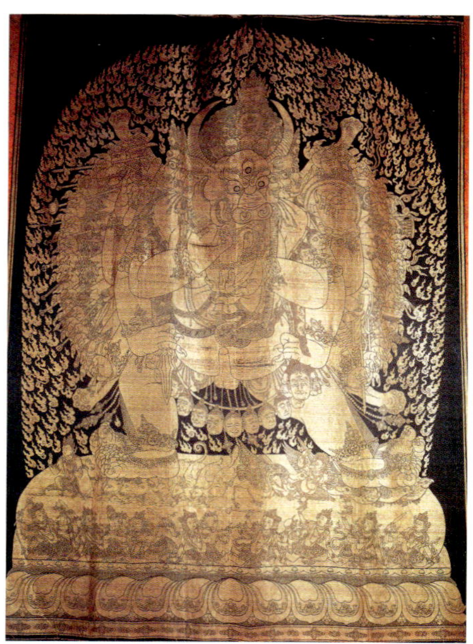

si thang in an earlier publication.[122] Deumar Geshe, in his brief history of Tibetan painting, discusses *si thang* as his first main painting style, using both spellings *zi thang* and *si thang*.[123]

Figure 1.35 depicts Thekchen Chöje as a highly revered transmitter of the Lamdre teachings. This sculpture would have been made in 1425, the year of his death, by people who had seen him or had seen accurate likenesses.

Figure 1.36 is a detail of a later sculpture made by Khyentse Chenmo, who had never seen Thekchen Chöje but attempted to depict his face true to life.

Thekchen Chöje's chief disciple was (Dzongpa) Kunga Gyaltshen, also known as Jamyang Trakpe Pal ('Jam dbyangs grags pa'i dpal, 1378–1442), whose biography is given by Mangthö Ludrup.[124] A more detailed biographical sketch of Thekchen Chöje is given by Ameshab in his *Sakya Genealogical History*.[125]

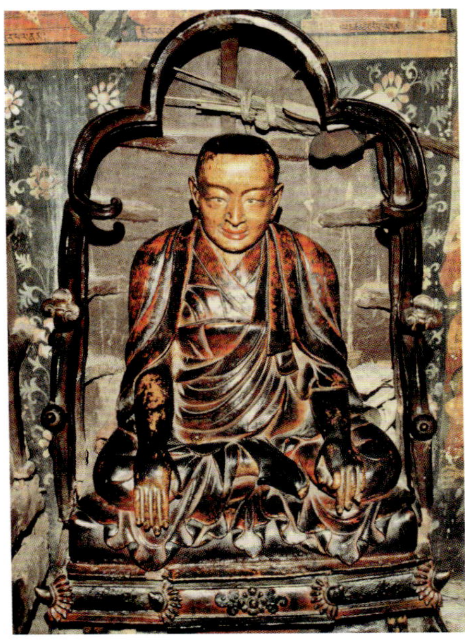

FIG. 1.35
Thekchen Chöje as Lamdre Master
H: 34 ⅝ in. (88 cm)
Gyantse, Lamdre Lhakhang, 1425
After: von Schroeder 2001, *Buddhist Sculptures in Tibet*, vol. 2, no. 204F

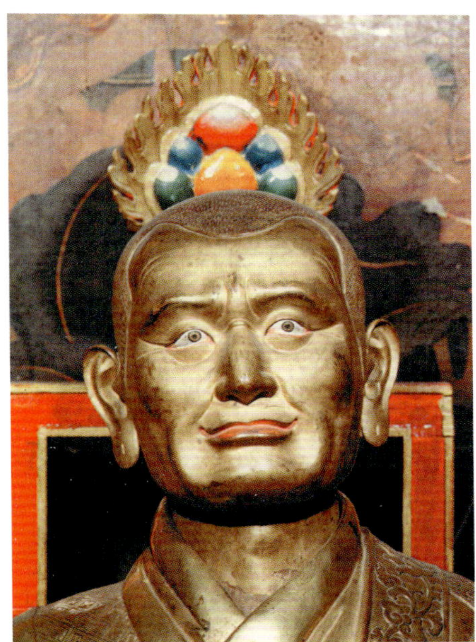

FIG. 1.36
Thekchen Chöje (detail)
Now in Mindröling, second half of the fifteenth century
After: von Schroeder 2001, *Buddhist Sculptures*, vol. 2, no. 241B

One of Thekchen Chöje's great claims to fame was his acceptance of the insistent invitation by the Yongle Emperor—whose generosity was legendary—to visit the Chinese court from 1413 to 1414.[126] The episode could hardly be overlooked by historians of the period. Kapstein, for instance, observed:

The Sakyapa were also beneficiaries of imperial largesse. When [Thekchen Chöje] Kunga Tashi visited the Yongle Emperor in 1413, for example, he was asked to initiate the monarch into the cult of the chief Sakyapa tutelary deity, Hevajra, and was awarded the titles: "Omniscient Gnostic, King of the Mahayana Doctrine, Most Virtuous in the West, All-Embracing Vajra, Buddha of Vast Light."[127]

Kapstein had similarly quoted another passage describing the stunning opulence of the Ming court when receiving a great lama from Tibet, the Fifth Karmapa. The reception of the Karmapa at the court is depicted in Fig. 1.37, in which the Yongle Emperor sits respectfully on a lower throne to the right, and two Chinese temples are in the background.

To welcome him, there were greeters with numberless ornaments, holding in their hands model palaces of silken fabric and of gold and turquoise, as well as parasols, banners, and ensigns—all the accouterments of worship beyond imagination. There was a white elephant, flanked by two more, making three, all caparisoned with trappings of gold. Three hundred other elephants bore various adornments, and the robed *sangha* numbered some 50,000, with flowers and various musical instruments in their hands. Led by the nine princes and their retainers, there were a hundred thousand officers of the court, who were surrounded by 1,200,000 soldiers, some of whom wore armor, some of whom held up canopies, and most of whom were armed with spears, while regiments each of one hundred men held golden mallets, battle axes, tridents, swords, and so on, and some four thousand held emblems of the sun and moon realized in gold, silver, and silken cloth. And then, at the door of the palace, the Emperor himself came to greet him.[128]

As explained by Heather Stoddard in *Early Sino-Tibetan Art,* Thekchen Chöje was one of the three most eminent lamas invited by the Yongle Emperor to the court; each was given a title "king (*rgyal po*) of dharma."[129] To convey the quality of the gifts, Stoddard helpfully published an image of a large embroidered silk thangka and several relevant sculptures.

The two other great lamas with the title "king" who visited the Ming court at this time—the Fifth Karmapa and Shākya Yeshe—received special black hats. Figure 1.38 depicts a Ming-period portrait of Shākya Yeshe wearing such a hat with five evenly spaced gold images of the five buddhas (*jinas*) of the mandala (*rigs lnga*) and a large red-jewel crest. But why do the standard sources never show Thekchen Chöje wearing a similar hat signifying his rank?

Figure 1.39 shows Thekchen Chöje in the only known example where he wears a different special hat, possibly the official hat (*las zhwa*) that he was granted by the Ming emperor. In this detail of a thangka that depicts Drakphukpa and Lama Dampa as Lamdre lineal teachers (see Fig. 1.31), he is shown as a minor figure. He is seated in a rocky landscape, with one hand in the teaching gesture, and surrounded by a halo of

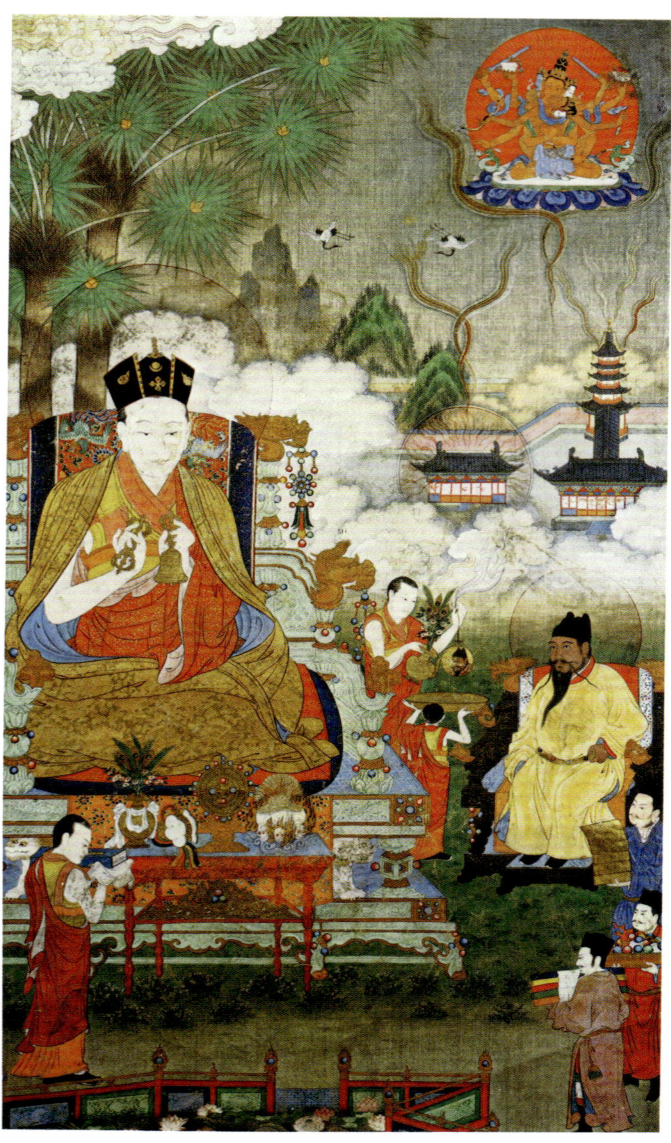

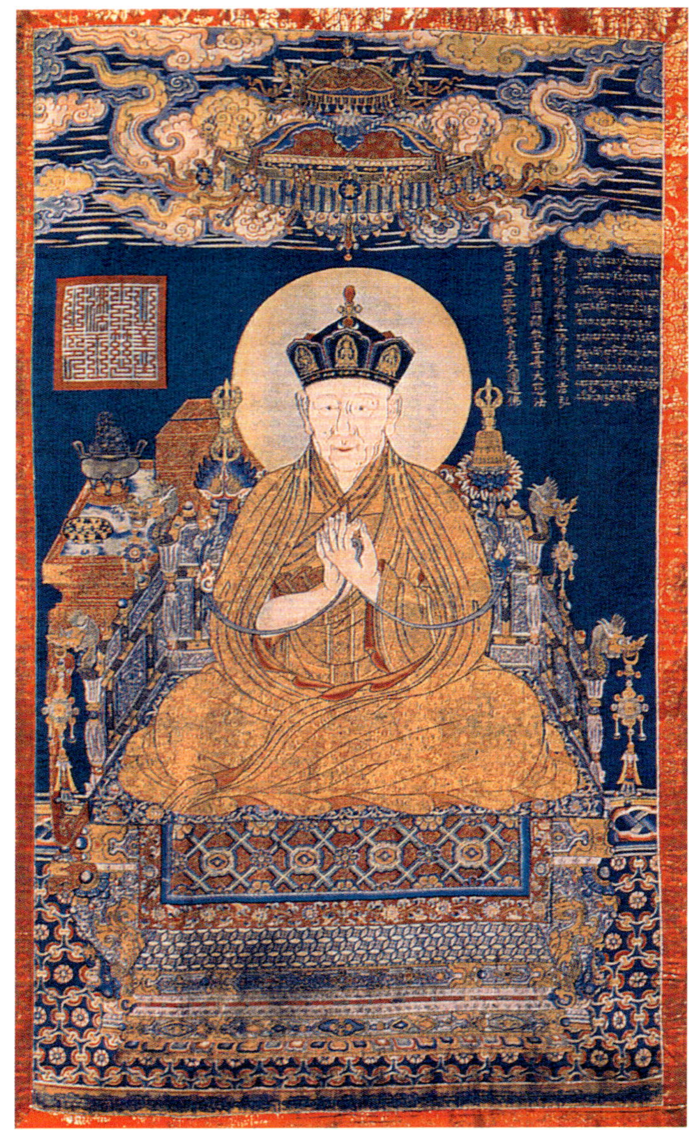

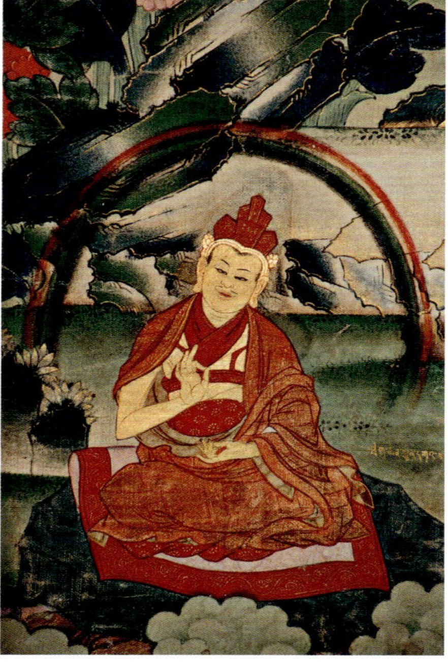

Fig. 1.37
Fifth Karmapa as sixteenth master of the lineage
late seventeenth century
39 ⅜ x 23 ⅝ in. (100 x 60 cm)
Private Collection
Literature: Pal 1984a, pl. 92; and Jackson 2009, fig. 9.16b

Fig. 1.38
Shākya Yeshe wearing a black ceremonial hat
Kesi silk weaving, Xuande period (1430s)
Norbulingka Palace, Lhasa
After: Henss 1997, fig. 15

Fig. 1.39
Thekchen Chöje wearing a special hat
Detail of Fig. 1.31
Collection of Cyrus Stearns

mystical light. His hat looks official and specially made for him, and it is unlike the usual lama hats in shape.

Sources on His Life and Other Connections with Yongle

In addition to the three accessible biographical sketches found in the Sakya family histories (*gdung rabs*) by Taktshang Lotsāwa and Ameshab (A mes zhabs) and the chronology of Buddhism (*bstan rtsis*) by Mangthö Ludrup, a biography of Thekchen Chöje also survives as an independent work. That work was seen by Leonard van der Kuijp in the early 1990s, who referred to two manuscripts of the same biography by Langthang Jennga (Glang thang sPyan snga), entitled *Theg chen chos rje'i rnam par thar pa kun tu bzang po'i rnam 'phrul nye bar mtshon byed ngo mtshar rgya mtsho'i gter*, that he saw in a Beijing library, though he also mentioned six manuscripts containing biographies that he saw but was unable to inspect.[130]

In another publication, Kurtis Schaeffer and Leonard van der Kuijp clarify that the available independent biography was written by a lama with the title Langthang Jennga (Glang thang sPyan snga), who was probably Kunga Gyaltshen Palzangpo (Kun dga' rgyal mtshan dpal bzang po, 1382–1446).[131] This same work was reprinted in 2008 in Nepal by the publisher Sa skya rgyal yongs gsungs rab slob gnyer khang, in one of three volumes of rare Sakya biographies: *Sa skya pa'i bla ma kha shad kyi rnam thar dang*.[132]

Schaeffer and van der Kuijp also mention van der Kuijp's sighting in Beijing: "A significant series of copies of some sixteen spiritual instructions-cum-letters [that] Kun dga' bkra shis, now Theg chen Chos rje, wrote for the Yongle Emperor and his sons between the years 1412 and 1417, as well as a copy of one unpublished edict, is found in

the *Ta'i ming rgyal po yab sras rnams la gdams pa*, of which there is a twenty-folio handwritten *dbu med* manuscript, C. P. N. [Cultural Palace of Nationalities] catalog no. [not given]."[133] Epistle no. 6 mentions "the great prince's son," no. 7 "the heir apparent (*rgyal bu tha'i tshe*) [Ch. *taizi*]" (perhaps the Hongxi Emperor), and no. 8, the layman prince Tenpe Dorje (Bstan pa'i rdo rje).

I found listed only one relevant work from Thekchen Chöje's collected writings. When I checked the relevant passage in the record of teachings of Dorjedenpa Kunga Namgyal (pp. 129–132), it was the penultimate work, entitled "Offered to the Emperor" (*rGyal po la phul ba*). Gongkarwa received the text transmission for these works from Drakthok Paldzinpa (Brag thog dPal 'dzin pa), who had received it from Thekchen Chöje's disciple Tai Gushri Yönten Gyatsho (Ta'i Gu shri Yon tan rgya mtsho).

Schaeffer and van der Kuijp also noted a passage in the history of the Sakya Khön family by Tsangpa Champa (Gtsang pa Byams pa), according to which Thekchen Chöje received patronage from the last Yuan emperor, Togön Temür (d. 1370), namely support for making a golden Kangyur and copies of the collected writings of the five Sakya founders and of Lama Dampa. But they add that this reference to Lama Dampa's collected works may be in error.[134] Togön Temür lost the Yuan throne in 1368, when Thekchen Chöje was just nineteen, but he remained khan of the Mongols until his death in 1370.

The Lamdre Silk Thangkas at Serdokjen: Khyentse Chenmo's Art?

It is well established that the Sakya hierarch Thekchen Chöje had direct contacts with China and its religious art. He was personally invited to the Chinese capital by the Yongle Emperor and in

1413 not only was honored with his title "King of Mahayana Dharma" (Thekchen Chögyal) but also was showered with religious gifts, including imperial commissions of the finest available religious ritual objects and art. When I first read about the existence of Lamdre *si thang* among lamas holding his tradition (such as in the life of Shākya Chokden by Kunga Drölchok), I suspected that the Yongle Emperor gave Thekchen Chöje a set of silk paintings depicting the Lamdre lineage. This would account for the distinctively Chinese styles in such paintings and their presence among the later followers of the Thekchen tradition.

But the actual process was more complex. Khyentse Chenmo, as an apprentice artist after learning the prevailing Indic, Beri style in Gyantse, also came to love and avidly copied Chinese paintings that included excellent landscape details, such as scenes of the life of the Buddha. Through copying and practice, he internalized the style to such an extent that it became second nature to paint in it. The Lamdre portraits that he made in Gongkar likely were a big success, and they would have been noticed and copied by nobles of Ü who were followers of Thekchen Chöje, such as at Gyama. So it seems that Khyentse Chenmo created the set of Lamdre "silk paintings" that Shākya Chokden hung in Serdokjen in 1506.[135]

Possible Examples of *Lamdre Si Thang*

When I first read Kunga Drölchok's reference to silk-thangka guru portraits for the Thekchen tradition of the Lamdre in the late fifteenth century, I had yet to see anything like that. Called "Lamdre silk thangkas*" (lam 'bras si thang)* in the histories, they imply the use of silk and a very Chinese style. In general, silk painting (*si thang*) was a rare genre of painting in central Tibet, almost unknown before Khyentse Chenmo's

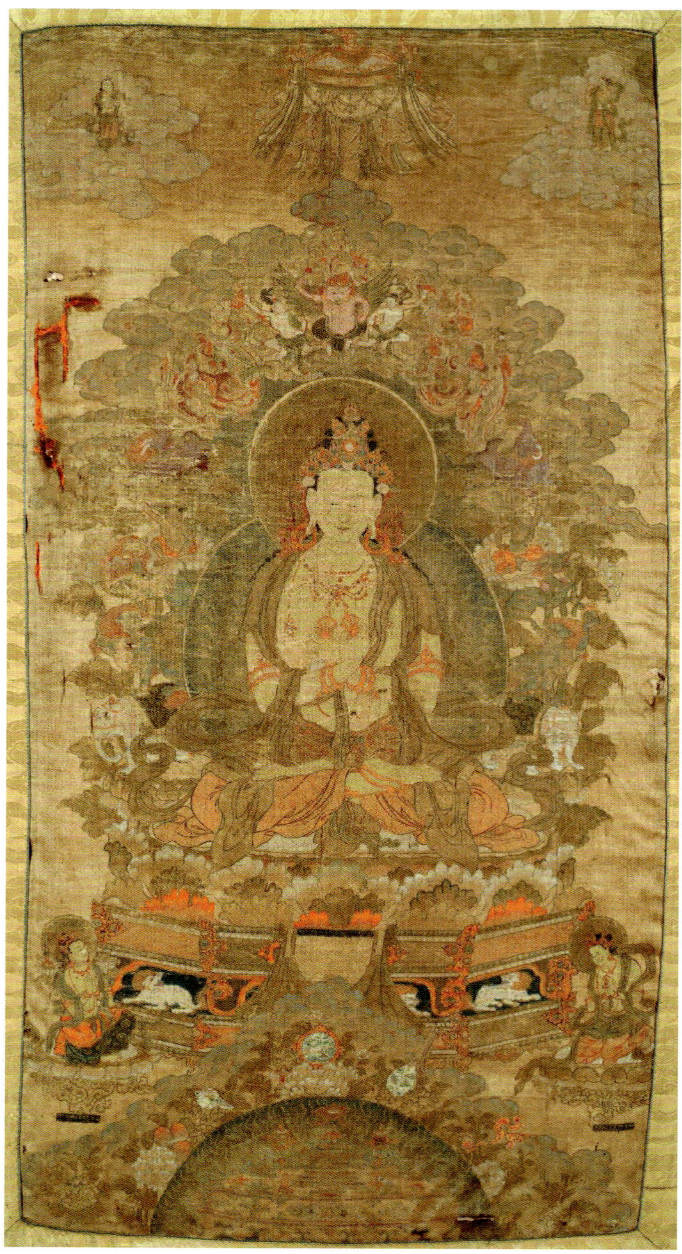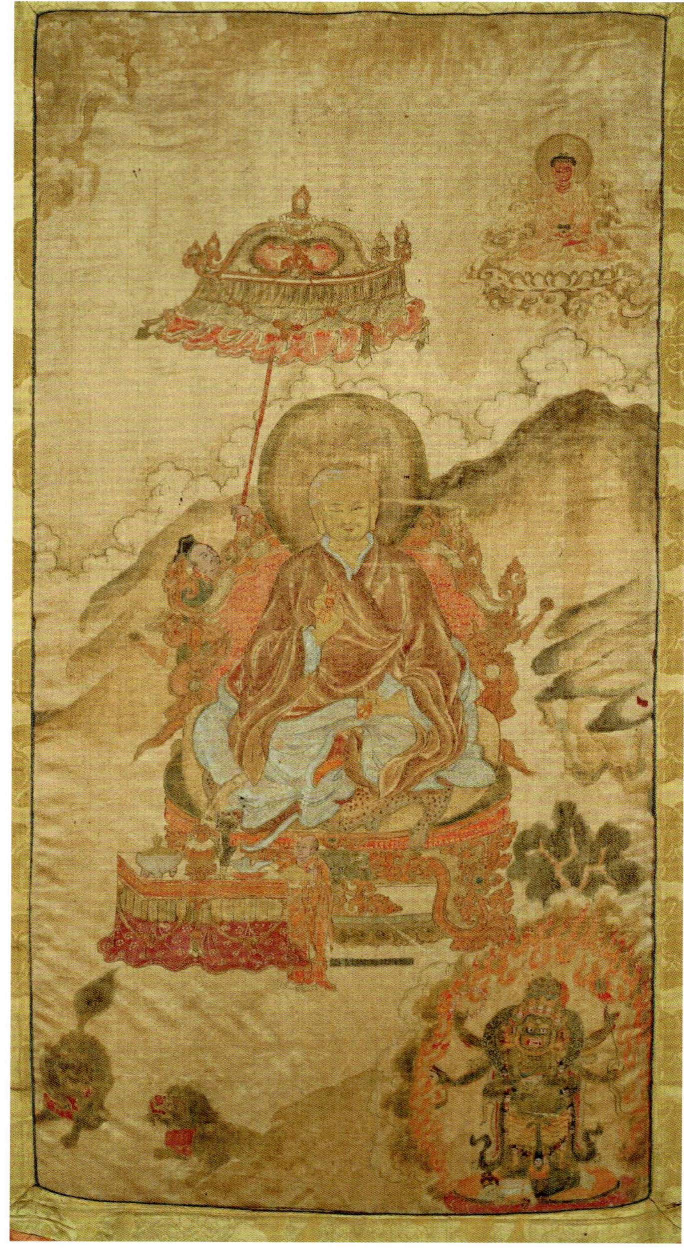

time. I subsequently located a few different sets of thangkas painted on silk, all of which represent uncommon painting types. In the following pages, I will present a few examples that depict the Lamdre lineage, to clarify what the Lamdre *si thang* looked like.

The first two paintings (Figs. 1.40 and 1.41) belong to a very rare set that is clearly both Lamdre and *si thang*. Each painting portrays a single lineal guru as the main figure and a Chinese-style landscape setting that is rendered on a silk background. In harmony with the painting's nature as a *si thang*, the painter avoided the thick coat of

gesso-like primer that paintings on cotton usually received. But he painted the skin of the major and minor figures gold, thus increasing their luminosity.

Figure 1.40 depicts Vajradhara, the primordial Buddha, as the first teacher of the Lamdre tradition. This is the central figure of the set, and the painting has a mainly iconic nature, reinforced by the formally kneeling bodhisattvas at the foot of the throne, evidently Mañjuśrī and Avalokiteśvara.

This depiction of Vajradhara is a standard subject for the Sakya school. But the painter or patron wanted to execute this set on an atypical material—not

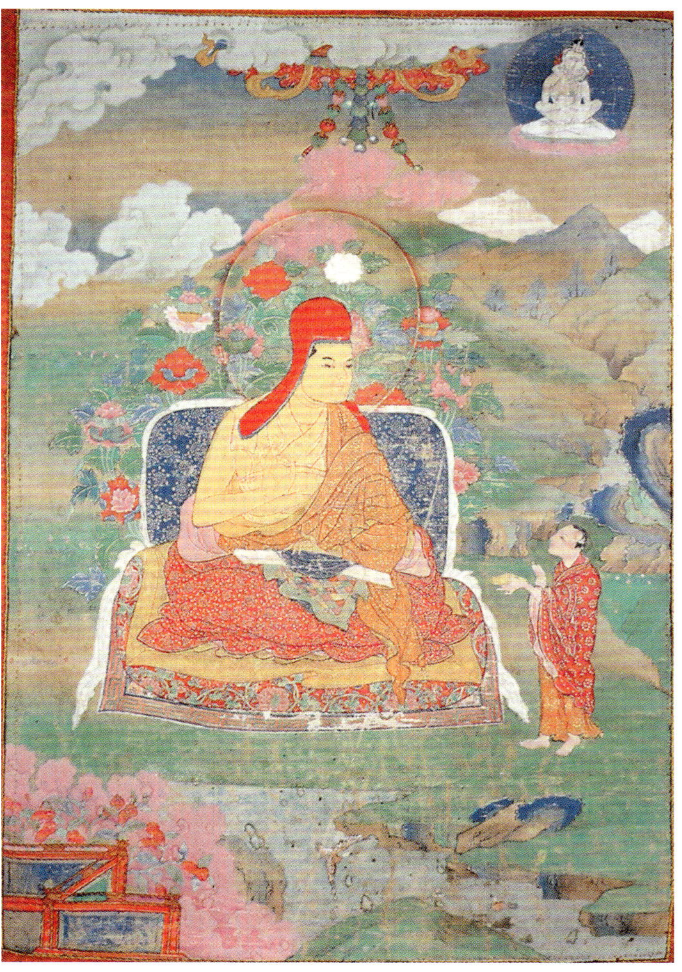 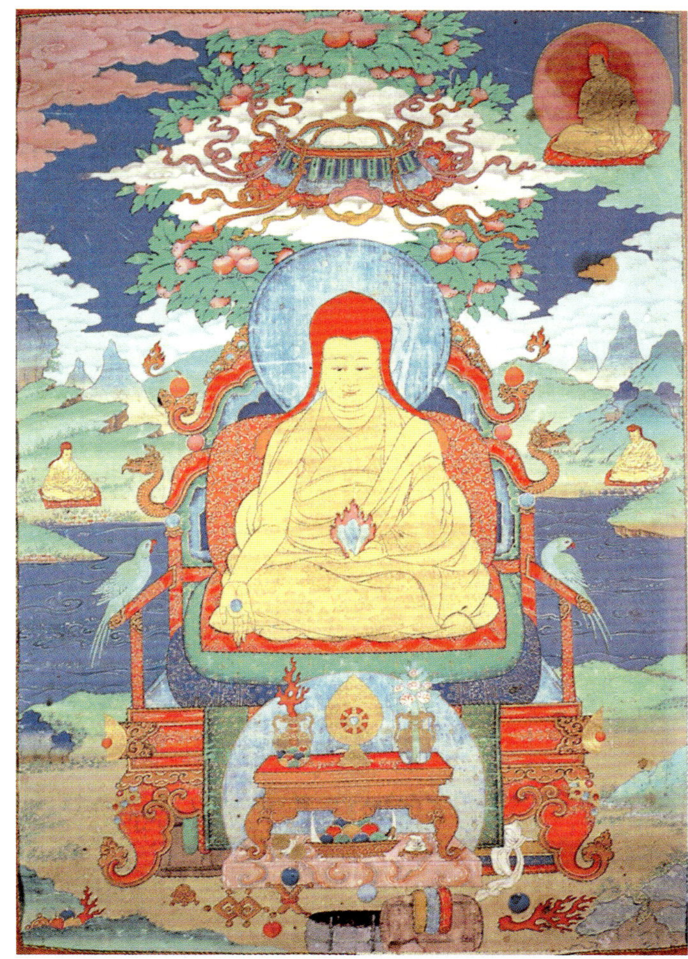

on cotton but on soft, unprimed silk. Similar to Chinese ink painting, the technique allowed only thin washes of ink or colors, except the areas of skin that were painted with gold. Some small areas of opaque white or orange color were also possible. The other opaque areas are the head and body nimbuses of the main figures, but even they were done through washes, just here applied thicker. Through this method and materials, the painting evokes an airy or luminous feeling.

In Figure 1.41, the painter has rendered an entire composition depicting the Lamdre guru Trakpa Gyaltshen on an unprimed creamy-gold background of plain silk. Like in a watercolor painting, all colors except gold have been applied in thin washes. But many parts of the painting received subsequent detailed outlining or fine details of gold. In all, the thangka conveys a light and elegant atmosphere.

These two paintings (Figs. 1.40 and 1.41) can be called Lamdre *si thang*. But they are not likely the kind of paintings that were hung in the temples of major Sakya monasteries. They are elegant and beautiful when viewed up close but are not impressive when viewed from afar.

The Lamdre *si thang* mentioned by Kunga Drölchok in the historical sources probably looked like Chinese paintings on silk, with full-color palettes. They would have been more colorful than the previous two examples (Figs. 1.40 and 1.41). In Figure 1.42, the tones of much of the landscape are still fairly pale but are better suited for public display than those in the true silk paintings above. Its main figure is a learned teacher, indicated by the opened book on his lap and his hand in the teaching gesture. This painting is linkable to Khyentse and his style by the see-through head nimbus of the main figure (a feature we shall explore in detail in chapter 8).

Figure 1.43 is another example of a more colorful type of landscape in late-fifteenth-century Lamdre *si thang* paintings.[136] The painting features brighter *si thang* colors and includes a background landscape with large areas of dark-blue skies and water. From the main figure's central placement and his iconography, it seems that this is the central painting of a set. (Several thangkas from the same set will be presented in chapter 7.) It probably depicts an eminent lama of Khyentse Chenmo's time. If the Lamdre tradition is being depicted, the main figure is possibly Gongkarwa Kunga Namgyal, suggested by the figure's *panzhu* (a hat of the Sakya pandit) and his youthful face. In that case, the figure in the upper right would be his Lamdre guru, Drakthok Chöje, and the two figures in the landscape in the middle of the painting may be the same guru, mediating in rocky settings.

Note the pair of green parrots perched on either side of the armrests of the main figure's throne. Such perfect bird depictions are a hallmark of Khyentse Chenmo's art. These green parrots might be meant to depict vernal hanging parrots (Loriculus vernalis) that are found in India, Nepal, and southeast Asia.[137] (As Khyentse's favorite bird they may have a special symbolic significance for him as artist, because of their powers of imitation.)

As mentioned above in connection with Figure 1.14, parrots are an established bird in both Chinese and Tibetan painting. Figure 1.44 shows parrots as typically depicted in China, illustrating two different poses: flapping its wings on the ground and flying.[138] Though not as important as some birds in Chinese art such as phoenixes or cranes, they were still a standard motif.[139]

Figure 1.45 illustrates seven drawings of parrots as shown in a modern book of Tibetan painting motifs.[140] This source depicts the birds in different sizes and poses at the top of a whole page devoted to "various birds," and dedicates the next page to examples of aquatic birds, including cranes. The earliest occurrence of a parrot in Tibetan painting that I know of was in a painting by Sakya Paṇḍita on the walls of Samye; there a two-headed parrot symbolizes

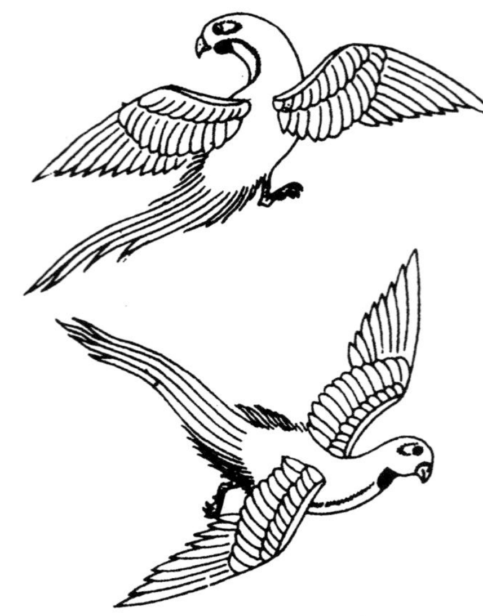

FIG. 1.44
Two Chinese parrots
After W. Eberhard 1990, p. 225.

FIG. 1.45
Tibetan drawings of parrots
After Khreng Hra'o-khrun et al. 2008, p. 51.

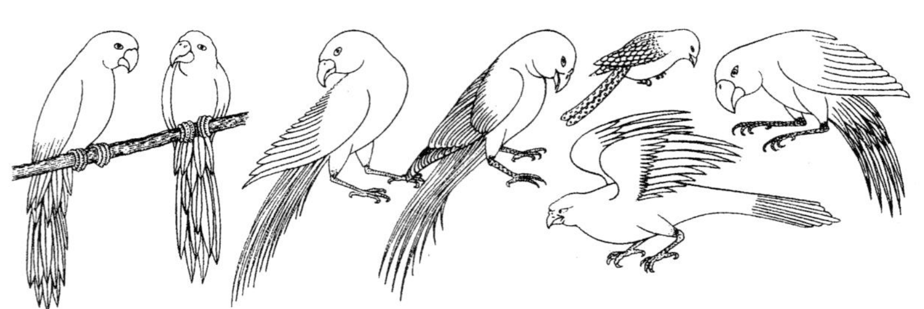

one of the great early translators of Tibet.[141]

Figure 1.46 presents a completely different type of silk painting. Rendered with dyes on a large piece of patterned damask, the elaborate centers of the lotus petals in this unusual thangka indicate a close link to Khyentse Chenmo's style. (See also Figs. 1.47, 9.2, and 9.3.) The painting mostly follows the models of Indic art, but the deities atop clusters of clouds to the upper right and left, pouring divine libations from vases, seem more Chinese. On the right margin near the bottom, Khyentse Chenmo may have added a special signature by painting a naturalistic, tiny, pitch-black bull as the protector's vehicle.

Though not recognized as such, Figure 1.47 was one of the first thangkas by Khyentse Chenmo or a close follower to be published in the West. It depicts Amitāyus surrounded by a constellation of deities in an orderly geometrical arrangement, without any landscape in the background. It illustrates well both the painter's special elaborate lotus petals (compare Fig. 9.2), on the main figure's throne, and his love of pastel colors. (I present it as a foretaste of what we shall see in chapter 4; compare Fig. 4.28 in Gongkar.) But even when using these colors in regularly placed columns, Khyentse maximizes through alternation the variety of colors of the body nimbuses and the contrasts between them.

Figure 1.48 is a depiction of Amitābha.[142] Through the dense field of repeated buddha figures, numerous peaked pagoda roofs can be seen. The muted colors are also unique; Khyentse usually employs brighter pastel colors such as pink, green, and blue (as in Fig. 1.47). But clearly he wanted to achieve a precise yet subtle and elegant effect. The painting exemplifies Khyentse

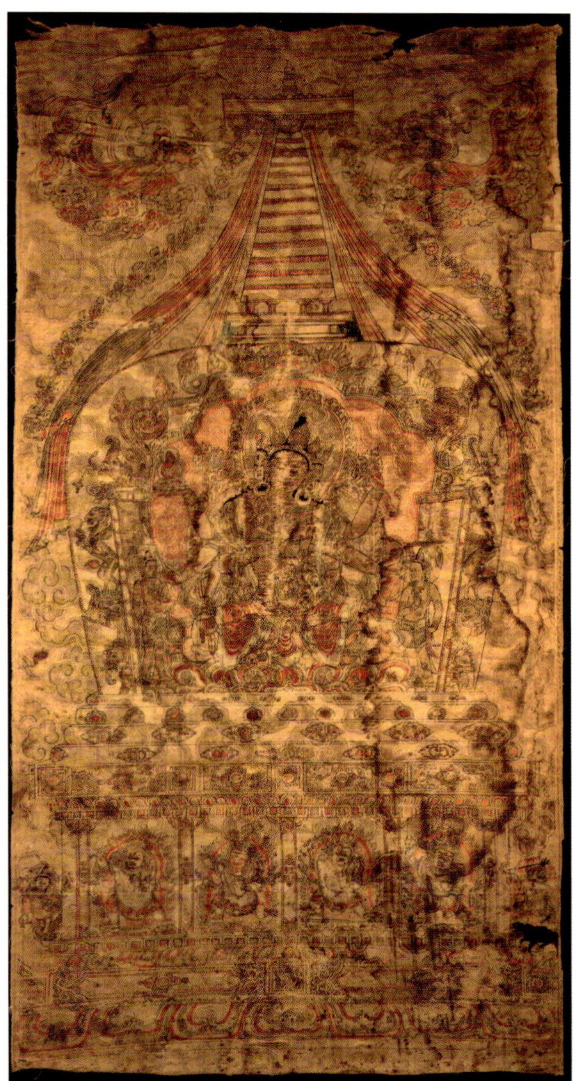

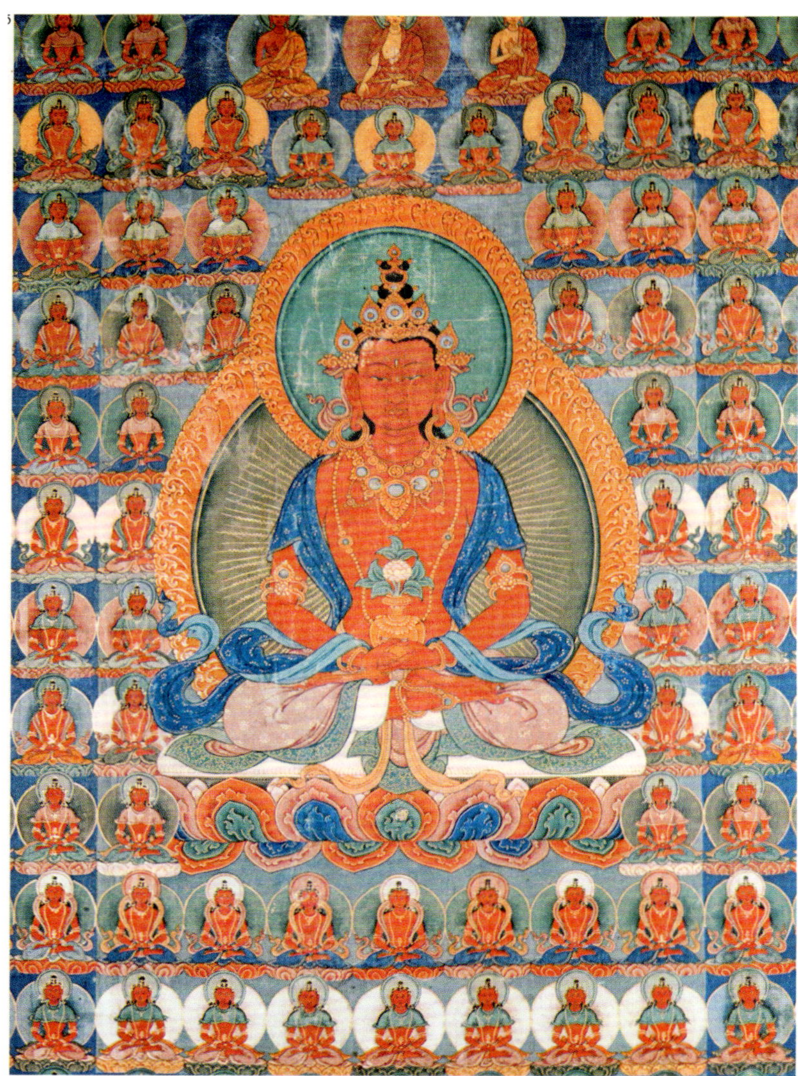

Fig. 1.46
Uṣṇīṣavijayā
Dyes and washes on silk (patterned damask)
second half of the fifteenth century
47 ⅝ x 25 in. (121 x 63.5 cm)
Private Collection

Fig. 1.47
Amitāyus
second half of the fifteenth century
Private Collection
Literature: Lauf 1976, no. 45; and Jackson
1996, figs. 78 and 79

Chenmo's artistic range. Few others could have painted such an understated yet impressive masterpiece.

An excellent painting of a white Tārā-like goddess holding a white vase (Fig. 1.49) can be linked to Khyentse Chenmo; he painted a pair of lifelike green parrots, nearly hidden in the tree at the upper left, almost as a kind of signature. To the left of the main figure is a striking pair of tigers, one with its tail wrapped around a thick tree trunk. Khyentse painted the beneficent central goddess and her surroundings very beautifully, but the threateningly dark wall of jungle trees that frame her is puzzling. (Two other paintings of goddesses in the same series survive in Boston.)[143]

Khyentse Chenmo's art will reveal many more surprises in the following chapters. He has been one of the most difficult artists to classify in terms of stylistic categories but is one of the most impressive virtuosos I have come across, from any time or any country.

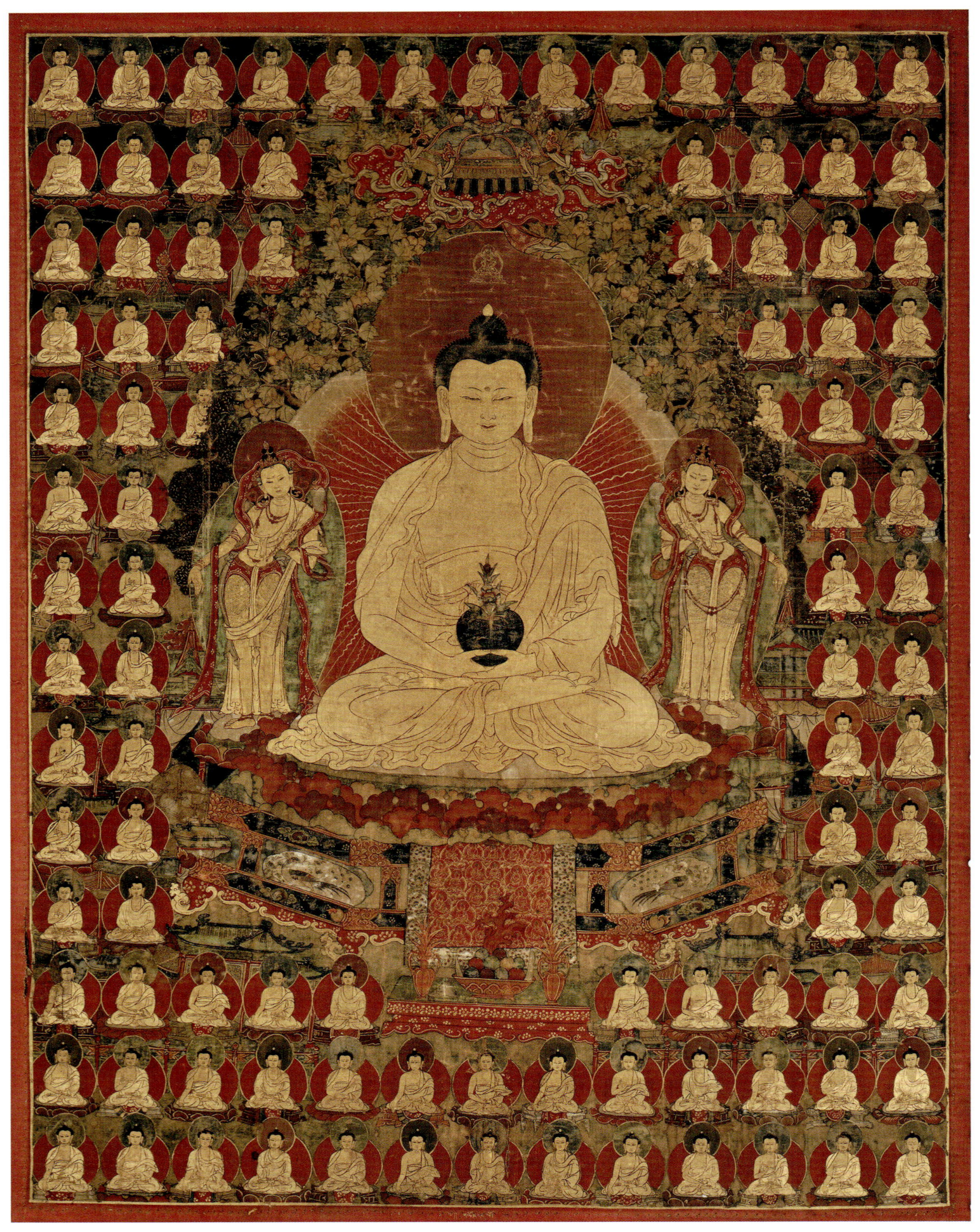

Fig. 1.48
Amitābha
second half of the fifteenth century
25 3/16 x 20 1/16 in. (64.0 x 51.0 cm)
Museum of Fine Arts, Boston (acc. no.
67.848), Gift of John Goelet (HAR 87235)
Literature: Toganoo 1986, no. III 2-3

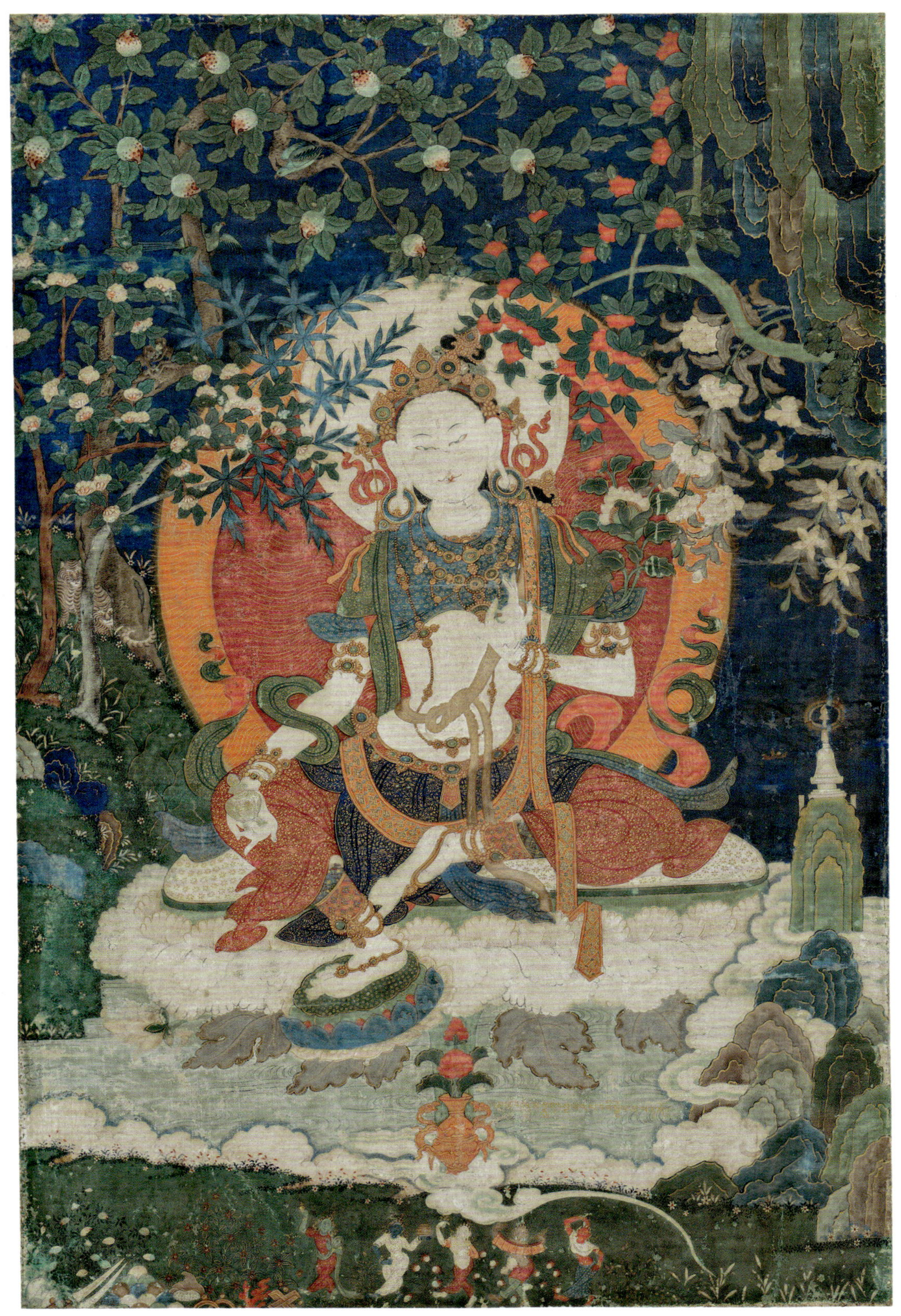

Fig. 1.49
White Goddess
second half of the fifteenth century
26 ⅜ x 17 ⅞ in. (67 x 45.5 cm)
Museum of Fine Arts, Boston (acc. no.
06.322), Ross Collection
Literature: Toganoo 1986, no. III 5-2

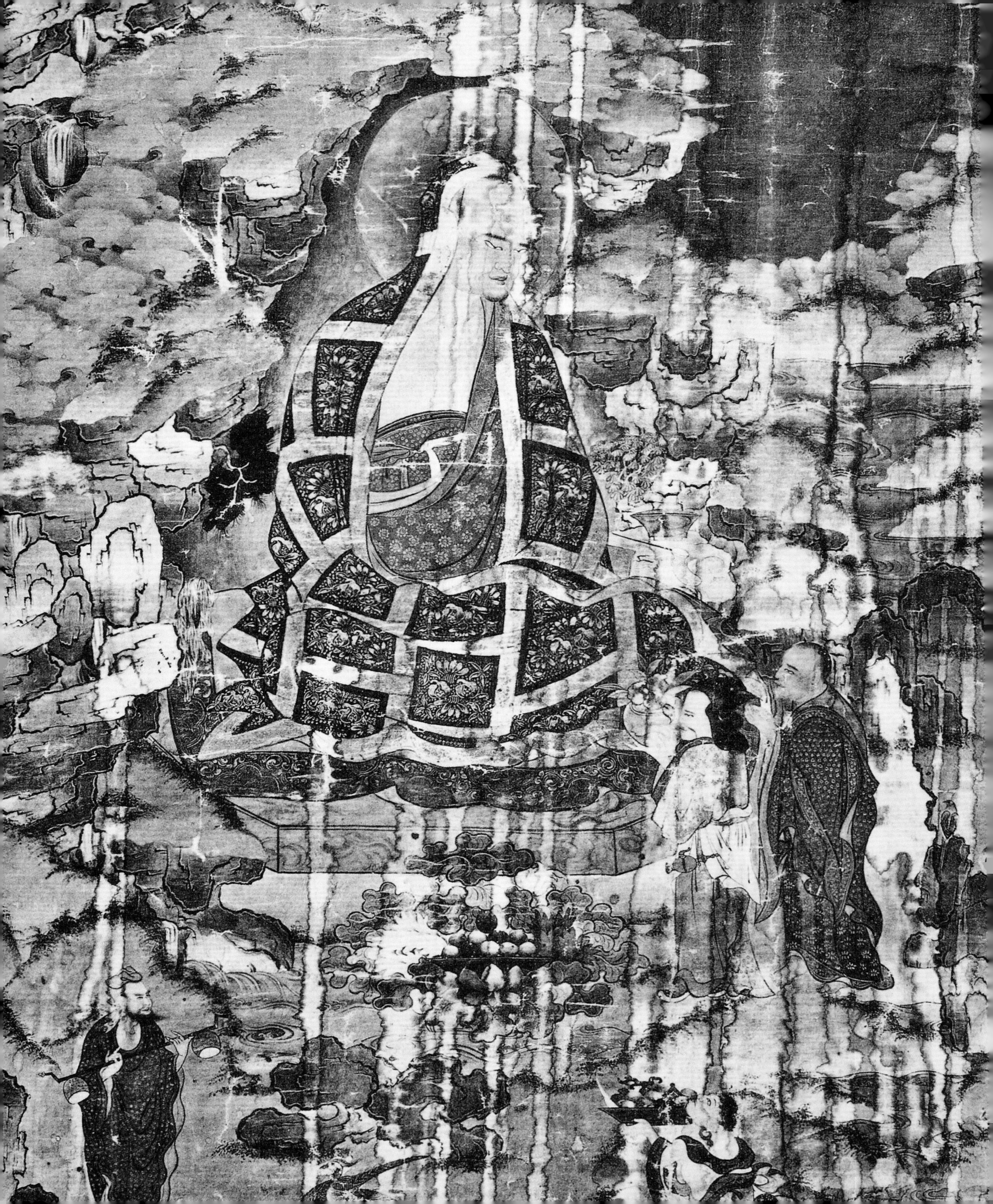

Previous Research

CHAPTER 2

THIS CHAPTER summarizes previous research on Khyentse Chenmo, Gongkar Dorjeden, and the Khyenri style.

TUCCI 1949

The history of Tibetan painting in the West began with the appearance of Giuseppe Tucci's book *Tibetan Painted Scrolls*. In this monumental work of two volumes and one portfolio, Tucci described Tibetan art, taking into account the relevant Tibetan historical sources and other written evidence that he could find. The book was a pioneering work, and its author did not know, for example, the existence of either the Menri or Khyenri painting styles. As preparation for this book, he had mainly done fieldwork, studying artistic sites of Ngari and Tsang provinces in the 1930s. When Tucci turned his attention to Ü province in the 1940s, he said that he did not expect to find anything new there.[144]

He did not know the traditional brief histories of Tibetan painting—for instance, those found in Kongtrül's *Encyclopedia* or the Desi's *gYa' sel*—but in one passage, he named several outstanding painters mentioned in historical sources, including the painter Menthangpa (sMan thang pa).[145] In another

passage, he also mentioned Menthangpa Jampeyang (sMan thang pa 'Jam pa'i dbyangs).[146] Although the name Khyentse Chenmo (mKhyen brtse Chen mo) does not appear in the book's index—where Tucci repeated the names of still more famous painters—he did mention once the name Tulku Khyentse (sPrul sku mKhyen brtse) of Gongkartö (Gong dkar stod), quoted from Sumpa Khenpo's list of artists.[147]

Tucci dated the great penetration and assimilation of Chinese landscapes in Tibetan painting several centuries too late. After briefly describing the remarkable achievements of the painters in Tsang who were responsible for the early- to mid-fifteenth-century murals in Tsang, especially those of the Gyantse stupa, Tucci believed that Tibetan painting traditions had subsequently remained quiescent and unchanged throughout the late-fifteenth, sixteenth, and seventeenth centuries, awaking again to Chinese influences only in the eighteenth century. In his words:

> The New Chinese Influence in the XVIIIth Century.
> No shock stirred Tibetan painting up to the new violent contact with China in the XVIIIth Century . . . A new Tibetan art developed which in a certain sense was a provincial echo of the Chinese XVIIIth century's smooth and ornate preciosity; this time, too, Tibet accepted suggestions from outside, but it did not remain passive, it worked out the Chinese style in its own way . . .[148]

Misled by his mistaken dating, Tucci thus overlooked three centuries of Tibetan painting history and did not take into account the advent of the Menri or Khyenri styles in any meaningful way. In central Tibet he also evidently never came across references to the third main Tibetan style, the Karma Gardri, and its founder, who were also omitted by Sumpa Khenpo and the Desi in their brief accounts of art.

The closing of Tibet in 1959 and the inaccessibility of Tucci's collection of Tibetan books and artworks in the 1960s and 1970s meant that for several decades most Western art historians of Tibet had to depend inordinately on Tucci's publications, especially *Tibetan Painted Scrolls*, whatever their limitations. His categories of painting styles were sometimes quite ad hoc, depending on the paintings he had chosen as prominent examples and his understanding or misunderstanding of them. For instance, most of the paintings he identified as examples of the Kham style actually came from Tsang province. The main set that he used for exemplifying the sixteen arhats (his plates 156–170, thangkas 121–136)—which he bought in Gyantse, a town of Tsang[149]—were actually examples of the local Tsangri style, not any style from Kham. (See Figs. 2.1 and 2.2.)

Little wonder, then, that Tucci elsewhere in his book could not recognize Figure 2.3, a painting of Vajradhara, as a masterful example of the Khyenri style. Placing it as thangka number 99 in his chapter devoted to various Tibetan stylistic schools, he believed it came from

FIG. 2.1
Arhat Ajita
Tsang, ca. eighteenth century
Acquired by Tucci in Gyantse
Museo Nazionale d'Arte Orientale
"G. Tucci," Rome
Literature: Tucci 1949, pl. 157

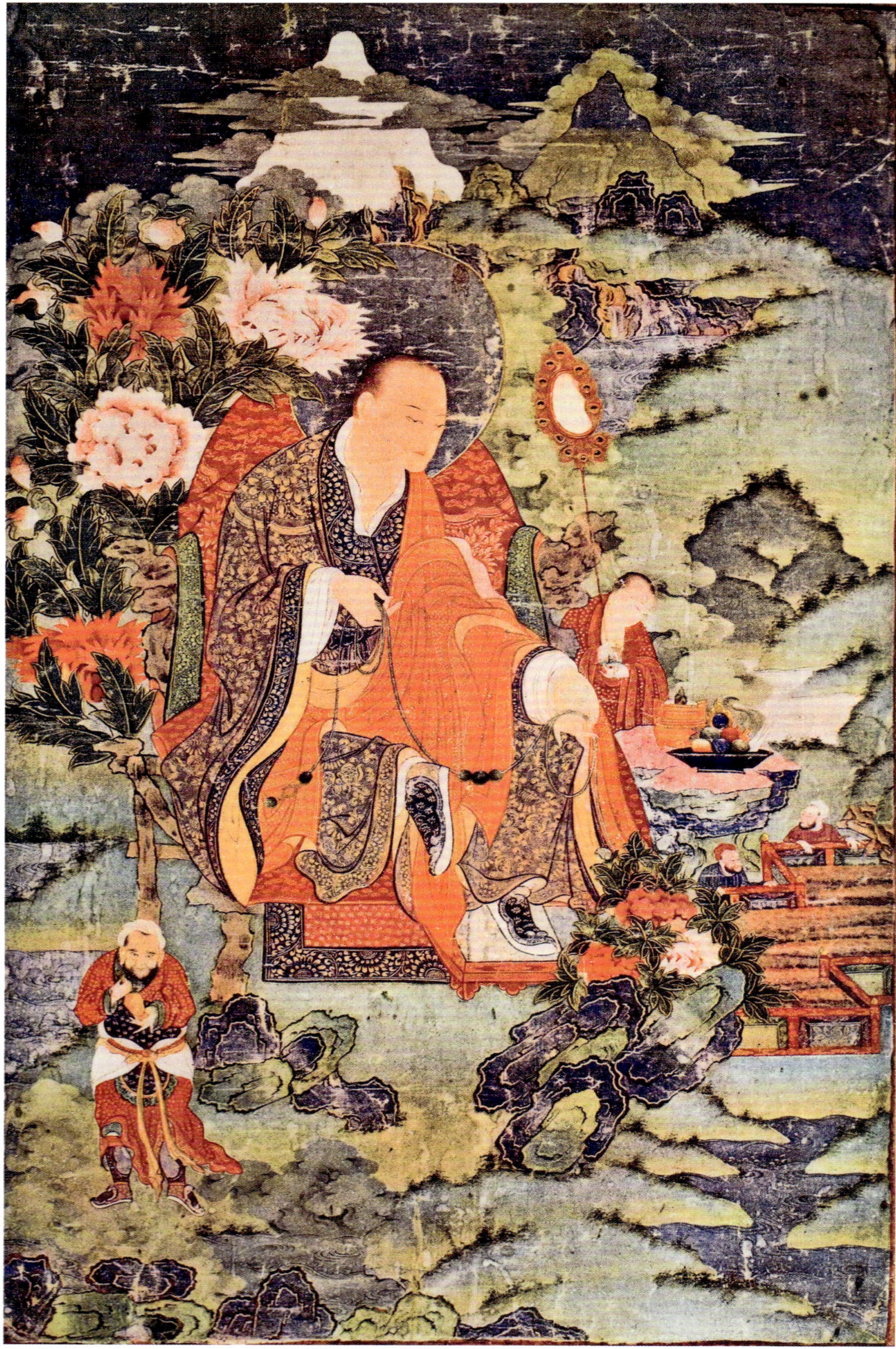

If the painting's donors came from Minyak, it is unclear why Tucci did not classify it as art from eastern Kham. In any case, this painting is a good example of the strong Chinese influence that we now know the Khyenri style could entail, so it could just as well be central Tibetan art. It could also date several centuries before the eighteenth century, but Tucci was not aware of that possibility.

Tucci 1956

Tucci had a chance in 1948 not only to travel to Ü province but also to visit Gongkar ("Kongkar") Dorjeden Monastery. He recorded this visit in his travel account, *To Lhasa and Beyond: Diary of the Expedition to Tibet in the Year MCMXLVIII*.[151] There, he recounted his impressions of the Dorjedenpa Tulku:

> In the meanwhile, the young incarnate went on dreaming and had built himself a secret, collected corner in a small garden aglow with flowers and blossoming trees. There he spent the long summer days lost in his musings, busily building his dream world like a poet or a child. The pent-up feelings of the young hermit found their outlet on the flowers, which he fondly tended as the companions of his captivity, as creatures born of his fancies and fed on his need of love.[152]

the Minyak district in the borderlands of Kham. He described the part of the painting that featured its donors:

> The most remarkable part of the tanka is the lower one, where the donors are represented, all in the typical costumes of Eastern Tibet and precisely of Mi nyag; they form an extremely lively picture, in which accurate design is joined by bright colours.[150]

Later Tucci wrote about Khyentse's art, giving a rare eyewitness account:

> I saw the assembly hall, where statues of the Buddhas of the Three Times were surrounded by the eight Bodhisattvas; and the circumambulation corridor with good frescoes of the Lord Buddha's life showing a marked Chinese influence. On the walls right and left

of the cell were painted the Lamas
of the Sakyapa sect and the main
events of their lives: dignified but
spirited and lively pictures, free
from the hieratic stiffness that too
often burdens Tibetan art.[153]

TUCCI 1967

In his book *Tibet, Land of Snows*, Tucci
again summarized his stylistic results:
"It is plain that we cannot speak of
schools of Tibetan art, or only in a very
general way."[154] A few pages later he
said, "Repeated journeys to Tibet have
yielded me with no more than three
score names of painters."[155] Tucci here
named three of the most outstanding:
Döndrup Gyatsho, who was praised as
a supreme painter by the Fifth Dalai
Lama; Chöying Gyatsho of Tsang; and
Menthangpa, along with his son. His
brief enumeration names two founders
of stylistic schools but not Khyentse
Chenmo.

SHAKABPA 1967

The first publication to name the three
most famous traditional painting styles
was by Tsepon W. D. Shakabpa, *Tibet:
A Political History*, but a misplaced
comma in the English translation erroneously divided the Gongkar Khyenri
(*gong dkar mkhyen ris*) into two: "Three
of the most prominent schools of painting are the Karma Gardre of Kham, the
Gongkar, Khyenri, and the Menthong
Ari of Ü."[156] Presumably the last should
be in Tibetan: Menthang Eri (sMan
thang E ris). The full Tibetan version
of Shakabpa's history, published in two
volumes in 1976, added nothing of significance on the Khyenri style.

HUNTINGTON 1968

The first monograph-length study
devoted to the subject of Tibetan
painting styles was the PhD dissertation
of John C. Huntington, which primarily
stressed the regional nature of Tibetan
painting. Taking his cue from the apparently geographical designations used by
Shakabpa 1967, he attempted to describe
the main regional styles, asserting:

> The method being proposed is to
> study the documents of the history
> of religion that we have in the
> extant scroll paintings and frescoes

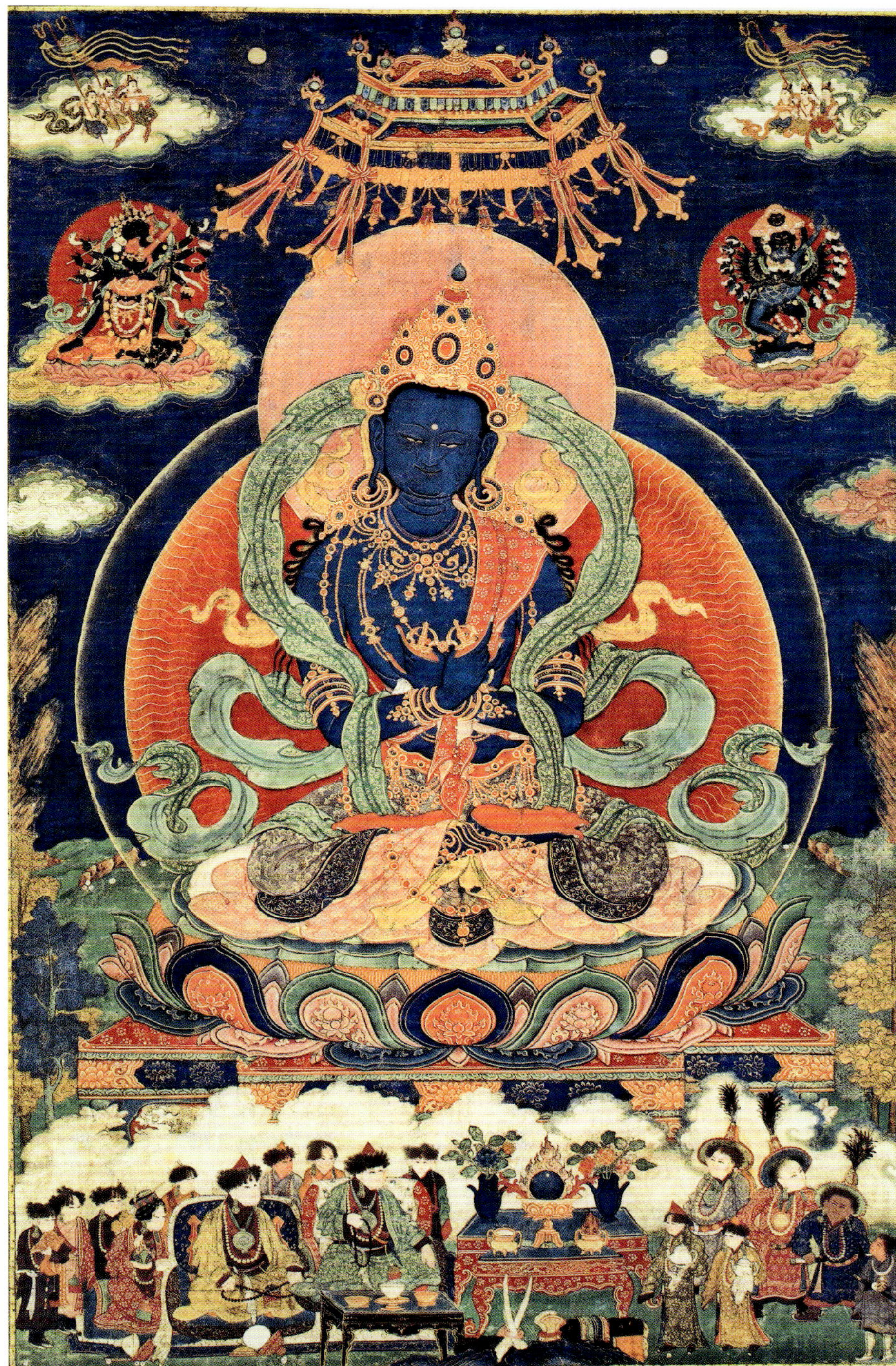

FIG. 2.3
Vajradhara
late fifteenth or sixteenth century
23 x 17 ½ in (58.4 x 44.5 cm)
Private Collection
Literature: Tucci 1949, 537, no. 9,
pls. 134 and O; and Rhie and Thurman
1991, no. 148

not as a unified whole but rather, separated into convenient regional classifications on the basis of style. The Tibetans give the following list of style designations: "Karma Gardre" in Khams district in Eastern Tibet (Karma sGar bris) which designates the painting of the Karma sect from the district of sGar in western Khams, "Gong kar" (Gong dkar) in dBus which may refer to either a monastery or an estate in the center of which is a town in the valley of the gTsang-po river in dBus, "Khen ri" (mKhan ris) of dBus and finally "Menthong [E]ri" (sMan-thang E-bris), of which "E" designates a district in dBus (Ü) . . . These are regional designations and indicate an awareness by the Tibetans of the regional nature of styles.[157]

Shakapa's misplaced comma misled Huntington into thinking that Gongkar and Khyenri should be separate styles. The four main regional styles that Huntington attempted to isolate and describe in the body of his work were those of western Tibet, central Tibet, Khams, and the Sino-Tibetan interface region.

SMITH 1970

The first Western scholar to make more extensive use of the indigenous written accounts on styles was E. Gene Smith. This he did in his English introduction to the *Shes bya kun khyab* encyclopedia of Kongtrül (Kong sprul). Later Western studies were heavily indebted to this contribution. Smith began his account of Tibetan art by presenting the relevant passage from Kongtrül's encyclopedia as a typical example of the latter's expository method.[158] After translating the basic verses and auto-commentary in notes 69 through 71, Smith rewrote and expanded the account into a form that would be more suitable for an entry

in a true encyclopedia.[159] About the two major schools of painting, he asserted:

[1] The sMan ris. It was founded by sMan bla don grub during the first half of the fifteenth century, and it was influenced by Yuan-dynasty temple banners, especially elegant embroideries. The sMan ris came to flourish in Tsang.
[2] The mKhyen ris. Founded in the sixteenth century by 'Jam dbyangs mKhyen brtse'i dbang phyug, it shows a degree of Chinese influence, though it differs from the sMan-ris. "The finer painters of Sa-skya and Ngor of the late sixteenth century represent this school at its best."[160]

Smith proposed that the great Menthangpa Menla Döndrup had flourished in the first half of the fifteenth century, following T. G. Dhongthog, who in a chronological compilation had dated the establishment of his school to 1400 and placed Khyentse in the mid-sixteenth century and Chi'u (Bye'u) similarly, as probably in the sixteenth century, though without any firm evidence.

Smith knew that his sources allowed only tentative chronological conclusions, stating, for instance: "The sixteenth century saw the birth of its second great school, the Khyenri (mKhyen ris), which takes its origins and name from 'Jam dbyangs mkhyen brtse'i dbang phyug (b. 1524)."[161] But in a footnote, he added that the relevant biographies were not yet available to confirm this provisional identification, noting several problems and speculating if it was possible he was dealing with two different personages. Subsequent Western scholars, however, for many years generally accepted this hypothetical chronology for the earlier Tibetan schools and also overlooked the doubts that Smith raised.

For years, Smith's introduction remained the only comparable

contribution by a Western scholar. Most who followed him were not in a position to recheck his assertions or sources, nor were reliable oral sources readily available. When summarizing Kongtrül's terse account of traditional style names, Smith made a number of mistakes in the information he added about each style, evidently based on oral information. The main errors relevant to the Khyenri style were: that Khyentse's full name was Jamyang Khyentse Wangchuk, that he was born in the sixteenth century, and that the finer painters of Sakya and Ngor of the late sixteenth century represented his school. These three mistakes were perpetuated within later Western scholarship.

DAGYAB 1977

Dagyab Rinpoche, in his sketch of the history of the main schools of Tibetan art that he published as chapter 14 in his book *Tibetan Religious Art*, mentioned the Khyenri tradition of Khyentse Chenmo of Gong dkar sGang stod.[162] His mention of the Khyenri is extremely terse, saying simply that this style was considered, together with the Menri, to be one of the two main painting traditions of Tibet.

DEMO 1979

The Tibet House society of New Delhi published a catalog in connection with the first art exhibition after the society moved into new premises. The text was written by Ngawang Gelek Demo, assisted by Gyaltsen Yeshey and Ngawang Phüntshok. In a section subtitled "A Brief History of Tibetan Art," Gelek Rinpoche summarized his description of the traditional painting styles, essentially rephrasing Smith's account of ten years earlier.[163] On Khyentse, Gelek Rinpoche followed the wrong chronology suggested by Smith and the erroneous suggestion that the famous Ngor Monastery paintings were a fine example of the Khyenri school.

CHOGAY TRICHEN RINPOCHE 1979

Chogye (Chogay) Trichen Rinpoche presented a brief sketch of Tibetan art history in his manual of monastic culture, published under the English title *Gateway to the Temple*. There he mentioned Khyentse Chenmo and his style:

> Further, in the time of Kun-dga'-rnam-rgyal, there came to the Gong-dkar rdo-rje-gdan monastic center from sGang-stod a great figure known as "sPrul-sku mKhyen-brtse chen-po." Because of the slight differences between his painting styles and that of sMan-lha-don-grub, there came about a painting style that was called "mKhyen style" (*mkhyen bris*) after him.[164]

Chogye Rinpoche thus specified for the first time Gongkar Monastery as the site of Khyentse's murals, saying that Khyentse had worked there as an artist during the time of the monastery's founder, Gongkar Dorjedenpa. He knew those paintings first-hand, having visited and taught at Gongkar, and he was the first person to alert me to their existence. I later found a rare photo of Chogye Rinpoche standing at Gongkar before one of its murals in the 1950s, taken during one of his brief visits there (Fig. 2.4).

HUNTINGTON 1980

When reviewing Detlef-Ingo Lauf's 1976 book, *Secret Revelations of Tibetan Thangkas*, John C. Huntington criticized Lauf for not using the traditional school names. He summed up his understanding of the traditional styles and their nomenclature:

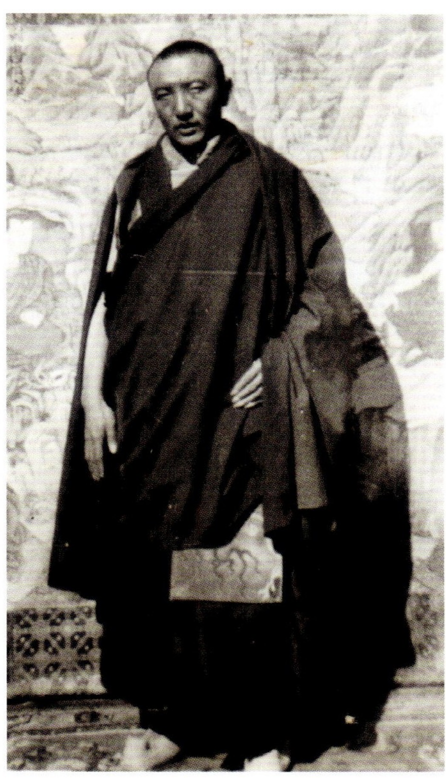

FIG. 2.4
Chogye Rinpoche while visiting Gongkar in the 1950s
Photo: unknown photographer; D. Jackson collection

3 mKhyen 'bris "drawing [in the manner of] mKhyen," may be seen in plate 24. In its pure form, this school is one of the rarest and most beautiful of all schools of Tibetan painting. mKhyen 'bris ser ma, the later outgrowth of mKhyen 'bris, also known as gTsang 'bris, may be seen in plates 9, 20, 27, 42 and 60.

We can now identify Lauf's plate 24 as a late Beri from Ngor Monastery dating to about the late fifteenth or early sixteenth century. Here Huntington may have been following Smith's erroneous link of the Khyenri with the late-sixteenth-century Ngorpa. Huntington also considered the Tsangri to be a later growth of the Khyenri, when in fact the Tsangri was a later branch of the Menri. In the thangka in plate 24, the centers

of the blue lotus leaves are quite ornate; the lineage depicted seems to be the Profound Path (Lam zab) Guru Yoga, continuing fourteen guru lineage generations after Sakya Paṇḍita, possibly to about the ninth or tenth abbot of Ngor.[165]

Figure 2.5, the painting illustrated by Lauf that Huntington cited as Khyenri, depicts as main figures two late-fifteenth-century masters from the Sakya school and a lineage of Ngor Monastery. Inscriptions identify these teachers as transmitters of an important Ngorpa lineage, such as the Profound Path (Lam zab) Guru Yoga.[166] The second main figure, guru number 20, whose name begins "Jamyang Könchok," is possibly the seventh abbot Könchok Phel (dKon mchog 'phel, 1445–1514, whose abbatial tenure was 1486–1513), in which case number 19 could be the sixth abbot, "the omniscient" Gorampa—note his Mañjuśrī emblems—and teacher number 18 would be Gyaltshap Kunga Wangchuk, the fourth abbot of Ngor. (See Diagram [B].)

REYNOLDS, HELLER, AND GYATSO 1986

This catalog presents the sculpture and painting in the Newark Museum's Tibetan collection of the mid-1980s; it is a revised edition superseding the original work of Eleanor Olson, who published between 1950 and 1971 the five-volume *Catalogue of the Newark Museum Tibetan Collection*. Assisting Valrae Reynolds with the catalog were Amy Heller, the source for most of the information on styles and iconography, and Janet Gyatso, the translator and adviser on more technical Tibetological and Buddhological questions. Regarding the Khyenri, the authors noted Smith's uncertainty about the school's founder; their publication was the first secondary source to do so.[167]

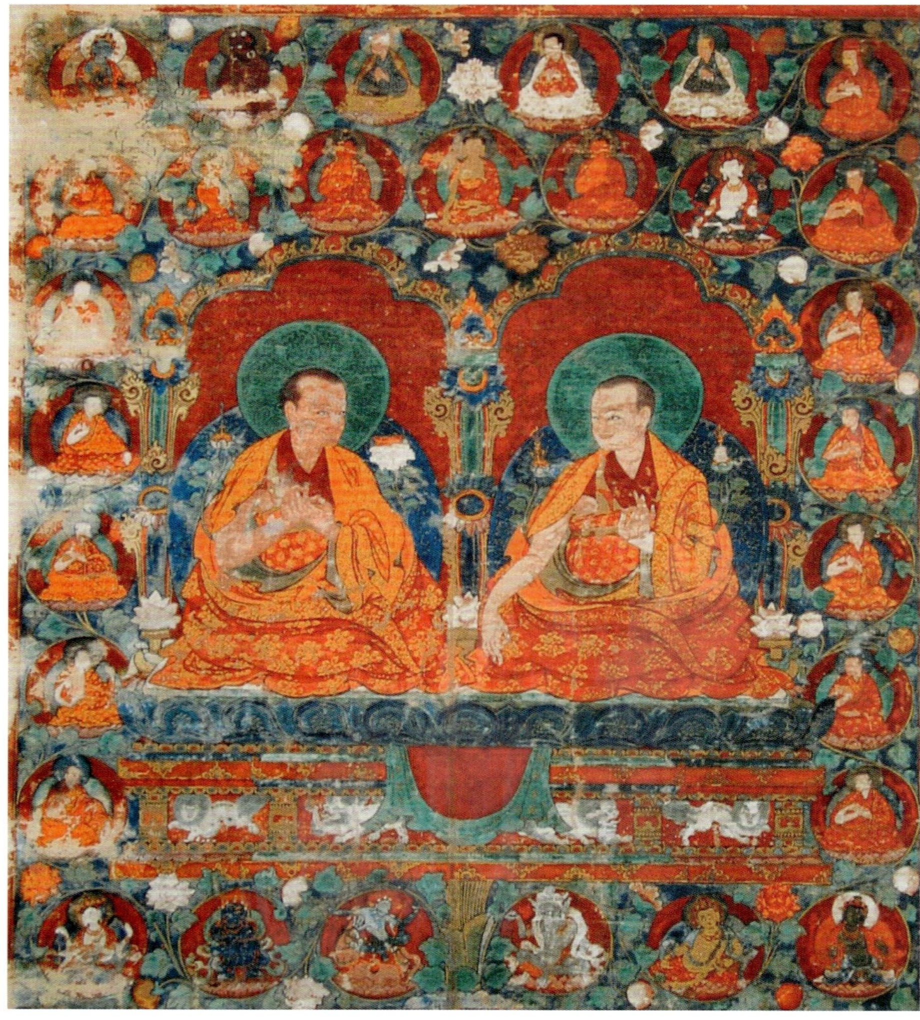

Fig. 2.5
Gorampa and Könchok Phel, Two Abbots
of Ngor
1480s–1520s
21 ⅝ x 19 ¾ in. (55 x 50 cm.)
Private Collection
Literature: Lauf 1976, pl. 24

Stephen Batchelor in *The Tibet Guide* devoted three pages to Gongkar Monastery.[168] He included a photo of a front view of the monastery (Fig. 2.6). Correctly noting that the monastery belongs to a lesser-known tradition of the Sakya school, he wrongly called the tradition Zung rather than the correct Dzongpa. When he visited the monastery, presumably in 1986, he could confirm the extent of the recent destruction:

> The main temple building remains more or less intact. During the Cultural Revolution all the statues were removed and the two upper stories with their gilded roofs taken down. The surrounding monastic buildings were either destroyed or turned to other uses.[169]

Batchelor sensed the importance of the mural paintings, devoting most of his text to them, but he was not aware of Khyentse Chenmo's role in making the older murals or of the painting school that he founded. He began by describing the much later murals of the main assembly:

> The murals that survive in the assembly hall and elsewhere are well worth seeing. Covering the two side-walls of the spacious assembly hall are some excellent scenes from the Buddha's previous lives, as told in the *Paksam Trishing*. Each scene is shown in minute detail, having been painted with very careful and delicate brush strokes, and bears a short numbered text in Tibetan beneath it.[170]

Batchelor went on to describe the murals nearest the new assembly hall: "Before entering the chapel at the rear, there are two other older-looking murals to either side of the doorway." He described the

[B]						
1	2	3		4	5	6
13	b	B	B	B	b	7
14						8
15		19		20		9
16						10
17						11
18						12
d	d	d		d	d	d

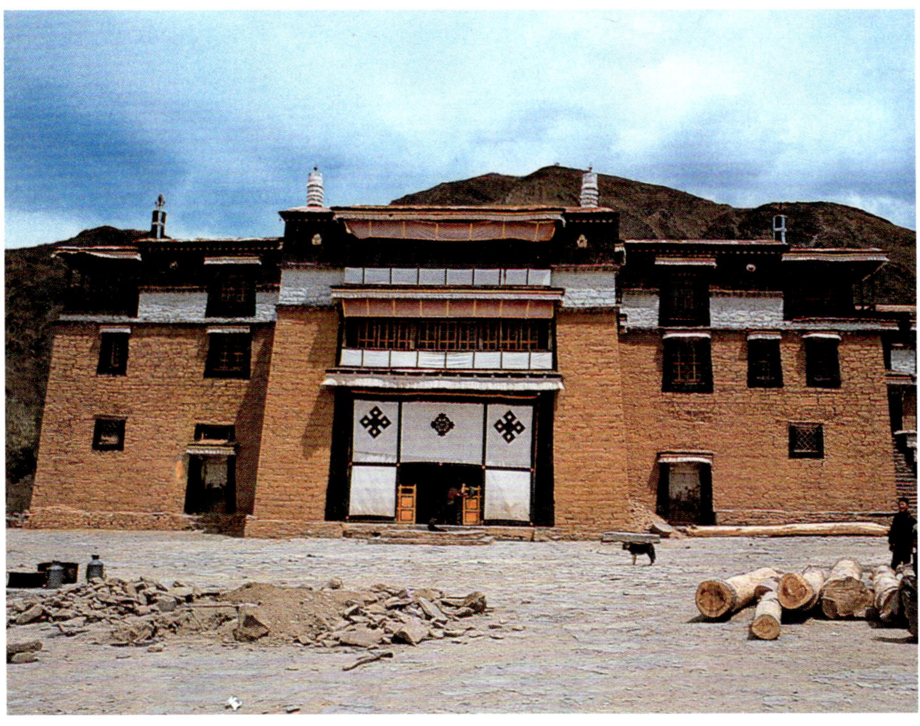

main figures of the Sakyapa triads as "Three White Ones" and "Two Red Ones," omitting the third Red One, Lama Dampa. Mentioning that the sixteen arhats were depicted "in the upper wall by the skylight," he spoke of two dimly lit protector's chapels to the left of the assembly hall; he said the farther of the two chapels is dedicated to "Gönpo Guru," that is, (Mahākāla) Gur gyi mGon po.[171] Next, he described the then noticeably incomplete inner sanctum, whose walls were still coated with whitewash:

> The large, high-ceilinged chapel to the rear of the assembly hall is now completely empty, its walls coated with whitewash to obscure the murals. It used to house a tall image of Shakyamuni, which was destroyed during the Cultural Revolution. If you look at the paneled ceiling you can make out lotuses with the mantra OM MANI PADME HUM written in Sanskrit on their petals. There is an inner circumambulation corridor around this chapel and it is just possible to recognize the twelve deeds of the Buddha painted on the inner wall and the Thousand Buddhas of the aeon on the outer wall.[172]

About the murals on the ground floor, Batchelor noted: "All . . . were whitewashed in the sixties. One can appreciate the careful and painstaking efforts the monks have made to remove this coat of wash so successfully, especially in the assembly hall."[173] He did not mention that in several other locations the removal of whitewash was not yet complete in 1986, such as in the circumambulation corridor.

Batchelor's high appreciation of the Gongkar murals did not flag when he came to a second-floor chapel:

> The Upper Storey of the monastery is largely empty and unused but contains the most remarkable Yidam Chapel. The walls of this small room are entirely covered with extremely well-painted images of the main tantric deities (*yidams*) of the Sakya tradition. The main image, which faces you as you enter, is that of Hevajra, in front of which used to be a full-sized statue of the deity. The colours of all these murals have been well preserved and the attention to detail is exceptional. Not only the main figures but also the smaller attendant deities and *dakinis* associated with their mandalas are shown, the artwork indicating a craftsman of considerable spiritual sensitivity.[174]

Dowman 1988

Keith Dowman briefly visited Gongkar Monastery in August 1986, when gathering material for his book, *The Power-Places of Central Tibet: the Pilgrim's Guide.* He described it in section 9, which described the south bank of the Tsangpo River. (See Fig. 2.7.) On pages 148 through 152, he briefly recounted what he had learned about Gongkar. He reported that only three of the buildings of the monastic complex had not been torn down during the Cultural Revolution—the main building, Drepung Tratshang, and Keuthang Lhakhang (College)—but actually it was the Kunzang Tse College that also survived. Restoration of the main building was almost complete in 1986, and the abbot was training about twenty monks then, but a number of the murals were still coated with whitewash, preventing visitors from properly seeing them.

Dowman made a few historical errors, such as saying that Lama Dampa (1312–1375) was Dorjedenpa's direct teacher and using the name "Jamyang Khyentse" for Khyentse Chenmo. Repeating the common misconceptions of Smith, more than once he dated the murals by Khyentse to the sixteenth century, one hundred years too late: "The murals of the Buddha's life in the

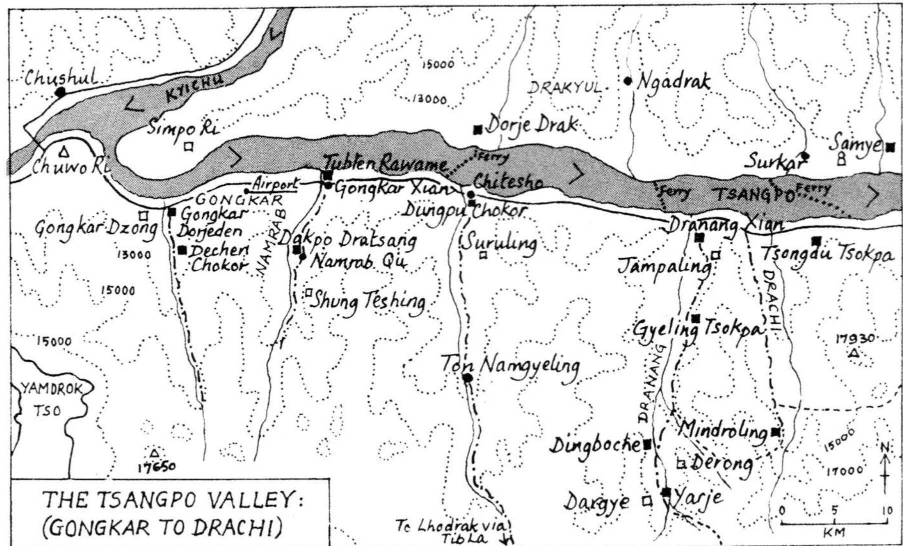

Fig. 2.7
Map of the Tsangpo Valley: Gongkar to Drachi
After: Dowman 1988, 149

lhakhang's *korsa* are said to be the original sixteenth-century work of artists painting in the Kyenri style, but the coat of whitewash permitted no judgment upon the date or style."[175] He added:

> Little is known of the sixteenth-century Jamyang Khyentse (b. 1524), otherwise known as Tulku Jamyang, who painted in the style later to be called Kyenri, except that he lived in Gongkar and painted murals in Dorjeden gonpa. Although highly stylized his work possessed a fluid vitality not to be found in later centuries of development of the Central Tibetan Menri style.[176]

Dowman did not realize that some mural panels on the second floor, in the room above the building's main entrance veranda, had been painted much later, in the 1930s or 1940s: "The murals above the *dukhang*'s portico contain four oval panels of early work in a good state of preservation. These murals are reputed to have been painted by the originator of the Kyenri style, Jamyang Kyentse, in the sixteenth century."[17]

Huntington and Huntington 1990

John Huntington, in the catalog that he co-authored with Susan Huntington, described Tibetan painting styles and their traditional terminology in more detail than he had in his 1968 and 1980 publications. His treatment of the later indigenous Tibetan schools was still quite brief, and understandably so, for his main subject was the early and heavily Indian-influenced Tibetan styles. When discussing the main later indigenous styles, he stressed the hypothetical nature of his identifications. On the Menri (sMan ris) and Khyenri (mKhyen ris), he stated, "No documentary or other direct evidence illustrates the features that can identify paintings of either the sMan bris or mKhyen ris schools."[178]

The situation was not quite as intractable as Huntington implied, since works of Khyentse's tradition, for example, survived in Tibet in situ at Gongkar, as reported by Dowman 1988. (Actually, Huntington had already mentioned the style in his dissertation, though in a garbled and misspelled form.) Huntington drew the following inferences from Smith's introduction and four Tibetan accounts:[179]

From the brief narrative of sMan's contributions, it would seem that

his alteration of the accepted Bal bris style was a major departure from the norm. From the even briefer description of the contribution of mKhyen [brtse] . . . , active in the late fifteenth and early sixteenth centuries, it would seem that he followed the direction of sMan [thang pa] in adding Chinese elements but also went further.[180]

He also pointed out that in in his examples, the overall coloration of the backgrounds "lends a conspicuous Chinese atmosphere to the surroundings of the deity and teacher."[181]

Huntington proposed not just examples of early Indian- and Nepal-inspired styles but also highly tentative attributions of the three main later Tibetan ones: those of Byi'u, Menthangpa, and Khyentse (his catalog nos. 121, 122, and 123). He thus attempted to use the traditional terminology introduced by Smith:

> Next there came mKhyen brtse who was born at Gong dkar sgang stod. He founded a style that branched off from that of sMan. The two, sMan and mKhyen, became as famed as the sun and moon, [of painting] in the land of snows (that is, Tibet).[182]

Referring to Smith's wrong explanation that he had been shown Sakya and Ngor (a Sakya subsect) paintings of the fifteenth and sixteenth centuries as examples of the Khyenri style, Huntington attributed his catalog number 123 to the Khyenri school. (See Fig. 2.8.) This painting depicts a twelve-armed, red, standing Ganeṣa; the thangka was then in the private Ford collection.

In retrospect, Huntington's mistake was too closely following Smith, who also had to depend on the limited oral information he obtained in India in the mid-1970s. Huntington rightly

stressed, "Even the most well-educated
and knowledgeable Tibetan informants,
when asked to identify examples of the
schools, indiscriminately will point out
virtually any Tibetan Bal ris painting
or Sa skya Bal ris painting."[183] Huntington's main informants from the
high-ranking Tibetan nobility and clergy
included Ngawang Gelek and Domo
Geshe Rinpoche, whom he had interviewed twenty years earlier, in 1969
and 1970.[184] Gelek Rinpoche told me,
when I interviewed him in New Delhi
in 1982, that among traditional Geluk
scholars in exile, the ability to confidently identify the early Tibetan painting
styles probably passed with the death of
Trichang Rinpoche (Khri byang Rin po
che, 1901–1981).[185] To a Tibetan historian who questioned him, Trichang Rinpoche also mentioned special features
of lotuses and clouds, but no clear-cut
examples were available to show West-
erners in India, and Gongkar itself was
inaccessible.[186]

RHIE AND THURMAN 1991

Although Marylin Rhie and Robert
Thurman happened to include a few
prominent examples of the Khyenri style
in their exhibition catalog, *Wisdom and
Compassion*; they did not expressly
address Khyentse Chenmo or the Khyenri style. Of the five main Khyenri
examples they published, two were
from the Musée Guimet, with entries
written by Gilles Béguin: number 19,
Arhat Rāhula; and number 90, "Eastern Tibetan Kagyu Lama, Shamarpa."
Béguin considered both examples to be
from Eastern Tibet or China and dated
them to the seventeenth or early eighteenth century. (See Fig. 2.9.)

Three Khyenri examples treated
by Rhie were number 8, "Śākyamuni
Buddha with Scenes from his Former
Lives"; number 17, a Dharmatrāta, from
Boston; and number 148, a Vajradhara,
from a private collection, seen above as

an illustration of Tucci 1949 (Fig. 2.3).
Rhie considered all three to come from
eastern Tibet, dating them between 1550
and the early eighteenth century. The
examples show a lot of stylistic diver-
sity; it would have been very difficult to
see a connecting stylistic thread without
studying several Khyenri-style sets of
different iconographic subjects.

EVERDING 1993

In his German-language Tibetan travel
guide, Karl-Heinz Everding devoted
about half a page to Gongkar Chöde,
observing that the traces of the destruction of the Cultural Revolution were
still clearly noticeable in the monastery.
All the statues had been either stolen or
destroyed and the building converted

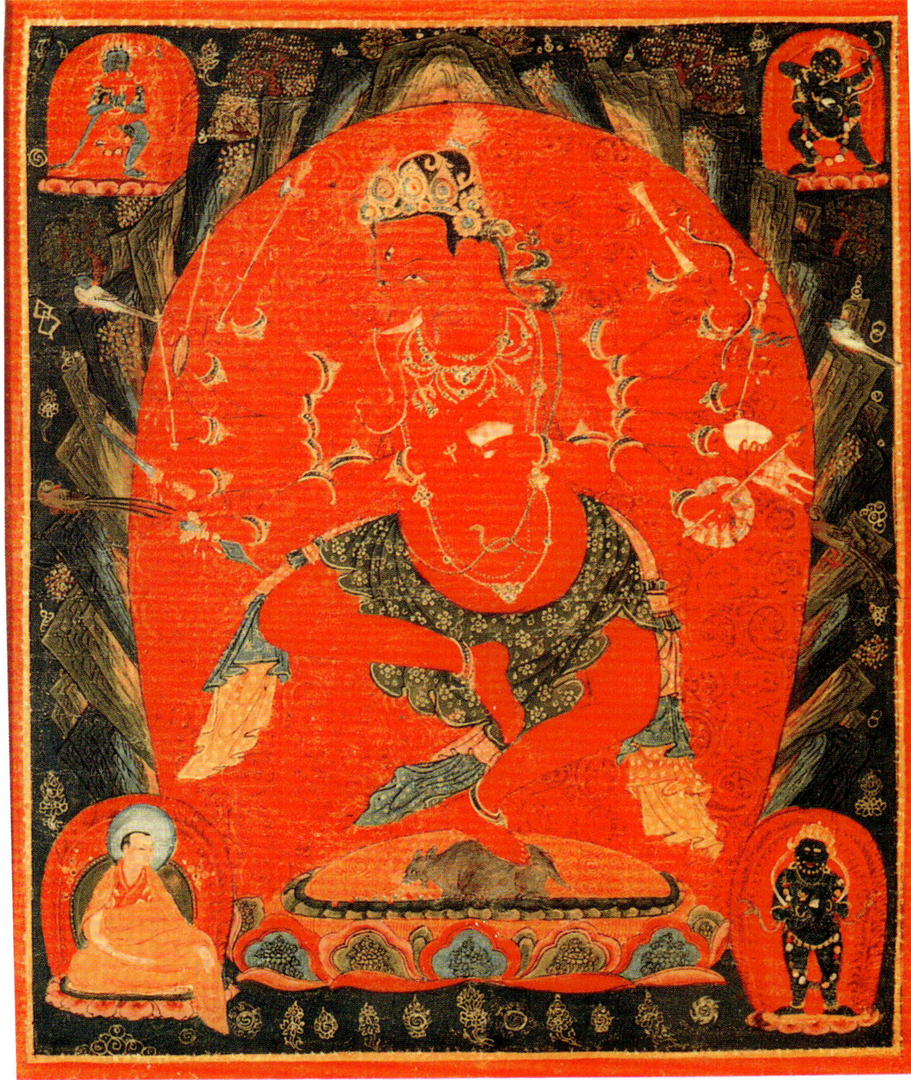

FIG. 2.8
Red Gaṇeśa
Private Collection
(HAR 89964)
Literature: Lauf 1976, pl. 54; Huntington
and Huntington 1990, cat. no. 123; and
Béguin 1995, 62, fig. 31

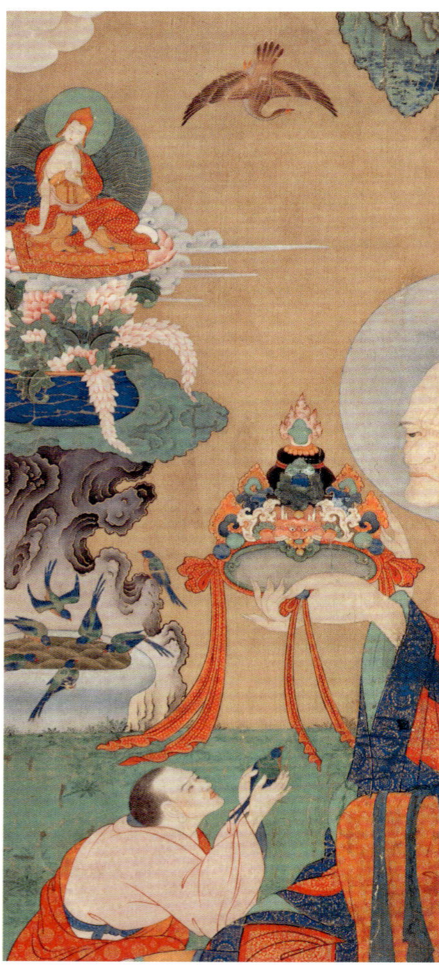

into a grain silo.[187] He added that the surviving original murals by the famous painter Khyentse Chenmo of the fifteenth century were well worth seeing, explaining that this artist had taken over the artistic decoration of the monastery that Dorjedenpa Kunga Namgyal had established in 1464. He stressed that travelers should not miss the murals of the tantric deities in the Hevajra Divine Palace (Kye rdor gZhal yas khang).

In the 2001 revised edition for the same art travelogue series, Everding enlarged his description of Gongkar considerably. Though now accepting the wrong birth date of Khyentse, 1524, he added details, such as that the smaller central assembly hall was a twentieth-century construction meant to compensate for the reduced number of resident monks; to make up for that, they also built the walls enclosing the new side temples.[188] The smaller assembly hall still remained visually full, but at the same time, several new shrine rooms and storage rooms came into existence.

The newly built walls in the new central assembly hall were actually also intended to strengthen the building's structure in the middle. The presence of the new walls also meant that some of the artistic treasures of the monastery—the original murals of Khyentse Chenmo on the old outer walls—were hidden within several small side rooms, where they survived the Cultural Revolution relatively intact. According to Everding, they depicted the iconographic cycle of the life story of the Buddha, his prior rebirths and deeds in previous lives.

Chan 1994

In his modern hiking and pilgrimage guide to Tibet, Victor Chan covered a fair amount of art history, thanks to the help of Roberto Vitali. Near the beginning of the book, Chan presented "A Short History of Tibetan Art," but he was not conversant enough with the main traditional styles, such as the Menri or Khyenri, to mention them much.[189] In his history, "The Rule of the Dalai Lamas (17th–19th centuries)," he referred to a stylistic revolution—the introduction of predominantly green Chinese landscapes in the backgrounds—that actually began in the mid-fifteenth century, but he characterized it as the spreading of the Üri style in the sixteenth century, from primarily Lhasa or Ü (dBus) provinces.[190]

Chan did mention the minor style of the Khyenri, correctly identifying Gongkar as one of its most important sites.[191] Rightly naming its founder Khyentse Chenmo, he nevertheless continued the misconception that Khyentse's murals dated to the sixteenth century. When describing Gongkar Chöde Monastery, Chan summarized what he had learned about the place, after more than one visit between 1984 and 1993:

This impressive, well-preserved monastery lies a few hundred meters off the main road. Its 16th-c. Kyenri murals are a rare and important find. This particular style of Tibetan painting was pioneered by Kyentse Chenmo, a 16th-c. native of Gongkar. According to tradition, the master personally painted all the murals in Gongkar Chöde. Not all survived but those that did are grouped in small pockets within the 64-pillar main hall, along the circumambulation corridor and in small rooms on the second floor. They are characterized by a pronounced Chinese influence. All the murals have been whitewashed by the Red Guards and have only recently been cleaned.[192]

Chan explained that the murals in the assembly hall showed the life of Śākyamuni according to the *Avadānakalpalatā*. Then he mentioned two murals flanking the entrance of the inner sanctum (*tsangkhang*): to the left, one portraying the Sakya founder Kunga Nyingpo, flanked by Trakpa Gyaltshen and Sönam Tsemo and, to the right, a panel depicting Sakya Paṇḍita and his nephew, Phakpa. Perhaps following Batchelor's account, he omitted Sönam Gyaltshen as the third of his trio of red-clad Sakya patriarchs.

Somewhat confusingly, Chan discussed the same murals a second time: "On the wall are lively paintings of the main lamas of the Sakya lineage: Sönam Gyaltshen, Sakya Paṇḍita, Phakpa, Drakpa Gyaltshen, Kunga Nyingpo, Sönam Tsemo, and scenes from their lives. These are freer and less rigid than the paintings from other monasteries in Central Tibet." The lamas actually appear with lineage lamas depicted above, not with episodes of their lives. Chan continued:

> The inner walls of the [circumambulation] corridor has Kyenri-style paintings depicting Śākyamuni's 12 deeds. On the outer wall are images of the Thousand Buddhas. The *gönkhang,* left of the main hall, has paintings of gruesome 'sky burials.' There are twelve divinities, Gönpo Gur's retinue (a form of Mahākāla highly revered by the Sakyapa), in an inner room.

Chan added that two rooms on the second floor contained excellent paintings by Khyentse Chenmo, mentioning the Hevajra Chapel's murals of tantric deities. He believed that the twentieth-century murals in the front were also old, saying: "The room directly above the front porch of the assembly hall has charming oval paintings; one shows the original monastic complex."

He also noted that to the rear of the main building was the then-ruined Lamdre Lhakhang, with atypical architecture: its first floor had four load-bearing pillars, the second had eight, the third, sixteen, and the top, thirty-two.[193] Near the end of his Gongkar account, he gave a brief lesson in art history, summarizing what he had heard about the Khyenri under the heading "Kyenri: paintings with Chinese influence":

> Murals in most monasteries of Central Tibet depict a central divine figure, a god or incarnation of some well-known saint, surrounded by other divinities. Scenes are painted in rigid symmetry on a large wall. Chinese influence, however, produced paintings in which the most important figures stand to the side, away from the center. Landscape enlivened and

permeated the whole composition. This freer style avoided the traditional stiffness of typical Tibetan temple paintings.[194]

Chan's observation is inaccurate, for Khyentse Chenmo did not typically place his main figures to the side in his thangkas, away from the central axis. Chan concluded with the assertion: "The Kyenri style is most apparent in Sakyapa and Karmapa monasteries of Kham (East Tibet), and it is unusual to find it in the Lhasa area." But actually it is most common in central Tibet, such as Lhokha, and almost never found in Kham.

Shalu Association 1994–95

One source of information on Gongkar Monastery and its recent conservation is the Shalu Association; the reports by this Paris-based organization are accessible online. The 1994 overview stated:

> The monastery of Gongkar belongs to the Zung branch of the Sakyapa school, and was decorated in the sixteenth century with beautiful wall paintings by the celebrated founder of the Khyenri school of Tibetan painting, Jamyang Khyentse Wangchuk (born 1524). Numerous wall paintings executed by him are still visible. These unique art historical documents will allow for the identification of this school which is known to have had a strong influence on later Tibetan painting, right up to the twentieth century. The monastery used to house one hundred and sixty monks, and now has about thirty. The main building is in good condition, and the exterior has been restored.[195]

The reports misdated Khyentse Chenmo to the sixteenth century and wrongly considered the Hevajra Divine Palace (Kye rdor gZhal yas khang) on

the second floor to be later than the rest of the structure.[196] The association believed it was part of a later, northern, three-floor addition or extension to the building.

The updated field report of May 1995—published as "Shalu Association: First Year Report, 1994–1995"—explained that the architect John Harrison visited Gongkar in May 1995. That report described the structure and the problems it faced:

> The sixteenth-century wall paintings with which Shalu Association is principally concerned are located in the assembly hall, the circumambulatory passage, and in the first floor (level 2) Yidam chapel of the northern extension. Apart from this northern extension, the building generally appears to be in fair condition structurally, and so the wall paintings in the *dukhang* and *khorlam* are not threatened by building failure. The high-level windows in the *khorlam*, however, are not glazed, only protected by inward-opening wooden shutters; rain penetration is a problem with the two windows on the south side, and thought should be given to replacing at least these shutters with glass windows. The paintings on both sides of the corridor have been extensively damaged in the past by rain penetration and roof leaks, but there have been no further leaks since the monks regained possession in 1985. The three-storey north extension has serious structural problems. It was built onto the outside wall of the original monastery and there appears to have been structural movement outwards over a considerable period of time.[197]

The May 1995 report continued: "An outer stone buttress wall had been added on the north and east sides 'a long time ago' to prevent these walls bulging outwards, and internally numerous posts and props have been added to support original columns and beams as they buckled and moved northwards." In addition to the printed annual reports up to this point, which provided photos and a simple floor plan of Gongkar Monastery, the report of October 1995 explained that members of the association could visit several parts of the monastery not seen before and could better estimate the difficulty of internal reconstruction or reinforcement, concluding: "The immense weight of the upper storey seems to have destabilized the building."[198]

The Shalu Association also successfully reinforced the structure on the other side, as reported in its news bulletin:

> Restoration of the Labrang Gönkhang, or upper Protector Chapel, is complete. As in the previous Yidam Temple project, all three levels have been taken into account. A pillar misalignment on the first floor was provoking imminent collapse of one entire section of the main building. Firstly the entire structure was lifted and consolidated from the base, with massive new pillars in the grain storage area below. The top floor was considerably lightened by removal of top-heavy stone roofing.[199]

Béguin 1995

Though Huntington's use in 1980 and 1990 of the traditional names for the styles found little resonance among most other scholars, they were carefully taken into account by Gilles Béguin, who also was trying to achieve a global overview of the stylistic development of Tibetan painting. Working for many years on the varied thangka collection of the Musée Guimet in Paris, Béguin published his catalog of that collection in 1995. Unlike many curators of that period, he rigorously investigated seventeenth- through nineteenth-century paintings and styles. Like Huntington, he could not read Tibetan, but he tried to employ as many indigenous stylistic names as possible, taking into account the description of the art-historical chapter from Kongtrül's encyclopedia, as summarized by Smith 1970.

Béguin in one passage briefly summarized his idea of the Khyenri style, mainly following Huntington and Huntington 1990.[200] He also suggested as a possible example a thangka of Pañjaranātha Mahākāla (Gur gyi mgon po) from the Fournier collection, as his catalog number 175, though that example is incorrect.[201]

Jackson 1996

In *A History of Tibetan Painting*, I tried to document as much as possible the art and career of Khyentse Chenmo as one of the most prominent artists of Tibetan history. Though few good photos of Gongkar murals were available to me, I tried to clarify the most relevant Tibetan-language sources. I corrected, for example, the translation of Kongtrül's brief account of the Menri and Khyenri styles:

> The Main Tibetan Traditions
> The painting lineage of the present day has spread as two traditions— the sMan tradition and the mKhyen style. [These were] the artistic lineages of [the artists] mKhyen brtse from the area of Gong dkar stod, and sMan bla don grub who was born in Lho brag sMan thang, the emanation of Mañjuśrī who [in a previous lifetime] when born in China painted the (silk?) scroll painting "Great Chinese [-style depiction of the Buddha's] Deeds" (*rgya mdzad chen mo*), and who [like mKhyen brtse] was one of two students of rDo pa bKra shis rgyal po who were more skillful than that master.

At that time, I thought Khyentse was less of a stylistic pioneer and radical innovator. I relied too much on one Tibetan traditional authority on art, the Thirteenth Karmapa, and his stylistic generalizations about the Khyenri, found in his work entitled *Little List for Appraising Things* (*dPyad don tho chung*).[202] The Karmapa asserted that Khyentse Chenmo preceded the great Menthangpa Menla Döndrup, crediting him for establishing the first excellent Tibetan style.[203]

Actually, Khyentse could not have antedated Menla Döndrup by more than a few years, for—according to a long-standing and plausible tradition—the two artists were contemporaries. In fact, according to the Desi Sanggye Gyatsho, both artists had studied under the same master painter, Dopa Tashi Gyalpo.[204] In chapter 6 of my 1996 book, I did not go beyond identifying a few reliable examples of paintings in the Khyenri style, nor was I in a position to adequately describe it.[205]

Figure 2.10, a painting depicting Four-handed Mahākāla, is an example of a Khyenri-style painting from the Jonangpa tradition in Tāranātha's time, which I did not make clear enough in my 1996 book. I did state that it resembles the Khyenri style in murals of *yidam* deities at Gongkar.[206]

Jackson 1997

In the essay "Chronological Notes on the Founding Masters of Tibetan Painting Traditions," I summarized what I knew about the dating of the great painters who founded schools of art. I discussed Khyentse Chenmo, and my two illustrations were of the Hevajra Chapel at

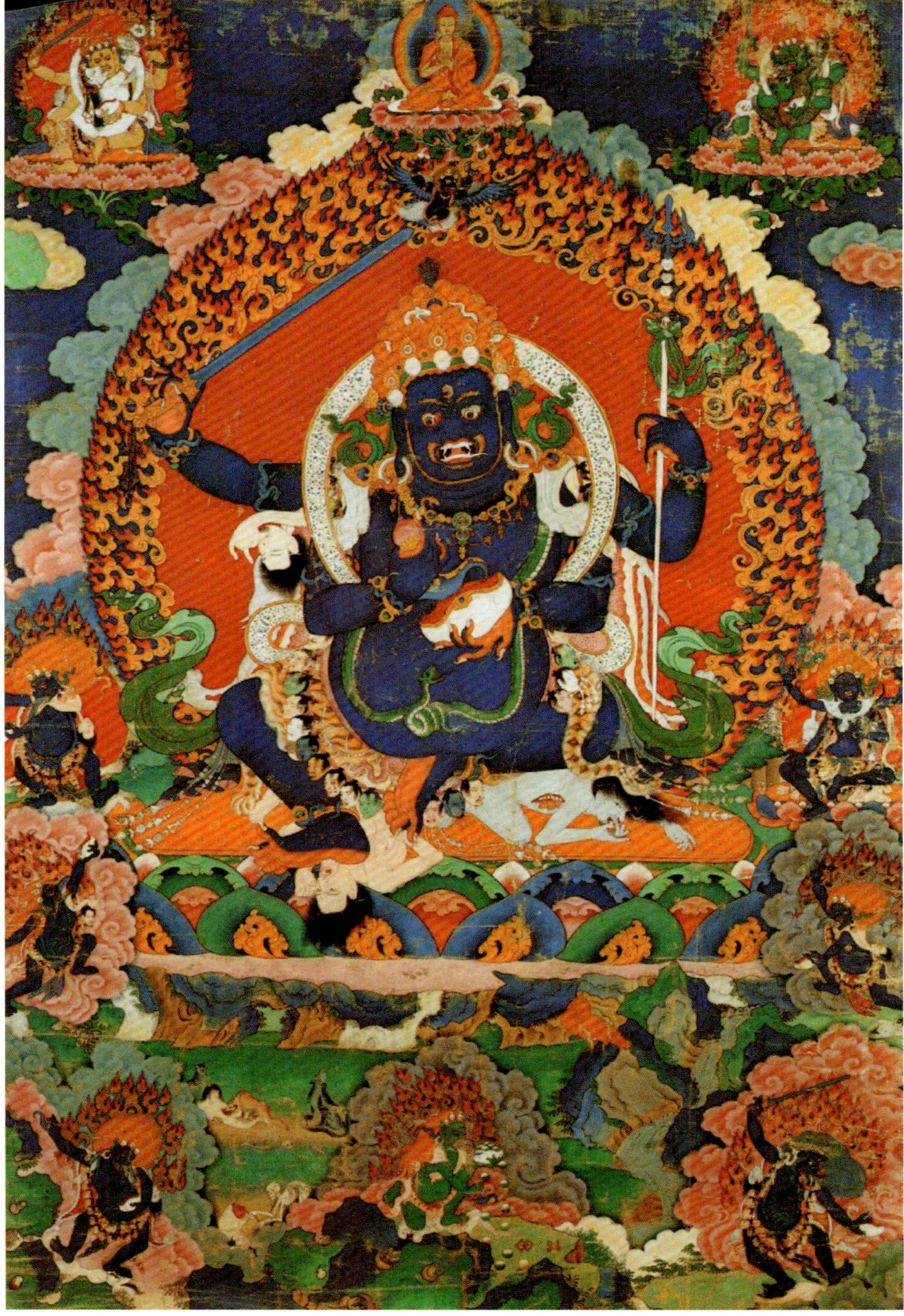

Gongkar.[207] I needlessly qualified the murals as at least the work of artists of the Khyenri tradition; I had heard erroneous reports that the chapel was part of a later addition on the northern side of the main building in Gongkar.

RHIE AND THURMAN 1999

Marylin Rhie and Robert Thurman, in their catalog of the Rubin collection, *Worlds of Transformation*, attempted to apply the three main traditional stylistic categories—Menri, Karma Gardri, and Khyenri—to thangkas.[208] Regarding the Khyenri style, Rhie mainly based her work on some of my 1996 findings, and she briefly introduced "the Master Khyenri Wangchuk (ca. 1420–1500)."

In a separate, later publication, I briefly discussed and suggested a few corrections to some of the stylistic identifications that Rhie made.[209] While three of her identifications as Khyenri (her catalog nos. 2, 95, and 165) cannot be accepted, one of her selections was apt (Fig. 2.11).

Rhie dated the painting in Figure 2.11 to the seventeenth century, describing it as:

> [reflecting] the Khyenri tradition in the large, handsome fierce form and in the gorgeous outer halo, features descended from the fifteenth century. The landscape is also uncommonly rich, and may also represent the Khyenri tradition as developed in the seventeenth century, possibly with some interaction with the New Menri and Karma Gardri styles. These, however, are not readily distinguished here. The fine drawing and modeling in the mountains and clouds impart a rather high degree of naturalism, which is then skillfully counteracted by the inclusion of unnatural, pastel colors. In totality, this is a brilliantly successful tangka of Guru Rinpoche.[210]

I do not see evidence of "interaction with the New Menri and Karma Gardri styles," here or elsewhere. Rhie also presented several paintings from the same sixteen-arhat set as in the Khyenri style: four thangkas, numbers 24 through 27, depicted arhats, and numbers 51 and 52 showed two guardian kings.[211]

Rhie detected a Khyenri connection in number 65, a monumental depiction of early Nyingma (possibly

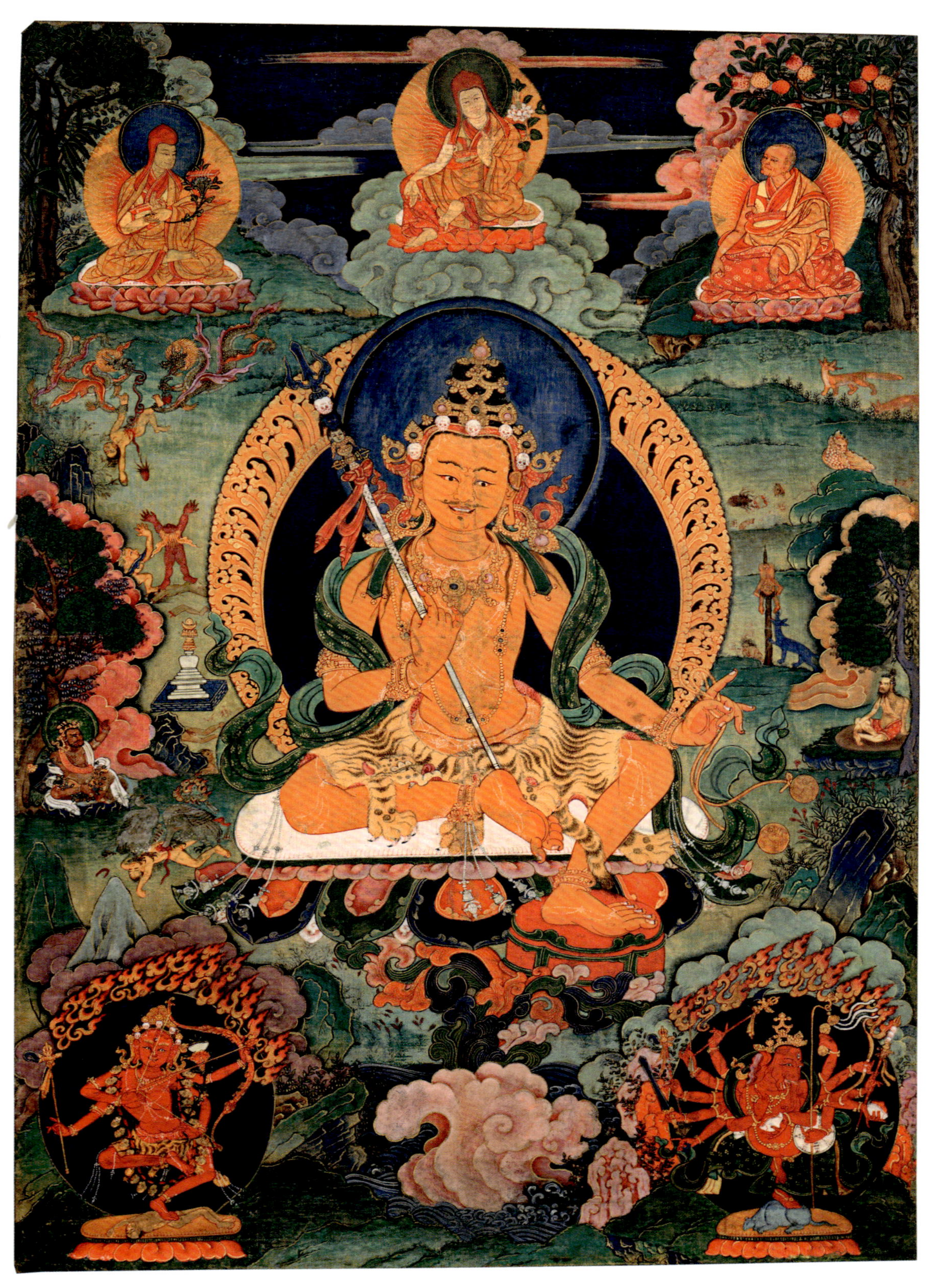

Fig. 2.11
Padmasambhava as Sūryaprabha (Nyima
Öser)
second half of the fifteenth century
30 x 21 ½ in. (76.2 x 54.6 cm)
Collection of Shelley and Donald Rubin
(HAR 675)
Literature: Rhie and Thurman 1999, no. 61

early Dzogchen lineage) masters, which I presented above as Figure 1.18. She commented about it:

> The density of the colors, the clarity of pattern, and the naturalism (as in the loose robes of the lama) along with the lyrical grace and mannered patterns of lines and shapes, reveal the eclecticism of the style, which at present is difficult to ascribe to a specific school. In the freedom of drawing, the solid tones of color, and the shapes of the mountains, this work has some resemblance to the set of arhats in the Khyenri tradition. [212]

GYURME DORJE 1999

In his *Tibet Handbook*, Gyurme Dorje mentioned the murals of Gongkar:

> Here there are still important murals typical of the free-flowing Khyenri school of painting, which were the original work of Jamyang Khyentse Wangchuk (b. 1524). . . . The murals of the assembly hall depicting the Twelve Deeds of Shakyamuni Buddha are relatively new, but there are original Khyenri-style murals of the Five Founders of Sakya and [Lama] Dampa Sönam Gyaltshen flanking the entrance to the central inner sanctum.[213]

The temple of Pañjaranātha, Gyurme Dorje says, contains "exquisite gold on black painted murals of Mahākāla in the form of Pañjaranātha and his retinue, the preferred protectors of the Sakya tradition." Moreover, "the walls of the circumambulatory walkway around the central inner sanctum have original murals depicting the thousand buddhas of this aeon." He mentioned seeing outside the second floor of the building, in the gallery, "fine murals depicting the Six Ornaments and Two Supreme Ones

of ancient India, and motifs of geometric poetry."

SMITH 2001

Three decades after his first contribution, in 1970, Gene Smith revised his introduction to Kongtrül's encyclopedia, correcting several errors. In his new version, he wrote:

> The mid-fifteenth century also saw the birth of the second great school (after the sMan ris), the mKhyen ris, which takes its origins and name from mKhyen brtse chen mo of Gong dkar. This style, too, shows a degree of Chinese influence and differs from the sMan ris in its greater realism, its complicated stylized lotuses and a few other details. The murals of Gong dkar of the late fifteenth century represent this school at its best. Examples of the mKhyen ris are much rarer than representative works of the other major schools, a fact that suggests that the style of painting declined along with the Sa skya schools in Central Tibet from the mid-1600s onward. But the style experienced a temporary revival thanks to the patronage of the Fifth Dalai Lama.[214]

Smith also stressed that Khyentse Chenmo should not be confused with Nesar Khyentse Wangchuk (gNas gsar mKhyen brtse'i dbang phyug, b. 1524), the prominent disciple of Tsharchen.[215]

LINROTHE 2004

In his *Paradise and Plumage* catalog, Rob Linrothe presented some arhat paintings that I believe were either painted by Khyentse Chenmo or copied from his works. One set is represented by a single painting, catalog number 9, Arhat Kālika, which he described

interestingly, as I quote below in chapter 9 in connection with Figure 9.9a.[216]

He dated another set, represented by catalog numbers 3, 15, and 19, to the seventeenth century. He also listed all known members of the entire set in the appendix. In chapter 10 I present the set below as a sixteenth-century copy (see Figs. 10.1–10.4.).

LINROTHE 2006

In his *Holy Madness* catalog, Linrothe presented numerous excellent paintings, including many from sets depicting the eighty-four siddhas. From among those, I now believe that we can identify three sets that were either painted by Khyentse Chenmo or copied from his work.

One of the excellent works that drew his highest admiration is Figure 2.12 (his catalog no. 40), a painting of three great adepts in the collection of the Rubin Museum of Art. I quoted the beginning of Linrothe's description of this work in an earlier publication:

> This painting is brimming with evidence for the artist's bravura performance of what must have been a well-known iconographic score. The accessories [of the three great adepts] appear next to each siddha in identical configurations in the murals of the Lükhang. . . . Although their forms are part of a stock, pattern-book type, the artist has gone to great lengths to instill each of the three figures with personality and to infuse their setting with tour-de-force details that only slowly reveal themselves. The painterly quality of the art is extraordinary and transcends that of the related murals by a large measure. The subtlety begins at the upper edge of the painting with the rose-tinted wash, which contributes a resonant blush of atmosphere to the inhabited space.[217]

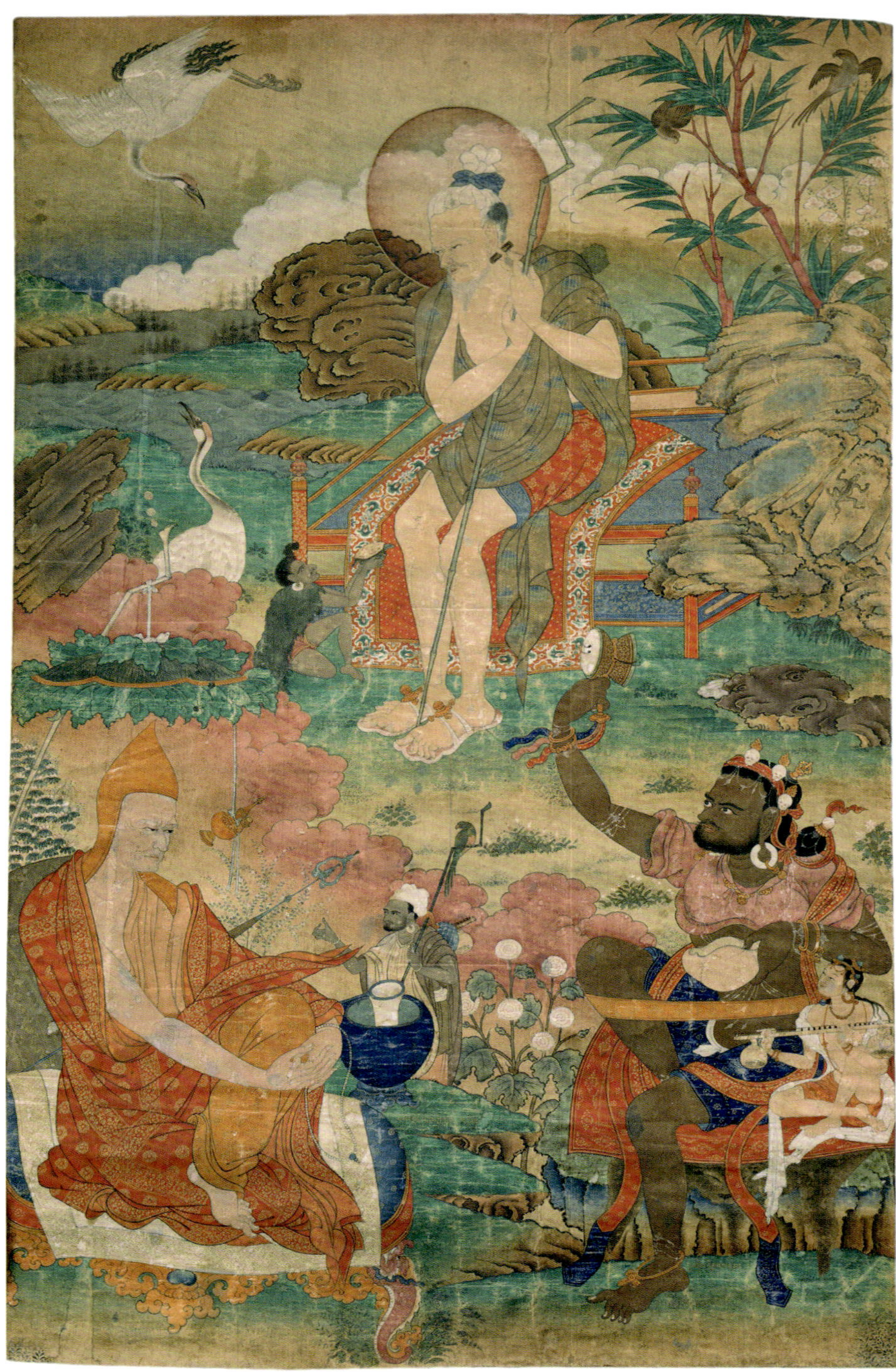

It is telling that Linrothe also used this painting for the front-cover image. I continue his apt description:

> The artist of this painting used a sharp eye, clever wit and expert drawing skills to create this painting, planting tiny surprises that reward the attentive viewer: the sutures on the skull held by Virāya, the sitar held by his consort that echoes that of Suvarṇadvīpa's interlocutor, the eyelashes on the head of the lion skin on which the couple sits, and above all, the patterns. This artist knew Chinese textiles and lacquer decoration, not to speak of bird-and-flower paintings. Details of Indian dress and tie-dyed decorations on Kamala's robe bespeak plausible familiarity with Indian customs as well.[218]

After noting the existence of a Japanese publication that illustrated eleven paintings of similar subjects, including one with an identical subject, Linrothe concluded:

> The artist's mastery of Chinese art and culture and the intense colors against a plain, unpainted upper background suggest an eastern Tibetan provenance. That these three mahāsiddhas could be so well imaged is a tribute to the artist's creative abilities …. [9]

Thus, when exploring this painting, we are continuously reminded of the artist's remarkable skills. What struck me when I saw it in person were the transparent head nimbuses, or the lack of them, and the pink clouds. Indeed, the use of pink was striking in three places: in the clouds, the upper garment of Ḍamarupa, and a front leg of the throne of Suvarṇadvīpa. Khyentse Chenmo's depiction of animals is masterful. He has portrayed two species of birds: two

Manchurian storks and three brown-green parrots, each in a different lifelike posture. Linrothe identified the two nesting in the tree as doves, but their tails are too long and their beaks too stubby. The chameleon lizard, crawling camouflaged on a rock outcropping above Ḍamarupa, has an almost human face. A living turtle is offered to one adept by a votary. The highly detailed throne of Suvarṇadvīpa features complicated legs and a decorative bottom edge.[220]

Another outstanding painting is Linrothe's catalog number 41, which depicts Śavaripa and Dārikapa. The painting bears three typical marks of Khyentse Chenmo's work: a pair of naturalistic birds perched in a tree, other lifelike animals, and unusually true-to-life poses and details of the major and minor figures (see Fig. 7.41).

Another intriguing set of paintings that now survives in Basel and Boston, numbers 20 through 25, follows the order of Vajrāsana. It contains some small details that are typical of Khyentse Chenmo, such as the foreign travelers or sadhus at the top of Figure 2.13 and the charnel ground scene, with two vultures, a crow, and a dog, at the bottom of his catalog number 25.[221] Such details are proof that the paintings were copied from thangkas created by Khyentse Chenmo.

In Figure 2.13, the white elephant is loaded with many jewels and other precious things such as branches of red coral, and is led by two travelers, one of which wears a white turban. Two other foreign rishis or travelers stand nearby; they should be holding *vīṇā*s, but the artist has wrongly copied them as long canes with bent ends and bundles attached. Also, the later artist has left out both resonating gourds of the instruments. Other Khyentse features in this painting are the ducks waiting at the edge of the lake and dragons emerging dramatically from a cluster of clouds. Similar Khyentse Chenmo details, in charnel grounds, are found at the bottom

of Linrothe 2006, catalog numbers 22 and 25.

Figure 2.14a depicts some other great adepts from the fixed group of eighty-four, the siddhas 10 through 12, as shown in the Sera set. It does not follow the Vajrāsana order as above but rather Abhayadattaśrī's collection of siddha hagiographies. In the tenth and twenty-seventh paintings of the Sera set, we find typical Khyentse details of charnel grounds and dragons emerging from

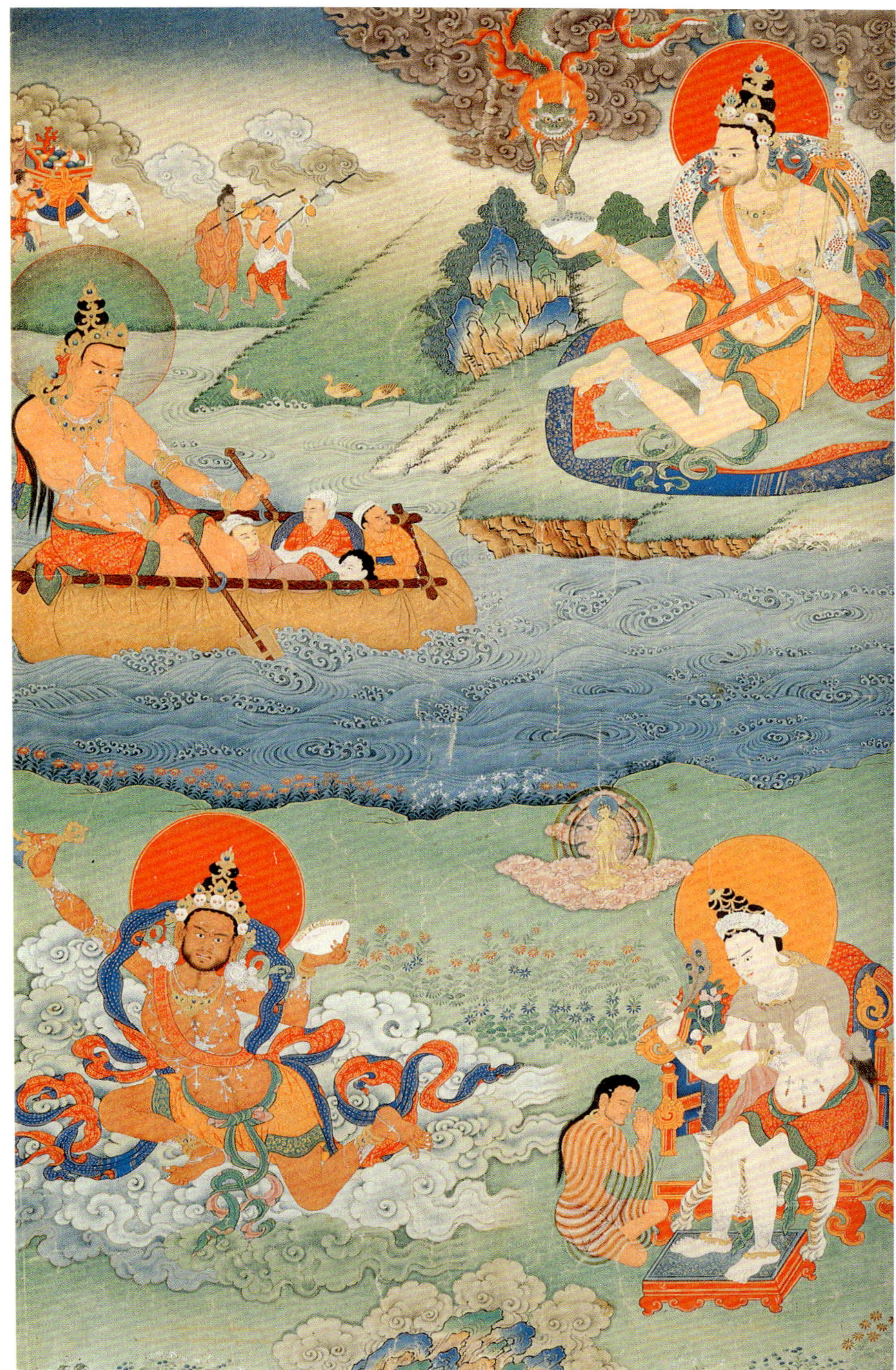

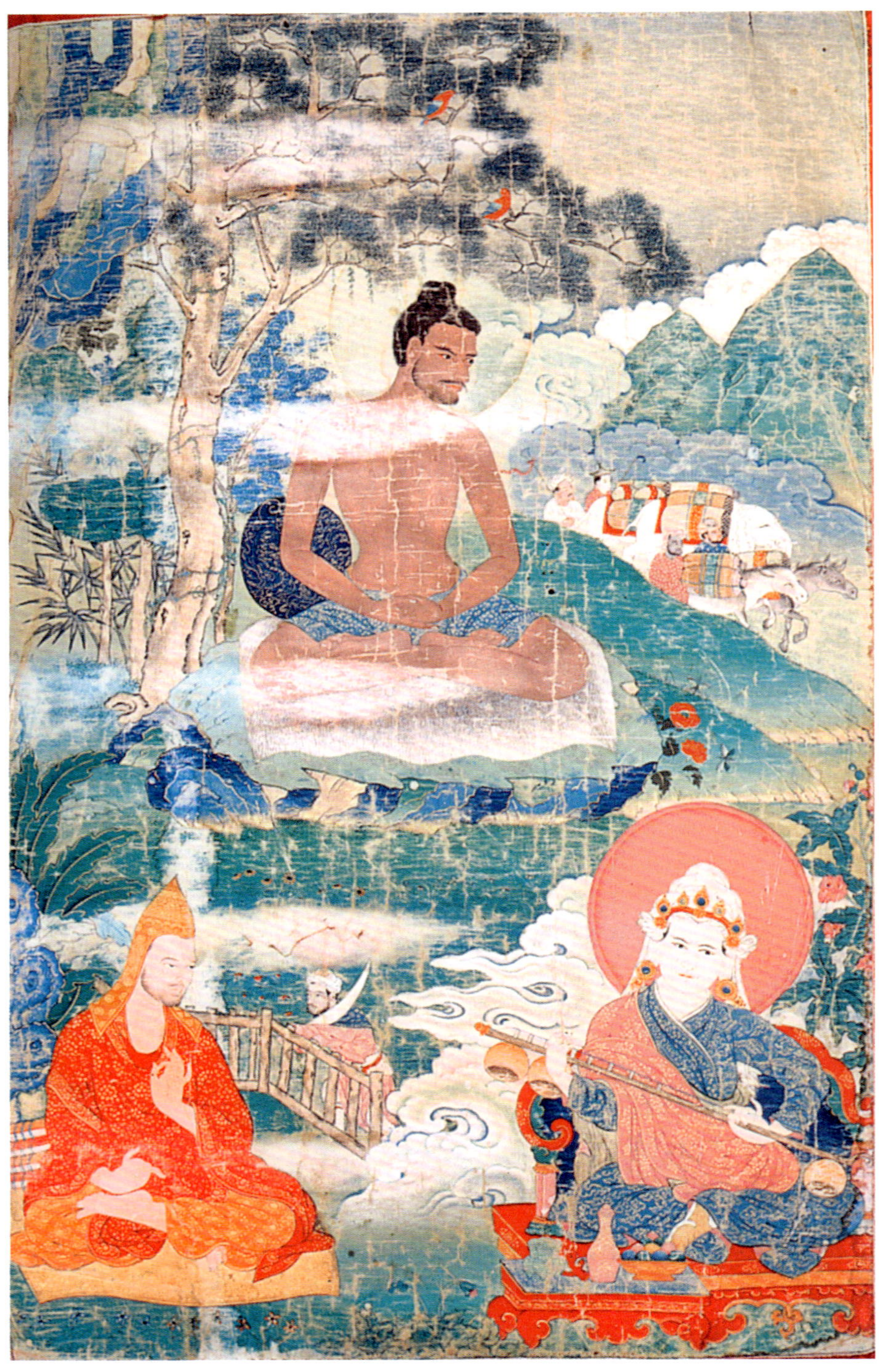

elephants and two horses carrying cargo. Below, next to Śāntipa, a traveling trader carries a whole elephant tusk in his arms. He also belongs to the caravan.

Thus both Figures 2.13 and 2.14a depict as prominent minor characters foreign traders traveling with white elephants loaded with jewels or cargo, a theme we shall also see below. In fact, the Indian "Ācārya leading an elephant" (Tib. *atsara glang 'khrid*) became in Tibetan mural painting a common decorative theme related to "The Mongol leading the Tiger" (*sog po stag 'khrid*). (See Fig. 2.14b.) Though considered a decorative motif, it had religious symbolism: the elephant stood for elephant-headed Gaṇeṣa, while the Indian ascetic for Vaiśravaṇa, both gods of wealth. The elephant here carries a load of radiant jewels that fills an ornate wooden box and which is secured like a saddle to the animal's back.

As Figure 2.14c shows, elephants carrying precious objects or carrying a boy on its back were typical Chinese motifs, showing us the origin of the jewel-laden elephant in Figure 2.13. In Chinese art elephants were also typically shown carrying a wish-fulfilling gem or the sacred alms bowl of the Buddha. In China, elephants symbolized strength and astuteness and were a common animal motif.[222]

JACKSON 2005B

I published a contribution to the *Die Welt der tibetischen Buddhismus* (The World of Tibetan Buddhism) exhibition catalog for the Museum der Völkerkunde in Hamburg. The English title of my article is "Traces of Tāranātha and his Previous Lives: Paintings from the Jonangpa School of Tibetan Buddhism." One of the main series of thangkas that I published in black-and-white plates, illustrations 2 through 18, was a set depicting the previous lives of Tāranātha. This major set of Khyenri portraits probably

clouds. Little Khyentse touches like those prove the ultimate origin of that set. I think the Basel paintings (like Fig. 2.13) were painted in a Drukpa Kagyu monastery in northeast Kham, such as Khampa Gar. Through their Drukpa Kagyu connections in central Tibet, they would have been able to get a Khyentse original or a close copy.

Above adept number 10, Tsoramgipa, is an approaching caravan of foreign travelers with their two white

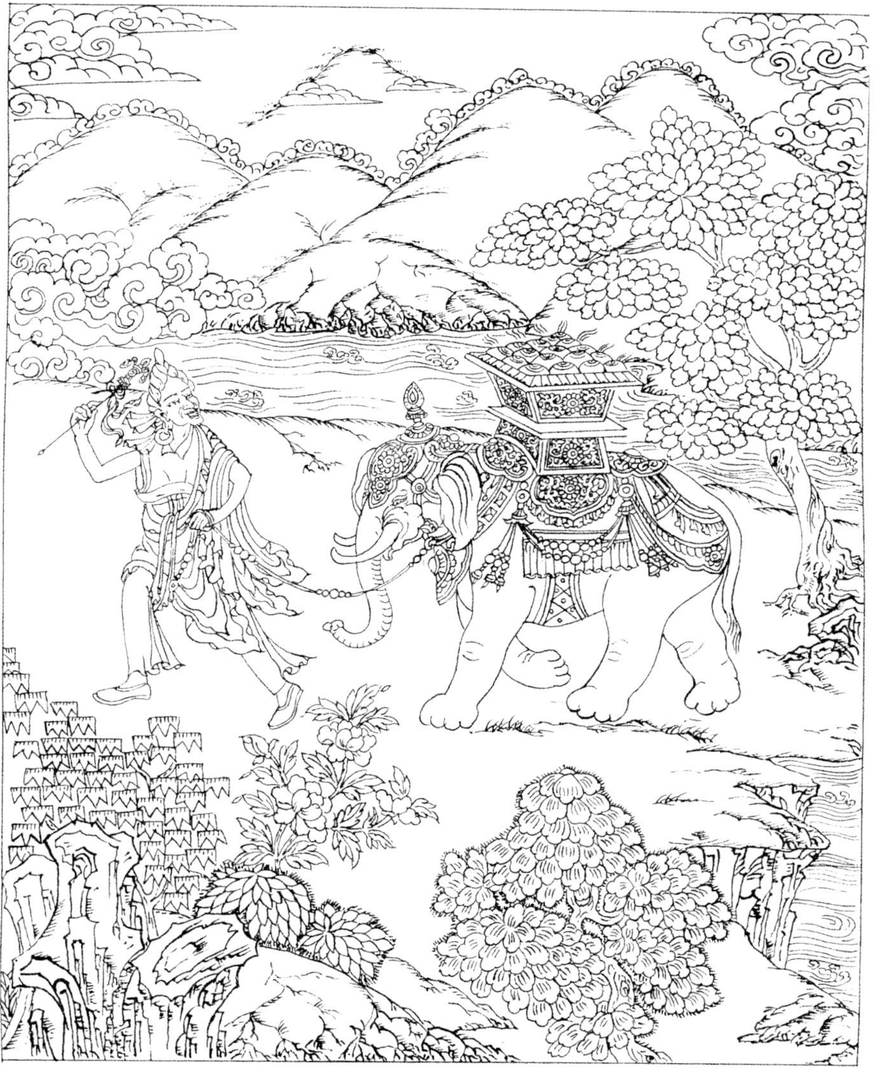

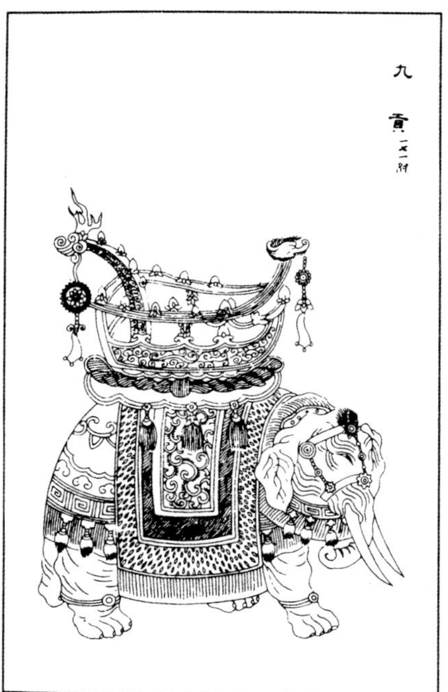

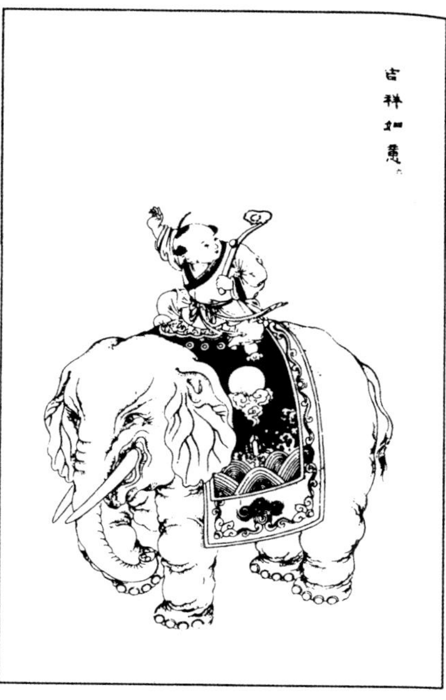

Fig. 2.14B
Ācārya leading an elephant
After: Awang Gesang 1999, p. 238.

2.14C
Two Chinese elephants
After: W. Eberhard 1990, p. 94

dates to the 1620s, that is, the lifetime of
Tāranātha (see Fig. 2.15). In one passage
I mentioned the existence of Khyentse
Chenmo's paintings at Gongkar and
Thekchen Chöje's tradition, including
the Lamdre *si thang* paintings.[223]

JACKSON 2007

In my contribution to the volume *The
Pandita and the Siddha*, I reconsidered a
number of stylistic identifications made
by Rhie and Thurman in their *Worlds of
Transformation*. I summarized in outline form the main Tibetan styles, using
those rubrics to classify a few paintings
in the private Rubin collection that I had
seen in the late 1990s. I presented three
brief sections on the Khyenri: the early
style of Khyentse Chenmo's time, the
seventeenth-century revival by the Fifth
Dalai Lama, and the establishment of a
branch of the painting school at Drigung
Monastery in the late seventeenth century.[224] I corrected the false use of names
and the statement that Khyentse painted
for the large Geluk monastic establish-
ments, Sera and Drepung, in Lhasa. I
accepted one of Rhie's identifications
as the Khyenri style (HAR 675) but
rejected two others.

FERMER 2009

Mathias Fermer's unpublished master's
thesis contains numerous long notes
relevant to Gongkar Dorjeden and its
art. For example, in note 191, Fermer
described the building of Gongkar, quoting the relevant Tibetan passage from
Gyatön Changchup Wangyal and adding

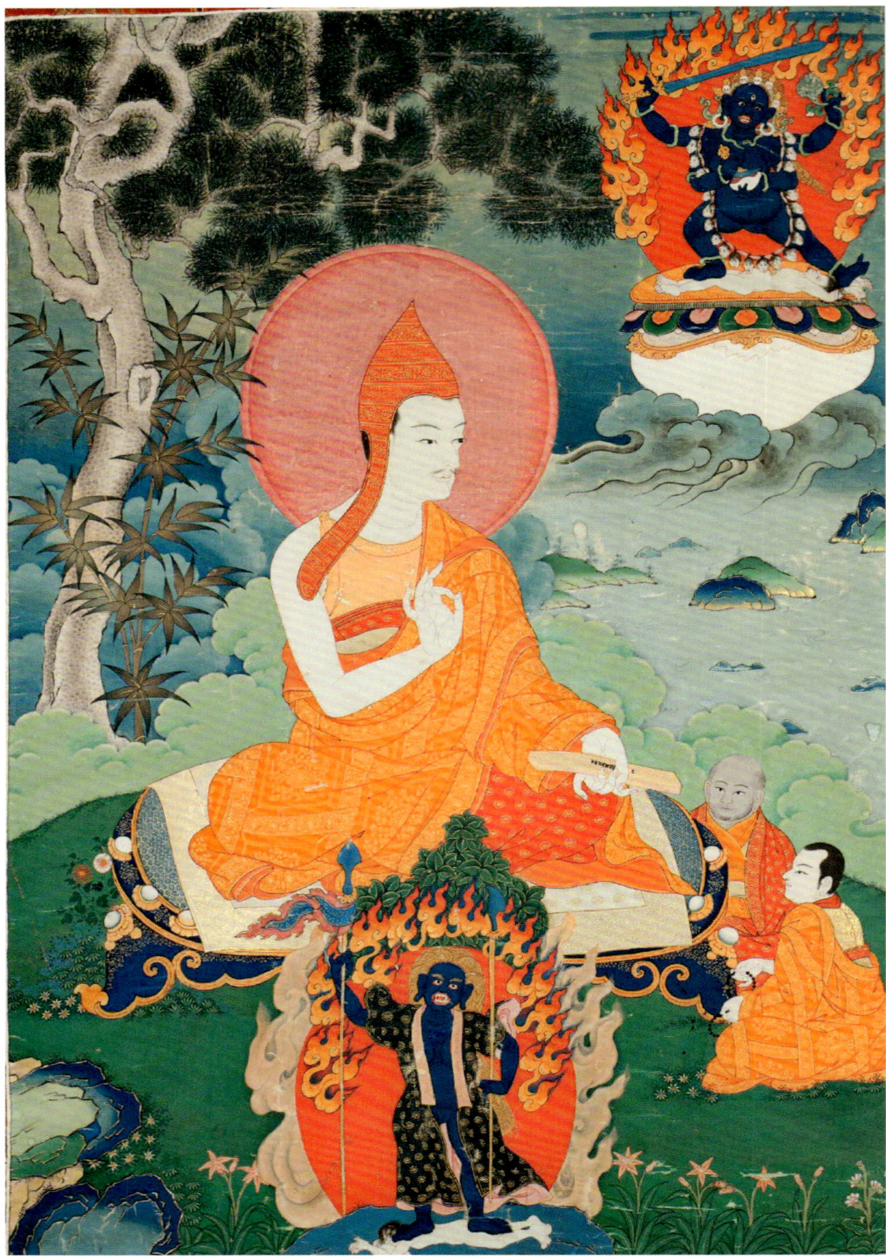

practitioner (*dge bsnyen*; *upāsaka*). In note 194, Fermer discussed Khyentse Chenmo's surviving murals at Gongkar:

> Some of Khyentse's fine murals have survived in a good condition up to these days, basically due to the foresighted undertaking of a monk who covered the painted walls with a layer of whitewash before new officials got hold of the monastery in 1959 [oral information given by Tenpa Gyatso]. Dorjeden is the original home of the mKhyen [b]ris painting style and "the greatest mKhyen ris paintings for later generations were, in fact, the murals of Gong dkar rDo rje gdan monastery."[225] A description of Khyentse's style and the tradition which emerged out of that is found in the fourth chapter of Prof. Jackson's survey of different Tibetan painting traditions.[226] Some of the murals which were executed by the illustrious artist from Gongkar can also be seen in the Japanese publication entitled *Chibetto mikkyô no shinpi: nazo no tera 'Konkaru Doruje den' ga kataru: kairaku no sora-chi'e no umi = Gong dkar rdo rje gdan*. This colorful book is basically a study of the Yi dam chapel located in the first storey of Dorjeden.[227]

information from the abbatial history of Shalu and Dungkar's modern dictionary. Fermer, in the same note, went on to describe the temple's main structure, listing its nineteen main chapels or rooms. He also enumerated several important Tibetan descriptions of Gongkar, such as the accounts of Kathok Situ and Situ Panchen, who visited the monastery as pilgrims, and a pilgrim's guide to Chuwo Ri (*Chu bo ri'i gnas yig*).

In note 192, Fermer listed Khyentse Chenmo among the disciples of Kunga Namgyal, as student number 91; he was, as his name tells us, a lay

Osada et al. 2010

In his illustrated guidebook to the Tibetan cultural realm, *Mapping the Tibetan World,* Yukiyasu Osada briefly mentioned Gongkar Monastery.[228] Describing the monastery correctly as the head monastery of the Gongkarwa subschool of the Sakya sect and as a fifteenth-century establishment, he also provided a map of Gongkar Monastery and its vicinity (Fig. 2.16).

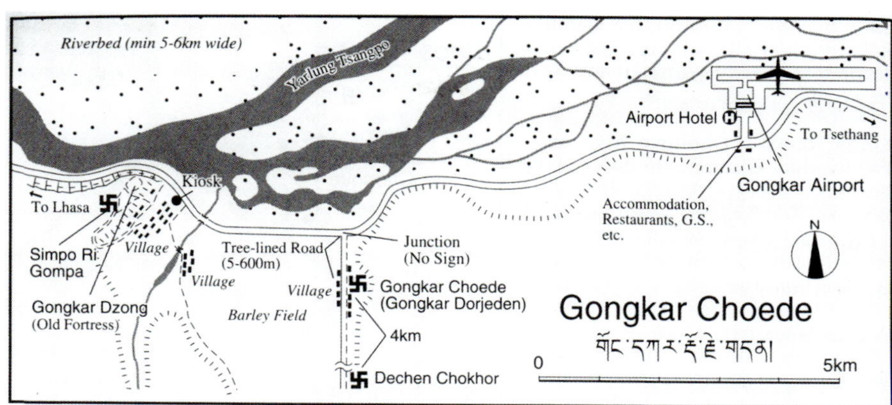

Fig. 2.16
Map of Gongkar Chöde and vicinity
After: Osada et al. 2010, 96

Fig. 2.17
Karmapa
second half of sixteenth century
59 ¼ x 42 ¼ in. (150.5 x 107.3 cm)
Rubin Museum of Art
C2005.20.2 (HAR 90005)
Literature: Pal 1984a, pl. 90; and Jackson
2009, fig. 5.13

JACKSON 2009

In my *Patron and Painter* catalog, I discussed a set of the eighty-four siddhas, now at Sera Monastery near Lhasa.[229] A Tibet University professor suggested that the set was in the style of Namkha Tashi, who flourished in the late sixteenth century, about a century after Khyentse Chenmo. However, the Vajradhara of that set possessed typical features of the Khyenri; I dated that work (catalog no. 5.12) to about the seventeenth century. But now, after reexamining it and other Karma Kagyu art from that chapter, I see evidence of the Khyenri style in works I had then considered very early Karma Gardri.

For example, in Figure 2.17, which because of its inscription we have to date to the late sixteenth century, Namkha Tashi's time, I noticed four carefully depicted pairs of birds.[230] They include pheasants, peacocks, large blue-and-green birds resembling doves, and green parrots, reminiscent of Khyentse Chenmo's unusual use of two parrots in human throne-backs.

The fine details of the landscape are also worthy of the art of Khyentse. Either this was painted by a brilliant Khyenri artist of the sixteenth century or an early Karma Gardri artist was putting birds in the backrest in ways that Khyentse would have loved.

I think Khyentse painted complete sets of the Karma Kagyu lineage, from

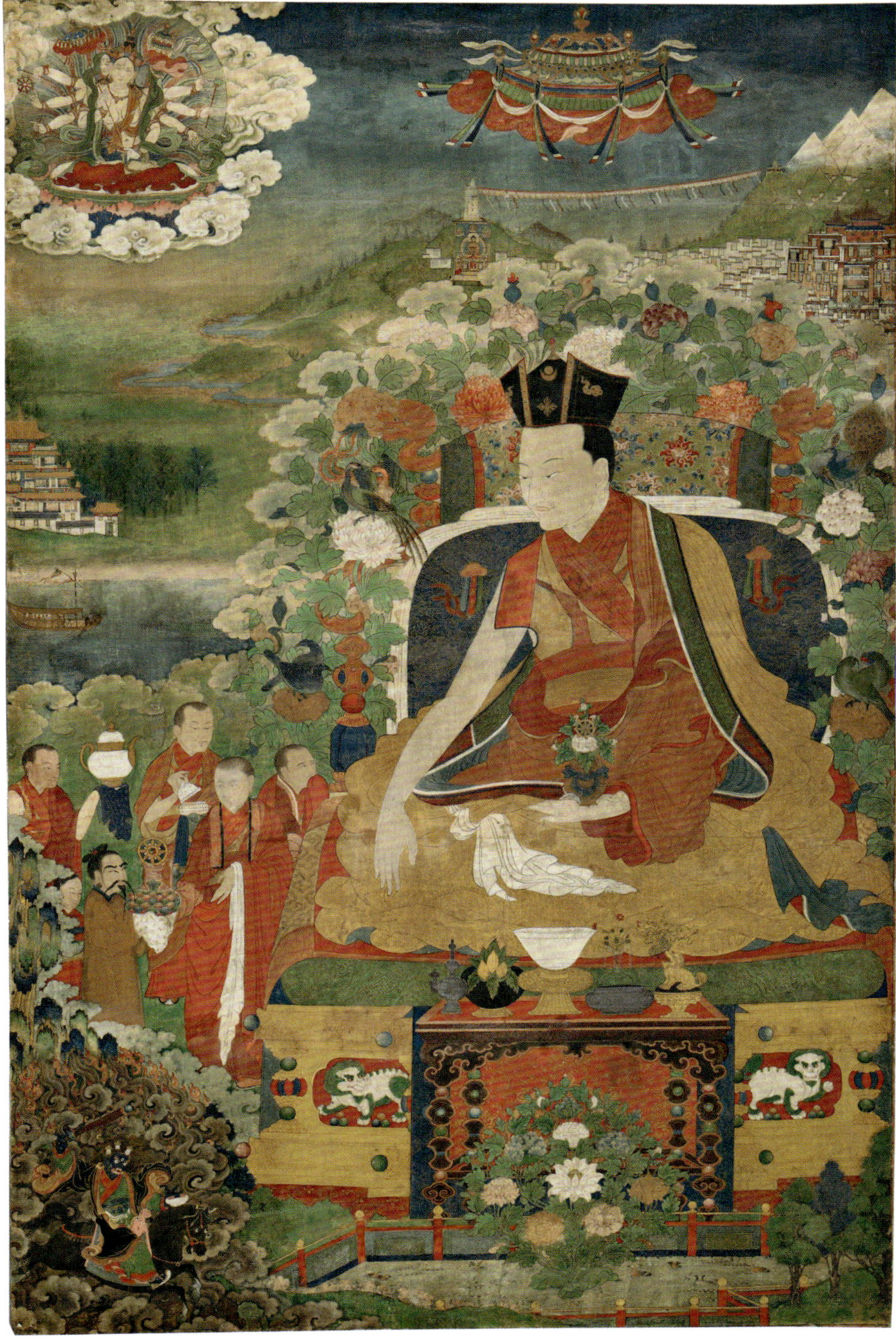

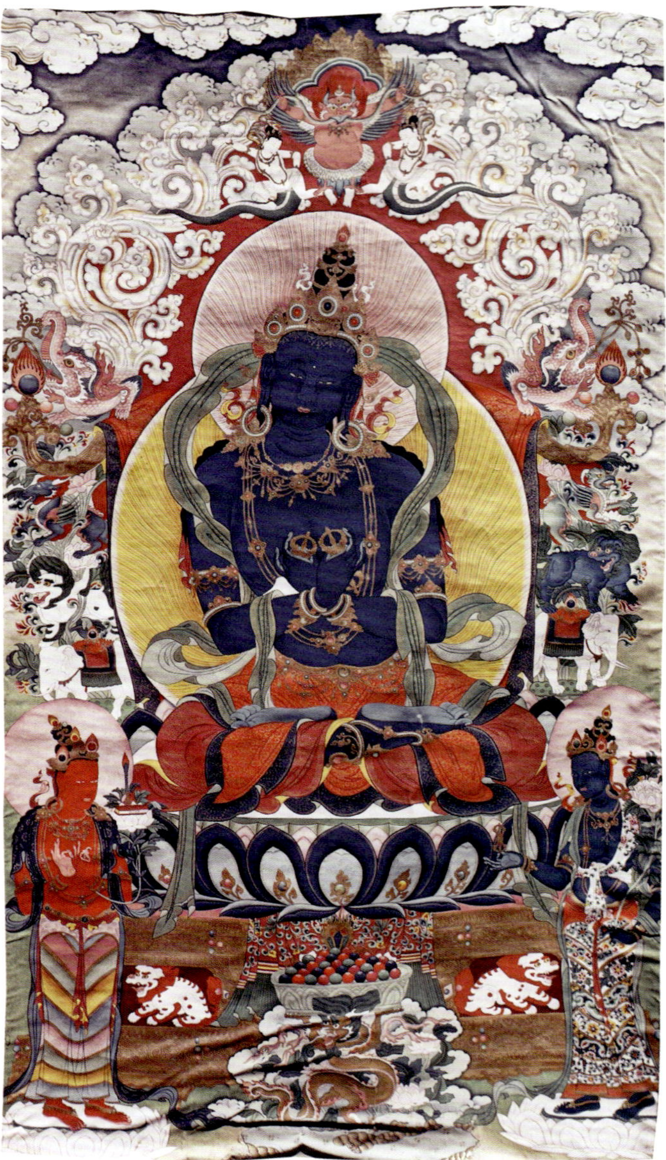

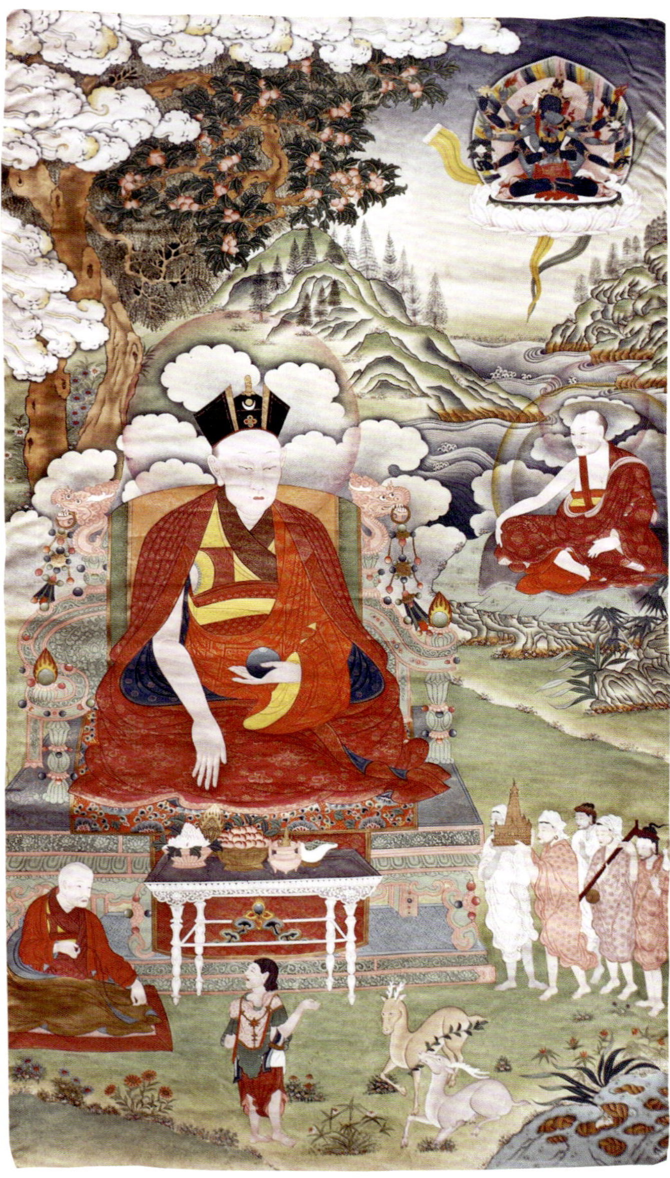

Vajradhara to the Seventh Karmapa, and that these existed and were copied within the tradition for a century or more. For a later copy of Vajradhara, see Figure 2.18.

Some of the existing Karma Kagyu art retained a few Khyentse characteristics that persisted after generations of copying, such as in Figure 2.19: the northern-Indian *vīṇā*-holding sadhu among the group of magically emanated Indian mendicants and the pair of kneeling deer, one holding a sprig in its mouth, at the foot of the portrait of the Fourth Karmapa, Rolpe Dorje. In this redrawn scene, the upper resonating gourd of the *vīṇā* is missing.[231] However,

the shape of the *vīṇā* neck, which the sadhu holds with both hands before him, is still recognizably different from a stick with a bag tied to it, held by the next yogi.

We find in another famous set of paintings, from Lhathok in Kham (depicting the eighty-four great adepts), a pair of Khyentse Chenmo sadhus depicted as minor figures (not illustrated). Similar to Figure 2.13, they have been recopied by painters who wrongly interpreted the *vīṇā*s to be sticks with cloth-bound bundles tied to them.

But a still earlier version of the same detail survives in a painting that I believe was by Khyentse Chenmo.

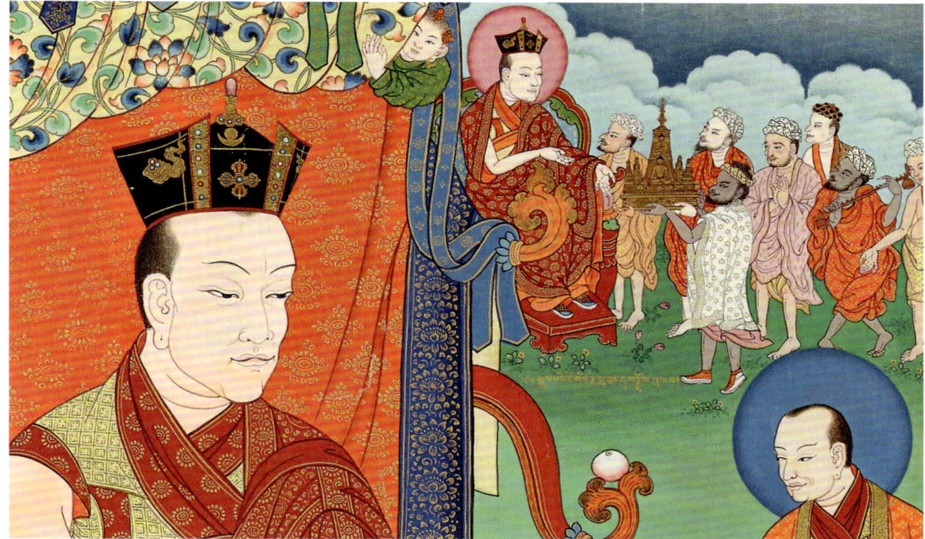

Figure 2.20 (a detail from Fig. 1.21) shows an episode in which Rolpe Dorje is offered a gilt *gaṇḍhola* shrine by a group of seven magically emanated Indian yogis at Tselhagang (rTse lha sgang), some with dark turbans and one clearly holding a *vīṇā*. So the origin of this motif, and of the major set of later paintings in which it is found, becomes clearer. Khyentse Chenmo likely provided original paintings for the Karma Kagyu lineage down to the Seventh Karmapa, including some of the striking historical details such as of the Fifth Karmapa visiting the Ming court. (See Fig. 1.37.)

JACKSON 2012

In *The Place of Provenance*, I briefly mentioned the Khyenri—"In the nineteenth and early twentieth centuries, the Khyenri also existed as a rare non-Menri minor tradition in Lhokha in southern Ü, near its main historical seat, Gongkar Monastery"—and the Driri as a possible continuation of the Khyenri.[232] This

revised my earlier statement that the Khyenri had died out in Lhokha by the early twentieth century.[233]

TSECHANG PENBA WANGDU 2010

Tsechang Penba Wangdu (rTse byang sPen pa dbang 'dus), in a 2010 article written in Tibetan, usefully summarized Khyentse Chenmo's life and art. Though the original version clarifies several points, its 2012 English translation by Amy Heller, available online, is not satisfactory. It omits his opening synopsis and refers to Khyentse Chenmo with the erroneous names "Khyentse Wangpo" and "Khyentse Wangchuk." Heller also made historical mistakes, writing, for instance, "As of 1472, there was the construction of two additional *chörtens* and mKhyen brtse was invited to Gong dkar once again."[234] The original passage in Tibetan tells about Khyentse Chenmo's painting murals not in two stupas but in a single one, and not at Gongkar but at Champaling. Heller translates another passage:

> Again, following this period, mKhyen brtse was requested to return to Gong dkar rdo rje gdan by his root lama Kun dga' rnam rgyal, where it was said that now mKhyen brtse was the only great

painter alive after the death of the painter sMan bla don grub.[235]

No source states that Khyentse Chenmo was requested to return to Gongkar. Moreover, Penba Wangdu took pains in his original article to reject the opinion of another art historian, who asserted without documentation, that Khyentse Chenmo was the only great painter alive after the death of the painter Menla Döndrup. Penba Wangdu stressed several times how little information was available about the great artist's life, and nowhere did he assert what Heller translates as, "It is thanks to the biography of the founder of Gong dkar, his root lama Kun dga' rnam rgyal that we have information about his activities spanning from roughly 1430 until 1500."[236] Because of such errors in the online version, Penba Wangdu's article of 2010 requires a new translation; I will retranslate two of the three main parts of that article in chapter 3.

JACKSON 2015

In chapter 6 of the *Painting Traditions of the Drigung Kagyu* catalog, I presented some paintings from the middle period of Drigung Kagyu art. They included nine thangkas in the Khyenri style (catalog nos. 6.8–6.16), such as seven that were preserved at Phyang Monastery, in Ladakh. Figure 2.21 exemplifies this series, showing the great Kagyu lineal guru Tilopa surrounded by five siddhas from the eighty-four great adepts.

HENSS 2014

In *The Cultural Monuments of Central Tibet*, Michael Henss briefly described Gongkar Monastery and its murals.[237] He followed me in accepting what he considered an early date, that is, the fifteenth century, for Khyentse Chenmo's murals in Gongkar.[238] Unlike many

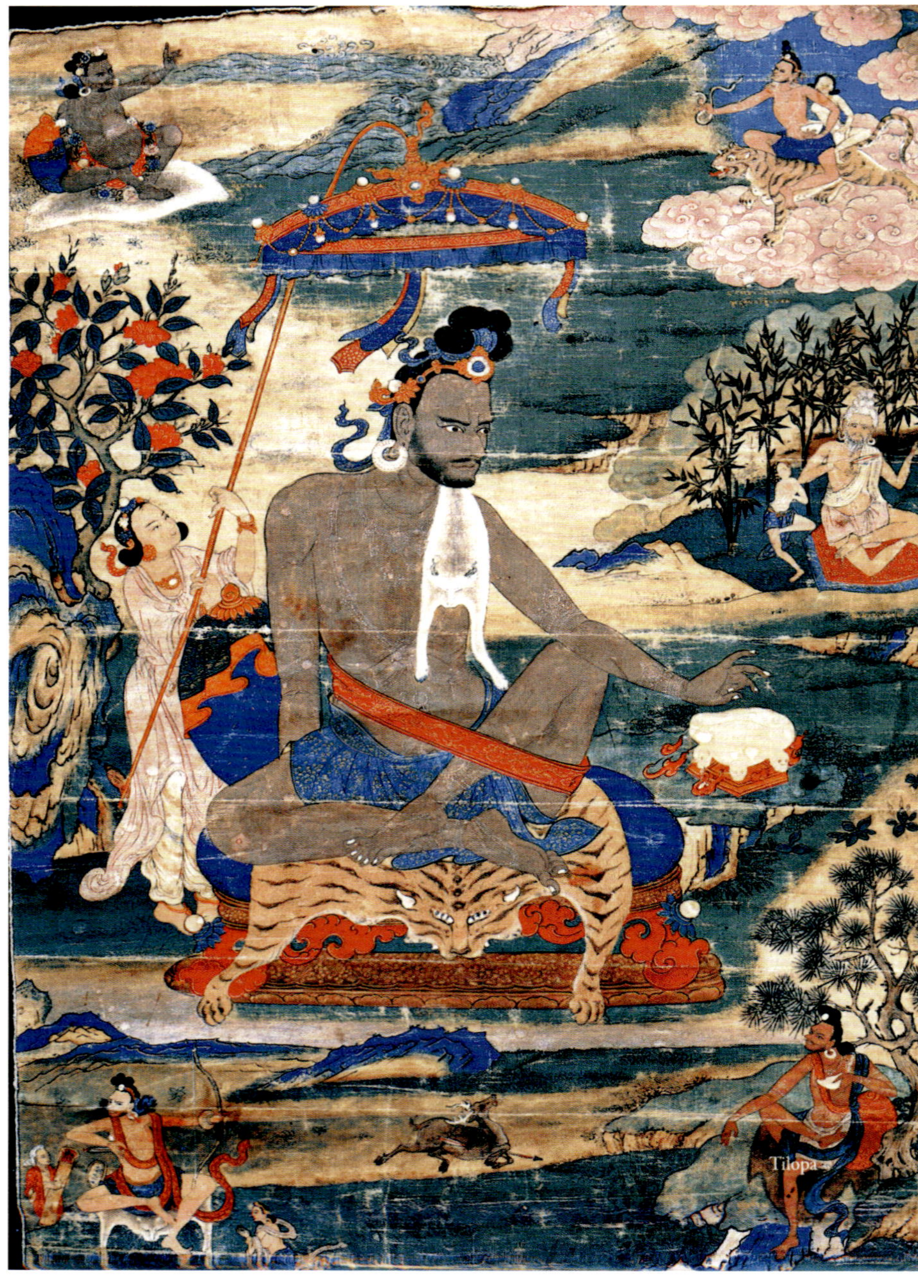

full of "realistic" landscape elements and three-dimensional
motifs. . . . Distinctive Chinese
influences such as trees and dragons, textiles and furniture, or rocky
landscapes are no longer isolated
"foreign" vocabularies, as in Gyantse (c. 1420/1440), but integrated
elements of a new overall style that
would become characteristic only
in the 16th century. Instead, in the
elegantly drawn and rather sche-
matic faces of the monks a new
sculptural and physical quality can
be discerned. And while in some
sections the color is gone due to
whitewashing and recent cleaning, a few surprisingly "realistic"
preparatory drawings of monk's
and men's heads are visible. . . .
Of the same highest artistic quality
and originality are the magnificent siddhas at the top of these
compositions.[239]

Regarding Khyentse's paintings of
the *Avadānakalpalatā* tales in another
part of the monastery, Henss judged
them to be ahead of their time and
unlike any painting elsewhere in Tibet
in the 1460s. He also characterized a
third group of paintings—depicting the
Twelve Great Deeds of the Buddha—as
innovative, using the terms *advanced*
and *modernism* loosely:

> In terms of stylistic chronology
> they are much more advanced and
> characterized by Chinese modern-
> ism, seen in landscape composition
> and scenographic architecture, and
> seem to indicate either another
> unorthodox "Khyentse idiom" or a
> different (later?) workshop.[240]

Henss considered the Hevajra
Chapel, or Divine Palace, on the second
floor to be a precious sanctuary. He
described the style of its murals (which
included Fig. 2.22; his no. 509), again

others, he avoided dating them to the
sixteenth century. He was impressed by
the murals' style, aptly commenting on
the panels that depict the Sakya founders, near the inner sanctum:

> Accepted as dating to the 1460s,
> these two large compositions mark
> a substantial break with the Tibetan
> painting tradition of the 15th cen-
> tury. Instead of a conventional
> emblematic layout of different
> registers with niches and *torana*
> settings for figures and narratives,
> there is now a spatial environment

using the term *modernism*, and asserted
that these painting were the "most
progressive" of any painting from that
period that survived anywhere in Tibet:

> Close to the Khyentse paintings
> on the ground floor, and though
> of a different stylistic idiom, char-
> acterized by a similar modernism
> in comparison with the preced-
> ing wall-painting tradition of the
> Gyantse wall-painting style. The
> traditional composition with rows
> and registers of deities framed by
> *prabha* niches remains the same,
> but is now partly combined with
> open-air scenes suggesting a much
> later style. Special motifs such as
> the lotus petals and haloes are of a
> highly ingenious graphic design,
> while for the clouds colour shading
> has replaced the conventional line
> drawing. By using a new palette of
> hitherto unseen shades of green and
> orange, the painter has gone beyond
> the traditional colour scheme.
> Whereas in Gyantse the highly
> refined decorative "Newar-Sakya
> style" had reached an unsurpassable
> mastery in the sense of what we
> may call a "synchronized" Tibetan
> identity, the Khyentse wall paintings
> have left those long-lasting tradi-
> tions behind, and if we accept a date
> of c. 1464 or within the second half
> of the 15th century, represent the
> most progressive Tibetan paintings
> still to exist in situ.[241]

When Henss calls Khyentse Chenmo's murals "advanced" or "most progressive," he refers to their place in the
progression of styles in Tibetan painting,
which had until Khyentse's time loyally
followed a conservative Indic style, the
Beri. As a revolutionary break with the
past and a great step forward, the change
to the new aesthetic seems almost modern. I am not sure what Henss meant
by the phrase "'synchronized' Tibetan

identity," but otherwise his descriptions
raised important points.[242] Henss also
mentioned that "extraordinary 1:1 scale
photographs of the Gongkar wall paintings in facsimile quality were made by
the American photographer Thomas
Laird."[243]

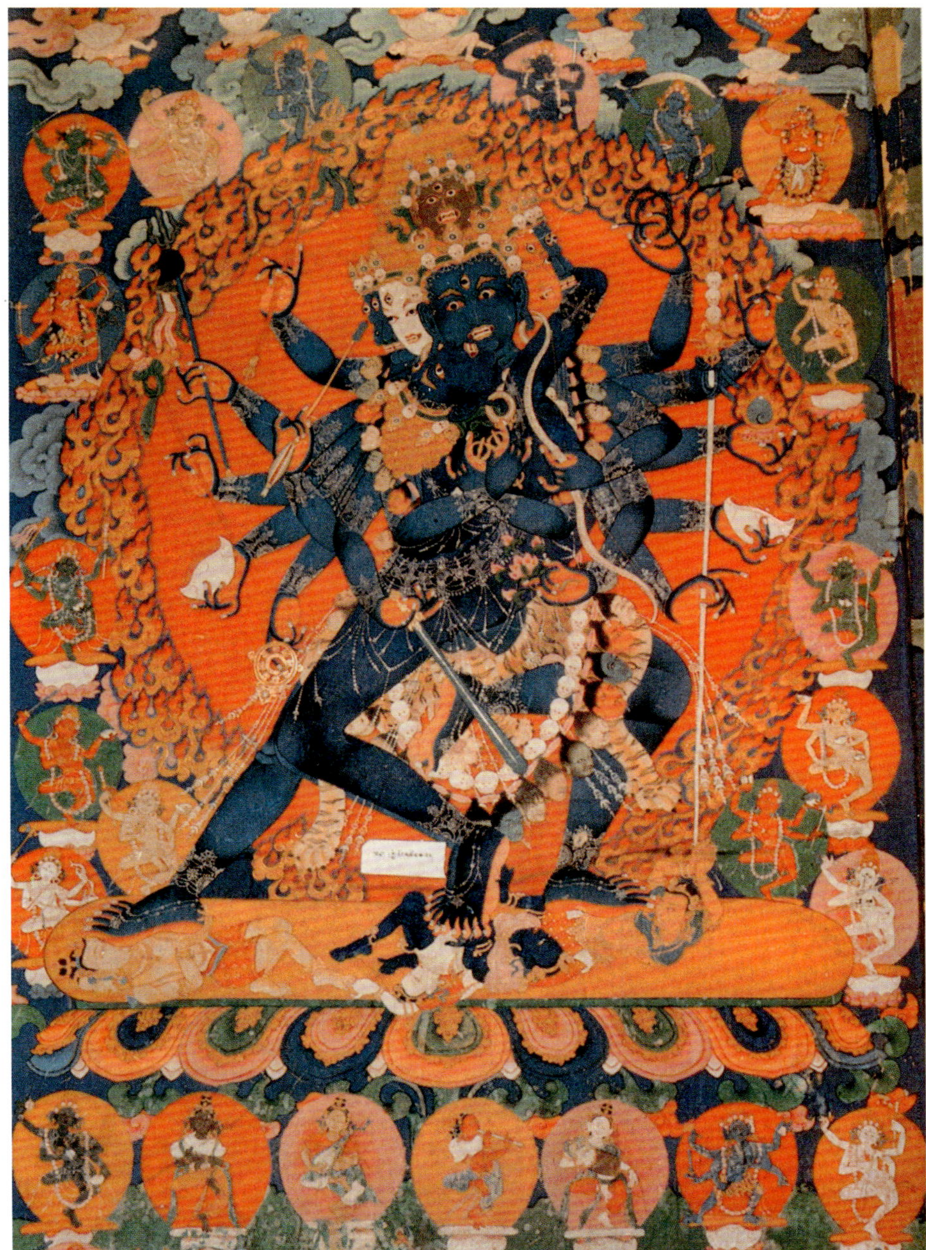

Fig. 2.22
Cakrasamvara
Hevajra Chapel, second floor, Gongkar
Monastery; 1464–1476
Literature: *Xizang Yishu* 1991, 95; and
Henss 2014, fig. 509

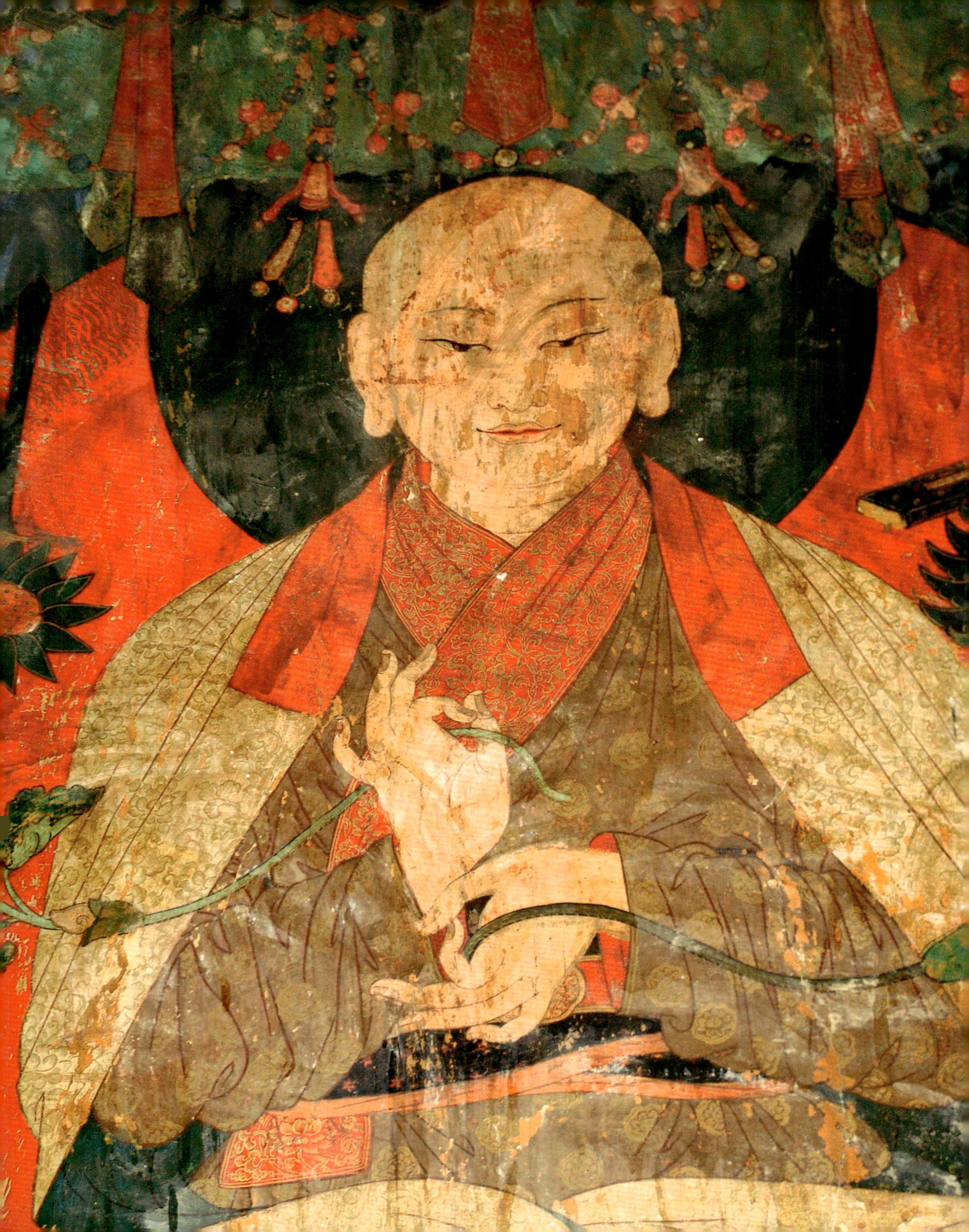

CHAPTER 3

A Recent Introduction of Khyentse Chenmo and His Art

THIS CHAPTER IS DEVOTED to the contributions of the Tibetan scholar Tsechang Penba Wangdu, who recently researched the life and art of Khyentse Chenmo in some detail. One of his contributions was mentioned above in chapter 2. In 2005, his brief article in the journal *Bod ljongs zhib 'jug* (*Tibetan Research*) sketched the life of Khyentse Chenmo and summarized some points about his artistry, based on the Gongkar murals.[244]

In 2010, he presented an updated version at the International Association of Tibetan Studies meeting in Vancouver. This revised article—whose title can be translated as "A Brief Discussion of Khyentse Chenmo Genyen Nampar Gyalwa of Gongkar Gangtö and the Special Features of the Khyentse Tradition"—usefully introduced Khyentse Chenmo's life and art, including some sources that he had not previously known. For instance, he pointed out the existence of a rare and unpublished manuscript recording the labeling inscriptions (*zhal byang*) of the *Kalpalatā* murals of Gongkar.[245] I believe Penba Wangdu's paper was first published without illustrations in the *Journal of Tibet University*.[246]

This 2010 Tibetan article was the basis for a "summary translation"

published online two years later.[247] As I mentioned in chapter 2, this English rendering, which is accessible online, has many mistakes and inaccuracies. In the following pages, I will retranslate much of it.

The paper in its Tibetan version begins with a synopsis, which I render as:

> The Khyentse Tradition, which is one of the five main established traditions or great schools of Tibetan painting, is a wonderfully beautiful (*mtshar tu mngar ba*) and indispensable tradition of painting not only in Tibet but also upon the stage of global art. That tradition has a history of over five hundred years. In this article I have critically discussed such topics as the history of the founder of this school, Khyentse Chenmo Genyen Nampar Gyalwa, the special features of the Khyentse painting tradition, and, further, in what condition several artworks of that school now survive.

The article addresses three main topics: the life of Khyentse Chenmo, the Khyenri style's distinctive stylistic features, and surviving artworks. In the first five pages, Penba Wangdu summarizes the life of Khyentse Chenmo; about one page of text deals with everything that is known about his birthplace, youth, and apprenticeship in Tsang. Penba Wangdu accepts the story of Dopa Tashi Gyalpo as the name of Khyentse's main teacher.

Penba Wangdu stresses how few

personal details are revealed by the original Tibetan historical sources. Yet he inserts into the narrative a few points about Khyentse's childhood that are not mentioned by the sources accessible to me. Possibly he took these details from the 2003 *Chinese-Tibetan Tibetan-Chinese Dictionary of Art* by Tenpa Rabten and Ngawang Jigme, his teachers. In their entry on Khyentse Chenmo, they write that he was "naturally skilled in painting as a child," adding that as a youth he was skilled in all fields of knowledge.[248] Such observations are not wrong, but they are things one can deduce about Khyentse Chenmo from knowledge of young artists in general, such as that he naturally loved to draw and sculpt.

Penba Wangdu's account becomes more detailed when he reaches the story of the works of art that Khyentse Chenmo produced at Gongkar. There, he lists the main chapels of that monastery, following the parallel passage in the life of Kunga Namgyal by Gyatön.[249]

Penba Wangdu concludes about the murals of Gongkar:

> As soon as we see those paintings, we react automatically and spontaneously with various emotions, such as faith and devotion or feelings of fright or trembling with terror, in accord with the subject matter of each painting. The objects of painting have a lively feeling and possess a nature even stronger than real life.[250] Thus from among the special paintings

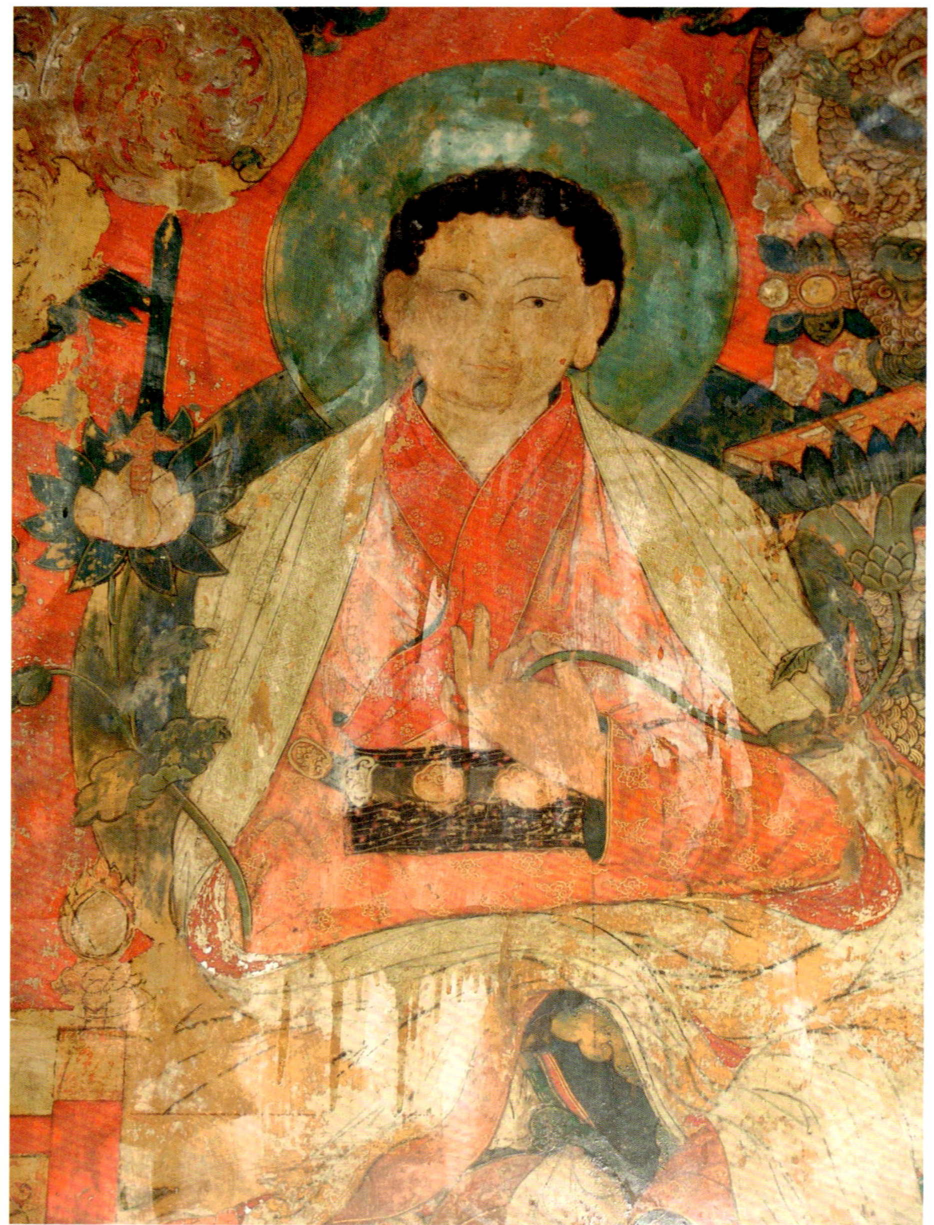

that was reputed to exist. Then he discusses and strongly rejects as unprovable the opinion of a modern scholar who quoted the history of Sumpa Khenpo to the effect that Khyentse Chenmo was still alive after the death of Menthangpa. He sums up his findings about when Khyentse Chenmo lived:

> If we consider such things as the dates or times of production of his paintings and sculptures, then we can know that he was a master artist who had become proficient in all aspects of painting and sculpture who lived from about the 1430s until the beginning of the sixteenth century. I think there is no harm if we have definitely established just that much for the present.

For the rest of this chaper, I present a new translation of the remaining two sections of his article, those dealing with the Khyenluk, or Khyenri, style and surviving artworks.[252]

and sculptures that once existed at Gongkar Monastery, the statues were destroyed during the previous ten years of unrest.[251] Most of the murals survive even now in Gongkar Monastery in a decrepit and dilapidated condition.

After that, in about one page, Penba Wangdu summarizes what is known about Khyentse Chenmo's art at three other sites—Champaling, Dra Dingpoche, and Yangpachen—from the traditional historical sources. He sums up Khyentse's known writings: a praise of Kunga Namgyal and a work on art

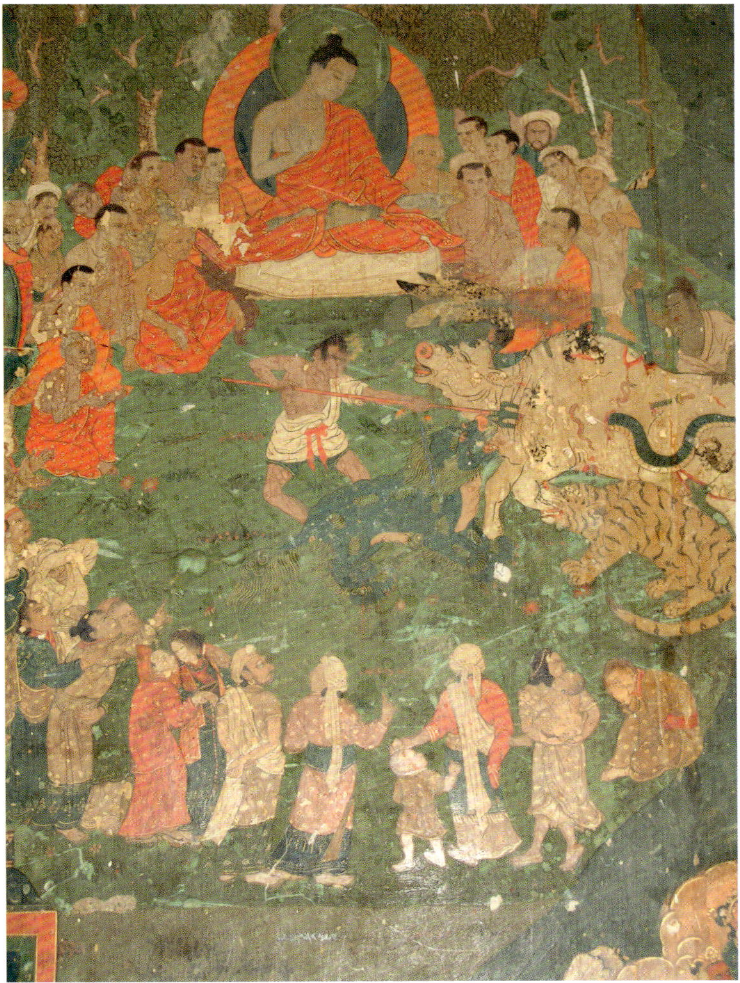
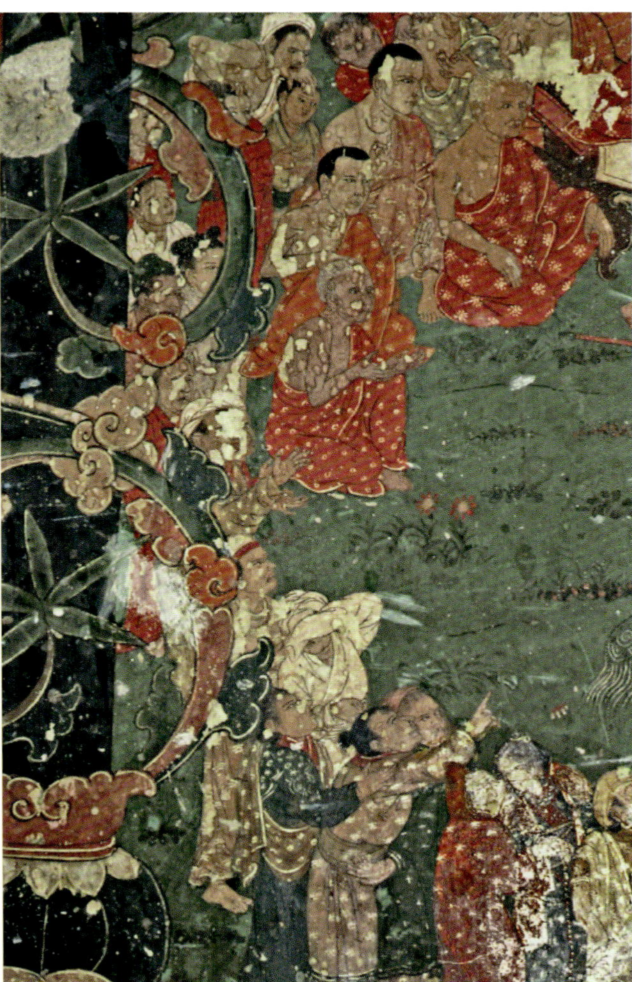

Section 2: An Explanation of the Special Features of Khyentse Chenmo's Tradition

by Penba Wangdu, translated by David Jackson

Regarding the main characteristics of the school of painting known as the Khyenri or Khyenluk tradition, there exists a widespread opinion, which is maintained, for instance, by the Fifth Dalai Lama: the Khyentse painting school was very good for depicting wrathful deities, but the school of Menthangpa was better for depicting peaceful deities.[253] But based on repeated visits to Gongkar Monastery and other sites of Khyenri murals, I have found another outstanding characteristic that points to the superiority of this school of painting: its realism. Khyentse Chenmo's art bears a close resemblance to real life.

See, for instance, the images illustrating the seventy-sixth chapter in the *Avadānakalpalatā* collection of moral tales, in which the water buffalo named Vidura, lying on the banks of the Ganges River, is being tortured by tigers, sea creatures, crows, and many insects (Figs. 3.3 and 3.4). The postures and activities of the people who have gathered to watch the spectacle are rendered extremely close to life: some are weeping; some are pointing their fingers at the activity, to communicate to others; and some are conversing with each other.

In portraits of lamas and gurus that were painted in earlier painting schools, such as that of the master Chiugangpa (Byi'u sgang pa, fl. early 15th century), usually both head nimbuses and throne backs are depicted. But in the Khyenri painting

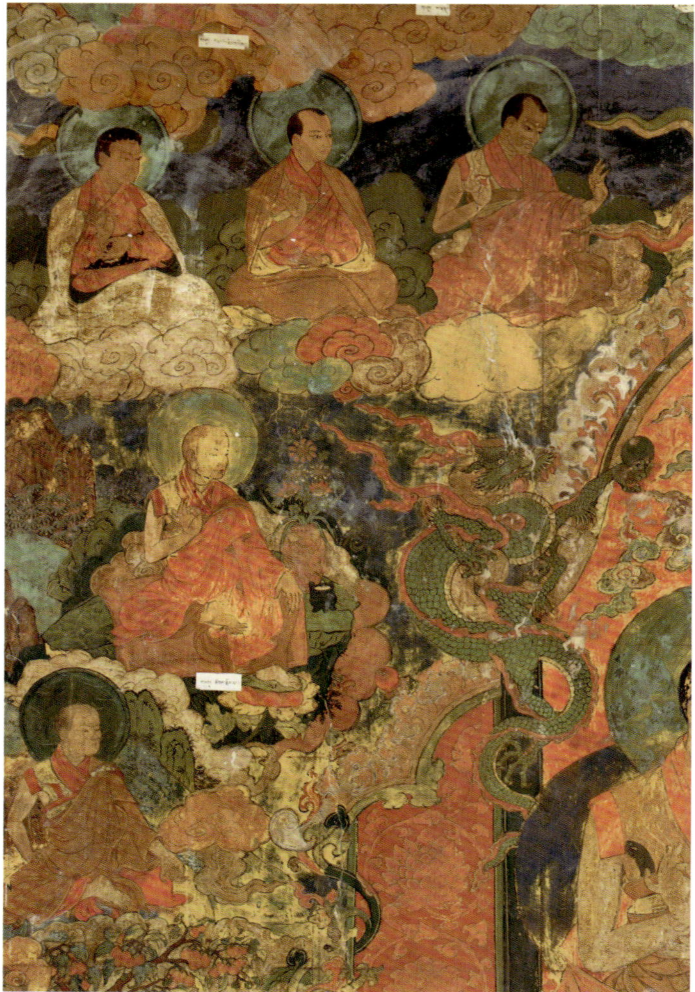

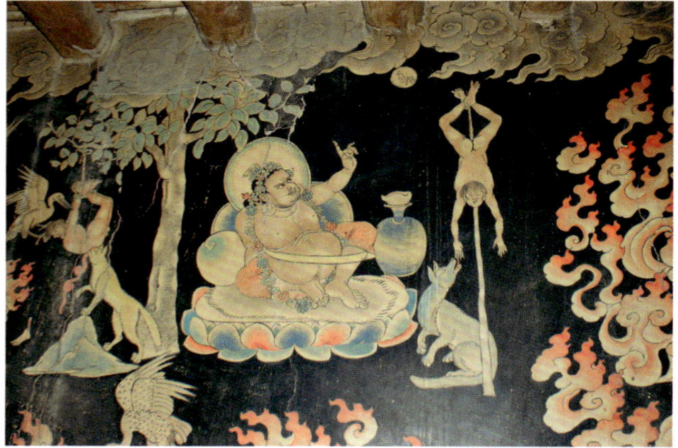

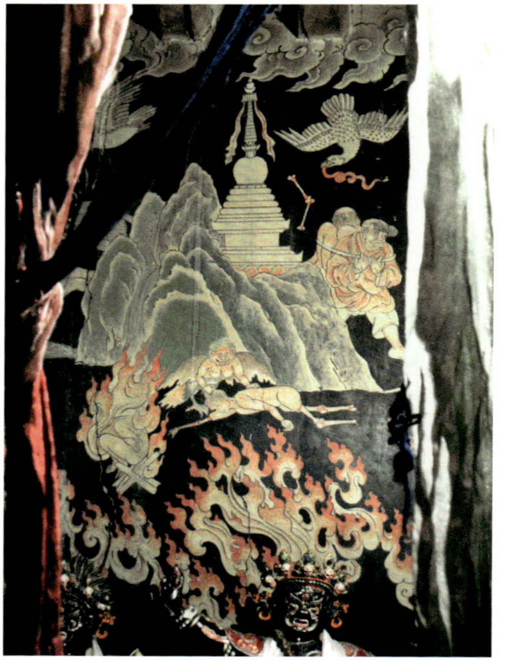

tradition, we find only head nimbuses. (See Fig. 3.5.) The face of each religious master is artistically rendered in accord with that teacher's highly individual features.

Also, the charnel-ground scenes in the Labrang protector's chapel and the Yamāntaka chapel instantly evoke actual charnel grounds (Figs. 3.6 and 3.7).[254] These artworks bear clear witness to the strongly realistic effect of Khyentse Chenmo's art, though the realism under discussion here is not at all an exact fidelity to life.

Though it is in some sense the original fidelity to real life, Khyentse's art reaches the pinnacle of art, surpassing real life. (See Figs. 3.8 and 3.9.) The artworks produced by Khyentse Chenmo's hands have reached such an extremely rarified stratum, possessing as they do such qualities as that great master's very high expertise, that it is almost superfluous to say that they possess such above-mentioned good qualities (as their strong realism).

When depicting a lama as the main figure in some thangkas and murals, Khyentse Chenmo slightly turns the figure, depicting a partial profile, and portrays the lama larger and with imposing elegance. Minor figures are not depicted at that large scale. And the depictions of the lamas' robes have more fold lines than that found in other traditions, another example of the fidelity to life.

Unlike in previous traditions of painting, here the faces of wrathful deities are a

Fig. 3.5
Lineal gurus depicted in landscape without backrests but with head nimbuses
1464–1476
right wall, entrance to inner sanctum, Gongkar Chöde; by Khyentse Chenmo,

Fig. 3.6
Virūpa and charnel grounds
1464–1476
east wall, Upper Protector's Chapel; by Khyentse Chenmo
Photo: Penba Wangdu
Literature: Penba Wangdu 2012, fig. 4a

Fig. 3.7
Details of gruesome charnel grounds
1464–1476
east wall, Upper Protector's Chapel
Photo: Laurent Dupeyrat
Literature: Penba Wangdu 2012, fig. 4c

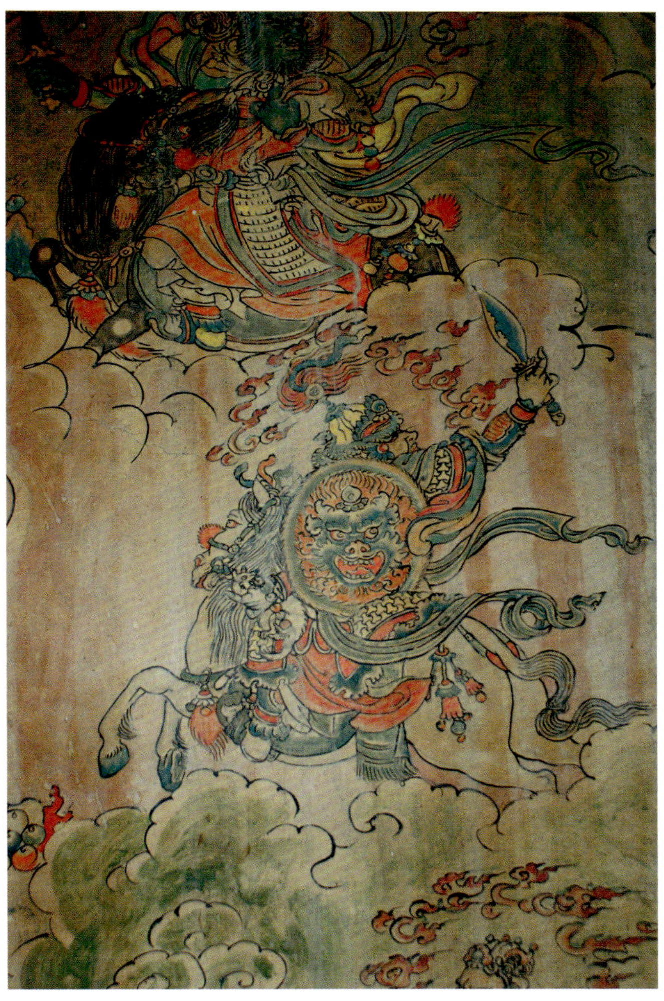 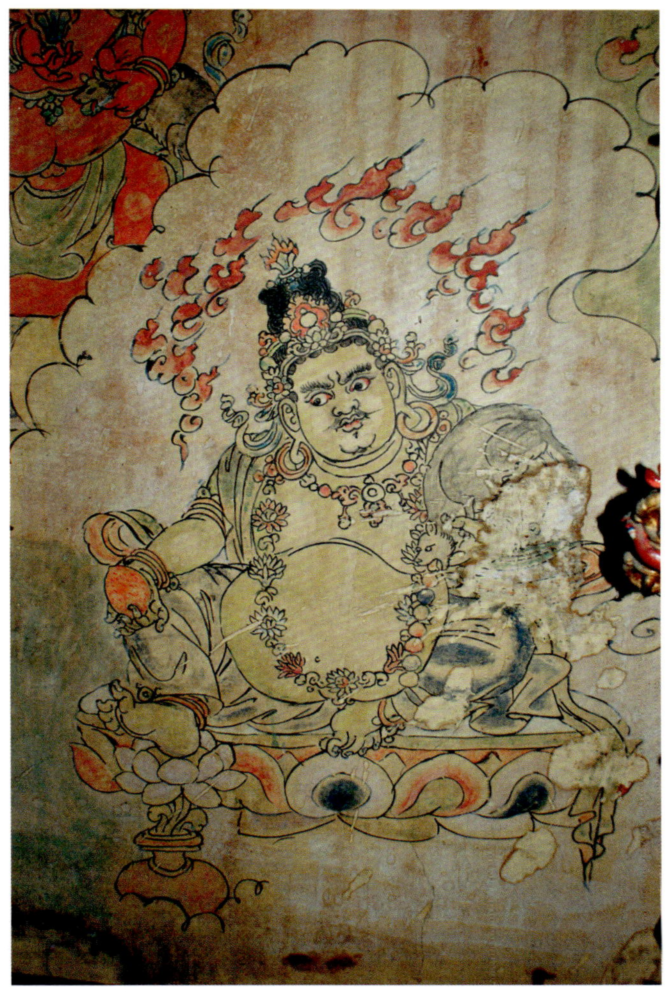

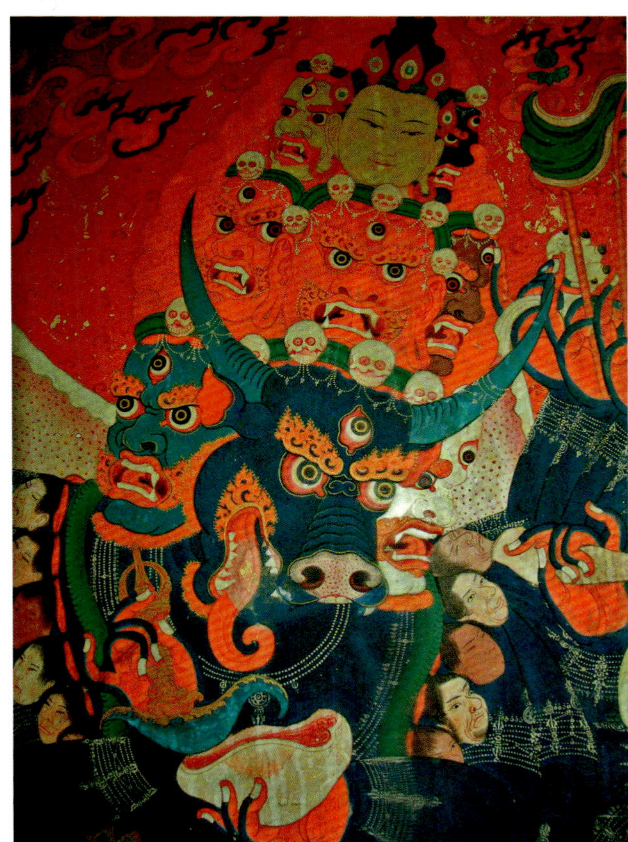

Fig. 3.8
Yakṣa Vaiśravaṇa and the Eight Horsemen
1464–1476
north wall, Upper Protector's Chapel; by
Khyentse Chenmo, 1464–1476
Photo: Penba Wangdu
Literature: Penba Wangdu 2012, fig. 5

Fig. 3.9
Jambhala, God of Wealth
1464–1476
north wall, Upper Protector's Chapel; by
Khyentse Chenmo
Photo: Penba Wangdu
Literature: Penba Wangdu 2012, fig. 6

Fig. 3.10
Vajrabhairava (detail of wrathful deity's
head)
1464–1476
west wall, Hevajra Chapel; by Khyentse
Chenmo,
Photo: Penba Wangdu
Literature: Penba Wangdu 2012, fig. 8a

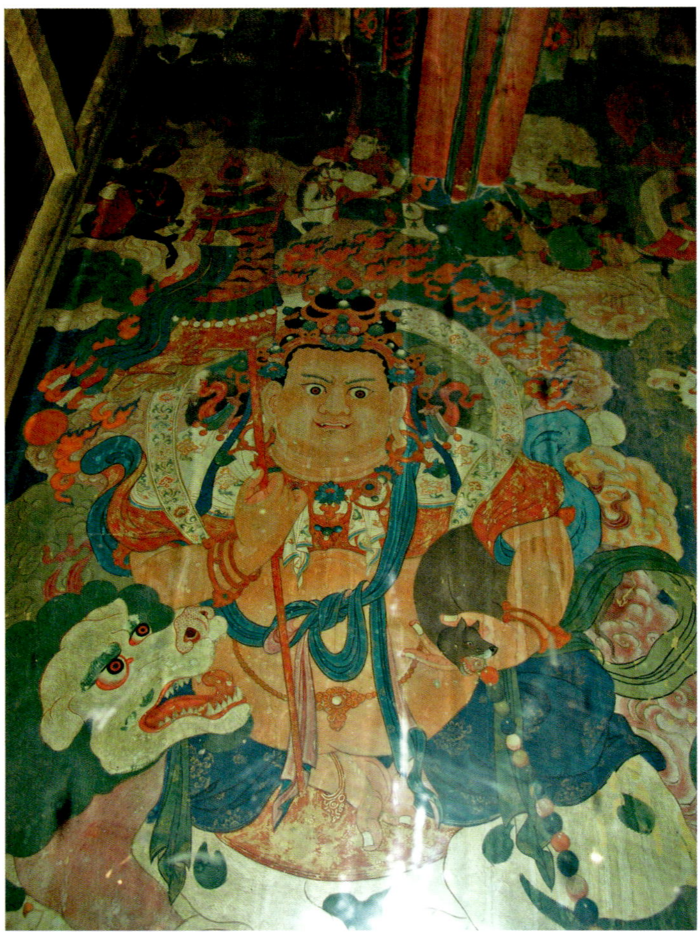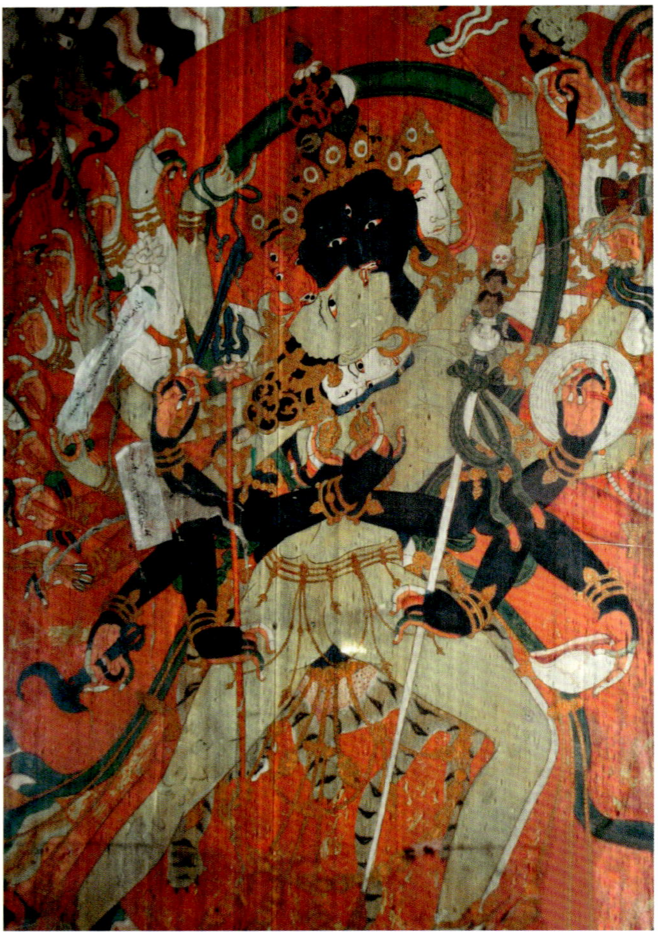

bit elongated, and the fangs protrude from open mouths in a more pronounced way. The veins of the eyes are painted solid red, and the whites and pupils of the eyes are clearly differentiated with white and black. The wrathful deities' postures are more exaggerated and appear angrier. When depicting flame nimbuses around the deities, they are painted not merely as flame scrollwork designs, but have a more realistic shape like real flames. Wrathful head ornaments, too, are not just scrollwork designs but are depicted having the shape of hair.

The body nimbuses for angered seers, such as Cakrasaṃvara, and wrathful gods and goddesses, such as the Ten Wrathful Ones (Khro bo bcu), sometimes feature discontinuous rings of flame, but which are represented by interrupted segments of fire designs that appear on and off around the edge of a background field of different base colors.[255]

When depicting such tutelary deities as Hevajra that possess many hands and feet, when such details are not fixed by the detailed description in the written *sādhanas*, Khyentse Chenmo does not paint them in a single unified way, but rather depicts them richly various in form, rendering their bodily postures and depictions of hands and feet in a flexible (that is, not in a mechanical) way. In particular, the bodies of goddesses are special in that they possess even more beautiful and attractive forms than those of other deities. (See, for example, Fig. 3.14, which depicts a goddess from a mandala of Hevajra.)

For the most part, Khyentse Chenmo paints angered seers (tantric *yidam*) and wrathful male and female deities lighter colors than what the texts call for, or he lightens the original colors by applying a network of fine gold lines (*gser gyis kha sel*) over them. For the retinue deities of Guhyasamāja, he depicts very round body nimbuses but

Fig. 3.11
Vaiśravaṇa
1464–1476
south wall, Hevajra Chapel; by Khyentse Chenmo
Photo: Penba Wangdu
Literature: Penba Wangdu 2012, fig. 7

Fig. 3.12
Kālacakra
1464–1476
west wall, Hevajra Chapel; by Khyentse Chenmo
Photo: Penba Wangdu
Literature: Penba Wangdu 2012, fig. 8b

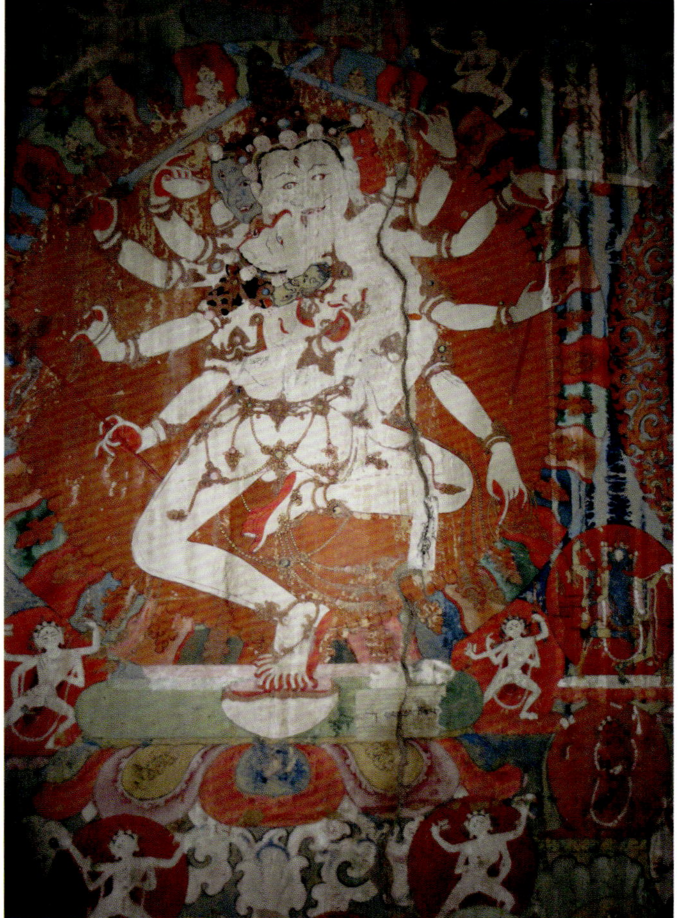

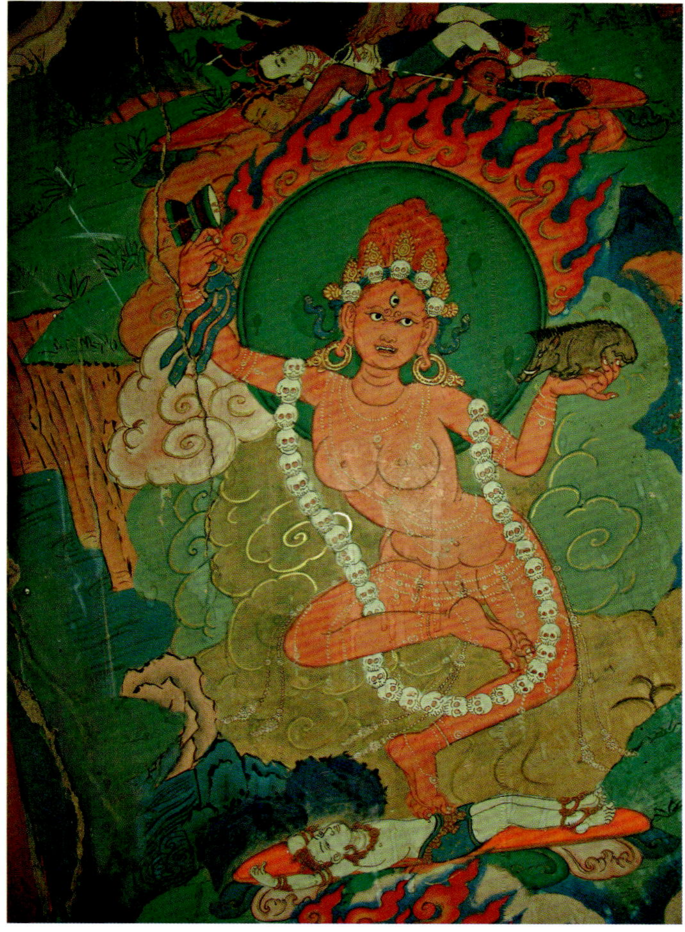

does not paint any head nimbuses. Sometimes in thangkas and murals, there are many clouds of lac-dye pink (*na ros*) depicted behind the deities or elsewhere.

Unlike in previous periods, Khyentse Chenmo outlines skin areas with lines of the same thickness; his clothing fold-lines are thick, with thin ends. He outlines leaves with a thicker middle line and thinner ends, and the inner lines are extremely thin and of even thickness, as if painted with a horse-tail brush. Rock outlines are sometimes thick and sometimes fat. Since there are many cases where those outlines change according to the particular situation, it is superfluous to mention them all individually.

Moreover, in the paintings of the Khyenri tradition, not only does Khyentse Chenmo employ numerous different scrollwork designs in such places as the head nimbus and throne backs of the main figures, but he also traditionally depicts each one with numerous special features even when depicting the same kind of image. For example, when painting in the Gongkar Dorjeden murals the buddhas who were the main deities of the *Avadānakalpalatā* cycle, not one has the same bodily form or the same robes as another. (See Figs. 3.15 and 3.16.) Even their lotus seats are depicted with variation, some with double layers of petals and others with triple layers. The colors and decorative scrollwork designs that he used are also extremely numerous and manifold.

Khyentse Chenmo also depicts landscapes as close to real life as possible. When showing the various sentient beings that inhabit those landscapes, he arranges them to conform to the main thematic content (*nang don*) of the picture. Some Khyenri-style arrangements of deities feature the main deity depicted larger in the center while the lesser deities are placed in straight vertical and horizontal registers and columns (arranged around the main figure), as was previously done in the Beri style; red

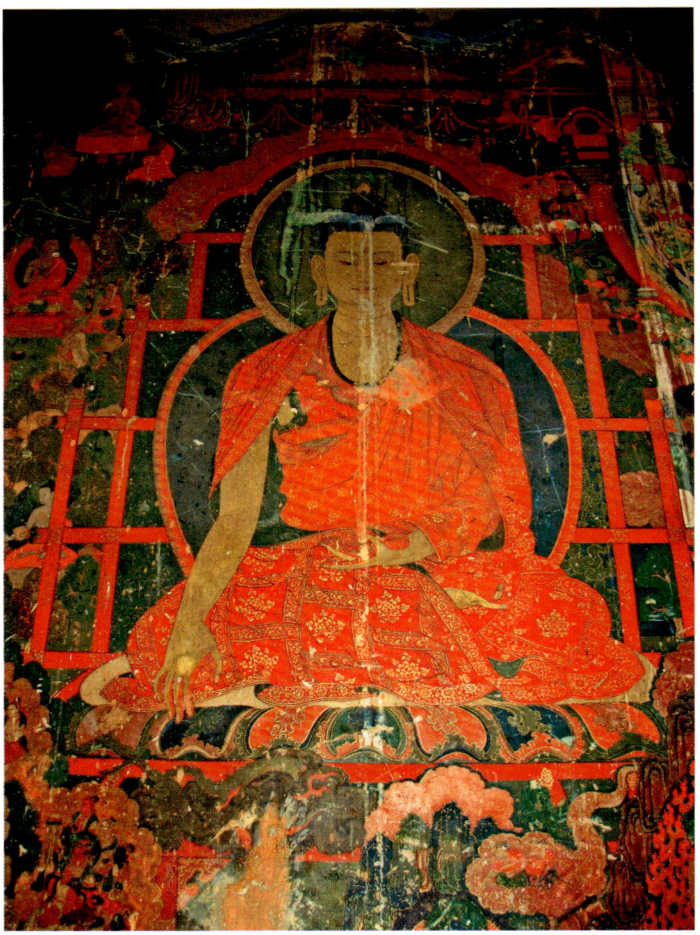 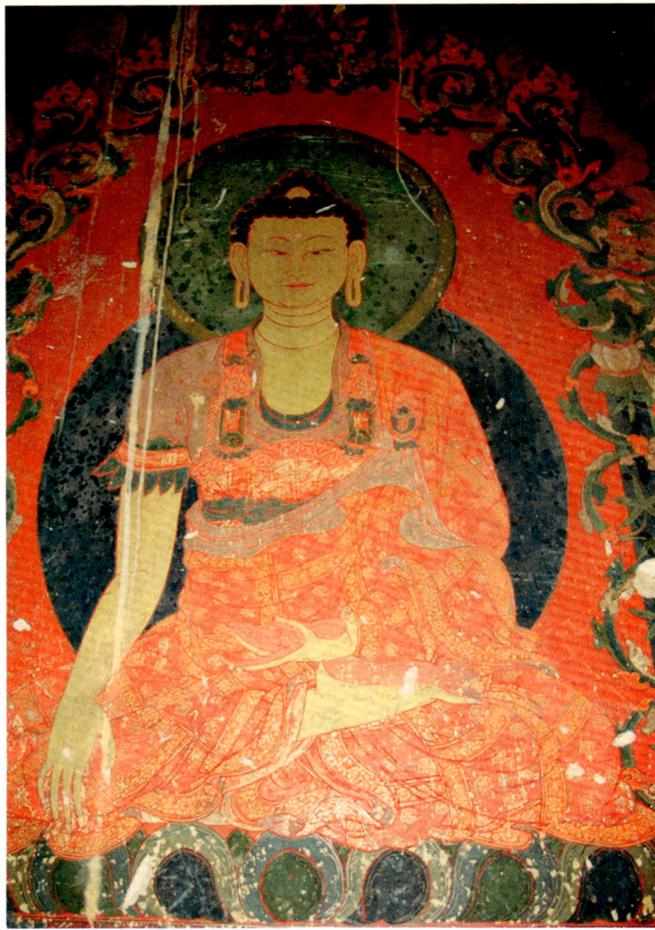

can be seen to dominate in their backgrounds. However, I do not consider these to be special characteristics of the Khyenri tradition.

Section 3: Surviving Examples of Khyentse Chenmo's Tradition of Painting

Surviving Murals

After searching for many years, mainly in Tibet but also in other countries, I found that quite a few artistic works in the Khyentse, or Khyenluk, tradition exist in Tibet. Some remain secret, as they are hidden from visitors in the various places where they now exist, while some are visible and accessible to people in every respect. The mural artworks that I was able to learn about mostly exist in the Ü and Tsang provinces of central Tibet, and their quality was good. They include:

(1) The murals of Gongkar Dorjeden Monastery, in Gongkar Dzong of the Lhokha region, that were painted in the fifteenth century.
(2) The murals of Phüntshokling Monastery, in the Lhatse region of Tsang, that were commissioned in 1615 by Jonang Tāranātha.[256] (See Figs. 3.17 and 3.18.)
(3) The murals of the assembly hall of Drepung in Lhasa, ordered repainted by the Fifth Dalai Lama in 1654. Murals of the sixteen arhats and some other sections

Fig. 3.15
Buddha Śākyamuni as main figure with
Avadāna tales
1464–1476
new side chapels (original assembly hall),
ground floor; by Khyentse Chenmo
Photo: Penba Wangdu
Literature: Penba Wangdu 2012, fig. 2a

Fig. 3.16
Buddha Śākyamuni as main figure with
Avadāna tales
1464–1476
new side chapel (original assembly hall),
ground floor; by Khyentse Chenmo
Photo: Penba Wangdu
Literature: Penba Wangdu 2012, fig. 2b

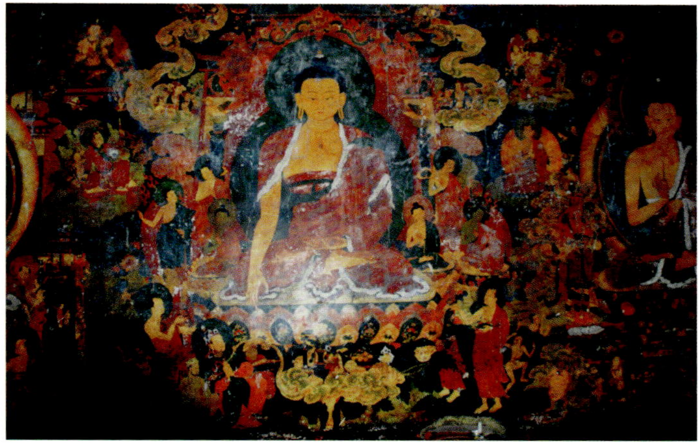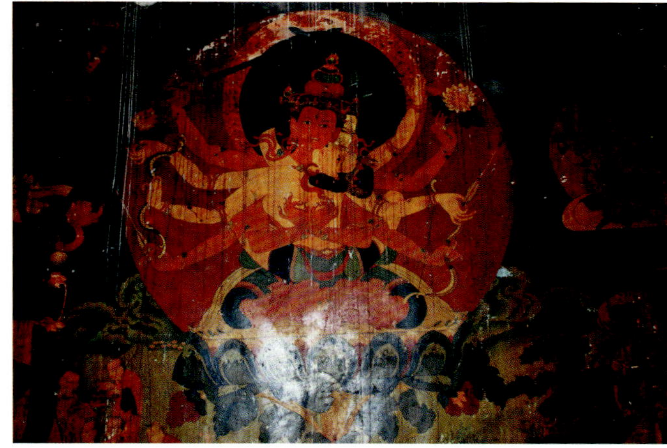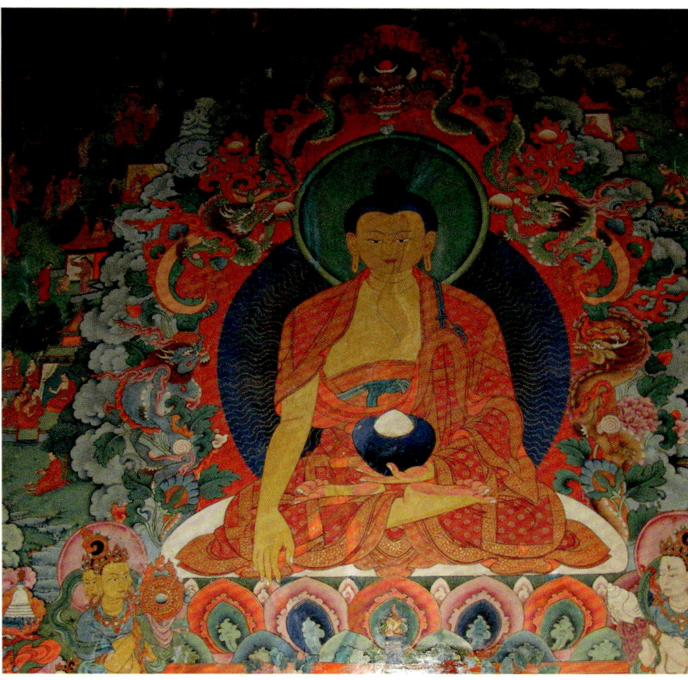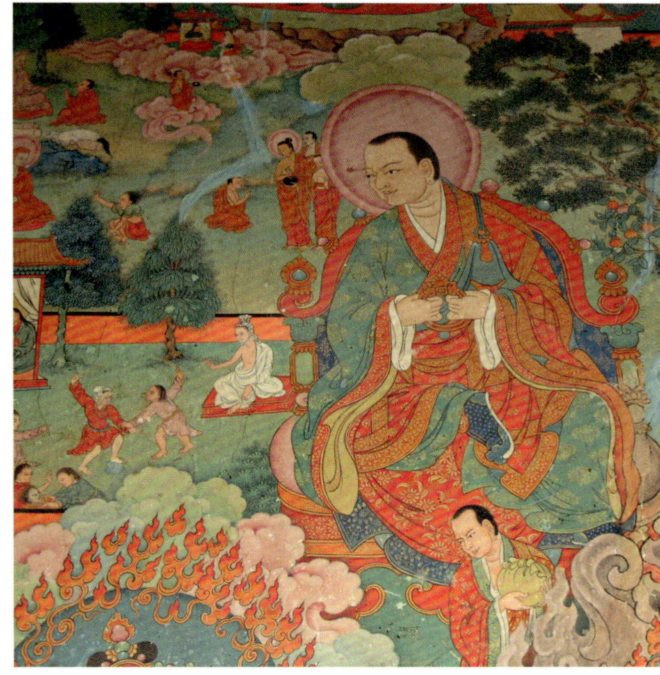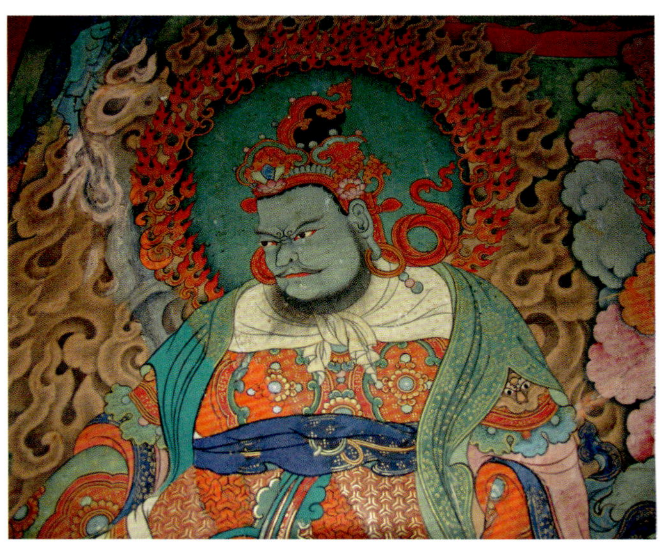

Fig. 3.17 (top left)
Buddha
Takten Phüntshokling Monastery
Photo: Kesang Tsering, 2009

Fig. 3.18 (top right)
Tantric deity
Takten Phüntshokling
Photo: Kesang Tsering, 2009

Fig. 3.19 (center left)
Buddha
Assembly hall, Drepung Monastery
Photo: Penba Wangdu

Fig. 3.20 (center right)
Arhat Rahula
Assembly hall, Drepung Monastery
Photo: Penba Wangdu

Fig. 3.21
Great King Vurūḍhaka
Assembly hall, Drepung Monastery
Photo: Penba Wangdu

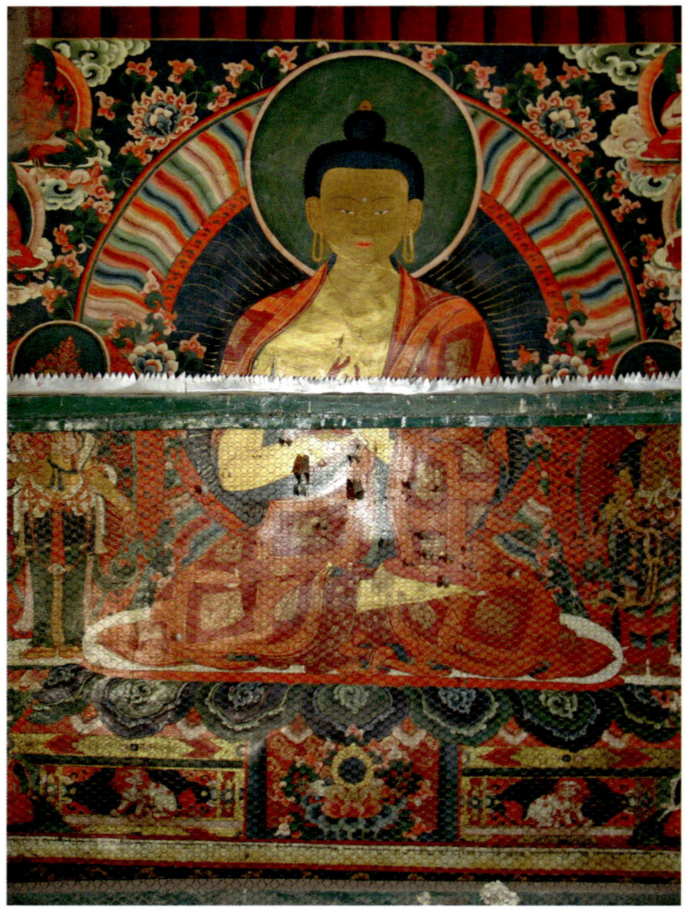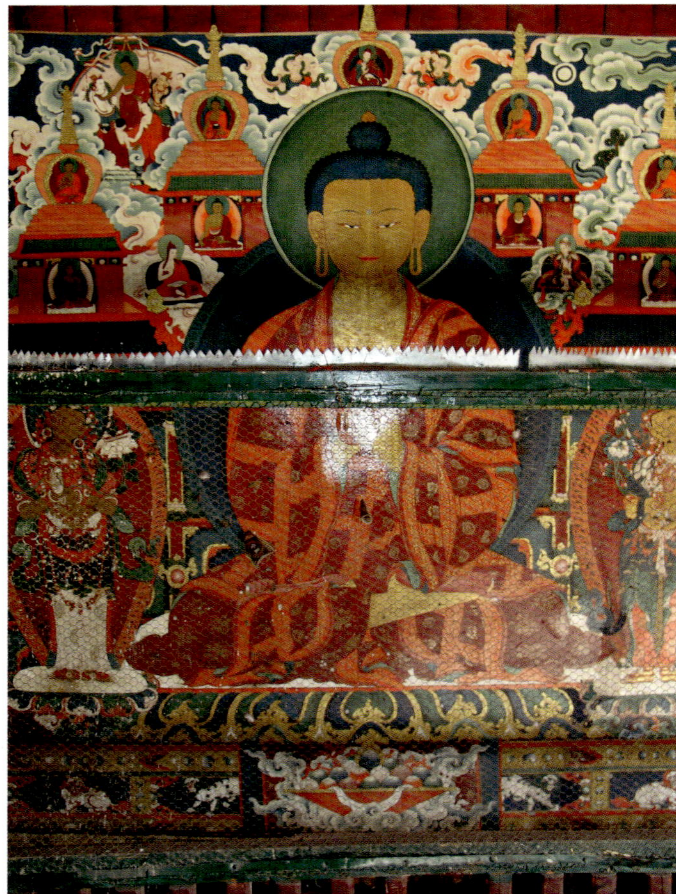

were then painted by a group of Khyenri painters led by Gongkar Sangngak Kharpa and Shora Gögö.[257] (See Figs. 3.19–3.21.)

(4) The murals in the Palkhor Chöde Tsuklakkhang assembly hall and Nyithok Barkhyam were commissioned about late 1890, during the period of the Demo regent (*srid skyong*) Trinle Rabgye ('Phrin las rab rgyas), during the repainting of certain old and damaged murals of Gyantse dating to the time of the king Rabten Kunzang Phak.[258] (See Figs. 3.22 and 3.23.)

(5) The murals at Mindröling (sMin grol gling) Monastery in Lhokha prefecture.

(6) The murals at Sakya Monastery in Shigatse.

There are even more that I could have enumerated, but I will leave it at that, not wanting my text to grow too long

Needless to say, the most valuable murals are those in Gongkar Monastery: firstly, they are the incredibly rare genuine paintings of none other than the founder of the Khyenri tradition, Khyentse Chenmo Nampar Gyalwa; secondly, they possess a history going back more than five centuries. Still, it is a matter of great sadness that among those murals, quite a few have been and continue to be damaged by natural and human causes: some have cracked, some have water damage, some have faded colors from exposure to sunlight, and some have collapsed. Like a rainbow vanishing into air, they are being destroyed before our eyes.

Fig. 3.22
Śākyamuni with Khyenri-style Lotus Petals
south side, Nyithok Barkhyam, Gyantse;
ca. 1890
H: 63 in. (160 cm)
Photo: Penba Wangdu
Literature: Penba Wangdu 2012, fig. 10

Fig. 3.23
Śākyamuni in Khyenri Style
south side, Nyithok Barkhyam, Gyantse;
ca. 1890
Photo: Penba Wangdu
Literature: Penba Wangdu 2012, fig. 11

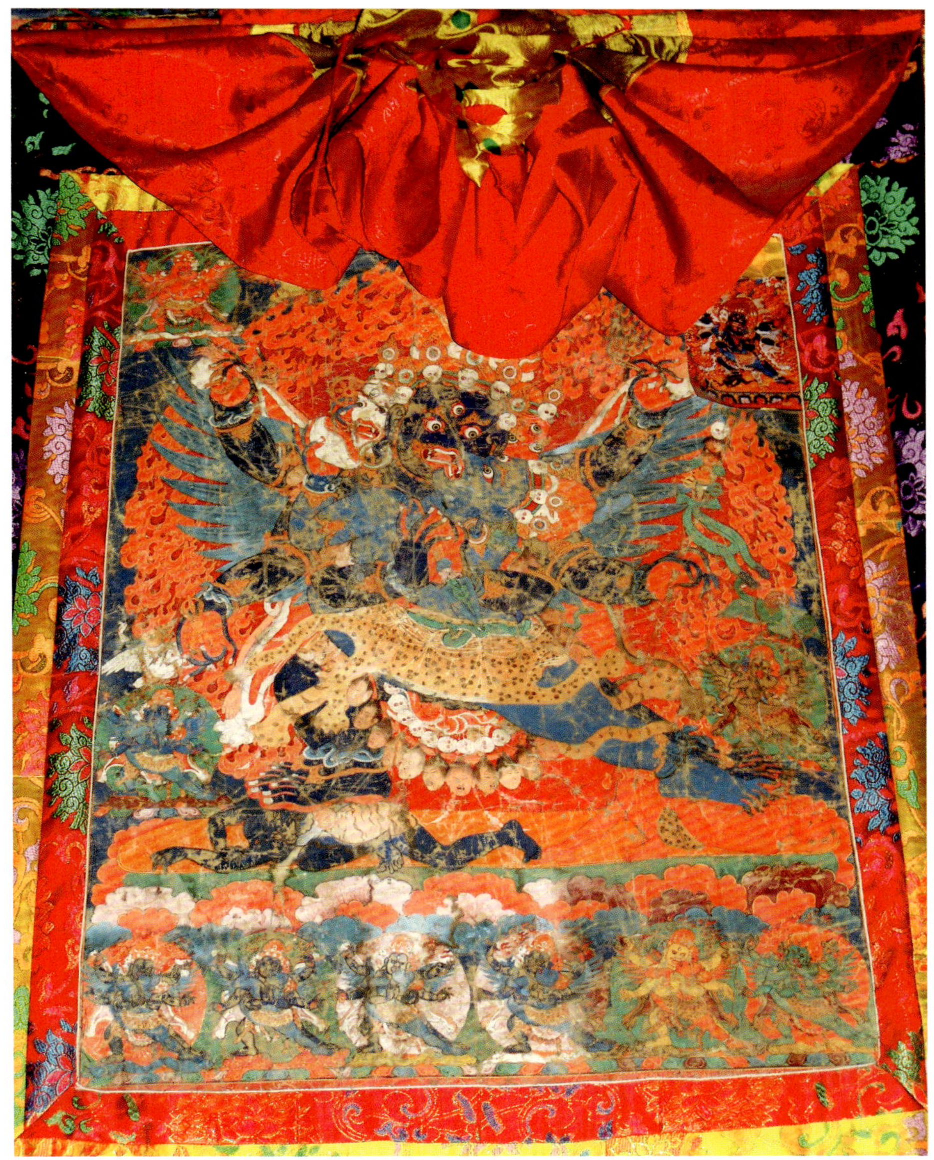

Surviving Thangkas

Quite a few Khyenri thangkas survive in museums and private collections:

(1) At Gongkar Monastery, there are thangkas dating to the fifteenth century, such as one depicting Vajrakīla (rDo rje Phur pa). (See Fig. 3.24.)

(2) At Sakya Monastery, thangkas dating to the seventeenth century depict lamas of the Sakya tradition.

(3) At Sera Monastery, there is a series of thangkas of the eighty-four great adepts, from the seventeenth or eighteenth century. (See Figs. 3.25 and 3.26.)

(4) In Beijing at the National Palace Museum, a series of the sixteen arhats dates to about the eighteenth century. (See Figs. 3.27 and 3.28, which depicts Aṅgaja, the first arhat, holding a censer and fly whisk.)

(5) In the Rubin Museum of Art, New York, thangka sets depict the eighty-four great adepts and Lamdre lineage masters dating to about the seventeenth century. (Here, Penba Wangdu refers to such paintings as Figs. 7.37–7.39.) One of them depicts Hevajra in a golden thangka. (See Fig. 3.29.)

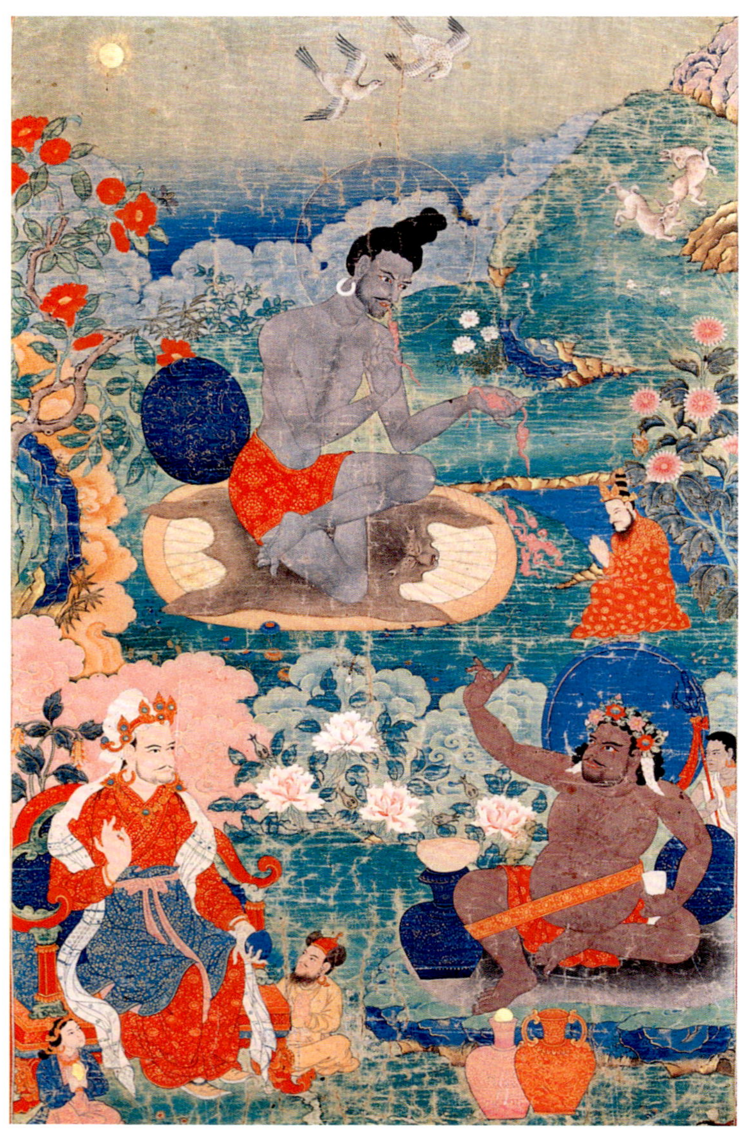

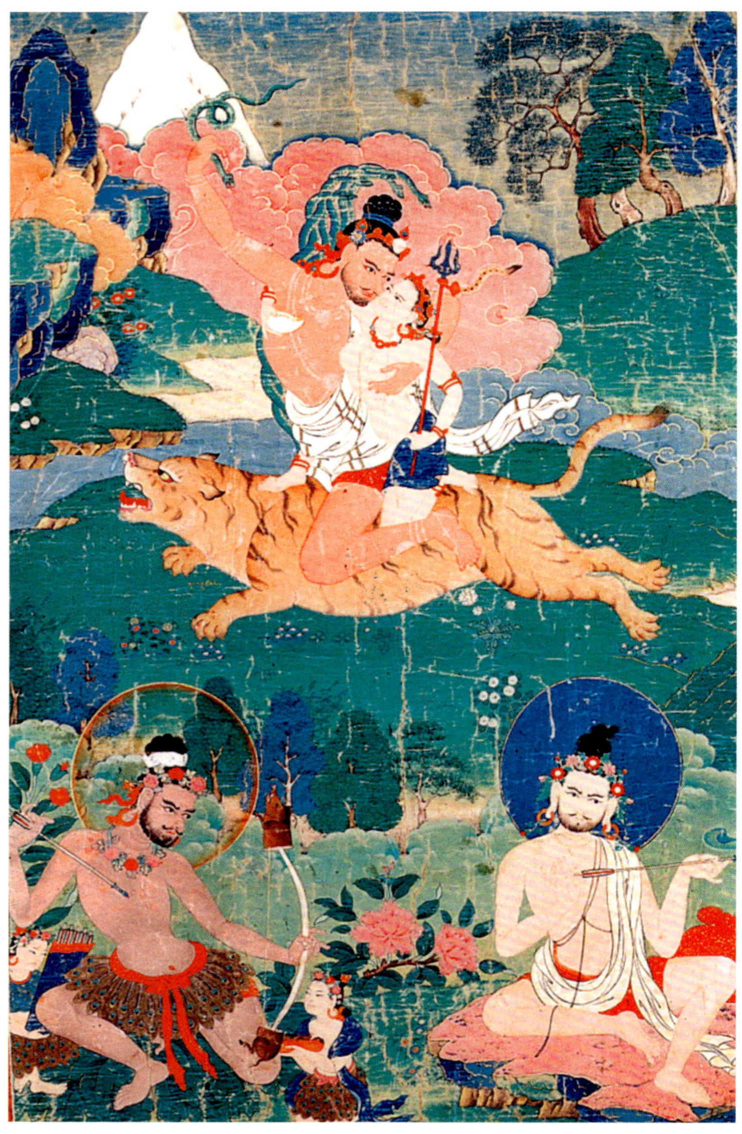

Fɪɢ. 3.25
Lūyipa and two other Great Adepts
pigments on cloth, preserved at Sera
Monastery
After: Tshewang Rinchen 2005, second
thangka

Fɪɢ. 3.26
Ḍombhi Heruka and two other Great
Adepts
pigments on cloth, preserved at Sera
Monastery
After: Tshewang Rinchen 2005, third
thangka

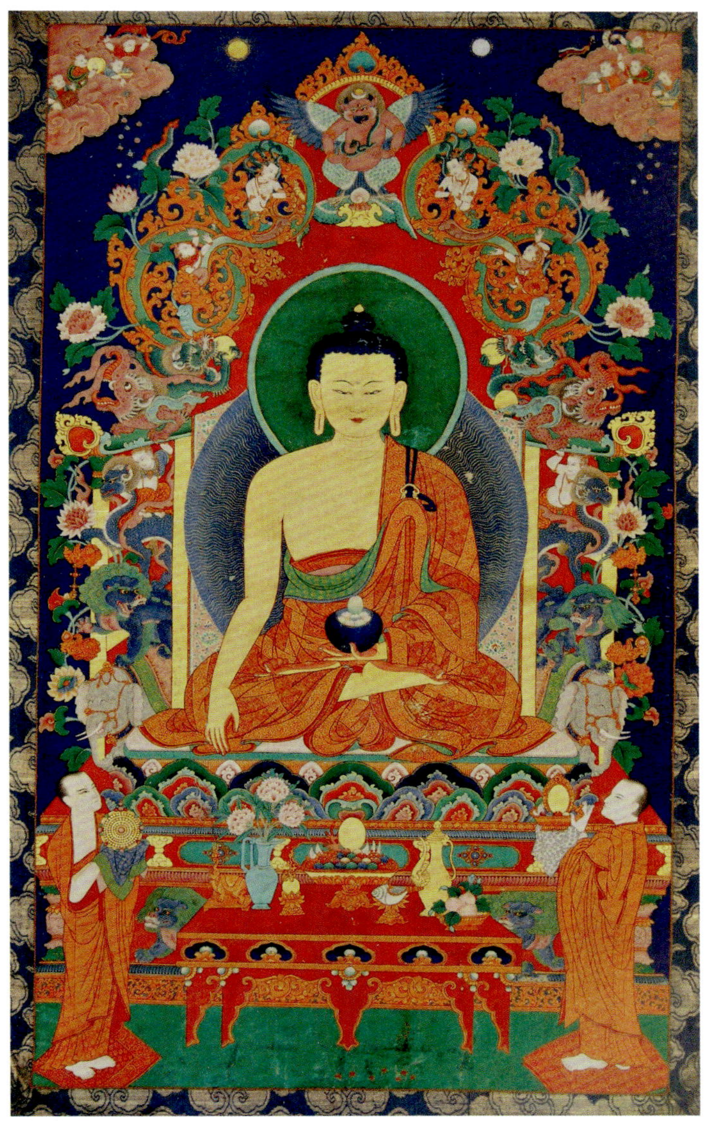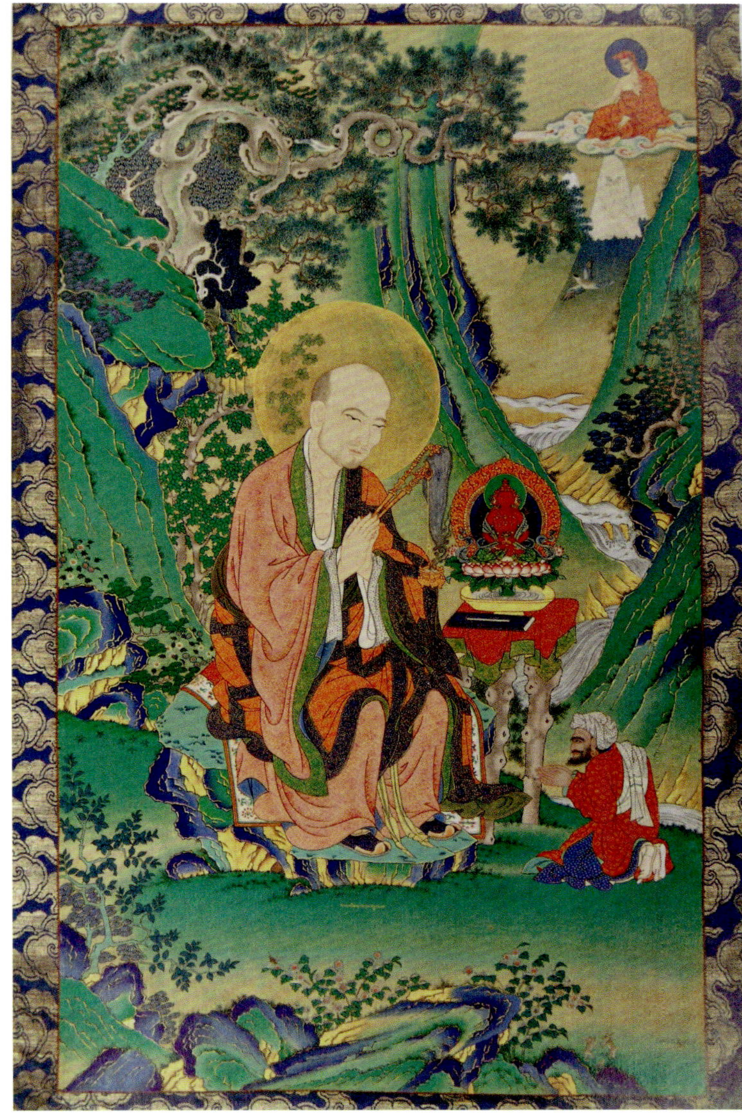

Fig. 3.27
Buddha Śākyamuni as the central painting
of the set
seventeenth or eighteenth century
pigments on cloth, preserved at the National
Palace Museum, Beijing.
Photo: Penba Wangdu
Literature: Penba Wangdu 2012, fig. 12

Fig. 3.28
Arhat Aṅgaja, First of the Sixteen Arhats
seventeenth or eighteenth century
pigments on cloth, preserved at the National
Palace Museum, Beijing
Literature: Penba Wangdu 2012, fig. 17a

Thangkas in the Khyenri style also can be found in museums in London and Paris. The thangkas survive in various states of repair. Some, though actually old, appear brand new in all their components, including their frames, as if just recently painted. Some survive with no damage to the thangka paintings but lack their original mountings. Some have abraded pigments and torn cotton painting supports. And some have become damaged through soiling, such as through oil stains.

This concludes my translation of Penba Wangdu's article. The paintings that he mentioned in his final section as surviving in New York, London, and Paris will be featured in the following chapters.

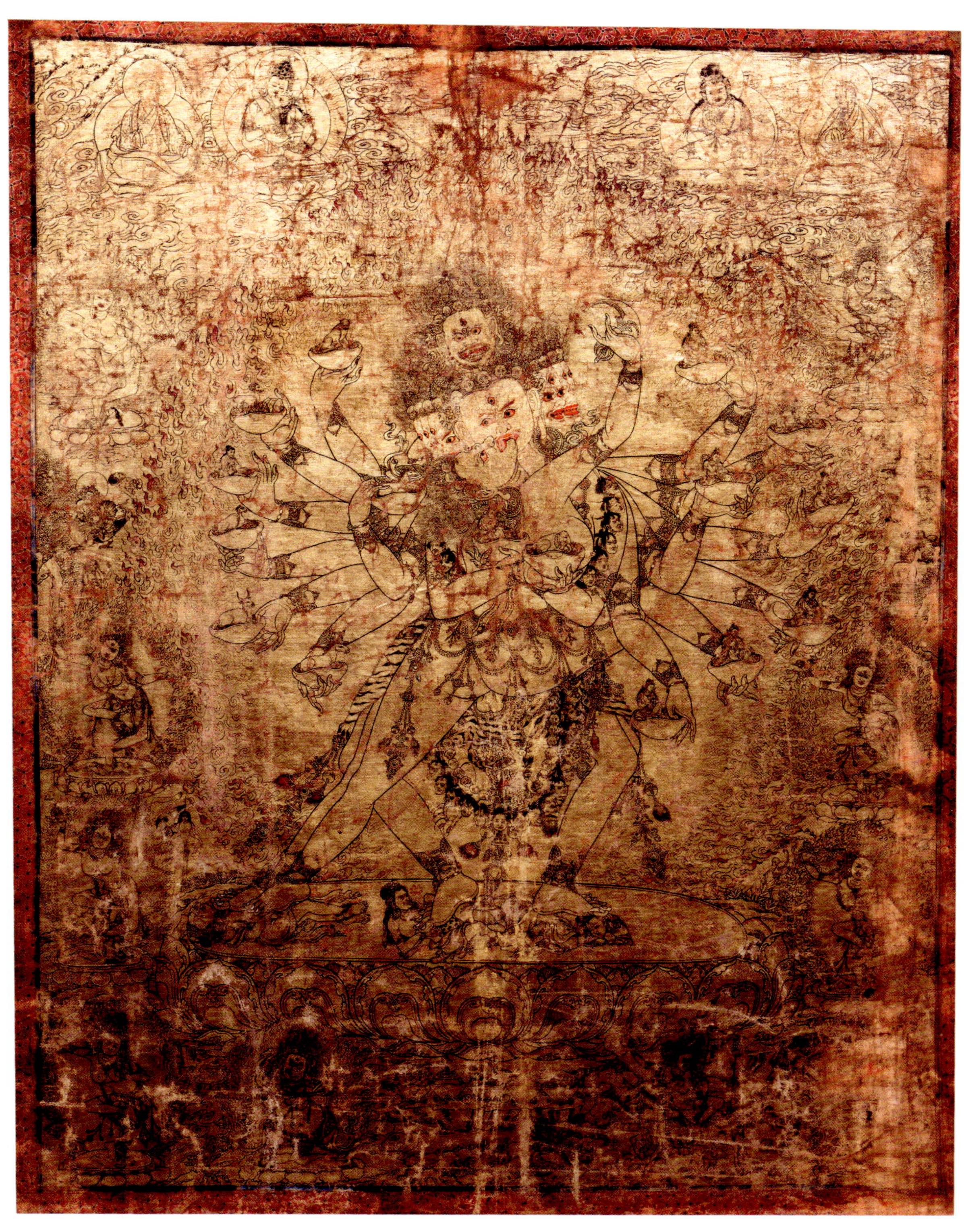

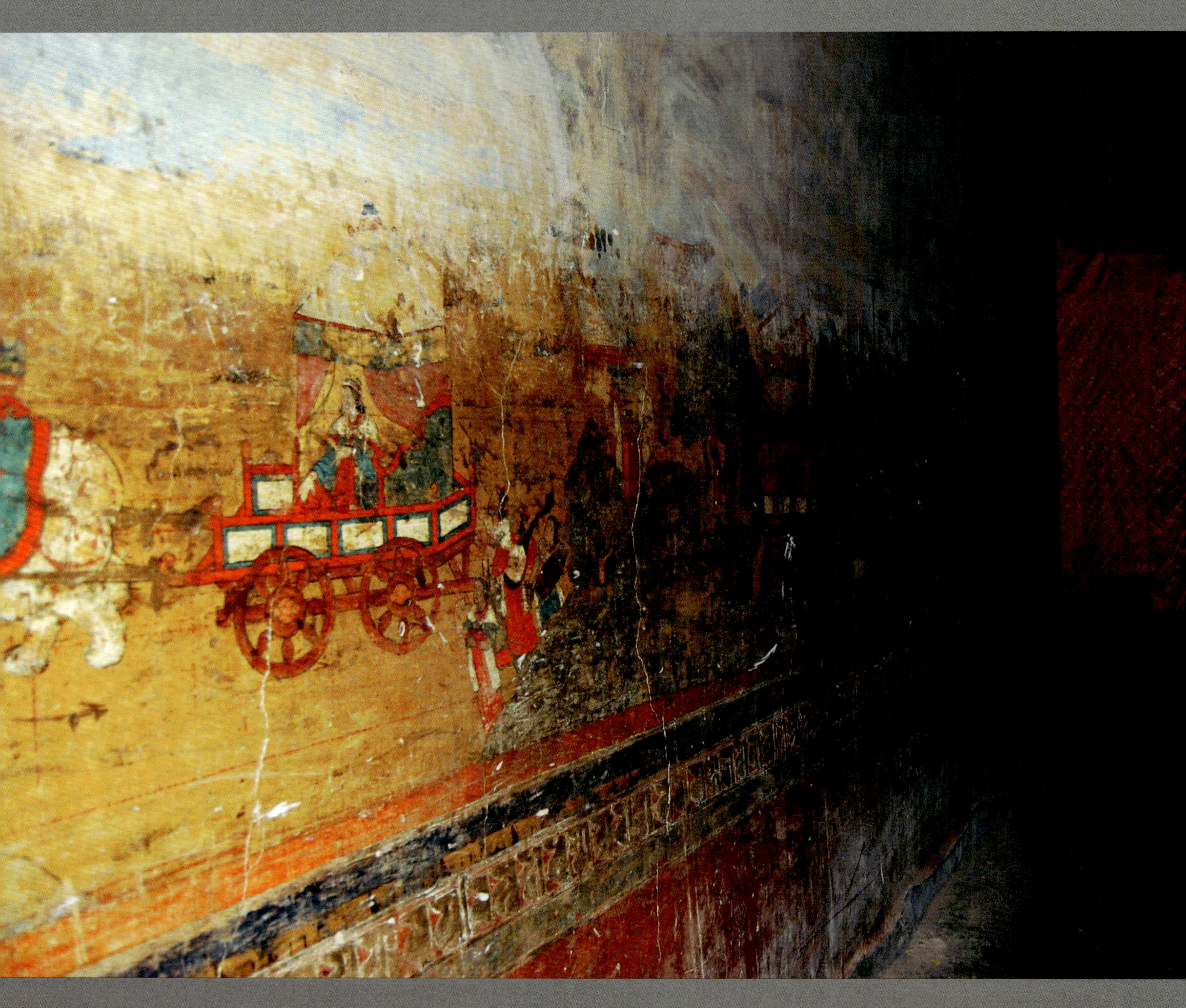

CHAPTER 4

Original Murals Surviving in Gongkar Monastery

PART I: *Original Paintings on the First and Second Floors*

THE MAIN SITE where murals by Khyentse Chenmo survive is Gongkar Dorjeden Monastery, which coincidentally stands near his birthplace.[259] He began these paintings about 1464 and worked on them and the Gongkar sculptures for twelve years, under the direction of the monastery's founder, Gongkar Dorjedenpa Kunga Namgyal (1432–1496). In this chapter, I present a selection of original paintings on the first and second floors of the main building. These murals are striking for their great variety of painting modes and hardly seem to be by the same artist. Michael Henss, for instance, in his summary of Gongkar after introducing the murals of Twelve Great Deeds of the Buddha as "Chinese modernism, seen in landscape composition and scenographic architecture," considered some other murals to be either another unorthodox "Khyentse idiom" or even the work of a different possibly later workshop."[260] Though I believe all the murals in question are by Khyentse, they are indeed hard to tie together stylistically, and each temple

FIG. 4.1
Queen Māyādevī traveling by an elephant-drawn carriage and some earlier episodes
1464–1476
first wall (south wall), near the middle, circumambulation corridor, ground floor
Photo: Kazuo Kano, 2007

can best be approached as incorporating its own mode of painting.

SURVIVAL OF MURALS

Several of the murals in Gongkar survived the damage of the Cultural Revolution with relatively little damage— astonishing visitors who saw them in the mid- to late 1980s—most strikingly Khyentse's paintings of tantric deities in the Chapel of Hevajra. In the early or mid-1960s, prior to the time of the worst political zealotry, the monks of the monastery painted over many murals with a layer of whitewash, which hid and protected those paintings until it could be carefully removed. In the 1980s, some of the murals were more or less restored, but some of the already worn or damaged murals still showed signs of pigment loss. In 1996, I wrote, "Some overhasty attempts at scrubbing off the coats of whitewash have already resulted in irreparable damage to the paintings below."[261] I was referring to parts of the murals in the circumambulation corridor; in 1986, pigment loss was noticeable, with sometimes just the underlying sketches left still visible. I now realize that some of that pigment loss probably predated the 1980s-era cleaning. But the continuing lack of clarity in photos in much of the circumambulation corridor's murals

may indicate the presence of a thin residue of whitewash in many places.

Original Structure of the Main Temple

In his biography of Gongkarwa, Gyatön Changchup Wangyal systematically described the main temple, with its numerous rooms and chapels. He also mentioned the corresponding interior sacred objects and main artistic contents, such as sculptures, wall paintings, and painted wooden shrines. Summarizing the structure of the main temple, he listed its nineteen main chapels or rooms in a peculiar order: not one floor at a time but one direction at a time, that is, listing the rooms in the east, north, south, and west sides of the main building:

> The main building rests upon one hundred thirty large pillars, in total. In the eastern part of [the ground floor of] the temple is (1) the Inner Sanctum (*dri gtsang khang*) with four large pillars and the main deity, Buddha Śākyamuni (pp. 113–116). Above, on the middle floor, is (2) the Vajradhātu Chapel (rDor dbyings Lha khang) with four large pillars and its main deity, Sarvavid Vairocana (pp. 116–119). Above that, on the top floor, is (3) the Guru Chapel (Bla ma Lha

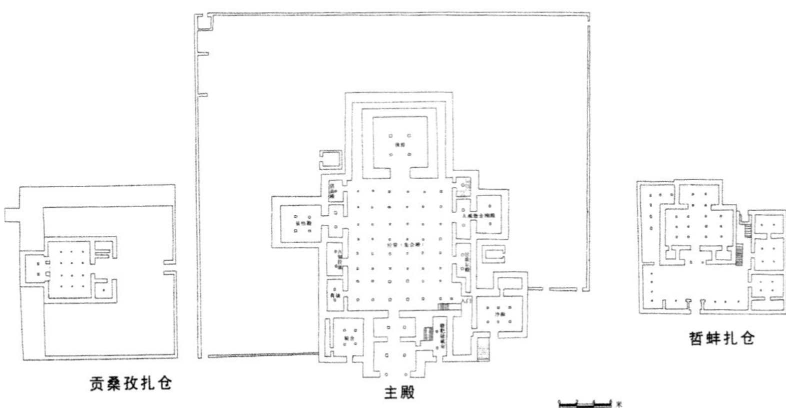

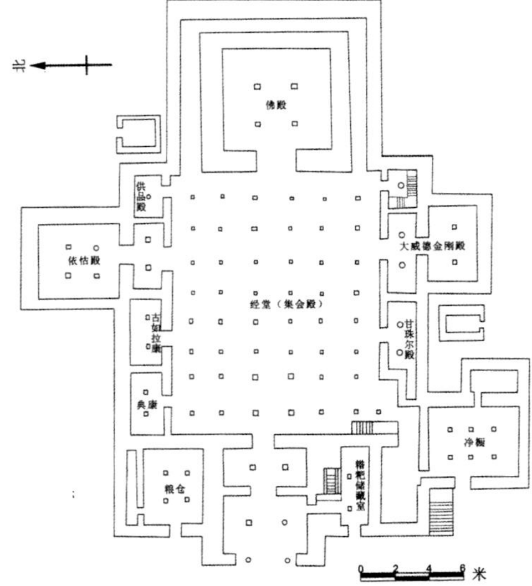

Fig. 4.0
Layout of Gongkar's main floor (north is to the left)
Diagram: after Xiong Wenbin 2012.

khang) with four long pillars
(*ka ring*) and its main sculptures
depicting the lineage masters of the
Lamdre transmission. The murals
depict lineages of various transmissions (pp. 119–125).

On the northern side of the
[ground floor of the] temple is
(4) the Great Protector's Chapel
(mGon khang Chen mo) with four
large pillars and its main deity,
Pañjaranātha Mahākāla (?) (pp.
125–129). Above, on the middle

floor, is (5) the Divine Palace
(gZhal yas khang) with four large
pillars and the nine-deity Hevajra
mandala (Kye rdor lha dgu) (pp.
129–132).[262] Above that, on the
top floor, is (6) the Chapel for
Worshiping the Face (Zhal ras Lha
khang); to its right, (7) the Library
(Phyag dpe khang) with four pillars (pp. 132–33), and to its left,
(8) a storage room for implements
of tantric ritual or dance (sNgags
chas khang pa) with four pillars
(p. 133).

On the southern side of [the ground
floor of] the temple is (9) the Great
Tantric Chapel or Yamāntaka
Chapel ('Jigs byed Lha khang

or sNgags khang chen mo, also
called Bla phyogs sNgags khang)
with two large pillars and its main
deity, Vajrabhairava (pp. 133–135).
Above, on the second floor, is (10)
the Lamdre Chapel (Lam 'bras lha
khang) with its main deity Mañjughoṣa and the sculptures of the
Lamdre instruction's lineage masters (pp. 135–37). Above, on the
top floor, is (11) the Kanjur Chapel
(bKa' 'gyur Lha khang).

On the western side of the [ground
floor of the] temple are (12) the
Great Assembly Hall (*khyams
chen*) with sixty-four large pillars
(pp. 137–39), (13) the Lama's
Private Quarters (*bla brang*) with
sixteen large pillars (pp. 139–46),
(14) the Chapel of the Great Kings
(rGyal chen khang pa), (pp. 139–
40), and (15) the Initiation Chapel
(dBang khang) with six pillars (p.
140). Above those, on the second
floor, is (16) the Protector's Chapel
(*mgon khang*) with six pillars
and its main deity, the Brahmin
(Bram ze) who was a great adept
of Mahākāla (Gur gyi mgon po)
(pp. 140–45?). Also (17) the Chapel
of Bronze Sculptures (Li ma Lha
khang) with two pillars (p. 145).

South of the lama's residence
quarters are (18) the kitchen (*rung
khang*) with nine large pillars
(p. 146) on the ground floor and,
above it, (19) the tea kitchen (*gsol
ja khang*) (p. 146).[263]

This chapter will concentrate on murals
surviving in three main areas of the
ground floor and two main chapels on
the second floor.

The Entrance to the Inner Sanctum

Important murals survive at the front
of the main assembly hall, on the walls

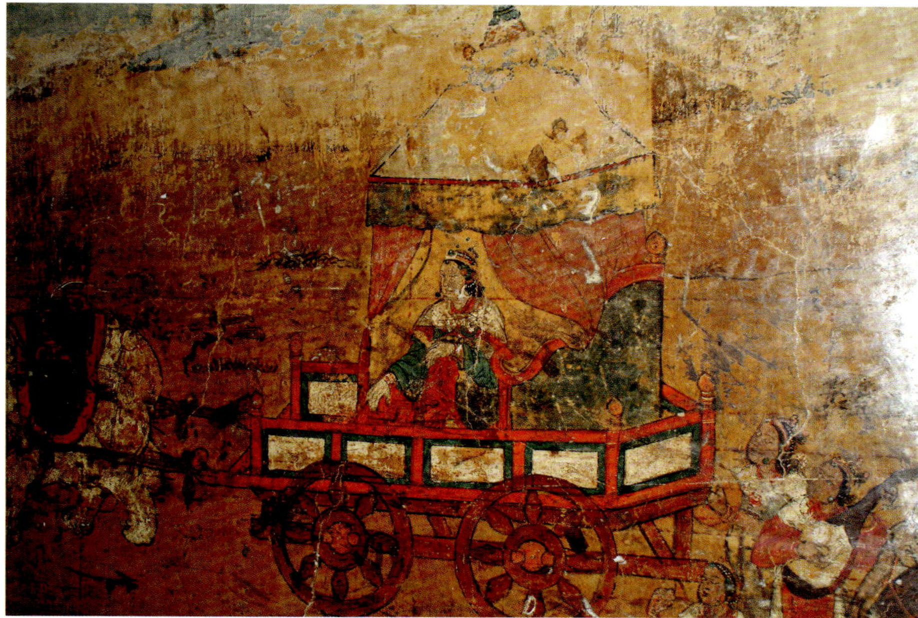

to the left and right of the inner sanctum's entrance. Those to the left depict the three white-clad founders of Sakya, surrounded by lineage gurus of the Lamdre instructions, while those to the right show the three red-clad founders of Sakya, surrounded by numerous lineal gurus. These significant murals will be described in part two of this chapter by Mathias Fermer in his independent contribution, "Mural Paintings of the Sakya Founding Masters with Two Hevajra Lineages."

The Circumambulation Corridor

A second important mural site is the circumambulation corridor (*bskor sa* or *bskor lam*) that surrounds the old inner sanctum on three sides. Pilgrims normally enter it through the opening to the left of the inner sanctum's entrance, walking in a clockwise direction. There, on the corridor's three inner walls, Khyentse Chenmo portrayed the Twelve Great Deeds of Buddha Śākyamuni, with large central buddha figures. I have numbered the walls first, second, and third, following the clockwise progression.

Gyatön states that those murals also contained six large images of the Buddha, in all.[264] But when I counted the large buddhas from the available photographs, I found more than six. These murals actually include twelve large buddhas, that is, not two but four on each wall; from the photos, I counted four buddhas each on the second and third wall and I am told there are also four on the first wall.[265]

The Twelve Great Deeds (*mdzad pa bcu gnyis*) of the Buddha are traditionally listed as:

1. leaving the divine realm of Tuṣita (*dga' ldan gyi gnas nas 'pho ba*)
2. entering his mother's womb (*lhums su zhugs pa*)
3. taking birth (*sku bltams pa*)
4. becoming skilled in arts and manual skills (*bzo yi gnas la mkhas pa*)
5. happily enjoying the company of his royal consort and her retinue (*btsun mo'i 'khor dgyes rol ba*)
6. renouncing lay life and becoming a mendicant (*rab tu byung ba*)
7. practicing austerities (*dka' ba spyad pa*)
8. going to the foot of the Bodhi tree (*byang chub snying por gshegs pa*)
9. overcoming the hosts of Māra (*bdud btul ba*)
10. becoming fully enlightened (*mngon par rdzogs par sangs rgyas pa*)
11. turning the wheel of dharma (*chos kyi 'khor lo bskor ba*)
12. passing into final, complete nirvana (*mya ngan las 'das pa*)

Though these murals in Gongkar are conventionally said to depict the Twelve Great Deeds, they actually include another twenty or thirty minor episodes. (For more detailed lists of episodes of the Buddha's life according to Tāranātha, see Appendix F.)

Only one of the twelve main deeds (number 7, practicing austerities) is illustrated in this catalog (Fig. 4.5). Figure 4.1, by contrast, depicts a minor scene, in which Queen Māyādevī travels by an elephant-drawn carriage, presumably returning to her maternal home for the impending birth (deed number 3). Other earlier episodes were depicted to the right of this scene. Note the cloudy residue that obscures much of the upper half of the mural; it could be a remnant of the whitewash applied in the 1960s.

At the middle of the first wall, immediately to the left of Figures 4.1 and 4.2, is a depiction of the third deed, the Buddha's birth in Lumbini. The first two deeds, the Buddha's leaving the divine realm of Tuṣita and his conception, entering his mother's womb while she dreamed of a white elephant, must have been depicted in the preceding half of this wall.

Figure 4.4 shows the first scene of the second wall. This episode depicts Prince Siddhartha leaving the palace by chariot and witnessing a man suffering from serious illness. The sick man is pictured lying in a small shed at the bottom left. To the right is Siddhartha's palace, with an imposing front gate. The

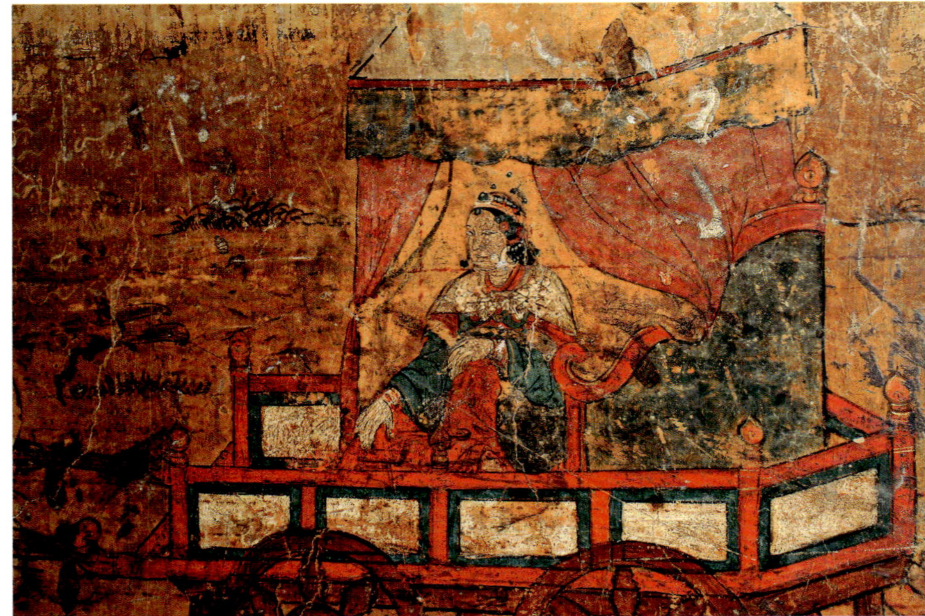

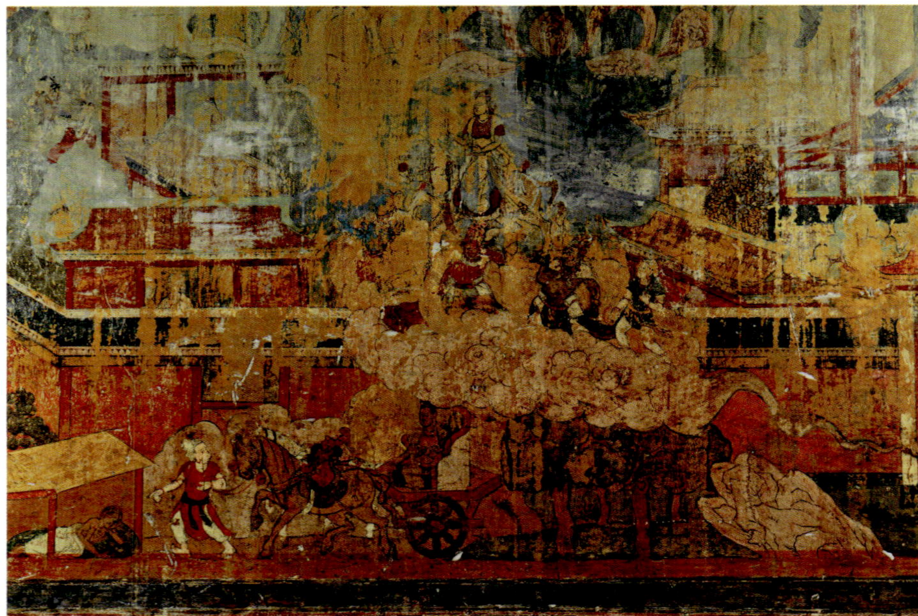

stick in the meditating Siddhartha's ear, who does not react.

After he had gone to the foot of the Bodhi tree, overcome the hosts of Mara, become fully enlightened, and turned the wheel of dharma, the Buddha miraculously tamed an elephant. Figure 4.6 shows five lions taming a single elephant. This episode may be based on an event in Śākyamuni's life in which a dangerous elephant named Nalagiri was set loose in the Buddha's path in an attempt to kill him, part of a conspiracy hatched by his wicked cousin and rival, Devadatta.[266] Higher up the wall, this painting's details are obscured by a white or gray film.

Part of a series of Chinese woodblock prints, Figure 4.7 portrays the same episode as Figure 4.6, but it shows five magically emanated lions taming five elephants, not one. The drawing of the lions and the layout of the vignette are typically Chinese. Khyentse Chenmo presumably saw his version in a detailed Chinese painted or printed depiction of the Buddha's life.

Figure 4.8 illustrates that the thin layer of whitewash or similar residue, which obscures much of the third wall, abruptly ends. Above that line, the original landscape can be seen: charming mountains and clouds and, at the upper left, a vignette featuring a small seated buddha at the edge of the rocky mountains, with a single standing disciple.

The Outer Walls: The Thousand Buddhas of the Fortunate Eon

The circumambulation corridor's three outer walls have been mostly ignored until now. The beginning of one of them can be seen slightly to the left of the middle of Figure 4.9, at the right-hand door leading to that side of the corridor. There we see a broad belt of thin white residue still coating the wall, with the final row of buddhas above the whitewash. From the otherwise blurred photos

Fig. 4.3
Queen Māyādevī's tent-covered upper carriage (detail)
first wall, circumambulation corridor
Photo: Rob Linrothe, 2007

Fig. 4.4
Prince Siddhartha leaving the palace by chariot and witnessing sickness
second wall (west wall), near the beginning, circumambulation corridor
Photo: Roberto Fortuna, 2011, courtesy Knud Larsen

last scene of the first wall, not pictured here, similarly shows him leaving his opulent palace by chariot and witnessing for the first time a person with old age. It is difficult to discern many other details, but Khyentse Chenmo obviously included a number of palaces with large, Chinese-style, gilt pagoda roofs in scenes of early deeds.

Figure 4.5 depicts Siddhartha undergoing extreme self-mortification, a deed that he accomplished after he ran away from his palace and renounced lay life. His practice is witnessed by two passing cowherds, one of whom pokes a

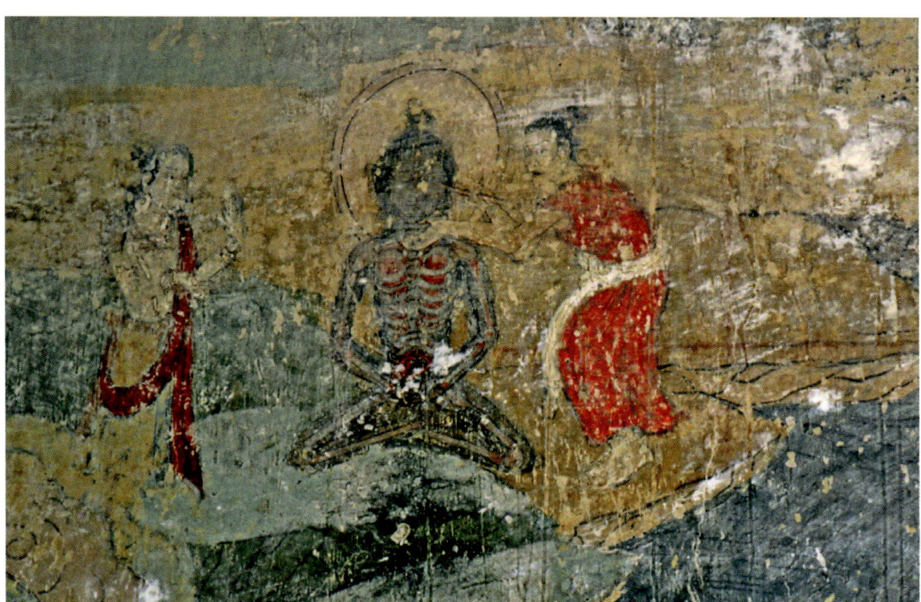

Fig. 4.5
Siddhartha practicing extreme austerities
second wall, circumambulation corridor
Photo: Lionel Fournier, 2008

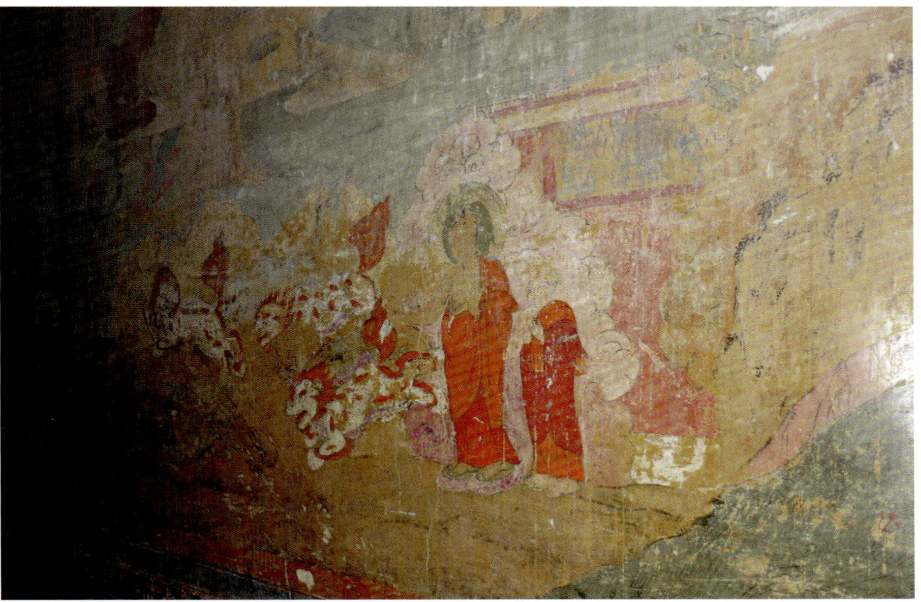

Fig. 4.6
The Buddha miraculously subduing an elephant by emanating lions
third wall (north wall), near the middle, circumambulation corridor
Photo: Mathias Fermer, 2014

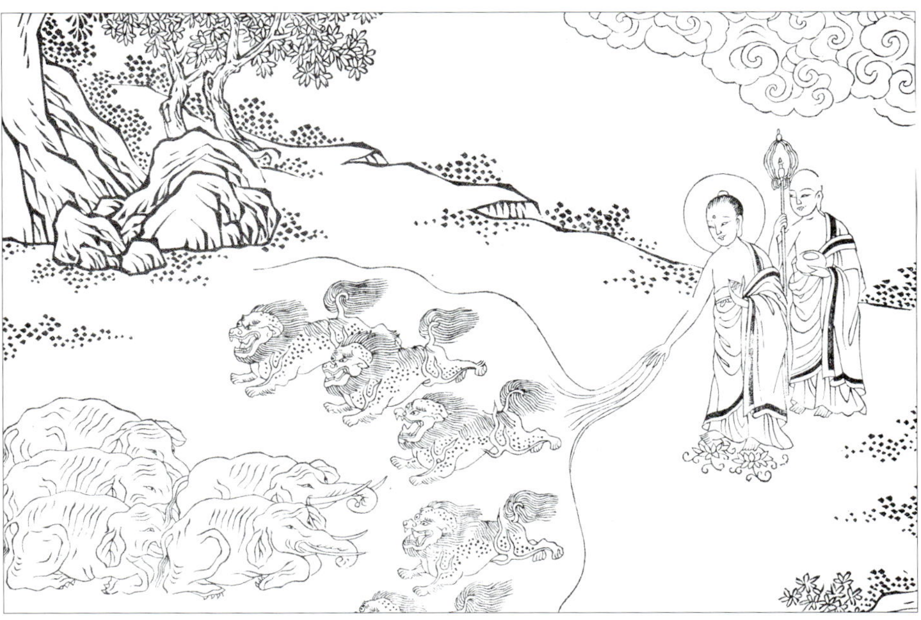

Fig. 4.7
The Buddha subdues threatening elephants
Chinese woodcut
After: Chandra 1972, no. 46

of this wall, I could make out five horizontal registers of large buddhas.

The subjects of these murals are repetitive, but the paintings are the work of Khyentse Chenmo. Here he depicted *The Thousand Buddhas of the Fortunate Eon* (Tib. *bskal bzang sangs rgyas stong*), arranging them in columns of larger and smaller images and painting them on a vermilion background. The Mahayana Sutra (Bhadrakalpika Sūtra; Tib. Bskal pa bzang po'i mdo) explains the fortunate nature of the present eon and enumerates the thousand buddhas (beginning with Buddha Krakucchanda; Tib. 'Khor ba 'jigs) that will appear.

Arhats in the Skylight Murals

Immediately after describing the circumambulation corridor, Gyatön mentioned the presence of paintings in the central assembly hall of the main building: "On the long walls of the central skylight openings, he painted murals depicting the Buddha with the sixteen arhats, with Hashang and Dharmatrāta supporting the ends."[267] These high murals are mostly overlooked, though Batchelor briefly mentioned paintings "in the upper wall by the skylight."[268] (See Fig. 4.10a.) From the photos, it seems they were painted in the 1930s.

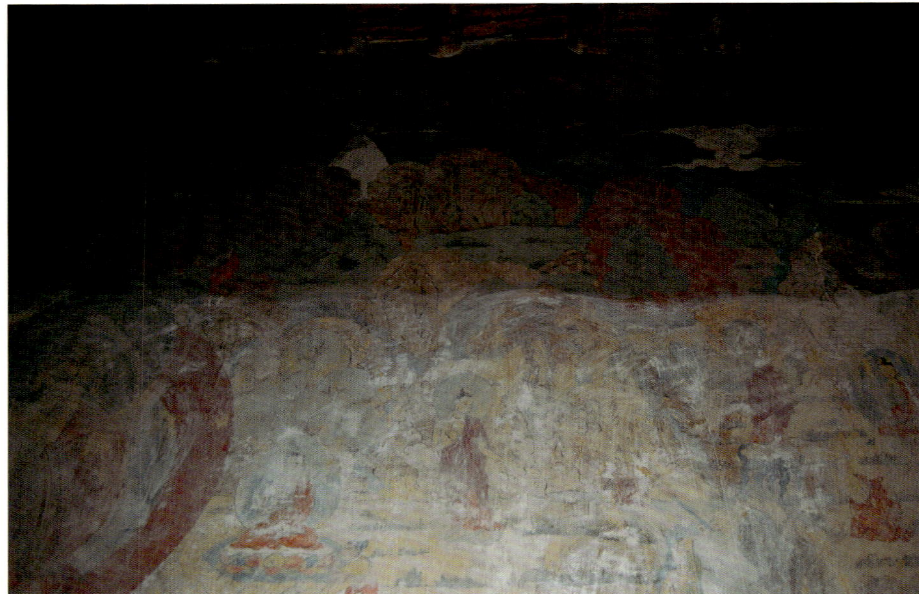

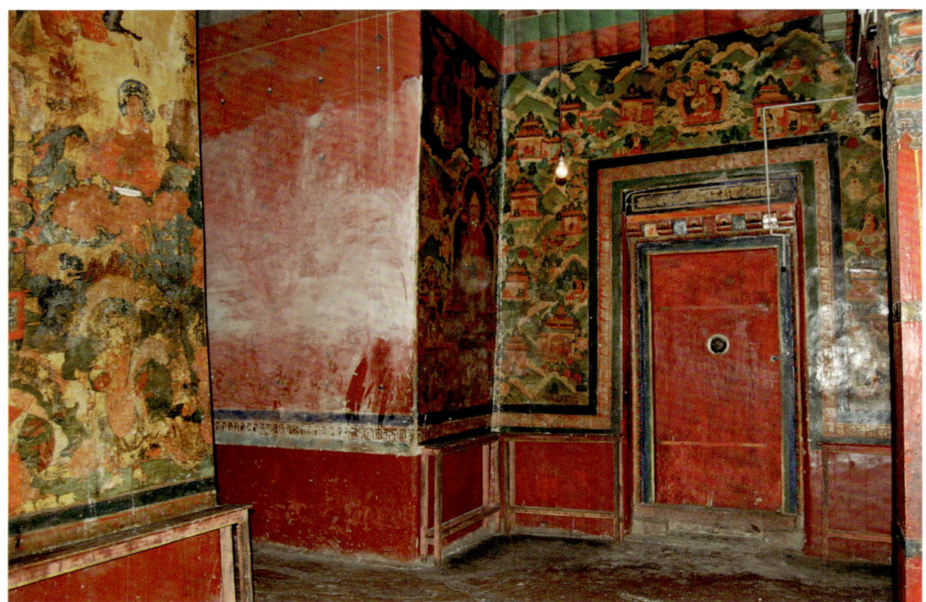

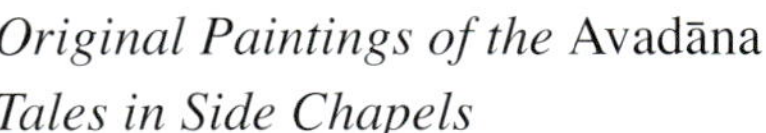

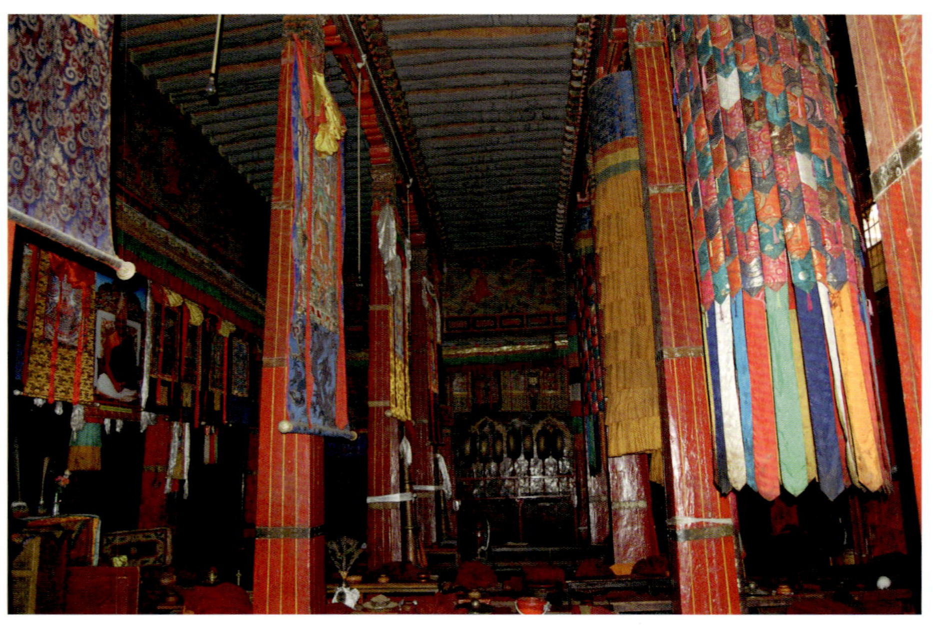

These skylight panels depicting the Sixteen Arhats do indeed date to the period of the 1930s renovation. They copy Khyenri models and are said to be the work of the Khyenri painting master Uchen Tenpa Gyatsho.[269] (See Figure 4.10b.) In this detail we note the presence in the landscape of a Manchurian crane and two tame rabbits being fed from behind the adjoining hillock, features that we shall see in later paintings.[270]

Original Paintings of the Avadāna Tales in Side Chapels

A second important group of surviving narrative murals by Khyentse Chenmo depicts in great detail the *Kalpalatā* (*dPag bsam 'khri shing*) cycle of moral tales. These paintings survive in the little side rooms on the ground floor to the right and left of the present assembly hall, on the formerly outer walls of the old assembly hall. Originally, out of one hundred thirty large pillars (*ka chen*), sixty-four pillars were devoted to depicting the Hundred Deeds (*mdzad pa brgya*) of the perfectly enlightened Buddha. "Hundred Deeds" was a common name not only for a detailed biography of the Buddha but also for what we have here: the more than a hundred moral tales of the *Bodhisattvāvadānakalpalatā*. This collection was composed in Sanskrit by the Kashmiri poet Kṣemendra—one hundred seven by him and a final one by his son.

The biography of Kunga Namgyal by Gyatön records that on the original outer walls of the assembly hall, "together with in the circumambulation way (*skor sa dang bcas pa la*)," Khyentse Chenmo painted the stories of the hundred eight moral tales.[271] His mention of the circumambulation way is confusing and probably in error since, as described above, those walls are filled with the story of the Buddha's life.

Khyentse Chenmo is said by Gyatön to have painted two episodes of moral tales for every larger buddha image. These murals include, in a band beneath each panel, several lines of inscriptions that give a simplified retelling of each tale, revised from the original full version of the text. Gyatön implies that either Khyentse or Kunga Namgyal wrote the new version; he does not mention anyone else's involvement. Luckily that simplified version survives as a separate text, which is attributed to "Lord Yangjenpa" (*rje yangs can pa*).[272]

Mathias Fermer discovered more about the text, such as that it was written by Gyatön Changchup Wanggyal, who was also called Yangpajenpa since he was from the monastic house of Yangpajen at Gongkar Chöde. The inscriptions were also copied and consulted by Ameshab for his *Avadāna* commentary, who greatly admired the layout of the original in Gongkar.[273] The published text of the Gongkar's *Avadānakalpalatā* inscription was originally discovered at Sakya Monastery. Since it lacks a colophon and verses of dedication, this work could in fact be Ameshab's transcription of the mural captions that he made while visiting Gongkar.

The rooms for the small side chapels were made in the 1930s, when two

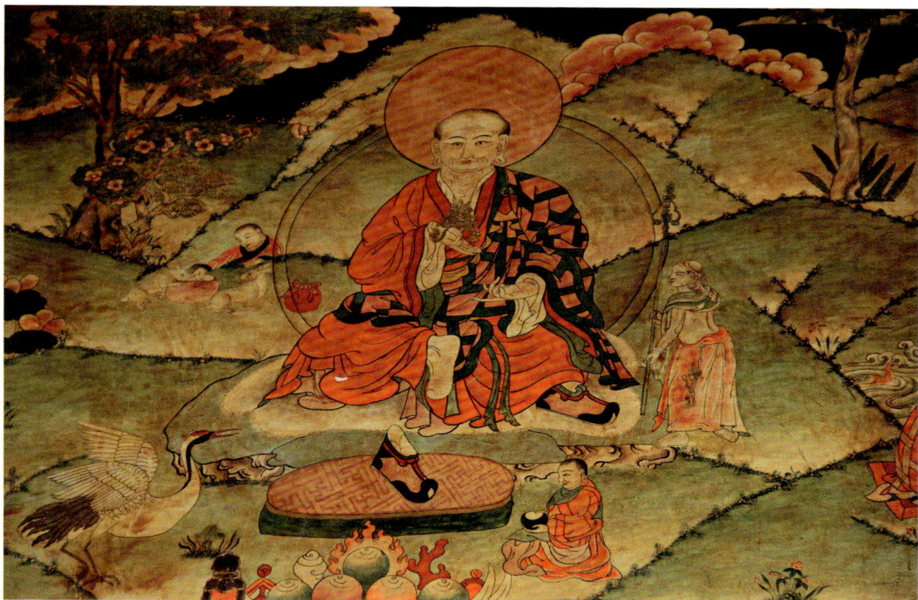

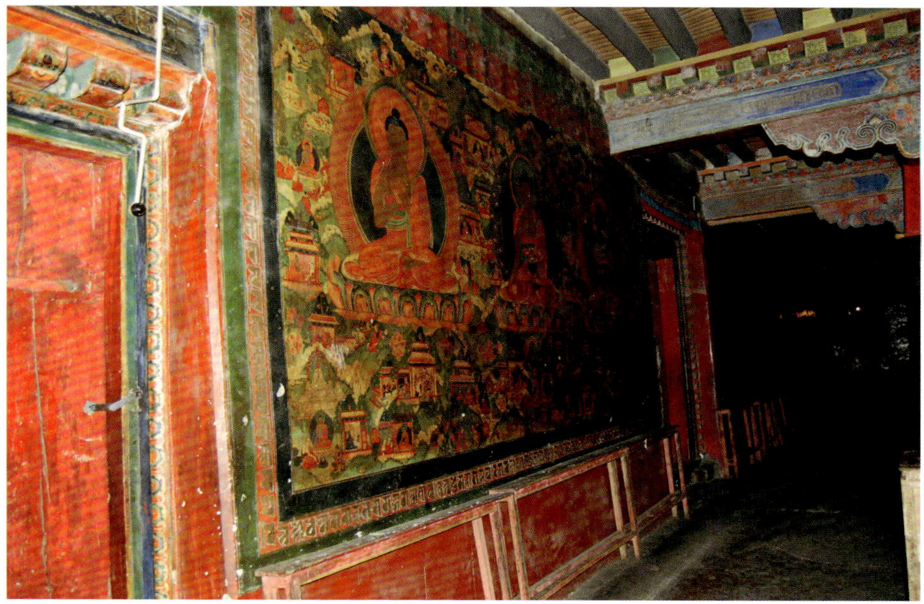

walls were added in the main assembly hall. Due to structural problems, the outside rows of pillars on either side of the old assembly hall were incorporated into a pair of new load-bearing walls, running east to west. This was done around eighty years ago, around 1934. It made the assembly hall much narrower, and new murals depicting the *Avadānakalpalatā* (*dPag bsam 'khri shing*) had to be painted to decorate the new inner walls. Figure 4.11 illustrates the new southern wall.

FIG. 4.10B
Arhat Rahula
New assembly hall, skylight panel, Gongkar; 1930s
Painted by Uchen Tenpa Gyatsho
Photo: Jampel Shedrub 2015, courtesy of M. Fermer

FIG. 4.11
South supporting wall
New assembly hall, Gongkar; 1930s
Photo: Kazuo Kano, 2007

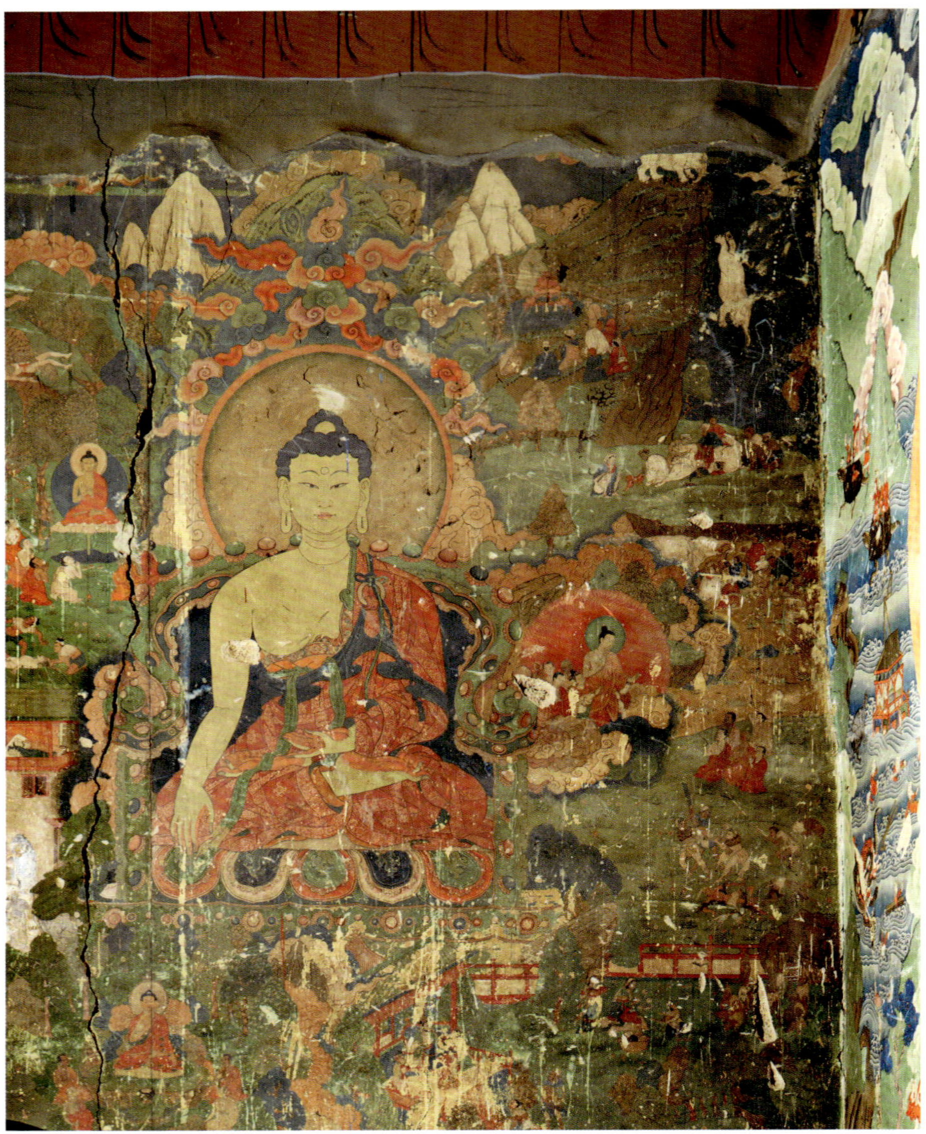

FIGURE 4.12
Buddha with *Avadāna* tale number 96
west wall, front-left storage room, ground
floor; 1464–1476
Photo: Roberto Fortuna, 2011, courtesy
Knud Larsen

Most of the original *avadāna* murals of Khyentse Chenmo were destroyed in the 1930s through a process of renovation. The few that still existed in the new side chambers hardly mattered, as they were the walls of storage rooms. When the Cultural Revolution struck, the remaining old paintings were in such dark and obscure places that no Communists saw the need to destroy or deface them.

According to a researcher who visited Gongkar in the 1990s, many of the surviving original murals by Khyentse were further obstructed by newly added shrines between November 1992 and October 1993. As of 1994, the spaces between the old and new perimeter walls that form the little chapel and storage rooms on both sides were still being finished and decorated.[274] Altars, statuary, and, in some rooms, even bags of grain had been pushed very near the old murals, making it difficult or impossible to see them. Some minor renovation at this time caused paint to be splattered here and there, but the old murals were left fairly intact though more difficult to photograph than earlier.

From Mathias Fermer's provisional research notes on these chapels, it seems clear that three small storage rooms or new chapels to the right, along the original northern wall, depict at least *avadāna* numbers 93 through 108 (that is, fifteen in all) while the three small rooms on the other side, along the old southern wall, contain at least stories number 62 to 76 (that is, fourteen in all) and perhaps a few more. It means that just a fraction of the original hundred eight stories survived, roughly no more than a third. The eighty or so now-missing tales must have been covered up by the new paintings added to the other ground-floor mural areas in the 1930s.

Figure 4.12 depicts one mural panel in the left-front storeroom. It shows a buddha, with *avadāna* tale 96 to his right. The central buddha's face and

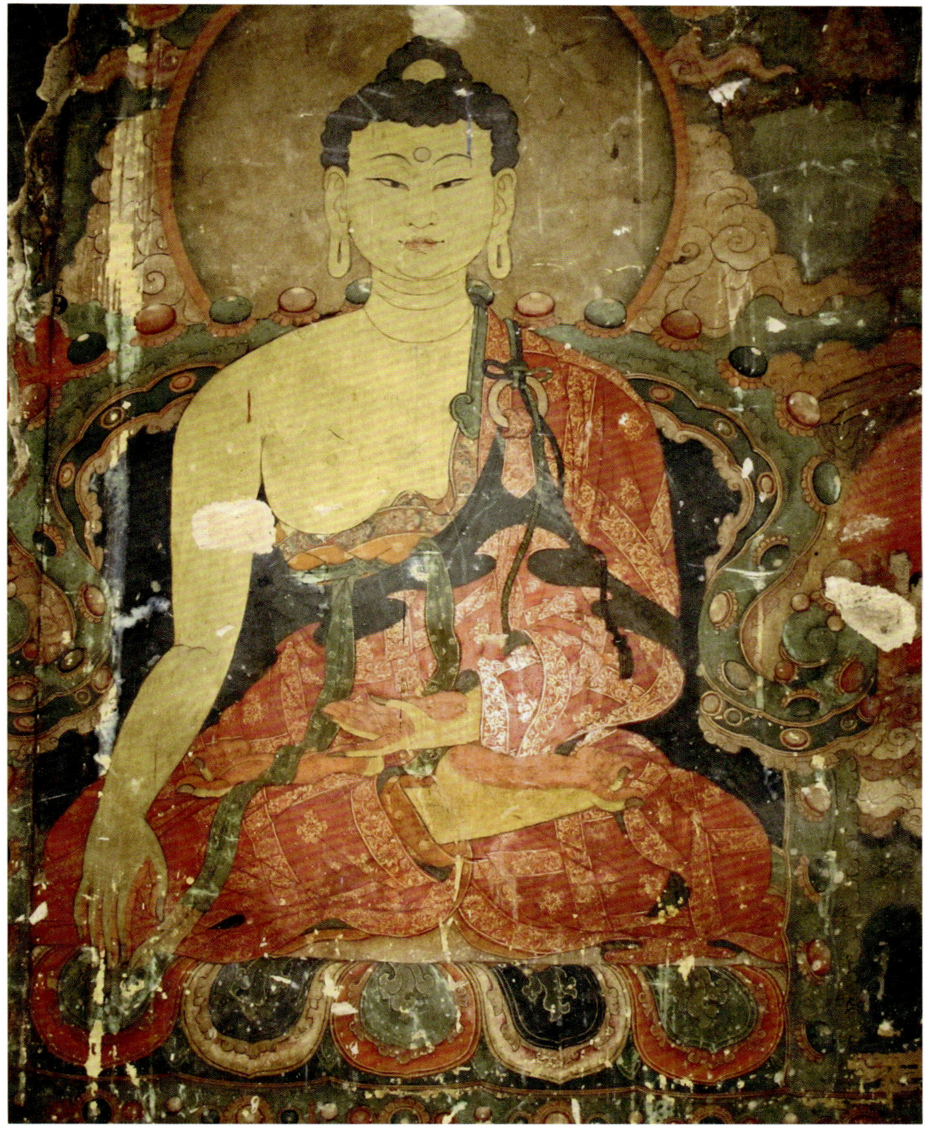

robes are exquisitely beautiful. The hair and head protuberance are Chinese in style, with many little bumps around the edges, and the center of the protuberance includes a golden jewel. The robes have several ornate details, including a large ring-shaped robe fastener hanging over one shoulder.

The western wall of this room depicts tales 93 through 96. The original murals were cut off by the new wall to the left, which was built in the middle of a buddha's body nimbus. Inscriptions can be seen below, but I have not translated them.

Generally in these murals, two stories are depicted between each large buddha. To the right of the buddha in Figure 4.12 are original murals of tale 95, about the tigress, and tale 96, about the compassionate and generous elephant. More recent events of both tales are depicted lower on each panel. The layout of the mural is given in Diagram [C].

Tales depicted: 93, the tale of Sumāgadhā; 94, the tale of Yaśomitra; 95, the tale of the starving tigress; and 96, the tale of the compassionate elephant.

The buddha in Figure 4.13 is one of the many that appear with this series of moral tales. Compare the large buddhas in Figures 4.15 and 4.16; it seems that Khyentse Chenmo prided himself on never depicting any of them in the same way.

Figure 4.14 depicts the mural panel to the left of Figures 4.12 and 4.13. This part of the mural depicts two moral tales: number 93, the tale of Sumāgadhā (Na ga dha bzang mo'i rtogs brjod), and number 95, the tale of the starving tigress (sTag mo'i rtogs brjod). The

details of the stories are fairly distinctive and can be located in the painting. I believe it will eventually be possible to locate below number 93 the details of number 94, the tale of Yaśomitra (Grags pa'i bshes gnyen gyi rtogs brjod).

Depicting one of the many central buddha figures in the moral-tale murals, Figure 4.15 was selected at random from available photographs, and I am not sure in which mural it appears. But this figure illustrates the variety of robes and lotus seats that Khyentse Chenmo employed. In this case, the head protuberance and robes represent not strongly Chinese models but more Indic ones: the protuberance has a more traditional shape and lacks a central jewel, and the upper robe covers both shoulders and lacks

anything resembling a ring-shaped robe fastener.

Figure 4.16 illustrates a mural depicting a buddha with *avadāna* tales, including number 76, which tells of the torture of the water buffalo Vidura. It was painted on the original southern wall of the assembly hall. It is now in the Kangyur Lhakhang, a different room than Figures 4.12 through 4.14. Compared with Figure 4.15, the buddha here is again very Chinese in certain respects, especially the head protuberance and robes. The protuberance seems shorter and more triangular in shape, and it has a central golden jewel. The robes have many complicated and colorful straps over both shoulders, and this buddha even wears a shirt with short fringed sleeves. Depicting

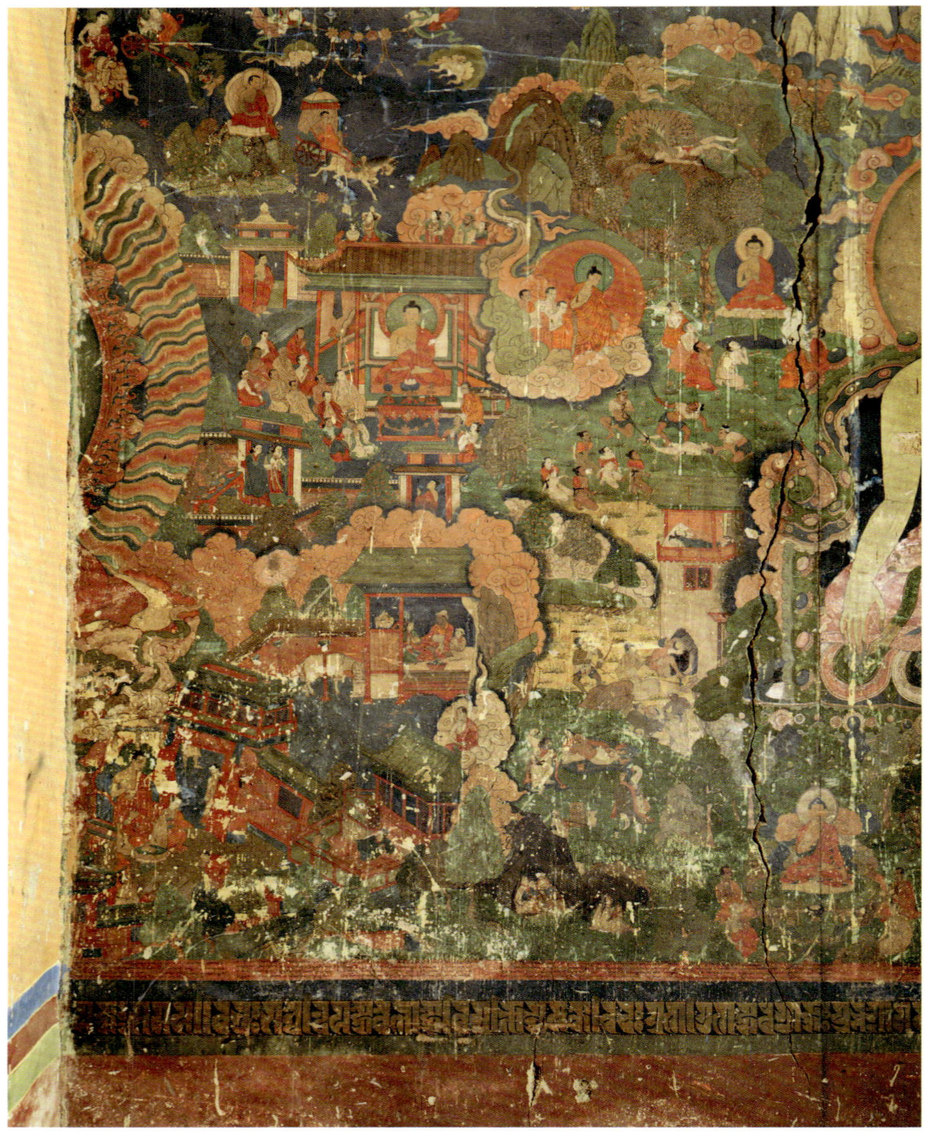

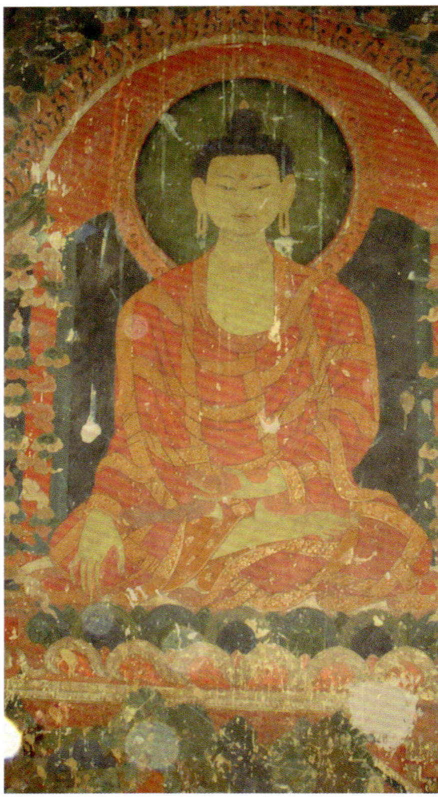

such an upper garment would be impossible on a buddha in an Indic style or setting (such as Fig. 4.15).

Figure 4.17 is a part of the previous mural (Fig. 4.16), showing in great detail the scene of the villagers who gathered to witness the torture of Vidura, with the somewhat reassuring presence of the Buddha. This mural was rightly chosen by Penba Wangdu as a striking example of Khyentse Chenmo's naturalism. (See Figs. 3.3 and 3.4.) In this rendition of the tale, two humans have joined in torturing the animal, driving swords into his back and a trident into his neck. A tiger and lion have also joined in the melee, oblivious to the humans brandishing sharp weapons. Twelve monks are also shown, accompanying the Buddha.

And twenty-three villagers are present, including many men wearing white turbans. In the foreground, the person at the far right seems to be a boy; he crouches and faces away from the scene, holding his hands over his face. To his left is a woman carrying a child on her back; she stares at the gruesome scene, but the child looks away, its view blocked by her body. The next pair may be another parent and child; the adult wearing a cloth turban is likely the father, who puts his hand on the standing child's head while the child looks up for assurance, clinging to the back of his father's robe. The next pair, wearing turbans, stands more casually, one pointing to something while the other listens, with his hands clasped behind his back. Next are two adult females who seem to be relatives or close friends, sharing their reactions to the scene; the one wearing red drapes her left arm over her companion's shoulders and holds her hand. These are just nine of the onlookers, an indication of the astonishing number of tiny naturalistic details in Khyentse Chenmo's paintings.

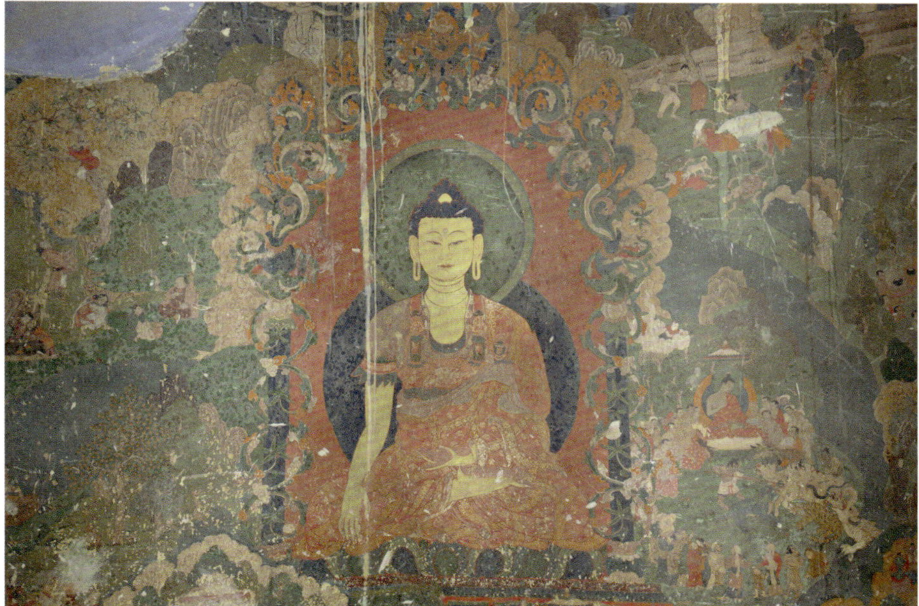

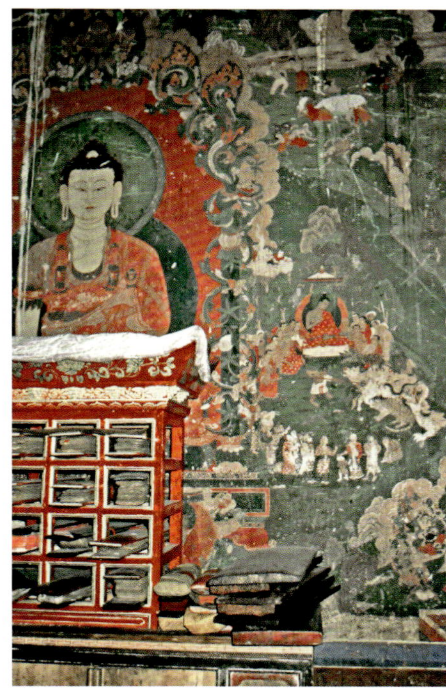

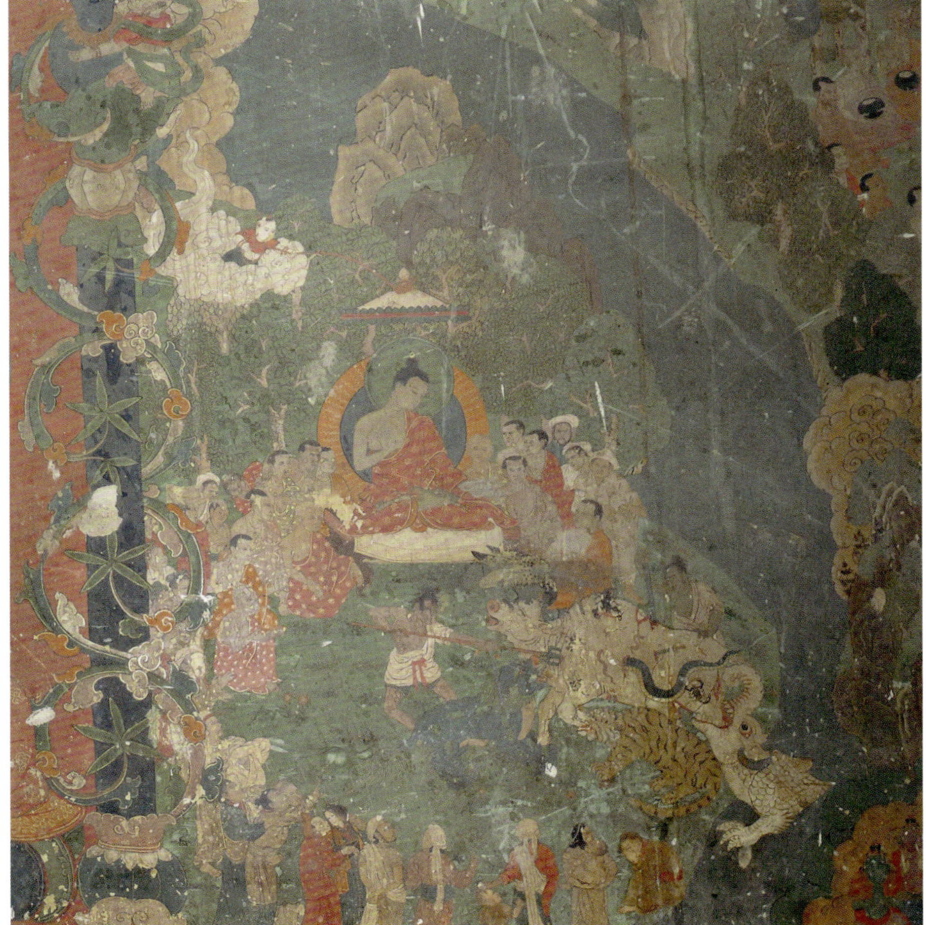

Figure 4.18 depicts the same mural with the moral tale of Vidura. The episode is visible to the right of a bookcase in a functioning chapel with enshrined sacred scriptures.

Great Protector's Chapel

The Great Protector's Chapel (Gönkhang Chenmo, dGon khang chen mo), with four pillars, also still exists in a room built by means of an extension wall to the north (Fig. 4.19).[275] Though this chapel is not a major mural site, it is decorated with detailed and accurate depictions of charnel grounds (Fig. 4.20).

I present Figure 4.20 as a comparison to the paintings of similar themes found in the Upper Protector's Chapel, on the second floor. Here, at the upper right, a vulture is carefully drawn, pulling the intestines from the open stomach of a human corpse. These paintings

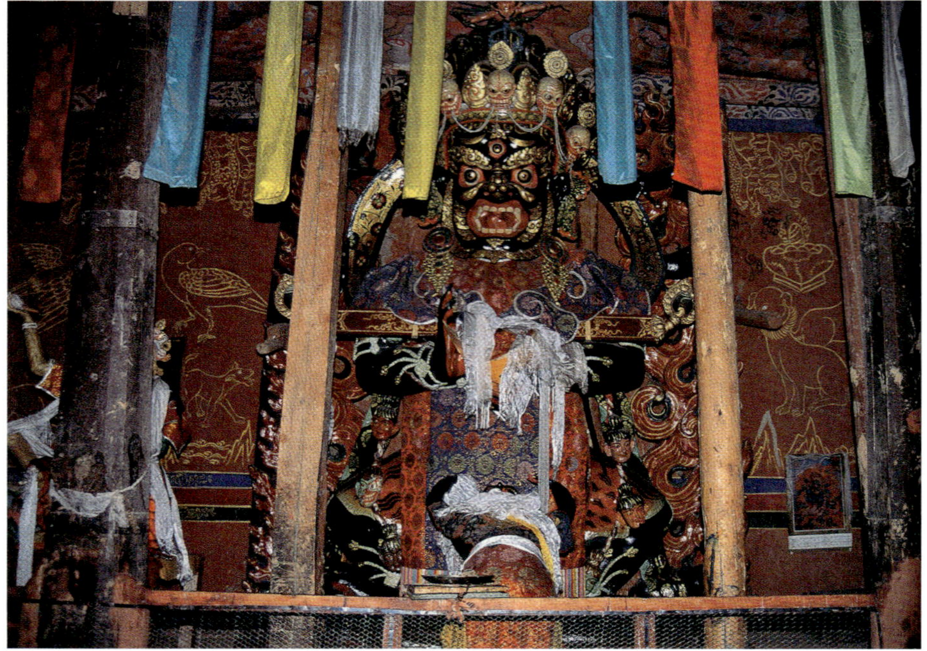

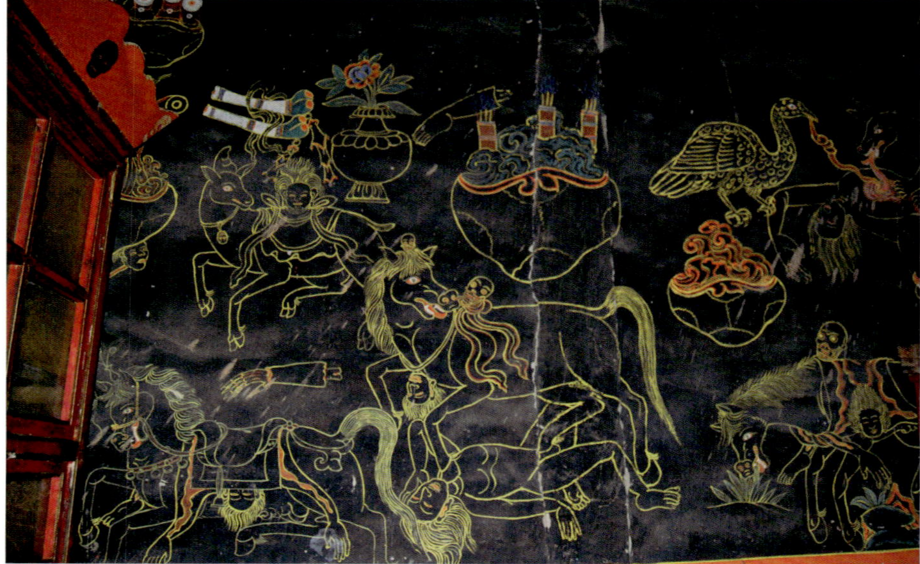

of Vajrabhairava was being made: Kunga Namgyal instructed Khyentse to insert the supporting pieces of wood of the main image, saying, "Since this image will be quickly achieved, please let me know when it is finished," and then he entered a retreat in the Ganden residence; Khyentse finished it well within one month.[276] This Vajrabhairava sculpture was the image that Tucci, completely ignorant of its special history, called the most terrifying image he had ever seen in Tibet.

The Hevajra Chapel

On the second floor, the most noteworthy wall paintings survive in the Chapel of Hevajra and the Upper Protector's Chapel (Gönkhang Tengma). The Hevajra Chapel, called the "Divine Palace" (*gzhal yas khang*) in the life of Gongkarwa, lies on the north side of the second floor. It has four pillars, and its main image was a gilt-copper sculpture of the nine-deity mandala of Hevajra by Khyentse Chenmo.

This chapel has many fine mural depictions of tantric deities with their retinues, including three types of Hevajra and even Vaiśravaṇa, Jambhala, and Kurukullā. Akira Masaki and Musashi Tachikawa published a small book about the chapel, in Japanese.[277] According to their temple diagram, the chapel possesses twenty-one main deities or mural panels, which they do not number.[278] They do not indicate Vimaloṣṇīṣa above the entrance or the two bodhisattvas to his right and left. According to Masaki and Tachikawa, there are five main deities on the southern wall, six on the western wall, four on the northern wall, and six on the eastern wall.

According to Gyatön, six main deities were depicted on three walls in this chapel. Their enumeration traditionally begins with the deity Hevajra of the Lamdre system (*man ngag lugs*), who is the first and central deity of the chapel.

are obviously not new—note the two prominent vertical cracks—but they do not possess the fine, lifelike details that Khyentse Chenmo's works normally do.

The Jigche Lhakhang

Penba Wangdu mentioned the presence of detailed charnel-ground depictions in the Jigche Lhakhang; Gyatön also mentioned it. Regarding the temple's main image, Gyatön records a remarkable cooperation by Kunga Namgyal and Khyentse when the main image of the Jigche Lhakhang, a sculpture

I list them here, following the order of Gyatön's description.[279]

The six deities on the northern wall are: 1. Hevajra, holding scull cups, in the center; 2. Vajraḍāka, one of Five *ḍāka* taught in the Vajrapañjara (rDo rje Gur) tantra, to Hevajra's left; 3. Sarvabuddha-samayoga (dPal Sangs rgyas mnyam sbyor); 4. Kālacakra; 12. Catuḥpīṭa (rDo rje gdan bzhi pa), to the right of the central Hevajra; and 13. Hevajra with weapons (*mtshon cha can*).

The six deities on the western wall are, from right to left: 5. Guhyasamāja Akṣobhyavajra; 6. Guhyasamāja Mañjuvajra; 7. Red Yamāri (Raktayamāri); 8. Yamāntaka; 9. Black Yamāri (Kṛṣṇayamāri); and 10. Mahācakra Vajrapāṇi.

The six deities on the eastern wall are, from left to right: 14. Cakrasamvara; 15. Vajrasattva of Sampuṭa (Tilaka?; dPal Kha sbyor [thig le]); 16. Mahāmāyā; 17. Blue Buddhakapāla; 18. Kurukullā (Lha mo Rigs byed ma); and 19. Bhūṭaḍāmara.

The six deities on the southern wall are: 11. Yangdak Thuk, to the right of the entrance door; 20. Vajrakīla (Dorje Phurpa), to the right of the door; 21. Large Yellow Vaiśravaṇa (rNam sras ser chen), also to the right of the door; 22a. Vimaloṣṇīṣa (dPal gTsug tor dri ma med pa)—a rare deity, evidently a wealth-granting peaceful *yakṣa*—above the door; 22b. Blue-clad Vajrapāṇi, in the tradition of Sugatigarbha (Phag na rdo rje 'Gro bzang [snying po'i lugs]), to 22a's right; 22c. Vajrapāṇi Kūṭāgāra ([Phyag rdor] Khang bu brtsegs pa), to 22a's left.[280]

Two murals were omitted by Gyatön, but two main deities are to the left of the door: 23. Yakṣa Vajramāradama (gNod sbyin rDo rje bdud 'dul), to the right, and 24. Samvara Vajraḍākārṇava (bDe mchog mKha' 'gro rgya mtsho), to the left.

I noticed a few discrepancies when comparing the north and south walls to

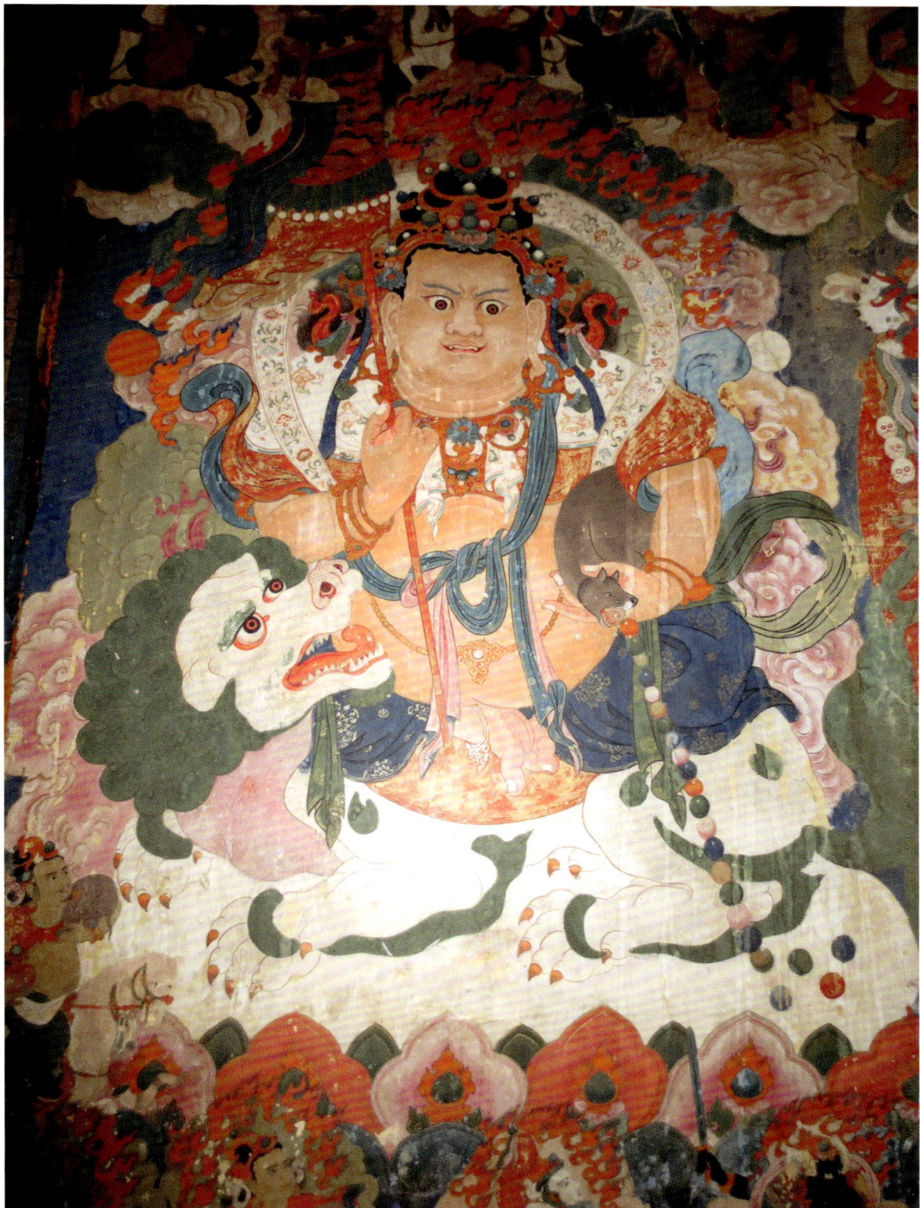

Masaki and Tachikawa's diagram, which includes measurements.[281] Their diagram lacks two deities to the left of the central Hevajra on the north wall, which is now a section of damaged mural but appears as numbers 2 and 3 in Gyatön's list. For the south wall, their diagram omits numbers 22a through 22c, above the door.

Figure 4.21 presents the deity Vaiśravaṇa, who has a peaceful, friendly visage. He is a yellow *yakṣa* who sits atop a white lion. In the mural, he appears with his full retinue of ten horse-riding *yakṣa*s, three above and seven below; they also appear in the Upper Protector's Chapel. In this detail image, parts of their bodies can be seen,

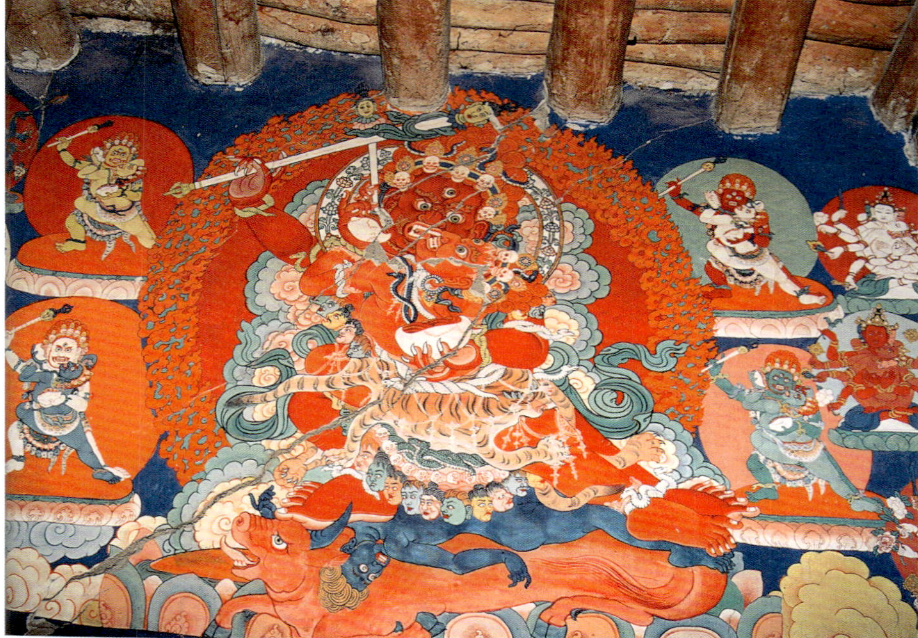

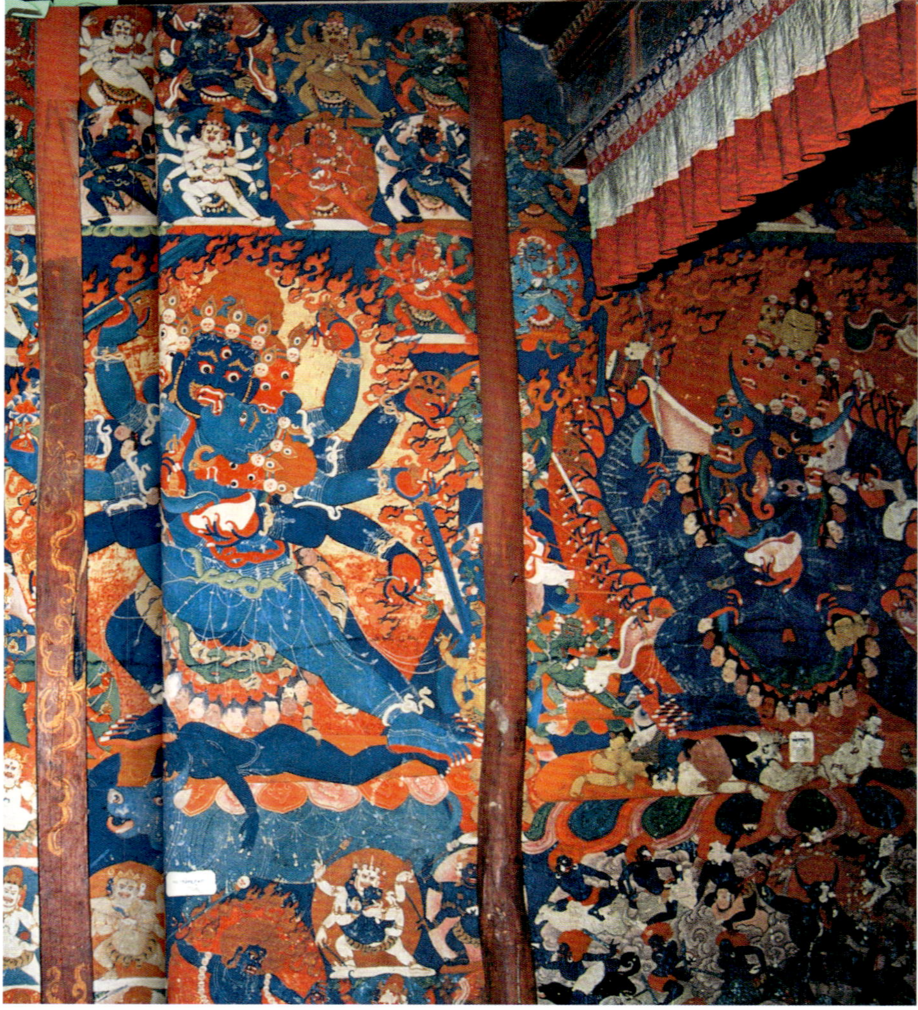

the horses above and the *yakṣa*s' heads below the deity. Since Vaiśravaṇa is a wealth-granting deity, it is no surprise to see his mongoose coughing up a continuous stream of jewels. Accordingly, Khyentse Chenmo adorned the centers of the lotus petals of the main figure's seat with a series of prominent flaming-green jewels.

Figure 4.22 illustrates a mandala of five deities, Red Yamāri with his four-deity retinue. The central figure is a wrathful *yidam* with bright-red skin standing on a blue corpse and a supine red bull that cranes its neck and seems to bellow. The artist painted a wreath of pastel blue clouds with pink centers behind the deity to divide and transition between two areas of red, the deity's body and the inner part of his body nimbus.

Yamāri and his retinue are placed against a contrasting solid-blue field. In the gaps of the main deity's body nimbus, a continuous ring of orange flames, the artist painted a contrasting pastel green. The body nimbuses of the four deities of the retinue are rounded ovals of solid colors, seen in other parts of this chapel: bright orange, bright red, pastel green, and pastel pink. It seems Khyentse Chenmo was fond of bright colors and pastel colors, and he also liked round body nimbuses for minor figures; here, he combines them.

Figure 4.23 depicts Black Yamāri and Yamāntaka with their respective retinues. Here, two supporting pillars partly block the view of the west wall of the

Hevajra Chapel. Yamāri is standing upon a corpse that lies on a blue bull with a gaping mouth. His body nimbus is made of repeated clusters of flames, with gaps between each cluster.

A detail of the heads of Black Yamāri and his consort shows more exactly the wrathful deity's mouths, eyes, and numerous head ornaments, including skeleton heads and tiny chains of dangling bone ornaments (Fig. 4.24).

The mural in Figure 4.25 depicts Hevajra surrounded by his retinue of eight goddesses, as taught in the Lamdre tradition. This tradition of Hevajra practice was also the subject of the chapel's main sculpture, which is now restored. The present mural shows Hevajra standing with his goddesses and subsidiary Hevajra deities in a charnel-ground setting. It is the only mural of this chapel that has a green Chinese-style landscape in the background.

Figure 4.26 shows the tremendous amount of detail that Khyentse Chenmo could fit into his background landscapes. This detail is from the painting of Hevajra with eight goddesses (Fig. 4.25), the only painting in this chapel to show charnel-ground scenes. They do appear in the Upper Protector's Chapel.

This image depicts a small landscape located between Hevajra and the two dancing goddesses, to the left of the main deity. Here, a vulture perched on a rock eyes a human corpse that has been impaled through its stomach on a huge wooden spike. On the ground, a flesh-eating demon with a three-pointed, spotted white hat crouches, munching on the intestine of a red-skinned, supine human corpse. This demon strokes the neck of and shares his meal with a long-tailed blue wolf or dog, whose muzzle is digging into the corpse's stomach

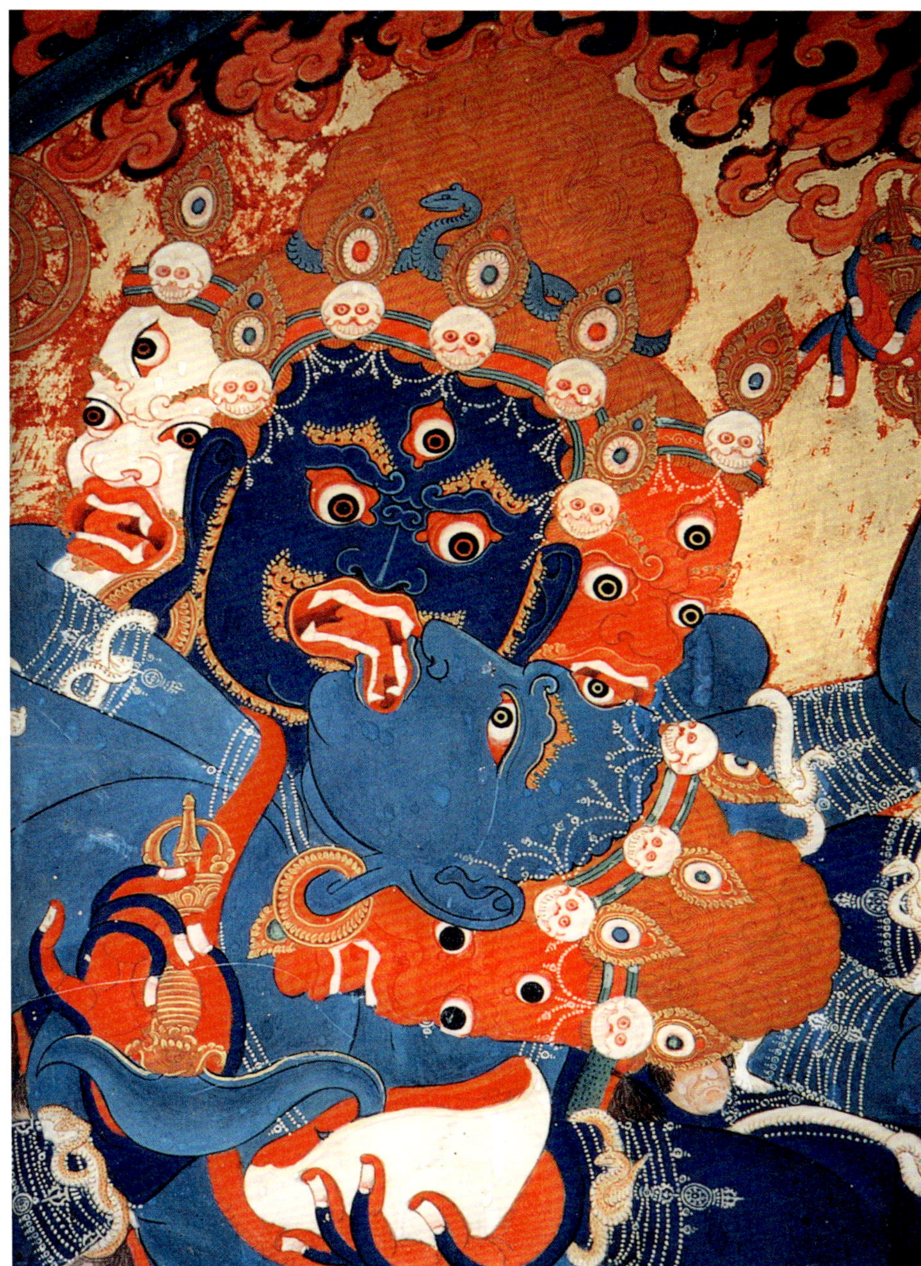

hole. Nearby, a smaller long-tailed fox approaches with raised ears, fully alert and waiting for its chance to feast once the larger animal leaves.

Figure 4.27, a detail of the bottom-left corner of Figure 4.25, depicts a White Hevajra, a minor form of Hevajra. There are several charnel-ground details: a crow, to the right of the body nimbus, and a brown dog, above the crow, which bites the foot of a corpse being carried to the charnel ground. Though both crows and dogs might be expected in charnel-ground depictions, they do not appear in the paintings of similar scenes in the Upper Protector's Chapel.

Figure 4.28 depicts a different form of Hevajra with a retinue of thirty-five minor deities. Here we have Hevajra "possessing weapons" (Tib. *mtshon cha can*), a type of the deity that is taught in the *Samputa Tantra* of the Hevajra tantric cycle. The main figure stands with legs far apart, unlike the form depicted in Figure 4.27. He is surrounded by a continuous ring of stylized orange flames on a ground of vermilion. The background is composed of a field of green below the main deity and a dark-blue sky, featuring stylized clouds of

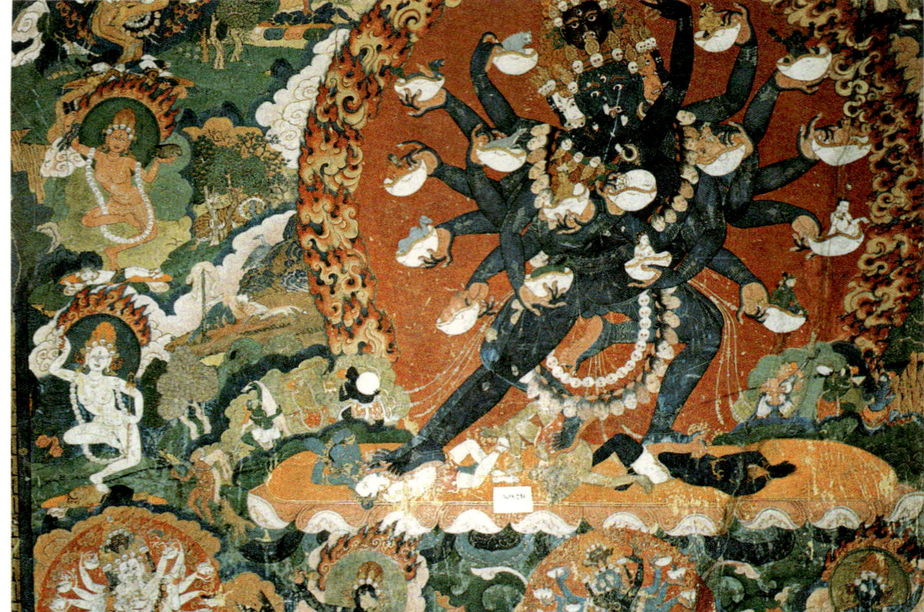

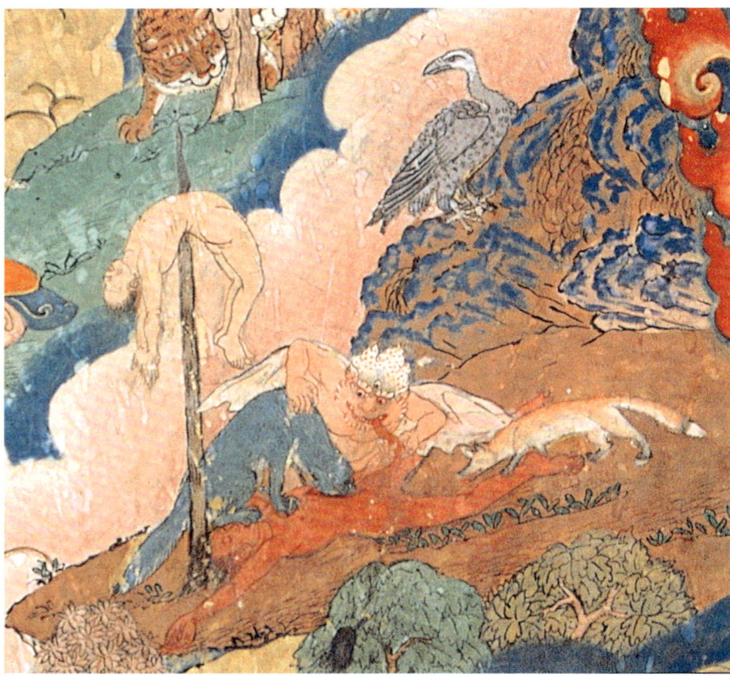

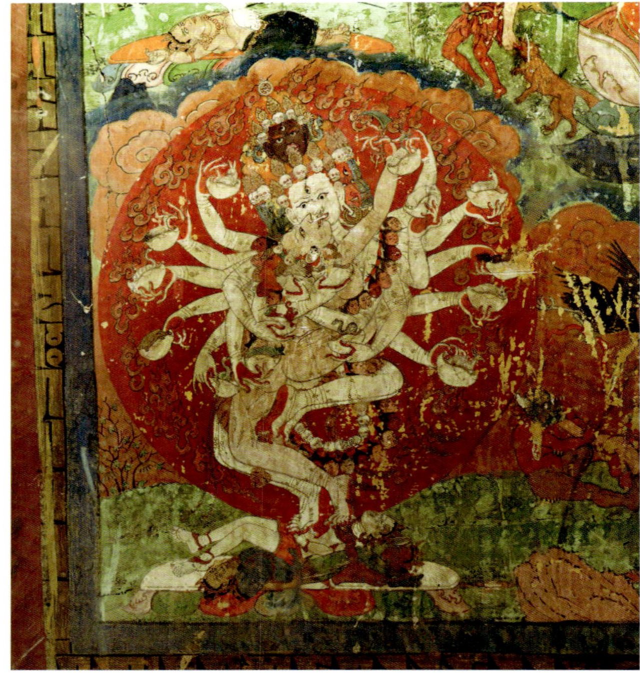

pastel green, blue, and pink. The body nimbuses of the numerous minor figures, which include additional deities of the Sampuṭa mandala, give the artist ample opportunity to use a variety of colors, including several pastels. The complicated petals on the lotus beneath the main figure often appear in other Khyentse Chenmo paintings.

Figure 4.29 depicts the tantric deity Kālacakra with his consort and a retinue of twenty-five multiarmed minor deities. He stands surrounded by a radiantly colorful body nimbus composed of repeated wavy bands of six colors; the nimbus and the red field within are strikingly round. The numerous implements or weapons that Kālacakra and his consort hold in their many hands allow the artist to demonstrate his masterful, exacting execution.

Figure 4.30 depicts the painted ceiling of the Hevajra Chapel. In the center are repeated square panels with eight-petal lotuses. Elsewhere are traditional, decorative floral motifs.

The Upper Protector's Chapel

The second main mural site of the second floor is the chapel with six pillars, on the western side of that floor, also called the Upper Protector's Chapel (Gönkhang Tengma). Its eastern walls depict highly naturalistic charnel-ground scenes, featuring Sachen and the great siddha Virūpa as minor figures.

Figure 4.31 depicts the corner of the eastern and northern walls of this chapel. The edges of some charnel scenes are

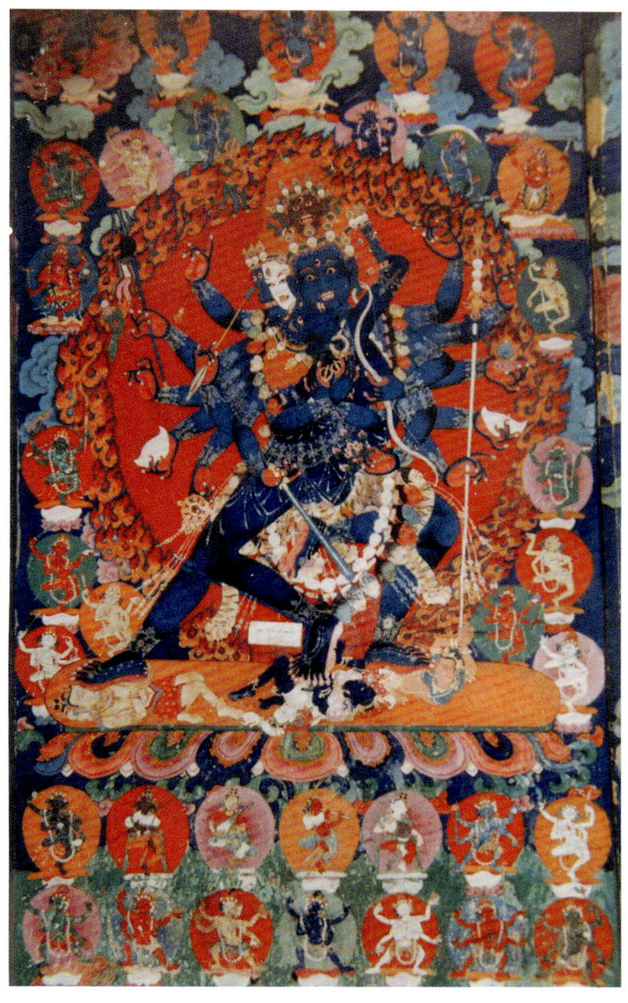

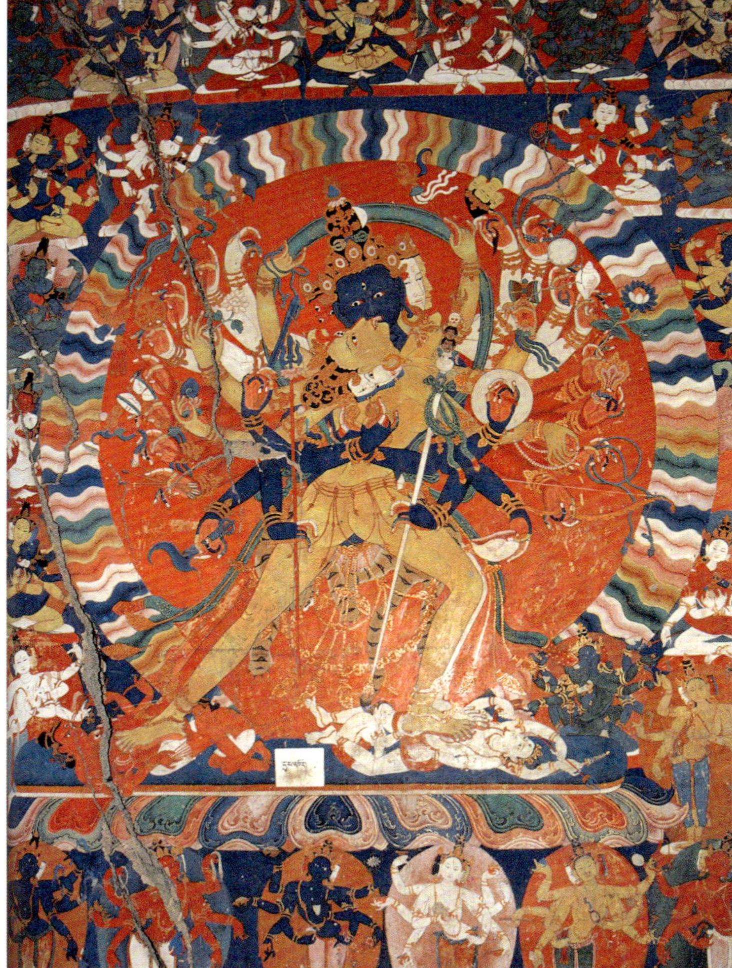

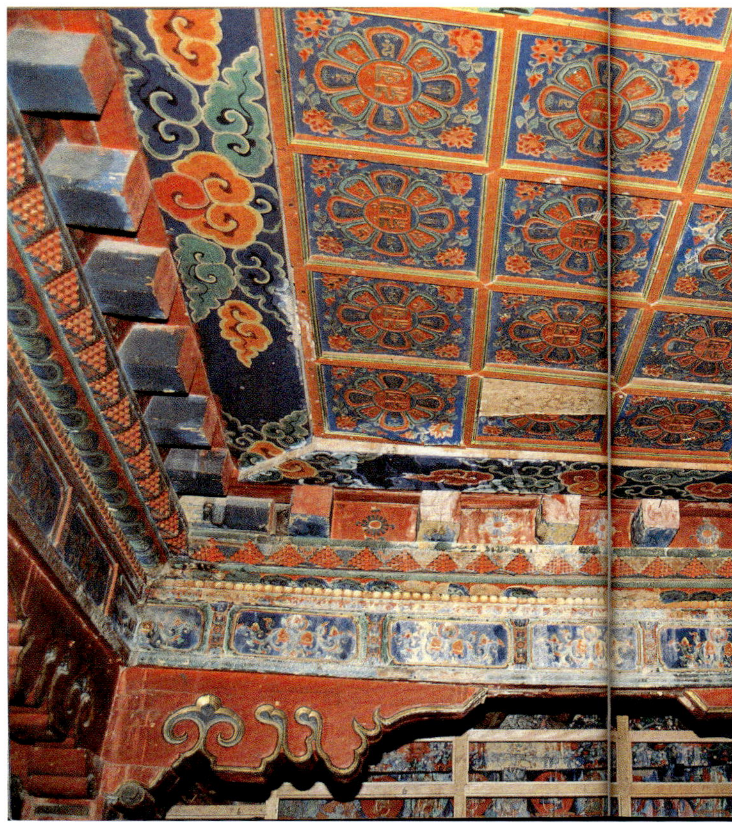

Fig. 4.28
Hevajra "with weapons"
north wall, Hevajra Chapel
Photo: Mathias Fermer, 2006

Fig. 4.29
Kālacakra
north wall, Hevajra Chapel
After: Masaki and Tachikawa 1997, 92

Fig. 4.30
Painted wooden ceiling
Hevajra Chapel
After: Masaki and Tachikawa 1997, 47

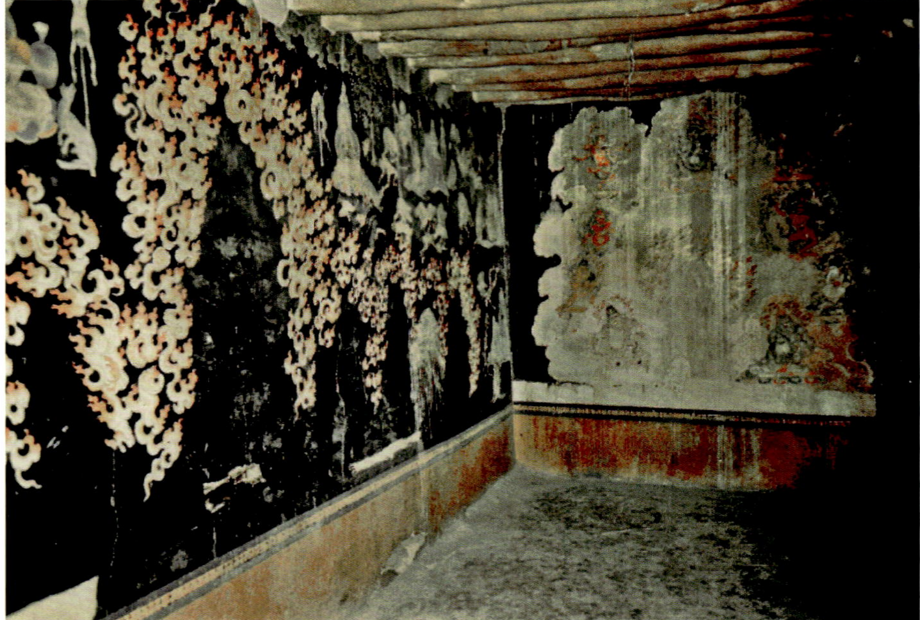

visible on the east wall. These paintings originally functioned as background murals for the sculptures that once were enshrined in the room. This is clear from the fact that the central part of the eastern wall features a painted flame nimbus that was meant to accompany a protector's sculpture. The center of the first panel on the north wall also comprises a nimbus of flames without a figure.

Since this photo was taken, sculptures have been installed in front of these murals. The original clay sculptures of this chapel, probably made by Khyentse Chenmo, are enumerated by Gyatön, beginning with Gurgyi Gönpo (Mahākāla) and his five attendants, and ending with images of Vaiśravaṇa and Twelve-handed Red Gaṇapati.[282]

For tantric deities and adepts, a charnel ground is a necessary environment. They were depicted twice before, in the Great Protector's Chapel downstairs and in the Hevajra temple, behind the Hevajra in the Lamdre tradition. But in the present chapel, the Sakya or Lamdre traditions of protectors are implied by the presence of the great adept Virūpa on one side and the great Sakya founder, Sachen, on the other side.

In the charnel-ground scene in Figure 4.32, both sky and earth are pitch

black. High above is a row of clouds, and fires burn here and there. From behind a rock, a frowning man carries a new corpse, tied like a large bundle on his back.

In this image, many animals and birds take part in a feast of corpse flesh. The most common are vultures and jackals. The flying bird with an intestine hanging from its beak may be one type of vulture.[283] Two herons or egrets also partake of the meal of human carrion. On the left side, a hedgehog investigates a corpse that a large snake has encircled. Above them, a gray wolf or jackal howls while two of its pack-mates eat from a corpse. On the right side, a heron clutches the head of a corpse hung from a tree by a rope while a jackal or fox digs into the corpse's belly with its snout. Before the large central rock crouches a female demon, which has evidently already nibbled away the flesh from the corpse limbs nearby.

Figure 4.33 depicts another corpse bearer at the bottom right, who is approaching the charnel ground, carrying the corpse of a youth tied on his back. The bearer is older, with a bald head and a look of annoyance or disbelief at the skeleton that stands ahead of him, blocking his path. A tongue of

flames emerges from the head of the skeleton, forming a ring of fire; appearing within are the hands of a sorcerer, holding ritual implements. Farther in the charnel ground, two or three types of vultures are most numerous among the natural animals; the one eagle tears apart a lump of flesh with its beak and talons. The birds and animals have unnatural competition: demonic flesh-eating beings that also carry off the corpses for food. One of the most gruesome details is a fully frontal corpse impaled on a long, sharp stake.

Figure 4.34 shows how wildly macabre and reassuringly mundane Khyentse's charnel-ground images can be. Vultures and jackals from the natural world are present, but they are joined by strange, chimerical, man-bird spirits, whose presence the vultures and eagle ignore. As a demon on the left side carries off a corpse, two jackals on the right side decide to rest, sitting together upon a corpse near a blazing cremation fire, in which a corpse is still unburnt. While one of the jackals dozes in the warmth of the fire, with eyes closed and head lowered, the other one yawns or yips, also with closed eyes.

The northern wall of the chapel has murals depicting such deities as the eight horse-riding *yakṣas* (*gnod sbyin rta bdag brgyad*) and Jambhala as the God of Wealth. These and the other deities painted on this wall were meant to accompany certain sculptures that no longer exist in this shrine. The eight horse-riding *yakṣas* are a standard group that appears as the retinue of a large yellow Vaiśravaṇa riding a lion (*rnam sras ser chen lha dgu*). The same group appeared as minor figures on the south

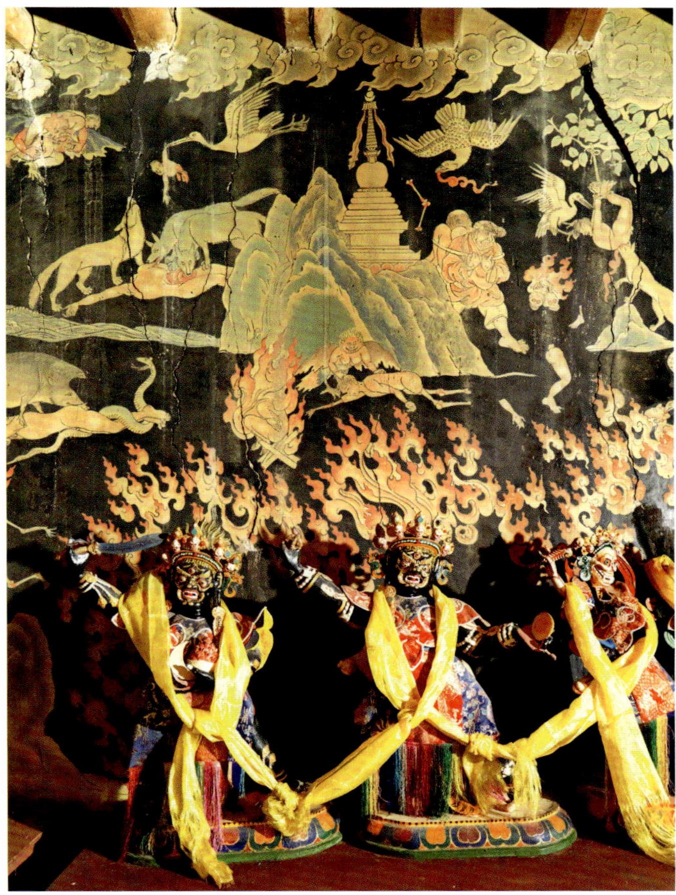 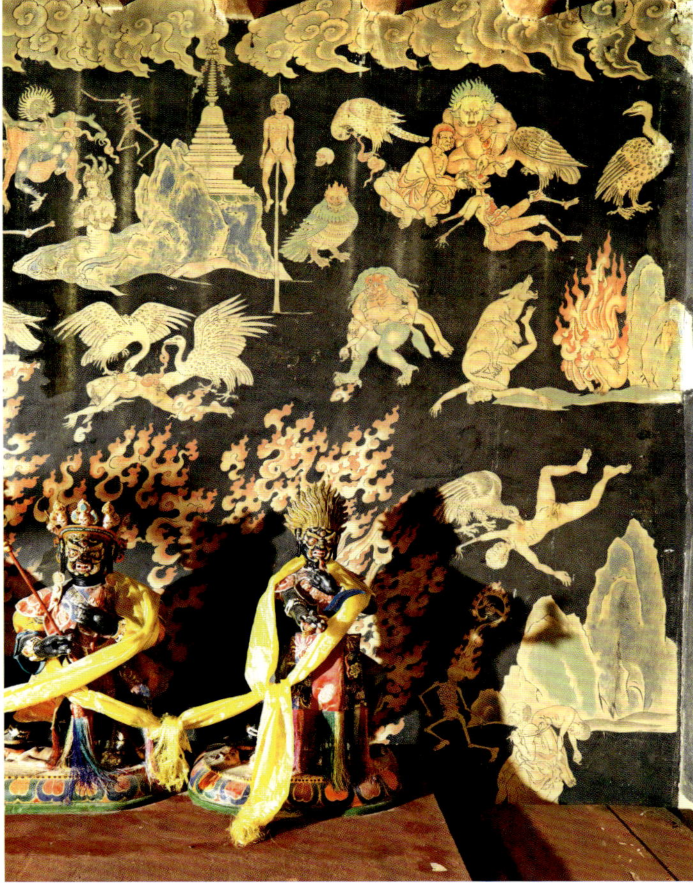

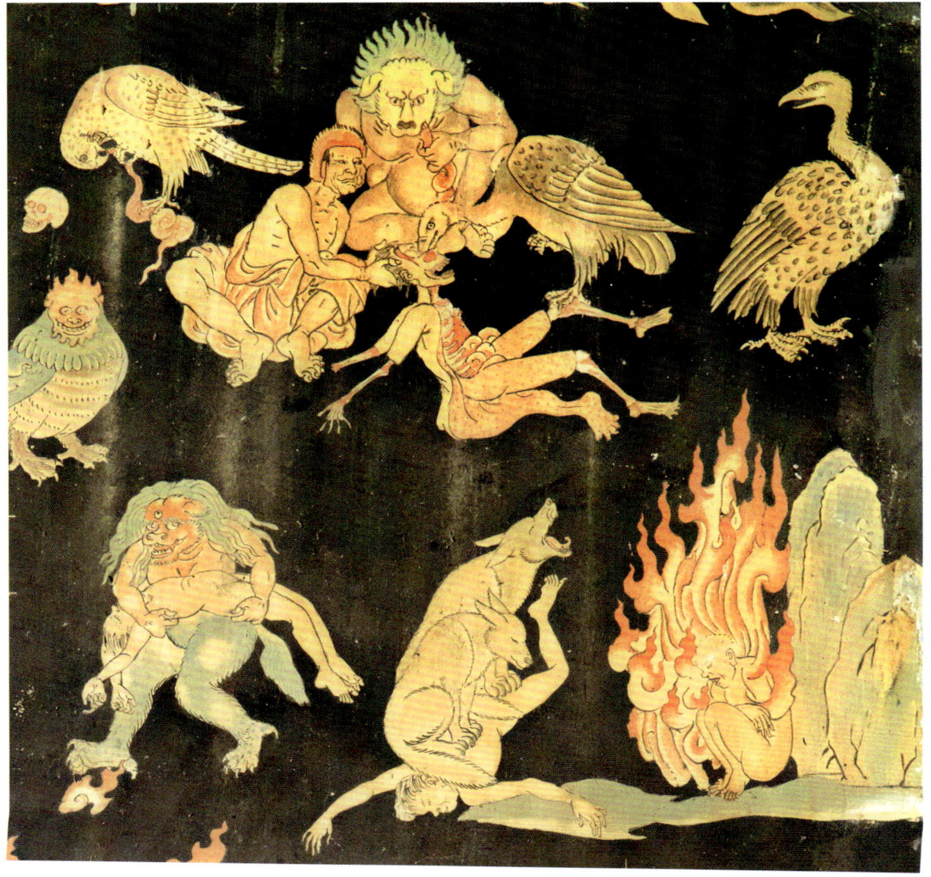

FIG. 4.32
Details of charnel-ground scene
east wall, Upper Protector's Chapel
Photo: Roberto Fortuna, 2011, courtesy
Knud Larsen

FIG. 4.33
Details of charnel-ground scenes
east wall, Upper Protector's Chapel
Photo: Roberto Fortuna, 2011, courtesy
Knud Larsen

FIG. 4.34
Charnel ground detail
east wall, Upper Protector's Chapel
Photo: Mathias Fermer, 2006

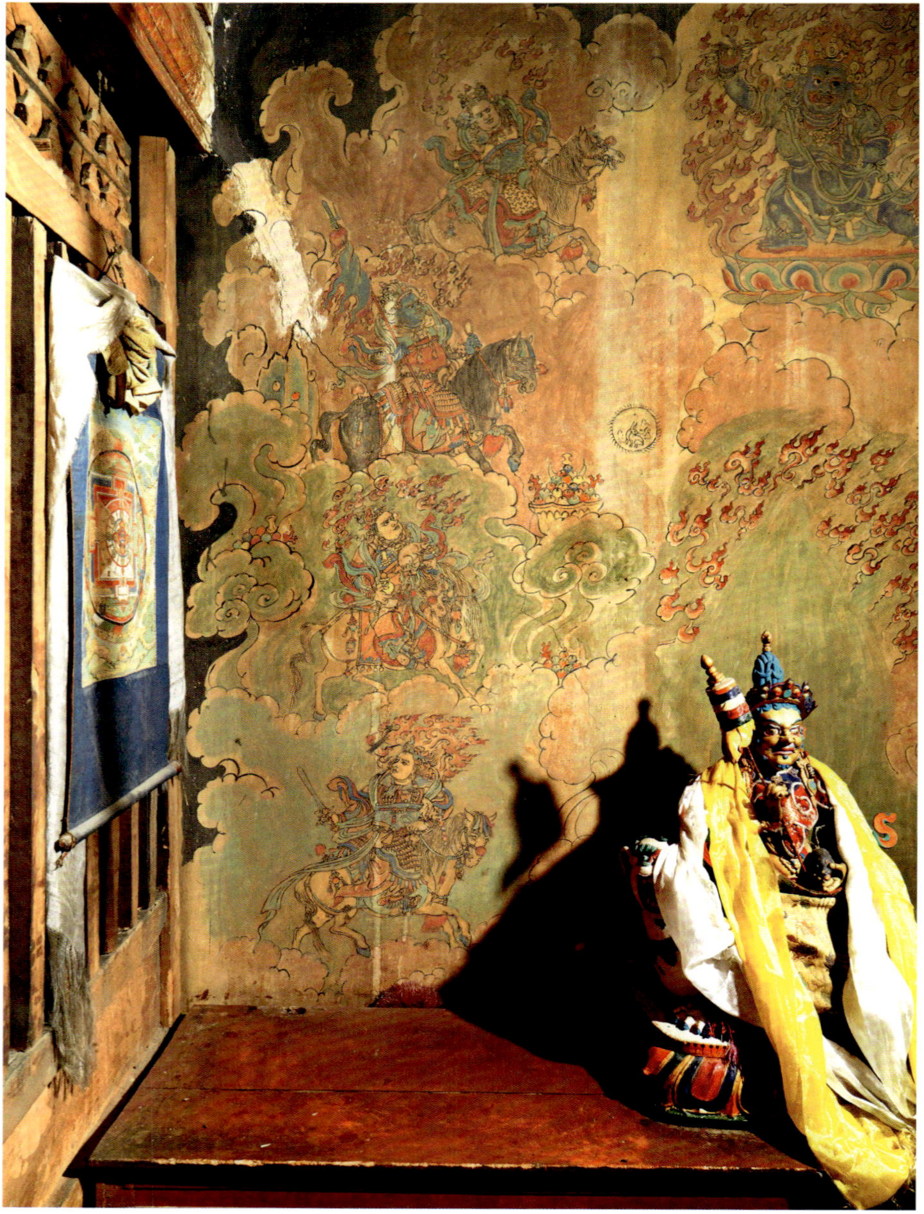

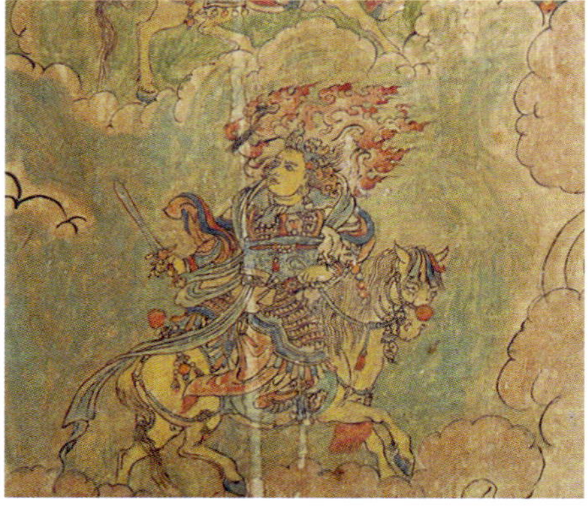

Each holds a treasure mongoose and
rides a horse of his own color.

Figure 4.35 depicts four of the
eight horse-riding *yakṣas* who make up
Vaiśravaṇa's retinue. The artist has chosen a characteristic pose, and repeated
it. (All four horses are basically the
same, except two are reversed with the
right leg lifted, two with the left leg
lifted.) They include (top to bottom):
Maṇibhadra, Āṭavaka, Pūrṇabhadra, and
Samjñāya. They are minor deities within
the chapel.

Figure 4.36 depicts the horse-riding *yakṣa* Samjñāya, who was the lowest
deity in Figure 4.35. This image exemplifies fairly lifelike representations of
horses painted by Khyentse Chenmo.
This *yakṣa* not only dresses like a general, with full body armor, but also grips
the hilt of a long steel sword. His horse
seems to be cantering, with both right
hooves raised. But it has turned, with tail
down and its ears back, probably in reaction to a tug on its bridle from its divine
rider, who holds the reins. The rider
looks at something behind him, holding
his raised sword in that direction.

The two deities shown in Figure
4.37 are a white four-armed Gaṇapati
and a standing blue *yakṣa* holding a
jewel-vomiting mongoose, who seems to

wall of the Hevajra Chapel. The eight
yakṣas are:[284]

1. yellow Jambhala, in the east,
   holding a jewel
2. yellow Pūrṇabhadra (Gang ba
   bzang po), in the south, holding a
   full jewel flask
3. white Maṇibhadra (Nor bu bzang
   po), in the west, holding a gem
4. black Kubera, in the north, holding
   a sword
5. yellow Samjñāya (Yang dag shes),
   in the southeast, holding a sword
6. black Āṭavaka ('Brog gnas), in the
   southwest, holding a jewel-red
   spear

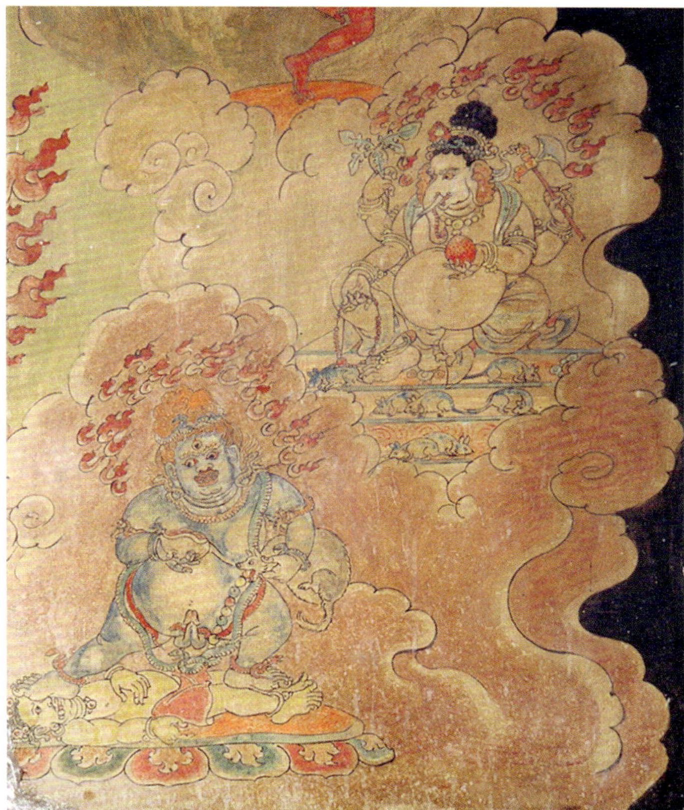

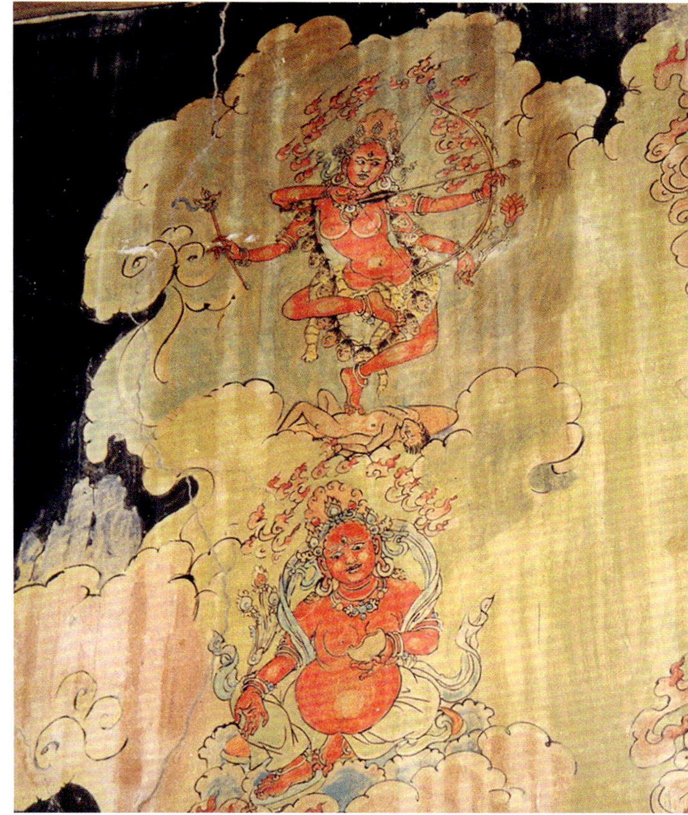

be Black Jambhala, who is ithyphallic. Note the beautiful details of Gaṇapati's elephant head with a trunk, his protruding belly, the different objects that he holds in each hand, and the rats scurrying about on his throne.

The part of the panel in Figure 4.38 depicts two goddesses, the higher of which is Kurukullā. She is iconographically distinct, with her red four-armed form, her dancing upon a corpse, and the flower-tipped arrow that she shoots.

According to Gyatön, the murals on the northern wall include Vajrapāṇi Kūṭāgāra, as in the Hevajra temple, together with the eight horse-riding *yakṣas*.[285] On the southern wall, Gyatön says, were painted Samvarodaya (bDe mchog lhan skyes), White Gaṇapati, and Red Two-armed Gaṇapati.

The paintings that we saw in the main murals of the ground and second floors are just a partial survival of what was once at Gongkar, with many murals painted over during the renovation of the 1930s. We saw two narrative modes of painting downstairs (and we shall see his distinct lineage mode in part II of this chapter), while the Upper Protector's Temple seems to have two different modes, distinct from that of the Hevajra chapel. Each and every chapel looked quite different. Though I attribute them all to the same artist, I cannot say what if anything unites all murals stylistically, beyond a love of variety.

Other Surviving Early Murals on the Second Floor

The old murals in the remaining chapels or rooms on the second floor are not in comparable condition. But one significant panel survives in a hall or passageway that depicts Sakya Paṇḍita as its main figure (Fig. 4.39). I will present that mural panel in chapter 6, as Figure 6.16.

Figure 4.40 shows a damaged mural that depicts the temples of Bodhgaya, the place of the Buddha's enlightenment in India.

Formerly Existing Chapels and Murals

As I mentioned above, the old descriptions tell of the Kanjur Lhakhang on the third floor, on the southern side, above the Jigche Lhakhang.On the eastern end, above the inner sanctum were: "In the murals of the four-pillar Vajradhātu Dorying Chapel and the four-pillar *'phrul ('phrul ka bzhi)*."[286] On the walls of these two rooms, there formerly existed paintings of nine hundred ninety-six bodhisattvas, such as Maitreya. Figure 4.41 is an outside view of the third floor.

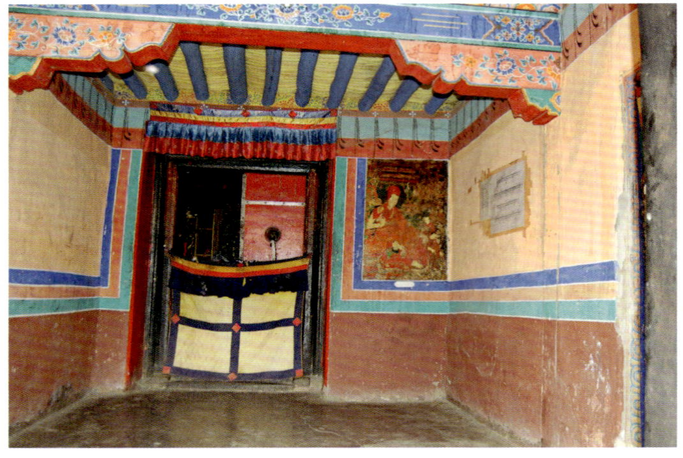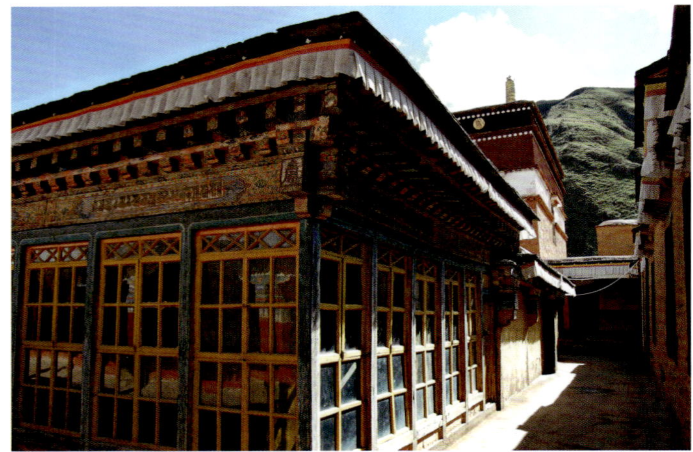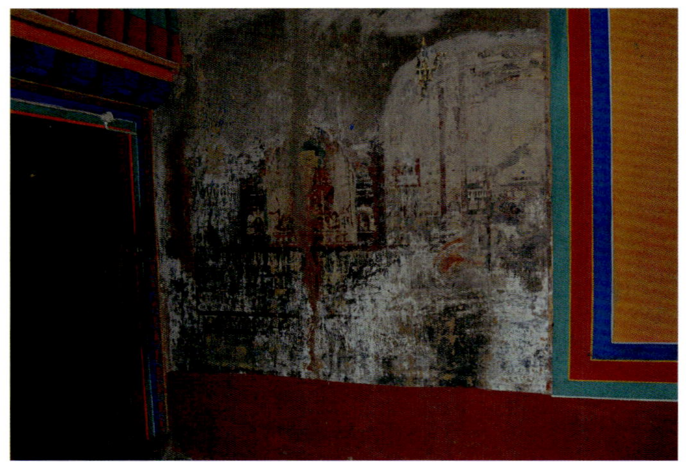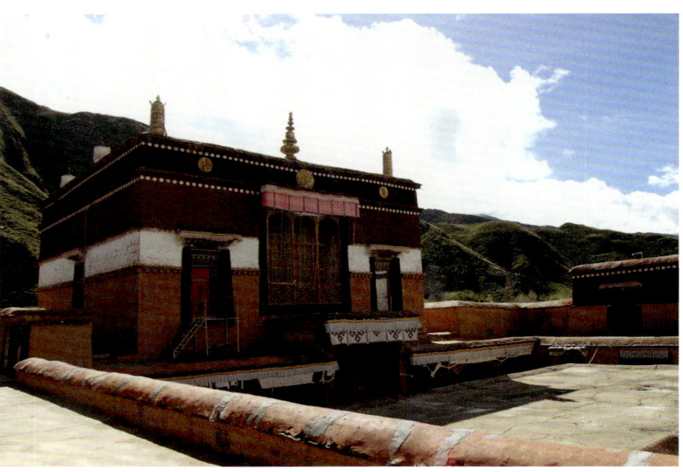

On the fourth floor, at the top of the building, on the eastern end above the Dorying Lhakhang, stood a Guru Chapel (Lama Lhakhang) with sixteen pillars, including four long pillars. Within, there formerly stood the reliquary stupa (*gdung rten*) of Kunga Namgyal. There was also a circumambulation place or path (*skor sa*) outside the chapel that enshrined the clay sculptures of the Lamdre guru lineage. Figure 4.42 is an outside view of the Guru Chapel, the taller structure to the rear.

Part ii: *Mural Paintings of the Sakya Founding Masters with Two Hevajra Lineages*

BY MATHIAS FERMER

INTRODUCTION

Among the surviving murals that date to the founding of Gongkar Chöde, two outstanding panels exist on the ground floor in the main assembly hall that illustrate Khyentse Chenmo's broad artistic range and genius. Monks who lived in the monastery before 1959 similarly assert that the old paintings decorating the front walls to the right and left of the entrance to the temple's central sanctum were painted by Khyentse Chenmo.

Each of those walls depicts a Hevajra lineage, one of which was for the crucial Lamdre practice of the Sakya school. When viewed together with the depictions of tantric deities and narrative scenes described earlier in this chapter, these murals demonstrate Khyentse Chenmo's mastery of another essential artistic subject: portrayal of Buddhist teachers, and, in particular, of tantric guru lineages.

The importance of these lineage murals as an iconographic subject is expressed by their position at the front of Gongkar Chöde's spacious assembly hall, where the entire community gathers regularly for collective rituals and prayer. (See Fig. 4.43.) The murals depict as their main subject two trios of prominent Sakya founding masters who enjoyed the highest veneration in the monastic tradition established by Gongkar Dorjedenpa Kunga Namgyal. (See Figs. 4.45, 4.52, and 4.54.)

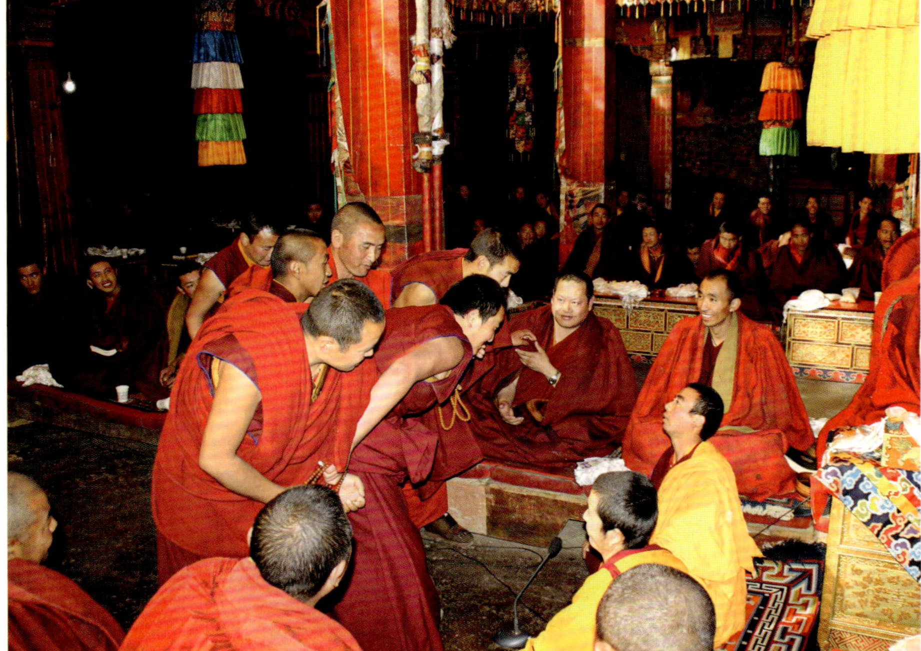

These paintings caught the attention of Giuseppe Tucci, the eminent Tibetologist who visited the monastery in the summer of 1948. No photos from his prolonged stay at Gongkar Chöde have so far been identified from among the surviving photographs of his journey.[287] But while he was there, the Italian scholar established a close relationship with the previous Gongkar Dorjedenpa Rinpoche Jampel Lungtok Chökyi Gyaltshen (For a tinted photograph of the previous Dorjedenpa *trulku*, see Fig. 12.10.) and repeatedly expressed his excitement about the high quality of art preserved here.[288] About the lineage paintings in the assembly hall, Tucci noted in his travelogue: "On the walls right and left of the cell were painted the Lamas of the Sakyapa sect and the main events of their lives: dignified but spirited and lively pictures, free from the hieratic stiffness that too often burdens Tibetan art."[289]

These two murals, which Tucci witnessed about seventy years ago in a state much closer to their original splendor, can be counted among the most important paintings that survive at Gongkar Chöde, documenting as they do

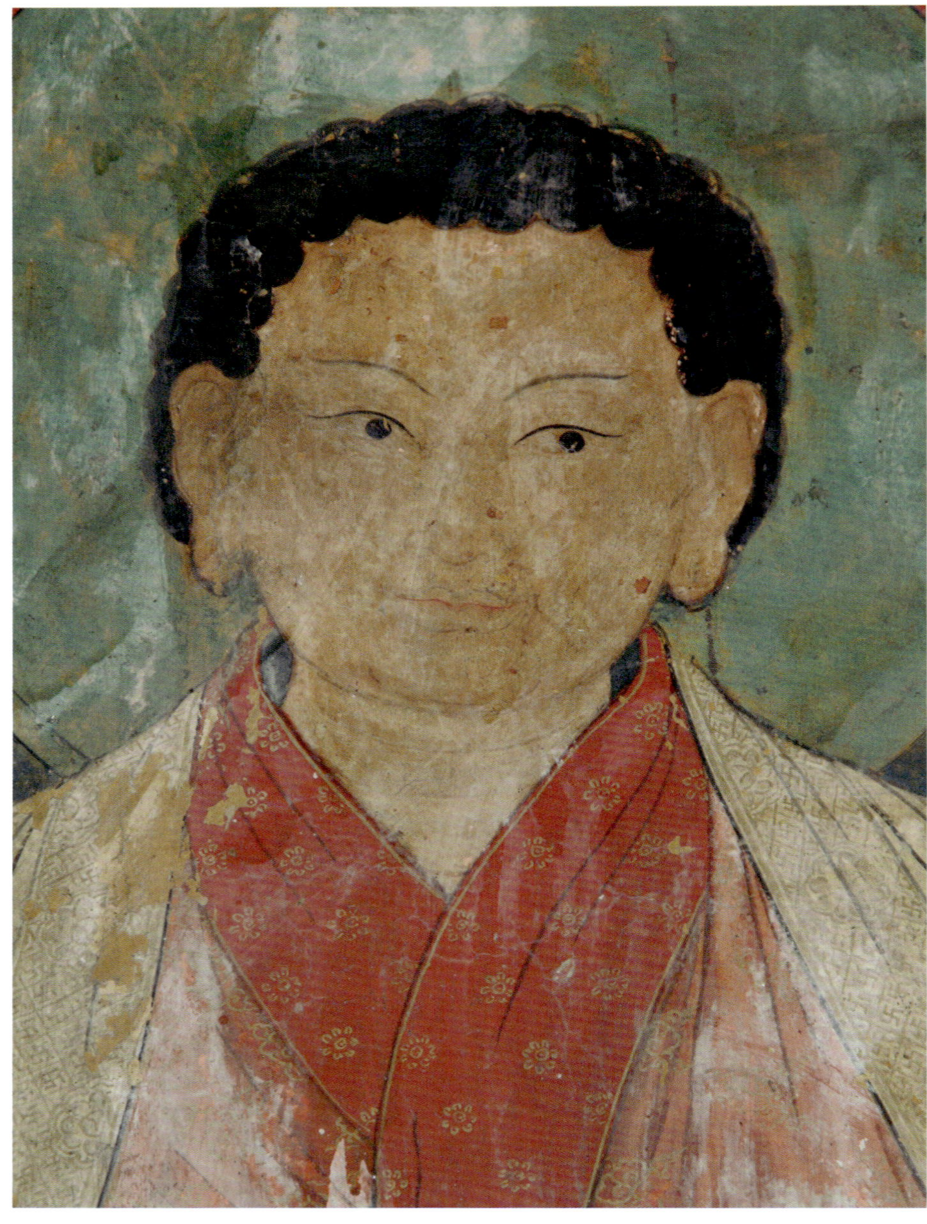

the origin and transmission of the community's main tradition of tantric instructions (the Lamdre) and its main tantric cycle (the Hevajra).[290] The walls to both sides of the inner sanctum's entrance were seen by all pre-1959 visitors who approached the central chapel to pay respects to its huge, two-story Buddha image (*thub chen*), the original of which was also crafted by Khyentse Chenmo.[291]

The thick walls and four large pillars of the inner sanctum are important parts of the building's structure. They support the chapels that lie directly above them on the upper floors: the Vajradhātu Chapel on the third floor, the

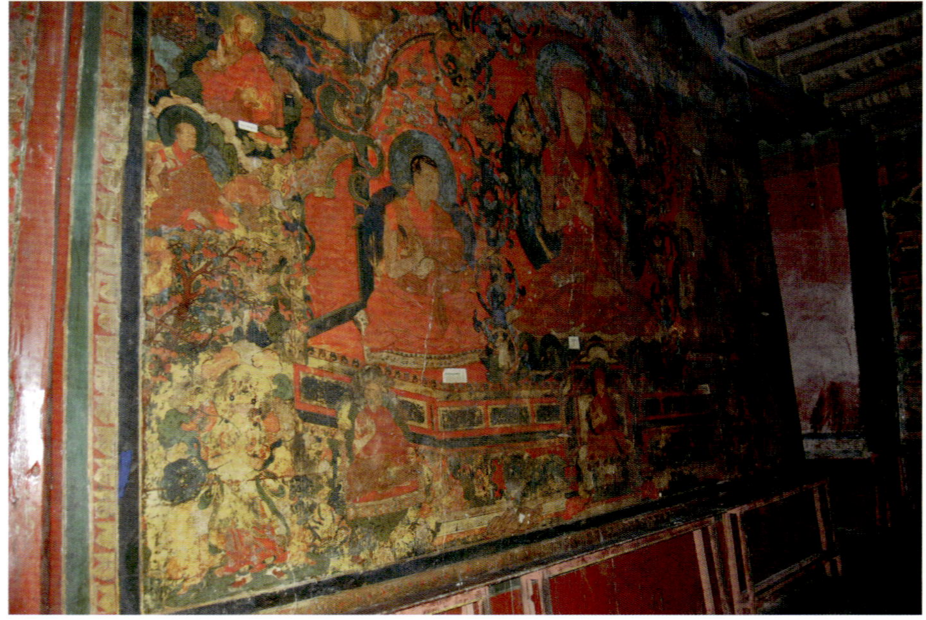

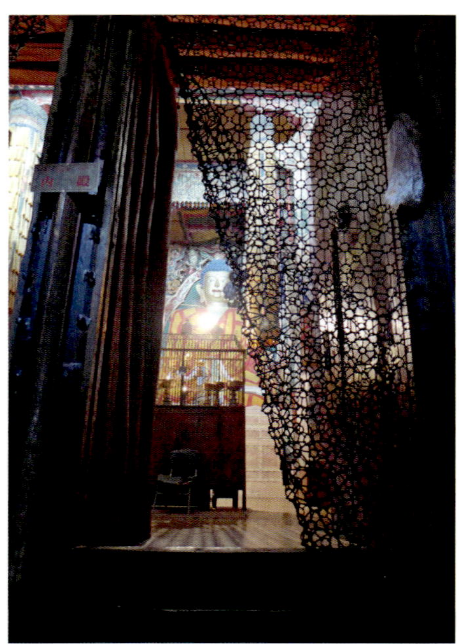

Guru Chapel, with images of the Lamdre
lineage masters, on the fourth floor,
and the (now missing) topmost chapel,
called the "line chapel" (*thig khang*),
which presumably provided a place for
preparing or practicing the basic lines of
mandalas.[292]

Condition of the Murals

The murals survive in a mediocre condition, with areas of pigment loss and
surface abrasion across the entire wall.
The lower parts, in particular, suffered
heavy abrasion, apparently due to their
being within the reach of worshippers
or pilgrims (before 1959) or due to mis-
treatment while the building was taken
over for more than two decades (during
the period 1960s–1984/85). During
those years the assembly hall was used
as collective grain storage (*gro khang*),
and the upper floors were emptied and
converted into offices for the local government. In 1985, when monastic life
was reintroduced at Gongkar Chöde,
the few monks who could return to their
monastery immediately began restoring the defunct temple. A young monk
who had then just joined the monastery
remembers that some of them began
restoring (*bskyar gso*) the covered walls
on the ground floor, even while government officials still retained offices in the
upper floors of the building. With just
water and a wet cloth, the young monks
tried to wipe off the layer of whitewash
(*dkar rtsi*) that had been protectively
applied to the walls before the monastery's confiscation.[293]

The overhasty removal of whitewash damaged the surface of the wall
and took away much of the mural's
original color and intensity. (See Fig.
4.47.) As a result of that forceful and
uneven cleaning, a light-brown ground
shows through in several locations. In
places, ornamental elements and even a
few minor lineal gurus disappeared, not
leaving a trace of the original pigment

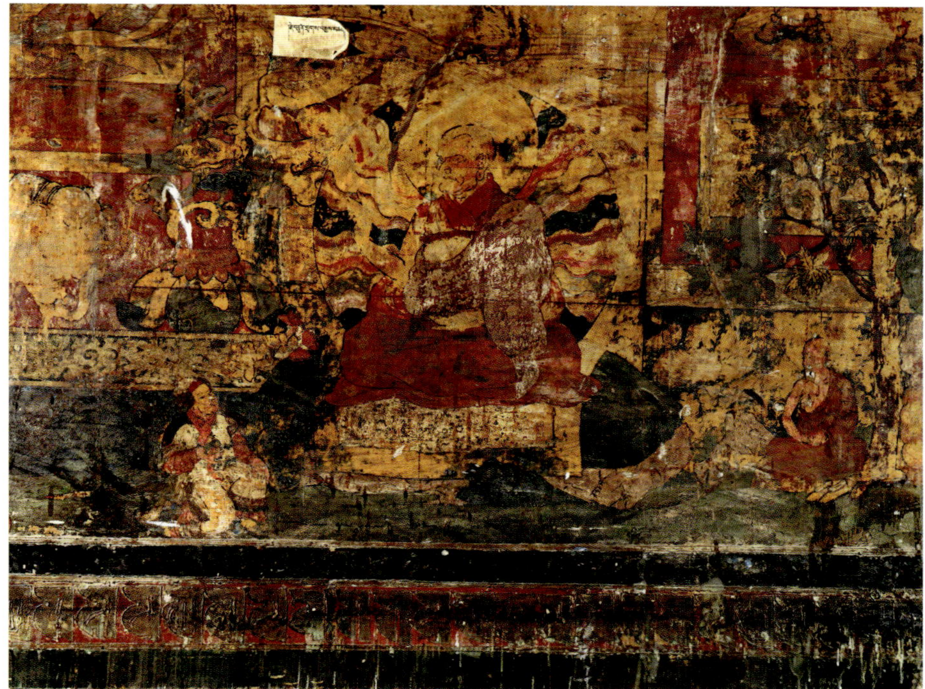

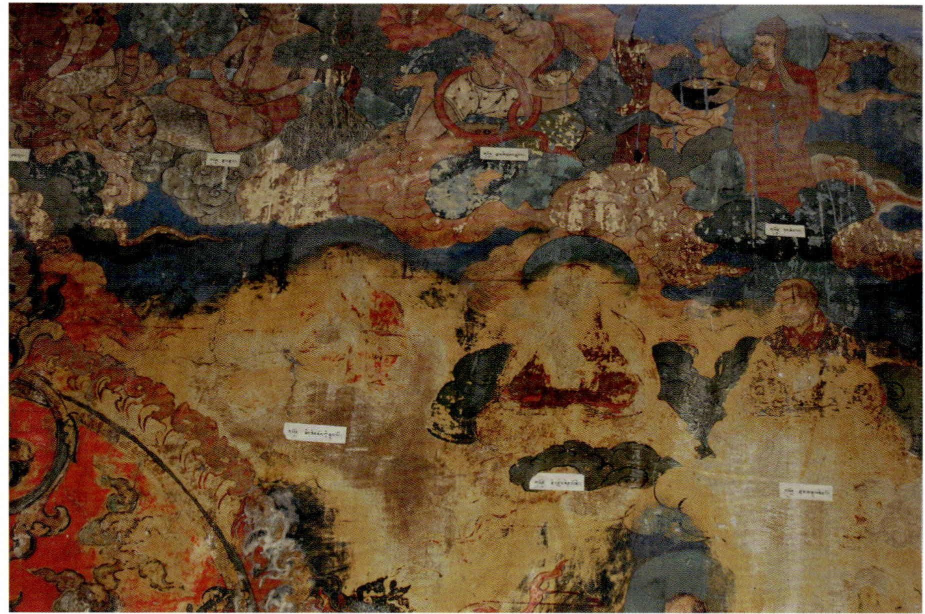

or even the underlying outlines (*phyi
thig*) or proportional measurements (*thig
tshad*). Figure 4.48 shows the worst spot
on the right wall, where gurus number
4, 6, 8, and 10 of the Hevajra Mūlatantra
Lineage are seen above, but three teachers are missing below: from left to right,
guru numbers 12, Ngari Salnying, 14,
Sachen Kunga Nyingpo, and 16, Jetsün
Trakpa Gyaltshen.

However, some damaged areas
provide a glimpse into the composition
of the murals. The exposed portions

Fig. 4.47
Damaged surface near the bottom of the
wall; this detail depicts Drakthokpa Sönam
Sangpo as guru number 22 in the Lamdre
Lineage
Detail, left wall, entrance to inner sanctum
Photo: Roberto Fortuna, 2011, courtesy
Knud Larsen

Fig. 4.48
Gurus from the Hevajra Mūlatantra
Lineage; damaged section
Detail, right wall, entrance to inner sanctum
Photo: Kazuo Kano, 2007

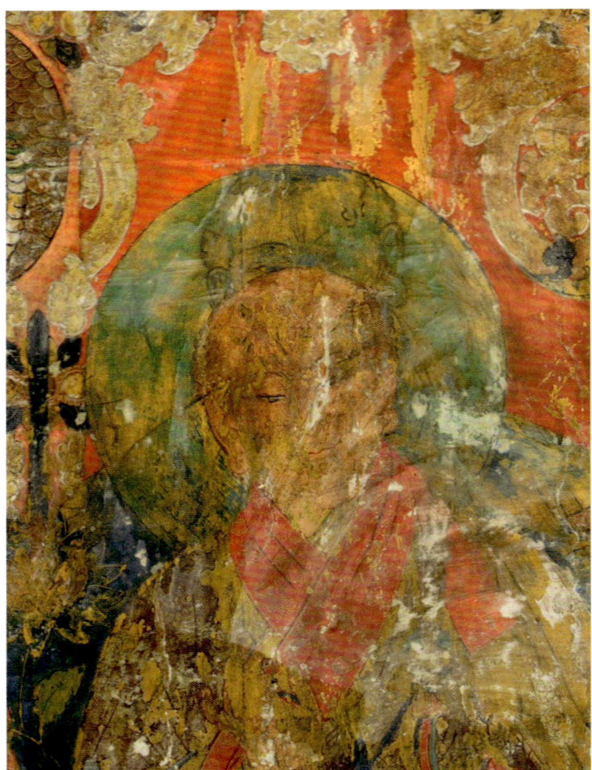

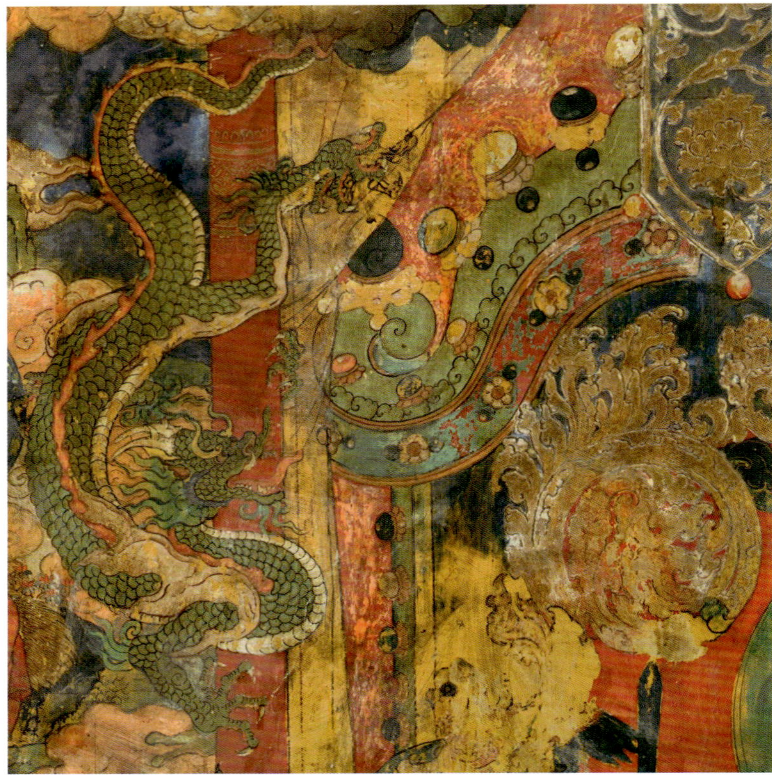

FIG. 4.49
The underlying sketch is visible in this detail depicting Trakpa Gyaltshen as one of the main figures
Detail, left wall, entrance to inner sanctum
Photo: Wang Peng, 2010

FIG. 4.50
Dragon with visible underlying lines
Detail, left wall, entrance to inner sanctum
Photo: Wang Peng, 2010

FIG. 4.51
Shang Dode Pal depicted in a landscape setting, as guru number 19 of the Hevajra Mūlatantra Lineage
Detail, right wall, entrance to inner sanctum
Photo: Mathias Fermer, 2010

reflect the different stages of the artist's work. If we look carefully, we can find facial outlines (*zhal thig*) of figures as well as the faded color code numbers or letters (*tshon yig*) that originally indicated which colors were meant to be applied. (In Figures 4.49 and 4.56, the Tibetan letter *pa* can be found as a color code where green pigment was applied to head nimbuses.)

Even while at a very early phase of his work, Khyentse seems to have modified his sketch fairly drastically, though the revisions were later hidden by the final coloring. For example, a reworked section is visible in the upper center of the left wall in Figure 4.50 (see the claws of the dragon's left leg and the green recoloring of the ornamental element to its lower right). In the same mural, the head nimbus belonging to the master

Trakpa Gyaltshen (1147–1216), who sits to the proper left of the large central figure, reveals an earlier (very similar) sketch of the same figure's face under the faded paint (as we see in Figure 4.49). The unskilled removal of whitewash in the 1980s thus brought to light here what are likely the rejected drawings of the master painter at work. Khyentse Chenmo, probably for artistic reasons, reworked his initial sketch of the face in order to position the master slightly lower in relation to the central figure.

In another case (Fig. 4.51) a prominent vertical and horizontal line shines through the worn-away pigment of a head nimbus. (Shang Dode Pal is depicted in a landscape setting, as guru number 19 of the Hevajra Mūlatantra Lineage.)

Fortunately, the lineage paintings on the ground floor were spared from repainting or recoloring (*mtshon gso*), while numerous murals on the second floor were "renovated" during the 2000s. The restoring of the lineage murals here involved just a little repairing in the form of filling cracks and minor background repainting along the upper parts of the two walls.

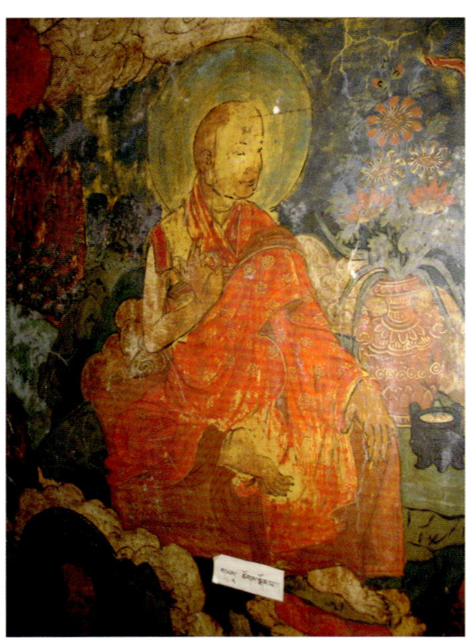

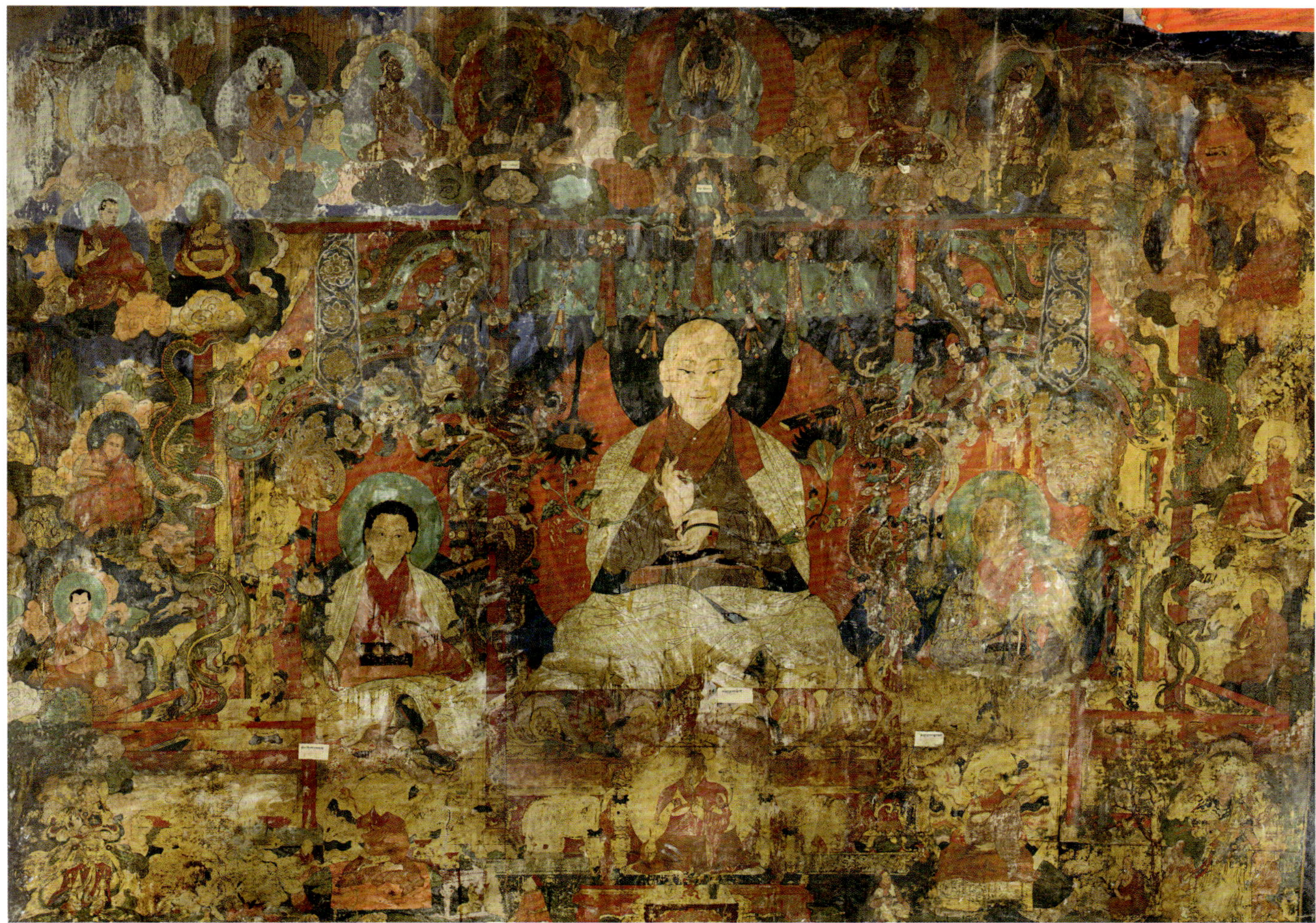

ICONOGRAPHIC THEME

The group of teachers that Tucci recognized as "Lamas of the Sakyapa sect" represent successive masters from two specific Hevajra lineages that are practiced or studied mainly within the Sakya school. Hugh Richardson in a brief survey of monasteries, temples, and forts in Tibet before 1950 mentioned Gongkar Monastery and its contents.[294] The lineage depicted in the great temple hall, he asserted, was that of "lama Rdo-rje gdan-pa," the monastery's founder, who commissioned the murals between 1464 and 1476. Although Richardson did not visit Gongkar Chöde personally, his statement about the lineage paintings was correct.

The mural paintings on the front wall of the inner sanctum consist of two separate panels, which we can call the left and right walls. They depict parallel compositions and are linked with each other through the identities of their main figures. Framed by the circumambulation path on their outer edges, they each measure approximately 420 centimeters (ca. 165 inches) high and 600 centimeters (236 inches) wide.

Each wall depicts three main central figures (*gtso bo*) seated on wooden thrones with elaborate throne backs. The largest main figure is flanked by two smaller masters depicted about half his size. On each wall the three main figures, together with the Indian adepts and other Tibetan lamas surrounding them, represent an unbroken transmission line of masters (*bla* [*ma*] *brgyud* [*pa*]; Skt. *guruparampara*) in the Gongkar tradition. The minor figures are arranged on five horizontal lines within a sketchy background landscape that surrounds the throne construction with the main figures. Both lineages begin at the top center and run in chronological order

down to a final master of the transmission in the bottom row. The lineage gurus descend alternating from left to right (relative to the viewer), while the transmission is interrupted by the main figures in the center.

The three main figures play a prominent role for the overall composition of each mural. Thanks to their distinctive iconography, they can be easily recognized as hierarchs from the Khön family who founded their tradition at Sakya Monastery.[295] On the left wall (Fig. 4.52) we see Sachen Kunga Nyingpo (1092–1158) and his sons Lobpön Sönam Tsemo (1142–1182) and

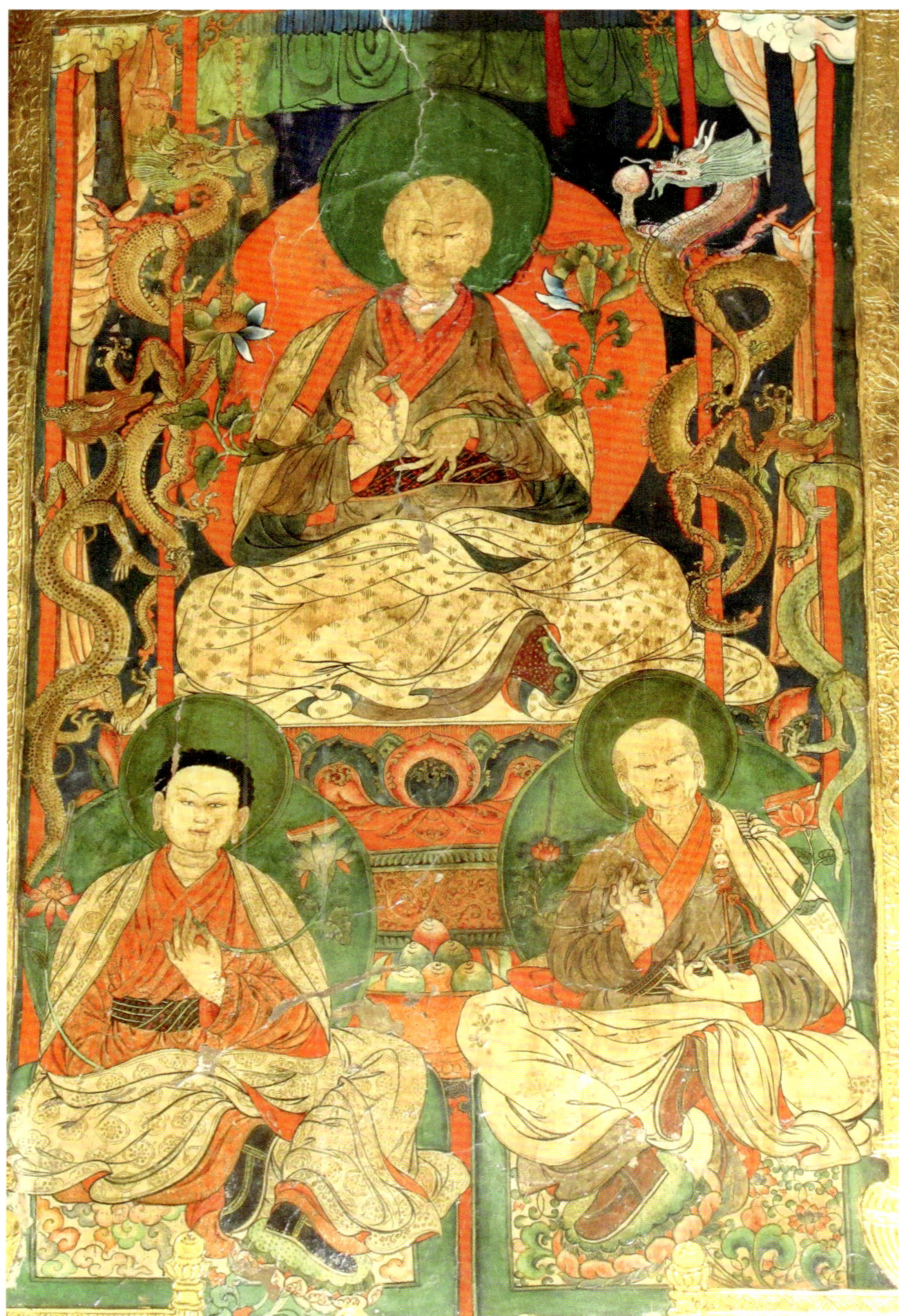

the illustrious "Five Founding Masters of Sakya" (*sa skya gong ma lnga*). (Fig. 4.53 is a much later mural of this same standard iconographic grouping in Kunzang Tse College of Gongkar Chöde. Note the pair of dragons to the right and left of Sachen, which were repeated.)

The backrest of the three early founders on the left wall features no fewer than six writhing dragons curling around the main supporting pillars. On the right wall, we will also see decorative dragons, but just two in all, one at the top of each outer vertical support, such as above Phakpa's left shoulder. (The two inner pillars of this mural feature little boys (*bu chung/mi chung*) who playfully clamber up the ornamental backrest to the left and the right of the central figure; the boys are depicted in a Chinese-looking manner and might be a motif adopted from Ming-period decorative arts.) Another key decorative feature of the left wall is the complicated silk canopy directly above the central figure, with elaborate tassels that hang so low that they impinge upon Sachen's head nimbus.

The right wall (Fig. 4.54) depicts a different trio of Sakya founding masters. Its central figure (Fig. 4.55) is Sakya Paṇḍita, who was Trakpa Gyaltshen's nephew and immediate follower on the abbatial throne of Sakya. To his proper right is his nephew Phakpa Lodrö Gyaltshen (1235–1280), his abbatial successor at Sakya. This pair of uncle and nephew (*sa paṇ khu dbon* or *sa skya pa khu dbon*) is famed for establishing a spiritual relationship with two different Mongol overlords, and they are also commonly called the "Two Red-Robed Ones" (*dmar po rnam gnyis*). Sakya Paṇḍita and Chögyal Phakpa were fully ordained monks and hence are portrayed wearing the red robes and lama vests of a Tibetan monk. They are also counted as the last two of the Five Founding Masters of Sakya.

Jetsün Trakpa Gyaltshen (1147–1216). All three are shown according to their standard iconography with long hair and wearing white garments that were permitted for lay adherents. The three first throne-holders of Sakya were not monks and hence are shown wearing inner garments with long sleeves colored faint purple or pink, in addition to their white capes and lower robes. Sachen and his two sons are traditionally known as the "Three White-Robed Ones" (*dkar po rnam gsum*), being the first three of

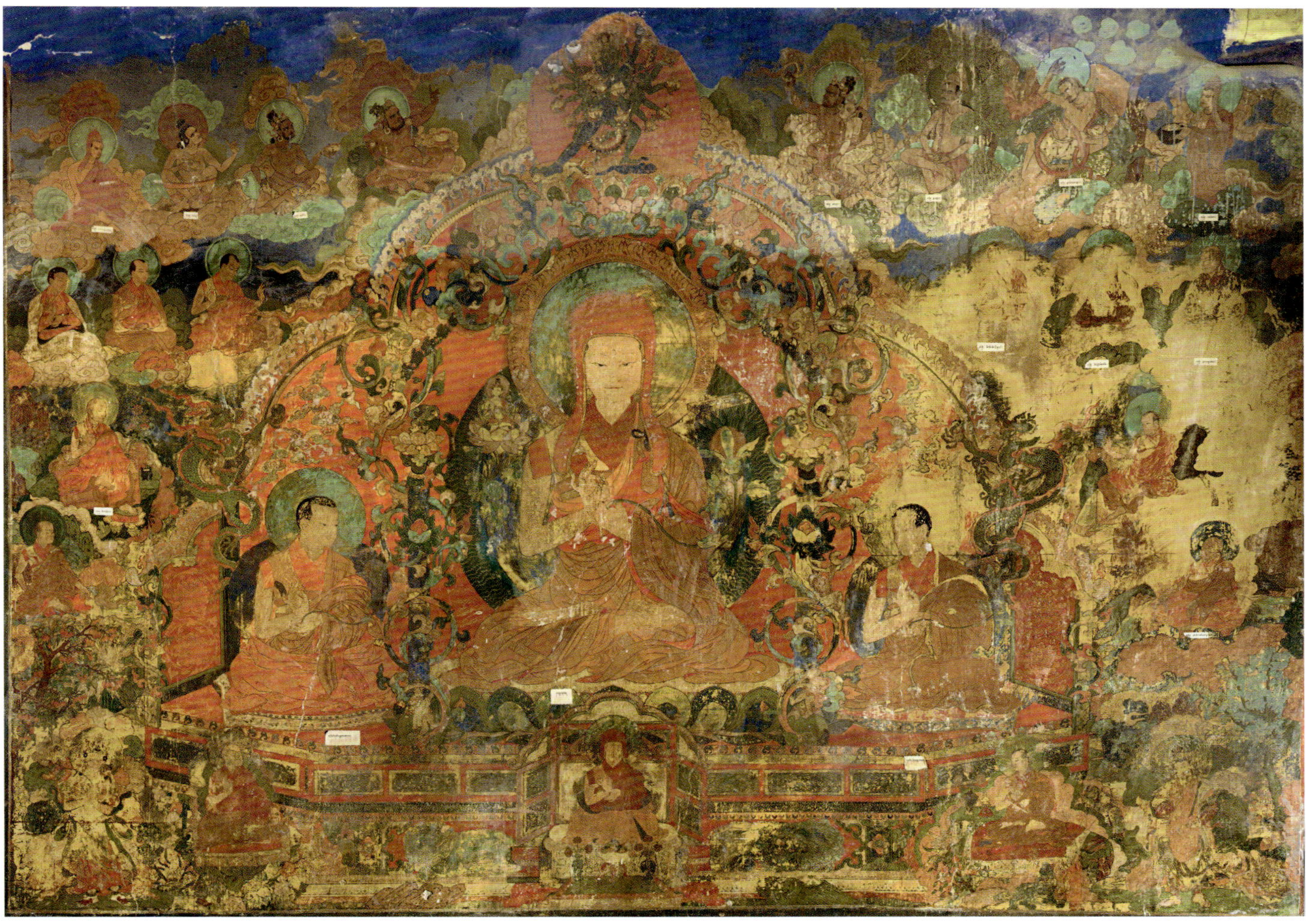

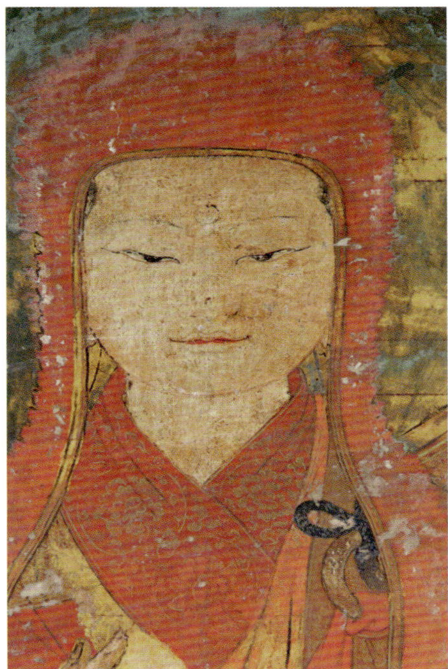

As its third main figure (Fig. 4.56), the right wall depicts Lama Dampa Sönam Gyaltshen (1312–1375). This outstanding master came from the Rinchengang Palace branch of the same Sakya Khön family, and he served as Sakya throne-holder around a century after Phakpa. He extensively traveled Ü province (dBus) of central Tibet and promoted Sakya traditions under the devoted patronage of the Phagmotrupa rulers at Nedong. Lama Dampa together with Sakya Paṇḍita and his nephew are typically called the "Three Red-Robed Ones" (*dmar po rnam gsum*) by Gongkar monks. Within their tradition, Lama Dampa enjoyed and still enjoys exceptional authority and veneration, comparable to that of the Five Sakya Founders. Dorjedenpa wrote annotations to at least two of Lama Dampa's works and is believed to have manifested as him in one of his previous existences.[296]

In particular, Sönam Gyaltshen's tantric exegesis was esteemed and followed by the monastic community at Gongkar Chöde. Early masters, including the monastery's founder, became involved in long doctrinal disputes with the Ngorpa sub-sect of the Sakya school. The proponents from Gongkar prominently quoted Lama Dampa's explanations in support of their positions, arguing that his understanding was no different from that of the Five Founding Masters. The authority of Lama Dampa and his exegetical tradition at Gongkar

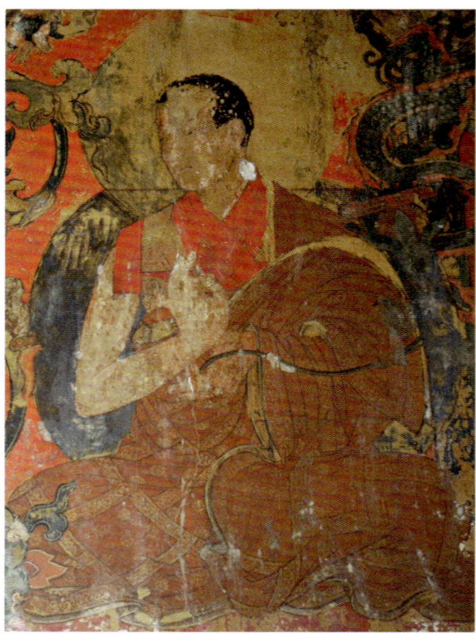

Fig. 4.56
Lama Dampa as one of the Three Red-Clad
Masters of Gongkar, as guru number 22 in
the Hevajra Mūlatantra Lineage
Detail, right wall, entrance to inner sanctum
Photo: Rob Linrothe, 2007

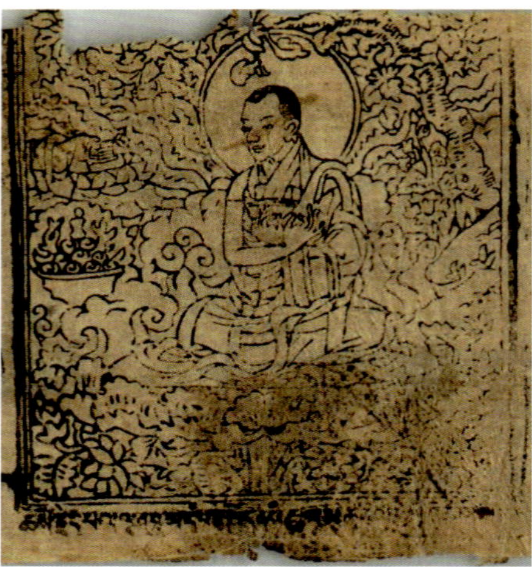

Fig. 4.57
Lama Dampa
Front-page Illustration of Xylograph, fol. 1v
right, block print of Gongkarwa's Hevajra
sadhana written in 1467; fifteenth century
Photo courtesy of Jampal Shedrup

also becomes evident in several of
Dorjedenpa's writings. In a versified refu-
tation of the Ngorpa system, compiled in
the form of a petition addressed to the
Five Founders, Kunga Namgyal explains
the "teaching tradition of the noble master" (here referring to Lama Dampa's
exegesis) to be the unsurpassed "tradition of the founders" (*gong ma'i lugs*).[297]
Lama Dampa is even prominently featured in an illustration at the head of a
Gongkar xylograph edition of a Hevajra
sadhana. (See Figure 4.57.)

The exceptionally high esteem in
which Kunga Namgyal and his followers held Lama Dampa reflected itself
artistically when Gongkar Chöde was
founded. This is the only explanation
of his appearing in the murals as the
third red-robed Sakya master, next to
Sakya Paṇḍita and Chögyal Phakpa,
on the same level and with the same
size as Phakpa. As he was added to the
group of the Five Sakya Founders as a
veritable sixth founder, Lama Dampa's
scriptural authority in the tradition found
iconographic expression in Khyentse's

respectful portrayal.[298] Gongkarwa, the
founder, must have decided to portray
him so, with Khyentse Chenmo following his directions, giving Lama Dampa's
exceptional status this iconographic
form for the first time.

At Gongkar Monastery, the
extended group of Five Sakya Masters
with Sönam Gyaltshen became a standard iconographic group. Depictions
of them were also preserved in a small
mural panel at Kunzang Tse College
(See chapter 5, Fig. 5.13) and on the
upper walls at Drepung College, where
they were worked into an arrangement
of eleven lineage gurus of the Lamdre
instructions. Though not mentioned in
the available texts from Gongkar, these
"Three Red-Robed Ones" remained an
important iconographic model for the
tradition (See Fig. 4.58).[299]

Lineage and Composition

Khyentse Chenmo's impressive lineage
murals have been researched for two
recent publications. In 2013, Zhong
Ziyin published the results of his art-
historical analysis in a Chinese-language

journal.[300] In his short article, he provides a diagram of the figure's placement and a listing of those teachers he
identified. By means of iconographic
comparison with parallel Sakya lineages,
Zhong established the chronology of
both lineages down to the painting's
main figures. He accurately identified
the first part of the respective lineages
(down to the second row) and linked
them with the central figures. Zhong
gave a valuable clue about the transmissions Khyentse depicted here, although
he wrongly assumed that the two transmission lines were connected through
the main figures in both murals.

Prior to that, in 2010, Tsechang
Penba Wangdu clarified the identity of
the two distinct lineages. In his article
on the life and art of Khyentse Chenmo,
Penba Wangdu quoted Changchup
Wanggyal on the lineage murals.[301]
Gyatön writes:[302]

> The right side of the inner sanctum
> (i.e., to the viewer's left) has the
> Three White-Robed Sakya Found-
> ers as main [figures], surrounded
> by the successive masters from the
> lineage of the Path with the Result,
> and the left side (i.e., to the view-
> er's right) [shows] the *mahāsattva*
> Sakya Paṇḍita, Phakpa Rinpoche,
> and Peldan Lama Dampa as main
> [figures], surrounded by the guru
> lineage from the transmission of
> the [Hevajra] Root Tantra.

According to this passage, the murals
in the front of the inner sanctum depict
two lineages from the Hevajra cycle:
to the left, for the meditative tradition
of the Lamdre known as the "Tradition
of Practical Precepts" (*man ngag lugs*),
and, to the right, for the exposition of
the Hevajra Mūlatantra (*rtsa rgyud*),
namely for the "Second Fascicle" (*brtag
pa gnyis pa*) of the Hevajra Root Tantra.
The crucial information provided by
Gyatön in his life story of Gongkarwa

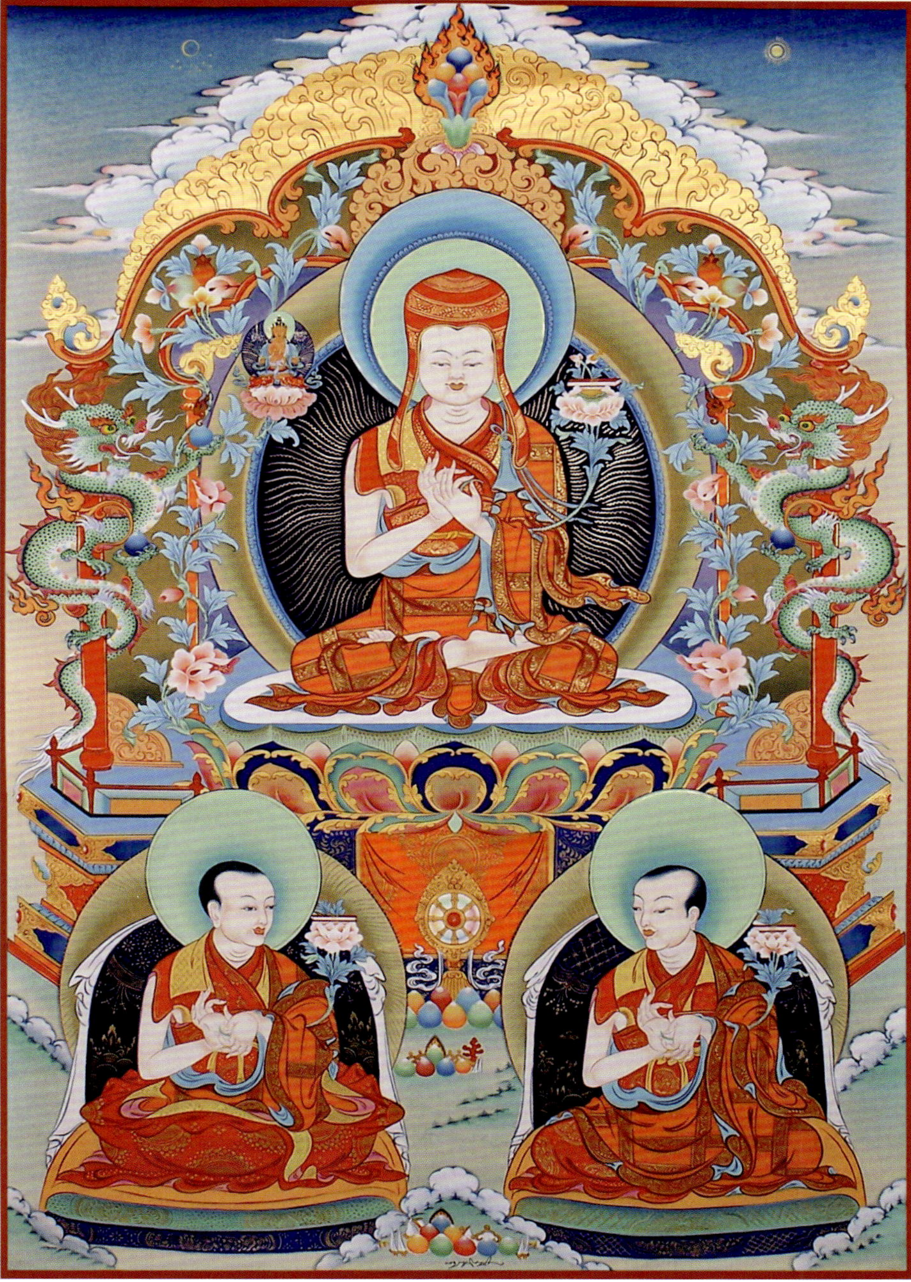

the temple hall are recorded in a handful of written works, which include most notably the monastery's main lineage prayer (*bla ma brgyud pa'i gsol 'debs*), Kunga Namgyal's record of teachings received (*gsan yig*), and his main life story by Gyatön. In the coming pages I will rely upon those sources, describing the two lineages and identifying their individual figures.

(1) The White-Clad Founding Masters and the Hevajra Lineage of the Lamdre

The wall to the left of the entrance of the inner sanctum depicts the three early founding masters, Sachen and his two sons, surrounded by the lineage gurus of the Path with the Result Instructions (*lam 'bras bla brgyud*). At Gongkar Monastery, the representation of lineal masters from the Lamdre was perhaps the most prominent iconographic theme of all. Not only do we find it featured here, but also the Lamdre Chapel on the second floor included a set of gilt-copper images (*gser zangs*) of the same lineage, while the Guru Chapel on the third floor also possessed realistic sculptures of this same lineage in clay (*'jim sku*).[304] Moreover, Changchup Wanggyal reports the existence of two Lamdre thangka sets in the biography of his master,[305] and a modern history of Gongkar Chöde mentions a lost set of gilt-copper sculptures of the complete Lamdre masters that formerly existed in the private chambers of the Dorjedenpa Trulku.[306]

Another group of murals showing Gongkarwa's main Lamdre lineage that survives in the Kunzang Tse College of Gongkar will be discussed in chapter 5. (See Figures 5.5, 5.8, 5.11, 5.16, 5.19–5.24.) Painted in around the 1930s or early 1940s, the local Khyenri artist at work here seems to have copied existing models such as older thangkas or Khyentse's magnificent interpretation

enables us to reconstruct Khyentse's lineage depictions, even though the murals lack inscriptions and several of the lineal gurus depicted are so damaged as to be unrecognizable. (Both paintings feature several pasted-on 1980s-vintage paper labels with names of Lamdre gurus, which I have ignored.)

Generally speaking, Tibetan teaching lineages, whether received and practiced by a single master or by his community, are documented by the histories and liturgies of those traditions.[303] In the case of Gongkar Chöde, the two Hevajra lineages publicly displayed in

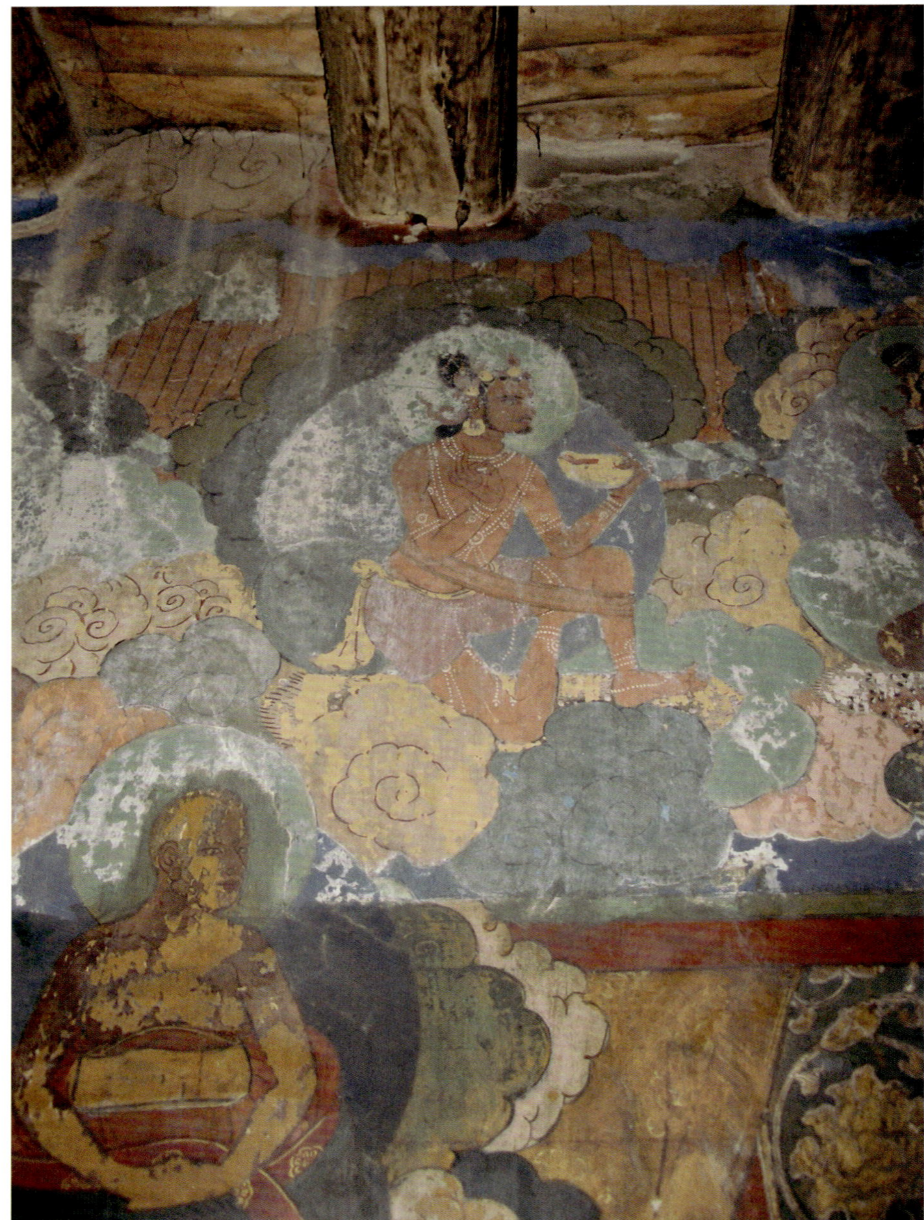

FIG. 4.59
Lineal Masters Avadhutipa and Shangtön
Chubar, as Lamdre Gurus number 6 and 10
Detail, left wall, entrance to inner sanctum
Photo: Mathias Fermer, 2010

of the subject matter in the great assembly hall.

Here also, the masters in the left wall's mural represent the main Lamdre lineage in the Gongkar tradition. The painting shows twenty-three gurus, including the three main figures and the twenty minor figures surrounding them. The main figures are Sachen Kunga Nyingpo (guru number 11; Fig. 3.1) in the center, flanked by his two sons—Sönam Tsemo (number 12; Figs. 3.2 and 4.44), to the right, and Trakpa Gyaltshen (number 13; Fig. 4.49), to the left. As I mentioned above, the three early throne-holders of Sakya in the white garments are shown in their role as the "Three White-Robed Ones" (*dkar po rnam gsum*) from among the Five Founding Masters (*gong ma lnga*). Each holds the stem of a lotus in both hands, and upon that flower rests a sword, to the right, and a volume of scriptures, to the left.

The lineage begins at the top center with the primordial teacher Vajradhara (guru number 1) and ends with Dorjedenpa Kunga Namgyal (guru number 23), the last master in the transmission. The lineage descends, alternating to the left and right, and ends at the bottom center. The lineage is interrupted in the middle by the three main figures, jumping from Shangtön Chubar (number 10) in the second row (Fig. 4.59) to Sachen (number 11) in the very center, from whom it passes to his elder son. (Fig. 4.60 might depict Nyenchenpa Sönam Tenpa as Lamdre guru number 17; note the realistic lines of his face and the individually drawn dragon scales to his right. This master holds a rosary with both hands, an iconographic feature that is otherwise

used for showing Namsa Drakphukpa; see Figures 1.31 and 4.61, row six of the right-side column.)

The line of transmission from Vajradhara down to Kunga Namgyal matches exactly the murals at Kunzang Tse College. As will be seen in the following chapters, this main Gongkar lineage of the Path with the Result was also followed in the murals of Drathang Monastery elsewhere in Lhokha.

In his record of teachings received, Kunga Namgyal lists the main lineage that he had received from Drakthokpa Sönam Sangpo, himself a follower of Thekchen Chöje from the Lhakhang Labrang at Sakya.[307] Down to Lama

Dampa's teacher (number 18, Namsa Drakphukpa) the lineage is identical with the main Lamdre lineages of Ngor.[308] Gyatön in his biography of Gongkarwa provides a slightly different line for the same transmission.[309] This variant version of the lineage (which omits 16b, Shang Könchok Pal, and 20b, Sakya Butön Wangchuk Dar) is depicted by Khyentse, as it evidently was the main and standard lineage for the Path with the Result instructions for his patron and teacher Gongkarwa. It is also followed in the Lamdre lineage recitations at Gongkar Chöde in India.[310]

The Gongkar lineage of the Path with the Result is as follows (The

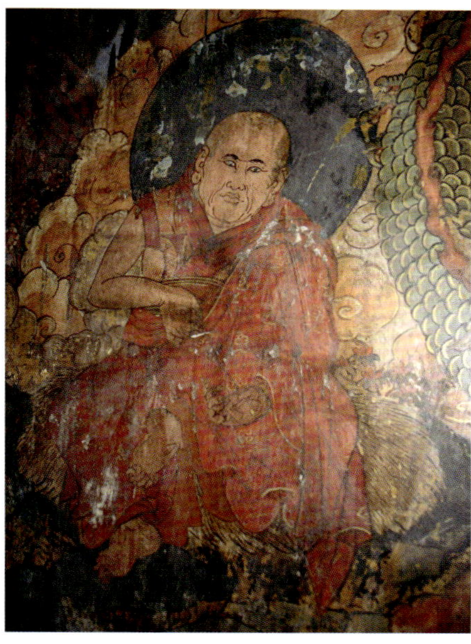

structure of the mural is given in Diagram [C-2]):

1. Vajradhara
2. Nairātmyā
3. Virūpa
4. Kṛṣṇapāda or Kāṇha (Shar phyogs Nag po pa)
5. Ḍamarupa
6. Avadhutipa
7. Paṇchen Gayadhara (d. 1103)
8. Drokmi Lotsāwa Shākya Yeshe (992–1072/77?)
9. Setön Kunrik (1025–1122)
10. Shangtön Chubar (1053–1135)
11. Sachen Kunga Nyingpo (1092–1158) (main figure)

12. Lobpön Sönam Tsemo (1142–1182) (main figure)
13. Jetsün Trakpa Gyaltshen (1147–1216) (main figure)
14. Sakya Paṇḍita (1181–1251)
15. Chögyal Phakpa (1235–1280)
16. Tshokgom Kunga Pal (1210–1307)
[16b. Shang Könchok Pal (Zhang dKon mchog dpal, b. 1240); according to the transmission recorded by Gongkarwa. He was also a teacher of 18.]
17. Nyenchenpa Sönam Tenpa
18. Namsa Drakphukpa Sönam Pal (1277–1350)
19. Lama Dampa Sönam Gyaltshen (1312–1375)
20. Sazang Mati Panchen (1294–1376)
[20b. Sakya Butön Wangchuk Dar]
21. Thekchen Chöje Kunga Tashi (1349–1425)
22. Drakthokpa Sönam Sangpo (d. mid-15th century)
23. Dorjedenpa Kunga Namgyal (1432–1496)

The Gongkar transmission of the Lamdre is also shown in a lineage thangka (*bla brgyud* [*kyi*] *sku thang*) of Hevajra that survives in a private collection (Fig. 4.61).[311] Except one guru, the succession of the twenty-three Lamdre masters in the painting matches exactly the Gongkar line of transmission above.[312] This early Khyenri thangka depicts the main lineage of the Path with the Result instructions, which Kunga Namgyal listed in his record of teachings received. It runs from Chögyal Phakpa

(guru number 15) through his disciple Könchok Pal from the Shang family (guru number 16b) down to the master Namsa Drakphukpa (here number 17) and Lama Dampa (number 18). Kunga Namgyal occupies position 22 in this condensed lineage, here prominently placed above to the left of the main deity. In the same row, to the right side he faces his lineal successor, who is the final guru in the transmission. This master with the number 23 can be identified as the great *upādhyāya* Chödrup Sengge (mKhan chen Chos grub seng ge, b. 1451), who headed the Gendungang (dGe 'dun sgang) community at Gyaling (rGyal [chen] gling) in Dranang (see Fig. 1.19 for earlier abbots of the Gendungang branch.).

(2) The Red-Clad Founding Masters and the Lineage of the Hevajra Mūlatantra

To the right side of the inner sanctum's entrance, the mural depicts Sakya Paṇḍita (guru number 17; Fig. 4.55), his nephew Chögyal Phakpa (number 18), and Lama Dampa Sönam Gyaltshen (number 22; Fig. 4.56) as the three main figures. Lama Dampa is portrayed here as the third of the "Three Red-Robed Ones" (*dmar po rnam gsum*), added to the common group of the "Two Red [Founding Masters]" (*dmar po rnam gnyis*). As pointed out above, the triad of Sakya Founding Masters wearing red monastic robes is special to the Gongkar tradition. The hands of each master are held in the gesture of teaching; each left hand grasps the stem of a lotus that supports a volume of sacred scriptures at shoulder level.

Around the main figures this mural depicts the guru lineage of the Hevajra Root Tantra (*rtsa rgyud*). Transmitted through the *siddha* Ḍombi Heruka (number 4), this lineage is also referred to as the "Tradition of Ḍombi" (*ḍom bhi* [*he ru ka'i*] *lugs*) or the "Commentarial Tradition" (*'grel pa lugs*) by lamas of Ngor

[C-2]								
8	6	4	2	1	3	5	7	9
15	10						14	16
17				11				18
19		12				13		20
(a)		21		23		22		(b)

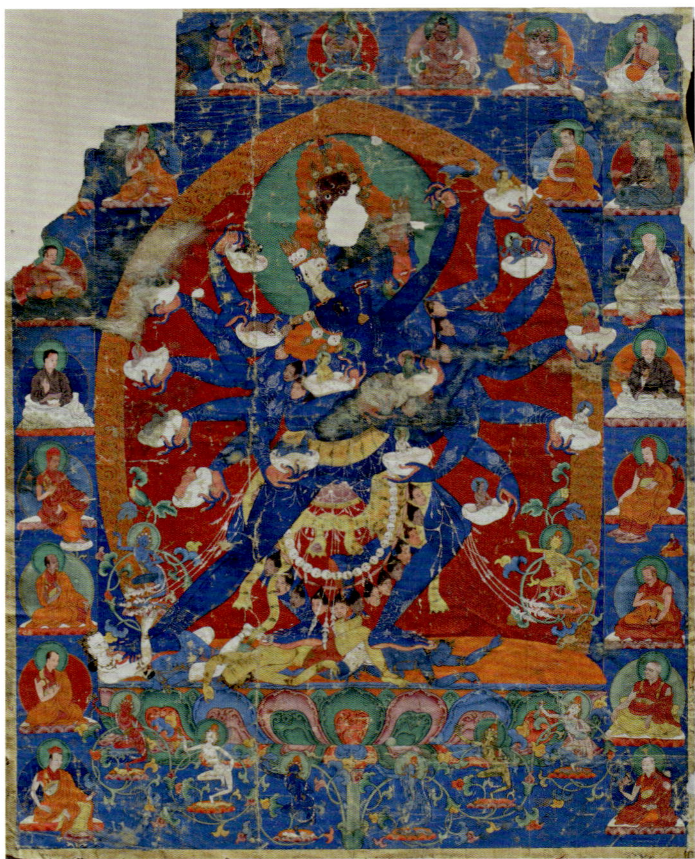

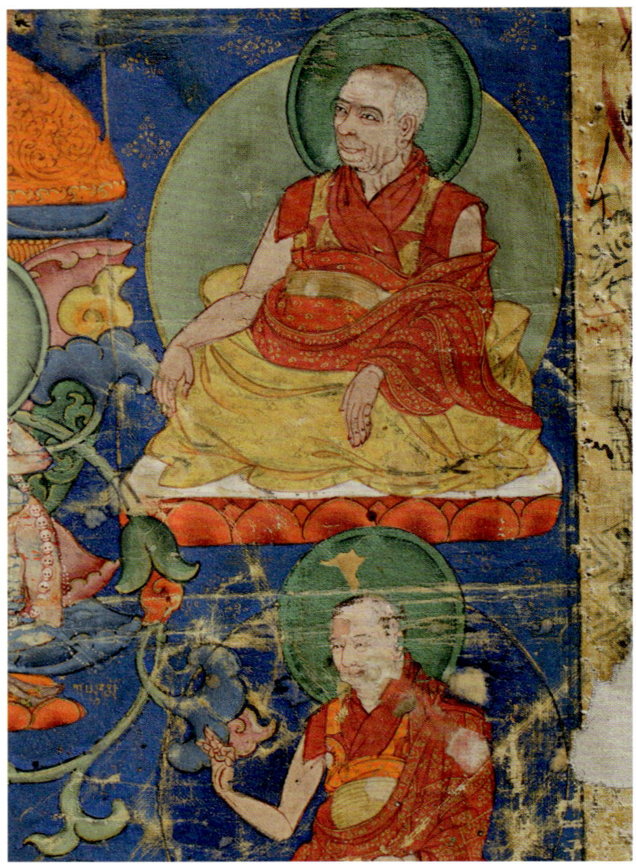

and Sakya monasteries.[313] (See Fig. 4.63 for Ḍombi Heruka depicted sitting on a tiger with his consort.)

The lineage consists of twenty-five masters, with three main figures and twenty-two minor figures surrounding them. It starts at the top center, with Nairātmyā (guru number 2) in union with Hevajra. For some unknown reason, the original Buddha Vajradhara, from whom the lineage originates, is missing in this painting.

The transmission alternates to the left and right, as in the previous mural. The sequence is interrupted twice by the main figures in the center. From Trakpa Gyaltshen (guru number 16) on the right margin of the second row, the lineage descends to Sakya Paṇḍita (number 17) and further to Chögyal Phakpa (number 18). Again, the transmission continues in right-left alternation until reaching Palden Sengge (number 21) at the left edge of row four. (See Fig. 4.66.) According to my interpretation, he passes the lineage to Lama Dampa

(number 22), who appears as a main figure, who then transmits it to the disciple just to his right, the great *upādhyāya* Shedorwa (number 23) (Fig. 4.67). The lineage then continues down to Dorjedenpa Kunga Namgyal (number 26), who is seated atop a rocky crag to the right side of the bottom row. Like the Lamdre instructions, he had also received the Hevajra Root Tantra explication from his chief teacher, Drakthok Chöje Sönam Sangpo (number 25).[314] He is shown with a round, very young-looking face (compare with Figures 5.24 and 12.7), which is correct for him. Though the lineage does not end in the middle of the bottom row as on the left wall, guru number 26 must be Gongkarwa. (See Fig. 4.68.) This slightly unusual placement in the right corner of the bottom might hint at his role as the commissioning patron.

If my identification and ordering are correct, number 25, Drakthokpa is depicted as central teacher on the lower row with his hands in the teaching

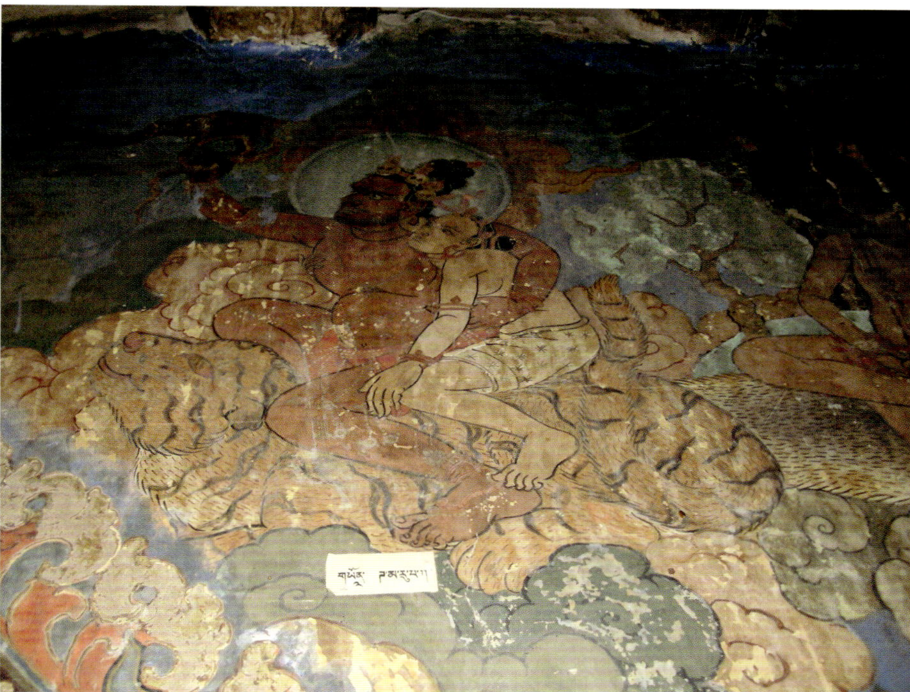

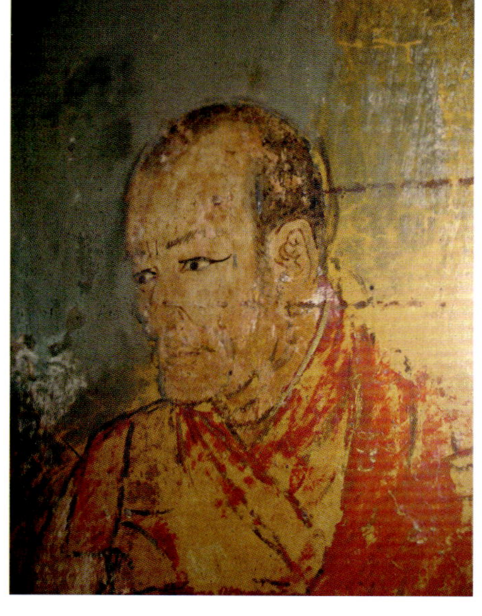

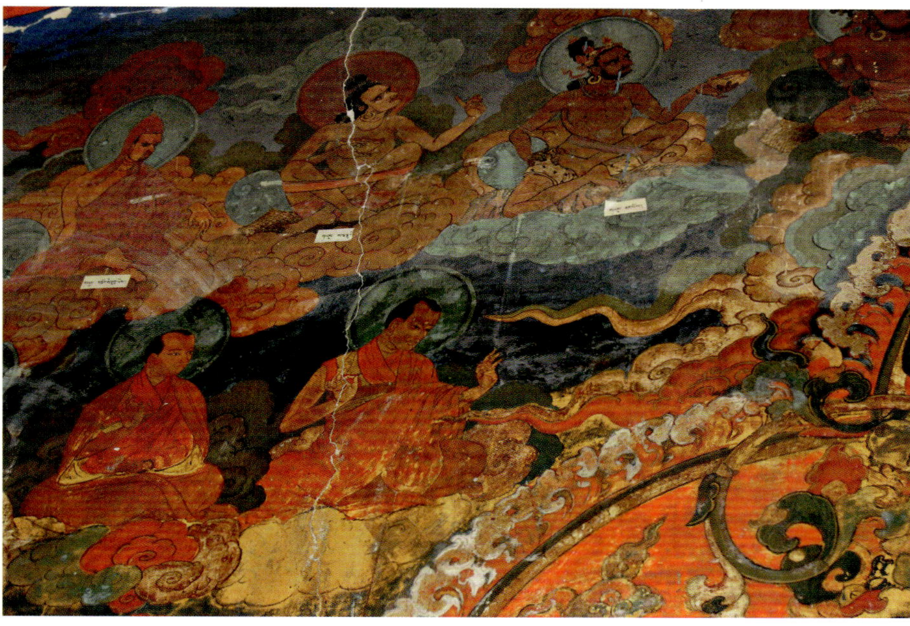

Fig. 4.63
Ḍombi Heruka as Hevajra Mūlatantra lineal
guru number 4
Detail, right wall, entrance to inner sanctum
Photo: Mathias Fermer, 2010

Fig. 4.64
Three Indian and Two Tibetan Teachers
from the Hevajra Mūlatantra (from left to
right guru numbers 9, 7, and 5, and
numbers 13 and 11 below)
Detail, right wall, entrance to inner sanctum
Photo: Mathias Fermer, 2010

Fig. 4.65
Lotsāwa Chokden or Jamkya Namkha Pal
as Hevajra Mūlatantra lineal guru
number 20
Detail, right wall, entrance to inner sanctum
Photo: Mathias Fermer, 2010

Fig. 4.66
Lama Palden Sengge as Hevajra Mūlatantra
lineal guru number 21
Detail, right wall, entrance to inner sanctum
Photo: Mathias Fermer, 2010

gesture. He is portrayed as an old master
wearing a red *pandita* hat with earflaps
tucked in (which is a common iconography for him, see Figs. 1.23 and 7.39.)
His prominent positioning in the center
of the bottom row I at first believed
indicated his role as current main teacher
of the lineage, but, here for identifying
him, facial appearance trumps his position in the lineage order.

The details of the depicted lineage can be established from Kunga
Namgyal's teaching record. However,
for the Hevajra Mūlatantra lineage, that
source omits three lineage gurus: 8.
Jayaśrījñāna, 15. Lobpön Sönam Tsemo,
and 22. Lama Dampa.[315]

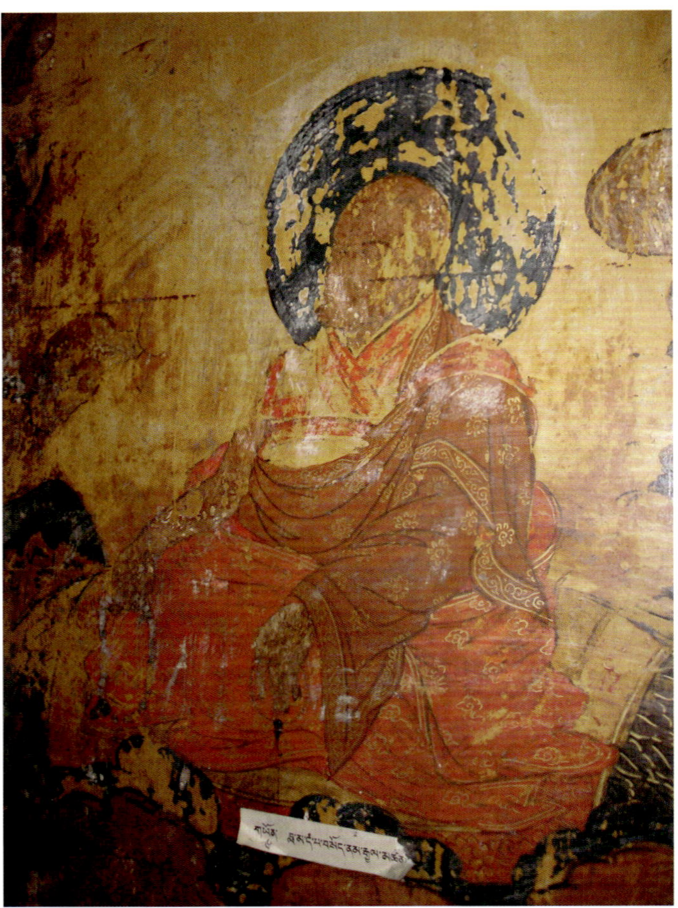 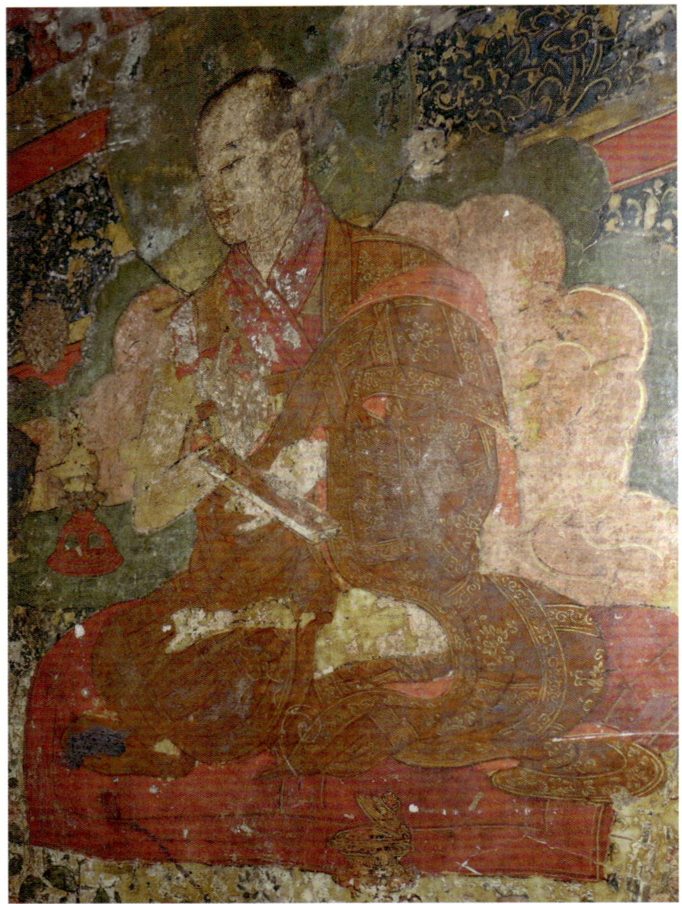

Problems with this transmission were also noticed by the Fifth Dalai Lama, who was a later recipient of the lineage passing through Gongkarwa. For the Hevajra lineage in the Ḍombi Tradition of the Sakyapa, the Great Fifth adds an explanatory gloss to his own lineage record, noting that although the Indian master Jayaśrījñāna was missing in the lineage as traced by Kunga Namgyal, that omission was probably an error since the name does appear in the record of "Thartsepa" (i.e., Drangti Panchen [1535–1602]) in the relevant passage. Though the Fifth Dalai Lama lists Sönam Tsemo in his correct position within the transmission, the lineage

he records does *not* pass through Lama Dampa.[316]

The later Gongkar master Trinle Namgyal also recorded the Hevajra Mūlatantra lineage passing through Dorjedenpa. His lineage gives Jayaśrījñāna and Sönam Tsemo in their correct positions, but it, too, skips Lama Dampa seven gurus later in the lineage.[317] I think that we can assume that an alternative transmission of the Mūlatantra exposition existed, which jumped directly from Lama Palden Sengge (guru number 21) to Khenchen Shedorwa (number 23). But could we expect the Gongkar lineage of the Hevajra Root Tantra to omit Lama Dampa? After all, he was portrayed here by Khyentse as a central figure on the same level as the two Red-Robed Sakya Founding Masters, Sapaṇ and Phakpa.

A solution to this is found in another section of Gongkarwa's record of teachings received. In the passage listing the teachings from Kangyurwa Shākya Gyaltshen (bKa' 'gyur ba

Shākya rgyal mtshan), Dorjedenpa records an alternative lineage of the Hevajra Root Tantra. This lineage omits Ngari Salnying (number 12) and Gyichuwa (number 13), and gives Khön Könchok Gyalpo ('Khon dKon mchog rgyal po, guru number 12b) as the one who passed on the Root Tantra to Sachen. Shang Dode Pal (here guru number 18), then passes it on to Jamkya Namkha Pal ('Jam skya Nam mkha' dpal, d. 1309), who transmitted it to Lama Palden Sengge, who bestowed it upon Lama Dampa.[318] (Note that Namkha Pal replaces Lotsāwa Chokden in the transmission; Fig. 4.65 showing lineal guru number 20 could thus depict either

Namkha Pal *or* Lotsāwa Chokden.) This alternative lineage, which also descends down to Gongkarwa, explains Lama Dampa's presence in the lineage depiction of the Hevajra Mūlatantra on the right wall, prominently shown as a Sakya Founding Master. The arrangement of the lineage of teachers is as in Diagram [C-3].

The lineage, according to Dorjedenpa's record of teachings received, is (with omitted masters restored between square brackets):

1. Vajradhara
2. Nairātmyā (in union with Hevajra)
3. Virūpa
4. Ḍombi Heruka
5. Alalavajra (A la la vajra)
6. Naktröpa (Nags khrod pa)
7. Garbharīpa (Garbha ri pa)
[8. Jayaśrījñāna (bSod snyoms pa rGyal ba dpal gyi ye shes); restored from other sources.]
9. Durgacandra / Durjayacandra (Mi thub zla ba)
10. Bhikṣu Vīravajra / Prajñendtaruci (dGe slong dpa' bo rdo rje or Shes rab dbang po mdzes pa)
11. Drokmi Lotsāwa Shākya Yeshe (992–1072/77?)
12. Ngari Salnying (mNga' ris gsal snying)
[12b. Khön Könchok Gyalpo (1034–1102); according to the alternative transmission. He was also a teacher of number 14.]
13. Gyichuwa Dralabar (sGyi chu ba dGra bla 'bar)
14. Sachen Kunga Nyingpo (1092–1158)

[15. Lobpön Sönam Tsemo (1142–1182); restored from other sources.]
16. Jetsün Trakpa Gyaltshen (1147–1216)
17. Sakya Paṇḍita (1181–1251) (main figure)
18. Chögyal Phakpa (1235–1280) (main figure)
19. Shang Dode Pal (Zhang mdo dpal) (fl. 13th century)
20. Lotsāwa Chokden (Lo tsā ba mChog ldan)
[20b. Lama Jamkya Namkha Pal (d. 1309); according to the alternative transmission.]
21. Lama Palden Sengge (Bla ma dPal ldan seng ge)
[22. Lama Dampa Sönam Gyaltshen (1312–1375)] (main figure); restored from the alternative lineage.]
23. Khenchen Shedorwa (mKhan chen Shes rdor ba)
24. Chögowa Chöpal Sherab (Chos sgo ba Chos dpal shes rab)
25. Drakthokpa Sönam Sangpo (d. mid-15th cent.)
26. Dorjedenpa Kunga Namgyal (1432–1496)

In the bottom-left and -right corners of both right and left walls, two additional deities seem to stand guard, which I have indicated through the letters (a) through (d) in the diagrams. They evidently depict the Four Great Kings (*rgyal chen rigs/sde bzhi;* Skt. *Caturmahārāja*). If so, they may be: (a) protector of the east, Dhṛtarāṣṭra (Yul 'khor srung; white-skinned); (b)

protector of the west, Virūpākṣa (Mig mi bzang; red-skinned); (c) protector of the north, Vaiśravaṇa (rNam thos sras; yellow-skinned); and (d) protector of the south, Virūḍhaka ('Phags skyes po; blue-skinned). Though some are too damaged to see their crucial iconographic details, number (a) does seem to be holding a plate with offerings in the left hand, and (b) has reddish skin but holds the handle of a censer. Number (c) grasps the stem of a lotus, but other details are lost, while (d), the final one, holds something thin and rectangular in his hand that could be the blade of a dark-blue sword.

[C-3]

9	7	5	3	2	4	6	8	10
15	13	11				12	14	16
19				**17**				20
21		**18**				**22**		23
(c)		24		25		26		(d)

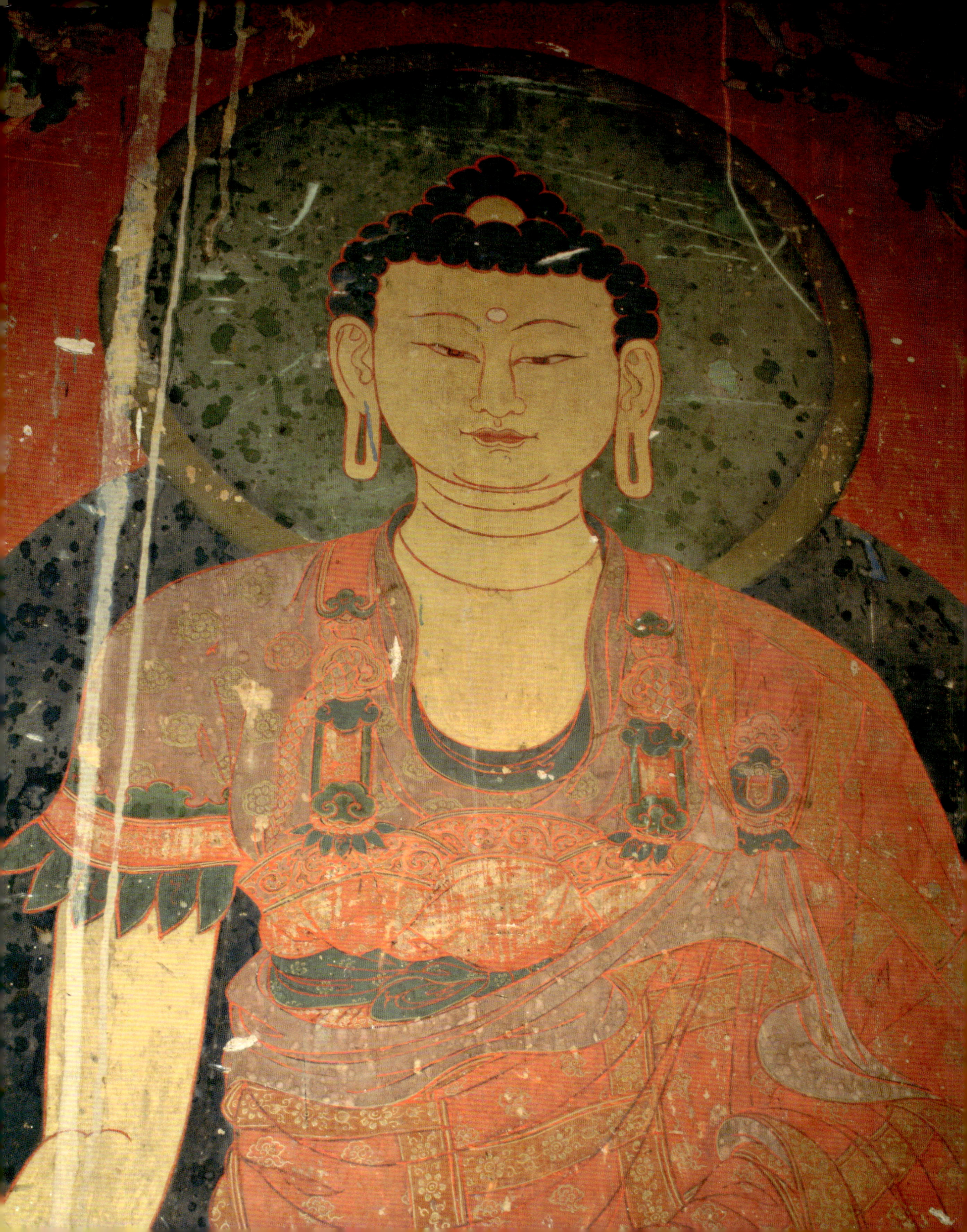

CHAPTER 5

Sculptures of the Lineage Masters from Drathang and Related Khyenri Paintings

ALL OF Khyentse Chenmo's many naturalistic sculptures at Gongkar were destroyed during the Cultural Revolution in the 1960s, when the monastery's main assembly hall was converted into a grain warehouse and the building's second floor was used mainly for offices of the Communist party. For several decades, historians believed that no sculptures made by Khyentse Chenmo remained anywhere. This chapter introduces a group of twenty surviving sculptures outside Gongkar that now can be attributed to him.

In this and the following chapter I will demonstrate how eight iconographically significant sculptures from that set are related to surviving murals in the Kunzang Tse College of Gongkar and at Drathang. I will also compare the statues to the most significant surviving thangka paintings in the Khyenri style. Finally I will present the conclusion of the Thekchen Chöje Lamdre lineage as it survives in the later murals of Kunzang Tse and Drathang.

THE KHYENLUK TRADITION OF SCULPTURE

In addition to his unrivaled mastery of painting, Khyentse Chenmo was also an extraordinarily skilled sculptor.[319] The style of sculpture he practiced can be called Khyenluk (*mkhyen lugs*, "Khyentse's tradition"). The chapels of Gongkar Dorjeden originally contained many

---

large sculptures that he had fashioned, some of them as high as from one-and-a-half to two-and-a-half stories tall. The images depicting fierce protectors were wonderfully terrifying.[320] Giuseppe Tucci, who saw the sculptures at Gongkar in the 1940s, was strongly affected by them: "A statue of Dorje Jiche in the Gönkhang, the most expressive I ever saw in Tibet, came close to frightening me out of my wits."[321] Khyentse's sculptures of the Lamdre lineage gurus at Gongkar Dorjeden were extremely naturalistic. According to Kathok Situ, who personally observed them when visiting Gongkar in the winter of 1918–1919, the sculptures were then still remarkably well preserved, remaining "as if freshly varnished."[322]

Khyentse's sculptures at Gongkar Monastery are also discussed at some length in the biography of Dorjedenpa. The author, Gyatön, reports the existence of a sculpture set depicting the Lamdre guru lineage (*lam 'bras bla brgyud*) on the top floor of the temple, in the Guru Chapel (Bla ma Lha khang), that was a little smaller than life-size (*sku tshad cung gzhon pa tshar gcig*). Gyatön devotes a passage to what turns out to have been two sets of portrait sculptures. He describes the first set as three-dimensional (*'bur dod*) images (*sku*) made of clay that depicted twenty-three lineal masters, whom he named one by one as highly revered teachers, concluding with his own guru, Dorjedenpa. He also mentions a second set, which was made of gilt copper and consisted of slightly smaller or "younger-looking" depictions

of those teachers and that included thrones and robes. Regarding the clay sculptures, Gyatön said:

When Khyentse Chenmo was making these images, he fashioned them below in a workshop, and after finishing them well, he brought them here, where it would be easier to modify [and give final touches to] them. But later, when he was making the life-size gilt copper image of the venerable master Kunga Namgyal—the sculpture that now stands in the middle of the temple (*kunga rawa*)—when he began to try to move the sculpture of Sakya Paṇḍita in front of the western *gomang* stupa for the sake of copying designs of its brocade robes and such things, no matter how he tried, he could not budge the sculpture, not even a tiny bit. Therefore the sculptures are an occasion of greatest amazement. The images that thus exist each has its own suitable bodily form that seems to the viewer that it is being directly perceived [as a living master, with a naturalism] that is so extremely wonderful that it exceeds wonder, conveying a feeling of the master portrayed changing the gaze of his eyes as he looks back at the viewer, as if caught in the midst of giving verbal teachings, glowing with spiritual blessing. The [clay sculptures] were each completed with robes of several layers made of brocade with special designs and a complete set of ritual implements, including a Chinese vajra and bell. [323]

The degree that Khyentse enthusiastically used Chinese elements in his art, including distinctive vajras and bells, is telling. He was very particular about which original elements he adopted for his art, even regarding the materials used for robes, *gos rgyud* ("brocade material"). The term *go ling* possibly refers to the decorative design elements in silk brocade. *Go ling* occurs a second time in Gongkarwa's biography in the phrase *go ling bzang po*, possibly meaning "excellent brocade designs," together with *gos dar yug sna tshogs*, "robes of various rolls of brocade."[324]

A SET OF SCULPTURES FROM DRATHANG

Gyatön's vivid and lively descriptions of the sculptures—such as that they possessed the feeling of the master being caught in the midst of actually giving teachings (*gsung gi sgra dbyangs stsal bzhin pa'i nyams dang ldan pa*)—also apply to one striking set of Lamdre lineal-guru sculptures that did survive in Lhokha. The set in question was brought from Drathang to Mindröling Monastery in 1990, its present home.

Amy Heller noted the set's existence, dated it to the sixteenth or seventeenth century, and described it as having "extremely expressive faces, much like the clay sculptures of the Mahāsiddhas from Gyantse."[325] In 1992, Ulrich von Schroeder photographed the sculptures in Mindröling; I helped document the historical background of that set.[326] In Kathok Situ's pilgrimage record, I noticed a passage regarding a large set of Lamdre lineage sculptures at Drathang. Kathok Situ wrote that he saw at Drathang, in 1918 or 1919, "a silver statue of Vajradhara and a set of nearly life-size gilt-copper statues depicting the guru lineage of the

Lamdre" (*rdo rje 'chang dngul sku dang / lam 'bras bla rgyud gser sku mi tshad tsam/*). The silver central Vajradhara was fairly distinctive, and I was convinced that the sculptures at Mindröling came from nearby Drathang Monastery. Believing that these sculptures were connected with the career of the lama Shalu Lotsāwa Chökyong Sangpo (1441–1528), who was also prominently mentioned by Kathok Situ, I dated them to between 1495 and 1528, based on the Kathok Situ passage and a few brief references to Chökyong Sangpo's other activities in Lhokha that I found in the Shalu abbatial history by Shalu Ribuk Tulku.[327]

Von Schroeder, having found "single undeciphered *Nagari* letters on the upper side of some images," considered the sculptures to have been made by Newari craftsmen and classified their style as "Nepalese schools in Tibet."[328] He dated the set to about 1495:

> It was only after the enthronement of Zhwa lu Lo tsā ba (1441–1528) as abbot of Drathang that the Lam 'bras doctrine was taught there. Therefore, it is probable that the set of twenty large embossed gilt-copper images were commissioned by Zhwa lu Lo tsā ba in 1495 or soon after. [329]

The Lamdre instruction was actually taught at Drathang in the decades before Shalu Lotsāwa, but von Schroeder could not have known this. So, his dating of the sculptures was not conclusive.

The Mindröling sculptures are also discussed in more detail in Lee-Kalisch et al. 2006, a catalog of an exhibition that brought ten of the twenty Mindröling sculptures to Germany and Japan. In an introductory section, Andreas Kretschmar, Bernadette Bröskamp, and Marit Kretschmar acknowledged that the set originated from Drathang, and they accepted the

identification of the final lama as Shalu Lotsāwa. They remarked on the figures' pronounced portrait-like character, which splendidly revealed the different personalities.[330]

They identified the depicted Lamdre tradition as "the lineage of the transmission of the Vajra verse."[331] That is correct if they meant the gurus of the main Lamdre lineage and not those of the nine ancillary traditions (*lam skor dgu*), each of which had its distinct lineage. They tried to identify which of the eighteen Lamdre traditions mentioned in some histories were depicted by the sculptures. When reconstructing the lineage, they wrongly added, after Lama Dampa, the lamas Palden Tshultrim and Ngorchen Kunga Zangpo, though these two represent a different tradition, the Ngorpa.

The authors basically followed von Schroeder, dating the sculptures to the early sixteenth century, but they specify that the silver Vajradhara seems to be from a different set.[332] They stressed the connections that Shalu Lotsāwa had with Gongkar Dorjedenpa, mentioning, for instance, that he visited Gongkar at age forty-two, in 1483, and received teachings from Dorjedenpa:

> We can suppose that Shalu Lotsāwa at that time came into contact with the artist Khyentse, who was then working there, or his students. The strong parallels in the presentation of the faces, folds in the robes, and flower decorations between the portraits of the Lamdre masters in the murals of Gongkar Chöde and the repousse figures here exhibited, suggests the conclusion that at least the twenty copper figures among the twenty-one sculptures made for Drathang Monastery are works in the Khyenri style.[333]

Thus they clearly sensed the presence of strong artistic links between the sculptures and Khyentse Chenmo's painting style.

Michael Henss also highly appreciated this set when he saw it in 1989, calling it "some of the greatest masterpieces of sculpture in Tibet."[334] For the set's date, he accepted the link with Shalu Lotsāwa but suggested it should be soon after that lama's death, that is, to the early sixteenth century. He noted how out of the ordinary the sculptures were:

> No stylistic parallels exist in monumental fifteenth-century sculpture for this characteristic Nepalese repousse technique, for the dynamic poses, the expressive and naturalistic portrait-style physiognomies, the ornamental vocabulary of headdresses and scarves, or for the design of the lotus petals.[335]

Suggesting the set was possibly inspired by the naturalistic Lamdre sculptures that once existed in nearby Gongkar, Henss noted correspondences of the style to those of the painted mahāsiddhas of Yamdrok Taklung and some thangka paintings of Lamdre lineages from Ngor. He, too, considered the central silver Vajradhara to be a later addition.

Reconsidering the Dating

The sculptures have until now been dated to the late fifteenth or early sixteenth century, about the tenure of Shalu Lotsāwa (d. 1528) as abbot of Drathang, or shortly thereafter. Yet if we examine the iconography of the lineal gurus, the set clearly depicts the Thekchen Chöje Lamdre transmission. Moreover, if we read a more detailed version of Shalu Lotsāwa's life story (which was not available to me in 2000), we find that Shalu Lotsāwa and his main guru, Khyenrab Chöje of Shalu and Nalendra Monasteries, both followed the Ngorpa tradition of the Lamdre instructions. Shalu Lotsāwa was the disciple of the fourth abbot, Kunga Wangchuk, and the ninth one, Könchok Phel while Khyenrab Chöje was the personal disciple of Ngorchen. A quick look in the detailed biography did not reveal any link between Shalu Lotsāwa and Thekchen Chöje's tradition.

Those facts forced me to discount the likelihood of Shalu Lotsāwa's involvement in the making of these sculptures, which clearly represent a distinctive non-Ngorpa lineage. Now it seems more likely that they were made about one generation earlier, that is, about the 1460s or 1470s.

The size, quality of the materials, and workmanship of the sculptures bespeak patronage by a rich nobleman; they are particularly fine and large, and the use of silver in the central Vajradhara is a sumptuous touch. Perhaps they were commissioned by a noble monk or with the support of a rich local lord, such as the Yargyap rulers. The patron might have been an eminent local lama of Lhokha and Drathang, who paid special homage to this non-Ngorpa lineage through these outstanding sculptures. The noble monk Champalingpa, who died in 1475, is known to have personally commissioned a smaller set of sculptures of the same Lamdre lineage in 1455. This larger set could have been commissioned in his or another Drathang abbot's honor. Khyentse Chenmo painted some murals of the Champaling stupa about that time; the artist was still living then, for he painted the murals of Yangpachen in 1503.

The sculptures lack naming labels. Based on their iconography, it is possible to identify many of them and to order the remaining ones provisionally. Correcting an earlier mistaken identification of a Tibetan lama as Gayadhara, I suggest that he could be a later Tibetan lineal lama, such as Tshokgom or Drakphukpa. In the surviving sculptures, as depicted in von Schroeder 2001, the one assumed to be the final master—who wears a distinctive crown—has also been assumed to be the main teacher present at the time the sculpture set was made. Instead of Shalu Lotsāwa, he could be an earlier local lama.

Until now, two sculptures depicting Tibetan lamas, probably later lineage gurus, were nameless or misidentified. I suggest that the unidentified sculptures may fill some of the gaps in the lineage after Phakpa but before Thekchen Chöje, including Tshokgom, Nyenchenpa, and Drakphukpa. According to a recent history of Drathang, one of the sculptures is a special very blessed depiction of Gongkarwa.[336]

Actually, another set of sculptures depicting Lamdre lineage masters survived in central Tibet: at Gyantse's Palkhor Chöde Monastery in Tsang province.[337] This set ends with guru number 21, Thekchen Chöje, but it omits numbers 19 and 20. In other words, it treats him as the final guru and as the direct disciple of his uncle Lama Dampa, which he was for many teachings. But for the Lamdre, his actual main teacher was Sazang Mati Panchen, and that lama is oddly lacking from the Gyantse set. To fulfill the strict rules of Lamdre for a valid and complete transmission, Sakya Butön could also be counted as another main guru who transmitted the tradition from Lama Dampa to Thekchen Chöje. Sakya Butön is indeed counted and fully present in Kunga Namgyal's record of teachings received, but he is bypassed in the Lamdre lineage sculptures of Gongkar Chöde, as they are described in Kunga Namgyal's detailed biography by Gyatön Changchup Wangyal, where the lineage passes from Lama Dampa to Sazang Mati to Thekchen Chöje.[338]

Of the twenty-one sculptures that survive in Lhokha, at Drathang and Mindröling, the central depiction of Vajradhara was made of silver and the remaining twenty were fashioned of sheets of embossed gilt copper. Newar craftsmen may have helped fashion the

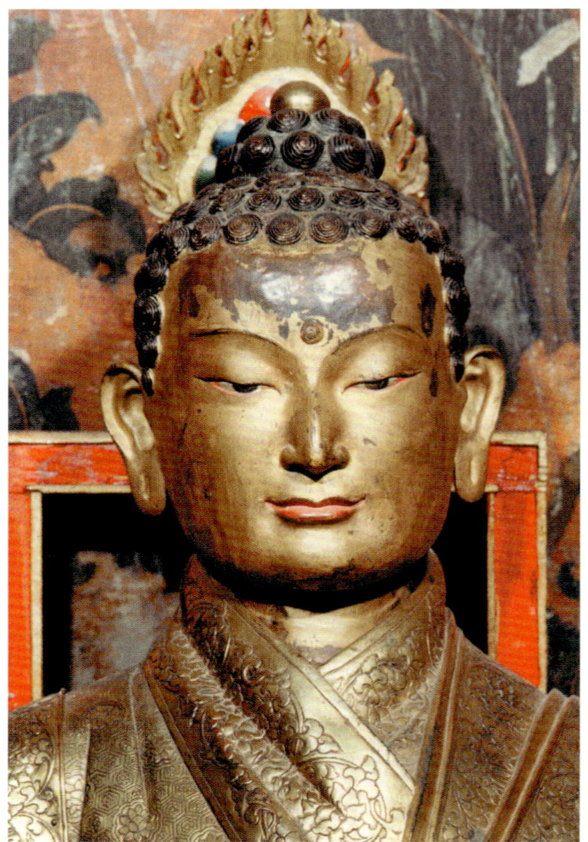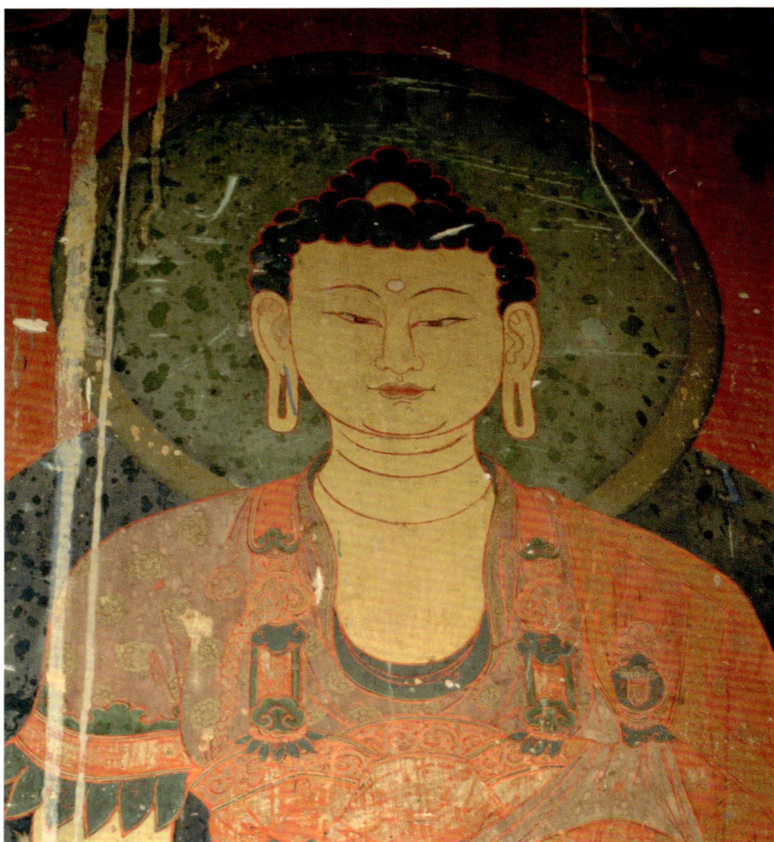

sculptures or to finish them with gold plating. I believe that the sculptures are in a strikingly true-to-life Tibetan style, one for which Khyentse Chenmo was famed. The artist was personally involved as the sculptor; the sculptures were not the work of some later disciples who followed his models.

In sum, these sculptures at Mindröling depict the Thekchen Chöje lineage and clearly establish Khyentse Chenmo's excellence as a sculptor. We can date them now to the 1470s, not the early sixteenth century.

Head Protuberances in a Sculpture, a Gongkar Mural, and a Nenying Thangka

The sculptures at Mindröling share some distinctive features with Gongkar murals. One iconographic detail of a Drathang sculpture can be traced both to an early Gongkar mural and to a thangka that was gifted by the Ming court to Nenying Monastery.

As noticed by Bernadette Bröskamp in Lee-Kalisch et al. 2006, the treatment of the *uṣṇīśa* in the Mindröling sculpture of Sakya Paṇḍita is distinctive (Fig. 5.1).[339]

Similar head protuberances occur in some of the depictions of buddhas that Khyentse Chenmo painted as main figures in the mural panels devoted to Kṣemendra's *avadāna* tales (Fig. 5.2). A painted image of the sandalwood buddha from the Ming court of China, now preserved at Nenying Monastery, features the same shape of *uṣṇīśa* (Fig. 5.3a). This shape is unique in Tibetan painting.

For comparison, the shape of the head protuberance of Sakya Paṇḍita in the set of Lamdre lineage sculptures surviving at Gyantse is completely different (Fig. 5.3b). The idiosyncrasy of certain iconographic details indicates that the metal Mindroling sculptures must have been made by Khyentse Chenmo. Since previously all of his sculptures were believed lost, the survival of at least one very impressive set of sculptures should be celebrated.

Iconographic Links to Later Gongkar Murals

The Drathang sculptures possess other important links to the portrait paintings made by later followers of the Khyenri style, which survive in Gongkar murals. For instance, the sculpture depicting the early Tibetan lineage master Shangtön Chöbar was clearly based on models

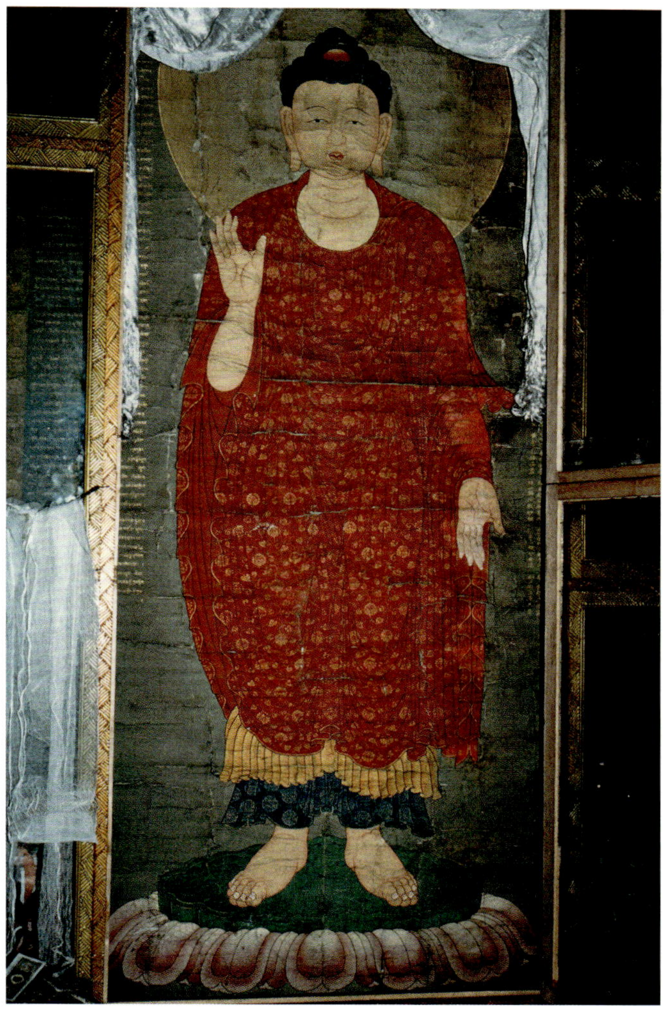

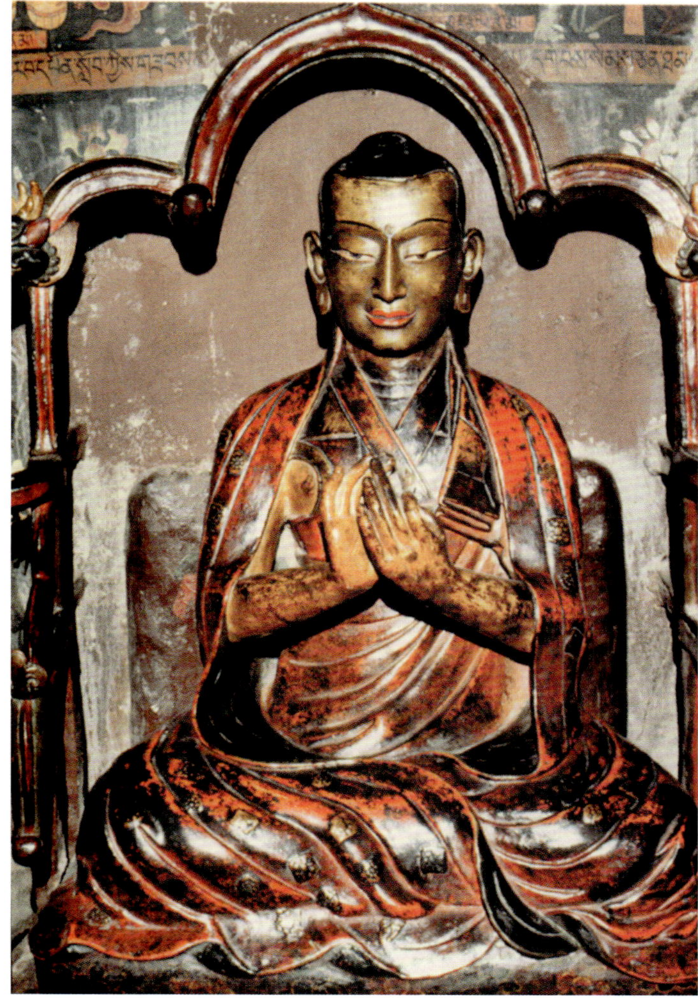

FIG. 5.3A
The Sandalwood Buddha of China
Detail of inscribed and dated Chinese scroll
painting
Made at Ming court, China; 1412
Photographed at Nenying Monastery, Tsang
province, Tibet
Photo: Helmut Neumann
Literature: Jackson 1996, fig. 42; and
Jackson 2012, fig. 8.19

FIG. 5.3B
Sakya Paṇḍita
Lamdre Lhakhang, Gyantse;
second half of the fifteenth century
Photo: U. von Schroeder, 1992
Literature: von Schroeder 2001, *Buddhist
Sculptures in Tibet*, vol. 2, pl. 204A

found in paintings in Kunzang Tse College. A few of the Drathang sculptures
closely follow the Kunzang Tse iconography. Compare, for example, the faces
and distinctive, protruding teeth in Figures 5.4, 5.5, and 5.6. They demonstrate
a close relationship between the artistic
motifs, at least when depicting the early
Tibetan Lamdre master Shangtön Chöbar.

Shangtön Chöbar was one of two
Shang (Zhang) brothers who were eminent disciples of Setön Kunrik. Both
were intelligent scribes who helped
Setön write and complete some sacred
Buddhist scriptures that he had previously commissioned. The sculpture in
Figure 5.4 depicts him with a rapt gaze,
wearing a meditation band around one
shoulder, and with his hands on his
lap in a gesture of meditation. Such
features proclaim his status as a great
contemplative.

Figure 5.5 depicts Shangtön

Chöbar in the murals of Kunzang Tse
College. Shangtön is said to have been
a monk, which might explain why his
hair was kept trimmed quite short. But
late in life, he was no normal monastic:
he lived as a hidden yogi, following a
layman's lifestyle in a village, with a
female consort.

In the painting, he gazes intently
into space. He is wearing the goatskin
that he wore when he met his disciple,
Sachen. The painting details the goatskin's hairs and its irregular lower-left
edge, near the carpet. Another notable
detail is his gray, cylindrical ear-lobe
plug. He sits with knees raised; beneath
him, a white goat with splayed horns
approaches, intently staring at him and
offering the flower held in its mouth.
Such details hint at his life as a shepherd.

Figure 5.6 depicts another version
of Shangtön, preserved in a Drathang
Monastery mural that dates to the 1930s.

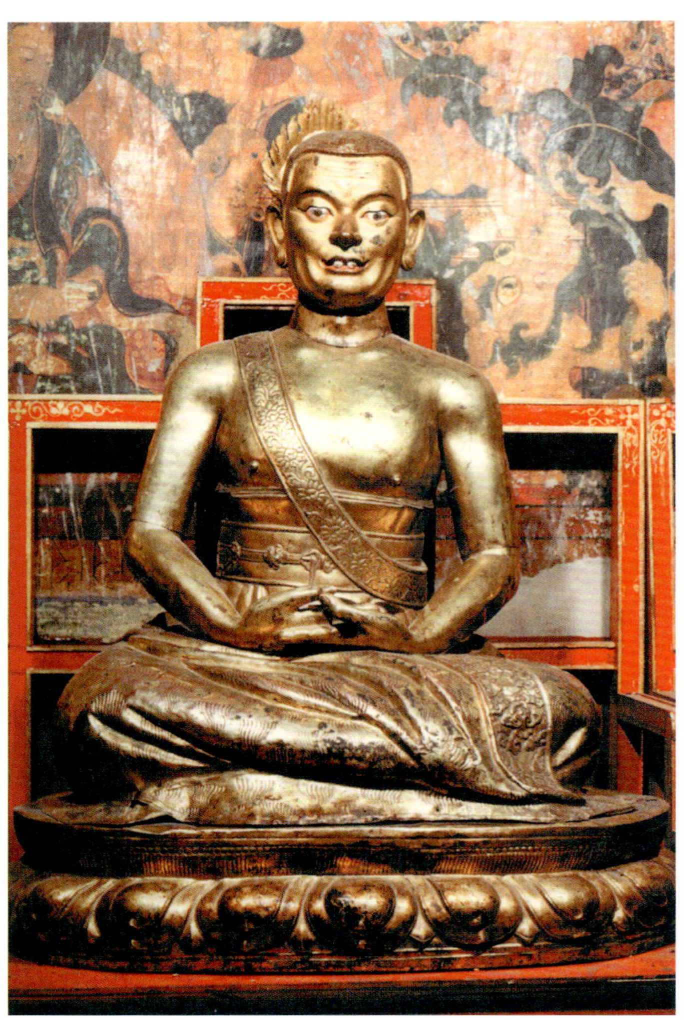

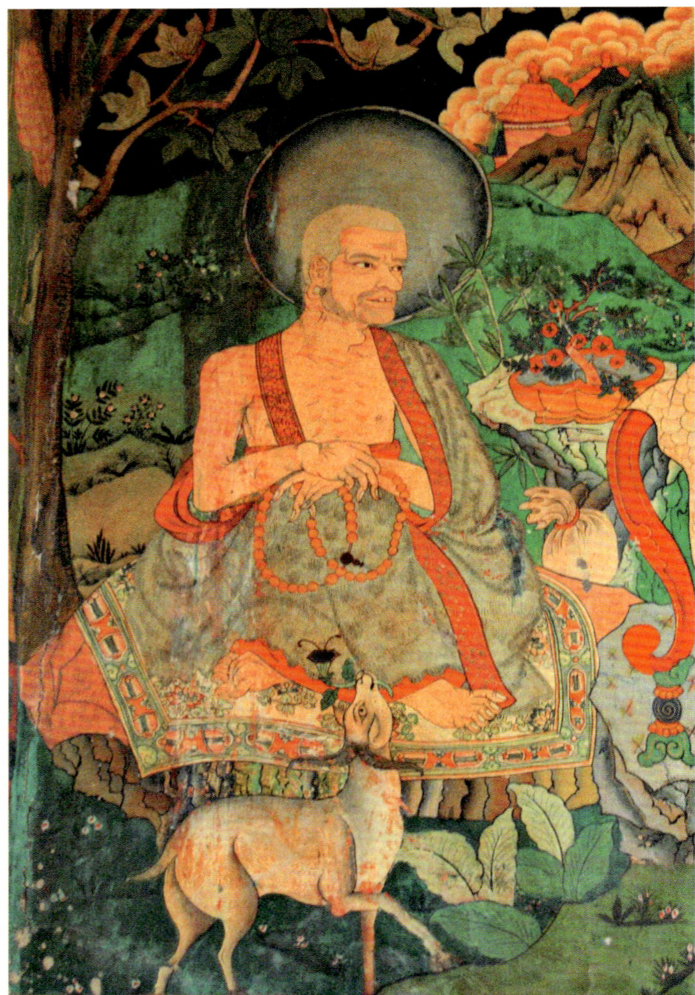

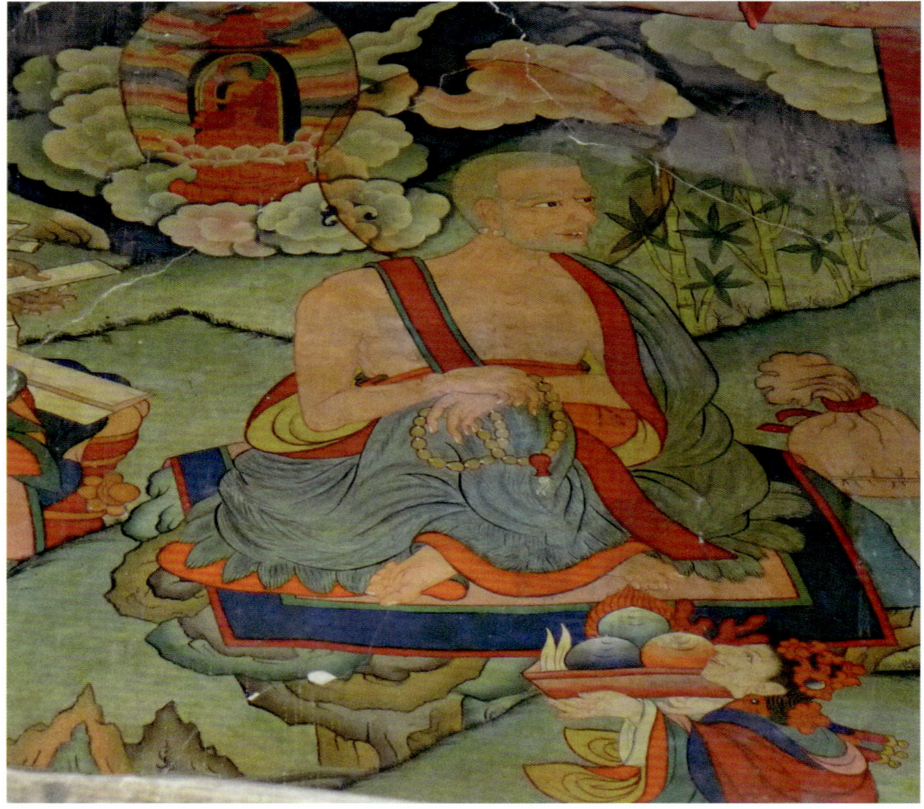

Fig. 5.4
Shangtön Chöbar
Gilt-copper
Mindröling; second half of the fifteenth
century
H: 36 ⅝ in. (93 cm)
Photo: U. von Schroeder, 1992
Literature: von Schroeder 2001, *Buddhist
Sculptures in Tibet*, vol. 2, pl. 239B

Fig. 5.5
Shangtön Chöbar
Mural, Kunzang Tse College, Gongkar;
ca. 1930s
Photo: A. Lustgarten, 2005

Fig. 5.6
Shangtön Chöbar
Mural, Drathang Monastery; ca. 1930s
Photo: Mathias Fermer, 2015

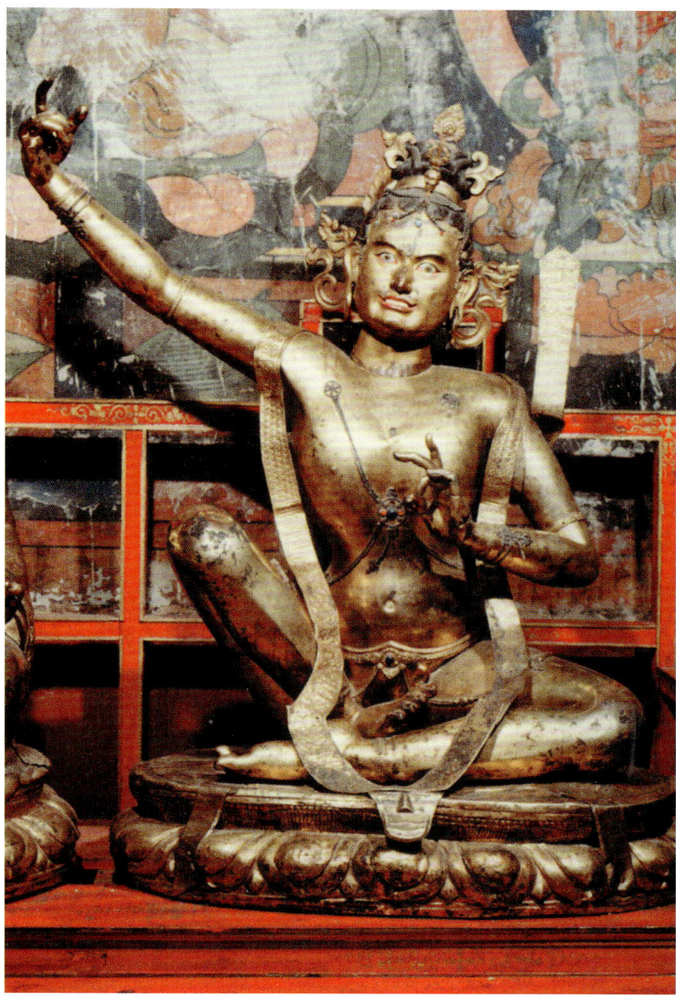

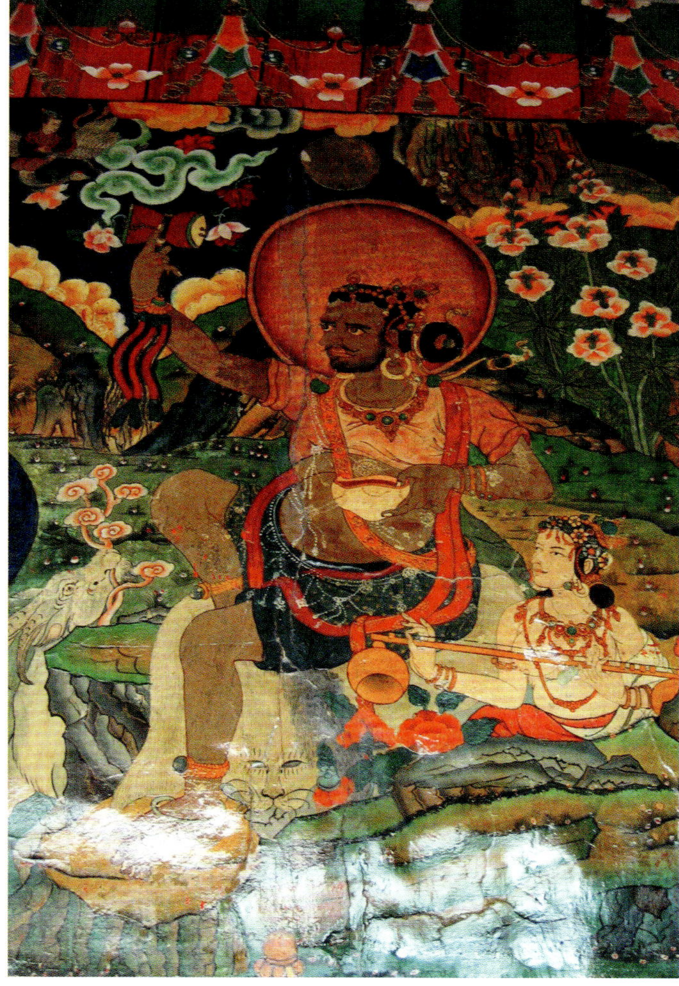

Many of the details of the main figure are so similar to those in Figure 5.5 that the Drathang and Kunzang Tse murals must have followed the same model. Here, once again, Shangtön wears a goatskin cloak with dentate edges. In both paintings, he holds a yellow-beaded rosary, possibly made of amber, and gazes to the right. Both images include a brown cloth or leather sack—possibly for holding food provisions—to the right of Shangtön's rectangular woven mat, on which he sits in the open air. But this painting omits the goat. The main figure's short hair and smile with protruding teeth show that this painting followed the same model as the two preceding examples.

Figure 5.7 depicts the adept Ḍamarupa as a guru of the Lamdre lineage. The hand-held *ḍamaru* drum is the defining characteristic of Ḍamarupa, yet the attribute is not depicted in the sculpture, only implied by the position of his raised right hand. This sculpture shows him staring intently at the viewer, wearing just bone ornaments and a long meditation strap or belt that hangs down over his legs.

Painted depictions of Ḍamarupa (such as Fig. 5.8) and the identically painted adept Virāya, from the eighty-four siddhas (Fig. 5.9a), provide more details than sculpted depictions. In both paintings, for instance, the main figure holds a *ḍamaru* drum. Both paintings contain other similarities that establish their common origins: the adept wears a cropped pink shirt and dark-blue shorts and not only a meditation band but also a long, thin band whose ends hang over his left thigh.

In both paintings, the adept is accompanied by a female consort (Figs. 5.8 and 5.9a). One striking detail is what she holds before her, in both hands: an

FIG. 5.7
The Great Adept Ḍamarupa as a Guru of the Lamdre
Gilt-copper
Mindröling; second half of the fifteenth century
H: 41 ¼ in. (105 cm)
Photo: U. von Schroeder
Literature: von Schroeder 2001, *Buddhist Sculptures in Tibet*, vol. 2, no. 237A

FIG. 5.8
The Adept Ḍamarupa
Mural, Kunzang Tse College, Gongkar; ca. 1930s
Photo: A. Lustgarten, 2005

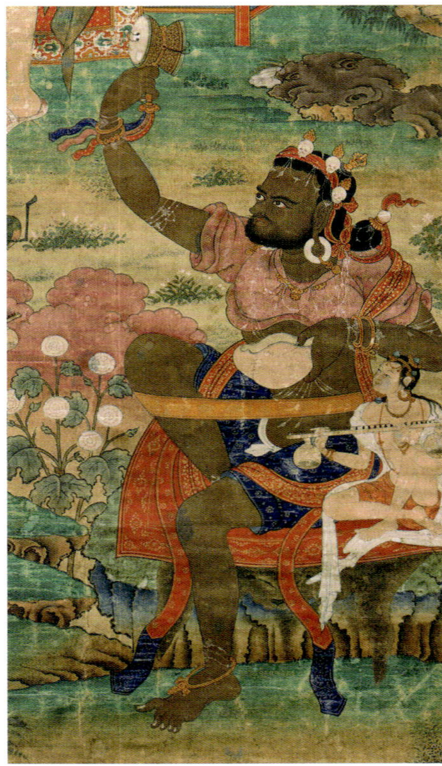

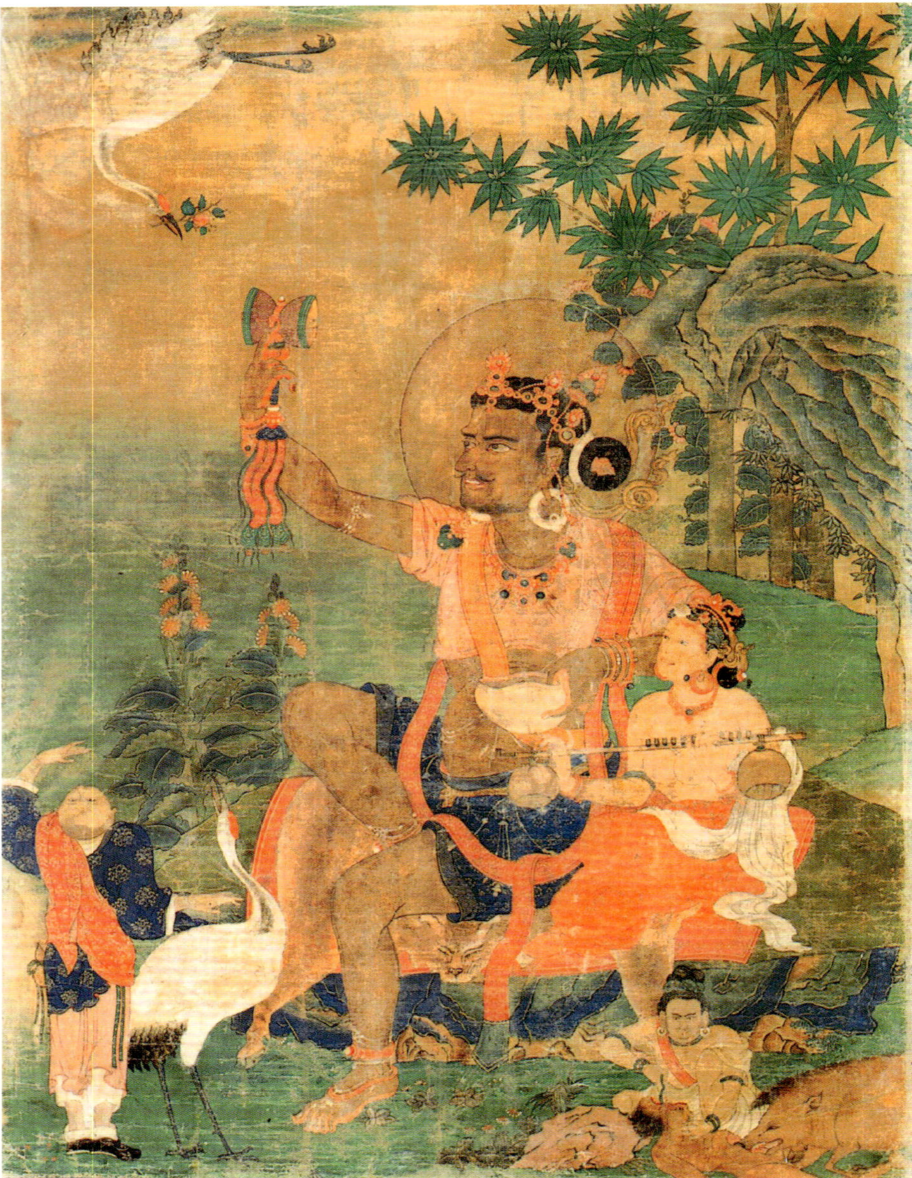

Indian *vīṇā*, a string instrument with resonating gourds prominently depicted on both ends. The consort and her instrument link the two paintings to a special Khyenri tradition.

Khyentse Chenmo had a fine eye for details. For instance, he made every effort to depict hair, dress, and other accouterments of his figures accurately, including the musical instruments they sometimes carried. For Indian adepts or seers, he seems to have preferred the Indian *vīṇā* over the Chinese or Central Asian lute. I will discuss both instruments in more detail in chapter 7 (Figs. 7.19–7.34).

Figure 5.9b confirms in many ways the presence of Khyentse Chenmo's hand in the preceding two examples. I think this painting is by Khyentse, or it is a careful later copy. This thangka depicts the great adept Ḍamarupa, again as a guru of the Lamdre lineage, and it may have belonged to one of the sets commissioned by Dorjedenpa. Ḍamarupa's *vīṇā*-holding consort is depicted larger and more beautifully than in the preceding painting (Fig. 5.9a). The artist added a striking pair of cranes with

bright-red crowns; even though their necks are mostly white, they are meant to be red-crown or Manchurian cranes, which have black necks. Cranes occur in several of Khyentse's known works; here, one stands on the ground near a minor human figure. Bird and man look up at the other crane flying in the sky, with a flowering twig in its beak. In this mostly peaceful landscape, Khyentse Chenmo radically changes the mood with a gruesome charnel scene in the bottom right corner. The scene includes a large wild boar eating the side of a human corpse while one of Ḍamarupa's fellow siddhas intently works on the head of the corpse.

FIG. 5.9A
The Adept Virāya as one of Eighty-four Great Adepts
Detail of Three Mahāsiddhas (HAR 65349)

FIG. 5.9B
The Adept Ḍamarupa as Guru of Lamdre Lineage
second half of the fifteenth century
Private Collection
(HAR 10813)

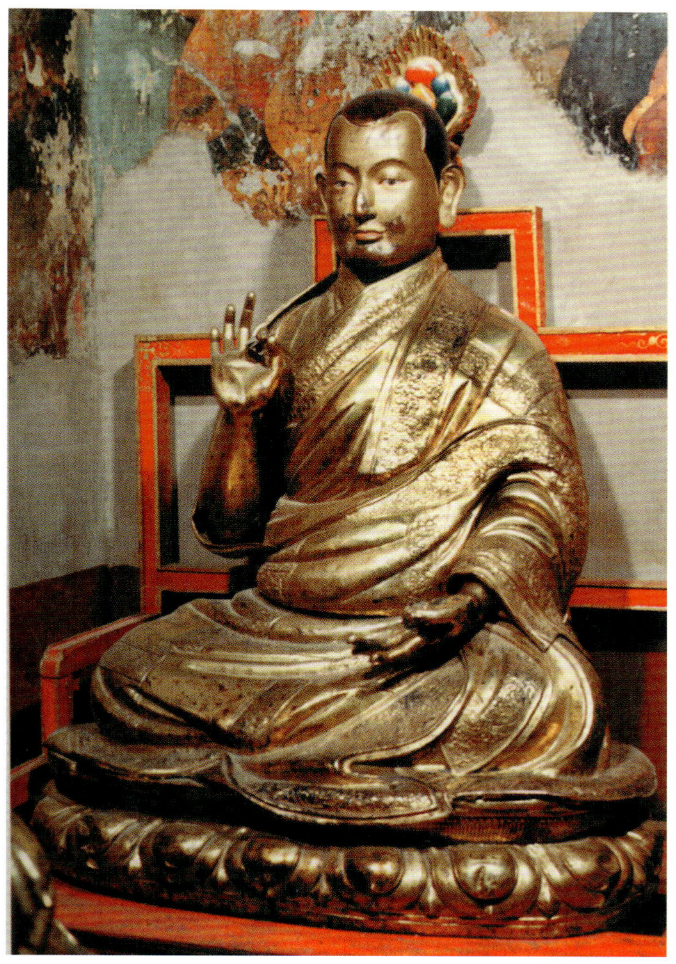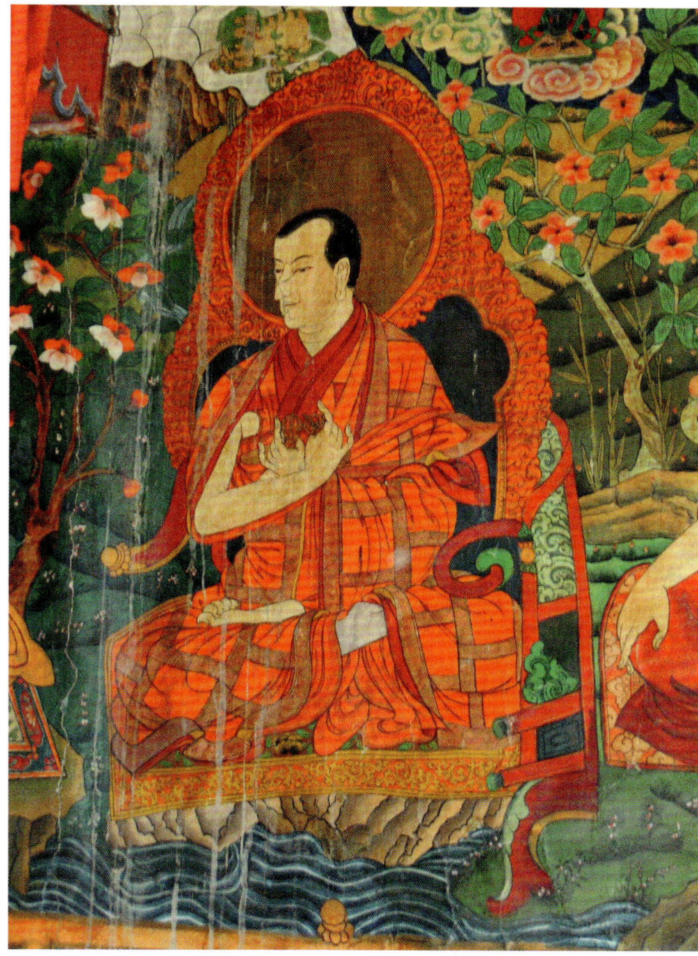

Depictions of Lama Dampa Sönam Gyaltshen

Another example of statuary from the set at Mindröling, Figure 5.10 belongs to a different iconographic type and nationality. He is not an Indian tantric adept but an ordained Tibetan Buddhist monk, whose youth is indicated by black hair. He holds his right hand in a gesture of teaching. No identification label is present, but I believe the sculpture depicts Lama Dampa as a guru in the Lamdre lineage. His rounded hairline is distinctive.

Lama Dampa was born a prince of the Sakya Khon family in Tsang, and his mother was from the Shalu Kushang nobility in Tsang. But later in life, and until his death in 1375, he was one of the most eminent spiritual teachers of the Phagmotrupa rulers in Ü province. Regarding Lama Dampa and his connection with the Phagmotrupa court, Leonard van der Kuijp provided many details in his study of the Lhorong

Chöjung. For instance, he mentions his links with Trakpa Changchup (Grags pa Byang chub) and the sudden passing of Jamyang Gushrī ('Jam dbyangs Gu shrī) in 1373. Van der Kuijp devoted two other articles to exploring the collected works of Lama Dampa.

Figure 5.11 depicts Lama Dampa Sönam Gyaltshen in a painting. Here, his hands hold a vajra and bell to his chest, like Vajradhara, symbolizing his mastery of Vajrayana teachings. His bare feet are visible, and he sits on a very ornate throne. His identification can be assumed because of his position as nineteenth guru in the Lamdre lineage.

Figures 5.12 and 5.13 illustrate Lama Dampa Sönam Gyaltshen's status as a highly esteemed figure in the murals of Gongkar. He appears regularly in the standard iconography because he was counted as one of the three red-robed founding masters of the Sakya tradition, with Sakya Paṇḍita and Chögyal

Fig. 5.10
Lama Dampa Sönam Gyaltshen
Gilt-copper
Now in Mindröling; second half of the fifteenth century
H: 38 ⅝ in. (98 cm)
Photo: U. von Schroeder, 1992
Literature: von Schroeder 2001, *Buddhist Sculptures in Tibet*, vol. 2, pl. 241A

Fig. 5.11
Lama Dampa Sönam Gyaltshen as Guru of Lamdre Lineage
Mural, Kunzang Tse College, Gongkar; ca. 1930s
Photo: A. Lustgarten, 2005

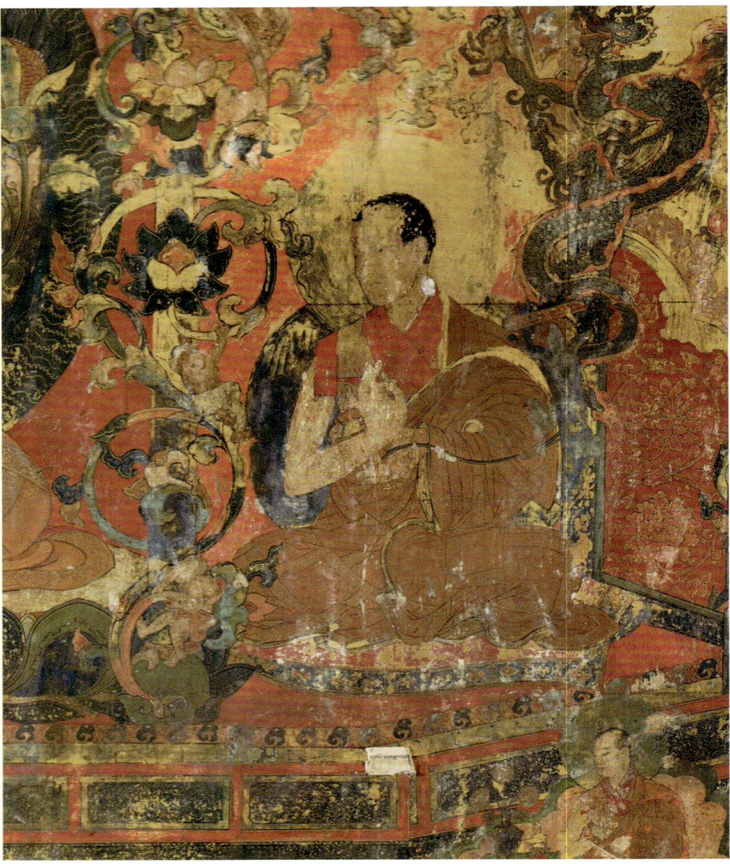
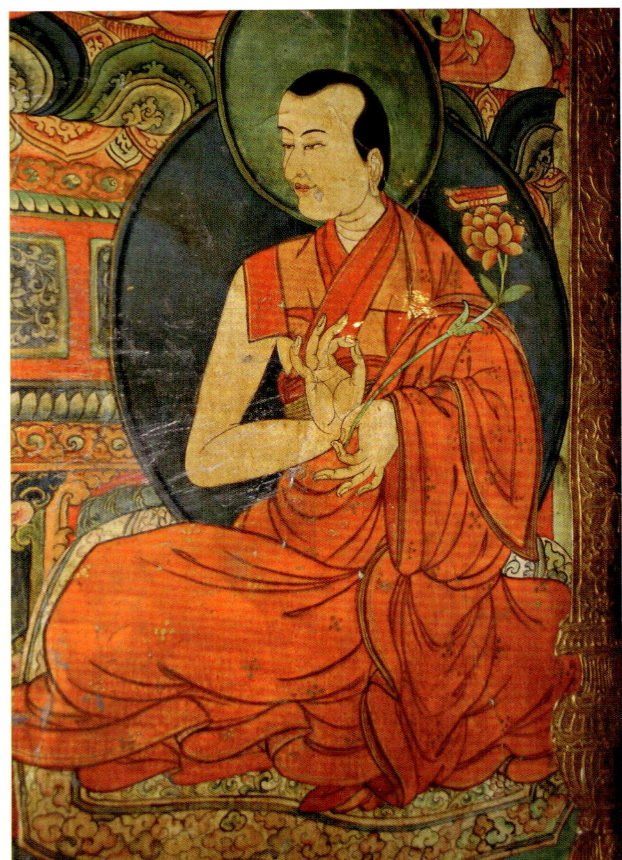

Phakpa. Figure 5.12 shows his depiction in a prominent mural by Khyentse Chenmo, on the first floor in the main building of Gongkar Monastery. Some details of his face can no longer be discerned.

Figure 5.13, too, depicts Lama Dampa as one of the three red-clad masters, in a later mural panel at Kunzang Tse College. It repeats Figure 5.12, a standard depiction at Gongkar and one of his well-known painted portraits. This later copy is valuable because it clearly preserves some details that are difficult

to see in the older and damaged original mural.

Figure 5.14 may be the best-known image of Lama Dampa outside Gongkar. In this painted sculpture in the Lamdre Lhakhang of Gyantse's Palkhor Monastery, he appears in a different posture: seated, with both hands hanging down, with robes covering both shoulders.

In general, paintings and sculptures of Lama Dampa from places other than Gongkar and from other periods vary widely in their faces and gestures. His original physiognomic traits are no longer recognizable in them. One early portrait with hand and footprints survived in the seventeenth century.[340]

DEPICTIONS OF THEKCHEN CHÖJE

Thekchen Chöje, until his death in 1425, was undoubtedly the most eminent lama of the Sakya Khön family and a key lama in the most important lineages of Gongkar Monastery, most notably his special transmission of the Lamdre.

Figure 5.15 depicts him in his role as a lineage lama, a venerable, fully ordained master with both hands on his knees, his most common pose. His hair is short and silver, descending slightly in the center of his forehead. He seems to smile, gently pursing his lips, with lines forming around his mouth.

Figure 5.16, a later Gongkar mural, depicts Thekchen Chöje similarly, in his role as a lineal guru. His posture, face, and dress are very similar to the sculpture, Figure 5.15. But this mural shows him sitting on a mat with a Chinese-style curved throne back. He smiles with kindly reserve, but his dress and the painting's setting are unremarkable.

Figure 5.17 also depicts Thekchen Chöje as a guru of the Lamdre. This later mural survives at Drathang Monastery and probably depicts him as number 21 in the lineage. Once again, he is portrayed as a silver-haired master who smiles with gently puckered lips, with lines forming around his mouth. But in

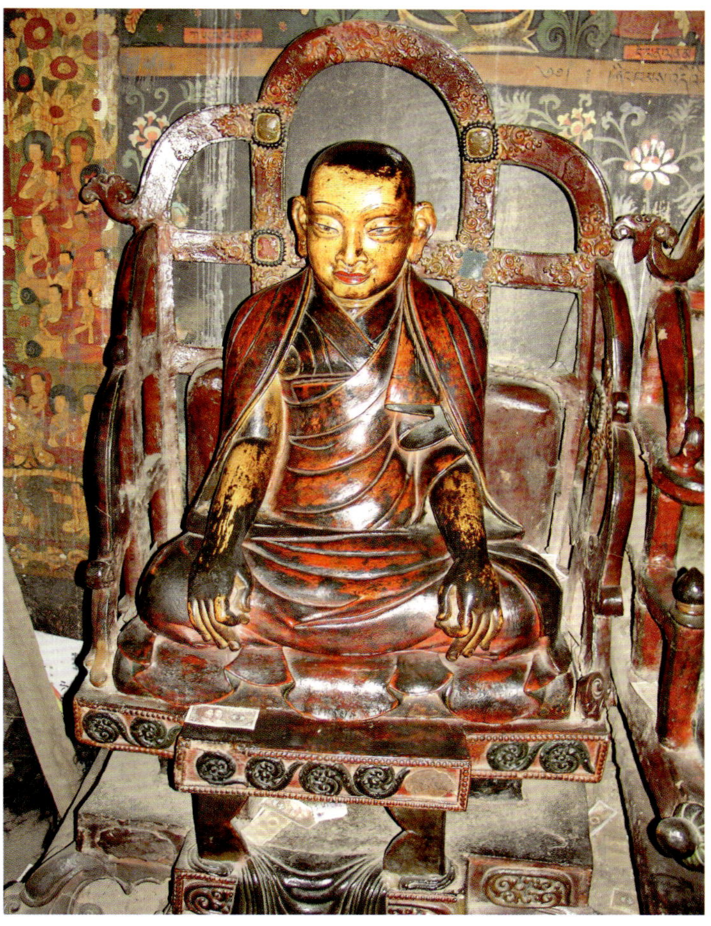

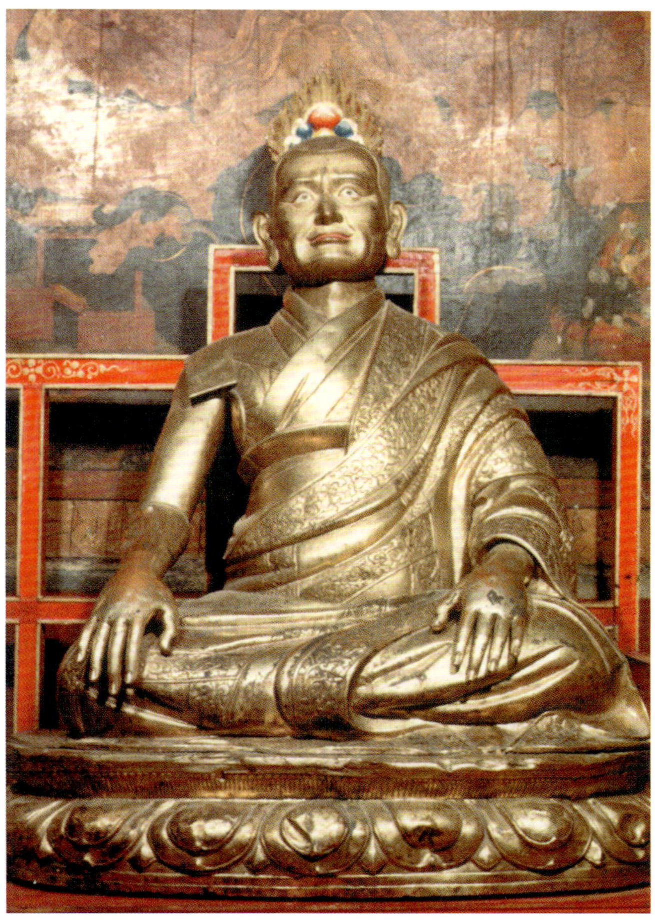

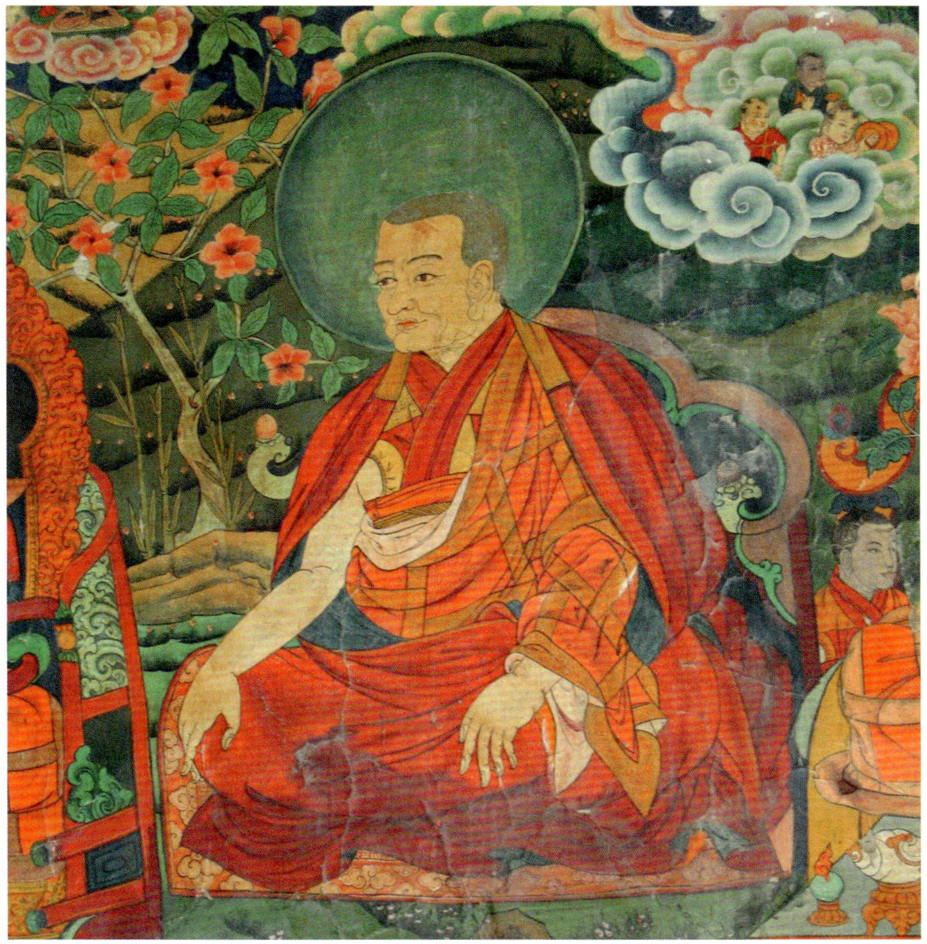

Fig. 5.14
Lama Dampa Sönam Gyaltshen
Gyantse, Tsuklakkhang, Lamdre Lhakhang;
1425
Photo: Tsechang Penba Wangdu, 2005
Literature: Lo Bue and Ricca 1990, pl. 178

Fig. 5.15
Thekchen Chöje
Gilt-copper
Now in Mindröling; second half of the fif-
teenth century
H: 36 ¼ in. (92 cm)
Photo: U. von Schroeder, 1992
Literature: von Schroeder 2001, *Buddhist
Sculptures in Tibet*, vol. 2, pl. 241C

Fig. 5.16
Thekchen Chöje
Mural, Kunzang Tse College, Gongkar;
ca. 1930s
Photo: A. Lustgarten, 2005

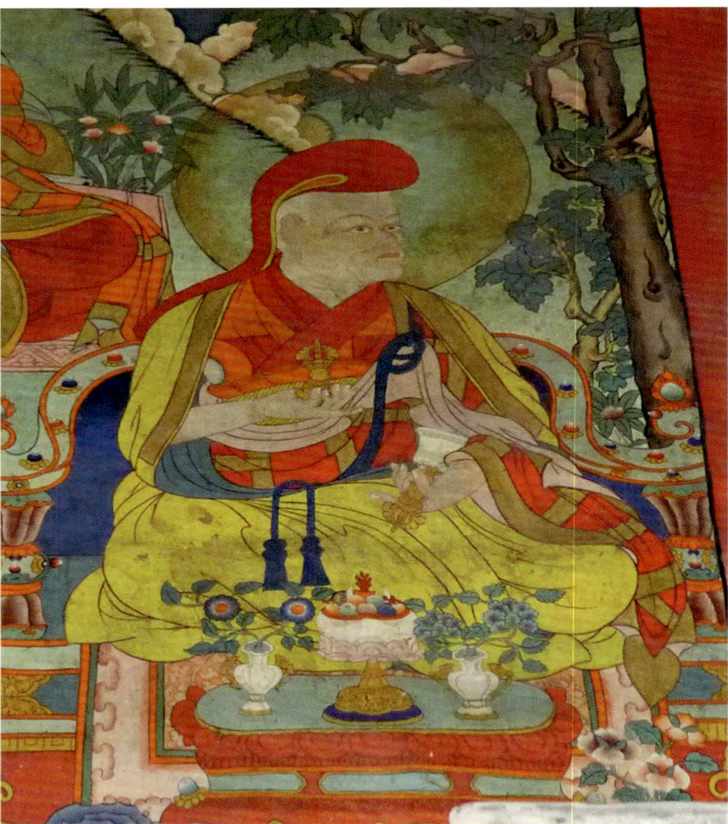

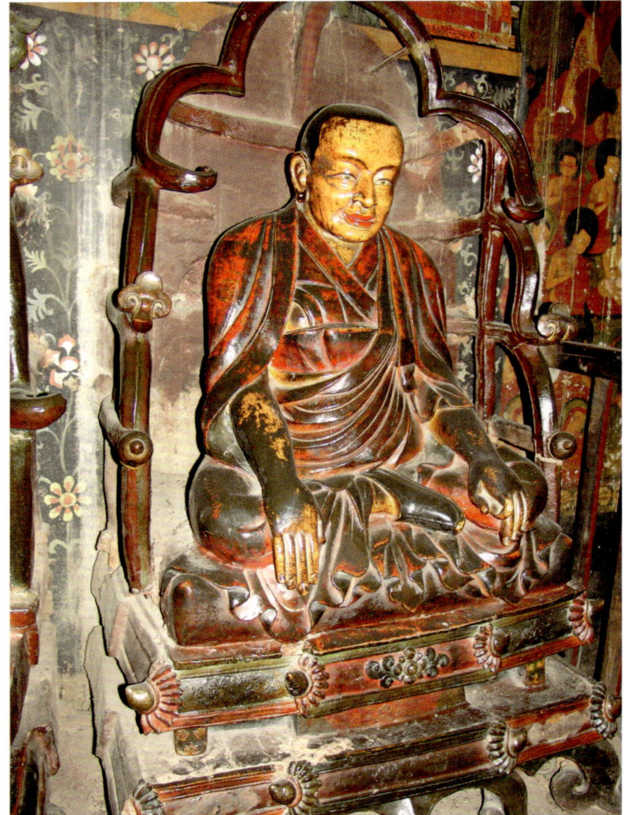

other respects, this painting differs from the preceding two examples and enriches the known repertoire of his depictions. Sitting on an expensive throne, he holds a golden vajra and bell, and he wears a Sakya-style pandit hat that is draped back, lying flat over his head. His robes, too, are decidedly more colorful here; they are fastened with heavy blue cords with blue tassels that drape over his yellow robe. The sumptuous quality of the portrait possibly reflects the fact that he was the recipient of the emperor's largesse, which included special robes. One of his biographies stressed the fact that

he possessed many fine things, including a vajra and bell made of gold, which he holds here.

Figure 5.18 shows a younger Thekchen Chöje Kunga Tashi as a painted non-metal sculpture. Located at Gyantse in the Tsuklakkhang, Lamdre Lhakhang, along the northern wall, it is the sole accessible portrait of Thekchen Chöje outside Lhokha. It demonstrates that his iconography at Drathang and Gongkar (Figs. 5.15 and 5.16) also prevailed in some circles of Tsang that were closely linked to him.[341]

Iconographic Links with Surviving Murals in the Kunzang Tse College

A complete set of murals at Kunzang Tse College depicts Kunga Namgyal's main Lamdre lineage. On page eight of Kunga Namgyal's record of teachings received, he was guru number 23 in the main lineage.[342] (See appendix B.) That written version counts Shang Könchok Pal as number 16 and Sakya

Butön as number 20. However, a second version of that lineage, by Gyatön, was followed in the Gongkar sculptures of Lamdre gurus. This features Tshokgom and Nyenchenpa as numbers 16 and 17 and omits numbers 16, Shang, and 20, Sakya Butön. But since Shang Könchok Pal was a major transmitter of the lineage and was Phakpa's main disciple, I include him as number 15b, in case Gyatön omitted him by mistake.

1. Vajradhara (rGyal ba Khyab bdag rDo rje 'chang)
2. Nairātmyā (dPal ye shes kyi mkha' gro bDag med ma)
3. Virūpa (mThu stobs kyi dbang phyug mGon po Shri Bi ru pa)
4. Kṛṣṇapāda or Kāṇha (Shar phyogs Nag po pa)
5. Ḍamarupa
6. Awadhutipa
7. Paṇchen Gayadhara
8. Drokmi Lotsāwa (sGra sgyur Bla chen 'Brog mi)
9. Setön Kunrik (Se ston Kun rig)
10. Shangtön Gönpawa Chubar

(Zhang dGon pa ba)

11. Sachen Kunga Nyingpo (Sa skya
    pa Chen po)
12. Lobpön Sönam Tsemo (Je btsun
    rTse mo)
13. Jetsün Trakpa Gyaltshen (rNal
    'byor dbang phyug Grags pa rgyal
    mtshan)
14. Sakya Paṇḍita (gNas lnga yongs
    su rdzogs pa'i Paṇ chen)
15. Chögyal Phakpa ('Gro mgon
    Chos kyi rgyal po)
[15b. Shang Könchok Palwa]
16. Tshokgom (Disciple of Sakya
    Paṇḍita)
17. Nyenchenpa (Disc. of Tshokgom)
18. Namsa Drakphukpa (Nam bza'
    Brag phug pa)
19. Lama Dampa Sönam Gyaltshen
    (dPal ldan Bla ma dam pa bSod
    nams rgyal mtshan)
20. Mati Panchen (Ma ti Paṇ chen)
21. Thekchen Chögyal (Theg chen
    Chos kyi rgyal po)
22. Drakthok Chöje Sönam Sangpo
    (Brag thog Chos rje bSod nams
    bzang po)
23. Gongkar Dorjedenpa Kunga
    Namgyal

The lineage murals in Kunzang Tse
College depict twenty-three lineal gurus,
from Vajradhara to Dorjedenpa. Based on
their style, I estimate that they date to the
first half of the twentieth century; their
dating to about the 1930s is explained
below in chapter 12. From the iconography, they follow the order listed immediately above: that of Gyatön's description
of the main sculpture sets at Gongkar.
The lineage is shared by all Lamdre
schools down to number 15, Phakpa, after
which they deviate slightly.

The Final Six Gurus at Kunzang Tse College

Here, the lineage is that of Thekchen
Chöje and of his uncle, Lama Dampa
Sönam Gyaltshen, who was highly

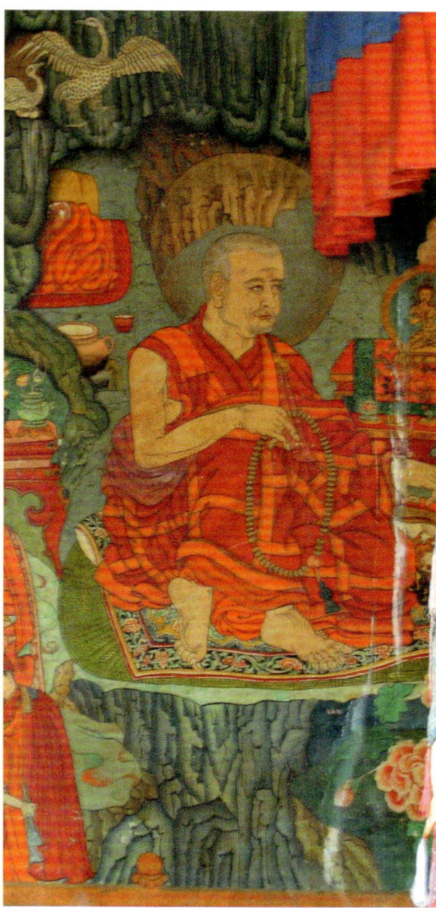

venerated by the Gongkar tradition as
one of the three red-robed masters (*dmar
po rnam gsum*) of the Sakya tradition—
they have virtually the same spiritual
status as the five revered founders (*rje
btsun gong ma lnga*). Murals depicting
this group of three masters survive at
Gongkar.

To consider the final six masters
who represent Gongkar's special lineage
in the Kunzang Tse College murals, I
present them individually in chronological order.

The eighteenth guru, depicted
in Figure 5.19 seated in a meditation
cave, must be Drakphukpa ("the yogi of
Namsa Cave"). He was a highly accomplished guru of Lama Dampa.

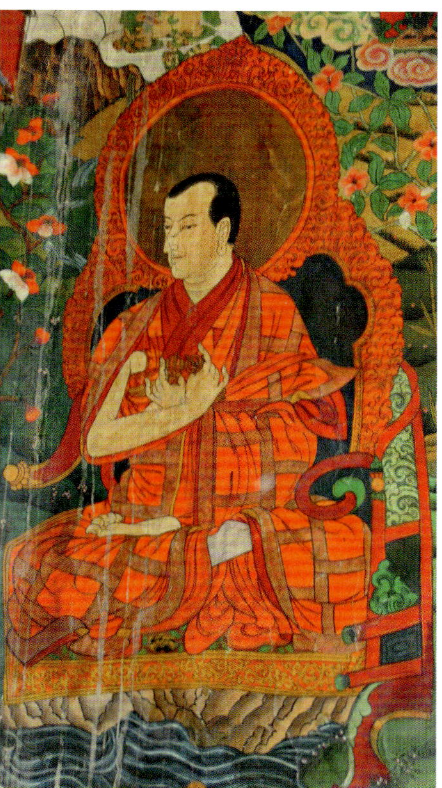

Figure 5.20 is the nineteenth guru
in this sequence. He agrees fairly closely
with the iconography of Lama Dampa,
as depicted in other Gongkar murals (see
Figs. 5.12–5.13). Note, for instance, the
same rounded receding hairline.

According to the version of the
Lamdre lineage in Kunga Namgyal's
record of teachings received, Figure
5.21 might depict the twentieth guru,
Sakya Butön Wangchuk Dar, who was
Thekchen Chöje's second Lamdre
teacher. Though he is a fairly obscure
lama in the histories, he might be
granted a place in the transmission,
thanks to his unbroken daily practice of
Hevajra, which was a prerequisite for
teachers of that lineage. He appeared as
a minor figure in Figure 1.31.

But the lineage here seems to skip
Sakya Butön, and the painting depicts

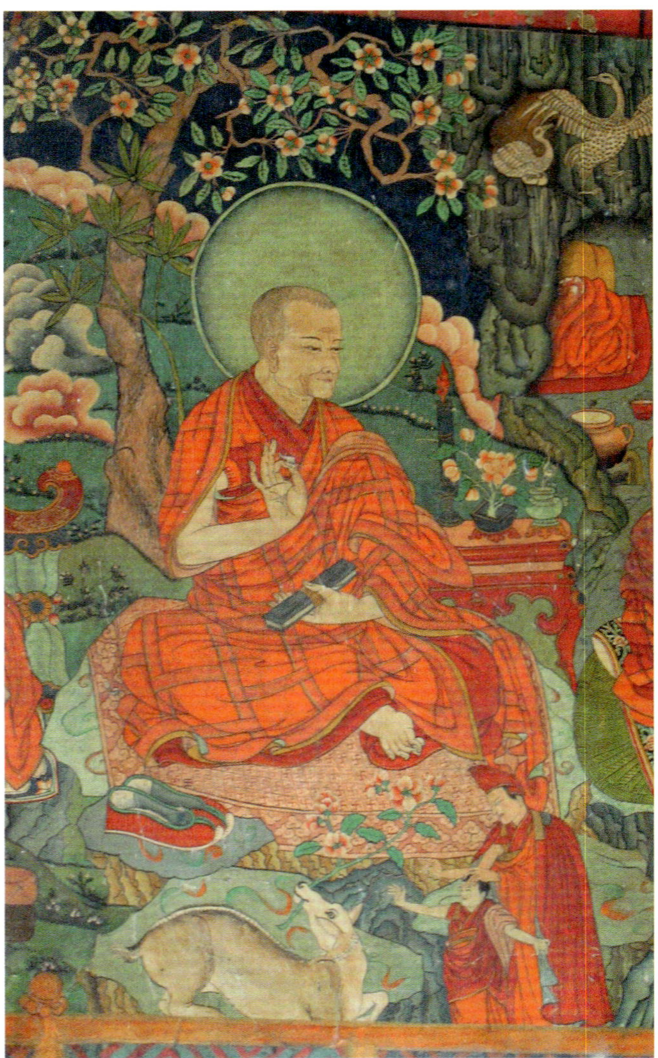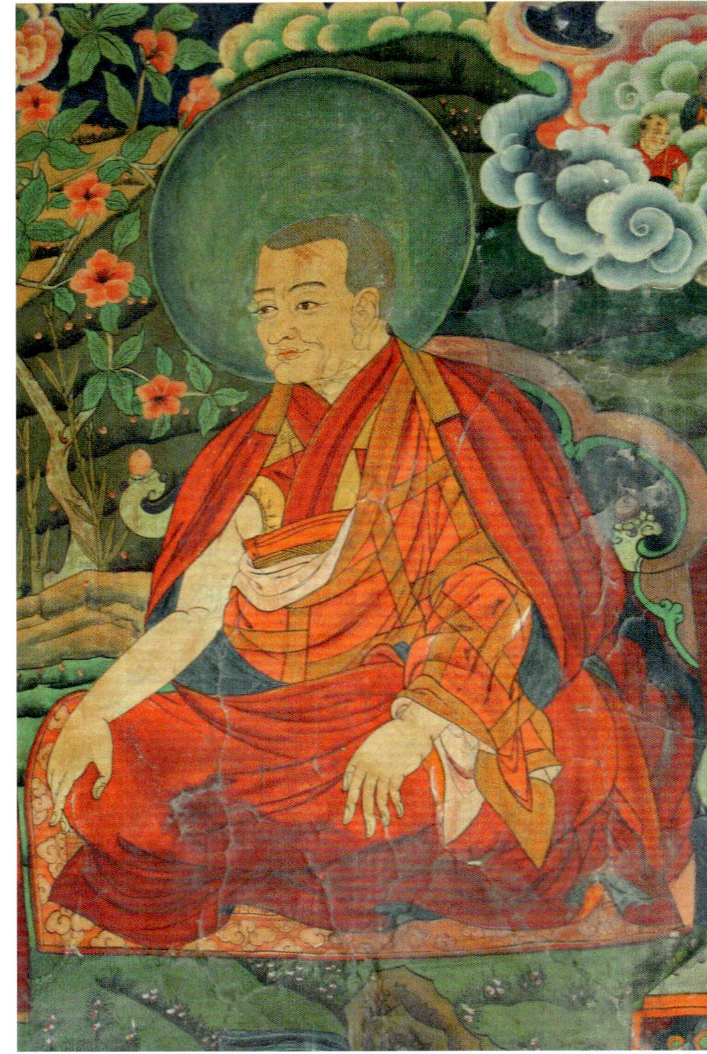

instead Sazang Mati Panchen, who was a more eminent teacher. Note that he holds a book, a symbol of great learning.

According to the lineage, Figure 5.22 must depict Thekchen Chöje Kunga Tashi, given his known iconography: a venerable master with both hands lowered, placed on his knees. His presence here proves that his special transmission of the Lamdre was the one practiced in Gongkar.

The lama depicted in Figure 5.23 is indubitably Drakthok Chöje Sönam Sangpo, Dorjedenpa's main guru for the Lamdre. Though no detailed biographies of him survive, he was acknowledged to be one of Thekchen Chöje's most eminent disciples in the realm of Lamdre practice.

The youthful-looking master of Figure 5.24 must be Gongkar Dorjedenpa Kunga Namgyal, who concludes the Lamdre lineage murals at Kunzang Tse.

Lamdre Lineage in Recent Murals of Drathang Monastery

The identities of some of the last six lamas depicted in the Kunzang Tse murals can be confirmed by their similar depictions in a pair of mural panels in Drathang Monastery that also date to about the 1930s. In the last two panels we find guru numbers 18 through 23, the same six as in the murals of Kunzang Tse College:

18. Drakphukpa
19. Lama Dampa
20. Sazang Mati Panchen

Fig. 5.21
Lineal Master Number 20, Sazang Mati Panchen
Mural, Kunzang Tse College, Gongkar; ca. 1930s
Photo: A. Lustgarten, 2005

Fig. 5.22
Lineal Master Number 21, Thekchen Chöje
Mural, Kunzang Tse College, Gongkar; ca. 1930s
Photo: A. Lustgarten, 2005

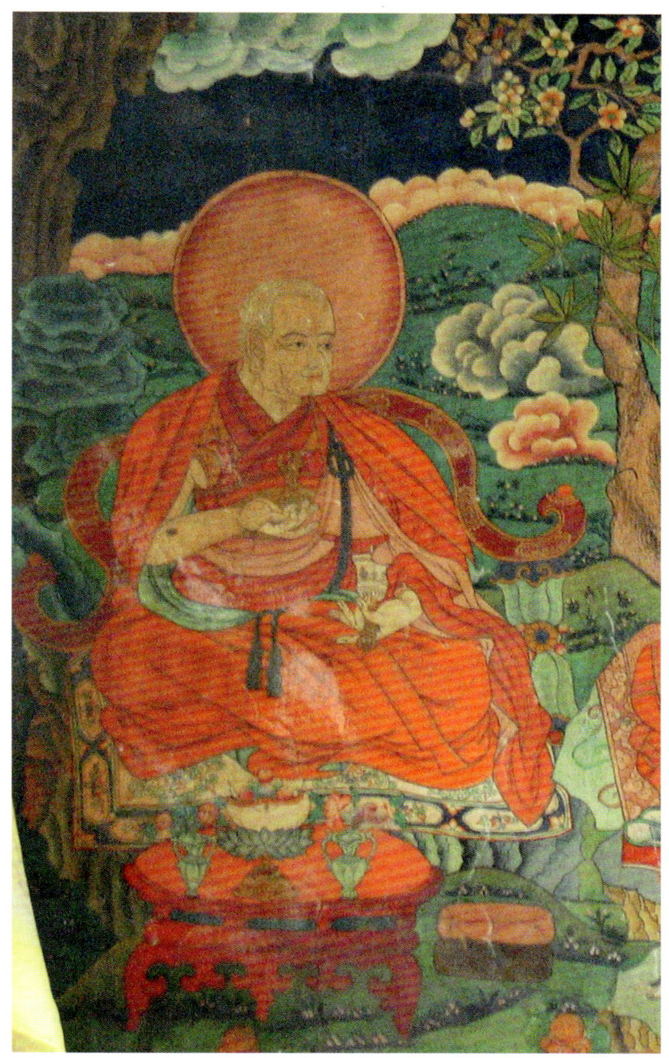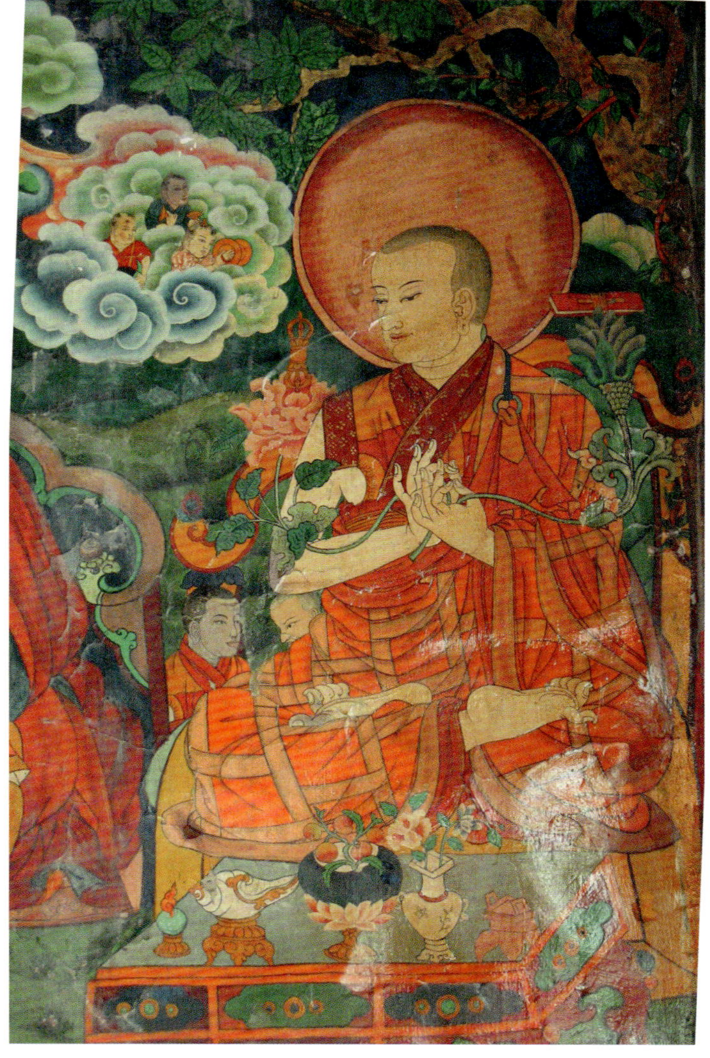

Fig. 5.23
Lineal Master Number 22, Drakthok Chöje
Sönam Sangpo
Mural, Kunzang Tse College, Gongkar;
ca. 1930s
Photo: A. Lustgarten, 2005

Fig. 5.24
Lineal Master Number 23, Gongkar
Dorjedenpa Kunga Namgyal
Mural, Kunzang Tse College, Gongkar;
ca. 1930s
Photo: A. Lustgarten, 2005

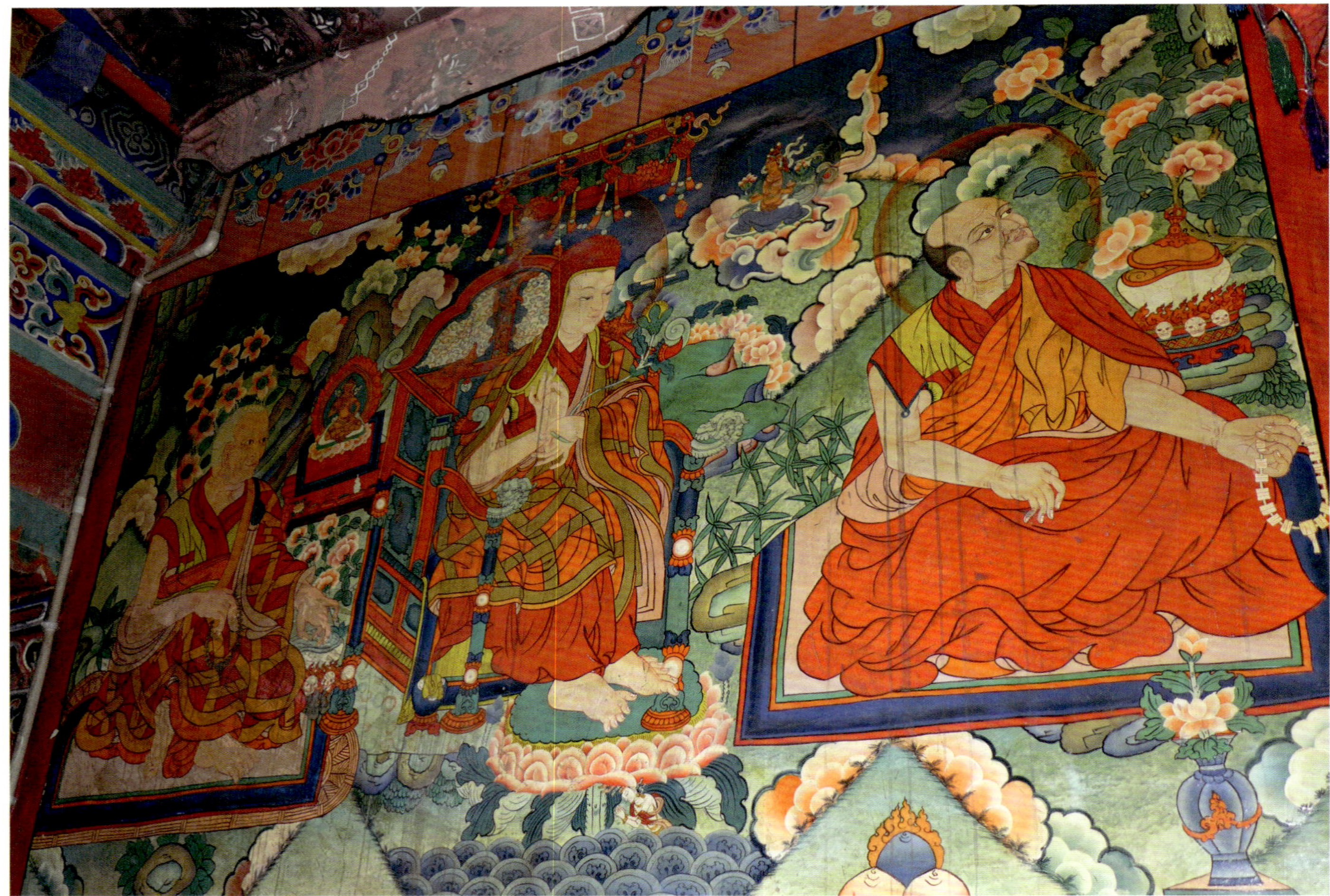

21. Thekchen Chöje
22. Drakthok Chöje
23. Dorjedenpa

The arrangement of the panels, however, is unorthodox and the ordering of gurus unexpected. (See Figs. 5.25 and 5.26 and Diagrams [D] and [E].)

Figure 5.25 depicts three gurus of the Lamdre, numbers 18, 19, and 22. (See Diagram [D].) Depicted in the center is guru number 19, Lama Dampa, with bare feet, wearing a red, rounded pandit hat, and seated on a throne. To his right, and oddly lower, is guru number 18, Drakphukpa, with both hands hanging down and his left hand holding a rosary. To the left is number 22, Drakthok Chöje, who holds a rosary in his right hand and extends his other hand down.

Figure 5.26 depicts three other gurus of the Lamdre lineage, numbers 20, 21, and 23. (See Diagram [E].) In the center is number 20, possibly Sazang Mati Panchen, who holds a book and has taken his slippers off. To his right is number 21, Thekchen Chöje, sitting on an elaborate throne. He holds a golden vajra and bell and wears special elaborate robes with special straps. To the left, the lineage ends with guru number 23, Gongkar Dorjedenpa. He looks youthful, with hands in the teaching gesture. He grasps the stem of a lotus flower topped by a book of holy scripture (*pustaka*), his identifying attributes.

Thus I have presented the final panels from two mural sets of Kunzang Tse and Drathang. They are two of the only surviving sets of murals depicting the final gurus of the Thekchen Chöje lineage, and they provide the only hope for eventually identifying the unnamed late lineal gurus in the uninscribed set of metal sculptures at Mindröling.

FIG. 5.25
Three Gurus of the Lamdre (nos. 18, 19, and 22)
Murals, Drathang Monastery; ca. 1930s
Photo: M. Fermer, 2015

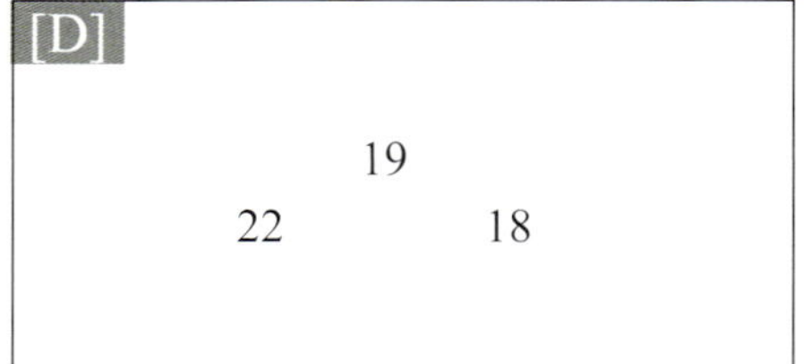

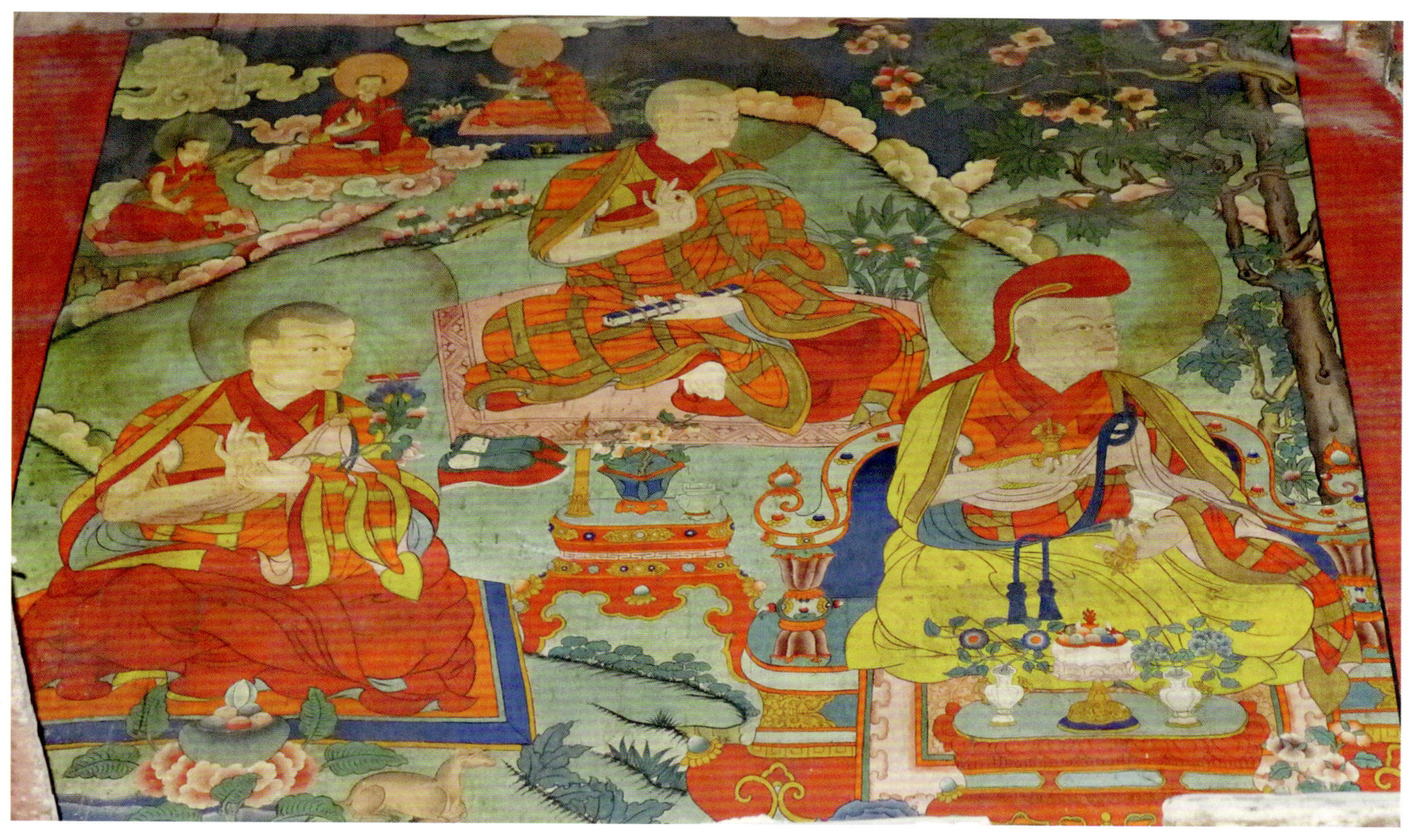

Fig. 5.26
Three Gurus of the Lamdre (nos. 20, 21, and 23)
Murals, Drathang Monastery; ca. 1930s
Photo: M. Fermer, 2015

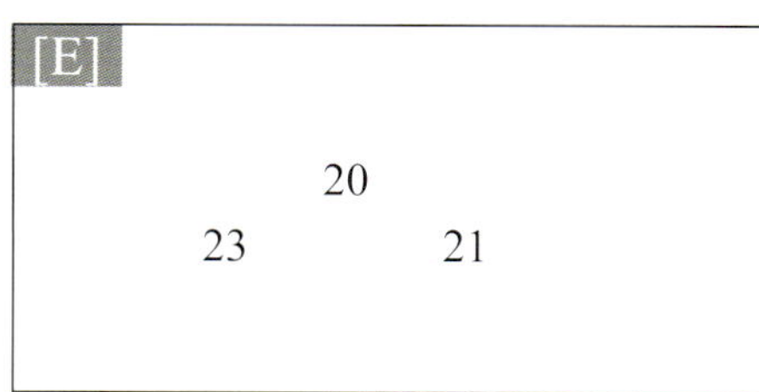
[E]
20
23   21

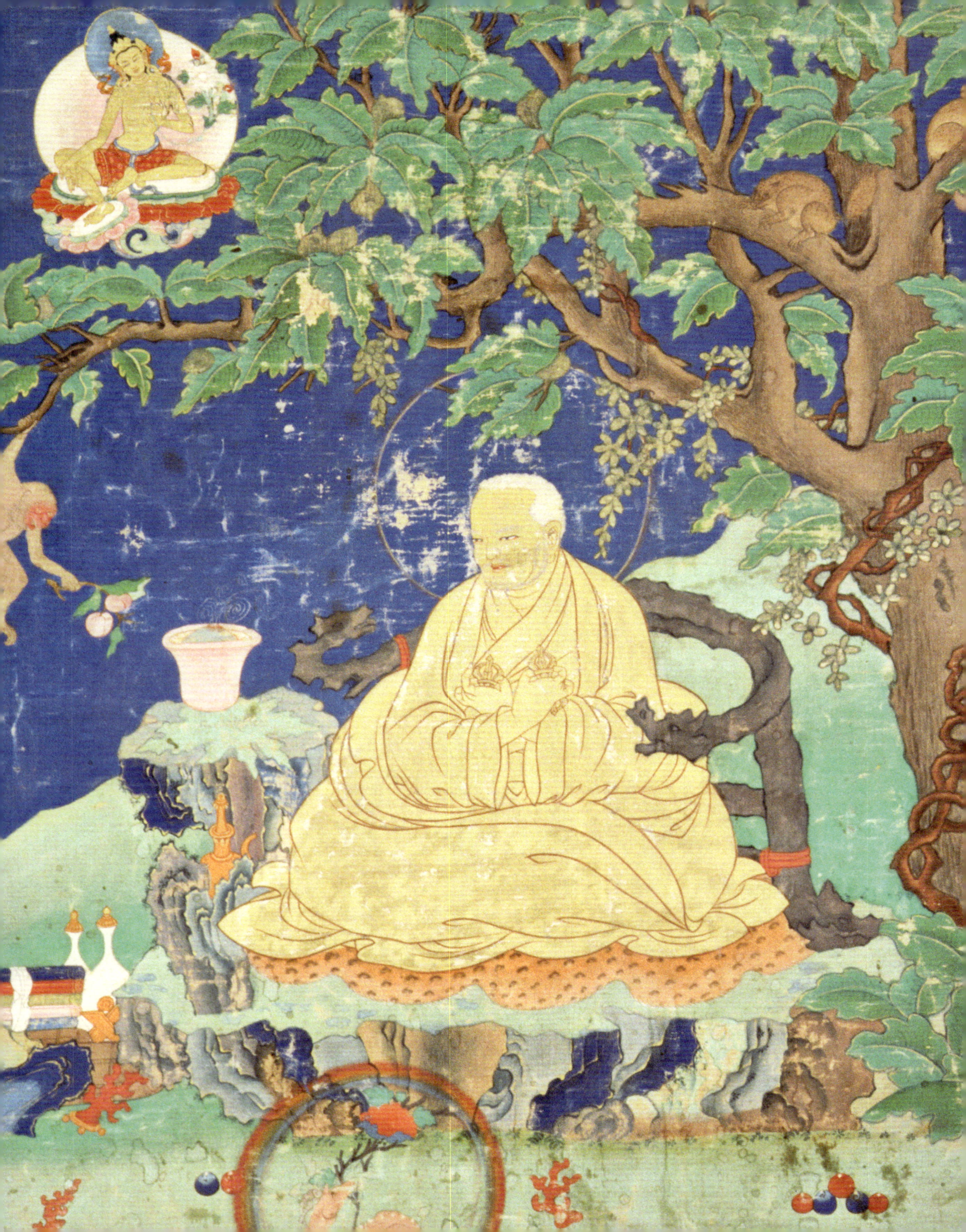

Four Sculptures from Drathang and Related Khyenri Paintings

THIS CHAPTER continues the investigation of chapter 5, presenting four more sculptures from the Drathang set of Lamdre lineal gurus, those portraying the great adept Virūpa, Jetsün Trakpa, Sakya Paṇḍita, and Chögyal Phakpa. These four sculptures provide a valuable point of departure for better understanding the iconography of paintings rendered in the Khyenri style. By examining a few examples of corresponding paintings, we can also appreciate Khyentse Chenmo's unusual penchant for depicting rich historical details.

In this chapter, I will also examine a few relevant later murals of Lamdre gurus from Kunzang Tse or Drathang that confirm the local survival of special iconographic traditions specific to Gongkar and Khyentse. As we shall see, the later murals can be linked not only with the iconography of the appropriate figure from the set of copper gilt sculptures, but can often be directly related in compositional details to early thangka paintings attributed to Khyentse (such as in Fig. 6.16, Sakya Paṇḍita, and Fig. 6.28, Phakpa).

REVOLUTIONARY FEATURE: TRANSPARENT HEAD NIMBUSES

Some of these paintings contain stylistic features that were revolutionary in the 1460s. Khyentse Chenmo filled his backgrounds with Chinese-inspired predominantly green landscapes, an innovation that both he and Menthangpa were famous for. He has based the setting on motifs and colors derived from Chinese painting such as blue-green mountains, gnarled trees, smooth ground plain with undercut escarpments, and faceted rocks. But Khyentse also encircled the heads of the main figures with nimbuses that seem to be transparent: they are depicted by a simple golden line (outlined with a single thin and almost invisible line of lac dye) and subtle shading while the interior of the nimbus continues the surrounding landscape. Such head nimbuses could be highlighted by a very thin application of lac dye, which made the presence of transparent nimbuses more noticeable. To my knowledge, transparent head nimbuses were never adopted by painters of the Menri school.

At times, Khyentse Chenmo omitted the head nimbus completely, that is, he did not even paint the golden ring; he frequently chose this approach, for instance, when painting great adepts. Leaving out the head nimbus was possible within the painting tradition that Khyentse learned as a student; his teacher, Paljor Rinchen of Nenying, did not paint head nimbuses on nine of the eighty-four great adepts in the Lamdre Lhakhang of Gyantse, but he never used transparent head nimbuses indicated by rings of gold, as Khyentse Chenmo did.[343]

DEPICTIONS OF VIRŪPA

The Sakya tradition features as many as six established forms for depicting Virūpa. According to the text "Notes on the Six Bodily Forms [of Virūpa]" (*sKu'i rnam 'gyur drug gi zin bris*), which is preserved in the collected writings of Ngorchen Kunga Zangpo (1382–1457), they are:

(1) Holding the sun as witness (*nyi ma gdeng bar 'dzud pa*). With a body reddish brown in color, he holds his right hand in a threatening gesture and with his left holds a nectar-filled skullcup to his heart, sitting in posture of royal dignity (*rgyal po rol pa'i stabs*; *rājalīla*).

(2) Turning back the Ganges River (*gangā bzlog pa*). His body color is dark blue; with the palm of his right hand, he presses on his seat; with his left, he makes a threatening gesture; and he sits in *sattvaparyanka,* the loosely cross-legged posture.

(3) Dharma teaching (*chos 'chad pa*). He holds two hands to his heart in the dharma-teaching posture and sits in the loosely cross-legged posture.

(4) Transforming things into gold (*gser 'gyur*). He presses his right hand on his seat, he holds his left in a fist on his left knee, and he sits in a slightly erect or upright (*krong nge ba*) posture.

(5) Splitting the image (*lha rten dgas pa).* He raises his right hand to his

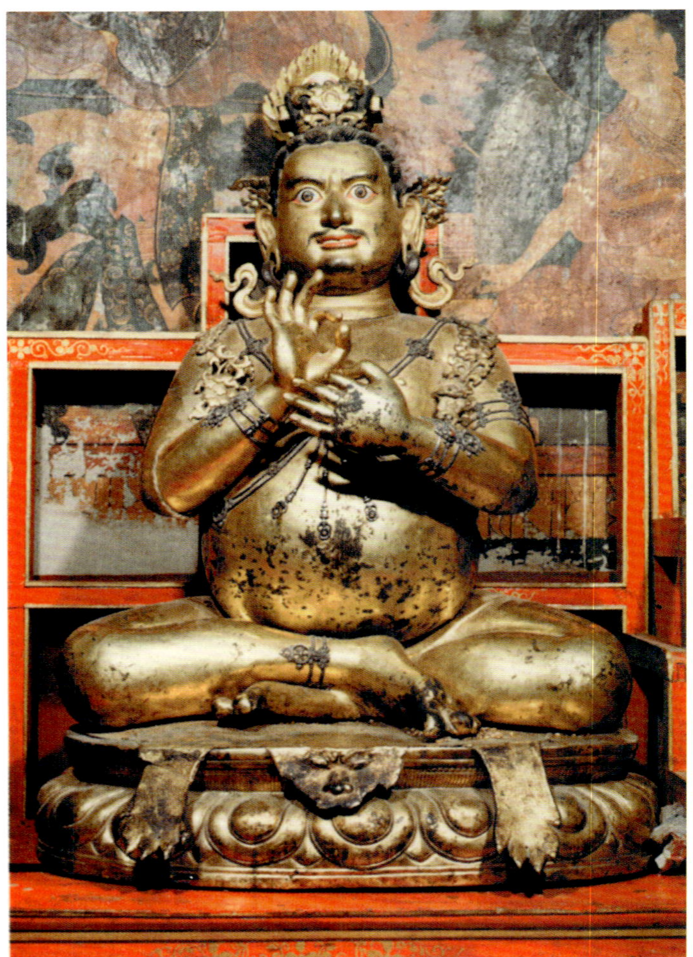

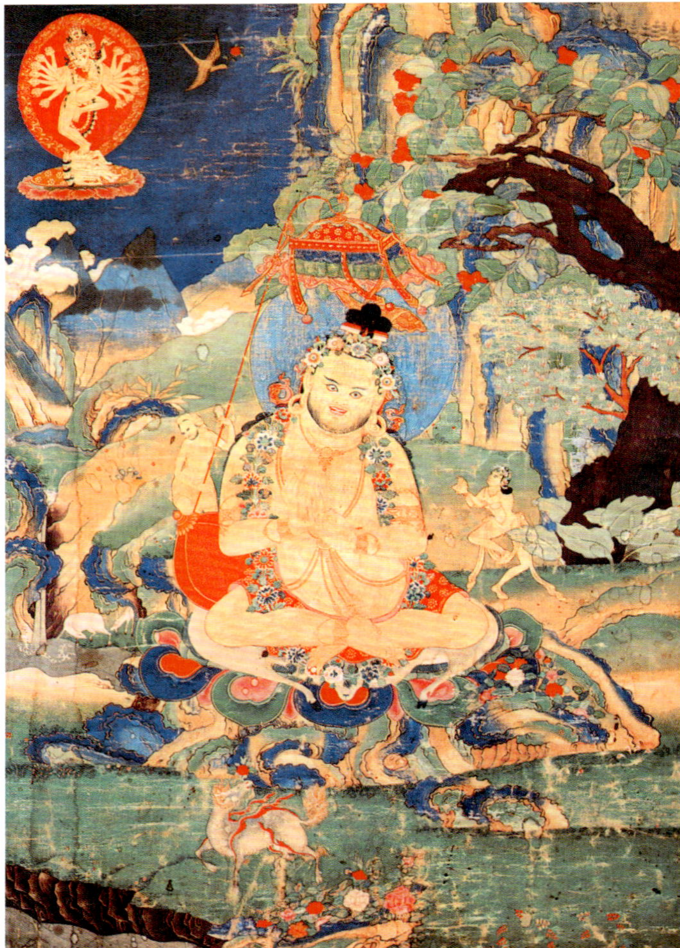

forehead in salutation, rests his
left hand on his seat, and sits in
the loose cross-legged posture.

(6) Subduing the non-Buddhist deity
(*mu stegs kyi lha mnan pa*). With
each thumb pressed against a
little finger, he performs the three-
pronged-vajra gesture; holding his
hands to his heart, he presses the
fourth toe of his left foot against
the fourth toe of his right one.[344]

Those writings specified that Virūpa's
skin in the first form is to be colored
reddish brown ("dark red," *dmar nag*),
but it may be either dark blue or light
blue for the remaining five forms.
This description of Virūpa's forms is
said to have been "compiled by the
Yogi Rinchen Dorje from the diverse
minor writings of the Sakya founding
masters."[345] All six forms are based
on prominent episodes from Virūpa's
biography.[346]

Figure 6.1 depicts the great adept
Virūpa as the third lineal guru of the
Lamdre teachings. He commonly appears
in two iconographic forms: hands in the
dharma-teaching gesture (here and in
Figs. 6.2 and 6.3), and one raised arm
to arrest the sun in the sky (Fig. 6.4).
This sculpture shows him gazing with
rapt attention, wearing siddha's bone
ornaments and holding his hands in the
gesture of teaching. His head and shoulders are decorated with long chains or
necklaces of flowers; according to his life
story, he stole them from a flower seller.
His long black hair is tied in a topknot,
which, surprisingly, holds a small volume
of sacred scripture.[347] He sits on an animal skin, the ends of which hang in front,
partly obscuring his lotus seat.

The thangka painting in Figure
6.2 also depicts Virūpa in the posture
of dharma teaching, that is, as a lineage
master of the Lamdre instructions. It is
not an ordinary thangka; gold pigment

colors the skin of Virūpa and the minor figures. But the long chain of flowers that adorn him, and refer to an episode in his life as a siddha, are easier to see here than in the gilt sculpture. The chain of flowers begins at the top of his head, passes over his shoulders, hangs down to his thighs covered by a red garment, and passes through his folded legs to the edge of his lotus seat. He wears a volume of scripture fastened in front of his three-lobed topknot of hair. Along his shoulders and upper arms are hints of the locks of hair that fall down his back.

Virūpa sits on an antelope skin, more obvious in this painting than in the sculpture. He leans against a red rounded cushion, behind which stands a white-turbaned Indian ascetic, who holds a staff supporting an elaborate tasseled canopy over the great adept's head. To his right stands a female yogini-consort, who offers him a skullcup filled with nectar. Virūpa is depicted fully frontal while the minor figures near him are depicted in three-quarter view, standing in quite lifelike poses.

Tastefully surrounding Virūpa are the rocks and trees of a Chinese-style landscape. On the right side, one larger and one smaller tree are intertwined. Near the upper left, a bird flies through the sky toward the right, where another bird is perched near the top of the larger tree. There are various shapes and sizes of blue-green rocks. Near the bottom of the painting, a deer-like mythical animal runs with tail erect, holding a twig of blooming red flower in its mouth and looking back toward Virūpa as if offering it to him. (The animal's blue-scaled deer body and bear tail identify it a *qilin* "unicorn" from Chinese art.)[348]

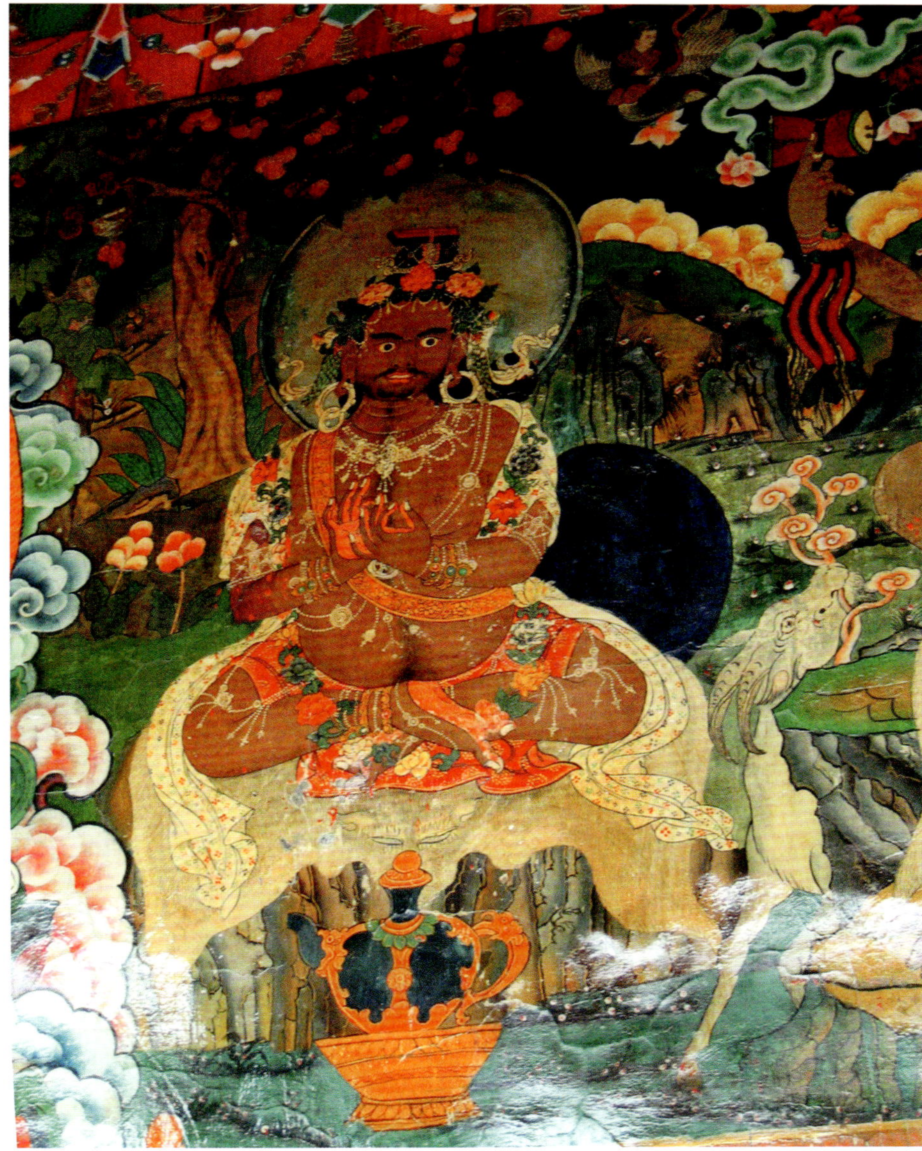

To the left of Virūpa's lotus seat, two small white deer cautiously approach a pool of water. On the horizon, a white cloud curls around one of the sharp, dark craggy peaks. In all, the painting is impressive artistically. It and its set could well have been a work by Khyentse Chenmo, though it would have been unsuitable for wide copying due to its extensive use of gold. Perhaps Khyentse was exploring his artistic range through such a painting and such a set.

Figure 6.3 is a much later depiction of Virūpa in a mural at Kunzang Tse College. It confirms that the teaching Virūpa became his standard depiction as a Lamdre lineal guru. The depiction of his body is quite close to that of Figure 6.2, with some differing minor details.

For instance, the book is positioned higher in his topknot, and his pillow is blue and placed to the right. Here, unlike the preceding two images, he wears an orange meditation band. A white robe covers his shoulders and falls along both sides of his body, around his knees.

Figure 6.4 also depicts Virūpa as its central figure. But here he is in his guise of a great adept working a miracle: holding the sun up in the sky as his witness and preventing it from setting. His face is turned slightly to the side, almost in three-quarter view. The minor figures around him stand or sit in various lively poses, with faces mostly in three-quarter view. But the face of the female consort at the bottom of the painting, holding the skullcup of nectar, is in profile. In the

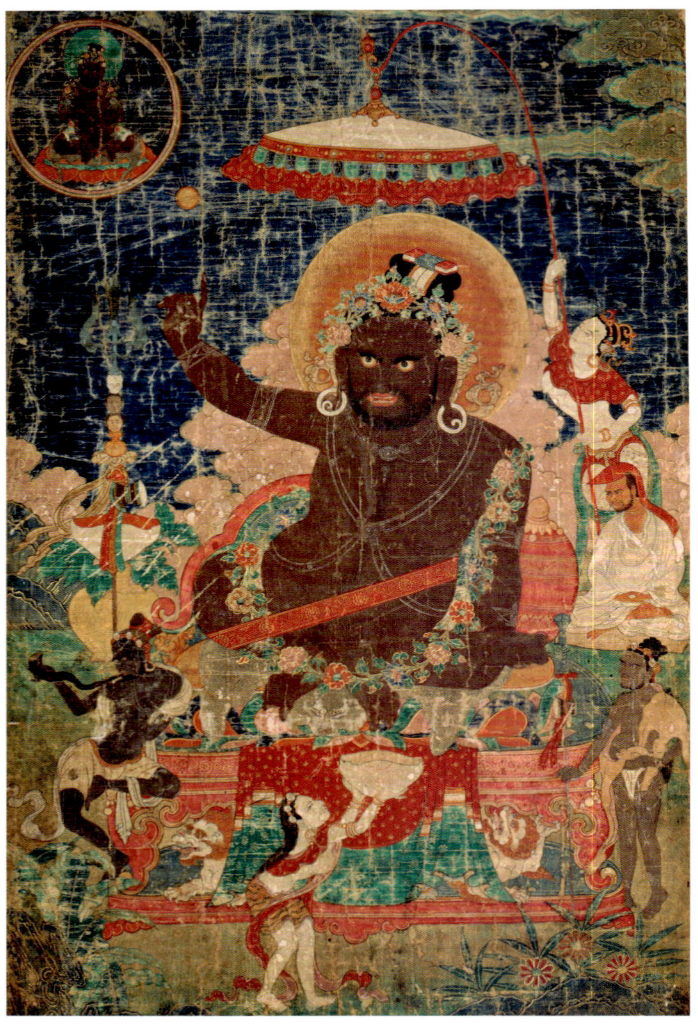
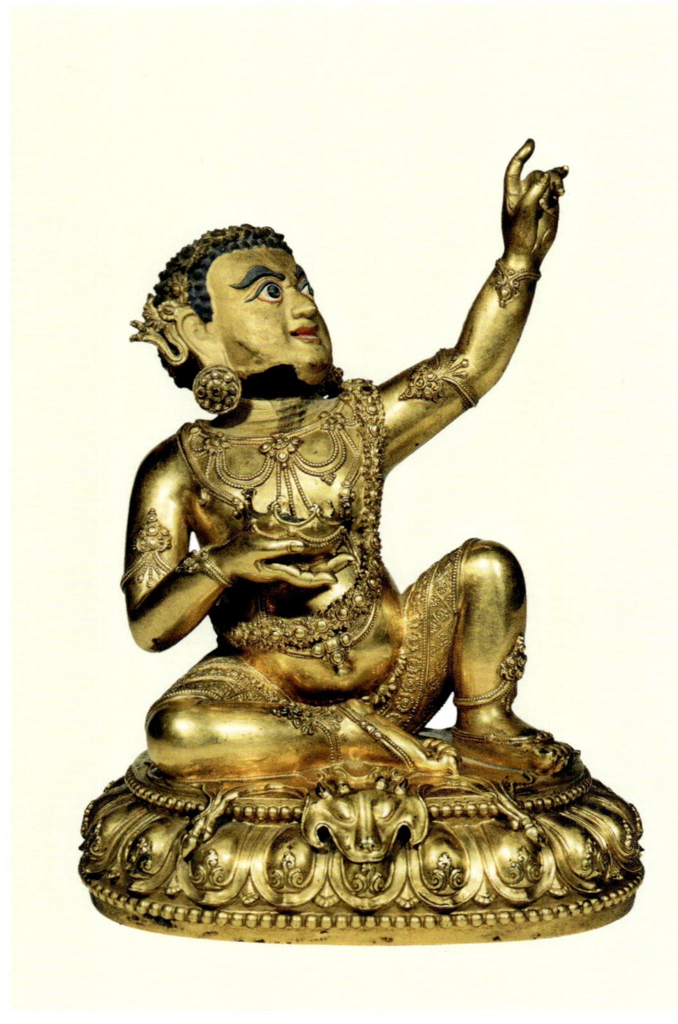

upper left, another image of the siddha floats in the sky, encircled by a rainbow nimbus.

On the back of the painting, the lowest line of inscriptions states that the painting was consecrated by Rinchen Sönam Chokdrup (1602–1681, Rin chen bsod nams mchog grub). According to its inscription, the thangka was commissioned in memory of Nyima Lingpa Tshutrim Tashi (Nyi ma Gling pa Tshul khrims bKra shis, fl. 17th century) of Gongkar by his student Yangchen Popa Zangpo, also of that monastery.[349] It was consecrated and blessed by Rinchen Sönam Chokdrup while he was the abbot of Shalu Monastery (Zhwa lu dgon), where his abbatial tenure was from 1659 to 1671. Given these facts, the thangka came from Gongkar Chöde and was painted by a Khyenri artist in the 1660s, the period of the Fifth Dalai Lama.[350]

Figure 6.5 depicts a sculpture of Virūpa in the same sun-arresting pose as the preceding painting (Fig. 6.4). It was commissioned by one of the Ming emperors. Given its specialized subject matter—sculptures of great adepts were quite rare as Ming art—this sculpture may have been commissioned to be gifted to a Tibetan lama who followed in Virūpa's tradition, that is, for a prominent Sakya lama such as Thekchen Chöje.

Depictions of Jetsün Trakpa

Figure 6.6 depicts in sculpture form Jetsün Trakpa as a lineal guru of the Lamdre. He stares intently, smiling at the viewer, radiating calm energy. The gestures of his hands imply they hold a vajra and bell. He wears layman's robes, and their long sleeves drape down over his knees on both sides.

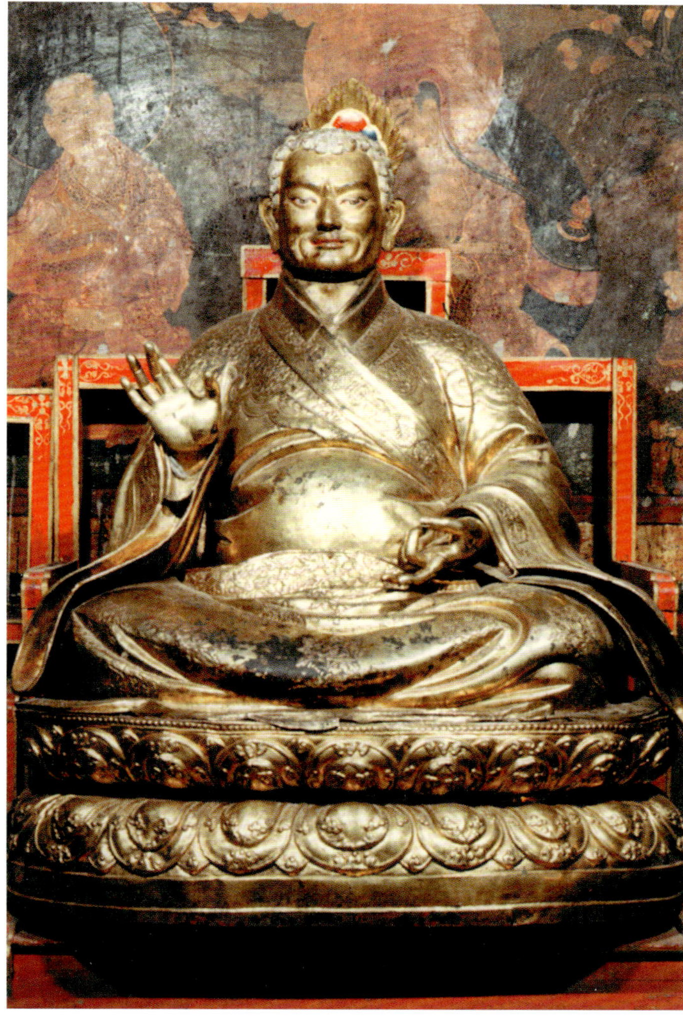

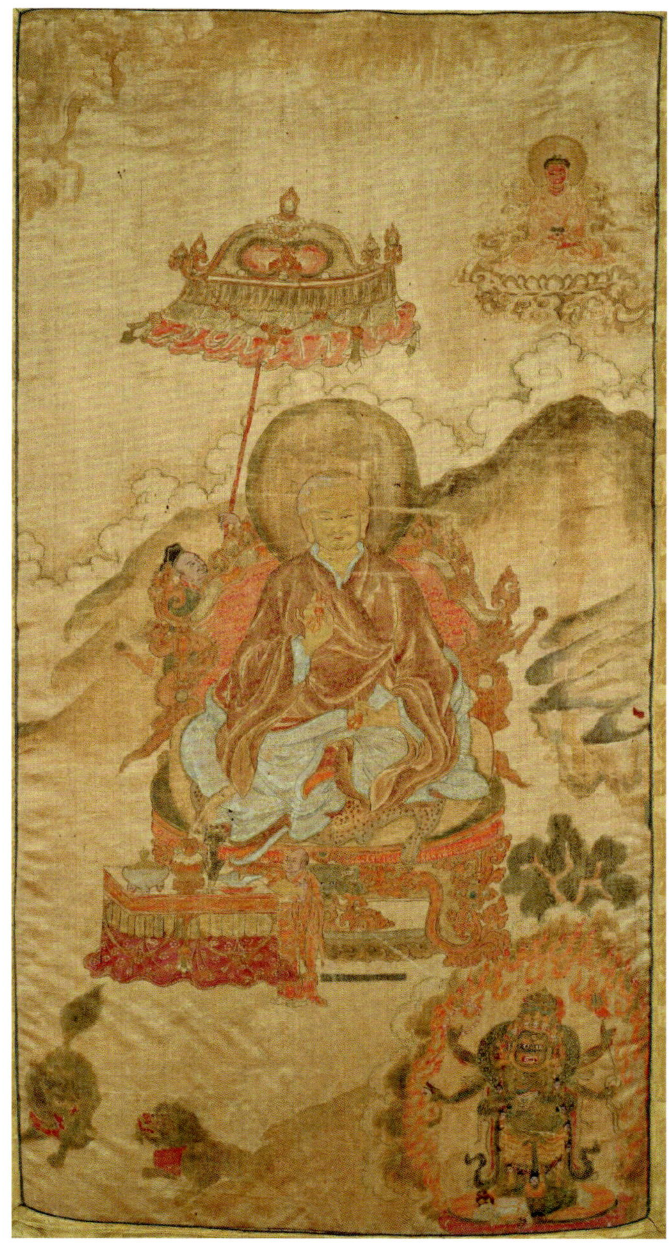

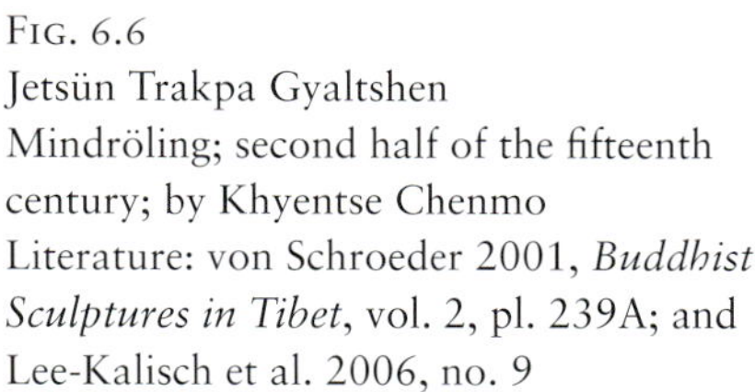

Among the available paintings that depict Jetsün Trakpa, the main figure's posture in Figure 6.7 is closest to that of the Drathang sculpture (Fig. 6.6). As in the sculpture, Jetsün Trakpa in this painting gazes benignly at the viewer. Here, his robes are depicted more clearly, and he holds a vajra and bell. His white inner and lower robes mark him as a layman. The long sleeves of his brown robe drape in pointed folds down to the spotted animal skin and mat upon which he sits. He also wears boots.

The artist has devoted much effort to depicting an elaborate wooden Chinese-style throne, including little dragons that curl around horizontal wooden members on both sides. To the lower left of the throne, two lions cavort in the grass. Another peers at the viewer from the middle of the throne base. Two minor figures also inhabit the foreground of the painting; both could be easily overlooked. The first is a monk— who could be mistaken as part of the throne—who holds a golden dish before the small offering table; note the trim at the bottom of the tablecloth swirling around and covering part of the monk's robe. The second is a person who wears what seems to be a black Chinese-official hat and holds the handle of a parasol

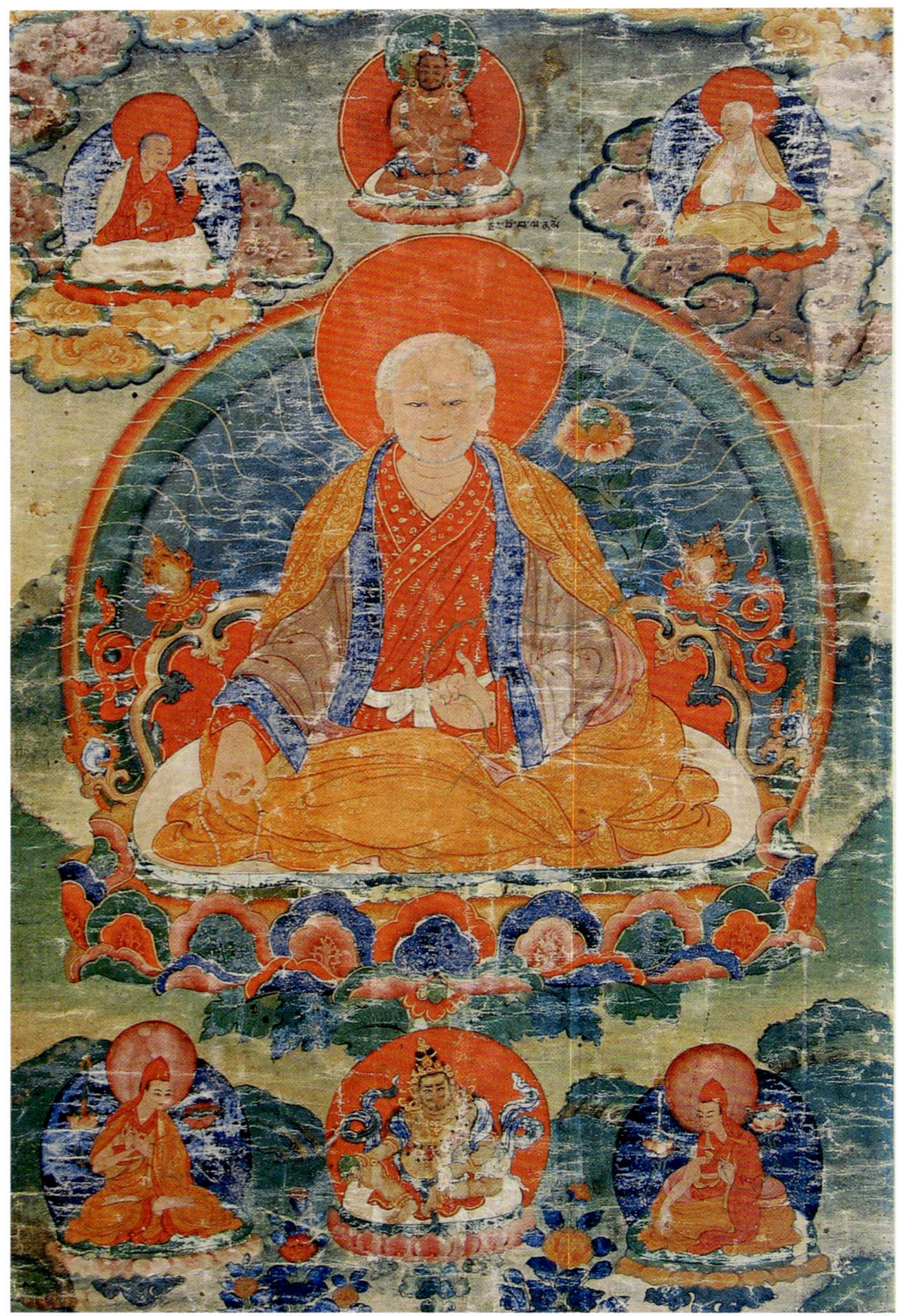

Fig. 6.8
Jetsün Trakpa Gyaltshen with the other
Four Great Founders of Sakya
sixteenth or seventeenth century
20 x 14 in. (50.8 x 35.5 cm)
Rubin Museum of Art
C2006.30.2 (HAR 100615)
Literature: Penba Wangdu 2012

that swirls above Jetsün Trakpa Gyalt-shen's head. Jetsün Trakpa and the two deities are depicted fully frontal, while the two attending humans are depicted in three-quarter views. This painting was seen above (Fig. 1.41) as an example of *si thang* or silk thangka; it features thin washes of color on silk, which were not usual materials among thangkas.

Figure 6.8 depicts Jetsün Trakpa Gyaltshen surrounded by Virūpa and four other great founders of Sakya: Sachen Kunga Nyingpo, Sönam Tsemo,

Sakya Paṇḍita, and Chögyal Phakpa. This full-palette (*rdzogs tshon*) painting, now preserved in the Rubin Museum of Art, embodies an early Khyenri style. It does not follow any known early or later model, but it seems to explore the pos-sibilities of portraying this great saint in the same spirit as the Drathang sculpture (Fig. 6.6).

The painting in Figure 6.9 depicts Jetsün Trakpa as a master of the Lamdre instructions, with an uncommon back-ground. The main figure sits on a mat of deep blue with golden brocade motifs, on an unusually broad Ming-style seat or a particular seat at his home temple, Sakya. A thick white cloak covers one shoulder and his folded legs. A modified one-point perspective is used to depict the offering table and the dais as if seen from above, while the figures are as if on the same level. This thangka is the first of two surviving paintings that por-tray essentially the same depiction of Jetsün Trakpa; though other details vary widely, the central figures are remark-ably similar. In fact, Figures 6.9–6.11 seem to correspond to particular "stan-dard" portrait of Trakpa Gyalshen, independent of the Drathang sculpture of him.

Here, Jetsün Trakpa is in the Sakya temple, on a certain occasion about 1208 or 1210, performing a miracle. Smiling mysteriously, Jetsün Trakpa Gyaltshen rings his bell. Meanwhile, to the left, his golden vajra floats in the air over the consecration vases.

Below him, to the right, stands a minor figure who may be his nephew Sakya Paṇḍita, with long black hair and a thick, white outer robe. This scene would date to the end of Sakya Paṇḍita's period as a "Sakya Jo sras," that is, as a long-haired, young noble layman; he was fully ordained as a monk in 1208.

Below him to the left, a kneeling horned demon humbly submits to the great master; his status as minor deity is indicated by the red cloud upon which

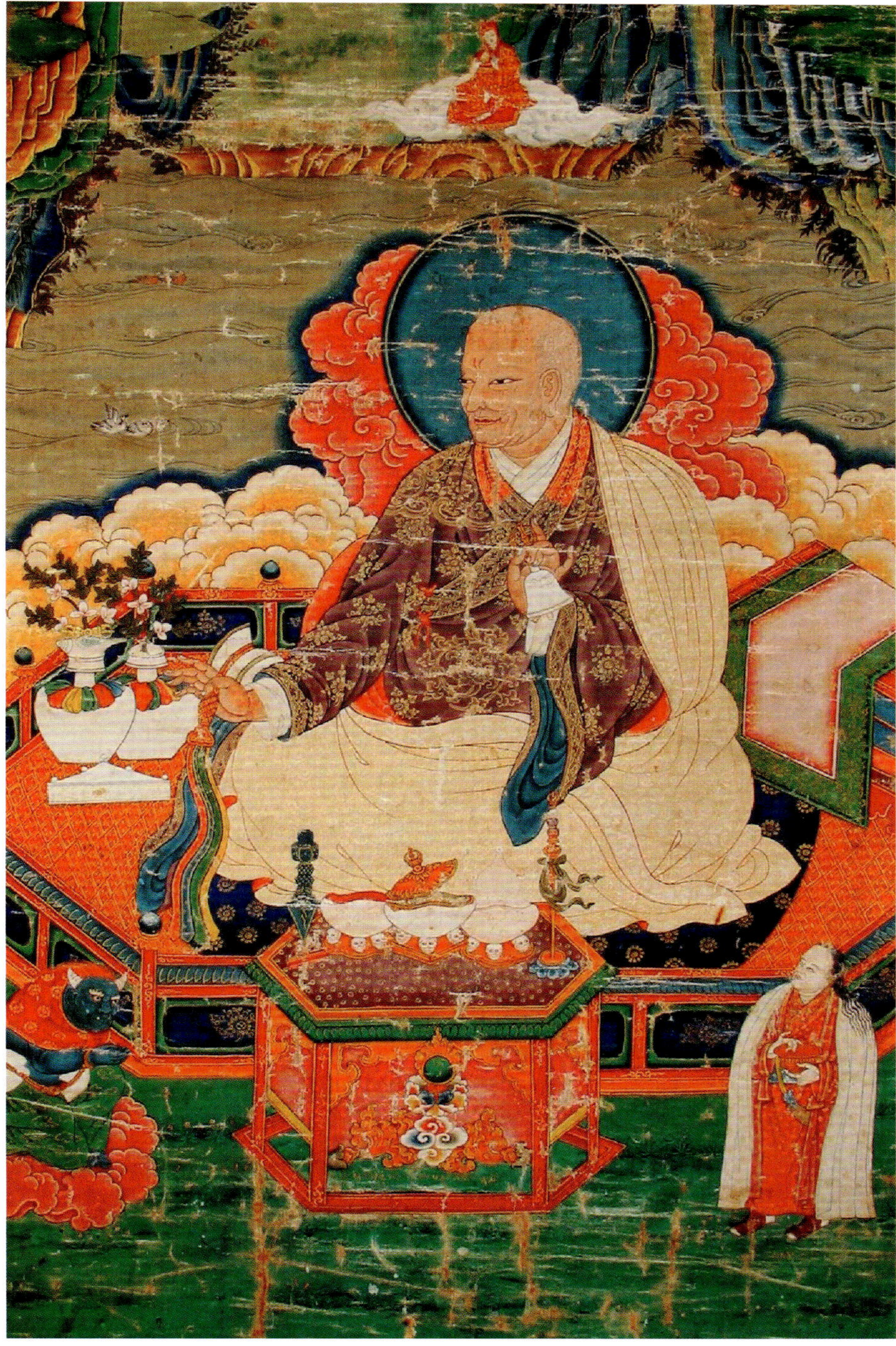

arrived in Sakya, the junior pandi-tas agreed beforehand, "He might be a great vajra-holder, but we are panditas famous in all parts of India, from east to west, so you should not return his prostration."

Following behind the pandita was . . . an evil spirit called Stack of Nine Goiters. When Drakpa Gyalt-shen saw him coming and placed his vajra and bell in space, exorciz-ing the impediment, the spirit could not retreat to India nor could he remain in Tibet . . .

As Drakpa Gyaltshen made pros-trations to the great pandita, the pandita returned them. When the junior panditas later questioned him about this, he said, "He is great Vajradhara in the mandala of Guhasamāja. Why should I not?"

The thangka is linked to the tradition of Gongkar, since it depicts Gongkarwa Dorjedenpa as a small lama above the main figure.[352] He may have been added by a later lama of Gongkar, who commissioned the later copy. The floating lama is depicted fully frontal while the other figures are depicted in three-quarter view. This later painting might have been copied from an early composition by Khyentse Chenmo. The atypical teal color in the head nimbus and the long-robed sleeves are possibly special touches by Khyentse.

In Figure 6.10, Jetsün Trakpa is again depicted as the central figure of a thangka painting. But in this simpler ver-sion, he is surrounded by different minor figures, and his skin is an eerie shade of purple-gray. He sits upon a light-colored wool rug with a cloud motif, and the armrest is ornamented with a prominent, golden dragon head. He wears robes of the same color as those in Figure 6.9, without the teal-colored interiors of the long pointed sleeves. Moreover, as he

he floats. This horned figure depicts a troublesome demon that Trakpa Gyalt-shen ritually subdued.

Two episodes of Jetsün Trakpa's floating vajra are told in a history of the Lamdre by Jamyang Khyentse Wang-chuk; this painting may refer to the first episode since it involves taming a demon.[351] According to a later history of the Lamdre:

When the great pandita of Kashmir

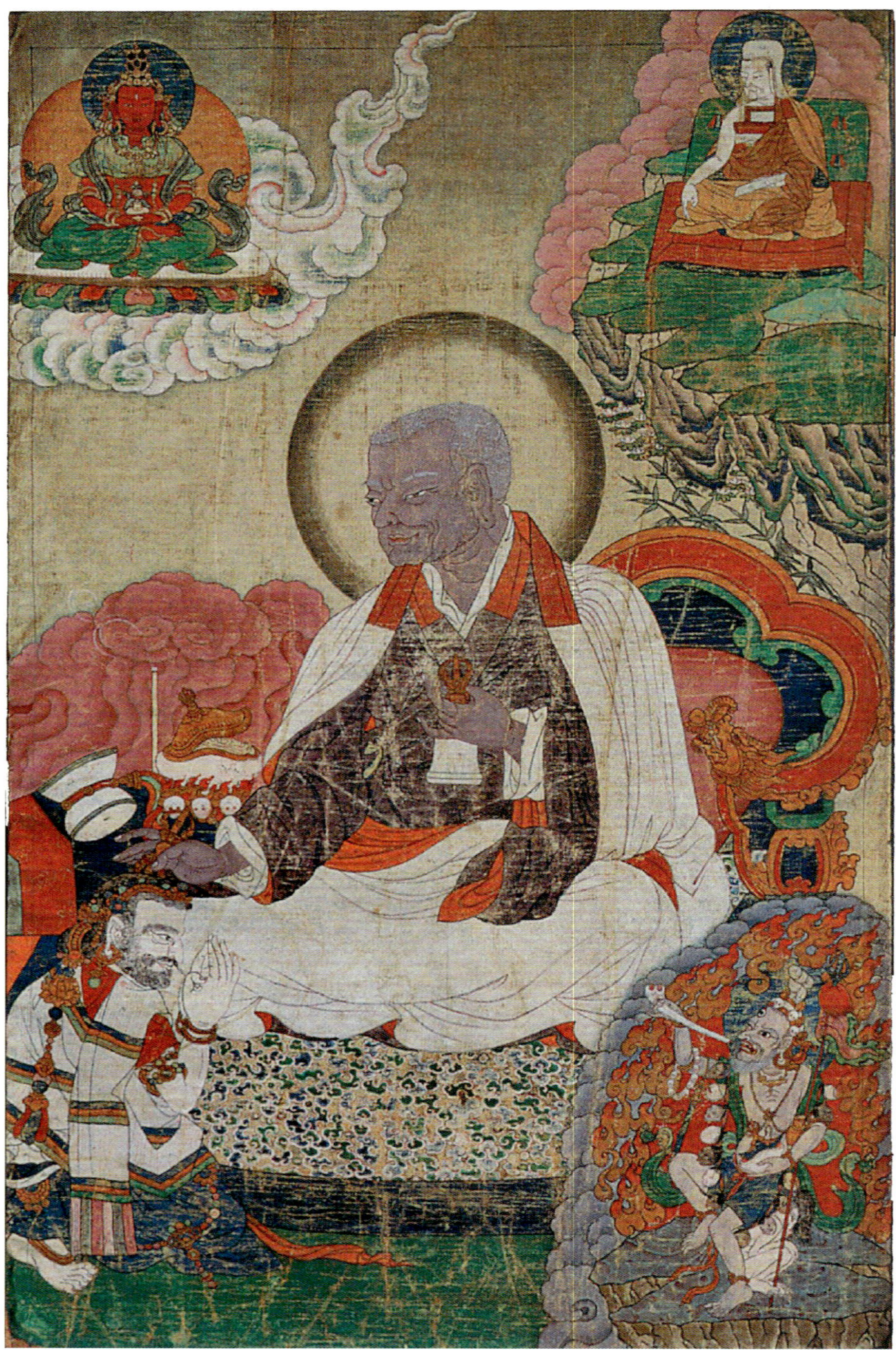

Amitāyus is portrayed fully frontal, the humans are in three-quarter view, and the submissive deity is shown in profile.

The Buddhist master at the upper right is probably an Indian pandit; he wears a yellow pandit hat, not a Tibetan lama's vest, as part of his monk's attire. I take him to be Śākyaśrībhadra, who was an important Kashmiri guru of Jetsün Trakpa Gyaltshen's nephew, Sakya Paṇḍita. They met at least once: the guru visited Sakya in 1210, spending the rainy season there.[353] He was also involved, directly or indirectly, when Jetsün Trakpa miraculously floated his vajra in the air, as mentioned in connection with Figure 6.9.

Figure 6.11, at Kunzang Tse College, confirms that the previous two portrayals of Jetsün Trakpa were standard enough to be copied in later murals of Gongkar. The color of his inner and outer robes here are the same as those in Figure 6.10, but here he sits on a mat with flower motifs. Note the identical backrest of his Chinese-style throne, with the same golden dragon head on the arm rest. Also, the pleats of his white outer cloak are remarkably similar in both paintings. Otherwise, this mural section is a simplified extract from a more complicated thangka composition.

Figure 6.12 shows Jetsün Trakpa in another painting, made about the time of Khyentse Chenmo. Again, the great lama is smiling, as if enjoying a spiritual mystery. He holds a vajra and bell together at his heart, like Vajradhara. The painting depicts him in gold, which is a more uncommon approach for a set of lineage portraits; it is difficult to do successfully. (This painting is from the same set as Figure 6.2, the golden Virūpa.) Besides lines drawn with lac dye, the only parts of the main figure painted with colors are his reddish-brown mouth, white eyes, white facial hair, and the wooly clumps of white hair atop his head. His face is portrayed in three-quarter view. Behind the main figure, the artist has

FIG. 6.10
Jetsün Trakpa Gyaltshen
seventeenth or eighteenth century
28 ⅞ x 18 ⅞ in. (73.3 x 47.9 cm)
Private Collection
(HAR 11566)
Literature: Sotheby's, *Indian and Southeast Asian Art*, New York (March 25, 1999), no. 99

rings his bell, he holds his vajra in his hand; it does not float in the air.

The minor figures include, at the lower left, an exotic deity who kneels in submission; perhaps he is the harmful spirit that Jetsün Trakpa tamed. In the sky, at the upper left, appears the Buddha Amitāyus, invoking longevity for the patron. At the lower right is a Brahmin blowing a thigh-bone trumpet; he may be the Sakya Mahākāla adept who appears in this form (Bram ze'i gzugs).

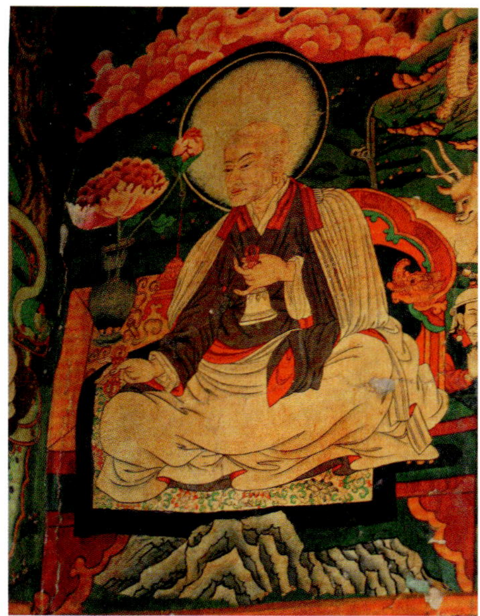

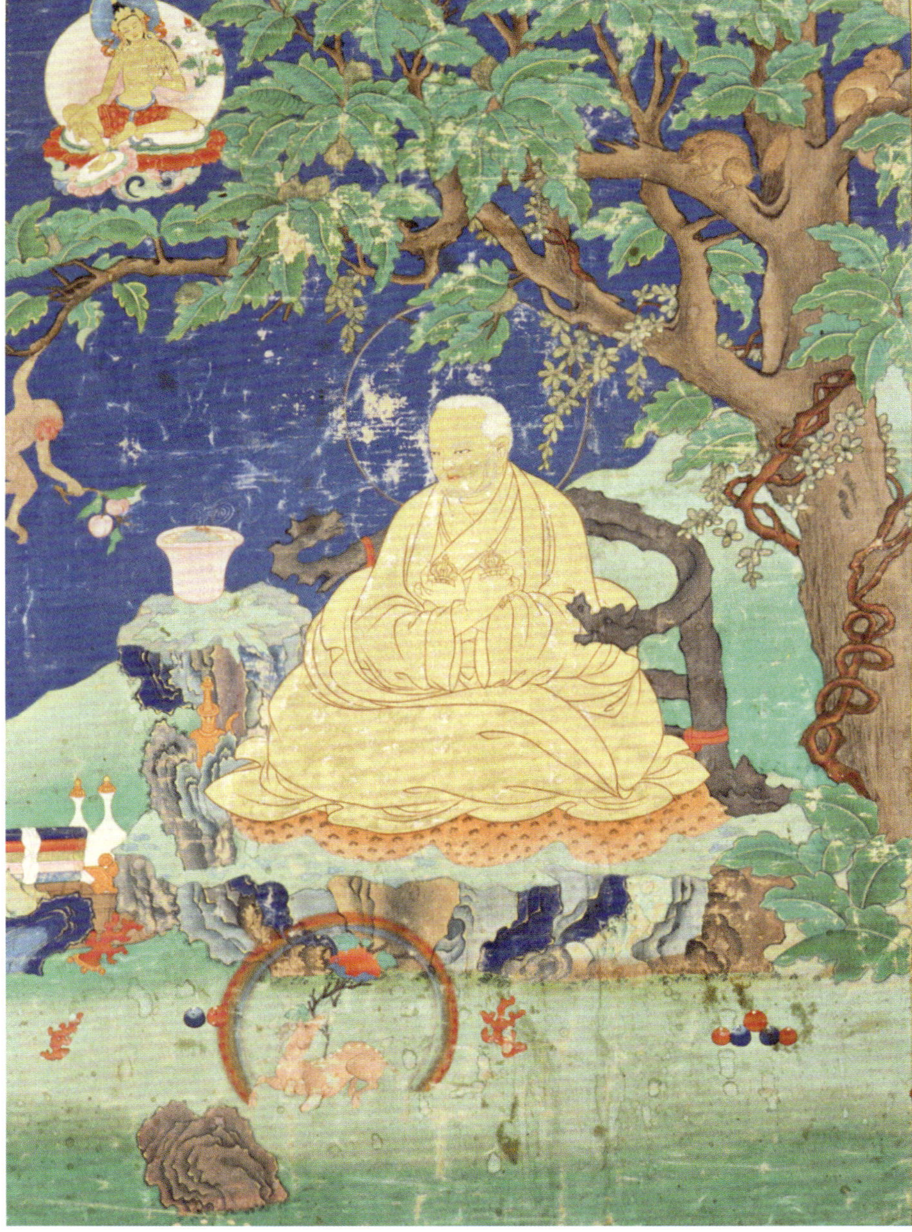

depicted a wooden throne, in which he has hidden a few dragon heads.

The artist did not fill the main figure's head nimbus with a solid color; he indicates the nimbus with a thin gold line, accented with an almost invisible line of lac dye, and nothing more. Meanwhile he challenges us to accept this minimal treatment of the main figure by dramatically outlining the mythical animal below, a very minor element, with a bright and radiant circle of light.

The copious use of gold for the main figure indicates that the patron of this set contributed a high level of religious donation. Gold also presents increased technical difficulty; it is a tricky material to use in large areas. Two subsequent paintings (Figs. 10.31 and 10.32) may be examples in which a Tibetan painter had copied the same Chinese original with golden main figures, seeing which parts should remain gold and which ones should be other colors for the best effect. Such copying could be a learning experiment for a young artist to gain competence and confidence. But in Figure 6.12, the painter's color and technique tell us that he does not acknowledge ordinary limitations.

By his style, the artist also shows he has mastered elements of Chinese landscape painting and could compose convincing settings from them. (He was using different brushes and formats and grounds, and to different effect, than Chinese landscape painters.) The restrained treatment of a vine around the tree suggests that he is aiming for subtlety. At the same time, he calls attention to his bravura performance in rendering the red-faced monkey that dangles from a tree branch at the far left. The primate reaches toward the master with his offering of a fruit-laden twig, pointing it at a large pink cup between them.[354] In addition to painting areas of solid gold, the artist surprises the viewer with some fine golden details, such as the wisps of incense smoke that whirl in the air above what is evidently an inverted bell-shaped incense burner with a rounded mound of

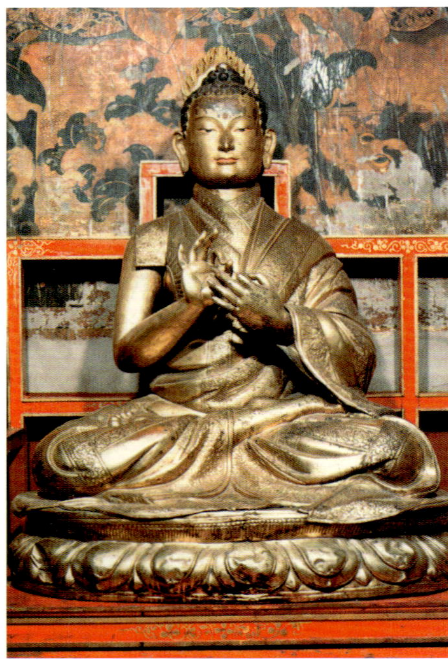

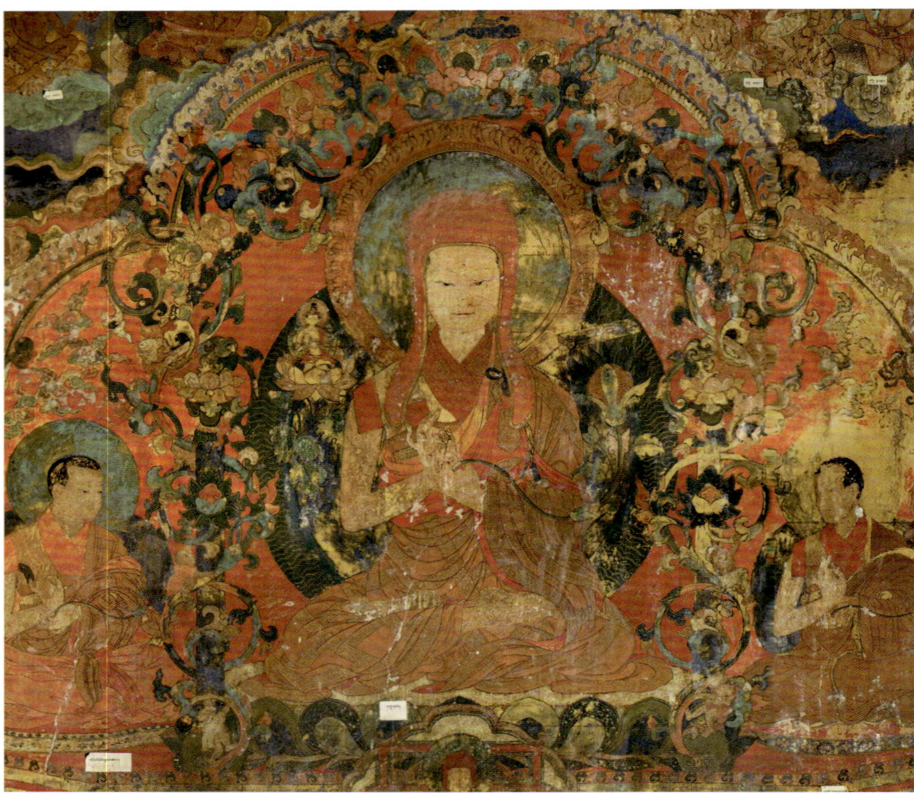

sand for incense sticks. The wispy vapors
are thus likely to be incense—in the Chinese manner, something that I have never
seen in Tibetan painting before or since.

Depictions of Sakya Paṇḍita

Depictions of the great scholar and
founding master Sakya Paṇḍita were
another beloved subject for portraiture in
Gongkar Monastery, with its traditions
of Thekchen Chöje and others. The two
most common types of portrait were as
a Lamdre lineal master and as one of the
three red-clad founders of Sakya.

Sakya Paṇḍita appears in Figure
6.13 as a lineal guru of the Lamdre in
a gilt-copper sculpture (also seen as a
detail in Fig. 5.1). Khyentse Chenmo
depicted his subject as an imposing
young monk, with hands in teaching
position and an atypical bumpy head
protuberance, unique to this artist.

Figure 6.14 depicts Sakya Paṇḍita
in another traditional role, namely as one
of the three most spiritually prominent
founders of the Sakya sect who wore
red robes as a sign of their full monastic ordination. Before Sakya Paṇḍita,
the three masters preceding him had
worn the white robes and long sleeves
allowed to laymen. In this original mural
by Khyentse Chenmo, he is shown as
the first of the three red-robed masters
of Sakya. Here he wears his special,
rounded, red pandit hat, holds his hands
in the position of teaching, and folds
his feet in mediation. He is depicted
fully frontal. Near his shoulders, a small
bodhisattva, who must be Mañjuśrī, and
a book of holy scripture rest on floating lotuses, whose stems he holds. The
yellow-trimmed flaps of his hat hang to
the edge of his lama vest. The right flap
partly covers a special ringed strap with

which he has fastened his monk's robe.

Figure 6.15 confirms that the
depiction of Sakya Paṇḍita as one of the
three red-robed masters was standard
at Gongkar. Here this mode appears in
the murals of Kunzang Tse College,
where the painter evidently copied the
corresponding part of an earlier mural
by Khyentse in the main building (Fig.
6.14). Most details of the iconography
are the same. Yet here we can see certain
details more clearly than in the original,
such as the special strap and ring used
to tie his robes on the right side, which
again is partly covered by a long flap of
his pandit hat.

Sakya Paṇḍita (or Sapaṇ, for short)
appears in Figure 6.16 playing a different iconographic role. This large and
impressive thangka shows him as the
fourteenth lineal master of the Lamdre.
It is believed to be the sole painting
known to survive from two complete
sets of twenty-three thangkas painted
for Gongkar Monastery by Khyentse
Chenmo.[355] (The set will be described
in more detail in chapter 7.) The painting depicts a dramatic event: Sapaṇ

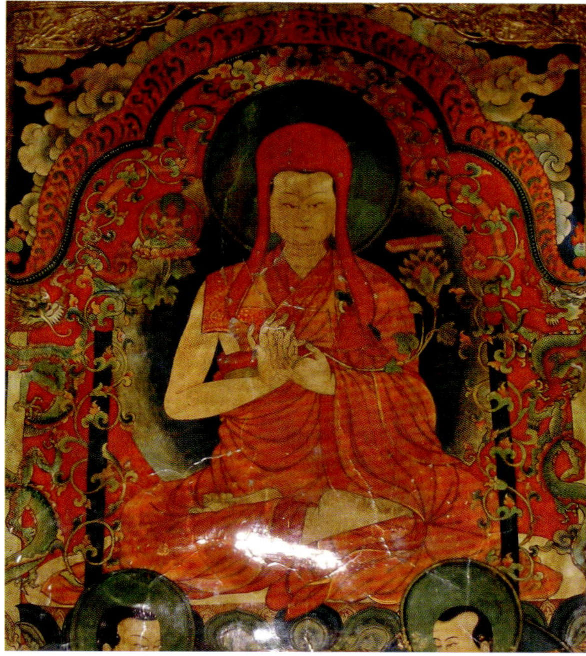

Fig. 6.15
Sakya Paṇḍita as First of the Three Red-
Robed Masters
Mural, Kunzang Tse College; ca. 1930s
Photo: M. Fermer, 2010

Fig. 6.16
Sakya Paṇḍita
1464–1476
Gongkar Monastery; by Khyentse Chenmo
31 ½ x 20 in. (80 x 50 cm)
Photo: M. Fermer, 2012
Literature: Penba Wangdu 2012, fig. 14

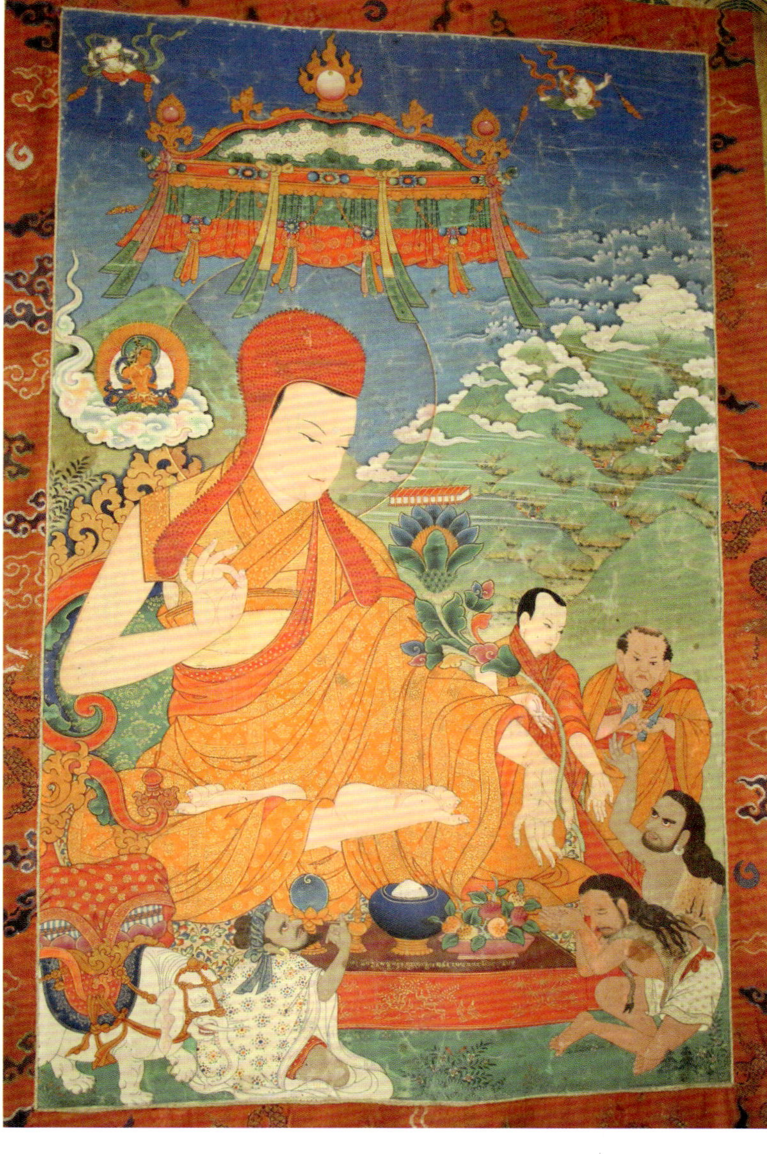

debating with the Indian non-Buddhist scholar Harinanda at Kyirong about 1240. As Sakya Paṇḍita recorded in a verse immediately thereafter, he actually debated six Indian sages and converted them to Buddhism; this survives in his collected writings, *Mu stegs kyi ston pa drug btul ba'i tshigs bcad*.[356] Khyentse included much true-to-life detail, both in the human subjects and in the landscape background. He depicts Sapaṇ's pandit hat not only with its precise shape but also with tiny dots that imitate the texture of the original cloth.

Compared to the previous two paintings (Figs. 6.14 and 6.15), Sakya Paṇḍita sits on a less elaborate throne, behind an offering table that seems distinctively Chinese with gold on red

(like lacquer) on its front. A simple, transparent nimbus graces his head; his sanctity and near divinity are also evoked by the canopy hovering in the air and the two minor divinities that hold its delicate metal chains. The Bodhisattva of Wisdom, Mañjuśrī, floats near Sapaṇ's shoulder, guiding and inspiring him. One of the Indian, non-Buddhist disputants kneels and bows with hands folded together in respectful submission. A second one still resists, with his hand raised. Two Tibetan lamas watch from the side; the one closest to Sakya Paṇḍita is perhaps his young nephew, Phakpa. The second, depicted fully frontal, watches distrustfully and uses a ritual dagger to magically subdue the resisting mendicant. A third mendicant

looks up in awe from the other side of the table, gesturing with his thumb. He might be an exotic traveler who has just arrived at the scene, leading his fully loaded white elephant. (Compare Figs. 2.14a and 2.14b.) He and the submitting ascetic are shown in profile.

For the landscape, Khyentse depicted the Himalayan hills above the southwest border area of Kyirong in detail. He not only showed three different kinds of clouds and bands of mist wreathing the mountains but also depicted several hermit huts, stupas, and a few anchorites standing here and there in the small valleys. For its time— indeed, for any time—this painting was a tour de force.

It is illustrative to compare the

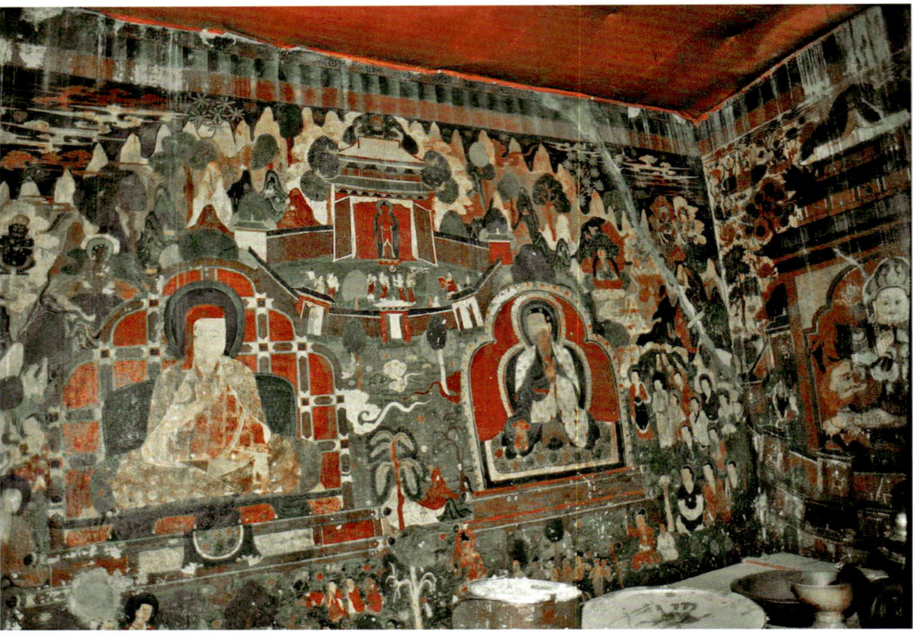

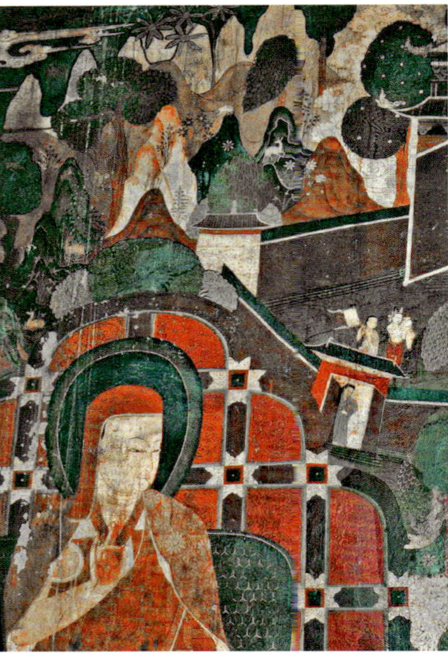

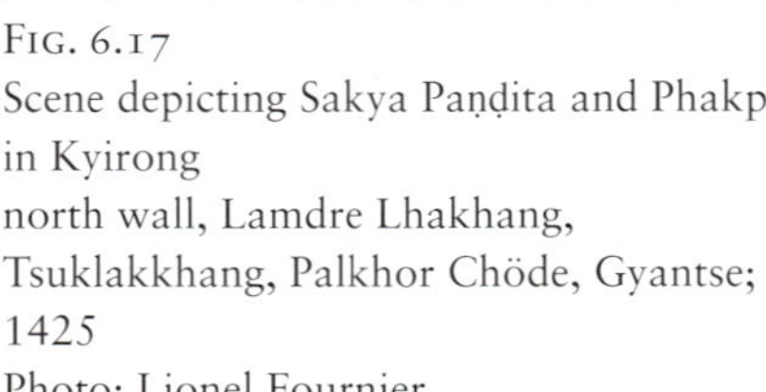

mural paintings in the Lamdre Lhakhang of Gyantse that depict a similar theme, namely Sakya Paṇḍita and Phakpa visiting Kyirong. According to Michael Henss, the mural on the right side of that chapel's northern wall depicts Chögyal Phakpa as if in dialogue with his uncle and predecessor, Sakya Paṇḍita, who wears a red pandit's hat. Between the two lamas is depicted a standing buddha within an enclosure. An inscription reveals that the scene depicts Sakya Paṇḍita and Phakpa visiting the famous Ārya Wati Zangpo or Kyirong Jowo buddha sculpture. (See Fig. 6.17 for the entire mural.) It is worth pointing out

that Chögyal Phakpa is not in monks's robes, presumably because he was very young and still wearing layman's robes before receiving tonsure.

The mountain panorama above this scene shows, in Henss's view, "how Tibetan painters copied and transformed Chinese landscape styles," referring to similar mountain scenes in the ground-floor circumambulation corridor at Shalu Monastery.[357] In just one generation, Khyentse Chenmo made a great stylistic jump in portraying these mountain scenes. (See also Fig. 6.18a, a detail of the landscape above Sapaṇ.)

These murals exist in the Lamdre Lhakhang of Gyantse, which—like the Neten Lhakhang and the rest of the Gyantse Tsuklakkhang—survived the Cultural Revolution relatively intact. Also, the imposing and lively set of lineal guru sculptures still exists. The set presents the Thekchen Chöje lineage of the Lamdre, but it omits two gurus between Lama Dampa and the final guru. More important, Khyentse Chenmo's teacher did not shy away from depicting such biographical scenes with complicated landscapes in the background.

Fig. 6.18b shows Phakpa in the scene depicting his meeting with Sakya

Paṇḍita in Kyirong, on the north wall of the Lamdre Lhakhang. Phakpa, a main figure, has the same hand gestures as in the preceding thangka (Fig. 6.16). The painting not only includes a nice background landscape, with Sachen, but also depicts, at Phakpa's feet, the group of Indian sectarians who had come to debate with his uncle. The painting is a clear reminder of Khyentse Chenmo's remarkable achievements in his depictions of both Sakya Paṇḍita and Phakpa, which surpass those of his teacher.

Figure 6.19 depicts the same composition as Figure 6.16, in a small mural to the side of a passageway door. (See also Fig. 4.39.) Again, Mañjuśrī floats near Sakya Paṇḍita's proper right shoulder. But here Sakya Paṇḍita extends his left leg, resting his foot on a small lotus, in a more convincing posture of debate; in the previous painting (Fig. 6.16), he was in a pose of meditation, with feet folded. In this mural, Hariranda and his colleague are not present. To Sakya Paṇḍita's right stand two smaller attendant monks. To the right of his dark-blue head nimbus, cherub-like minor deities float in the clouds. In the bottom left corner, parts of the exotic traveler or trader leading his small white elephant can be seen. It appears the new bands of paint

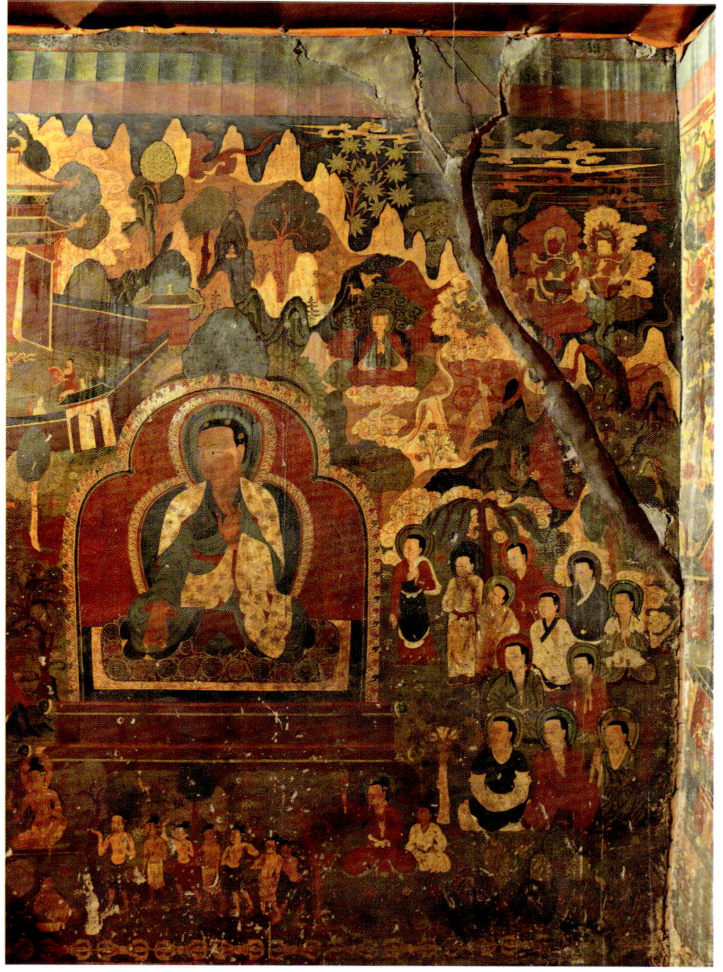

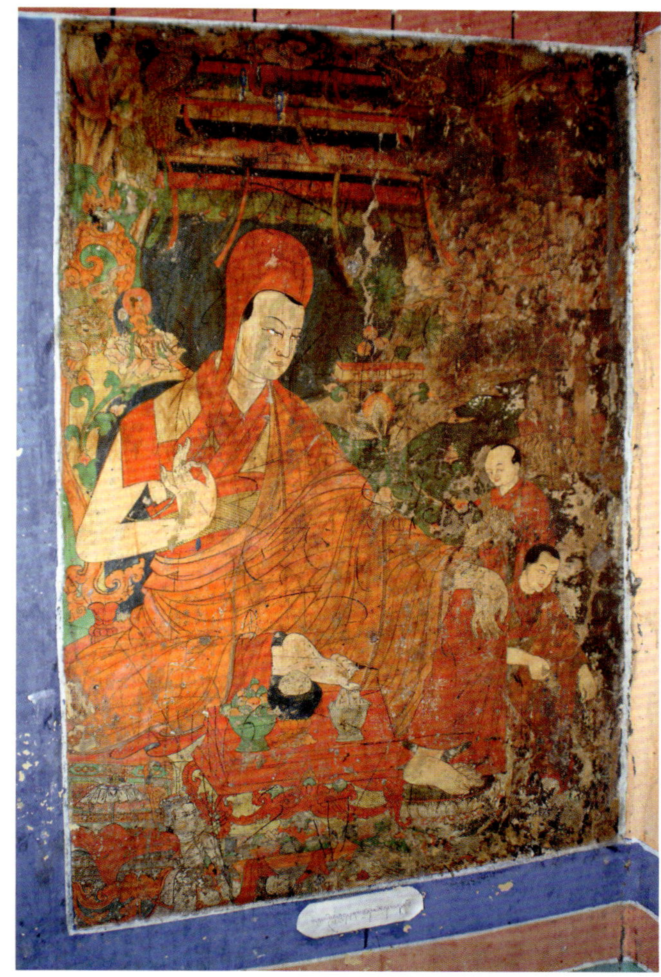

conceal the bottom edge of the old mural.

A variation on the same theme, Figure 6.20 depicts Sakya Paṇḍita as a Lamdre guru, in a closely related Khyenri painting tradition but in a thangka. Here Sapaṇ sits on a chair with both legs down, like Maitreya, his bare feet resting on a large white lotus. At the bottom left, one standing Tibetan monk attends the guru. The artist has expended a lot of energy on the throne behind Sapaṇ and the offering table to the right, with all their tiny details.

Figure 6.21 is yet another painted depiction of Sakya Paṇḍita, who was a standard subject in Gongkar. In this later mural at Kunzang Tse College, his body posture follows his depiction in Figure 6.19, an original mural in the main building. But the artist of this panel moved Mañjuśrī to a more prominent place in the upper-right side of the sky. Behind Sakya Paṇḍita is what seems to be the

curved outer frame of a Chinese-style throne; where one would expect to find a solid backrest, the artist has depicted the landscape behind the throne.

Figure 6.22 depicts the same subject as Figure 6.16, Sakya Paṇḍita debating Harinanda. But it shows a mid- or late-seventeenth-century treatment, from a set of thangkas depicting the previous lives of the Panchen Lamas; the pointed pandit hat would become acceptable by the seventeenth century. It is painted in a sumptuous Tsangri or New Menri style. Featuring many impressive details, such as the debating mendicant at the lower right and the Phakpa Wati shrine in the landscape to the left, this painting, too, was a masterpiece for its time.

Portraits of Sakya Paṇḍita continued to be painted at Gongkar in the seventeenth and eighteenth centuries. Figure 6.23 illustrates a depiction of Sakya Paṇḍita from about that time, as

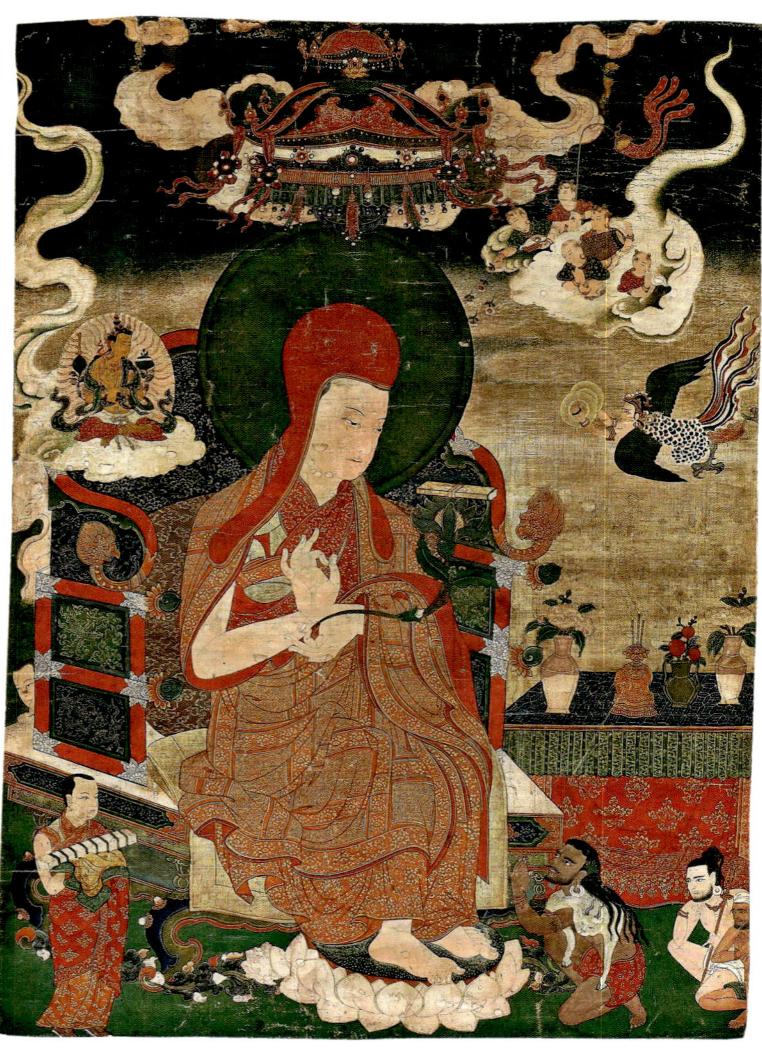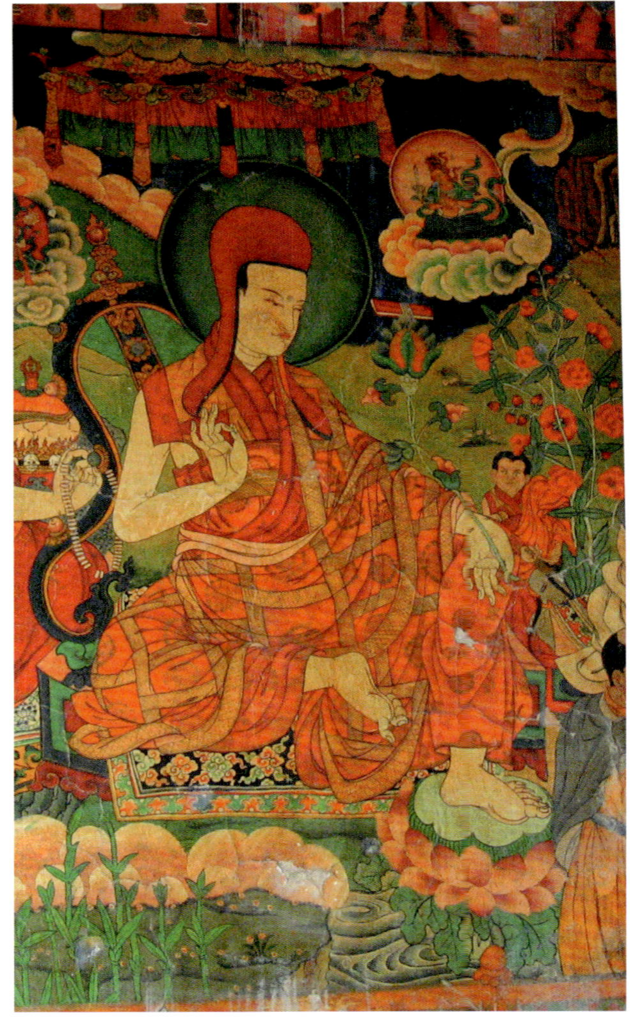

Fig. 6.20
Sakya Paṇḍita as a Lamdre Guru
late fifteenth or sixteenth century
29 ⅛ x 21 ½ in. (74.0 x 54.5 cm)
British Museum, inventory no. 1980
12–20 01

Fig. 6.21
Sakya Paṇḍita as Lineal Guru
Mural, Kunzang Tse College, Gongkar;
ca. 1930s
Photo: A. Lustgarten, 2005

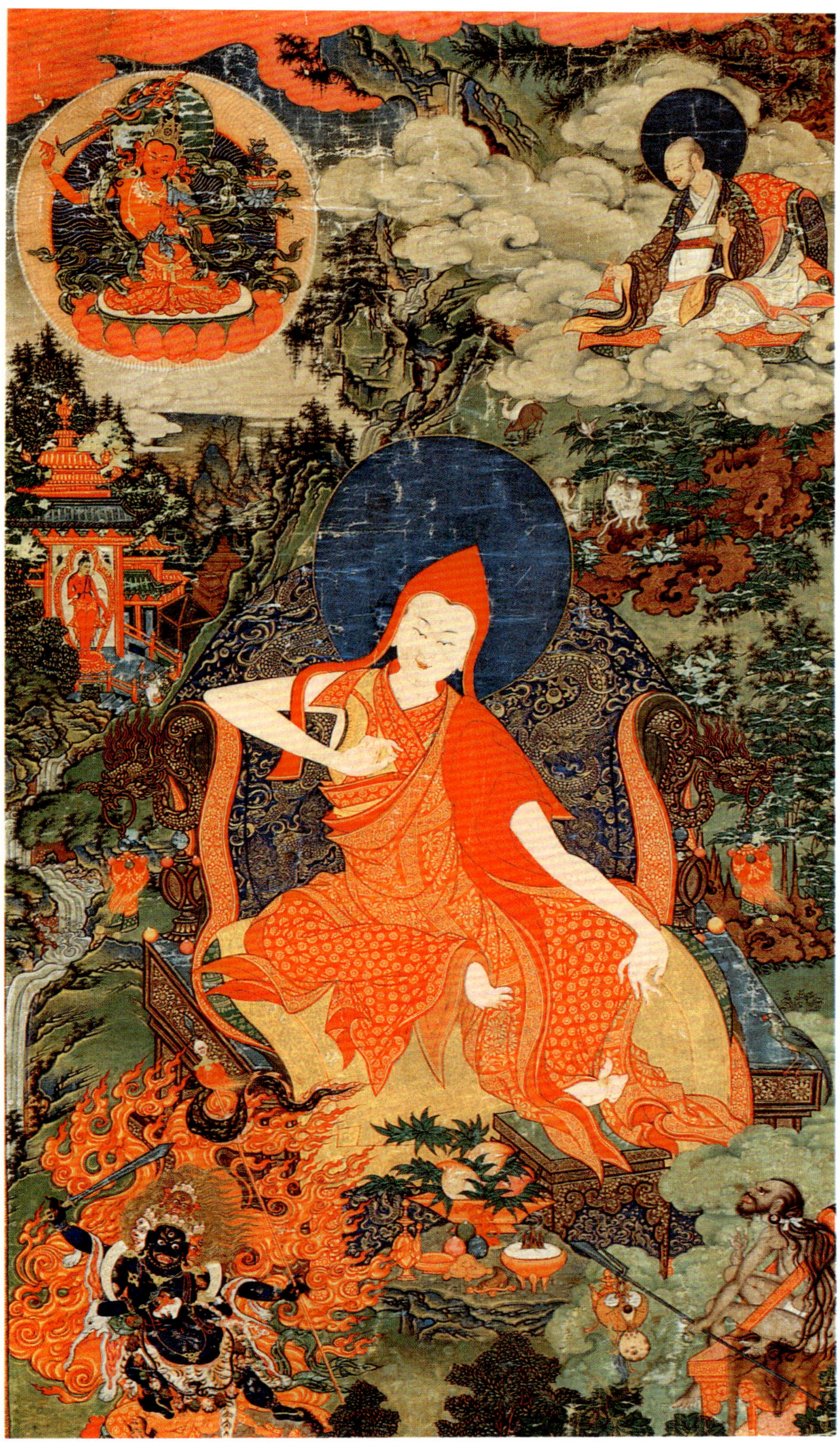

the teachers is gold. The mixture of fully frontal and three-quarter views with both main and minor figures is rare.

The distinctively Khyenri elements include Sapaṇ's lotus seat, the transparent and various head-nimbus colors, including pink, pastel green, and bright orange. The painting is marked "third on the left" (*g.yon gsum pa*), that is, number 7 in the set. Inscribed in gold under the two main figures: *bdag nyid chen po sa skya paṇḍi ta la na mo// chos kyi rgyal po 'phags pa blo gros rgyal mtshan la na mo//*. The structure is shown in Diagram [F].

Inscriptions: 3. *rje btsun*; 4. *sa paṇ*; 5. *'phags pa*; 6. *dam pa kun dga' grags*; 7. *sa paṇ*; 8. [name not found]; 9. *a gnyan dam pa*; and 10. *bdag nyid chen po.* The minor figures depict part of a lineage for Mahākāla Pañjaranātha, including the great Tibetan adepts of the Sakya/Yuan period Dampa Kunga Trak (Dam pa Kun dga' grags) and Ga Anyen Dampa (sGa A gnyan Dam pa).

DEPICTIONS OF CHÖGYAL PHAKPA

The Sakya founding master with the most varied surviving portraits is Chögyal Phakpa, Sakya Paṇḍita's nephew and main successor. The life of Phakpa obviously fascinated Khyentse Chenmo, and in thangkas he depicted some impressive historical details of the Yuan imperial court.

In sculpture form, Figure 6.24 depicts Chögyal Phakpa as a guru of the Lamdre lineage. Here, he holds his right hand down in the earth-witness posture and lays his left hand on his lap. He has black hair with a straight hairline, and his jaw is squarish. He wears the robes of a fully ordained monk; his upper robe is fastened at the right shoulder with a ring that hangs on a cord. That robe fastener—a feature of Chinese, not Tibetan, monk robes—is also found on the back of the same shoulder. Such a fastener appeared as a special feature of Sakya

one of two main lineage masters. He is depicted with a transparent head nimbus. As in Figure 6.22, his hat has a point, unlike the rounded pandit hats found in earlier depictions. Here, his proper right arm is covered with a robe, like Figures 6.17 and 6.20. The painting is special because the skin color of all of

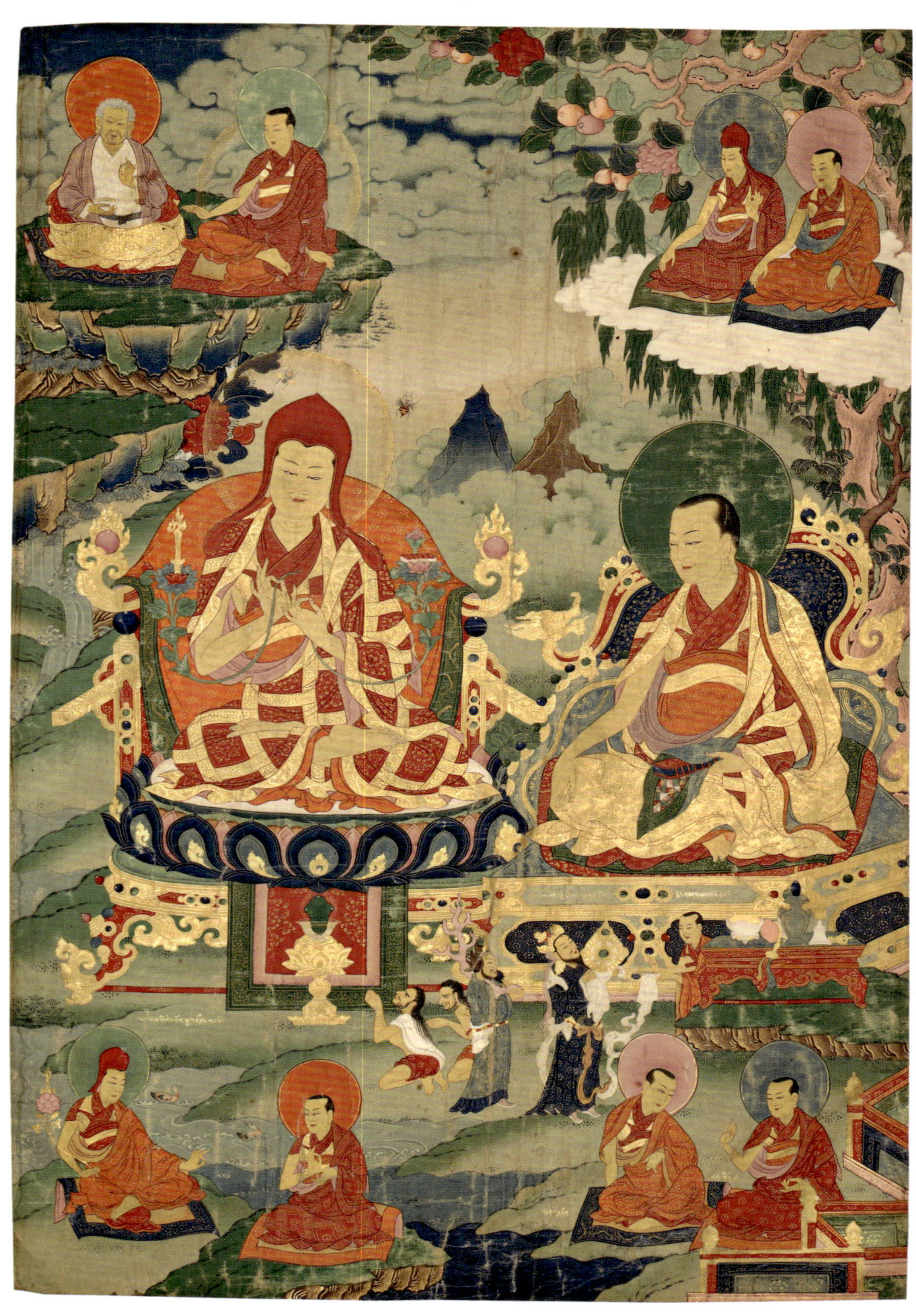

FIG. 6.23
Sakya Paṇḍita and Chögyal Phakpa with
Mahākāla Lineage Masters
seventeenth century, originating from
Lhokha
31 ¼ x 22 ¼ in. (79.4 x 56.5 cm)
Rubin Museum of Art, Gift of Shelley and
Donald Rubin
C2006.66.23 (HAR 695)

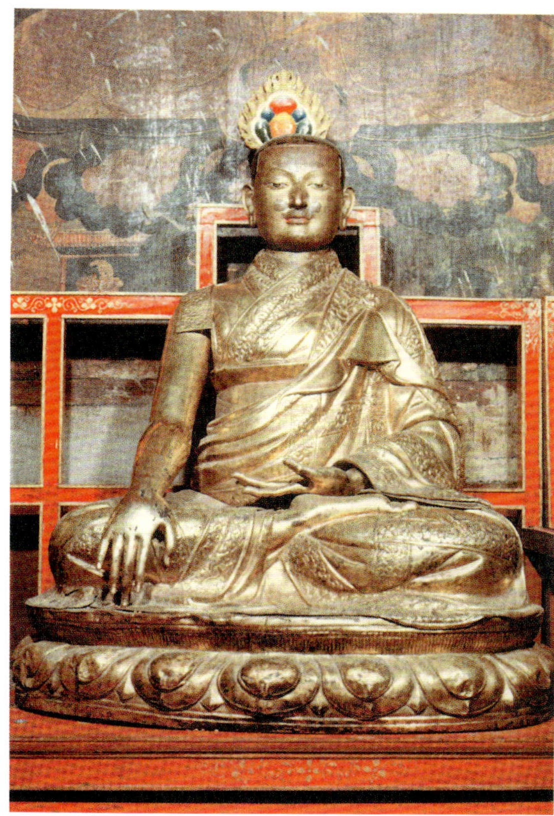

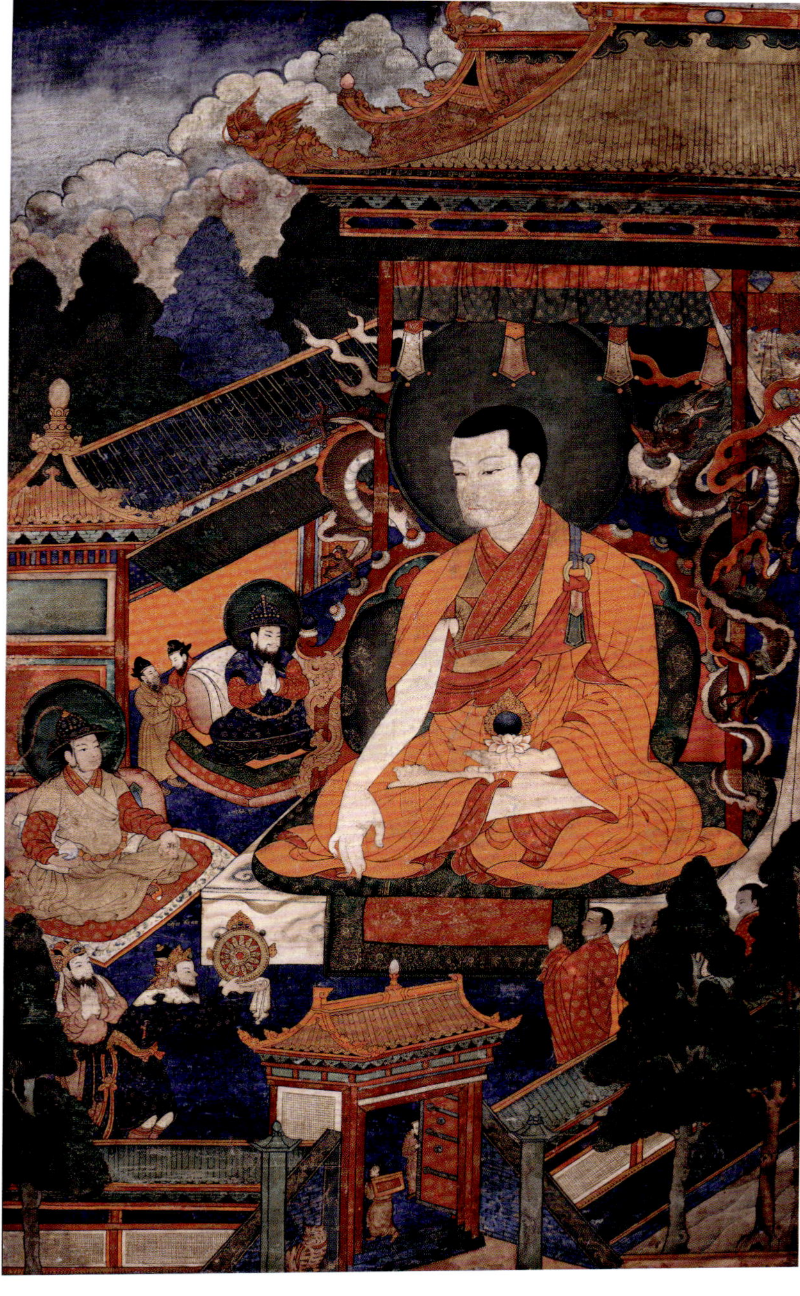

Paṇḍita's robes in two Gongkar murals, Figures 6.14 and 6.15, partly hidden behind the flap of his hat.

Figure 6.25 depicts Chögyal Phakpa in a painting as lineal guru of the Lamdre; his body and robes are the same as in Figure 6.24. Depicted around the main figure, however, is a Chinese imperial-court scene. It was copied from a Khyentse composition and may date to a century or two after him. It seems that Khyentse for his Lamdre lineage thangkas (presumably in consultation with his guru, Gongkarwa), chose to depict several prominent Sakya founding masters—such as Jetsün Trakpa, Sakya Paṇḍita, and Chögyal Phakpa—within telling episodes to illustrate their spiritual career and importance. The background of Figure 6.25 illustrates one or more striking episodes related to Phakpa that occurred at the Yuan imperial court, and we shall see something similar in Figure 6.28.

This painting of Phakpa as eminent Lamdre guru shows him seated on a high throne. Pictured much smaller and seated to the left is his main imperial patron, the bearded Qubilai Khan, wearing a black, safari-like, Mongolian official hat and pressing his hands together in respect. To his right stand two lesser figures, wearing Chinese robes and hats, making comments to each other; they are probably high ministers.

Besides Qubilai, another person—depicted larger than the emperor—wears a Mongolian hat with a long feather projecting from its tip, which suggests he is an equally important Mongol official. Yet, from the inscription beneath him (*'gro mgon phyag na*) he is Phakpa's younger brother, Drogön Chakna Dorje (Phyag na rDo rje 1239–1267)! Chakna was famed for wearing Mongol clothing; a prominent Tibetan cleric of Tsang, Jomden Raltri (bCom ldan Ral gri) of Narthang, famously grumbled in a versified epistle of the 1270s that, among other things, Phakpa had become Mongol in his dress.[358]

Figure 6.26 illustrates a painting of Qubilai Khan from closer to his time. Here, too, he wears a distinctive black hat.

Chögyal Phakpa was clearly very important for Qubilai, the first Yuan emperor. In 1260, when Qubilai declared himself supreme khan of the Mongols at a great assembly in Kaiping (Shangdu or Xanadu in present-day Inner Mongolia), Phakpa led his enthronement. In 1271, Qubilai established the Yuan dynasty of China, with its capital at Daidu (Dadu, present-day Beijing).

Qubilai conferred numerous high titles and honors upon Phakpa, awarding him the title of state preceptor (*guoshi*) in 1260. In 1270, he awarded him the still more prestigious position of imperial preceptor (*dishi*). This second title was grander, entailing a huge cash award.

Phagpa was again honored by Khubilai, who bestowed on him the title of "Prince of Indian Deities, Miraculous Divine Lord Under the Sky and Above the Earth, Creator of the Script, Possessor of the Five Higher Sciences, Phagpa, the Imperial

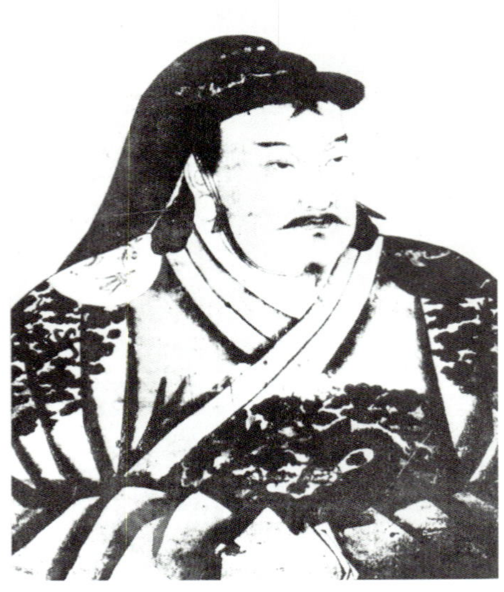

Preceptor." The customary gifts included 1,000 shoes (ingots) of silver and 59,000 rolls of silk. [359]

When Phakpa was in his teens, he and his younger brother, Chakna Dorje, accompanied his uncle, Sakya Paṇḍita, to the camp of the Mongol prince Köden. As Kapstein tells it:

Sakya Paṇḍita's visit did establish a precedent of sorts, and it led to some factions of the Mongol court insisting upon Sakyapa's authority in Tibetan religious affairs, even if the temporal dimensions of the relationship were not yet fully formed. Moreover, and perhaps most important for the future, it meant that Sakya Paṇḍita's two young nephews, Phakpa and his brother Chakna, who accompanied him, spent their formative years among the Mongols. The former would become the Tibetan preceptor of Khubilai Khan (1215–1294) and in 1264 was elevated to the religious and secular leadership of

Tibet. This occurred when, as the offering bestowed by the khan on the occasion of his receiving formal tantric initiation, he granted to Phakpa lordship over the thirteen myriarchies of central Tibet and Tsang, together with western Tibet, Amdo and Kham. As the preeminent Tibetan clergyman in the eastern Mongol empire, which in 1271 adopted the Chinese dynastic title Yuan, Phakpa would be instrumental in the formation of the Mongol-Sakyapa alliance.

Phakpa's service to Khubilai Khan included the creation of a new writing system . . . He also conferred tantric initiation on the emperor, thereby symbolically anointing him as a Cakravartin . . . universal monarch.[360]

Another source similarly states that Qubilai received initiation from Phakpa on two occasions; once, he offered him the rule of Tibet as part of his initiation offering.[361]

The layout of Figure 5.25 is highly unusual. Phakpa is depicted sitting on an elaborate throne, outside of a Chinese-style, gilt-roof pavilion or temple. His throne has a unique base made of white stone with marble-like veins and with large dragons on both sides. The white stone is continued in architectural elements to his right, which resemble curving sides of pillar bases and a long white stone capital. When visiting Xanadu, Marco Polo reported that one of Qubilai Khan's main palaces was made of marble. As one historian of the Mongols described it:

There was of course a Xanadu–Shang-tu, on a southern spur of the Khitan Mountains, where Khubilai's marble palace stood, surrounded by the slow paths and padding beasts of his parklands,

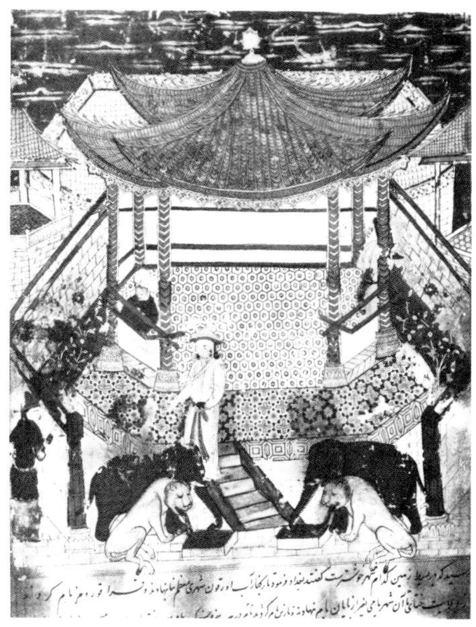

and where with an architectural obeisance to his nomad past he had erected a vast tent, its roof and uprights gilded and its hundred supporting ropes of glittering silk, a structure mobile in theory, but in practice never taken down. [362]

The two thin, red supporting pillars to the right and left of Phakpa are also distinctive. As reported by Marco Polo, the Cane Palace was another of Qubilai's palaces, a marvelous structure made of lengths of painted or gilt bamboo that, when fitted together, connected the bodies of dragons, possibly intertwining ones.

In this painting (Fig. 6.25), tassels of a canopy hang from the pavilion behind Phakpa, overlapping his dark-green head nimbus. The gathering seems to take place in an imperial courtyard. Three religious attendants stand to the lower right, partly obscured by a wall and two trees that grow outside it. At the bottom of the painting, a standing man guards the open courtyard gate, through which passes a man bearing a

rectangular load. An animal resembling a tiger sits outside the gate, restrained by a red rope. The courtyard is walled in on the left side, behind the great patron, Qubilai. At the lower left are two foreign rulers, perhaps from Persia or Central Asia, offering to Phakpa a golden wheel, symbolizing political rule.

Such a unique tableau—the first such composition in the history of Tibetan painting—must have been created by Khyentse Chenmo, an artist who loved to include as many true-to-life details as possible. Perhaps we will one day know better the Yuan artistic sources that he copied here.

Figure 6.27 illustrates a Mongolian khan's luxurious pavilion at the old capital, Karakorum, in the thirteenth century, the time of Ögedei (1229–1241). Note the pairs of elephants and tigers at either side of the of the entrance stairs.

It seems that Khyentse Chenmo depicted two different Yuan court scenes, both of which must have been telling in the career of Chögyal Phakpa (Figs. 6.25 and 6.28). Presumably Khyentse adapted older paintings of such scenes, or he reconstructed the imperial court after studying other paintings of it. The first key event may have been Phakpa's receiving the Pearl Edict (*'Ja' sa mu tig ma*) in May 1264. This named him head of Buddhist affairs for the Yuan empire and granted him rule over Tibet, as symbolized by a wheel. The second key event may have been Phakpa being named imperial preceptor (*dishi*) about 1269 to 1270. I suggest that Figure 6.25 shows the first event in 1264, when Chakna was still alive, and Figure 6.28 depicts the second event. Since Khyentse Chenmo painted two complete sets of the Lamdre lineage for Gongkar, he could have depicted Phakpa differently in each one.

In Figure 6.28, Chögyal Phakpa appears as a teacher of the Lamdre lineage, in the Mongol court setting. Again he is shown seated on an elaborate

throne, but here his hands are differently positioned. He may be giving teachings or manifesting miracles in the presence of the emperor and empress or conferring initiations upon them. The small figure at the bottom left seems ready to hand a scroll to Phakpa.

In this painting, Qubilai wears a hat with a white top and cloth neck guard in back (Fig. 6.29). It is closer in shape to the hat in a later portrait, Figure 6.30, which depicts Qubilai as he appears in a Yuan imperial album.

The layout of the second thangka portraying Phakpa (Fig. 6.28) is idiosyncratic. Here, the main figure is placed to the right of the central axis. It is unexpected to see a Tibetan lama depicted in the foreground of an elaborate and minutely depicted imperial-court scene, but it seems Khyentse Chenmo welcomed such a challenge.

Another noteworthy difference between this portrait of Phakpa and Figure 6.25 is that Phakpa's younger brother, Chakna Dorje, is not present here. Also striking is the presence of a Mongol noblewoman wearing a distinctive red hat and sitting next to Qubilai. She is his wife, Empress Chabi, who was a devoted disciple of Phakpa and did much to make her husband more sympathetic to Buddhism and receptive to Phakpa as his religious teacher. Figure 6.31 shows Empress Chabi's formal portrait in a Yuan imperial album.

One historian of Mongolia described Chabi:

> His wife, Chabi, a devout Buddhist, clearly affected his attitudes and policies toward Buddhism, but the lama Phagpa (1235–1280), the chief figure in the Sakya order, made the most profound impression on the Great Khan. The Tibetan lama had not only developed a projected written language . . . but had also instructed Khubilai in the tenets of Tibetan Buddhism.

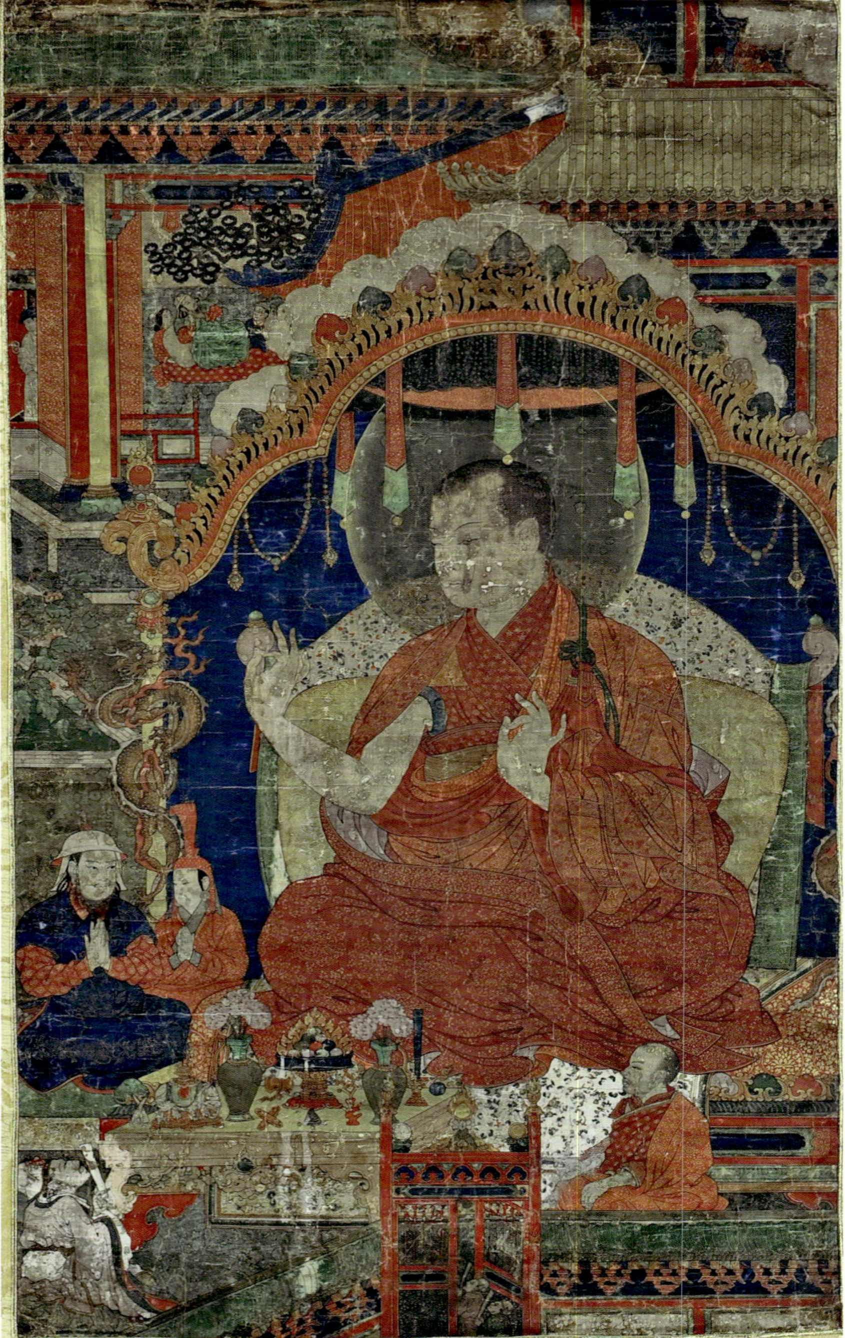

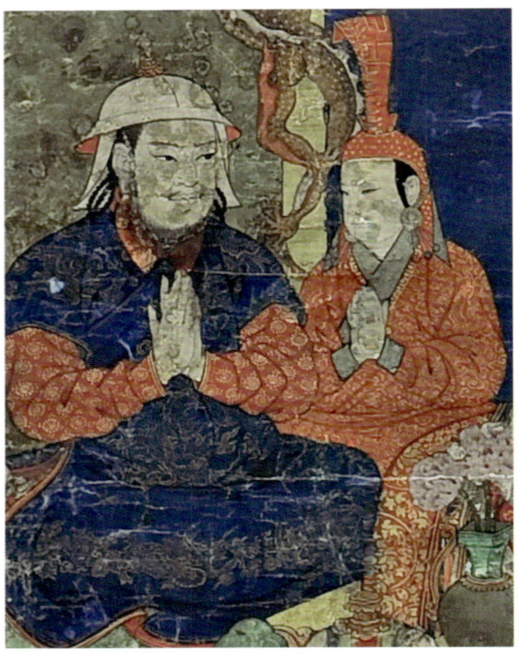

FIG. 6.28
Phakpa as Teacher of the Path with the
Result at the Yuan Court
by Khyentse Chenmo
second half of the fifteenth century
32 ¼ x 20 in. (82 x 50.8 cm)
Art Gallery of Greater Victoria, British
Columbia.
Literature: Fisher 1997, pl. 155

FIG. 6.29
Qubilai and Chabi
Detail of Fig. 6.28

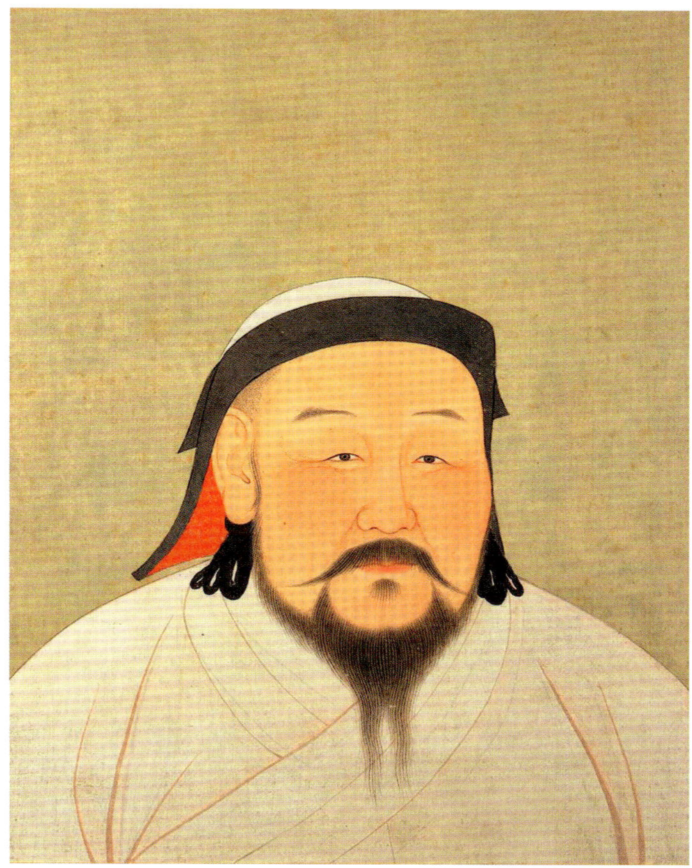

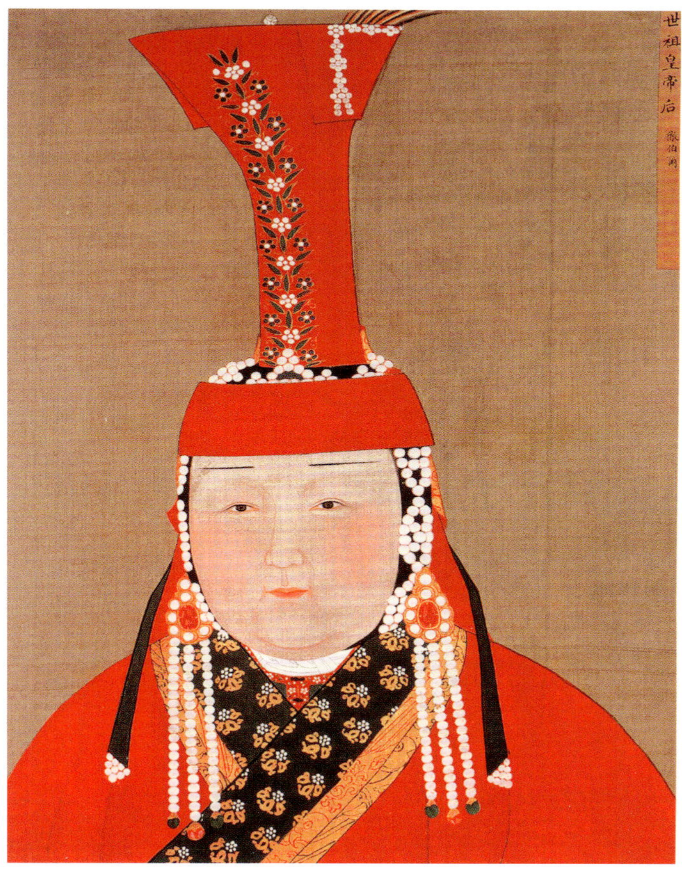

Fig. 6.30
Qubilai Khan
album leaf; ink and colors on silk, second
half of the thirteenth century
23 ⅜ x 18 ½ in. (59.4 x 47.0 cm)
National Palace Museum, Taiwan
Literature: Rossabi 1995, fig. 3

Fig. 6.31
Empress Chabi, Consort of Qubilai Khan
album leaf, ink and colors on silk; late
thirteenth century
24 ¼ x 19 in. (61.5 x 48.0 cm)
National Palace Museum, Taiwan
Literature: Rossabi 1995, fig. 7; and
McCausland 2015, no. 28

Perhaps as critical, Khubilai ordered his Tibetan instructor to tutor Zhenjing, his son and heir, in a more systematic way in the precepts of the faith.[363]

Chabi (1227–1281) was an Onggirat Mongol who, as wife of Qubilai Khan, became empress consort of the Yuan dynasty in China. According to *The Secret History of the Mongols*, she was the favorite wife of Qubilai and his valued unofficial counselor throughout his reign. Exemplifying the high role of women in Mongol culture, she was politically and diplomatically very influential as Qubilai's spouse and adviser, especially in gaining the sympathy of the Chinese common people through a policy of reconciliation. She also promoted Buddhism in the upper levels of government.[364]

Chabi was eight years older than Phakpa, and she died a year after he did, in 1281. One source says that Phakpa conferred upon Qubilai and others a tantric initiation already in 1253.)[365] Chabi was a major patroness of many Buddhist projects.[366] She sponsored the carving of Yuan xylographs (*hor par ma*) for printing Tibetan Buddhist sacred writings, such as those of Chögyal Phakpa's uncle, Sakya Paṇḍita.[367] Her distinctive red hat, *boghtaq*, was a symbol of high status among Mongol noblewomen. (See Fig. 6.32.)

In his recent book on Yuan visual art, Shane McCausland featured Empress Chabi three times, including the album portrait in Figure 6.31 as both a full image and a detail.[368] His third illustration was Figure 6.33, a detail from a scroll painting attributed to Liu Guandao, in which she is depicted on horseback, hunting with Qubilai in the spring of 1280.

McCausland referred to Chabi's personal integrity: "The official Chinese source portrays Chabi as fully deserving of her honorary title, granted in 1273: as Chaste and Good, Bright and Sagacious, Compliant to Heaven, Wise in Culture,

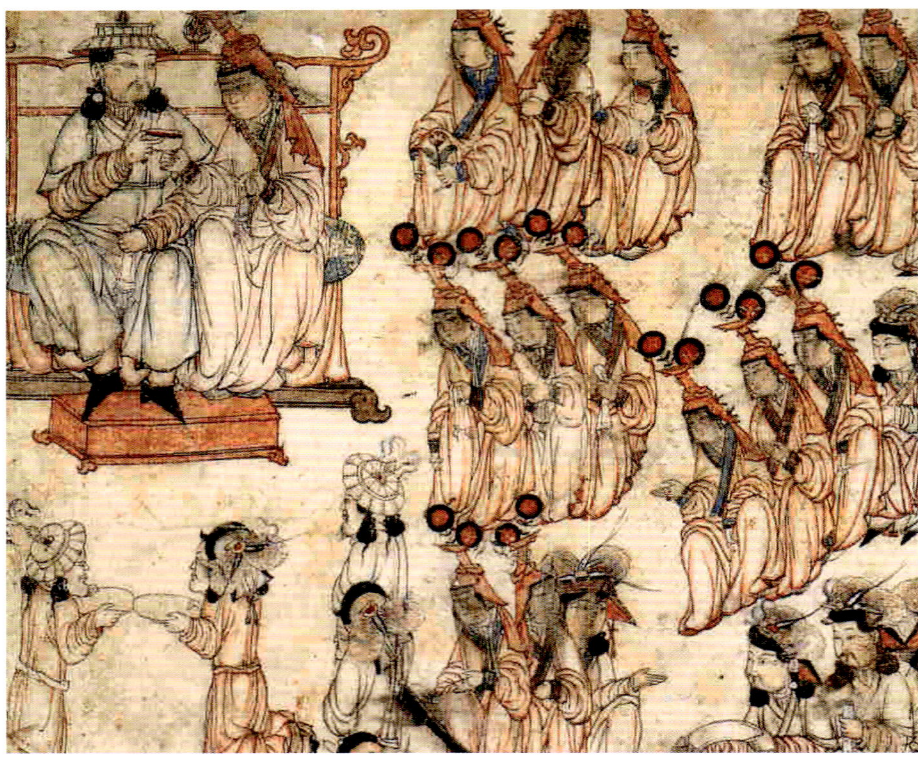

Brilliant in Responsiveness Empress."[369] And he described her exceptional character:

> According to Chabi's official Chinese biography in the *Yuan shi*, then, in 1276 after the defeat of the Southern Song, Khubilai had the former boy emperor, Gongdi (r. 1274–1276) and remnants of the Song royal family brought to court in Shangdu where he held a great feast to celebrate the victory. Everyone was enjoying the occasion to the full. Only the empress Chabi was unhappy—worried by the demise of the Songs and about the future of her own descendants, the future rulers of the Yuan dynasty. She was certainly deeply concerned for the welfare of the Song empress dowager, who was unhappily forced to reside in the capital, for her own safety, by Khubilai. To lift his wife's spirits, Khubilai ordered the antiquities (*guwu*, ancient things) of the Song palace treasury brought to Dadu and he had a huge display of them in the palace for Chabi to look at. She came, examined them, and departed. Seeing the wealth that would never be handed down the Song royal line, and thinking of her own progeny, she said she was so moved by the Song's defeat that she was unable to pick out anything for herself.[370]

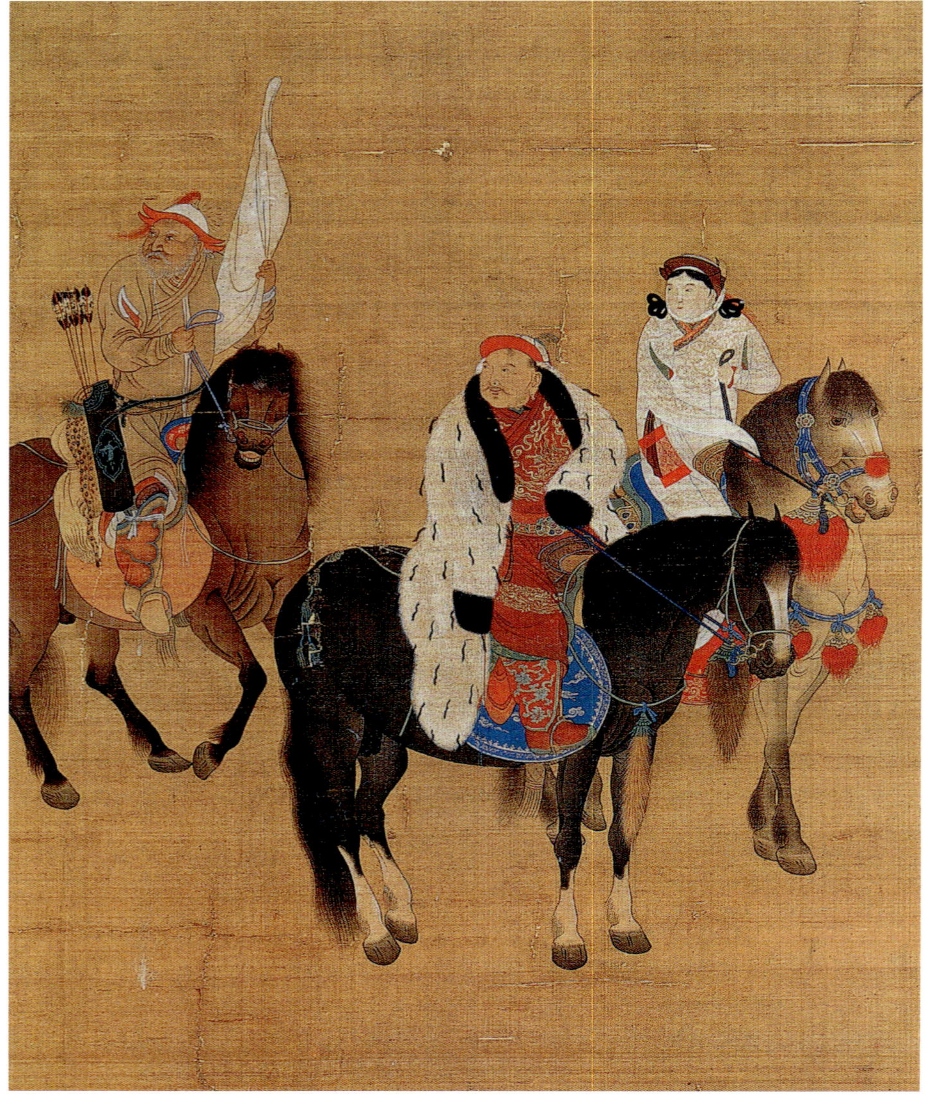

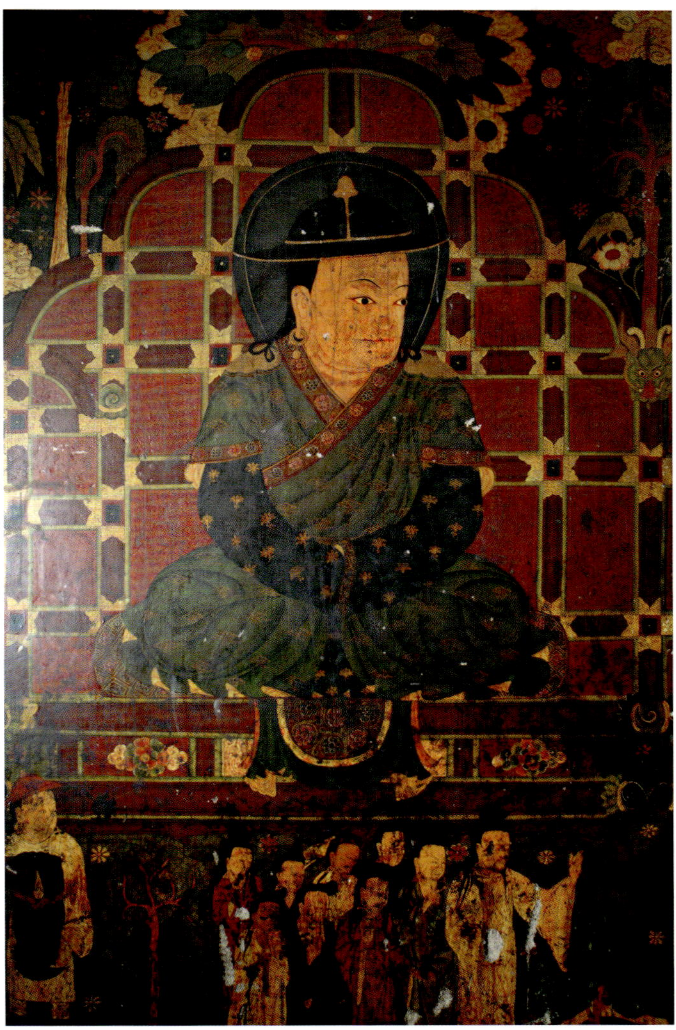 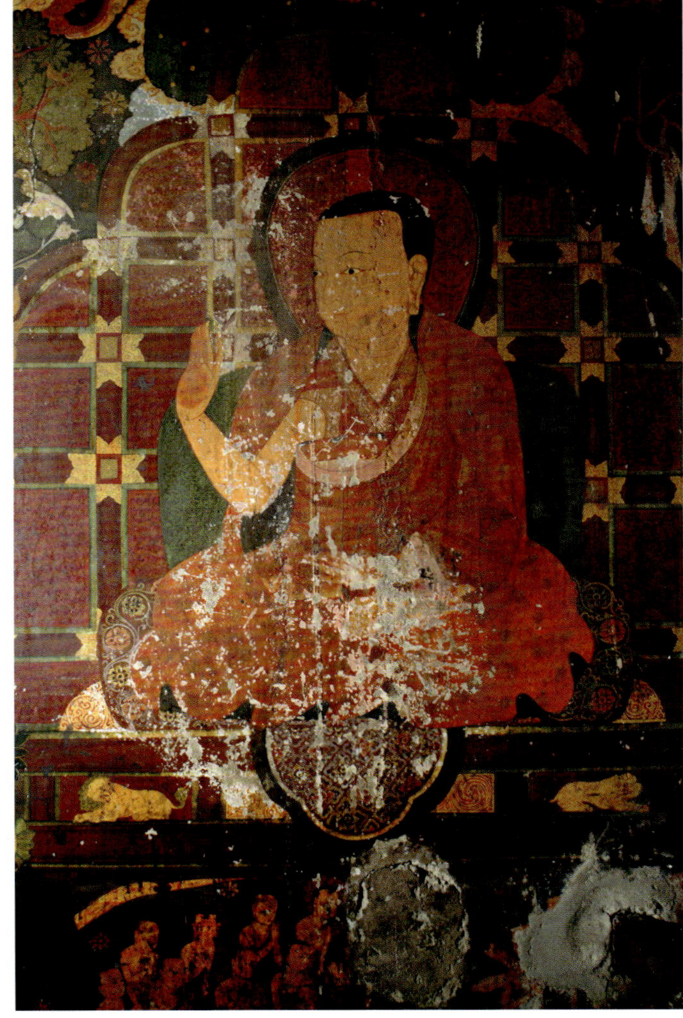

On another, perhaps earlier, occasion Chabi picked from the Tai Fujian war spoils, in southeastern China, some fine silk "inners and outers." But Qubilai scolded her, saying that such plundered goods belonged to the military and official departments and were not for members of the royal family. After that, she exercised diligence and frugality, setting a high example for the women of the palace. She was also remarkably resourceful: once, when Qubilai was blinded by the sun while out shooting, "she invented a hat with a brim to shade his eyes, a design that was thereafter adopted widely."[371] She may have devised the distinctive brimmed hat that Qubilai wears in such Tibetan portraits as Figure 6.25.

Another significant mural that portrays Chögyal Phakpa and Qubilai together is in the Lamdre Lhakhang on the second floor of the main temple of the Palkhor Chöde Monastery in Gyantse (Figs. 6.34a and 6.34b). Michael Henss notes the presence of many Sakya biographical scenes there.[372] He stresses, in particular, the presence of such famous biographical episodes as Sakya Paṇḍita with young Phakpa in Kyirong and Chögyal Phakpa at the Yuan court with Qubilai Khan. He also mentions fifteen relevant illustrations in a Chinese publication (*Zhongguo*, pls. 75–90).[373]

For details of Qubilai and his hat, see Figures 6.35 and 6.36.

Corresponding scenes also exist in a published thangka set depicting the life of Phakpa, which was painted in Sakya in the late seventeenth or eighteenth century.[374] The relevant painting was also shown in a 2006 catalog that discussed the eleventh in the series of twenty-odd paintings, showing details of events of

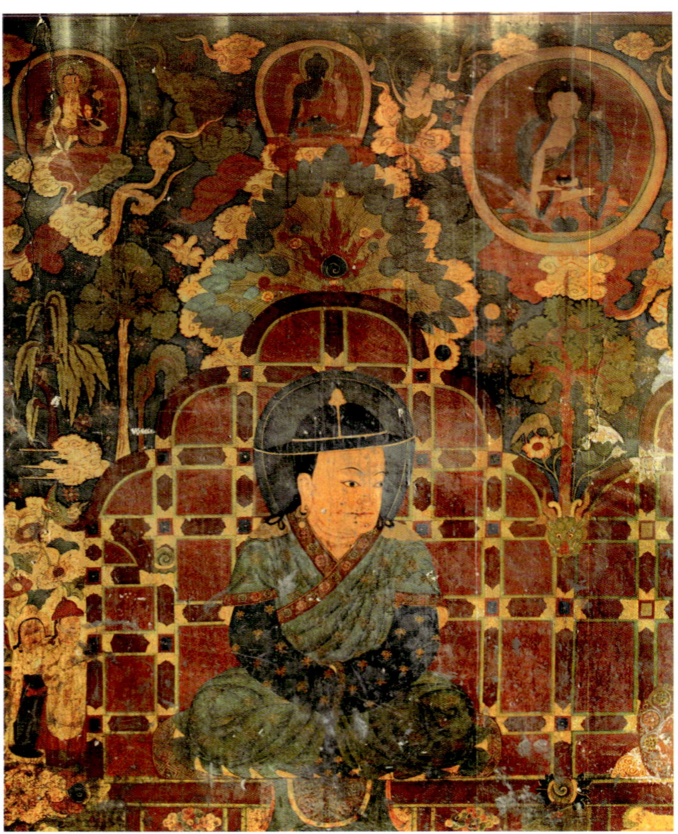
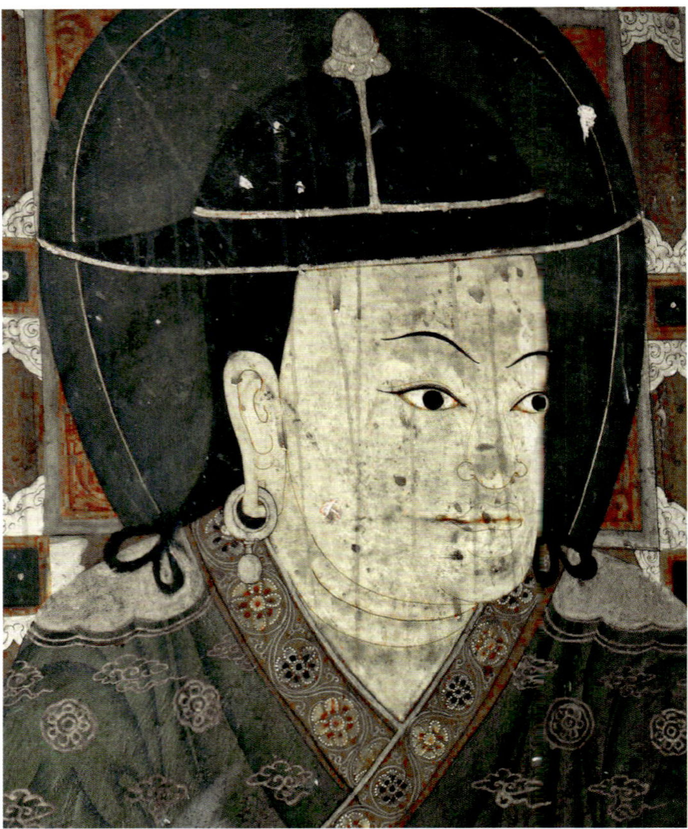

Phakpa's life involving Qubilai.[375] The catalog shows two details of the khan and his court, sitting in two palaces; Qubilai wears a white broad-brimmed hat with a golden crest ornament (*tog*). None of the details of these biographical paintings or the murals of Gyantse bears any resemblance to the Yuan court scenes painted by Khyentse Chenmo.

Figure 6.37 depicts Chögyal Phakpa as a lineal teacher of the Lamdre. This later mural at the Kunzang Tse College confirms that the unusual depictions in the two main thangkas discussed above (Figs. 6.25 and 6.28) were well-established traditions at Gongkar that either went back to a copy of a Khyentse original (as in Fig. 6.25) or were a Khyentse original (as in Fig. 6.28). Here the iconography of the central figure is exactly that of Figure 6.28, with both hands raised distinctively in the presence of his two great patrons.

Figure 6.38 is another thangka portraying Chögyal Phakpa as a lineal master of the Lamdre. The painting is not in good condition. Though his face is not clear in the available photograph, he appears youthful, with both hands on his knees. He is seated on an elaborate black-and-gold throne, without the usual court around him.

A female protective deity, Green Tārā, is directly above Phakpa, and from her hang two long blue scarves. Below her, a red canopy hovers, with long tassels fluttering in the breeze. A gust catches the middle of the canopy, which reveals the golden fabric underneath.

The painting's background also depicts clouds and a landscape that includes birds and animals. Noteworthy are, at the left leg of the throne, the deer-like beast that holds a special fungus of longevity in its mouth and, in the lower-right foreground, the pair of long-legged and long-tailed blue birds that hop about.

Interestingly the Yuan-court setting was not forgotten from this painting. A detail (Fig. 6.39) depicts Qubilai's capital of Xanadu from a bird's-eye view. At the center is a gilt-roof temple or palace, where Phakpa is seated, perhaps with his patron; Phakpa's holy presence is indicated by the red canopy floating above the pagoda-like roof. Around the complex are numerous gates and towers with exotic shapes. Inside the walls are various people, some wearing black official hats.

The central structure features uncommon white elements: two curved shapes in the upper-right and -left corners of the room where Phakpa sits and the squarish shape on the floor above. At first

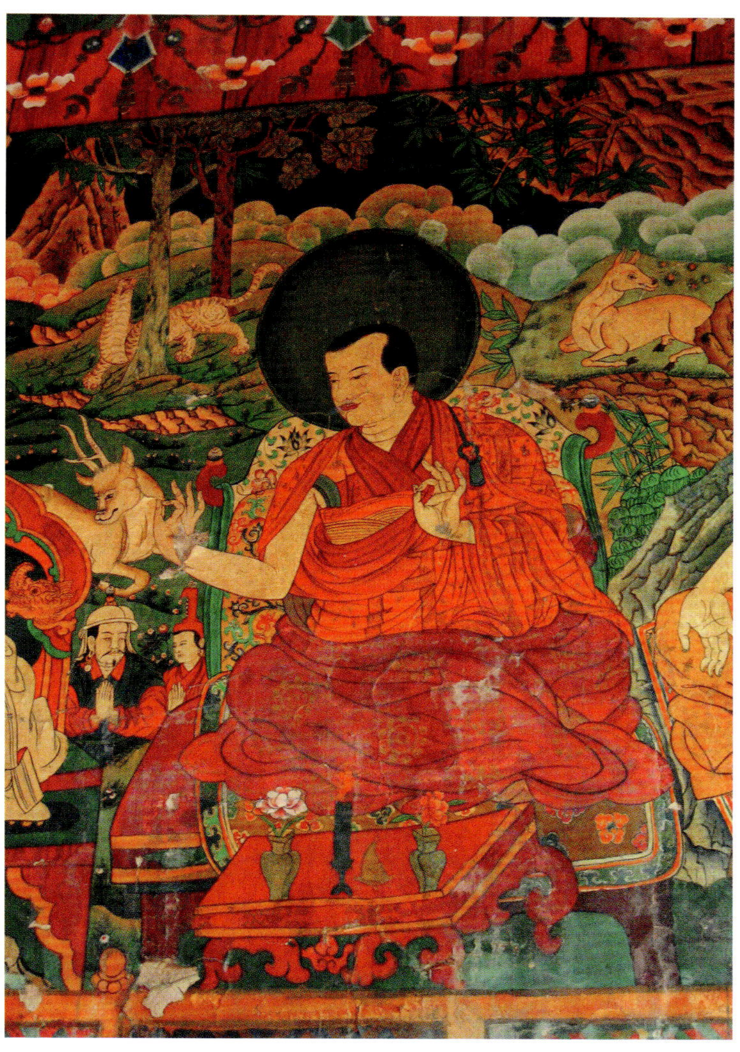

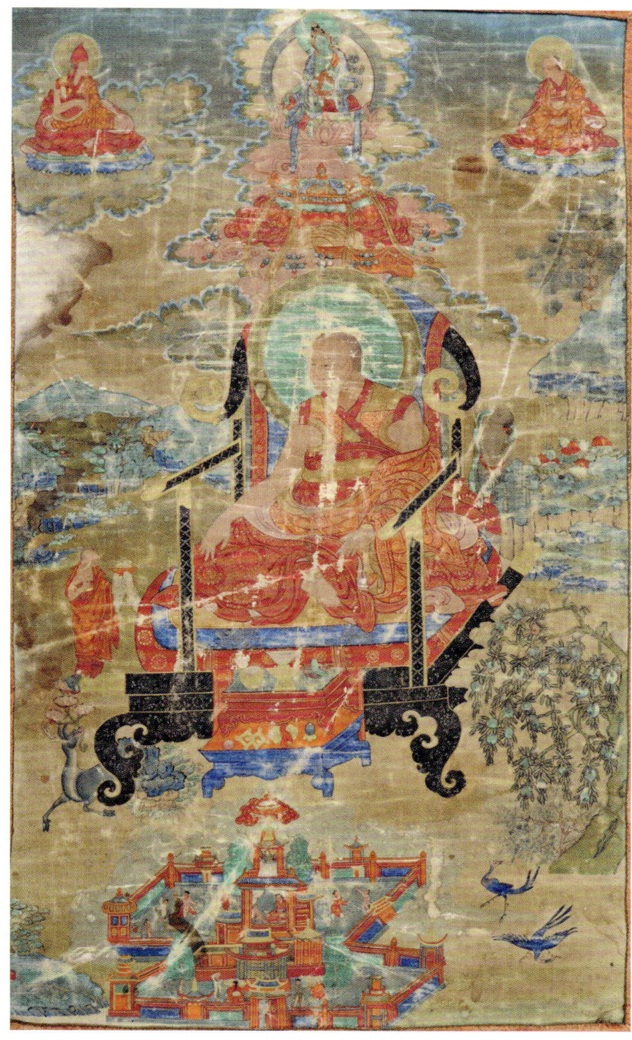

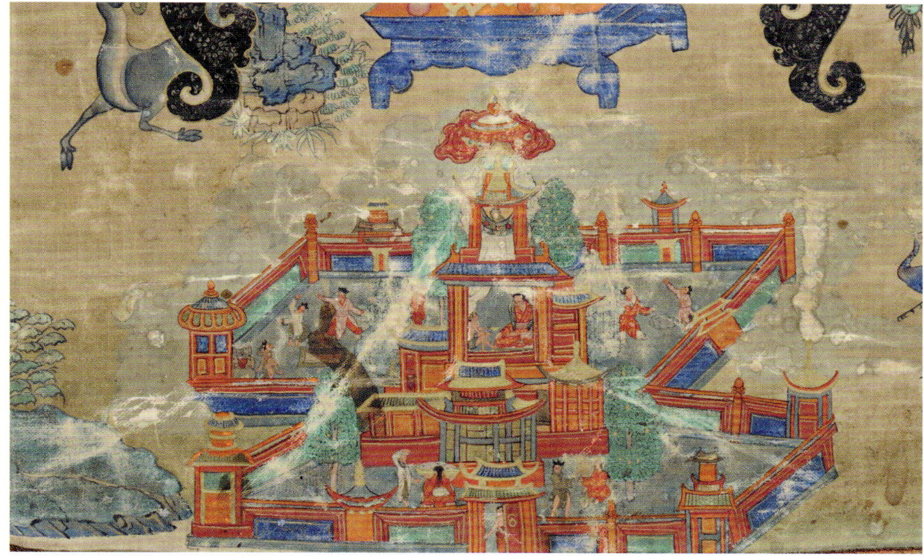

Fig. 6.37
Chögyal Phakpa as Fifteenth Guru of Lamdre
Mural, Kunzang Tse College, Gongkar; ca. 1930s
Photo: A. Lustgarten, 2005

Fig. 6.38
Chögyal Phakpa as Teacher of the Path with the Result Lineage
pigments on cloth, second half of the fifteenth century
17 ¾ x 10 ¾ in. (45.2 x 27.3 cm)
Burke Museum 80.0-517

Fig. 6.39
Bird's-eye view of Xanadu
Detail of Fig. 6.38

glance I thought that these might depict the white marble of Qubilai's palace. But they are more likely white curtains, pulled back to reveal the gray-green interior of the ground-floor room and hanging out of the second-floor window.

Figure 6.40 offers an example of the Yuan imperial pavilions' elaborate backdrops of curtains with white grounds and colorful floral designs. The painting's main subject, the Fourth Karmapa Rolpe Dorje (1340–1383), visited the Yuan court for three years; one episode is depicted by the main figure on his special throne and the patterned curtains. In a smaller episode below, the Karmapa sits in a pavilion with pale green curtains.

Figure 6.41 portrays Chögyal Phakpa in a Khyenri-style thangka with a completely different composition. Here the lama is depicted with his right hand touching the robes at his right knee and his left in a gesture of teaching. He sits on a stack of mats, with a complicated throne behind him. The throne, offering table, and offerings are depicted in great detail. The painting could be a later copy of a Khyentse Chenmo composition.

Phakpa is shown with a transparent head nimbus, which Khyentse and his followers were known for. Behind and mostly obscured by the throne back, three foreign nobles or Yuan-court functionaries stand, each wearing a distinctively different official hat and each waving a different honorary banner above Phakpa. In the upper right, as a minor figure, sits the learned saint from Kashmir, Śākyaśrībhadra, who was a teacher of Phakpa's uncle, Sakya Paṇḍita.

Here, Phakpa's appearance is extremely youthful. The justification for depicting him so young, as if in his twenties, may lie in historical fact: in 1260, when Phakpa became ruler of Tibet, he was just twenty-five years old. And he was just nineteen when he first became Qubilai's religious teacher.[376] It is wonderful that so many of his portraits have survived.

Fig. 6.40
The Fourth Karmapa
second half of the fifteenth century
British Museum
BM no 1906,1226,0.13.

Fig. 6.41
Chögyal Phakpa
ca. sixteenth century
27 ½ x 22 in. (70 x 56 cm)
Essen Collection, Museum der Kulturen, Basel
(HAR 3314520)
Literature: Essen and Thingo 1989, no. I–74

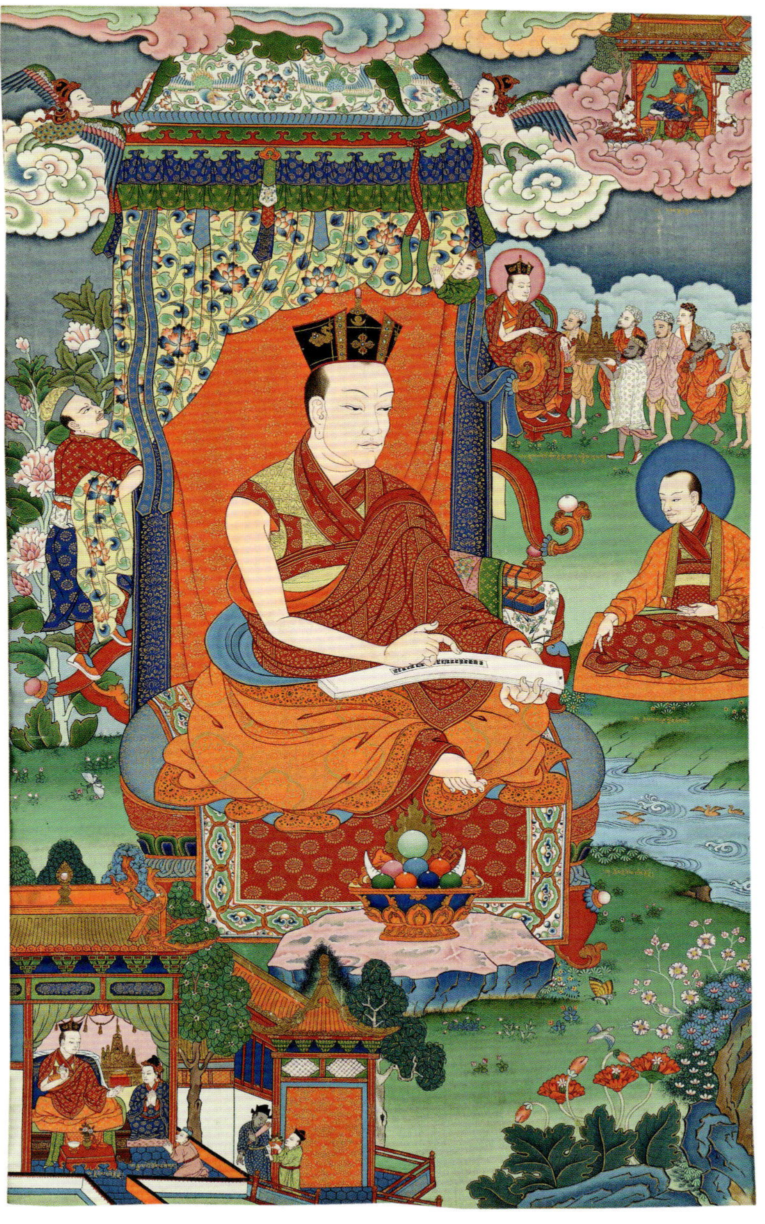 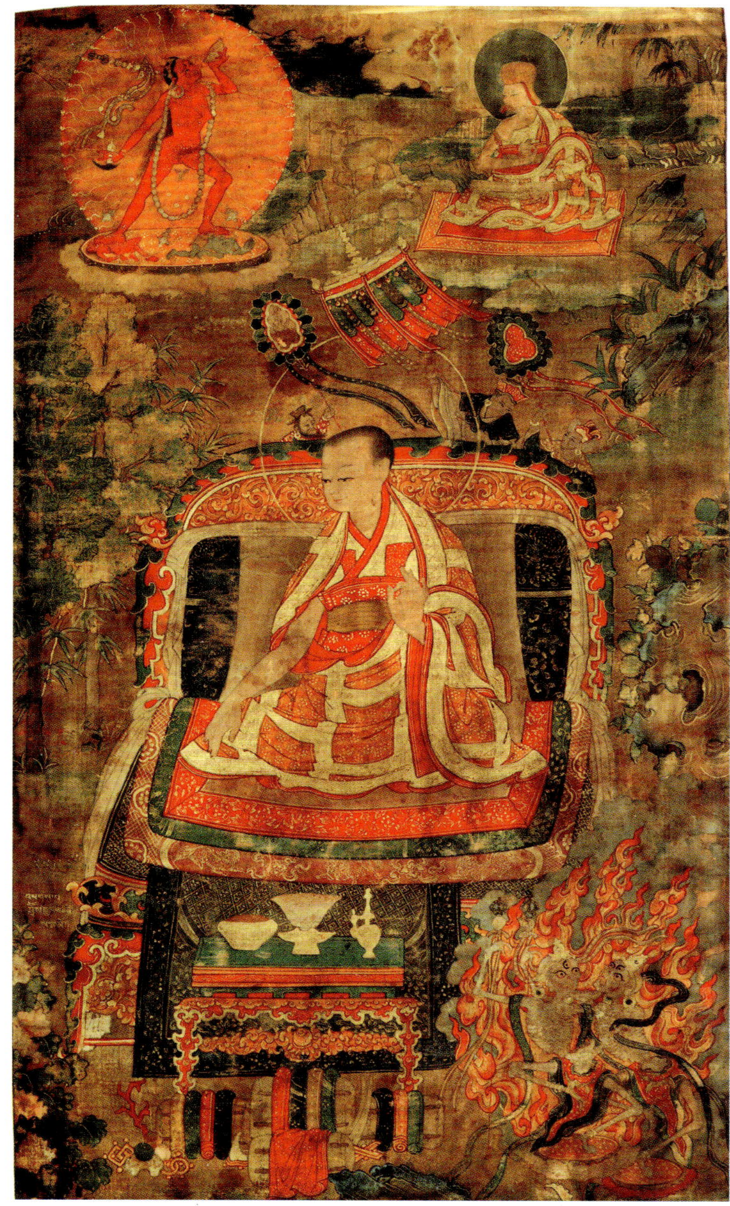

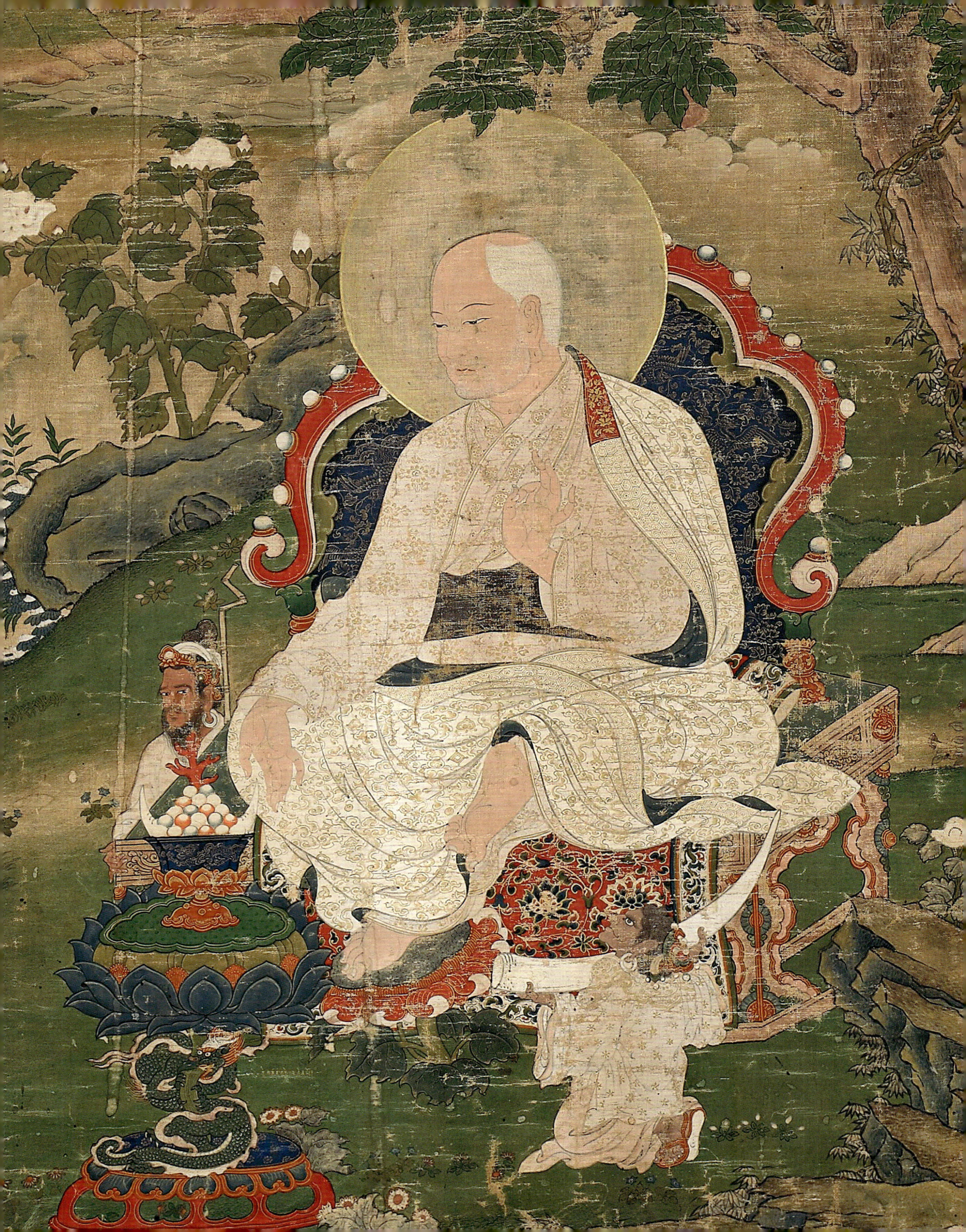

CHAPTER 7

Thangka Sets Depicting the Lamdre Lineage by Khyentse Chenmo

BASED ON SIMILARITIES with the Gongkar murals and with other sets of thangkas, I have been able to identify almost thirty surviving thangka sets that are indisputably in the Khyenri style. Often the central painting of Buddha or Vajradhara provided the stylistic evidence for those identifications. The main known sets can be divided temporally into three periods: early, from Khyentse Chenmo's time; middle, from about the sixteenth century; and late, from about the seventeenth century or later.

Chapters 7 through 9 will present the earliest painting sets, dating to the mid- or late fifteenth century, that I believe were by Khyentse Chenmo himself. Thus the present chapter will investigate thangka sets by Khyentse Chenmo that depict the Lamdre lineage.

I was able to find evidence of about twenty-one sets of Khyentse Chenmo's paintings, originally comprising several hundred individual paintings. These earliest sets can be divided by theme into eight groups, according to subject: 1. Lamdre lineage masters (4 sets); 2. the Shambhala kings (2 sets); 3. the sixteen arhats (8 sets); 4. the eighty-four great adepts (1 set); 5. the *jātaka* (1 set); 6. the Buddha's life (2 sets); 7. Nyingma lineage lamas (1 set); and 8. Kagyu lineage lamas (2 sets). This chapter features the four sets depicting Lamdre lineage masters, painted by Khyentse Chenmo or his very early successors.

TEACHERS OF THE *LAMDRE* LINEAGE

In Chapters 5 and 6, when comparing several gilt-copper sculptures from Drathang to the main corresponding Khyenri-style thangkas and murals, I presented several paintings that depict Lamdre lineage masters, including a number of very early ones. Some individual paintings are the sole known surviving fragments of important thangka sets.

Gyatön, in his biography of Dorjedenpa, mentions "two sets of wonderful paintings of the Lamdre lineage masters" among the most treasured paintings kept at Gongkar.[377] They must have been painted by Khyentse Chenmo. Gyatön enumerated them at the head of the list of one hundred forty thangkas of larger and smaller sizes that existed in Gongkar Monastery at Gongkarwa's time. I assume that many of the later thangka and mural paintings depicting the Lamdre lineage at Gongkar were based on these two lost or dispersed sets of thangkas.

1. Lamdre Set 1: Sakya Paṇḍita (in Gongkar Dorjeden)

Figure 7.1, discussed in detail as Figure 6.16, is the sole thangka from Khyentse Chenmo's two main sets that survive at Gongkar Dorjeden Monastery. The thangka depicts Sakya Paṇḍita as a teacher of the Lamdre lineage. According to Penba Wangdu, its dimensions are 80 centimeters tall by 50 centimeters wide.

Figure 7.2, though slightly larger than Figure 7.1, may come from the same set. Here, Khyentse Chenmo depicts the Sakya founding master Sönam Tsemo (bSod nams rtse mo) as a lineage master of the Lamdre instructions. Tiny gold letters under the main figure identify him—*bso nam tse mo* (*bsod nams rtse mo*)—otherwise, it would have been hard to guess his identity without also knowing the Kunzang Tse murals. Khyentse devoted much care to portraying the main figure, a long-haired Tibetan lay master in his twenties or thirties, sitting in a Chinese-style landscape. The fact that Khyentse omitted the main figure's head nimbus heightens the stylistic effect.

Sönam Tsemo comes across as a cultivated and intelligent young nobleman-lama (Fig. 7.2). His dark brown hair is either tied back or cut short. He wears a pink long-sleeved upper rope with a green collar, which he wears inside a white brocade upper cloak (Tib. *zla gam*) and lower robe. The cape has a rectangular red collar. He wears colorful boots and sits in an ornate chair; two contrasting cloths are draped over the rounded chair back. On all the textiles, the artist has painted gold brocade designs. On the white table to the right lay three colorful scroll-like objects, a small red box, and a plate of four golden peach-like fruits, possibly adopted by Khyentse from some arhat depiction.

Khyentse Chenmo has also minutely depicted the other figures and the landscape background. The three figures seem to be minor teachers of Sönam Tsemo, whose main teacher

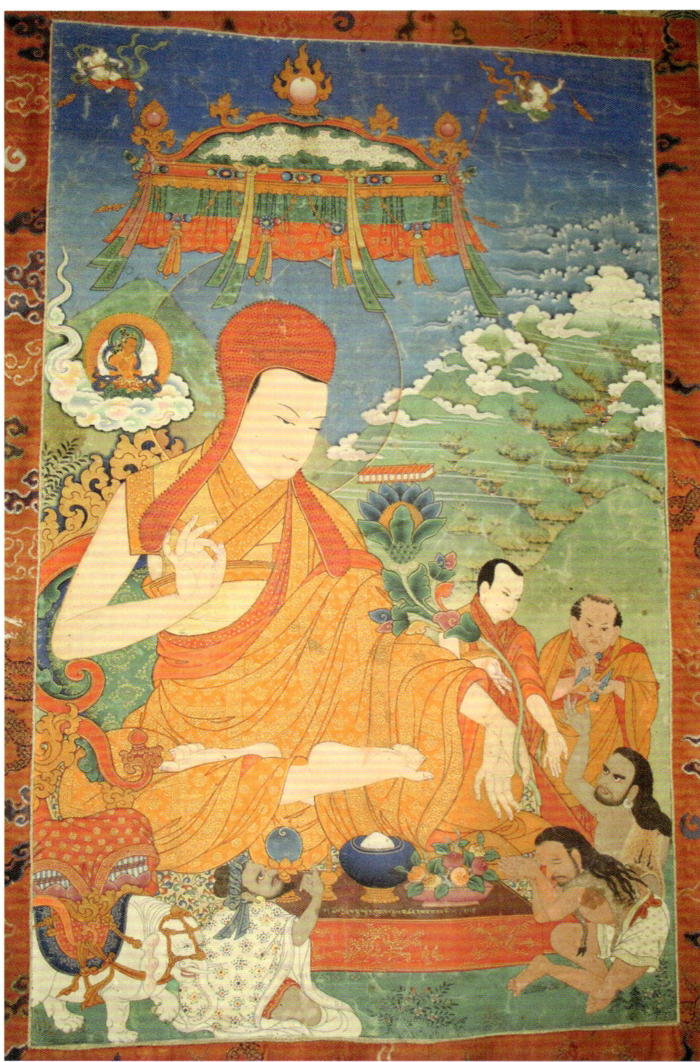

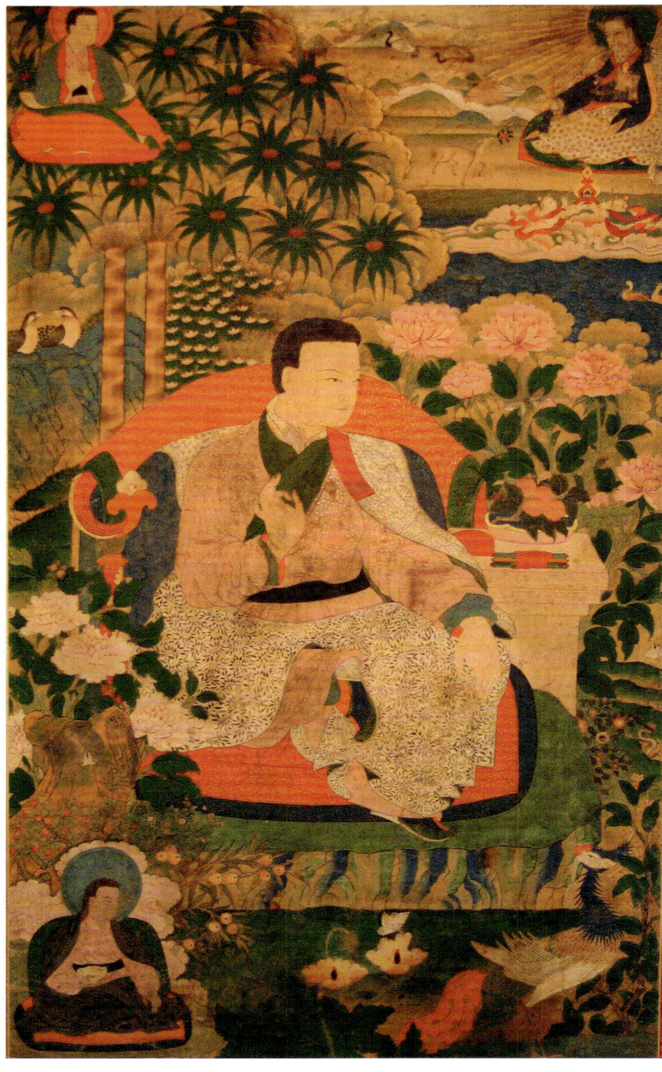

was his father, Sachen. One of his more noteworthy minor teachers was the great dialectician Chapa Chöseng (Phywa pa Chos kyi seng ge). Dominating the middle ground of the landscape are peonies, pink ones to the right of the main figure and lighter pink ones to the left. Four different species of birds stand out from the landscape: a long-tailed phoenix struts in the foreground, a pair of dove-like birds are perched on the rocks behind the chair, a pair of ducks swim in the lake above the pink peonies, and a pair of tall cranes stalk on the distant horizon—though they are too large for being so far away. Several different types of butterflies or other insects are attracted to the nine or ten types of blooming plants. The details are overwhelming; the treatment of the minor deities in the clouds above the lake and

the beaming golden rays of the sun, in the upper right, would alone have been an impressive display.

Seeing this painting's elegant Ming-period landscape in the mid-1990s, I thought it might be an example of Chinese-style paintings of Lamdre masters (*Lam 'bras si thang*) mentioned in a Sakya biography. But it is surely Khyentse Chenmo's work, either belonging to or based on the sets he painted in Gongkar.

The iconography of Sönam Tsemo in Figure 7.2 is the same as his depiction in a surviving mural at Kunzang Tse (Fig. 7.3). Note the cape draped over the same shoulder and the same shoe-clad feet. In the mural, the presence of flowers is reconfirmed. The mural adds an intriguing minor figure, to the lower left of Sönam Tsemo, grasping a small offering table of tantric offerings in both hands.

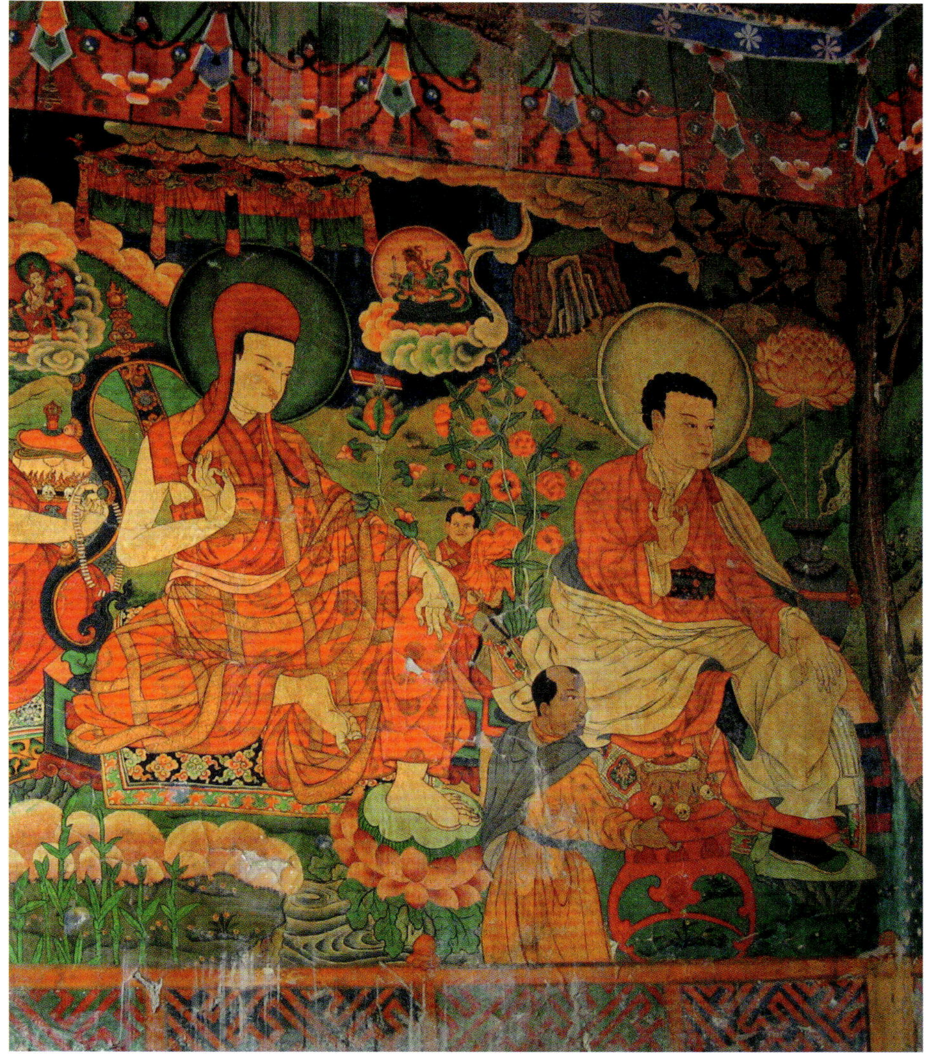

2. Lamdre Set 2: Phakpa (in Victoria, British Columbia)

In Figure 7.4, discussed in detail as Figure 6.28, Khyentse Chenmo depicted the lineage guru of the Lamdre after Sakya Paṇḍita, Chögyal Phakpa Lotrö Gyalt-shen. The eminent lama is portrayed as the main figure in three-quarter view, seated on a broad throne with an ornate backrest. Chögyal Phakpa is distinctly depicted at the Yuan imperial court: to the left sits Qubilai Khan and his main wife, Empress Chabi. There is no ornate canopy over Phakpa's head, but a similar element with tassels has been worked into the top of the bejeweled backrest.[378]

This thangka is somewhat smaller than Figure 7.23; the two paintings evidently came from different sets. The landscape treatments can vary a lot within a single set by Khyentse

Chenmo.[379] Another probable member of an early Lamdre lineage set is the painting of Ḍamarupa, presented earlier in Figure 5.9b.

3. Lamdre Set 3: Three Paintings (in the British Museum, London)

The next set depicting the gurus of the Lamdre is known through three thangkas in the British Museum. It, too, is closely related to the sets painted by Khyentse Chenmo at Gongkar. The paintings are shorter than the three early paintings just discussed but are about the same width as the painting of Sönam Tsemo (Fig. 7.23). The three paintings once belonged to Hugh E. Richardson, a British diplomat who visited Tibet in the 1940s, when the set was divided.

Figure 7.5 depicts Paṇḍita

Gayadhara as a Lamdre lineal guru. It portrays him as an intense teacher, caught while explaining a difficult point of practice. Here, Khyentse has taken care to get his details right. The subject is an Indian learned man with brown skin. His prominent red pandit hat appears to be made of Indian silk, with long earflaps hanging down. Unlike most pandits in Buddhist lineage paintings, he is a layman, hence he wears a white upper robe, such as those typically made of plain Indian cotton. His meditation band and rosary, which he holds in his left hand and which he seems to go on absent-mindedly fingering even while teaching, show that he is a specialist of yogic practice. Since he is an Indian, his upper chest is bare and he wears a pair of sandals made of red leather set with a few jewels—he is no penniless beggar-sadhu.

In this painting, the pandit is not alone. Behind him sits a foreign-looking disciple or helper who wryly smiles as he offers with both hands a large bowl of nectar. On the table before the yogi are an Indian book and a silver initiation vase. But the master does not need to consult his book; he has not even opened it. He presses his right thumb and middle finger together, as if about to snap his fingers to emphasize his point of yogic practice. His spiritual insight seems to be conveyed by his transparent head nimbus, ringed in gold.

Before him, a horned, blue deer-like beast approaches, holding a large cluster of white, auspicious long-life fungus in its mouth. The lifelike bend of

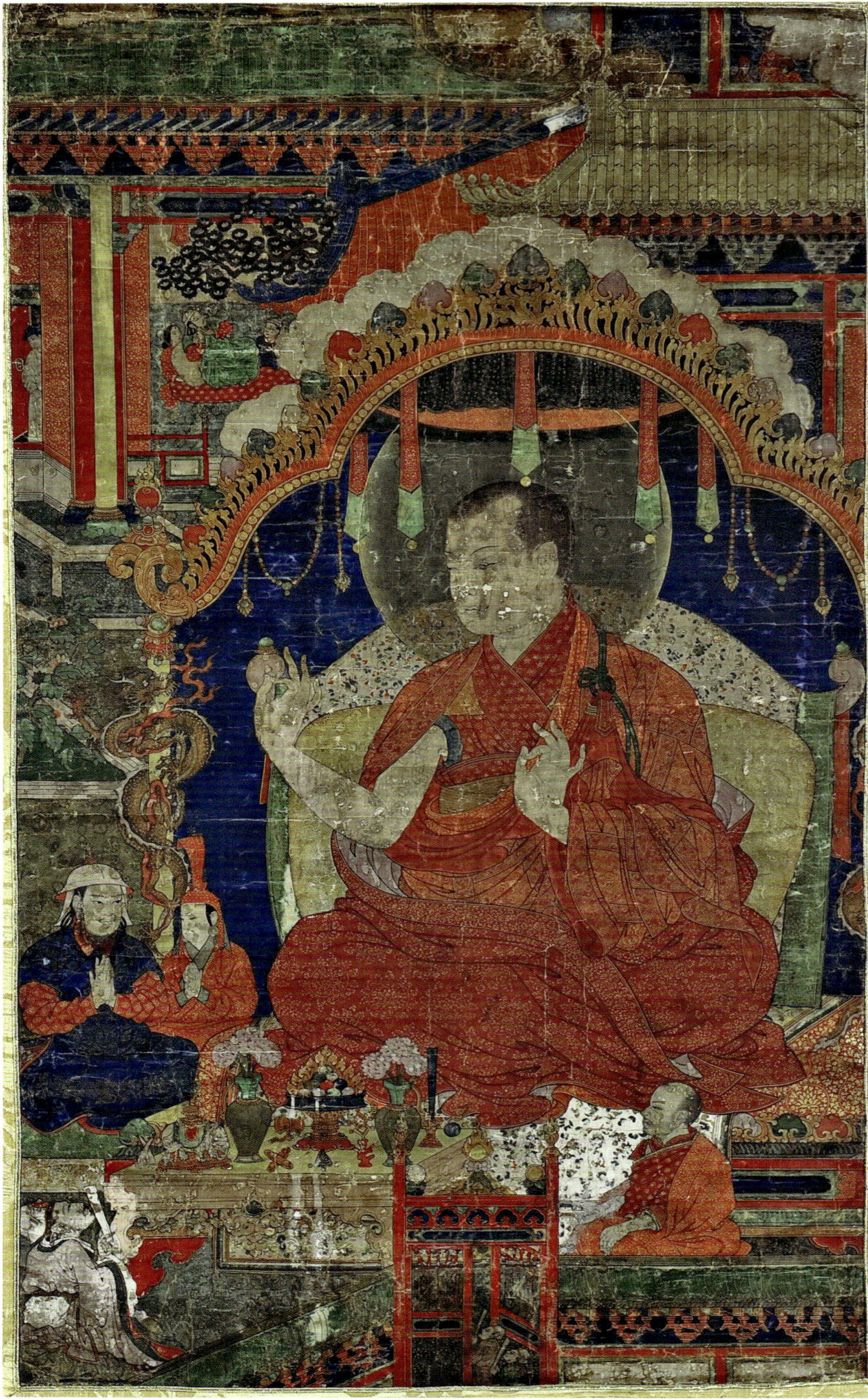

saw the painting in the 1990s, I found no labels or inscriptions, but the main figure was doubtless Pandita Gayadhara, based on the iconography. His portrayal in the surviving lineage-guru murals in the Kunzang Tse College is almost identical, lacking only the silver vase on the table and the fungus-bearing animal (Fig. 7.6).

Figure 7.7 depicts Sachen Kunga Nyingpo as a Lamdre guru, also from the same set. Under the main figure, gold letters state his name, "The Venerable Kind One" (*rje btsun brtse ba chen po)*, a common epithet of Sachen.

The thangka portrays the revered founder of the Sakya school seated on an elegant throne in a tasteful Chinese-style landscape. Khyentse Chenmo has carefully depicted Sachen as a kindly white-haired master, partially bald. His receding hairline features forward and upward points, like little horns, and a few wisps of hair in front. The grayish-green head nimbus contrasts subtly with his relatively smooth pink face, and his thin white beard is effectively indicated. His cape and lower robes of white brocade contrast not only with the dark-blue brocade backrest but also with the dark-blue, broad belt around his waist and with the red brocade collar on the cape, behind his neck; this red is repeated on the rounded edge of the throne and the carpet on which he sits. (The same red trim on a white cape was seen in the portraits of Sönam Tsemo, Figs. 7.2 and 7.3.) His bare feet projecting from the lower robe seem perfectly normal, as does the little lotus pad upon which one foot rests. In all, the painting evokes a gentle and benevolent spiritual presence.

this animal's raised front hoof conveys a feeling of tenderness. Farther away, in the upper right, two small white deer keep their distance, hiding in the distant rocks above a small stand of bamboo. The Chinese-style landscape suggests an Indian or sub-tropical place, reinforcing an exotic atmosphere and feeling of wonder.

Gayadhara's posture is atypical; his torso is turned away and only one

foot is visible. The painter shows a little of Gayadhara's right eye, even though his chin, nose, and brow strongly suggest his profile. The disciple holding a bowl of nectar is depicted in full profile, staring up.

This painting (Fig.7.5) has been previously published twice; the British Museum correctly identified its main figure as Pandita Gayadhara.[380] When I

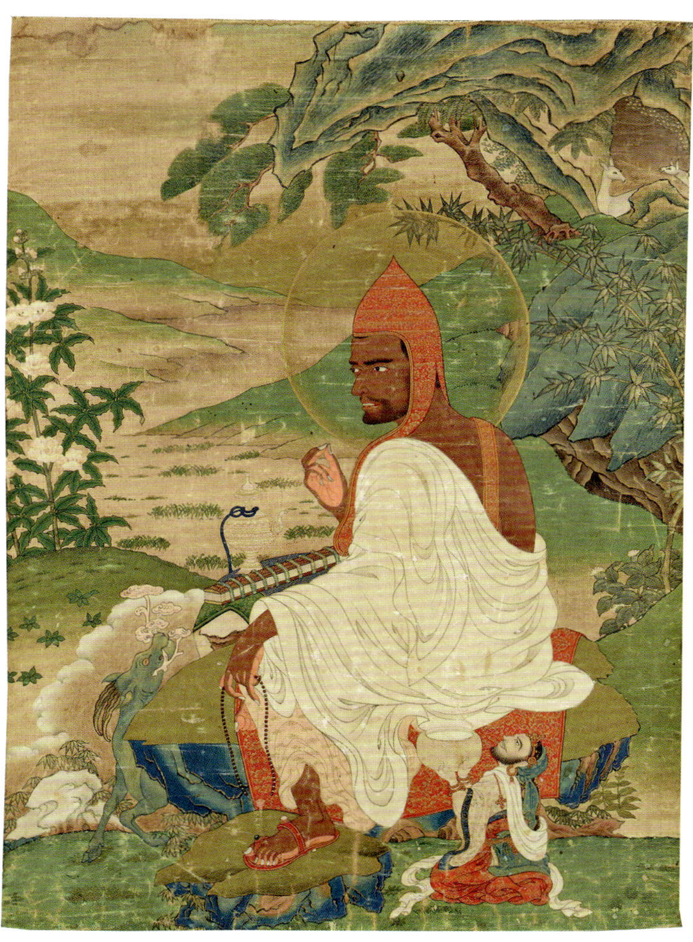

FIG. 7.5
Gayadhara as Path with the Result Guru
late fifteenth or early sixteenth century
28 ½ x 21 ⅞ in. (72.5 x 55.5 cm)
British Museum, inventory no. 1980
12 20 03.
Literature: Zwalf 1985, 142, pl. 195; and
Snellgrove 1987, cover

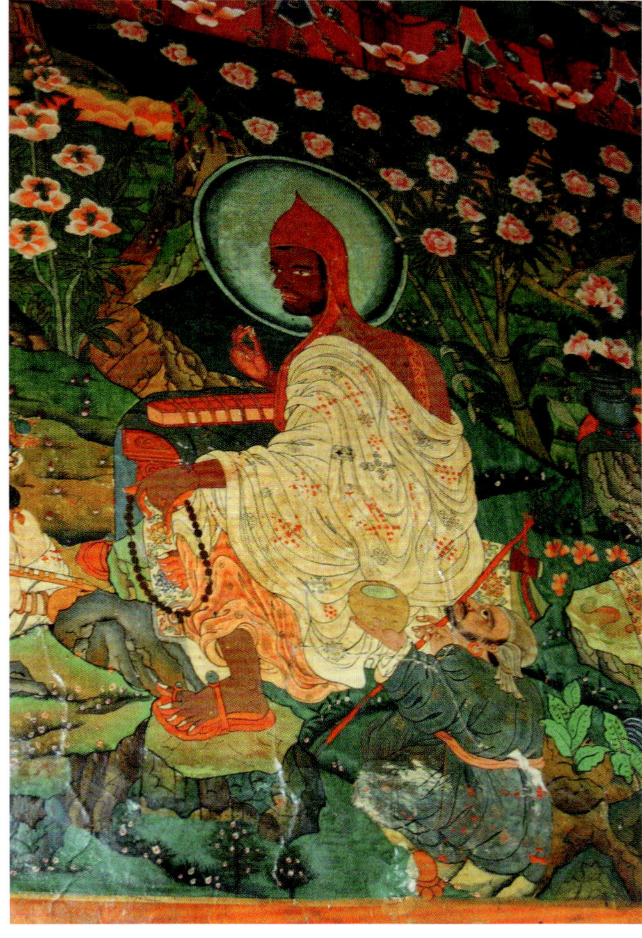

FIG. 7.6
Pandita Gayadhara
Mural, Kunzang Tse College, Gongkar;
ca. 1930s
Photo: A. Lustgarten, 2005

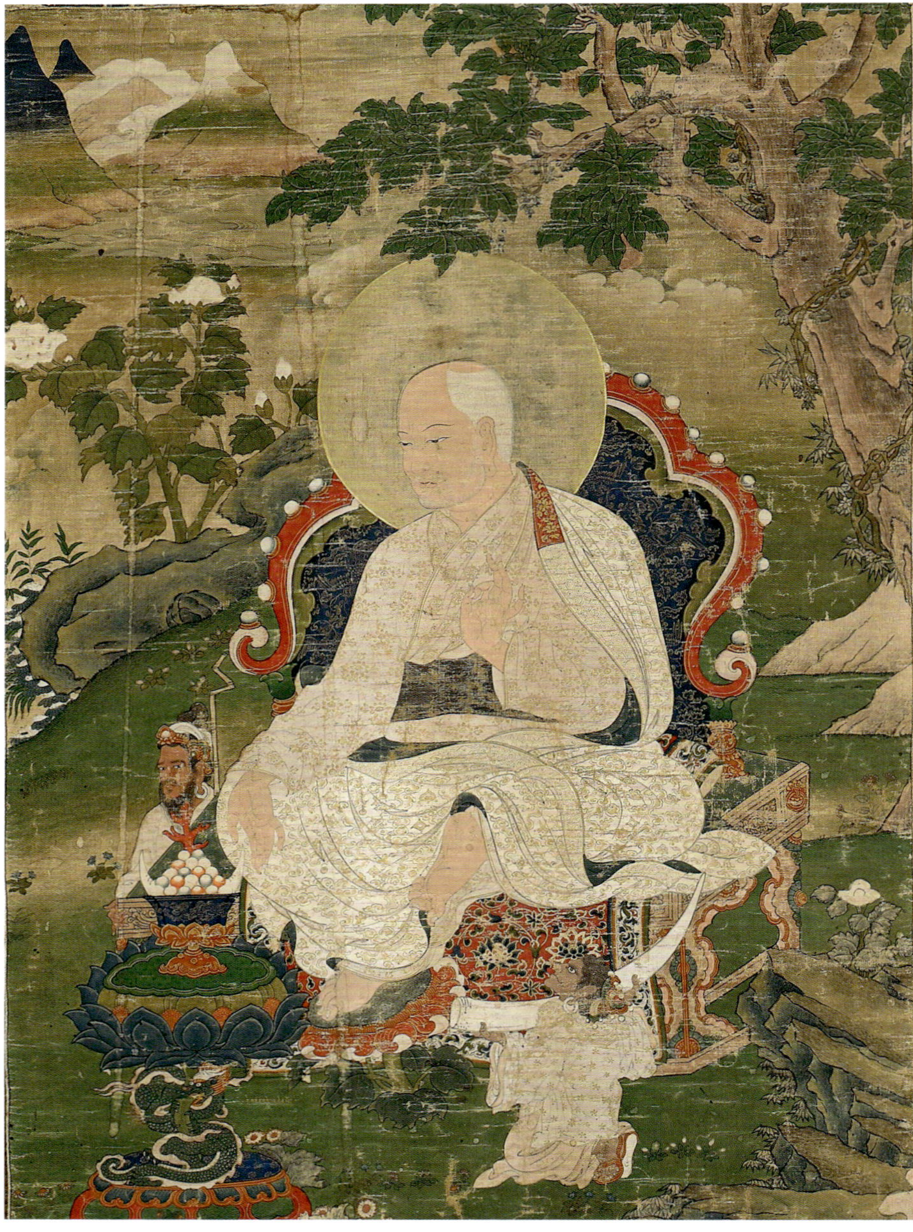

attributed to Yan Liben [d. 673] in the Palace Museum, Taipei.) It seems that Khyentse appropriated not just the trees and hills but the entire visual repertoire of the arhat landscape, including the minor characters, but such details feel forced in this painting. The mature vine-draped tree to the right seems distinctly Chinese, but it is balanced by the Tibetan feeling evoked by the distant snowy peak at the upper left. The clouds encircling a mountain, the peony flowers and buds, and the chain of jewels punctuating the edge of Sachen's chair were all introduced by the artist to combine elegantly with the white elements at the center.

Figure 7.8, which shows Sachen as depicted in the Kunzang Tse murals, proves that this manner of portraying Sachen in a painting was standard in Gongkar.

Figure 7.9, described earlier as Figure 6.20, depicts Sakya Paṇḍita as a Lamdre guru. The inscription on the lotus under the main figure identifies him as *sa paṇḍi ta*. This and the preceding two thangkas belonged to a set of paintings that depicted the Lamdre lineage masters in the tradition of Gongkar Monastery and Khyentse. Each painting is still framed in its original dragon-brocade silk mount, with worn silk face-covers (*zhal khebs*) that hang about eight inches (20 cm) past each painting. I hope that the publication of these three paintings will stimulate the emergence of others of the same set from their present places of concealment.

4. Lamdre Set 4: With Main Figures in Gold

Among the paintings of the Lamdre lineage masters in Chinese landscapes, this set features a striking abundance of gold. All of the major, minor, divine, and human figures are painted gold, a rare technique for later Menri painters. Several paintings from this impressive set are preserved in the Musée Guimet, the

The minor figures are characters that appear in other paintings by Khyentse. Below Sachen, the foreign traveler or trader who presents an ivory tusk, though strange iconographically, makes visual harmony, given the multiple white elements: Sachen's hair and robes and the foreigner's robes, earrings, and white-soled sandals.[381] Another foreigner in a white turban appears to the left of Sachen's seat, looking at the viewer askance with curious, insistent eyes. (Foreign travelers presenting an ivory tusk no doubt derived from Chinese painting; as Rob Linrothe informed me, one prominent example that features this motif several times is a Tang handscroll

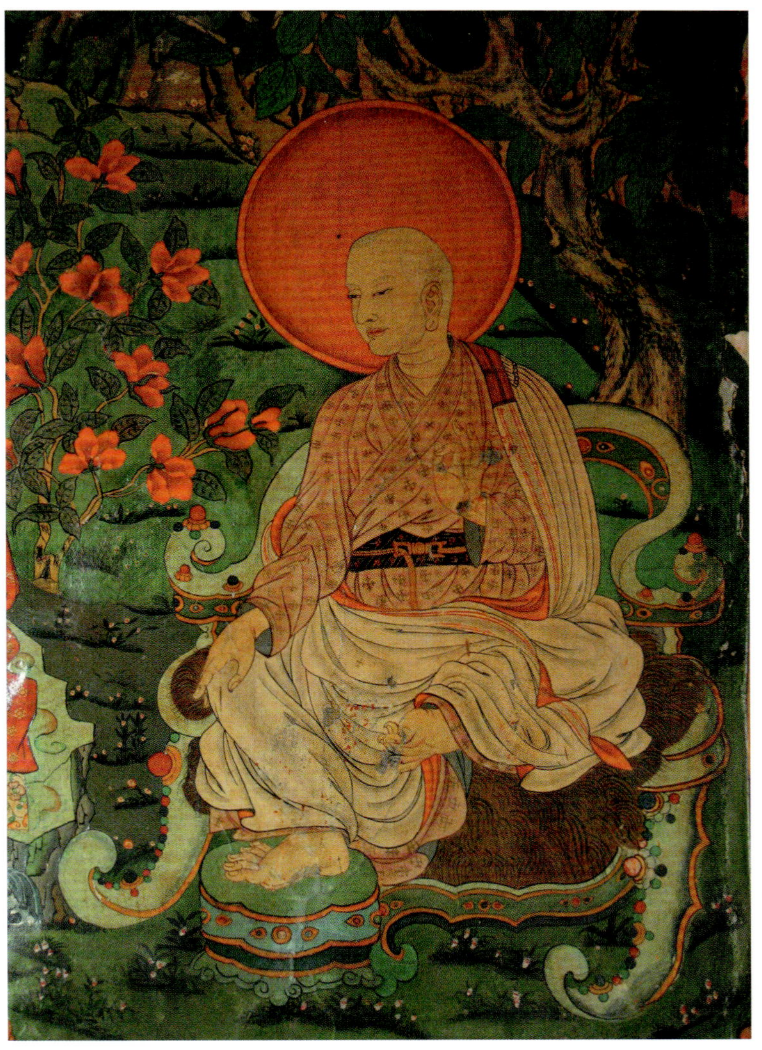

FIG. 7.8
Sachen
Mural, Kunzang Tse College, Gongkar;
ca. 1930s
Photo: A. Lustgarten, 2005

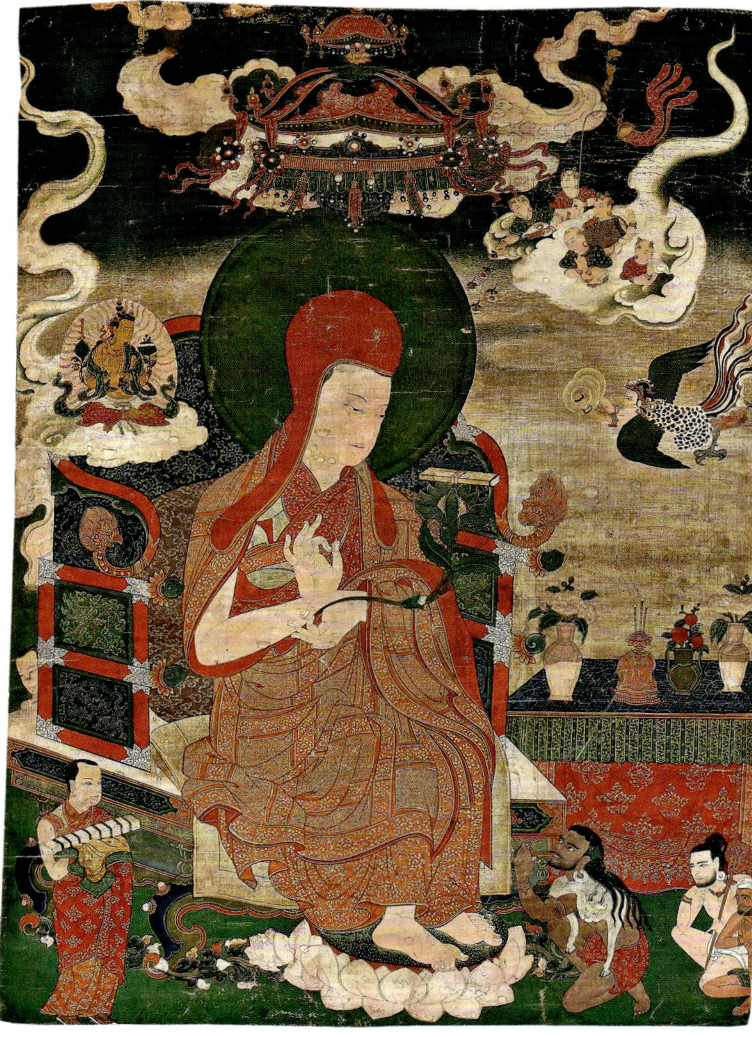

FIG. 7.9
Sakya Paṇḍita as a Lamdre Guru
late fifteenth or early sixteenth century
29 ⅛ x 21 ½ in. (74.0 x 54.5 cm)
British Museum, inventory no. 1980
12–20 01

Khyentse used gold fairly often to paint the skin of his human and divine major and minor subjects.

Figure 7.10, described earlier as Figure 6.2, is a masterful portrait of Vir-upa. As a guru of the Lamdre, he holds his hands in the teaching position, one of the six standard hand positions. The landscape has pale hues like a *si thang* that harmonize with the central golden figure. A *qilin* Chinese mythical beast (with blue-scaled deer's body and bear's bushy tail) frolics in the foreground,[382] and a light-brown male dove or swallow flies toward the right with a flowering twig, to its paler mate in the tree.

This is one of four paintings from this set, now preserved in the Musée Guimet and from the private collection of Jean Mansion (1932–1992). Béguin described them separately in a catalog that he published in 1994, considering them one of the high points of that collection.[383]

Figure 7.11 portrays Kāṇha as a teacher of the Lamdre. He is shown in an exotic landscape meant to be a wooded wilderness of India. He blows a thigh-bone trumpet, attended by his consort. Both sit on true-to-life animal-skin mats. Curled up at his feet is a sleeping tiger. In the foreground, two brown-and-white ducks splash in the water. In the upper register of the painting, a blue-headed, long-tailed white bird like a magpie flies toward the left, to its mate on the hill above Kāṇha.

Béguin in his 1977 catalog noticed similarities between this painting and Ming-period paintings, pointing out the resemblance of the elongated rocks, on the left, to certain landscapes by Li Tsai. Béguin also asserted in his 1994 and 1995 catalogs that the paintings began as block prints on cloth that had later been colored, but I could not confirm that statement.[384]

Figure 7.12 portrays Ḍamarupa as a guru of the Lamdre. It is interesting to compare it to the depictions discussed in

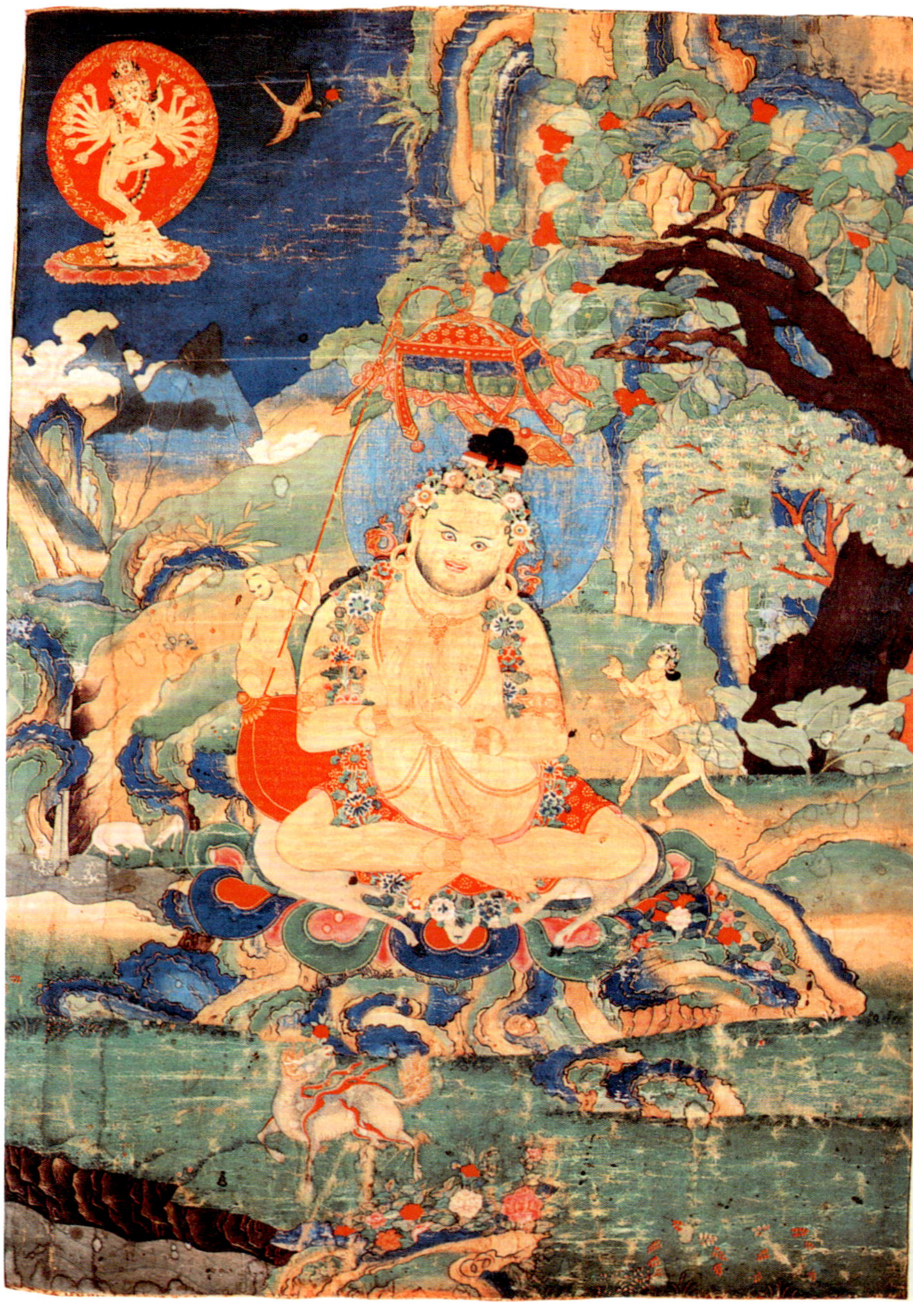

Fig. 7.10
Virūpa as Teacher of the Lamdre
second half of the fifteenth century
25 ⅜ x 18 in. (64.5 x 45.8 cm)
Musée Guimet, MA 6004
Literature: Béguin 1994, no. 25; and Béguin 1995, cat. no. 275

Burke Museum in Seattle, and the Ford private collection. (Two from the set were also sold at auction in Switzerland; see above Figs. 1.42 and 1.43.)

Though no doubt the set was painted by an excellent painter, it is different in some respects from other paintings that I attributed to Khyentse. But after examining several pieces individually, I was convinced by the technical mastery displayed by the painter, such as his depiction of a smoking incense holder in the painting of Jetsün Trakpa (see Fig. 7.18). I also now believe that

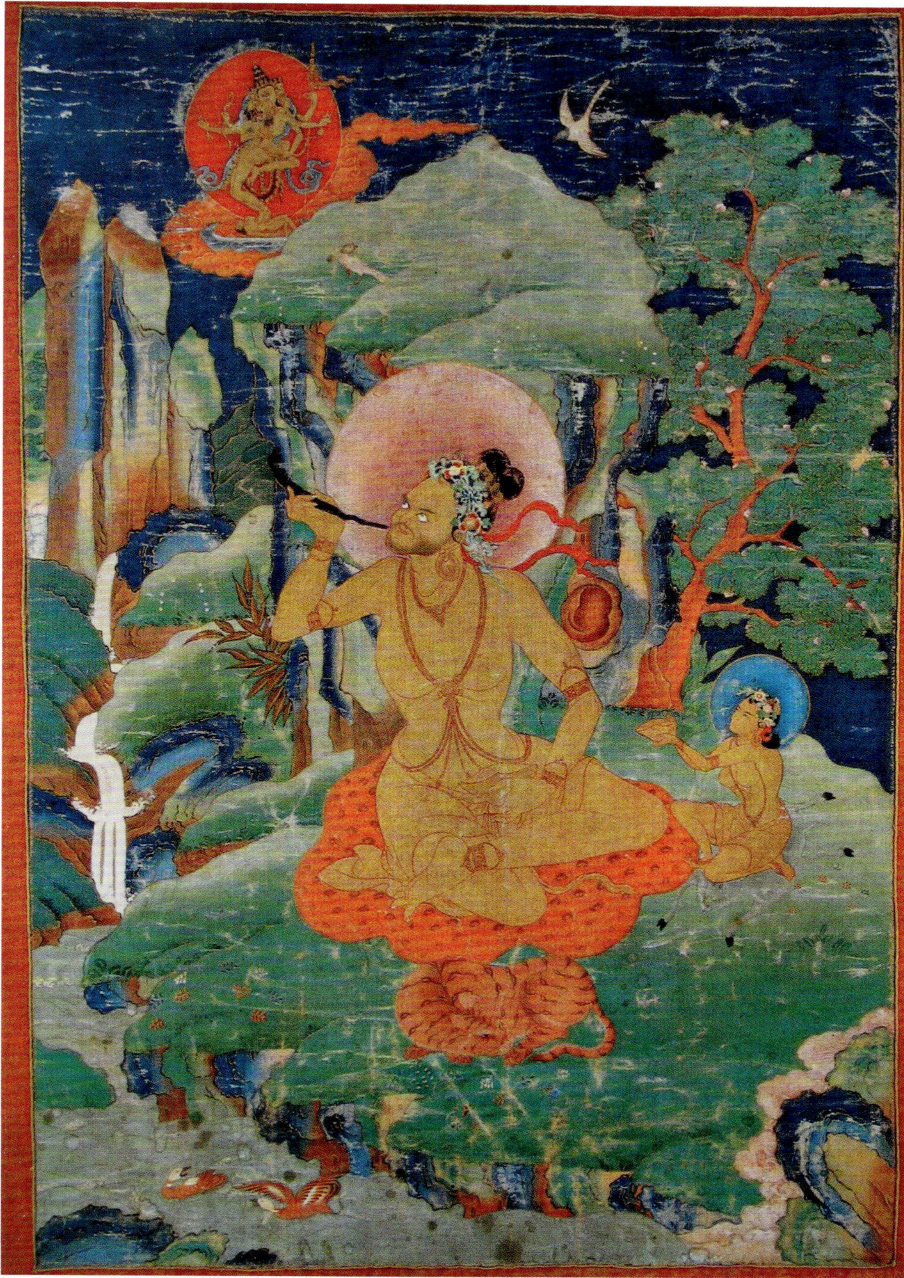

Lamdre, seated within a pale-gold landscape, like a *si thang*. A sense of mystic clarity is enhanced by the transparent head nimbus. The great adept has lost himself in non-conceptual mystic abstraction and doodles in the dust before him with a stick. His siddha attendant and a little boy join him in drawing. In this peaceful scene, no fewer than three pairs of birds are depicted. In the tree at the left are two long-tailed white birds like magpies. At the lower right, two white-headed brown ducks rest on the sandy ground near the water. And near the adept's attendant are two exotic multicolored parrots—one about to peck the ground before it—that seem more deliberate and intent than the humans!

Figure 7.14 depicts the Indian pandit Gayadhara as a lineage teacher of the Lamdre instructions. The small figure before him, offering a heap of gold, may be his Tibetan disciple Drokmi Lotsāwa (992-1072?). They are sitting in an exotic semi-tropical landscape, but Himalayan snow peaks loom above, to the right; the scene could be in Nepal. Elegant garden balustrades, which are common in Chinese painting, form a decorated enclosure around a garden behind them, and lotuses bloom from nearby pools of water. The tree behind Gayadhara is colored a light, golden brown that harmonizes with the other gold areas in the painting. Its leaves overhang and block most of the head nimbus. Upon one branch, a long-tailed, white-bellied black bird like a magpie perches. It looks toward its mate, in the dark-blue sky above the tree.

Setön Kunrik, the great early Tibetan layman yogi of the Lamdre, is depicted in Figure 7.15. He holds a rosary in both hands and speaks to an attendant while seated on a light gray-green mat in an open landscape that likely depicts the border of a remote nomadic place in Tibet. To the right are a few final rocks and small trees. Between

chapter 5 (Figs. 5.7–5.9b). The painting is noteworthy for showing the adept in a quite different way, holding up both ḍamaru and bell and with a seated consort not holding a *vīṇā*. The pastel-pink clouds and head nimbus provide contrast against the gold bodies. In the foreground, four interesting animals appear. To the right rests a pair of large deer, the doe with her head on the ground. In the roiling gray water, a large brown catfish swims on the surface; to the left, a green dragon emerges, eying the great adept.

In Figure 7.13, Khyentse portrays the adept Awadhutipa as a guru of the

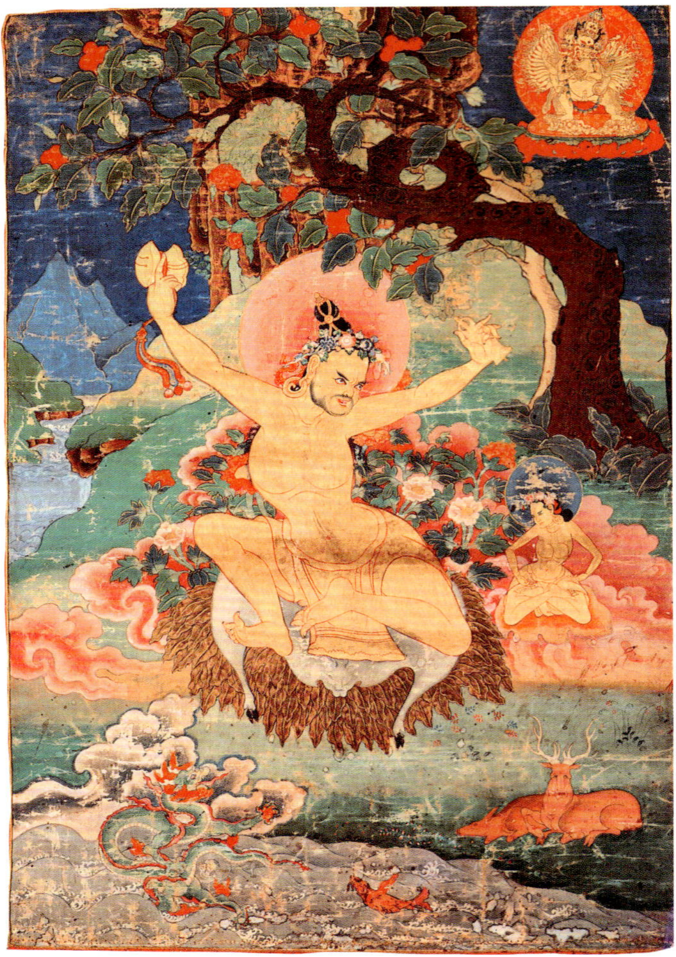 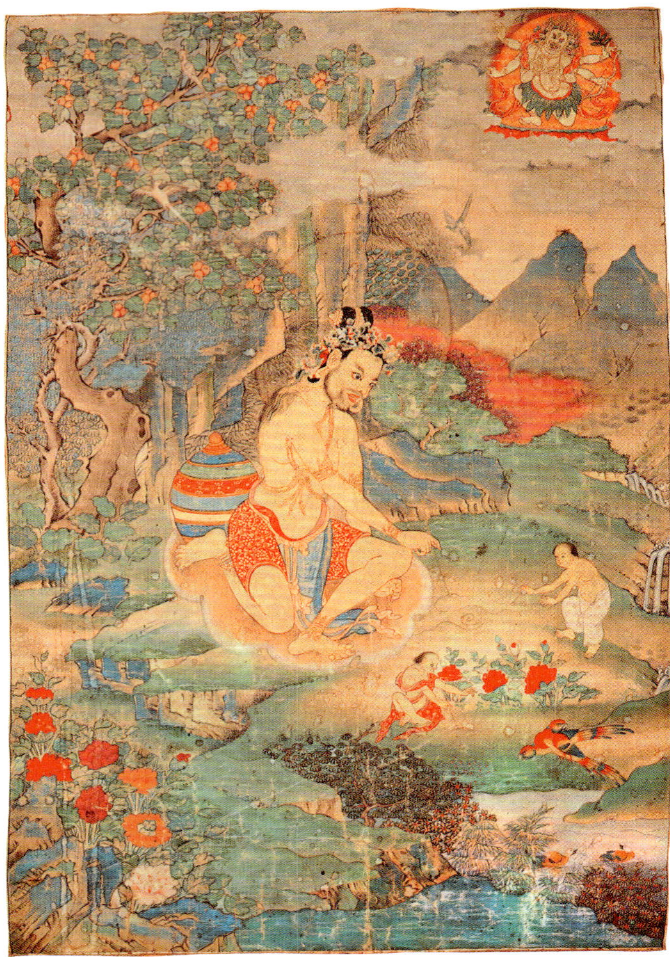

the rock outcropping and Setön, a pair of pale-brown deer approach, the doe with her ears pointing back and the buck with his head held upright.

This portrayal of Setön's face and hair is close to that in a Gongkar Kunzang Tse College mural (see Fig. 7.16). But in the mural, Setön sits alone, with hands folded in his lap in meditative concentration. The mural painter followed a different model for the landscape.

Figure 7.17 portrays Sachen Kunga Nyingpo as a master of the Lamdre lineage. Like all of the paintings in this set, the figures of Sachen, deity, and attendant are painted gold. What is striking about the composition is the white mountain behind Sachen—a symbol of his home, Sakya, which literally means "whitish earth" (*skya sa*). The stream flowing to the left may be the Tromchu River, the local river in Sakya.

In addition to the impressive presence of gold, the painting features

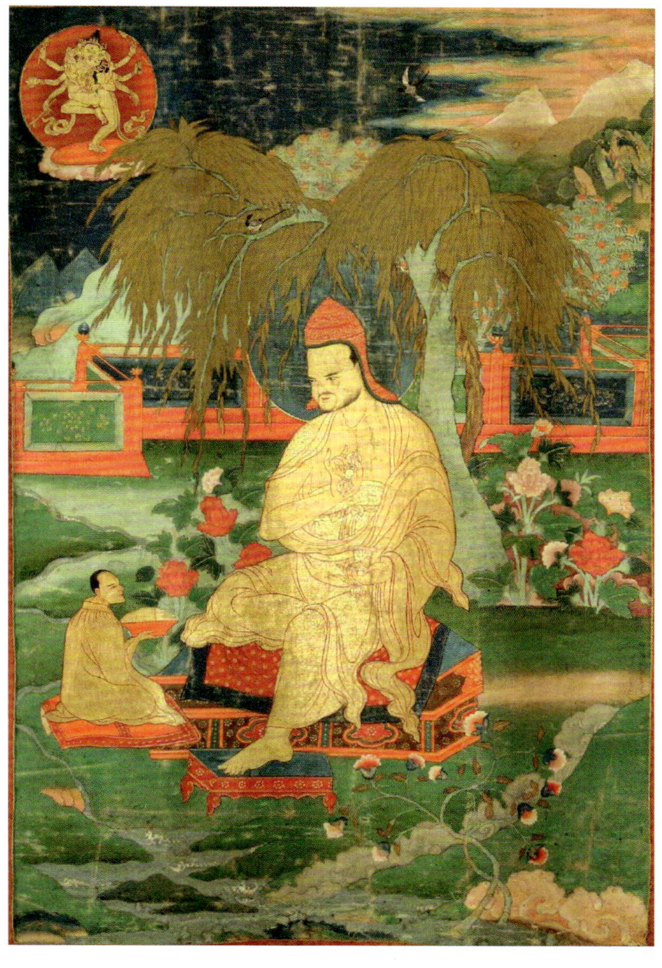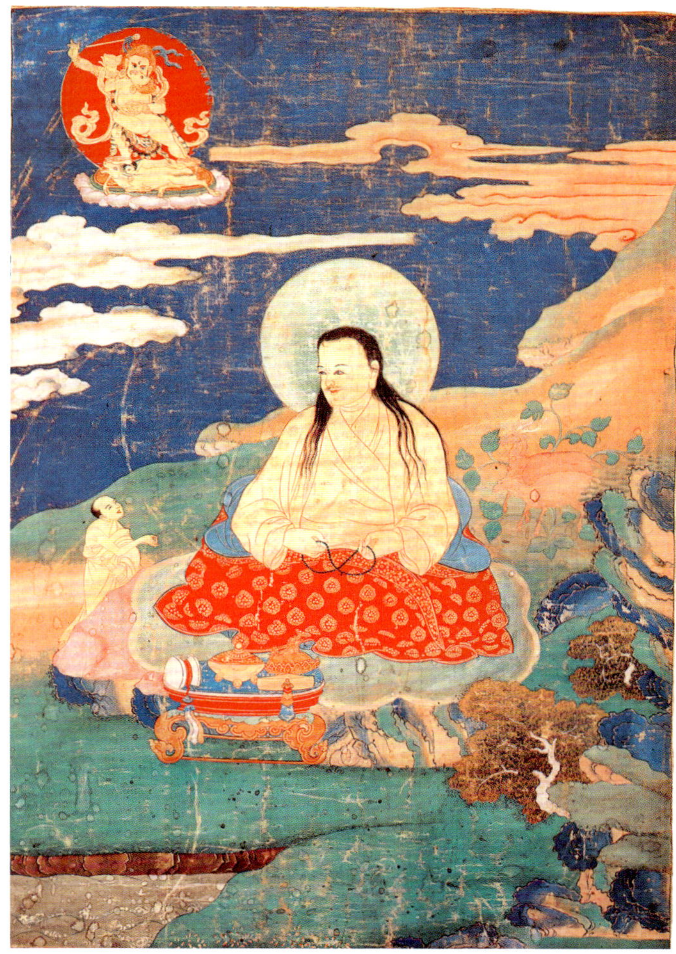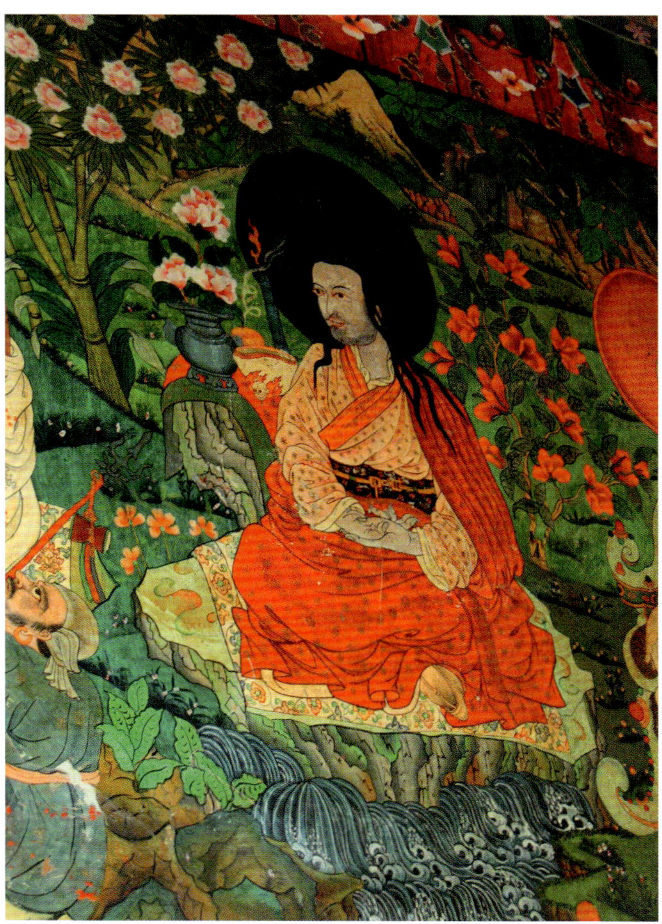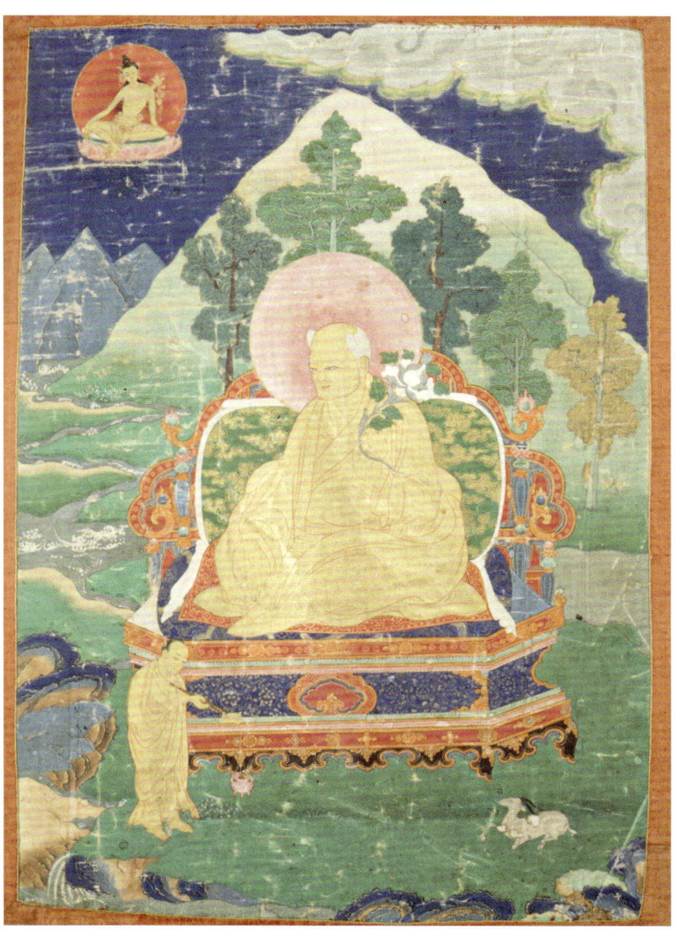

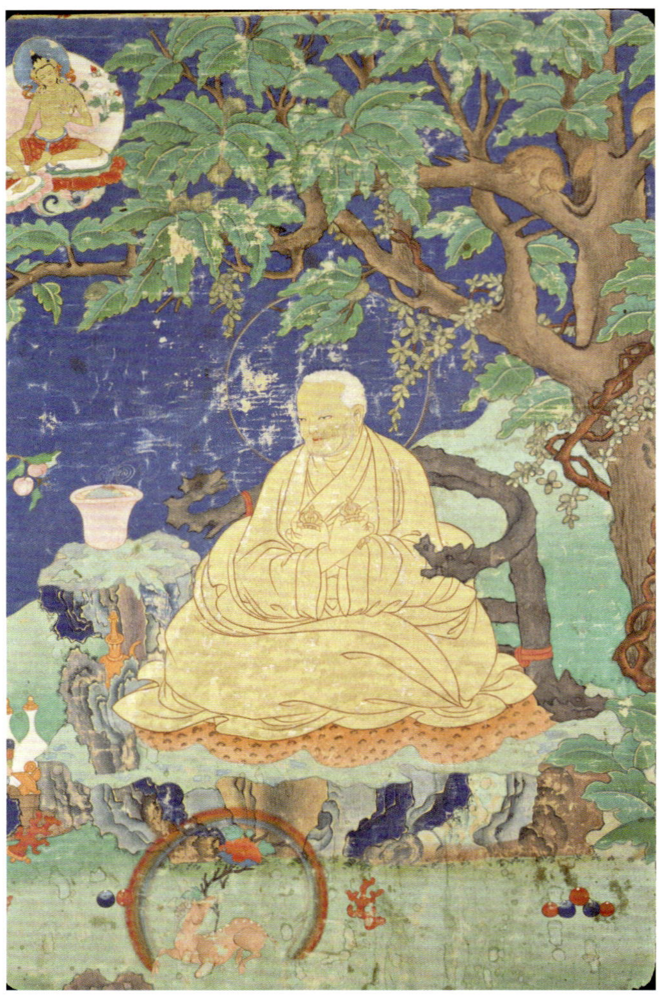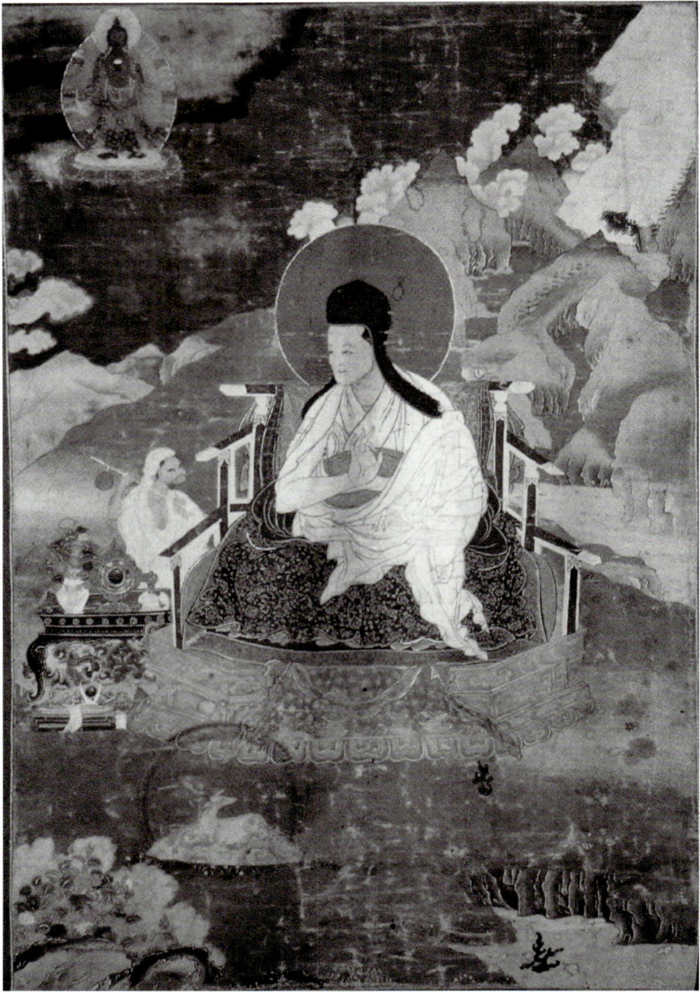

a variety of hues in the row of five identically shaped trees behind Sachen, pastel-pink accents in his head nimbus and the incense holder below his throne, and a rare green color in the mat behind him.

Figure 7.18, discussed earlier as Figure 6.12, depicts Jetsün Trakpa as a teacher of the Lamdre lineage. Both the guru and deity figures are colored gold. The light-pink color of the smoking incense-holder and the nearby fruit is striking. Also notable are the transparent head nimbus of the main figure, the fat brown squirrels in the trees, and the accents of red corals and jewels in the foreground.

An unidentified Tibetan teacher of the Lamdre wearing a red pandit hat is depicted in Figure 7.19. He may be Lama Dampa, who is commonly depicted with such a hat, throne, and visage. In the foreground to the left, a deer quietly kneels, ringed with a soft rainbow nimbus; it pays homage to the lama by its presence.

At the left side of the throne stands an Indian seer (*rishi*) carrying a two-gourd *vīṇā*, with just one of its resonating gourds visible. He is here as a stock character, almost a part of the landscape.

*Vīṇā*s as Preferred Musical Instruments

The appearance of the *vīṇā* in Figure 7.19 is an example of the instrument's common presence in Khyentse Chenmo's paintings. With images of the consorts of Ḍamarupa and Virāya (see Figs. 5.8 and 5.9), Khyentse accurately depicted the north-Indian *vīṇā*. It would be interesting to trace whether his later Khyenri followers continued painting that particular instrument in a number of contexts—such as in the hands of female

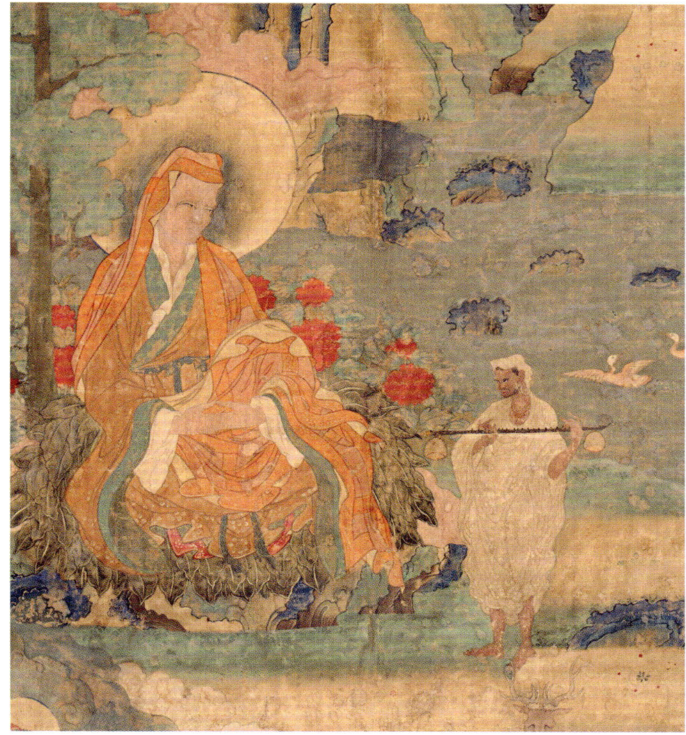

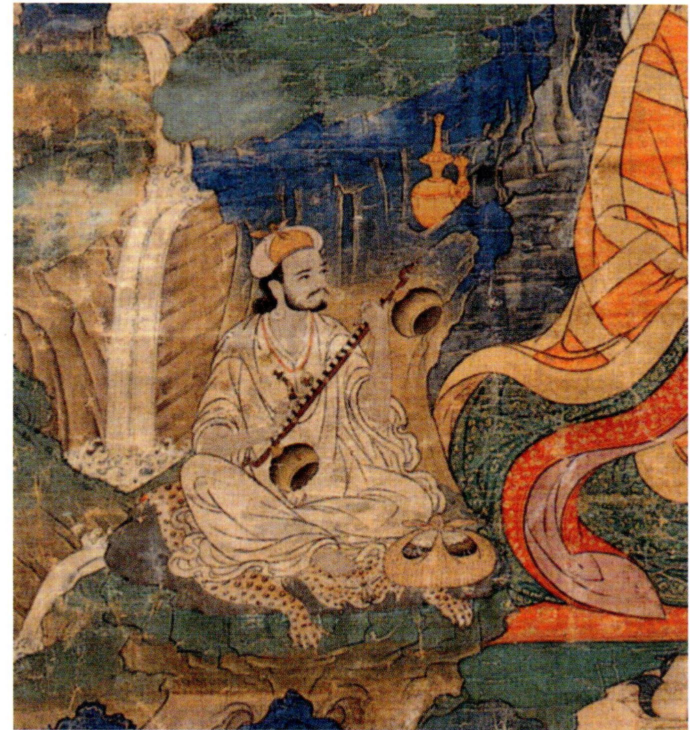

musicians or music-playing attendants or goddesses—where Menri artists nowadays usually depict the Chinese lute (*pipa*; Tib. *pi wang*).[385]

Besides being played by female consorts, another common appearance of the *vīṇā* in Khyentse Chenmo's paintings show it being held by cotton-clad Indian seers (*rishis*), as in Figure 7.19. In Khyenri-style paintings, *vīṇā*-toting Indian seers turn up with some regularity.

Figure 7.20 presents a detail of a painting of the arhat Ajita. Seated with hands folded in meditation and head covered, he is accompanied by the standing, white-cloaked Indian seer Uśīra, who holds a *vīṇā*. According to a verse of praise attributed to Śākyaśrībhadra: "On Rishi Mountain in Crystal Cave is the noble elder Ajita, surrounded by one hundred arhats; homage to him with two hands placed in meditation."[386] Here

Ajita sits on a pile of leaves near the base of a single tall tree.

The north-Indian *vīṇā* is a distinctive instrument, with two resonating gourds on opposite ends of a thin wood neck. According to an online source, it is different from the *vīṇā* used in south-Indian Carnatic music, which is a type of lute:

> The design of the *veena* has evolved over the years, probably from the form seen in Indian Medieval paintings and temple sculpture: a string instrument with two gourd resonators connected by a central shaft, possibly of bamboo, and held diagonally from lap to shoulder. The North Indian *rudra veena* and *vichitra veena*, technically zithers, demonstrate this genealogy."[387]

At some point in his career, Khyentse Chenmo chose a model for a north-Indian *vīṇā* and carefully repeated its details in his paintings, including its resonating gourds. Later artists of the Khyenri style also commonly depicted

*vīṇā*s but not with the same accuracy.

Figure 7.21 shows the most detailed version of a *vīṇā* that I have found, held in the hands of the seer Uśīra, who accompanies the arhat Ajita as a minor figure (see Fig. 9.8). Note the true-to-life representation, with the instrument held at a slant, from lap to shoulder.

In Figure 7.22, a detail of a thangka that depicts the eighty-four great adepts, a standing minor figure wearing a white turban and a light-red robe carries a *vīṇā* with both hands. Riding a lion, the main figure balances on his shoulder a staff to which is connected a cloth bag, for carrying food that he begs for as a mendicant.

Robert Beer helpfully illustrated and differentiated the instruments in a pictorial index.[388] He first illustrates the lute (*pi wang*), calling it the Central Asian or Chinese lute (Fig. 7.23).

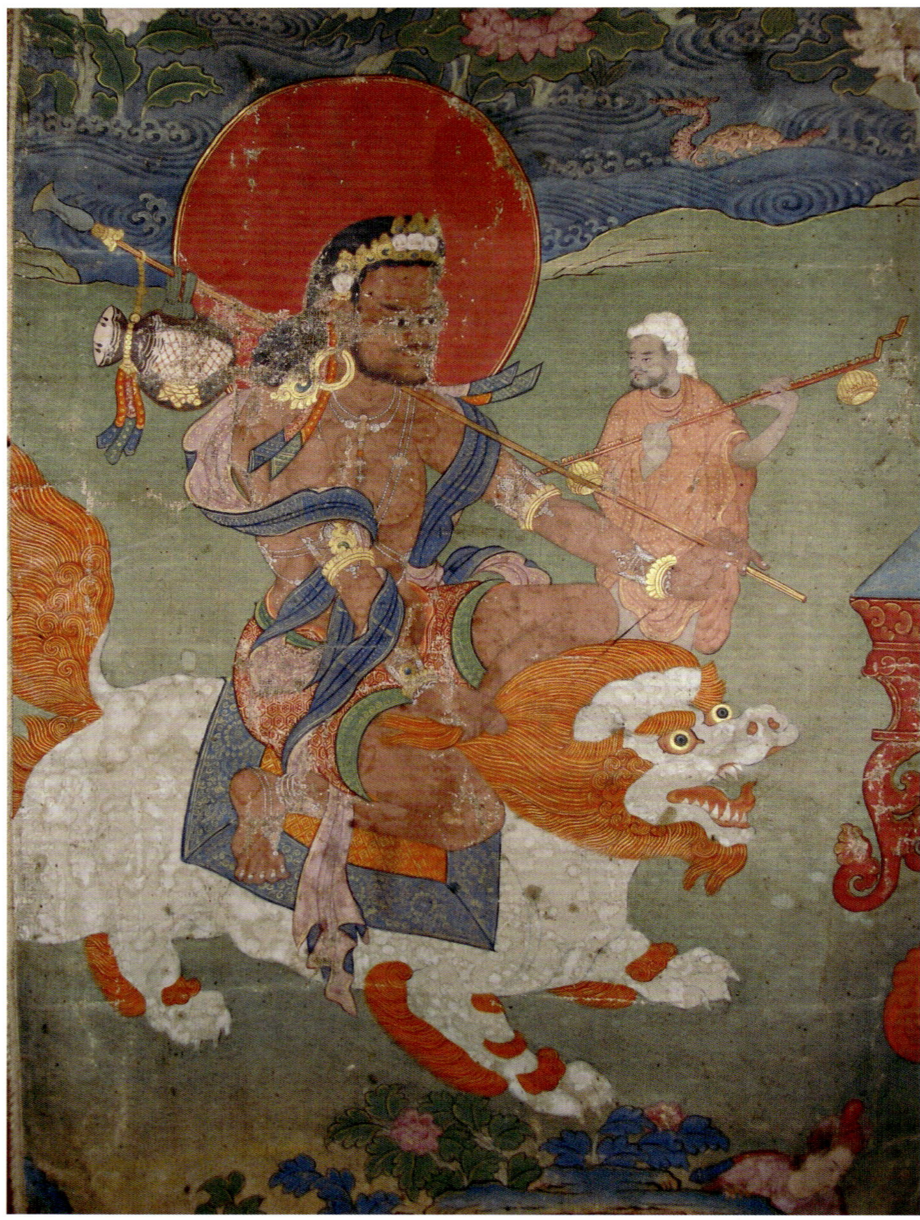

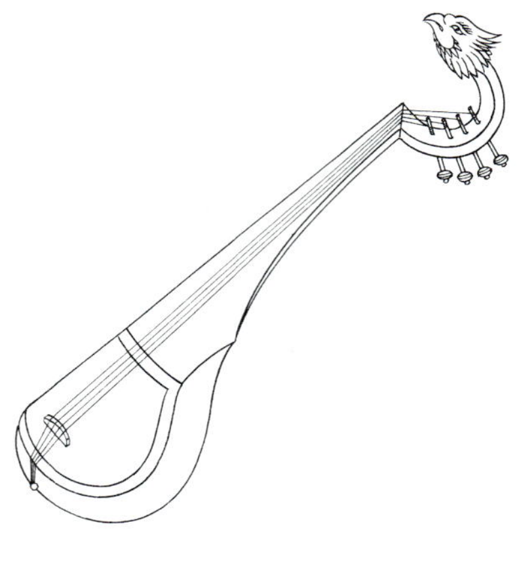

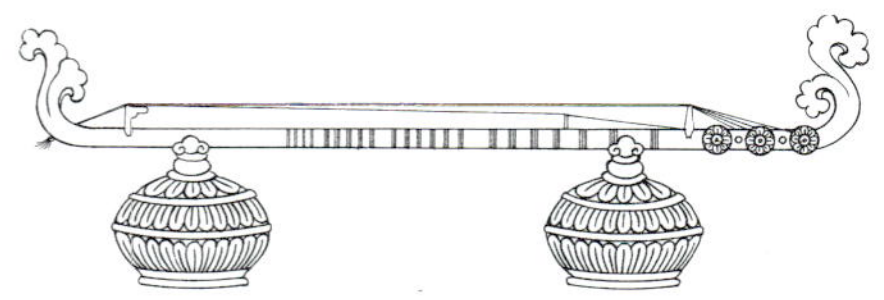

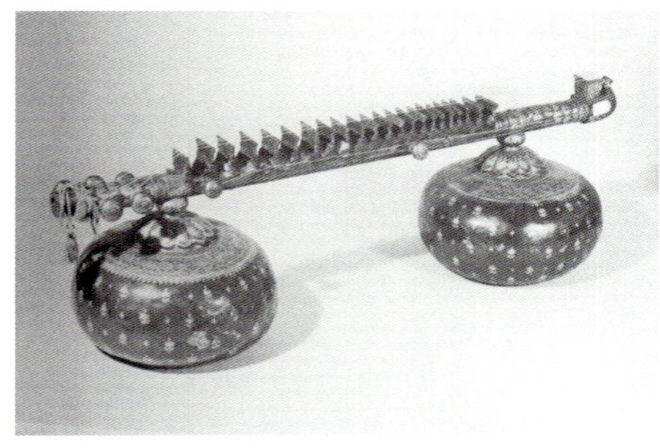

Fig. 7.23
Central Asian or Chinese Lute
After: Robert Beer, in Willson and Brauen
2000, 569, fig. 52a

Fig. 7.24
North-Indian Vīṇā
After: Robert Beer, in Willson and Brauen
2000, 569, fig. 52b

Fig. 7.25
North-Indian Vīṇā
After: Ravi Shankar 1968, 34

The second instrument he illustrates is the *vīṇā* (Fig. 7.24), correctly called in Tibetan *rgyud mang/mangs* ("many-stringed"). Beer calls it by its Indian name, *vīṇā*, and says that "they are often depicted interchangeably in Tibetan art, depending on whether the imagery follows a Chinese or an Indian style." Though that is basically correct, it gives the impression that both instruments are equally current in Tibetan painting. My impression is that the *vīṇā* has become an iconographic rarity; it is seldom depicted nowadays, even in Indian styles or contexts, and it probably had been infrequent in the past century or two. The only depiction of a *vīṇā* that I could find in modern Tibetan-art publications was among various lute-like stringed instruments in a compilation of artistic motifs.[389] It had been copied from Robert Beer's drawing.

Beer's illustration (Fig. 7.24) presents a side view of the *vīṇā*. The drawing is very accurate in many respects, but it would be hard for a Tibetan artist who had never seen the instrument to know how it should be held or how large its gourds should be in relation to the musician, adept, or deity depicted holding it.

The *vīṇā* depicted by Khyentse Chenmo resembles most closely an instrument in Ravi Shankar's book, *My Music, My Life* (see Fig. 7.25).[390] Captioned "North Indian *veena* with a peacock at the end of the resonating tube," this inlaid *vīṇā* is in the collection of the Metropolitan Museum of Art. Pictured alongside it in Shankar's book is a "South Indian ivory-inlaid *veena* with a belly somewhat like a Western lute."

Figure 7.26 provides a depiction of a north-Indian *vīṇā* in an Indian painting. In this late-seventeenth-century painting from Rajasthan, an Indian ascetic is holding the *vīṇā* at a naturalistic diagonal angle. Its resonating gourds are nearly as large as the musician's head.

Figure 7.27 depicts a detail of a painting of three great adepts within a set of eighty-four mahāsiddhas believed to be by Khyentse Chenmo; the thangka was discussed earlier as Figure 2.12. In the Kunzang Tse murals in Figures 5.8 and 5.9, the female attendants of Ḍamarupa and Virāya play double-gourd *vīṇās*. In this painting, Ḍamarupa's consort also holds a *vīṇā*. The white-turbaned Indian ascetic standing between Suvarṇadvīpa (Serlingpa) and Ḍamarupa carries a *vīṇā* on his back, but only its end is visible. A parrot perches on a nearby staff. Khyentse teases the viewer by painting white flowers of similar shapes and sizes near the ascetic.

Figure 7.28 is a detail of a painting in the same set as Figure 7.27; the entire set was published in 2005.[391] Here, one would expect a fairly good depiction of a *vīṇā*: it shows the thirteenth siddha,

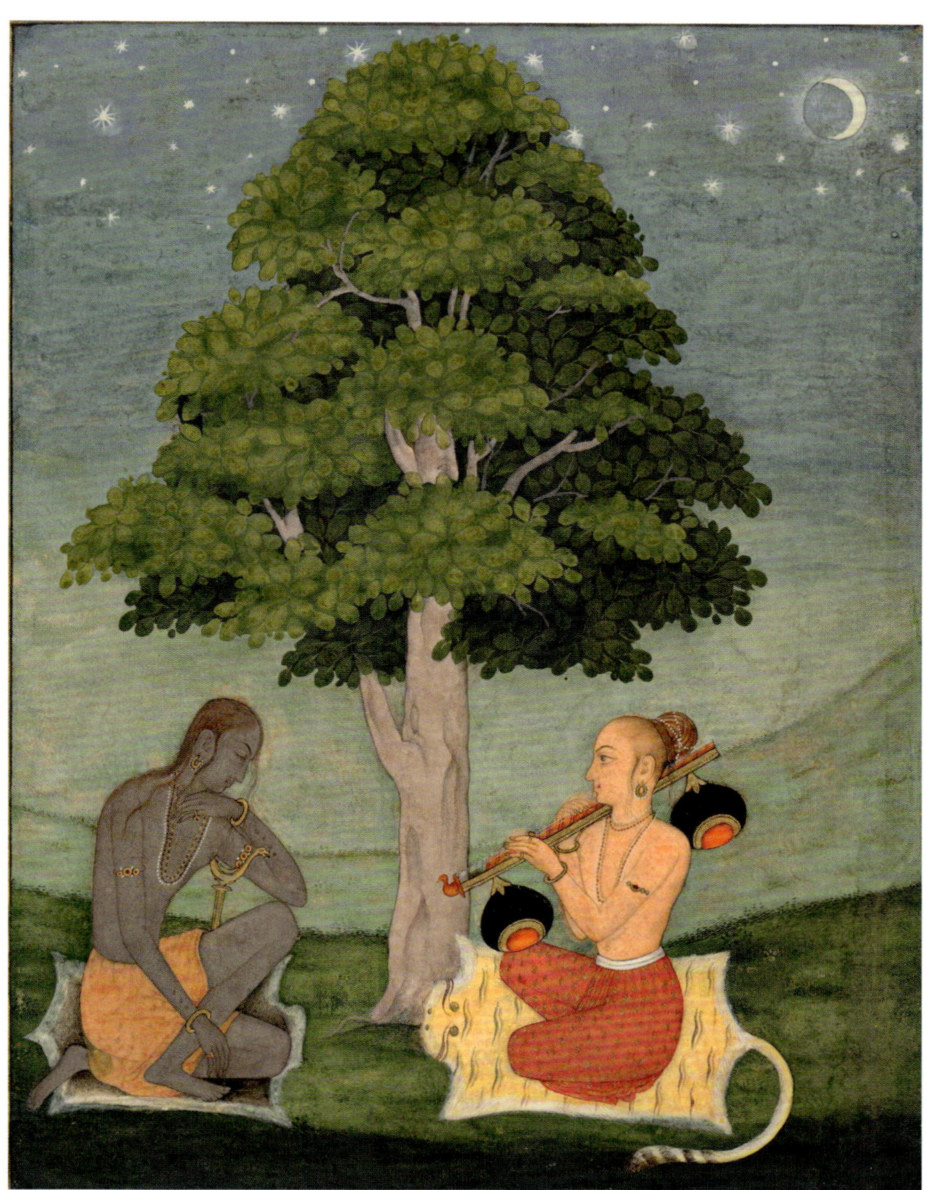

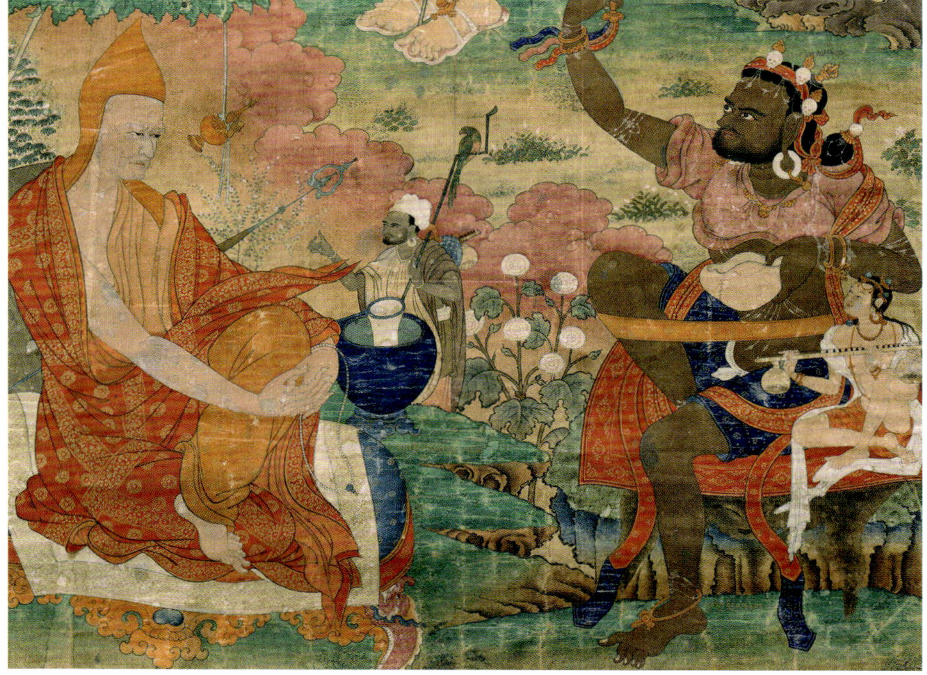

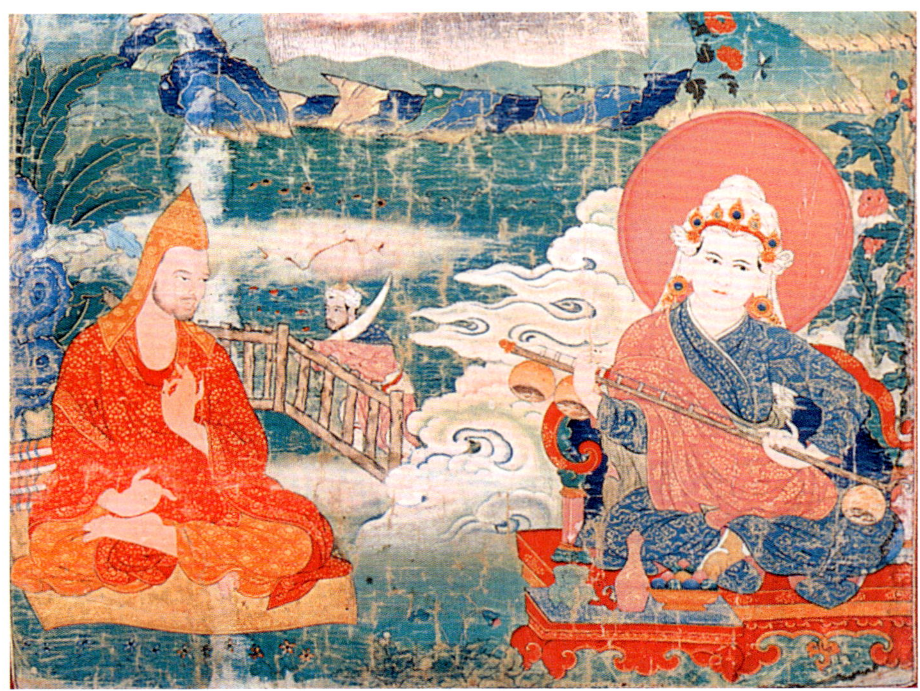

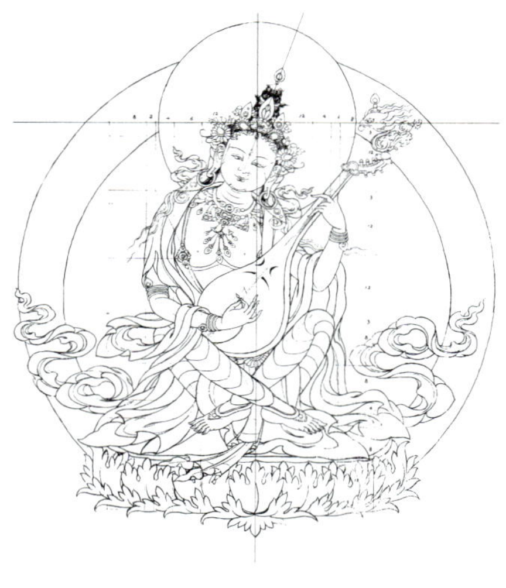

Fig. 7.29
White Sarasvatī Playing a Lute, proportional drawing
After: Kachen Losang Phüntshok 1993, 78, Zla gi lha mo dByangs can ma dkar mo

Binapa (Vīṇāpa), the prototypical *vīṇā* player. The synopsis of his life relates that when he was a small child, he often heard the rhythmic strumming of the tamboura, a stringed instrument; he was soothed by that sound and focused completely on it.[392] He later became obsessed with the music of the *vīṇā* and with playing it. Here Khyentse Chenmo depicts, in the hands of Vīṇāpa ("Vīṇā-man"), the instrument after which he was named. Yet, strangely enough, he holds a three-gourd *vīṇā*.

I have yet to find the two-gourd *vīṇā* depicted by any current painter of the Menri style. These artists seem to prefer depicting the Central Asian or Chinese lute, even as Sarasvatī's instrument. It is the lute (Tib. *pi wang*; *tam bu* or *sgra snyan*; according to Goldstein, "a Chinese stringed instrument") that White Sarasvatī and the protector Great King Dhṛtarāṣṭra are shown holding or playing, for instance in a drawing by the great Tsangri master, Kachen Losang Phüntshok, in Figure 7.29.[393]

Figure 7.30 is the single image of Sarasvatī holding an Indian *vīṇā* in recent Tibetan art that I have found. It is an example of eighteenth-century Kham art, from Derge.[394] But the artist seems unsure of how the instrument should look and be held. It is too small for the figure of Sarasvatī, which reduces the effect.

Another rare representation of the two-gourd *vīṇā* outside the Khyenri style is shown in Figure 7.31. It reveals that the instrument was depicted in some Tsangri paintings held by an Indian seer accompanying Ajita, as in the Khyenri style. Thus, the *vīṇā* did appear occasionally in that central Tibetan tradition.

Drawn in the Karma Gardri style by the more recent painter, Gega Lama, Figure 7.32 shows Sarasvatī playing the Chinese lute, not the *vīṇā*.

In Khyentse Chenmo's time, there were fairly accurate depictions of *vīṇās*, including some paintings that depicted two different string instruments in the same scene. In Figure 7.33, the young ladies of Prince Siddhartha's entourage play music outdoors while he sits within a garden pavilion, listening. The musicians all stand, and the one strumming the *vīṇā* holds it in a reasonably lifelike way.

At the same time, as Figure 7.34 demonstrates, an Indian *vīṇā* has no place in a true Chinese-style painting. Here, in the corresponding scene from a detailed painting of the Buddha's life, a flute, a Chinese lute, cymbals, and drums are played, but there is no *vīṇā*; Prince Siddhartha holds a white conch shell.

Thangkas Portraying Two or More Main Figures

Here I include two paintings in the hope that they will help to confirm the identity of gurus in similar works. Figure 7.35 shows two gurus of the Lamdre linage, possibly Drakphukpa and Lama Dampa, numbers 18 and 19 in the transmission. A pair of white long-tailed birds flies in the sky toward the left, the leading one looking back at its mate. However, the lama on the left may be Sangye Rinchen if I have read the blurred reproduction of the inscription correctly.

Figure 7.36 depicts three central figures, probably Drakphukpa, Lama Dampa, and Mati Panchen, his main disciple in the Thekchen tradition of the Lamdre (gurus 18, 19, and 20). The small figures in the upper register

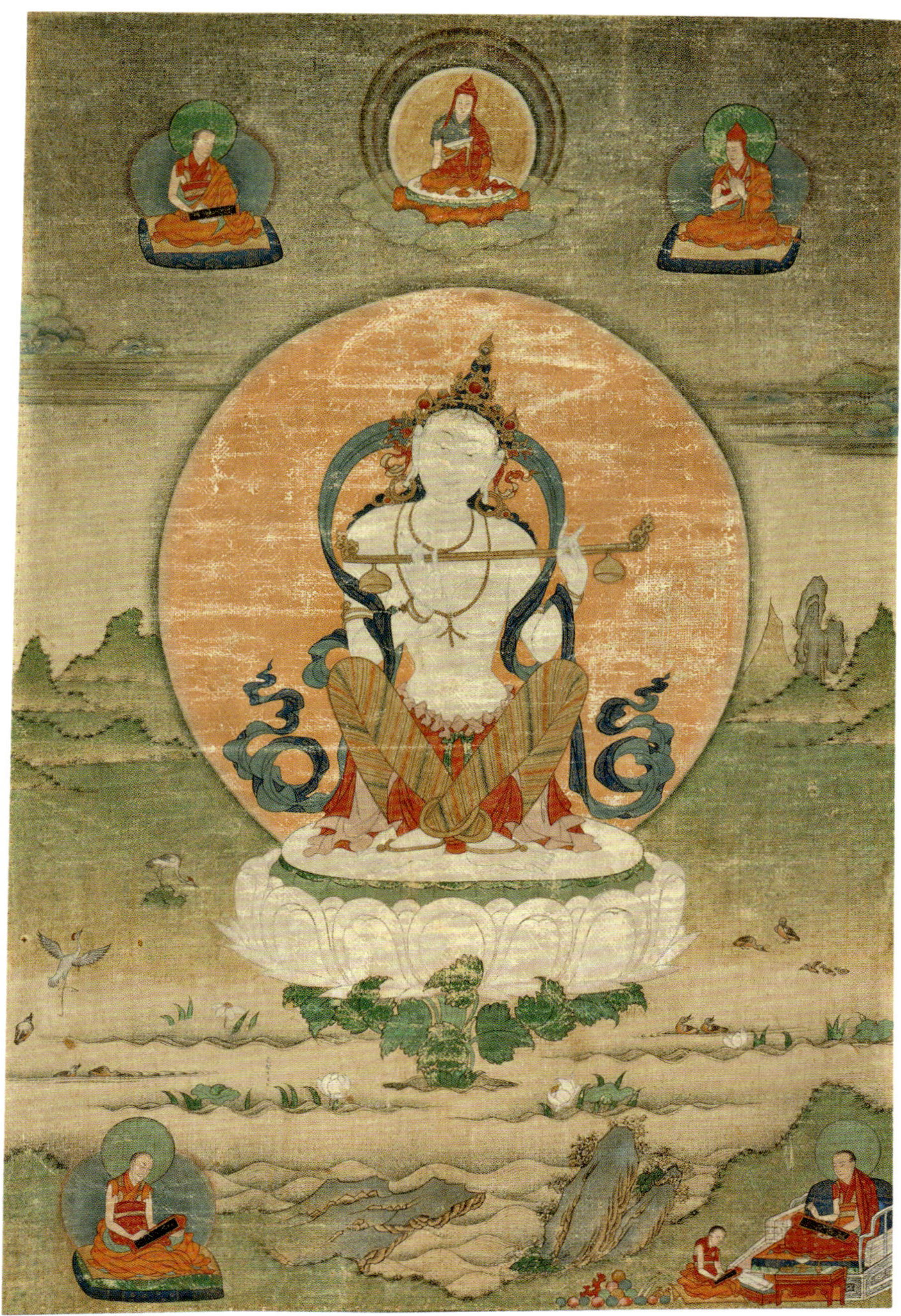

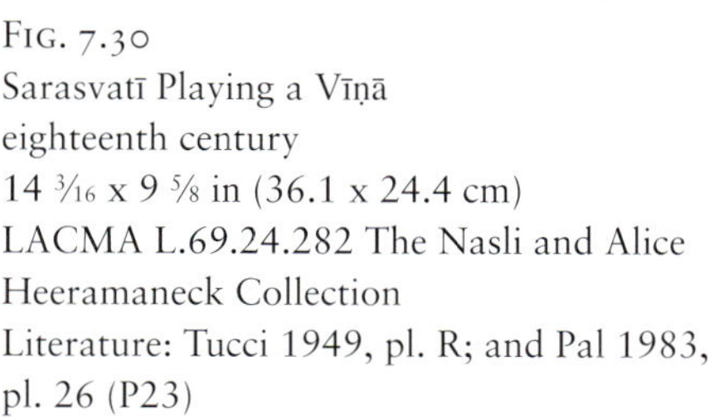

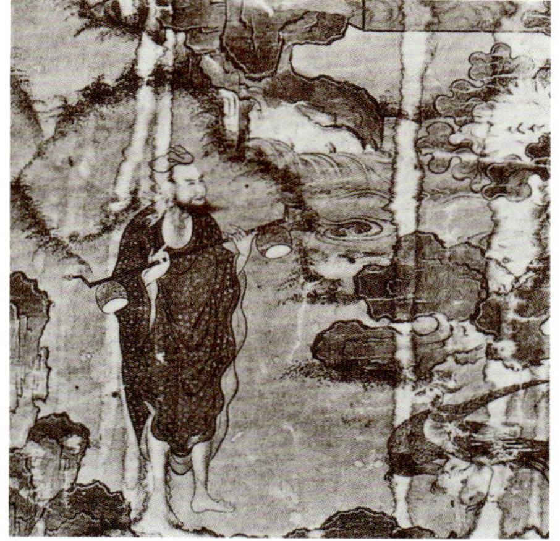

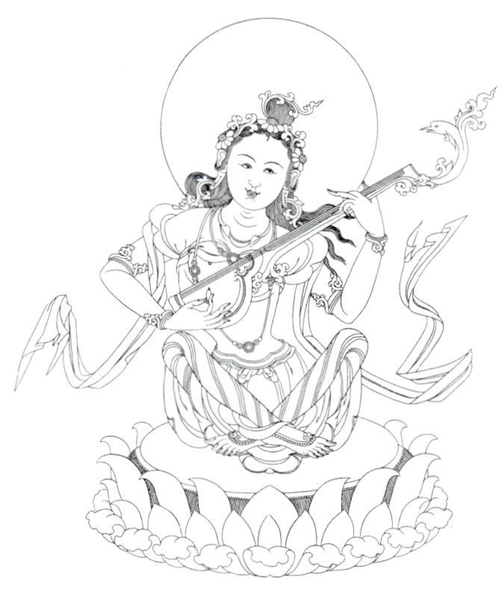

Fig. 7.30
Sarasvatī Playing a Vīṇā
eighteenth century
14 ³⁄₁₆ x 9 ⁵⁄₈ in (36.1 x 24.4 cm)
LACMA L.69.24.282 The Nasli and Alice
Heeramaneck Collection
Literature: Tucci 1949, pl. R; and Pal 1983,
pl. 26 (P23)

Fig. 7.31 (detail of Fig. 2.1)
Arhat Ajita
Tsang, ca. eighteenth century
Acquired by Tucci in Gyantse
Museo Nazionale d'Arte Orientale
"G. Tucci," Rome
Literature: Tucci 1949, pl. 157

Fig. 7.32
Sarasvatī Playing Her Lute
Drawing in the Karma Gardri style
After: Gega Lama 1983, 225

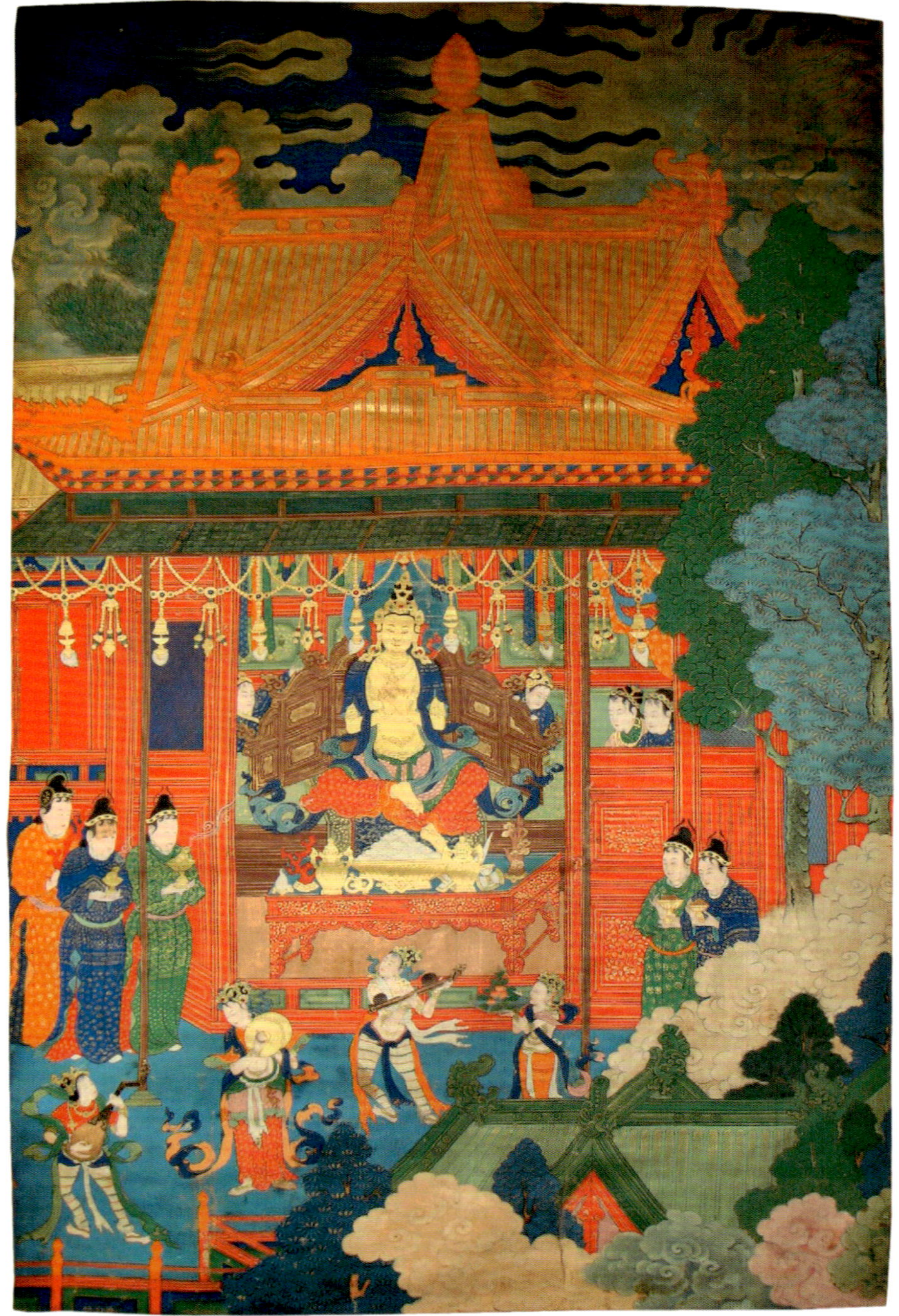

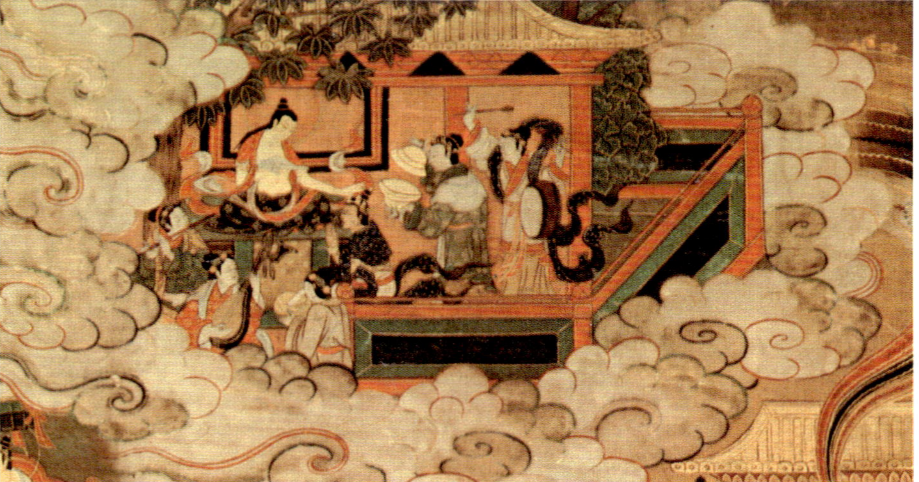

are Śākyamuni, Atiśa to the left, and Lotsāwa Rinchen Sangpo—with a readable inscription—to the right.

Three Paintings from a Later Set Depicting Lamdre Gurus

This set, which is now preserved in the Rubin Museum of Art, is relatively late—from the sixteenth or seventeenth century—but it follows the iconography of the older models from Gongkar.

The first painting of the set portrays Phakpa as a teacher of the Lamdre lineage (Fig. 7.37, discussed earlier as Fig. 6.25). This may be a later copy of one of two slightly different portraits of Phakpa by Khyentse Chenmo (the second being Fig. 6.28). It is difficult to date accurately; the abundant details put its date closer to Khyentse's time. For example, note the several kinds of animal heads on the roof.[395]

Like the other Phakpa painting, this one has a small entrance gate below, middle.

Figure 7.38 depicts an unidentified lineage guru of the Lamdre instructions. He is shown wearing a red pandit's hat with earflaps amid many craggy rocks (*brag*), and he wears a special robe clasp. This could be an alternative, somewhat younger depiction of Drakthok Chöje. In the known murals, he is hatless and holds the vajra and bell; he is also seated before or amid many craggy

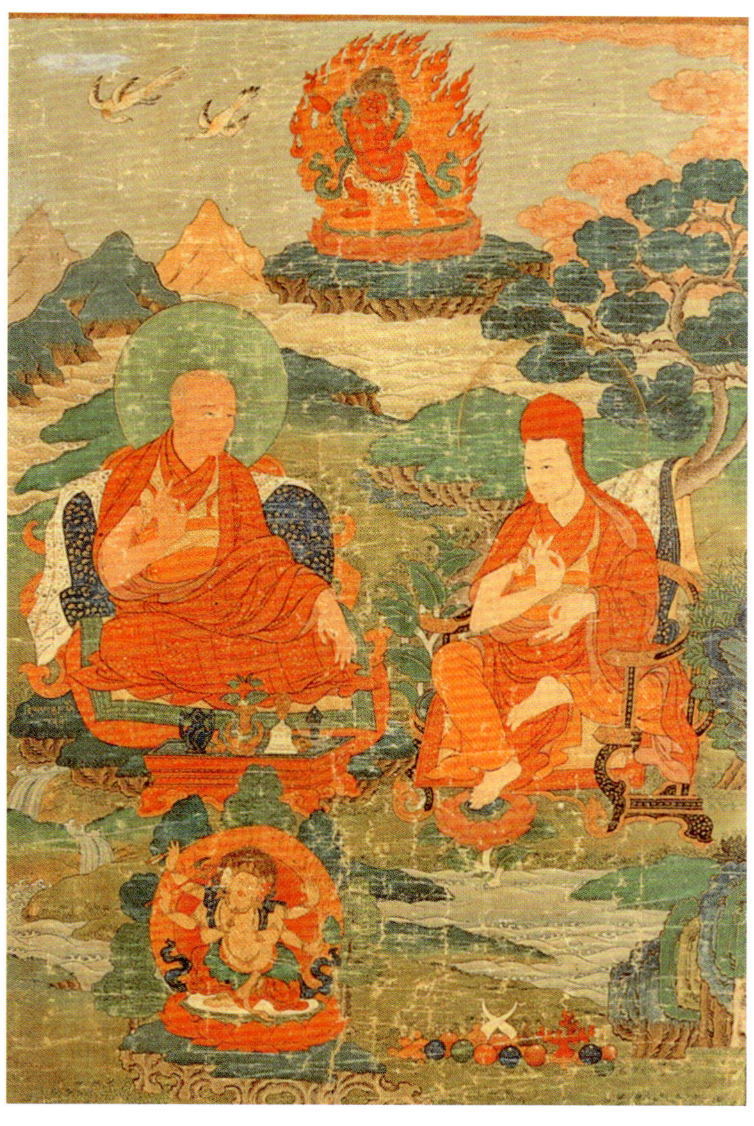 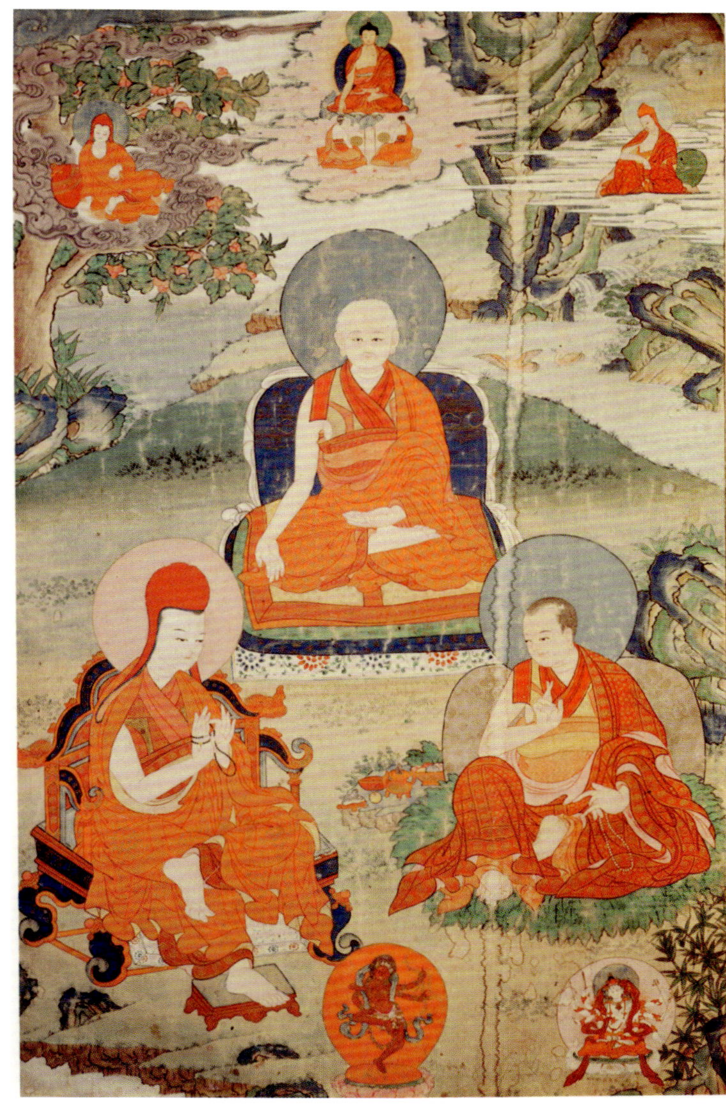

Fig. 7.35
Two Lineage Masters of the Lamdre
second half of the fifteenth century
26 ⅜ x 18 ½ in. (67 x 47 cm)
After: *Koller Asiatica* (Nov. 27, 1985),
no. 24

Fig. 7.36
Three Lineage Masters
second half of the fifteenth century
33 ½ x 22 in. (85 x 56 cm)
Private Collection
After: Pal 1984a, pl. 85

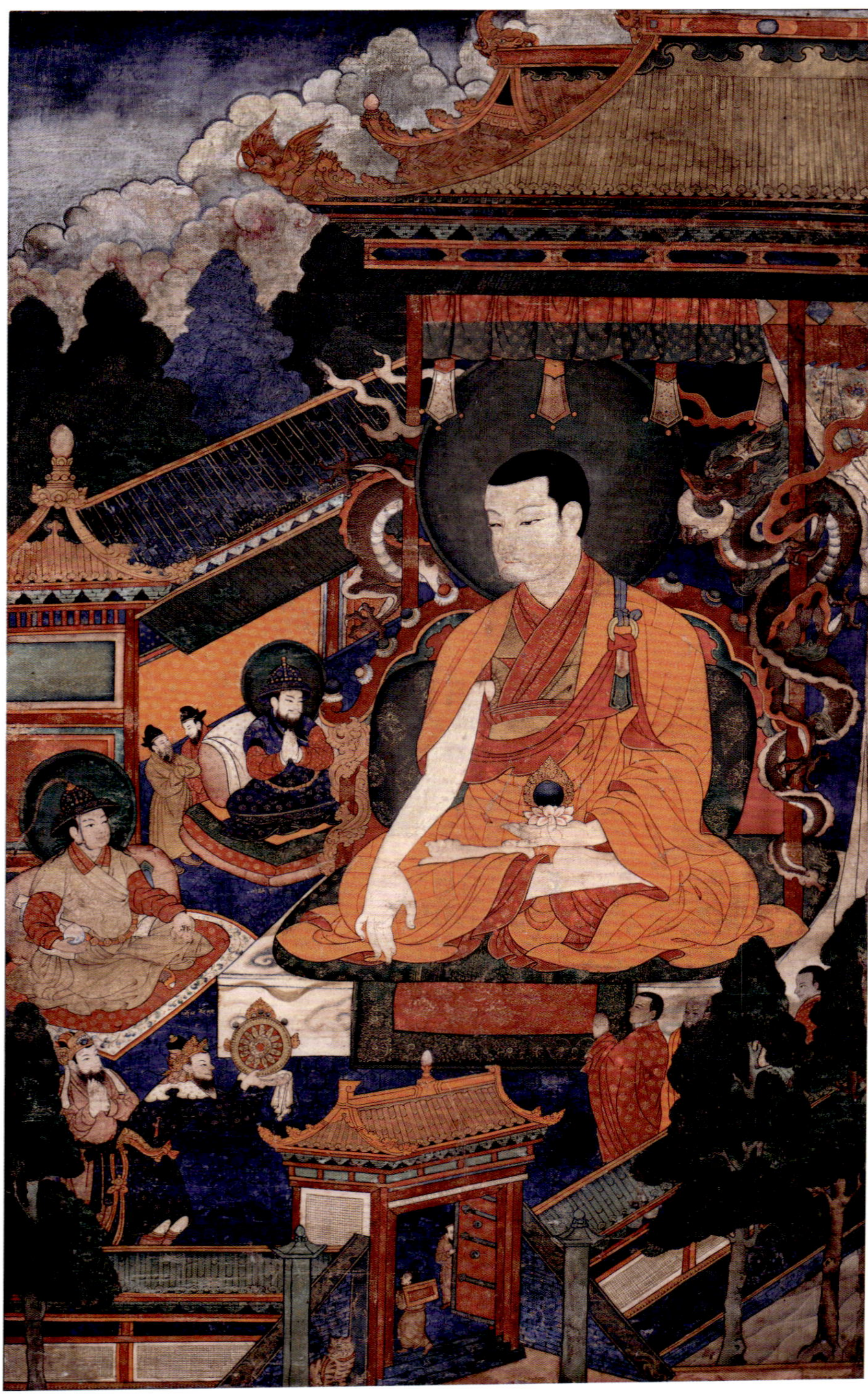

beard and mustache. Though his robes and handheld emblem of holy scripture are imposing, the saint's expression is slightly wistful, as if reflecting a hint of his deep insights.

As in the preceding thangka, an honorary canopy floats magically in the sky above the main figure; its central tassel slightly overlaps the top of the throne back. The artist has included very fine details, such as the golden dragon-brocade pattern in the dark-blue mat with a colorful border, under the main figure.

Two Paintings of Great Adepts

Two outstanding paintings seem likely to be works of Khyentse Chenmo. I am adding these two late discoveries here, at the end of this chapter. Both have certain typical features of the artist, such as naturalistic depictions of different and sometimes untypical types of birds and animals, excellent landscape details, and

rocks. Elsewhere he also wears a special robe clasp over one shoulder.

To the left, Mañjuśrī rides a lion, and the central figure is also mounted on two blue-green lions with lifelike poses. The transparent, rainbow-edged body nimbus of the central figure is echoed by that of Mañjuśrī. The lamas floating above are probably two prominent gurus of the central figure.

Introduced earlier with its detail (Fig. 1.23), Figure 7.39 depicts another unidentified lineal guru from the same set, evidently as a last central figure. It is likely Gongkar Dorjedenpa, who would appear in this lineage beneath his two most prominent gurus, Champa Lingpa and Drakthok Chöje; both are clearly labeled. The central figure appears to be a master in his forties, with a faint

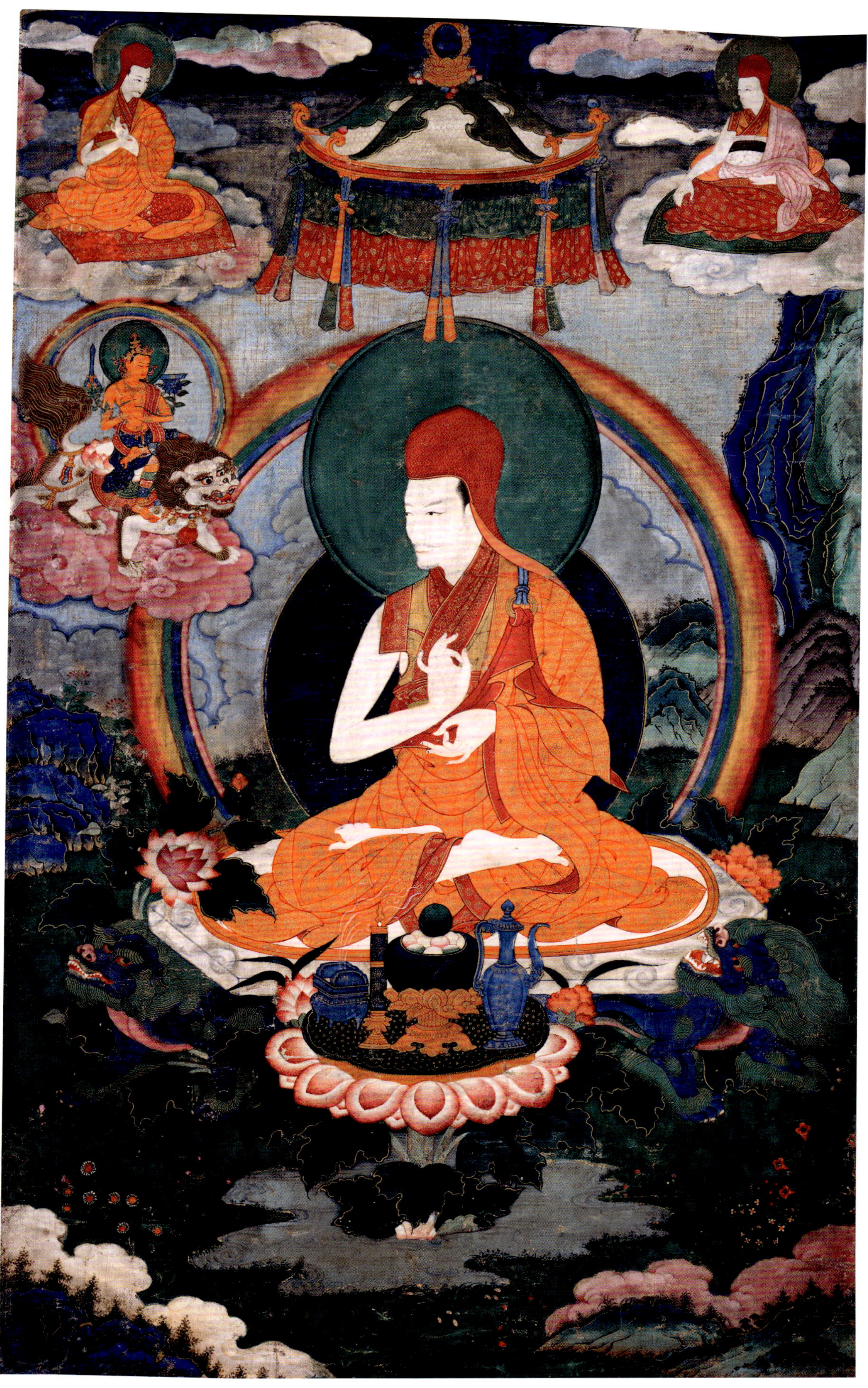

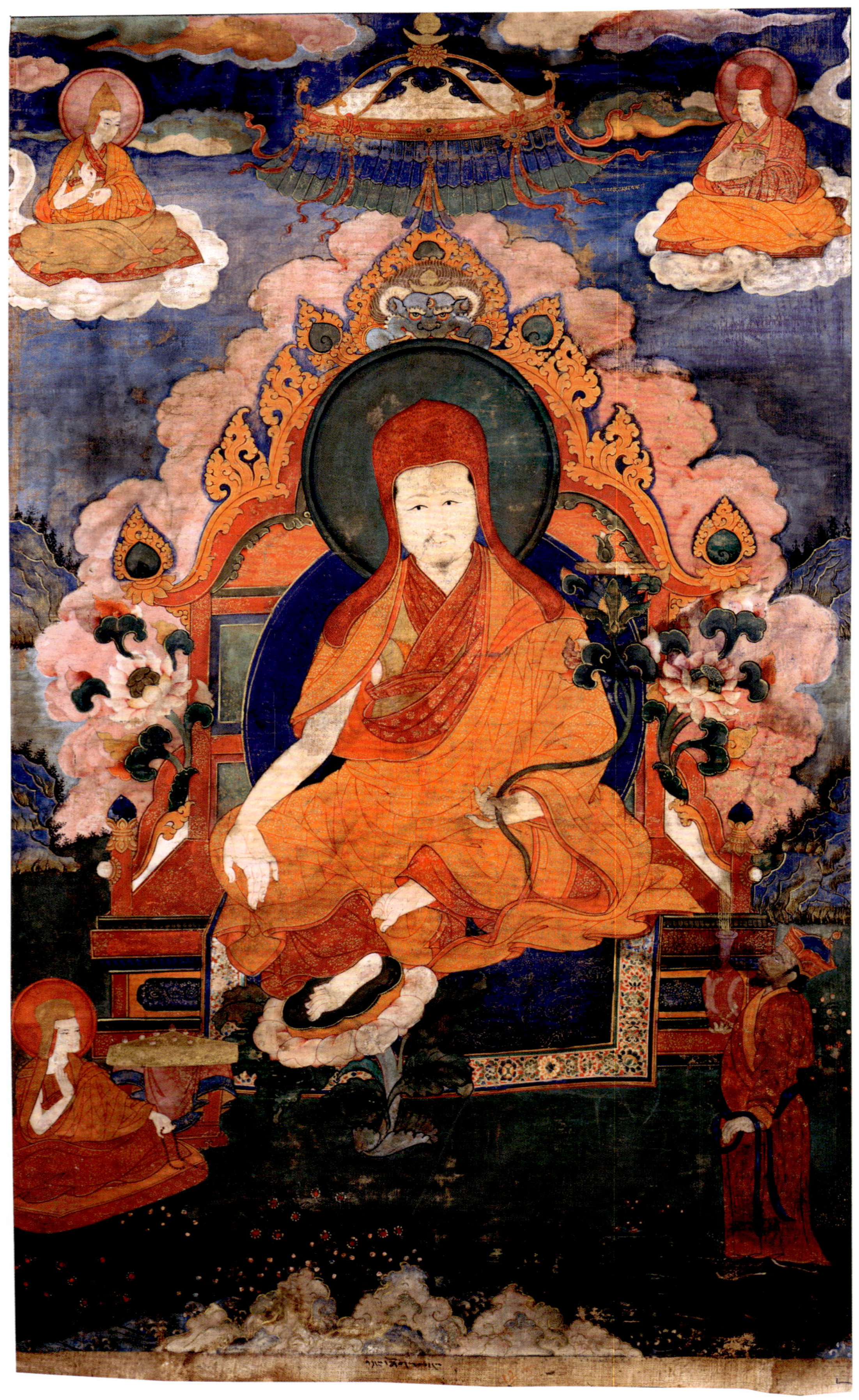

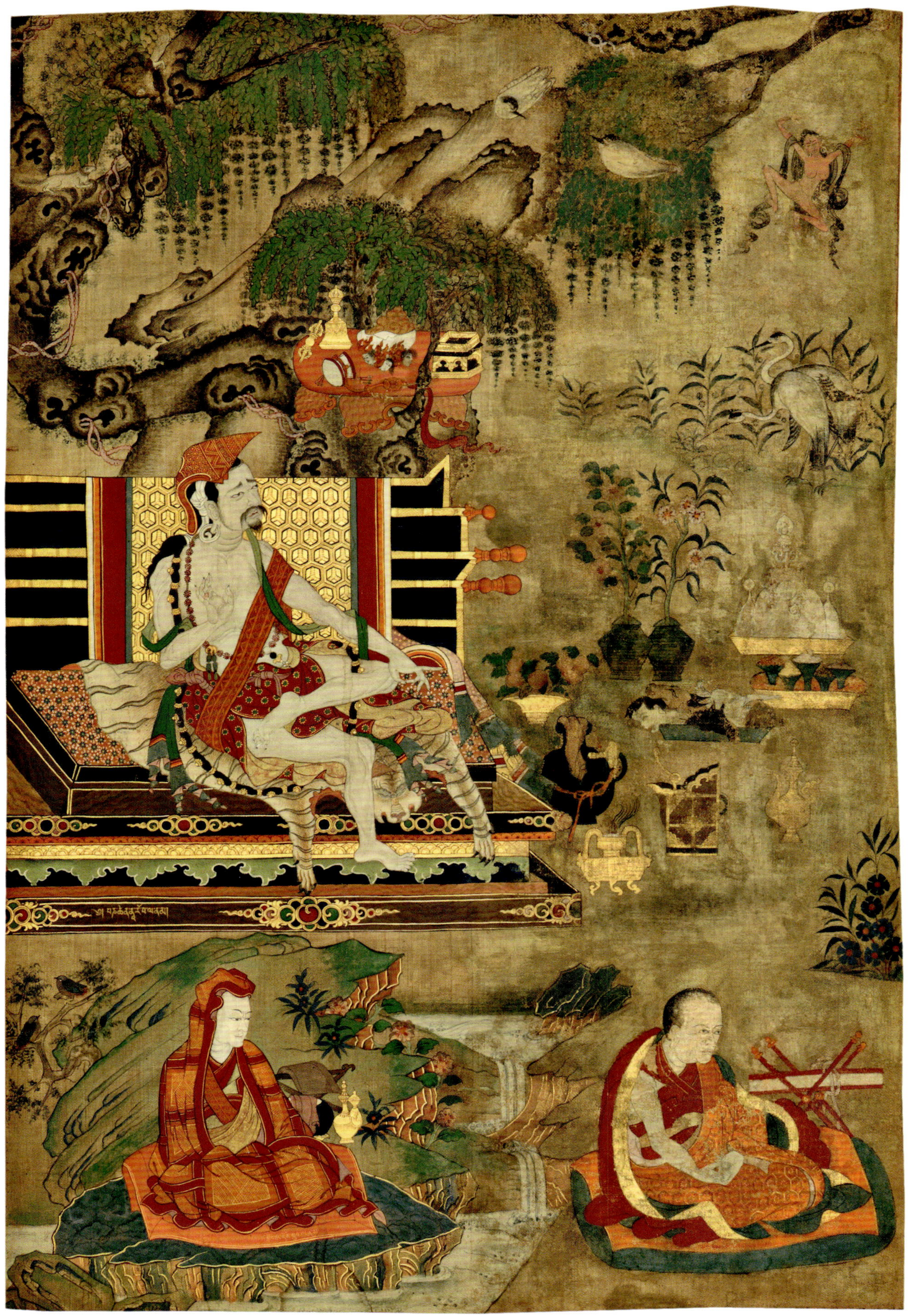

unusually lifelike poses of minor human figures. Though not defining stylistic marks strictly speaking, such elements rarely appear together in the same Tibetan painting.

Figure 7.40, a painting in the Chinese *si thang* style, depicts the great pandit-siddha Nāropa with uncommon iconography: a pointed yellow pandit hat lies flat on his head. He appears here as a lineal master or as one of the eighty-four great adepts. Below are two Tibetan lamas, presumably later lineal gurus. The depiction of the main figure has many unusual details, such as the elaborate and colorful animal skin and wooden throne and the two rosaries that he wears, one with large dark-brown beads that hangs lower than usual, below his thigh.

The painting includes two pairs of birds: two storks standing together to the right and another species in the crags and bushes above. In the upper-left corner, two small gray squirrel-like animals climb along the contorted tree trunk. The landscape includes trees with gnarls like sharp-edged scabs, and a skinny-legged yogini floats in the air above right, seemingly smaller than the nearby birds. The painting is very stylized--precious and mincing.

Figure 7.41, depicting the great adepts Śavaripa and Dārikapa, was probably part of a set of Vajrāsana's great adepts, as numbers 27 and 28. At the top of the landscape, in the upper-left corner, the artist depicts a pair of lifelike, long-tailed birds perched in a small tree. He also very convincingly portrays a fleeing deer—diving toward the left edge of the painting—and a dead boar being carried in the middle of the picture. The major and minor figures are unusually true-to-life in their poses and details of dress and accouterments.

Rob Linrothe captures the mood and contents of the painting well:

[In] this moody and atmospheric painting, the figures in the upper half appear to be dancing gracefully and languorously underwater, while in the lower half the figures seem to be settling into the ocean floor. The deer, its ears pricked, dashes for its life, diving out of the left side of the picture. Śavaripa, the hunter, is accompanied by two of his consorts (named Padmalocanā and Jñānalocanā). One of them balances a slaughtered wild boar upside down on her back; the other looks coyly out at us,

her legs twisting in space as she holds a quiver of arrows. As his quarry escapes, Śavaripa (A5, V27) watches impassively, perhaps even sadly, but not nearly as mournful in expression as the king on the throne below.

According to an inscription, neatly written in gold on the lower edge of the odd bench-like throne, the lower siddha is the king Dārikapa (A77, V28). Eyes tilt upward, his mustache droops. It is a haunting face, expressive of character. Dārikapa's salmon-colored outer cloak spreads over his lap, closely mimicking Chinese satin embroidered with auspicious motifs. The midnight-blue sleeves of his robe have an appropriately royal dragon motif. That his activities are tantric in nature is underscored not only by a poem in the *Caryāgīti* associated with him, but also by the ritual implements around him, including a bone *ḍamaru* drum looped around his chest.[396]

FIG. 7.41
The Great Adepts Śavaripa and Dārikapa
second half of the fifteenth century
25 ¾ x 15 in. (65.4 x 38.1 cm)
The Walters Museum of Art, the John and Berthe Ford Collection, Baltimore (F.110)
Literature: Linrothe 2006, no. 41

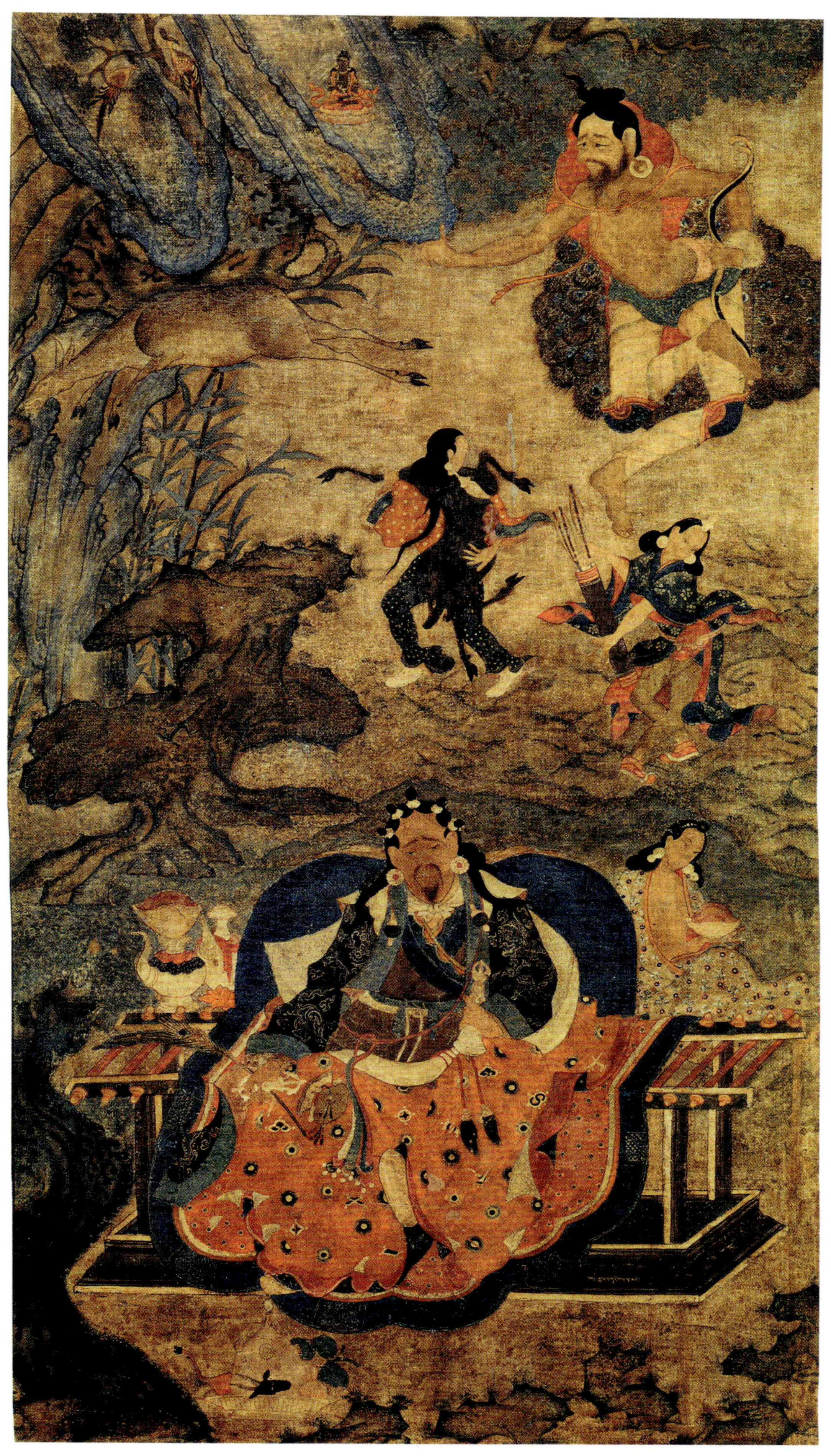

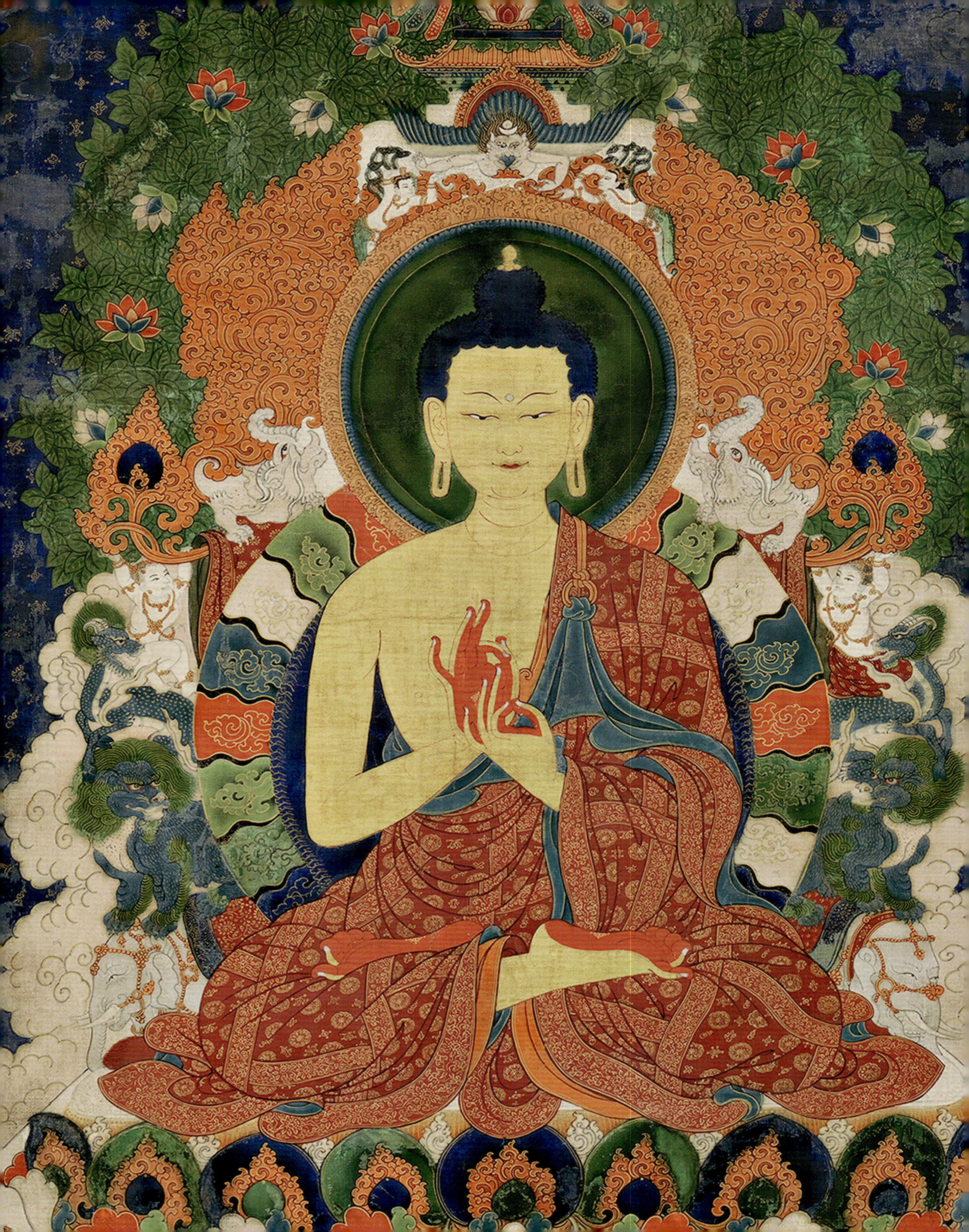

CHAPTER 8

Paintings of the Kings and Kalkins of Shambhala by Khyentse Chenmo

THIS CHAPTER concerns an intriguing set of thangkas, now preserved in the Museum of Fine Arts, Boston (MFA), that depicts the kings and Kalkins ("wisdom-holders") of Shambhala as single figures. When I saw a few of its paintings in 1997, I noted that the style of the central Buddha was similar to the Khyenri mode of painting. Curators have long considered the set to be Sino-Tibetan, and some scholars even speculated that the paintings originated from China. It is a pleasant surprise to realize that these thangkas may well have been painted by the founding master of the Khyenri style.

I propose this based on many formal qualities and motifs shared by this set of paintings with the murals known to be by the artist at Gongkar. As is often the case with early Khyenri-style sets, the ornate body nimbus or lotus seat in the central painting provides a vital stylistic link with those murals of Gongkar. Other decisive characteristics include the ring used to affix the Buddha's upper robes, the transparency of some of the nimbuses, the variety of nimbuses, and the pairs of birds in the settings.

However, those crucial central Buddha or Vajradhara paintings have rarely been published or even adequately photographed. The entire set of the Boston Shambhala kings has rarely been exhibited. Until now, the most prominent exposure of the set was the publication of a single painting in Pratapaditya

Pal's 1984 book, *Tibetan Paintings*. Pal praised that painting:

> Two other thangkas by unknown artists, one portraying a Karmapa hierarch and another, from a set depicting the kings of Shambhala, are just as elegantly painted as the portraits by Karshu Gönpo Dorje. The draughtsmanship is equally accomplished and the landscapes are just as reposeful. . . . While the mountains behind the king are entirely imaginary and follow conventional forms, the landscape passages with the river, the boat and the monasteries are much more realistic . . . .[397]

The set of Shambhala king paintings was first briefly owned by Denman Waldo Ross (1853–1935), an American painter, art collector, and professor of art at Harvard University who was also an active and generous donor of art to the MFA. He reputedly bought these paintings in Paris a year or two before he donated them in 1906.[398] With the donation, Ross stipulated that the paintings not be allowed to leave the museum.

As preparation for an exhibition in 2012, the paintings were removed from the Japanese wooden panels they had been mounted on for decades and remounted by the MFA conservation team. In the process, the identifications and order of the paintings could be determined. Using infrared reflectography, the conservators identified preliminary sketches and shorthand color code

annotations on the paintings from the master painter to his apprentices.

After being exhibited in Boston in 2012, the entire set was made available online as digital images. The *Shambhala Times* reported:

> The Rigden Thangkas are not allowed to leave the Museum of Fine Arts—a request of the donor—and are almost impossible for the public to view as they are not on permanent exhibit. There were not sufficient funds in the museum's budget to produce an exhibition catalog, and the museum was more than willing to enable Shambhala to make images of the thangkas available on our website.
>
> The Rigden Thangkas are part of the Denman Waldo Ross Collection of the Museum of Fine Arts comprising many thousands of works from all over the world that were donated by Mr. Ross in 1906. He purchased this set of paintings in Paris, and for a number of years it was believed that the thangkas were painted in Mongolia. However, research and special photography revealed written instructions in Tibetan script under the paint, and Jacki Elgar, the exhibit's [conservator], was able to determine that the thangkas are of Tibetan origin.[399]

The set has been dated by the museum to the second half of the seventeenth century, and it was previously described in Japanese in a catalog by Shozui M. Toganoo in 1986, as images III 10–2 through III 10–18. That author dated the set to the seventeenth or eighteenth century and omitted five paintings. In this chapter, I refer to the romanized text and numbers for his main identifications and dating of the set.

Two Traditions of Iconography

The Boston set represents one of two main iconographic traditions that existed in Tibet for painting the seven dharma kings of Shambhala and the twenty-five Kalkins. One tradition—presumably of the Khyenri and Menri in central Tibet—was that followed by both Khyentse Chenmo and a standard Tibetan pantheon; its crucial iconographic information is conveyed by black-and-white drawings in a 1972 work edited by Raghu Vira and Lokesh Chandra. These revealed that handheld implements or symbols (*phyag mtshan*) were decisive; body color may also have been important.

The second tradition was that of Situ Panchen at Palpung Monastery, near Derge in Kham. If we compare what the figures hold in their hands, we can see that, though the dharma kings are similar in both traditions, most of the handheld implements of the Kalkins differ. Thus the physical appearance of the one tradition—for example, the Kalkins of Khyentse—cannot be compared with that of the other tradition—the Kalkins of Situ—for identification purposes. Both use the same iconographic language but have assigned different symbols to the respective Kalkins. In one coincidence, three figures hold the same wheel and conch in both Khyentse and Situ traditions: Shambhala king number 3 and Kalkins 3 and 22.

The first tradition seems to be earlier. I do not believe it was based on ritual texts with physical descriptions, such as exist for the sixteen arhats. Situ

Panchen may have derived his tradition with the help or inspiration of Kathok Rigdzin Tshewang Norbu, and it may be based on a special written description of the deities, such as by Kathok Rigdzin, which is rumored to exist. The only relevant text that I found in Kathok Rigdzin's collected works was a list of the names of the dharma kings and Kalkins; volume 4 of his writings also contains two Kālacakra *sādhanas* and one brief instruction.

The following passages describe a few of the most striking features of this set.

The first painting, Figure 8.1, depicts Buddha Śākyamuni in the central painting of the set. It was originally identified by Toganoo.[400] The painting includes some noteworthy and rare decorative details in the colorful body nimbus of the main figure, which are also found in the murals of Gongkar Dorjeden in the Hevajra Chapel. (See Fig. 3.13.) Also distinctive is the thick double cord holding a ring-shaped robe fastener that hangs over the Buddha's proper left shoulder. (See Fig. 4.13.)

The scene of this painting is relatively simple. The background sky is dark blue with eight minor deities flying with divine offerings. In the foreground, two figures sit to the right and left; one of them holds his hands together above his head in supplication. Both are probably highly realized teachers of the tradition; perhaps they are the first king, Sucandra, and the first Kalkin, Mañjughoṣa Yaśas.

Figure 8.2 depicts Sucandra as the first dharma king of Shambhala, holding a vajra and bell. He was originally identified by Toganoo, who noted agreement with Vira and Chandra 1972, part 20, number 258b. The MFA similarly identifies him as "the first dharma religious king of Shambhala."[401]

Sucandra is depicted sitting outside on a rug, evidently within a royal park, with a small table for books at one side.

The surrounding landscape is complex. The viewer is invited to enter it through the wide opening at the bottom right, where a supplicant or attendant is shown humbly kneeling, offering a book to the king. Two other figures—probably highly realized masters—float before the edges of the main figure's body nimbus; the overlap pushes them forward in the pictorial space. Above the king stands a golden-roofed temple amid a grove of trees. Far in the distance looms a row of sixteen dentate snow peaks with a blue sky behind them. We have reached the sacred realm of Shambhala, as the artist imagined it.

Figure 8.3 depicts a king or Kalkin of Shambhala who holds a staff with a simple jeweled tip and a rope with a hook on the end. In his 1986 catalog, Toganoo identified this figure as the fourth Kalkin, Vijaya. The MFA identifies him differently, as "Sureśvara, Lha dbang, . . . second dharma religious king of Shambhala."[402] However, he seems to be neither Vijaya (rNam par rgyal, Kalkin 4) nor Sureśvara (Lha yi dbang, king 2): both of them, like Kalkin 13 and 21, should hold special axes and ropes with hooks on the ends. Here the iconography matches more closely that of Somadatta (Zla bas byin), fourth dharma king of Shambhala, based on Vira and Chandra 1972, part 20, number 259a, where this king is shown holding a jewel-headed staff and a chain with a hook on the end.

In this painting, the king is shown seated on a green rug on a royal throne with a colorful and elaborate back, leaning on a white patterned bolster. The surrounding scene is extremely simple. Above the plain field of green grass in

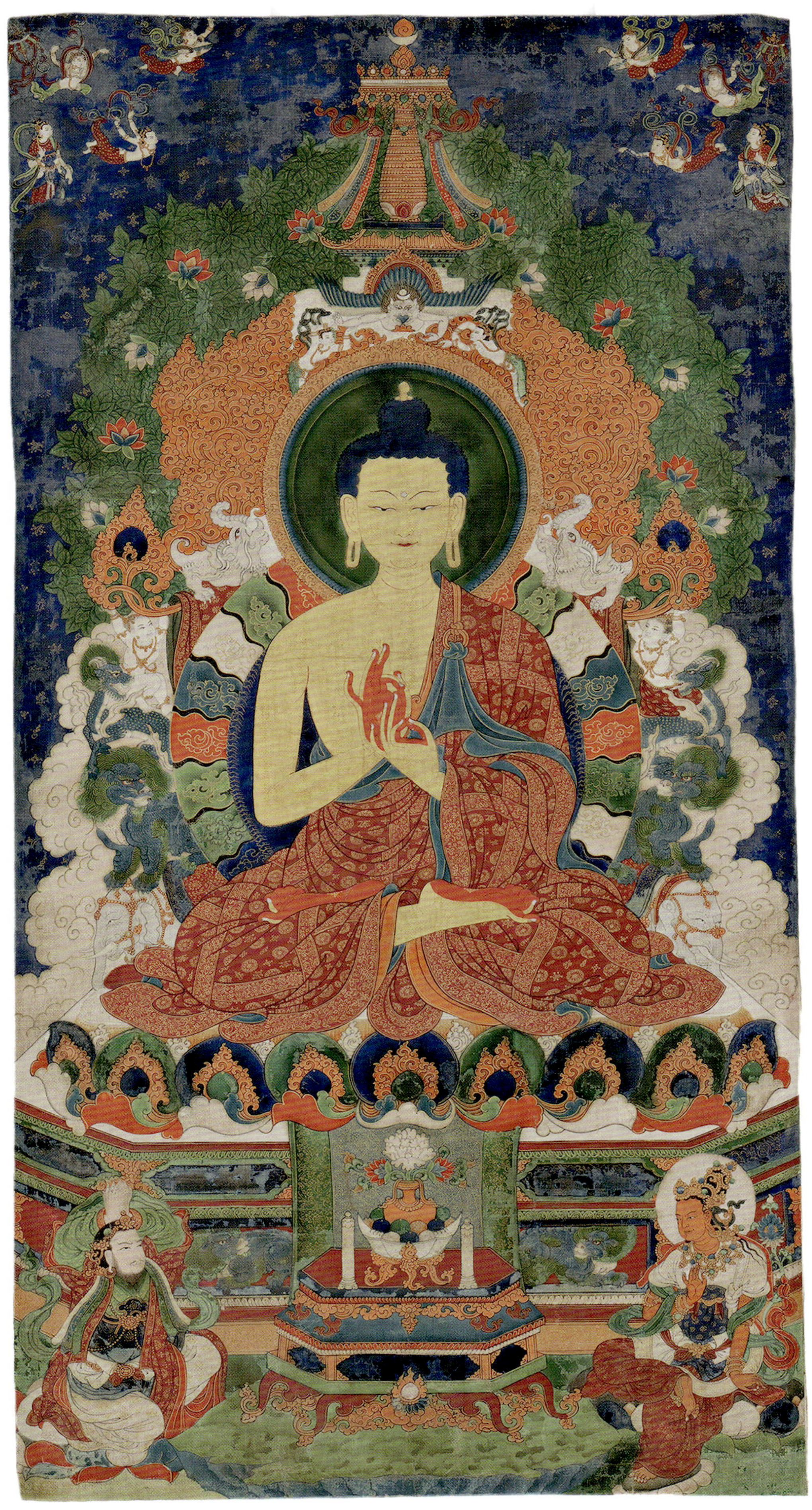

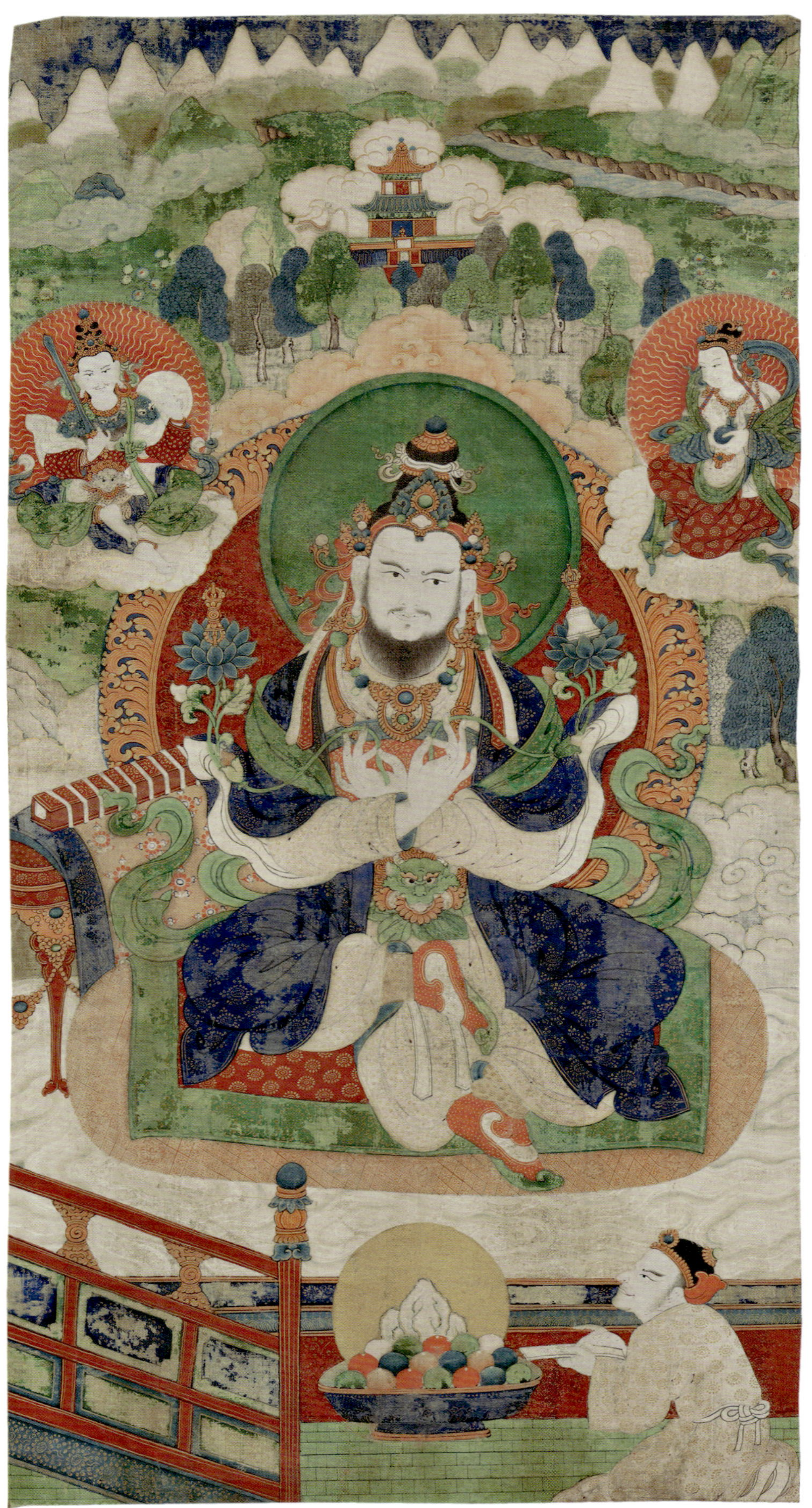

Fig. 8.2
Sucandra, First Dharma King of Shambhala
second half of the fifteenth century
31 ⅞ x 17 in. (80.9 x 43.3 cm)
MFA, Boston, Ross Collection (06–329)
Literature: Toganoo 1986, no. III 10–3

Fig. 8.3
Somadatta(?), Fourth Dharma King of
Shambhala
second half of the fifteenth century
31 ⅞ x 17 in. (80.9 x 43.3 cm)
MFA, Boston, Ross Collection (06–340)
Literature: Toganoo 1986, no. III 10–9

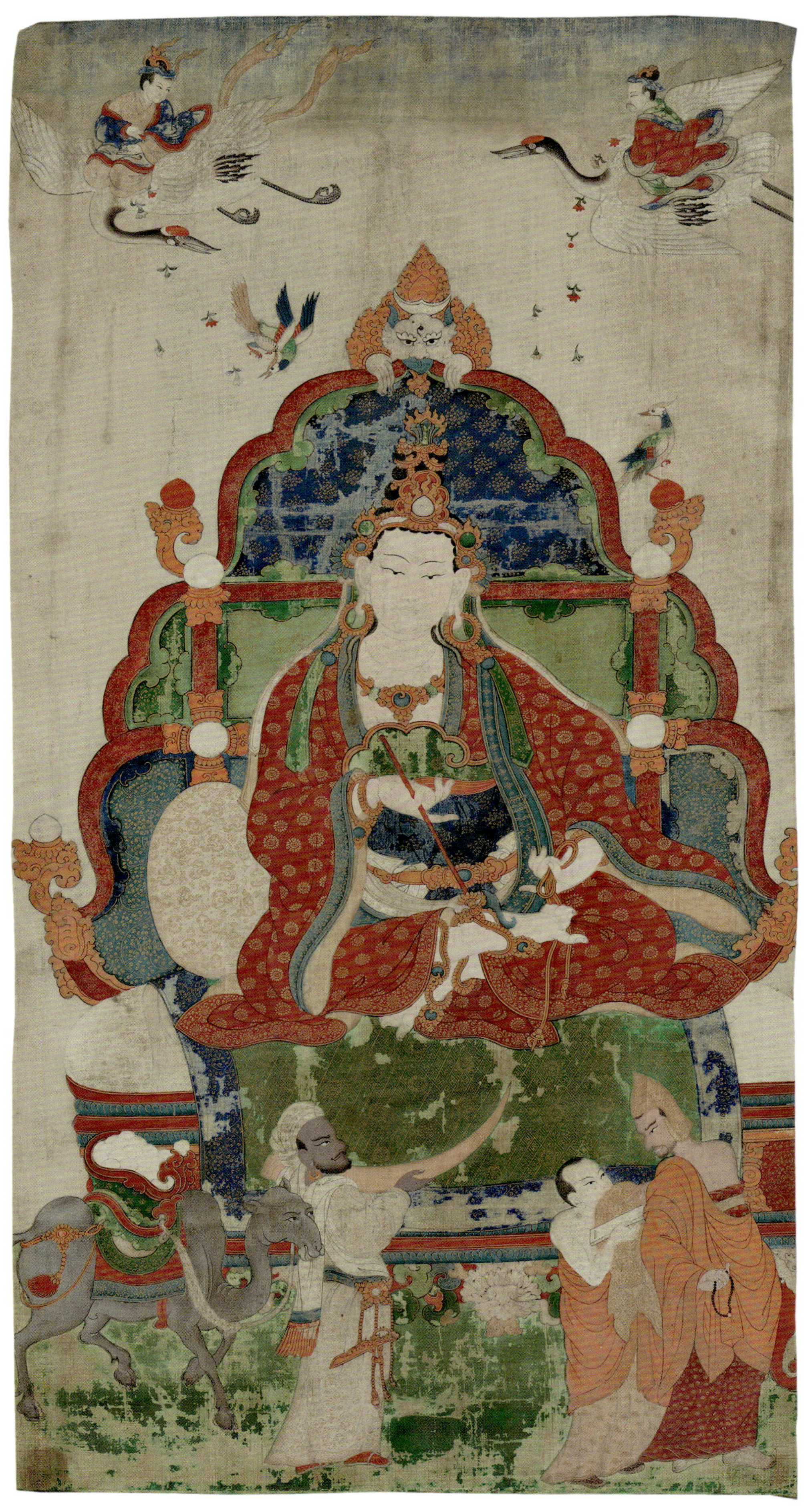

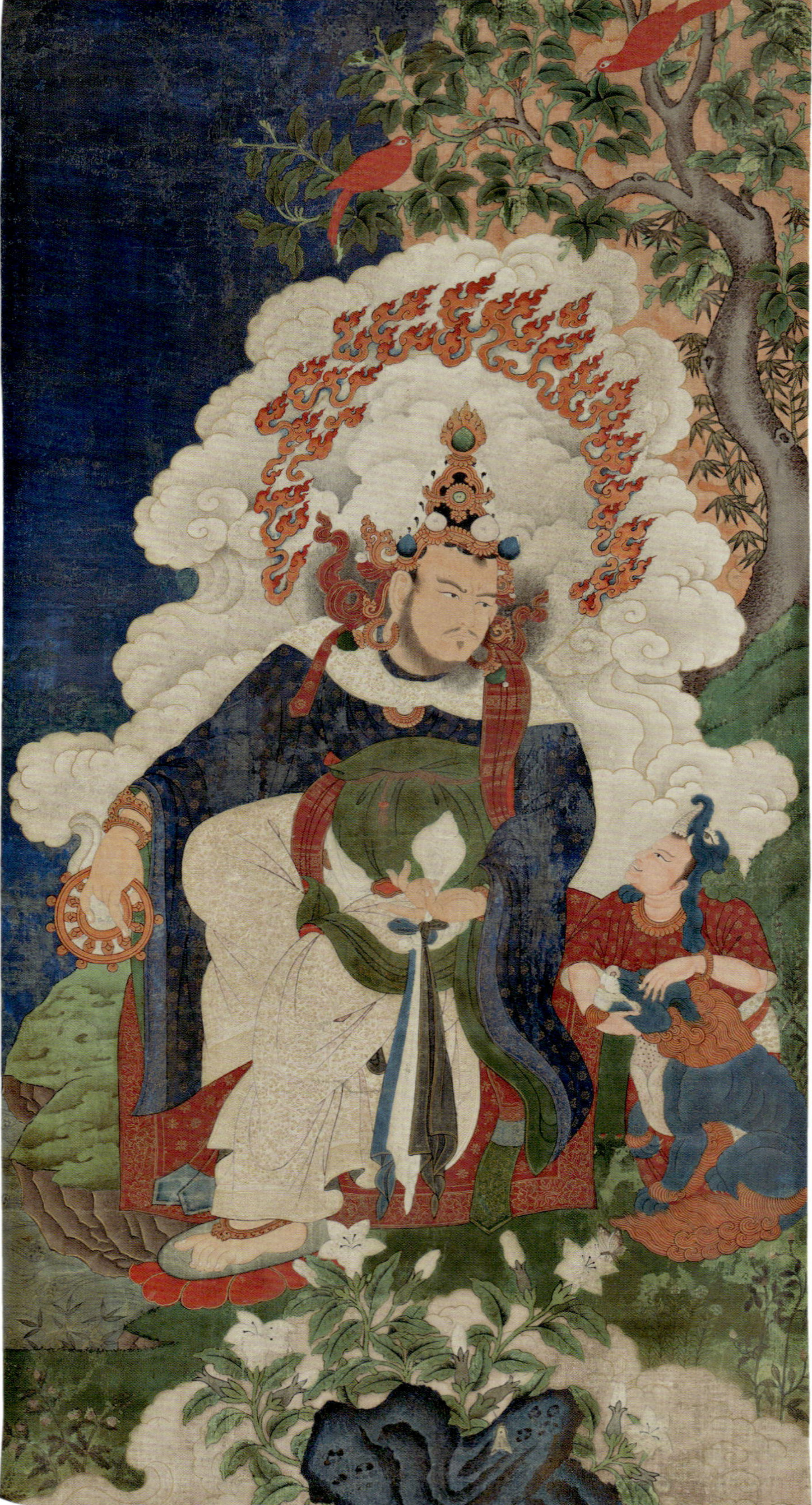

the foreground is a very low, indistinct horizon. At the top edge of the painting, a thin wash of light indigo lends the only color to the sky. Though faintly colored, the sky is not empty. Two minor deities ride on large cranes, sprinkling a few divine flowers (*lha yi me tog*) as they pass. The red crests and black-and-white necks suggest they are red-crowned cranes. To the left of the top of the throne, a large crested bird—possibly a kingfisher, with its white breast and blue-and-green throat—swoops acrobatically, catching one flower and eyeing another as if to see whether it is edible. Its mate watches intently from where it is perched on a single leg, on the right side of the throne.

In the foreground stands a white-turbaned Indian or other foreign trader, staring up at the king. Accompanied by his camel, which looks thoughtful, the trader balances a large ivory tusk on one shoulder. Meanwhile, standing to the right, a novice holding a book and a Buddhist holding a rosary and wearing a yellow pandit hat with tucked-in earflaps seem engaged in conversation. Such details inject human interest into the otherwise simple foreground.

Figure 8.4 depicts Tejin (gZi brjid ldan), Third Dharma King of Shambhala, holding a wheel and white conch. He was originally identified by Toganoo, who pointed out that the painting agreed with the iconography of that king in Vira and Chandra 1972, part 20, number 258d. The MFA also identifies him as "third dharma religious king of Shambhala."[403]

This king appears in a landscape before a cluster of white cumulus clouds, which contrast dramatically with the deep blue of his robe and the large triangular

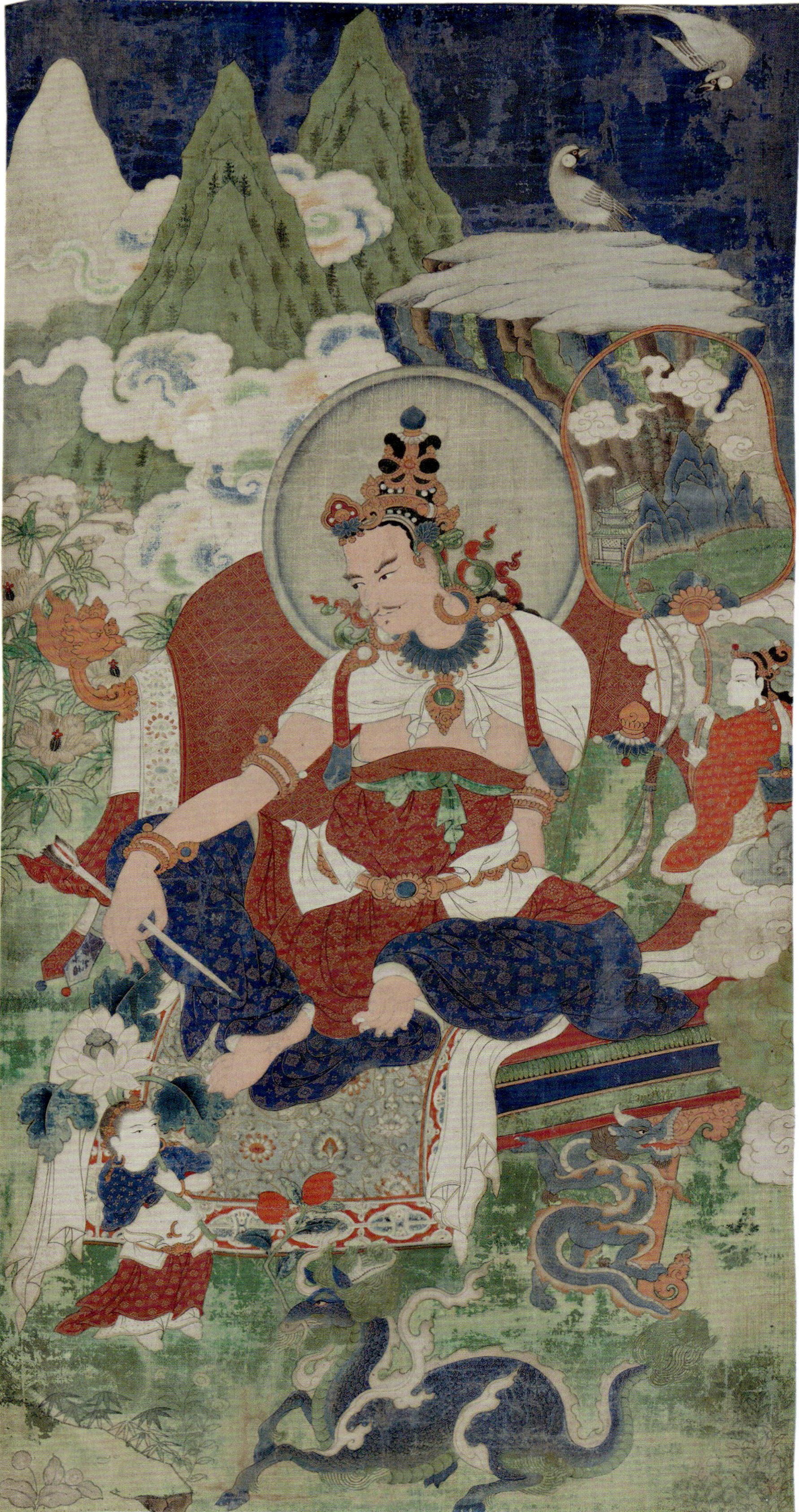

field of sky to the left. He seems to be at the edge of a forest, represented by the trees to the right. He looks intently toward the right, holding a wheel in his left hand. Reinforcing the circular theme, an arc of flames forms a type of head nimbus. In this painting set, Khyentse Chenmo employed as many as eight ways to depict nimbuses; some main figures are without nimbuses. In seven cases, he painted a solid-color disc, with a border created by an inner ring of indigo. He also commonly employed a brightly colored disc, such as orange, without a border. Other types of nimbuses include a solid-color disc with a gold edge, a solid-color disc with an indigo outline, a transparent disc with a gold outline, a transparent disc with an indigo outline, a transparent disc without an outline, and, as in this painting, a ring of flames.

This king seems to be standing in a wilderness without a throne or shelter. But he is seated, with his right knee pulled up; a red carpet hangs from his otherwise invisible seat. He seems to be conversing with an interlocutor to the right, a man wearing a red robe and *makara* helmet who stands looking up at the king as if expecting his next remark. (This figure grasps the head of a blue lion, with an auburn mane and stylized tail that seems reptilian.) Below him, a butterfly rests on a white trumpet-shaped flower of a bush growing behind a blue craggy rock. At the top of the painting, two red birds with long tails look at each other, perched on different branches of the tree.

Figure 8.5 is probably a depiction of Sureśvara (Lha yi dbang phyug), Fifth Dharma King of Shambhala. As originally identified by Toganoo, his bow and arrow agree with his iconography in

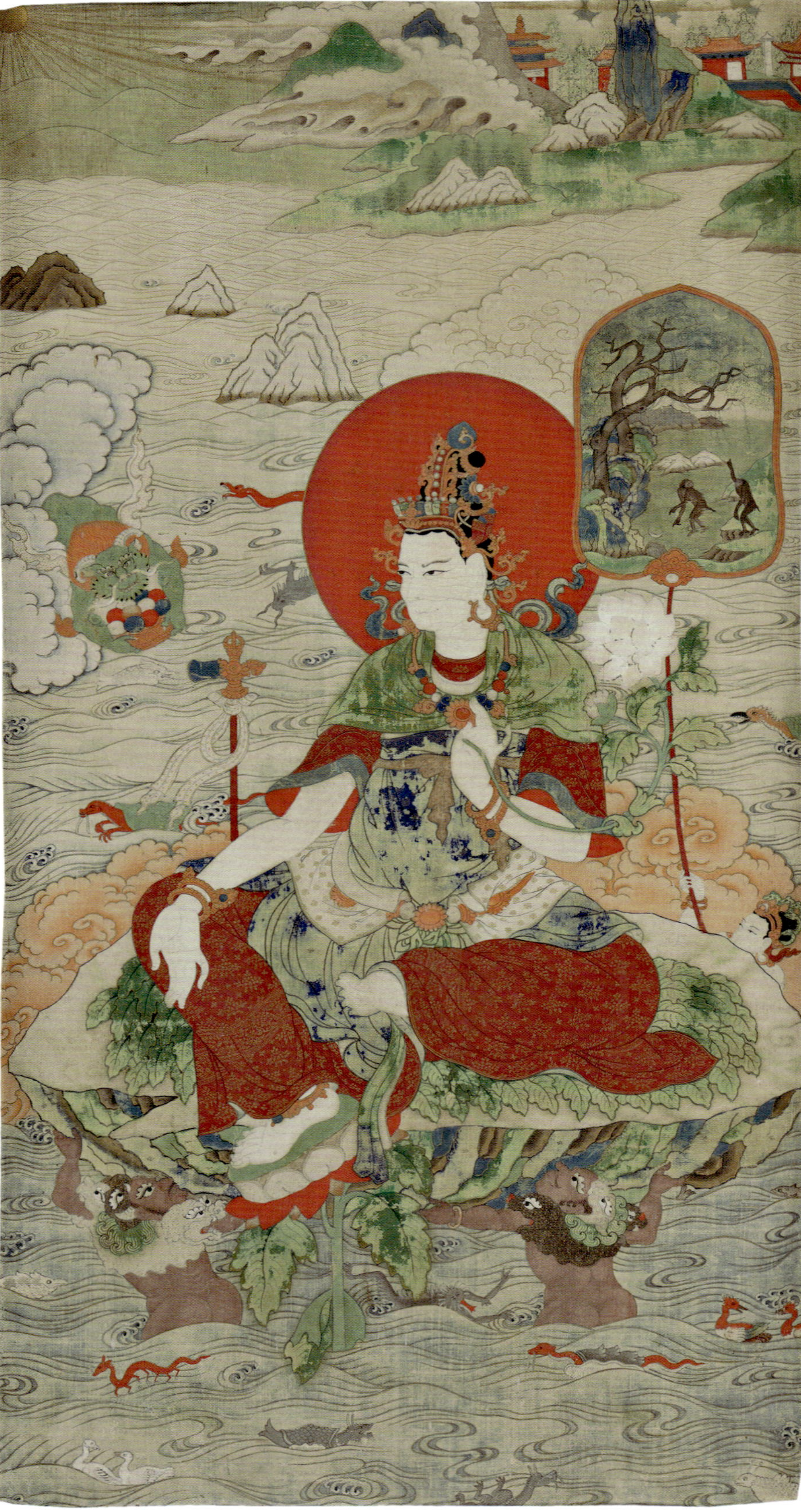

Vira and Chandra 1972, part 20, number 259b. The MFA also identifies him as "fifth dharma religious king of Shambhala sureshvara."[404]

The king sits on a throne in a wilderness in which three distant but imposing cone-shaped mountains rise, two verdant and one snowy. Two clusters of clouds create spatial depth between the main subject and the green mountains, which feature tiny pine trees. Beyond them is deep-blue sky, the same color as the king's lower robe. In the upper-right corner, a gray bird with a stubby finch-like beak seems to somersault through the air; it possibly represents a Himalayan snowcock or large gray partridge. Its mate is perched on the flat gray top of a blue-green outcropping. The landscape to the right of the king's head nimbus is hidden by a large painted fan, held by a red-robed female divinity. The fan depicts a landscape with similarly stylized clouds with trailing tails. The fan's background mountains line up perfectly with the blue-green structure of the mountain "behind" it, as if the surface of the fan were transparent. This painting within a painting, a device meant to baffle the eye, is fairly rare (though we shall see it again in the following painting). In the foreground, a little boy stands near the base of the king's rug, holding the stem of a huge flower. At the bottom of the picture, a magical blue-scaled *qilin* from Chinese art rests on the ground, clenching a fruit-laden twig in its mouth that it has brought as an offering.

Figure 8.6 depicts a king or Kalkin of Shambhala with an unusual hammer-tipped staff, holding the stem of a large lotus. This agrees with the fairly rare iconography of the fifteenth Kalkin, Anantamitra (mTha' yas gnyen). Toganoo

identified him as Anantamitra, yet the
MFA now identifies him as the "sixth
dharma religious king" (sNa tshogs
gzugs).[405] I agree with Toganoo, who cited
as evidence the similar drawing in Vira
and Chandra 1972, part 20, number 263d.

This painting has the most complicated landscape in the set and depicts
the central figure seated on a piece of
land surrounded by a vast gray sea, an
uncommon setting. The king sits on a mat
of green tree leaves. His small island is
held aloft by two standing monsters, their
bare bottoms pointing toward the viewer.
There are many dangerous and fantastic
creatures in the sea around him. To give
the scary scene a more normal cast, Khyentse depicted at the bottom left a pair of
ordinary white ducks, who rapidly swim
away, eyes glued on each other. On the
right side, mostly hidden by the island, a
minor divinity—possibly a *nāga*—holds
the long handle of a fan that depicts a
detailed landscape with two apes, one of
which gesticulates to the other at a nearby
tree. To the left of the main figure's
head, a remarkable green dragon seems
to move toward the front of the picture
plane, holding in its claws a cluster of
eight magical balls in a bowl.

In the far distance, at the top of the
painting, floats the land of Shambhala
or another beautiful place, with golden-roofed pagodas and a hilly landscape,
wreathed in clouds. In the upper-left
corner, a golden sun blazes, illuminating
a few rolling hills. For comparison, a
golden sun blazing from the corner was
one of the striking features in a portrait
of Sönam Tsemo (Fig. 7.2).

Figure 8.7 depicts a king or Kalkin
who holds the sword and shield of the
Seventh Dharma King, Sureśāna (Lha'i

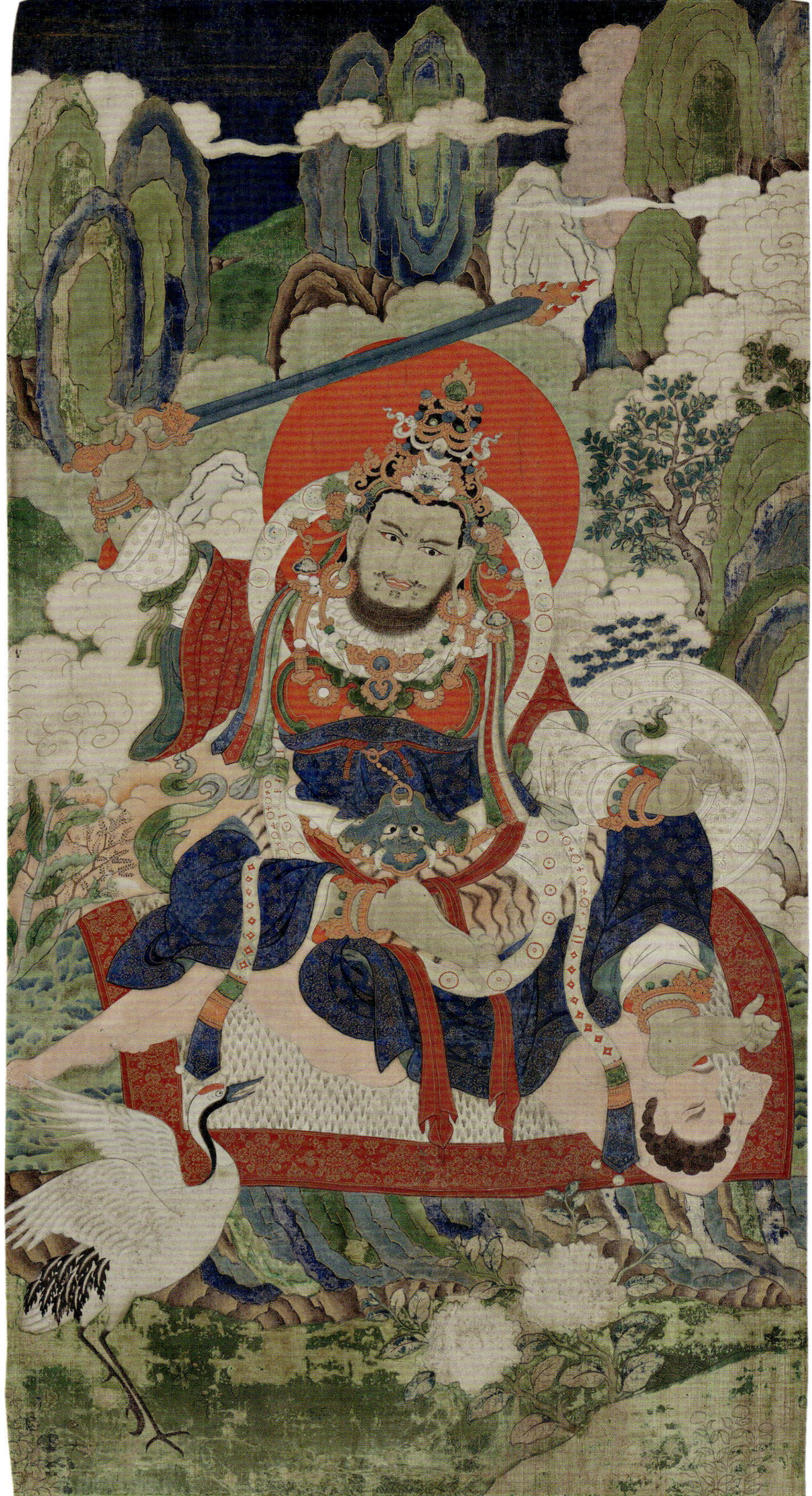

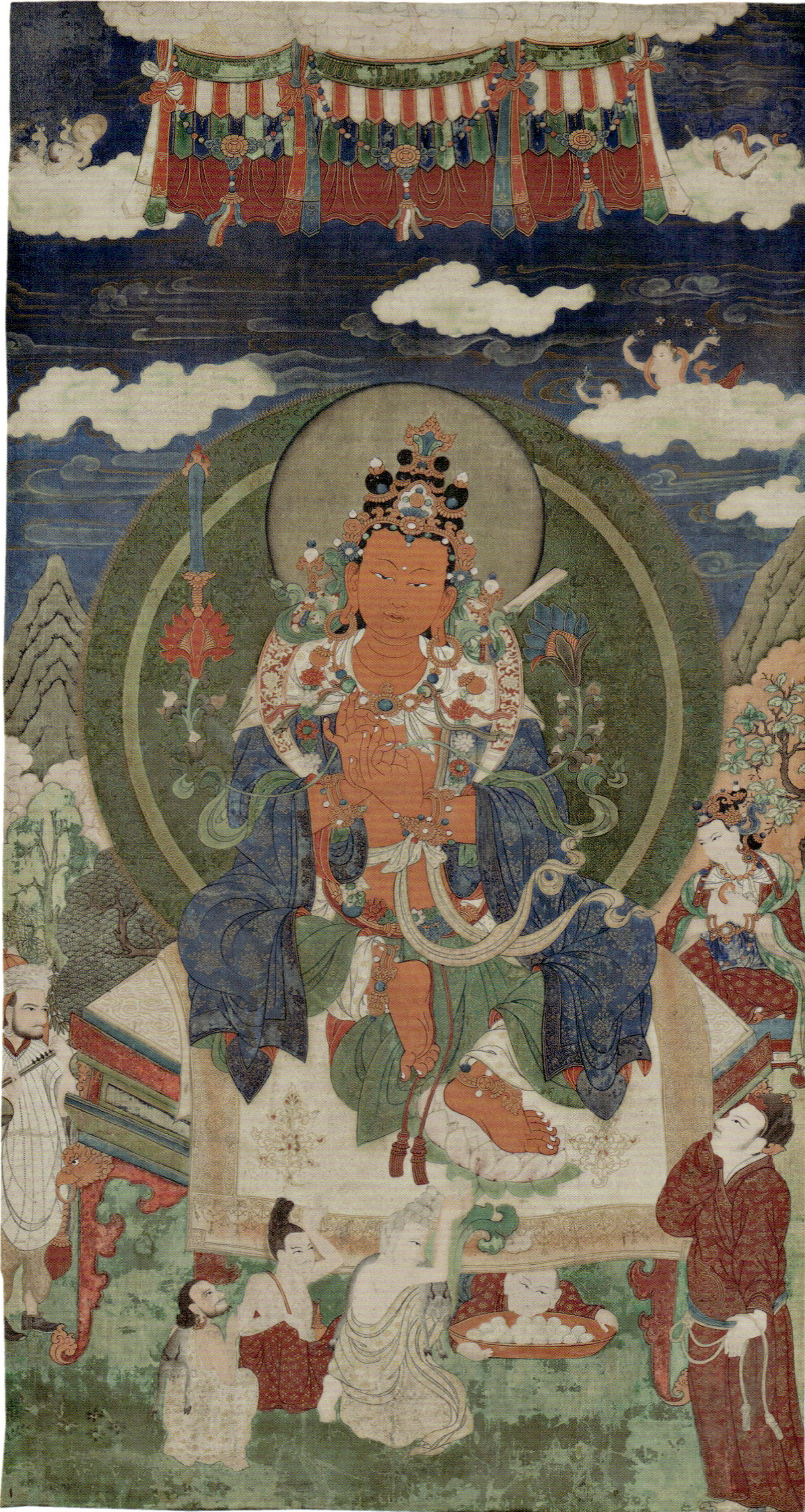

dbang ldan); both Toganoo and the MFA identified him as such.[406] Toganoo was supported by the similar iconography found in Vira and Chandra 1972, part 20, number 259d.

The king's sword is tipped with the flame of gnosis, but his posture evokes a martial feeling. He holds his shield at the ready and sits on what appears to be the flayed skin of a human enemy. At the bottom left, a single Manchurian crane—nicely painted with a black-and-white neck and red crown—flaps its wings, as if squawking in alarm and about to fly away. In the distance, at the top of the painting, a dark-blue sky is partially obscured by pink and white clouds that meander between three clusters of craggy mountains; one crag is white. This landscape contains more colors of craggy rock than any other painting in the set: green, blue-and-green, brown, and white. The rocks also appear under the red-bordered carpet upon which the king sits, like a fringe. In all, the landscape evokes a threatening mood.

Figure 8.8 no doubt depicts the First Kalkin, Mañjughoṣa Yaśas (Jam dbyangs grags pa), an orange-skinned Mañjuśrī-like figure. He was originally identified as such by Toganoo, who compared his iconography in Vira and Chandra 1972, part 20, number 259d, where the figure holds a small lotus topped by a small sword and a book. The MFA identifies him as Manjushri Yashas.[407]

A divine canopy floats in the sky above the central figure, and he is honored by several minor deities who cavort like children, partly hidden by white clouds on both sides. A single steep mountain on each side demarcates the horizon. Though the landscape is fairly simple, the foreground teems with minor figures. In the middle, a group of Indian mendicants is paying respect. One Indian male stands to the far left, holding a North-Indian *vīṇā*. Meanwhile three other minor figures from Shambhala are present: the female to the right is perhaps the First Kalkin's consort, at the bottom right stands a man dressed in a red robe, and, under the throne, a youth crawls on the ground with a tray filled with large jewels.

Figure 8.9 depicts a king or Kalkin of Shambhala who holds a special tantric ax and a rope. Those attributes are shared by Shambhala king number 2 and Kalkin numbers 4, 13, and 21. Toganoo identified this figure as Shambhala king number 2, Lha dbang, Sureśvara, comparing his iconography with Vira and Chandra 1972, part 20, number 258c. The MFA identifies him differently, as the "fourth *vidyadhara* wisdom-holder," that is, the Fourth Kalkin.[408]

The Kalkin sits on a throne surrounded by a wilderness. Two distant mountains, one rocky and the other snowy, are in the upper-right corner. On the left side, a pair of birds with white heads, blue shoulders, orange breasts, and long green tails perch on a rocky outcropping, one of them perhaps spying a butterfly below. Meanwhile, to the right of the king's face, a pair of gray rabbits cavorts in a grassy meadow, one looking back at its mate; the same jumping rabbits appear in the second painting of the Sera set of eighty-four siddhas, next to Lūyipa (see Fig. 3.25). In a pool of water at the bottom right, a *nāga* pays respects while, on the ground to the left, a blue-skinned, white-maned beast looks

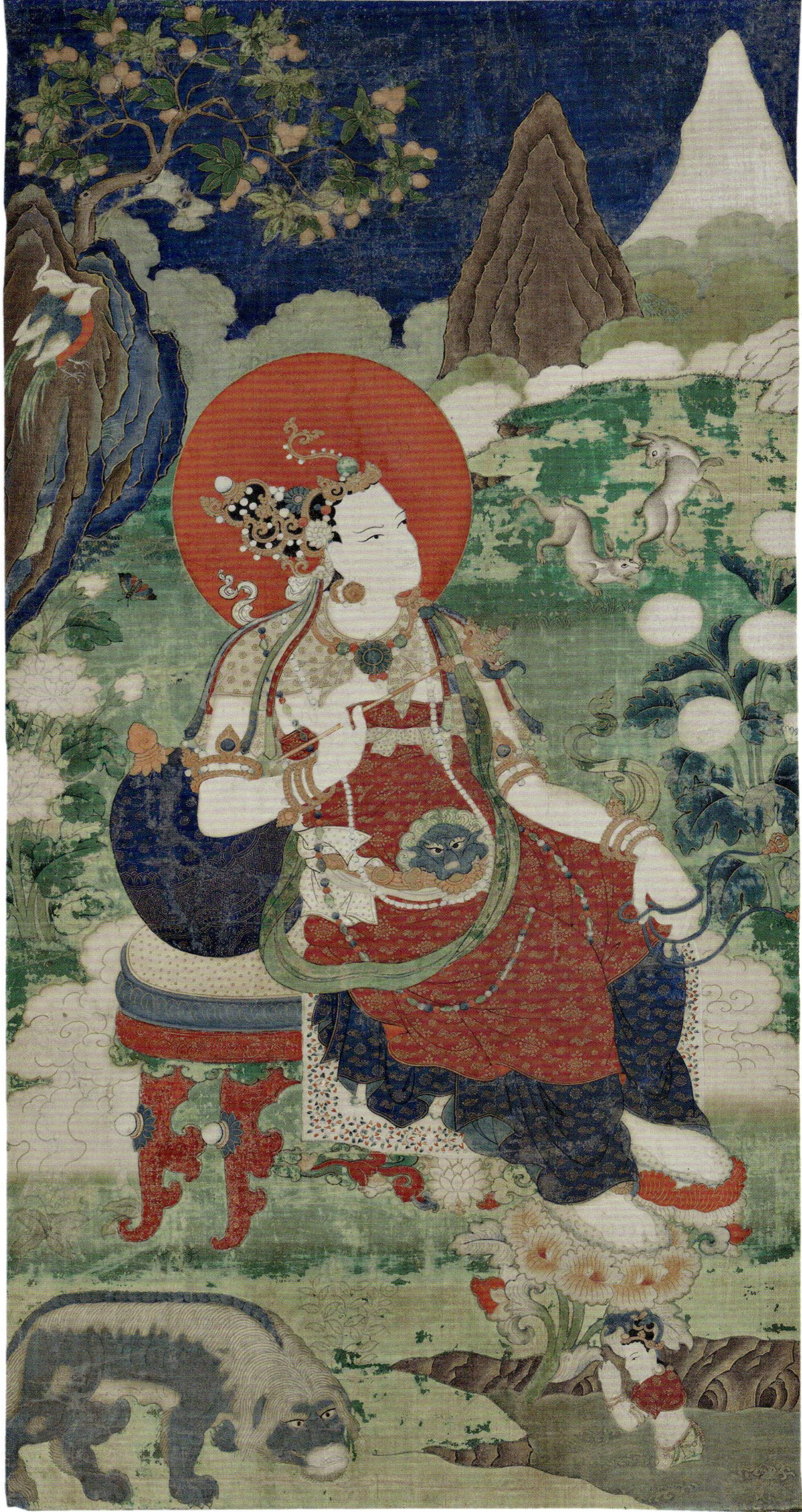

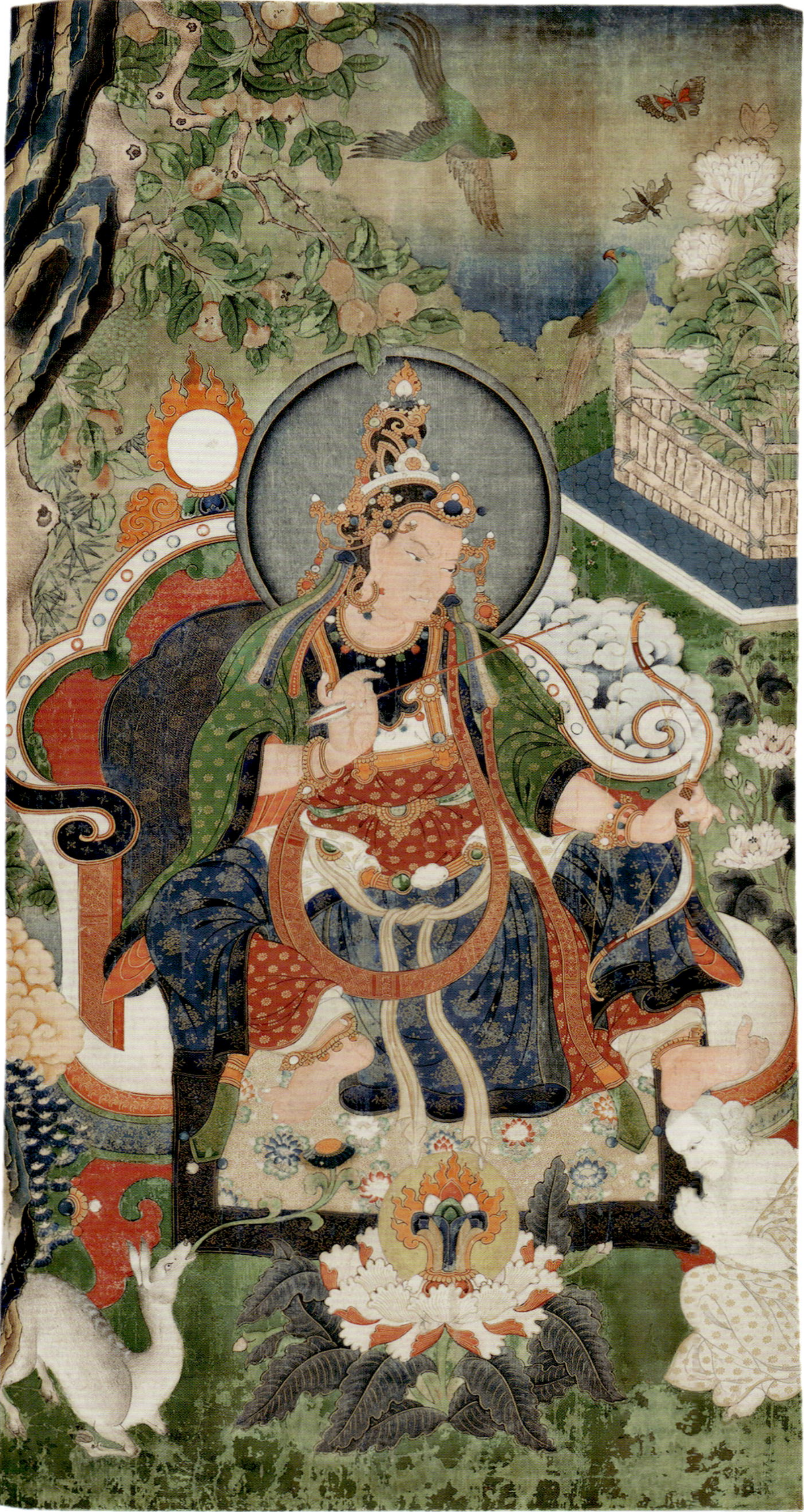

on. Overall, the mood is peaceful and bucolic.

In Figure 8.10, the main figure holds a bow and arrow, attributes shared with the Fifth Dharma King and the Fifth Kalkin, Sumitra. Toganoo first identified him as Sumitra, comparing the iconography in Vira and Chandra 1972, part 20, number 261a; the MFA agrees with this identification.[409]

In this very beautiful painting, full of amazing details of every kind, the setting is unusual. The Kalkin sits on an elaborate throne, possibly at the edge of a forest. To the right are the walls of a palace garden, surrounded by what appears to be a blue canal. In the upper right, the sky is rendered with a gradient that begins with indigo at the top, fades to beige, and reemerges with a brighter blue below, beyond some rocks. A large green parrot—perhaps a Derbian parakeet—flies toward the right to its mate, who sits on the fence. Both birds are probably eyeing the fruit hanging in the branches to the left. The scale of the birds, butterflies, and nearby flowers is too large to convincingly exist in the fenced garden. In the bottom-left corner, a spotted deer kneels before the main figure, holding a curving lotus stem in its mouth as an offering to the Kalkin. (In pure Chinese art the deer would have been holding a special fungus of immortality.)[410]

In Figure 8.11, the Kalkin is depicted with a vajra and bell, the attributes of Kalkin numbers 6, 18, and 24 and the First Dharma King. This painting was not discussed by Toganoo, who identified the similar figure (in III, 10–15) as "Kal 18 Seng ge." The MFA identifies him as "the sixth or eighteenth

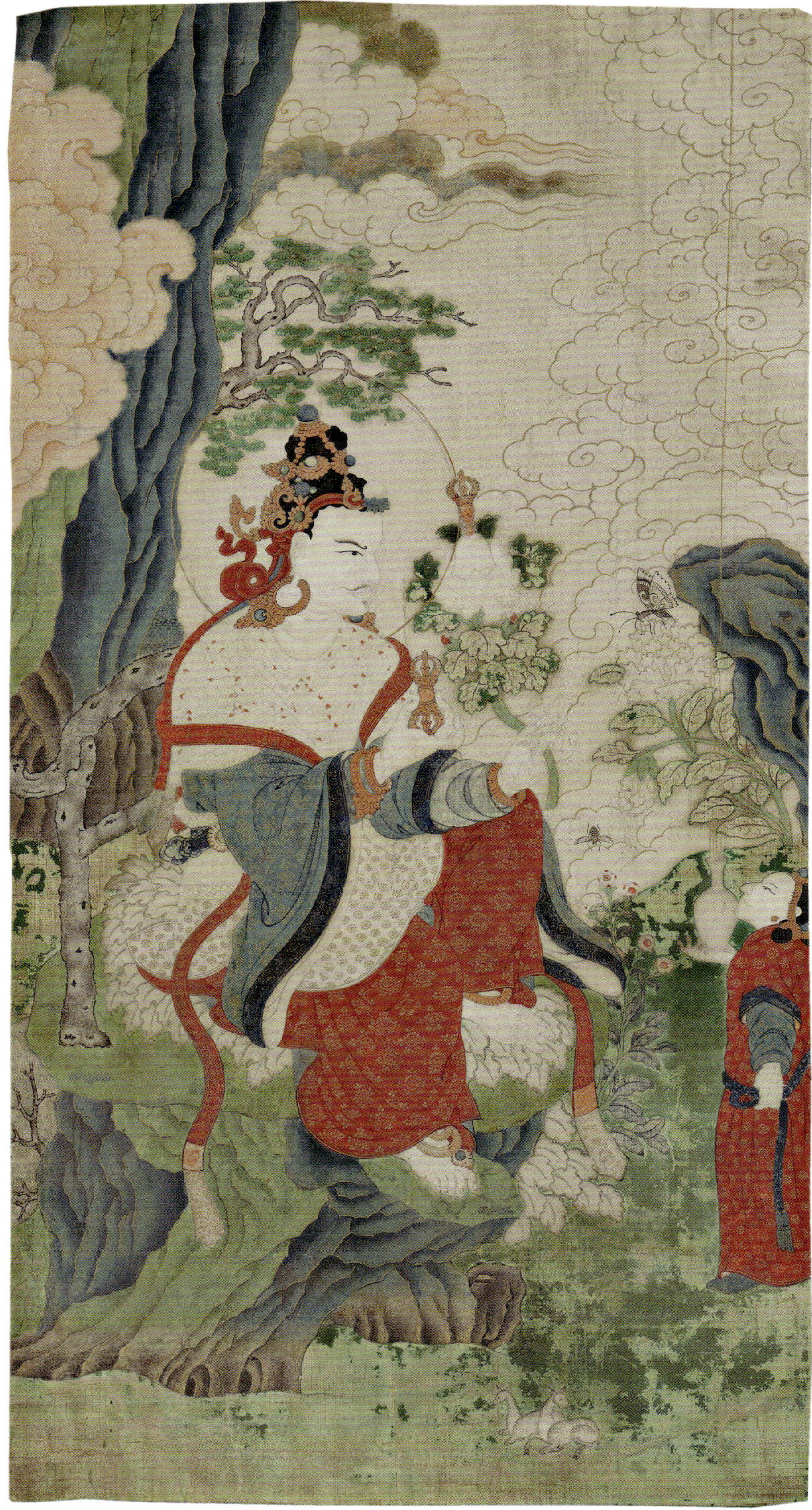

vidyadhara."[411] That would make him either the Sixth Kalkin, Raktapāṇi (Rigs ldan Phyag dmar), or the eighteenth, Hari (Seng ge). The comparable iconography is found in Vira and Chandra 1972, part 20, numbers 261b and 264a.

The main figure sits on a mat of white leaves on a throne with a back made of gray branches and a seat of green turf. His skin is white, as are two of his robes. The white bell seems to float in space directly before his intently gazing eyes, but it actually rests on a lotus, his rare emblem or handheld implement (*phyag mtshan*). The landscape around him is out of the ordinary for its depiction of mountain mists and clouds, near and far, creating a sense of airiness. The large area of sky behind him is off-white while most of the clouds are white or pale colors. I have never seen another depiction of sky like this, of white clouds in a white sky, in Tibetan painting. To emphasize the mood of misty clarity, the artist has created a transparent head nimbus, with only a golden line to demarcate it from the sky.

In the right foreground appears a tiny pair of deer, far too small to be convincing; their scale is suitable for representing mice. To the right of the main figure, a butterfly rests on a white peony, and a bumblebee approaches smaller pink flowers below.

Another uncommon element of this thangka is the orientation of the figures' heads. In this painting, both the main and minor figures are depicted in full profile. Khyentse Chenmo regularly depicted minor figures in profile, but this practice was rare in Tibetan painting. I have found one or two idiosyncratic

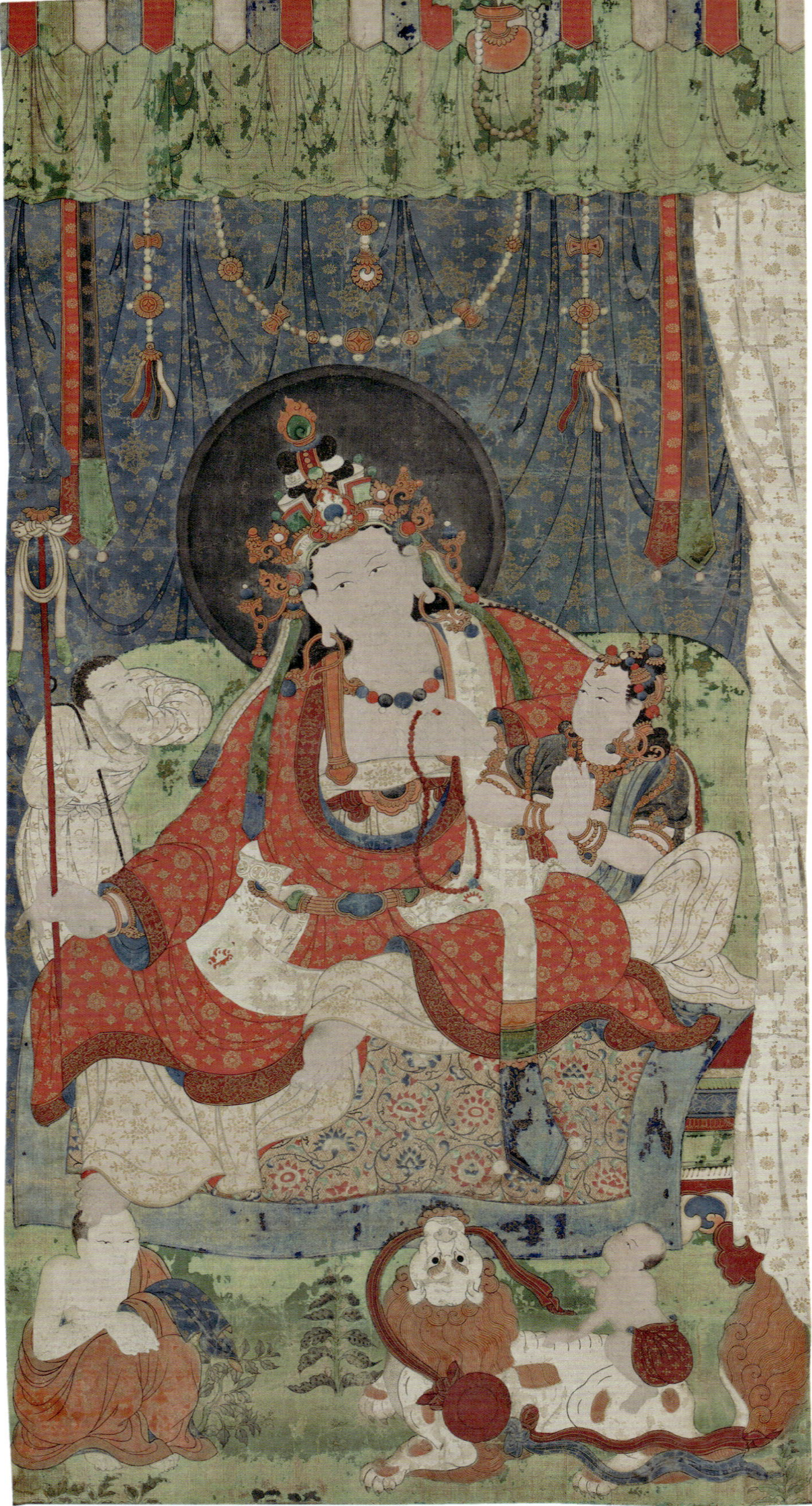

profile depictions of main figures—
once in this Shambhala king set, which
illustrates a broad range of depictions,
from fully frontal to profile, attesting to
the artist's love of variety. Such profile
depictions, though fairly rare in later
Tibetan art, were occasionally used by
Khyentse's probable teacher, Paljor
Rinchen of Nenying: when depicting the
eighty-four siddhas, he used profiles for
two adepts.[412] Khyentse Chenmo painted
seven mahāsiddhas in profile in his set
of eighty-four adepts.[413]

The main figure of Figure 8.12
holds a blue-trident-headed staff and a
rosary, a rare iconography, found only
with the seventh Kalkin. Comparing his
iconography to Vira and Chandra 1972,
part 20, number 261c, Toganoo identified him as Kalkin 7, Viṣṇugupta (Khyab
'jug sbas pa); the MFA names him the
"seventh *vidyadhara* wisdom-holder."[414]

This Kalkin is depicted in an atypical setting, seated on a rug in a fancy tent
or enclosure created by curtains and canopies. This is the most domestic setting of
all the Shambhala king and Kalkin paintings in this set, with a consort or wife to
the right, a child in the foreground, and a
servant standing to the left, respectfully
covering his mouth with a long sleeve.
The child, perhaps representing the
youngest son of this Kalkin, climbs on an
orange-maned and -tailed lion that stares
upward at the Kalkin and patiently submits to being mounted.

The central figure of Figure 8.13
holds a sword and shield, like the seventh dharma king, Sureśāna (Fig. 8.7).
But this iconography is also that of the
ninth Kalkin, Subhadra (Shin tu bzang),
the "ninth *vidyadhara* wisdom-holder,"
as identified by Toganoo—citing Vira

and Chandra 1972, part 20, no. 262a—
and the MFA.[415]

The setting is in nature, as suggested by the large curving coniferous tree to the right, the blue-green rocks below the central figure, and the mass of clouds across the middle ground. From the upper left, a dragon dramatically descends from a cloud, holding a bright-red jewel of magical power before it. On the right, two birds crouch on limbs of the pine tree, as if about to fly off. Meanwhile, at the lower right, a minor deity or forest dweller approaches, holding the long stem of a lotus flower, on which the Kalkin's right foot rests. In the foreground is a pool of water from which luxuriantly flowering vines emerge.

In Figure 8.14, the main figure holds a staff with a special ax with curved knife and gold knob or jewel as its head and a rope, the iconography of Kalkins 11, 13, and 21. The MFA identifies him as "the eleventh *vidyadhara* wisdom-holder," that is, as Kalkin 11, Ajita (rGyal dka'), which seems reasonable.[416] The painting was not discussed by Toganoo; the iconography should be compared to Vira and Chandra 1972, part 20, number 262c.

This setting is also within nature, represented by a large leafy tree on the right and three triangular peaks in the upper left. The Kalkin's throne is unexpected. He sits on an open, elaborate sedan chair carried by two white elephants. By Tibetan standards, both elephants are naturalistically depicted, but they are too small for the scale of the chair. In the foreground, a tortoise pauses, extending its neck with curiosity at the spectacle. To the left of the main figure, two rabbits calmly sit, one of

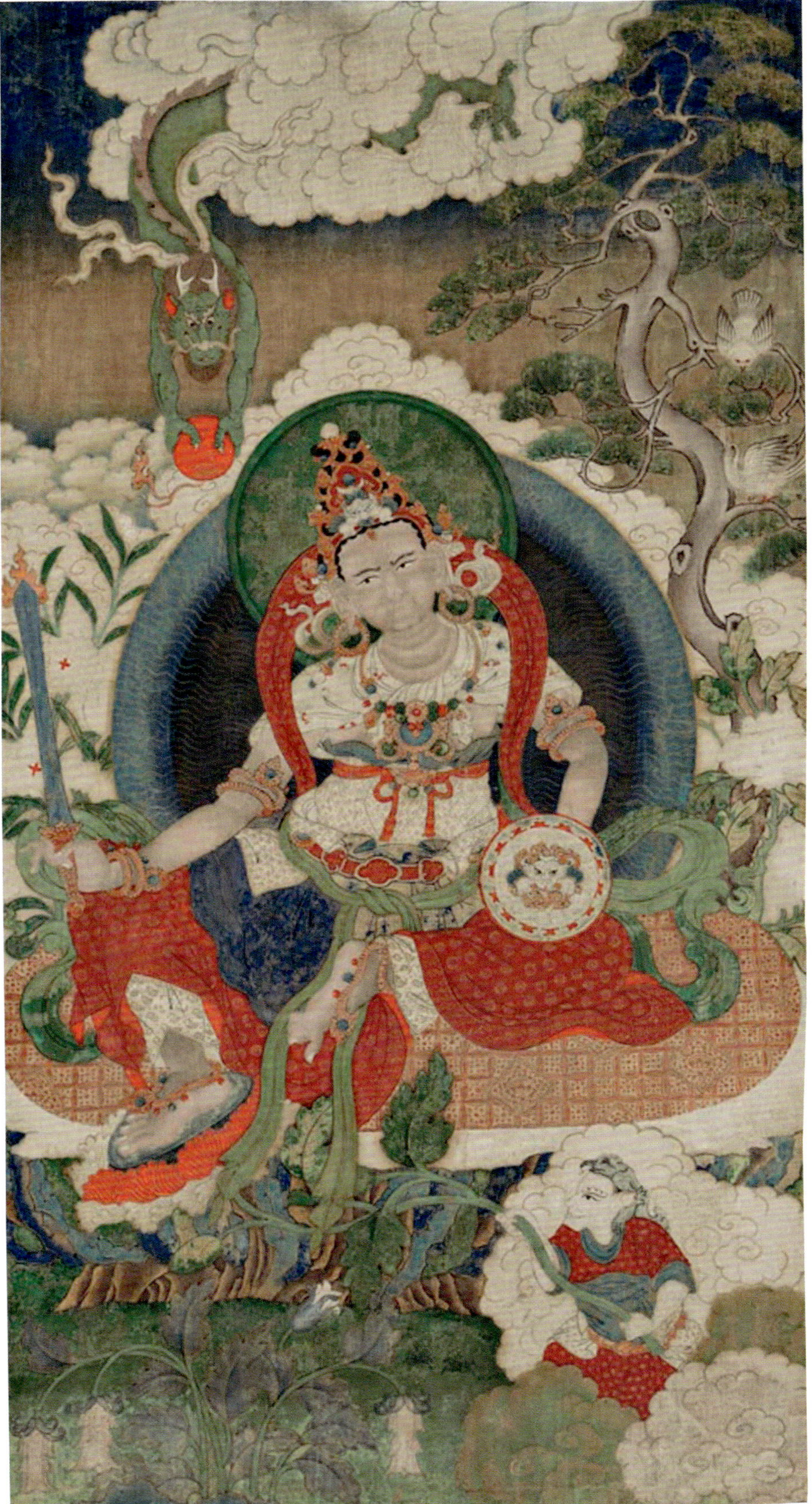

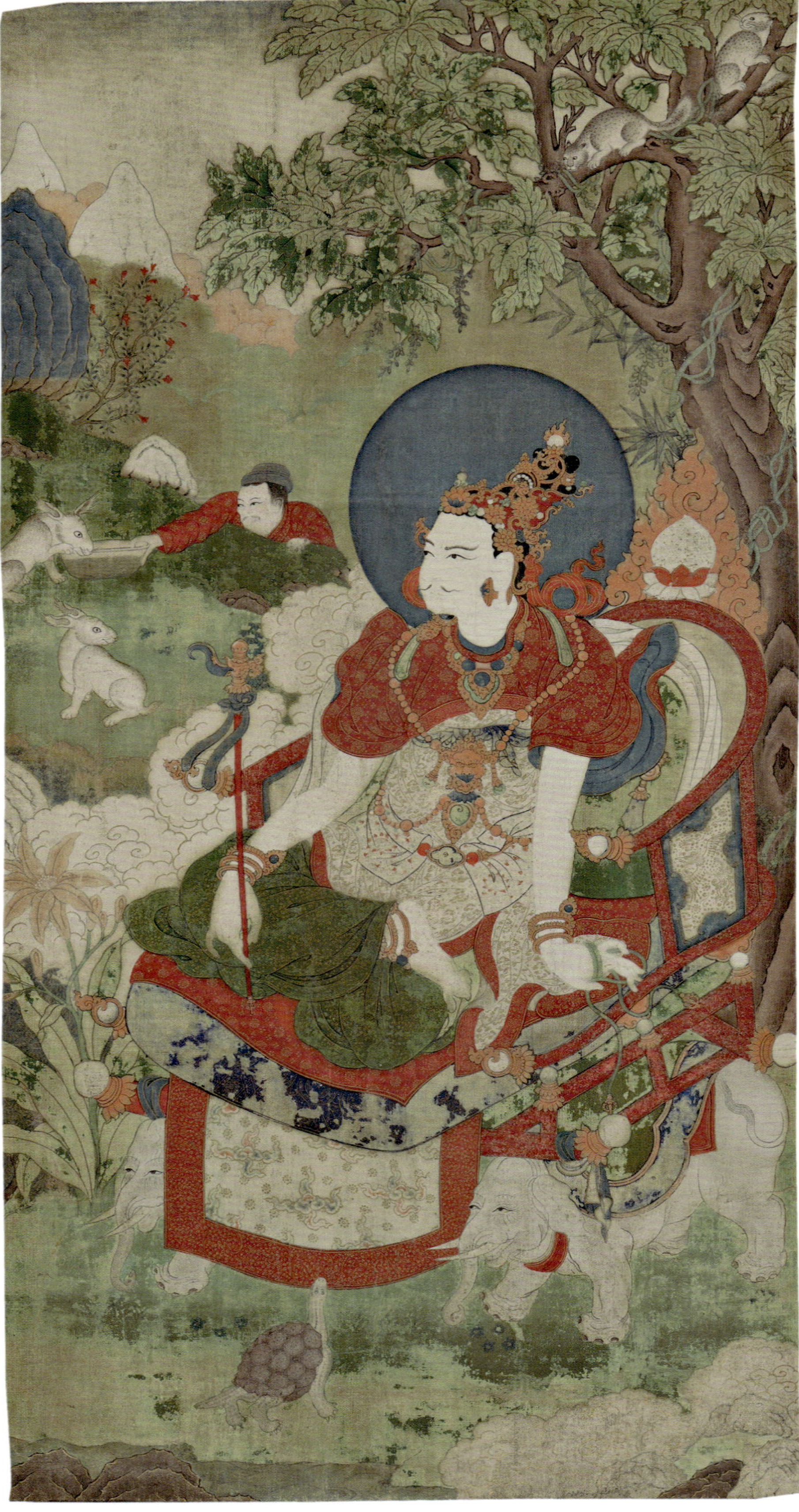

them accepting food in a bowl offered by a youth. High in the tree in the upper right climbs a pair of furry, long-tailed animals, perhaps martens. The mood of the painting is light and peaceful.

The main figure in Figure 8.15 bears a special ax and a rope, an iconography shared with the second dharma king and with Kalkin numbers 4, 13, and 21. He was not presented by Toganoo, but the MFA identifies him as "the thirteenth *vidyadhara* wisdom-holder," that is, as Kalkin 13, Viśvarūpa (sNa tshogs gzugs).[417] In that case, the comparable iconography is found in Vira and Chandra 1972, part 20, number 263b.

The setting is not ordinary: the Kalkin is seated with his consort or wife in a garden pavilion within a walled palace garden. Behind him, three of the pavilion's screen-like panels feature a painted landscape while the top-central one depicts a buddha.

Khyentse depicted the two side panels of the landscape painting at an oblique angle suggesting illusionistic spatial perspective. In the center foreground, a gray deer or antelope humbly kneels, offering a flower-laden sprig to the Kalkin. To its right, a *nāga* pays obeisance, emerging from a pool of water and showing much of its snake tail.

In Figure 8.16, the main figure holds a wheel and a conch, an iconography shared with the third dharma king and Kalkin numbers 3, 14, and 22. Toganoo identified him as Kalkin 14, Śaśiprabha (Zla ba'i 'od), and the MFA agrees that he is "the fourteenth *vidyadhara* wisdom-holder."[418] Toganoo referred to the similar iconography of Vira and Chandra 1972, part 20, number 263a.[419]

Here the regal Kalkin sits outside in a misty, mountainous forest after sunset, and the mood is somber and stormy. The sky is dark blue-black. The small pond at the bottom has roiling waves, and its water is dark gray. The Kalkin sits on a blue patterned mat on a platform of rock. He seems to be summoning a dragon at the lower right. Emerging from the water amid a cloud of mist, the dragon grasps a jewel with its claws. Hardly noticed within the dark, threatening scene are two large dark-green parrots with beige throats and bellies. They roost next to each other on blue-green rocks, seemingly finding shelter from the storm. On the right side of the painting, a tiger sleeps, partly hidden behind two trees.

In Figure 8.17, the main figure holds a vajra and bell, which are the attributes of Kalkin numbers 6, 18, and 24. Toganoo identified him as Kalkin 18, Hari (Seng ge). The MFA suggests he is "eighteenth or sixth *vidyadhara*," both of which are possible.[420] In any case, Toganoo cited Vira and Chandra 1972, part 20, number 263d, as an example of similar iconography.

The setting is atypical. The rocks and plants of the foreground show that the Kalkin is traveling outside. He rides in an elephant-drawn chariot, with two male attendants or younger relatives behind him. One elephant holds a lotus stem in its trunk. This chariot has elaborately carved sides, a curtain back, and a tasseled and bejeweled canopy, resembling a portable royal tent. In the upper right, the area of dark blue with golden flower motifs seems to be a curtain or cloth divider, but its position suggests that it depicts the sky.

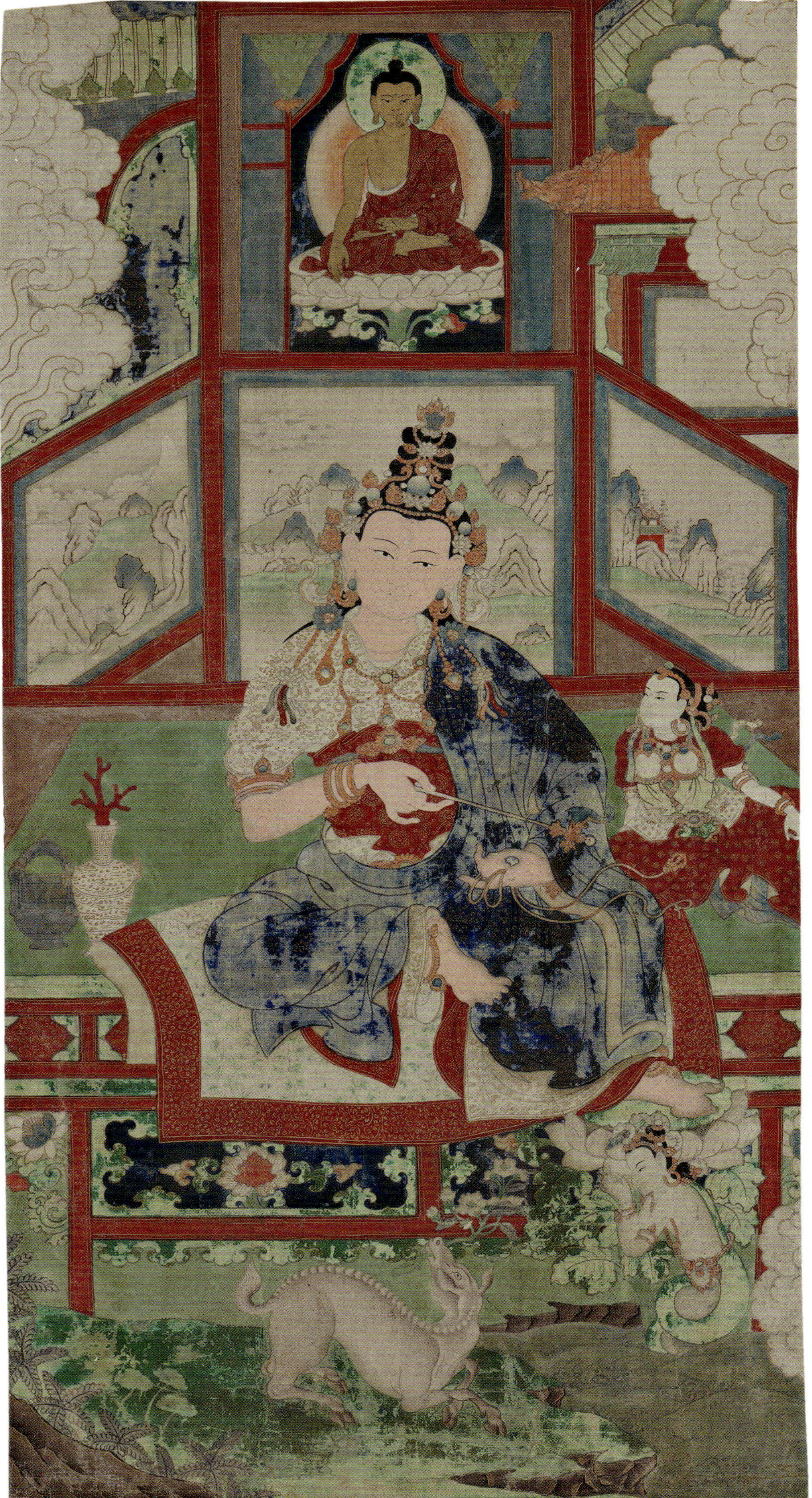

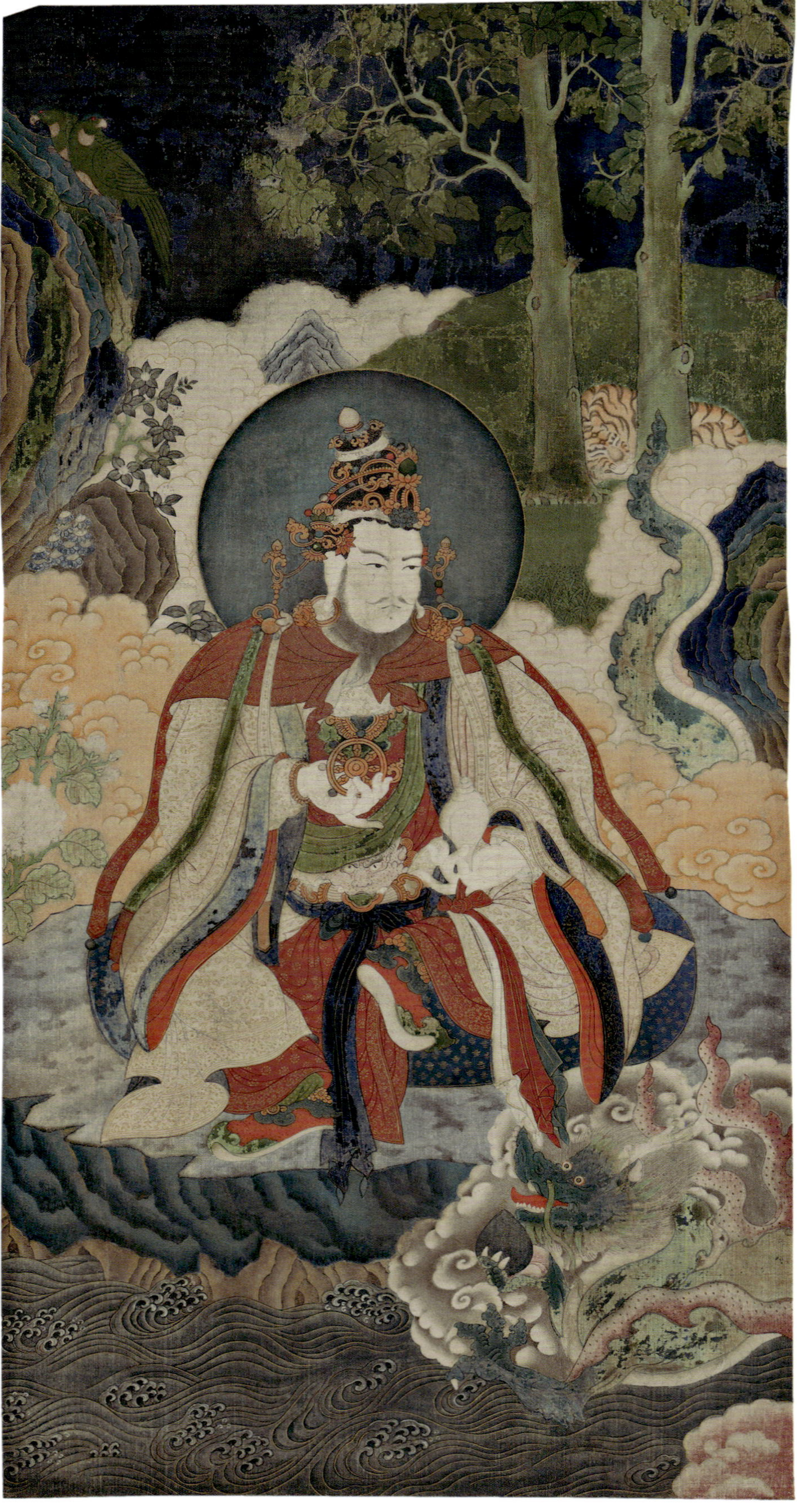

In Figure 8.18, the main figure holds a jewel-headed staff and a chain, which is the iconography of the fourth Shambhala king and Kalkin numbers 11 and 19. This painting was not presented by Toganoo; the MFA suggests the main figure is Kalkin 19, Vikrama (rNam par gnon), "the nineteenth *vidyadhara*."[421] In that case, the comparable figure would be Vira and Chandra 1972, part 20, number 264c.

The Kalkin sits in a natural setting in semitropical mountain foothills, by a pool of water in the lower left foreground. The large leaves of a flowering banana plant fill the upper left corner of the painting. To the right, farther away, two cranes stand near a body of water, one lowering its head to search for prey; they seem to be the black-necked cranes of Tibet, as they appear in the wild. Behind them, a cluster of snowy peaks stands against a pale sky. To the left of the main figure, two birds with gray wings and tails and white bellies are present, one perched on a rock and the other standing in shallow water. In the foreground, two large and complicated lotuses bloom, emerging from the water to the left. On the ground to the right of the water, two colorful butterflies hover near a cluster of red flowers. Above them, almost hidden by the lotuses and the patterns of the Kalkin's rug, a forest spirit with sideburns respectfully kneels, holding a white jewel in his left hand and staring up at the Kalkin.

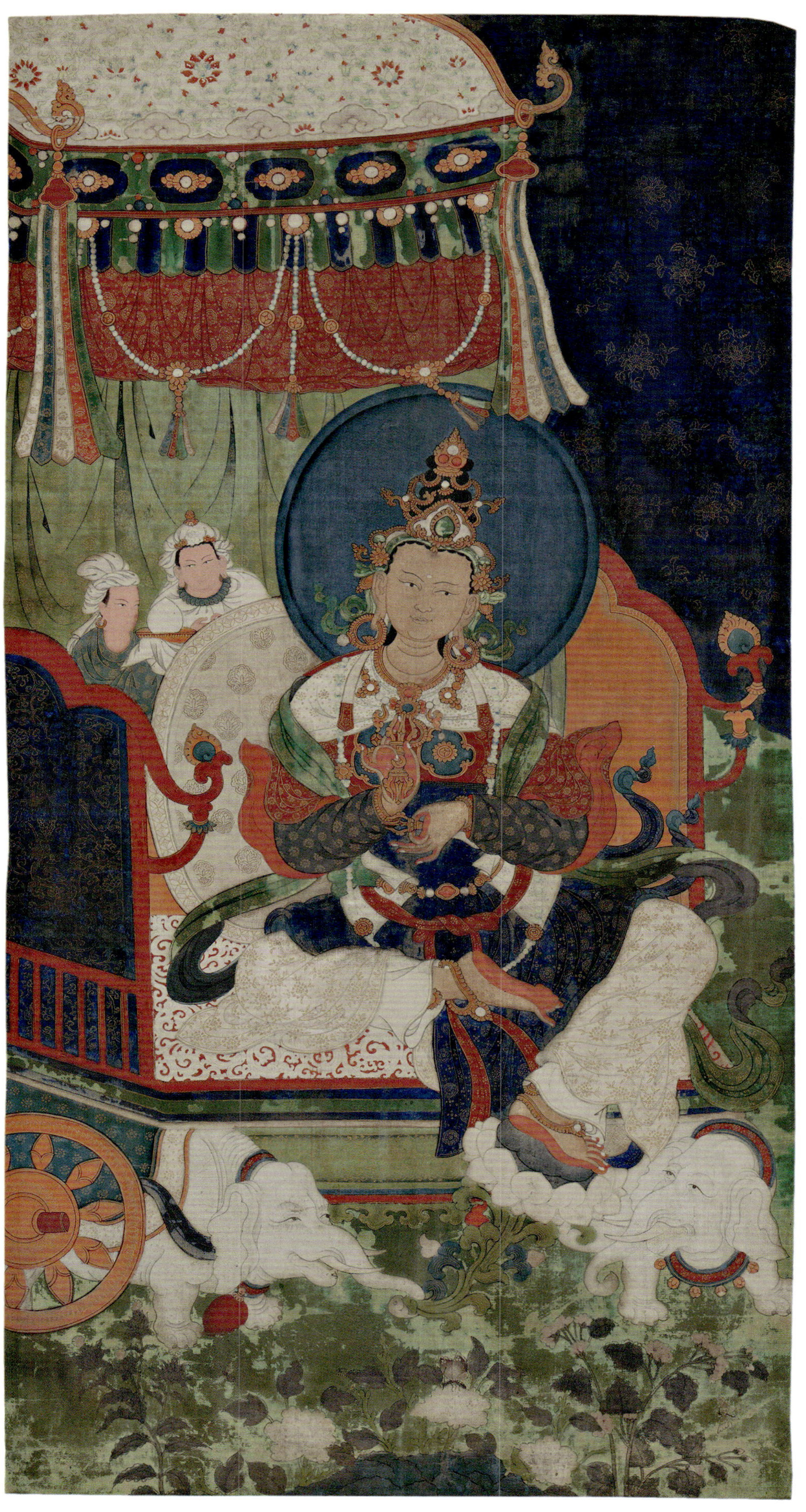

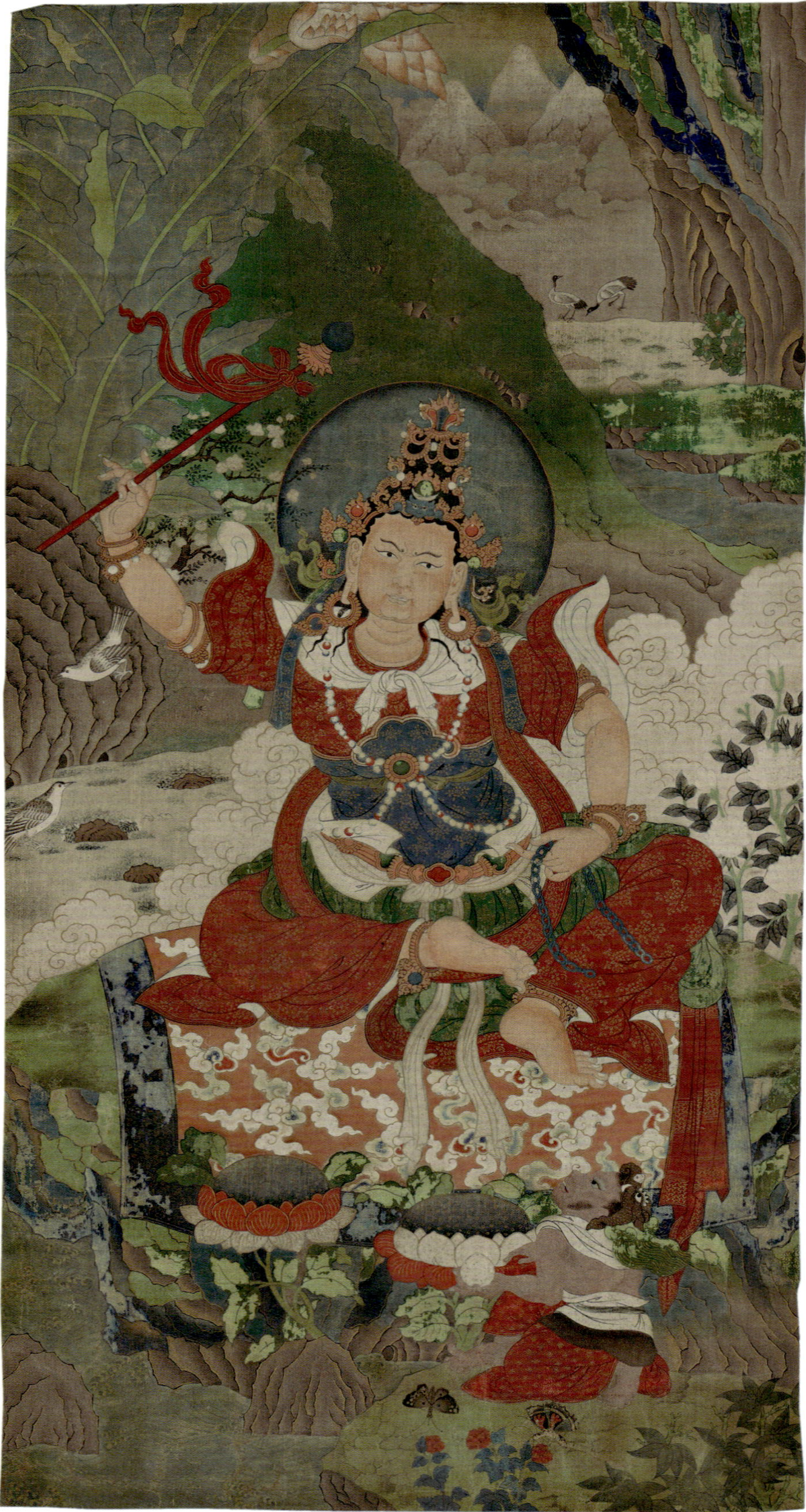

In Figure 8.19, the main figure holds a special axe and rope, iconography shared with Kalkin numbers 4, 13, or 21. He is not discussed by Toganoo; the MFA identifies him as Kalkin 21, Aniruddha (Ma 'gags pa), "twenty-first *vidyadhara*."[422] Comparing him with Vira and Chandra 1972, part 20, numbers 263b and 265a, the main figure could be Kalkin 13 (sNa tshogs gzugs) or 21 (Ma 'gags pa).

This Kalkin sits on a carpet outside; the wild setting is represented by the large tree and blue-green rock behind him. The area of the sky is unpainted, as is the transparent head nimbus. An attendant or fellow adept of Shambhala stands respectfully to the left, hands held together with index fingers pointing up. On the right, clusters of red, blue, and green clouds echo the colors of the carpet border. In the foreground, a gray lion strides toward the right, his attention focused on the main figure. On limbs of the fruit tree behind the Kalkin, two birds with white bellies and blue-and-green wings and tails have landed.

Here, in Figure 8.20, the main figure appears with a wheel and a conch, an iconography shared by the third dharma king and Kalkin numbers 3, 14, and 22. I agree with Toganoo's identification as Kalkin number 22, Narasiṃha (Mi yi seng ge). The MFA identifies him as "the twenty-second or twelfth *vidyadhara*."[423] However, in Vira and Chandra 1972, Kalkin number 12 is shown with a *ḍamaru* and jewel.[424]

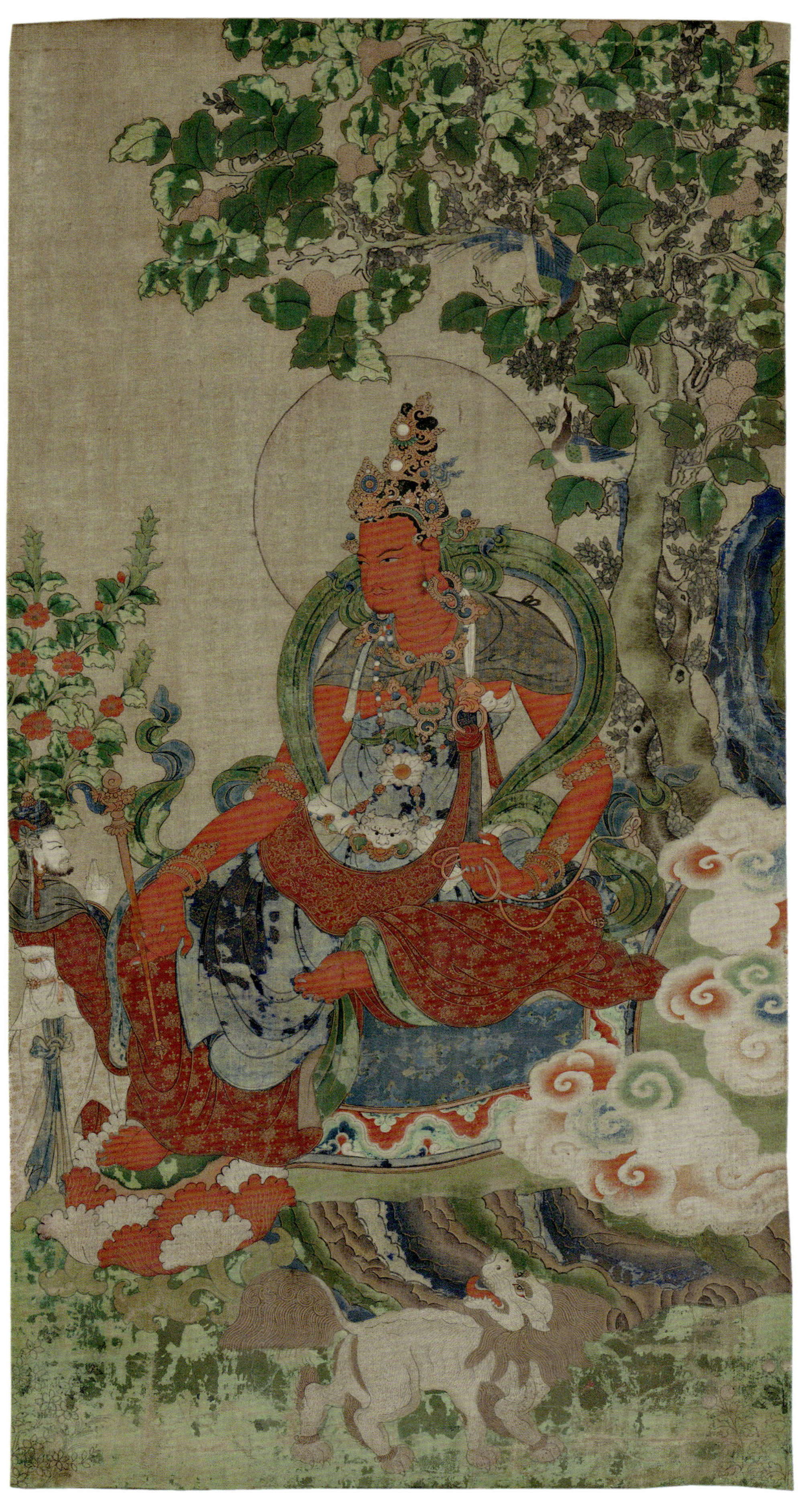

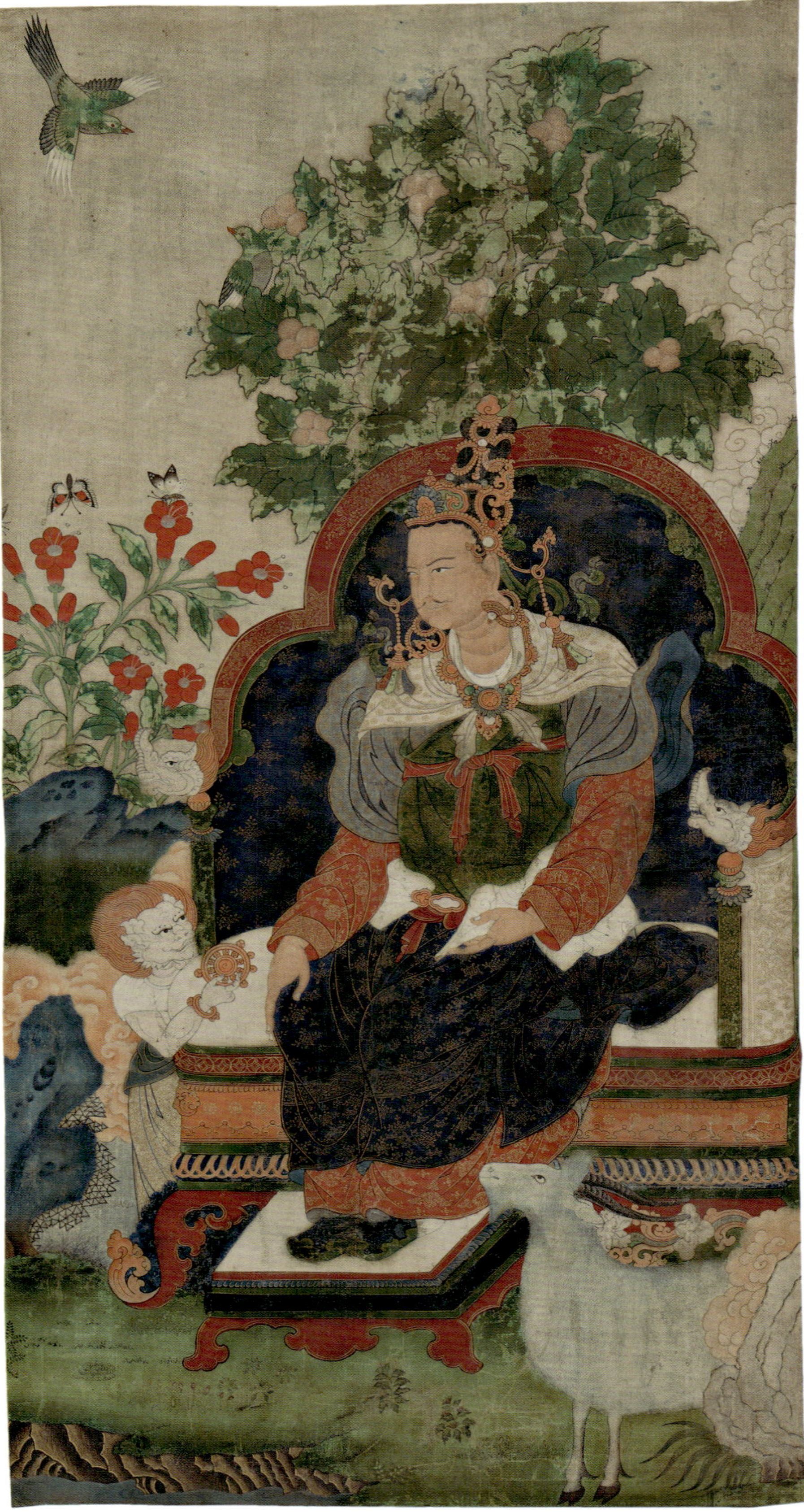

Fig. 8.20
Narasiṃha
second half of the fifteenth century
31 ⅞ x 17 in. (80.9 x 43.3 cm)
MFA, Boston, Ross Collection (06–335)
Literature: Toganoo 1986, no. III 10–16

The Kalkin sits on a large and elaborate throne placed outside, as represented by the tree behind him, the edge of a craggy mountain to the right, and the bit of water visible in the bottom-left corner. In the upper left, a large green bird with white wingtips, perhaps a magpie, flies to its mate perched in the fruit-laden tree, above the main figure. To the left of the Kalkin, butterflies are attracted to red flowers. To the left of the throne, a horned demon offers a golden wheel to the Kalkin. To the right in the foreground, a bearded goat with long horns stands with head raised, staring at the Kalkin as if waiting for some reaction.

In Figure 8.21, the central figure holds a sword and shield, as do the seventh king (Fig. 8.7) and the ninth Kalkin (Fig. 8.13). The painting is not discussed by Toganoo. The MFA calls him "the twenty-third *vidyadhara* wisdom-holder," that is, Kalkin number 23, Maheśvara (dBang phyug chen po).[425] This Kalkin holds a small sword on a lotus and a full-size shield in Vira and Chandra 1972, part 20, number 265c.

The mountainous landscape includes a series of snowy peaks across the upper register and rivers or lakes to the right and left. The Kalkin sits with his consort, on a rug on a flat stone platform. Though he raises a flaming sword, the martial mood is lessened by the rainbow behind it. In the foreground stands a large pheasant with a red belly, long brown tail feathers, and a light-green band around its neck. To the right, butterflies or other insects are drawn to a blooming peony.

In Figure 8.22, the main figure holds a vajra and bell, attributes

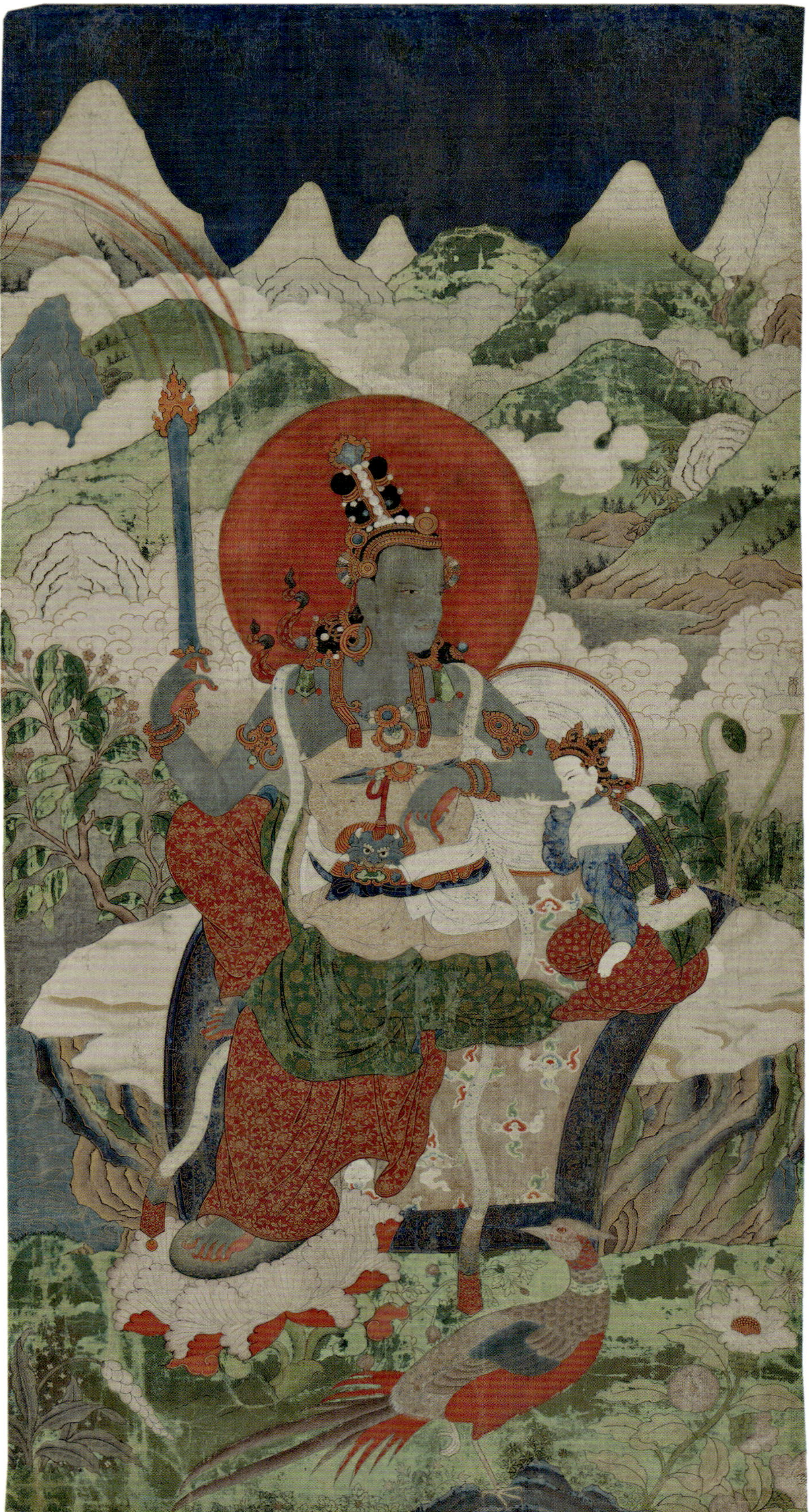

associated with Kalkin numbers 6, 18, and 24. Toganoo accordingly identified him as Kalkin number 24, referring to Vira and Chandra 1972, part 20, number 265d, as a similar example. The MFA agrees, calling him "the twenty-fourth *vidyadhara* wisdom-holder."[426]

This Kalkin is seated in a natural setting of forested hills. This landscape is one of the most beautiful in the set, with delicately colored clouds and carefully rendered trees growing on crags behind the Kalkin. His seat is the orange top of an enormous blue lotus that emerges from a pool of water beneath him. The centers of the lotus petals feature elaborate shapes that Khyentse Chenmo also used in some Gongkar murals. The lotus seat includes elements of a more typical throne, such as a dark-blue rounded backrest and a round white cushion to the left. In the lower right corner is a large bird with long wavy tail feathers and unusual back feathers; standing on one leg, it looks up at the Kalkin. It is a phoenix, a mythical creature that combines parts of many different birds. Khyentse Chenmo has colored it with light gray hues, in harmony with the two gray rocks on the left side of the foreground.

In Figure 8.23, the main figure is fighting on a battlefield with an army. He wears a helmet and armor, brandishes a long red spear in his right hand, and holds a white shield in his left. Referring to a different depiction in Vira and Chandra 1972, part 20, number 266a, Toganoo identified him as Kalkin number 25, Raudracakrin, with which the MFA agrees.[427]

Figure 8.24 proves the existence of a second set of thangkas depicting the

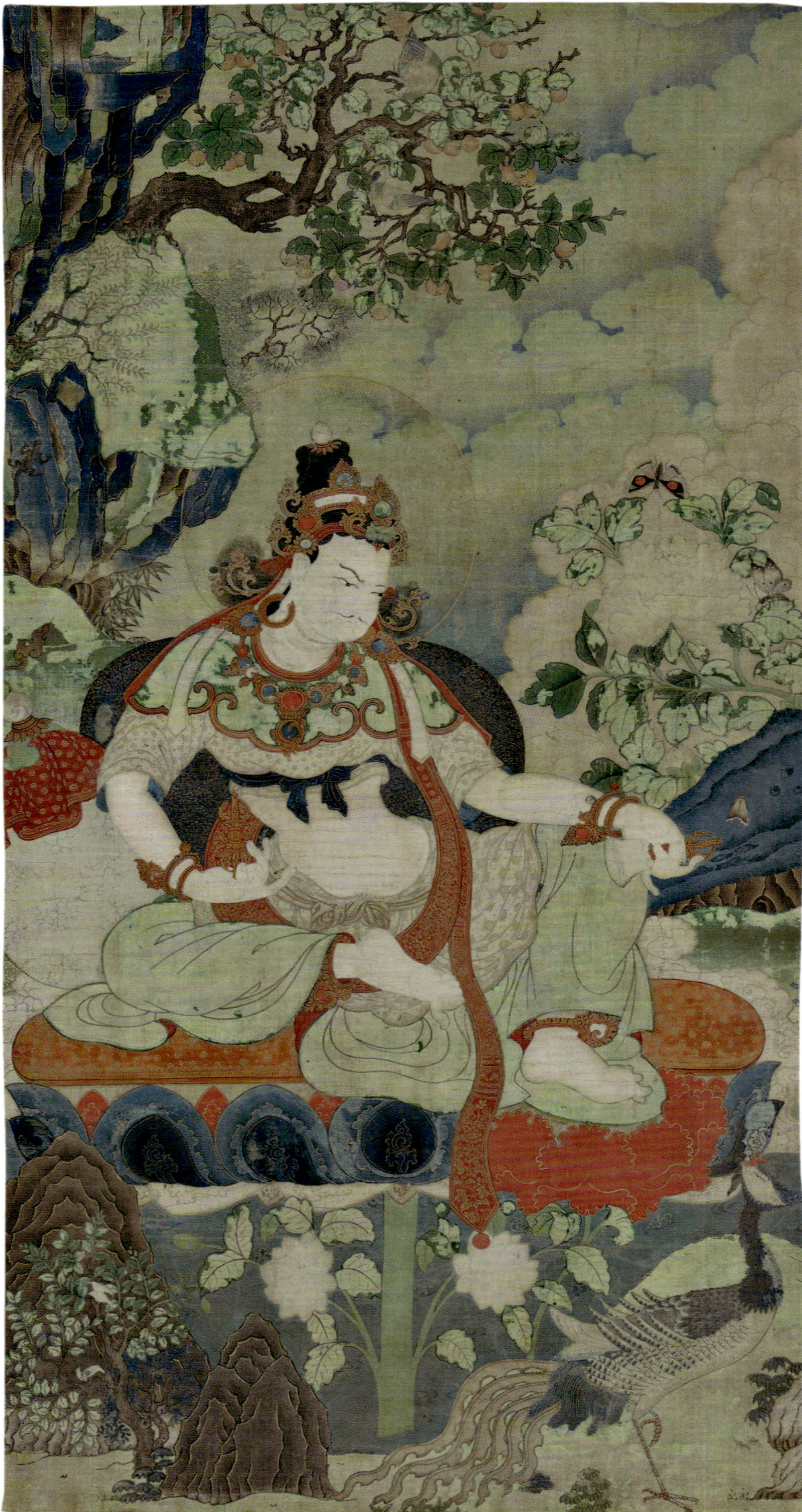

Shambhala kings and Kalkins by Khyentse Chenmo or one of his close followers. Its main figure is the second Kalkin,
Puṇḍarika, who is missing from the Boston set. Though similar in style to those
paintings, its subject is different: instead
of depicting one main figure, it depicts
one large Kalkin in the center and two
smaller ones below. The two smaller figures hold attributes—a bow and arrow,
and a wheel and a white conch—that are
common iconography among Kalkins.
This painting was shown in the exhibition *Compassion and Reincarnation
in Tibetan Art* (1995–1996), in Austria,
Switzerland, and Germany; it was
described in a subsequent English-
language publication.[428]

A List of the Shambhala Dharma Kings and Kalkins

For the sake of future comparison, I list
here the Shambhala kings and Kalkins
as they occur in the other main tradition,
that of Situ Panchen.[429] Situ Paṇchen's
guru Kathok Rigdzin Tshewang Norbu
lists the seven Shambhala dharma kings
and twenty-five Kalkins (Rigs ldan),
thirty-two kings in all, in a minor work
entitled *Shambha la'i chos rgyal rigs
ldan nyi shu rtsa lnga ste sum bcu rtsa
gnyis*.[430] Hiroki Fujita provided a list of
the same thirty-two deities, with illustrations in Situ Panchen's style.[431]

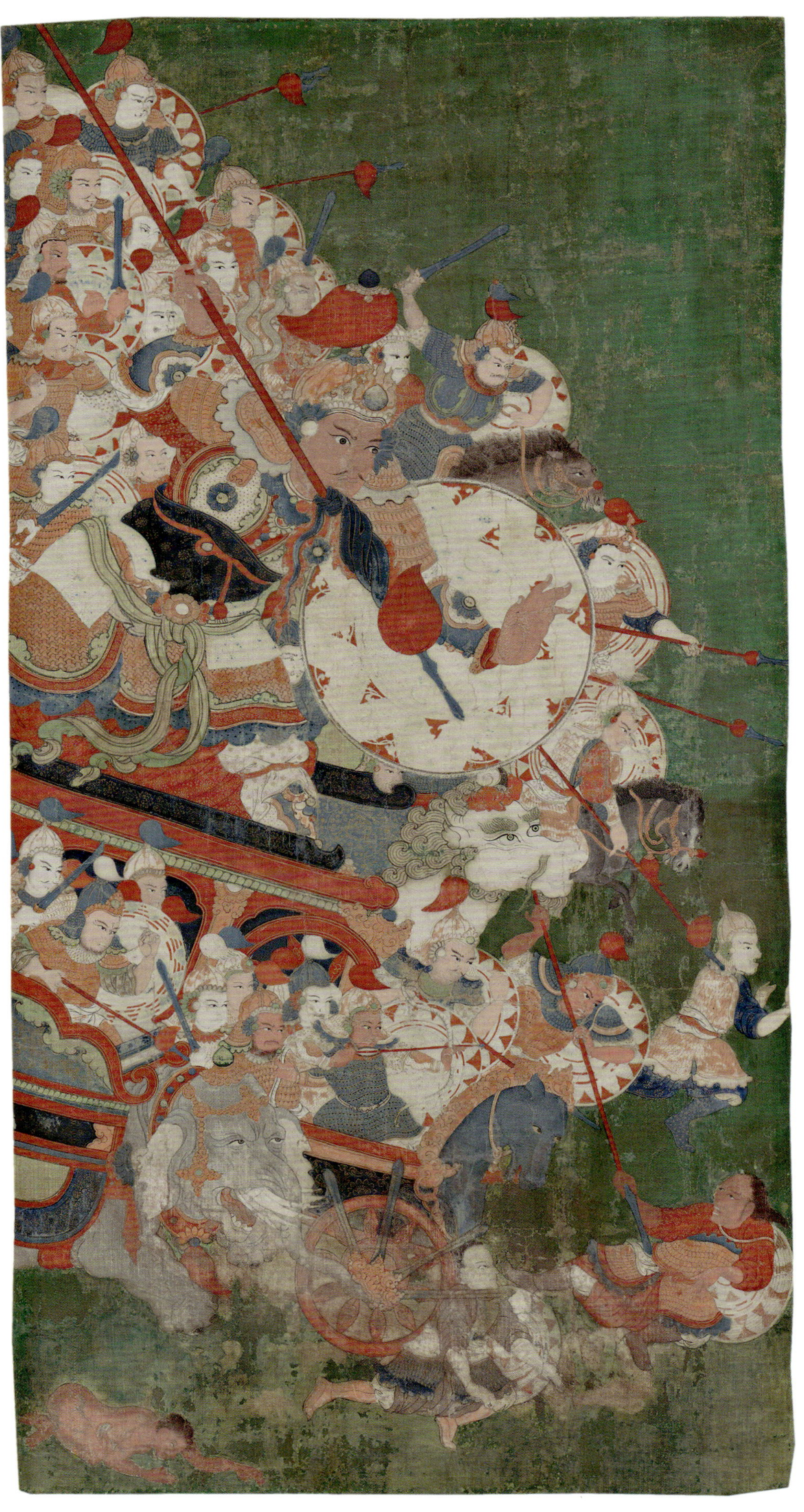

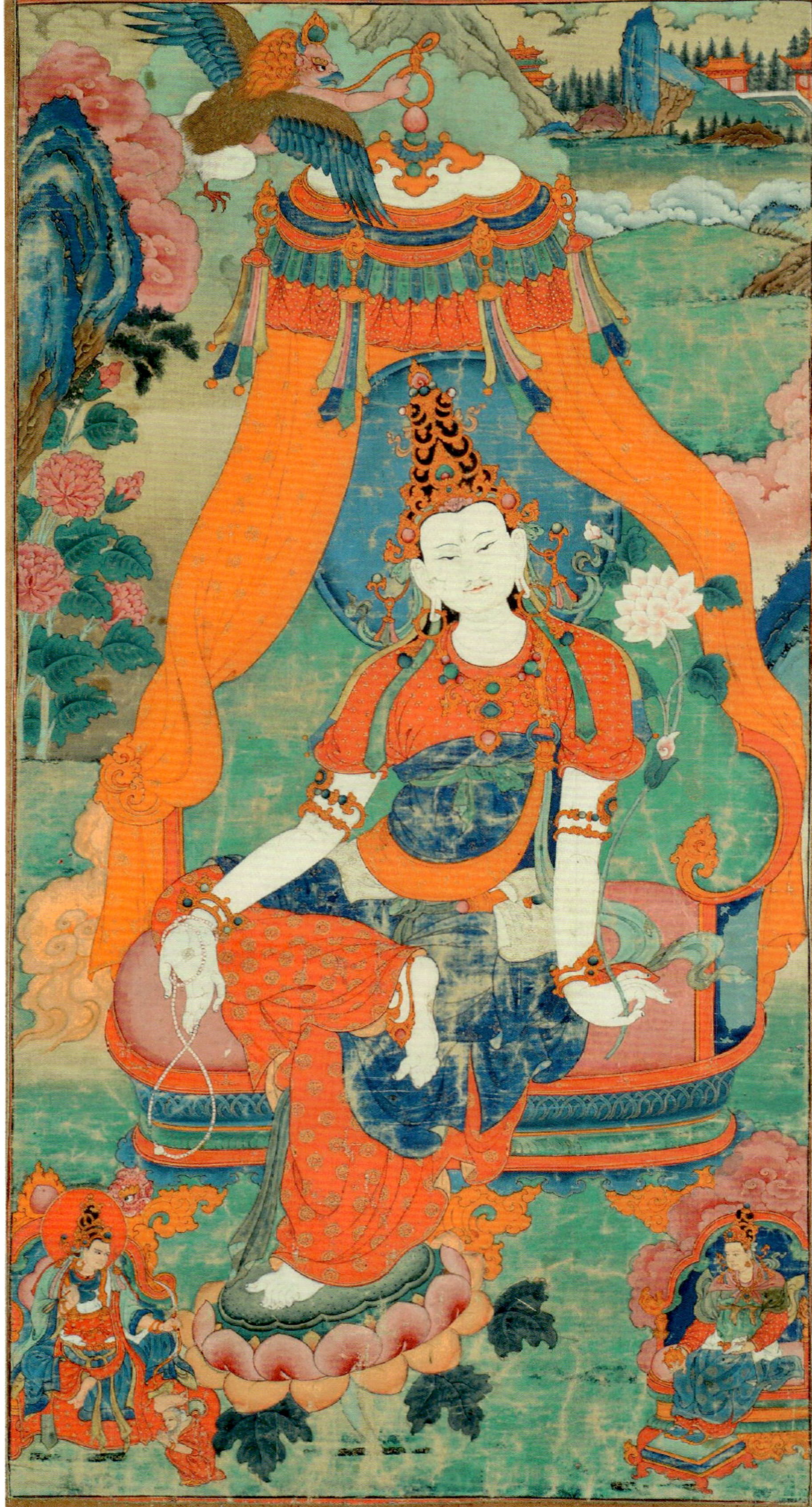

The Seven Shambhala Dharma Kings:

1. Sucandra, (Chos rgyal) Zla ba bzang po
2. Sureśvara, (Chos rgyal) Lha dbang
3. Tejin, (Chos rgyal) gZi brjid can
4. Somadatta, (Chos rgyal) Zla bas byin
5. Sureśvara, (Chos rgyal) Lha yi dbang phyug
6. Viśvamūrti, (Chos rgyal) sNa tshogs gzugs
7. Sureśāna, (Chos rgyal) Lha'i dbang po

The Twenty-five Kalkin (Tib. Rigs ldan) Kings of Shambhala:

8. Mañjughoṣa Yaśas, [Kalkin no. 1] Rigs ldan 'Jam dbyangs [=dpal] grags pa
9. Puṇḍarika, [Kalkin no. 2] Padma dkar po
10. Bhadra, [Kalkin no. 3] bZang po
11. Vijaya, [Kalkin no. 4] rNam rgyal
12. Sumitra, [Kalkin no. 5] bShes gnyen bzang po
13. Raktapāṇi, [Kalkin no. 6] Rigs ldan Phyag dmar
14. Viṣṇugupta, [Kalkin no. 7] Rigs ldan Khyab 'jug sbas pa
15. Arkakīrti, [Kalkin no. 8] Nyi ma grags
16. Subhadra, [Kalkin no. 9] Shin tu bzang
17. Samudravijaya, [Kalkin no. 10] rGya mtsho rnam rgyal
18. Ajita, [Kalkin no. 11] rGyal dka'
19. Sūrya, [Kalkin no. 12] Nyi ma
20. Viśvarūpa, [Kalkin no. 13] sNa tshogs gzugs
21. Śaśiprabha, [Kalkin no. 14] Zla ba'i 'od

22. Ananta, [Kalkin no. 15] mTha'
    yas
23. Mahīpāla, [Kalkin no. 16] Sa
    skyong
24. Śrīpāla, [Kalkin no. 17] dPal
    skyong. (Not: Sa skyong again)
25. Hari, [Kalkin no. 18] Seng ge
26. Vikrama, [Kalkin no. 19] rNam
    par gnon
27. Mahābala, [Kalkin no. 20] sTobs
    po che
28. Aniruddha, [Kalkin no. 21] Ma
    'gags pa
29. Narasiṃha, [Kalkin no. 22] Mi yi
    seng ge
30. Maheśvara, [Kalkin no. 23] dBang
    phyug chen po
31. Anantavijaya, [Kalkin no. 24]
    mTha' yas rnam rgyal
32. Raudracakrin, [Kalkin no. 25]
    Rigs ldan Drag po 'khor lo can

The set that Fujita published was
nearly complete; a whole set, with
two main figures per painting, would
depict thirty-two main deities in sixteen
paintings. In Fujita's book, the Shambhala kings numbers 4 and 5 (Somadatta
and Sureśvara) are missing, the final
Kalkin appears twice, in two different forms, and one extra *vidyarāja* is
present.

As Fujita stated:

There is no fixed style for depicting the kings of Śambhala. But
in the case of King Sucandra, an
incarnation of Vajrapāṇi, King
Yaśas, an incarnation of Mañjuśrī,
King Puṇḍarika, an incarnation of
Avalokiteśvara, and King Raudracakrin, a reincarnation of King
Yaśas and an incarnation of Mañjuśrī, it is general to depict them
holding the same implements as
the deities of which they are incarnations. Thus, for example, in the
present set of thangkas King Yaśas
is shown holding a Buddhist text
and a lotus supporting an upright
sword [i.e. the usual characteristics
of Mañjuśrī]. . . .

But, as was mentioned previously,
neither the *Kālacakra-tantra* nor
the *Vimalaprabhā* specify in regard
to the remaining kings of Śambhala
which king is an incarnation of
which bodhisattva or *vidyārāja*.
Therefore it is not possible to
determine their characteristics by
the original deities of whom they
are incarnations.[432]

Noting the presence of both wrathful and
peaceful forms among Kalkins, Fujita
suggested that it reflects the Kalkin's status as a *vidyārāja* or bodhisattva.[433]

For a list of the depictions of
Shambhala kings and Kalkins in Situ
Panchen's tradition, including body col-
ors and lineal lamas, see appendix C.

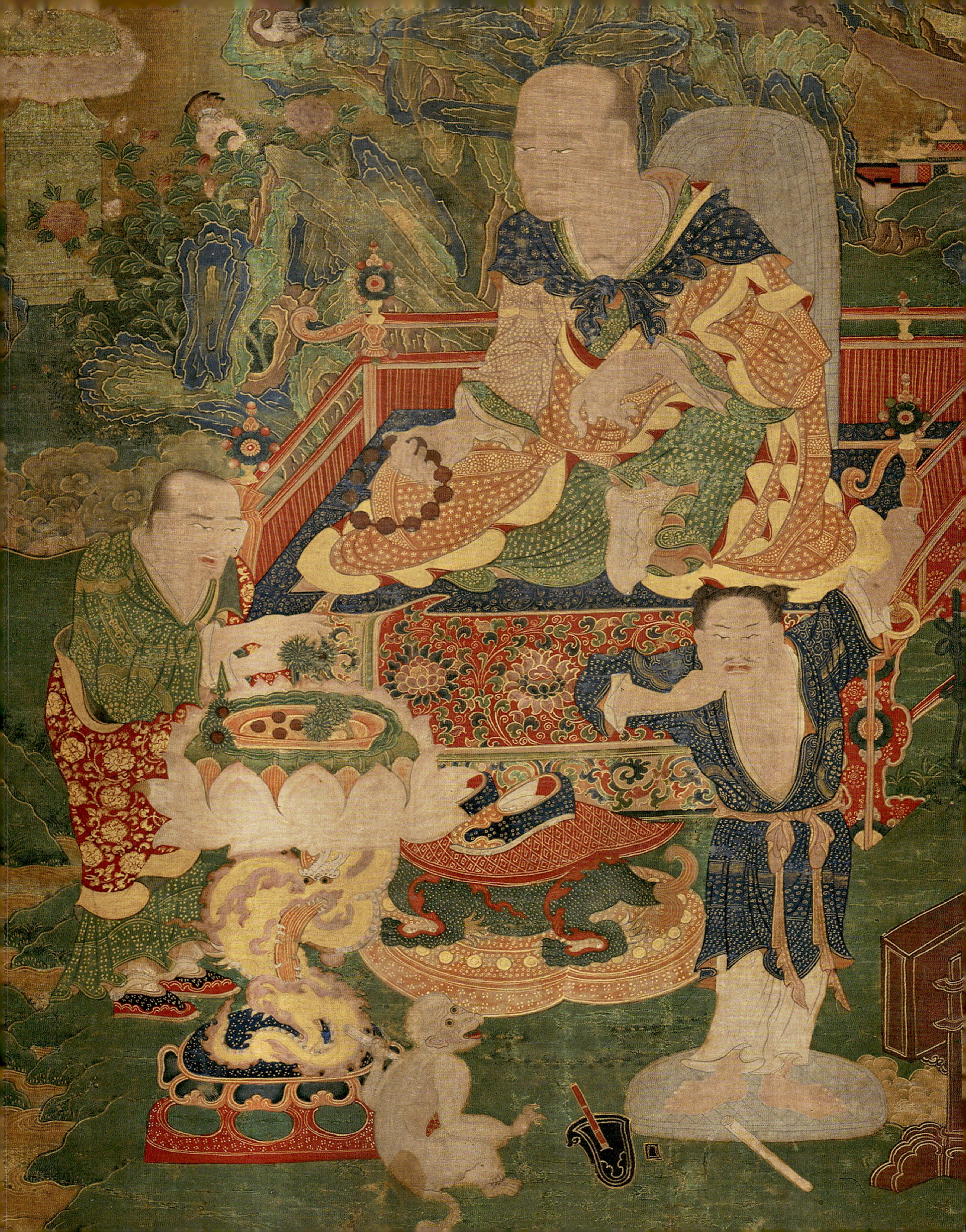

CHAPTER 9

Paintings of the Sixteen Arhats by Khyentse Chenmo

IN A TIBETAN BUDDHIST temple, Śākyamuni, the four guardians of the directions, and the sixteen arhats form an almost obligatory iconographic group. Artistically the arhats are of great interest. Since they were introduced to Tibet from China, they often embody very striking Chinese elements. This chapter presents nine early Khyenri-style sets of thangkas that depict the sixteen arhats as single main figures. A tenth set of arhat paintings in the Cleveland Museum of Art depicts two arhats as its subject. I will discuss one example of that tenth set below, as Figure 9.31.

Khyentse Chenmo probably painted dozens of sixteen arhat sets in his long career. He seems to have copied landscape and numerous background details, such as minor almost picaresque humans, from Chinese originals (as seen above in his Lamdre and Shambhala king paintings in chapters 6 through 8). He also prominently provided the background landscapes with pairs of birds and with distinctive animals.

ARHAT SET 1: FIVE PAINTINGS IN THE MUSEUM OF FINE ARTS, BOSTON

Of an important set of twenty-three paintings, just five thangkas have survived. These paintings, like the set of Shambhala kings in chapter 8, were largely unnoticed for many years in the Museum of Fine Arts in Boston.

DETAIL OF FIG. 9.5

They were donated in 1908; four of them came from a special donation and one, the central Buddha, came from the Denman Waldo Ross collection.[434] These paintings embody a high level of workmanship. Indeed, I would argue that they are by Khyentse Chenmo or a close follower, though the stylistic clues are not as clearcut with the sixteen arhats as with such iconographic subjects as Lamdre gurus and Shambhala kings.

Figure 9.1, the central Buddha, lacks the typical ring robe fastener (as in Fig. 9.2), but another feature links it unmistakably to the paintings of Khyentse Chenmo at Gongkar.[435] The form of the floral volute in the centers of the lotus-seat petals—vaguely resembling a fleur-de-lis—is distinctively Khyenri. Similar volutes appear at the centers of petals in the lotus seats of certain Gongkar murals. For comparison, see the lotus seat of Buddha Śākyamuni (Fig. 9.2) and that under the tutelary Yamāntaka (Fig. 9.3).

Other decorative details of Figure 9.1 include the elaborate tassels of a canopy above the central figure and the elaborately tasseled cloths that hang from the offering table before the Buddha. At the bottom of the painting stand two of the Buddha's chief monk-disciples. The one to the right is depicted in a rare fashion: he stares at the offering table, seemingly intent on laying his plate of offerings with the others. On the backrest of the Buddha's throne, the mythical animals have been rendered not just naturalistically but also asymmetrically: the lions and little boys

on both sides are looking in the same direction. In each upper corner of the painting, a group of four minor deities floats on clouds, making offerings to the Buddha.

Figure 9.4, one of the better-known paintings in the set, depicts Dharmatrāta as an attendant of the sixteen arhats.[436] Marylin Rhie described this thangka with sensitivity, noticing prominent stylistic features deriving from Ming-period China and seeing in the painting an opportune mixture of Chinese and Tibetan styles:

[Here] the landscape is far more delicate and subdued, and recedes farther into the distance. The dominant color is malachite green; its cool and inviting tonality draws the viewer into the setting. We move readily from object to object in a zigzag path from the lower left, where a mysterious "foreign"-type male figure offers up to Dharmatrāta two blue jewels from his place beneath rocky ledges and a lavender cloud.[437]

This lavender cloud or mist somewhat obscures the thin blue strip at the bottom of the painting that depicts a body of water. The foreign-looking male may be a serpent spirit, a minor divinity believed to haunt such pools, though he does not have the classic *nāga* iconography. But he seems to lurk, partly submerged, near the edge of the water, intending to grant Dharmatrāta two jewels from his fabulous *nāga* treasure.

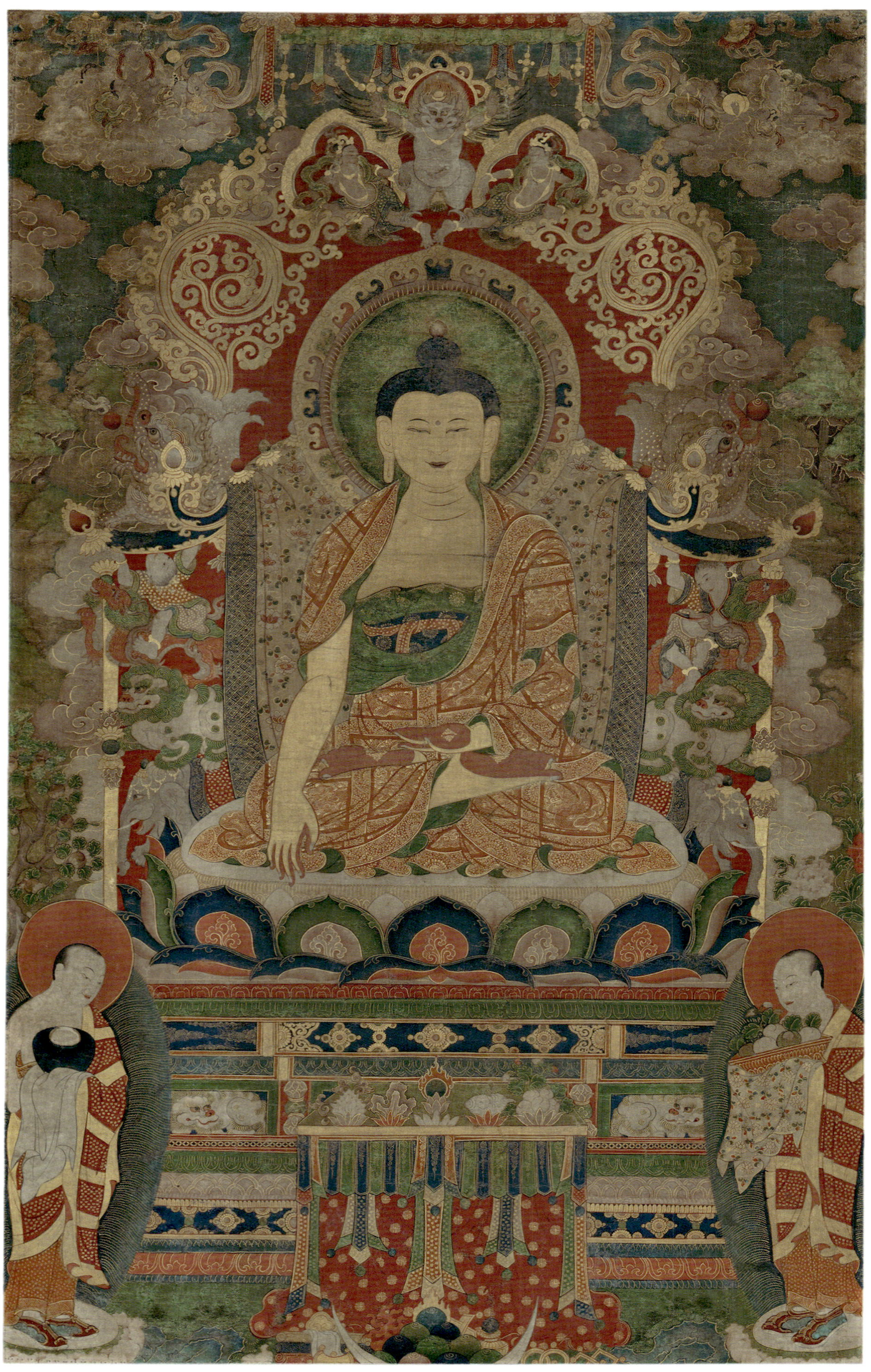

Fig. 9.1
Central Buddha
second half of the fifteenth century
31 ⅜ x 20 ⅛ in. (79.8 x 51 cm)
Museum of Fine Arts, Boston (acc. no.
08.174) Denman Waldo Ross Collection
Literature: Pal and Tseng 1969, no. 7; and
Toganoo 1986, III 6–1

Fig. 9.2
Buddha Śākyamuni
Detail of *avadāna* murals, ground floor,
Gongkar; 1464–1476

Fig. 9.3
Detail of a lotus seat under the deity
Yamāntaka
Hevajra Chapel, second floor, Gongkar;
1464–1476
After: Masaki and Tachikawa 1997, 53
bottom

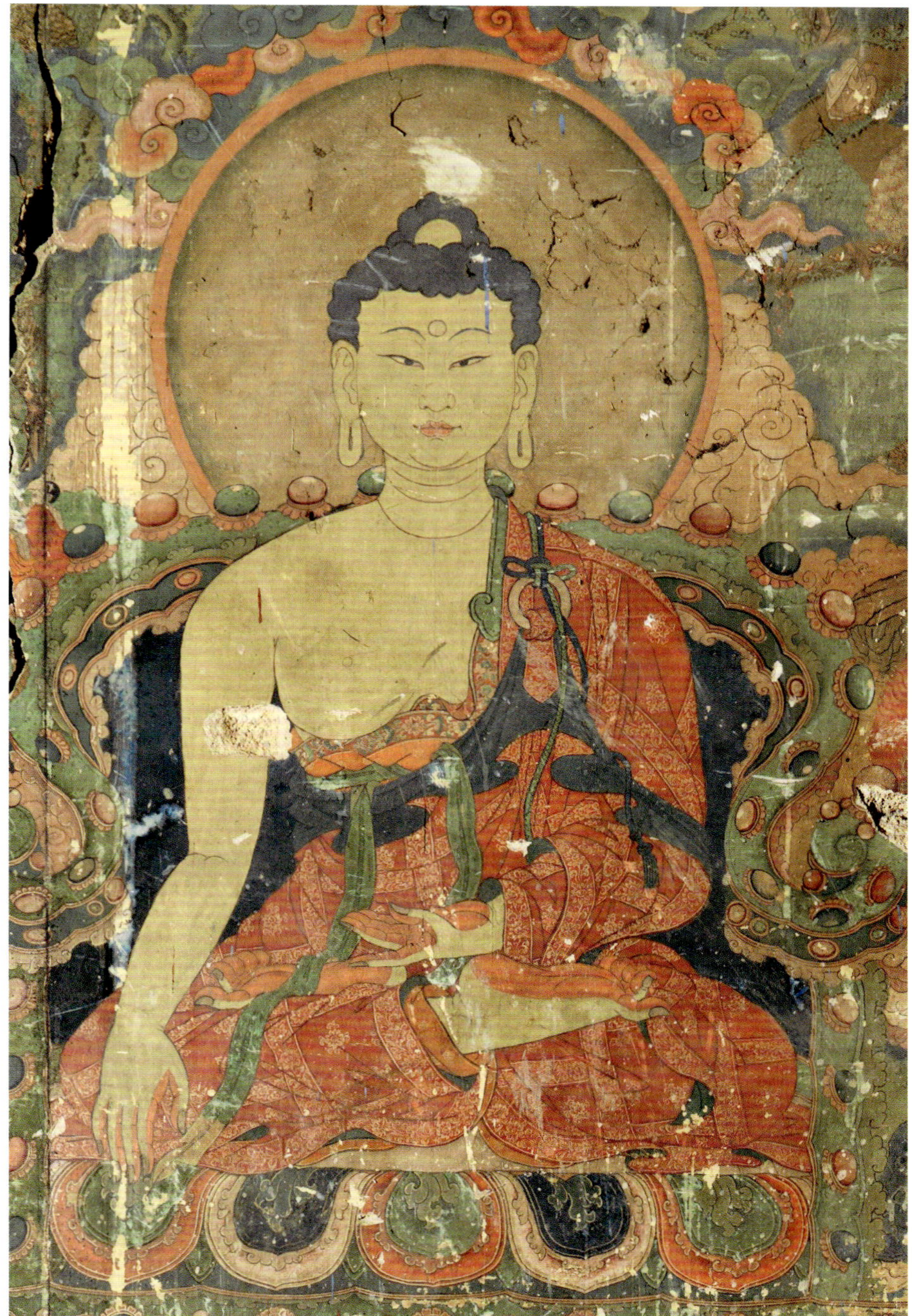

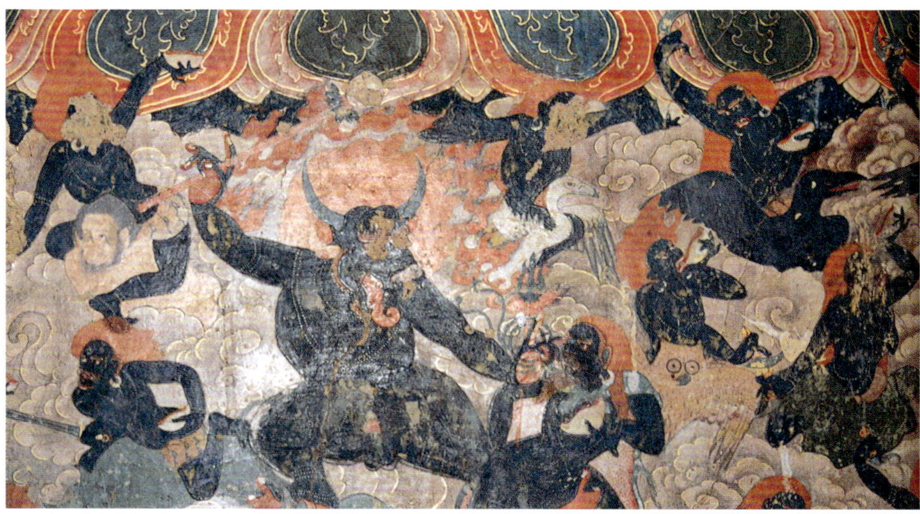

Another large lavender cloud and a beautiful leafy tree reinforce the central position of Dharmatala. From here we are drawn through the breaks in the rocks to the deities and clouds that float in the pale, murky sky. An offering deity in brilliant garb hovers above the white-robed Amitābha.[438]

It is strange that Khyentse Chenmo depicted the winged minor deity so colorfully and prominently in the sky, almost between Dharmatrāta and the Buddha Amitābha. He is too large to be worshipping Amitābha. Perhaps he was meant to be a divine accompaniment for the pilgrim Dharmatrāta, announcing his approach through the ringing of his bell.

This kind of landscape—with beautifully detailed naturalistic elements (such as the large tree), the spatial composition and ground plane, and the pastel coloring of the clouds and the green landscape—is related to Chinese Buddhist painting of the Ming dynasty (1368–1644), particularly of the 16th century. The atmospheric illusions in the painting seem to suggest a relationship with middle Ming-period painting, before the crisp clarity of the late Ming ushers in a more precise definition of space, as seen in the Ford thangka [Rhie's catalog no. 18]. Despite the similarities with Chinese painting, the distinctively Tibetan artistic style emerges in the clarity and sharpness of the primary figures and the latent power of the two-dimensional representation, which injects its own potent kind of reality. It gives the ethereal landscape a vigor and intensity more Tibetan than Chinese. The painting does reveal, however, a fortuitous merging of the Chinese styles with the Tibetan expression.[439]

Following the opinion of the time, Rhie considered the painting to come from eastern Tibet; most art historians equated strong Chinese stylistic elements with a provenance in Kham or Amdo. She dated the painting to the second half of the sixteenth century, about a century too late. Regarding three paintings from the same set, she also observed that they were "exceptionally fine works of great delicacy, refined detail and beauty of color."

The second painting from this set to be published was Figure 9.5.[440] Pratapaditya Pal in 1969 described it with remarkable insight and flair:

A votary offers flowers at a lotus font supported by a dragon, while another stands with his left arm raised and appears to be chanting. In the background is a visionary landscape with blue-green rocks, through which we are given a glimpse of a palace or a temple and a tree with contorted, twisted branches. Above the building, a bodhisattva, rendered in the Nepali manner, is ensconced in the rocks, and to the right of the Arhat is a water font from which an animal seems to be drinking.[441]

Pal attributed this set to Tibet or China, noting the charm and humor of its distinctively "Lamaist," that is, Tibetan, rendering:

Although the forms are strongly Chinese, such visionary landscapes were developed by painters, both Tibetan and Chinese, especially for arhat paintings. The basic vocabulary of such paintings, particularly of blue-green rocks, stylized scrolls or expressively rendered trees, is derived from the more traditional repertoire, but the ultimate visualization remains distinctively Lamaist.[442]

Here Pal compares the painting to a Chinese one (his cat. no. 4, by Chao Meng-fu), asserting that they possessed both basic similarities and profound differences. He continued:

There seems almost a purposeful attempt here to contrast the forms. The attendants appear to be agitated, the dragon contorts itself to support the font, the rocks and branches seem to reflect strong tensions, and amidst all this the Arhat sits in total tranquility and introspection. The details, however, are carried out with great charm, especially the rendering of a flying crane and two butterflies near the water-font, while the monkey in the foreground adds a touch of humor, both by its posture and expression.[443]

Pal was impressed by the excellence of this painting. In conclusion, he referred to the persistence of the forms of both the water font and decorative floral scroll in the arhat's chair, which also occurred in Chinese works published in his catalog (no. 25 and fig. 2).

Pal identified the arhat as Cūḍapanthaka (Tib. Lam phran brtan). But the arhat depicted here does not hold his two hands in meditation gesture, as would be usual for that arhat. Rather, he prominently holds a rosary of stone beads. Hence, I suggest that he is Kanakavatsa (Tib. gSer be'u), the seventh arhat.

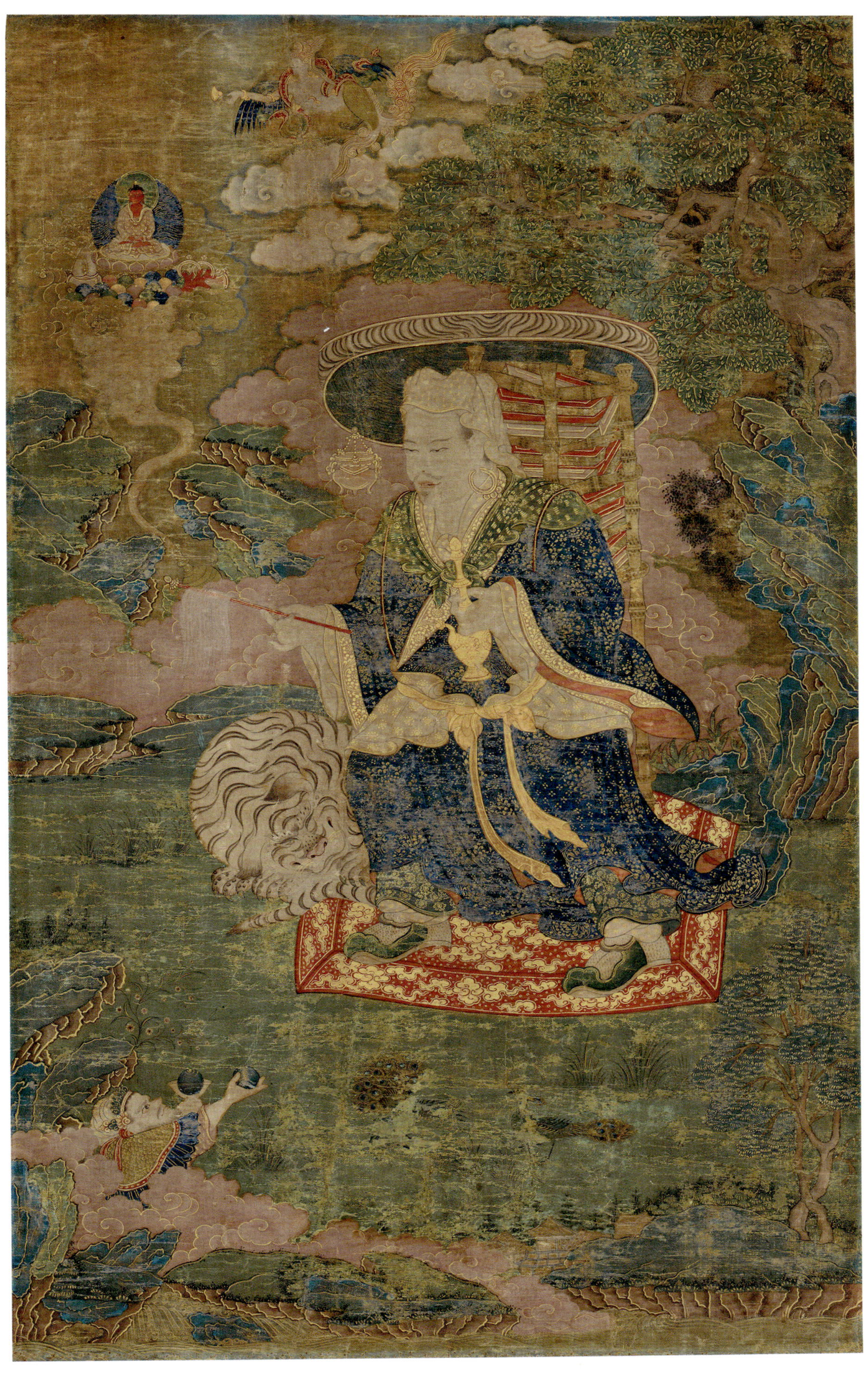

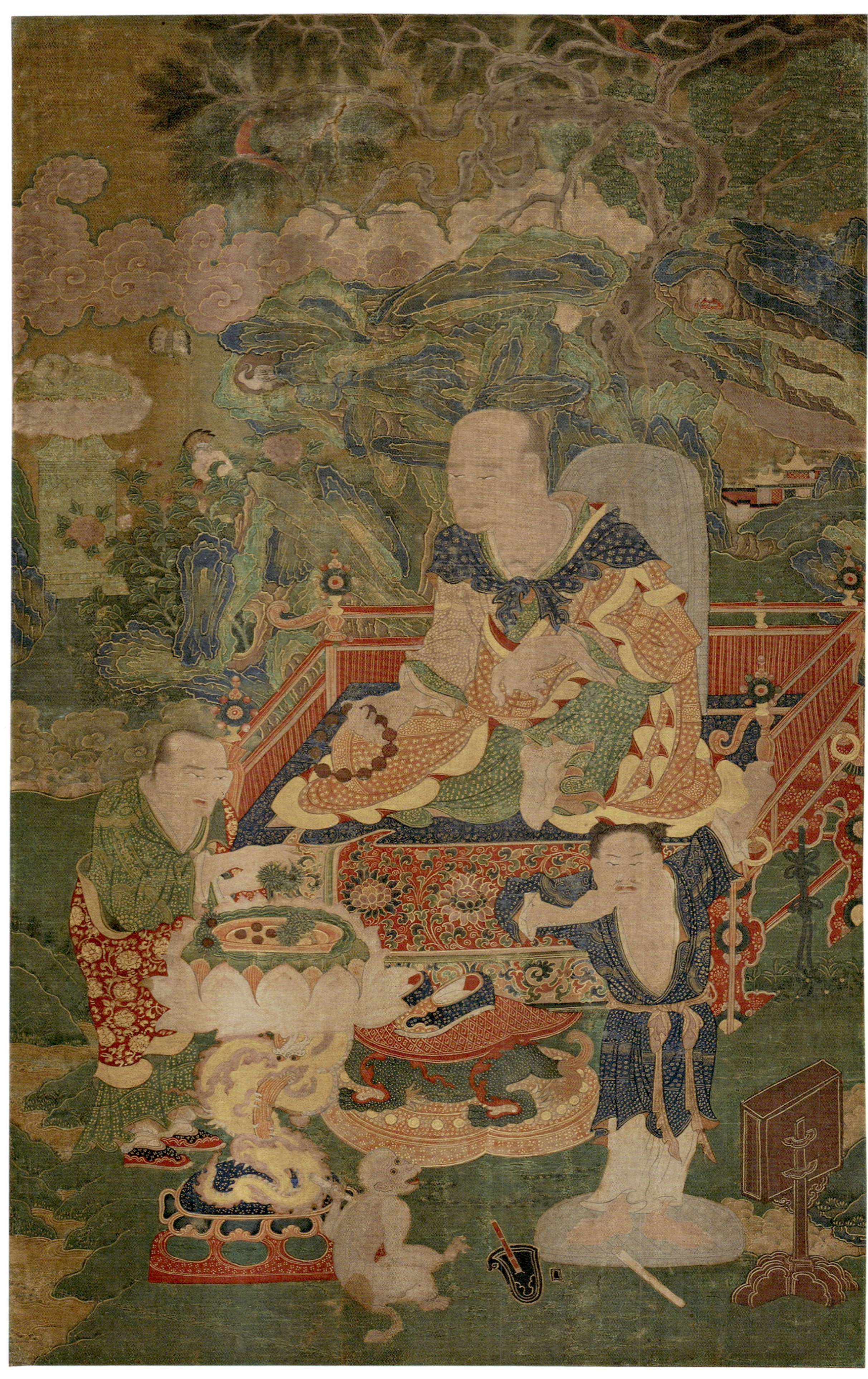

He typically holds a "string of precious stones," according to his praises attributed to Śākyaśrībhadra, here represented by a rosary of twelve large beads held in his proper right hand.[444]

The two minor votaries mentioned by Pal are evidently attendants of the meditating arhat in his mountain retreat. One of them is opening green thorny-skinned fruits or nuts and laying their chestnut-brown centers on a plate. The other had been quietly at work, rubbing a stick of ink on an inkstone preparing to paint. Now he stands, shouts, and raises his left arm to scare off an over-curious monkey that has snuck up and grabbed a roll of paper, which the primate impishly holds in his left hand, looking around to see what else he can grab.[445]

Toganoo in his 1986 catalog presented two more of the same set of arhats, calling them "Rakan in a chair" and "Rakan seated under a gnarled tree."[446] (*Rakan* or *arakan* means "arhat"

in Japanese.) Both paintings are the same size, and Toganoo described them as a continuation of the set. The first arhat, in Figure 9.6, leans on his right arm against his chair back and extends his left arm, his palm facing up on his lap. Such gestures do not resemble those of any known arhat in the praises attributed to Śākyaśrībhadra.

On an ornate chair with dragon-head finials, the arhat seems to sit in peaceful concentration, oblivious to the others near him. The painting is rich with human activity; no birds or animals appear. To the right, one of the arhat's attendants, or some local villager, is at work conducting water via pipes from its source to a square reservoir, which feeds the pond at the arhat's feet, from which lotus buds and blooms emerge. Two other attendants or villagers are in the foreground, one dozing off while reading a book and the other about to rouse and scold his comrade, to whom he gestures dismissively with one hand.

Figure 9.7 depicts the "Rakan seated under a gnarled tree" mentioned in Toganoo's catalog.[447] The arhat holds a book in his left hand and grasps the limb of a tree with his right. These gestures do not agree with those of Panthaka, whose hands usually form the gesture of dharma explication and hold a book. This figure is more likely to be Gopaka if his iconography follows the system of the arhat praises attributed to Śākyaśrībhadra; there, arhat number 15, Gopaka (Tib. sBed byed), simply holds a book in one hand.

Here the arhat has found a peaceful perch in a gnarled tree, not heeding the presence of those around him. Two humans stand near the trunk of the tree: one seems to be a young attendant, wearing monk robes and holding a mendicant staff, who greets a long-haired visitor to their forest retreat. The visitor, a forest inhabitant, turns to answer the attendant and has brought an offering, a large golden-shelled turtle that he holds

before him with both hands. In the sky, in the upper-left corner, is a goddess, possibly White Tārā. Below, to the left of the arhat's feet and a slight distance away, is a pool of water from which emerges a *nāga* serpent spirit, who offers the arhat a flaming jewel in a bowl.

ARHAT SET 2: THREE PAINTINGS

Two closely related Khyenri-style arhat paintings are preserved at the Rubin Museum of Art. The first, Figure 9.8, is the sole known surviving member of a set of paintings that are similar but slightly larger than those of the Boston set. I believe this masterwork was probably painted by Khyentse Chenmo. It depicts Ajita (Tib. Ma pham pa) and a number of finely executed minor figures and splendid landscapes. Ajita is shown sitting before an overhang or shallow cave, truly in "a lush and exotic paradise of Rishi Mountain."[448]

The two minor figures to his right and left dressed like Indian ascetics are *rishi* who probably live nearby on the same mountain; one of them is the *rishi* Uśīra. Rhie in her 1999 catalog noted the *vīṇā* instrument in the hands of one seer but went too far in identifying them as the great adepts Vīṇāpa and Śavaripa, who would be completely out of place here. This painting's masterfully depicted *rishi* on the left outdoes even the great adept Vīṇāpa as an impressive *vīṇā* player (see the detail, Fig. 7.21).

In the foreground, three wild elephants offer Ajita branches of red coral, paying tribute. One gently lays his branch of coral on the ground, and another has already left his and begun his slow retreat backward, still observing Ajita. These two elephants are an oddly dull gray; they originally may have been painted silver. Some water damage has occurred to the painting: the body nimbus of the Buddha in the upper-left corner was originally green.

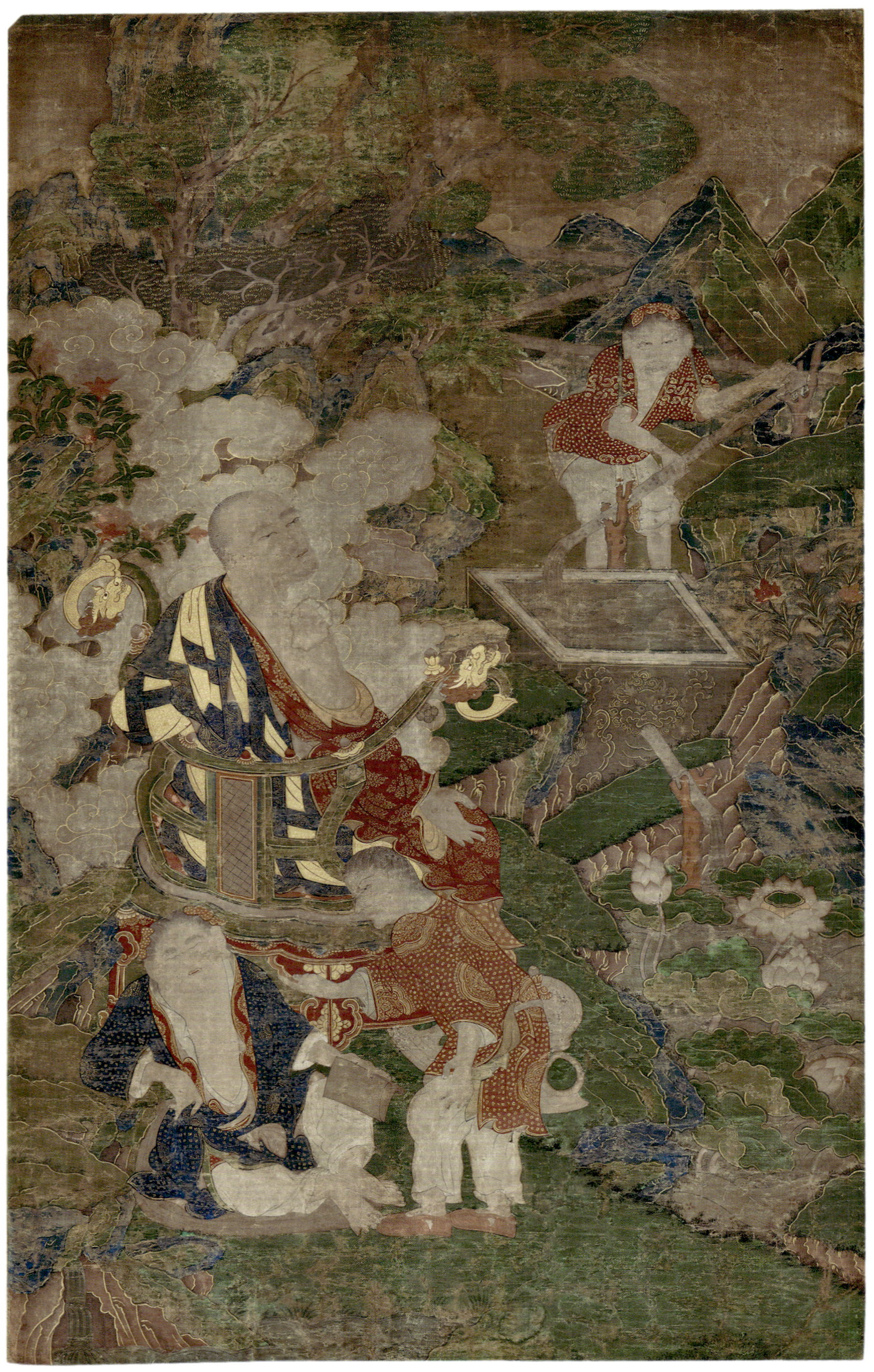

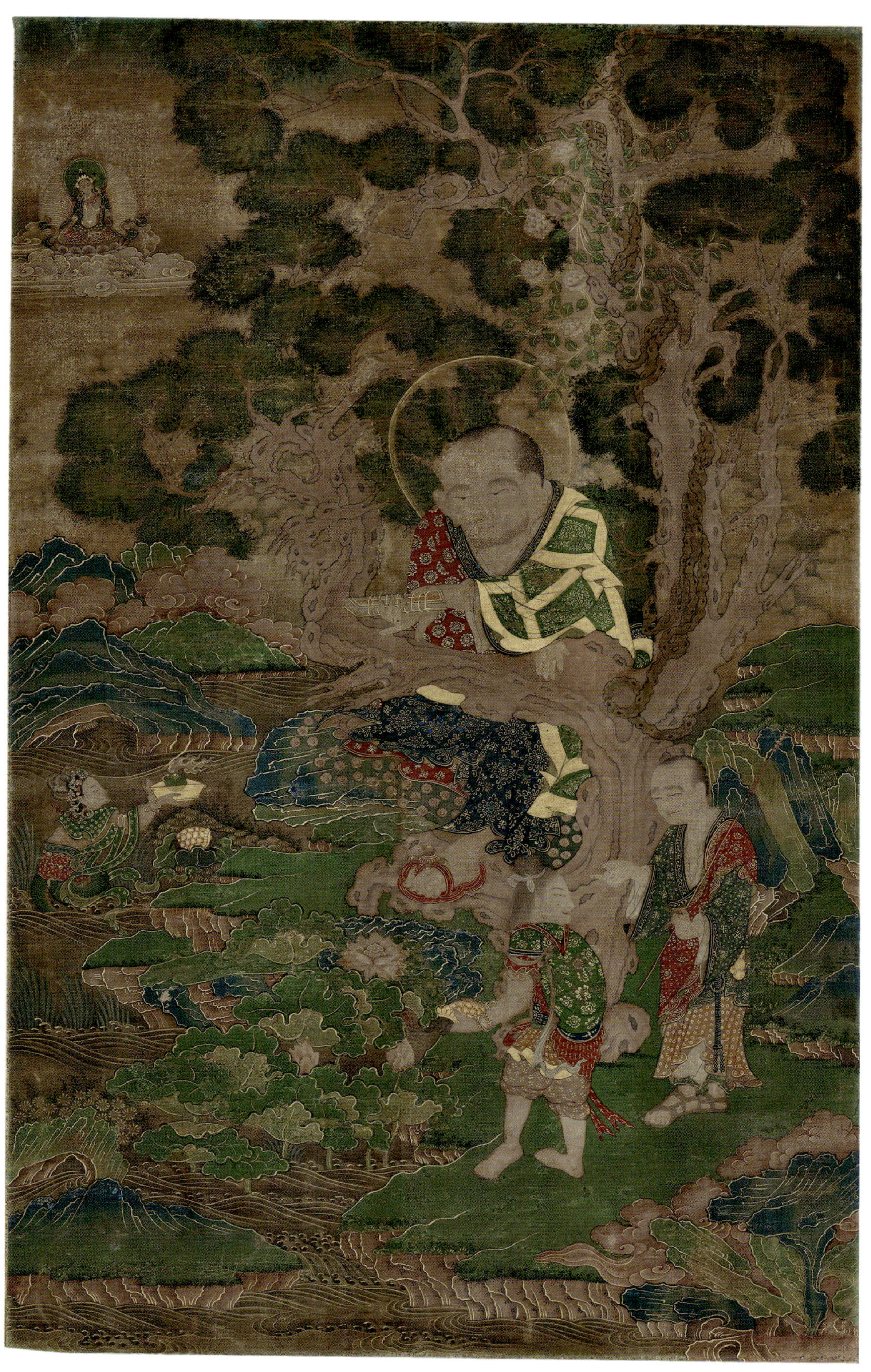

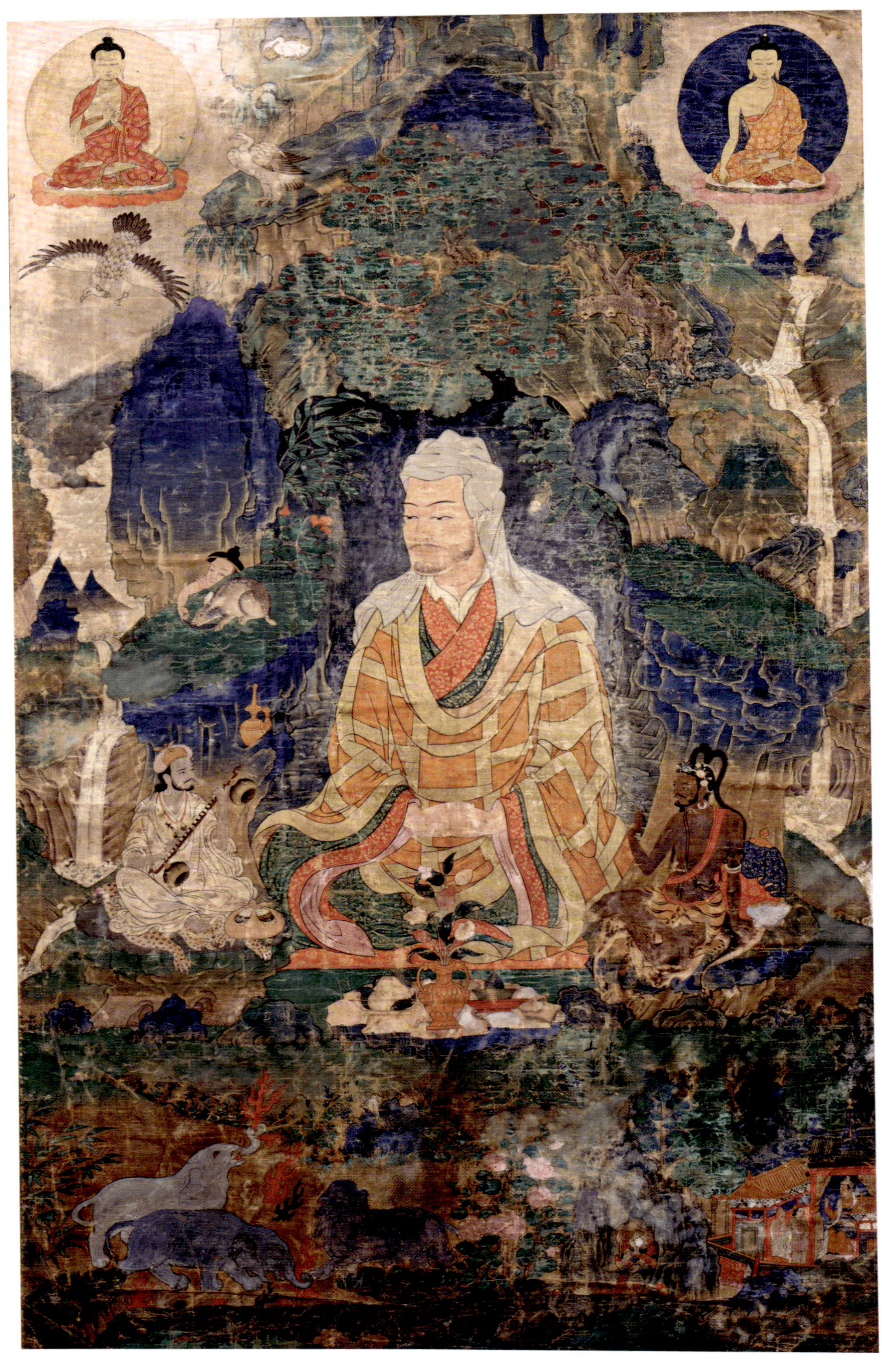

Fig. 9.8
Arhat Ajita
second half of the fifteenth century
36 x 23 in. (91.4 x 58.4 cm)
Rubin Museum of Art
F1997.9.2 (HAR 122)
Literature: Rhie and Thurman 1999, no. 20

In a fine vignette in the bottom-right corner, two other seers or mendicants are visiting a king in his pagoda-roofed retreat. Elsewhere, as Rhie aptly describes:

> Three striking lammergeier vultures are shown, one nesting, one standing and one swooping down from the cliffs above the cave. A young attendant with a black cap offers a fish to a rabbit on an outcropping, adding further drama to the scene at the left, while cataracts of waterfalls enliven the right side of this symmetrically balanced composition.[449]

The black-capped attendant may be offering the rabbit something vegetal, like a thin leaf, rather than a fish. Rhie insightfully compared this painting's trees and main figure to the Boston MFA painting of Dharmatrāta (another Khyentse set that she knew from her previous publications), adding: "The composition of fantastic rocks piled high and the brilliant blue-green coloring reflect styles of the later period of Ming painting from around the mid-sixteenth century."[450] But her date for the painting is a century too late.

The depiction of arhat Kālika in Figure 9.9a was also I believe probably painted by Khyentse Chenmo. It contains a number of elements that he was fond of: a prominent flying pair of birds and lifelike human attendants or accompanying minor figures. At the bottom right is a wild goat offering an auspicious flowering twig, which also appears in the background of a Kalkin painting and in a mural of Shangtön Chöbar.

Rob Linrothe described this painting:

> [This] Kālika has a number of Tibetan genre elements. The face and the bare arm of the arhat are quite closely observed in terms of anatomy. The parallel lines

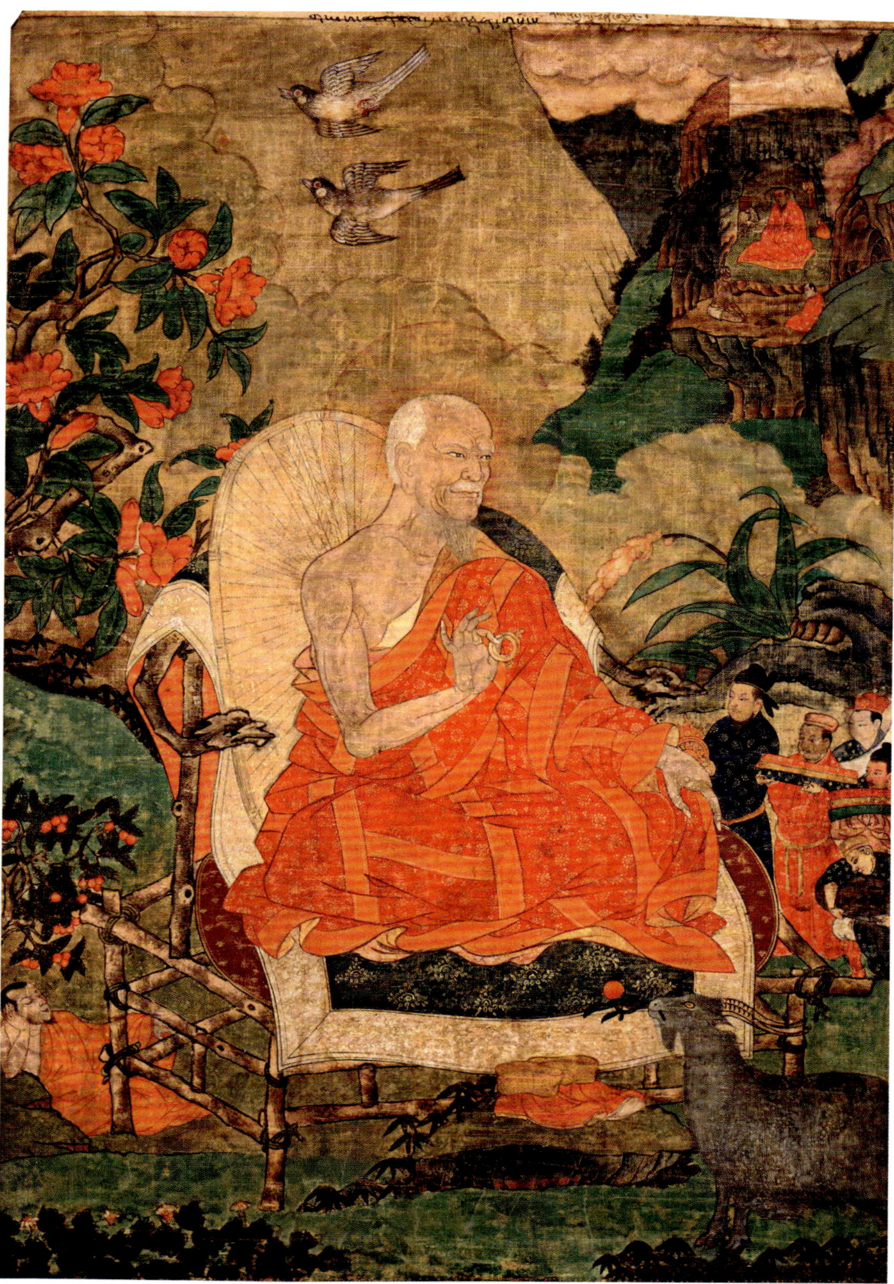

FIG. 9.9A
Arhat Kālika
second half of the fifteenth century
21 ¼ x 15 ¼ in. (54 x 38.7 cm)
Rubin Museum of Art
C2006.66.484 (HAR 948)
Literature: Linrothe 2004, no. 9

etched around his mouth are impressively rendered. The lazy monk daydreams below the chair (left), tapping his fingers distractedly on one of the wooden struts. A younger monk with a beard, which, except for its dark color, resembles the Arhat's, instructs a nearly naked ascetic and another monk in front of his cave-retreat (top right corner). Before the Arhat stand five men. The nearest one, in an archaic Chinese-style imperial headgear, offers the Arhat a golden

wheel. Of the four others, two offer
brocade-wrapped books, a third an
ivory tusk, and a fourth seems to
overturn a reed basket of the type
used to cage birds.[451]

Linrothe describes the animal that
has joined the respectful human donors
in bearing pious gifts:

> At the lower right, by the Arhat's
> boots—with the upturned soles
> revealing stitched soles—a gray
> goat, yellow-eyed, stands immo-
> bile, offering the Arhat an extraor-
> dinary, round, scarlet fruit or
> flower, the stalk of which the goat
> holds in his mouth.[452]

Linrothe goes on to explain the Chinese
qualities of the painting:

> The wild goat's offering from the
> natural world recalls the *ruiying,*
> or auspicious signs, discussed
> [earlier] as an important Chinese
> mode of thought adopted into
> Arhat painting. Among the many
> other Chinese elements in this
> painting are the renderings of the
> branches of what resembles hibis-
> cus flowers and, in particular, the
> chair on which the Arhat sits. It is
> made of knotty branches of wood
> roughly lashed together, and in
> design, if not material, the form is
> comparable to the chair in which
> Lu Wen-ding sits [in Linrothe's cat.
> no. 8].[453]

Figure 9.9b is probably also by
Khyentse Chenmo. The arhat depicted
here holds a fly whisk and a censer, so
he is probably Aṅgaja, the first of the
sixteen. Though previously identified as
Gopaka, he lacks that arhat's characteristic book. Above, amid the masterfully
rendered trees and mountains of the
landscape, a prominent black-and-white
long-tailed bird, perhaps a magpie, flies

to its mate, which is just visible in a
crook of a branch ahead of it. At the bottom left, in the foreground, stands a wild
beast with gray-blue hair that droops its
head sadly and looks like a long-haired
dog; similar creatures also appear in the
foregrounds of other Khyentse paintings,
such as his painting of the fourth Kalkin.
Also distinctive are the lifelike minor
figures in the foreground; these often
occur in Khyentse's arhat paintings.

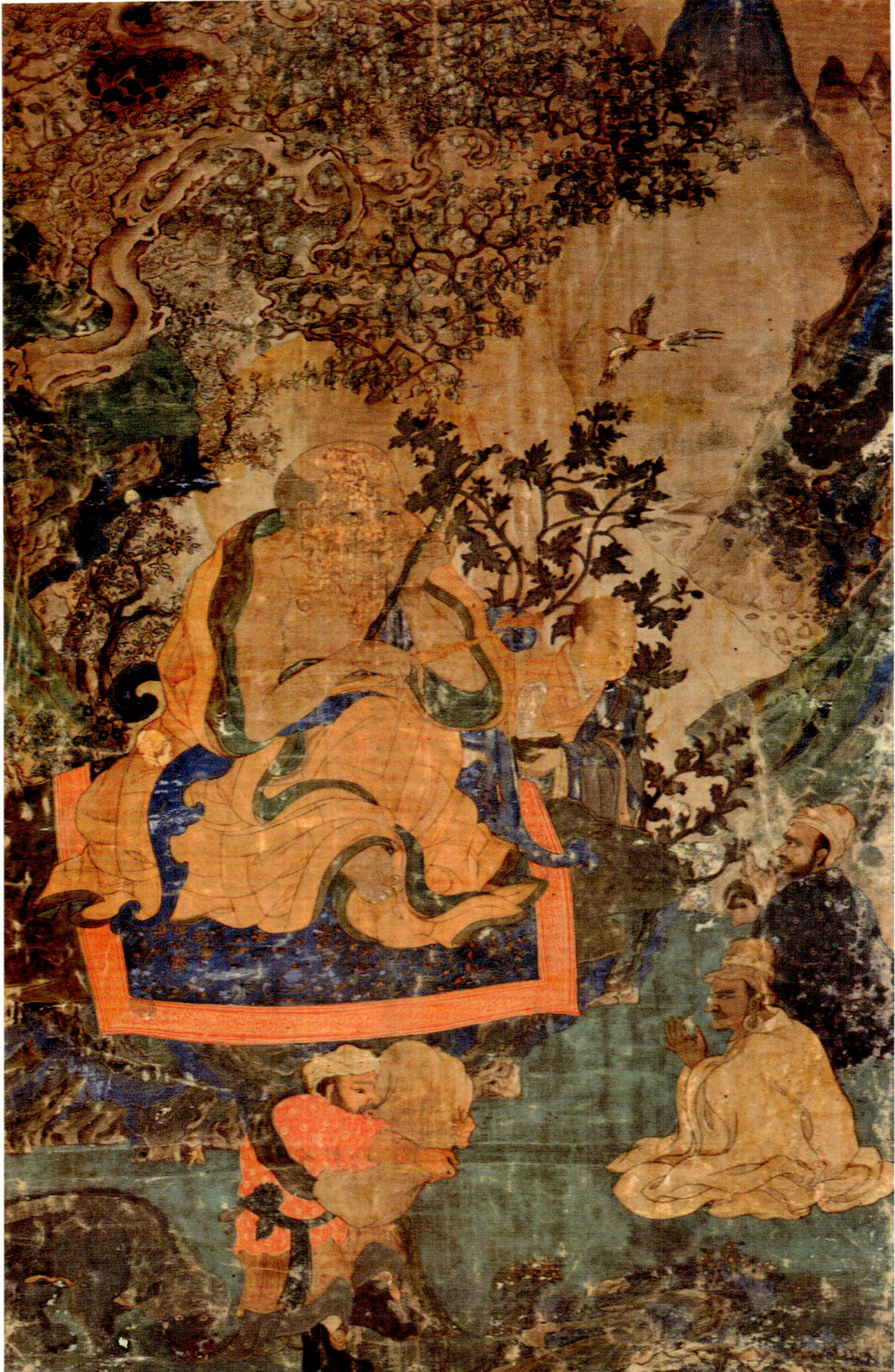

Figure 9.10 is the sole known surviving painting of its set. Depicting the arhat Rāhula, this painting is larger than that in Figure 9.8. It is also the largest known painting of an arhat in the Khyenri style; its set must have been sumptuous. As Rob Linrothe kindly informed me, a more complete set of paintings based on the same compositions by the eighteenth-century court painter Yao Wenhan (active during the reign of the Qianlong emperor, Qing dynasty) exists in the National Palace Museum, Taipei.[454]

Gilles Béguin, in the *Wisdom and Compassion* catalog, introduced this masterpiece as a work made through Tibetan techniques, perhaps for a Chinese monastery, that had been strongly influenced by Chinese decorative painting of the Ming period (1368–1644). Béguin finds here a successful synthesis of two well-known methods of illustrating arhats in China: "The expressive face is reminiscent of Guan Xiu (832–912), and the noble attitude as well as the magnificence of the environment, of Li Longmian (ca. 1040–1106)."[455]

The rocky landscape is the habitat of two kinds of wild birds. One soars high above, looking for its mate nesting within a high craggy cliff. (They may depict lammergeier vultures, though their beak is not vulture-like and the tail feathers of one are not fanned out.) At the left side of the painting, six green-and-blue birds that resemble magpies drink from a tub of water. The arhat's young attendant has managed to catch another of these birds; he cups it gently in his hands to show to Rāhula, who seems wrapped up in his thoughts. Meanwhile in the foreground, a foreign visitor crouches, holding a large ivory tusk, waiting for the arhat's attention. Such exotic travelers or merchants holding white tusks are favorite minor characters for Khyentse, who seems to work

them into compositions with or without a reason. But a face in profile offers a good opportunity to highlight outlandish features—this foreigner may be from India—as do aspects of costume, such as this visitor's sandal-clad left foot, with widely splayed toes.

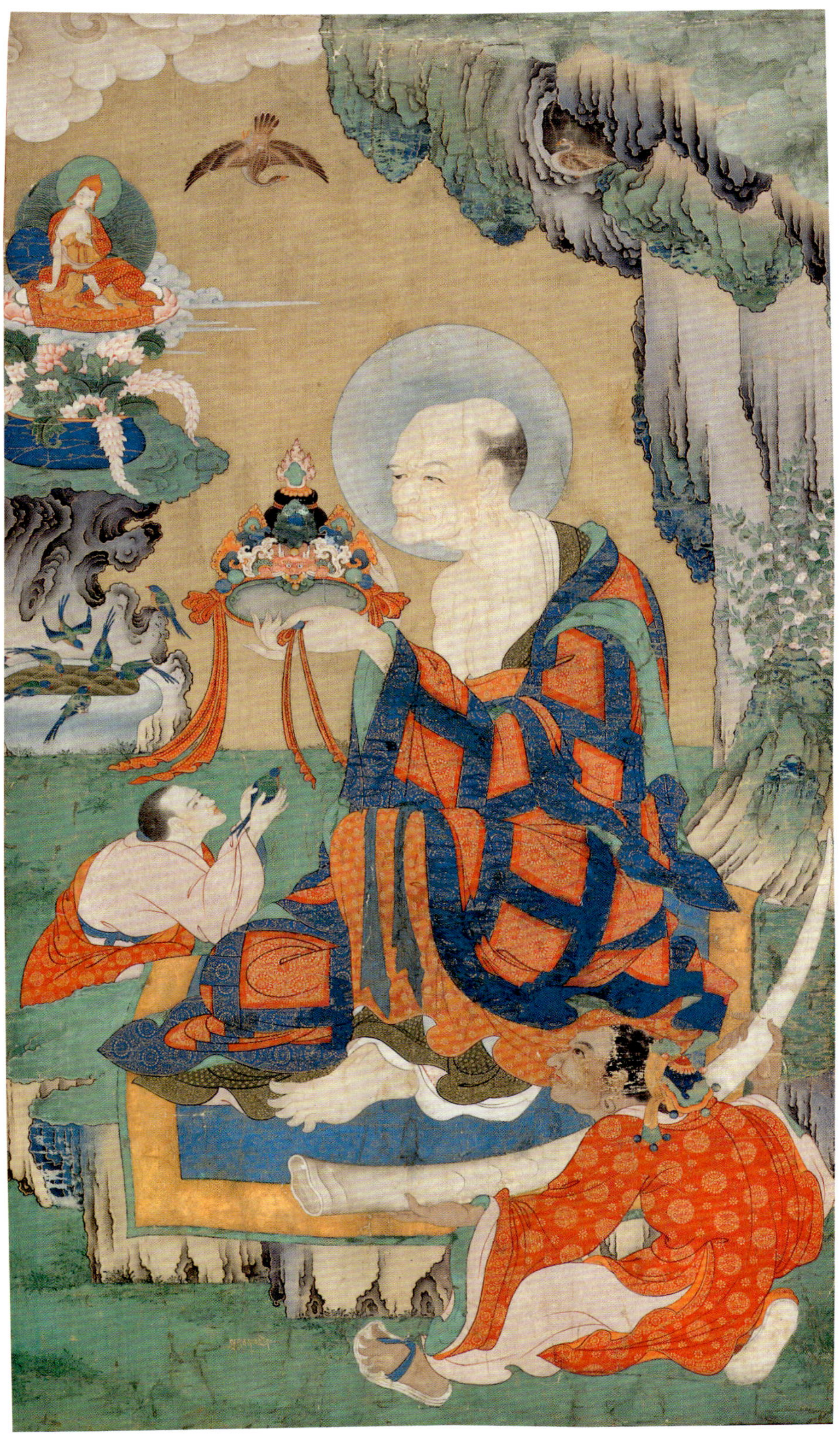

FIG. 9.10
Arhat Rāhula
second half of the fifteenth century
43 ¼ x 25 ¼ in (110 x 64 cm)
Musée Guimet
Literature: Rhie and Thurman 1991, no. 19; and Béguin 1995, Rāhula, cat. no. 263

Arhat Set 4: One Painting in the British Museum

In the British Museum, there exists a painting of a single large guardian of the direction from among the Four Great Kings, belonging to a set of the sixteen arhats, namely Dhṛtarāṣṭra (Fig. 9.11). It is slightly smaller than Figure 9.10 but still impressively large. A prime example of the early Khyenri style, it is presumably by Khyentse Chenmo or a very close early follower. The artist carefully depicts a Chinese or Central Asian five-string lute, with frets and a bent neck. The upper-left corner of the painting is graced by a figure of Śākyamuni, whose presence is highlighted by rainbow-colored streams emanating from his body in three directions, seemingly from his heart.

Arhat Set 5: Three Paintings in Phyang, Ladakh

The following three paintings of arhats are preserved in the Drigung Kagyu monastery of Phyang in Ladakh. They may have been painted by Khyentse Chenmo or a very close follower; note the ring-shaped robe fasteners worn by both Aṅgaja and Vajrīputra. These thangkas were considered by Ācārya Ngawang Samten in his 1986 catalog to be seventeenth-century paintings rendered in the Karma Gardri style. I presented two of them in earlier catalogs as puzzling cases, as possibly a lesser-known type of Drigung art from the sixteenth century that may have been brought to Ladakh from central Tibet.[456]

In Figure 9.12, the arhat Aṅgaja is depicted fully frontal, gazing peacefully and holding a fly whisk in his right hand. The painting contains a number of idiosyncratic features, including, at the foot of the painting, a tiny lama depicted in a transparent body nimbus like a bubble. The arhat's seat is unique, with two ornamented posts behind him and a dragon-head handrest directly in front. In the upper right, a pair of snowy peaks signifies the glacial abode of Aṅgaja. To the right of the arhat stand a buck and doe; the doe's ears point forward in curiosity. At the bottom right, the arhat's young attendant wears robes similar to Aṅgaja's, including the ring-shaped fastener hanging over his left shoulder. The attendant reaches out to

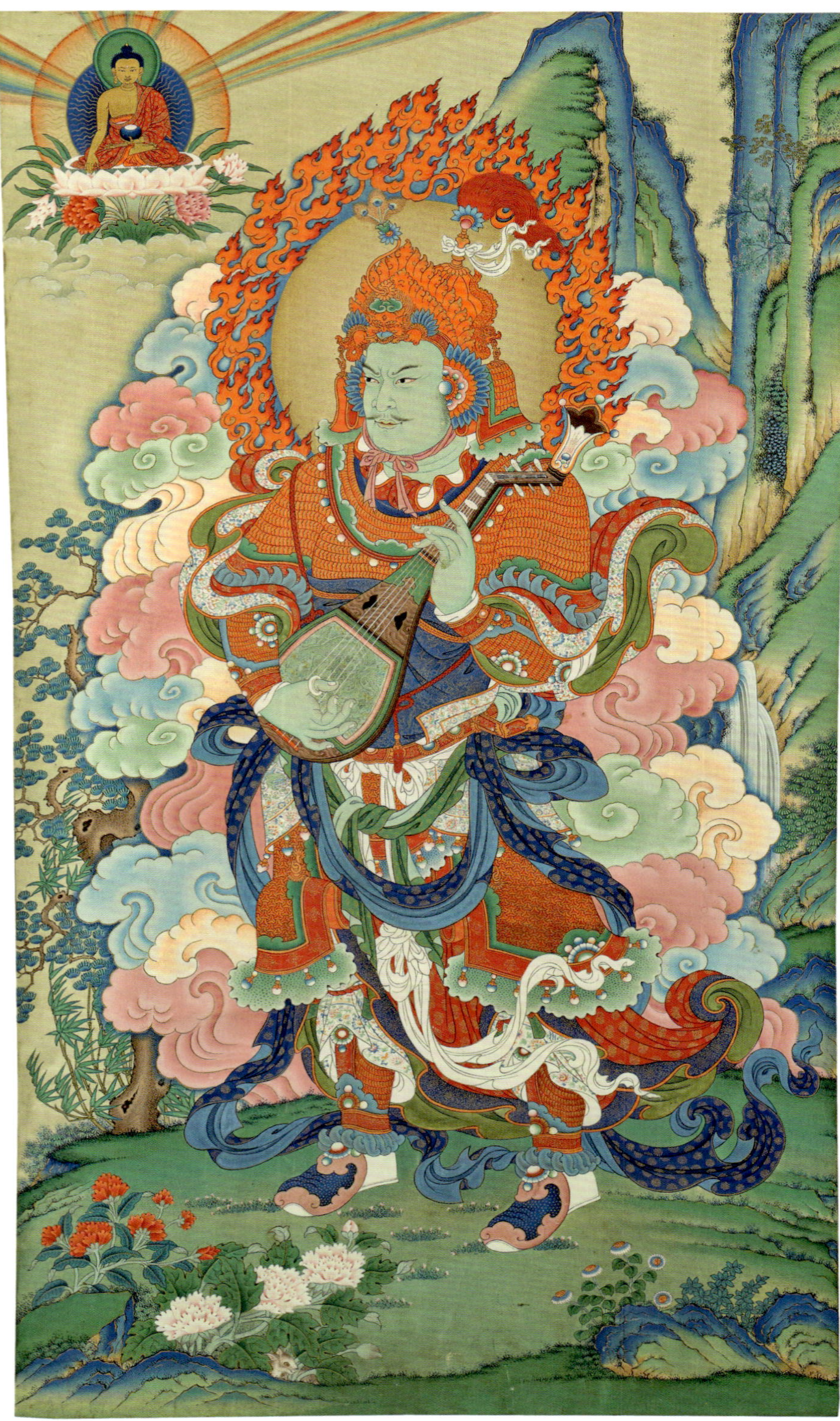

Fig. 9.11
Dhṛtarāṣṭra, the Guardian King
second half of the fifteenth century
40 ½ x 24 ⅜ in. (103.0 x 61.8 cm)
British Museum, no. 1906,0718,0.13
Literature: Willis 1999, 30

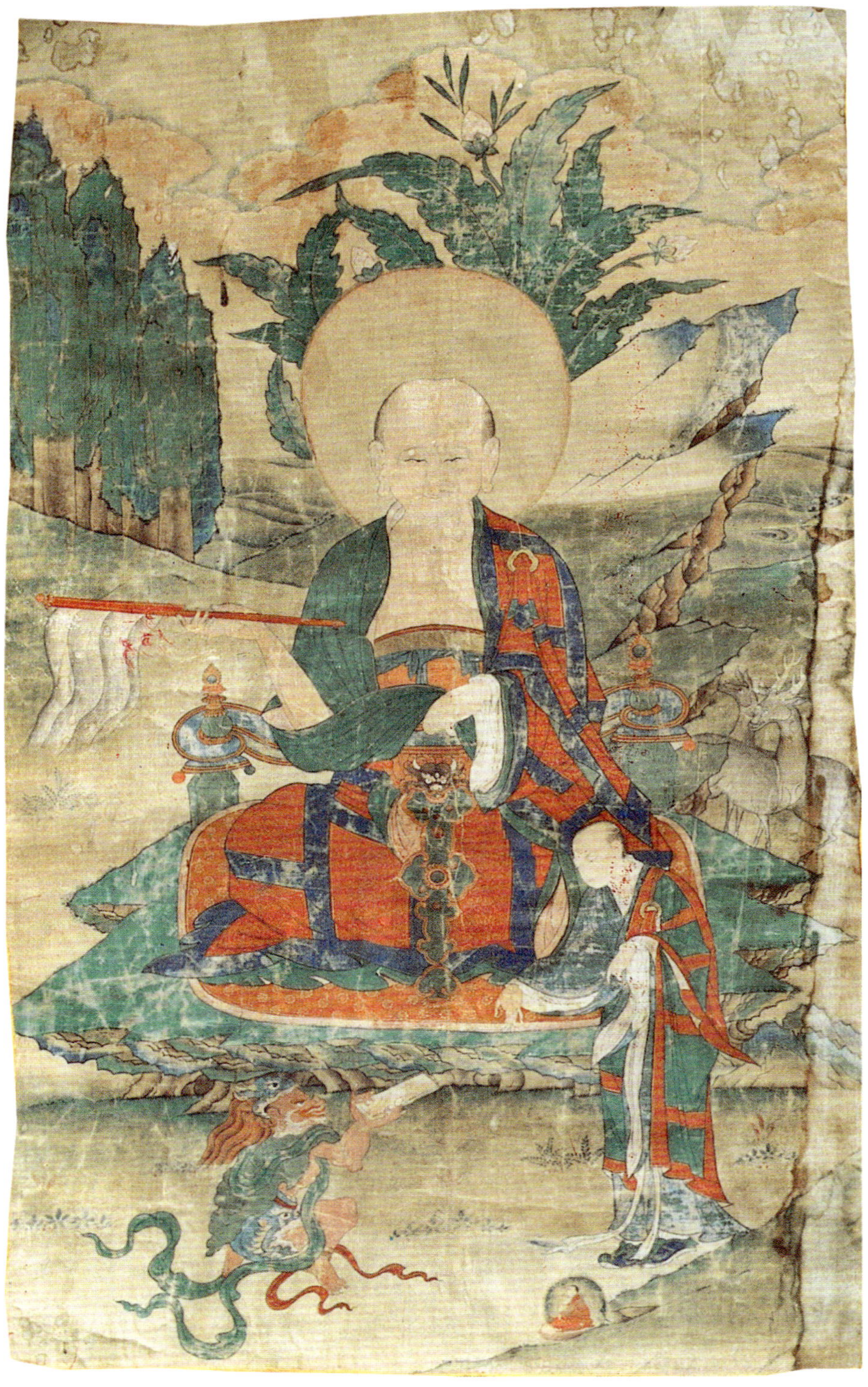

phoenix heads, that fills much of the painting. The elegant jewel-crested red brocade backrest fills the space where a head nimbus would be. Below him, to the left, stands his attendant in similar robes, bending slightly forward and offering a volume of sacred scriptures. In the bottom-right corner sit two royal patrons, possibly a king and queen of Sri Lanka, the island realm where Vajrīputra dwelled. Though the blue-robed king looks regally past the arhat, the queen and attendant focus their attention on the venerable arhat.

In Figure 9.14, the arhat Nāgasena sits on a mat, wearing colorful boots and holding a long bamboo staff. He radiates such calm that he has tamed a tiger, which has approached the arhat's right hand, as if to be petted. But the arhat's young attendant is not as confident, partly hiding himself behind a nearby tree and staring at the beast. In the lower-right foreground is a minor figure, a white-horse-riding protector, or *yakṣa*, holding a flag in one hand and possibly a sword in the other.

The areas of sky in all three surviving thangkas from this set are mostly bare of pigments. This feature may have caused Ācārya Ngawang Samten to classify the set as the Karma Gardri style in 1986. To confirm this, we need to see more examples from the set, for Khyentse Chenmo's treatments of skies can vary a lot within a given set.

ARHAT SET 6: SIX PAINTINGS IN THE MUSÉE GUIMET

There is an interesting but neglected set of arhat paintings in the Musée Guimet, in Paris, that seemingly dates to Khyentse Chenmo's time or soon thereafter. Its central Buddha painting, which would establish a Khyenri link more clearly, is no longer extant. Though some thangkas in this set are damaged, more than half of the original set has been kept together: fifteen paintings depicting

receive the object offered by the respectfully crouching, animal-headed minor divinity, whose headgear and short pants seem to be made of dragon mouths.

Figure 9.13 depicts the arhat Vajrīputra, with a fanlike fly whisk over his right shoulder. Here a Chinese-style robe fastener hangs prominently over his left shoulder. He sits on an ornate throne, with tassels hanging from golden

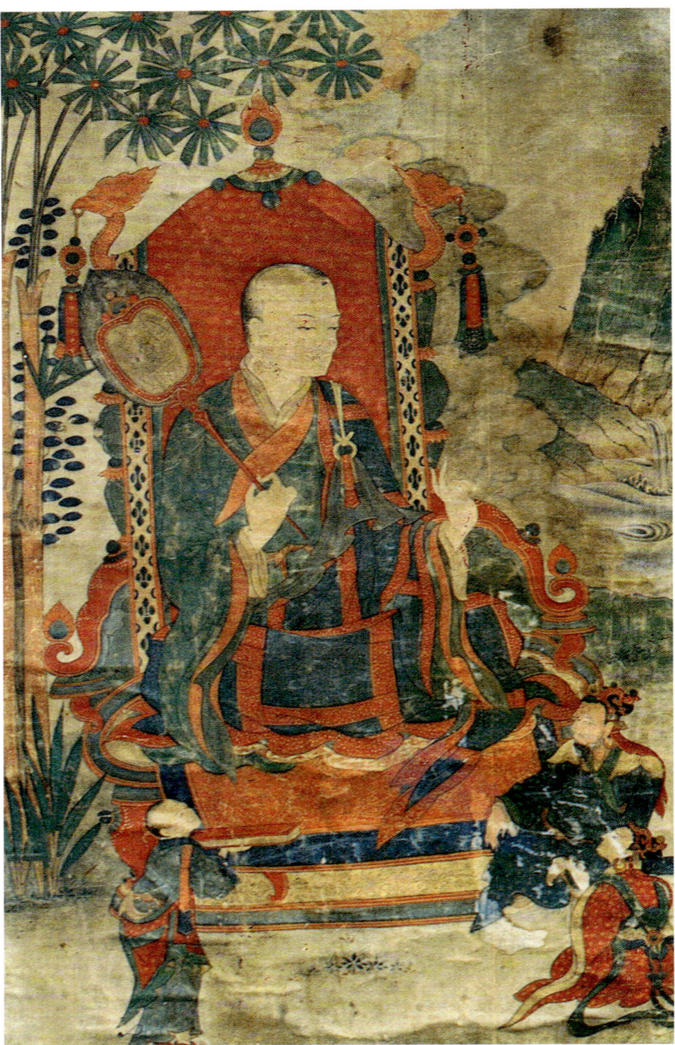

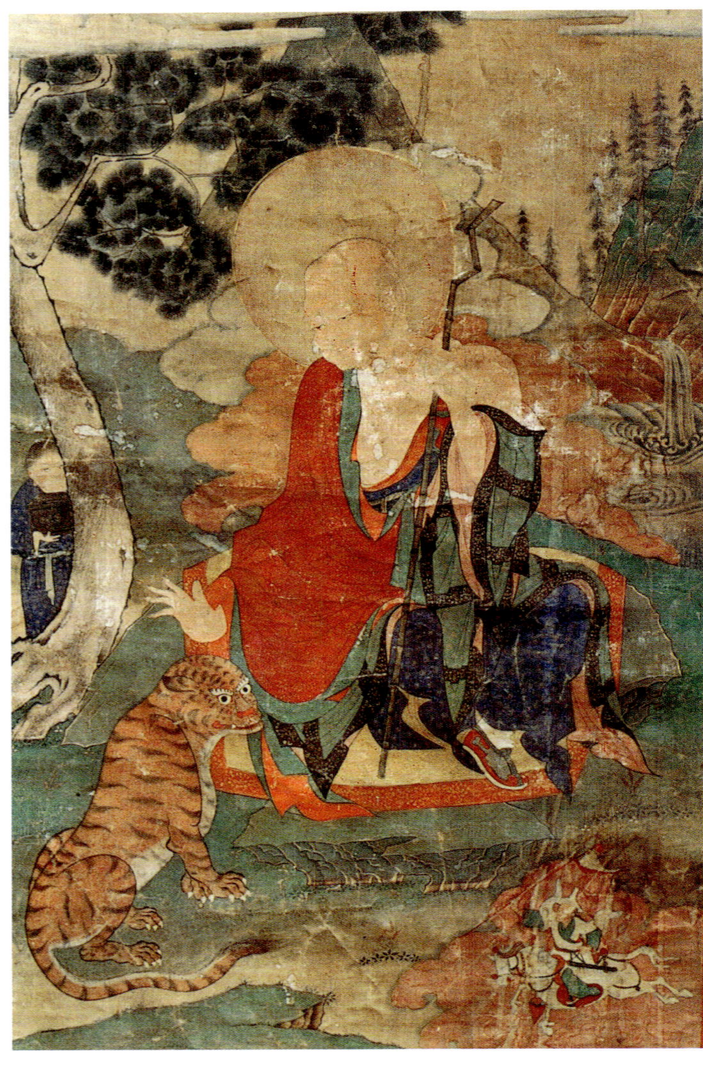

eleven arhats, two arhat attendants, and two guardian kings.[457]

The provenance of the set is unknown; it is part of the "Ancien fons" collection. Though previously dated to the seventeenth century, it seems to represent a Khyenri-style work of about Khyentse Chenmo's time or soon thereafter. Béguin remarked on the fine workmanship of the set: "The extreme meticulousness of the design and the relatively somber coloring link this arhat set to the refined and eclectic art of central Tibet of the seventeenth century, strongly influenced by the strongly China-influenced aesthetic of eastern Tibet (the new Menri style)."[458]

In these thangkas, it seems the painter tried to recreate the feeling of *si thang* paintings, often opting for light or thin colors and leaving large areas unpainted. One arhat (Fig. 9.17, Kanakavatsa) wears a robe with a special clasp, and that same thangka features a buddha with a special clasp typical of the very early Khyenri style. For that and other reasons, this previously overlooked set should be considered among the sets of arhats possibly painted by Khyentse Chenmo.

In addition to depicting an arhat as the main figure, each painting includes a bodhisattva or buddha in the sky, of which not all could be identified. Béguin also noted the regular appearance of a minor deity at the foot of each painting, which he identified as a deity of the elements, a Hindu god, or one of the twelve *yakṣa* companions of Vaiśravaṇa.[459]

It seems characteristic of Khyentse Chenmo's art that he often depicted minor deities at the bases of the paintings at a smaller than usual scale. In this set, they are painted in lifelike poses. Of the fifteen paintings, eight are in better condition, disregarding the water damage that some clearly have. Among them, I have selected six for discussion.

Figure 9.15 presents Ajita (Tib. Ma pham pa), the second arhat. Depicted with hands folded in meditation and head covered, he is seated on a mat of leaves. He lives with the white-cloaked seer Uśīra, standing to his right. According to his verse of praise, attributed to Śākyaśrībhadra: "On Rishi Mountain in Crystal Cave is the noble elder Ajita, surrounded by one hundred arhats; homage to him with two hands placed in meditation."[460] According to Dagyab Rinpoche, the seer Uśīra once lived practicing meditation with five hundred followers. Owing to his altruistic wish that they all have good places to practice meditation, his body was magically transformed into Rishi Mountain.[461]

In the lower right, a pair of deer reclines in a nearby meadow, the doe resting her head on the ground and closing her eyes; the buck keeps its head erect and eyes open, facing fully frontal. The buck's ten-point horns are depicted with slight asymmetries. To the right of Uśīra, a pair of waterfowl flaps and swims in the turbulent water.

One of the minor deities is a buddha in the upper-right corner. Béguin identified the minor deity mounted on an elephant in the bottom-left corner as Indra, the king of the gods and the guardian of the east, in the group of guardians of the directions called *dikpāla*.[462]

Figure 9.16 probably depicts Kālika (Tib. Dus ldan), the fourth arhat, since he wears prominent golden earrings. (This might be a quirk of Khyentse to depict him so.) According to his praises in a liturgy attributed to Śākyaśrībhadra: "On the copper island (Tamradvīpa) of the Jambudvīpa continent is the noble elder Kālika, surrounded by 1,100 arhats; homage to him who holds golden earrings."[463] He is said to have taught the Buddhist doctrine to

deities, who in return gratefully offered the ornaments.

Behind the arhat to the right stands a brown-skinned demon with sharp fangs that brandishes a red jagged-edge sword. In the landscape, Khyentse depicts two pairs of birds true to life. In the pool of water directly before Kālika swims a pair of ducks, one of them submerging its head. In the large tree, above and behind the arhat, perches a pair of beautiful long-tailed birds; they look like either small-beaked parakeets or magpies. Béguin identified the minor

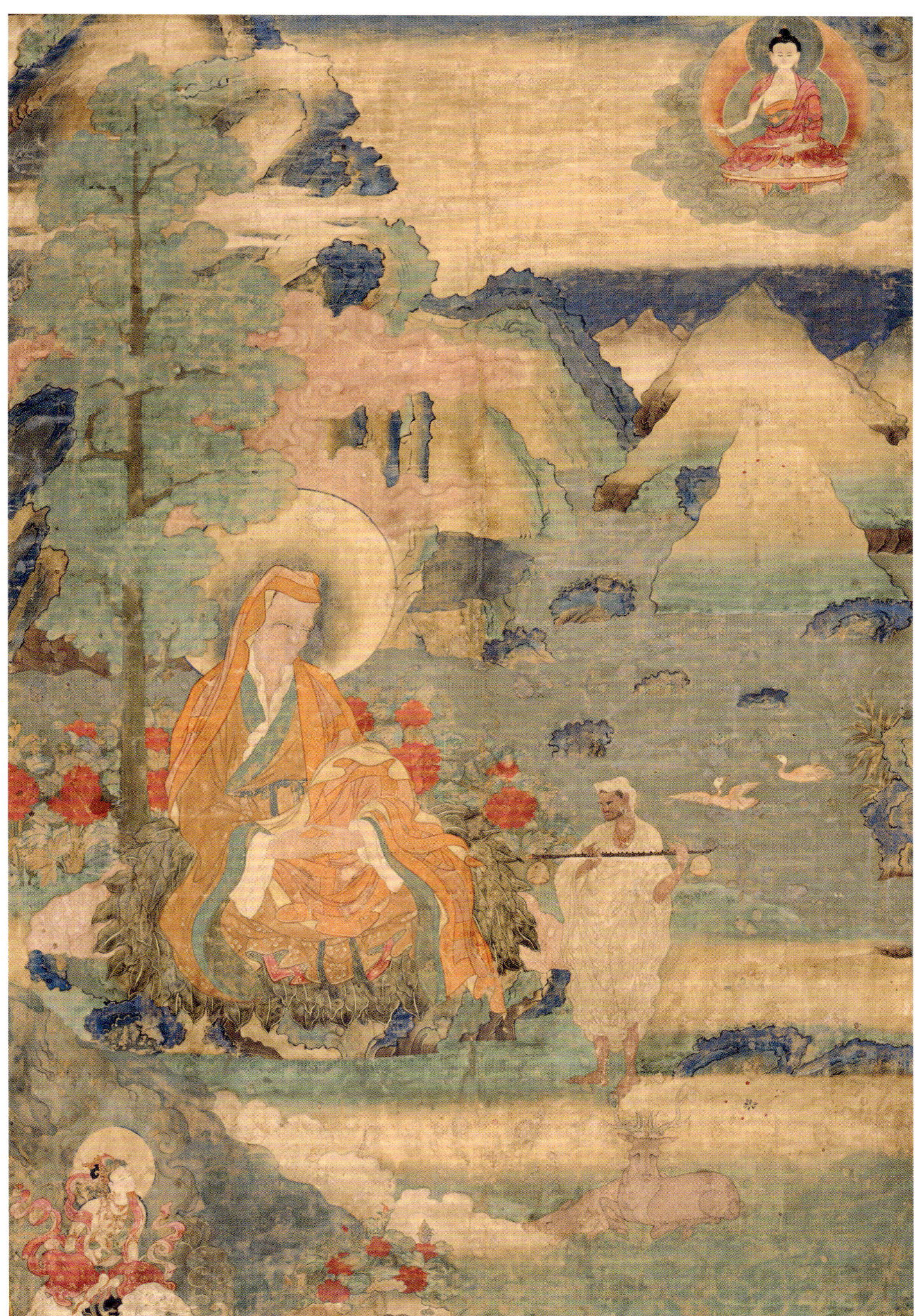

Fig. 9.15
Arhat Ajita
second half of the fifteenth century
23 ¼ x 15 ⅞ in. (59.0 x 40.5 cm)
Musée Guimet, MA 22825
Literature: Béguin 1995, no. 245

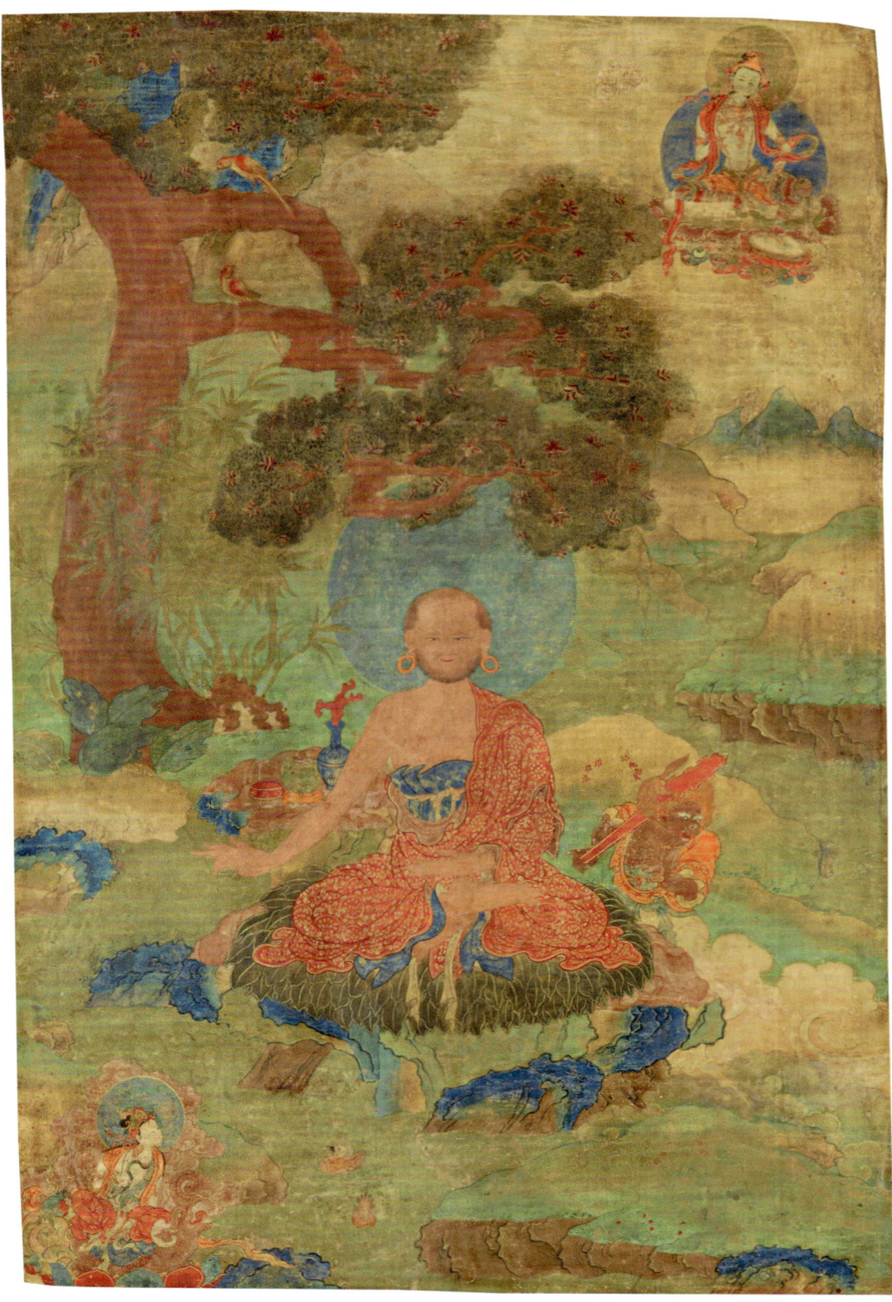

Fig. 9.16
Arhat Kālika
second half of the fifteenth century
23 x 15 ⅞ in. (58.3 x 40.4 cm
Musée Guimet, MA 22830
Literature: Béguin 1995, no. 247

deity in the upper right as the bodhisattva Vajravidāraṇa and the deity mounted on a *makara* in the bottom-left corner as Varuṇa, who was the god of the ocean and the guardian of the west.[464]

Figure 9.17 depicts Kanakavatsa (Tib. gSer be'u), the seventh arhat. He typically holds a "string of precious stones," here represented by a long chain of small golden beads that he holds in his right hand. It is one of many costly objects on a large blue platter that a regal-looking figure is offering. Meanwhile the arhat's attendant at the lower left has uncorked a magic bottle: a small

cloud emerges from it, filled with six small deities, including one playing cymbals, who observe the scene with approval from behind the arhat.

According to his praises, attributed to Śākyaśrībhadra: "On the holy spot of Kashmir (Khache) is the noble elder Kanakavatsa surrounded by his retinue of five hundred arhats; homage to him who holds a string of precious stones."[465] Béguin identified the deity in the upper right as Śākyamuni and the green deity mounted on a gazelle in the lower left as Vāyu, the god of air and the guardian of the northwest.[466]

Figure 9.18 depicts Piṇḍola Bharadvāja (Tib. Bha ra dvā dza bsod snyoms len), the twelfth arhat, since he holds a book and a begging bowl.[467] Smiling, the arhat holds a volume of sacred scripture in his left hand while his long-haired lay attendant approaches, carrying a larger volume of scriptures before him with both hands. Meanwhile, in the foreground is a pair of cranes or egrets on two little islands of a nearby lake; one stands on one leg while the other looks at it and flaps its wings. (They are the black-necked cranes of Tibet, as Khyentse could have seen in nature, and not red-crowned Manchurian cranes with their black and white necks copied from Chinese art.) In the upper-right corner is a white-skinned bodhisattva, and in the bottom-left corner is a dark-blue-skinned *yakṣa* holding a vajra-tipped staff and a gem-vomiting mongoose, a companion of Vaiśravaṇa.

Figure 9.19 depicts Nāgasena the Elder (Tib. Klu'i sde), the fourteenth arhat. He sits on a high, ornate black chair with a footrest. He grimaces as he strokes the head of a tiger, who appears as calm as a housecat and stares past him with yellow-green eyes. The arhat's young attendant, holding a vase with a large red coral branch, turns to watch what might happen. There are no birds or small animals in the landscape.

As mentioned in his traditional

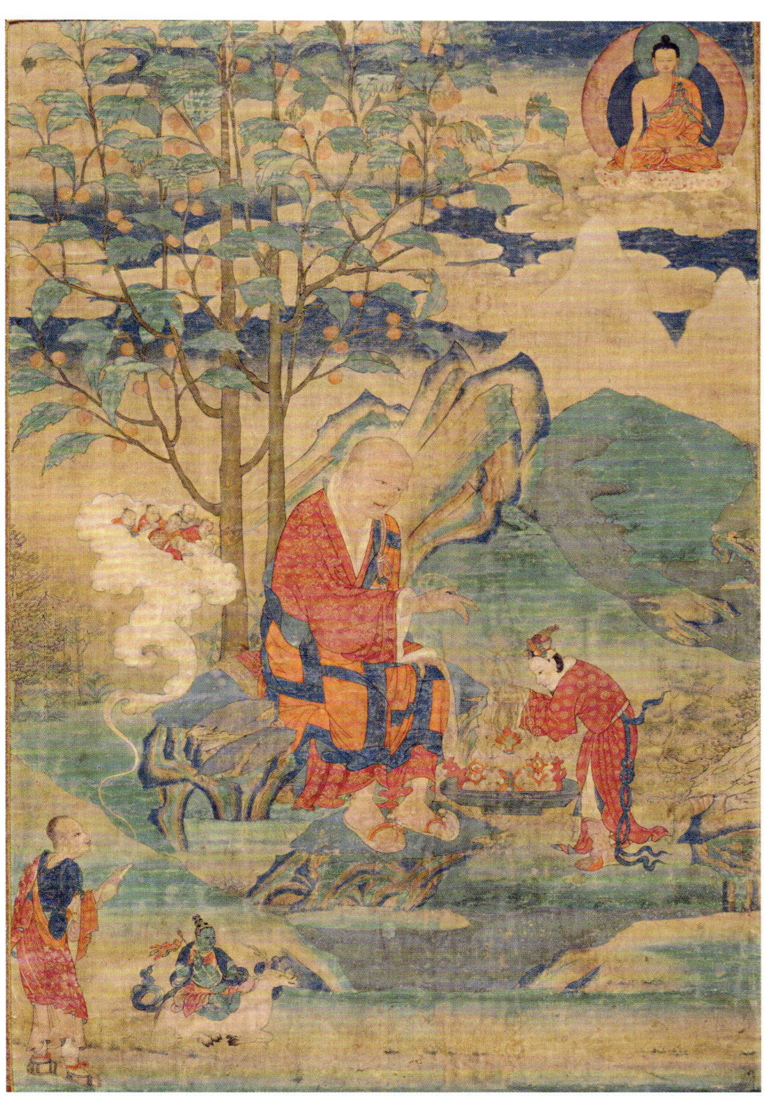

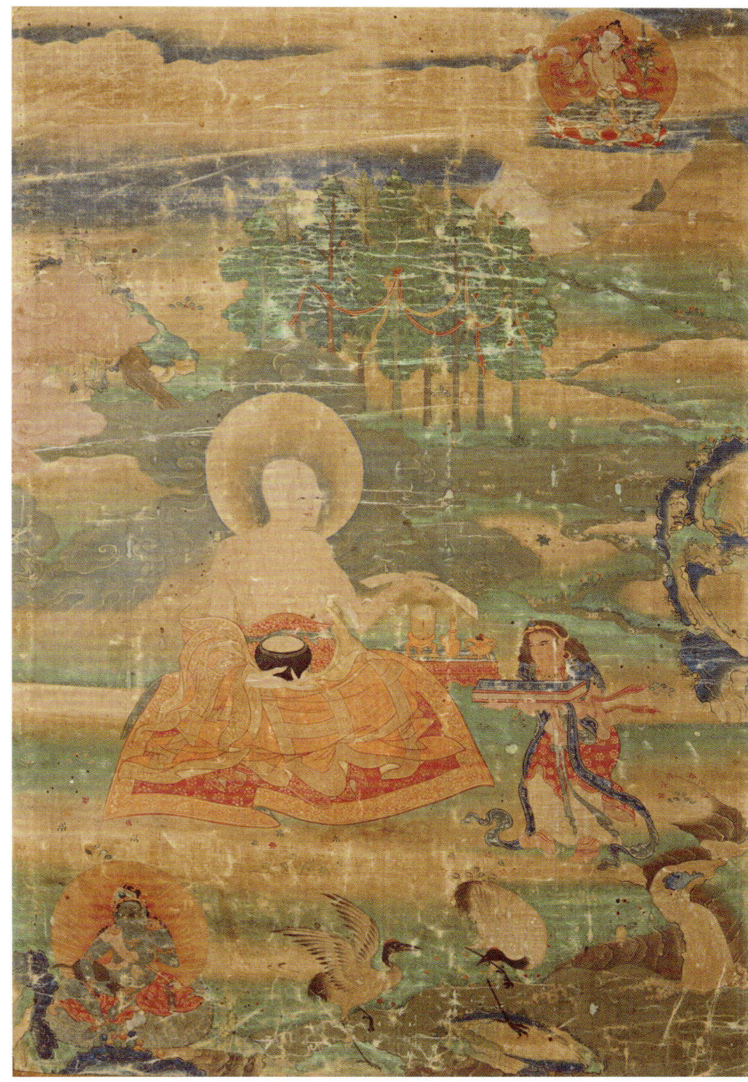

FIG. 9.17
Arhat Kanakavatsa
second half of the fifteenth century
23 x 15 ⅞ in. (58.5 x 40.5 cm)
Musée Guimet, MA 22828
Literature: Béguin 1995, no. 249

FIG. 9.18
Arhat Piṇḍola Bharadvāja
second half of the fifteenth century
23 ⅛ x 16 in (58.7 x 40.8 cm)
Musée Guimet, MA 22834
Literature: Béguin 1995, no. 252

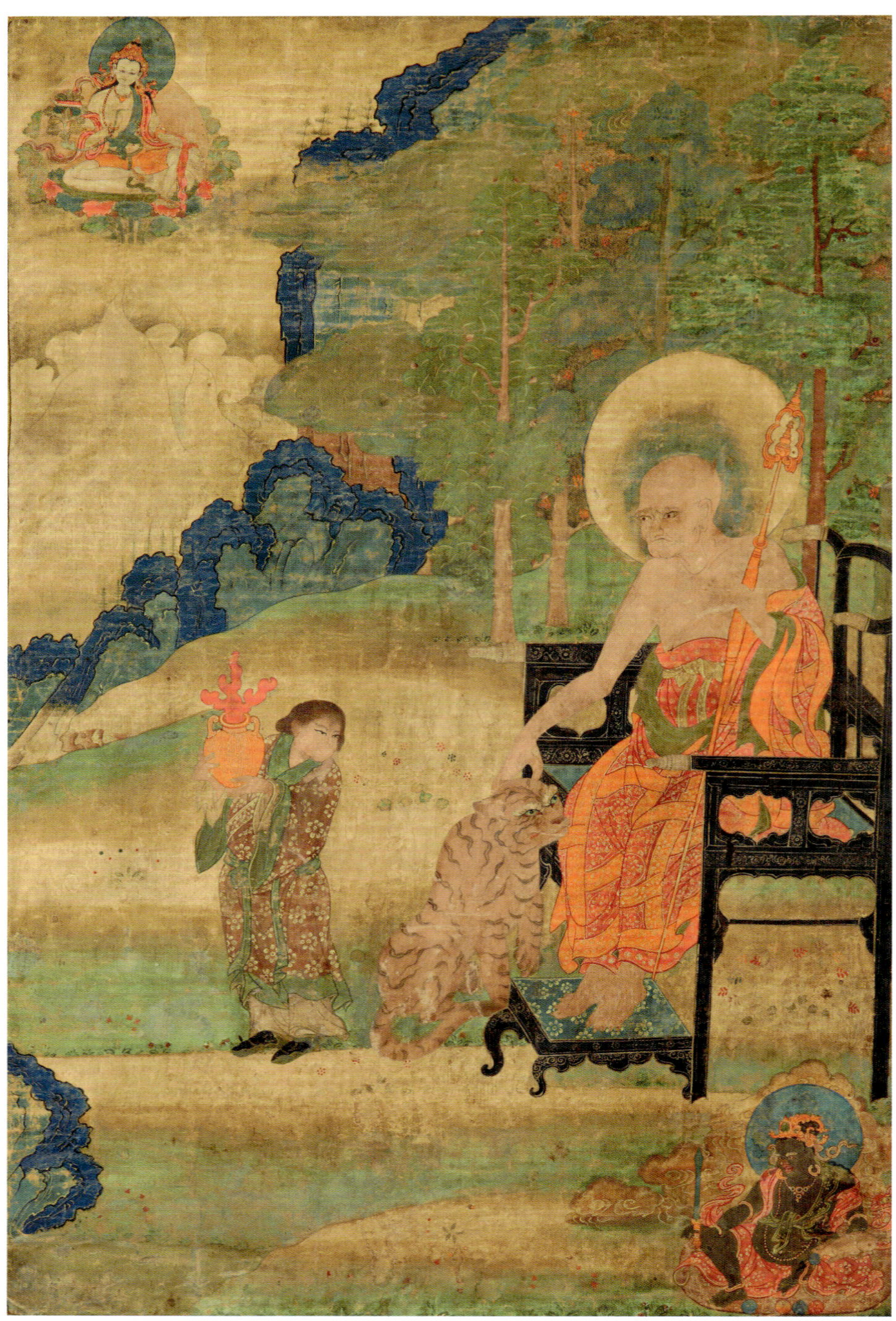

Though Béguin in his 1995 catalog identified the main figure in Figure 9.20 as "Abheda," the iconography matches the traditional verse of praise of Bhadra (Tib. bZang po), the sixth arhat: "On an Island in the Yamuna river is the noble elder Bhadra, surrounded by twelve hundred arhats; homage to him who performs [the gestures] of Dharma explanation and meditation."[470]

Seated and seen in profile, Bhadra looks calmly at a dramatic scene. His barefoot young attendant holds a golden bottle with a pointed spout; he looks and points up at a dark cloud of smoke that contains a gyrating golden dragon, which emerged from the bottle. The dragon holds a crystal vase with jewels and coral.

In the foreground, a white elephant lumbers along, also looking up at the dragon. He may have brought one or several bright-red coral branches that lay on the ground as offerings. The elephant is quite lifelike, with tusks and curving raised trunk. Béguin identified the deity in the upper left as a bodhisattva and the deity in the bottom right as one of the five companions of Vaiśravaṇa.[471] This yellow-skinned *yakṣa* has the distinctive iconography of holding a jeweled-tipped staff in his right hand and a jewel-producing mongoose in his left.

One element that is unusual about this set compared to almost all the other ones attributed to Khyentse is that the main figures are relatively small and more distant from the picture plane, which I believe may have expressed his desire to try this standard composition in a fresh way. Rob Linrothe, in a personal communication, doubted my attribution of this set to Khyentse, seeing, for instance, a consistency in the way the features of the faces were pushed into the lower third of heads and a much more exaggerated jagged edge and silhouette of the blue-green rock forms that looked like a completely different brush manner, compared to most of the other

verse of praise attributed to Śākyaśrībhadra, "On the King of Mountains, Vipulopa, is the noble elder Nāgasena, surrounded by twelve hundred arhats; homage to him who holds a vase and a mendicant's staff."[468] Béguin identified the deity at the upper left as possibly the bodhisattva Mañjuśrī, and the deity in the bottom-right corner as Raktadhūsaravajra, the companion of Vaiśravaṇa.[469] This brown-skinned *yakṣa* holds a sword in his right hand and a jewel-vomiting mongoose in his left.

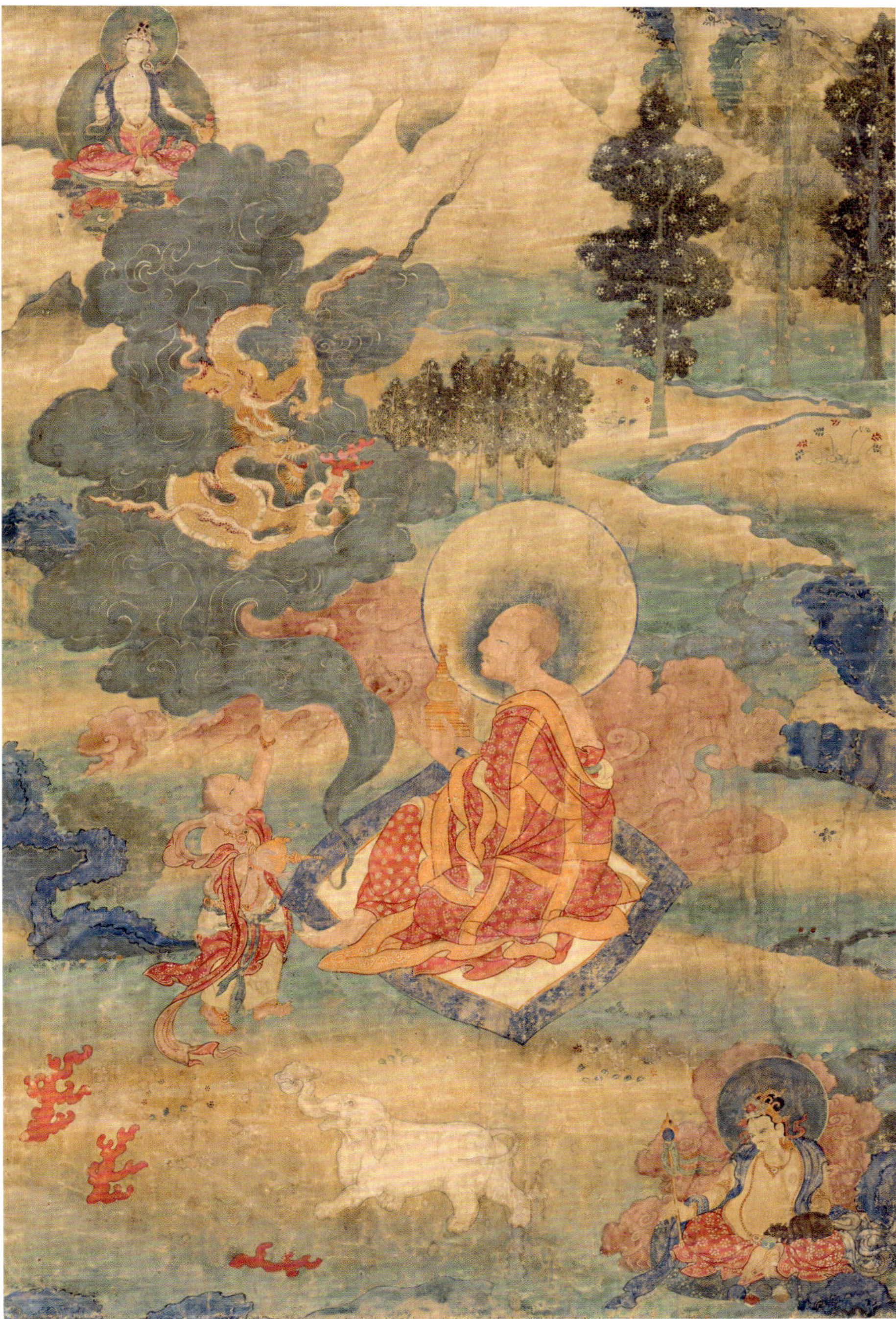

was made soon after the original and the artist must have followed it very closely.

ARHAT SET 7: FOUR PAINTINGS IN THE NATIONAL PALACE MUSEUM, BEIJING

Another impressive set of sixteen arhats is in the National Palace Museum in Beijing. I know of it from Penba Wangdu, who published five of the paintings (see also Figs. 3.27–3.28).[472] They were originally published by Wang Jia Peng in 2011.[473] From reproduction images, I took them to be the works of Khyentse Chenmo, but they are evidently much later copies of his originals. Tsechang Penba Wangdu, who has seen the actual thangkas, dates them to the eighteenth century.

Figure 9.21 is an understated tour de force. It seems at first glance to be a skillful yet orthodox treatment of an ordinary theme: Buddha Śākyamuni with his two main monk disciples as the central painting in a set of twenty-three thangkas. The buddha's robe has a distinctive strap and clasp over one shoulder, a typical choice of Khyentse Chenmo. In the upper-right and -left corners, clusters of pink clouds in the sky hold minor deities; each is naturalistically depicted in an activity of praise, such as playing an instrument, waving a banner, and tossing jewels from bowls.

The petals of the Buddha's lotus seat are colorful and frilly, with pastel purple and green colors. But the stance of his two attendants is more dramatic than usual: they stand on red mats and carefully hold large golden offerings draped with cloths of different colors and patterns. The disciple on the right— one of the Buddha's Supreme Pair of Śrāvaka Disciples (Tib. *mchog zung*), namely Śāriputra, who was among disciples supreme in insight or wisdom)—is depicted in full profile, offering a golden oval-shaped jewel that seems to glow within its frame. In the throne base,

attributions. Granting that Khyentse was creative and able to change his mode, Linrothe still wondered why the artist was here suddenly so different in both small things and large, suggesting to him that in this set someone else was working with a group of designs associated with Khyentse, but putting a different stamp on it. Though I have not seen the original paintings, I still feel that the treatment of details such as minor deities in the foreground is distinctively Khyentse, and if it is a later copy, then it

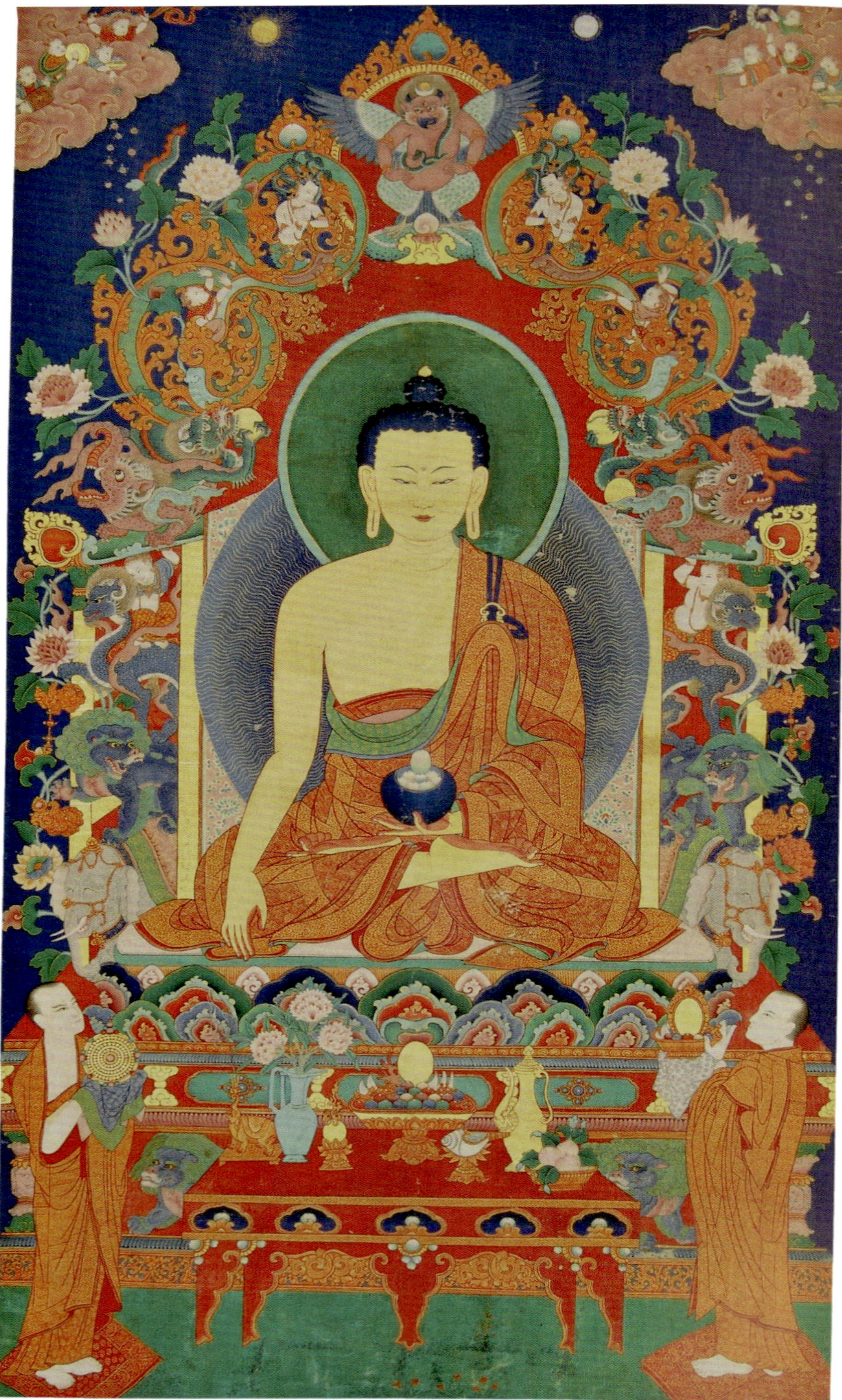

lively blue lions are partly hidden by the table of offerings; both face the same direction yet look at different things.

The careful observer can usually find asymmetrical features in Khyentse Chenmo's depictions of ornate throne backs of central buddhas. Here, the two little boys riding on griffins are both looking in the same direction. Near the Buddha's head nimbus, three golden orbs are held by two dragons, and dragon tails stream near the top, like warning flags, outside the zone above the *makaras*, which are normally reserved for *nāgas*. Dragon heads and tails are strange things to add to a classic backrest, but it was the dragon's orb-like golden jewels that the artist had worked into the offerings held by one chief disciple below. Only Khyentse Chenmo would have attempted such a thing.

Figure 9.22 depicts the arhat Panthaka (Lam bstan) who is explaining the dharma and holding a book. He sits in an extremely detailed landscape that stretches behind him to distant pointed mountain peaks, some snow-covered. In the sky above, a small buddha floats on a cloud toward a divine realm at the top center of the painting. In the foreground to Panthaka's right stands a long-haired layman with bare feet who wears colorful robes and holds a blue flower-filled vase while gazing up at the arhat.

In Figure 9.23, the arhat Gopaka holds a book with both hands. This painting, too, features an extremely detailed landscape, with coniferous trees, fruit-laden deciduous trees, and little flowering bushes at the center of the foreground that are attracting a few butterflies. To the right of the arhat's mat and slippers, a tiger has curled up, resting its head on its paws that it has crossed in front of its body, peacefully and almost lovingly looking up at the arhat. Meanwhile, at the bottom-left corner of the foreground, two tiny deer are gamboling about, despite the presence of the huge predator cat.

Figure 9.24 depicts the Great King Virūpākṣa, who is red in color and holds a stupa. At the bottom right, a snake-hooded *nāga* king has emerged from the water. Near him, a red and a yellow giant sea snake—each wearing a golden necklace, being the rulers of their kind—have raised their heads out of the water. The *nāga* king has placed a tray loaded with precious jewels at the great king's feet.

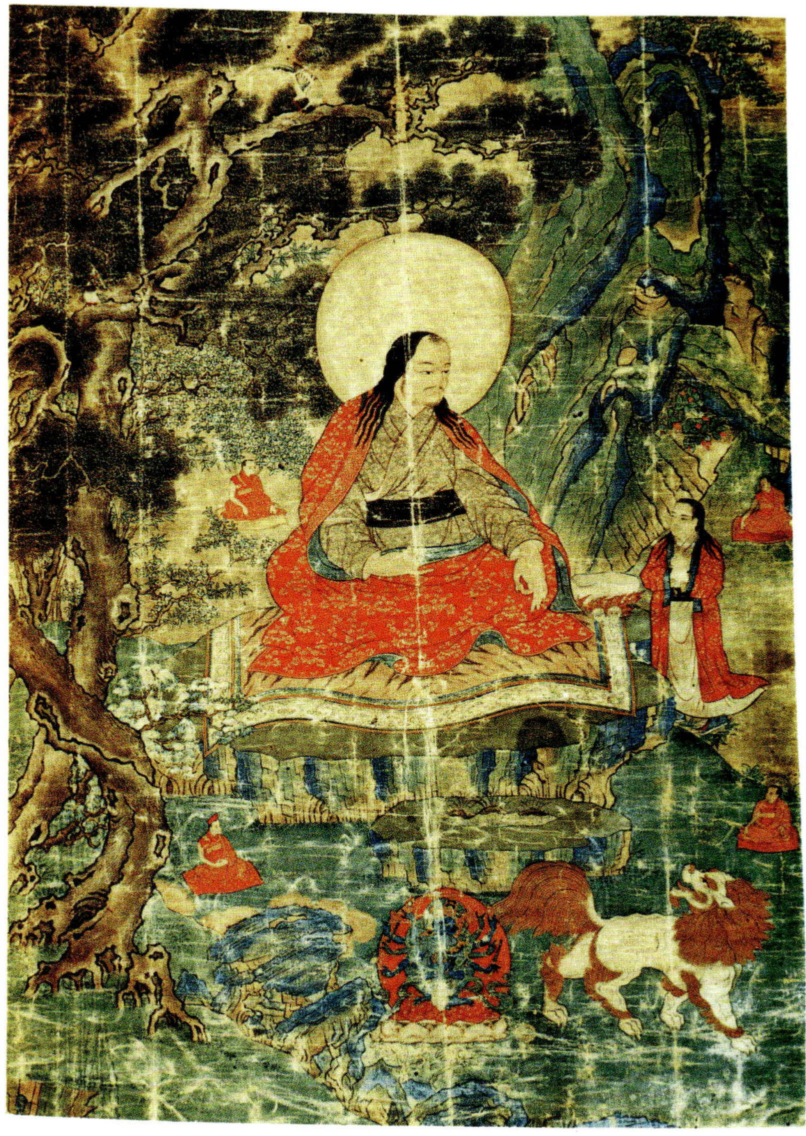

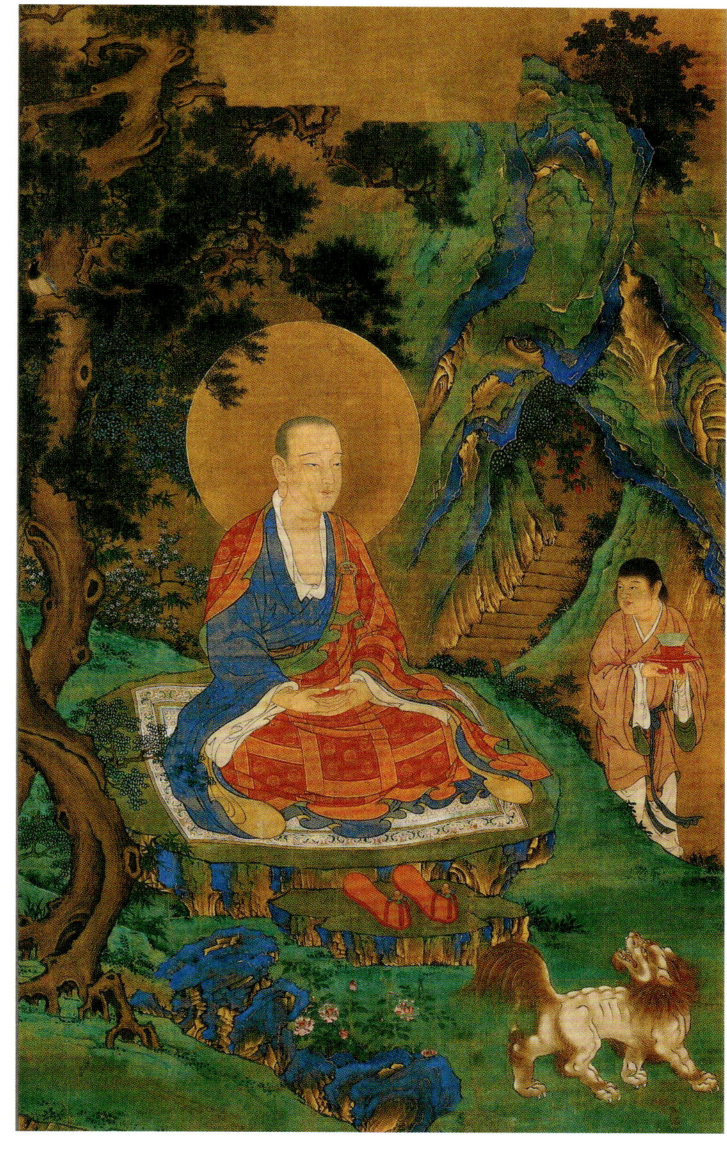

Fig. 9.25
Tantric Lama
distemper on cotton
second half of the fifteenth century
27 ½ x 19 ¾ (70 x 50 cm)
Literature: Burawoy 1976, no. 9; and
Jackson 2009, fig. 5.18

Fig. 9.26
Arhat Ajita
China, Yongle period; distemper on silk
(1402–1424)
30 ¾ x 19 ¾ in (78 x 50 cm)
Collection of Robert Rosenkranz and
Alexandra Monroe
After: Jackson 2009, fig. 5.19;
K. Debreczeny 2012, fig. 3.12.

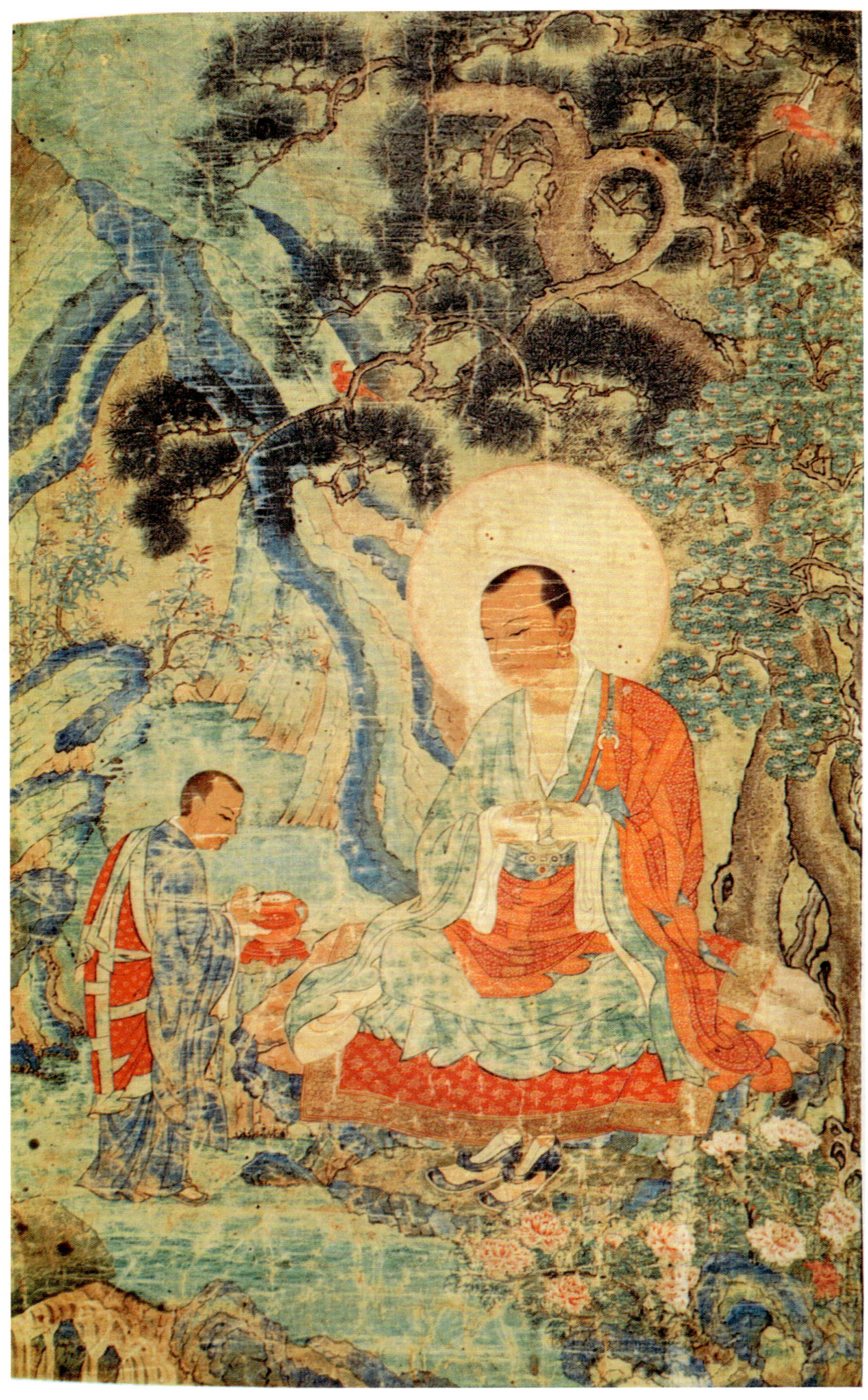

The stunning painting of two arhats in Figure 9.29 has previously been dated to the fourteenth century; considered Sino-Tibetan, it was dated to the Yuan period. But, according to my knowledge, Khyentse Chenmo was the first to paint like this in Tibet. The upper arhat is Panthaka, holding a book on his lap and his right hand in the teaching gesture, and the other is Nāgasena, holding a begging staff. Because of extensive damage to the paint in certain places—most areas of dark green and blue are lost—the painting looks old, though the overall effect is elegant and attractive.

I suggest that it dates to a much more recent period—the second half of the fifteenth century—and that we consider Khyentse Chenmo as the painter of this and its beautiful companion piece (depicting Hashang and Dharmatrāta) in Cleveland. Note the highly naturalistic minor figures, such as the attendant of the upper arhat, crouched and dramatically holding up his hands before a writhing animal on the ground, and the ring-shaped robe fastener worn by the arhat. The depictions of the dragon and the standing attendant by the lower arhat are also superb. I suspect that this arhat set was meant to be in a *si thang* style, but it was made more impressive through a liberal addition of subtly applied gold to the human faces and bodies and to the dragon. As a proof of his technical mastery, the artist even used gold in subtle shading behind the clouds ringing the lower arhat's head, creating a transcendent halo effect.

this painting Sino-Tibetan, from the seventeenth century. Its landscape includes many blue-green crags and a rushing stream to the right. Two birds are carefully depicted; one flies through a valley to its mate that is perched in a tree. The white-turbaned minor figure, kneeling and in profile, is a Khyentse Chenmo trademark (see Figure 3.28, also of Aṅgaja).

Two Modes of Portraiture

Generally speaking, beginning no later than the ninth century, two main ways of portraying arhats existed in China, which continued down to the present and also spread to Tibet. As Rob Linrothe explains:

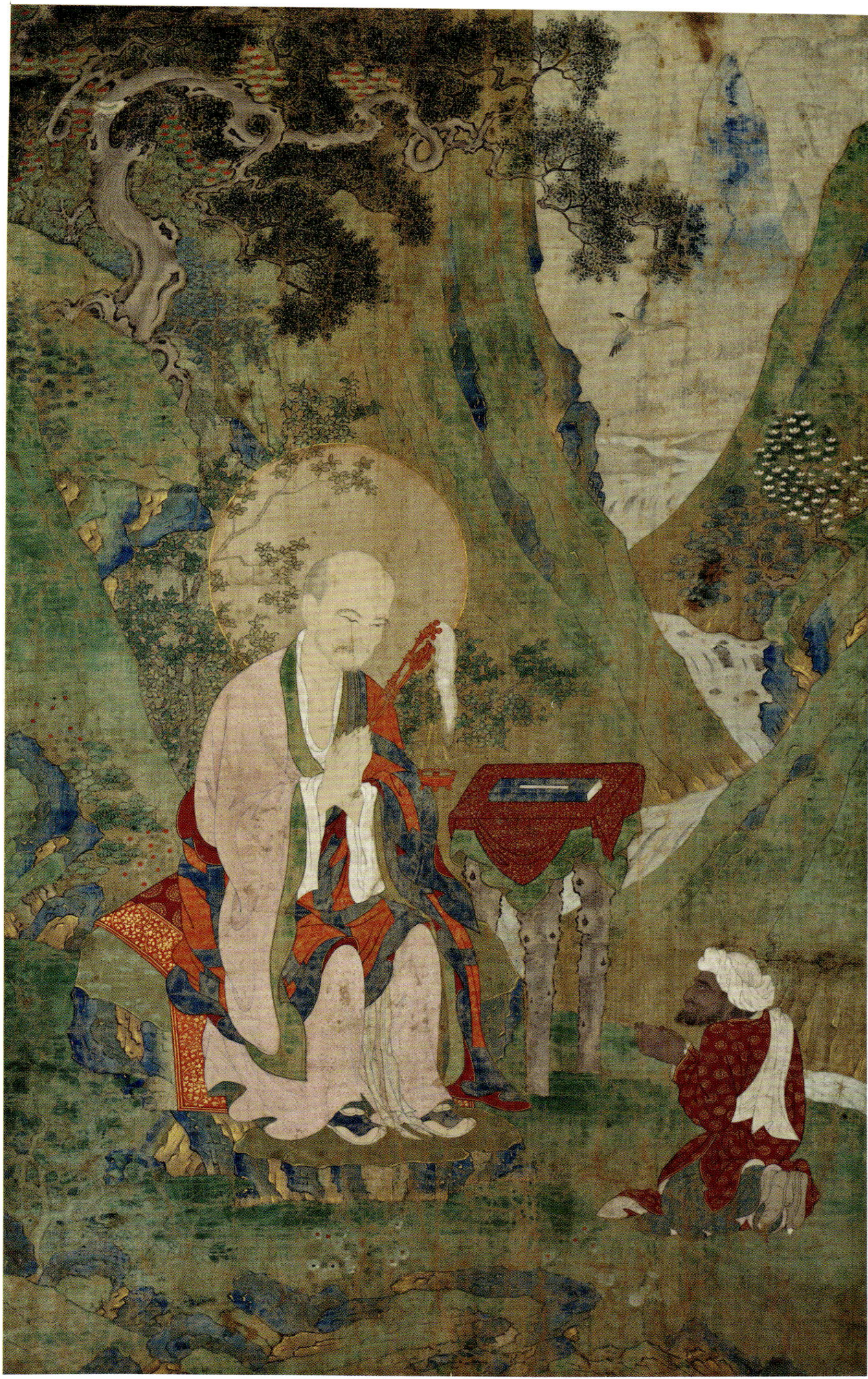

THE ICONOGRAPHY OF THE SIXTEEN ARHATS: MAIN LITURGIES

Three main scriptural or liturgical traditions of sixteen-arhat worship existed in Tibet: the Maitreya prophesy; verses of praise from Śākyaśrībhadra or his translator, Trophu Lotsāwa; and a liturgical tradition from the Kadam tradition.

(1) The Maitreya prophesy

The earliest tradition was based on the Maitreya prophesy (Byams pas lung bstan). Richard Kent explained the origin of the arhat cycle:

> The scriptural basis for the worship of a select group of sixteen "great" lohans in China is the *Da aluohan Nandimiduoluo suo shuo fazhuji* (A Record of the Abiding of the Dharma Spoken by the Great Arhat [Lohan] Nandimitra), a short sūtra that originated sometime between the late third and early sixth centuries CE and was first translated into Chinese in the mid-seventh century. The sūtra's characterizations of these sixteen lohans points both to the iconography used to depict them and to the basis for the enduring popular devotion they inspired in China.
>
> The sūtra is spoken by the dying lohan Nandimitra to console his followers, the monks and nuns who have gathered in the capital of the realm of Prasenajit (ca. 3rd–4th century CE), then ruler of what is now Sri Lanka. In the opening

The first mode emphasizes the Arhats' human nature by giving them an appearance correlated to the dignified, ordinary though idealized monks of China or Tibet. . . . They wear monk's robes traditional to China or Tibet.

If the first mode emphasizes the idealized but natural, the second mode underscores the Arhats' supernatural aspects by giving them a grotesque, sometimes caricatured appearance, exaggerating physiognomic characteristics. Foreign features seem to recall the Indian origins of Arhats, but through a stereotyping East Asian lens.[474]

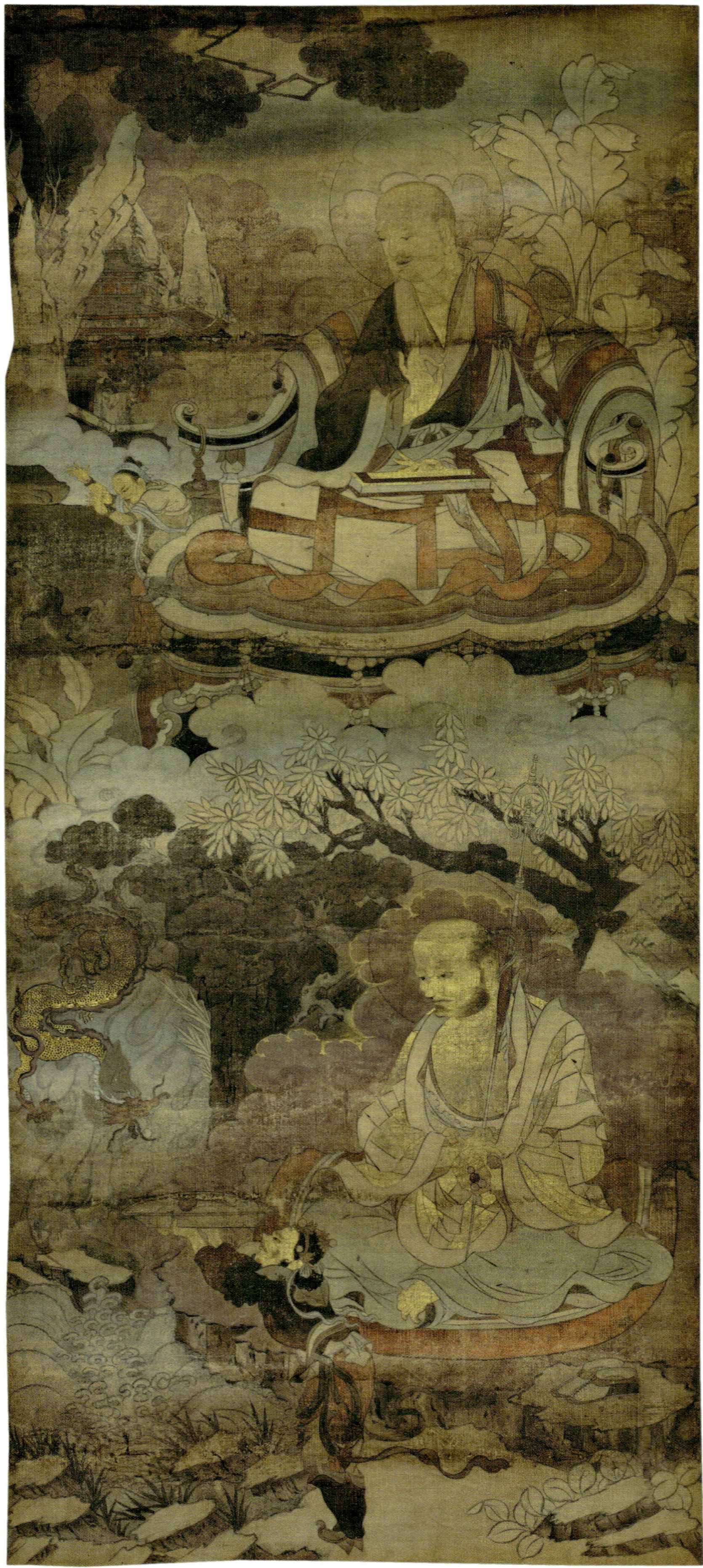

portion of the sermon Nandimitra states that eight hundred years before, when the Buddha was approaching his death or nirvana (release from rebirth) he had entrusted the protection of the Buddhist law to sixteen great lohans. These lohans, through transcendent powers, could extend their lives and thus keep the law secure until the arrival of the Future Buddha Maitreya, at which time they too would be able to enter nirvana. [475]

Kent implied in his introduction that the text had specific iconographic content. Then he clarified how limited that content was: "Nandimitra's pronouncement is chiefly a catalog of the names of the sixteen and their respective mythical abodes." Tucci also discussed this basic text, calling it the "Revelation Concerning the Duration of the Law, revealed by the great Arhat Nandimitra," and referring to its translation's place in the Tibetan canon.[476] In the Peking edition of the Kanjur, it is considered a sūtra.[477] Though rare as a practiced tradition, it was preserved at least as a text in the Drukpa Kagyu. A liturgy of that tradition was published in Hemis, Ladakh (rGod tshang sgrub sde'i tshogs pa), from xylograph blocks, which were carved in 1969.[478]

(2) Verses of praise ascribed to Śākyaśrībhadra or transmitted by Trophu Lotsāwa

The tradition of the Maitreya prophesy of Nandimitra is almost never practiced by Tibetan Buddhists nowadays. Instead, all use in their liturgies a collection of verses in honor of the sixteen arhats that was ascribed to Śākyaśrībhadra. For instance, L. S. Dagyab *Tibetan Religious Art* treated as one of his main sources a traditional liturgy that is known to Tibetan monks of various schools, including Geluk and Sakya. He listed two similar works in his bibliography, which seem to be different titles of the same work. Dagyab Rinpoche also translated the relevant verses for each arhat, treating it as one of his key sources.[479]

Tucci, when comparing the surviving lists of arhat names and locales taken from different versions of the main surviving arhat liturgies, seems strangely ignorant of this work.[480] Nevertheless, he mentioned as a source a work having similar place names, saying it was by a certain D-Tro Lotsāva.[481] Though Tucci did not identify this source further, it was probably a work composed by or transmitted by Trophu Lotsāwa Champe Pal. In the record of teachings received of the Fifth Dalai Lama we find, among a collection of various instructions by or transmitted by him, a prayer to the sixteen arhats.[482] Though some works in this group are clearly attributed to Śākyaśrībhadra, many are not, including this one. Still, I suspect that this might have been the origin of the prayer to the sixteen arhats often attributed to Śākyaśrībhadra.

(3) The Kadam tradition, tracing its roots to Atiśa and transmitted by the abbots of Narthang

The Fifth Dalai Lama lists in his record of teachings received a liturgy of sixteen-arhat worship in the Kadam tradition, which included a detailed liturgy by Chim Namkha Trak.[483] That lineage traced its roots back to Atiśa and was transmitted by such abbots of Narthang as Chim Namkha Trak. Sakya authors of arhat liturgies knew the text of Namkha Trak, saying he was correct to begin the praises with Aṅgaja, but that, in the ordering of the arhats within the mandala, it was correct to begin with Rāhula, as Namkha Trak does. In the Sakya versions and probably in others Hashang is omitted, but a final verse is dedicated to Dharmatrāta. Another Kadampa master, Se Jilphuwa (Chökyi Gyaltshen, 1121–1189), was also famed for his devotion to the sixteen arhats.[484]

Tucci's Main Arhat Set

In *Tibetan Painted Scrolls*, Tucci noticed the existence of two main traditions in Tibet regarding the ordering of the names of the sixteen arhats.[485] The first went back to Nandamitra's prophecy, and the second, handed down by Tibetan authors, he believed went back to the tradition of Atiśa. Furthermore, Tucci concluded that in their liturgies, Tibetans substituted the earlier Indian names with those of the tradition of Atiśa and Chimtön (mChims stön), thanks to the authority of those two authors and the influence of their hymns—of their verses of praise—upon the liturgies of the arhat cycle.[486]

However, Tucci was not aware of the verses of praise attributed to Śākyaśrībhadra as one of the competing sources. Nevertheless, he does note the existence of praises attributed to Trophu Lotsāwa, the Tibetan translator who invited Śākyaśrībhadra to Tibet.[487] The places of arhat residence listed there are the same as in the so-called "Śākyaśrī's prayers to the arhats." Tucci summarized the iconography in chart form, basing himself on a ritual text by an author he called "Jennga Chödrak Gyaltshen," who turns out to be the famous Sakya scholiast Yongdzin Ngawang Chödrak.[488]

The set of sixteen arhats that Tucci illustrates as his plates 156 through 170 is out of order. He wrongly presents the image of plate 159, Kālika, as the first

(pl. 156, Aṅgaja). He similarly presents the image of plate 169 (no. 15, Gopaka) as plate 167, which should be the thirteenth, Panthaka.

According to Tucci, his examples were of the "Kham style" that he bought in Gyantse.[489] But only his three final paintings are probably from Kham: black-and-white plates 171 and 172, and color plate R. The set he presents is actually in a handsome Tsangri style, the predominant Menri style in Gyantse in the seventeenth century. Sometimes the paintings feature interesting parallels to the Khyenri arhats. For Ajita, for example, it shows a very similar *vīṇā*-carrying Indian seer, but his robe is brown instead of the Khyenri white (see Figs. 2.1 and 7.31).

List of the Sixteen Arhats from the Praises Attributed to Śākyaśrībhadra

The sixteen verses of praise traditionally attributed to Śākyaśrībhadra (also known as Khache Paṇchen) are found in most Tibetan liturgies of sixteen-arhat worship. (I did not find this work among the several works ascribed to Śākyaśrībhadra in the Peking Tangyur (Kanjur) canon.) The recent Sakya liturgical compilation that I have compared repeats the praises of the sixteen arhats on p. 21ff and again on p. 82ff.[490] These two Sakya rituals, like all versions of this prayer, include Dharmatrāta as a seventeenth arhat, but they omit Hashang as the eighteenth. Here the wording of the Dharmatrāta prayer differs slightly from that in the Geluk liturgies, but the sense remains the same.

For a list of the sixteen arhats taken from the verses attributed to Śākyaśrībhadra, together with their iconographic attributes, see appendix D-1. For the related source in Tibetan, see appendix D-2.

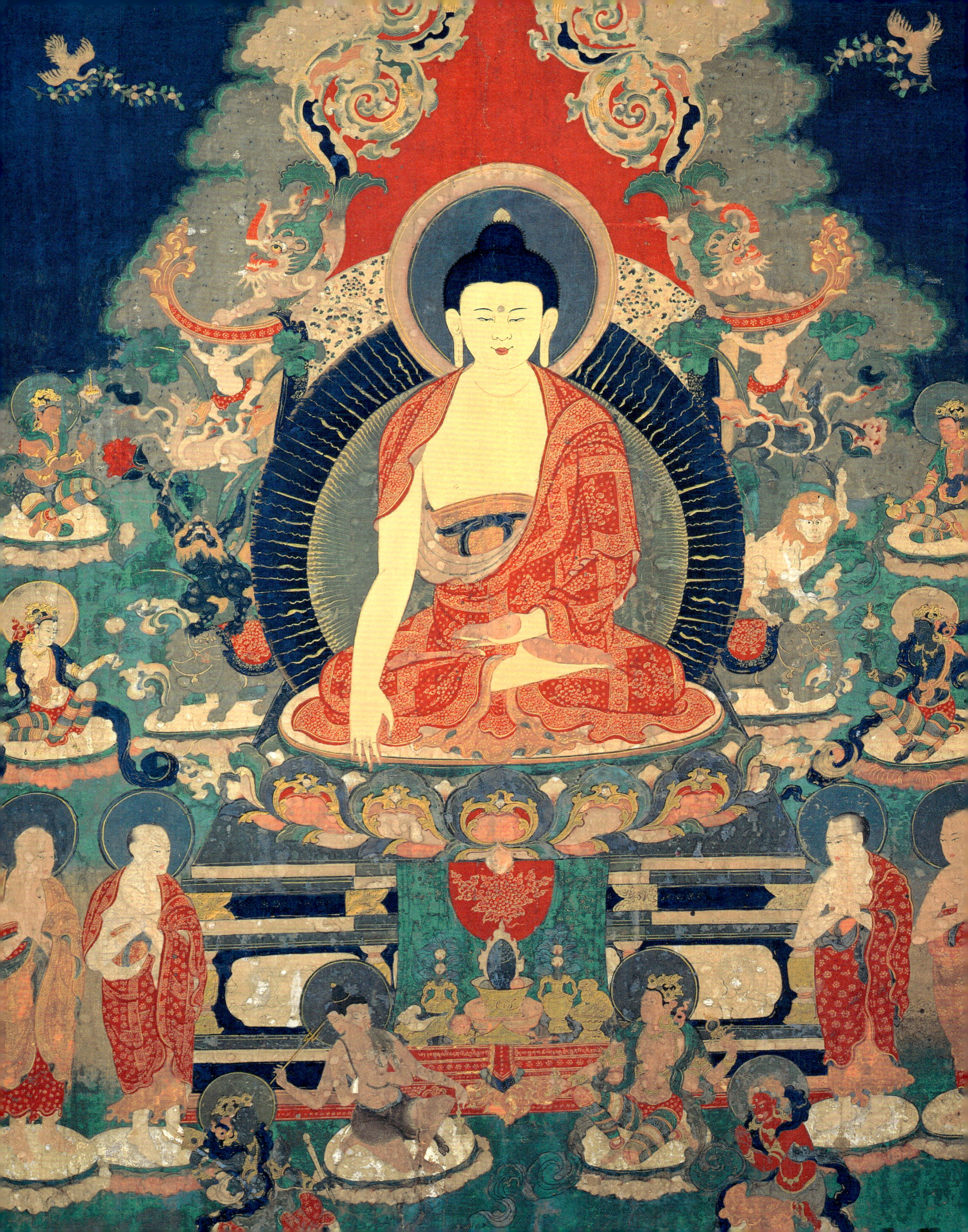

CHAPTER 10

Khyenri-Style Thangka Sets from the Sixteenth Century

THIS CHAPTER presents six thangka sets in the Khyenri style that date to the sixteenth century, after the life of Khyentse Chenmo. They include several excellent sets of single and double arhats, a Drukpa Kagyu lineage, and thangka sets depicting the life of Buddha Śākyamuni. In an earlier publication, I discussed a seventh set of thangkas, depicting the Drigung Kagyu lineage in Phyang, Ladakh.[491]

A DARKLY COLORED ARHAT SET

This is a beautiful and intriguing set of large paintings with dark-blue skies and dark-green landscapes. Marylin Rhie in 1999 said this set was in the Khyenri style. However, it has almost no similarities with the known sets attributed to Khyentse Chenmo, except one arhat whose robes feature the circular robe clasp (Fig. 10.1).

In 2004, Rob Linrothe presented the eighteen available paintings of the original set of twenty-three.[492] The central image, portraying Buddha Śākyamuni, was said to survive in damaged condition in a private collection. I believe that the painter or patron wrongly identified some of the arhats through erroneous labels.

Figure 10.1 is said to be the arhat Cūḍapanthaka. However, according to the iconography in the praises by Śākyaśrībhadra, the fact that he holds a string of jewels indicates he is

Kanakavatsa. Interesting here is a minor figure, a kneeling bearded man wearing a sort of crown, who offers a large ivory tusk to the arhat; he may be a rich trader or traveler. Next to him is his beast of burden, a white lion—not an elephant or camel as normally expected (see Fig. 2.14a). The rendering of the lion suggests that the artist followed a tracing that he could not understand parts of. A mistaken tracing may also explain the porcelain vase being held instead of a *vīṇā* by the standing figure wearing a white turban and robes. (However, *vase*-holding bearded and white-turbaned foreigners do exist in Chinese-inspired arhat paintings.)[493]

In the same set, with dominant dark-green landscapes and dark-blue opaque skies, Figure 10.2 is said to depict the arhat Bakula. In this case, though, the main figure does not hold the mongoose typical of that arhat in Śākyaśrībhadra's tradition; instead, he holds an opened Chinese handscroll on his lap. A crane stands behind him that is solid white, a color that Khyentse did not normally use for cranes. Visiting Bakula and his monk attendant is a bundle-carrying traveler with long black hair and a kind of begging bowl strapped across his torso. Here the painter, working from a tracing, may have mistaken the *vīṇā*, a rare object. I could not find any *vīṇā*-toting standing sadhu in the paintings of the set (besides the possibly mistaken one in Figure 10.1).

Figure 10.3 is said to depict Rahula, but it would be better to identify him as Nāgasena, who holds a monk's staff in

the usual iconography. Earlier, Khyentse Chenmo twice depicted the same composition, with the arhat petting a tiger, as seen in examples from Ladakh and the Musée Guimet (Figs. 9.14 and 9.19).

The arhat in Figure 10.4 must be, according to his normal iconography, Vajrīputra. We have seen the same arhat composition in the Phyang set (Fig. 9.13) but reversed, left to right. This may be the result of painting from a tracing, without an original to check against. The hat of the regal-looking donor to the left is more distinctly Chinese than that in Figure 9.13; the artist may have copied it from another painting.

In sum, this set of paintings is not in a known Khyenri style. Indeed the artist may have been following a distinctively non-Khyenri approach with his thick and dark colors. However, I think it is too soon to exclude it from the corpus of possible sixteenth-century copies of Khyentse Chenmo's paintings. If we ignore the proposed identifications and compare their iconography and details of their surroundings, we see in the major and minor figures and even the animals quite a few familiar features. But some details may have been lost or mistaken due to working from tracings.[494]

A DOUBLE ARHAT SET

This set, which depicts two arhats per painting, survives as four known paintings. It may date to the sixteenth century; the painter remains true to the Chinese style or silk-painting atmosphere inherited from Khyentse. He also

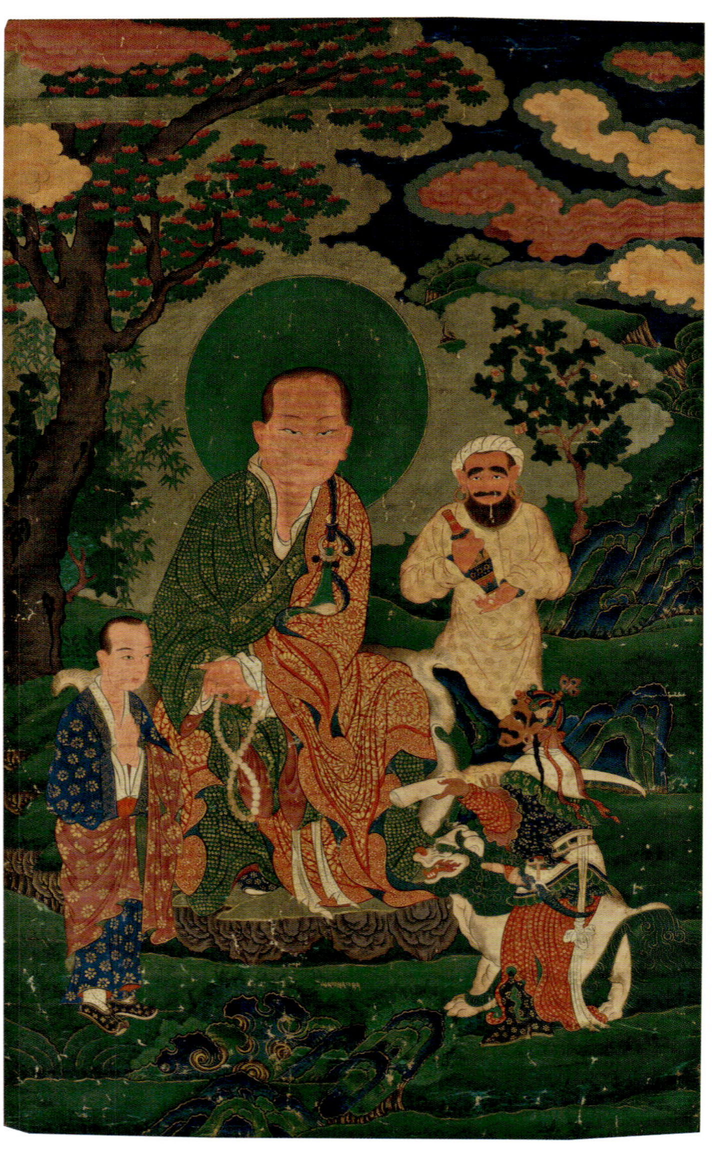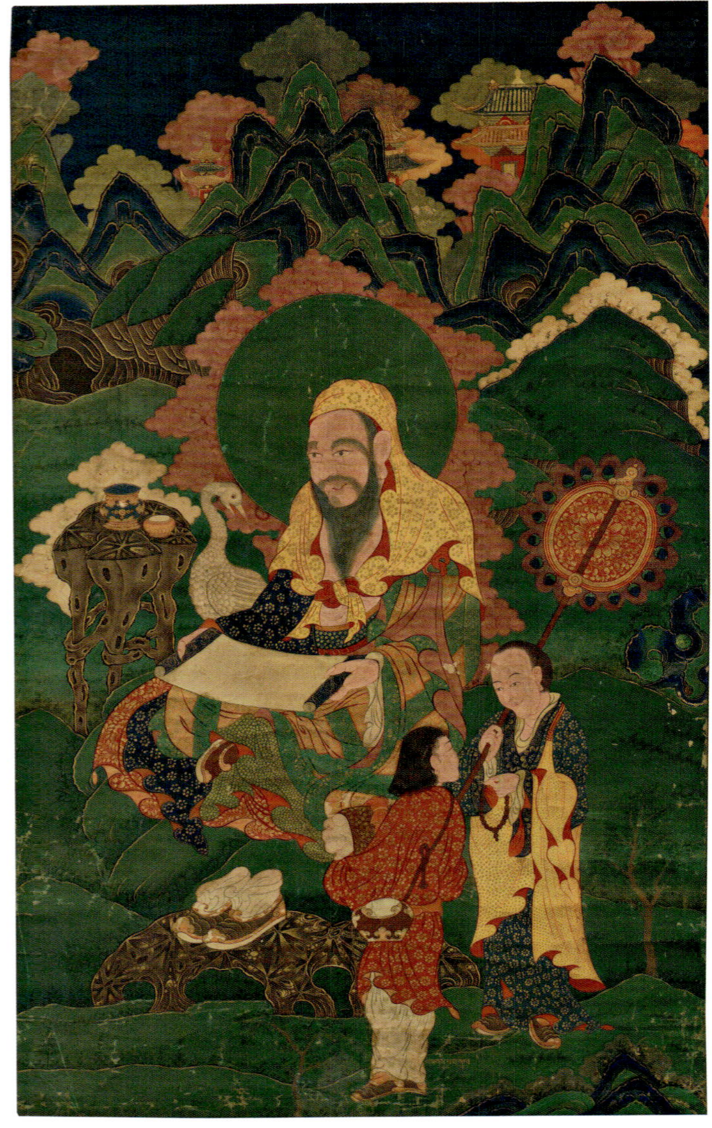

Fig. 10.1
Arhat Kanakavatsa
sixteenth or seventeenth century
38 x 25 in. (96.5 x 63.5 cm)
Collection of Shelley and Donald Rubin
(HAR 165)
Literature: Linrothe 2004, 100, no. 11

Fig. 10.2
Arhat "Bakula"
sixteenth or seventeenth century
27 ½ x 23 ½ in. (95.3 x 59.7 cm)
Collection of Shelley and Donald Rubin
(HAR 166)
Literature: Linrothe 2004, 99, no. 6

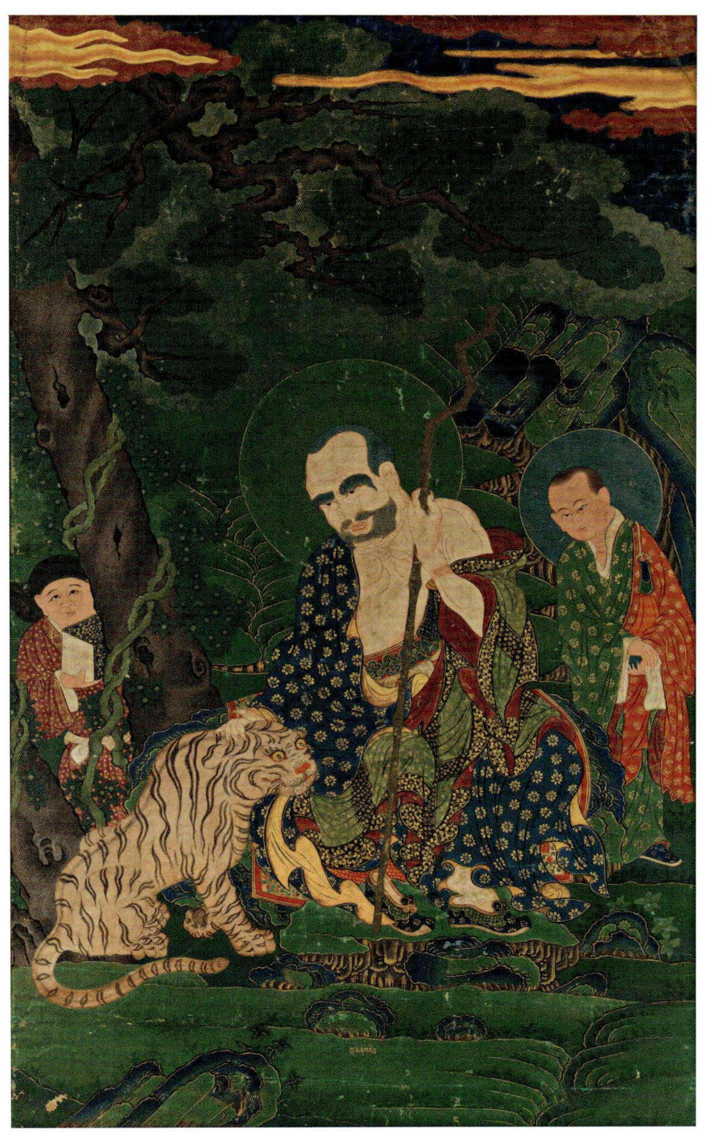 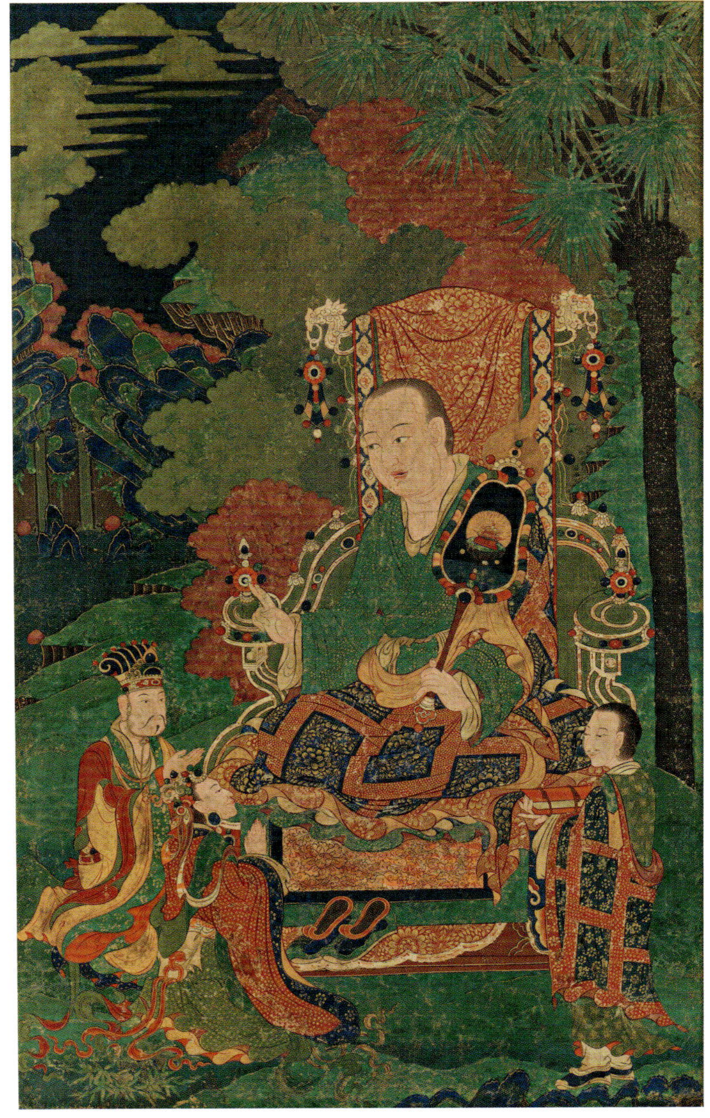

Fig. 10.3
Arhat Nāgasena
ca. sixteenth century
37 ½ x 23 ½ in (95.3 x 59.7 cm)
Collection of Shelley and Donald Rubin
(HAR 245)
Literature: Linrothe 2004, no. 3

Fig. 10.4
Arhat Vajrīputra
ca. sixteenth century
36 ½ x 22 ¾ in. (92.7 x 57.8 cm)
Collection of Shelley and Donald Rubin
(HAR 246)
Literature: Linrothe 2004, 99, no. 10
"arhat"

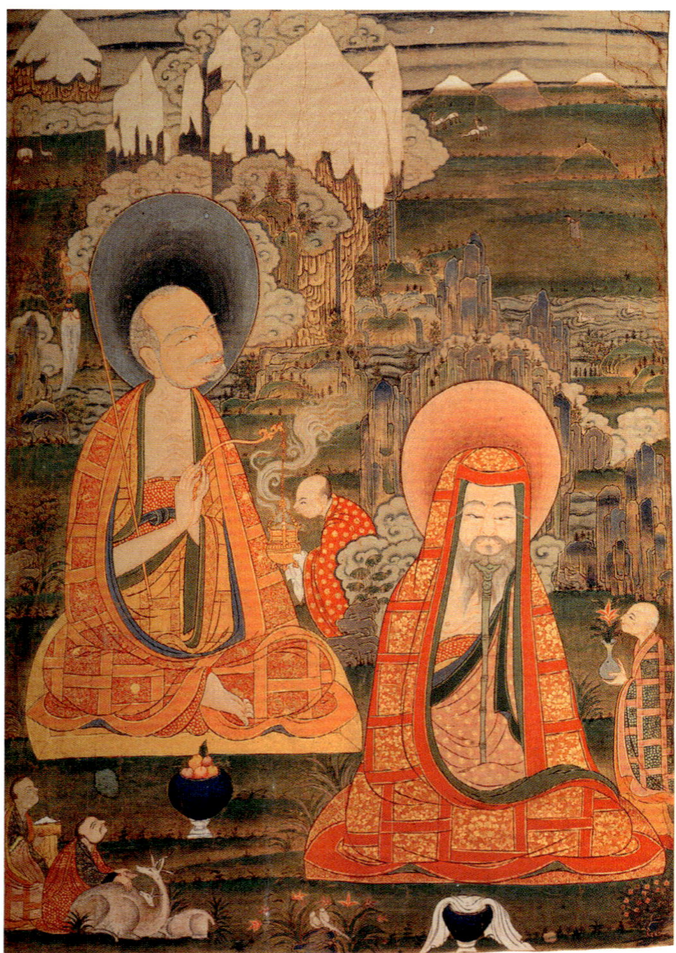

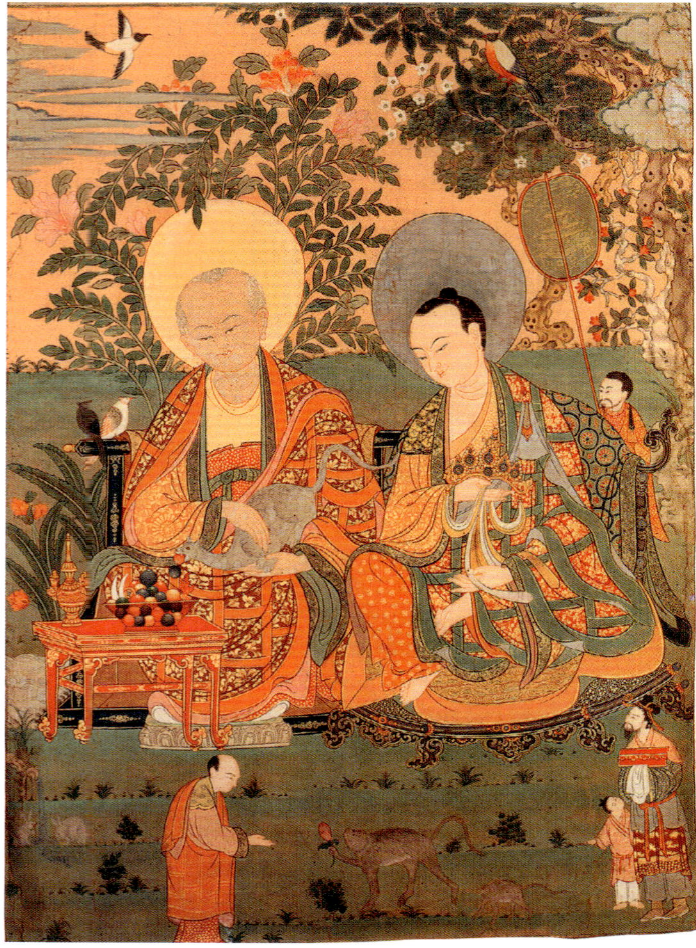

reproduces many wonderful birds, forest animals, and other special features of the landscapes, such as an Indian-style *gaṇḍhola* temple and heavenly palaces floating in the sky. My guess is that this set was copied from an original set by Khyentse Chenmo.

Figure 10.5 depicts the arhats Aṅgaja and Ajita. Behind Aṅgaja looms a beautifully rendered cluster of glacial peaks, one dominating the rest; they refer to Mount Kailash, this arhat's abode. In the distant alpine meadows, to the right, a herdsman tends sheep while a pair of white ducks swims in the nearby lake.

Aṅgaja's attendant holds a smoking censer, and some deer kneel tamely before him, one of them allowing a human to lay his hand upon its back. In the middle foreground, a pair of white birds peacefully roosts in a clump of vegetation. Ajita rests his chin on a meditation prop, and his attendant stands by, holding a vase with a flower in it.

Figure 10.6 depicts the arhats Bakula and Rahula. As usual, Bakula holds a jewel-vomiting mongoose, and Rahula holds a royal crown. Behind Rahula stands a mustached attendant, with a large Chinese fan. The landscape is teeming with birds and wildlife. In the foreground a monkey, followed by its tiny offspring, approaches an attendant to hand him a fruit while to the right a pair of rabbits calmly sits. Birds fly in the sky or perch on a tree branch; one white and one black bird are so fearless that they roost on one corner of Bakula's wooden throne back.

Figure 10.7 depicts the arhats Cūḍapanthaka and Piṇḍola Bharadvāja. Here Cūḍapanthaka sits in meditation, with his attendant approaching from the left with a sacred book. He is seated in the hollow of a large tree. Several birds are drawn to him, including three that perch on the branches of the tree and three large peacocks, two of which strut nearby on the ground, while a third has jumped up to perch on the side of the tree next to the arhat. Piṇḍola Bharadvāja holds a volume of scripture and a begging bowl. Behind him a wonderfully naturalistic landscape includes a large Buddhist *gandhola* shrine and

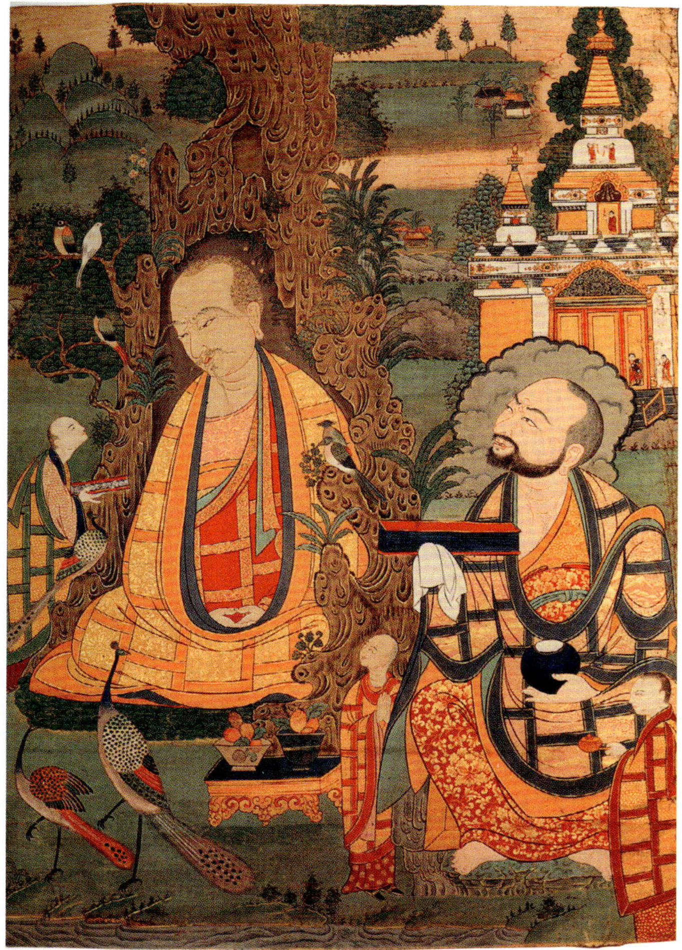

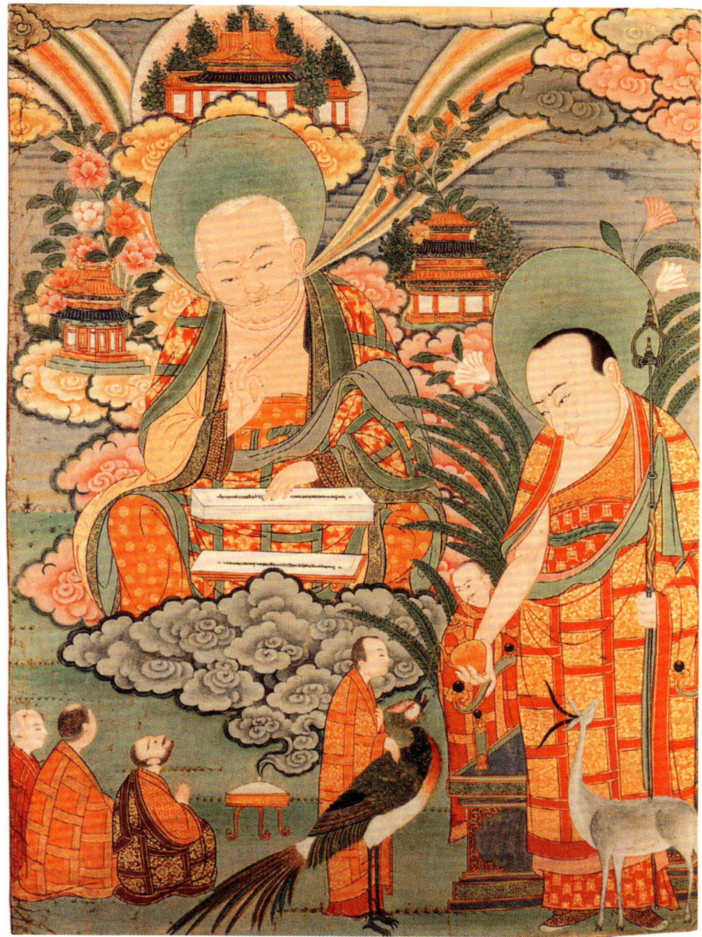

village houses and banana trees in the distance, as they exist in the subtropical Himalayan foothills.

The arhats Panthaka and Nāgasena are depicted in Figure 10.8. Panthaka is shown in the heavens—floating on clouds and with several divine mansions behind him. His mouth emits bands of mystical rainbows. Meanwhile Nāgasena stands on the ground, holding a begging staff and a flask. Before him a large phoenix has approached, so tame that an attendant can put his hand on its back. To the bird's right, a white goat with splayed horns waits peacefully, gazing up at Nāgasena. The artist has made a painting as factually accurate and finely detailed as one by Khyentse: the manuscript of Panthaka is written in Indian Vartula script, and the inner robes of Nāgasena feature an auspicious Chinese character for longevity (*shou*) woven into the fabric.

A Double Arhat Set in Boston

Another set in the Museum of Fine Arts, Boston, consists of eleven paintings, with two arhats depicted per thangka; I will discuss the seven better-preserved ones. Judging from the black-and-white photos, I consider them to be later copies of a Khyentse Chenmo set, possibly dating to the sixteenth or seventeenth century. The order of the set is:

1. Buddha Śākyamuni, the central painting (acc. no. 59.286)
2. Aṅgaja and Vanavāsin (acc. no. 59.276)
3. Ajita and Cūḍapanthaka (acc. no. 59.277)
4. Vajrīputra and Kanakavatsa (acc. no. 59.279)
5. Bhadra and Kanaka-Bharadvāja (acc. no. 59.282)
6. Bakula and Kālika (acc. no. 59.283)
7. Rāhula and Piṇḍola (acc. no. 59.284)
8. Panthaka and Gopaka (acc. no. 59.278)
9. Nāgasena and Abheda (acc. no. 59.280)
10. Dharmatrāta, Virūpākṣa (sPyan mi bzang), and Vaiśravaṇa (rNam thos sras) (acc. no. 59.281)

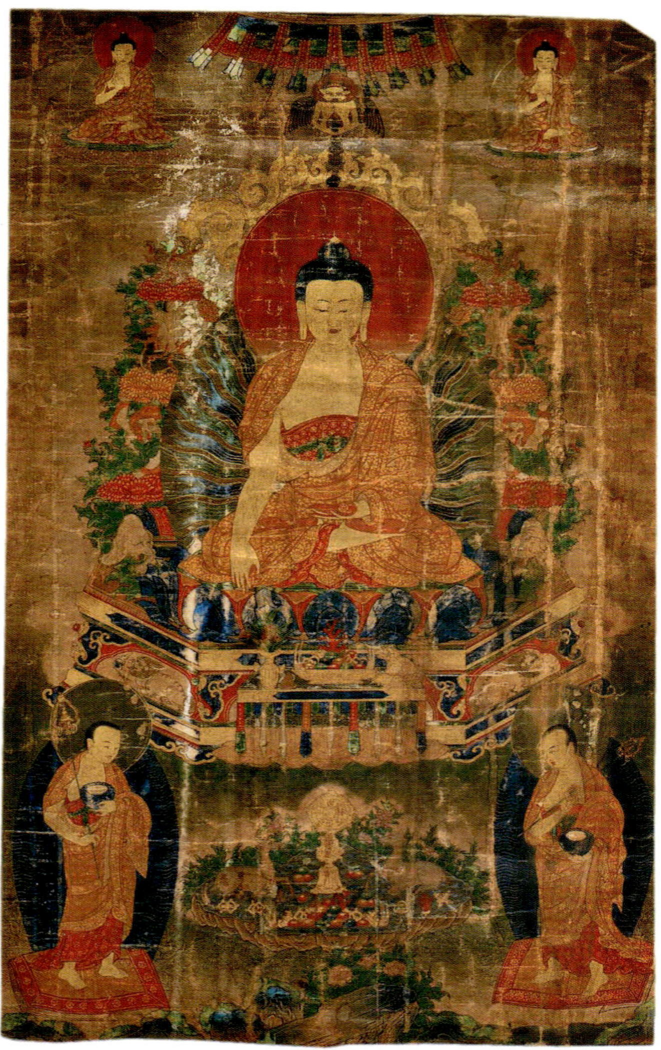

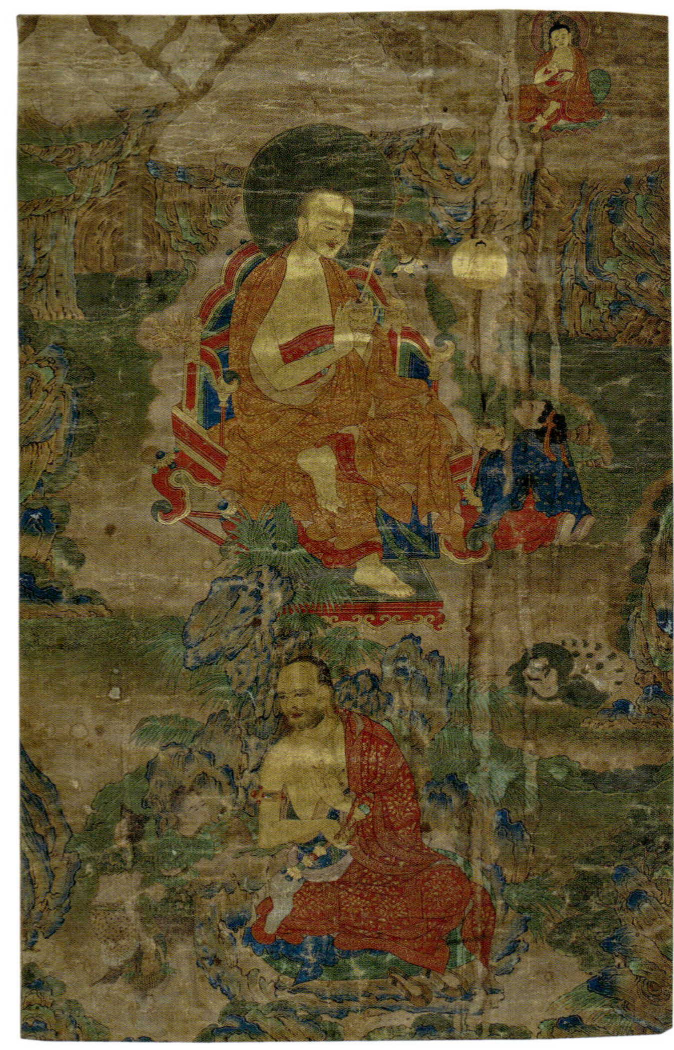

FIG. 10.9
Buddha Śākyamuni
ca. sixteenth or seventeenth century
26 ¾ x 17 in. (68 x 43 cm)
Museum of Fine Arts, Boston (acc. no.
59.286) Gift by the Asiatic Curator's fund
in 1959
Literature: Toganoo 1986, no. III 6–6

11. Hashang, Dhṛtarāṣtra (Yul 'khor srung), and Virūḍhaka ('Phags skyes po) (acc. no. 59.285)

Buddha Śākyamuni is the central figure of the set (Fig. 10.9). Before him, his two greatest monk disciples are carefully depicted holding begging bowls and staffs with different hand positions. In the foreground, a pair of antelopes kneels, each with a single foreleg raised, to the right and left of a golden wheel

of dharma (*dharmacakra*) on a stand. On the backrest, mythical animals are supported and separated by flowers of alternating red and orange, with frilly gold-edged petals.

The second painting in the set, Figure 10.10 depicts the arhats Aṅgaja and Vanavāsin. To the right of Aṅgaja kneels a long-haired, foreign-looking man depicted in profile, holding a vase from which issues a cloud with a buddha. (A fish or some other aquatic creature is nearby on the ground.) Vanavāsin's name means "forest dweller"; he is accompanied by a young man wearing clothing made of leaves and offering fruit.

Figure 10.11, the third painting of this set, depicts the arhats Ajita and Cūḍapanthaka. Here, Ajita is served by a young attendant holding a vase before him; Ajita's usual companion, a

FIG. 10.10
Arhats Aṅgaja and Vanavāsin
ca. sixteenth or seventeenth century
26 ⅝ x 17 in. (67.6 x 43 cm)
Museum of Fine Arts, Boston (acc. no.
59.276) Gift by the Asiatic Curator's fund
in 1959
Literature: Toganoo 1986, no. III 6–8

vīṇā-toting *rishi*, appears with Panthaka in this set (Fig. 10.13). In the foreground before Cūḍapanthaka, a monk kneels humbly.

Figure 10.12 depicts the arhats Rāhula and Piṇḍola as the seventh painting of this set. Rāhula is not served by any human attendant, but below him is an ox or water-buffalo in the water nearby. Here Piṇḍola is attended by a bearded layman wearing a white turban, dancing and clapping his hands.

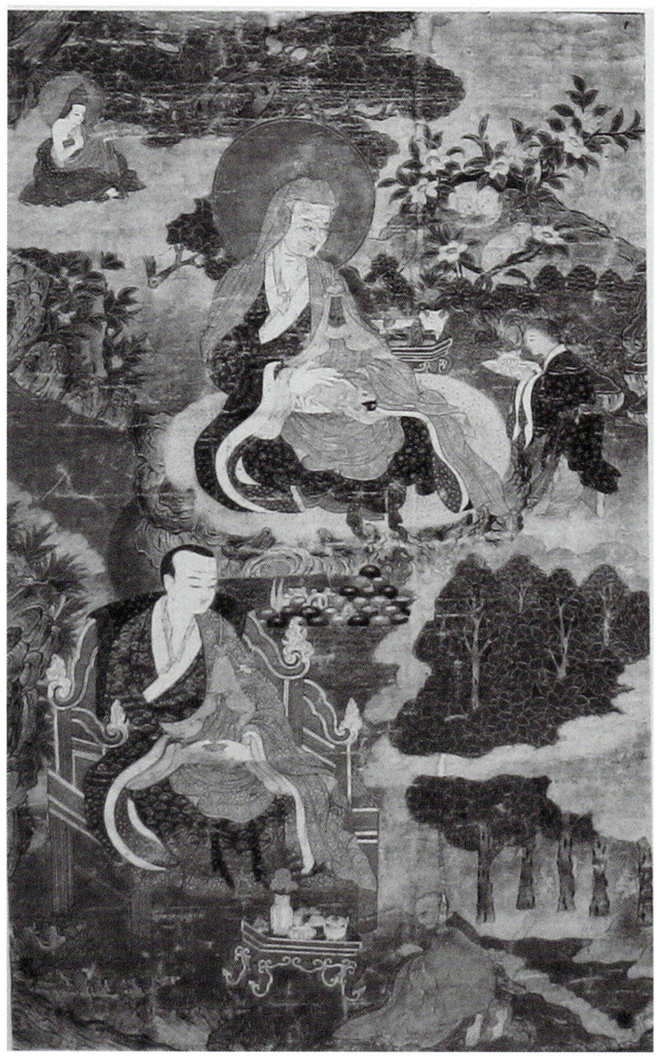

Depicting the arhats Panthaka and Gopaka, Figure 10.13 is the eighth painting of this set. Panthaka is accompanied by a standing *rishi* who holds a *vīṇā* before him with both hands. Here, Gopaka is writing with ink brush or pen on small sheets of paper, and his attendant stands very near, observing with hands joined.

Figure 10.14 depicts the arhats Nāgasena and Abheda in the ninth painting of the set. Nāgasena holds a vase that emits a cloud with a buddha image. He is attended by a water demon, standing to the left and holding a tray loaded with food or jewels; something emits golden tendrils of steam. To the right are two resting deer, the doe with her head on the ground.

Here, Abheda is attended by a standing, long-haired layman who holds a vase with flowers. A deer sits nearby with a flowering sprig in its mouth.

Figure 10.15, the tenth painting of the set, depicts three main figures: the lay follower Dharmatrāta with the great kings Virūpākṣa (sPyan mi bzang) and Vaiśravaṇa (rNam thos sras). To the left of Dharmatrāta, a striped tiger lays curled on the ground, staring at him with wide-open eyes. In the lower left, a *nāga* king and a demon hold large trays of jewels for the two great kings.

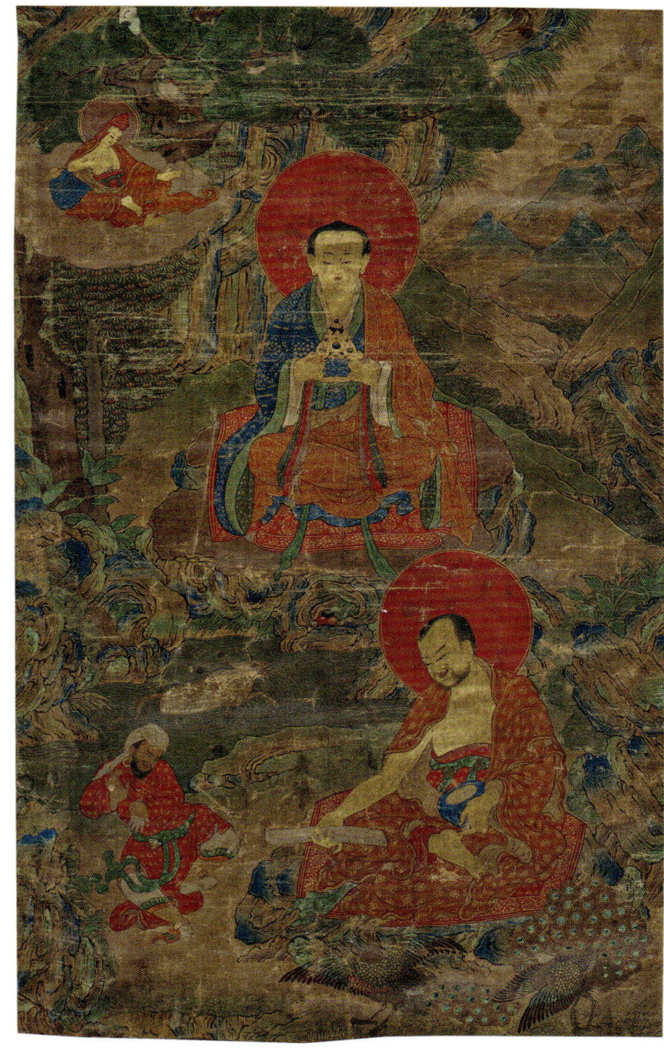

The eleventh thangka of the set, not illustrated here, also depicts three main figures. When the central buddha painting is placed in the middle of the set, the remaining paintings form an even number of symmetrical flanking thangkas.

A Quintuple Arhat Set

Figure 10.16 is a finely detailed thangka from another set, one that depicts five arhats per painting. At the center

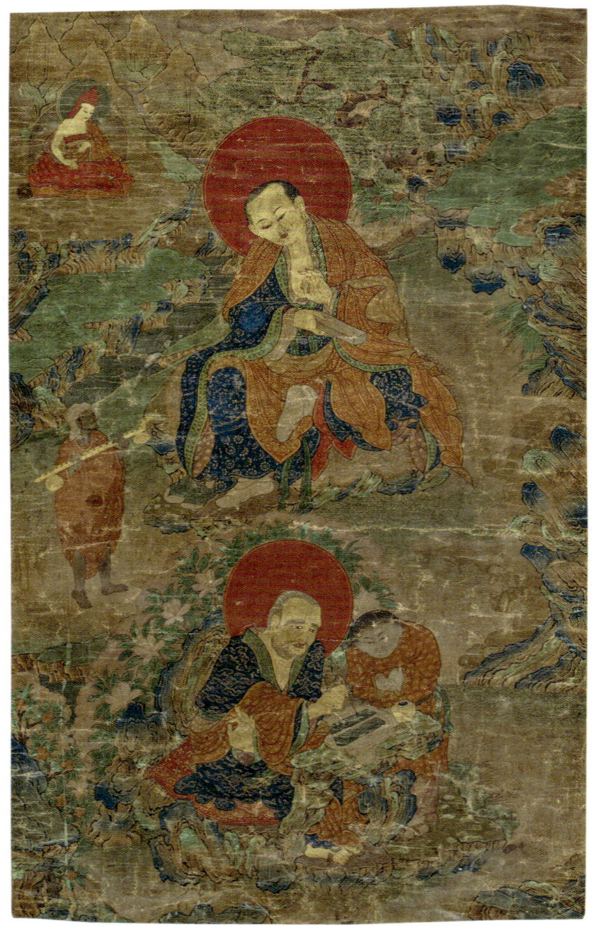

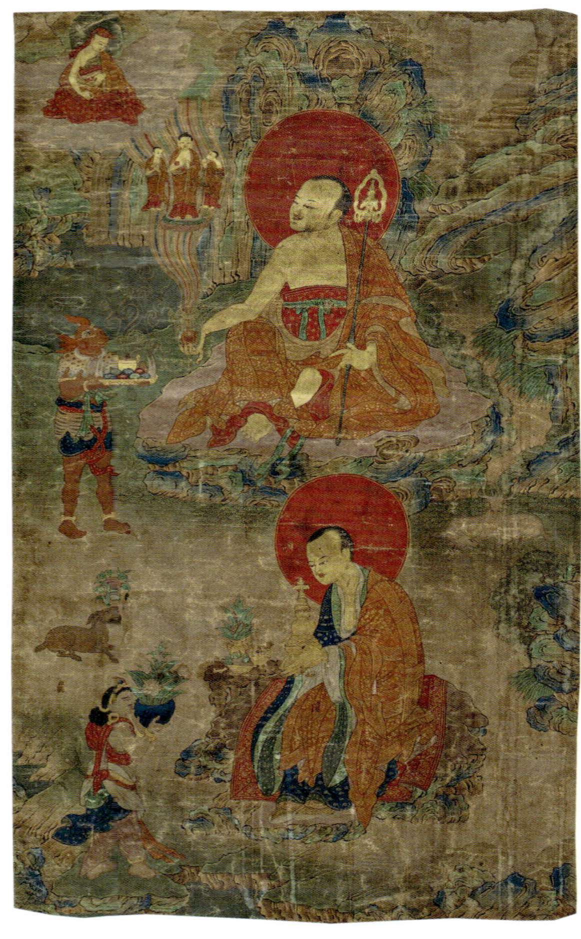

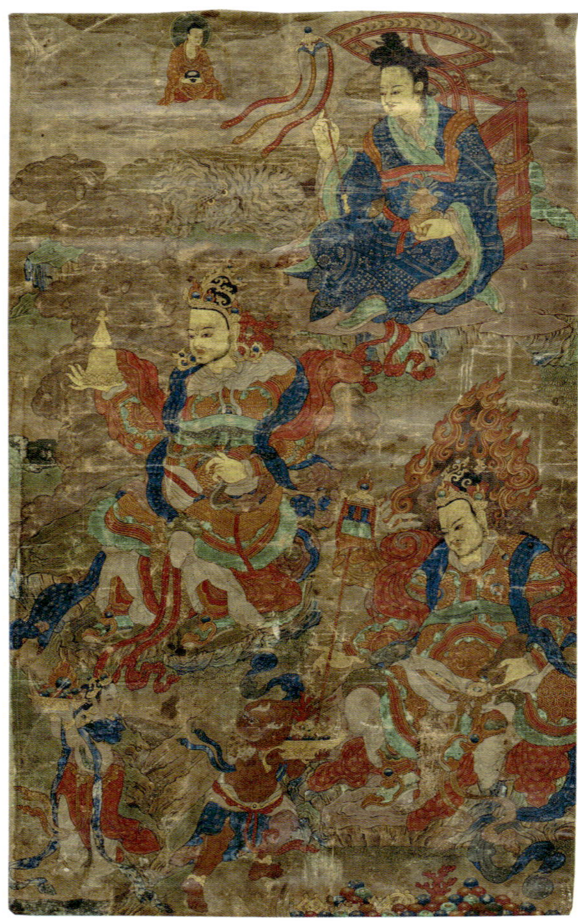

Fig. 10.13
Arhats Panthaka and Gopaka
ca. sixteenth or seventeenth century
26 ⅝ x 17 in. (67.7 x 43 cm)
Museum of Fine Arts, Boston (acc. no.
59.278) Gift by the Asiatic Curator's fund
in 1959
Literature: Toganoo 1986, no. III 6–10

Fig. 10.14
Arhats Nāgasena and Abheda
ca. sixteenth or seventeenth century
26 ⅝ x 17 in. (67.7 x 43 cm)
Museum of Fine Arts, Boston (acc. no.
59.280) Gift by the Asiatic Curator's fund
in 1959
Literature: Toganoo 1986, no. III 6–12

Fig. 10.15
The lay follower Dharmatrāta, and great
kings Virūpākṣa and Vaiśravaṇa
ca. sixteenth or seventeenth century
26 ¾ x 17 in. (68 x 43.2 cm)
Museum of Fine Arts, Boston (acc. no.
59.281) Gift by the Asiatic Curator's fund
in 1959
Literature: Toganoo 1986, no. III 6–13

it depicts the arhat Ajita, with hands
folded in meditation, who is accompanied by the *vīṇā*-toting, white-robed,
and red-turbaned *rishi* standing at the
bottom of the painting. At the top right
is the arhat Kālika, holding earrings to
his chest. To the left, he is accompanied
by a white-turbaned, kneeling, bearded
foreigner shown in profile. At the upper
left sits Vanavāsin, holding a fly whisk
in his left hand and accompanied,
below, by a dancing, bearded foreigner
with a white turban. At the bottom left
is Vajrīputra, holding a fly whisk over
his right shoulder; he is accompanied
by an attendant who serves him a cup of
tea. At the bottom right is Bhadra, who
is accompanied, above, by a man with
a sea-creature head covering and a pot
from which a dragon in a pink cloud
emerges. This painting and Figure 9.8,
depicting Ajita as a single arhat, are
related iconographically and stylistically
but were not created by the same artist.
I estimate that Figure 10.16 was painted
by an adherent of the Khyenri style,
about a century or two after Khyentse
Chenmo's time.

A Set Depicting Drukpa Kagyu Lineage Masters

One of the sets that I provisionally
identified as Khyenri depicts a Drukpa
Kagyu lineage.[495] It first became known
thanks to a 1977 publication of Vajradhara and two prominent lineal lamas,
Gampopa and Milarepa.[496] I published
preliminary notes on the set in 2008,
describing it as a sixteenth-century series
of Drukpa Kagyu lineage masters.[497]
Omitting only number 11, which I had
not yet seen, I reported that this set may
provide crucial evidence about the iconography of both Ling Repa (Gling Ras
pa) and the complete Ralung Drukpa
lineage down to the time of Drukchen
Pema Karpo ('Brug chen Padma dkar
po, d. 1592), noting that the set has for
many years not been properly identified.

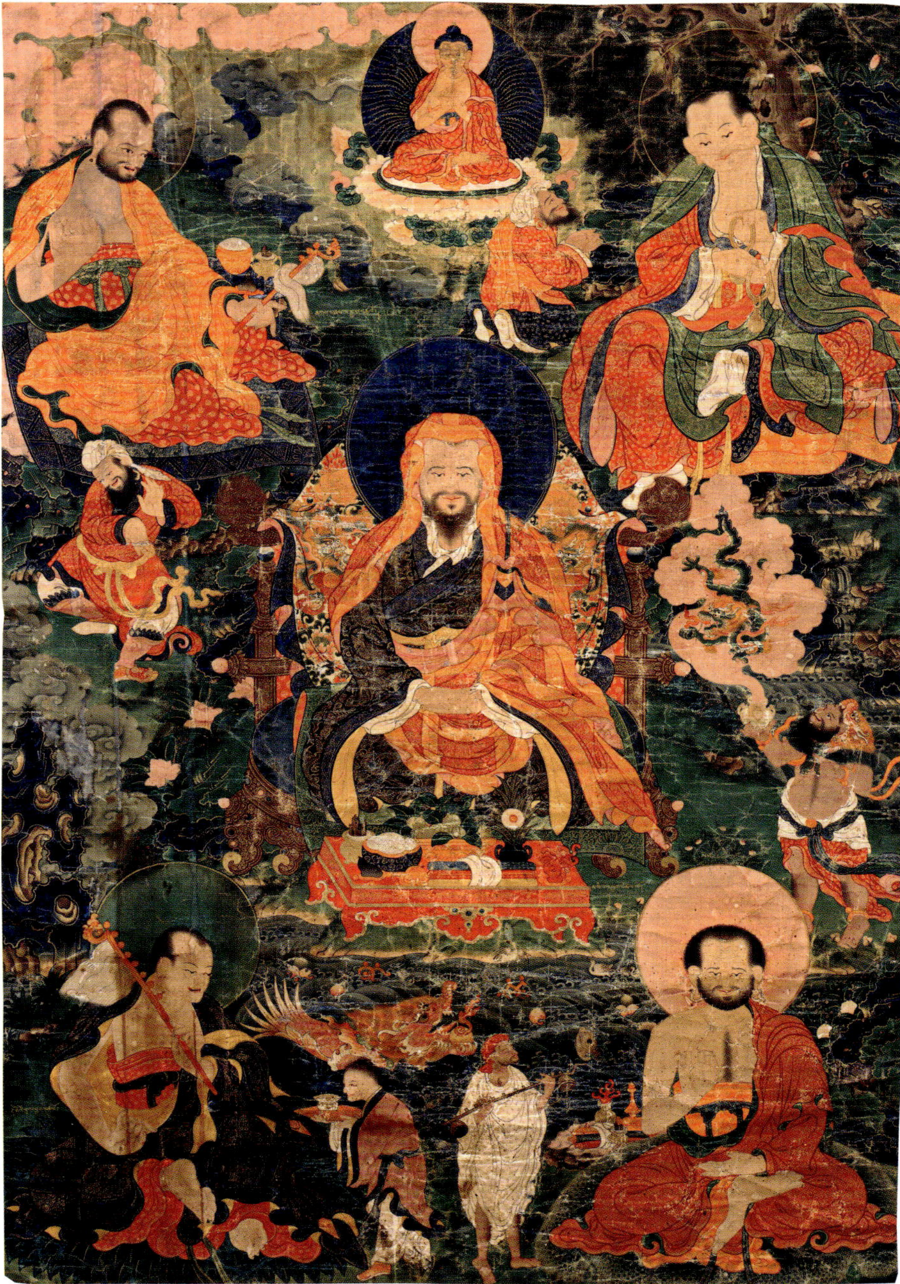

This series was originally mistaken for abbots of the Taklung Kagyu,
a Dakpo Kagyu branch with a seat in
northern Ü province. The distinctive
portrait of Ling Repa, at the Los Angeles
County Museum of Art, belongs to this
set as its eighth thangka; about eleven
thangkas in two private collections also
belong to this set. The Zimmerman collection contains ten in all (according to
Rhie and Thurman 1991) and was the
original source for single paintings elsewhere. This set exemplifies the need to
treat scattered lineage paintings from the

Fig. 10.16
Five Arhats (center: Ajita; top right: Kālika;
top left: Vanavāsin; bottom left: Vajrīputra;
bottom right: Bhadra)
sixteenth or seventeenth century
29 x 20 ½ in. (73.7 x 52.1 cm)
Rubin Museum of Art
F1998.10.3 (HAR 640)

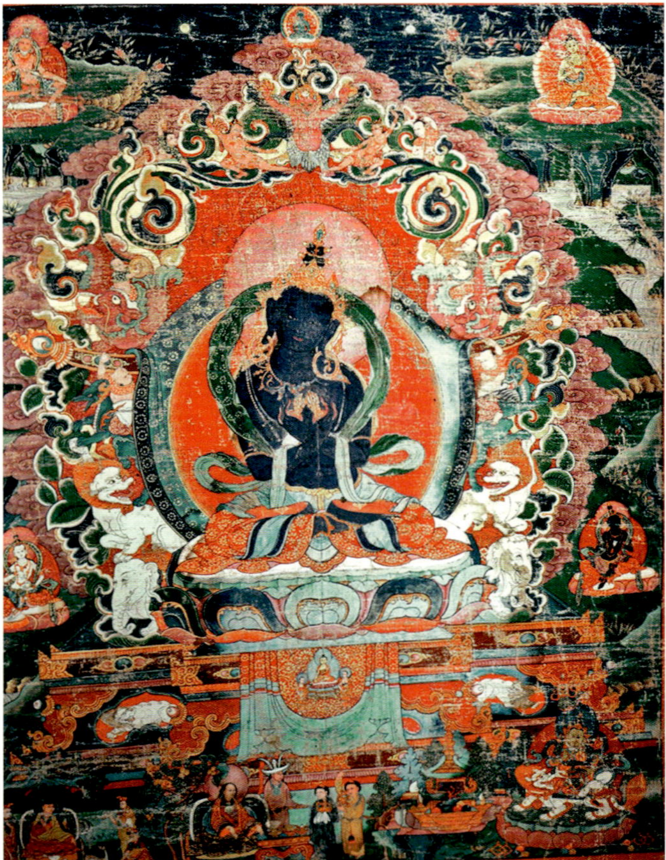

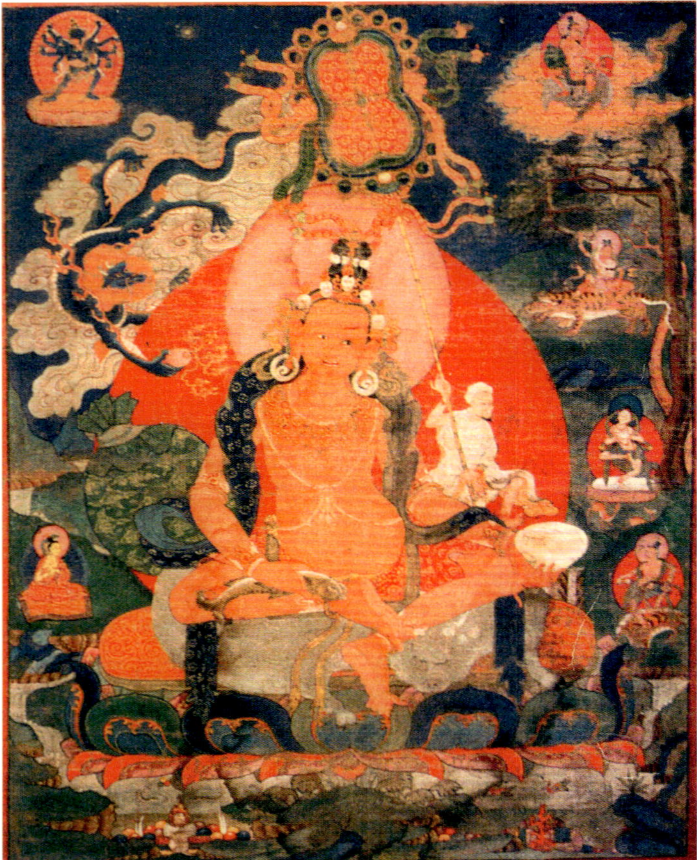

FIG. 10.17
Vajradhara
mid- or late sixteenth century
23 ¼ x 20 in. (59 x 51 cm)
Zimmerman Family Collection
Literature: Béguin 1977, no. 275; and Heller 2012, no. I

FIG. 10.18
Tilopa
mid- or late sixteenth century
23 ¼ x 20 in. (59 x 51 cm)
Zimmerman Family Collection
Literature: Heller 2012, no. II

same set together, if they can be found, and not individually.

The lineage portrayed by the thangka set begins:

1. Vajradhara (rDo rje 'chang) (Fig. 10.17)
2. Tilopa (Fig. 10.18)
3. Nāropa (Fig. 10.19)
4. Marpa Lotsāwa (1012–1096) (Fig. 10.20)
5. Milarepa (Fig. 10.21)
6. Gampopa (Dwags po Lha rje bSod nams rin chen, 1079–1153) (Fig. 10.22)
7. Phagmotrupa (Phag mo gru pa rDo rje rgyal po, 1110–1170)

For notes about subsequent paintings in this set (not illustrated in this catalog), namely, thangkas number 7 through 14, see appendix G.

After my 2008 article, I was told that there was a fourteenth painting in the set; it would be the seventh to the right and would portray the fourteenth lineal master of the Drukpa Kagyu. If the third Drukchen Chökyi Trakpa is the last master of the series, then this is a fairly reliable indication that the entire set dated to the mid- or late sixteenth century, the time of Pema Karpo. There is no evidence that the set dated to the eighteenth or nineteenth centuries, as previously conjectured by Béguin and Lauf. I saw the set only once, examining only four or five of the later paintings. I then read the inscriptions of numbers 10, 12, and 13, which were decisive for dating the set.

Regarding the provenance of the entire set, an important Drukpa Kagyu center such as Ralung, in the upper Nyang valley of central Tsang province, would be a better guess than Phenyül in northern Ü province, which Lauf suggested in 1976. Nevertheless, the Ralung-based Drukpa Kagyu was widely spread also in the southern borderlands of Ü during the period of Pema Karpo and his disciples. Perhaps a careful investigation of the whole set will one day yield more reliable clues about the set's patrons and provenance.

There is also no evidence that the set or its patrons were connected with Minyak (Mi nyag) in the far eastern borderlands of Khams, as also previously conjectured, based on the portrayal of costumes. The set seems to be a distinctive, atypical Khyenri style of the

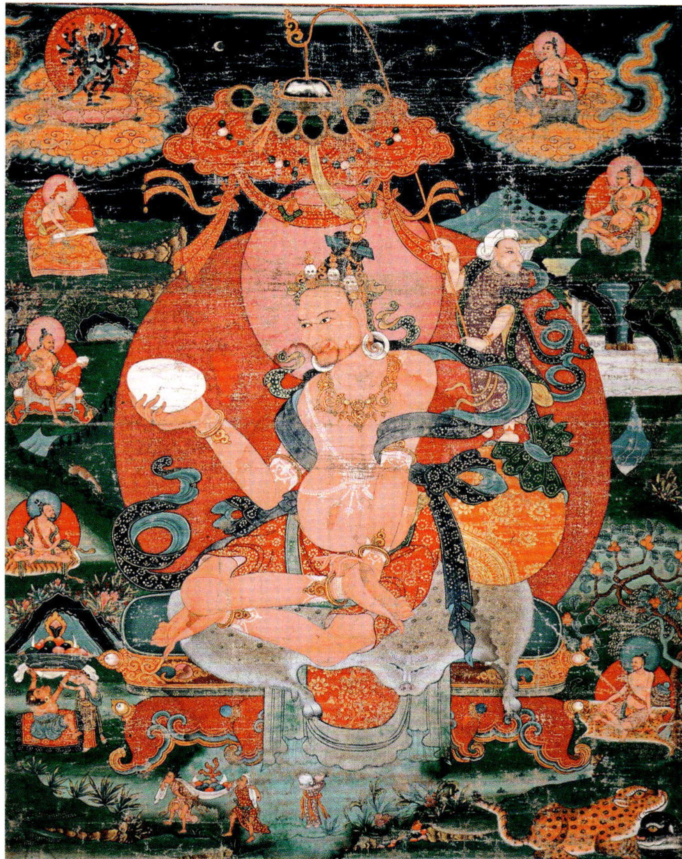

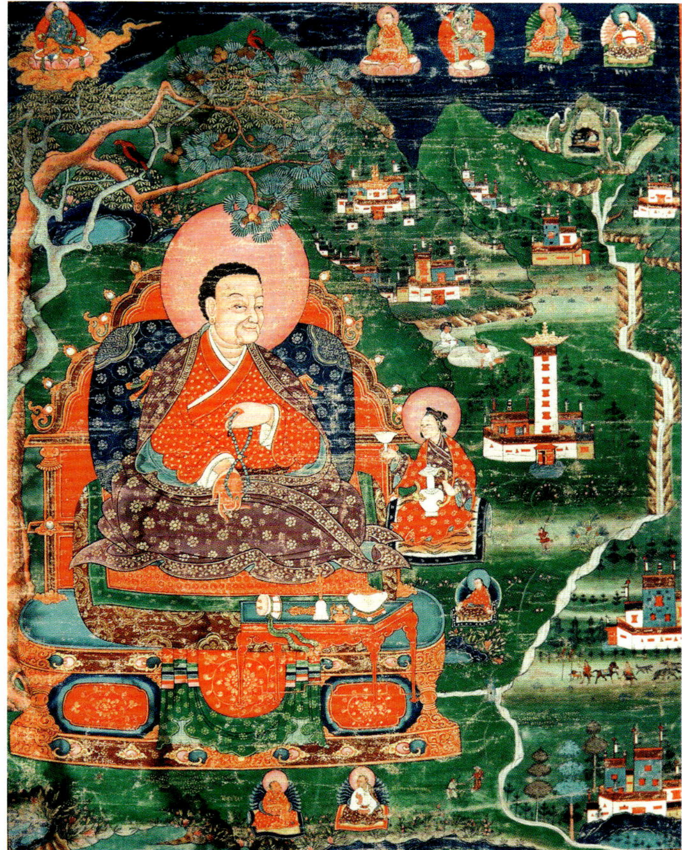

mid- or late sixteenth century. I have reconstructed the order of the set to be:

1. center: Vajradhara (rDo rje 'chang)
2. first to the right: Tilopa
3. first to the left: Nāropa
4. second to the right: Marpa Lotsāwa (1012–1096)
5. second to the left: Milarepa
6. third to the right: Gampopa (Dwags po Lha rje bSod nams rin chen, 1079–1153)
7. third to the left: Phagmotrupa (Phag mo gru pa rDo rje rgyal po, 1110–1170)
8. fourth to the right: Lingre
9. fourth to the left: Tsangpa Gyare

10. fifth to the right: *g.yas lnga pa rje rin po che ngag dbang chos rgyal* (the second 'Brug chen Ngag dbang chos rgyal, 1464/65–1540)
11. fifth to the left: unidentified
12. sixth to the right: *g.yas drug pa bstan 'dzin nor bu* (bsTan 'dzin nor bu, flourished mid-16th century)
13. sixth to the left: *g.yon drug pa rje chos kyi grags pa*
14. presumably seventh to the right, if in order

The existence of a fourteenth painting would mean that the set was not balanced to the right and left of Vajradhara, when the whole set was hung.

In addition to my 2008 article, there also exists a discussion of the set by Amy Heller, who illustrated fourteen thangkas from it in an online journal.[498] Heller asserts that the set includes several Bhutanese hierarchs but adduces no evidence, except in one case: lama number 12 has the same personal name

as a much later Je Khenpo of Bhutan. The fact that the Drukpa Kagyu was the paramount tradition in Bhutan many decades later has no relevance here, unless we can prove the names through inscriptions.

Heller said I identified several paintings of the series in two articles but that my research was compromised because I did not study the full series and all of the inscriptions, and thus the order I proposed was inaccurate.[499] Actually, as described above, I listed and identified twelve out of possibly fourteen paintings of the set. Heller also described one painting (her cat. no. X, now in Virginia) as "unidentified" and

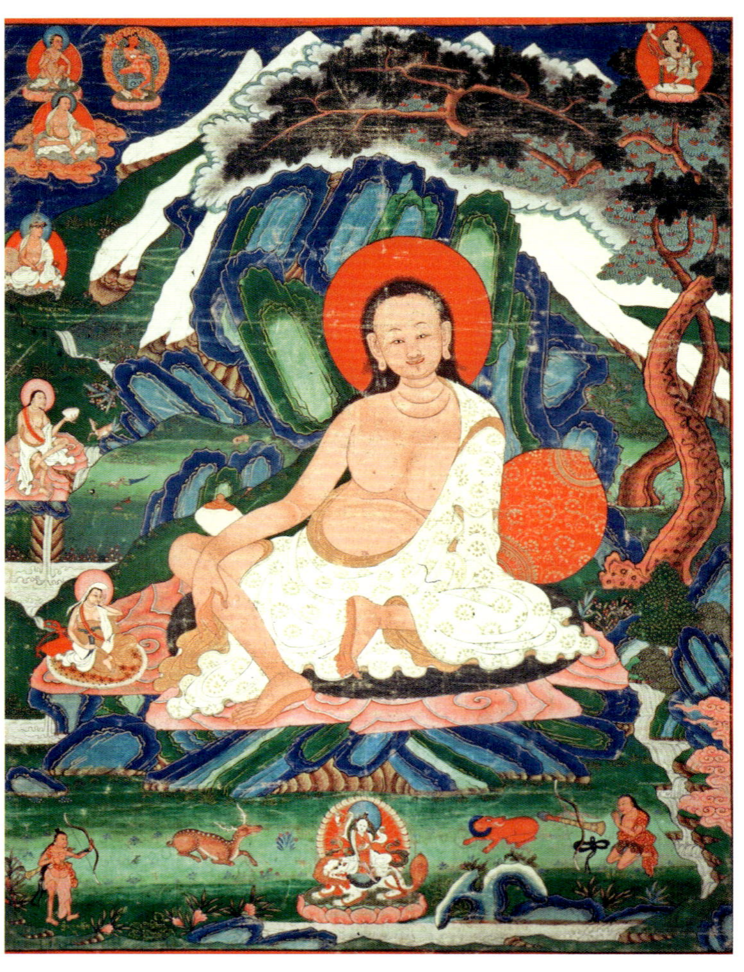 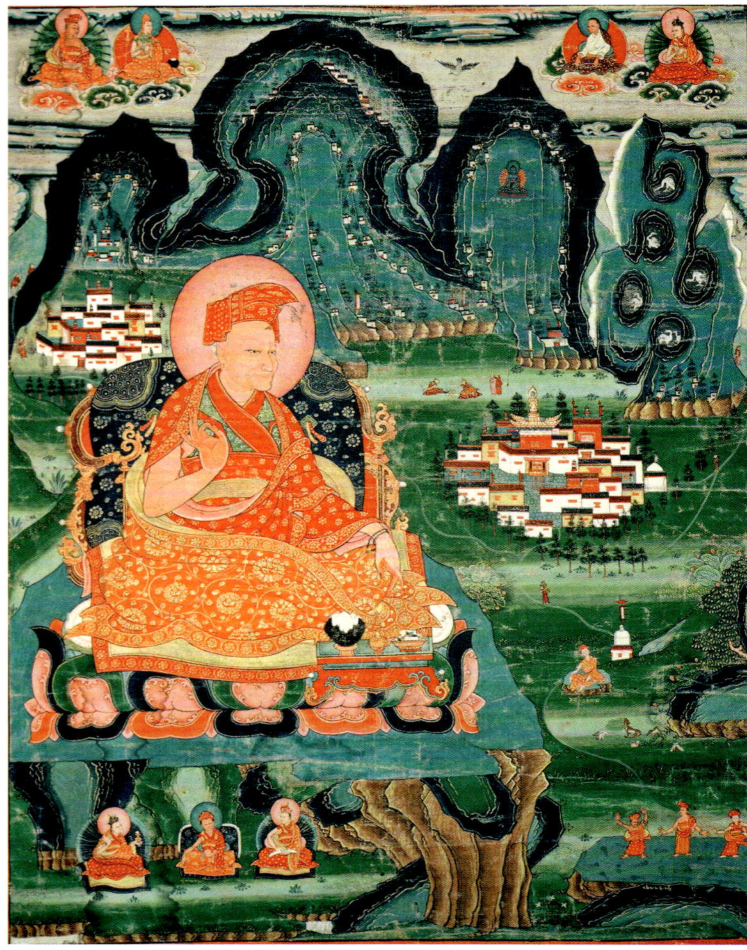

Fig. 10.21
Milarepa, as the fifth linage master of the
Drukpa Kagyu
mid- or late sixteenth century
23 ¼ x 20 in. (59 x 51 cm)
Zimmerman Family Collection
Literature: Heller 2012, no. V.; Pal 1983

Fig. 10.22
Gampopa, as the sixth lineage master of the
Drukpa Kagyu
mid- or late sixteenth century
23 ½ x 19 ¼ in. (59.8 x 49.9 cm)
Zimmerman Family Collection
Literature: Heller 2012, no. VI; also
Rhie and Thurman 1991, 246, pl. 84
("sGam po pa")

her number XIV as "missing," which does not bring us any closer to identifying the main lamas portrayed.

Heller focused on the donor figures:

> The key to accurate chronological attribution is the main donor figures that are represented on the first painting and the last painting, an aristocratic gentleman accompanied by two slender women whose short hair and distinctive woven garments are characteristic of the typical Bhutanese costume (see [Figs. 10.23 and 10.24]). The man is to be identified as Miwang (*mi dbang*) Pho lha nas, the lay ruler of Tibet, ca. 1730–1747, with his two wives who hailed from an illustrious Bhutanese family who settled near Gyantse after their ancestors were driven out of Bhutan in the aftermath of the [creation of the Bhutanese state by] Zhabdrung Ngawang Namgyal (Zhabs drung Ngag dbang rnam rgyal, 1594–1651) during the first half of the seventeenth century.[500]

Heller in her note to her figure 1 stated: "Lower center — aristocratic man with an attendant and 2 women: no inscription. Comparative research allows identification as the lay ruler of Tibet of mid-18th c., Mi dbang Pho lha nas bsod nams stobs rgyas, 1689–1747, and his 2 wives of Bhutanese origin."[501] But actually the aristocratic man that she mentions is not shown with an attendant. The man standing behind with the very distinctive hat and a thin sheathed blade tucked into his belt would seem to be another aristocrat, perhaps his younger brother. And it is not clear what makes two figures identifiable as female because Tibetans of both genders wore long hair.

Heller believes that the two figures—one holding a teapot and the other

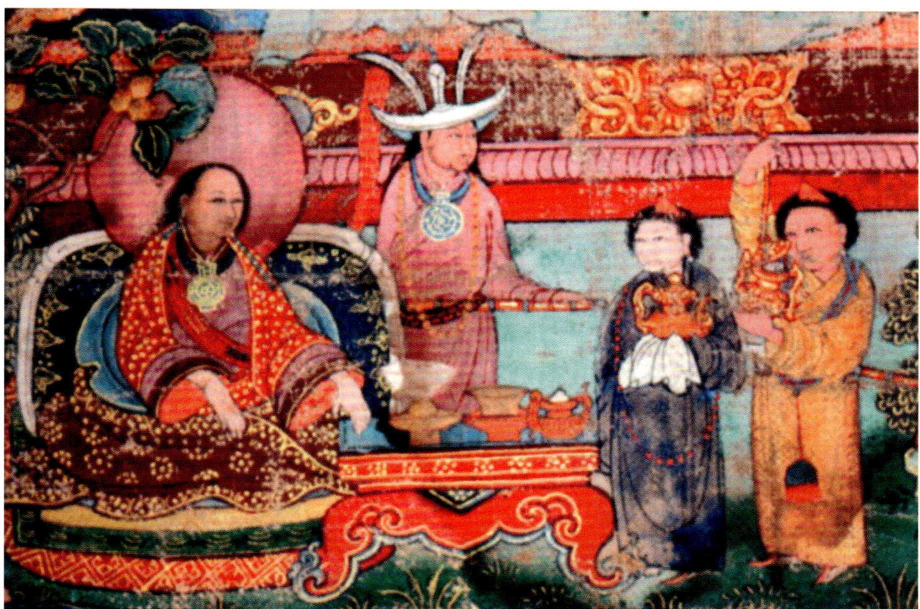

a censer—are Pholhane's wives because they wear distinctive Bhutanese textiles. Yet nothing even remotely like that can be found in the garments of the much smaller pair of standing figures she refers to, who stand before the patron in both first and last paintings, one serving tea and the other swirling a censer. In the last painting, they wear garments with textiles similar to the main patron, and in the first painting, the cloth they wear is plain but has brighter base colors. Perhaps they were servants. Heller further states:

> The identification of Miwang Pholhane is further confirmed thanks to the portrait of him and his wives which are mural paintings in the La mo temple near Lhasa, consecrated during his reign (see [Fig. 10.25] the mural painting of the La mo temple, photograph by Françoise Pommaret, 2006).[502]

Heller imagines that if Pholhane's wives had ancestors who came from Bhutan, they would continue, even two generations later, to wear highly distinctive Bhutanese textiles in their formal robes. But nothing of the kind can be found in the illustrations that Heller provides.

Thus Heller's confused dating of the set to the eighteenth century remains

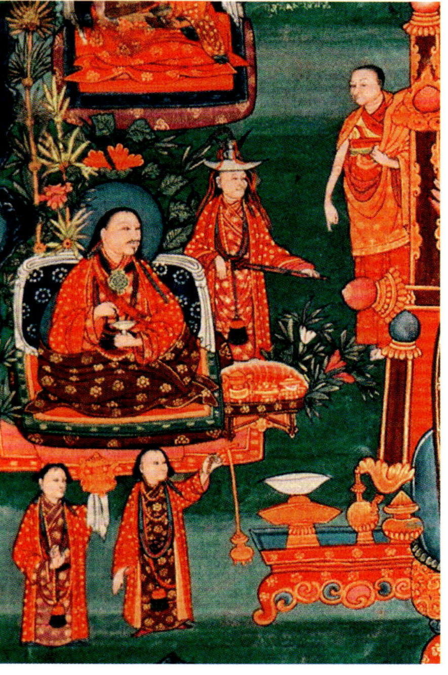

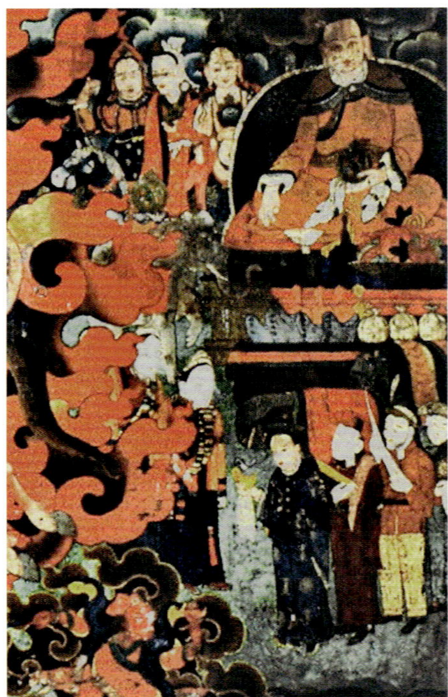

unproven. In dating this set, I am very reluctant to jump over several lineal guru generations—such as Pema Karpo— to land two centuries later, in eighteenth-century Bhutan.[503] Also, with my knowledge of the development of Tibetan painting styles, it is hard for me to assign a middle-period, Khyenri-hybrid style to such a late date. All things considered, the set should be dated to the late sixteenth century, that is, Pema Karpo's period or a generation later, at the latest.

THE DETAILED LIFE OF BUDDHA IN TWENTY-THREE THANGKAS

This set of sixteenth-century thangkas consists of twenty-three paintings, and I believe it was made after the life of Khyentse Chenmo, probably the sixteenth or even seventeenth century. It may be the most detailed painting of the Buddha's life now in existence. (For the many episodes of the Buddha's life according to Tāranātha's writings, see appendix F.)

The set was given to Tada Tokan (1890–1967) by the Thirteenth Dalai Lama, and it survives in the Hanamakishi Museum of Iwate, Japan. The set is discussed in a 1996 book to which eight authors contributed, including Hajime Nakamura and Yamaguchi, Zuiho.[504] In 1958, with Shuki Yoshimura, Tada also published a related bilingual book with the English title *Tibetan Pictorial Life of the Buddha*, which I have not seen.[505]

Tada was a Japanese priest and Tibetologist. As a Buddhist country, Japan was motivated to better understand Buddhism by studying the Tibetan religion. An exemplary early Japanese monk-explorer was Kawaguchi Ekai, whose travelogue was published in English under the title *Three Years in Tibet* (1909). Through his secret travels and later important publications, Kawaguchi established himself as a sort of Sarat Chandra Das of Japanese Tibetologists.[506] Tada followed in his footsteps. He stayed in Tibet from 1912 to 1916, the same time that the Japanese Buddhist priest Aoki Bunkyo did, representing the count Otani Kozui.[507] But the previously promising Tibetan-Japanese relations came to nothing in 1914, when Otani was disgraced.[508]

I believe that in Figure 10.26 the artist has copied an original painting of Śākyamuni by Khyentse Chenmo but made a few small changes. Note the use of different colors for the pairs of lions and *sharabha* antelopes (or *qilin* beasts) on both sides of the central buddha's backrest: white on one side but dark blue on the other. Similar alternating colors appear in the central Vajradhara of the Karma Kagyu lineage thangkas.[509] (See above, Fig. 2.18.)

I present Figures 10.27 and 10.28 as examples because they are the only two of this set that preserve the ring-shaped robe fasteners on the shoulders of the buddhas depicted as main figures.

Both buddhas are surrounded by colorful body nimbuses and sit on lotus thrones with unusually broad petals, which are different shapes but the same general size in both paintings. These lotus petals do not closely resemble the elaborate ones painted in the Gongkar murals by Khyentse Chenmo.

Figure 10.29 depicts Śākyamuni Buddha as a main image of the set. I believe that the artist copied this from a Khyentse Chenmo original, as he did in Figure 10.26. The backrest behind the central figure is striking for the unusual tropical bamboo leaves and the large long-tailed birds that perch in them, just below the bright-red peonies, one on either side. Few painters other than Khyentse would have included such a thing and pulled it off gloriously.

OTHER DETAILED DEPICTIONS OF THE BUDDHA'S LIFE

Figure 10.30 is a Chinese-style painting that portrays the life of the Buddha in many episodes. That is, it exemplifies the Hundred Deeds (*mdzad brgya*) or "Great Chinese [Painting] of the [Buddha's] Deeds" (*rgya mdzad chen mo*), a crucial iconographic theme for the young Menthangpa and Khyentse. But not in a Khyenri style.

Figures 10.31 and 10.32 are early Khyenri-style copies of another Chinese painting of the Buddha's detailed life. Both have a distinctive ornate central lotus petal in the lotus seat beneath the main buddha, a feature that we have already explored in the Gongkar murals discussed above in chapter 4. (It is remarkable that only the middle petal

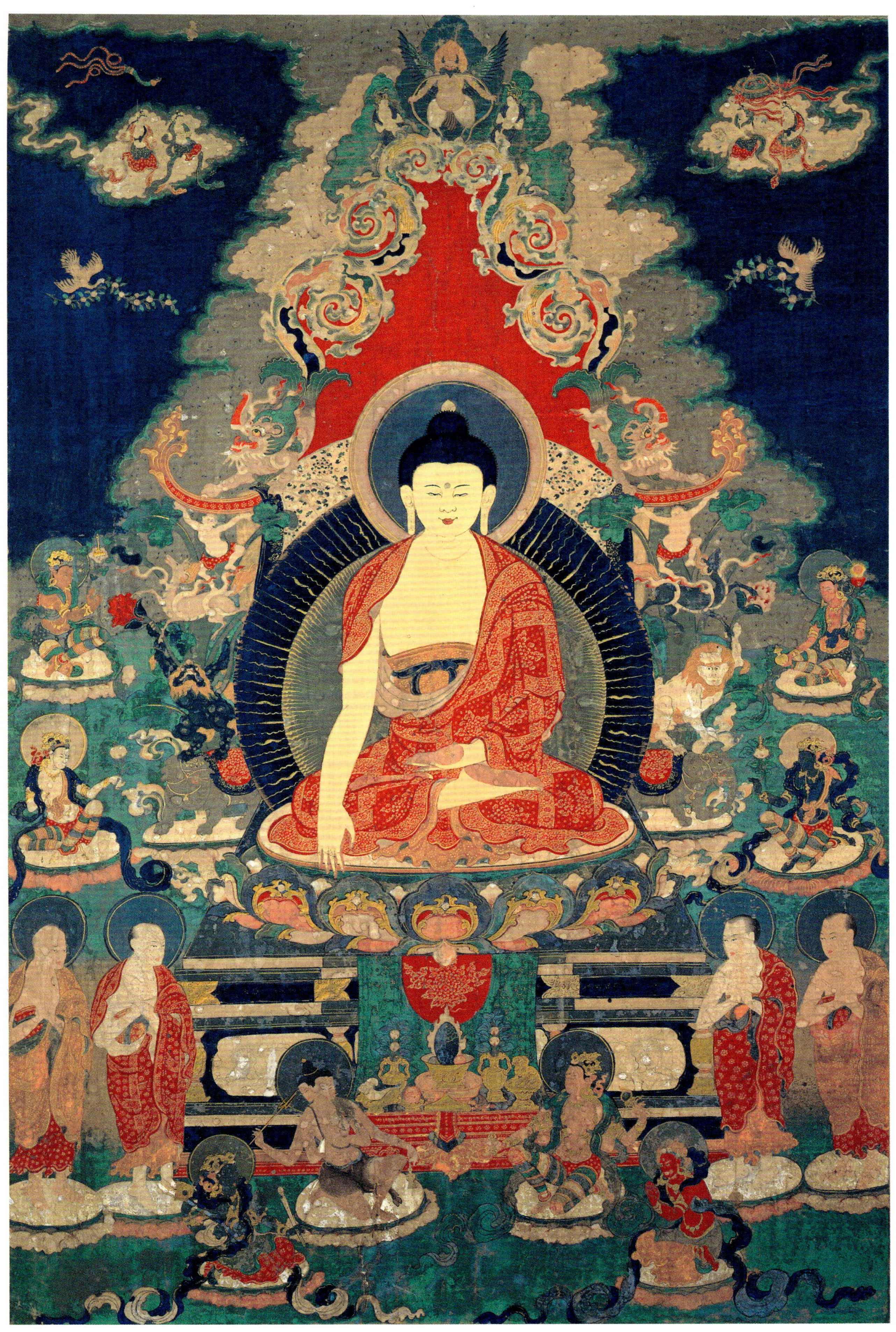

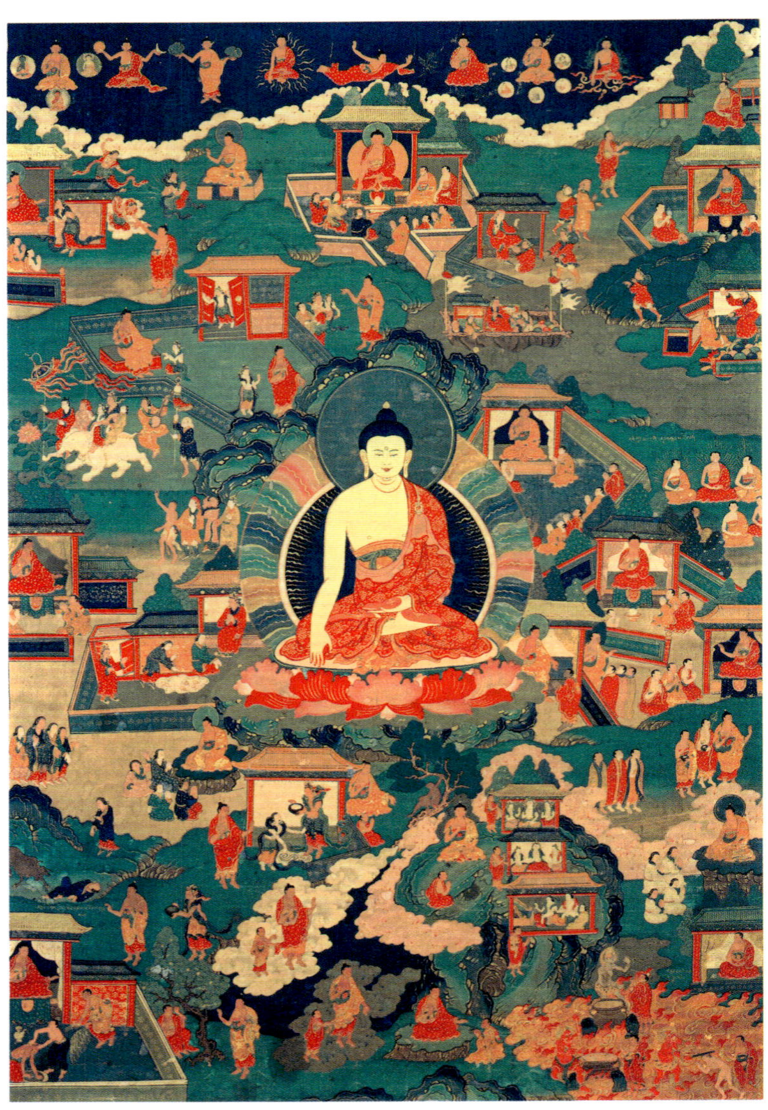

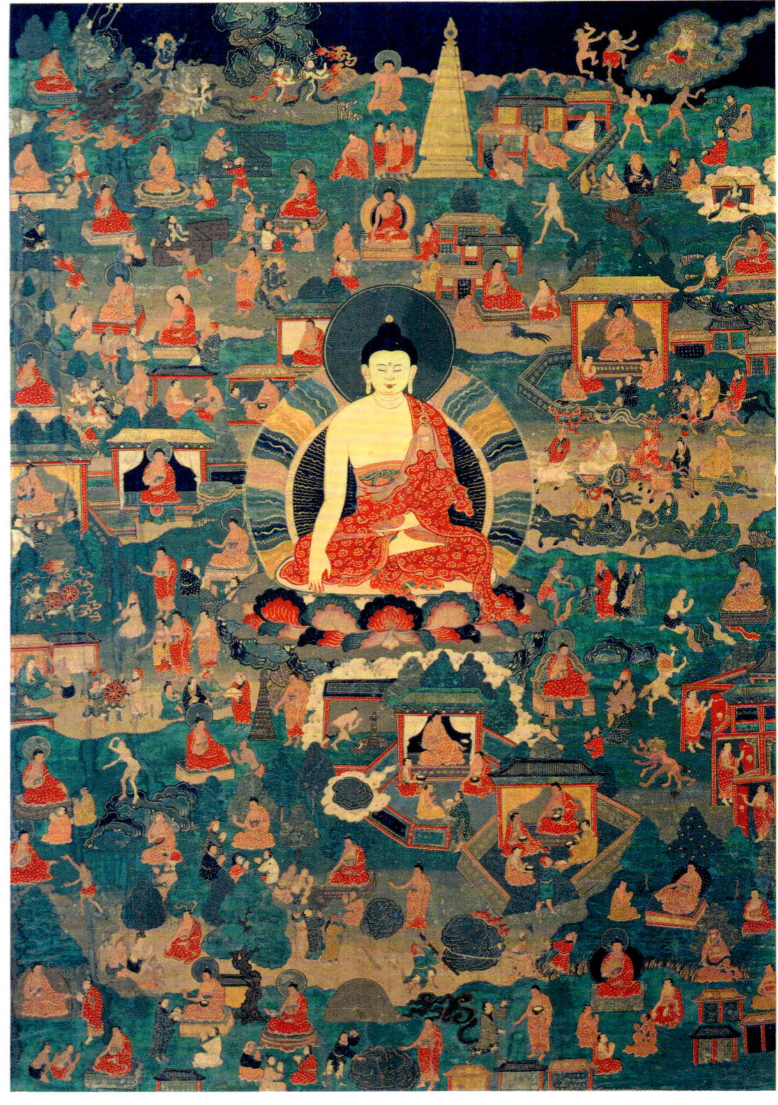

FIG. 10.27
Episodes from the Life of the Buddha
(ninth painting in set)
ca. sixteenth or seventeenth century
Tada Tokan collection, now in Hanamakishi
Museum, Iwate, Japan

FIG. 10.28
Episodes from the Life of the Buddha
(twentieth painting in set)
ca. sixteenth or seventeenth century
Tada Tokan collection, now in Hanamakishi
Museum, Iwate, Japan

FIG. 10.29
Episodes from theLife of the Buddha
(last thangka in set)
ca. sixteenth or seventeenth century
Tada Tokan collection, now in Hanamakishi
Museum, Iwate, Japan

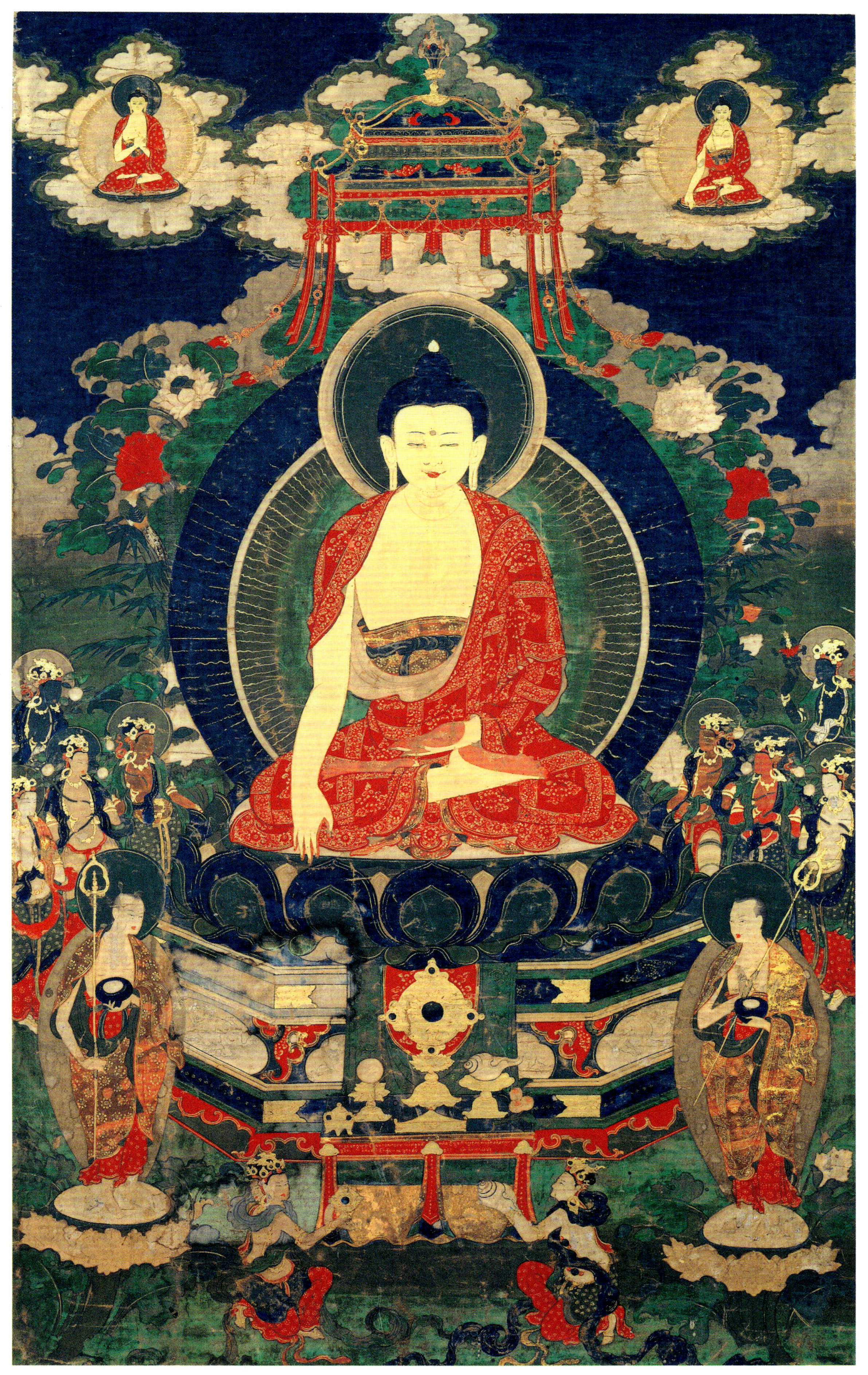

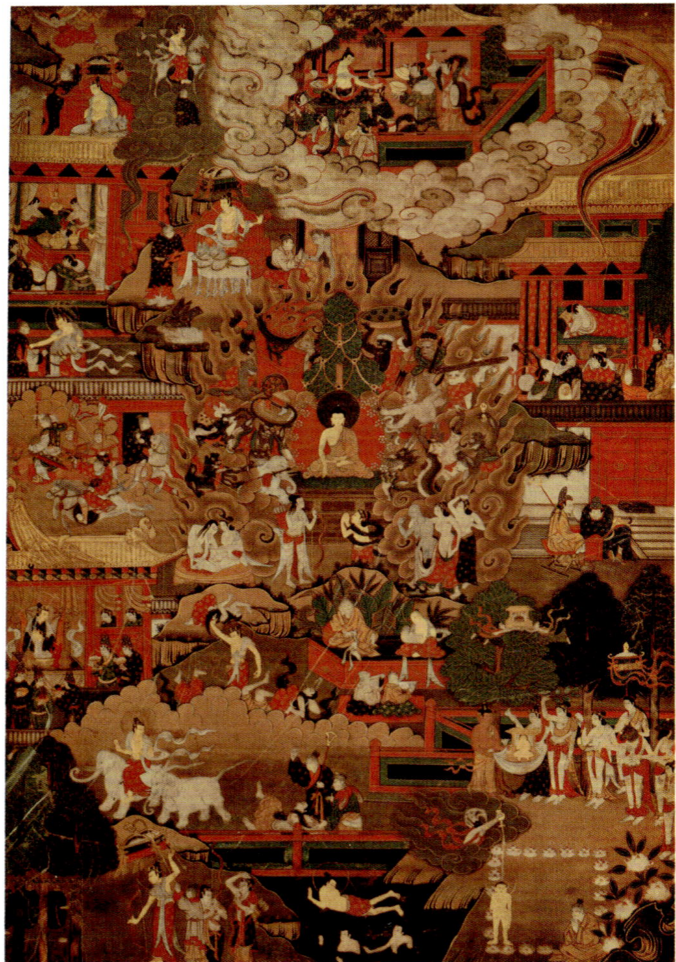

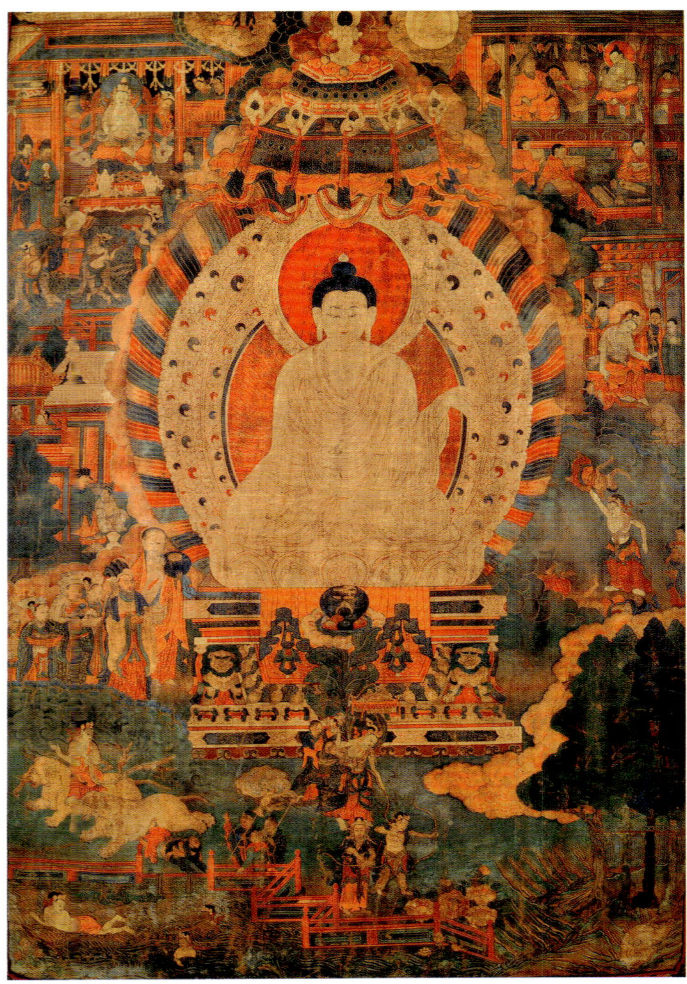

is furnished with the fancier petal.) The artist, who may have been Khyentse or one of his early followers, possibly made two copies of his original. Some details in the second (Fig. 10.32) are improved, such as the treatment of palms, soles, and the body nimbuses.

These two paintings, long separated, help convey the sort of copying of Chinese style detailed lives of the Buddha that Khyentse presumably did as a young artist in Gyantse and even later, in his maturity. Detailed lives of the Buddha were part of his main artistic repertoire. These Khyenri style paintings are also noteworthy for the large amount of gold used.

Figure 10.33 is an enlargement of a single episode, depicted in the upper-left regions of the preceding two paintings. It shows how each episode from this detailed narrative could be recast as the composition of a whole painting. I imagine that Khyentse Chenmo might have made it and many similar paintings as a master, not as a student, for a set of thangkas depicting this theme. It may have been requested by one of his noble lama-patrons, who similarly paid minute attention to the visual reconstruction of the life of the Buddha in a new by Tibetan standards strongly Chinese mode.

What is "Chinese" about this painting? Though the musicians are not wearing Chinese pants, the two women staring out the window of the façade certainly look Chinese, due to their demure faces and shapes. The architecture, furniture, and the incense burners (lions on a lotus) all seem Chinese. But the clouds and the odd uniform direction of the beams extending at the roof line are less so. The misunderstood *biwa* (with an extra angle to its neck), might be Chinese, though the *vina* is not.

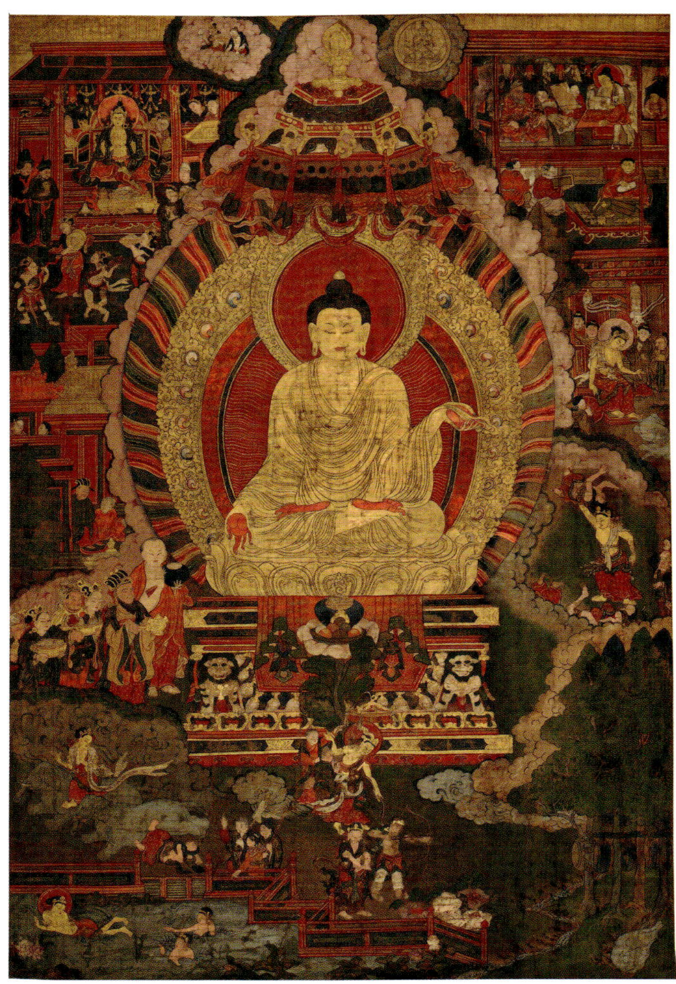

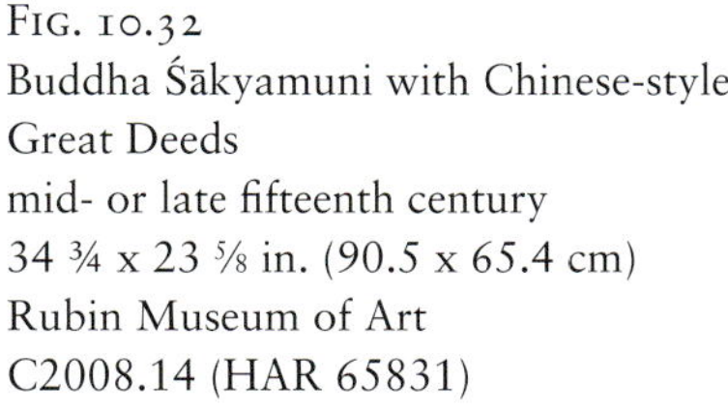

Fig. 10.32
Buddha Śākyamuni with Chinese-style
Great Deeds
mid- or late fifteenth century
34 ¾ x 23 ⅝ in. (90.5 x 65.4 cm)
Rubin Museum of Art
C2008.14 (HAR 65831)

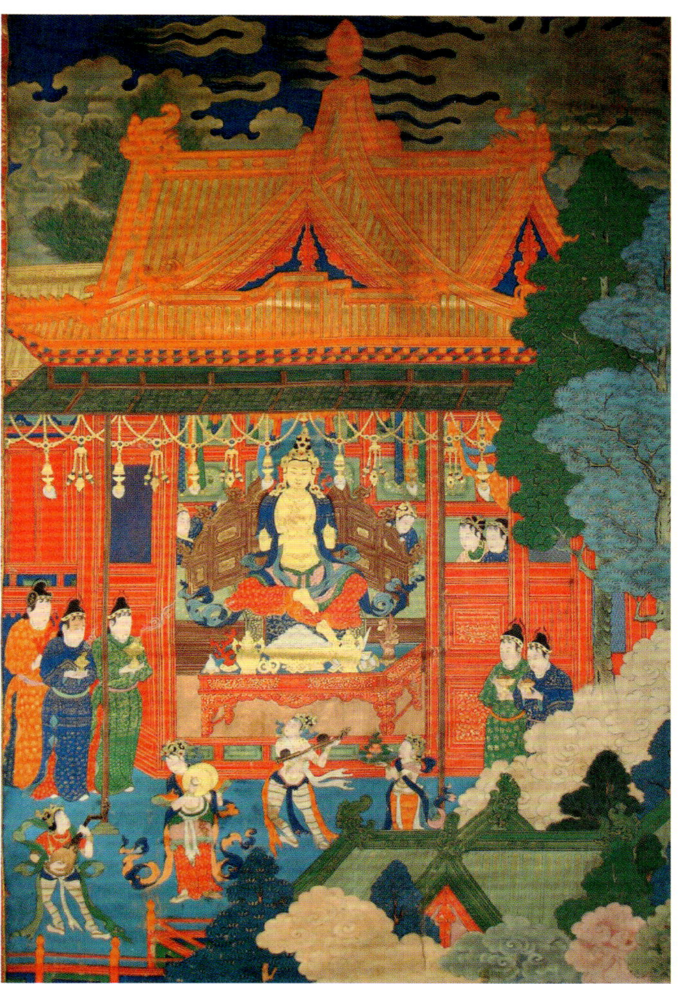

Fig. 10.33
Detailed Life of the Buddha in Chinese Style
mid- or late fifteenth century
Private Collection
After: Pal 1984a, pl. 70

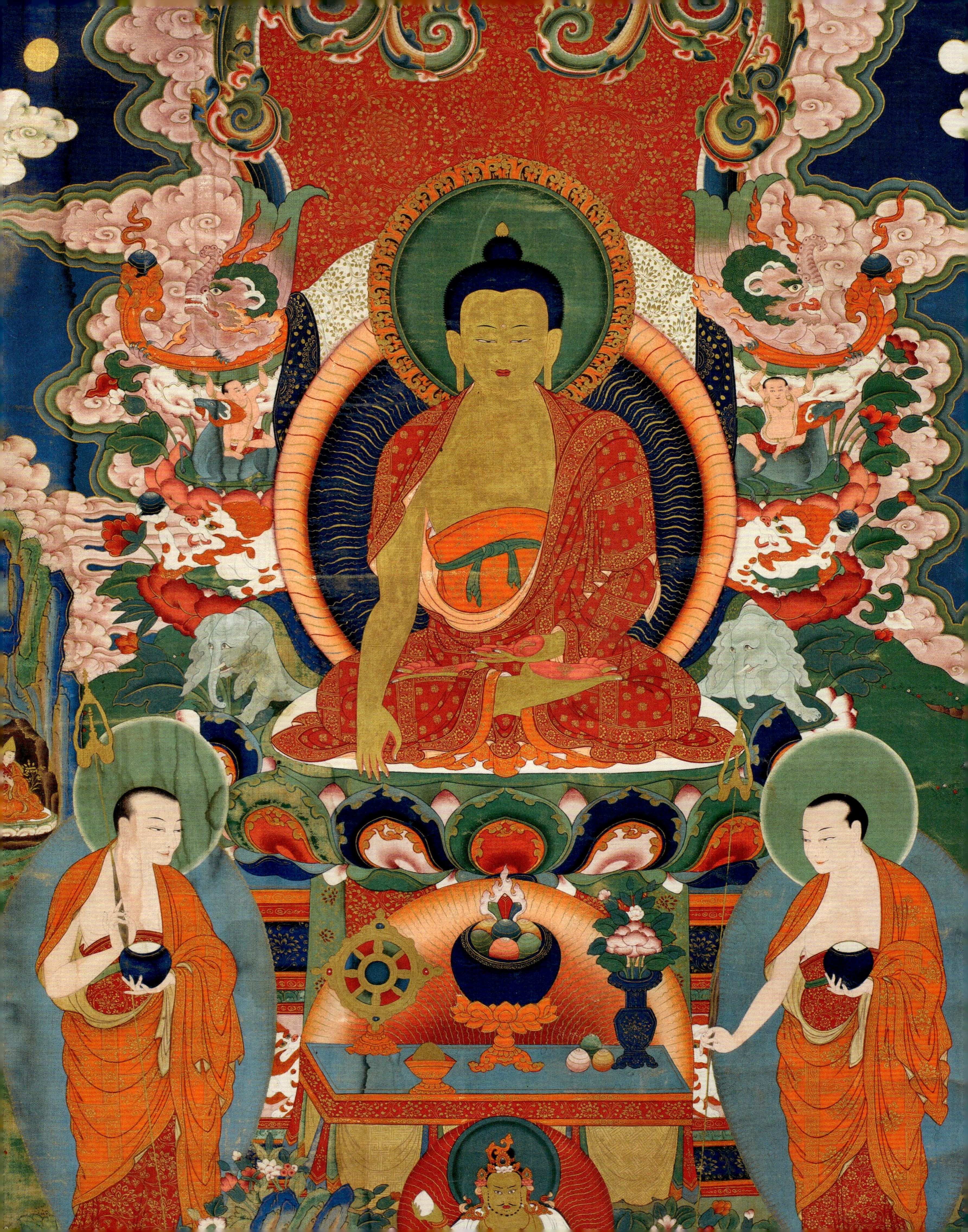

CHAPTER 11

Khyenri-Style Thangka Sets from the Seventeenth Century

THIS CHAPTER presents several Khyenri-style thangka sets that date to the seventeenth century. Five sets are discussed in detail; for an example of a sixth painting set from the Jonangpa tradition, see the discussion of Figure 2.10.[510]

The first two sets that we investigate have important connections with the life and patronage of the Fifth Dalai Lama. In the present chapter I thus describe in detail the patronage of paintings in the Khyenri style by the Fifth Dalai Lama. But I begin by enumerating accounts of several other important late-sixteenth- or seventeenth-century commissions of art in Khyentse Chenmo's style that are mentioned in Sakya histories or biographies.

CONTINUATIONS OF THE KHYENRI IN Ü AND TSANG IN THE SIXTEENTH AND SEVENTEENTH CENTURIES

For several centuries, the Khyenri tradition was continued in central Tibet by a series of outstanding painters who were mainly based in Ü province but occasionally also in Tsang. An example of such patronage by the Sakya tradition in Tsang is found in the autobiography of the eminent master Mangthö Ludrup Gyatsho (Mang thos Klu sgrub rgya mtsho, 1523–1596). His autobiography recorded that he commissioned in the 1580s excellent murals by a painter of

the Khyentse tradition (*mkhyen lugs*). In 1582 he had Trulku Dorje (sPrul sku rDo rje) paint two mural panels in a monastery in Tsang, one that depicted the sixteen arhats in the Chinese silk-thangka tradition, in accordance with the artistic tradition of Khyentse, and another showing Amitāyus surrounded by the Six Ornaments.[511] He sponsored three murals by that same artist between 1582 and 1586, including a mural of Padmasambhava, surrounded by early translators and panditas, that included gold leaf (*gser shog ma*).[512] In 1585 he sponsored some murals depicting an excellent image of Sakya Paṇḍita; the mural included episodes from the life of that saint, including his defeating the long-haired Harinanda (*'phrog byed ral pa tshar bcad pa*) and his spiritually favoring the Mongol king Göden (*hor rgyal po go brtan rjes su bzung ba*). The latter biographical murals, which included the application of gold leaf, were painted by the Menthangpa-tradition artist Trulku Ganggyüpa (sPrul sku sGang brgyud pa).[513]

In the early seventeenth century, a discerning lama-patron in Tsang, then the seat of the ruler of Tibet, commissioned works by outstanding painters of the Khyenri from Ü province and at Jonang (Jo nang) Monastery or at the monastic seat of Jonang Jetsün Tāranātha (1575–1634), Phüntshokling. Some Jonangpa masterpieces from this period were thus painted in the Khyenri style.[514]

References to the Khyenri as a living style continue to turn up in written sources throughout most of the

seventeenth century. In 1630, for example, the great Drukpa Kagyu ('Brug pa bKa brgyud) master Paksam Wangpo (dPag bsam dbang po, 1593–1651) sponsored works of Khyenri and other styles when he had the murals at Tashi Thongmön (bKra shis mthong smon) repainted.[515] Similarly the Nyingma master Surchen Chöying Rangdröl (Zur chen Chos dbyings rang grol 1617–1682)—who was a prominent guru of the Fifth Dalai Lama—painted around 1644 in the Khyenri as well as the Menri style.[516]

LATER EMULATIONS OF KHYENTSE CHENMO'S ART AT SAKYA

The Gongkar thangkas depicting Lamdre lineage gurus were also highly esteemed by some of the most eminent lamas of the Sakya school, even the heads of Sakya itself. Some of them went so far as to commission copies of them. For example, in his classic history of the Sakya Khön lineage, Ameshab relates the late-sixteenth-century commission by his father, the Sakya Dagchen and throne holder Ngakchang Trakpa Lotrö (sNgags 'chang Grags pa blo gros, 1563–1617, tenure 1589–1617): "For thangkas, [he commissioned] the Lamdre lineage of the Dzong tradition, copying the great Chinese-style thangkas (*rgya thang chen mo*) that were in Gongkar Dorjeden."[517] Though his reference to the paintings is somewhat vague—it does not mention Khyentse Chenmo as artist—he refers to commissioning a copy of the whole Lamdre lineage, not a single large thangka, calling them by a name by which they were evidently known in Sakya, "great Chinese-style thangkas" (*rgya thang chen mo*). He must have meant one of the famous sets of large paintings of Lamdre masters in a strongly Chinese style at Gongkar, namely the two main sets painted by Khyentse Chenmo for Gongkarwa from 1464 to 1476.

As a historian, Ameshab knew the Lamdre traditions very well. Though he called the lineage depicted in these thangkas the Dzong tradition, the more general name, he certainly meant the Thekchen tradition and its offshoot, the Gongkar tradition (Gong dkar lugs), the lineage of Gongkar Dorjedenpa.

Ameshab adds that Trakpa Lotrö framed this and several other newly completed thangka sets with costly silk brocades and also commissioned one of the finest sets of *jātaka* paintings in central Tibet, with exquisite frames; wonderful flowers rained down at the consecration ceremony (*rab gnas*) for these thangkas.[518] Trakpa Lotrö was in the position to borrow such paintings or have copies of them painted in Gongkar; as a highly respected Sakya throne holder, his influence upon all Sakyapa branch monasteries was very strong. Ameshab elsewhere records that his father's disciples included high monastic officials (*slob dpon and dbu mdzad*) of Gongkar.[519]

In the late sixteenth and early seventeenth centuries, Khyentse Chenmo's sculptures were also prized as examples for copying by leading masters of the Sakya school. For example, when the eminent Sakya throne-holder Kunga Rinchen's son, Ngakchang Trakpa Lotrö (sNgags 'chang Grags pa blo gros, 1563–1617), built at Sakya the Düdül Buk (bDud 'dul sbug) shrine dedicated to the protector Mahākāla Pañjaranātha and his retinue, he is said to have had the figures of the main images modeled after those by Khyentse in the Protector's Chapel (mGon khang) at Gongkar.[520]

Leading masters of Sakya in the sixteenth century also highly valued the later Gongkar-based sculptors who followed in Khyentse Chenmo's tradition. For instance, when the great Ngakchang Kunga Rinchen (sNgags 'chang Kun dga' rin chen, 1517–1584), the twenty-fourth throne-holder of Sakya, commissioned an image of Mahākāla— in connection with his restorations at Sakya, begun about 1576—the main artist was the Gongkar Trulku Jinpa Namgyal (Gong dkar sPrul sku sByin pa rNam rgyal), who pitched his tent in the *thig khang* of the Great Southern Temple (Lha khang Chen mo).[521] His making of the sculpture was marked by an exceptional sign: a sudden, great windstorm.

Khyenri Paintings Associated with the Fifth Dalai Lama

About a generation later, the Fifth Dalai Lama (Ngag dbang blo bzang rgya mtsho, 1617–1682) also highly appreciated the work of Khyenri artists. Through his patronage and that of the regent Desi Sanggye Gyatsho (1653–1705), painters executed many works in a later Khyenri style that survive in the Potala Palace.[522] A highly discerning patron, the Fifth Dalai Lama preferred the Khyenri artists when commissioning paintings that depicted wrathful deities and mandalas.

Thus Khyenri artists contributed in important ways to large projects sponsored by the Fifth Dalai Lama— and later by his regent, Sanggye Gyatsho—on which some of the greatest Menri painters also worked. In 1648, painters of the Khyenri tradition—led by a master named Khedrup (mKhas grub)—painted for the Fifth Dalai Lama the murals of gurus, tutelary deities, and protectors of both "New" and "Old" tantric lineages in the Sangngak Gatshal (gSang sngags dGa' tshal) temple at Chökhor Gyal (Chos 'khor rGyal) in Ölkha ('Ol kha).[523] Six years later,

in 1654, the Khyenri masters Gongkar Sangngak Kharpa (Gong dkar gSang sngags mkhar pa) and Shora Gögö (Zho ra dGos dgos) were among the five artists who led a group of sixty-eight Menri and Khyenri painters in renovating the main assembly hall and other chapels at Drepung ('Bras spungs), under the patronage of that same Dalai Lama.[524] (See chapter 3, Figs. 3.19–3.21.)

About 1669, the Fifth Dalai Lama sponsored a set of thangkas in a Khyenri style depicting the Lamdre guru lineage—showing the lineage of Kha'u Drakdzongpa (Kha'u Brag rdzong pa) after Müchen Sempa Chenpo (Mus chen Sems dpa' chen po, 1388–1469)—a set of paintings commissioned in the memory of and dedicated to the recently deceased former abbot of Pökhang (sPos khang mKhan po Zur pa) named Bumrampa ('Bum rams pa). The chief supervisor of the project was Langbu (Glang bu), and the head artist was Sangngak Kharpa (gSang sngags mKhar pa), who was the chief artist (or chant leader, *dbu mdzad*) of the Gongkar Monastic Center.[525]

Another interesting reference to the Khyenri style from the autobiography of the Fifth Dalai Lama refers to the commissioning about 1670 or 1671 of a set of thangkas depicting mandalas (*dkyil thang*) from the Vajrāvalī cycle. The political ruler (sDe pa) undertook sponsoring the large project and set up a workshop for it. Since Menthangpa had expertly painted peaceful deities and Khyentse fierce deities and mandalas, in the Fifth's opinion, it was essential that both traditions be sustained. In the time of Depa Sönam Rabten (sDe pa bSod nams rab brtan, d. 1657) there were few painters who could work in the Khyenri style, but now a skillful group was called together, led by the high monastic official of Gongkar Monastery, Sangngak Kharpa. Their main examples for copying were thangkas from a set that had belonged to Gongkar Dorjedenpa Kunga Namgyal himself. Presumably the paintings were by Khyentse Chenmo. To guarantee the accuracy of the paintings, a team of four scholars compared the Tibetan translations of the Indian sources *Vajrāvalī* and *Kriyāsamuccaya* as well as the liturgical works of Ngaripa Tshulö (mNga' ris pa Tshul 'od, possibly fl. 15th century) and Thartse Paṇchen ('Brang ti Paṇ chen Nam mkha' dpal bzang, 13th abbot of Ngor, 1535–1602).[526] Differences and points of doubt were referred to the Shalu (Zhwa lu) abbot Kagyurwa Gönpo Sönam Chokdrup (Zhwa lu mKhan po "bKa' 'gyur ba" mGon po bsod nams mchog grub, 1603–1659)—a learned teacher of the Dalai Lama, especially for Tsharpa lineages within the Sakya school—for his decision.[527] Some queries were also directed to the Fifth Dalai Lama himself. The Indian basic text and the model thangkas (*thang dpe*) were taken as the decisive authorities; the few slight deviations were noted as annotations in red letters in the ritual texts. The master Thöncha Goné (Thon bya sgo nas) supervised the work, and the paintings were completed in the eighth lunar month of the iron-pig year (1671).[528]

In 1673, the extensive repainting of the murals at Lhasa Ramoche (Ra mo che) temple began. More than fifty painters participated in this project, including: the two chief directors of painting work (*bris pa'i dbu chen*), Gongkar Chöde's Sangngak Khar Chödze Shönnu (Gong dkar Chos sde gSang sngags mkhar Chos mdzad gZhon nu) and Drepung Lobpön Ngawang Trinle ('Bras spungs sLob dpon Ngag dbang phrin las); the three mid-level painter overseers (*dbu 'bring*), Dranang Bükhyimpa or Pükhyimpa Ngawang Sichö (Gra nang sBus khyim pa [or sPus khyim pa] Ngag dbang sri chod), Shöra Gyalpo (Zhos ra rGyal po), and Sangkhar Tshephel (gSang mkhar Tshe 'phel); and the junior painter overseer (*dbu chung*), Bükhyimpa (or Pükhyimpa) Norwang (Nor dbang).[529] At least two painters

associated with Sangkhar (gSang mkhar, short for gSang sngags mkhar) worked in the Khyenri style.

The Fifth Dalai Lama's Khyenri commissions included two more, which I had not noticed in my 1996 history but which I add here for the sake of completeness. In the first volume of his autobiography, the Fifth Dalai Lama mentions a group of Nyingma thangkas in a Khyenri style that were commissioned at Yargyap.[530] Later in the same volume, he mentions that on another occasion several skillful artists from Gongkar paint mandalas (Yogatantra and Amitāyus).[531]

PROJECTS AFTER THE PASSING OF THE FIFTH DALAI LAMA

In the mid-1690s, during the delayed building of the reliquary stūpa and temple for the deceased Fifth Dalai Lama (d. 1682), a large group of Khyenri painters worked under government support alongside a larger group of Menri painters and a substantial contingent of Newar metal workers. The foremost of these Khyenri tradition (mKhyen lugs) masters were: the artist of highest rank Sangngak Khar Tshephel (gSang sngags mkhar Tshe 'phel), the artist of medium rank Pükhyim Ngakdröl (sPus khyim Ngag grol), and the two artists of lower rank, Ngawang Söten (Ngag dbang bsod brtan) and Champa Gyaltshen (Byams pa rgyal mtshan). Under the direction of these four painters worked sixty-three ordinary painters of the Khyenri tradition, all of whom are mentioned by name in Desi Sanggye Gyatsho's account. This list can be seen as a sort of census of the four leading Khyenri painters and sixty-three ordinary artists in the 1690s and their seventeen home communities, which were specified: gSung gling, rNam rab, Gongkar Chos sde, Tsher shing, bDe chos, Zho ra, rGyal gling, Yul chos, rDza rong, Gling, Brag ram, sPus bde, mNyes thang, bKra shis

Chos sde, Hor, sNye mo, and bKra shis rtse Chos sde.[532]

Elsewhere in the same work, Sanggye Gyatsho mentions again Sangngak Kharwa Tshephel (gSang sngags mkhar ba Tshe 'phel), the master and director of the Khyenri tradition painters (*mkhyen lugs dbu chen*), and Ngakdröl (sPus khyim Ngag grol), his junior painter overseer in the Khyenri tradition.[533] The Khyenri artists clearly flourished in the 1690s, at the turn of the eighteenth century, in southern Ü province, especially in or near Khyentse's birthplace, Gongkar in Lhokha.

A THANGKA SET OF THE PRINCIPAL DEEDS IN THE LIFE OF BUDDHA ŚĀKYAMUNI

The first seventeenth-century Khyenri-style set to be discussed survives in the Tibet House, in New Delhi. The set depicts in seven paintings more episodes than the usual Twelve Great Deeds of Buddha Śākyamuni's life. The total number of large and small episodes, in which the Buddha appears, is about fifty. (For the many episodes of the detailed Buddha's life according to Tāranātha's writings, see appendix F.)

This set of paintings was described in a 1969 Tibet House Society catalog, which gives the dimensions of the thangkas as 21 ½ x 15 ⅝ inches (54.5 x 39.5 cm); it omits thangkas 2 and 5, and the order of the remaining five paintings is sometimes confused.[534]

Stylistically, the central buddha thangka is not as distinctive as many of the earlier Khyenri sets. Yet one distinctive Khyenri feature in every painting is a canopy floating above and encroaching upon the top of the central buddha's head nimbus.

Figure 11.1 is the first thangka of the set. It depicts three figures that help establish a historical context for dating the set. At the top proper left (from the perspective of the Buddha) is

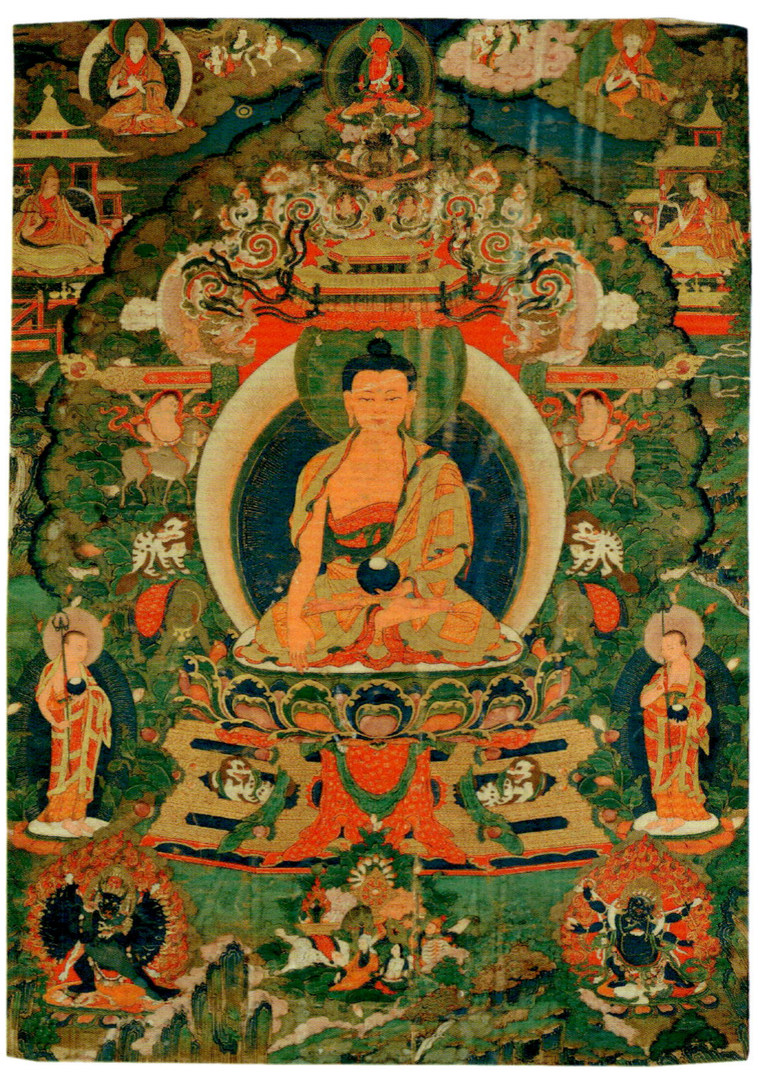

FIG. 11.1
Principal Events in the Life of Buddha
Śākyamuni
seventeenth century
21 ½ x 15 ⅝ in. (54.5 x 39.5 cm)
Tibet House, New Delhi
(HAR 72043)
Literature: Tibet House Society 1969,
"thangka one"

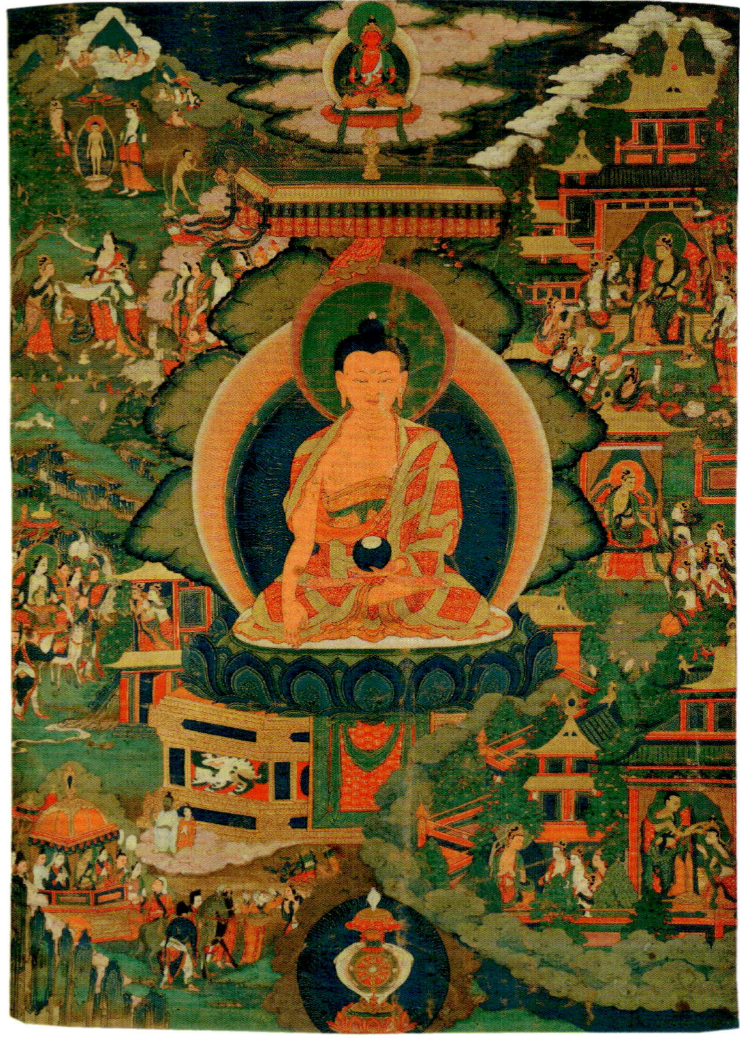

FIG. 11.2
Principal Events in the Life of Buddha
Śākyamuni
seventeenth century
21 ½ x 15 ⅝ in. (54.5 x 39.5 cm)
Tibet House, New Delhi
(HAR 72044)
Literature: Tibet House Society 1969,
"thangka two"

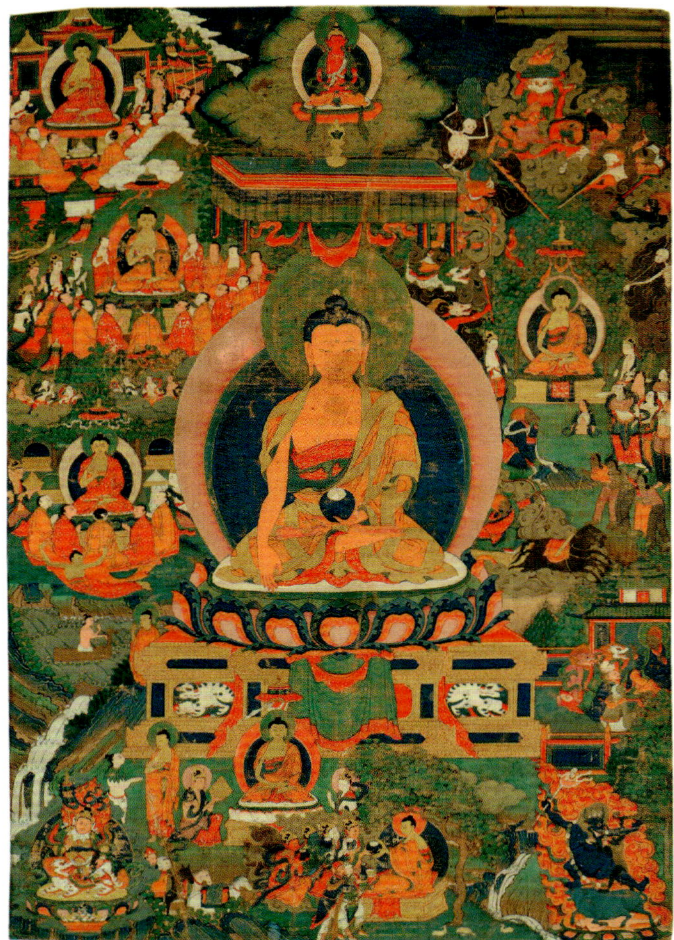

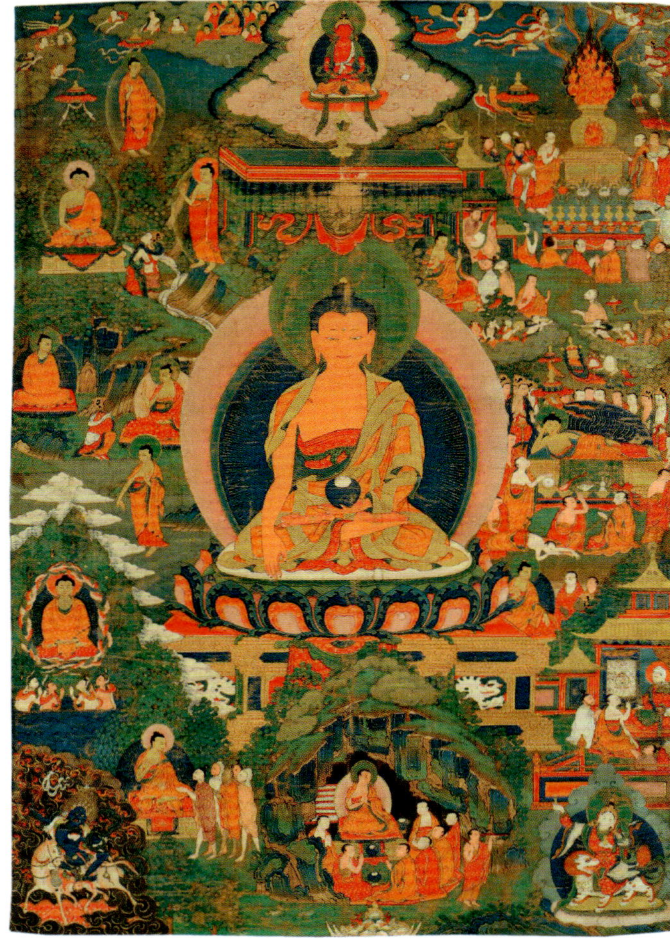

Losang Chögyen (Blo bzang chos kyi rgyal mtshan), the First Panchen Lama (1567–1662). Below him is Könchok Gyaltshen, who the 1969 catalog is identified as "principal disciple of the First Panchen Lama." Above to the right are Tsongkhapa and Ngawang Losang Gyatsho, the Fifth Dalai Lama. Thus the set dates to the time of the Fifth Dalai Lama, since he is the latest lama portrayed. The set was presumably made for his longevity, since Amitāyus,

the Buddha of Long Life, also regularly appears at the top center of each painting.

In Figure 11.2, the second painting of the set, the birth from Māyādevī at Lumbini takes place in the upper left corner, and episodes of the Buddha's immediately preceding life as a god in Tuṣita are depicted on the right side of the painting.

The Tibet House catalog mixed up the numbering of two thangkas of the set. Figure 11.3, which was called "thangka seven" in the catalog, is actually number 6 in the series. It depicts many late events in the life of the Buddha, including in the upper-right corner his manifesting of miracles.

Figure 11.4, called "thangka five," is actually the final thangka for the set, that is, number 7.[535] It shows in the upper right quarter the Buddha's final passing into nirvana and cremation.

A Thangka Set Depicting Jātaka Stories

This seventeenth-century thangka set is a nearly complete series of Ārya Śūra's *Jātakamālā* in a Khyenri style. Now preserved in the Saint Louis Art Museum in Missouri, the set includes thirteen thangkas. We can see a link with the Khyenri style most obviously in the central buddha painting (Fig. 11.5). In some other paintings in the set, the buddha robes and petals also resemble those of the Khyenri.[536]

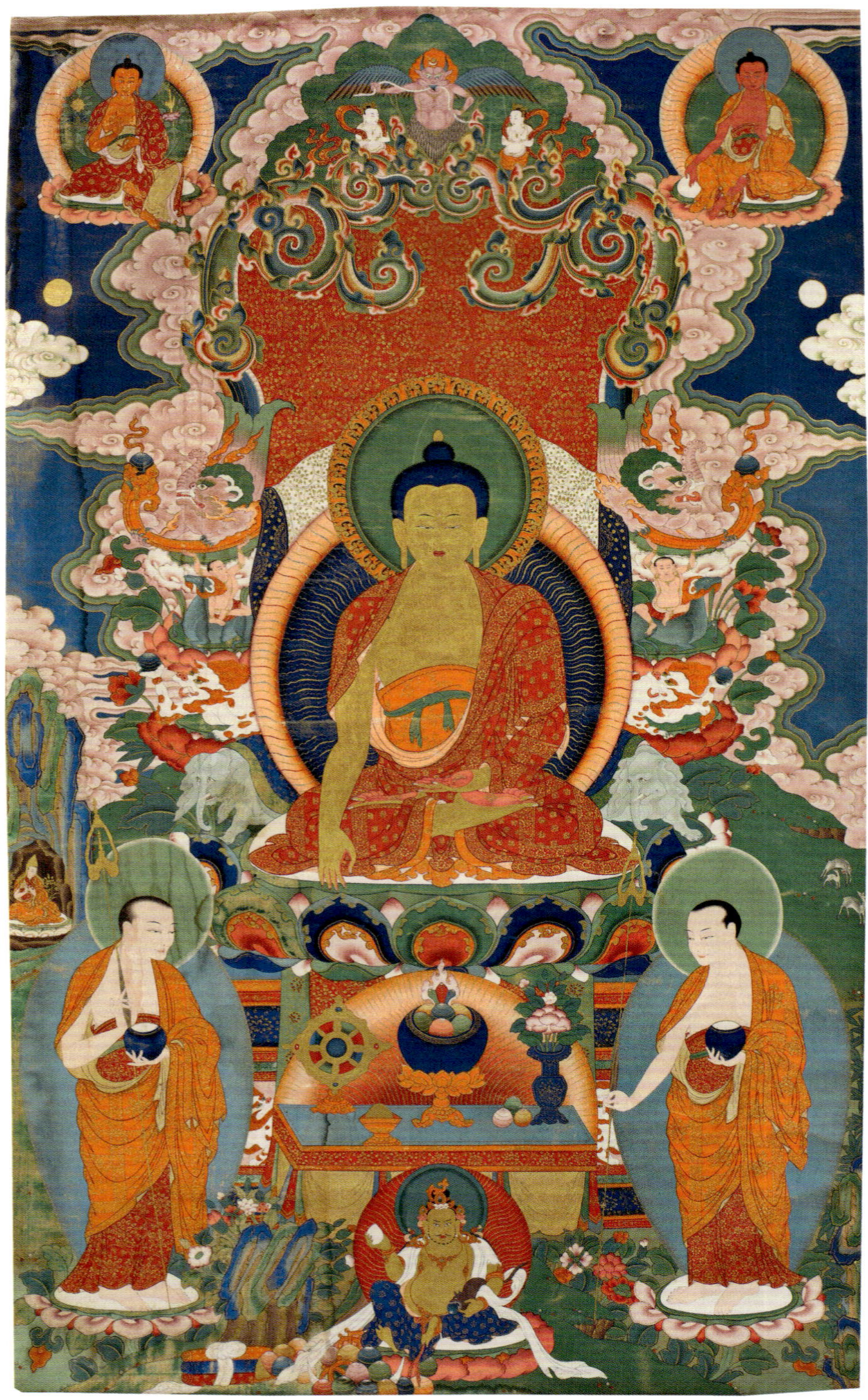

Edna Bryner, in *Thirteen Tibetan Tankas*, documented almost the entire set of thangkas. She presented the central buddha (Fig. 11.5; Bryner's "Tanka 1") in color on the cover and the frontispiece. She illustrated thirty-one *jātaka* through thangka numbers 2 through 13. She believed that two paintings were missing from the series: "Twenty-nine of his thirty-four tales . . . are portrayed."[537] Yet actually only one painting—which

would have been number 10, illustrating *jātaka* numbers 24 through 26—is missing. So of the thirty-four *jātaka*, thirty-one were illustrated by her thangkas 1 through 13.[538] She makes up for the iconographic gap by adding thangkas A and B, later in the book.[539]

Bryner dated the set to "certainly after the seventeenth century, probably along the way toward the twentieth," that is, to the eighteenth or nineteenth century.[540] I now date the set to the late seventeenth century and the period of the Fifth Dalai Lama. One hint about the Geluk sectarian origin of the series is the repeated depictions of single yellow-hatted masters, who usually have the iconography of Tsongkhapa. These figures have been placed into almost every painting's landscape, often in the sky or in caves.

Bryner did not mention these masters or remark about their possible significance. Even more obvious regarding the set's patronage is a great Gelukpa lama who is prominently depicted in the final thangka (Fig. 11.6; Bryner's "Tanka 13"). Immediately to the left of the central buddha, he sits on a high throne receiving homage from Tibetan monk-servants in a double-pagoda-roofed pavilion. In size, he is on a par with the royal characters of the *jātaka*, and he holds his right hand in the gesture of teaching. His identity as the learned Fifth Dalai Lama is implied by the painted setting and iconography. The set may have been commissioned in his honor, perhaps with prayers for his longevity. The painting likely dates to the end of his life (d. 1682) or during the regency of Desi Sanggye Gyatsho (d. 1705).

The set was believed to come from the "famous Stael-Holstein Tibetan Art Collection, lately sold, after the great collector's death, in America."[541] The collector mentioned here was Baron Alexander Staël von Holstein (1877–1937), who lived and taught in Beijing

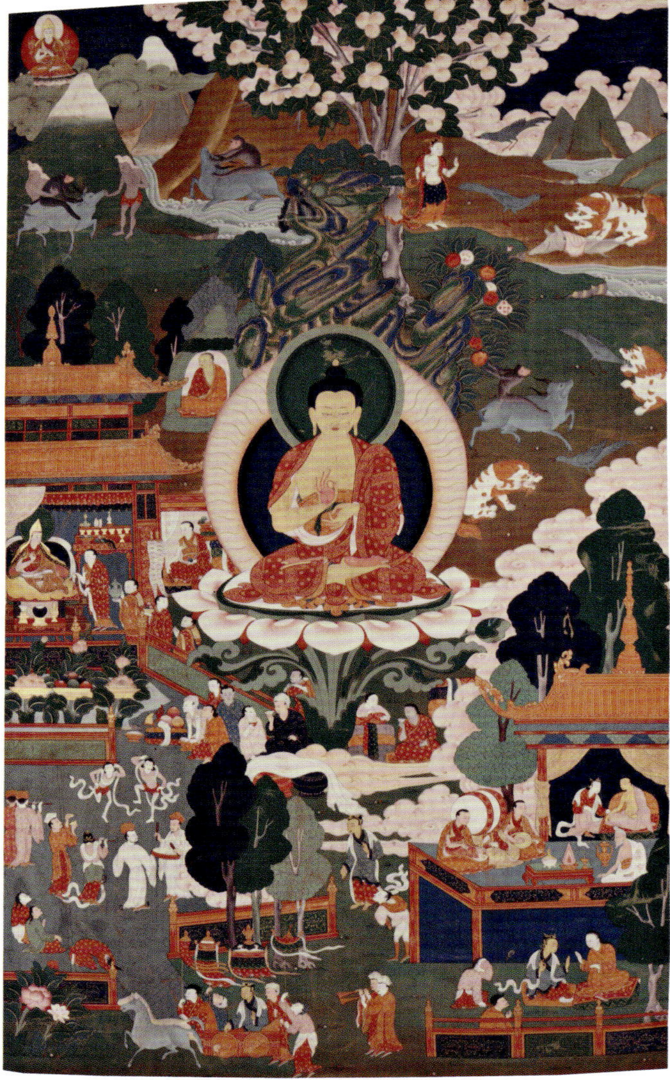

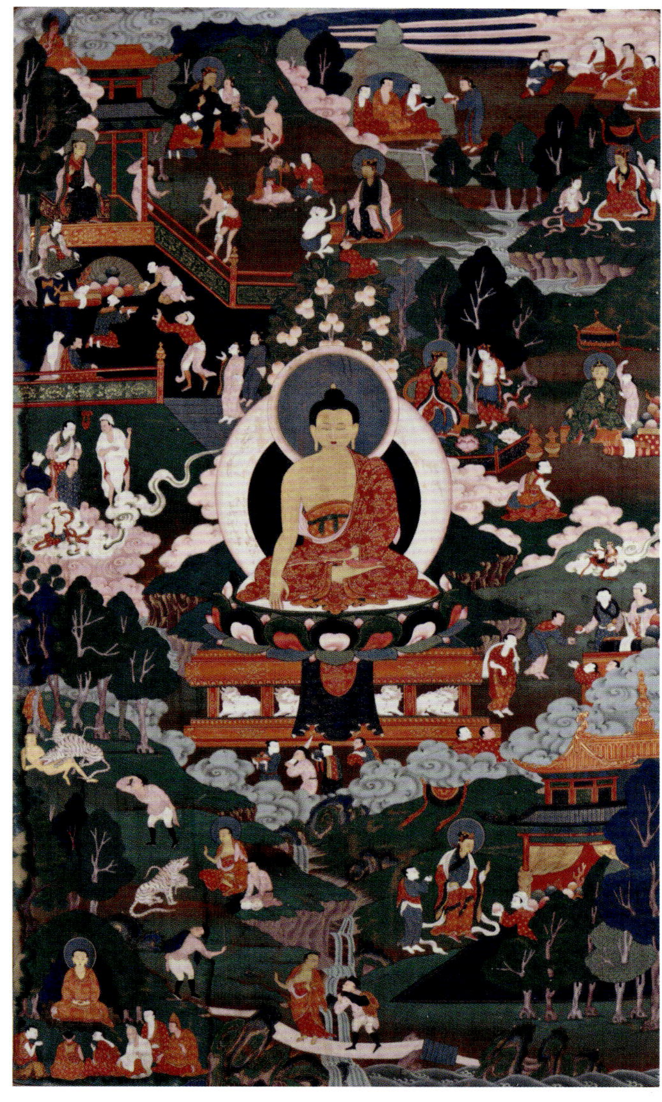

for more than two decades, dying there in 1937.[542]

Bryner observed the direction of the narrative, illustrating it with the second painting in the series (Fig. 11.7):

> On each tanka the picturing always begins at the bottom and mounts artfully upward. So, on Tanka 2, the story about the tigress begins in the lower left corner, with the Bodhisattva's sitting in his forest retreat, teaching all who came to him, before he starts off with a disciple to the plateau where he sees the starving young mother and gives his body to her. The second story begins on the lower right with the bestowal of gifts by the excessively charitable King of the Śibis. Other scenes of giving carry the story up and across the banner to the top.[543]

However, my investigation of the individual thangkas did not confirm this episodic ordering in all of the paintings. Some tales in other thangkas proceed in other directions, following a completely different sequence and arrangement.

Figure 11.8 depicts thangka number 10, with *jātaka* 22, "Born as the golden king of geese." Bryner beautifully summarizes the story depicted in the thangka:

> What delicacy there is in the picturing of the snare that Nishāda made, fit only for its Golden Captive, with its artless looping against the ground and the curving of its

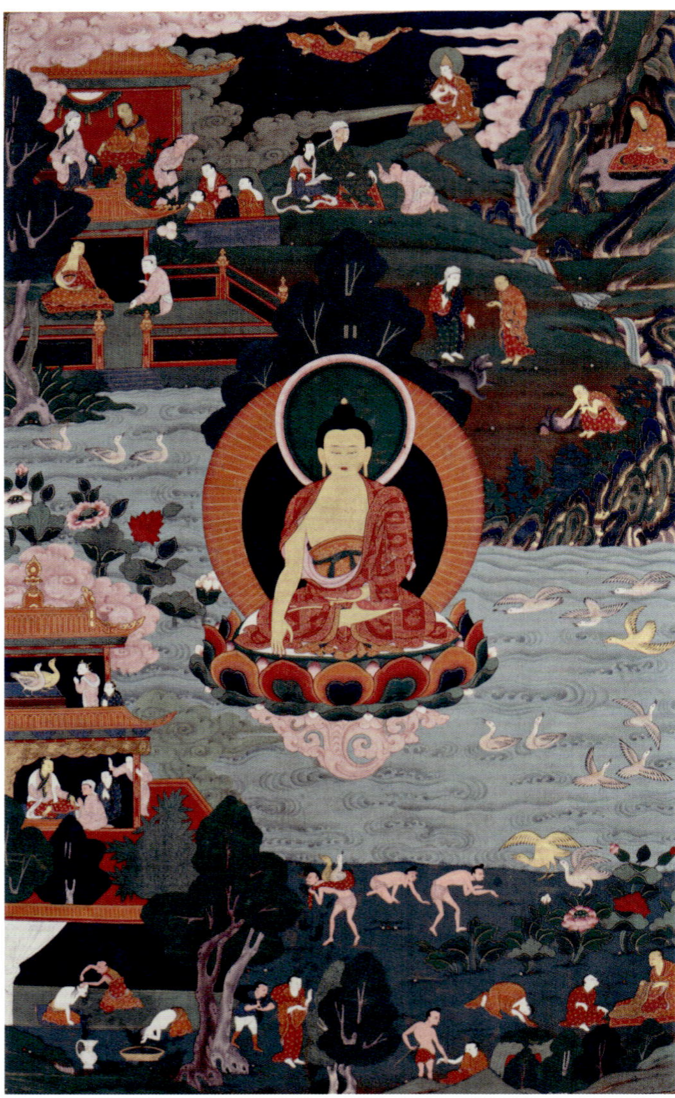

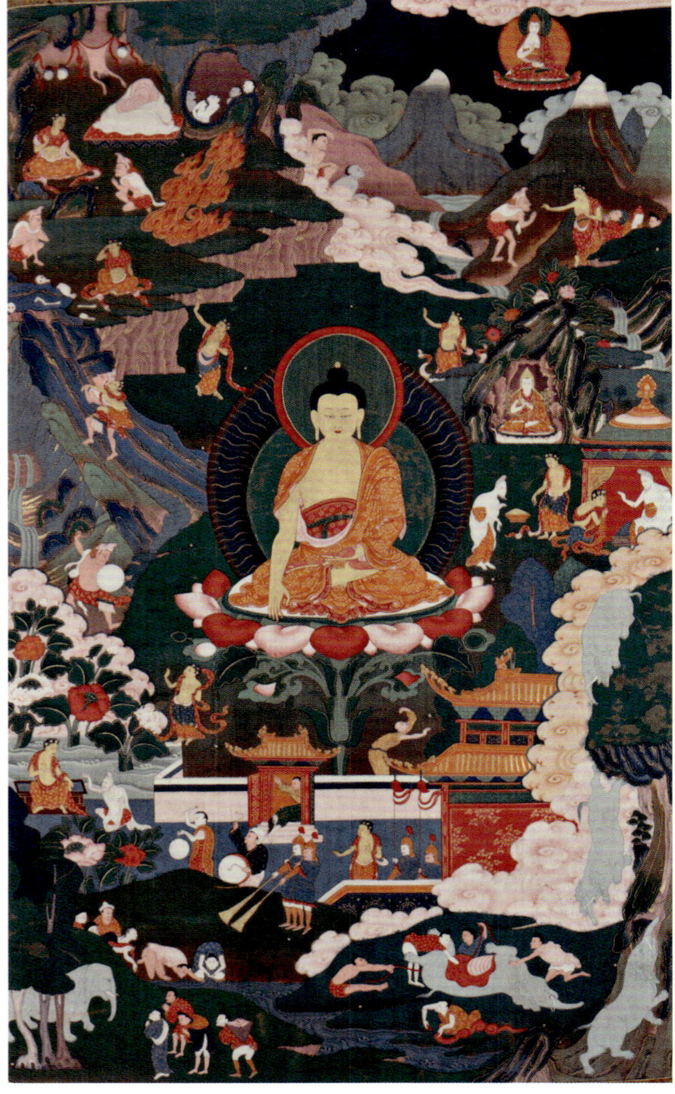

Fig. 11.8
Three Tales from the Jātakamālā (no. 21-23)
mid- or late seventeenth century
Tibetan Tanka 203:1950.
Saint Louis Art Museum, W. K. Bixby Fund.
Literature: Bryner 1956, "Tanka 10"

Fig. 11.9
Two Tales from the Jātakamālā (no. 30
and 31)
mid- or late seventeenth century
Tibetan Tanka 200:1950.
Saint Louis Art Museum, W. K. Bixby Fund.
Literature: Bryner 1956, "Tanka 12"

dainty hooks, secured at both ends with a golden pin!

In the snare the Bodhisattva caught his foot, but in spite of pain from the injury he did not utter the "cry of dangerousness" until his flock had finished eating and so, well fed, could fly away in a great hurry.[544]

As Bryner observed, "The artists surely sketched the scenes on the tankas freehand, so very supple were they in their handling of the iconographic images they had to use."[545] As she added (concerning Fig. 11.7):

> Sophistication toward the events of daily life and a tender sharing of them are subtly displayed in the rich, ever varying shades of pastel blues and greens, reds and yellows, together with generous amounts of gold that make a shimmering surface atmosphere.

Witness the adroitly free manner of placing more than fifty figures on Tanka 12, bearing scenes from the two Jātakas. At the bottom is the Bodhisattva as the Great White Elephant, in five attitudes: meeting the lost strangers and telling them what to do; climbing the cliff above the watering place to which he has directed them by a different easy way; on top of the cliff, ready for his plunge downward in sacrifice; the plunge itself; his dead body being used, as he had counseled, for food and for skins in which to carry water for the rest of the journey.[546]

It is good that Bryner focused on and described these scenes in such detail (see Fig. 11.9). By good luck, the same episode with the kind and altruistic white elephant survives in fragments of several other *jātaka* sets and in an original mural of Gongkar, depicting the *Avadāna* tale as told by Kṣemendra (depicted above in chapter 4).

ANOTHER JĀTAKA SET

A third set of eight seventeenth-century Khyenri-style thangkas also depicts *jātaka* and was formerly in the private Ford collection.[547] One painting is still in that collection; several others have been donated to the Walters Art Museum, the Newark Museum, the Los Angeles County Museum of Art, and the Freer Gallery of Art.[548]

In Figure 11.10, depicted to the left of the central Buddha is tale number 30, of the Buddha-to-be as the compassionate white elephant that jumped to his death from a cliff so that people could feast on his body. At the bottom right, in tale number 33, he is a wild water buffalo who explains that he will not seek revenge on a monkey that had tormented him.[549]

Figure 11.11 depicts the Buddha surrounded by *jātaka* numbers 24 through 28. Tale 26 is told on both sides of the central buddha. The episodes are mapped in Diagram [G]: number 25, "The Sharabha antelope" (here evidently painted as a Chinese *qilin* mythical beast); number 26, "The Ruru deer"; number 27, "The monkey king"; and number 28, "Kṣāntivāda."

OTHER KHYENRI JĀTAKA SETS

Another main group of seventeenth-century thangkas is preserved in two locations: two paintings in the Rubin Museum of Art and one in a private collection. The one in the private collection seems to be the only known survivor from its set, which seems to represent an earlier date than the two in the Rubin. Based on the available photography, it

may be the workmanship of Khyentse Chenmo. It evidently belongs to a large set of one hundred *jātakas* such as the *sKyes rabs brgya rtsa*.

Figure 11.12 depicts *jātaka* numbers 42 through 45. At the lower right is story number 42; at the lower left is number 43, "The brahmin and the rabbit"; at the bottom center is number 44; at the top center is number 45. Note the detailed treatment of the throne back and the large pagoda roofs in the painting.

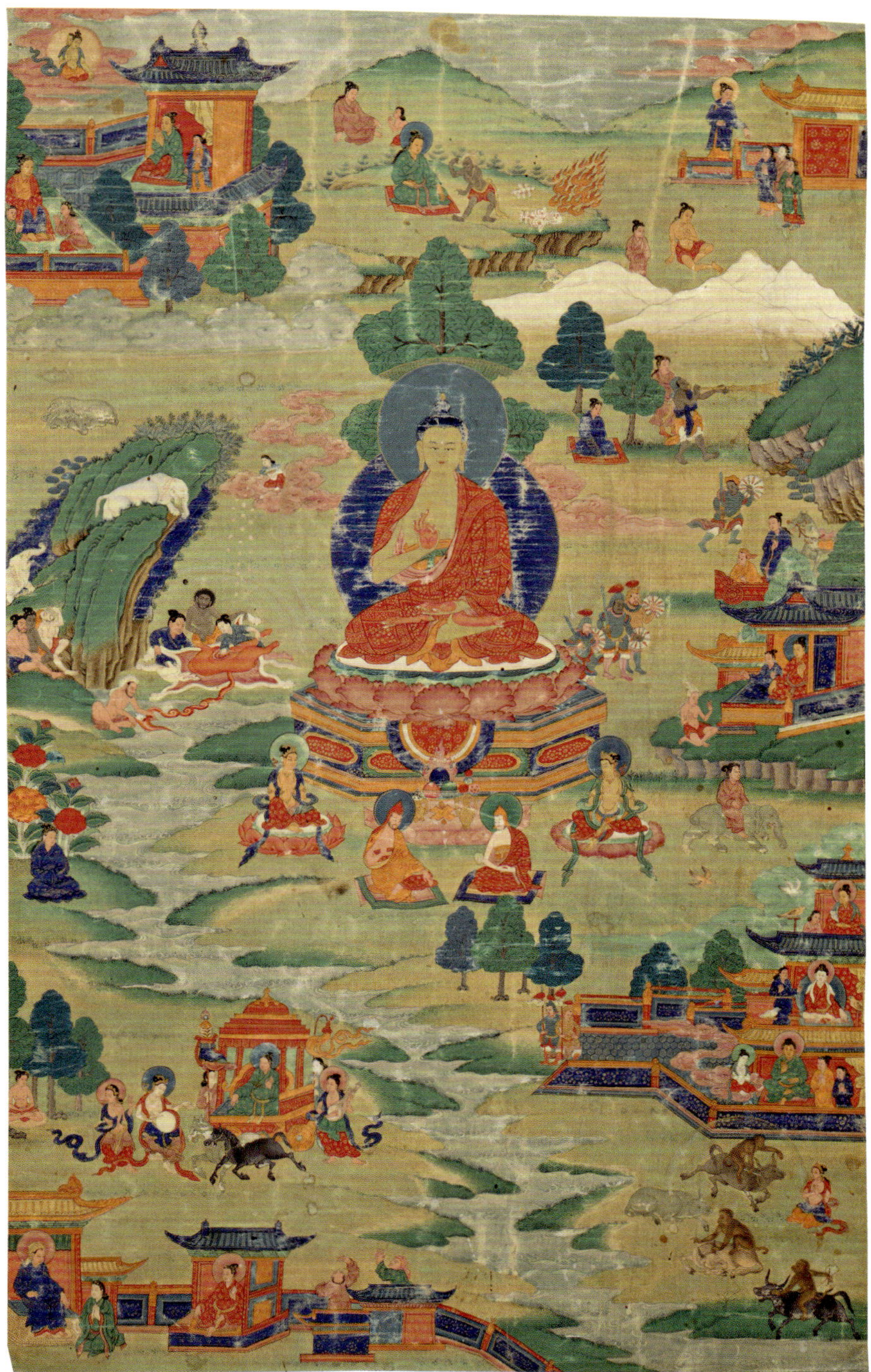

Fig. 11.10
Buddha with Jātaka Tales
seventeenth century
25 ⅞ x 16 ⅝ in. (65.7 x 42.3 cm)
Walters Art Museum, Baltimore, accession no. 35.140

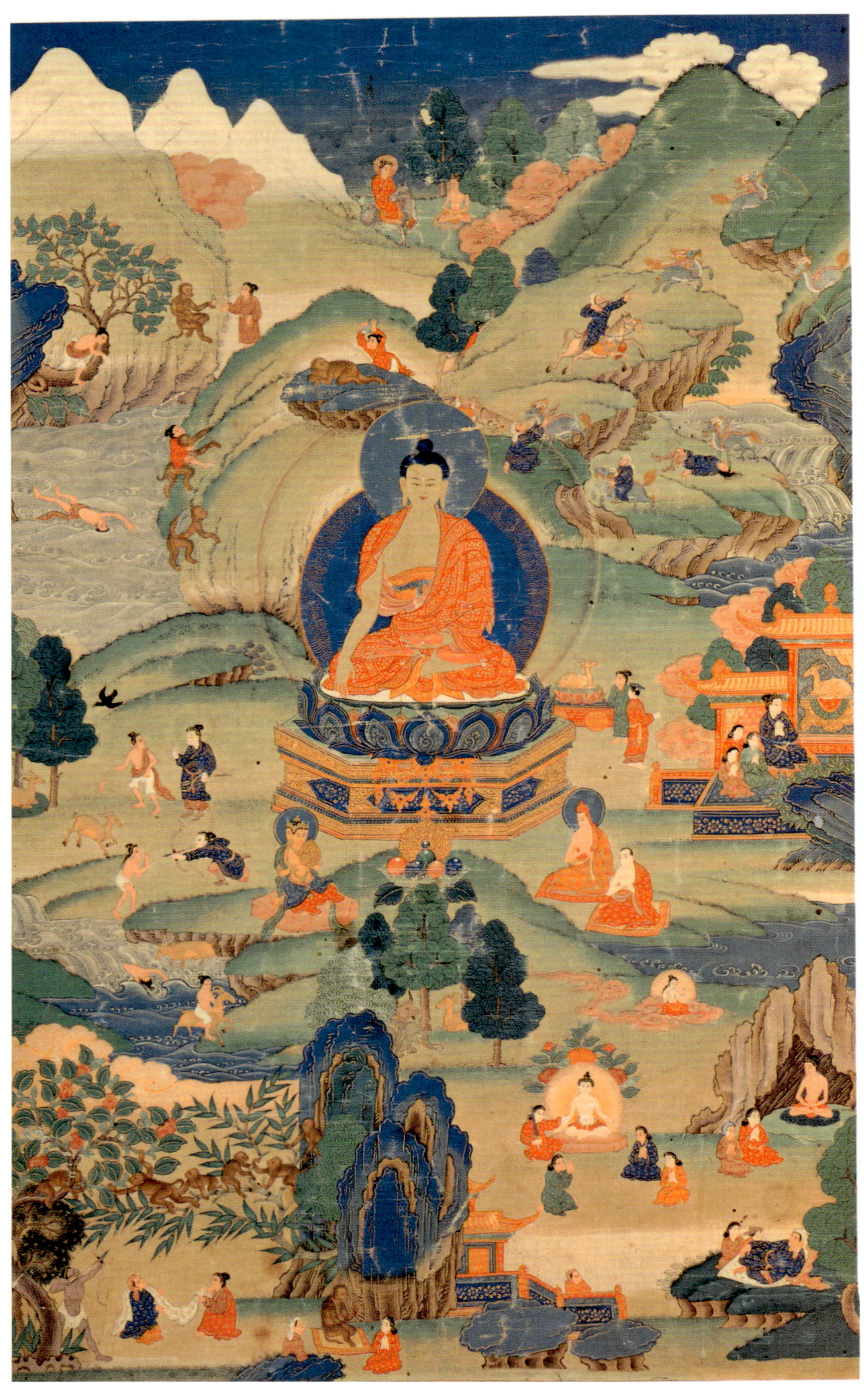

Fig. 11.11
Buddha with Jātaka Tales
seventeenth century
26 x 16 ½ in. (66 x 42 cm)
John and Berthe Ford Collection
Literature: Rhie and Thurman 1991, no. 8

The two stylistically related *jātaka* paintings in the Rubin Museum of Art belong to a later Khyenri set. Figure 11.13 is the sixth in a set of perhaps as many as twenty-five paintings. It depicts *jātaka* numbers 28 through 32. For their arrangement, see Diagram [H]: at the top left is story number 28, "The teacher of restraint," a tale of patience; at the lower right is number 29, "A visitor from Brahma"; at the top right is number 30, "The white elephant," a tale of self-sacrifice; at the bottom left is number 31, "Sutasoma"; at the middle left is number 32, "The prince of the iron house."

Figure 11.14 continues the sequence of tales, after Figure 11.13. This painting includes the last tale in *Jātakamālā*, number 34, which proves that this painting belongs to a larger set. At the lower left is number 33, "The buffalo," a tale of patience; at the lower right is number 34, "The woodpecker," which tells of kindness without thought of reward. Then the series continues at the top left with number 35, "The lion king"; at the top right is number 36, "The trader Mahāvīrya"; and at the bottom center is number 37, "King Suvarṇavarṇa." See Diagram [I] for the placement of the tales.

Figures 11.13 and 11.14 reminded Rob Linrothe of the murals in the San 'dzin lha khang in Nyentok village of Rebgong, which was also a set of murals with Buddhas and Jātaka.[550] I hope those similarities will be possible to verify in the future.

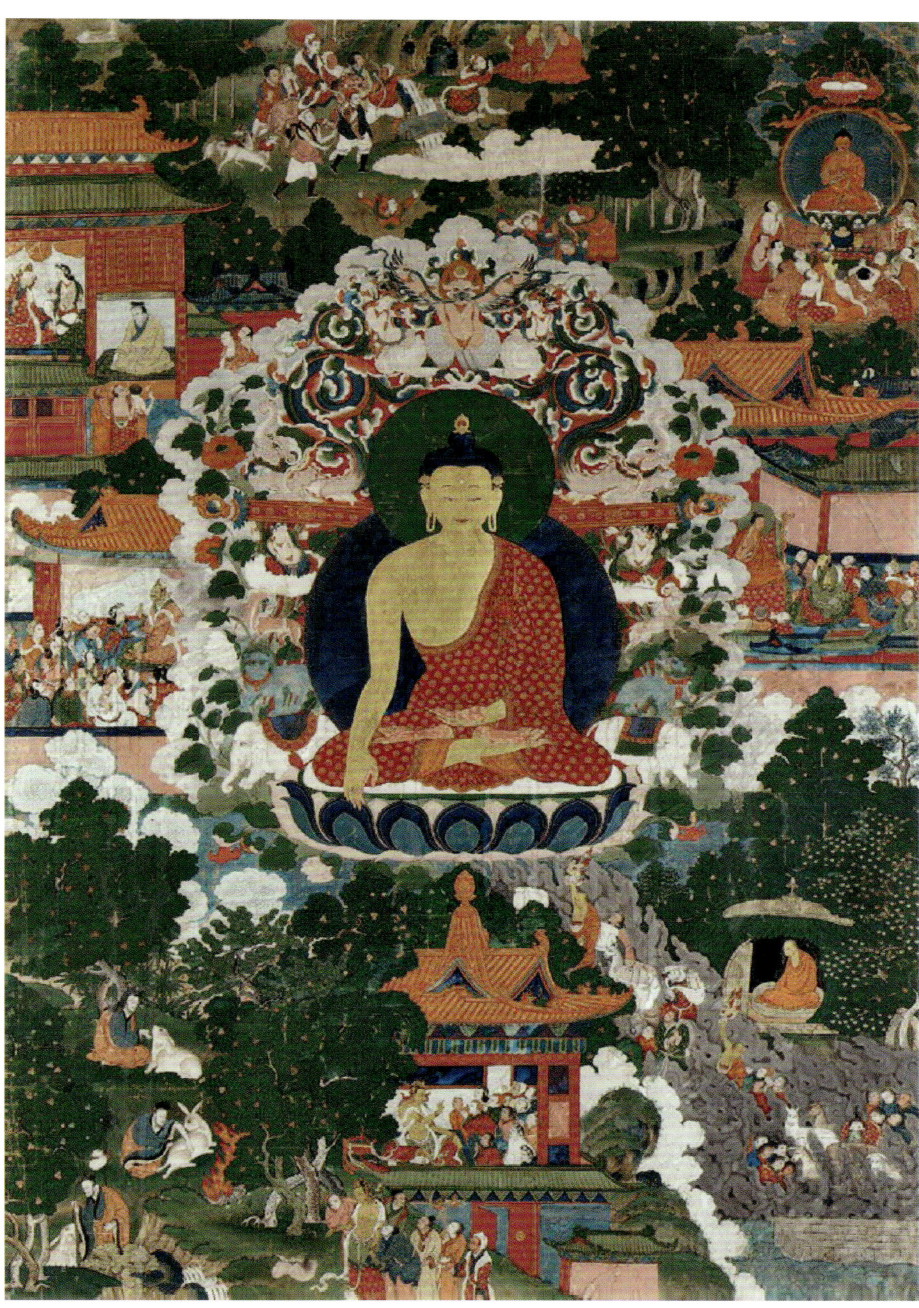

Fig. 11.12
Buddha with Jātaka Tales
late fifteenth or sixteenth century
Private Collection (HAR 81408)

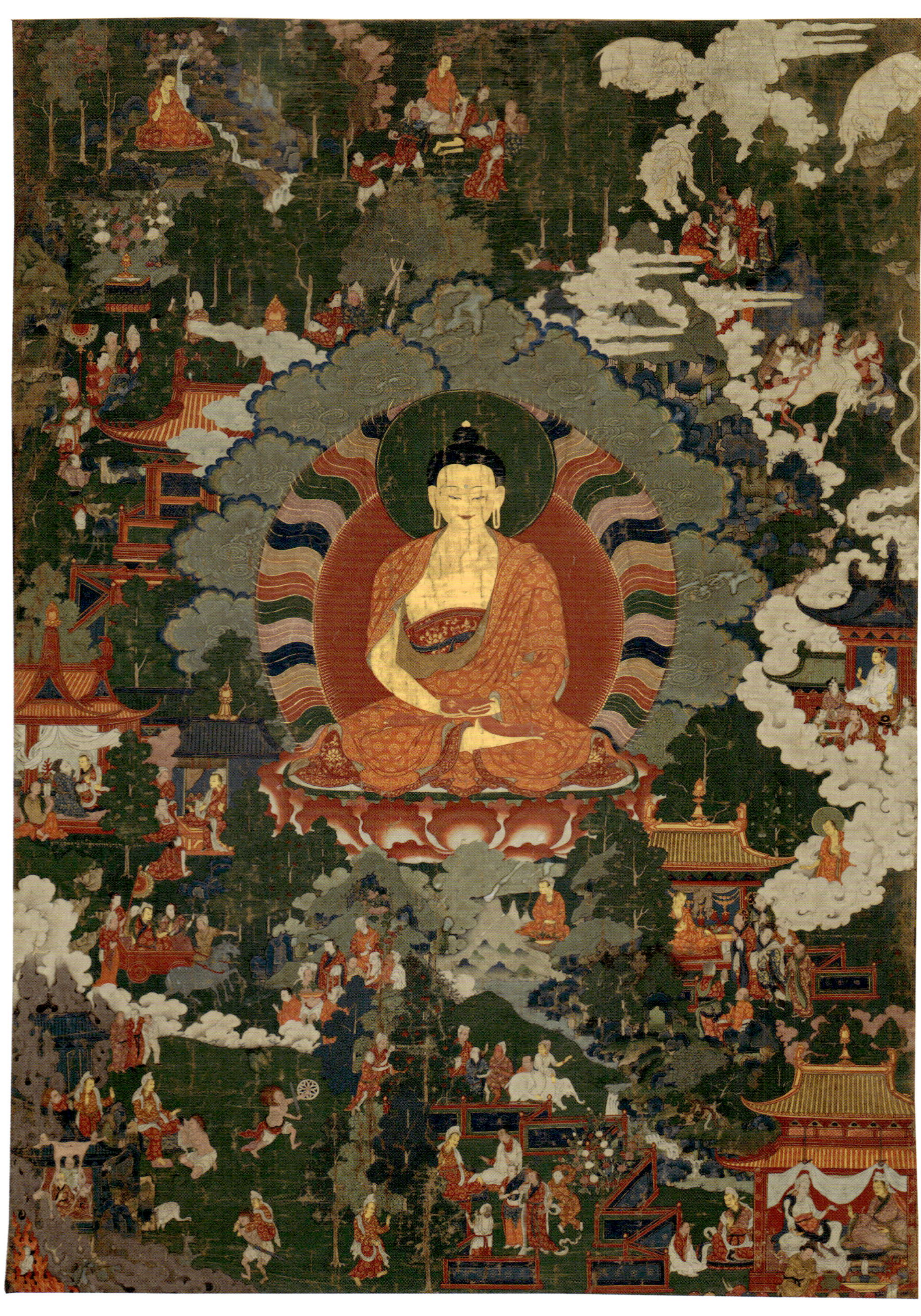

[H]

28. bzang smra ba'i ...

30. glang po che'i ...

B

32. lcags kyi khyim na ...   29. tshangs pa'i ...

31. [unclear] ...

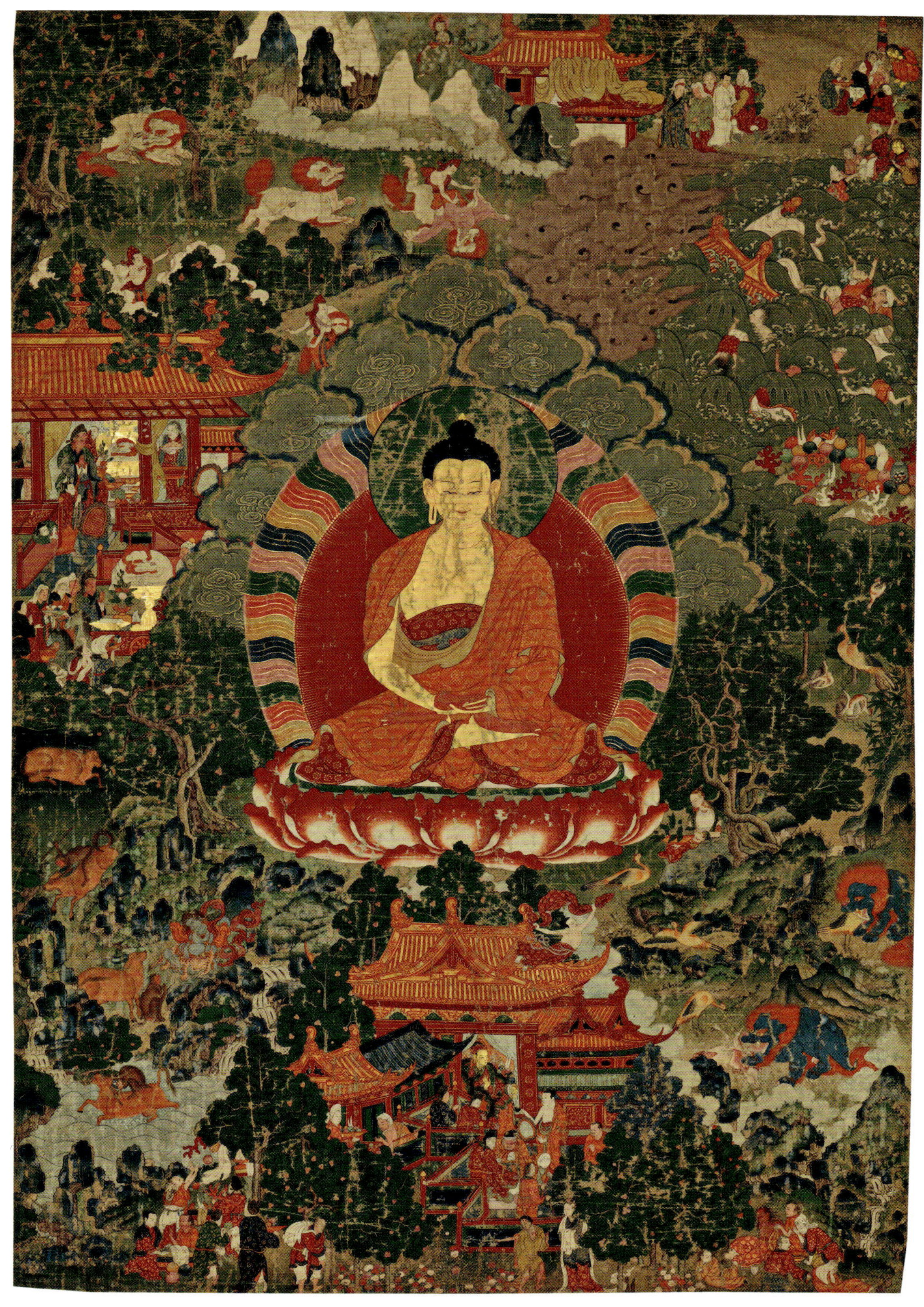

Fig. 11.14
Buddha with Five Jātaka Tales (no. 33-37)
seventeenth century
36 x 25 in. (91.4 x 63.5 cm)
Rubin Museum of Art
C2007.33.1 (HAR 65816)

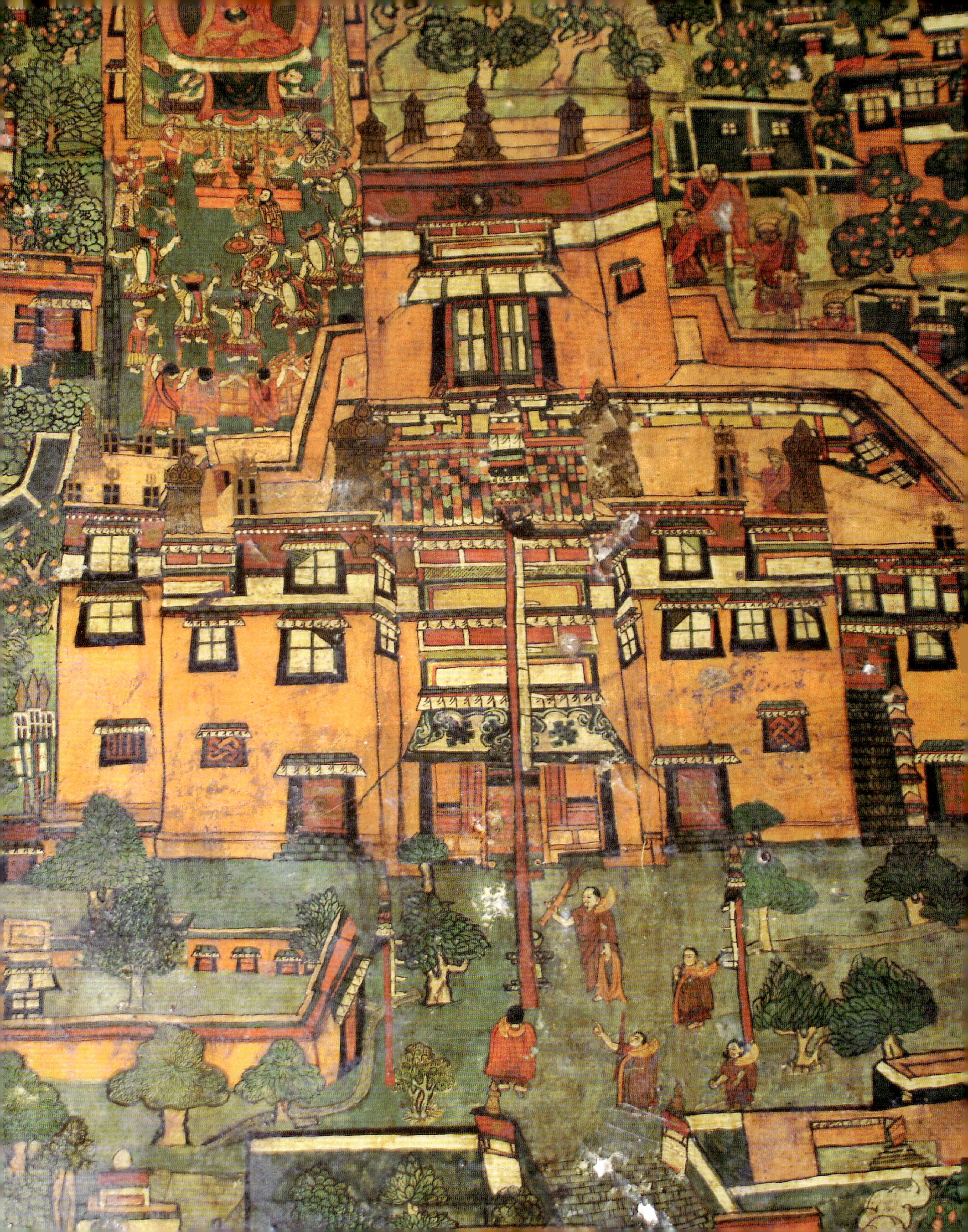

CHAPTER 12

Yeshe Tendzin, a Twentieth-Century Painter from Gongkar

BY MATHIAS FERMER

INTRODUCTION

Elder monks of Gongkar commonly say that around two hundred to two hundred sixty monks lived at Gongkar Chöde before 1959.[551] When Kathok Situ visited the area in winter of 1918/19, he reported a slightly lower number—one hundred sixty—apparently because he did not count those monks residing temporarily at the monastery's several branch temples or at estate holdings nearby.[552] By the first half of the twentieth century, Gongkar Chöde's population had fallen substantially, when we consider that it once housed as many as a thousand resident monks, as Kathok Situ also informed us in his pilgrimage record.[553] During the mid-seventeenth century, the time of the Fifth Dalai Lama, Gongkar Dorjeden was still a large monastic center, renowned for its wide tantric learning, excellent ritual and dance, and fine painting in the style of Khyentse Chenmo. At that time, within Gongkar's monastic compound, the monk residence ([grwa] shag; shag tshang) of Sangngak Khar was a stronghold of Khyenri painters. Gifted artists from this monastic house, including such master artists as Chödze Shönnu and Tshephel, gained trans-regional fame and worked for large projects under state patronage.[554]

The decline in the monk population that occurred in the eighteenth or nineteenth century eventually led to the dying out of the special Khyenri

painting tradition at Gongkar Monastery. In the 1930s, the size of its old assembly hall with sixty-four pillars was reduced partly as the consequence of its much smaller monastic community.[555] (The main building was also sagging in places, which the two new walls were meant to remedy.)

In around the mid-1930s, the walls of the new main temple hall, which was reduced to just forty-nine pillars in size, were decorated with scenes from the *Avadānakalpalatā* moral tales (*dPag bsam 'khri shing*), the same subject that had also graced the outer walls of the old assembly hall.[556] Painted in a variety of the usual predominant central Tibetan Menri style (the Eri of Lhasa), the new rendering of the *Kalpalatā* was, judging by its style, probably done by outside artists with at most just a few Gongkar monks or local painters helping. A few slightly more elaborate lotus petals under some of the thirty-two buddhas as main figures and a few other details are the only hints of a limited involvement of Khyenri artists in the new ground-floor murals dating to the 1930s.

Figure 12.2 illustrates three buddhas as main figures with lotus petals as they were typically painted by Menri painters of central Tibet. However, in Figure 12.3 the lotus petal centers of the left-hand buddha approach the kind of elaborate lotus petals that might be found as a special feature of the Khyenri style. (The sleeveless inner garments worn by the first and third buddhas in this illustration are also unusual and evocative of the Khyenri.)

Figure 12.4 depicts one buddha with a cluster of clouds in the landscape that have the typical "cloud-eyes" of the Eri style of Lhasa. (This panel also depicts the Fifth Dalai Lama and two Sanskrit scholars above.) The clouds and the typical peonies mark it as the work of Menri artists.

The fact that the artists almost all painted in a fairly orthodox Menri style of Ü province seems to reflect that the Khyenri style by the 1930s was no longer significantly present at Gongkar Monastery. David Jackson in his *History of Tibetan Painting* of 1996 asserted that "by the early 20th century, the style of mKhyen-brtse chen-mo and his followers had apparently died out as a separate living tradition."[557]

Nevertheless, we now know that a few Khyenri artists still lived in Lhokha in the 1930s. Jackson did not then know about the survival of a very small number of Khyenri artists in Lhokha such as Uchen Tenpa Gyatsho (1882–1959), whom I will come to discuss later, and three of his sons to whom he had passed on his knowledge. Tenpa Gyatsho's disciple Tshewang Dorje (1933–2002) and his artistic career are presented below in appendix E. As briefly mentioned above in chapter 4, Tenpa Gyatsho's murals of the Sixteen Arhats still survive in skylights high above the main assembly hall. (See Figs. 4.10A and 4.10B.)

As seen above in chapter 5, Kunzang Tse College of Gongkar also preserved murals in a late Khyenri style that date to the 1930s or early 1940s, the time of the seminary's general

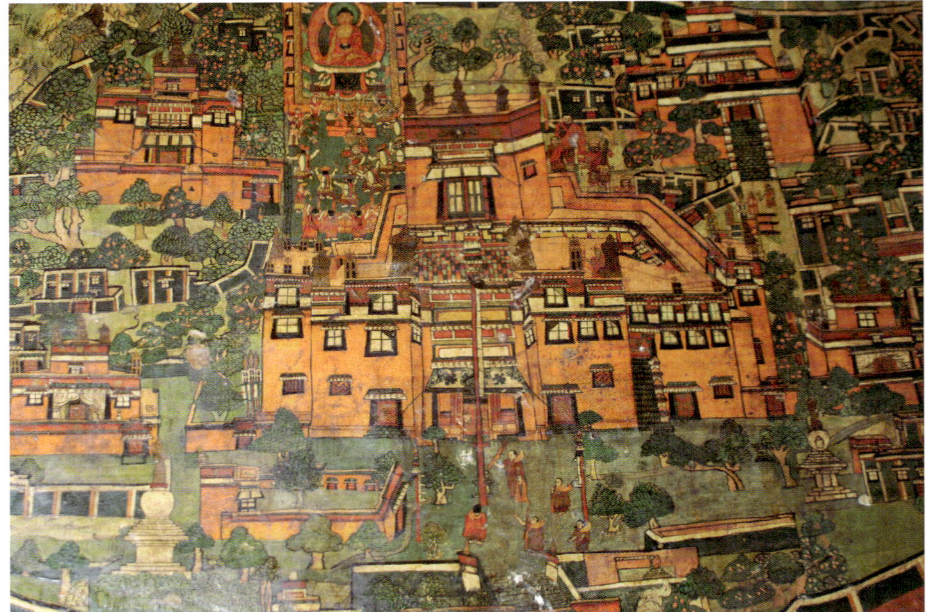

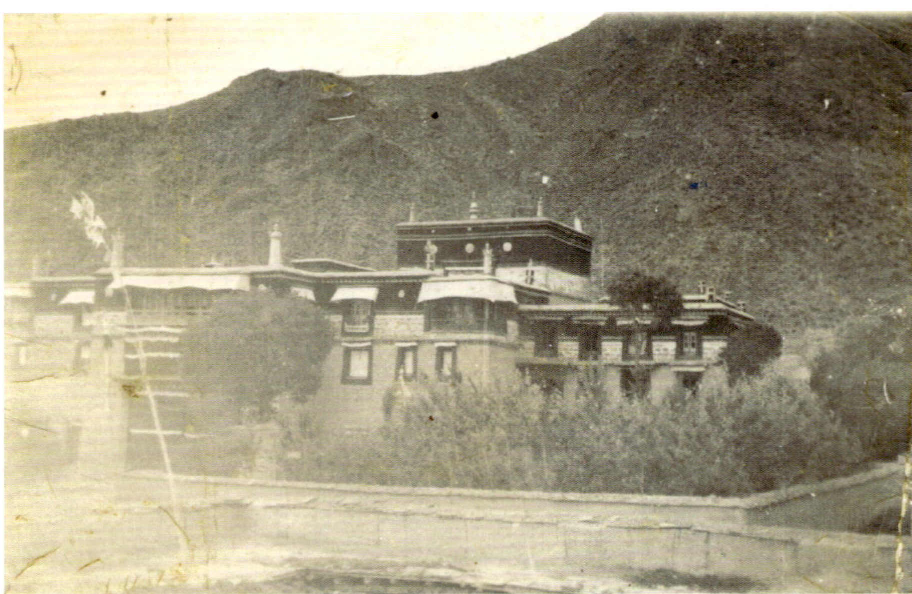

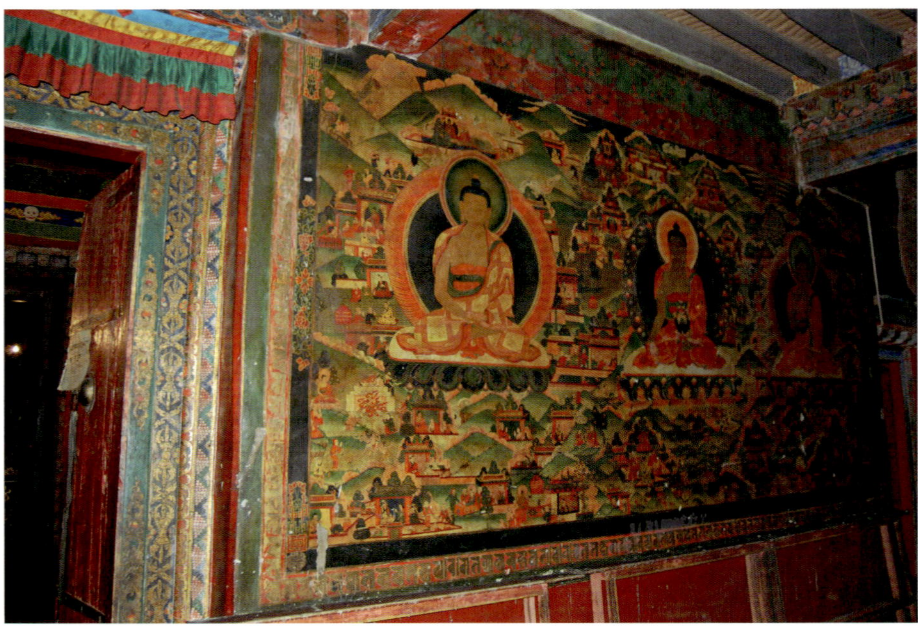

Fig. 12.0
Gongkar Chöde's Main Temple before 1959
Mural, second floor, main building,
Gongkar; painted by Yeshe Tendzin, 1940s
Photo: Rob Linrothe, 2007

Fig. 12.1
Gongkar Chöde's Main Temple before 1959;
lama's private quarters in the upper front;
photograph taken from the *trulku*'s summer
residence southwest of the main building
Photo courtesy of Chögyal-la, Dharamsala,
India

Fig. 12.2
Three Buddhas with *Avadāna* Tales
Murals, New Assembly Hall, Gongkar;
1930s
Photo: Kazuo Kano, 2007

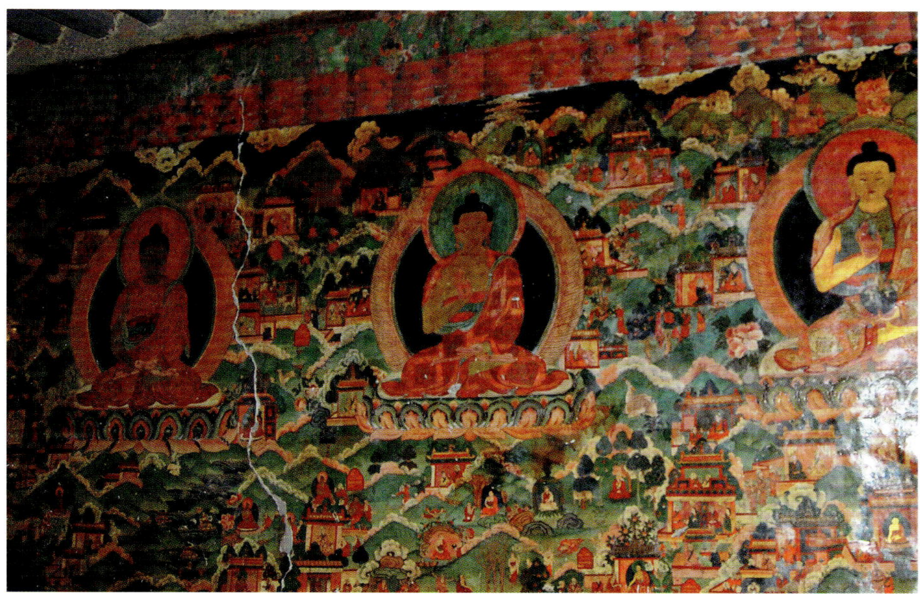

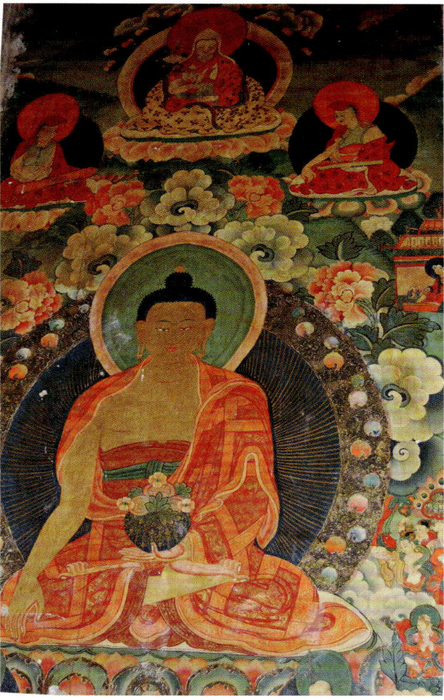

renovation. The impressive murals on the upper walls (*khyams*) of that twelve-pillar temple hall depict the complete Lamdre lineage in the Gongkar tradition. (See Figure 12.5 and Figures 5.5, 5.8, 5.11, 5.16, 5.19-5.24, 6.3, 6.11, 6.21, 6.37, 7.3, 7.6, 7.8, 7.16) These may have been the work of Tenpa Gyatsho or another local Khyenri artist. Figure 12.6 illustrates the same artist's work in an adjoining mural panel of Kunzang Tse that depicts three bodhisattvas in form of the "Protectors of the Three Families" (*rigs gsum mgon po*). (Upper garments cover the upper torsos and upper arms of the bodhisattvas, as is usual in the Khyenri.)

Moreover, the same lineage of the Lamdre, passing down to Dorjedenpa, Gongkar Chöde's founder (who was guru number 23 in the transmission), was depicted in a mural series at Drathang Monastery. These wall paintings, which are in style and iconography similar to the Kunzang Tse murals, can be dated to the time of the restoration of the main temple that was initiated by the Fifth Reting Rinpoche (1912/19–1947) in the late 1930s.[558] When we investigate the surviving art from Drathang, most prominently these well-preserved lineage murals and the related set of gilt sculptures that were presented above, in chapter 5, we find a close connection with the iconography of Gongkar Chöde. Moreover, the fact that the Drathang murals represent the same sequence of the Lamdre guru lineage points to similarities with the teaching system at Gongkar and reflects the strong historical ties between the two monasteries from the fifteenth century onward.[559] Figure 12.7 is taken from this set of mural panels at Drathang. (All three masters have transparent Khyenri head nimbuses, which we never see in Menri paintings.)

Another Sakya monastery in the vicinity of Gongkar preserved murals by Lhokha artists working in a late Khyenri style. Rawame (Rwa ba smad) Monastery in Kyishong (sKyid gshongs), just twenty kilometers (twelve miles) downstream from Gongkar Monastery, shows some Khyenri elements in its murals. Depicting the Indian and Tibetan teachers in the upper wall above the assembly hall, the murals can be dated slightly earlier than Kunzang Tse and Drathang, to around the 1920s or 1930s, as they portray the Thirteenth Dalai Lama (1876–1933), who I assume was then alive. The restoration was directed by the Rawame abbot Palden Losang (dPal ldan blo bzang), who was thirty-seventh in the abbatial succession. The artist or artists came from Dechen Chökhor Monastery (bDe chen chos 'khor), the large Drukpa Kagyu establishment in the upper valley to the south of Gongkar Chöde. (This intriguing reference to local artists comes from lHag tshing 2004, a publication that also included a brief history of Rawame and the life of Khenchen Paljor Yeshe [mKhan chen dPal 'byor ye shes, 1935–1998].) As mentioned above in chapter 11, Dechen Chökhor was one of the seventeen sites of Khyenri artists in the late seventeenth century, at the time of the Fifth Dalai Lama's passing.[560]

The new Rawame murals in the upper part depicted Buddha Śākyamuni

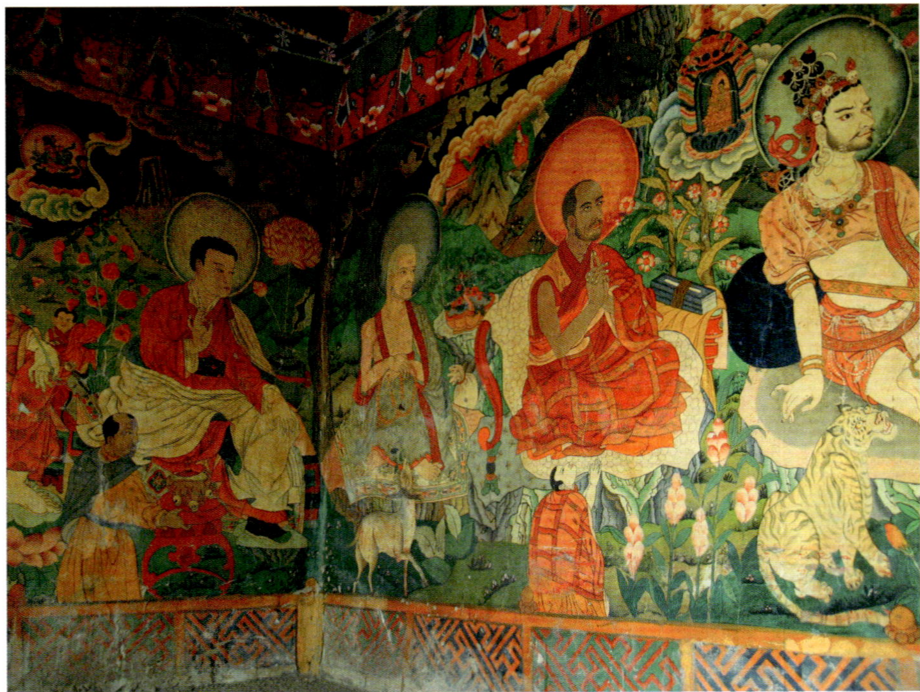

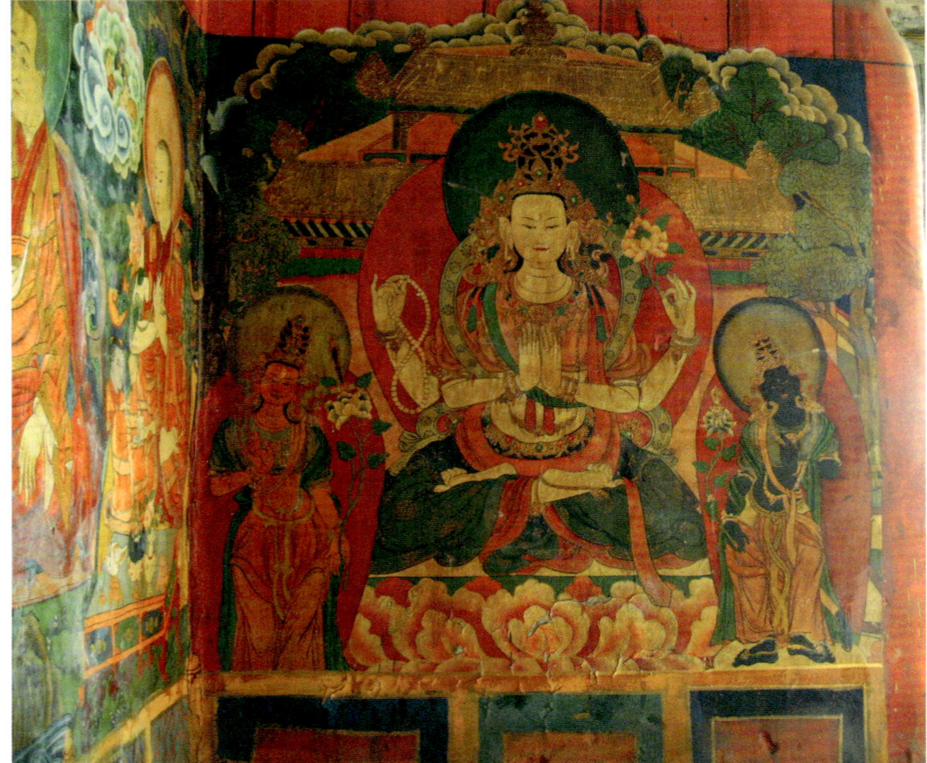

YESHE TENDZIN OF GONGKAR[562]

When Yeshe Tendzin (1915/16–1971) joined Gongkar Chöde in the early 1930s, no Khyenri painters were still active at the monastery. David Jackson in his brief introduction of Yeshe Tendzin in his book of 1996 characterized him as a twentieth-century reviver of the Khyenri style who "used to study and copy the old murals of mKhyen-brtse" and "imitated them in his own paintings,"[563] implying that he did not encounter a Khyenri painting master to learn from at Gongkar Monastery. My own sources and findings support that same conclusion, though we now know that as late as the 1930s some Khyenri artists were still based just south of Gongkar at Dechen Chökhor and others were still based in Chushül.

Background

Originally from Nyemo (sNye mo) in present-day Lhasa prefecture, Yeshe Tendzin was born into his mother's family of the Yakde Simkhang (g.Yag sde gzims khang). His father was from Lhasa and descended on his own father's side from the Chöchang Simshak (Chos byang gzims shag) family.[564] Later in life Yeshe Tendzin was once told by a fortune teller (*pra babs mkhan*) that in his previous life he had been the chief attendant of the famed Rime master Jamyang Khyentse Wangpo ('Jam dbyangs mkhyen brtse'i dbang po, 1820–1892),

with his two chief disciples, the Eight Medicine Buddhas, and the Six Ornaments with the Two Excellent Ones. (See, for example, Fig. 12.8.). The same murals also show the Five Sakya Founders, Atiśa with his chief disciples, the current (i.e., Thirteenth) Dalai Lama, and the Öntrül Trulku Champa Losal Tenpe Gyaltshen (Byams pa blo gsal bstan pa'i rgyal mtshan) from Yarlung Tashi Chöde.[561] These paintings regularly use pink in body nimbuses, and we find here elaborate lotus petals beneath the buddhas, which are both probably Khyenri touches. (For the painted portrait of the Öntrül Trulku, see Fig. 12.9.)

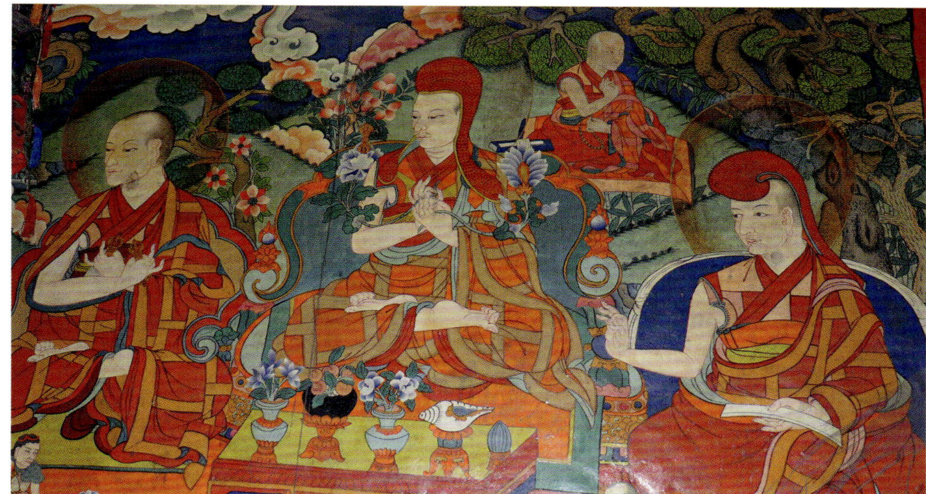

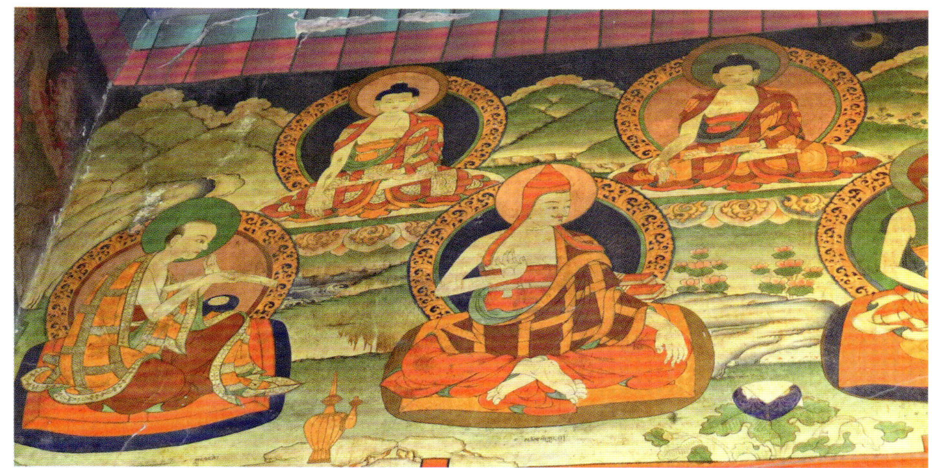

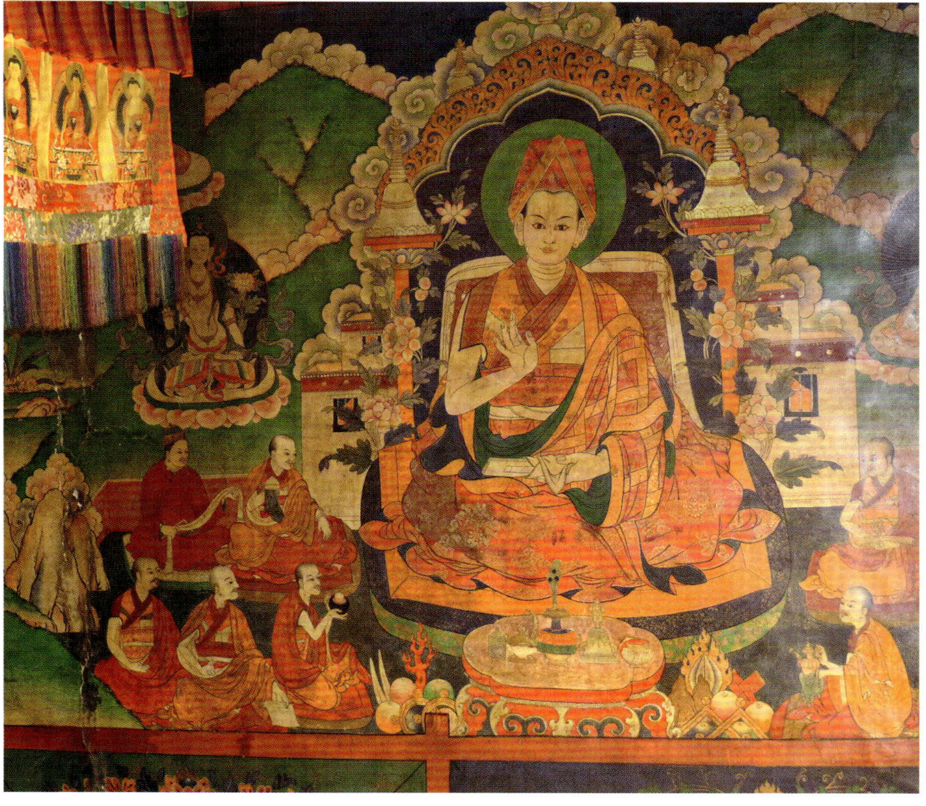

FIG. 12.7
Three Lamdre Lineage Masters: Lama
Dampa (left), Dorjedenpa (center), and
another lama
Mural, upper wall, right, Drathang
Assembly Hall; late 1930s
Photo: Mathias Fermer, 2015

FIG. 12.8
Nāgārjuna (left) and Dignāga (right) from
among the Six Ornaments
Mural, upper wall, front, Rawame Assembly
Hall; early twentieth century
Photo: Mathias Fermer, 2015

FIG. 12.9
Portrait of the Tenth Öntrül Trulku
Mural, upper wall, right, Rawame Assembly
Hall; early twentieth century
Photo: Mathias Fermer, 2015

who was named Tshultrim. The fortune
teller from Kham also prophesied that
he would be reborn in his next life in the
pure land of Shambhala.[565] At an early
age, Yeshe Tendzin was sent to Lhokha
to study painting. Somewhere east of
Gongkar on the southern banks of the
Tsangpo River—probably at Yarlung,
Tsethang, or Chonggye—he received
training in the painting tradition of
Menthangpa (*sman thang lugs*).[566] Later,
in the 1930s, he was ordained as a monk
at Gongkar Chöde, where in the following years he extensively learned recitations and rituals. His monastic house
was Tönden Ling (Don ldan gling
gzims shag).[567]

Showing talent in the monastery's
liturgy, Yeshe Tendzin was appointed
chant-leader at one of the colleges (i.e.,
grwa tshang dbu mdzad or *dbu mdzad
'og ma*),[568] most likely at Kunthang College, to which he belonged. At Tönden
Ling, as a young monk he took over the
administration (*gzims shag nyar red*),[569]
apparently thanks to the sound secular
education he had received before he
became a monk. Later, he was appointed
as the chamberlain (*gsol dpon*) of the
Dorjedenpa Trulku Jampel Lungtok
Chökyi Gyaltshen ('Jam dpal lung rtogs

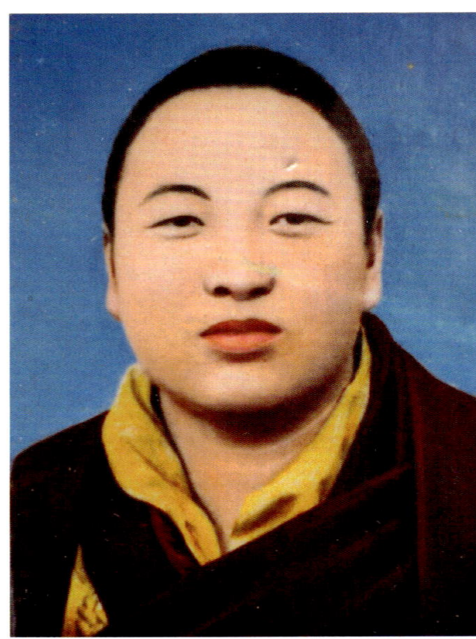

chos kyi rgyal mtshan, 1928–1959).[570] (See Fig. 12.10.) Yeshe Tendzin is said to have been personally chosen for this post by the young *trulku*, while he was painting somewhere at the monastery.[571] Having served the boy *trulku* for a while, he was then promoted to steward (*phyag mdzod*) of the lama's estate (*bla brang*).[572]

At around this time, the Dorjedenpa *trulku* set up a small scriptural seminary (*bshad grwa*) at the monastery. "Chamdzö-la" (*phyag mdzod lags*)—as Yeshe Tendzin was then called as steward—had to pay for the twenty-five students who were pursuing the new course of study under Minyak Kyorpön (Mi nyag skyor dpon, d. 1956?), a scholastic teacher (*geshe)* from the Geluk monastery of Drepung who also had some links with the Sakya school.[573] In connection with his administrative duties, he travelled several times to northern India (and possibly also to Bhutan) on business trips for the lama's estate. In around 1953 on one of his trading journeys, he disrobed and left Gongkar Chöde after his return.[574] He then settled in the

neighboring valley of Shung Namrab (gZhung rNam rab) at Treshing (sPre'u zhing). He took a wife from a family with the name "Bepa" (Brag pa?). At Treshing he lived as a lay painter, though he was still addressed by his former title as "Bepe Chamdzö" (Brag pa'i phyag mdzod).[575] Following the tragic events of March 1959, he and his family fled into exile, leaving Tibet for India.

Life as an Artist

Before coming to Gongkar Chöde, Yeshe Tendzin had first learned painting under a Menri-style master in Lhokha.[576] In the mid-1930s, at about age twenty (he was born in 1915 or 1916), Yeshe Tendzin is said to have assisted in painting the inner walls of the resized assembly hall of Gongkar.[577] Could he have been among the Menri artists who painted the new walls? One oral source states that a Menthangpa artist from the monastery of Dungphü Chökhor (rDo/gDung phud chos 'khor), who was then painting the new murals in the entrance hall (*sgo 'byor*) of Gongkar's main temple, became his teacher.[578] The small Sakya monastery in Chideshöl (lCe bde zhol) also underwent restoration at around the same time, during which two monks from Dungphü Chökhor painted the new murals.[579] Thus Yeshe Tendzin may have received his initial Menri training by the monks from Dungphü Chökhor and may have studied at that monastery. (It is not known whether he was already a monk by the time he learned from them.)

Later, as a monk of Gongkar and stimulated by the rich artwork there, he adopted the style of Khyentse Chenmo, which nobody in the monastery was practicing. As models he took the old murals and sculptures by the great master. He copied what he saw and imitated some features in his own paintings.[580] It is said that he learned the Khyenri divine proportions by tracing the sketch lines (*thig*) from the back of old *thangkas*.[581]

When serving as personal attendant to the Dorjedenpa Trulku, he must have had access to masterpieces by Khyentse Chenmo. While working as the lama's chamberlain, he painted as much as time allowed and gradually developed his style through self-study and painting at the monastery.[582]

By around the 1940s, sometime after the ground floor restorations were completed, he painted several small decorative murals in the second floor of Gongkar's main temple.[583] In the "Chapel of Bronze Sculptures" (Li ma lha khang) near the front of the main building's second floor, he painted, for instance, a small panel depicting the monastic compound of Gongkar with all four colleges and the surrounding monk's residences, also labeling each building with small inscriptions. (See Figs. 12.0 and 1.27B).

Yeshe Tendzin also painted, in the same outside areas of the second floor, decorative murals depicting such auspicious themes as the Four Harmonious Friends (*mthun po spun bzhi*) and the Six Symbols of Long Life (*tshe ring rnam drug*).[584] The painting of the longevity symbols (Fig. 12.12.) is noteworthy for the many animals and birds depicted in the landscape, somewhat reminiscent of Khyentse Chenmo's art. The six symbols of longevity are: "the rocky crag of longevity," "the old man of longevity," "the tree of longevity," "the water of longevity," "the crane of longevity," and "the deer of longevity."

Figure 12.13 illustrates yet another mural of similar size, style, and location, this one depicting the Sakya founder Sachen Kunga Nyingpo in a landscape setting, again with a multitude of birds and animals. The artist took the ornate throne and depiction of Sachen seated on it from a Khyenri depiction of Sachen (compare Fig. 7.8). The inclusion of small exotic-looking minor figures at the base of the painting is something that Khyentse Chenmo also commonly did. (See also the similar minor figure that

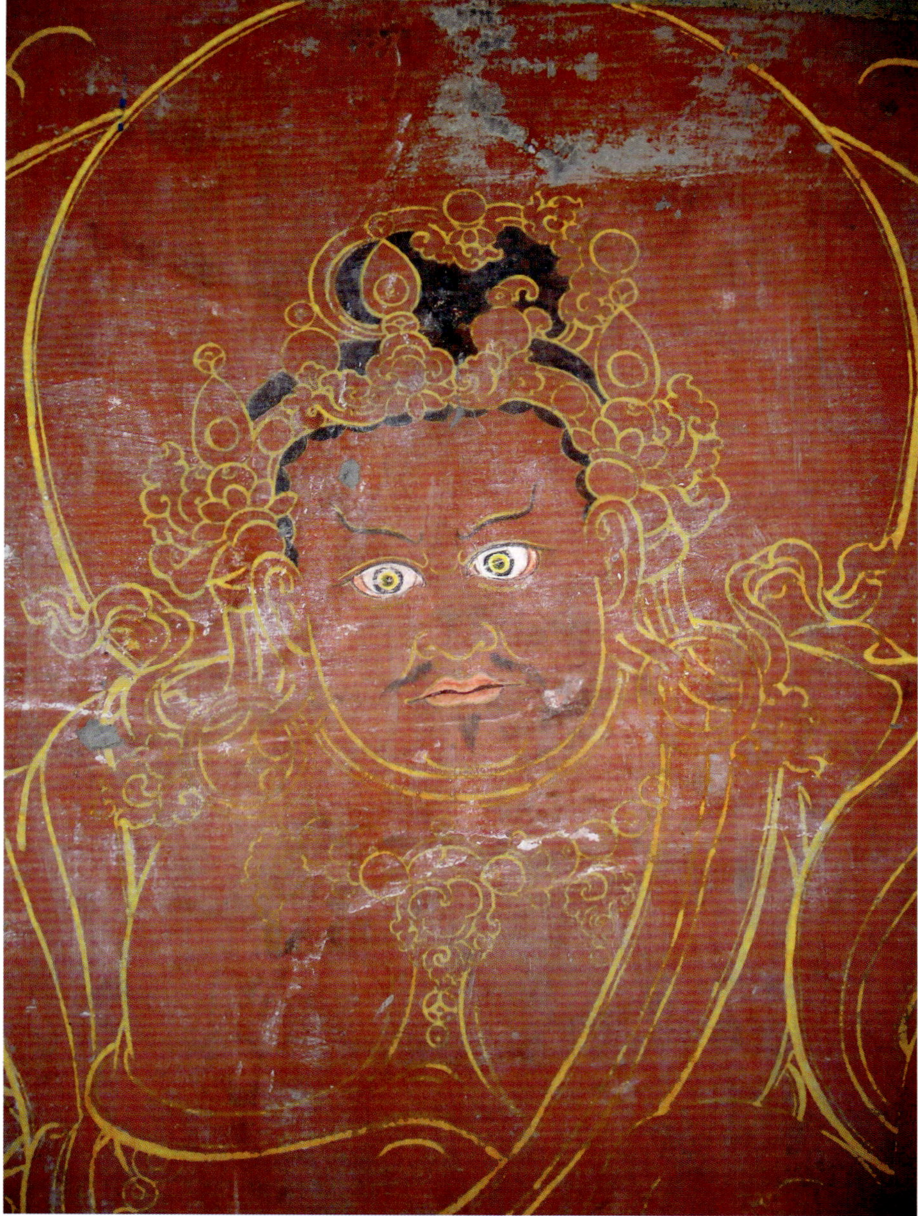

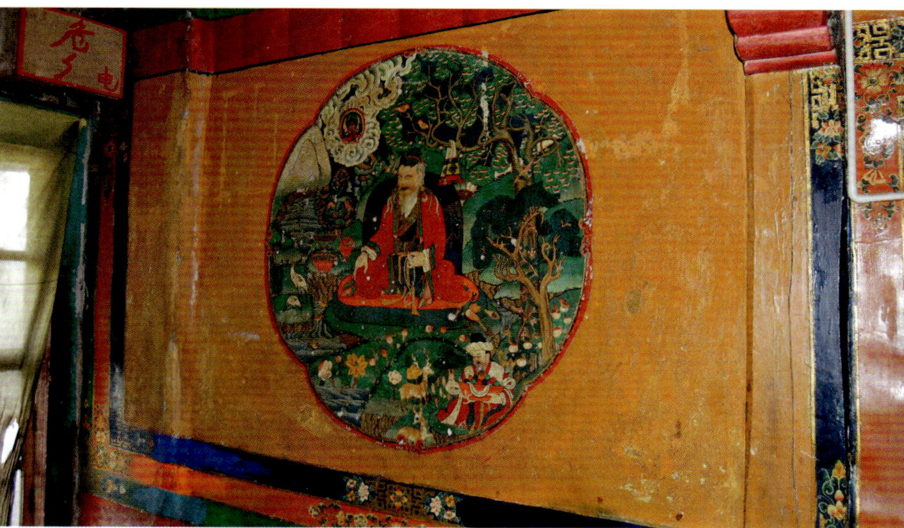

Fig. 12.11
Jambhala
Detail, mural, lower wall, Drepung College,
Gongkar Monastery; 1940s
Photo: Mathias Fermer, 2010

Fig. 12.12
Six Symbols of Long Life
Mural, second floor, main building,
Gongkar Monastery; 1940s
Photo: Kazuo Kano, 2007

pops up unexpectedly at the base of Fig. 12.12.)

Figure 12.14 depicts part of yet another small mural, but this detail shows Virupa's face and headdress. Yeshe Tendzin (if he was the artist of this mural) did seem to have painted its details with knowledge of Khyentse Chenmo's paintings and sculptures of the same adept. (Compare Figs. 6.1, 6.3. and 6.4)

Later, at the end of the 1940s, Yeshe Tendzin or "Chamdzö-la" painted the walls of the restored twelve-pillar temple hall at Drepung College of Gongkar.[585] Drepung College, to the south of the main temple, was the last college to be renovated at Gongkar Chöde (See Fig. 1.28 for an outside view the building.).[586] He painted the upper front wall with some lineage masters from the Path with the Result. On its side walls he depicted the Sixteen Elders (*gnas brtan bcu drug*) in an "Indian style," as my sources told me in Tibet.[587] What is referred to here is a special naturalistic painting style that Yeshe Tendzin is said to have discovered and admired when visiting India in the 1940s or early 1950s.[588]

See Figures 12.15 and 12.16, which depict arhats Bakula, holding a mongoose, and Piṇḍola Bharadvāja (Bha ra dhwa dza bsod snyoms len), holding a book and an alms bowl. (Note the faint pink and pastel orange base colors of the head nimbuses.)

Except its back wall, no murals survive on the lower walls of Drepung

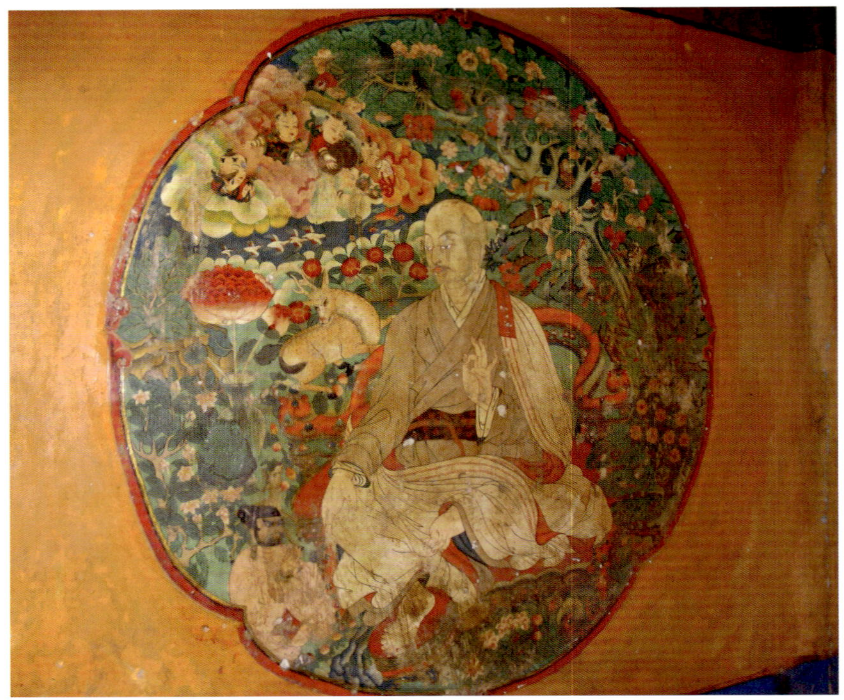

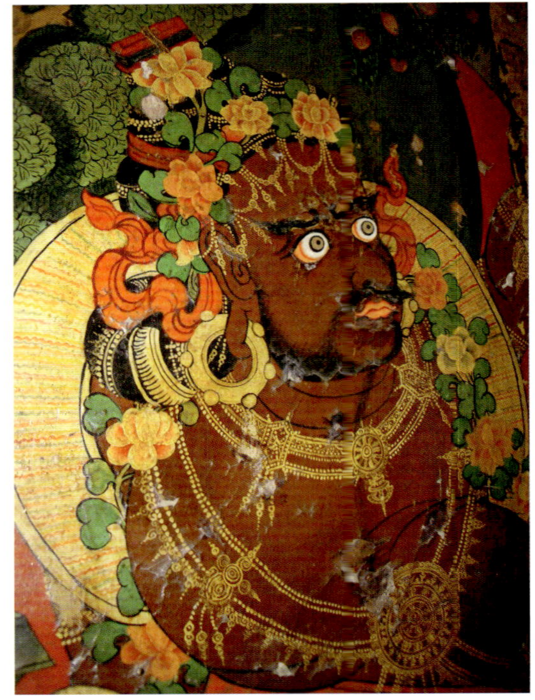

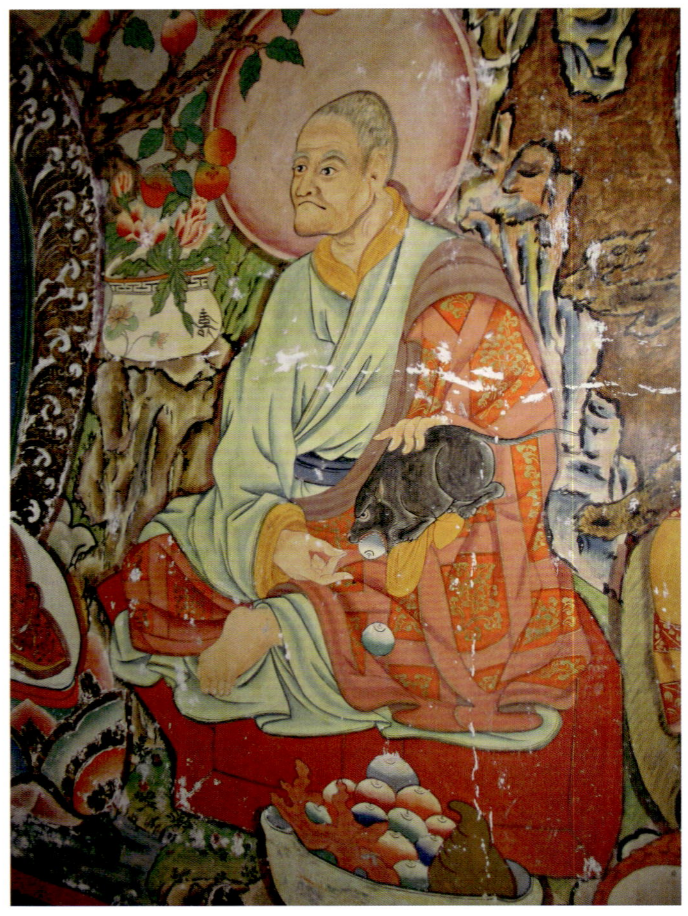

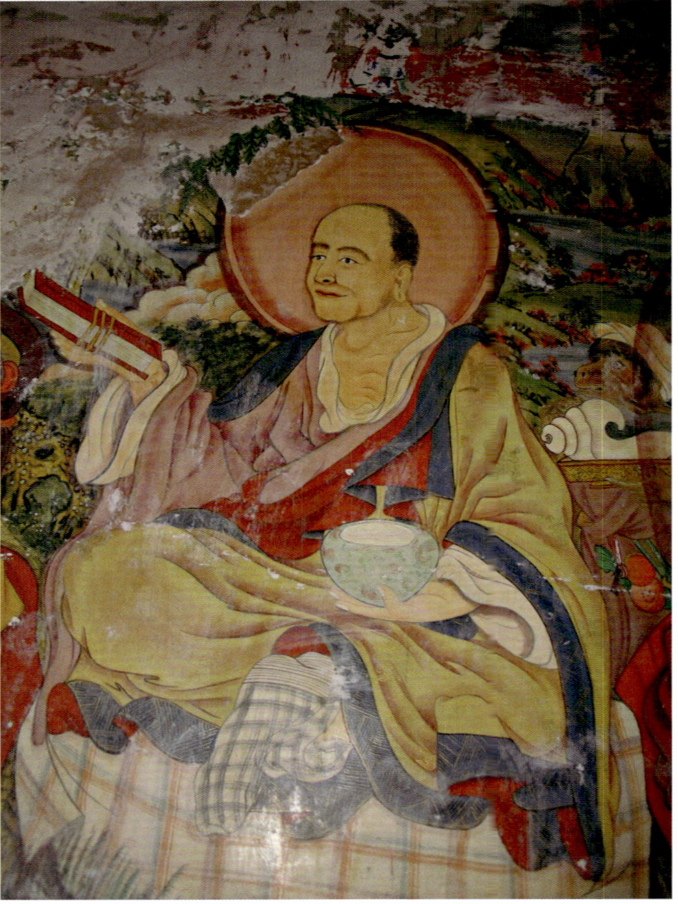

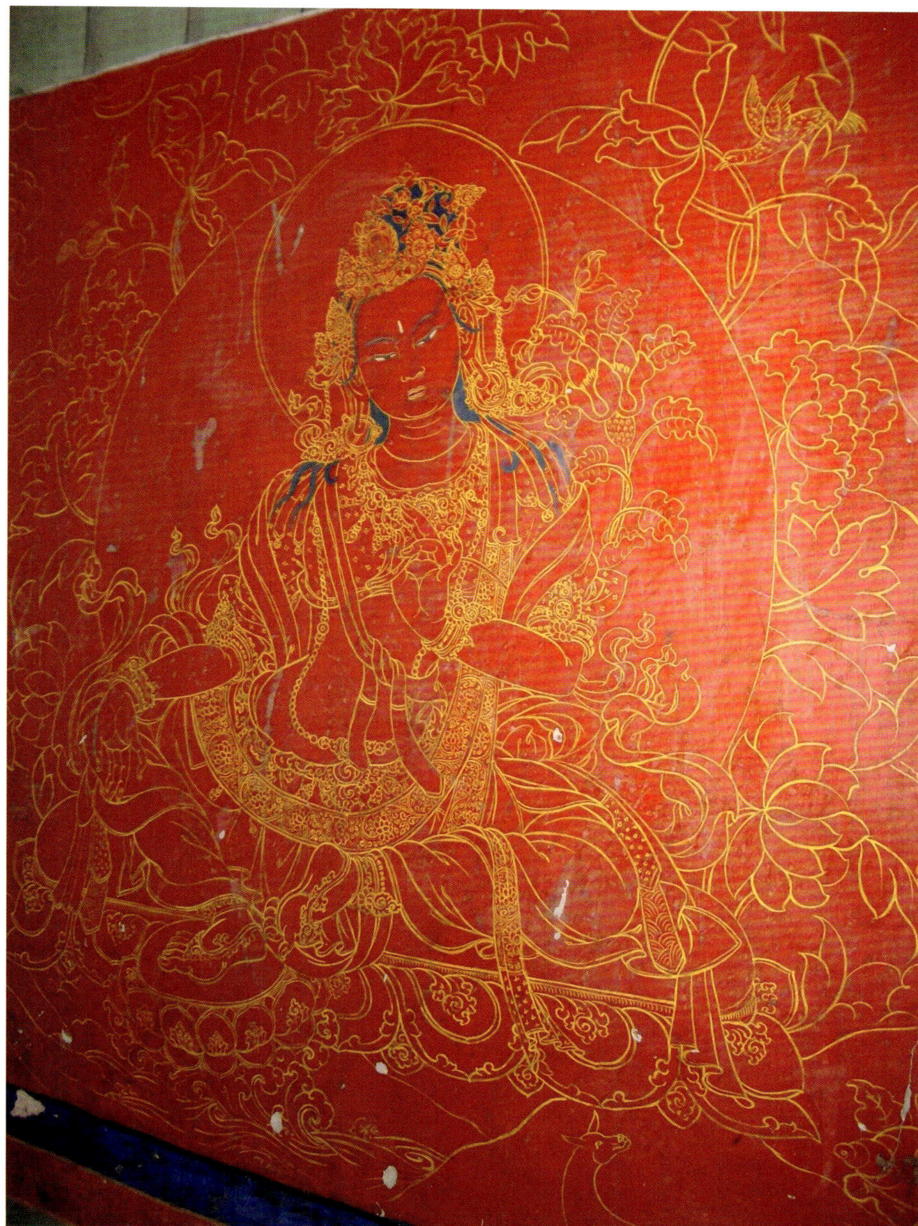

College. The back wall depicts, to the left and the right of the entrance, Gaṇapati (Tshogs bdag glang chen) and Jambhala (Dzam bha la) (see Fig. 12.11), both painted on a red background. No trace survives of the murals he painted in the outer entrance portico of the Four Great Kings (*rgyal chen rigs bzhi*).[589]

Similar murals on a red background that were probably the work of Yeshe Tenzin still survive at Öphu Estate ('Od phub gzhis ka), a short distance up the Gongkar valley. (See Fig. 12.17.) Gongkar Chöde maintained here an estate with a small branch temple and one caretaker monk. The second floor of this multistoried building once accommodated a Kanjur Chapel (bKa' 'gyur lha khang). The chapel still contains yellow-lined paintings on a red ground that depict the Twenty-One Tārās (*sgrol ma nyer gcig*) and masters from the Gelugpa and Sakya sect, including Dorjedenpa

and his chief lama, Drakthokpa Sönam Sangpo. The murals, which date to the 1940s or 1950s, are preserved in surprisingly good condition.

Once in around the 1940s, while he was still in charge of the *trulku's* estate at Gongkar, Yeshe Tendzin is said to have met with Uchen Tenpa Gyatsho (dBu chen bsTan pa rgya mtsho, 1872–1959), another contemporary Khyenri painter from Lhokha. According to one oral account, Tenpa Gyatsho served as the steward at the Jaksam Labrang (lCags zam bla brang) near Gongkar in the 1930s or 1940s and invited Yeshe Tendzin there to do some artwork.

However, as both of them then had the responsible positions of monastic stewards, this is believed to have been just a pretext for the two artists to briefly meet and learn from each other.[590]

Tenpa Gyatsho himself was born in the Upper Valley of Dranang into the family of the Simsha Tago (gZims shag rta mgo).[591] He was a well-known master artist who worked in both Menri and Khyenri styles, having studied under the Khyenri painter Sönam Chokden (bSod nams mchog ldan) and the Menthangpa masters Gen Tsöndrü (rGan brTson 'grus) and Gen Palden Trinle (dPal ldan 'phrin las).[592] His painting was

highly appreciated in Lhasa circles and
by members of the Ganden Phodrang
government. In around the 1920s, the
Thirteenth Dalai Lama commissioned
several *thangkas* in the Khyenri style
from him, and he was hired by the
Medical College in Lhasa (sMan rtsis
khang) to copy (*'dra bshus*) old Khyenri
thangkas and complement available
Menri-style compositions with Khyenri-
style renditions. He also painted at
Thangtong Gyalpo's main seat of
Jaksam Labrang and other monasteries
in Lhokha.[593] At Gongkar Chöde, Tenpa
Gyatsho painted the Sixteen Arhats
in the upper skylight panels (*khyams*)
of the main assembly hall (See Figs.
4.10A and 4.10B).[594] Several of his
works survive at Drepung Monastery,
where he worked at an earlier stage of
his career. The Thirteenth Dalai Lama
acknowledged Tenpa Gyatsho's extraordinary style about which he reportedly
said: "[His painting contain] 80 percent
of the Khyenluk and 20 percent of the
Menri."[595] Tenpa Gyatsho had seven
children by three different wives. He
passed on his knowledge of painting as
a lay tradition to three of his sons: Jinpa
(sByin pa), Tshering (Tshe ring, 1929–
2002), and Phüntshok (Phun tshogs),
who is still alive. Another student of
Tenpa Gyatsho was Tshewang Dorje
(1933–2002), whose life is summarized
below in appendix E.

In the early 1950s, when Yeshe
Tendzin was in his late thirties, he gave
up his monastic and official duties and
continued to paint. Then, as a lay artist
living in Treshing, he began for the first
time to train a few students in the style
that he had mastered over the years.
Those who learned painting from him
included a few monks from the monasteries Dakpo Tratshang (Dwags po grwa
tshang) and nearby Serthok Labrang
(Ser thog bla brang) in Namrab, a single
monk from Gongkar Chöde, and a monk
from Sungrapling (gSung rab gling) in
the Dol Valley.[596]

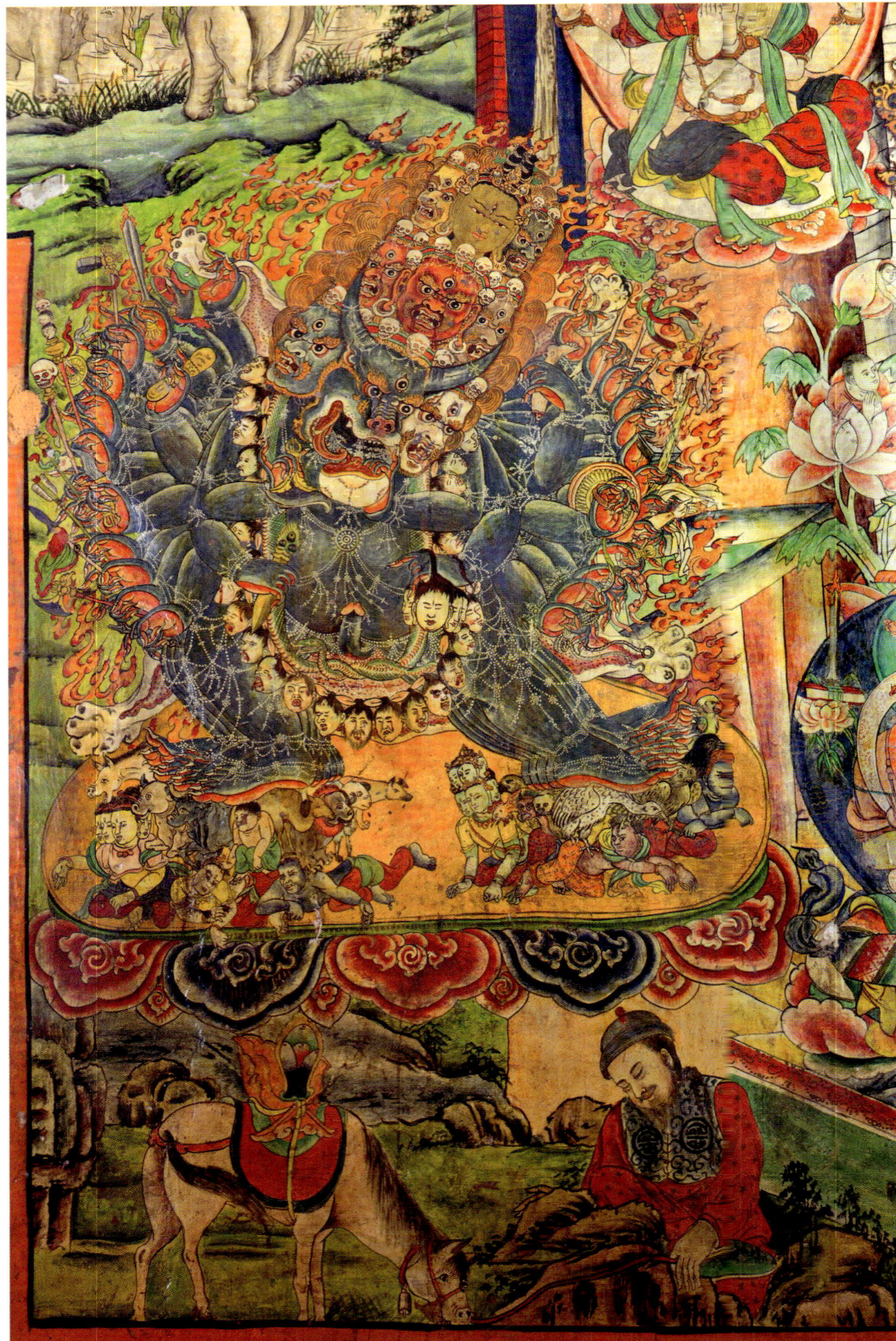

In 1958 (Earth-Dog year), about
five years after he had given up the
monastic vows, Yeshe Tendzin was
asked to repaint the inner sanctum at
Dakpo Tratshang (Dwags po grwa
tshang), the largest monastery in Namrab,
just beneath from where he had settled.
Within about a month, he painted the
murals in a casual, easygoing mood
(*snang ba med pa'i thog nas*).[597] (See
Figs. 12.18-12.20.) The underlying
enthusiasm with which he painted is

Fig. 12.18
Yamāntaka
Mural, right of entrance, Inner Sanctum,
Dakpo Tratshang; 1958
Photo courtesy of Dakpo Tratshang, 2012

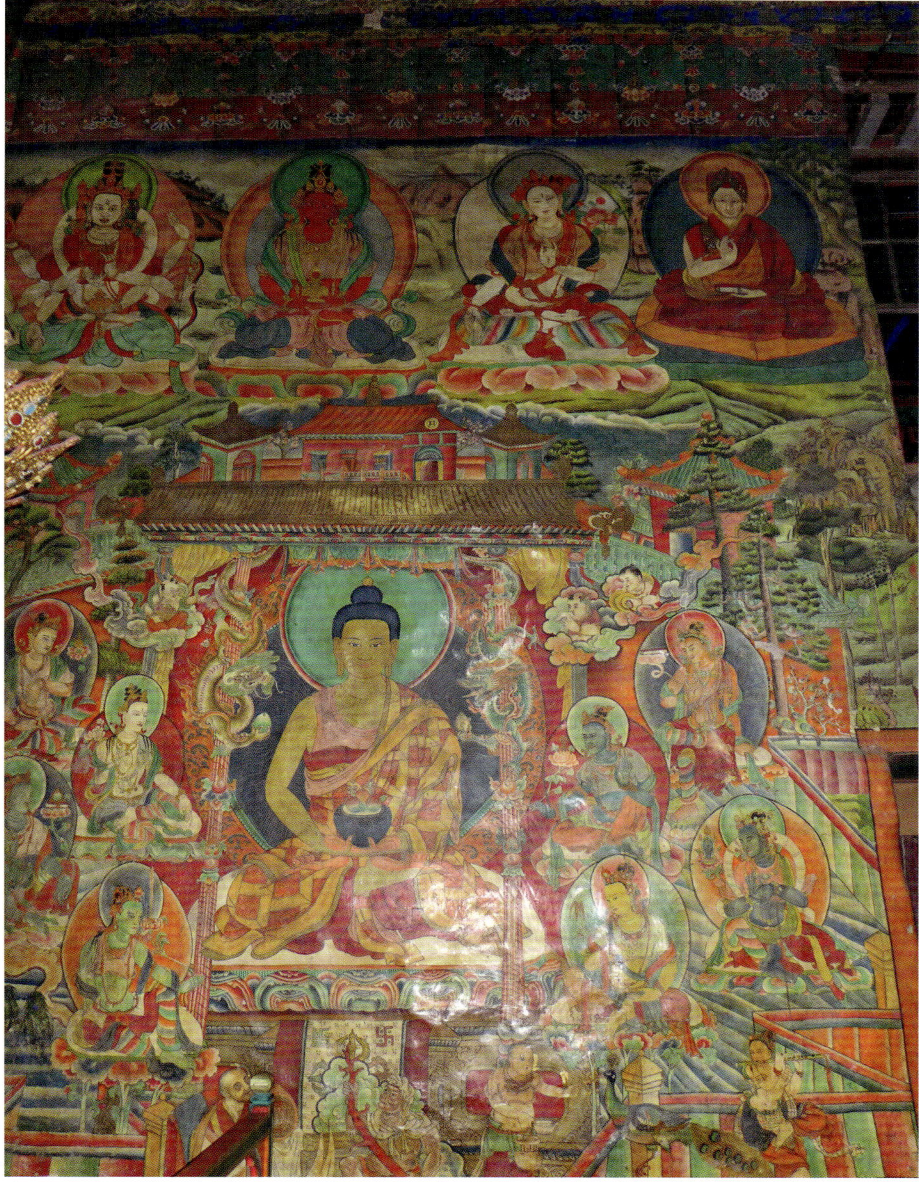

reflected in the lively murals he then created in that chapel. His composition effectively assembles numerous deities from the tantric pantheon and masters from all Tibetan Buddhist traditions. A detailed panel with inscribed label (*mtshan byang*) below the frescos reveals that Bepe Chamdzö (as he was then usually called) was the master artist responsible for it and was assisted by four painters who did the coloring (*tshon gtong mi bzhi*), two helpers (*lag g.yog mi gnyis*), a manager, and a cook (*gnyer pa mar chen gnyis*).[598]

Figure 12.18 features under the main figure ornate lotus petals as in the Khyenri style of Gongkar. Also we find striking exotic-looking minor figures and animals at the base of this panel.

In Figure 12.19 the artist employed unusual colors, including many rare ones, such as bright olive green or chartreuse. Note the distinctive upper garments hanging down over the shoulders and upper torsos of all the deities in the top row. The central buddha, Amitabha, is depicted wearing a pink sleeveless upper garment. Dragons and minor offering deities floating in clouds and playing divine music flank the central buddha. Several exotic figures stand at the base of the panel, including one who holds a large tusk-like curved object that is not ivory but a branch of red coral.

In Figure 12.20 the depiction of Ngaklo Rinpoche (1892–1959) of

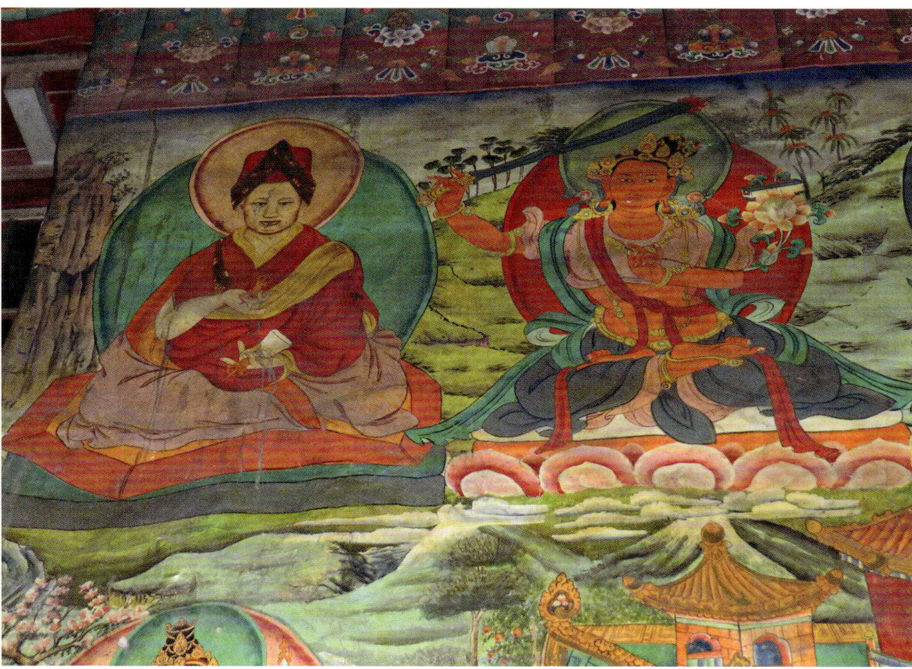

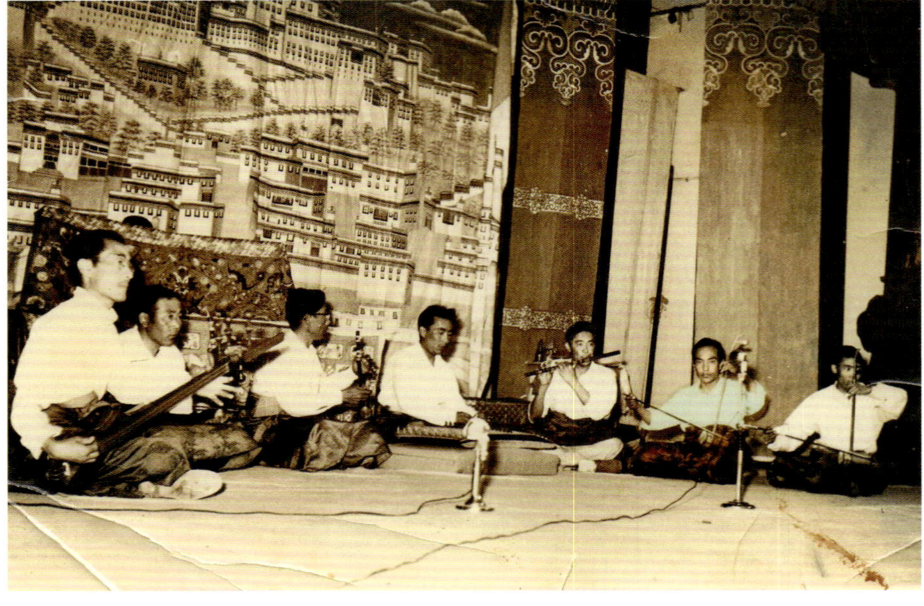

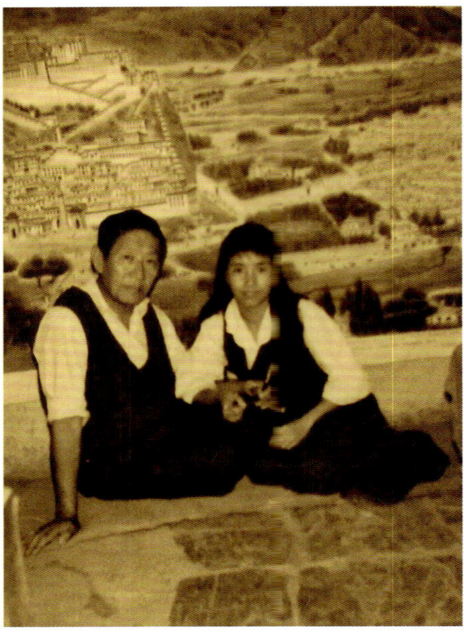

Nalendra is quite naturalistic—almost as in a photograph. (Compare the less true-to-life painting of a contemporary local lama in Figure 12.9.) Note also the pink upper garment worn by Mañjuśrī.

Indian Exile

A year later, in March 1959, Yeshe Tendzin donated his goats and sheep to Dakpo Tratshang and set off with his family to India as refugees.[599] As some of the first arrivals from Tibet, they found shelter at Buxa Fort (sBag sa chos sgar), a former army camp in northeastern India that was used as the main reception and holding center for refugees coming from or through Lhokha.[600] Later, the family moved to Dharamsala, where the Tibetan government-in-exile had relocated shortly before, in May 1960. There, Yeshe Tendzin found work at the recently established Tibetan Institute of Performing Arts (Zlos gar tshogs pa) or "TIPA."[601]

For seven or eight years (until about 1967 or 1968), Yeshe Tendzin designed the large cotton backdrops (*ras yol chen po*) that were needed for the performances of the TIPA troupe.[602] He painted those background scenes in a naturalistic style (*'dra bris; par bris*) and depicted such scenes as the Potala Palace, the Jokhang Temple, Samye Monastery, episodes from the life of Tibet's Three Early Buddhist Kings (*chos rgyal mes dbon rnam gsum*), and scenes of nomad or village life (*bzo zhing 'brog gsum*).[603] When painting and coloring the large-size backdrops, he was assisted by his wife, Lobsang Chödrön, who had learned the basics of painting from him. In 1984 all old backdrops of the Dharamsala drama troupe were destroyed by a fire in the auditorium hall (*tshogs khang*). However, a few of his background scenes that had been captured on old black-and-white photographs were reproduced in a book commemorating the fiftieth anniversary of the institute in 2009.[604]

While working and living at the Tibetan Institute of Performing Arts, Yeshe Tendzin also busied himself with other projects. On behalf of the government-in-exile's publishing house (the Shes rig par khang) in Dharamsala, he illustrated the Tibetan school textbooks, the first edition of which was published in 1963 by letter press and for which an enlarged edition was published in 1967. In addition to the book covers, his drawings of religious and secular personalities (*bla dpon mi sna*), places (*sa gnas*) and everyday items (*'tsho thabs*) illustrated the various aspects of Tibetan life and culture within each book, a modern feature that traditional Tibetan books lacked.[605] Every Tibetan child who received his or her schooling in the exile-government schools in India or Nepal knew his drawings, such as those of Tibet's Three Early Buddhist Kings, which were reproduced on the covers of editions even as late as the 2000s (Fig. 12.23).

Among Tibetan painters in exile, Yeshe Tendzin was one of the most capable for naturalistic paintings and drawings. Before leaving Tibet, he is said to have admired Indian highly naturalistic paintings. We can assume that while still in Gongkar he also admired the naturalism of Khyentse Chenmo, who was unrivaled for his true-to-life and expressive paintings and sculptures.

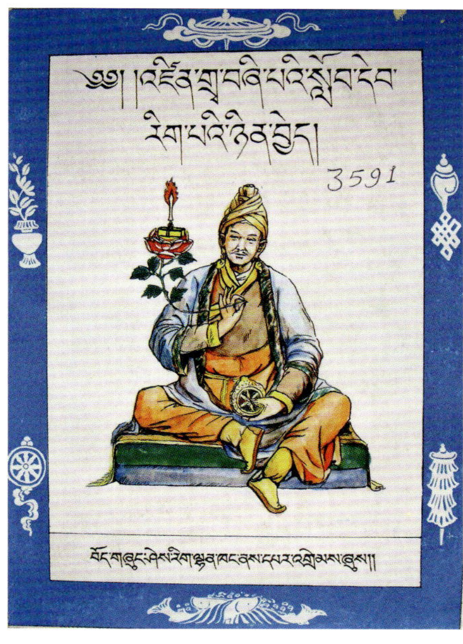

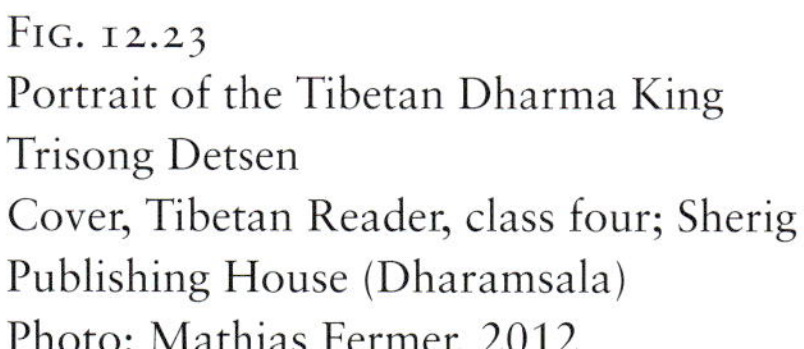

Fig. 12.23
Portrait of the Tibetan Dharma King
Trisong Detsen
Cover, Tibetan Reader, class four; Sherig
Publishing House (Dharamsala)
Photo: Mathias Fermer, 2012

Fig. 12.24
Tibet's Three Early Buddhist Kings
Pigment on cloth, 99 ¼ x 70 in.
(252 x 178 cm); painted by Amdo Jampa,
1983
Now in the Kashag office (bKa' shag las
khungs), Tibetan government-in-exile
Photo courtesy of Ven. Jinpa Gyatso,
Dharamsala, India
Literature: Clare Harris 1999, pl. 17.

Fig. 12.25
Green Tārā
Detail, pigment on cloth
11 ¼ x 14 ¼ in. (28.5 x 36.5 cm)
painted by Amdo Jampa, 1980s
Private Collection, Dharamsala, India
Photo: Mathias Fermer, 2010

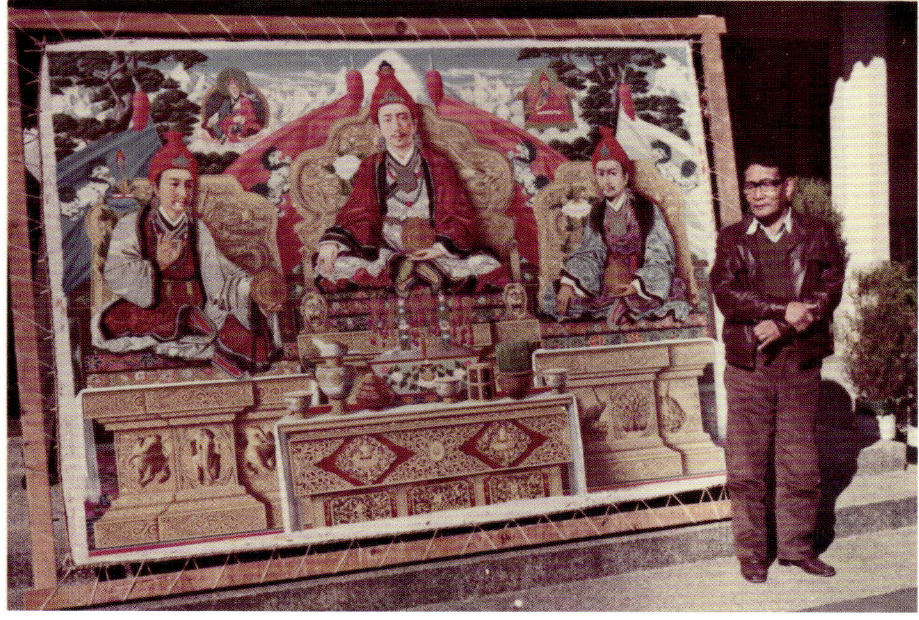

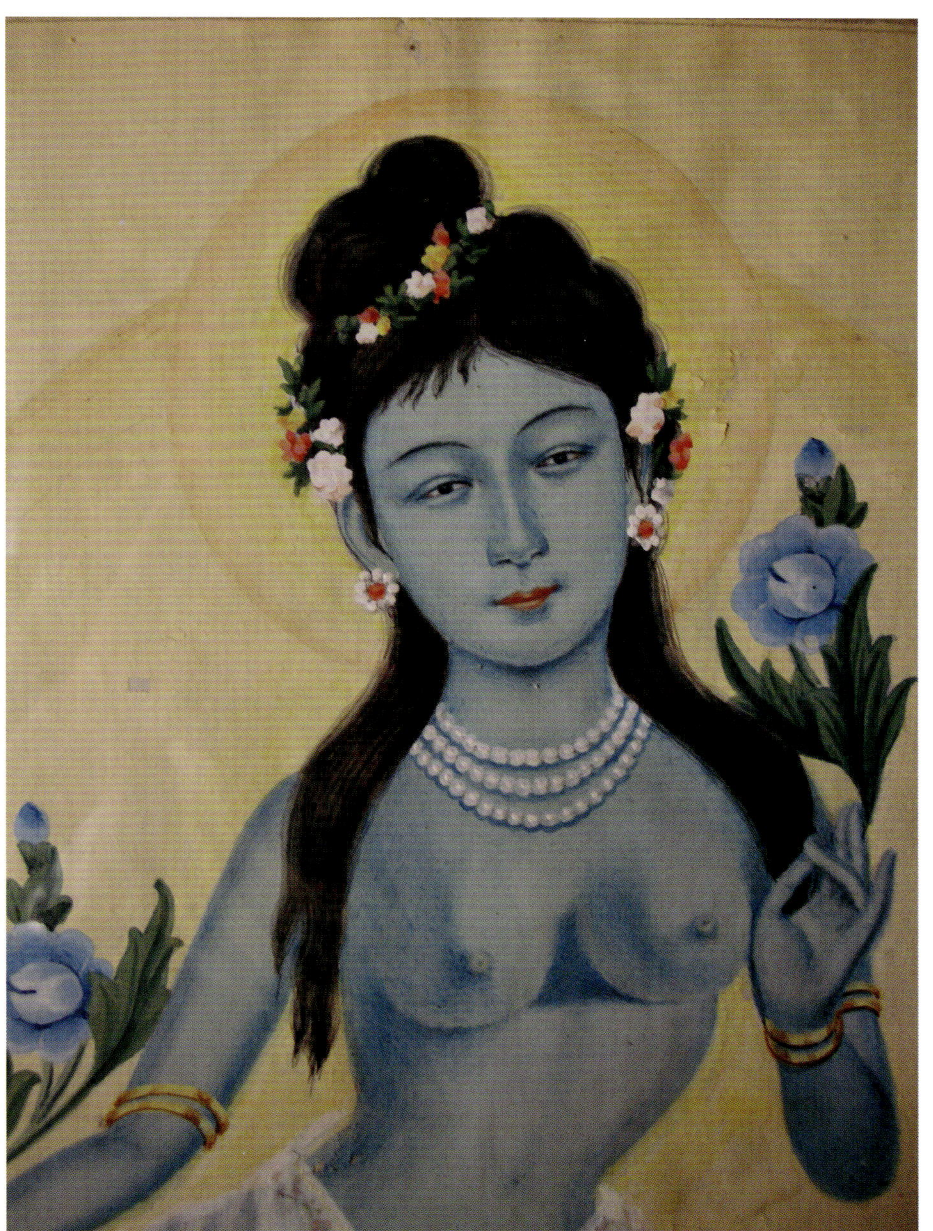

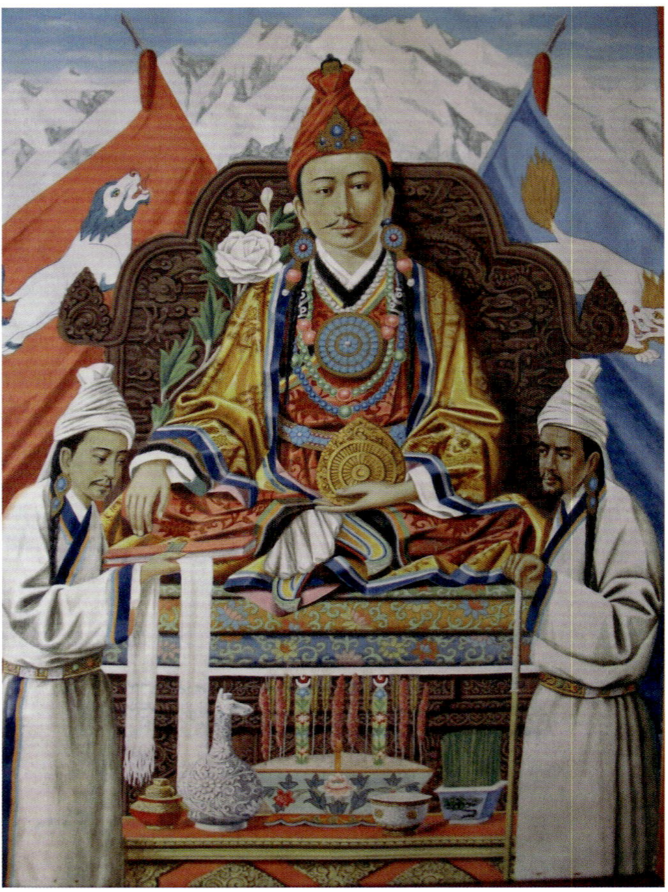

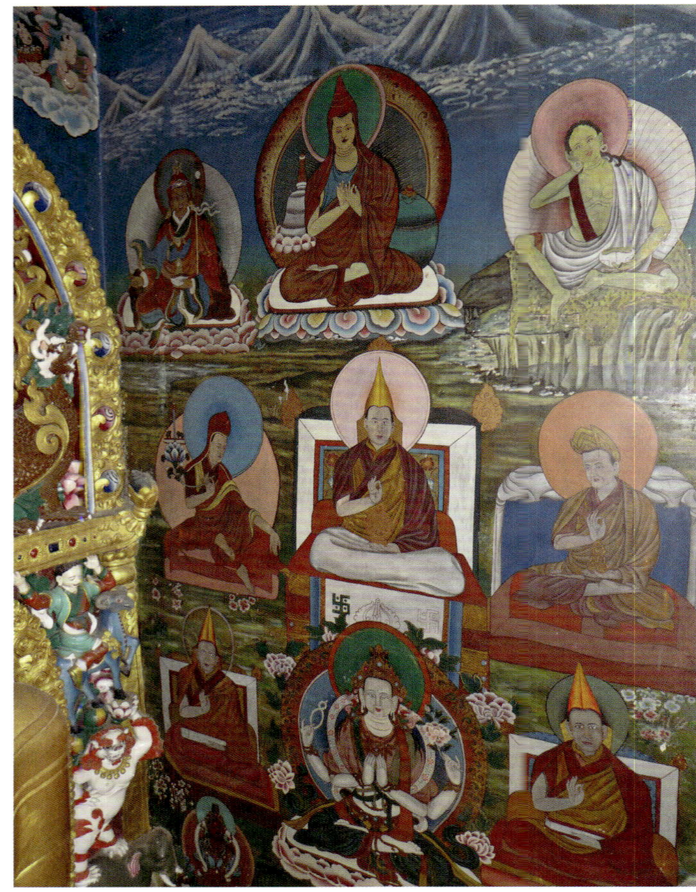

In Lhasa in the twentieth century the painter most famed for naturalism or realism (*dngos bris*) of Yeshe Tendzin's generation was Amdo Jampa Tsheten (1911–2002).[606] Like Yeshe Tendzin, Amdo Jampa also painted for the Tibetan exile community in Dharamsala. In the early 1980s, during a longer visit at the Dalai Lama's seat in India, he produced several large paintings for the Tibetan government-in-exile institutions and private people. Compared to Yeshe Tendzin, Amdo Jampa's painting style was less traditional and more radical when portraying religious figures. Many traditional-minded refugees found his style too close to the Socialist Realism of Communist China (see Figs. 12.24–12.26).

In 1964/65, Yeshe Tendzin was invited to the Buddhist holy place Sarnath by Gen Gose (1924–2004), who was finishing decorating the main temple of his monastery there. The construction of that monastery, which Tibetans call just "Bö Gönpa" (Bod dgon pa), was begun as early as 1955, but the decoration of the larger temple hall was completed about ten years later. On this occasion, Yeshe Tendzin was invited to decorate the tall walls of the temple's central sanctum.

Similar to his paintings at Dakpo Tratshang in Tibet, in Sarnath, Yeshe Tendzin painted portraits of leading lamas from the four main schools of Tibetan Buddhism. (See Fig. 12.27.) They appeared on the right wall, where we also find depicted the Fourteenth Dalai Lama and his two principal tutors (Ling Rinpoche and Trichang Rinpoche). In this panel a row of snowy white peaks seems to float in the distant dark-blue sky. The left wall featured Tsongkhapa with his two chief disciples (*rje yab sras gsum*).

In 1970, after retiring as the background painter of the TIPA troupe, Yeshe Tendzin was requested to paint the murals for a prayer wheel chapel (*ma ṇi lha khang*) that was evidently built by the Tibetan community in Manali, a hill-station town of present-day Himachal Pradesh.[607] Here again, he depicted a mixed assembly of tantric deities and lineage masters from different traditions in the upper parts of the wall and reserved the lower parts for the chapel's main theme, the Twelve Deeds (*mdzad pa bcu gnyis*) of the Buddha (Fig. 12.28) and an Eight-armed Avalokiteśvara (Fig. 12.29). The

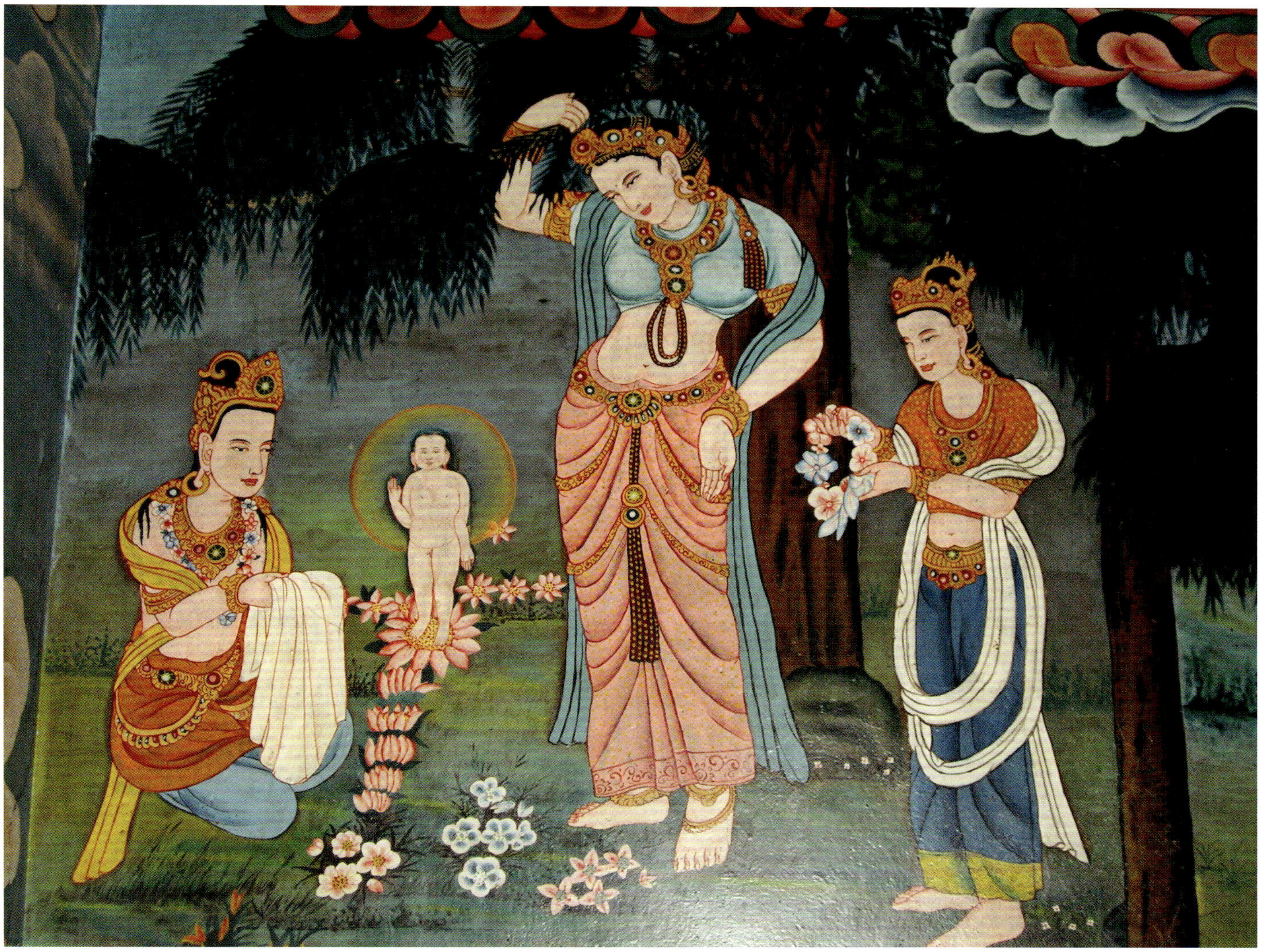

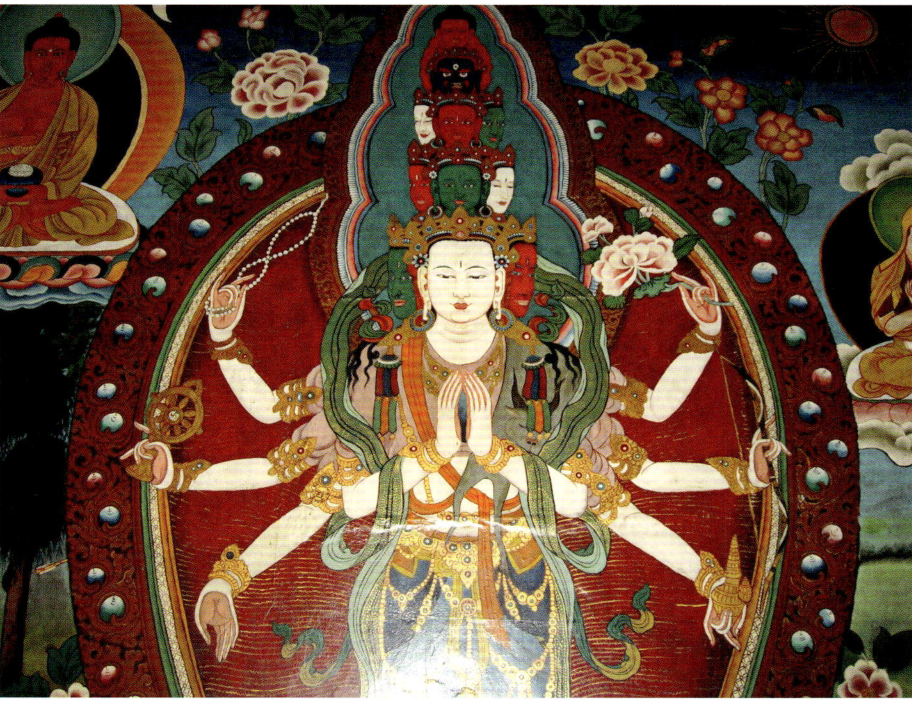

FIG. 12.28
Birth of the Buddha in Lumbini, One of the
Buddha's Twelve Great Deeds
Detail, mural, Prayer Wheel Chapel,
Manali; 1970
Photo courtesy of Chögyal-la, Dharamsala,
India

FIG. 12.29
Eleven-headed and Eight-armed
Avalokiteśvara
Detail, mural, Prayer Wheel Chapel,
Manali; 1970
Photo courtesy of Chögyal-la, Dharamsala,
India

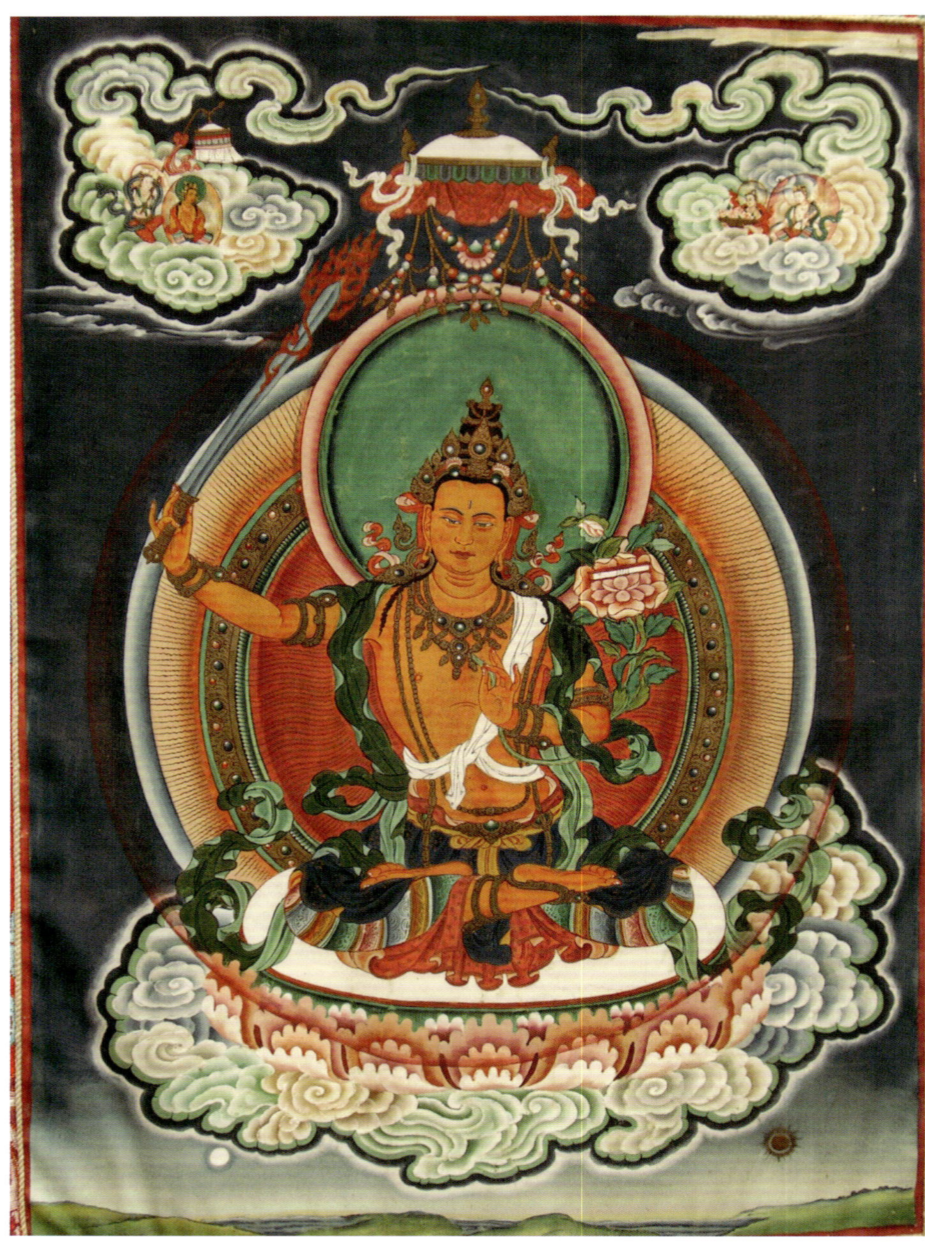

bodhisattva's upper torso and upper arms are covered by a faint pink garment.

Yeshe Tendzin was a highly respected artist within the Tibetan exile community in India. Until his death in 1971, he painted thangkas and larger paintings for private patrons. Some of the most noteworthy people who commissioned works from him were Freda Bedi (1911–1977), Dr. Yeshi Dondhen (b. 1927 or 1929), and Mrs. Kalsang Takla. Figures 12.30 and 12.31 give a good idea of the thangkas he painted during this period. The first, which depicts the Bodhisattva Mañjuśrī, incorporates several classic elements of Khyentse Chenmo's style (such as the silk parasol floating in the sky above the bodhisattva's nimbus and the four minor divine deities floating within clouds in the sky to either side, one holding his own parasol) that make the painting a poignant evocation of the art tradition that Yeshe Tendzin had left behind in Gongkar. The depiction of Thangtong Gyalpo (Fig. 12.31) is powerful and more naturalistic than usual. The lotus petals beneath him have elaborate centers. Two smaller female goddesses below, the White and the Green Tārā, wear pastel-blue and faint-pink upper garments that completely cover their upper arms and upper torsos.

Yeshe Tenzin was frequently approached by patrons requesting that he paint so-called "birth-sign" (*skyes rtags*) memorial thangkas. Painted on behalf of those who had recently died, such sacred depictions were meant to facilitate a good rebirth. For commissioning a small memorial thangka of this type, people then often donated as little as ten or fifteen Indian rupees, and for larger paintings, up to fifty rupees.[608] (See Figure 12.32.) Yeshe Tendzin did not demand a particular price and accepted whatever he was offered.[609] Quiet and humble, he preferred not to paint for well-to-do foreign patrons, if possible, thinking first of the Tibetan refugee community around him.[610] Through his painting he earned himself and his family a simple living in the harsh early years of the Tibetan diaspora.[611]

Yeshe Tendzin was a dedicated artist who emphasized the sacredness of his occupation. At times he explained to his daughters the heavy responsibility of being a painter, saying, "It would be sinful for people to worship a badly depicted painting" (*zhal ras yag po ma mjal pa yin na sdig pa red*).[612] More of his paintings probably survived in private homes of Dharamsala, in the private residence (*gzims chung*) of the present Dalai Lama and in the larger Tibetan monasteries of South India.

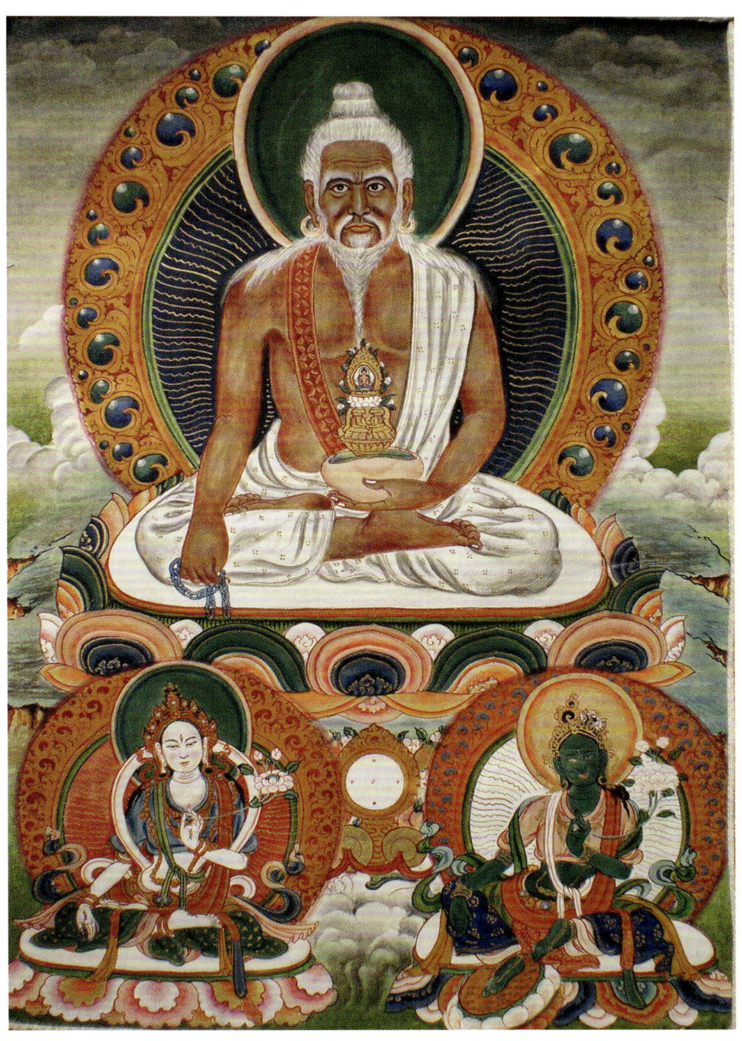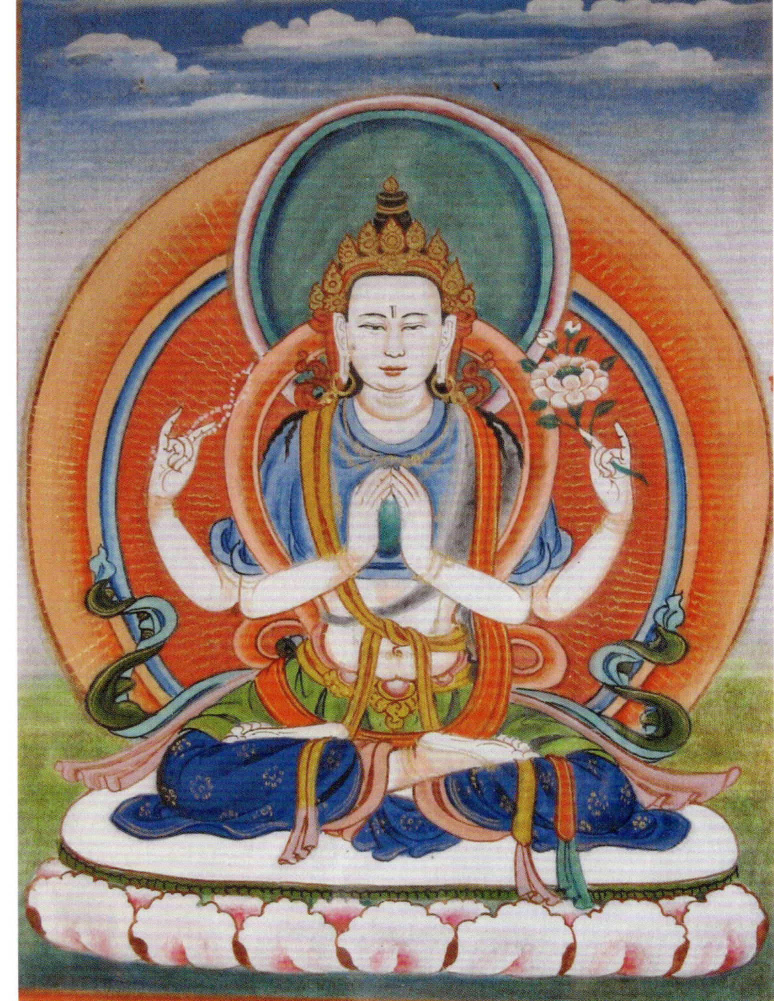

Fig. 12.31
Thangtong Gyalpo
Pigment on cloth, 9 ⅝ x 13 ⅜ in.
(24.5 x 34 cm); 1960s
Now in Nyungne Temple (sMyung gnas lha
khang), Dharamsala, India
Photo: Mathias Fermer, 2012

Fig. 12.32
Four-armed Avalokiteśvara
Pigment on cloth, commissioned as a
memorial thangka; 1960s
Private Collection, Dharamsala, India
6 ¾ x 8 ⅝ in. (17 x 22 cm)
Photo: Mathias Fermer, 2012

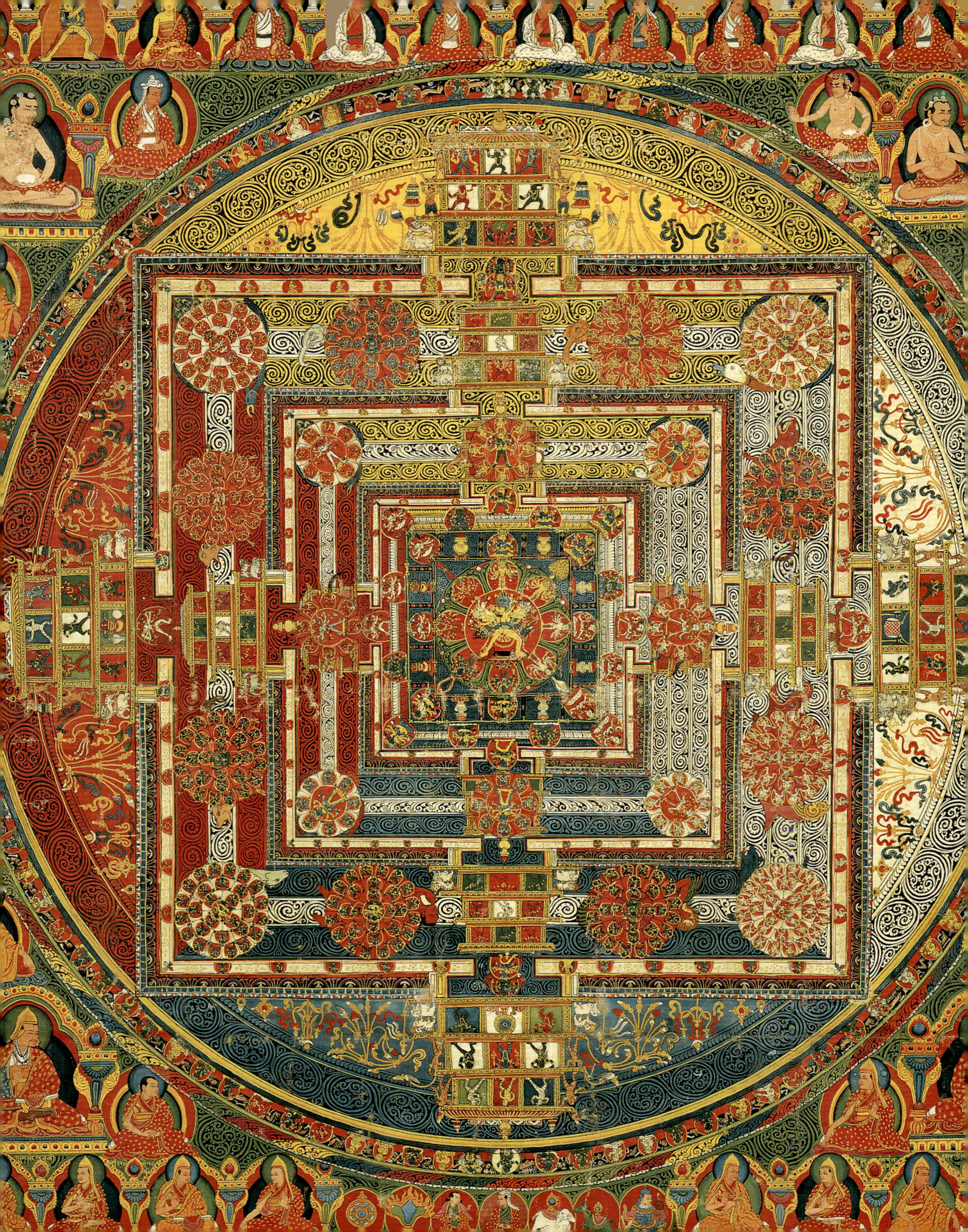

CHAPTER 13

The Possibilities and Limitations of Dating Tibetan Art

GIVEN THAT SO MANY portable works of Tibetan art have been scattered in recent decades, the difficulty of dating them might appear insurmountable.[613] But this problem may reflect more the elementary stage of present art-historical research than the presumed impossibility of dating. Exact dating is of course usually not attainable—at least not in the narrow sense of dating to the precise day, month, or year; such exact dating is also not possible for many works of medieval European art that were removed from their original contexts. Yet chronological precision is relative, and in a scholarly discipline such as Tibetan art history, in which some scholars deem precision to be virtually impossible, establishing the date of a work within a generation or two is to be welcomed as wonderfully exact.

In this chapter, I offer a few suggestions for improving the accuracy and reliability of dating Tibetan art works. Tibetan painting developed through a historical sequence of styles, which no competent art historian ever disputed. By comparing those styles, many individual paintings can be dated to an approximate century, give or take a few decades. In these respects, the study of Tibetan Buddhist art does not differ fundamentally from that of traditional European religious art, but it has not yet reached the same level of connoisseurship. The history of Tibetan painting, in particular, has until now mostly been left to those who lacked the necessary qualifications as historians.

A Few Fundamentals

Though the broad outline of the stylistic development of Tibetan painting has been known since Tucci's *Tibetan Painted Scrolls* appeared in 1949, the detailed historical sequence of the various styles could only be established more recently because few paintings had been accurately dated or otherwise placed in a precise historical context. Scholars working in the field since the appearance of Tucci's seminal book have often overlooked such vital historical evidence as labels, inscriptions mentioning patrons or datable historical figures, the structure and contents of lineages, and mentions of important artworks, or their patrons or painters, in the external historical record.

Two different methods of dating can be applied, depending on how much evidence of historical people can be found in a given painting. A historian has two alternatives: to date by interpreting internal evidence relating to datable people, or to provisionally date paintings that lack such internal evidence by comparing their styles to paintings datable through the first method.[614] Obviously, the first method is primary and necessary; without it, the second cannot exist.

The first method entails assigning a date to a painting through gathering and interpreting the internal and external evidence relating to datable people.[615] Internal evidence may be written or iconographic clues that relate to datable persons within the painting. Written evidence begins with the careful deciphering and copying of all labels or inscriptions on the front and back of the painting and its mount. It leads to the extracting of names and identifying persons and places named. Iconographic evidence can be the identification of famous founding or lineage masters through the iconography of their portrayals. It can also entail identifying the lineage through structural analysis and through identifications, sometimes hypothetical, of series of individual masters.

External evidence relevant to chronology can mean information that helps identify and date the historical figures portrayed, such as: life histories of individuals in biographies and biographical sketches, records of religious lineages of transmission (*thob yig*), and histories of religious schools (*chos 'byung).* External evidence from histories may be records of commissioning or painting of thangkas or murals. Evidence may come from similar or related paintings, such as other paintings from the same set that exist elsewhere. Often the final painting of a set is the most useful chronologically, especially if it portrays and names the patron. There may also exist a clear link with the activities of an otherwise documented artist, patron, or another person.

We can interpret the historical evidence in order to reach a chronological judgment. The main task is to link up the people mentioned in the internal evidence to records about them in the external historical record. The identification of even a single figure will allow at least one chronological limit or terminus to be established (for example, "It cannot have been painted earlier than Master _____"). The evidence also makes possible important non-chronological conclusions. The identification of founding masters will often link the painting to a particular school, tradition, or even monastery.

The presence of inscriptions and naming labels should always be noted the first time a thangka is cataloged or systematically described. Each new study can document internal evidence by recording inscriptions. If done carefully, this need not be repeated by subsequent studies. Pains should be taken to decipher and copy accurately, which may require a more qualified consultant. Copies should be literally exact, and one should resist the natural tendency to correct irregular spellings. Many difficult inscriptions will never be interpreted correctly if they are not first published in complete form, accurate to the original.

Inscriptions can be divided into two chronological types: the majority was contemporaneous with the completion of the paintings, and a smaller number were later additions. Besides the labels that identify individual figures, inscriptions may reveal lineages or fixed iconographic themes or communicate details about the painting's commissioning, painting, consecrations, or ownership. On very old or highly revered paintings, an inscription referring to the consecration (*rab gnas*) of the painting by a specific master may have been added several generations later, and its reliability should be confirmed by a careful stylistic analysis of the painting.

One should examine not only the front and back of the painting but also the brocade mount for labels. On mounts of thangkas belonging to sets, the position of the painting within the set is often indicated by conventional shorthand notations on the mount or on a loosely attached strip of cloth. These should not be thrown away or overlooked; they can be crucial for establishing the place of a painting within a series or set.

For paintings with complex compositions, one should provide a diagram that indicates the position of each figure or episode. If a detailed iconographic description is intended, even a preliminary and arbitrary chart that numbers each figure is helpful. If a lineage can be identified and interpreted, the diagram's numbers should correspond to the order of the lineage.

With the first method, the key to reaching a reliable judgment is the presence of internal evidence that can be interpreted chronologically, that relates to dateable historical people, whether in the inscriptions or iconography. The main task in assigning a date is to link the internal evidence, mentions of people in the painting, to external evidence, records of them in the historical sources. Note that the proposed identification is not only a possibility, but it is also historically probable. If a name in the inscription is common, the burden of proof rests with the person asserting the identity. With unusual names, the identity can be more readily assumed.

There may be a few cases—such as wall paintings without inscriptions or identifiable masters—in which external evidence from the written record (for example, a history of the temple or biography of its founder) gives a convincing date. In this event, the painting should still be compared with more securely dated pieces and examined for evidence of later repainting.

"Art history," a sage once said, "is art plus history." In the past, many who have tried to bring Tibetan art and history together have been handicapped by the fact that dating was often based on one stylistic comparison after another. They will not fail to appreciate the almost revolutionary implications of dozens of new datings based on historical evidence: we finally have something more substantial to compare.

Ranking by Quality of Evidence

One way to refine this method is to rank paintings according to the quality of their internal evidence. By assigning thangkas to five descending classes (such as A through E), we can specify more clearly the reliability and exactitude of a thangka's dating and hence its value for chronology. Underlying this ranking system is the relative richness of the painting as a historical source, established by answering key questions: Does it contain a colophon-like inscription to help date it? Does it contain a recognizable lineage? Are the individual figures labeled? Is the figural iconography distinctive? Can any other evidence be noted?

I suggest the following five classes to rank paintings as historical evidence, from strongest to weakest:

A. Contains excellent historical evidence. This is a painting in which the name of the patron or his teacher is revealed by a colophon-like inscription, ideally confirmed by a labeled lineage and other inscriptions.
B. Contains good evidence. This is a painting in which the name of the last lineal guru is known from inscriptions, ideally with a fully labeled lineage.
C. Contains mediocre historical evidence. This is a painting depicting lineage masters; the final teacher can be roughly estimated with iconography. Here, ideally a whole lineage is present, but it is not inscribed. At least one teacher can be identified from distinctive iconography.
D. Contains weak evidence. This is a painting for which only uncertain

conclusions can be drawn from its internal evidence.

E. Contains no historical evidence. This is a painting for which no interpretable historical evidence is recognizable, leaving only stylistic comparison and technical means to date it (for example, C14 or pigment testing).

EXAMPLES OF THE DIFFERENT CLASSES

With a little luck and a certain amount of effort, the two methods will help us to date existing thangkas to within a generation or two.[616] But the thangkas must contain sufficient and relevant internal evidence and should be studied in connection with the history and lineages of the Tibetan Buddhist traditions that gave them birth.[617] Thangkas cannot be studied in a historical vacuum. The best practice is to start by investigating sets and stylistic or iconographic corpuses together, beginning with those bearing labeled lineages and other inscriptions.

EXAMPLES OF CLASS D

Here are several examples from the above five classes, beginning with those that contain the poorest or least evidence; there is no point exemplifying class E paintings, which lack any internal evidence. From a class D painting, one may identify a dateable historical figure, such as a famous lama, that can establish a chronological limit: the painting cannot be dated earlier than that lineage master. Yet this piece of evidence does not reveal how much time passed between that dateable figure and the patronage of the painting.

Figure 13.1, for example, depicts two members of an important ordination lineage: the Kashmiri abbot

Śākyaśrībhadra and probably one of his Tibetan disciples. The surrounding squares depict episodes from Khache Paṇchen's life in India before he came to Tibet. No internal evidence has yet been found in this painting that would date it more precisely than after the time of its main subjects, the first of whom died in 1225.

The presence of a tentatively identified lineage can also lead to provisional conclusions about the dating. The next example, Figure 13.2, portrays the tutelary deity Yamāntaka as its main figure, but I am not sure which lineage it shows; evidence is lacking. If we provisionally assume that it is the common tradition of Ra Lotsāwa (Rwa Lo tsā ba) as transmitted to Ngorchen, then generation 17, the last lineal guru shown, would have been that of Mati Paṇchen, and the patron would have belonged to generation

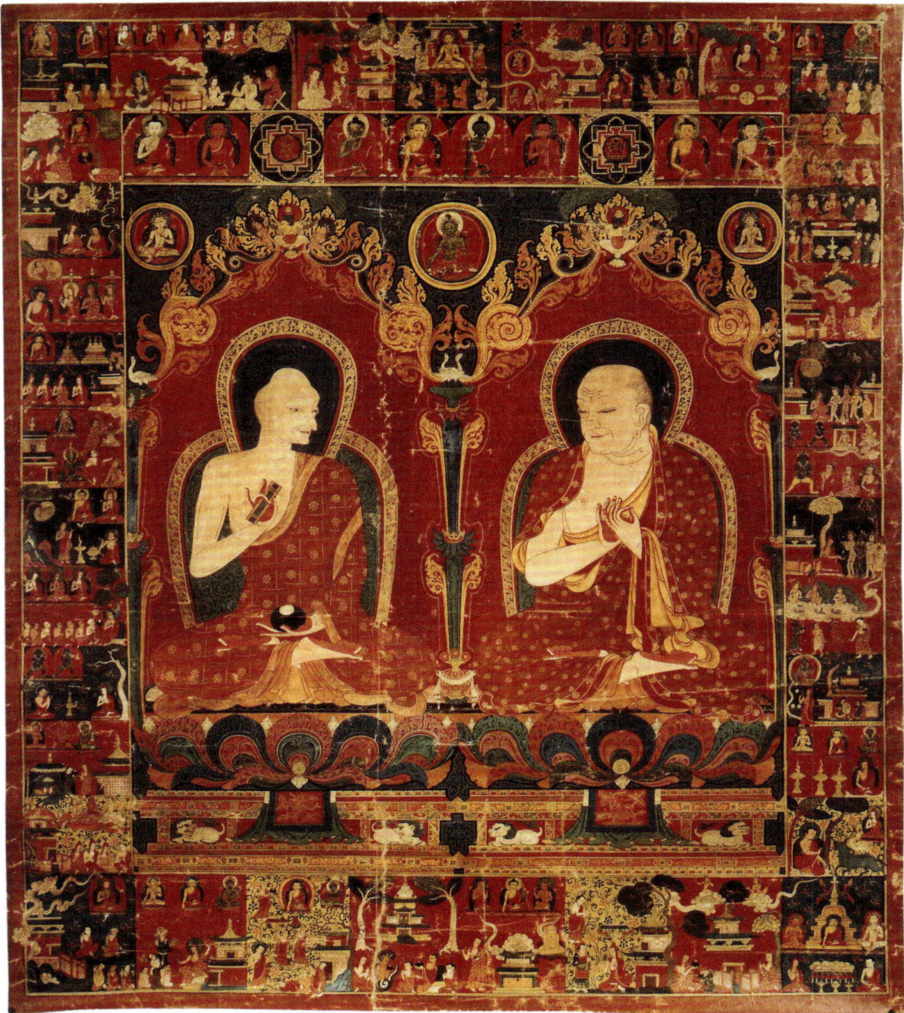

FIG. 13.1
Śākyaśrībhadra with His Life Episodes and Disciple
ca. mid- to late fourteenth century
28 ⅜ x 32 ¼ in. (72 x 82 cm)
Private Collection
Literature: A. Heller 1999, 85f, no. 64; Jackson 2010, fig. 7.4; and Jackson 2011, fig. 1.2

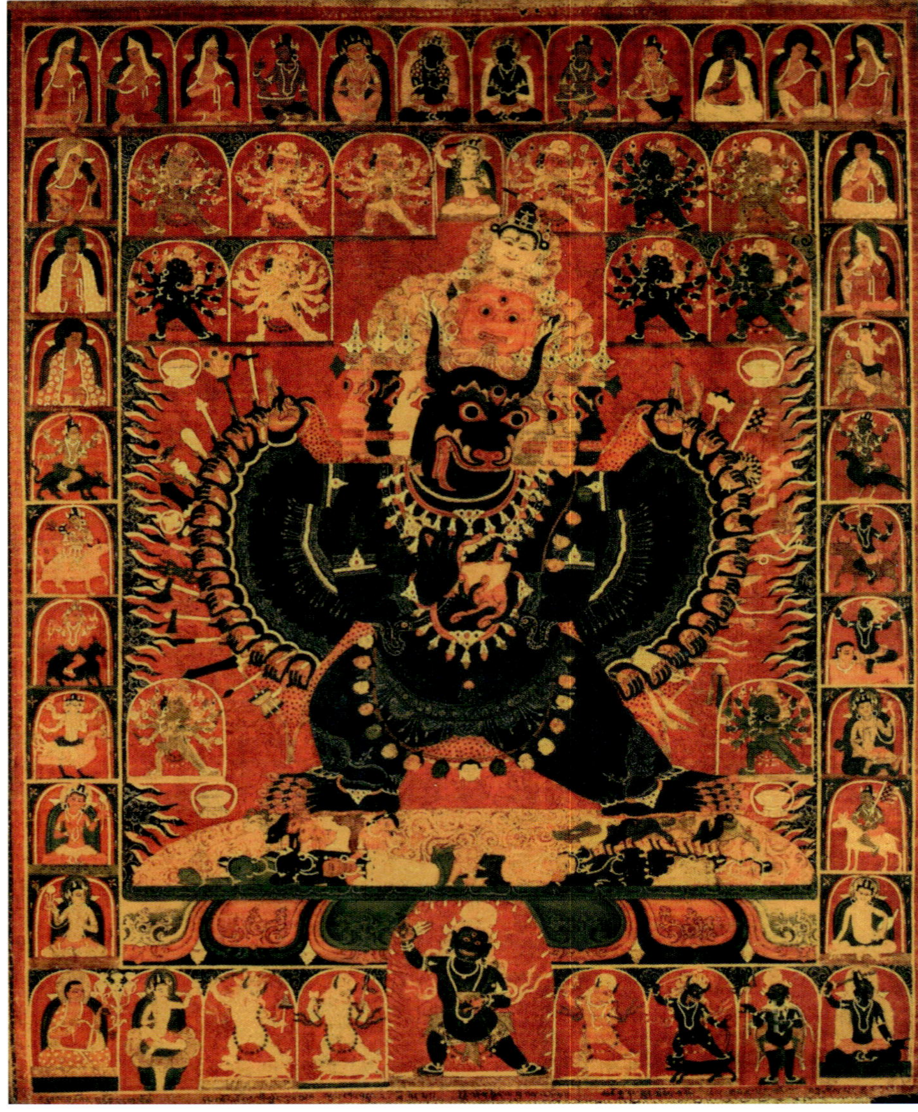

are present, but they are not inscribed. At the very least, one or more founding gurus can be identified thanks to their distinctive iconography.

One example is Figure 13.3, which I described as an "Eastern Indian" style painting, but its lineage is not the Karma Kagyu.[618] Its main deity is Hevajra, depicted here in the lineage passed down by Marpa to his disciple Ngoktön (rNgog ston), a tradition esteemed and cultivated by some later Karma Kagyu lamas. The Ngokpa was a hereditary religious lineage, and the first three teacher-generations after Ngoktön are portrayed accordingly as long-haired laymen (6, 7, and 8), whereas the final three figures (9, 10, and 11) are monks, reflecting the introduction of monastic ordination in the later generations. The structure of the thangka is shown in Diagram [J].

Though it lacks inscriptions, the painting presumably shows the standard Ngokpa (rNgog pa) lineage, down to the first half of the fourteenth century:

1. Vajradhara
2. an Indian siddha
3. another Indian siddha
4. Marpa
5. rNgog Chos sku rdo rje
6. rNgog Zhe sdang rdo rje alias rNgog mDo sde (b. 1090)
7. rNgog Seng ge sgra alias gTsang tsha Jo tshul Tshul khrims shes rab (1115–1158)
8. rNgog Kun dga' rdo rje (the last layman) (1157–1234), founder of the monastery Treshing
9. rNgog gZi brjid grags pa (the first monk) (1202–1281)
10. rNgog Rin chen bzang po (1243–1319)
11. Chos kyi rgyal mtshan (1283–1359)

The last three masters enjoyed greater than usual longevity, and the first two flourished during most of the

Yamāntaka with Lineage
ca. second half of the fifteenth century
35 ⅜ x 32 ¼ in. (90 x 82 cm)
Collection R. R. E.
Literature: Ernst 2001, fig. 8a; and Heller 1999, no. 80

18, that of Ngorchen's teacher, Sazang Phakpa Shönnu Lodrö (Sa bzang 'Phags pa gZhon nu blo gros, 1358–1412), who flourished in the first quarter of the fifteenth century. The frequent use of yellow hats for the Tibetan masters may be a sign that the patron and his teacher were Gelukpa, some of whom practiced this cycle avidly. If the lineage could be identified more definitively through its iconography, the painting would be raised to the C class.

EXAMPLES OF CLASS C

In a class C painting, lineage teachers are not inscribed, but some may be identified from distinctive iconography. Lineage teachers, ideally a whole lineage,

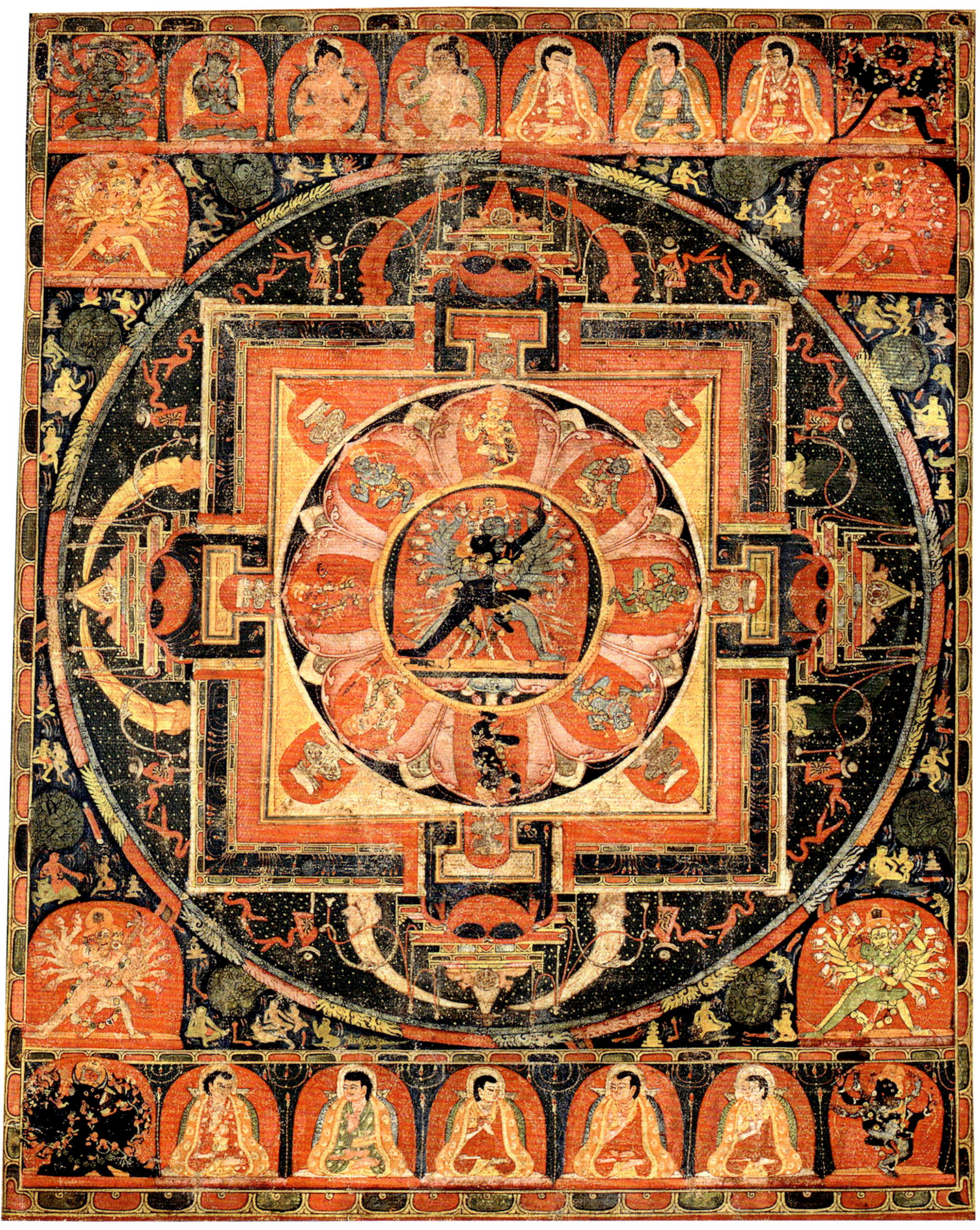

FIG. 13.3
Mandala of Hevajra in the Tradition of
Ngoktön
first half of the fourteenth century
13 x 12 in. (33.0 x 30.5 cm)
Michael J. and Beata McCormick Collection
Literature: Leidy and Thurman 1997, no.
15; and Jackson 2009, fig. 4.5

	d1	1	2	3	4	5	6	d2
	d3	7	8	9	10	11		d4

thirteenth century. The life spans of the
final two masters reached two and nearly
six decades into the fourteenth century.
The last master portrayed here, number
11, Chökyi Gyaltshen (Chos kyi rgyal
mtshan, 1283–1359), was presumably the
eldest son of Ngok Chödor (rNgog Chos
rdor, 1246–1311). He traveled to Kham,
where his disciples included the abbot
of Riwoche. During his visit, the senior
abbot of Riwoche would have been his
younger contemporary, Chöku Orgyen
Gönpo (1293–1366). If this is Kham art
from Riwoche, it may have been commissioned by that illustrious abbot.

The *Blue Annals* relates the history
of this Ngok (rNgog) family lineage,
explaining that in the life of Ngok
Kunga Dorje (Kun dga' rdo rje, 1157–
1234), the family established its monastic seat at Treshing (sPre zhing) in the
Lhokha district of central Tibet, west of
Gongkar.[619] The same or similar Hevajra
lineages were transmitted from Marpa
and Ngoktön through the Fourth Shamar
and Situ Paṇchen down to Kongtrül
(Kong sprul) and Loter Wangpo (Blo
gter dbang po), as listed in the record
of teachings received for the *Compen-
dium of Tantras (rGyud sde kun btus)*
collection.[620] After Ngok Kunga Dorje,
the lineage merges with the Mahāmāyā
lineages in the *Blue Annals*, including
one variant that passes through Situ
Paṇchen.[621]

The painting possesses a few
archaic features that have not yet been
attested in fourteenth-century mandalas,
such as the plain bases of the multicolored vajras. Perhaps the artist was copying an older model here.

Figure 13.4 illustrates another
surviving early thangka from the Ngok
tradition. Published in 1993, this painting
is said to possess inscriptions, including
one that names Marpa, but they cannot
be read from the plates.[622] The painting's
structure is mapped in Diagram [K]. Here
we find eight generations of Tibetan masters, starting with Marpa (12), the same

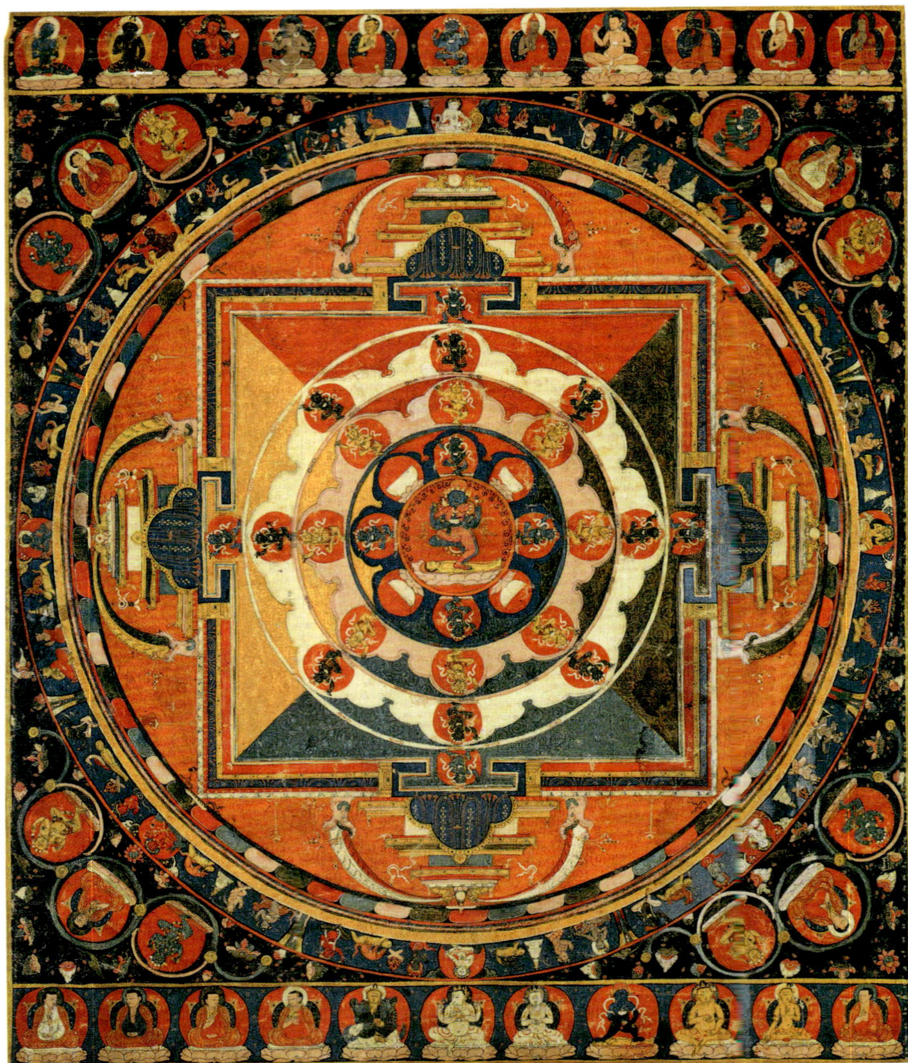

[K]										
1	2	3	4	5	6	7	8	9	10	11
		12					13			
		14					15			
16	17	18	19	d1	d2	d3	d4	d5	d6	20

as in the mandala from the McCormick collection (Fig. 13.3). Hence it suggests a date in the second quarter of the fourteenth century. But there are three final monks (18, 19, and 20), and the two lamas shown upside down (14 and 15) seem to resemble monks in their dress. Here the painters clearly have painted in the Beri style: note the thin yellow strips along the edges.

Figure 13.5, published in the same source (Singer 1993), portrays the mandala of the goddess Nairātmyā. An inscription mentions a certain Changchup Pal (Byang chub dpal) as a patron. The authors identify him as the early ordination abbot from the Khache Paṇchen Śākyaśrībhadra lineage, who was mentioned in the *Blue Annals* (1071f). But that lineage is not relevant here, and a date of the early or mid-thirteenth century seems too early. It seems more likely that Changchup Pal had a link with the Ngokpa lineage. I suggest the patron was the renowned Ngokpa (rNgog pa) lama, Treshing Rinpoche Changchup Pal (sPre'u zhing Rin po che Byang chub dpal), who flourished two centuries later and was the teacher of Gö Lotsāwa in the mid-fifteenth century.[623] To come to any more lasting conclusions, we will have to gather and analyze many more thangkas of the Ngok tradition.[624]

Examples of Class B

Ideally a class B thangka portrays a complete lineage, whose teachers' names are labeled. A single thangka would be class B if the lineage and its last two or three generations of teachers can be identified. If the painting belongs to a set of guru-lineage portraits, it is essential to identify the last painting of the set, which would raise the whole set to B class.

An example of a class B painting, Figure 13.6 is a black thangka from the Drigung Kagyu tradition that depicts the wrathful deity Yamāri of the Gya

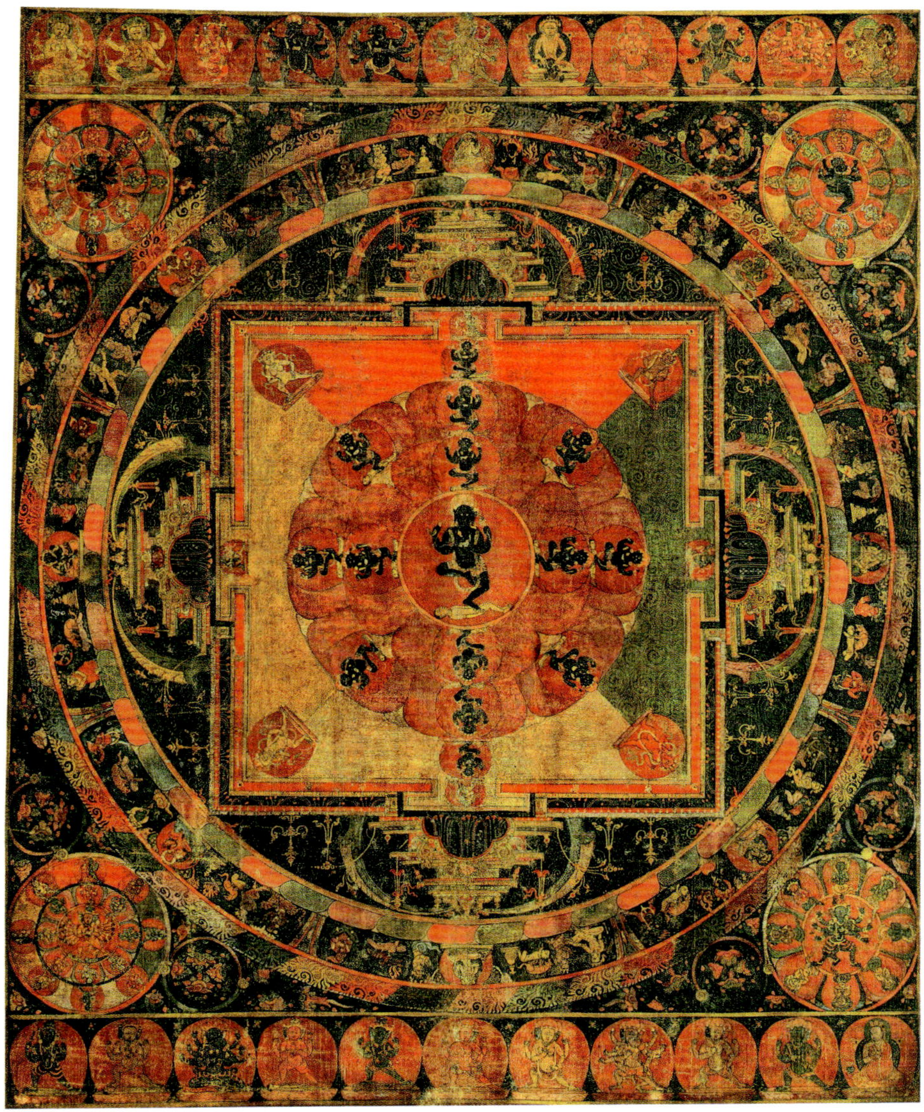

Shangtrom tradition as its main figure. In 1989, Essen and Thingo dated it to the eighteenth century.[625] They did not identify it as from the Drigung school, but they noted the Nyingma origin of this lineage.[626] The order of lamas is indicated by Diagram [L].

The last six lineal teachers are:
20. Don grub Chos rgyal (1704–1754)
21. Phrin las bZang po (1656–1718); out of order
22. dPal gyi rGya mtsho
23. bsTan 'dzin 'Gro 'dul (1724–1766)
24. dPal ldan mGar chen pa
25. Chos kyi Nyi ma (1755–1792)

FIG. 13.5
Nairātmyā Mandala from the Ngokpa Tradition
fifteenth century
Literature: Singer 1993

The painting may have been commissioned by a disciple of Chökyi Nyima (Chos kyi nyi ma, 1755–1792, twenty-ninth abbot of Drigung), that is, in the late eighteenth century, more or less the date proposed by Essen and Thingo. If the birth and death dates of the last master in a lineage are not known, one can assume that each generation spanned about twenty-five years. Here, we ignore the possibility that a patron was more than a generation younger than his teacher or lived to great old age, though such cases should be watched for when the dates of lineal teachers are well documented.

Figure 13.7 is a second example of a class B thangka. Also from the Drigung Kagyu school, it depicts Samvara (bDe mchog) in two-armed form (Sahaja-Samvara, Lhan skyes bde mchog) with four other deities (*bDe mchog lha lnga*), accompanied by a lineage of Drigung masters. Lineage analysis indicates it probably dates to one generation later than the twenty-ninth abbot, Chökyi Nyima. Preserved in a private collection, this painting was previously dated as "circa late eighteenth or early nineteenth century" thanks to an understanding of the lineage.[627] The lineal structure is indicated by Diagram [M].

The last three lineal teachers are: 32, dPal ldan 'Gar chen pa; 33, dKon mchog ting [=bstan!] 'dzin Chos kyi Nyi ma (twenty-ninth abbot of Drigung, 1755–1792), or Chos kyi Nyi ma, for short; and 34, dKon mchog Ting [=bsTan!] 'dzin Phrin las rNam rgyal. The last lama was not an abbot, and he was a contemporary of the thirtieth abbot of Drigung (tenure 1788–1810). He and his patron thus lived about one generation after those of the previous thangka (Fig. 13.6). I conclude that this thangka's date is between the 1790s and the 1820s. These two examples from the same school and period illustrate how the dating of nearly

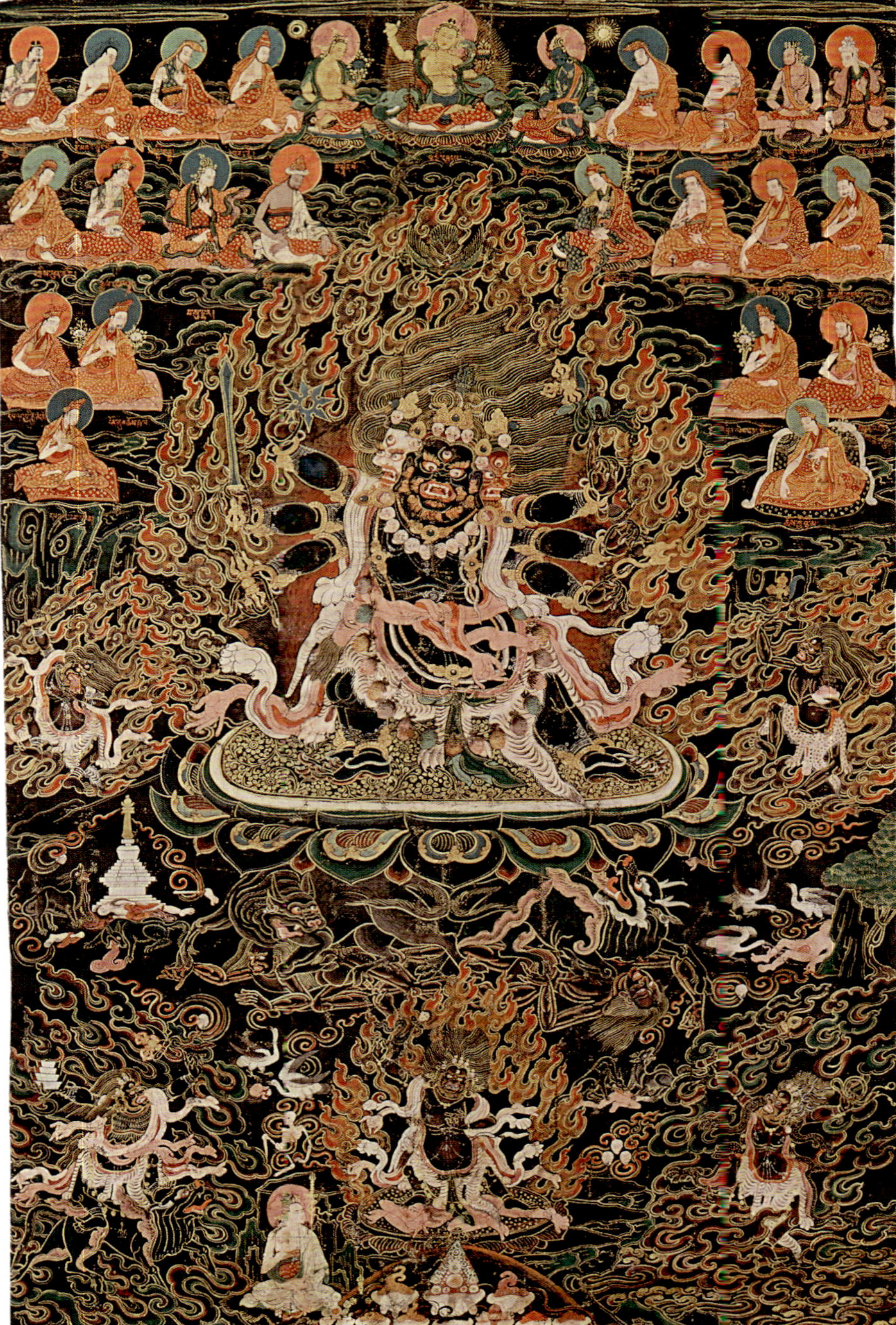

10	8	6	4	2	1	3	5	7	9	11
18	16	14	12				13	15	17	19
22	20								21	23
24										25

Fig. 13.6
Yamāri of the Gya Shangtrom Tradition
with Drigung Kagyu Lineage
mid- or late eighteenth century
(1760s–1780s)
19 ⅛ x 15 ¾ in. (48.5 x 40.0 cm)
Museum der Kulturen Basel, Essen Collection
Literature: Essen and Thingo 1989, vol. II, no. 331; and Jackson 2015, fig. 8.27

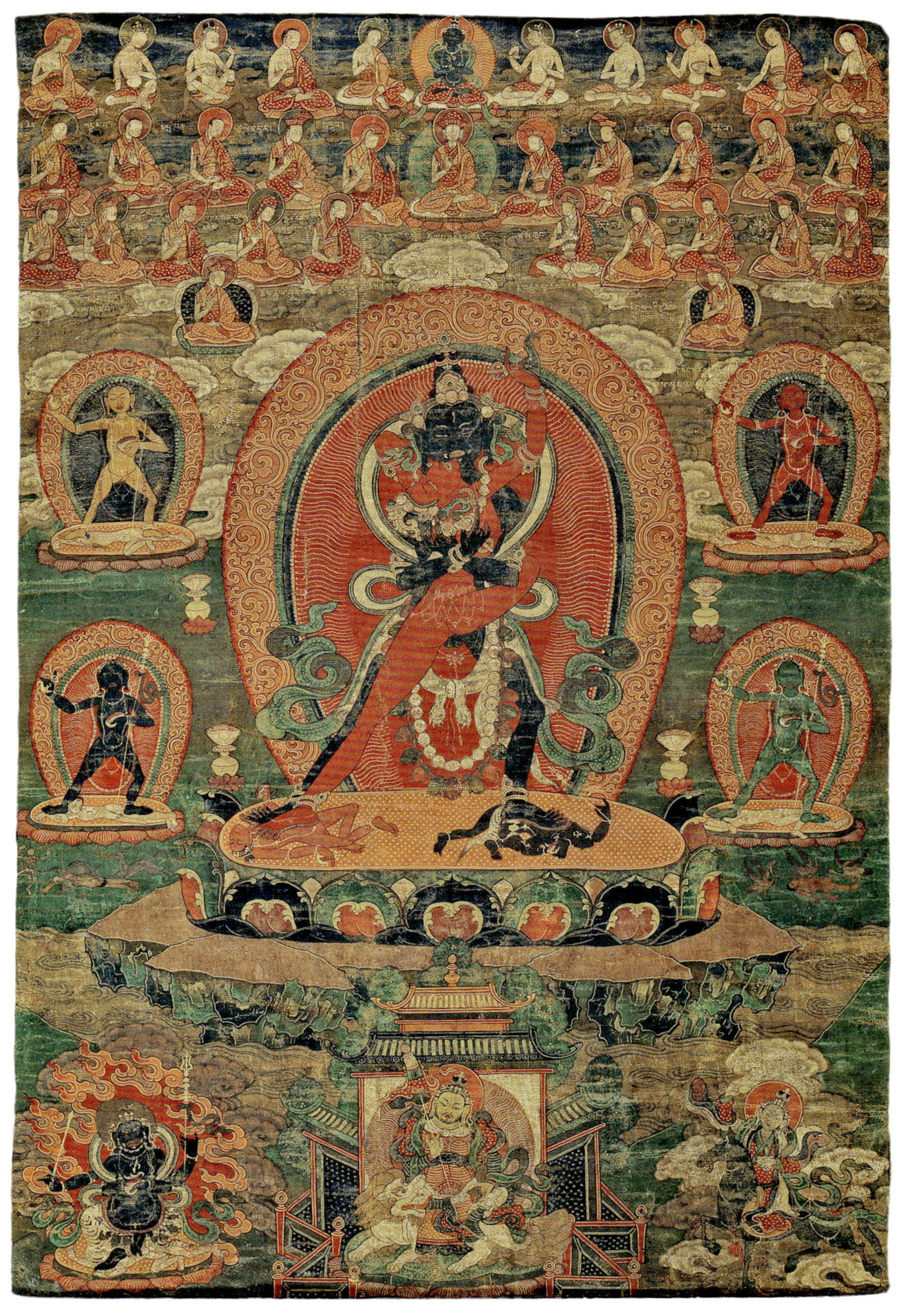

[M]

10	8	6	4	2	1	3	5	7	9	11
21	19	17	15	13	12	14	16	18	20	22
31	29	27	25	23	24	26	28	30	32	
				33		34				

Fig. 13.7
Sahaja-Samvara with a Drigung Kagyu
Lineage
late eighteenth or early nineteenth century
(1790s–1820s)
22 ⅞ x 15 ¾ in. (58 x 40 cm.)
Private Collection
Literature: Jackson 1996, 343, pl. 64; and
Jackson 2015, fig. 8.7a

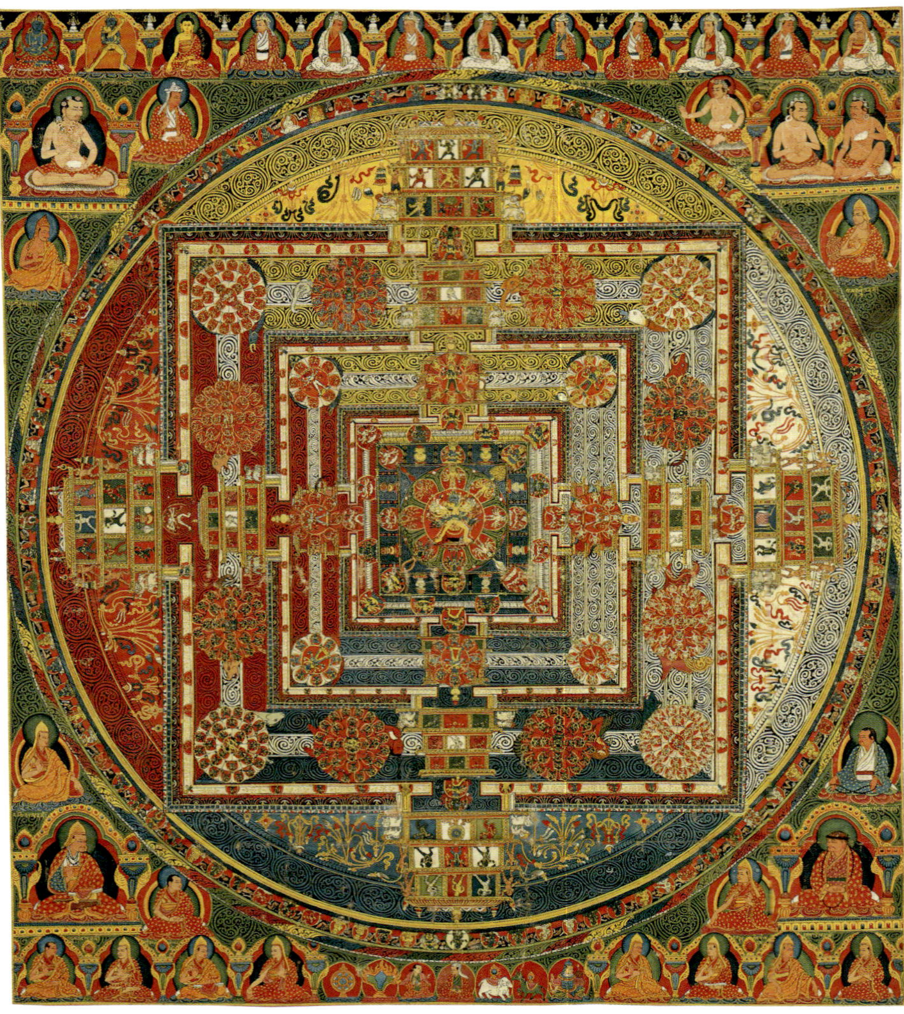

and the patron died in 1602, the painting can be confidently dated to the period between those years.

Figure 13.9, another example of a class A thangka, has a rich historical background from Tibet; it has also been discussed at some length as the subject of a 1980s legal suit in Switzerland concerning possible forgery.[629] The basic problem of the case, as now, was how to date the painting reliably. Several expert witnesses submitted widely differing dates to the court, in part because the thangka contained both distinctly earlier and later stylistic elements, which nobody could explain. Basing their dates mainly on style, the experts could reach no consensus; they did not, however, refer to the rich internal historical evidence present in the painting in the form of inscriptions and lineages.[630]

I will first present the inscriptions and lineage structure of this thangka, shown in Diagram [N], and then interpret these within the historical context of the tradition that produced the painting. The inscriptions identify the main figures (27 and 28) as Ngor abbots and include a verse in praise of Kunga Wangchuk (27): *rgyud sde kun gyi de nyid gzigs// smin grol dga' ston phyogs bcur 'gyed// phrin las dbang phyug 'dul ba yi// 'dren pa dam pa de la 'dud//*. The second verse, in praise of Gorampa (28), begins: *rgya chen bsod rams lus stobs rab rgyas te// de gshegs gsung rab seng ge'i nga ro yi// log smra'i ri dags mtha'*. The second verse is incomplete.

A smaller inscription to the bottom right names the thangka's patron and explains his purpose: *lam 'bras [b]rgyud pa'i kha skong 'di rig pa 'dzin pa lha mchog seng ges bzhengs.*/ "This continuation of the Path with the Fruit lineage thangkas was made by the mantra practitioner Lhachok Sengge."

The last four teachers in the lineage are:

27. rJe btsun Kunga Wangchuk (1424–1478)

contemporaneous pieces can be done once two or three examples have been properly documented.

Examples of Class A

A painting in the A class typically has a colophon-like inscription that specifies the name of the patron, his teacher, or both. Ideally, this inscription is confirmed by a labeled lineage. A thangka is class A only if the names of its historical figures have been properly identified.[628]

The first example of a class A painting is Figure 13.8. Its date is established by a brief inscription at the bottom, which states that it was reverently commissioned by the Drangti monk Namkha Palzang in memory of his deceased teacher, Vajradhara Sanggye Sengge. Since the latter died in 1569

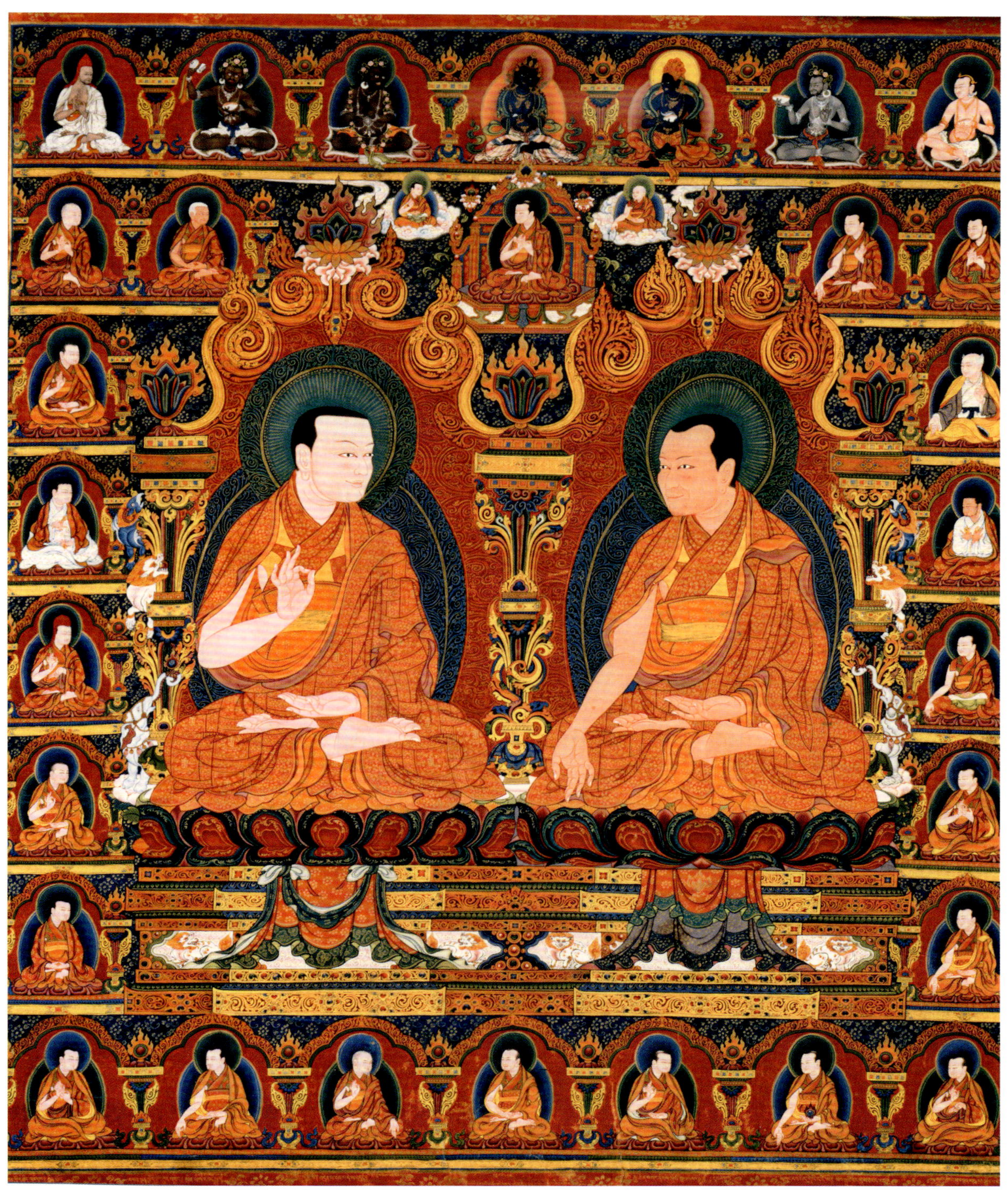

Fig. 13.9
Two Abbots of Ngor
early sixteenth century
33 ⅞ x 30 ⅞ in. (86 x 78.5)
Collection of Ravi Kumar
Literature: Brauen 2003, 6, fig. 1

7	5	3	1	2	4	6
8	26a	24b?	25	24c?	26b	9
10						11
12						13
14						15
16		**27**		**28**		17
18						19
20	22	23	24	29	30	21

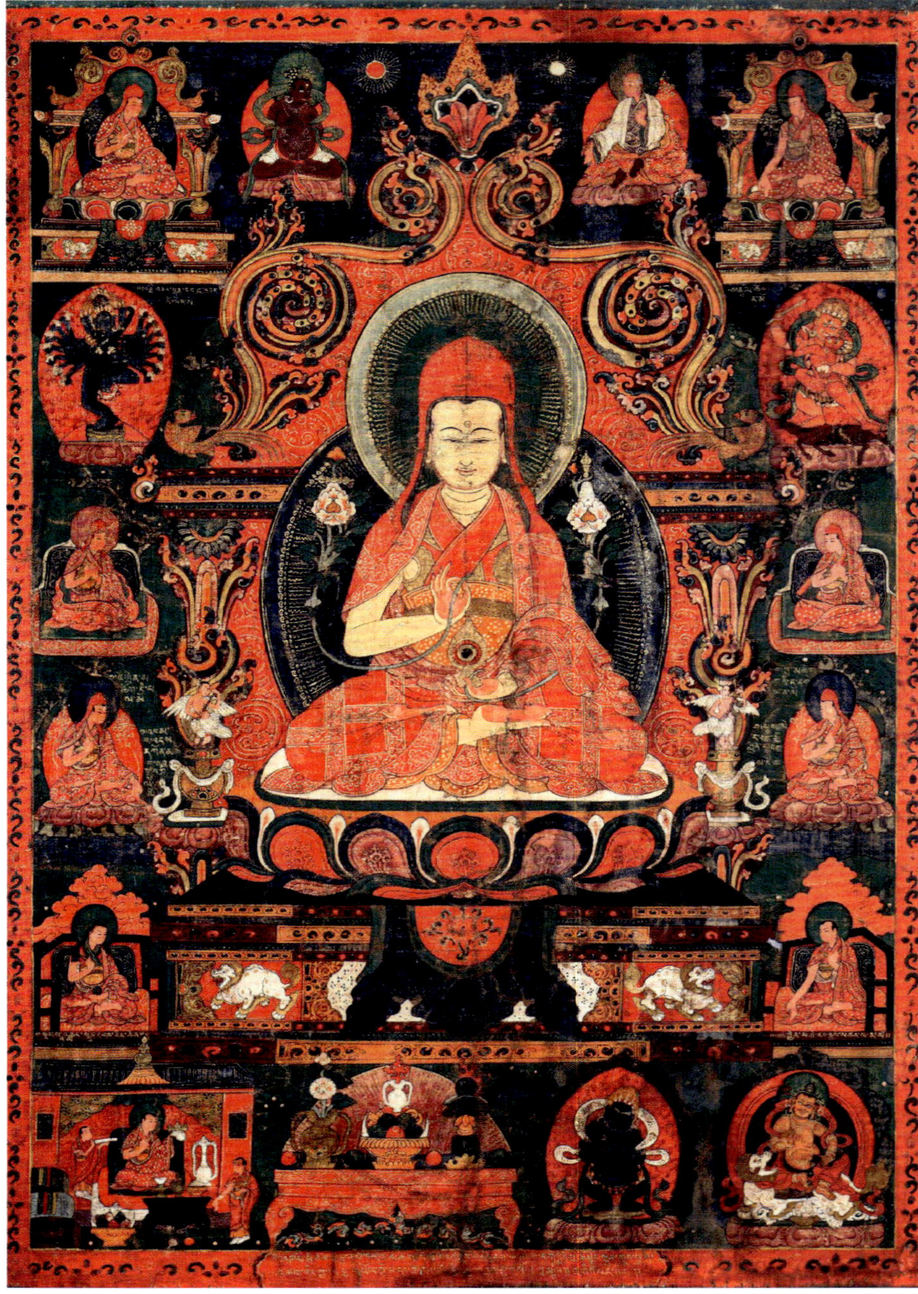

Lhachok Sengge, a major figure at Ngor in the early sixteenth century, commissioned many paintings during his abbatial tenure (1524–1535); by his time, the old sets of lineage thangkas painted at Ngor in the period of its founder, Ngorchen, needed to be brought up to date.[632] We know that Lhachok Sengge was involved in carrying out at least one such completion (*kha skong*), that is, of this set of Lamdre lineage thangkas, as explicitly stated in the inscription. Thus this stylistically puzzling painting, with its portraits of the Ngor abbots Kunga Wangchuk (1424–1478) and Gorampa (1429–1489) as the main figures, was meant to continue a venerable set depicting the lineage masters of the Lamdre.[633] This continuation presumably consisted of three thangkas, each portraying a pair of lineage-master abbots: one showing Ngorchen (25) and Müchen (26), the present one showing Kunga Wangchuk (27) and Gorampa (28), and a third one showing Müchen Sanggye Rinchen (Mus chen Sangs rgyas rin chen; no. 29) and Könchok Phel (30).

The painting's short inscription eliminates much style-based speculation. It also has art-historical implications: since the patron was continuing an older set, he might have shown his artists the fifteenth-century original when commissioning the updated set in the 1520s or 1530s. Later analysis of the cloth supports showed that the painters were provided with older cotton to paint on.

A key stylistic element that supports the dating of Figure 13.9 to the early sixteenth century is the wavy golden rays in the head nimbuses of the main figures, also seen in Figure 13.10. Such rays occur in other Ngorpa and related paintings of the sixteenth century.[634] No convincing case has been made that the painting in Figure 13.9 is a twentieth-century fake because of iconographic mistakes.[635] The iconography of the lineage teachers, including the

28. Gorampa Sönam Sengge (1429–1489)
29. Müchen Sanggye Rinchen
30. possibly Könchok Phel[631]

The colophon-like inscriptions point unmistakably to the participation of the Ngor abbot Lhachok Sengge (Lha mchog seng ge, 1468–1535) in the commissioning of this thangka. The lineage structure independently confirms that the patron belonged to generation 31, that of Könchok Phel's disciples. The date indicated by the lineage and the inscriptions is therefore the early sixteenth century.

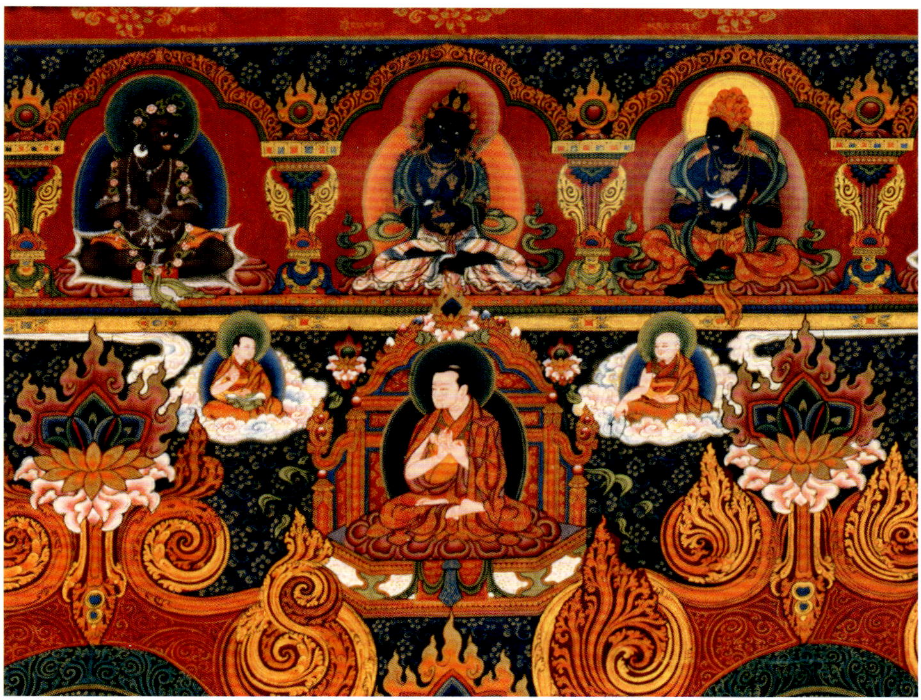

adept Virūpa and goddess Nairātmyā, is correct, but note that the positions of Virūpa and Nairātmyā are erroneously reversed in the lineage. In the detail (see Fig. 13.11), both are shown as teachers of the Lamdre instructions, and Virūpa's hands are in the gesture of teaching, the third of six standard postures in which he is depicted (as enumerated in chapter 6). The same depictions of Virūpa and Nairātmyā appear in Figure 13.13, a detail of Figure 13.12.

Since the patronage inscription accounts well for the stylistic elements found in the painting, we hardly need to consider whether the thangka could have been a recent fake merely because of stylistic inconsistencies.[636] To assert it is inauthentic would require stronger prima facie evidence and a plausible motive. A forger's usual intention is to extract from a buyer as much money as possible. No right-minded forger would devote the exquisite effort to produce this slightly hybrid style on a fifteenth-century cloth support with faultless inscriptions, iconography, and lineage—all indicating an origin with a Ngor abbot of the early sixteenth century—to flog it on the market as a work of the nineteenth century.

In the past three decades, the study of Tibetan painting has made significant progress by exploiting the internal historical evidence—lineages and inscriptions—of individual paintings in ways that conform to high professional and scholarly standards. But some educational work is still needed. Even fairly recently, a correct and carefully reasoned date based on internal evidence was still mistaken as one more contribution to the formerly prevailing guesswork.[637]

But to keep this in methodological perspective: Not long ago, the prevailing wisdom (or prevailing confusion) about post-fifteenth-century Tibetan painting styles and their dates was based mainly on secondary style comparisons; hardly any thangkas had been accurately dated through sound internal evidence. Too few primary internal-evidence-based datings had been performed for secondary stylistic comparisons to be well founded. But now the field is in a position to distinguish the two types of dating methods and to perform

more primary dating based on internal evidence. In 1990, a few later Ngorpa thangkas had been dated by internal evidence.[638] In 1996, two main sets of important early Ngorpa painting sets commissioned by its founder, Ngorchen, were identified.[639] And by 2010, many more Ngorpa paintings were documented and dated.[640] Three decades ago, nobody had seriously tried to establish when the predominantly Indic, mainly red-colored Beri aesthetic changed to the Chinese-style blue-and-green landscapes. Now we know the change began in the middle of the fifteenth century, with the stylistic revolution led by Menthangpa Menla Döndrup and Khyentse Chenmo.[641] The stylistic dissonance of the puzzling Ngorpa thangka in Figure 13.9 embodies this aesthetic sea change in a fascinating way.

Few people thirty years ago knew that connoisseur-patrons in Tibet sometimes commissioned works in intentionally archaic styles or copies of famous older models. Now we know several examples from the written record.[642] One comes from the same Ngorpa tradition.[643] Thirty years ago, almost nobody thought the stylistic development of the Tibetan schools from the mid-fifteenth century or later was worthy of serious study. Now at least preliminary investigations of this period have begun.[644] Previously, for many experts, the post-Menthangpa or post-Menri developments in Ü and Tsang provinces formed a single amorphous category, under such vague terms as "recent" or "circa eighteenth or nineteenth century," or even, at unguarded moments, as "modern," leading one jokester to remark that Tibet was the only country where modern art began in the fifteenth century.

Hence, in the 1980s, the majority of experts dated the thangka in Figure 13.9 between the seventeenth and nineteenth centuries; such later datings were encouraged by the nearly immaculate condition of the painting. It is interesting that the most accurate date for the

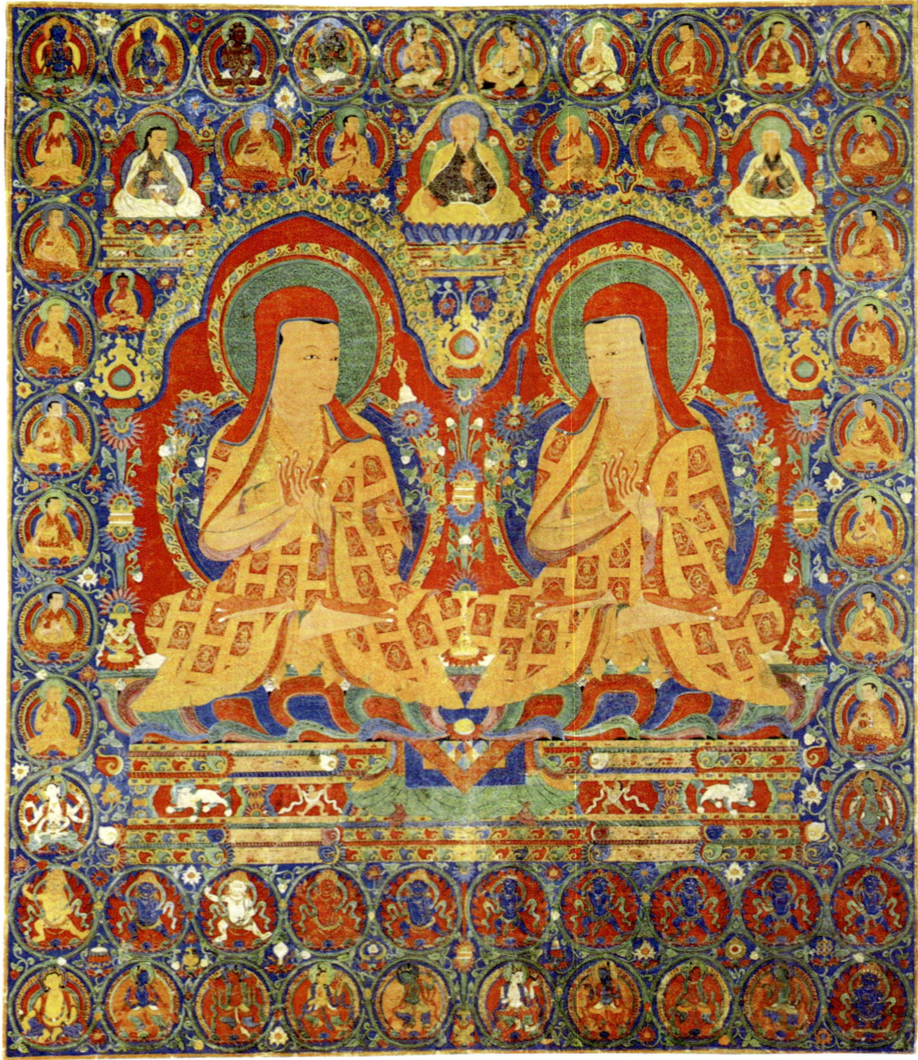

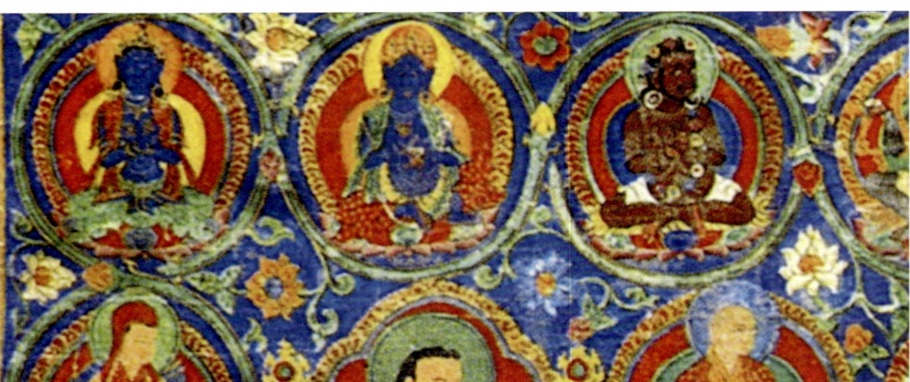

might use today—namely, the investigation of inscriptions and lineages—since
none of the past experts took these decisive factors into account. It is possible to
date a richly inscribed piece of Tibetan
religious art with a reasonable degree
of certainty—in the case of Figure 13.9,
to the period between 1510 and 1535.
There is no harm if the strict standards
of proof from criminal jurisprudence are
not attained, such as certainty "beyond
the shadow of a doubt."[645] Historiogra-
phy aims at establishing the probability
of a historical assertion, not its plausibility, possibility, or certainty.[646]

Accuracy of Dating

How precise is dating based on internal
evidence or one that uses comparison of
style? In my experience, primary dating
based on internal evidence can be accurate enough for most art-historical purposes, but they are only as precise as the
internal evidence they contain. Class A
thangkas with rich historical contents—
with colophon-like inscriptions naming
their patron and his or her historically

court case—the first half of the seventeenth century—was made by a French
museum curator with most experience
cataloging post-fifteenth-century thangkas, who took later Tibetan periods
seriously. His basic description of the
style as sixteenth century was correct.
His revised suggestion of 1600–1650
was only one century too late, which is
an acceptable result for dating a work

purely through stylistic comparison at
that time.

This stylistically puzzling Ngorpa
thangka and its attendant court case
demonstrate the near-impossibility for
the experts in the late 1980s to reach
a reliable date. But no general conclusions can be drawn from that case about
the accuracy or reliability of the dating
methods that a competent historian

known deceased teacher, for instance—can produce very precise dates. These sometimes specify the date that a painting was made, but that is rare. The dates of paintings of class B and stronger examples of class C are usually reliable within two generations, that is, plus or minus twenty-five or thirty years.

The methods of dating depend upon certain suppositions, such as that an abbot identified in the inscription as patron probably commissioned more works toward the end of his life and particularly during his abbatial tenure. In the analysis of lineages, it is reasonable to presume that the patron was the disciple of the last lineage master depicted, and that he commissioned the painting in the last two decades of that master's life or in the first two decades after the master's death.

The accuracy of secondary comparison-based dating depends on a continuous series of paintings—drawn from the relevant artistic and religious traditions—that have been reliably dated through internal evidence. Ideally, two or three firmly dated paintings of each main subject should be available for comparison from each generation. When styles change quickly, as they do in certain periods, comparison dating is more accurate. But with slower rates of stylistic change, there is greater room for chronological error.

Assuming that a continuous series of internal-evidence-based datings has been made, based mainly on paintings of A and B classes, I believe dating by comparing styles can approach accuracy within one or two generations, that is, plus or minus twenty-five to fifty years, at best. In the worst case, the accuracy of stylistic comparison can achieve that of some of the best connoisseurs today, that is, plus or minus seventy-five to one hundred years.

Higher degrees of probability—nearing or reaching 100 percent certainty—can also be achieved for certain chronological judgments. For example, a thangka must have been painted in or after the lifetime of any historical figure portrayed. But the earlier the figure, the longer the period encompassed by the anterior limit; hence the value of complete lineages, which provide not only anterior but also posterior limits.

Greater certainty can be gained at the cost of diminished accuracy. One can assume, for instance, that most paintings with both a complete lineage and a depicted patron were painted in the last thirty years of the last lineal teacher's life or in the thirty years following his death. The probability that such a painting was made in the last forty years of the last master's life or in the forty years after his death is, of course, still higher. Such a thangka was almost certainly painted within the last seventy years of its last master's life or in the seventy years after his death.

Carbon 14 Dating

For dating surviving works of art, one should also take into account radiocarbon (carbon-14 or ^{14}C) analysis results, if they are available. The possibilities and limitations of this method have been summed up by Richard Ernst:

> ^{14}C analysis is the only truly quantitative method available for paintings. But it has numerous inherent limitations: (i) The dating refers to the support material, which could be older than the painting itself. This is of particular relevance for wooden objects where the ^{14}C date reflects the date of growth of the part of the tree stem that has been used. (ii) The precision of the ^{14}C content measured by accelerator mass spectroscopy limits the accuracy usually to plus or minus 50 years, depending on the period to be dated. (iii) Contamination by more recent insoluble material, for example, deposits from the smoke of butter lamps, dust or material from recent attempts of conservation may lead to a too recent dating. (iv) An inherent source of uncertainty is the irregular production rate of ^{14}C in nature. It can cause grave ambiguities in the dating. This unfortunate fact of nature may be appreciated by the calibration curve [in the illustration, for the years 1000 to 2000]. The dating is hampered particularly in the ranges 1000–1150, 1260–1420 and 1460–1620. In these periods, the dating uncertainty is grave. For paintings [that date] after about 1660, dating by ^{14}C analysis is virtually impossible. Often, it is merely possible to distinguish material produced before and after the nuclear bomb testing of the 1950s. [647]

Pigment Analysis

Another possible source of chronological clues is the paint material of the thangka. Through most of their history, Tibetan artists used a limited, fixed palette of pigments and dyes derived from minerals and plants or insects.[648] Yet a rare pigment can give clues for dating and provenance. Some test cases investigated by Richard Ernst produced interesting results; the examination of a small number of paintings revealed the presence of such unexpected pigments as smalt (a blue cobalt glass) and Prussian blue.[649] Gilles Béguin presented pigments found in the sixteenth-century Ngorpa Lamdre teacher and abbot series, "sMra ba'i seng ge" (=Lha mchog seng ge), and some other Beri (Bal bris) paintings; the pigments that differ significantly are those for the colors white, green, blue, and orange.[650]

Conclusions

Tibetan religious art developed under particular historical circumstances. So did every other traditional religious art in the world, and there is nothing uniquely difficult about dating paintings from north of the Himalayas. The methods I have sketched above are commonsensical and can be applied to historical relics from any highly literate society, so why not to those from Tibet?

A good historian will remain cautious and critical, whether faced by doubtful evidence or overly simple methods. But I would stress careful attention to inscriptions and lineages, for they are most likely to yield valuable anterior or posterior limits for the dating of many thangkas. Any serious description of a Tibetan painting will include and record all inscriptions—with the possible exception of the commonly repeated consecration formula on the rear. In studies of thangkas that depict lineages, the documentation should include: a diagram showing the arrangement of figures found in the painting, using numbers for each figure belonging to a lineage or lineages; and a sequential list of the names of the figures in the probable lineage or lineages—as far as it can be established—with numbers matching those in the diagram.[651]

I once assumed that such basic elements of documentation were self-evident and was surprised to find how seldom these steps have been followed systematically. To this day, such thorough documentation remains rare; realistically, only a handful of people will employ this method in all its aspects. In order to reach an accurate historical interpretation of a thangka based on internal evidence, a good knowledge of its tradition may be required for all but the simplest cases. Precise interpretation thus depends on a high level of competence in art, history, and written Tibetan. Who can spare the many years of study needed to become expert in all three

areas? Dating through stylistic comparison, by contrast, does not require the same constellation of skills and should be available for a larger number of practitioners, once a sufficient number of paintings have been reliably dated and documented as points of comparison.

Thus the accurate dating of Tibetan paintings remains perfectly possible for a small number of competent specialists, but every case will vary in terms of precision and ease. The main task at present is to thoroughly document as many thangkas as possible, concentrating first on important sets and obvious masterpieces. The work should proceed from the paintings that have rich documentation to those that lack documentation. Individual minor paintings, collected almost at random for ethnographic museums, are usually not significant, but even those should be possible to date approximately and classify stylistically as soon as there is an adequate corpus of well-documented and reliably dated paintings for comparison. But until the richly inscribed main masterpieces have been studied with more care, it is premature to speak of the impossibility of dating them.

Postscript

In this Masterworks of Tibetan Painting series, each catalog was meant to have a chapter treating a different aspect of scholarly method. Chapter 13, on the methods of dating, fulfills that purpose here. Though I had originally meant to present it in a later catalog, I decided to place it here to make sure it appeared in the series at all.

Ironically, in the foregoing study of Khyentse Chenmo and his school, I used dating through lineage analysis much less frequently than I had in several other catalogs. When identifying the thangkas by Khyentse Chenmo and his stylistic followers in the main body of this book, I relied mainly on stylistic

similarities with the surviving murals of Gongkar. No thangkas with rich inscriptions or complete lineages were available.

Nevertheless, two complete lineages did survive in the murals of Gongkar Monastery, as explained by Mathias Fermer in chapter 4b (see Figs. 4.52 and 4.54). Those two lineages confirmed the dating of the surviving original murals of Gongkar Monastery to the generation of Gongkarwa Kunga Namgyal, its founder. Moreover, his biography established that the murals were painted in the years 1464–1476, and hence those firmly dated original murals could serve as my main point of departure for later stylistic comparisons.

In this catalog, I presented only a single surviving thangka from Gongkar that possessed a colophon-like inscription that named an identifiable historical person. That was Figure 6.4 (Virūpa), a painting commissioned in memory of the seventeenth-century Gongkar lama Nyima Lingpa Tshultrim Tashi. One other thangka (Fig. 1.14), Khyentse's masterful depiction of Pandita Vanaratna, could be identified and dated fairly accurately to the late 1470s, though not with the help of inscriptions; its dating was based on its being mentioned in a contemporary biography. It means that the patron depicted at the base of the painting was probably Lochen Sönam Gyatsho (1424–1482).

Two later Khyenri-style sets could be dated through the presence of contemporaneous historical figures, both to the mid- or late seventeenth-century. The first (see Fig. 11.1) contained a few eminent Geluk lamas with inscribed names. For the second set (especially Fig. 11.6, and see here Fig. 13.14), I deduced from the artistic context that the great lama prominently depicted in the landscape of the set's last painting was the Fifth Dalai Lama.

In chapters 5 through 7, I was able to link and date fairly convincingly the

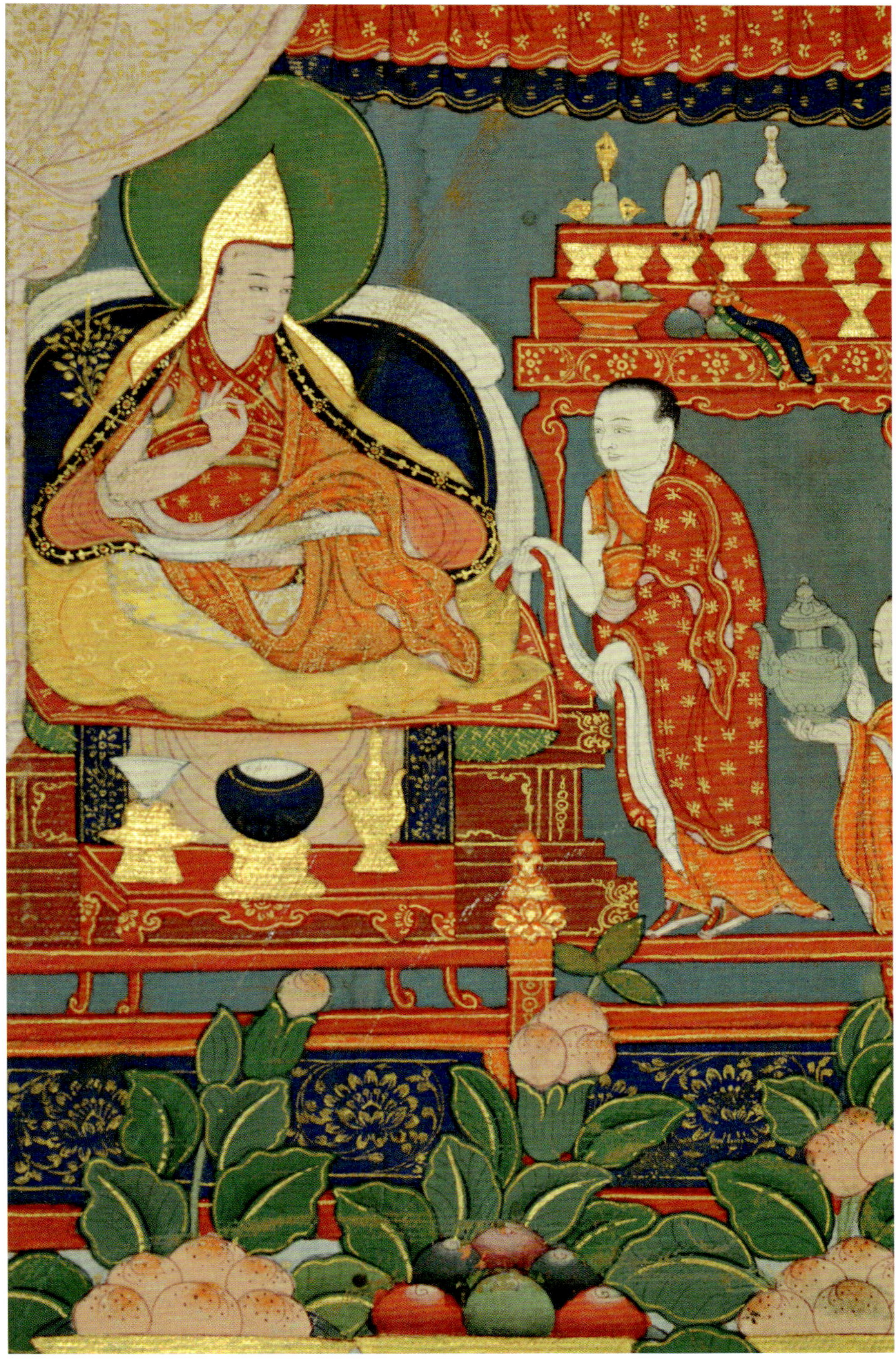

details could be linked in various ways with the previous more securely datable works of art. In chapter 9, too, the arhat sets lacked datable humans and hence were historically linkable to other paintings merely by stylistic evidence. (The comparisons were further complicated by the fact that most of the sets survived in just five or fewer thangkas.) So in chapter 9, too, I mainly used the second stage of dating, employing telling stylistic similarities to relate these paintings to more securely dated examples.

In conclusion, no single method is applicable for every case. One has to make the best use of whatever is available, which is what I tried to do in this catalog. I regret not having the time to identify and describe the background animals and pairs of birds in more detail. It would also be good if those and other China-inspired aspects of Khyentse Chenmo's art could be treated more thoroughly in the future by someone who knows both Tibetan and Chinese art well, something like Karl Debreczeny investigated the art of the Tenth Karmapa in his *The Black Hat Eccentric*. But none of that would change the main datings I reached.

Lamdre painting and statue sets, since their figural iconography was highly specific to Gongkar. Here the identifications of individual lamas were helped by the fortuitous survival of complete Lamdre lineage murals at both Kunzang Tse and Drathang.

In chapter 8, the whole Shambhala king set lacks any datable historical figures. Still, the set is useful for detailed stylistic comparison, because it was nearly complete and its background

A Nyingma Lineage Thangka at Mindröling, Described by Kathok Situ

As mentioned in chapter 1, this is the contents of the Nyingma lineage thangka set at Mindröling that was seen by Kathok Situ.[652] (See Fig. 1.18.)

1. Vajrasattva and (Sambhogakāya) Five families of Buddhas (rDor sems Rigs lnga). Dzogchen lineage masters no. 2 and 3.[653]

2. Garab Dorje (dGa' rab rDo rje) as main figure. Garab Dorje was Dzogchen lineage master no. 4 and guru of Mañjuśrīmitra.[654]

3. Tertön Dangma Lhüngyal (lDang ma Lhun rgyal or Lhun gyi rgyal mtshan) as main figure, with minor figures Jetsün (lCe btsun) and Zhang.[655] Jetsün Sengge Wangchuk was Dangma Lhüngyal's main disciple, while Shangtön Tashi Dorje (Zhang ston bKra shis rdo rje) was Jetsün's main disciple.

4. Melong Dorje (Me long rDo rje) as main figure, with Pema Ledrel (Padma Las 'brel) and Kumārādza as minor ones. Grub thob Me long rdo rje (1243–1303). His main disciple was Rigdzin Kumārādza (Rig 'dzin Ku mā rā dza, 1266–1343). Pema Ledrel is Pema Ledrel Tsal (Padma Las 'brel rTsal, 1248 or 1231/2–1307?).

5. Trinle Lhündrup (gSang bdag Phrin las Lhun grub of gNyos, b. 1611) as main figure, with Natshok Rangdröl (sNa tshogs Rang grol) as minor one.

6. Tendzin Trakpa (bsTan 'dzin Grags pa) with minor figures, such as Thukse Dawa (Thugs sras Zla ba rgyal mtshan, 1499–1587).

7. Urgyen Rinpoche (U rgyan Rin po che), i.e., Padmasambhava, as main figure, with king Khri srong [lde'u btsan] and [Yeshe] mTsho rgyal as minor ones. Padmasambhava is Dzogchen lineage guru no. 8.[655]

8. Śrīsiṃha as main figure, with Vimalamitra, Jñānasūtra, and Chöku Kunzang Öbar (Chos sku Kun bzang 'Od 'bar) as minor ones. Śrīsiṃha is Dzogchen lineage guru no. 6, while Vimalamitra is Dzogchen lineage no. 9, and Jñānasūtra is Dzogchen lineage no. 7.[657]

9. Khepa Nyibum (mKhas pa Nyi 'bum, 1158–1213, his father was Shangtön Tashi Dorje) as main figure, with minor figures, such as Jober (Jo 'ber).

10. Khedrup Dongak Tendzin (mKhas grub mDo sngags bsTan 'dzin of gNyos, father of Trinle Lhündrup) as main figure.

11. Kunkhyen Longchen Rabjampa (Kun mkhyen Klong chen Rab 'byams pa, 1308–1363) as main figure, and Sangdak (bSang bdag) and Kumārādza as minor ones.[658] Kumārādza is Rigdzin Kumārādza (Rig 'dzin Ku mā rā dza, 1266–1343)

12. Terchen Rinpoche (gTer chen Rin po che) as main figure.

For this set, most of the masters can be recognized and parallel Nyingma lineages can be found in the Fifth Dalai Lama's record of teachings received; for example, he gives a similar Nyingma Kama (bKa' ma) lineage, with Nyang Ben after Vimalamitra, down to Longchen Rabjampa and beyond.[659] The lineage given by the Fifth Dalai Lama for a certain Nyingma initiation and seventy tantras matches the lineage of the Dzogchen Guru thangka set in the middle.[660] The end of the lineage of the Dzogchen thangka set down to the Mindröling lamas can also be found; it matches the lineage the Fifth Dalai Lama gives for a certain Nyingma initiation and seventy tantras.[661]

The Main Lamdre Lineage of Dorjedenpa Kunga Namgyal

Kunga Namgyal was number 23 in the main lineage, according to page 8 of his record of teachings received (published in 2005 by the rGyal yongs sa chen in Bodhnath, Kathmandu):

1. Vajradhara (rGyal ba Khyab bdag rDo rje 'chang)
2. Nairātmyā (dPal ye shes kyi mkha' gro bDag med ma)
3. Virūpa (mThu stobs kyi dbang phyug mGon po Shri Bi ru pa)
4. Shar phyogs Nag po pa
5. Ḍamarupa
6. Awadhutipa
7. Paṇchen Gayadhara
8. sGra sgyur Bla chen 'Brog
9. Se ston Kun rig
10. Zhang dGon pa ba
11. Sa skya pa Chen po
12. Je btsun rtse mo
13. rNal 'byor dbang phyug Grags pa rgyal mtshan
14. gNas lnga yongs su rdzogs pa'i Paṇ chen
15. 'Gro mgon Chos kyi rgyal po
16. Zhang dKon mchog dpal
17. Nam bza' Brag phug pa
18. dPal ldan Bla ma dam pa bSod nams rgyal mtshan
19. Ma ti Paṇ chen
20. Sa skya Bu ston dBang phyug [also a disciple of 18]
21. Theg chen Chos kyi rgyal po [a disciple of both 19 and 20]
22. Brag thog Chos rje bSod nams bSod nams bzang po
23. Kunga Namgyal

His lineage is repeated in a section describing the sculpture set of lineal masters (pp. 120–122):

1. Vajradhara (rGyal ba Khyab bdag rDo rje 'chang) [in the center] [Then, alternating to the right and left:]
2. Nairātmyā (dPal ye shes kyi mkha' gro bDag med ma)
3. Virūpa (mThu stobs kyi dbang phyug mGon po Shri Bi ru pa)
4. Shar phyogs Nag po pa
5. Ḍamarupa
6. Awadhutipa
7. Paṇchen Gayadhara
8. 'Brog mi Shākya ye shes
9. Se ston Kun rig
10. Zhang ston Chos 'bar
11. Sa skya pa Chen po Kun dga' snying po
12. sLob dpon Rin po che bSod nams rtse mo
13. rJe btsun Rin po che Grags pa rgyal mtshan
14. Sakya Paṇḍita Kun dga' rgyal mtshan dpal bzang po
15. Chos kyi rgyal po 'Phags pa Rin po che Blo gros rgyal mtshan dpal bzang po
16. Tshogs sgom pa Kun dga' dpal [gSan yig: Zhang dKon mchog dpal]
17. Nyan chen pa bSod nams brtan pa
18. Brag phug pa bSod nams dpal
19. dPal ldan Bla ma dam pa bSod nams rgyal mtshan
20. Sa bzang pa Blo gros rgyal mtshan (Ma ti Paṇ chen)

[Not shown: Sa skya Bu ston dBang phyug, who was also a disciple of 18.]
21. Theg chen Chos kyi rgyal po Kun dga' bkra shis [a disciple of both 19 and 20]
22. Brag thog Chos rje bSod nams bSod nams bzang po
23. Kunga Namgyal

The Shambhala King Thangka Set at Palpung

To supplement my description of the Shambhala kings and Kalkins described above in chapter 8, I would like to present here information about the other main tradition, that of Palpung Monastery in Kham. (On that set, see also Jackson 2009, Figs. 6.14 and 6.15.)

Thirty-seven of the thirty-nine-thangka set of the Shambhala and Kalkin kings have survived at Palpung. Note that the designations *right* and *left* refer to the proper right and proper left of the central figure, that is, they are opposite the viewer's standpoint. According to the copies of the inscriptions recently made by Palpung monks, the second thangka of the series is a prominent portrayal of Chos rgyal Nyi ma'i 'od, placed directly to the Buddha's right, with the lineage lama Dus zhabs pa 'Jam pa'i rdo rje above. I cannot explain this Shambhala king's presence, as his name is absent from the accessible lists. Nor can I explain the fact that several lineage lamas are far out of order.

1. Buddha Śākyamuni [central thangka]

The seven Shambhala kings:

2. Chos rgyal Nyi ma'i 'od [possibly a Shambhala king; 1st right]. Above: lineage guru 2, Dus zhabs pa 'Jam pa'i rdo rje

3. Chos rgyal Zla ba bzang [1st Shambhala king, blue, 1st left]

4. Chos rgyal Lha dbang rdo rje [2nd Shambhala king, yellow, 2nd right]

5. Chos rgyal gZi brjid can [3rd Shambhala king, yellow, 2nd left]

6. Chos rgyal Zla bas byin [4th Shambhala king, yellow, 3rd right]. Above: lineage guru 6, 'Bro lo Shes rab grags pa

[7. *missing*] Chos rgyal Lha yi dbang phyug [5th Shambhala king, 3rd left]

8. Chos rgyal sNa tshogs gzugs [6th Shambhala king, white, 4th right]. Above: lineage guru 8, sGo ston Nam brtsegs

9. Chos rgyal Lha yi dbang ldan [7th Shambhala king, blue, 4th left]

The twenty-nine Kalkin (Tib. Rigs ldan) kings of Shambhala:

10. [Kalkin no. 1] Rigs ldan 'Jam dpal grags pa [orange, 5th right]. Above: lineage guru 10, Chos kyi dbang phyug

11. [Kalkin no. 2] Rigs ldan Padma dkar [white, 5th left]

12. [Kalkin no. 3] Rigs ldan bZang po [blue, 6th right]. Above: lineage guru 24, Grub chen Kun blo [out of order]

13. [Kalkin no. 4] Rigs ldan rNam rgyal [green, 6th left]

14. [Kalkin no. 5] Rigs ldan bShes gnyen bzang [white, 7th right]. Above: lineage guru 14, Chos rje 'Jam gsar Shes rab 'od zer

15. [Kalkin no. 6] Rigs ldan Phyag dmar [blue, 7th left]. Above: lineage guru 13, Grub thob Se mo ba

16. [Kalkin no. 7] Rigs ldan Khyab 'jug [red, 8th right]. Above: lineage guru 34, Chos rje Ngag dbang phrin las [out of order]

17. [Kalkin no. 8] Rigs ldan Nyi ma grags [blue, 8th left]

18. [Kalkin no. 9] Rigs ldan Shin tu bzang [blue, 9th right]

19. [Kalkin no. 10] Rigs ldan rGya mtsho rnam rgyal [orange, 9th left]

20. [Kalkin no. 11] Rigs ldan rGyal dka' [white, 10th right]. Above: lineage guru 22, Phyogs las rnam rgyal

21. [Kalkin no. 12] Rigs ldan Nyi ma [green, 10th left]

22. [Kalkin no. 13] Rigs ldan sNa tshogs gzugs [orange, 11th right]

23. [Kalkin no. 14] Rigs ldan Zla 'od [white, 11th left]

24. [Kalkin no. 15] Rigs ldan mTha' yas [blue, 12th right]

25. [Kalkin no. 16] Rigs ldan Sa skyong [red, 12th left]. Above: lineage guru 26, mKhas pa Nam mkha' chos skyong

26. [Kalkin no. 17] Rigs ldan dPal skyong [blue, 13th right]. Above: lineage guru 28, 'Jam dbyangs chos skyong bzang po

27. [Kalkin no. 18] Rigs ldan Seng ge [yellow, 13th left]. 29. Above: lineage guru, rJe btsun Kun dga' grol mchog

28. [Kalkin no. 19] Rigs ldan rNam gnon [yellow, 14th right]. Above: lineage guru 30, mKhan chen Lung rigs rgya mtsho

29. [Kalkin no. 20] Rigs ldan sTobs po che [white, 14th left]. Above: lineage guru 31, 'Jam mgon Tāranātha Kun dga' snying po

30. [Kalkin no. 21] Rigs ldan Ma
’gags [white, 15th right]

[31. *missing*] [Kalkin no. 22] Rigs
ldan Mi yi seng ge [15th left]

32. [Kalkin no. 23] Rigs ldan dBang
phyug chen po [blue, 16th right]

33. [Kalkin no. 24] Rigs ldan mTha’
yas rnam rgyal [white, 16th left]

34. Rigs ldan ’Jam dpal grags pa
[orange, 17th right]

35. Rigs ldan Chad tshangs pa [red,
17th left]. Above: lineage guru 12,
sPrul sku Jo ’bum [out of order]

36. [Kalkin no. 25] Rigs ldan Drag po
’khor lo can [orange, 18th right].
Above: lineage guru 16, Kun
spangs Thugs rje brtson ’grus [out
of order]

37. Rigs ldan Lha dbang [white, 18th
left].[662] Above: lineage guru 36,
Rig ’dzin Tshe dbang nor bu

38. Rigs ldan ’Od srung [green, 19th
right]. Above: lineage guru, bKa’
brgyud phrin las shing rta

39. sByin bdag rDo rje ’chang Chos
kyi ’byung gnas. Si tu Paṇ chen
(1700–1774) as patron and great
guru of the series and tradition.
[19th left, no. 37 in the lineage]

Because of the immense work involved
and the specialized subject matter of
this thirty-nine-thangka set from Palpung, few later copies would have been
commissioned. Still, a few copies were
made, and one survived until at least
the 1920s at Lha thog Khams pa sgar.[663]
Kaḥ thog Si tu, when visiting there, saw
a series of forty-one-thangkas depicting
the “Kalkin kings following the Palpung

model” (*rigs ldan dpal spungs ltar*).[664]
Seventeen paintings from a different set
were photographed elsewhere in Kham
in the 1980s, and the slides are now in
the Shechen Archives collection (Himalayan Art Resources, nos. 15411–15457).

Three thangkas from another,
probably later copy of this set have
been published. Two appeared in the
calendar, *Iconographie de l’art sacré du
Tibet. Calendrier d’art Tibétain 1995*
(Paris, Editions Médicis-Entrelass, 1994;
original German edition by Wolfgang
Jünemann, Schneelöwe Verlagsbera-
tung): the first Shambhala king, mTha’
yas rnam rgyal/Anantavijaya, on the
January page; and the ninth Shambhala
king, Zla ba bzang po/Sucandra, on the
September page. They subsequently
appeared in D. Jackson 1996 and 1999,
including Sucandra, the first Shambhala
king (Rubin no. 305). Sucandra was the
earliest recipient and transmitter of the
Kālacakra Tantra. Above in the sky is
the Tibetan adept “grub chen Kun bzang
po.”[665] Another stray painting from the
set was published in *Chö-yang, Year of
Tibet Edition* (Dharamsala: Council of
Religious and Cultural Affairs, 1991),
page 291, plate 7, but incorrectly captioned, “A Bodhisattva.” Also known
are thangkas that depict more than
one Kalkin (Rigs ldan) each. See, for
instance, Himalayan Art Resources number 65082, which portrays eight Shambhala kings or Kalkins; the complete set
would have consisted of five paintings.

The Sixteen Arhats Listed in the Praises Attributed to Śākyaśrībhadra

Here is a list of the sixteen arhats or Sthaviras (Tib. *gnas brtan bcu drug*) taken from from the praises attributed to Śākyaśrībhadra, together with their iconographic characteristics.[666]

1. Aṅgaja (Yan lag 'byung; who holds a censer and a fly whisk)
2. Ajita (Ma pham pa; who is depicted in meditation)
3. Vanavāsin (Nags na gnas; with *sdigs mdzub* threatening gesture and fly whisk)
4. Kālika (Dus ldan; holding golden earrings)
5. Vajrīputra (rDo rje mo'i bu; with *sdigs mdzub* gesture and fly whisk)
6. Bhadra (bZang po; with gestures of explaining the teaching and meditation)
7. Kanakavatsa (gSer be'u; holding a string of jewels or a "precious noose")
8. Kanakabharadvāja (Bha ra dhwa dza gser can; shown in meditation)
9. Bakula (Ba ku la; holding a mongoose)
10. Rāhula (sGra gcan zin; with a jewel crown)
11. Cūḍapanthaka (Lam phran bstan; shown in meditation)
12. Piṇḍola Bharadvāja (Bha ra dhwa dza bsod snyoms len; holding a book and an alms bowl)
13. Panthaka (Lam bstan; explaining the teaching and holding a book)
14. Nāgasena (Klu'i sde; holding a flask and a monk's staff)
15. Gopaka (sBed byed; holding a book)
16. Abheda (Mi phyed pa; holding a stupa of enlightenment)

Added to the sixteen elders are:
17. Upāsaka Dharmatrāta (dGe bsnyen Dharma; holding a fly whisk and a flask)
18. The Chinese monk Pu tai Hoshang (Hashang, Hwa shang; holding a rosary in his right hand and a bag in his left)

The Four Great Kings (*caturmahārāja, rgyal po chen po sde bzhi*):
1. at the east gate is Dhṛtarāṣṭra (Yul 'khor srung; white and holding a lute)
2. at the south gate is Virūḍhaka ('Phags skyes po; blue and holding a sword)
3. at the west gate is Virūpākṣa (Mig mi bzang; red and holding a serpent noose and a *stupa/caitya*)
4. at the north gate is Vaiśravaṇa (rNam thos sras; yellow and holding a banner marked with a wish-granting gem and a mongoose)

The praises following this tradition were included in many liturgical compilations (*mchod spyod*) of Tibet. For the full text of the praises of the sixteen arhats in Śākyaśrībhadra's tradition, see Appendix D-2.

Regarding the arhats in China, C. A. S. Williams 1976, pp. 161-168, summarized and illustrated one standard recent iconography of the eighteen *lohans*.

Tibetan Text of the Praises of the Sixteen Arhats Attributed to Śākyaśrībhadra

These are the praises attributed to Śākyaśrībhadra in Tibetan. Here I extract from a ritual liturgical compilation of the Geluk school entitled *Ser byes mkhas snyan grva tshang gi zhal 'don chos spyod rab gsal* (ACIP S02121.txt), p. 174b:

gangs ri chen po ti se la // 'phags pa gnas brtan yan lag 'byung //
dgra bcom stong dang sum brgyas bskor // spos phor rnga yab 'dzin phyag 'tshal //
bla ma'i sku tshe brtan pa dang // bstan pa rgyas par byin gyis rlobs //

drang srong ri yi ngos shel na // 'phags pa gnas brtan ma pham pa //
dgra bcom brgya phrag gcig gis bskor // phyag gnyis mnyam gzhag mdzad phyag 'tshal //
bla ma'i sku tshe bstan pa dang // bstan pa rgyas par byin gyis rlobs //

lo ma bdun pa'i ri phug na // 'phags pa gnas brten nags na gnas //
dgra bcom stong dang bzhi brgyas bskor // sdigs mdzub rnga yab 'dzin phyag 'tshal //
bla ma'i sku tshe brtan pa dang // bstan pa rgyas par byin gyis rlobs //

'dzam bu gling gi zangs gling na // 'phags pa gnas brtan dus ldan ni //
dgra bcom stong dang chig brgyas bskor // gser gyi rna kor 'dzin phyag 'tshal //
bla ma'i sku tshe brtan pa dang // bstan pa rgyas par byin gyis rlobs //

singga la yi gling na ni // gnas brtan rdo rje mo yi bu //
(175a1) dgra bcom stong phrag gcig gis bskor // sdigs mdzub rnga yab 'dzin phyag 'tshal //
bla ma'i sku tshe brtan pa dang // bstan pa rgyas par byin gyis rlobs //

chu bo ya mu na'i gling na // 'phags pa gnas brtan bzang po ni //
dgra bcom stong dang nyis brgyas bskor // chos 'chad mnyam gzhag mdzad phyag 'tshal //
bla ma'i sku tshe brtan pa dang // bstan pa rgyas par byin gyis rlobs //

gnas mchog dam pa kha che na // 'phags pa gnas brtan gser be'u //
dgra bcom chen po lnga brgyas bskor // rin chen zhags pa 'dzin phyag 'tshal //
bla ma'i sku tshe brtan pa dang // bstan pa rgyas par byin gyis rlobs //

nub kyi ba glang spyod gling na // bha ra dhva dza gser can ni //
dgra bcom chen po bdun brgyas bskor //phyag gnyis mnyam gzhag mdzad phyag 'tshal //
bla ma'i sku tshe brtan pa dang //bstan pa rgyas par byin gyis rlobs //

byang gi sgra mi snyan na ni // 'phags pa gnas brtan pa ku la //
dgra bcom chen po dgu brgyas bskor // phyag gnyis ne'u le 'dzin phyag 'tshal //
bla ma'i sku tshe brtan pa dang // bstan pa rgyas par byin gyis rlobs //

pri yang (175b1) ku yi gling na ni // ‘phags pa gnas brtan sgra gcan ‘dzin //
dgra bcom stong dang chig brgyas bskor // rin chen prog zhu ‘dzin phyag ‘tshal //
bla ma’i sku tshe brtan pa dang // bstan pa rgyas par byin gyis rlobs //

bya rgod phung po’i ri bo la // ‘phags pa gnas brtan lam phran bstan //
dgra bcom stong dang drug brgyas bskor // phyag gnyis mnyam gzhag mdzad phyag ‘tshal //
bla ma’i sku tshe brtan pa dang // bstan pa rgyas par byin gyis rlobs //

shar gyi lus ‘phags gling na ni // bha ra dhva dza bsod snyoms len //
dgra bcom stong phrag gcig gis bskor // glegs bam lhung bzed ‘dzin phyag ‘tshal //
bla ma’i sku tshe brtan pa dang // bstan pa rgyas par byin gyis rlobs //

lha gnas sum cu rtsa gsum na // ‘phags pa gnas brtan lam bstan ni //
dgra bcom chen po dgu brgyas bskor // glegs bam chos ‘chad mdzad phyag ‘tshal //
bla ma’i sku tshe brtan pa dang // bstan pa rgyas par byin gyis rlobs //

ri yi rgyal po ngos yangs la // ‘phags pa gnas brtan klu yi sde //
dgra bcom stong dang nyis brgyas bskor // bum pa ‘khar gsil ‘dzin phyag ‘tshal //
bla ma’i sku tshe (176a1) brtan pa dang // bstan pa rgyas par byin gyis rlobs //

ri yi rgyal po bi hu la // ‘phags pa gnas brtan sbed byed ni //
dgra bcom stong dang bzhi brgyas bskor // phyag gnyis glegs bam ‘dzin phyag ‘tshal //
bla ma’i sku tshe brtan pa dang // bstan pa rgyas par byin gyis rlobs //

gangs can ri yi rgyal po la // ‘phags pa gnas brtan mi phyed pa //
dgra bcom stong phrag gcig gis bskor // byang chub mchod rten ‘dzin phyag ‘tshal //
bla ma’i sku tshe brtan pa dang // bstan pa rgyas par byin gyis rlobs //

dge bsnyen dharm’a ta la ni // ral pa’i thod bcings glegs bam ‘khur //
snang ba mtha’ yas mdun gnas shing // rnga yab bum pa ‘dzin phyag ‘tshal //
bla ma’i sku tshe brtan pa dang // bstan pa rgyas par byin gyis rlobs //

yul ‘khor srung dang ‘phags skyes po // spyan mi bzang dang rnam thos sras //
rang rang ‘khor ‘dul sgo bzhi bsrung // rgyal chen bzhi la phyag ‘tshal lo //
bla ma’i sku tshe brtan pa dang // bstan pa rgyas par byin gyis rlobs //

The Life of the Khyenri Artist Tshewang Dorje

One of the very few representatives of the later Khyenri style, Tshewang Dorje (1933–2002), is known to have been active in Lhokha in the generation after Yeshe Tendzin (whose life was summarized above in chapter 12). He learned art in Lhokha in the 1950s, after Yeshe Tendzin's departure for India. His career is described in a recent art dictionary by Tenpa Rabten and Ngawang Jigme.[667] According to that source, his teacher in the 1950s was head artist Tenpa Gyatsho (who painted the Sixteen Arhats in the skylight panels of the central assembly hall of Gongkar in the 1930s and in the 1950s was living in Gongkar). (See Figs. 4.10a and 4.10b.) In the 1990s, very late in his career, he published an article on special features of the Khyenri style.[668]

In his 2007 history of Tibetan art, Tenpa Rabten gives a few more details of Tshewang Dorje's life.[669]

The expert artist Tshewang Dorje— who was proficient in painting, sculpture, and carving—was born in Lhokha khul of Lhasa [Lhaden] in 1933 as the son of Tashi Phünt-shok, his father, and Achung, his mother. His father had been born in Chongye Dzong [in Lhokha], while his mother was born in Gongjo Dzong [in Kham]. When he was around nine years old his parents sent him to a privately established school. There, he very diligently learned such things as writing, recitations, and the memorization of correct orthography. From a young age he was particularly fond of drawing pictures. As a carry-over of habits from a previous life, every free moment that he had he filled with drawing with charcoal crayons or lead pencils such things as various flowers or animals, drawing them on wooden boards or sheets of paper. When his parents brought him to a temple to worship the holy images there, he just sat there, wholly engrossed in looking at the mural paintings of the temple. After finishing the temple visit and returning home, he would draw from memory such things as birds and game animals, and since the pictures he drew were good, people who saw them were immediately surprised.

Later on, after his parents moved to Lhokha and he was living there, he continued to learn and practice alone, painting and making sculptures from clay. But, thinking that it would be difficult to properly understand the key points of painting and sculpture merely through self-study and without learning under a qualified master, at age nineteen [1952] he took as his teacher the great artist of the Khyenri tradition named Uchen Tenpa Gyatsho [1872–1959], who was living at Gongkar in Lhokha. Not only did he exactly follow—with full concentration of body, speech, and mind—everything his teacher told him, but he also offered his teacher the highest possible respectful service. As a result, he completely mastered the arts of painting and sculpture, and after much energetic practice, he quickly became an acknowledged master in those fields. He also researched the arts of clay sculpture, stone carving, and the making of seals.

After that, Tshewang Dorje worked for several years as art teacher of the middle school of Gongkar Dzong of Lhokha. Subsequently, he was invited by the Lhokha district art association, and after going to work there, he took responsibility for art planning. Similarly, he was a member of the Tibetan artist association and also served as a member of the national artist association of China.

His main traditional art works were three larger and smaller Lamdre lineage thangkas that he painted for Dophü Chökhor monastery in Jedeshö (lCe bde zhol), and also a thangka depicting the nine-deity mandala of Hevajra. Many other thangkas that he painted are owned by the Tibetan public. Similarly, in Dorjedrak, Rawame Monastery, and Dakpo Namrab Tratshang, many of his clay sculptures are said to exist.

Among the many carved objects
that he made, many are said to still
exist in Lhasa, Lhokha, and Nepal.

Moreover, among the many modern artworks that he made, some
of the more exemplary ones were
[the titles] "A Bird's Fresh Song
on a Riverbank," "Getting a Good
Harvest Again on High Ground,"
[and] "The Monkey and the Cave,"
[and the subjects] Tibetan King

Songtsen Gampo, Thangtong
Gyalpo, and Sakya Paṇḍita, which
were published in the modern
Tibetan art journal. In brief, the
above-mentioned wonderful works
of art that he made remain visible
by all, and they are still widely
praised.

Following the orders of the Lhokha
district government, Tshewang
Dorje kept several art students,

teaching them mainly the practice
of painting together with its practical instructions. Those students
that he trained became independent
artists, and nowadays they are
strongly represented within the specialized profession of Tibetan art of
Lhokha district. He passed away in
2002, at the age of sixty-nine.

Episodes of the Buddha's Life, According to Tāranātha

As mentioned above in chapter 4, Khyentse Chenmo is said to have painted the Twelve Great Deeds of the Buddha in the circumambulation corridor of Gongkar Monastery. Those murals are detailed enough to be legitimately called the Hundred Deeds. Tucci in *Tibetan Painted Scrolls* (1949) mentioned the "hundred deeds" *(mdzad brgya)*, and he cited a relevant Chinese work detailing the Buddha's life.[670] Following are two lists in Tibetan of the episodes of the Buddha's life, both composed by Tāranātha: first, fifty-six episodes that were meant to be painted; and second, 125 episodes from a detailed biography.

For the Tsang king, Tāranātha compiled these lists in a guide to painting the Buddha's life *(bris yig)* in fifty-six sections or chapters (up to section *li*); it was titled *A Guide for Painting the Hundred Deed Life Story of Our Teacher, the Lord of the Śākyas.*[671]

1. (ka), p. 339.4: dga ldan nas 'pho ba
2. (kha), p. 342.1: lhums su zhugs pa dang gtam [bltam] pa [actually 2 major deeds]
3. (ga), p. 343.3: sgyu rtsal mkhas par bstan pa
4. (nga), p. 34.1: btsun mo'i 'khor tshogs
5. (ca), p. 348.2: nges par 'byung ba
6. (cha), p. 349.4: dka' ba spyod pa
7. (ja), p. 350.1: byang chub snying por gshegs pa
8. (nya), p. 350.4: bdud 'dul ba
9. (ta), p. 351.3: mngon pa byang chub pa
10. (tha), p. 353.4: wa ra nā sir chos 'khor bskor ba
11. (da), p. 359.2: mchog zung gnyis rab tu byung ba
12. (na), p. 360.5: ka tya na'i sde tshan
13. (pa), p. 364.5: 'phags pa ka tya na bsngags te grong khyer 'phags rgya du rgyal po rab snang la sogs pa skye bo thams cad dge ba la 'god par mdzad pa
14. (pha), p. 365.4: me skyes lung bstan
15. (ba), p. 369.6: rgyal bu rgyal byad gyi tshal bzhengs shing/ rgyal po gsal rgyal la dad pa la bkod pa
16. (ma), p. 374.4: yab sras 'jal ba
17. (tsa), p. 381.1: grong khyer ser skyar 'gro don mdzad pa
18. (tsha), p. 386.1: grong khyer glog ma can du gshegs pa dang/ 'od zer can gyi zhing khams su byon pa
19. (dza), p. 387.4: yul 'dod pa mthun par bram ze padma'i snying po 'khor bcas brtul ba
20. (wa), p. 389.6: klu dga' bo dang nyer dga' brtul ba
21. (zha?), p. 393.1: gnod sbyin 'brog gnas brtul ba
22. (za), p. 394.4: 'brog gnas su dbyar gnas pa mdzad cing lag rgyud bden pa la bkod pa
23. ('a), p. 399.3: rgyal po u tsa yā na bris skus brtul zhing grong khyer sgra sgrogs su bstan pa dar ba
24. (ya), p. 400.3: byis pa gnyis lung bstan cing seng ge ral pa can brtul ba [2 themes]
25. (ra), p. 402.2: nya pa lnga brgya brtul zhing dgra bcom pa la bkod pa
26. (la), p. 404.2: 'od bsrung chen po bden pa la bkod pa sogs
27. (sa), p. 411.4: cho 'phrul chen po bstan pa [12 wonders are enumerated]
28. (ha), p. 415.5: lha las 'babs pa
29. (a), p. 418.1: grong khyer bzang byed du bshegs pa
30. (ki), p. 420.2: khyim bdag dpal sbed la sogs pa brtul ba
31. (khi), p. 422.6: gnod sbyin ma 'phrog ma brtul ba
32. (gi), p. 424.6: rgyal po ka bi na 'khor bcas brtul ba
33. (ngi), p. 430.3: yul kau shambhirar bshegs shing/ khyim bdag gdengs can gyi kun dga' ra ba phul ba dang/ rgyal po shar pa la sogs pa yul de'i skye bo rnams dge ba la bkod pa
34. (ci), mtsho byed gzhon nu pos 'phags pa'i gnas la bkod pa
35. (chi), p. 432.5: me skyes rab tu byung zhing dgra bcom pa thob pa
36. (ji), p. 434.6: rgyal po'i bu mo mu tig can gyi lo rgyus bden pa la bkod pa ["a continuation of the above"]
37. (nyi), p. 439.4: grong khyer bu ram shing 'phel du byon cing/ ma gha dha bzang mo la sogs pa skye bo dpag tu med pa bden pa la bkod pa
38. (ti), p. 445.1: dge 'dun gyi dben byung zhing mchog zung gcig gis bsdum pa
39. (thi), p. 457.3: glang chen smyon pa brtul ba
40. (di), p. 453.3: rgyal chen bzhi bden pa la bkod cing/ drang srong

ke na'i bu dang/ drang srong ro bo
'khor ? bden pa la bkod pa

41. (ni), p. 454.6: sor mo phreng ba
brtul ba

42. (pi), p. 457.3: las kyi rgyu? ba?
lung bstan pa

43. (phi), p. 462.3: ston pa dang chos
la sdig bsags pas sdug bsngal
myong tshul lhas sbyin la dper
mtshon pa

44. (bi), p. 465.1: rgyal po ma skyes
dgra dad pa la bkod pa

45. (mi): de dag ? can rnams 'jigs pa
las skyob pa sogs

46. (tsi), p. 472.3: mi dang mi ma yin
pa'i 'gro ba dpag tu med pa yang
dge ba'i lam tu bkod pa ste/ byang
phyogs kyi rgyud du gshegs pa

47. (tshi), p. 474.1: bcom rlag dang o
ta sogs su byon pa

48. (dzi), p. 477.1: grong khyer sgra
mthar dbyar gnas pa

49. (zhi), p. 481.2: klu a mra chu
ngogs pa brtul ba'i bkod pa ste/
chu srin gyis pa gsod kyi ri la
bzhugs pa la sogs pa

50. (zi), p. 482.5: 'ga' zhig byang
chub mchog tu lung bstan pa

51. ('i), p. 483.2: shākya lhag ma
rnams bden pa la bkod pa

52. (yi), p. 485.6: rgyal po'i khab
dang yangs pa can gyi gdul bya
mthar phyin pa

53. (ri), p. 492.1: mya ngan las 'das
pa nye bar bstan pa

54. (li), p. 494.4: sku gdung cha
brgyad du bgos pa

55. (shi), p. 496: 'od srung gi mdzad
pa bka' bsdu dang po

56. (?), p. 498.5: nyer sbas kyis bdud
brtul zhing sa steng dgra bcom pas
khyab par mdzad pa

The life of the Buddha by
Tāranātha (*Jo nang mdzad brgya*) was
even more detailed; it comprises one
hundred twenty-five sections. Tāranātha
gives its main points summarized
(*sdoms*) on page 5.2 and listed them

again on page 7.1. Tucci devotes three
pages of *Tibetan Painted Scrolls* (pp.
355–357) to listing those hundred twenty-five sections of the holy biography.
He also refers to studies by Hackin of
Musée Guimet thangkas depicting the
Buddha life stories (p. 357, and note 48),
and elsewhere (p. 612, note 48) he refers
to Ernst Waldschmidt, *Die Legende vom
Leben des Buddha.*

1. The Buddha was in dGa' ldan
[Tuṣita], Dam pa tog dkar po,
Śvetaketu (tog dkar 'gyur)

2. History of the Śākya family, the
highest family lineage (rigs
mchog)

3. The five things he saw (gzigs pa
lnga)

4. The descent from dGa' ldan
[Tuṣita] and the entrance into his
mother's womb (lhums su 'jug)

5. Sojourn in his mother's womb
(lhums na bzhugs)

6. His birth in the garden of Lumbinī
(bltams)

7. Entrance into the city of Ser skya
(Kapilavastu) (se skyar bshegs)

8. Prophecy of the soothsayer Nyon
mongs med (Araṇa) (lung bstan
sogs)

9. He learns various arts (bzo yi gnas
la sbyangs)

10. He competes in his skills (sgyu
rtsal 'gran)

11. He marries Grags 'dzin ma
(Yaśodharā) (grags 'dzin)

12. Story of the tree dGe ba'i snying
po (Udumbara) born when the
Buddha appeared (dge ba'i snying
po)

13. He marries Sa 'tsho ma (Gopā) (sa
'tsho ma)

14. He sees three things that
encouraged renunciation: an old
man, a sick man, and a corpse
(nges 'byung rkyen gzigs)

15. Meditation in the field and vision
of the cemetery (ting nge 'dzin
bsgrubs pa)

16. Story of Ri dwags skyes (Mrgajā)
who, having seen him from a
window, threw a pearl necklace to
him (ri dwags skyes)

17. The palace is guarded by sentries,
lest the prince should go out
(srung 'khor)

18. Flight from home (khyim nas
byung)

19. He assumes a monk's apparel (rab
byung)

20. The quest for truth in the company
of heretics (lam tshol)

21. The seven ways of asceticism (?)

22. He abandons asceticism and
restores his body to strength with
milk-soup (sku lus mthu bskyed)

23. He goes to Bodhgayā (byang chub
snying por gshegs)

24. He subdues Māra (bdud bcom)

25. He obtains supreme gnosis (ye
shes mchog brnyes)

26. He rests in the forest (dal bar
bzhugs)

27. On Brahmā's and Indra's request,
he goes to Benares (gsol btab)

28. First teaching of the Dharma, to
his first five disciples (thog ma'i
chos 'khor bskor)

29. Yaśas and the four others are
converted (nye ba'i lnga sde sogs)

30. From Benares to Magadha (lam
bar gtam)

31. Conversion of Mahākāśyapa and
one thousand other ascetics (ral pa
can stong)

32. Invited by the king Bimbisāra
(gzugs can snying pos bsu)

33. Conversion of Śāriputra and
Maudgalyāyana, his two chief
disciples (mchog zung)

34. The serpent spirit Elāpatra's
conversion (e la'i 'dab)

35. Kātyāyana sent to convert the king
Pradyota of 'Phags rgyal (Ujjayin)
('phags yul dgongs)

36. Story of Me skyes btsas pa
(Jyotiṣka) (me skyes btsas)

37. The Buddha, in a flaming cave,
preaches to Indra and other gods

(’bar ba’i brag phug brten)

38. Anāthapiṇḍada’s sees the truth of the Dharma (zas sbyin chos mthong)

39. Anāthapiṇḍada builds the Jetavana (rgyal byed tshal bzhengs)

40. The Buddha travels to Śrāvastī (mnyan yod gshegs)

41. King Prasenajit comes to believe in the Buddha (gsal rgyal dad la bkod)

42. Meeting of the Buddha with his father, Śuddhodana, on the former’s return to Kapilavastu (yab sras mjal)

43. Sermon to the Śākya women (shāk rigs bud med)

44. Nanda’s ordination (dga’ ?)

45. Gautamī and other women are admitted to the order of fully ordained nuns (dge slong ma)

46. Story of Pūrṇa (tshogs slob ma can)

47. Maudgalyāyana goes to the ’Od zer can (Prabhāvatī) world, to find his mother, who had been reborn there (’od zer can byon)

48. Conversion of the Brahmin Padma snying po (Padmagarbha) (padma’i snying po btul)

49. Story of two boys, a Kṣatriyā and a Brahmin, the first of whom, through his wisdom, obtains good luck and is converted (khye’u gnyis)

50. The Buddha sends Maudgalyāyana to convert the two nāgas Nanda and Upananda (klu zung)

51. The Buddha protects Prasenajit from the nāgas’ attacks (gsal rgyal gnod las skyob)

52. Conversion of the yakṣa ’Brog gnas (Āṭavaka) (’brog gnas)

53. Lag rgyud (Hastaka) is taught the truth (lag brgyud)

54. Story of Utrāyana (Rudrāyaṇa) and Rauraka (sGra ’grogs) (sgra sgrogs)

55. Submission of the lion Ral pa can (Keśarin) (seng ge btul) (shed bu)

56. Birth of Ser skya (Kapila) as a sea monster (ser skya’i gtam)

57. The Brahmin Nya gro dha skyes (Pipalāyaṇa) marries a woman resembling the golden sculpture he has made, lives with her chastely, and is ordained as a monk by the Buddha (’od srungs che --)

58. The Buddha invites Mahākāśyapa to sit with him on the same seat (stan phyed rtsal)

59. Ānanda has a part in each of the Buddha’s acts (lhan cig gnas pa tshol)

60. An ape offers honey (spre’u gnyis)

61. Story of the great Śrāvastī miracle (cho ’phrul che)

62. Conversion of five hundred ascetics (drang srong sde)

63. Reconciliation between the two kings of Pañcāla (lnga len) (lnga len gnyis bsdums)

64. Conversion of a thousand *pissāca* flesh-eating spirits (sha za stong btul nas)

65. The great assembly in Kapilavastu when demons and creatures of all kinds gathered (’dus pa che sogs)

66. Conversion of five hundred Śrāvastī merchants saved from a storm (tshogs pa lnga brgya gnyis)

67. The descent from heaven (the fifth miracle) (lha babs)

68. Entry into the city of bZang byed (Bhadramkara) (bzang byed gshegs)

69. Conversion of dPal sbed (Śrīgupta) (spal sbed)

70. Ordination of Me skyes (Jyotiṣka) (me skyes rab byung)

71. Story of ’Phrog ma (Harīti) (’phrogs ma)

72. King Kapina of gSer gyi sa (Suvarṇabhūmi) in the south becomes an arhat (ka pi na)

73. He reveals the truth to gDengs can (Ghoṣila) of Kauśāmbī (gdengs can bden mthong)

74. gDengs can (Ghoṣila) invites the Buddha to Kauśāmbī; the king’s conversion (kau shambir byon)

75. Story of Mu tig can (Mālikā), daughter of the king of Simhala (mu tig can)

76. Mā ga dha bzang mo (Sumāgadhā) invites the Buddha to Bu ram shing ’phel (Puṇḍavardhana) (bu ram shing ’phel)

77. Magic displayed by Lhas sbyin (Devadatta) (lhas sbrin sgyu ’phrul)

78. Reunites the schism of the monk assembly (dge ’dun dben bsdums mdzad)

79. Sinful deeds of king Ma skyes dgra (Ajātaśatru) (rgyal po’i log spyod)

80. Devadatta attempts in vain to hurt the Buddha (lhas sbyin sgrub)

81. The dangerous elephant Nor skyong (Dhanapāla) is subdued (nor skyong ’dul mdzad)

82. Establishes ’Tsho byed (Jīvaka) on the level of an *arya* or saint (’tsho byed phags sar bzhag)

83. The rgyal chen and a thousand seers (*rishi*) see the truth (rgyal chen drang srong bcas)

84. Submission of Sor mo phreng (Angulimāla) (sor ’phreng)

85. Story of ’Phags pa legs ’ongs (Svāgata) (Legs ’ongs)

86. The Buddha passes the summer on the mountain Chu srun byis pa gsod (Śiśumāra) (byis pa gsod)

87. King Pasenajit honors Mahākāśyapa (’od srungs mchod)

88. He prophesies that a poor woman will become a buddha (dbul mo lung bstan)

89. He pacifies king Prasenajit’s ambitious pretensions (rgyal po’i nga rgyal bsal)

90. He restrains Ma skyes dgra from offending (ma skyes dgra skyabs)

91. He induces Ma skyes dgra to have faith (de nyid dad la bkod)

92. Prophesy of Devadatta (Lhas sbyin) (lhas sbying lung bstan)

93. Story of Śāriputra and Maudgalyāyana visiting there (mchog zung der byon gtam)

94. Events on the way to Vaiśālī (yangs par 'jug)

95. Establishes the inhabitants of Vaiśālī in happiness (spong byed bde bar mdzad)

96. He visits Maithila and other places (mi thil sogs)

97. He subdues the Malla (rdo 'phags)

98. He goes to the village of Nyagrodha (nya gro sogs)

99. Visits the Brahmins' village (brams ze'i grong sogs)

100. Conversion of the northern populations (de bzhin byang phyogs btul)

101. Visit to bCom rlag (Mathurā) (bcom rlag bskor)

102. Visit to O ta la (Story of Kajangalā) (o ta lar byon sogs)

103. He passes the summer in dGra mtha' (Parāntaka) (dgra mtha')

104. Events on the way to lnga len (Pañcāla) (lnga len lam)

105. The story of the poor Brahmin (dbul po sogs)

106. The prophecy about the course of deeds (rgyu na lung bstan)

107. He guides the remainder of the Śākya people toward liberation (shākya lhag ma grol)

108. He prophesies to the Brahmin Gang po (Pūrṇa) that he will attain enlightenment (bram ze gang po)

109. List of the seven indestructible causes (mi nyams pa'i rgyu) (mi nyams rgyu bdun)

110. Events on the way to Vaiśālī (spong byed lam zhugs)

111. Sojourn in the wood of simsapa trees, to the north of 'Od ma can (Beluva) (sha ba'i tshal bzhugs)

112. Story of Nor can (Dhanika) (nor can)

113. Renouncing the vital *samskāra* ('du byed btang)

114. On the way to rTsa can (Kuśa) (rtswa can lam)

115. Deeds while in Kuśa (rTsa can) (der bzhugs mdzad pa)

116. Conversion of Rab dga' ba (Supriya), king of the *gandharva* (Dri za) spirits (rab dga')

117. Rab bzang (Subhadra) becomes an arhat (rab bzang)

118. Passing into Parinirvāṇa (myang 'das)

119. The relics (zhugs la bzhen)

120. The relics are divided into eight lots (cha brgyad bgos)

121. Account of the first council (bka' bsdu)

122. 'Od srung chen po's nirvana ('od srungs zhi)

123. Ordination of Sa na'i gos can (Śāṇāvāsin) (sha na'i gos)

124. Kun dga bo's final deeds (kun dga'i mtha')

125. The second council (bka' bsdu gnyis pa)

A Thangka Set Depicting a Drukpa Kagyu Lineage

This appendix gives more information about the thangka set depicting a Drukpa Kagyu lineage that I introduced above in chapter 10, in connection with Figures 10.17–10.25. The lineage begins:

1. Vajradhara (rDo rje 'chang) (Fig. 10.17)
2. Tilopa (Fig. 10.18)
3. Nāropa (Fig. 10.19)
4. Marpa Lotsāwa (1012–1096) (Fig. 10.20)

It continues:

(5.) Milarepa as the fifth linage master of the Drukpa Kagyu. This thangka from the Zimmerman collection was published by P. Pal in his catalogue of 1983.

(6.) Gampopa as sixth lineage master of the Drukpa Kagyu. Zimmerman collection, see also M. Rhie and R. Thurman 1991, p. 246, plate 84 ("sGam po pa"), which is from the same series.

(7.) Phagmotrupa as seventh lineage master of the Drukpa Kagyu. That this series in the Zimmerman collection was wrongly considered "Taklungpa" goes back to Detlef-Ingo Lauf's erroneous identification of a painting in the Ford collection.[672] Here, based on the single inscription "sTag lung thang pa" under a minor figure above, far left, and without taking the other numerous inscriptions into account, Lauf jumped to wrong conclusions about the contents, provenance, and dating of the series. After him, for many years nobody read the other inscriptions or examined the entire set. Here the main figure seems actually to be Phagmotrupa as a guru of a Middle Drukpa (Bar 'brug) or sTod 'brug lineage. If so, he would be number 7 in the series, perhaps third from the left. Note that the Indian siddha Virūpa and Sakya master Sachen Kunga Nyingpo, who was an important teacher of Phagmotrupa, are also pictured above, but this by no means indicates that the entire set is from the Sakya school.

(8.) Ling Repa as the eighth lineage master of the Drukpa Kagyu. The iconography and other details of another published thangka now in the Los Angeles County Museum of Art indicate that the main figure is Ling Repa. It was published by Pal as "A Mahāsiddha and Taglungpa Lamas."[673] Lama Zhang is shown as a minor figure, as are other lamas contemporary with Ling Repa. Based on his iconography, the Tibetan master shown as the main figure was previously misidentified as an Indian adept, but with his white robe he is definitely a "cotton-clad yogi" (*ras pa*). In the context of the whole set, he can hardly be anyone other than Ling Repa. The inscriptions on the backs of thangkas in the Zimmerman collection reveal not only the main figures' identities but also their position in the lineage. The following notes are from my examination of those works.

(9.) Tsangpa Gyare as the ninth lineage master of the Drukpa Kagyu. Here I failed to record in my notes the position of the thangka in the overall set, but the rest of the rear inscription on the mount said *rgya ras*. In this context, he would be expected to be the ninth.

(10.) The second Drukchen, Ngawang Chögyal, as the tenth lineage master of the Drukpa Kagyu. This thangka has never been exhibited. The inscription on the reverse of the mount reads: *10. g.yas lnga pa rje rin po che ngag dbang chos rgyal* [fifth on the right, the second Drukchen Ngawang Chögyal (1464–1540)].

(11.) The fifth painting on the left is the eleventh master of the Drukpa Kagyu lineage.

(12.) Tendzin Norbu as the twelfth lineage master of the Drukpa Kagyu: This thangka has never been exhibited. The inscription on the reverse of the mount reads: *12. g.yas drug pa bstan 'dzin nor bu* (bsTan 'dzin nor bu).

(13.) Drukchen Chökyi Trakpa ('Brug chen Chos kyi grags pa) as the thirteenth lineage master of the Drukpa Kagyu: This thangka has never been exhibited. Inscription on the reverse of the mount reads: *13. g.yon drug pa rje chos kyi grags pa* [the third Drukchen Chökyi Trakpa].

(14.) A fourteenth painting is reported to exist.

The Lamdre Lineage of Ngor

This is the detailed lineage of the Ngorpa tradition of the Lamdre that is depicted in Figure 13.9, down to the abbot Könchok Phel. Since not all inscriptions were photographed, I supply a few names within square brackets from context. In this lineage, the third and fifth abbots of Ngor, 'Jam dbyangs shes rab rgya mtsho (1396?–1474) and dPal ldan rdo rje (1411–1482), seem to have been omitted. The small figures to Ngorchen's right and left (marked in the diagram as 24b? and 24c?) may be his two other main teachers, Sharchen and Sazang Phakpa. (Note the presence of Lama Dampa as number 22.)

1. rDo rje 'chang (Vajradhara)
2. bDag med ma (Nairātmyā)
3. Birwapa (Virūpa)
4. Nag po pa (Kṛṣṇapāda)
5. Ḍamarupa
6. Awaduti pa
7. Gayadhara
8. Bla chen 'Brog mi Lo tsā ba (992–1072?)
9. Se mKhar chung ba
10. Zhang dGon pa ba [Zhang ston Chos 'bar]
11. Sachen Kun dga' snying po (1092–1158)
12. bSod nams rtse mo (1142–1182)
13. rJe btsun Drakpa Gyaltshen (1147–1216)
14. Sa paṇ (1182–1251)
15. Phakpa (1235–1280)
16? [Zhang dKon mchog dpal (b. 1240)]

17? [Tshogs bsgom Kun dga' dpal]
18. Nyan chen pa [bSod nams brtan pa]
19. Brag phug pa [bSod nams dpal] (1277–1352)
20. dKar po brag pa Rin chen seng ge
21. Bla ma Blo gros brtan pa (1316–1358)
22. Bla ma dam pa [bSod nams rgyal mtshan] (1312–1375)
23. dPal ldan tshul khrims (1333–1399)
24. Buddha shrī (1339–1419)
25. [Ngor chen Kun dga' bzang po (1382–1456)]
26a. [Müchen dKon mchog rgyal mtshan (1388–1469)]
26b. [Mus pa chen po, repeated]
27. rJe btsun Kunga Wangchuk (1424–1478)
28. Gorampa Sönam Sengge (1429–1489)
29. Müchen Sanggye Rinchen
30. [Könchok Phel?]

Chapter 1: Part I

1   See sDe srid 1971, vol. 1, 583.1; and De'u dmar 1970, 17. Kaḥ thog Si tu 1972 mentions him on p. 175.2 (fol. 88a) as *mkhyen brtse chen mo* and on p. 230.1 (fol. 115b) as *'gran gyi do med lha bzo sprul sku mkhyen brtse chen mo*. Zhu chen 1973, 149.5, calls him *"mkhyen brtse chen po."* Klong rdol 1973, 415, calls him *"sprul sku mkhyen brtse ba."*

2   See the life of Gongkar Dorjedenpa by Gyatön Changchup Wangyal 2001, 173.

3   Cf. for instance Rhie and Thurman 1999, 31; 74, note 52; and 497.

4   See Jackson 1996, 139, and Jackson 1997, 257. Cf. Smith 1970 and Rhie and Thurman 1999.

5   sDe srid 1971, vol. 2, 643 (255b).

6   Jackson 1996, 108.

7   Jackson 1996, 134, note 255.

8   Henss 2014, 559, mentions Paljor Rinchen of Nenying in connection with Nenying Monastery and its artists.

9   Ricca and Lo Bue 1993, 20, quoting 'Jigs med grags pa, 132–141, and the *Myang chos 'byung* 1983, 52 .

10   See Lo Bue 1992, 570; Lo Bue and Ricca 1990, 412; and Ricca and Lo Bue 1993, 23. Lo Bue in a personal email communication, June 1994, described these murals: "In my opinion that is the finest wall painting in the whole of the Gyantse compound."

11   Lo Bue and Ricca 1990, 412, note 119. Tib.: *ri mo mkhas pa gnas rnying pa dpon mo che dpal 'byor ba dpon slob kyis gzabs nas bris so//.*

12   These murals are mentioned also in the *Myang chos 'byung* 1983, 62. For the date of the murals, see Lo Bue and Ricca 1990, 70.

13   Jackson 1996, 108, note 256.

14   Tucci 1941, pt. 2, 42. Tib.: *pir thog rgyal po dpal gnas rnying pa dpon mo che dpal 'byor rin chen pa dang dpon dge bshes bsod nams dpal 'byor.*

15   From the list extracted from Tucci 1932–41. See also Ricca and Lo Bue 1993, 20, 250, and 290, on Paljor Rinchen; and 250 and 303, on Sönam Paljor.

16   The Tibetan: *dpal gnas rnying pa dpon mo che dge bshes bsod nams dpal 'byor ba*. See also Lo Bue and Ricca 1990, 261 and 412f; Tucci 1941, pt. 2, 112.

17   Tucci 1941, pt. 1, 217. See also Tucci 1941, pt. 2, 70: gnas rnying pa mkhas pa'i dbang po rin chen dpal 'byor dang de'i sras.

18   I am indebted to Franco Ricca for discussing these inscriptions with me by email in 1995.

19   'Jigs med grags pa, 166.

20   See ibid., 241 and 244. On p. 240, he also gives a detailed description of the plan of the great thangka and of the symbolism of its various elements.

21   Lo Bue and Ricca 1990, 27, mention that Gyantse at certain times also exercised political control over Lho brag, which could also have been a factor contributing to sMan bla don grub's going there.

22   His biography is found in the *gNas rnying chos 'byung*, vol. 2, fols. 41a–46a. His statue flanks that of the Kha che paṇ chen Śākyaśrībhadra in chapel 4/10 of the Palkhor stupa. See Lo Bue and Ricca 1990, 342. It is possible he is sPos khang pa 'Jam dbyangs Rinchen rgyal mtshan of the same period. Cf. Lo Bue and Ricca 1990, 343. The *gNas rnying chos 'byung* ("History of Nenying") is a compilation in *sKyes bu dam pa rnams kyi rnam par thar pa rin po che'i gter mdzod*. (2 vols., xylograph dating to the 1520s.) The contents of the two volumes are: vol. 1, fols. 1a–17a (A. sTon pa'i byon tshul/ B. Kha ba can rgyal po'i gdung rabs) and vol. 2, fols. 1a–88b (C. gNas rnying gi chags tshul/ D. Bla ma'i byon rim/ and E. dByil gyi gdung rabs). Ricca and Lo Bue 1993, 22, suggest that he was identical with Rinchen grub (1403–1452), but this is impossible.

23   *gNas rnying chos 'byung*, vol. 2, fol. 45a: *bzo'i chag tshad/ lha'i gral dkod/ kha rtog gi spel/ gras tshems kyi zhal bkod/ rje rang nyid kyis ji ltar mdzad pa sngar [=ltar?] bris bzo ba lag len pa rnams kyis zhabs tog bgyis te/ gos sku chen mo 'gro ba yongs kyis mthong thos dran reg gi mig ltos dge ba'i lam po che'i srol [b]tod cing/.*

24   Ibid.: *ma the ba dpon dpal 'byor rin chen dang/ dbon [or: dpon?] bkra shis mgon bris gras la mkhas pa du ma zhig bsags nas/.*

25   This no doubt refers to the mission of Rab brtan kun bzang 'phags to the Chinese court in 1413. At that time the abbot of Nenying was said to have received the rank of *gu shri*. See the "Chronicles of Gyantse" translated in Tucci 1949, vol. 2, 665.

26   Cong rdo may have been the old Yüan name for Zhongdu, one of the capital cities near present Beijing, as I was kindly informed by Leonard van der Kuijp in a personal communication.

27   *gNas rnying chos 'byung*, vol. 2, fol. 45b: *yang rje nyid kyi rab dkar gyi snyan pa rgya nag rgyal po'i snyan du grags pa la rten nas chen po dngos grub rin chen pas/ rgya nag chos kyi rgyal po'i bka' dang du blangs nas rgya nag cong rdor byon ste/ gnas rnying mkhan po brgyud par bcas pa la/ sa chen dbang bsgyur shel gyi dam kha/ 'ja' sa mnga' ris kyi gnang sbyin dang/ lag rtags dang/ gos phyi nang dang bcas pa gnang ba blangs nas phul te/ rje nyid kyi phrin las kyi mthu dpal lo//.* On this mission to the Ming court, see also Tucci 1949, vol. 2, 665, who quotes the "Chronicles of Gyantse," fol. 18a.

28   This large Chinese painting of a standing Buddha Śākyamuni, with Tibetan and Chinese inscriptions to the left and right, survives as one of the monastery's great treasures, as I was first informed by H. Neumann in London, 1994. The painting is devoid of any background landscape. According to its description in a brief article by the investigation team of the Cultural Relics Management Committee of Tibet (1991), the painting measures 2.5 by 1.3 meters and bears a Chinese inscription dating it to the 17th day of the 4th month of the Yongle Emperor's ten year of reign (i.e., to the year 1412).

29   As I previously mentioned (Jackson 1996, note 46), the putative teacher of both great artists, rDo pa bKra shis rgyal po, if he existed, may well have been from Lhokha. The "rDo pa" element of his name seems to indicate he was from Do (rDo), a few miles east of Samye (bSam yas) in Lhokha, as Yeshe Sherab also suggests (Ye shes shes rab 1990, 15). It would make sense that Gongkar Khyentse at least would apprentice himself to someone from a nearby district, but no evidence supports this.

30   Ricca and Lo Bue 1993, 243, also mention a painter named Tashi from Shagtshal near Lhatse. He turns out to have the full name Tashi Zangpo. See Ricca and Lo Bue 1993, 238 and 284.

31   Gyaltshenpa decorated I.20= rNam rgyal khang, 1Sa'. The other artists from Nenying included no. 19, Tsan nes, bTsan nes of Nenying (II.9, 11.11, 11.12); Rinchen Paljor of Nenying (IV.2=, mKhyen rab lha khang 4S2); and no. 33, dPal 'phel ba of Nenying (dome 2, campana, upper cella 1, 2, 3, 4, 5, 11).

32   *gNas rnying chos 'byung*, vol. 2, fol. 56a.

33   Ibid., fol. 56a–b.

34   Ibid., fol. 63a.

35   Ibid., fol. 72b. Elsewhere (fol. 49a) the *gNas rnying chos 'byung* mentions the famous statue-makers, La stod dPon mo che bKra

shis Rinchen (who made a gilt image of the Buddha ca. 1452), and (fol. 56a) Lha bzo ba Rin bsam (active in 1472). About ten years later, bKra shis Rinchen was invited by dGe 'dun grub pa to Tashilhunpo, but he was not released by Thang stong rgyal po.

36   Cf. Rhie and Thurman 1999, 31. Thurman imagined that a "Ganden Renaissance" took place as a mass movement in Tibetan religious culture from about 1400 to the 1640s. By contrast, the art historian Rhie did not adopt the Ganden Renaissance as a period or descriptive category in her own essays. The period in question does not represent a coherent phase or development in art history. It overlaps two major art-historical epochs, beginning in the pre-Menthangpa, heavily Indic, Beri style. It includes the transitional styles of the Gyantse stūpa (1430s–1440s), undergoes the Khyentse and Menthangpa revolution (from the 1450s or 1460s), and ends in a Sinicized style of the later Menri (mid- to late seventeenth century).

37   See, for instance, Heller 1999, 142–44, and Fisher 1997, 183–88.

38   On the importance of the Yongle Emperor for the patronage of Buddhist art, see Weidner 1994, 52 and 107. On Tsongkhapa's declining of the imperial court's invitation, see Sperling 1982, 105–07.

39   Cf. Rhie and Thurman 1999, 31.

40   Jackson 2011, 94.

41   Ehrhard 2004, 264, mentioned the possibility that the two teachers inside roundels and wearing red hats might be Gö Lotsāwa and Trimkhang Lotsāwa.

42   See Ehrhard 2004, 256.

43   Ehrhard 2002, 89.

44   Ehrhard 2002, 90, note 51.

45   The Mongolian author Jampal Dorje ('Jam dpal rdo rje) includes a number of birds in his illustrated materia-medica. On p. 226a we find ne tso, parrots illustrated, and they are said to come from Kham or the Indian and Chinese borderlands. On p. 223a: ka lanta is the very first bird. This is the phoenix "which appear at very auspicious times." A separate section is devoted to raptors and carrion-eating birds vultures (bya rgod) 240c. (See pp. 240-242.) On p. 225b we find ri bya "mountain bird," which looks like a pheasant.

46   In my experience parrots are in general fairly rare in Tibetan painting. Yet Khyentse painted them in landscapes quite often. What is even more special about Khyentse is that he would sometimes add them to the throne-backs of human gurus, which I never saw before or after him. (Compare Figs. 1.43.)

47   P. Welch 2008, p. 89, note 52. See also Terry Hurley, "The Symbolism of Parrots in Ancient Chinese Culture," LoveToKnow website (http://antiques.lovetoknow.com/Antique_Chinese_Parrots). Accessed Dec. 12, 2015. As Hurley explains: "For hundreds of years the parrot has held a place of honor in ancient China. Often kept in the living quarters of women, parrots were considered the keeper of their secrets. Throughout the years parrots have come to symbolize several different things in the Chinese culture: During the Hongshan culture of the Neolithic period, the migration of the birds to their breeding spots

was a sign that it was time to plant the crops. The birds in flight signaled that the rains were coming. In ancient China a beautiful colorful parrot was kept in the palace by Emperor Xuanzong during the Tang Dynasty. The bird, excellent at mimicking people's voices was so loved by Emperor Xuanzong that parrots have since been known as the Divine Bird. Traditionally parrots and other birds symbolized freedom and long life. A parallel is often drawn between a bird and the life experience and wisdom that come with old age. A pair of parrots symbolizes affection, fidelity and deep, enduring love. In the ancient Chinese art of feng shui the parrot is a powerful symbol of opportunity and the bearer of good news. It draws positive energy while keeping away the negative. Many types of parrots have feathers that represent the colors of the elements of life, fire, water and the sun."

48   LACMA collection number M.77.19.3. See also entry 29, "Mahasiddha Vanaratna Receiving Abhishekha from White (Sita) Tara," in Huntington and Bangdel 2003, 143–45.

49   According to Fermer 2009, a detailed description of this vision is given in rGya ston Byang chub dbang rgyal, Ngo mtshar gter mdzod: 95.15–97.7. See also A mes zhabs, mGon po chos 'byung, 298.2–299.3; Jackson 1984, 12; and Jackson 1996, 139.

50   A mes zhabs 1979, vol. 2, 97.2–99.1 (fols. 49a–50a). The passage concludes: de dag gi sku'i bkod pa 'phral du bri ba'i slad du zhabs 'bring pa rnams la ras gzhi zhig gi rtsol ba bgyis bka' rtsal pa/ mtshan mo de ma thag ras gzhi chung ngu tsam las .na rnyed pas/ rje nyid kyis de ka la sku'i deyibs ji lta ba'i skya ris gnang/ nang par nas rig byed mkhyen brtse bas/ tshon bris rdzogs par mdzad cing/ shin tu gces spras kyi nang nas mchod gtor gyi dbus su yun du bzhugs pa las/ nam zhig na nye gnas chen mo brgya sbyin pa sku khams ma bde ba'i dus bris sku 'di'i ster.g nas rjes gnang tshar 'ga' gnang/ re zhig sngas srung gi tshul du bzhugs pa las/ dus phyi's yang khong pa'i sger gzhis rnam rgyal rab brtan na rten gsum kun gyi [fol. 50a] gtso bor bzhugs so//.

51   Mathias Fermer 2009, in a very long note 191, described the building of Gongkar, quoting the relevant Tibetan passage from Gyatön Changchup Wangyal, adding information from the abbatial history of Shalu and Dungkar's dictionary: rGya ston Byang chub dbang rgyal, Ngo mtshar gter mdzod: pp. 112.16–113.7: […] lo skor gcig tsam gyi bar la gtsug lag khang rten dang brten par bcas pa ma lus shing lus pa med par bar chad kyi mtshan [p. 113] ma tsam yang med par yongs su grub par mdzad la/ de yeng dbyar dgun gyi bye brag gis las byed pa kho na'i yun ni de'i yang phyed tsam du gyur pas/ des na da lta'i dus su ni grub pa'i 'bras bu phra mo tsam la'ang rgyu tshegs/ 'bad rtsol/ yun ji tsam 'gor sogs la dpag na sprul pa'i rdzad pa kho na ma gtogs/ tshur mthong gi blo'i gzhal byar ci 'gyur blo gros dang ldan pa rnams kyis rtogs pa nyid do. See also Zhwa lu Ri sbug sPrul sku 1971, 175.6–176.1.

52   Dung dkar Blo bzang phrin las 2002, 530: chos sde chen po 'di'i rten dang brten gnas yongs rdzogs grub par lo skor gcig ste lo bcu gnyis 'gor zhing […], as pointed out by Mathias Fermer.

53   For Menthangpa in Tsang, Shigatse as a

cultural center was coming into its own and eventually could vie with Gyantse. Menthangpa's best known early patronage began in the 1450s, when Gendun Drup invited him to Tashi Lhunpo Monastery in central Tsang.

54   Smith 1970, 44, note 75, stated that Khyentse's paintings included "figures from the tantric cycles in which the Sakya schools specialized." But the relevant passage from bDud 'dul rdo rje's dPyad don tho chung accessible to me does not mention the Sakyapas, in particular.

55   Kaḥ thog Si tu 1972, 261.4 (fol. 131a): sne gdong rgyal po'i rten gnas brtan mkhyen bris shin tu spus dag mtha' ljang can nyer gsum.

56   See Jackson 2015, chap. 6.

57   bsTan 'dzin padma rgyal mtshan 1977, 401 (composed 1808–09): lha bris la sbyangs pa mdzad pas shin tu mkhas shing da lta 'bri gung 'dir mkhyen lugs kyi ri mo rje 'dis [='di'i] zhal slob kyi rgyun yin. I owe this reference to Tashi Tsering. Karma rin chen dar rgyas also mentions a dKon mchog phrin las on p. 247, though he would seem to have lived much later.

58   Kaḥ thog Si tu 1972, 183.2 (fol. 90a): bka' brgyud gser phreng mkhyen brtse chen mo'i phyag bris rgyu tshon bkod phul gyur 'ja' shar ba 'dra ba thog sleb ma snang ba gyur thub pa gsum.

59   See Linrothe 2012, 186–88.

60   Kaḥ thog Si tu 1972, 229.5–230.2 (fol. 115a-b), enumerates the contents of the set and concludes by describing them as: 'gran gyi do med lha bzo sprul sku mkhyen brtse chen mo'i lugs/.

61   See Khempo and Gomchen 1975, no. 29.

62   See dPa' bo gTsug lag phreng ba, mKhas pa'i dga' ston (1986 ed.), p. 1148 : de nas yangs pa can du... steng 'og thams cad du ri mo'i bkod pa khyad par can sman thang pa sman bla don grub yab sras dang mkhyen brtse bas bris/ gtsug lag khang phyi nang thams cad lhan cig tu grub pas grub mgyogs pa dang dngos gtsang ba dang bla gab che ba 'di lta bu sngon ma byung zhes bdag chung ngu'i dus sgrog cing snang/. Bla gab means "upper cover" and is possibly a term for roof; bla cab can, "possessing an upper cover," is a word for house.

63   Si tu Paṇ chen and 'Be lo 1972, vol. 1, 621.6 (da 311b).

64   See also Jackson 2009, fig. 5.15.

65   D. Jackson 2009, 88f.

66   See Karma Thinley 1980, 65. See also Sperling 2004, 231–33. Sperling clearly establishes the incomparable prestige of Rolpe Dorje at the Yuan court at the time of his second visit.

67   See Si tu Paṇ chen 1968, 90.5 [fol. a 45b]): gong dkar rdo rje gdan du gtsug lag khang gi dbu rtse gong mar rdo rje gdan pa'i sku gdung ril por bzhugs dngul gyi mchod rten la mkhyen brtse chen mos bzos pa'i lam 'bras bla brgyud kyi lder tshos bskor ba/ 'og mar mkhyen brtse bas bzos pa'i yo ga'i lha tshogs kyi lder tsho khyad thon// li ma khang du li ma sna tshogs gcig tu thugs dam rdul tshon

g.yogs pa'i kye rdor blos bslang rdo rje gdan pa rang gi khyad chos can bzhugs pa sogs mchod khang bcu grangs dang mgon khang steng 'og rnams su sku dang rten mdos sogs brjid bags can dang/ rdo rje 'jigs byed 'khor bcas kyi lder tsho ngo mtshar can sogs mdor na mjal rgyu mang zhing dngos gtsang ba dang bris 'bur mtha' dag mkhyen brtse ba rang gi phyag bdar ma yin pas bzo khyad phul du byung ba dper 'os pa 'dug cing/ kho bos dang por mjal dus khams pa a jo ba'i [fol. 46a] de mthong gis brnyes bcos log ge ba zhig las zhib mjal kyi skabs ma rnyed kyang sog po'i chos rje da las kho thug tu byams pa gling gi mkhan po gnang skabs yin pa 'dir pheb nas gong dkar ba'i slob dpon nam mkha' mdzod pa la chos khrid 'ga' re gsan gyi 'dug pa nged dang sngar thugs 'gris kyi stabs gzigs ma thag ngo mkhyen nas bzhugs khri las har bzhengs te pheb byung nas nged la khams 'dri 'dra mdzad 'dug pa kh[o]ng tshos gzigs nas slar nam mkha' mdzod pa rang gis yang skyar nged khrid de mchod khang rnams zhib mor mjal/.

68 That acquaintance happened to be in Gongkar receiving teachings from the Gongkar Lobpön Namkha Dzöpa. As soon as he saw Situ and recognized him, he suddenly stood up and politely greeted him. After that, Namkha Dzöpa personally accompanied Situ to the shrines.

69 See Jackson 1996, part II, chap. 4.

70 See bDud 'dul rdo rje as quoted in Smith 1970, 43, note 73, referring to the old Menri (sman rnying) as compared to the original Khyenri: cung zad tshon srab nyams gyur de bas che // "[The old Menri] had slightly thinner pigments and was more expressive than the [Khyenri]."

71 Tucci 1956, 151.

72 Tucci 1956, 151.

73 K. Debreczeny 2012, 124 who rightly calls that Karmapa "a painter of birds."

74 Kaḥ thog Si tu 1972, 175.2 (fol. 88a): mkhyen brtse chen mo'i phyag bris kyang snang/.

75 Ehrhard 2002, 86.

76 Gyatön Changchup Wangyal 2001, 173.

77 Padma dkar po, Li ma brtag pa'i rab byed, 306 (ka cha fol. 7b): mkhyen brtse dbon po tshe dbang kun mkhyen dang/ mkhas skor ba rnal 'byor nyams dga' blo bde'i ched du bkod pa.

78 Padma dkar po, Sems dpa' chen po, vol. 1, 511 and 521.5 (ga nya fols. 89a and 94a). The first passage runs: gong dkar rdo rje gdan nas mkhyen brtse dbon po ba rgyud la dogs gcod du rkang gtad slebs pa sogs la chos dang/ dogs gcod kyi re ba bskangs/. These passages were cited by Shakabpa 1976, vol. 1, 107, as pp. 83b.6 and 88b.5.

79 Ameshab 1980, 61b.5: de yang gong dkar sprul sku sbyin pa rnam rgyal gyis lha khang chen mo'i thig khang du dur gur phab nas/ mgon po'i rus shing dang span 'dzugs la 'jim pa phal cher g.yogs grub mtshams glo bur du rlung mar chen po lang ste/.

80 Such a work is attributed also to Khyentse in a list of Tibetan sources on iconometry by Kong sprul 1970, part 1, 573.6 (oṃ fol. 209b): sman mkhyen rnam pa gnyis/ bu ston dang rje

81 This is mentioned third in a list of sources on p. 28 in the publication Bris sku rnam bzhag mthong ba don ldan (Dharamsala: Shes rig lhan khang, n.d. [ca. 1980?]). The sources listed were treatises of: (1) Tsong kha pa, (2) Menthangpa, and (3) Gong dkar ba bShes gnyen rnam rgyal, (4) An anonymous author of a prose treatise on iconometry (mdzad byang med pa'i cha tshad kyi gzhung tshig lhug par byas pa cig), and (5) [A kyā yongs 'dzin?] (a.) Tshigs su bcad pa yod pa dag dang, and (b.) Lag len mthong ba brgyad pa'i man ngag. I am indebted to Mr. Tashi Tsering for this reference.

82 Henss 2014, 479. Henss dates these murals to the 15th or 16th century.

83 See Jackson 2015, figs. 6.8–6.13, and 6.16; and Linrothe 2012, fig. 9.5.

84 See HAR 73267-73269. http://www.himalayanart.org/search/set.cfm?setID=2958. According to the web entry: "In one small chapel at the side of the main monastery are several well preserved wall murals. These paintings are believed to have been created during the time of Ngagchang Jamyang Lodro in the late 17th century. This prominant teacher of Rebkong was a student of the 5th Dalai Lama and Trichen Lodro Gyatso."

85 See Tsechang Penba Wangdu 2010. Gyatön Changchup Wangyal, rDzong pa kun dga' rnam rgyal rnam thar, 2001 ed., 173, lines 6–13: gzhan yang rje btsun dam pa de sangs rgyas kyi bstan pa la bya ba rlabs po che mdzad pa'i slad du/ rje nyid kyi mkhyen rab kyi cha shas rig byed kyi rnam par shas bas [=shar bas?] rab 'byams kyi rgyal ba'i dkyil 'khor ma lus mngon sum pa lta bur gang gi lag sor la skrun par byed pa'i sprul pa'i skyes chen mkhyen brtse ba dge bsnyen rnam par rgyal ba khu dbon snga mas ngo mtshar 'khri shing zhes pa'i sku bstod cig mdzad.

86 According to Fermer 2009, its full reference is: 'Bras spungs dkar chag, p. 1532, no. 017278, Phyi ra ? (MS, 10 fols., 8 x 45cm).

87 Gyatön, in Tsechang Penba Wangdu 2010, 115.

88 Gyatön, in Tsechang Penba Wangdu 2010, 115: byang chub sems dpa' chen po brgyad rnams sku'i dbyibs rgya dkar nag/ bal po/ kha ba can gyi rig byed mkhas pa rnams kyi lugs so so dang mthun par sku'i rnam 'gyur/ na bza'/ rgyan phreng sogs de dang de'i tshul ma ma 'dres par bzhugs pa'o//.

89 I summarized the following biographical sketch from Jackson 1983, 10–12.

Chapter 1: Part II

90 For a list of its branches see Jackson 2015b. Gongkar Monastery appears among a published list of 375 Sakya monasteries in Tibet: Gangs ljongs chol kha gsum du gnas pa'i dpal sa skya'i ring lugs 'dzin pa'i dgon sde dang/ ri khrod/ lha khang (gnas shul) khag gi mtshan byang dkar chag gzig bder bkod pa. Gangs ljongs sa skya pa. gNa' deng lo rgyus rig gnas

'tshol bsdu tshogs chung. Lhasa: 2006.

91 Stearns 2004, 752.

92 Fermer 2009, 163.

93 See Cassinelli and Ekvall 1969, 409.

94 An unreliable description of the main temple, its contents, and the four colleges is also given by Chödze Delek, Lho kha'i lam yig gsar ma, A Brief History of Gongkar Chöde, fols. 5a–10b.

95 Kunga Namgyal, Record of Teachings Received (Bodhnath, Kathmandu: rGyal yongs Sa chen publishers, 2005), 8.

96 van der Kuijp 1993a, note 13. The work of Ameshab (A mes zhabs) was entitled in Tibetan dPal ldan sa skya pa'i bstan 'dzin ngor rdzong rnam gnyis kyi gsung ngag rin po che'i phyag len gyi rim pa 'ga' zhig las brtsams te so so'i bzhed srol rnams legs par bshad pa lugs gnyis zab don gsal ba'i nyin byed (Rajpur: Sakya College, 1985).

97 Fifth Dalai Lama 1971, vol. 1, 247b: **rdzong lugs** ni/ 'phags pa yan spyi ltar la/ de nas zhang ston pa/ brag phug pa/ yang na 'phags pa nas/ tshogs nyan gnyis/ brag phug pa/ brag phug pa/ chos rje bla ma dam pa/ sngags 'chang gzungs kyi dpal ba/ thugs sras bzang po rgyal mtshan/ mtshungs med rgyal mtshan dkon cog/ mus srad pa rtsang/ (rus ming) byams pa rdo rje rgyal mtshan/ rje dkon cog dpal/ 'jam dbyangs chos dpal 'byor/ rje byang chub dbang rgyal/ paṇ chen bde ba'i rdo rje/ rje lha dbang 'phrin las/ rje tshul khrims bkra shis/ zha lu mkhan chen khyab bdag rin cen bsod nams mchog grub/ des bdag la'o/ yang na 'jam dbyangs chos dpal 'byor nas/ byang chub dbang rgyal/ shākya kun dga'/ dbang phyug rgyal mtshan/ paṇ chen bsod nams mchog ldan/ zha lu pa chen po/ des bdag la'o/ yang na bla ma dam pa nas/ bla ma dpal ldan tshul khrims/ yang na brag phug pa nas/ ri khrod pa blo brtan/ bla ma dpal tshul ba/ [p. 248a] / /yang na nyan chen pa/ dkar po brag pa/ bla ma dpal tshul ba/ thugs sras bzang po rgyal mtshan man sngar ltar/.

98 Fifth Dalai Lama 1971, vol. 1, 244a: / /nams mchog grub/ des bdag la'o// **gong dkar ba lugs** ni/ 'phags pa rin po che nas/ ('di nas bla ma dam pa'i bar gyi brgyud pa rnams ngor pa dang mthun pa don gyis thob kyang 'dir rdo rje gdan pa'i gsan yig sor gnas bzhin bris pa yin/) paṇḍi ta rdo rje shes rab/ bla ma 'phags pa rgyal mtshan/ bla ma rin cen dpal bzang/ bla ma dam pa bsod nams rgyal mtshan/ mkhan chen shes rab rdo rje/ bla ma chos sgo ba/ brag thog pa bsod nams bzang po/ thams cad mkhyen pa rdo rje gdan pa kun dga' rnam rgyal dpal bzang po/ mkhas grub rnam rgyal rin cen/ yongs 'dzin shākya kun dga'/ bla ma dam chos gling pa ye shes dbang po/ bla ma nyi ma gling pa tshul khrims bkra shis/ rdo rje 'chang mgon po bsod nams mchog ldan/ des bdag la'o//

99 Fifth Dalai Lama 1971, vol. 1, 248a: **gong dkar ba** lugs ni/ bla ma dam pa nas/ gangs khrod pa/ de las bzang ma ti dang sa skya bu ston dbang phyug dar gyis zhus/ de gsum ga la theg chen rin po che/ brag thog pa/ kun mkhyen rdo rje gdan pa/ rgya ston byang chub dbang rgyal man gong bzhin no/.

100 Pal 2003, no. 156, "Mahasiddha Virupa."

101 Pal 2003, 293.

102 See Jonang Kunga Drölchok, 213.

103 See Caumanns 2015, 319.

104 Jonang Kunga Drölchok, 54. See Caumanns 2015, 372–77, for Janglungpa's life and dates.

105 Jonang Kunga Drölchok, 52. On the differing ages of sPyang lung Rin po che according to two different references in Shākya Chokden's biography, see Jonang Kunga Drölchok, 51.5 and 72: sPyang lung pa was also a teacher of the Drukpa Gyalwe Wangpo (rGyal ba'i dbang po, 1428–1478) for esoteric tantric lineages; he seems to be the master mentioned in Pema Karpo's *History of Buddhism* (*Chos 'byung*), 458, line 1, as "lCang lung pa gZhon nu blo gros." He is apparently also the one called "Chos sdings pa" by Shākya Chokden (from his residence at Chos sdings).

106 Jonang Kunga Drölchok, 52.

107 Ibid., 190.3.

108 Ibid., 57.

109 Ibid., 72.

110 Ibid., p. 78.

111 Ibid., 165.

112 Ibid., 189. Shākya Chokden remarked at the time that he used the long Hevajra *sādhana* by Lama Dampa Sönam Gyaltshen (as in the Thekchen tradition). He had consulted Ngorchen as a young monk about whether he should switch to the one commonly used by Ngorchen's disciples, and Ngorchen replied that it was fine to continue use it, and that indeed he used it himself for his personal practice.

113 Ibid., 192.1.

114 Mangthö Ludrup, *bsTan rtsis*, 197.

115 Ibid., 198.

116 See also the Lamdre history by Jamyang Khyentse Wangchuk, translated in Stearns 2006, 242.

117 The statue was made of *gshed snying*; the *Sakya Genealogical History* says *sher shing* ("of *sher* wood") according to the editor Mangthö Ludrup.

118 On the woven gifts of the Yongle Emperor, see Henss 2008, 51–53. See also Henss 1997, 26–39. On gifts by Chinese emperors to Tibetans, including mainly eminent lamas, see also Berger 2003.

119 Mangthö Ludrup, 198.

120 *dGa' ldan se'u thang* is the name of a woven silk image preserved at Ganden.

121 Dagyab 1977, 40.

122 Jackson 1996, note 248. The word *si btags dngos rdzas* means "silk fabrics" in modern literary Tibetan.

123 See Jackson 1996, 49.

124 Mangthö Ludrup, p. 216.

125 See Ameshab 1986, 332–55: many prominent disciples listed on p. 347.

126 Concerning Theg chen Chos rje visits to the Ming court, see Kun dga' rgyal mtshan, *Chos kyi rgyal po'i rnam thar byin rlabs rnam par*

rol pa, p. 201, with mentions of offerings on p. 202.

127 Kapstein 2006, 126.

128 Kapstein 2006, 125.

129 Stoddard 2008, 66–89 and 96, chart of three kings of Dharma and five princes (*rgyal bu*).

130 van der Kuijp 1993a, 155, note 12. In the Nationalities Library, Cultural Palace of Nationalities, Beijing, the two manuscripts were C.P.N. no. 002775 (10), ms. in 23 fols., and C.P.N. no. 002775 (10), 18 fols.

131 Schaeffer and van der Kuijp 2009, 31.

132 See Kunga Gyaltshen Palzangpo, *Theg chen chos kyi rgyal po'i rnam thar rgyas pa* (comprising pages 199 through 240; Thekchen Chöje's visit to the Ming court is mentioned on pages 233 through 236.

133 Ibid., 31, note 66.

134 Ibid., 30.

135 This Chinese-style set is mentioned in the appropriate passage of Shākya Chokden's life by Caumanns 2015, 319.

136 Though the Koller catalog identified him as "Chögyal Chokdrup," I doubt that is reliable, given that it also misidentified the preceding thangka from the same set as the Sakya lama Sönam Tsemo.

137 Vernal hanging parrots have mainly green plumage, white eyes, a light red bill, red rump, and upper-tail coverts. The slaty-headed parakeet (Psittacula himalayana), common in the Himalayas, has a dark-gray head.

138 W. Eberhard 1990, p. 225.

139 A. S. Williams 1976, p.315, reports that parrots mainly come from south China and repeats a provincial legend in which a merchant was saved from his faithless wife by a speaking parrot and hence the birds were seen as a symbolic warning to women to be faithful to their spouses. Hean-Tatt Ong 1993, p. 284, adds that the parrot is also the bird of the goddess of mercy, Kuan Yin, and is often found perched on her side, and was also believed to be the symbol of the Nimbus or Yin-Yang.

140 Khreng Hra'o-khrun et al. 2008, p. 51.

141 Jackson 1996, fig. 13, *sDom gsum dam pa* or *'Jam dbyangs phyag mtshan ri mo*.

142 The online entry from the Museum of Fine Arts states: "On reverse, in red and black ink, a drawing of a stupa with a long inscription in small Tibetan print—yet to be read. Also on the inscription is a line of cursive Tibetan script—also yet to be read. Provenance: donated by John Goelet, New York, NY, in 1967 (probably purchased in India or Nepal in the 1960s)."

143 See the black-and-white photos in Toganoo 1986, nos. III 5-3 and III 5-4.

CHAPTER 2

144 Tucci 1949, 208.

145 Tucci 1949, 208.

146 Tucci 1949, 293.

147 Menthangpa is mentioned by Tucci 1949 on 292 and 299.

148 Tucci 1949, 283.

149 Recorded in Tucci 1949, 546.

150 Tucci 1949, 537.

151 Tucci 1956, 149–151.

152 Tucci 1956, 150.

153 Tucci 1956, 151.

154 Tucci 1967, 106.

155 Tucci 1967, 111.

156 Shakabpa 1967, 11.

157 Huntington 1968, 9–10.

158 Smith 1970, 38–41.

159 Smith 1970, 42–51.

161 Smith 1970, 44.

162 The five main Tibetan works Dagyab cited as sources on Khyentse include an art manual by Shuchen Tshultrim Rinchen, the Lhasa Tsuglag Karchag by the Fifth Dalai Lama, and Kongtrul's Encyclopedia; his fourth source, Sumpa Khenpo, misspells Gong dkar as Gos dmar.

163 Demo 1979, 2–3.

164 Chogay 1979, 60.

165 The plates Huntington listed for this group represent several quite distinct styles: Lauf 1976, plate 9, of a style not evident to me; plate 20 is in the Üri or Eri; plate 27 has a Ngorpa lineage down to Drangti Panchen and is painted in a Tsangri style; plate 42 (Second Dalai Lama) is painted in a Eri or Üri style; and plate 60's style is also not evident to me.

166 Inscriptions on the front: 1. [rdo rje 'chang], 2. [bi ru pa], 3. sa chen, 4. rtse mo. 5. grags pa, 6. sa pan [After Sakya Paṇḍita, Phakpa is omitted, evidently by mistake.] 7. tshogs sgom, 8. nyan chen pa, 9. brag phug pa, 10. [bla ma dam pa] bsod nams rgyal mtshan, 11. dpal ldan tshul khrims, 12. bsod nams ... [illegible], 13. ye shes rgyal mtshan, 14. [buddha shrī], 15. [kun dga'] bzang po, 16. mus chen [sems dpa' chen po], 17. byams pa thugs rje, 18. [illegible], 19. [illegible], and 20. 'jam dbyangs dkon mchog ['phel?].

167 Reynolds et al. 1986, 25, note 48.

168 Batchelor 1987, 223–25.

169 Batchelor 1987, 223.

170 Batchelor 1987, 223.

171 Batchelor 1987, 224.

172 Batchelor 1987, 224.

173 Batchelor 1987, 224.

174 Batchelor 1987, 225.

175 Dowman 1988, 151.

176 Dowman 1988, 152.

177 Dowman 1988, 151.

178 Huntington and Huntington 1990, 299.

179 He used Tāranātha's *History of Buddhism*

in India, Kongtrül's *Encyclopedia*, Dagyab's *Tibetan Religious Art*, and Gega Lama's bilingual art manual of 1983.

180 Huntington and Huntington 1990, 299.

181 Huntington's chronology was not accurate, for Menthangpa and Khyentse were actually contemporaries. His statement (p. 289) that both Menthangpa and Khyentse were Tsang painters was also miseading—they were both natives of Ü province, having been born in Lhodrak (Lho brag) and Lhokha, respectively—unless he was alluding to the fact that they both learned how to paint in Tsang. Huntington also asserted (p. 299) that no sculptures were produced by the schools founded by Menthangpa and Khyentse, but in fact Khyentse was highly adept as a sculptor.

182 Huntington and Huntington 1990, 289.

183 Huntington and Huntington 1990, 299.

184 Huntington and Huntington 1990, 306, note 25. Both Ngawang Gelek Demo and Domo Geshe Rinpoche had been active at the Tibet House in New Delhi from 1969 to 1970.

185 The late Trichang Rinpoche had mentioned typical features of the Khyenri—for instance, that the ends of wrathful deities' eyebrows curved up at the ends, and that artists of the school were fond of painting lotuses with a mauve pink (*zing skya*). For Gelek Rinpoche's account of styles, see Demo 1979, 2–3.

186 Tsepon (Tsipon) Wangchuk Deden Shakabpa also told me in March 1982, in New Delhi, that another typical feature of the Khyenri mentioned by Trichang Rinpoche was particular treatments of the edges of clouds—perhaps a series of dark bumps. Trichang Rinpoche had moreover mentioned to Shakabpa seeing a thangka in Calcutta with an inscription identifying it as created by a mKhyen ris artist. Shakabpa in writing his *Tibet: A Political History* also consulted Trichang Rinpoche.

187 Everding 1993, 236.

188 Everding 2001, 197.

189 Chan 1994, 47–57.

190 Chan 1994, 57.

191 Chan 1994, 479.

192 Chan 1994, 479.

193 Chan 1994, 479.

194 Chan 1994, 480.

195 "Overview," Shalu Association, accessed December 5, 2015, http://www.asianart.com/associations/shalu/gongkar/index.html.

196 The overview of 1994 went on to explain: "The wall paintings in the circumambulatory are of fine and delicate execution, but are in the greatest danger of being repainted or badly restored, since the monastery does not appear to come under the protection of any government office. Three different groups of paintings of remarkable quality require urgent attention: those mentioned above, which are in a poor state of conservation, and therefore most in danger, together with the series of portraits on the back wall of the assembly hall. The entire Yidam chapel, on the first floor, containing ten large panels depicting tantric deities, is in a different style, perhaps

a little later, but of excellent execution. Some restoration dating to recent times is visible there, though it is not too disastrous. Shalu Association proposes to help with reinforcing the structure in the Yidam chapel, where a forest of support pillars were propping up the main beams."

197 "May 1995," Shalu Association, accessed December 5, 2015, http://www.asianart.com/associations/shalu/gongkar/index.html.

198 "October 1995," Shalu Association, accessed December 5, 2015, http://www.asianart.com/associations/shalu/gongkar/index.html.

199 "Ongoing project: Gongkar Monastery," Shalu Association New Bulletin, May–September 1999, http://www.asianart.com/shalu/bulletin.html. The bulletin continues: "In this way the unique fifteenth century wooden structure on the middle storey has been saved, together with the fine wall paintings attributed to Khyentse in the fifteenth century. Here, superbly macabre cemetery scenes dominate the chapel, while Vaishravana and his eight horsemen and Vajrayogini adorn either end."

200 Béguin 1995, 62.

201 See also Béguin 1995, 269, MA 5184.

202 Jackson 1996, 139 and 142.

203 Smith 1970, 43, note 73, quotes the Tibetan: *mkhyen brtses bod ris legs pa'i srol btod cing// lhag tu rgyud sde'i sku ni ches cher 'phags//.*

204 sDe srid 1971, vol. 1, 582.4 and 583.1. This point seems to have eluded Zhu chen and Kong sprul, whereas De'u dmar 1970, 17, and Shakabpa 1976, vol. 1, 106, were clearly aware of it.

205 Henss 2014, 416, note 12, rightly pointed this out.

206 Jackson 1996, 191.

207 Jackson 1997, 257, figs. 299 and 300.

208 I contributed an independent chapter to that catalog; see Rhie and Thurman 1999, 75–127.

209 See also Jackson 2007.

210 Rhie and Thurman 1999, 249.

211 One was originally published in Pal 1984a, and Linrothe 2004, 99–101, presented the available paintings, eighteen out of twenty-three.

212 Rhie and Thurman 1999, 252.

213 Gyurme Dorje 2004, 167; and Gyurme Dorje 1999, 161.

214 Smith 2001, 254.

215 Smith 2001, 335, note 857.

216 Linrothe 2004, 61.

217 Jackson 2009, 98.

218 Linrothe 2006, 272.

219 Linrothe referred to the book by Hemmi Baiei 1975, *Chūgoku Ramkyō bijutsu taikan* (1975).

220 These inscriptions are found: *grub thob birwa pa la na maḥ// gser gling pa dharma? kirti .*

221 The last painting in Basel also contains a scene of Tshembupa flying over the River Ganges, with the river water loaded with various highly realistic water fowl and fish. See Essen and Thingo 1989, vol. 1, no. I-58.

222 See W. Eberhard 1990, p. 93f. C. A. S. Williams 1976, p. 169, illustrates an elephant carrying the sacred alms bowl of the Buddha on its back and also explains that one tradition depicted it carrying a wish-fulfilling gem. Hean-Tatt Ong 1993, p. 232f., adds much lore, including the importance of ivory as a material and mentioning that the future Buddha was born as a White Elephant.

223 Jackson 2005b, 630.

224 Jackson 2007, 100.

225 Jackson 1996, 142.

226 Cf. Jackson 1996, 139–68.

227 See Masaki and Tachikawa 1997.

228 Osada et al. 2010, 95.

229 Jackson 2009, 97–100, figs. 5.9–5.12.

230 Jackson 2009, 101f.

231 See Karma Thinley 1980, 60.

232 Jackson 2012, 53.

233 Jackson 1996, 164.

234 Penba Wangdu 2012.

235 Penba Wangdu 2012.

236 Penba Wangdu 2012.

237 Henss 2014, 346–49.

238 Henss 2014, 416, note 12.

239 Henss 2014, 347.

240 Henss 2014, 347f

241 Henss 2014, 349–51.

242 Henss 2014 also pointed out later (p. 551, note 127) that I "reconstruct Menla Döndrup's style solely on a textual basis . . . the artistic profile remains remarkably faint." Though that is true, he also is aware of the difficulty of photographing the only known surviving murals of Menthangpa at Tashilhunpo Monastery, which are highly reflective—almost solid black—since he did not reproduce a single one.

243 Henss 2014, 416, note 11. Thomas Laird's forthcoming *The Murals of Tibet* (Taschen) will present some murals of Gongkar.

CHAPTER 3

244 See brTse byang sPen pa dbang 'dus 2005.

245 Tsechang Penba Wangdu 2010, note 11, for manuscript (*bris ma*) written by "Lord Yangpajen" (rJe Yangs pa can), *Gong dkar rdo rje gdan gyi gtsug lag khang gi logs bris dpag bsam 'khri shing gi zhal byang.*

246 Tsechang Penba Wangdu 2010.

247 Penba Wangdu 2012.

248 Tenpa Rabten and Ngawang Jigme 2003, 445.

249 Tsechang Penba Wangdu 2010, 2, line 10, through 4, line 7. In his footnote, Penba Wangdu cites rGya ston Byang chub dpal (2001 ed.), *rDzong pa kun dga' rnam rgyal rnam thar*, p. 173, line 6.

250 I here have corrected *bsod nyams* to *gson nyams*.

251 The "ten years of unrest" refers to the Cultural Revolution.

252 See Tsechang Penba Wangdu 2010, 5–10.

253 See the Fifth Dalai Lama 1983 (his autobiography), vol. 2, *Dukula'i gos bzang*, 176.

254 Those in the Yamāntaka chapel are mentioned by Gyatön. I do not know if they survive.

255 Rob Linrothe in a communication of Jan. 2016 observed that one thing that stuck him about the Khyenri style of paintings of tantric yidam in the Hevajra divine palace was a consistent way of arranging the headdresses that was quite visible in Figs. 3.12 and 3.13. There was a high piled, but relatively thin chignon that is wrapped as if by thick bands of filigree. Same with Fig. 3.11 (Vaiśrāvaṇa) but the chignon was a little fatter and orange and black. Not the same in the Mahasiddha paintings illustrated by Figs. 3.25 and 3.26, but very close to what you see in the Jonang Phüntshokling porch.

256 Penba Wangdu 2012, note 6, referred to Dung dkar blo bzang phrin las 2002, *Dung dkar tshig mdzod chen mo*, entry 2330.

257 Penba Wangdu 2012, note 7, referred to the Fifth Dalai Lama's autobiography (1991 ed.), vol. 1, p. 443. Though new murals are mentioned in this passage, it does not refer to any specific chapels painted by the Khyenri artists, so their existence was ascertained through Penba Wangdu's research.

258 Penba Wangdu 2012, note 8, referred to: "1998 (6): 66, *Annals of 1890 for Gyantse Prefecture* (in Chinese)."

Chapter 4: part i

259 For two descriptions of Gongkar Dorjeden Monastery by Tibetan pilgrims of the past, see Kaḥ thog Si tu 1972, 156–160 (fols. 78b–80b), and Si tu Paṇ chen 1968, 90.5 (fol. a 45b). Both were impressed by Khyentse Chenmo's art. Shakabpa 1976, vol. 1, 106. On Gongkar Dorjedenpa and the founding of the Gongkar monastic center, see Zhwa lu 1971, 175. On other religious patronage by Gongkar Dorjedenpa, see Jackson 1983, 7–16, and Jackson 1987, 74.

260 Henss 2014, 347f

261 See Jackson 1996, 139.

262 This chapel was called Kye rdor khang by Kathok Situ.

263 Fermer 2009, note 191: rGya ston Byang chub dbang rgyal, *Ngo mtshar gter mdzod*, pp. 113.11–146.8. I have emended Fermer's translation.

264 Gyatön 2001, 139: *skor sa'i nang gi ngos la thub pa'i dbang pos zhing 'di mdzad pa bcu gnyis kyi bstan pa'i bkod pa ji lta ba la gtso bo sku che ba drug dang bcas pa/*.

265 Mathias Fermer could recently photograph all twelve larger Buddhas, as the whitewash on the upper parts had been removed further between 2010 and 2015.

266 See Bhikkhu Ñāṇamoli 2001, 263.

267 See Gyatön 2001, 139: *gung gi mthong g.yab kyi ngos rings la/ ston pa gnas brtan bcu drug hwa shang dang dhharma ta la gnyis kyis mtha' brten pa/*.

268 Batchelor 1987, 224.

269 Mathias Fermer, email of January 15, 2016.

270 Cf. the similar rabbits found below in Figs. 8.14 and 9.8.

271 Gyatön 2001, 138: [...] *gnas de'i phyi'i ngos rings skor sa dang bcas pa la ston pa yang dag par rdzogs pa'i sangs rgyas kyi skyes pa'i rabs shin tu rgyas pa dpag bsam 'khri shing du grags pa yab rgyal po dge ba'i dbang pos mdzad pa'i sa bdag rab gsal gyi rtogs brjod nas/ khyim bdag zas gtsang gi rtogs brjod kyi bar yal 'dab brgya phrag gcig dang bdun la bkra shis kyi grangs kha skong ba'i slad du sras zla ba'i dbang pos mdzad pa'i brgyad pa sprin gyi bzhon pa'i rtogs brjod de brgya rtsa brgyad tshang ba'i yal 'dab gnyis gnyis la gtso bo sku tshad [p. 139] che ba re sku'i 'gyur ba khri rgyab yol sogs rnam grangs tha dad pa bzhugs pa rnams la skyes rabs nyid nas bsdus shing go bder ɔkrol ba'i so sor kha byang dang bcas te bkod pa ni/*.

272 A transcript of Gongkar's *Avadānakalpalatā* inscriptions was published in India in 2013. As Mathias Fermer informed me, it was published by the Gongkar monks in the compilation *dPal ldan rdzong pa'i chos 'byung dang rnam thar gces btus*, Saṃ bho ṭa'i dbon brgyud dpe tshogs, vol. 1, pp. 1–157. Fermer also has an input version made by the monks in India.

273 Cf. A mes zhabs, *rGyal ba'i rtogs brjod dpag bsam 'khri shing gi don 'grel legs par bshad pa tshogs gnyis bsam 'phel nor bu'i phreng mdzes*, who mentions it in the colophon (fol. 357.2-3): *gong dkar rdo rje gdan gyi 'du khang gi logs bris la dpag bsam 'khri shing gi zhing bkod yod pa'i zhal byang/ 'jam dbyangs byang chub dbang rgyal gyis mdzad pa nyid yal 'dab so so'i gsal byed du sbyar zhing / gong dkar rdo rje gdan gyi gtsug lag khang gi logs bris dpag bsam khri shing gi zhal byang rje yangs pa can pas mdzad pa/*. The same work is also mentioned in A mes zhabs's biography; cf. Byams pa bsam gtan rgya mtsho, *dPal sa skya pa sngags 'chang bla ma thams cad mkhyen pa chen po ngag dbang kun dga' bsod nams grags pa rgyal mtshan dpal bzang po'i rtogs pa brjod pa ngo mtshar yon tan rin po che 'dus pa'i rgya mtsho*, A mes zhabs gsung 'bum (2000 ed.) , vol. 28 (sa): *'du khang chen mo'i ldebs ris la dpag bsam 'khri shing nas 'byung ba'i rgyal ba'i skyes rabs shin tu legs pa bris nas yod pa rnams la thugs rtog zhib dpyod mdzad de/ phyis su yang gong dkar chos sde'i ldebs ris la yod pa'i 'khrungs rabs kyi bkod pa de gzhan las rmad du byung ba zhig yod ces yang yang gsungs shing / de dus 'khrungs rabs so so'i zhal byang ldebs ris la yod pa de zhal bshus mdzad/*.

274 Marilyn Kennell, letter of October 1994.

275 Concerning the term *Glo 'bur*, the Tibetan-Tibetan dictionary, *Tshig mdzod chen mo*, English transl. p. 569: "buttress, projecting bay, projection." Henss 2014, 833, defines *Lobur* (*glo 'bur*) as "nave" and "annex building."

276 Gyatön 2001, 134.

277 Masaki and Tachikawa 1997.

278 Masaki and Tachikawa 1997, 63.

279 Gyatön 2001, 130.

280 On the two forms of Vajrapāṇi, see Willson and Brauen 2000, nos. 159 and 160.

281 Masaki and Tachikawa 1997, 101.

282 Gyatön 2001, 141–43.

283 Lammergeiers (bearded vultures) only eat bones and bone marrow, Himalayan vultures disdain offal and only eat old carrion flesh, and cinereous vultures (Eurasian black vultures) eat all kinds of carrion.

284 On "Yakṣa Vaiśravaṇa and the Eight Horsemen," see also the deity "Large Yellow Vaiśravaṇa with Eight Horsemen" (*rnam sras ser chen lha dgu*) in Willson and Brauen 2000, no. 300; on p. 320, they describe this group of eight horse-riding *yakṣas* in detail.

285 Gyatön 2001, 143.

286 See Gyaton 2001, 116, last line: the expression *'phrul* in this context is unknown to me.

Chapter 4: part ii

287 The photographic collection of the expedition's main photographer, Pietro Francesco Mele (b. 1923), is accessible at the ethnographic museum in Zurich (VMZ), while photographs from other expedition members survive in the Tucci Archives in Rome. The Mele collection in Zurich does not contain a single image taken at Gongkar Chöde, though it was a major destination during Tucci's final journey to Tibet. Likewise, the large collection of black-and-white negatives and photo prints from the 1938/39 Schäfer-expedition (i.e. BArch Bild 135) does not include photographs taken at Gongkar Chöde; research visit, German Federal Archive, Koblenz, November 2015.

288 Tucci 1956, *To Lhasa and Beyond*, 150f.

289 Ibid., 151.

290 Before 1959, the annual Hevajra practice (*kye rdor sgrub mchod*) took place on the ninth and the tenth day of the eighth Tibetan month at Gongkar; see Gendün Rabsal, *Gong dkar chos sde dgon pa'i lo rgyus rags bsdus rin chen do shal*, 15b.

291 The main Buddha sculpture by Khyentse Chenmo is mentioned in the context of Ameshab's visit at Gongkar Chöde in his extensive biography compiled by Jampa Samten Gyatsho (Byams pa bsam gtan rgya mtsho); see *dPal sa skya pa sngags 'chang bla ma thams cad mkhyen pa chen po ngag dbang kun dga' bsod nams grags pa rgyal mtshan dpal bzang po'i rtogs pa brjod pa ngo mtshar yon tan rin po che 'dus pa'i rgya mtsho*, (Ameshab, Collected Works 2000, vol. 28), 399: *chos sde chen po de'i rten gyi gtso bo mkhyen brtse chen mo'i phyag bzo thub chen 'khor bcas/* [...] *la rten mjal legs par mdzad/*.

292 On the main temple's structure, see chapter 4a.

293 Interview, Dehradun, 2015.

294 H. Richardson 1998, "Some Monasteries, Temples and Fortresses in Tibet before 1950," 315.

295 Chan 1994, 479; Dowman 1988, 151; Tsechang Penba Wangdu 2005, 107.

296 Gyatön, 12f. and 159.

297 Gongkar Dorjedenpa, *rJe btsun sa skya pa gong ma rnams la zhu ba'i 'phrin yig* [Petition to the Venerable Sakya Founders], 467: *des na dpal ldan bla ma yi/ /lugs 'di mchog tu gong ma'i lugs/ /yin na sdang zhugs can ma gtogs/ /dam pa su zhig 'di mi byed/*. Also *ibid.*, 469: *spyir na rje btsun gong ma dang / bla ma dam pa mi mthun med/*. In his biography Kunga Namgyal is described as a major proponent of Lama Dampa's teaching system; Gyatön, 12f.

Among the Sakyapa, the authority of Lama Dampa's writings was widely discussed in the seventeenth century; see Jonang Tāranātha (1575–1634), *sTag lung zhabs drung gi gsung lan* (Collected Works 2008, vol. 36), 466: *bla ma dam pa'i 'khrid yig 'di glegs bam rang dang mthun nges lags shing / rtsom pa po gang zag gi dbang du byas na'ang / mkhas btsun bzang gsum gyi yon tan 'gran zla med cing / gong ma lnga gsung rab kyang mi zhan pa yin/ /dge bshes phal pa ma yin sprul pa'i sku yin par 'dug pas/ rang re khong gi 'khrid yig la rtsis po cher byed pa yin lags/*. Moreover, Ameshab's collected writings contain two treatises that each discuss and juxtapose the Ngorpa and the Dzongpa traditions' exegesis of the Hevajra and the Lamdre, respectively; see Ameshab, Collected Works 2000, vol. 24, 1–302 and 303–528.

298 David Jackson mentioned elsewhere that the choice of the main figure/s in a painting is directly linked with the "immediate spiritual wishes or priorities" of the patron commissioning the work; Jackson 2005c, 9, 13.

299 Gyatön, for instance, does not refer to them by this term in Gongkarwa's life story; see Gyatön, 137f. (as in note below) . The only written source that lists three instead of the two later red-robed Sakya founders is Longdol Lama's (1719–1794) biographical history, i.e., *sKyes bu rgya bod ming gi rnam grangs*; see A. Vostrikov 1970, 65, n. 186.

300 Zhong Ziyin 钟子寅 2013, "Lamdre Patriarch Lineage Murals in the Main Hall of Gongkar Chöde Monastery in Shannan of Tibet and Their Significance in Art History." [in Chinese], 法音 (*The Voice of Dharma*), no. 350 (2013), 35-39.

301 Tsechang Penba Wangdu 2010, section on Khyentse Chenmo (*Gong dkar sgang stod mkhyen brtse chen mo'i skor/*).

302 Gyatön, 137f.: *gtsang khang gi ngos g.yas la/ rje sa skya pa dkar po rnam gsum gtso bor gyur pa la gsung ngag rin po che lam 'bras bu dang bcas pa'i brgyud pa'i rim pa'i bla ma rnams kyi (sic!) bskor ba dang / [138] g.yon ngos la bdag nyid chen po sa skya paṇḍi ta/ 'phags pa rin po che/ dpal ldan bla ma dam pa rnams gtso bor gyur pa la rtsa rgyud kyi brgyud pa'i bla ma'i rim pa rnams kyis bskor bar bzhugs so/*.

303 This was noted long ago by D. Jackson 1990, 133.

304 See chapter 4, part I, *Original Structure of the Main Temple* and chapter 5, *The Khyenluk Tradition of Sculpture* respectively.

305 Gyatön, 146. Also chapter 7, *Teachers of the Lamdre Lineage*.

306 Gendün Rabsal, *Gong dkar chos sde dgon pa'i lo rgyus rags bsdus rin chen do shal*, 8b4: *de'i nub tu gzim chung chen po'i gzim dkyil la gtso bo brdzi khyim gyi thub dbang dang kun mkhyen rin po che'i yab rgyal ba shes rab kyi 'dra sku/ gser zangs kyi lam 'bras bla rgyud cha tshang [...]*

307 Gongkar Dorjedenpa, *Record of Teachings Received*, 6-8. See also Gongkar Trinle Namgyal, *Record of Teachings Received* (ed. 2008), 22f.

308 See, for instance, Ngorchen's record of teachings received; see D. Jackson 1990, 133f.

309 Gyatön, 120–123; 135 and Fermer 2009, 381f. See also chapter 5, *Iconographic Links with Surviving Murals in the Kunzang Tse College* and appendix B.

310 See *gSung ngag rin po che lam 'bras bu dang bcas pa'i bla ma brgyud pa la gsol ba 'debs pa dngos grub rin po che'i char 'bebs* [Lamdre Lineage Prayer] (16 fols., modern computer input, Gongkar Chöde, Dehradun), 2-6.

311 I am very grateful to Christian Luczanits (SOAS, London), who provided his personal photos of the painting for this catalog. Moreover, he kindly shared with me the draft of a forthcoming paper in which he discusses this thangka and its iconographic and historical links with the Lamdre repoussée sculptures from Drathang, that are dealt with in chapter 5.

312 An inscription below guru number 19 identifies him as Chang[chup] Tse[mo] (Byang [chub] rtse [mo], 1303–1380), a close disciple of Lama Dampa and another important teacher of Thekchen Chöje. As above in the main Gongkar lineage, one would expect Sazang Mati or Sakya Büton in this position. This is reinforced by the fact that Thekchen Chöje is recorded to have received the Lamdre from Mati Panchen and Butön Rinpoche Wangchuk Dar, but not from Changchup Tsemo; see *Theg chen chos kyi rgyal po chen po'i gsan yig ngo bshus* [Record of Teachings Received], 9a and 18a-b. Instructions (other than the Lamdre) that he obtained from Lochen Changchup Tsemo are recorded in ibid., 12b-15a, and in Thekchenpa's life story by Dzongpa Kunga Gyaltshen; see Kunga Gyaltshen Palzangpo, *Theg chen chos kyi rgyal po'i rnam thar rgyas pa*, 211f., 220.

313 The Gongkar transmission of the Hevajra Root Tantra after Phakpa through gurus 19, Shang Dode Pal, and 20, Lotsāwa Chokden, and so on down to Lama Dampa is not exactly identical with the main Ngorpa and Sakya lineages. See D. Jackson 1986, 185-187; and J. Sobisch 2008, 77-79. (Sobisch, 79, inserts Lama Dampa between Drakphukpa and Palden Tshultrim, but Ngorchen records a separate line for Lama Dampa beginning with Phakpa's disciple Jamkya Namkha Pal and continuing to Palden Sengge, Lama Dampa, and Palden Tshultrim. See Jackson 1986, 191.) Ngorchen's lineage is recorded by his record of teachings received; see D. Jackson 1986, 190f.

314 Gyatön, 41 and Gongkar Dorjedenpa, *Record of Teachings Received*, 3.

315 Gongkar Dorjedenpa, *Record of Teachings Received*, 3: *kyai rdo rje ḍombhi (gloss: rgya dper gdol pa mo ma ḍoṃ bhi ni 'dug pas 'di yang ḍoṃ bhi thob bam/) he ru ka'i lugs kyi dbang / de'i dkyil chog rje btsun rtse mos mdzad pa'i steng nas thob pa'i brgyud pa ni/ [1] rdo rje 'chang / [2] bdag med ma/ [3] birwa pa/ [4] ḍombhi ba/ [5] a la la badzra/ [6] nags khrod pa/ [7] garbha ri pa/ [8] [missing] [9] mi thub zla ba/ [10] dpa' bo rdo rje/ [11] 'brog mi lo tsā ba/ [12] mnga' ris pa gsal snying / [13] sgyi chu ba dgra bla'bar/ [14] sa chen pa/ [15] [missing] [16] rje btsun pa/ [17] chos rje sa paṇ/ [18] bla ma 'phags pa/ [19] zhang mdo sde dpal/ [20] lo tstsha ba mchog ldan/ [21] bla ma dpal ldan seng ge [22] [missing] [23] grub chen sher rdor ba/ [24] bla ma chos sgo ba/ [25] pha chos kyi rje/ des [26] bdag la'o/*. A *dbu med*-manuscript (287 fols.) of Gongkarwa's record of teachings gives the same corrupted lineage; see *rJe btsun rdo rje gdan pa thams cad mkhyen pa kun dga' rnam rgyal dpal bzang po'i gsan yig yongs su rdzogs pa*, 3a-b.

316 Fifth Dalai Lama's *Record of Teachings Received* (vol. 1), 381f.: *rje btsun sa skya pa yab sras la kye rdor bka' babs bzhi bzhugs pa [382] las rnal 'byor dbang phyug birwa pa dang ye shes kyi mkha' 'gro gnyis kyis dngos su byin gyis brlabs pa'i grub chen ḍombhi he ru kas legs par bkral ba'i kye rdor ḍombhi lugs su grags pa lha dgu'i ras bris kyi dkyil 'khor du theg chen rin po ches mdzad pa'i mngon rtogs yan lag drug pa las dang po pa 'jug bde dang dkyil chog kye rdor rnam par rol pa la brten nas dbang bzhi rdzogs par nos pa'i brgyud pa ni/ rdo rje 'chang/ bdag med ma/ birwa pa/ ḍombhi he ru ka/ a na (sic!) la badzra/ nags khrod pa/ garbha ri pa/ dza ya shrī dznyā na/ (gloss: 'di gong dkar ba'i gsan yig na mi 'dug kyang thar rtse pa'i gsan yig na snang bas chad dam snyam/) mi thub zla ba/ dpa' bo rdo rje/ 'brog mi lo chen/ mnga' ris pa gsal ba'i snying po/ 'khon sgye chu ba dgra lha 'bar/ sa chen/ rtse mo/ rje btsun pa/ sa paṇ/ 'phags pa rin po che/ zhang mdo sde dpal/ lo tsā ba mchog ldan/ bla ma dpal ldan seng ge/ mkhan chen shes rab rdo rje/ chos sgo ba chos dpal shes rab/ brag thog pa bsod nams bzang po/ kun mkhyen rdo rje gdan pa/ [...]*

317 Gongkar Trinle Namgyal, *Record of Teachings Received* (*dbu med*-manuscript), fascicle 1, 15a-b: *kye rdor rgyud lugs su grags pa gsum gyi dang po/ ḍombhi he ru ka'i lugs dgyes pa rdo rje phyag bcu drug pa lha dgu'i rdul tshon gyi dkyil 'khor du/ mngon rtogs slob dpon rtse mo/ dkyil chog theg chen chos rje'i nas/ dbang bzhi rdzogs par thob pa'i brgyud pa ni/ rdo rje 'chang / bdag med ma/ birwa pa/ ḍombhi pa/ a la la badzra/ nags khrod pa/ garbha ri pa/ bsod snyoms pa rgyal ba dpal ye shes/ mi thub zla ba/ dpa' bo rdo rje/ 'brog mi lo tsa/ mnga' ris pa gsal snying / sgyi chu ba dgra bla 'bar/ bla ma sa skya pa chen po/ slob dpon rin po che/ rje btsun rin po che/ 'jam dbyangs sa paṇḍi ta/ 'gro mgon chos rgyal 'phags pa/ zhang mdo sde dpal/ lo tsa ba mchog [15b] ldan/ bla ma dpal ldan seng ge mkhan chen shes rab rdo rje/ chos sgo ba chos dpal/ rje btsun brag thog pa/ thams cad mkhyen pa rdo rje gdan pa/ mkhas grub rnam rgyal rin chen/ yongs 'dzin shākya kun dga'/ kun spangs rin chen dbang sgrol/ (gloss: yar rgyab pa'i zhal ngo btsun mo/) bla chen ye shes dbang po/ g.yu lo bkod*

pa rgyal mtshan rdo rje/ rtsa ba'i bla ma paṇ chen bsod nams mchog ldan/ des bdag la'o/. Also Gongkar Trinle Namgyal, *ibid.* (2008 ed.), 20.

318 See Gongkar Dorjedenpa, *Record of Teachings Received,* 176f.: *gnyis pa/ kyee rdo rje'i skor la/ rtsa ba'i rgyud/ bsdus pa'i rgyud/ rgyud phyi ma/ phyi ma'i phyi ma/ bshad pa'i rgyud/ snying po'i rgyud/ 'bras bu'i rgyud bdun gyi dang po/ rtsa ba'i rgyud kyee rdo rje 'bum phrag lnga pa las bsdus pa'i kyee rdo rje zhes bya ba'i rgyud kyi rgyal po/ brtag pa dang po la le'u bcu gcig pa/ brtag pa gnyis pa le'u bcu gnyis pa/ paṇḍi ta ga ya ya dha ra* [177] *dang / lo tsā ba 'brog mi shākya ye shes kyis bsgyur ba/ 'di la dkyil 'khor drug yod do/ / gnyis pa/ de'i thun mong ma yin pa'i bshad rgyud/ mkha' 'gro ma rdo rje gur zhes bya ba le'u bco lnga pa 'gyur byang snga ma dang 'dra'o/ / 'di la dngos su dkyil 'khor bcu gtso bo 'pho ba'i dbye bas drug cu rtsa gnyis su 'gyur ro/* (gloss: *rtsa bshad 'di gnyis/ pha chos kyi rje* [i.e. Drakthokpa Sönam Sangpo] *las thob pa'o/*) */de gnyis kyi brgyud pa ni/* [1] *rdo rje 'chang /* [2] *bdag med ma/* [3] *birwa pa/* [4] *ḍom bhi ba/* [5] *a la la badzra/* [6] *nags khrod pa/* [7] *garbha ri pa/* [8] *bsod snyoms pa rgyal ba dpal gyi ye shes/* [9] *mi thub zla ba/* [10] *dge slong dpa' bo rje/* [11] *'brog mi shākya ye shes/* [12] *'khon dkon mchog rgyal po/* [13] *sa chen kun snying /* [14] *slob dpon bsod nams rtse mo/* [15] *rje btsun grags pa rgyal mtshan/* [16] *chos rje sa paṇ/* [17] *'phags pa rin po che/* [18] *zhang mdo dpal/* [19] *'jam skya/* [20] *bla ma dpal ldan seng ge* [21] *bla ma bsod rgyal/* [22] *mkhan chen shes rdor ba nas gong bzhin no/.*

Dorjedenpa received the same transmission of the Hevajra Mūlatantra (from Vajradhara down to Khenchen Shedorwa) also from Ngoktön Sönam Döndrup (rNgog ston bSod nams don grub); see ibid., 416.

Chapter 5

319 I have adapted these introductory paragraphs on Khyentse's statues from Jackson 1996, 139 and 142.

320 Kaḥ thog Si tu 1972, 156 (78b): *mgon khang ka brgyad ma na mkhyen brtse chen mo'i phyag bzos 'bur sku 'jigs rung nyams mtshar 'dom phyed gsum tsam re.*

321 Tucci 1956, 151.

322 Kaḥ thog Si tu 1972, 159.5 (80a): *bla ma dngos yin snang skye ba/ pra rtsi legs po snum nas bton ma thag pa lta bu sha stag/.*

323 The Tibetan text, in Gyatön Changchup Wangyal 2001, 123: *sku 'di dag ni sgrub dus bzo khang mthil du bgyis te legs par grub nas/ gnas 'di ru bca' bde bar spyan drangs pa yin pa la/ phyis rjes btsun dam pa nyid kyi gser sku sku tshad ma da lta kun dga' rwa ba'i dbus na bzhugs pa 'di bzhengs dus/ gos rgyud la sogs pa'i dpe blang ba'i phyir/ bdag nyid chen po sa skya paṇḍi ta'i sku 'di nub kyi sgo mang mdun du spyan 'dren par brtsams pa na/ thabs 'phrul ji ltar byas kyang cung zad tsam yang g.yo bar ma nus pas/ ngo mtshar rmad du byung ba'i gnas su gyur pa yin no/ / de lta bzhugs pa so sor gang 'os kyi sku'i rnam 'gyur ngo mtshar ba las kyang ches ngo mtshar ba'i mngon sum pa'i snang tshul spyan gyi gzigs pa sgyur ba dang / gsung gi sgra dbyangs stsal bzhin pa'i nyams dang ldan pa*

byin rlabs [B:39a] *kyi gzi 'od dang bcas pa rnams la go ling khyad par can gyi na bza'i brtsegs du ma dang / rgya'i rdo rje dril bu sogs mchod cha tshang ma re dang bcas pa/ gzhan yang rin po che gser zangs las grub pa'i bla ma de dag gi sku tshad cung gzhon pa tshar gcig khri na bza' dang bcas te bzhugs* [A:124] *pa'o//.*

324 *bstan pa'i gtso bo mnyam med shākya'i rgyal po'i sku mtshan dang dpe byad kyi spras pa/ lta bas chog mi shes pa dzambu chu bo'i gser lan brgyar byugs pa lta bu'i 'od zer kun nas 'phro ba la/ go ling bzang po'i na bza' padma rā ga'i mdog can/ gos dar yug sna tshogs pa rnams dbang po'i gzhu ltar bkra bas snyan shal mdzes par byas pa/ lha dang bcas pa'i 'gro ba rnams kyi bsod nams kyi zhing dam par lham me lhan ne lhang nger bzhugs pa'o/ /.* Maybe *go ling* is a variant or misspelling of *'go ling* or *mgo ling* (*mngon brjod*), a rare term meaning "branch" (*yal ga*).

325 Heller 1999, 128.

326 von Schroeder 2001, vol. 2, 972.

327 See von Schroeder 2001, vol. 2, 972, notes 926 and 927.

328 von Schroeder 2001, vol. 2, 911-993.

329 von Schroeder 2001, vol. 2, 974.

330 Lee-Kalisch et al. 2006, 120.

331 Lee-Kalisch et al. 2006, 121.

332 Lee-Kalisch et al. 2006, 121.

333 Lee-Kalisch et al. 2006 122, my translation.

334 Henss 2014, 370–72.

335 Henss 2014, 371.

336 See Ngag dbang phun tshogs 1994, p. 50, which mentions a blessed statue of Kunga Namgyal among the gilt statues of the Sakyapa Lamdre masters: *sa skya'i lam 'bras kyi sku gser zangs las grub pa rdo rje gdan pa kun dga' rnam rgyal gyi zku byin can mi tshad tsam.*

337 For the Palkhor Chöde set, see von Schroder 2001, vol. 2, 874–81, plates 201–204.

338 The need for Sakya Butön in the lineage is also discussed in Stearns 2006, 242, translating a passage from Jamyang Khyentse Wangchuk's history of the Lamdre.

339 Bernadette Bröskamp was BB in the catalog of Jeong-hee Lee-Kalisch et al. 2006. At LIRI in Lumbini I also saw a draft of a paper she later gave at a conference in Beijing in 2009

340 The autobiography of the Fifth Dalai Lama 1983, vol. 1, 673, mentions a thangka, portraying Lama Dampa Sönam Gyaltshen with his footprints and hand prints, that was given to the Fifth Dalai Lama.

341 See also the mural painting of Thekchen Chöje at Gyantse stupa, Lam 'bras Lha khang, chapel 4/2 (southern wall) as published in Lo Bue and Ricca 1990, plate 92. The available photo does not clearly show his head or hat.

342 Kunga Namgyal's record of teachings has been published in 2005 by the rGyal yongs sa chen in Bodhnath, Kathmandu.

Chapter 6

343 See von Schroeder 2006, nos. 13, 15, 17.

344 Naljorpa Rinchen Dorje, *sKu'i rnam 'gyur drug gi zin bris* ("Notes on the Bodily Forms of Virūpa"), Collected Writings of Ngorchen Kunga Zangpo 1, 533, fol. 264r–264v.

345 Colophon: *zhes pa rnal 'byor pa rin chen rdo rjes gong ma'i gsung thor bu pa rnams las btus pa'o.* Cf. Himalayan Art Resource, http://www.himalayanart.org/search/set. cfm?setID=1988.

346 See Stearns 2006, 143.

347 The sacred volume is said to have been either a Hevajra Tantra or volume of the Prajñāpāramitā Sūtra; see C. Stearns 2006, *Taking the Result,* 146.

348 P. Welch 2008, p. 140. A *qilin* (Jap. *kirin*) is also sometimes called a unicorn, because it is sometimes shown with one horn, though it can also have two or three. See W. Eberhard 1990, p. 303. C. A. S. Williams 1976 also calls it a unicorn and stresses its gentle and benevolent nature, listing it with phoenix, tortoise, and dragon as one of the four intelligent creatures. Hean-Tatt Ong 1993, 115–119, adds much lore about this mythical beast, such as that it is considered the prince of mammalian beasts.

349 Mathias Fermer pointed this out in an email, July 2015.

350 Mathias Fermer also explained to me that Tshultrim Tashi was a contemporary of Gongkar Trinle Namgyal ('Phrin las rnam rgyal), author of the record of teachings received *Thob yig bum pa bzang po* that I saw in Gongkar in 1986, and who was from the same residence (*gzims shag*) of Nyimaling (Nyi ma gling) in Gongkar. Yangpachen (Yangs pa can) was the residence (*gzims shag*) where Gyatön Changchup Wangyal (Gongkarwa's biographer) resided a century or two earlier.

351 See Stearns 2006, 234.

352 The inscription below the main figure reads: *rje btsun rin po che rdo rje 'dzin pa grags pa rgyal mtshan la na mo/.* Below the small lama: *rje btsun kun dga' rnam rgyal la na mo/.*

353 Jackson 1987, 27.

354 Cf. Debreczeny, fig. 4.4, "monkey stealing a mushroom," an arhat composition in which a monkey similarly dangles from a limb.

355 During an interview in October 2003, one of the lamas of Gongkar told me that they had so far only located one thangka from the old set: this portrait of Sakya Paṇḍita, hanging high above the seats in the main assembly hall.

356 See van der Kuijp 1993a, 149 and note 2.

357 Henss 2014, 524.

358 For the exchange of letters between Phakpa and Jomden Raldri, see Schaeffer and van der Kuijp 2009, 7, and note 11.

359 Shakabpa 1984, 68.

360 Kapstein 2006, 111.

361 See also Franz-Karl Ehrhard 2004, 245, note 2. He cites the published Paris lectures of Seyfort Ruegg 1995, and the *Hor chos 'byung* of Jigme Rigpe Dorje, p. 114.16.

362 Brent 1976, 105.

363 Rossabi 1995, 33.

364 This paragraph is based on the Wikipedia entry, "Chabi," https://en.wikipedia.org/wiki/Chabi, from the source Stearns et al., "The Last Great Nomadic Challenges: From Chinggis Khan to Timur," *World Civilizations: The Global Experience* (AP ed., 6th ed.), 2011, 327–28.

365 Shakabpa 1984, 64.

366 van der Kuijp 1993c, note 3, refers to a forthcoming study, van der Kuijp 2004. Van der Kuijp 2004, 9, mentions Chabi and in note 27 refers to the contribution of M. Rossabi, "Khubilai Khan and the Woman in his Family," *Studie Mongolica: Festschrift für Herbert Francke* in *Münchner Ostasiatische Studien* 15, ed. W. Bauer, 1979, 157–170.

367 van der Kuijp 1993c, 280. The excellent king of Dharma (Chos kyi rgyal po bzang po) mentioned in the first colophon as the project's main inspiration is probably Chögyal Phakpa; the line below alludes to him as the one who clearly knows all objects of knowledge, referring to the title of the treatise he composed for Chabi's son, the crown prince.

368 See McClausland 2015, 6, frontispiece; no. 21, detail from Khubilai Khan hunting; no. 28, anon.; 62, "Empress Chabi." Another valuable summary of Tibetan Buddhist art in the Yuan dynasty is given by Casey 2014, which mainly investigates a set of painted *tsakli* initiation cards, now in a private collection.

369 McClausland 2015, 62.

370 McClausland 2015, 62.

371 McClausland 2015, 62.

372 Henss 2014, 524.

373 Henss 2014, 550, note 64. Henss explains these murals: "Sakya iconography predominates on the side walls, whose wall-paintings, though of considerable historical interest in view of the biographies of Sakya Paṇḍita and Phagpa Lama, and like all other statues and paintings in this chapel dating to the foundation year 1425, have not yet received serious attention and deserve detailed documentation. The central group on the left southern wall [his fig. 751, no. 24], depicts Phagpa Lama (1235–1280), who had in 1253 initiated his later imperial patron, the Great Khan (1264) and Chinese emperor (1279) Khubilai Khan (1215–1294), sitting opposite on the left . . . ."

374 See Yang 1987, 55, fig. 8-1.

375 See Lee-Kalisch et al. 2006, no. 46.

376 Shakabpa 1984, 64.

Chapter 7

377 Gyatön Changchub Wangyal 2001, 146: *lam 'bras kyi bla ma brgyud pa'i bris thang ngo mtshar ba cha gnyis.*

378 I was told that the Art Gallery of Greater Victoria acquired this painting from a minor private collector in 1965, without other paintings from the same set.

379 This painting was never published, except its appearance in Sotheby's auction catalog, (for Indian and Southeast Asian Art, New York, Dec. 5, 1992).

380 Zwalf 1985, 142, pl. 195, and on the cover of Snellgrove 2013. According to the British Museum online database, the painting was purchased from Hugh E. Richardson in 1980, funded by the Brooke Sewell Permanent Fund; eighteen Tibetan paintings (1980.12-20.01–018) were bought from Richardson at this time.

381 In a large depiction of an arhat that we shall see later, Figure 9.24, the same tusk-bearing character wears bright red robes and no earrings; he also appears early in the Shambhala king series and in the fifth thangka of the Sera mahāsiddha set, between Śāntipa and Vīṇāpa.

382 P. B. Welch 2008, 140.

383 See Béguin 1994. Béguin also referred to two paintings in the Ford collection, both previously published (by Lauf 1976 and by himself), adding that one painting also appeared on the cover of *Arts of Asia* 5, no. 6 (1975).

384 The paintings were originally bought by Jean and Lise Mansion, in Paris 1974; through the Jean Mansion bequest, four of the set were donated to the Musée Guimet in 1993.

385 W. Eberhard 1990, 178, calls the Chinese *pipa* (*bi ba*) a mandolin or lute, while calling (p. 172) the *qin* a "lute (guitar.)" See also p. 199, where Eberhard lists the five types of musical instruments of classical China. C. A. S. Williams 1976, p. 286, no. 3, calls it a "balloon guitar."

386 Cf. Dagyab 1977, 75.

387 "Instruments in Indian Classical Music," http://www.sahajayogaportal.org/en/music-arts/indian-classical-music/instruments.html. Accessed November 19, 2015.

388 Willson and Brauen 2000, 569.

389 Khreng Hra'o-khrun 2008, 90.

390 Shankar 1968, 34.

391 See Tshewang Rinchen 2005.

392 The *tambura* is an essential droning instrument in Indian music. As Shankar 1968, 37, explains, it comes in any size, and its function is: "to sound the tonic repeatedly though-out a composition so that both the performer and the listener are always aware of the basic note of the raga." It needs no frets, and its strings (from four to six) are plucked continuously, one after the other, with the fingers without using a plectrum. In the *Tshig mdzod chen mo*, the Tibetan word *tambu ra* is defined as *rgyud mang*, "many-stringed instrument," though *rgyud mang* is actually the Tibetan word for *vīṇa*.

393 See Kachen Losang Phüntshok 1993, 78, Zla gi lha mo dByangs can ma dkar mo [Sarasvatī]; and 102, Yul 'khor srung.

394 Pal 1983, pl. 26. In Jackson 2009, fig. 8.2, no. 11, Vinapa, is an example of the Indian *vīṇā* outside the Khyenri style but not held by Sarasvatī, nor by a Menri painter, nor from central Tibet. In this painting, the great adept Vīṇāpa holds a north-Indian *vīṇā* with two gourds; the artist depicted it a bit too small and in a simplified side view.

395 Could it have been badly restored? That might explain why it has some excellent features but mostly has a kind of blankness.

396 Linrothe 2006, 273.

Chapter 8

397 Pal 1984a, pl. 89; the painting is discussed on p. 156.

398 After signing an agreement in Lhasa in 1904, a small British military ("Younghusband") expedition returned that year. Someone on the expedition could have brought the Khyenri sets from Tibet to British India and then have sent them to Paris for sale.

399 "Rigdens in Boston," *Shambhala Times*, April 3, 2014, http://shambhalatimes.org/2014/04/03/rigdens-in-boston/.

400 See Toganoo 1986, no. III 10–2.

401 http://www.mfa.org/collections/object/the-first-dharma-religious-king-of-shambhala-sucandra-beautiful-moon-8501.

402 http://www.mfa.org/collections/object/the-second-dharma-religious-king-of-shambhala-8512.

403 http://www.mfa.org/collections/object/the-third-dharma-religious-king-of-shambhala-tejin-beautiful-one-8503.

404 http://www.mfa.org/collections/object/the-fifth-dharma-religious-king-of-shambhala-sureshvara-divine-king-8496.

405 http://www.mfa.org/collections/object/the-sixth-dharma-religious-king-of-shambhala-8497.

406 http://www.mfa.org/collections/object/the-seventh-dharma-religious-king-of-shambhala-sureshama-divine-power-8498.

407 http://www.mfa.org/collections/object/the-first-vidyadhara-wisdom-holder-king-of-shambhala-manjushri-yashas-beautiful-radiant-fame-8499.

408 http://www.mfa.org/collections/object/the-fourth-vidyadhara-wisdom-holder-king-of-shambhala-8500.

409 http://www.mfa.org/collections/object/the-fifth-vidyadhara-wisdom-holder-king-of-shambhala-sumitra-8514.

410 P. Welch 2008, 118.

411 http://www.mfa.org/collections/object/the-sixth-or-eighteenth-vidyadhara-wisdom-holder-king-of-shambhala-8516.

412 Cf. the adepts in von Schroeder 2006.

413 Cf. Tshewang Rinchen 2005.

414 http://www.mfa.org/collections/object/the-seventh-vidyadhara-wisdom-holder-king-of-shambhala-vishnugupta-8518.

415 http://www.mfa.org/collections/object/the-ninth-vidyadhara-wisdom-holder-king-of-shambhala-subhadra-great-right-8508.

416 http://www.mfa.org/collections/object/the-eleventh-vidyadhara-wisdom-holder-king-of-shambhala-8517.

417 http://www.mfa.org/collections/object/
the-thirteenth-vidyadharas-wisdom-hold-
er-king-of-shambhala-8515.

418 http://www.mfa.org/collections/object/
the-fourteenth-vidyadhara-wisdom-hold-
er-king-of-shambhala-shashiprabha-moon-
light-8506.

419 However, it also occurs to me that this figure
looks very regal. If that is iconographically
significant (and I am not sure whether it is),
he would make a very imposing third Dharma
King, and the current candidate for that would
become the present Kalkin (i.e., Kalkin number 14).

420 http://www.mfa.org/collections/object/the-
eighteenth-or-sixth-vidyadhara-wisdom-hold-
er-king-of-shambhala-hari-8504.

421 http://www.mfa.org/collections/object/
the-nineteenth-vidyadhara-wisdom-hold-
er-king-of-shambhala-vikrama-8511.

422 http://www.mfa.org/collections/object/the-
twenty-first-vidyadhara-wisdom-holder-king-
of-shambhala-8510.

423 http://www.mfa.org/collections/object/the-
twenty-second-or-twelfth-vidyadharas-wis-
dom-holder-king-of-shambhala-8507.

424 Compare Vira and Chandra 1972, part 20, nos.
262b (Kalkin 12) and 265b (Kalkin 22).

425 http://www.mfa.org/collections/object/
the-twenty-third-vidyadhara-wisdom-hold-
er-king-of-shambhala-maheshvara-8509.

426 http://www.mfa.org/collections/object/
the-twenty-fourth-vidyadhara-wisdom-hold-
er-king-of-shambhala-anantavijaya-in-
finite-victory-8502.

427 http://www.mfa.org/collections/object/the-
twenty-fifth-vidyadhara-wisdom-holder-king-
of-shambhala-rudra-chakrin-8513.

428 Tibet House Museum 1999.

429 See Jackson 2009, 125, fig. 6.14.

430 Kaḥ thog Rig 'dzin Tshe dbang nor bu,
1973–82.

431 Fujita 1984, 168.

432 Ibid., 171.

433 Ibid., 171.

CHAPTER 9

434 "Tibetan Art: An Unusual Exhibition
at the Museum of Fine Arts, Boston,"
Art & Antiques, May 2012, http://
www.artandantiquesmag.com/2012/05/
tibetan-art-museum-of-fine-arts-boston/.

435 MFA says "14th century." http://
www.mfa.org/collections/object/
shaka-on-a-throne-with-two-attendants-8788.

436 MFA says "Eastern Tibetan, 15th–16th century." (http://www.mfa.org/collections/object/
arhat-dharmatala-8789.)

437 Rhie and Thurman 1991, 114, fig. 17.

438 Rhie and Thurman 1991, 114, fig. 17.

439 Rhie and Thurman 1991, 114, fig. 17.

440 MFA says "about 1500" and "in *Buddhist
Arts of Asia*: 30, pg. 94." http://www.mfa.org/
collections/object/arhat-cudapanthaka-8790.

441 P. Pal and H.-C. Tseng 1969, p. 42.

442 Pal and Tseng 1969, 42.

443 Pal and Tseng 1969, 42.

444 Cf. Dagyab 1977, 89: "On the holy spot
of Kashmir (Khache) is the noble elder
Kanakavatsa surrounded by his retinue of five
hundred arhats; homage to him who holds a
string of precious stones."

445 Cf. K. Debreczeny, fig. 4.4, "monkey stealing
a mushroom," and fig. 4.14, "teaching a monkey to read or write."

446 Toganoo 1986, III 6–4 and III 6–5. MFA
entry on first painting: http://www.mfa.org/
collections/object/rakan-in-a-chair-8830.

447 The MFA says "14th century." http://
www.mfa.org/collections/object/
rakan-seated-under-gnarled-tree-8831.

448 Rhie and Thurman 1999, 175.

449 Rhie and Thurman 1999, 175.

450 Rhie and Thurman 1999, 175.

451 Linrothe 2004, 61.

452 Linrothe 2004, 61.

453 Linrothe 2004, 61.

454 The two sets were discussed in Patricia
Berger 2003, *Empire of Emptiness: Buddhist
art and political authority in Qing China*
(Honolulu : University of Hawaii Press), pp.
143–146, figs. 45–46, and plate 14.

455 Rhie and Thurman 1991, 119.

456 Jackson 2012, fig. 7.23: and Jackson 2015,
fig. 6.16.

457 See Béguin 1995, cat. nos. 245–58.

458 Béguin 1995, 337.

459 Béguin 1995, 337. Béguin also noted that
those twelve deities occur as a group in the
pantheon of the Mongol Tengyur canon, referring to Chandra 1991, 151–53, nos. 303–14.
See also the deity "Large Yellow Vaiśravana
with Eight Horsemen" (*rnam sras ser chen
lha dgu*) in Willson and Brauen 2000, no. 300;
on p. 320, they describe this group of eight
horse-riding *yakṣas* in detail, as I listed above
in chapter 4.

460 Cf. Dagyab 1977, 75.

461 Dagyab 1977, 78.

462 Béguin 1995, 337.

463 Cf. Dagyab 1977, 80.

464 Béguin 1995, 338.

465 Cf. Dagyab 1977, 89.

466 Béguin 1995, 339.

467 Cf. Dagyab 1977, 102. According to
his praises in a liturgy attributed to
Śākyaśrībhadra: "In the eastern continent
Lus 'phags gling dwells Piṇḍola Bharadvāja
surrounded by his retinue of twelve hundred
arhats; homage to him who holds a book and
an alms bowl."

468 Cf. Dagyab 1977, 107.

469 Béguin 1995, 341. Chandra 1991, 151, no.
303.

470 Cf. Dagyab 1977, 86.

471 Béguin 1995, 342. See Chandra 1991, nos.
303, 308, 309, 312, and 313.

472 See Penba Wangdu 2012, figs. 12 and
17a–17d.

473 Wang Jia Peng 2011.

474 Linrothe 2004, 15; p. 41, footnote 25, cited
Tucci 1949 and Kent 1994 as his main sources
for the two main types of portraiture.

475 Kent 1994, 184.

476 Tucci 1949, 615, note 248.

477 See Peking cat. 1011, *'Phags pa byams pa
lungs bstan pa* (translated by Jinamitra and
Kawa Paltsek) in the *mdo sna tshogs* section.

478 As listed in the Library of Congress online
catalog, the work was entitled: *Byams pa lung
bstan lugs kyi gnas bstan phyag mchod*.

479 Dagyab 1977, 72–114. The Sakya liturgy is
cited as Khache Panchen Śākyaśrī, *gNas brtan
phyag mchod*, as cited by Dagyab 1977, biblio
no. 144.

480 See Tucci 1949, 565–67.

481 Tucci 1949, 566.

482 Fifth Dalai Lama 1971, vol. 2, 83a. This is
the passage listing the minor works associated
with Triphu Lotsāwa: *bsod snyoms kyi kun tu
spyod pa rgud pa rnam sel/ chab gtor dri ma
med pa'i gzhung mar me mdzad ye shes kyis
mdzad pa rkan ston legs pa'i shes rab kyis
zhus pa/ 'phags pa'i gnas brtan bcu drug gi
gsol 'debs/ klu sgrub yab sras kyi bstod pa/
thugs rje chen po snying gi dug sbyong gi man
ngag/ dpal sgrol ma dkar mo'i 'chi ba blu ba'i
sgrub thabs slob dpon ngag dbang grags pas
mdzad pa/ de'i bstod pa/ chos rje lo ts'a bas
rang la smod cing gshung ba'i tshigs brgyad/
bha su ke'i gtor ma'i man ngag /*

483 The Fifth Dalai's record of teachings received
records this lineage for a detailed liturgy for
invoking the sixteen arhats. See Fifth Dalai
Lama 1971, vol. 1, 113a: *mchims nam mkha'
grags kyis mdzad pa'i 'phags pa'i gnas brtan
bcu drug gi sgrub yig rgyas pa'i iung nos pa'i
brgyud pa ni/ jo bo chen po/ dha na shr'i/
rngog byang chub 'byung gnas/ po to ba/ sha
ra ba/ 'chad ka ba/ spyil bu ba gr,yis/ 'bre lhas
pa rdo rje dpal/ sangs rgyas sgom pa/ mchims
nam mkha' grags/ slob dpon bsod ye/ bsod
grags pa/ bar 'dir bla ma gsum bzhi zhig ma
rnyed/ spyan snga lha bsod nams lha dbang/
spyan snga ngag dbang chos grags/ brag
dgon spyan snga gzhon nu chos dpal bzang
po/ rdo rje 'chang pa bong kha pa dpal 'byor
lhun grub/ zur kun mkhyen chos dbyings rang
grol/ des bdag la'o//. See also Ngorchen 1968,
102b: gnas brtan bcu drug gi cho ga'i brgyud
pa ni / jo bo rje bod du byon ba'i phyags phyi
la / sems tsam rnam brdzun [Fol. 102c] gyi
grub mtha' 'dzin ba'i paṇḍi ta gcig la / rngog
byang chub 'byung gnas kyis zhus / de las
dge bshes bu to ba / shar ba / 'chad ka ba /
se sbyil bu ba / 'dre lhas ba / rgan mo lhas pa
/ chos rje 'dzim pa chen po / chos rje spang
sgang ba / chos rje 'phags pa gzhon nu blo
gros / de las bdag gis bla ma nyid kyis mdzad
ba'i lung dang bcas pa legs bar zhus so.*

484 Gö Lotsāwa, *Blue Annals* (Roerich 1949–53), 340: *spyil bur tshul zhugs cig gi dus su gnas brtan bcu drug dngos su byon pasl 'gro ba'i mgon po la gnas brtan bcu drug gis bskor ba'i thang sku yang mang du 'phell dbyar gnas kyi tshe gnas brtan bcu drug dngos su byon pasl 'gro ba'i mgon po la gnas brtan gsol 'debs kyang byedl.*

485 Tucci 1949, 567.

486 Tucci 1949, 568.

487 Tucci 1949, 566.

488 Tucci 1949, 560.

489 Tucci 1949, 546, 555–570, pls. 156–170, thangka nos. 121–136.

490 See Ngag dbang legs grub 2011.

CHAPTER 10

491 Jackson 2015, figs. 6.8–6.16.

492 Linrothe 2004, 99–101.

493 K. Debreczeny, fig. .4.5.

494 For more discussion of the set, see Linrothe 2004, nos. 3, 15, 19, and appendix.

495 Note that Khyenri art was commissioned by great Drukpa hierarchs, and one thangka from another Drukpa ineage set is found in the RMA (HAR 874), which depicts Jennga Ngagki Wangchuk and four of the eighty-four great adepts. Another stray thangka from a stylistically different Drukpa Kagyu lineal guru set is documented by Tanaka 2003, pl. 43, "Grub chen Blo gros mchog ldan."

496 See Béguin 1977, nos. 273–75. Individual paintings were also published: a portrait of Ling Repa in Pal 1983, 27; of Milarepa in Pal 1991, no. 110, 94; of Gampopa in Rhie and Thurman 1991, no. 84: and of Phagmotrupa in Lauf 1976, pl. 37, Ford collection.

497 Jackson 2008, 213–16.

498 Heller 2012.

499 Heller 2012, para. 1.

500 Heller 2012, para. 1.

501 Heller 2012.

502 Heller 2012, para. 1. In note 6, Heller says: "I am grateful to Françoise Pommaret for kindly providing this photograph. See Kapstein 2006: 152, figure 20, for a black and white photograph of this same mural painting. Kapstein identified the seated hierarch as Miwang or perhaps his son, however in the light of the research presented here, the identification as Miwang is certain. Kapstein's photo was made in 2004, when the mural had slightly less water damage than in 2006 when Pommaret made her photograph."

503 Heller moves numbers 12 and 13 out of order, confusing the set's obligatory order of "sixth to the right" and "sixth to the left." Where is the proof that no. 12, Tendzin Norbu, should be identified as a much later Bhutanese lama? Both Tendzin and Norbu are fairly common name elements.

504 Nakamura et al. 1996.

505 According to the Library of Congress catalog, that was a bilingual book, with its main Japanese title as: *Chibetto butsuga Shakuson den* (Tokyo: Tibet Bunka Senyokai), 1958.

506 A history of early Tibetan studies in Japan and the contributions of its main scholars until the mid-1970s is given by Gadjin Nagao in his article, "Reflections on Tibetan Studies in Japan," *Acta Asiatica* 29 (1975), 107–28.

507 Hisao Kimura as told to Scott Berry, *Japanese Agent in Tibet: My Ten Years of Travel in Disguise* (London: Serindia, 1990), 105.

508 Scott Berry, *The Japanese in Tibet, in The History of Tibet—The Medieval Period: c. 850–1895,* ed. Alex McKay (Cornell University, 2003), 311.

509 Jackson 2009, fig. 9.1, which has other Khyenri features.

CHAPTER 11

510 See also Jackson 2005b, "Spuren ...," Abb. 2–18. One previously published "Jonang" painting is clearly Khyenri: Jackson 1996, pl. 30. It dates to the early seventeenth century, the period of Tāranātha.

511 See the autobiography of Manthö Ludrup Gyatsho, *Rang gi rnam par thar pa yul sna tshogs kyi bdud rtsi myong ba'i gtam du byas pa zol zog rdzun gyis ma bslad pa sgeg mo'i me long, Lam 'bras slob bshad rnam thar,* vol. ga (klu sgrub), p. 495: *sna tshogs zhes pa chu pho rta'i [1582] lo dbyar gyi cha la sprul sku rdo rjes* **gnas bcu si thang lugs mkhyen brtse'i phyag srol bzhin** *dang/ tshe dpag med rgyan drug gis bskor ba'i zhing khams gnyis/ mkhan rin po che blo gros rnam par rgyal bas gnang sbyin sogs bdag rkyen mdzad nas bzhengs/.*

512 Ibid.: *sa skyong zhes {p. 496} pa shing mo bya [1585] lo o rgyan pa'i zhing khams sngon gyi lo paṇ gyis bskor ba dang/ mi zad pa zhes pa me pho khyi [1586] lo grub thob brgyad cu'i zhing khams gser shog ma gnyis bzhad nas khang pas sbyin bdag byas nas bzhengs/ ri mo mkhan o rgyan pa'i zhing kha[m]s sprul sku rdo rje'i* **mkhyen lugs** *dang/ grub thob brgyad cu'i zhing khams sprul sku bstan rgyan gyi* **sman lugs** *ri mo yin.*

513 Ibid.: *sa skyong zhes pa shing mo bya [1585] lo sa paṇ gyi sku brnyan shin tu legs pa/ 'phrog byed ral pa tshar bcad pa dang/ hor rgyal bo go brtan rjes su bzung ba sog kyi rnam thar zhing bkod gser shog dang bcas pa rong 'tsho nas 'byor lags sku mched kyi sbyin bdag mdzad nas bzhengs/ ri mo mkhan sprul sku sgang brgyud pas* **sman lugs** *yin/.*

514 See Jackson 1996, 190, plate 30.

515 Macdonald and Vergati Stahl 1979, 32, refers to dPag bsam dbang po, *dPal 'brug pa rin po che rgyal dbang thams cad mkhyen pa dpag bsam dbang po thub bstan yongs 'du'i dpal gyi sde'i rnam par thar pa,* xylograph, fol. 101a.

516 Fifth Dalai Lama 1979, fol. 76a.

517 See Ameshab 1986, 499–500: *bris thang la rdzong lugs kyi lam 'bras brgyud pa gong dkar rdo rje gdan na bzhugs pa'i rgya thang chen mo la 'dra shus gnang ba dang/.*

518 See also Ameshab 1986, 500, for references to renovations of certain temples.

519 Ameshab 1986, 447.

520 Kaḥ thog Si tu 1972, 443.6 (222a): *gangs [sic] dkar mkhyen brtse'i phyag bzor dper mdzad pa'i gur zhal [222b] lcam sogs lha bcu gsum thog sleb khyad 'phags/.*

521 A mes zhabs 1980, 61b.5: *de yang gong dkar sprul sku sbyin pa rnam rgyal gyis lha khang chen mo'i thig khang du gur phab nas/ mgon po'i rus shing dang span 'dzugs la 'jim pa phal cher g.yogs grub mtshams glo bur du rlung mar chen po lang ste/.*

522 See also the numerous thangkas that are described as New Khyenri ("mKhyen gsar") in Bod ljongs po ta la do dam khru'u 1996.

523 Fifth Dalai Lama 1983, vol. 1, 283 (*ka* 142a): *gsang sngags dga' tshal du mkhyen lugs mkhas bsgrubs* [sic] *kyis gsang sngags gsar rnying gi bla ma yi dam chos srung gi ldeb bris dngos gtsang/.*

524 Ibid., 445 (*ka* 223): *mkhyen brtse ba'i dbu mdzad gong dkar gsang sngags mkhar pa.*

525 Ibid., vol. 2, 163.3 (*kha* 82a): *spos khang mkhan po zur pa 'bum rams pa rdo rje btsun mo'i zhing khams su gshegs pa'i bsngo rten du glang bu nas kyis do dam byas pa'i lam 'bras brgyud pa'i zhal thang mkhyen ris dngos gtsang ba zhig byung ba mus chen sems dpa' chen po man kha'u brag rdzong pa'i brgyud rim gong dkar chos sde'i dbu mdzad gsang sngags mkhar pa can gyis bris te bsabs/.* See also Fifth Dalai Lama 1989–91, vol. 2, 157. It is possible that the word *dbu mdzad,* translated in the main text as "chief artist," here has the more usual meaning of "precentor" or "chant leader," a monastic office.

526 mNga' ris pa Tshul khrims 'od zer seems to have been the lama mentioned as "lnga rig paṇ chen" Tshul [khrims] 'od zer in an inscription to a thangka, now in Los Angeles, depicting three mandalas. See Pal 1983, 260. The inscription also mentions the patron as one rGyal mtshan 'od zer, who may be the dMar ston rGyal mtshan 'od zer who is mentioned in the *Blue Annals* as an important early master in the transmission of the *Kriyāsamuccaya* tradition in Tibet, evidently a student of Ngorchen Kunga Zangpo. See Roerich 1949–53, 1054. A certain mNga' ris rab 'byams Tshul khrims is also mentioned in Nash et al. 1994, in an inscription to a mandala thangka from the early fifteenth century: "... Donated by mNga' ris rab 'byams Tshul khrims to fulfill the vows [that is, in memory of?] Shes rab bzang po."

527 A brief biography of Kangyurwa appears in Zhwa lu Ri sbug sprul sku 1971, 329–337, and his full-length biography by the Fifth Dalai Lama is preserved at the end of vol. 4 (*nga*) of the *Lam 'bras slob bshad* biographies (Derge ed.).

528 Fifth Dalai Lama 1989–91, vol. 2, 176: *'phreng ba'i dkyil thang bzheng dgos yod pa sde pas dang dod kyis khur bzhes te las grwa 'dzugs pa'i sgo dod/ de'ang zhi ba'i rigs la sman thang pa dang khro bo dang dkyil thang la mkhyen brtse ba byang chub pas lugs gnyis ka ma nub pa zhig dgos rgyur sde pa bsod nams rab brtan gyi dus mkhyen brtse phyogs kyi ri mo bas go ma lo ba lta bus ha cang mang rgyu mi 'dug rung gong dkar chos*

*sde nas slob dpon gsang sngags mkhar pas
thog drangs mkhas bsgrags bos/ ma dpe kun
mkhyen rdo rje gdan pa'i thugs dam thang
ka la gtso bor bzung/ 'phreng ba kri ya gnyis
kyi rgya gzhung/ mnga' ris pa tshul 'od dang
paṇ chen thar rtse pa'i yig cha rnams mthun
mi mthun gyi go 'dur dge slong 'jam dbyangs
grags pa/ gnas gsar 'jam dbyangs bstan 'dzin/
phun tshogs legs 'byor/ dkar brag pa ngag
dbang byams pa bzhis byas nas mi gcig pa
rnams zha lu mkhan rin po cher dogs gcod
dang 'di gar yang dris shing gtso bo rgya
gzhung dang thang dpe btsan pa byas/ 'then
'khyer cung zad byung ba 'thor bur yig cha la
dmar mchan phab nas gzhis ka'i sgo lcog lho
mar 'dri ba'i do dam thon bya sgo nas kyis
byas te 'go btsugs pa lcags phag hor zla brgyad pa'i nang du gegs med par grub/.*

529 Ibid., vol. 2, 326.

530 Ibid., vol. 1, 218: *che mchog gi rag sku gcig
/ phyag drug pa sogs chos srung gi gser
sku bzhi / mtshan brgyad / brag dmar / ma
ning dang bcas pa'i thang kha yar rgyab tu
bzhengs pa'i mkhyen ris khyad mtshar gra
tshar bcu gcig /.*

531 Ibid., vol. 1, 716: *gong dkar chos sde nas ri
mo ba mkhas pa kha shas kyis brag sgo ka ki
na'i gnam rgyan la ngan song sbyong rgyud
kyi dkyil 'khor bcu gnyis dang dbus su tshe
dpag med lha dgyu'i dkyil 'khor rnams bris /.*

532 sDe srid 1990, 271.

533 sDe srid 1973, vol. 1, 420.4. The same work
later mentions (p. 421.2) a mixed group of
Menri and Khyenri artists (*bris pa sman
mkhyen 'dres pa*) and also (p. 421.4) the masters and ordinary painters in a mixed group
of Menri and Khyenri painters (*sman mkhyen
'dres pa'i dbu byings*).

534 Tibet House Society 1969, 17–23. Images
of the seven paintings of this set are available on the Himalyan Art Resource website,
www.himalayanart.org. See HAR nos.
72043–72050.

535 Tibet House Society 1969, 21.

536 See, for instance in Bryner 1956, in thangka
4, the ornate petals of the lotus seat of the
central buddha.

537 Bryner 1956, 17. See also Bryner 1956, 69:
"Two tankas in the St. Louis series are lacking, presumably bearing the other five tales."

538 Bryner 1956, 51.

539 One from the set was previously published on
cover of Peter Khoroche's book, citing it as
"Tibetan Tanka 197: 150. The Saint Louis Art
Museum, W. K. Bixby Fund."

540 Bryner 1956, 8.

541 Bryner 1956, 9.

542 According to Wikipedia, he started his
academic career in 1909 when he was
appointed assistant professor of Sanskrit in the
University of St. Petersburg and the member
of the Russian Committee for the Exploration
of Central and Eastern Asia. In 1912, he
studied Sanskrit at Harvard for some time. He
was in China when the Bolshevik Revolution
in Russia broke out. The government of the
new Estonian Republic, established in 1918
after the Versailles treaty, left him only a
small part of his inherited estate. He then
accepted an Estonian citizenship but remained
in Beijing. With the recommendation of his
friend Charles Eliot, then principal of the
University of Hong Kong, he was invited by
Hu Shi to teach Sanskrit, Tibetan, and History
of Indian Religion at Peking University, as
lecturer from 1918 to 1921 and as professor
from 1922 to 1929. He helped set up the Sino-
Indian Institute in Beijing in 1927. In 1928 he
was a visiting scholar at Harvard, helping the
Harvard-Yenching Institute to collect books.
Source: Serge Elisseeff, "Stael-Holstein's
Contribution to Asiatic Studies," *Harvard
Journal of Asiatic Studies* 3, no. 1 (April
1938), 1–8), https://en.wikipedia.org/wiki/
Alexander_von_Staël-Holstein.

543 Bryner 1956, 26.

544 Bryner 1956, 22.

545 Bryner 1956, 14.

546 Bryner 1956, 15.

547 According to my 1995 notes, the third painting I saw was the final one. It contained an
elaborate court scene of the patrons: lama, lay
nobleman, Sakyapa patrons, etc. Dimensions:
26 x 16 1/2 in. (66 x 42 cm).

548 For another member of the same set of
thangkas, see LACMA, Gift of Mr. and Mrs.
John G. Ford (M.84.219), cited in P. Pal, *Art
of Tibet*, expanded ed. (Los Angeles County
Museum of Art, 1990). See also Newark
Museum, acc. no. 85.411; Gift of Mr. and Mrs.
John Gilmore Ford.

549 Compare the depiction of tale numbers 32–34
in Bryner 1956, 66, tanka 13.

550 Rob Linrothe, personal communication. See
also HAR 73267-73269. http://www.hima-
layanart.org/search/set.cfm?setID=2958.

CHAPTER 12

551 Gendün Rabsal, himself a pre-1959 monk of
the monastery, mentions two hundred sixty
monks in his history; see *Gong dkar chos sde
dgon pa'i lo rgyus rags bsdus rin chen do
shal*, 11a.

552 On the branches of Gongkar Chöde, see D.
Jackson 2015b.

553 Kaḥ thog Si tu (2001 ed.), 145: *sngar grwa
stong phrag da lta brgya dang drug cu yin/.*

554 On the Khyenri artists during the Fifth Dalai
Lama's time, see chapter 11.

555 Everding 2009 (5. Auflage), 197. The grand
renovation of the main temple and the resizing
of the assembly hall is also reported by pre-
1959 monks of Gongkar Chöde; *inter alia*
Chögyal-la, interview, Dharamsala, 2010. For
the year 1939, the German expedition team
under Ernst Schäfer (1910–1992) reported
a population of 300 monks at Gongkar
Chöde; see German Federal Archive, Berlin-
Lichterfelde, R 135/56, *Routenbeschreibung*,
52 (here: Kongka Tschödeng)

556 See chapter 4, part A. The rendering of
the *Kalpalatā* was researched by Xiong
Wenbin; see Xiong Wenbin 熊文彬 2012, "A
Preliminary Study on Murals Representing
Stories from dPag bSam vKhri Shing
(Kalpalata) in the Assembly Hall of the Main
Temple, Gong dKar Chos sDe, Gong cKar
County, TAR," *China Tibetology* (Chinese
version), no. 2, 176–187.

557 D. Jackson 1996, 164.

558 Ngag dbang phun tshogs 1994, 52. The
restorations were still going on when
E. Schäfer and his team visited the
monastery in April 1939; German Federal
Archive, Berlin-Lichterfelde, R 135/56
Routenbeschreibung, 47 (here: Daitang).

559 Jamgön Ameshab (1597-1659) reports in
his master's biography that Drathang also
followed the Gongkar tradition of ritual dance;
see Ameshab, *Khyab bdag 'khor lo'i mgon
po dpal sa skya pa chen po sngags 'chang
bla ma thams cad mkhyen pa ngag dbang kun
dga' bsod nams grags pa rgyal mtshan dpal
bzang po'i rnam par thar pa ngo mtshar yon
tan rin po che'dus pa'i rgya mtsho'phel bar
byed pa phun tshogs bdud rtsi'i char rgyun*,
(Collected Works 2000, vol. 27), 709: *der yod
rnams dang phyogs nas 'dus pa'i skye bo khri
phrag tu longs pa la dbang mo che daag thugs
rje chen po'i bsgom lung gi bka' drin yang
stsal cing / grwa tshang pa dpon slob rnams
kyis kyang gong dkar rdo rje gdan gyi phyag
len dang mthun pa'i las mkhan ru 'dren dang
bcas pa'i gar 'cham dang /* […]

The German expedition identified Drathang's
sectarian affiliation by the design of the
temple's outer walls that showed the
characteristic blue-gray, red and white colors
of Sakya; see German Federal Archive, Berlin-
Lichterfelde, R 135/56, *Routenbeschreibung*,
47: "Ebenso ist die Westwand des großen
Klosters mit waagerechten, rotweißblauen
Streifen, graublauweiß im Wechsel,
angebracht. Es sind dies die Farben der Sakja-
Sekte und das Zeichen dafür, daß viele der
hiesigen Einwohner zu ihr gehören."

560 See sDe srid Sangs rgyas rgya mtsho, *mChod
sdong* (1990 ed.), 271.

561 On the temple's restoration and enlargement
under Palden Losang, see lHag tshing 2004, 88.

562 My findings on Yeshe Tendzin's background
and his life as an artist are largely derived
from interviews I conducted inside and
outside Tibet. I am particularly grateful to
Chögyal-la (Dharamsala, India) and Jampal
Khyentse (Swayambhunath, Nepal), who were
both monks at Gongkar Chöde prior to 1959.
Chögyal-la, in particular, spent hours with me
discussing the art and customs of Gongkar
Monastery before the Chinese occupation.
For Yeshe Tendzin's years in Indian exile I
am very thankful to his daughters, Ngawang
Lhamo (Boston) and Kalsang Kaiser
(Winterthur, Switzerland), who generously
shared with me some of their early memories.
Moreover, I would like to thank numerous
other informants from Lhokha, who remain
unnamed here but who have tremendously
helped in this investigation with various
means of assistance.

563 D. Jackson 1996, 164f.

564 Chögyal-la, interview, Dharamsala, 2010.

565 Ibid. In fact, an attendant (*nye gnas*) named
Tshultrim Gyatsho did accompany Khyentse
Wangpo on his pilgrimage to central Tibet.
He is mentioned several times in Khyentse
Wangpo's biography; see M. Akester 2012,
82, 139, and 144.

566 Chögyal-la, interview, Dharamsala, 2010.

567 Ibid. Chögyal-la also explained to me that Yeshe Tendzin belonged to Kunthang College of Gongkar; communication, 2016.

568 Ibid. Also D. Jackson 1996, 165.

569 Interview, Rawame Monastery, Tibet 2015.

570 Chögyal-la, interview, Dharamsala, 2010. Also D. Jackson 1996, 165.

571 Chögyal-la, interview, Dharamsala, 2010.

572 Ibid. Also D. Jackson 1996, 165.

573 Chögyal-la, interview, Dharamsala, 2010. On the establishment of a scriptural seminary at Gongkar Chöde before 1959, see also M. Fermer 2009, xv, xvi.

574 Chögyal-la, interview, Dharamsala, 2010. Also D. Jackson 1996, 165.

575 Interview, Dakpo Tratshang, Tibet 2015.

576 Chögyal-la, interview, Dharamsala, 2012; Jampal Khyentse, interview, Swayambhunath, 2010. Also D. Jackson 1996, 165.

577 According to Chögyal-la, interview, Dharamsala, 2012.

578 Jampal Khyentse, interview, Swayambhunath, 2010.

579 Interview with a Dungphü Chökhor monk, Dehradun, 2015. The restoration of Dungphü Chökhor in the late 1930s was reported by the Schäfer expedition; see German Federal Archive, Berlin-Lichterfelde, R 135/56, *Routenbeschreibung*, 50 (here: Dombang Dschökar). The extensive restoration was also noted by G. Tucci in his travel diary, see *To Lhasa and Beyond*, 148 (here: Dambuchokor).

580 Chögyal-la, interview, Dharamsala, 2012; Jampal Khyentse, interview, Swayambhunath, 2010.

581 Jampal Khyentse, interview, Swayambhunath, 2010.

582 Chögyal-la, interview, Dharamsala, 2010.

583 Ibid.

584 Ibid.

585 Chögyal-la, interview, Dharamsala, 2010; Jampal Khyentse, interview, Swayambhunath, 2010.

586 Ibid.

587 Interviews, Rawame and Lhasa, Tibet 2015.

588 See D. Jackson 1996, 165: "While there [i.e., in India] he also took a great interest in realistic Indian painting styles." Back at the monastery Yeshe Tendzin is said to have copied images that were brought from India; Interviews, Rawame and Lhasa, Tibet 2015.

589 Jampal Khyentse, interview, Swayambhunath, 2010.

590 Interview, Rawame, Tibet 2015. Jaksam Labrang also underwent extensive restoration in the late 1930s; see German Federal Archive, Berlin-Lichterfelde, R 135/56, *Routenbeschreibung*, 28 (here: Dschaksam). Here, the account from the German expedition conveys that the construction of a larger temple at Jaksam monastery was begun in 1938 ("Dschaksam ist ein größerer Klosterort mit z.Zt nur kleinem Klostertempel. Der Bau eines großen Tempels wurde im Jahr 1938 begonnen. Bauholz liegt am Eingang und in der Hauptstraße des Ortes, in dessen Mitte ein größerer Tschorten steht.").

591 I am deeply indebted to the contemporary painter Tshering Norbu for sharing with me a three-page handwritten draft on Uchen Tenpa Gyatsho. Most of the information given here is derived from this biographical sketch entitled *mKhyen lugs mkhas pa bstan pa rgya mtsho lags kyi lo rgyus mdor bsdus/*. Tshering Norbu, a native from Takar (rTa dkar grong mtsho) in Chushül, had studied under Tenpa Gyatsho's son Tshering (1929-2002) in the 1980s. He is an active painter of both Menri and Khyenri styles, and runs a thangka school in Lhasa, the Thangka Center of China (Krung go'i thang ga'i lte gnas).

592 As is summarized by his disciple Tshewang Dorje (1933–2002); cf. Tshewang Dorje 1998, 99f.: *lugs 'di'i [i.e., mkhyen lugs] 'byung khungs gong dkar mkhyen brtse'i slob ma mchog 'gyur lnga'i phyi ma bsod nams mchog ldan bya ba dang de'i slob ma nyes dus kyi ri mo'i sgyu rtsal mkhas can bstan pa rgya mtsho lags zhes grags pa kun du khyab pa de* [100] *yin/ khong gi bris pa'i ri mo dang ga dang ldebs bris rnams mkhyen lugs gtsang gtsang yin 'dug kho bos gong gsal sman thang gtsang ma bris mkhan rgan brtson 'grus lags dang / sman lugs sam e ris kyis bris lugs phyag bzhes mdzad mkhan rgan dpal ldan 'phrin las lags khong rnam gnyis sa nas 'bri srol khag gnyis kyi ri mo'i shes bya slob sbyong zhus pa dang / [...]*

593 Also Interview, Rawame, Tibet 2015.

594 Jampel Shedrub, communication, January 2016.

595 Tshering Norbu, *mKhyen lugs mkhas pa bstan pa rgya mtsho lags kyi lo rgyus mdor bsdus/*: [...] *sku phreng bcu gsum pas khyed kyi brtsams bya de dag la dmigs bsal khyad chos 'dug de'i nang brgya cha brgyad cu mkhyen lugs dang / brgya cha nyi shu sman lugs kyi khyad chos ldan 'dug pas/ lugs de la "mkhyen gsar" zhes thogs cig ces bka' slob yang gnang ba'i lo rgyus kyi shod srol 'dug.*

596 Interview, Dakpo Tratshang, Tibet 2015.

597 Interview, Dakpo Tratshang, Tibet 2015.

598 The ending of the inscription on the left wall of the entrance reads: [...] *lha bris dbu chen gong chos ye shes bstan 'dzin la sogs tshon gtong mi bzhi lag g.yog mi gnyis gnyer pa mar chen gnyis bcas kyis zla gcig zhag grang gnyis gsum tsam la bzhengs sgrub/.* The two inscription panels on the left and the right side of the inner sanctum's entrance mention all figures depicted, as well as the occasion of the restoration and the means through which this mural painting project was realized.

599 Interview, Dakpo Tratshang, Tibet 2015.

600 Chögyal-la, interview, Dharamsala, 2012.

601 Ibid.

602 Ibid. Also D. Jackson 1996, 168, n.358.

603 Tashi Tsering 2002, 25f.: *shes rig zlos gar tshogs pa'i bzo zhing 'brog gsum/ chos rgyal mes dbon rnam gsum gyi mdzad thang / rtse pho brang po tā la/ jo khang / bsam yas sogs kyi ras yol chen po dag kyang khong nas 'dra bris sam par bris lugs ltar bris yod/.*

604 See Tashi Tsering ed. 2010, 563, 564, 566, 568, 569, and 571.

605 Tashi Tsering 2002, 25: *btsan byol du 'byor rjes phyi lo 1961 nas bzung bod gzhung shes rig slob gra'i klog deb nang gi zhal thang gi ri mo'i thig rtsa dang mtshon don gtan 'bebs yod pa dang mi 'dra ba'i bla dpon mi sna dang / sa gnas/ 'tsho thabs mtshon pa'i ri mo mang che ba gong dkar phyag mdzod ye shes bstan 'dzin (1915-1971) lags nas bris gnang 'dug.*

606 See Clare Harris 1999, *In the Image of Tibet*, 50ff.

607 Chögyal-la, interview, Dharamsala, 2012. Also D. Jackson 1996, 168, n.358.

608 Chögyal-la, interview, Dharamsala, 2012.

609 Ibid.

610 Kalsang Kaiser, communication, 2014.

611 Chögyal-la, interview, Dharamsala, 2012.

612 Ngawang Lhamo, communication, 2014.

CHAPTER 13

613 In this chapter, I revise and expand an earlier paper. See Jackson 2003a.

614 Cf. S. Kossak in Kossak and Singer 1998, 26.

615 The basic method of dating was also summed up by Stoddard 1996, 27: "Most often the central figure is *not* identified (being too obviously well known at the time of painting), whereas all those surrounding him often are. The dating depends largely, of course, on the latest historical person represented. Although this only gives an approximate limit, we are now in a better position to judge from the style as well. Other inscriptions allow us an approximate upward date limit."

616 See for instance the results reached through lineage and inscription analysis in Jackson 1986, 1990, 1993, 1996, 1998, and 1999a. Since the mid-1990s, a few other scholars have noticed the potential usefulness of this method, including Singer 1994, Singer and Denwood 1997, and Tanaka 1996, 6–9. See also C. Luczanits 2001 and C. Luczanits' chapter 6 in D. Jackson 2011.

617 See for instance Jackson 1999, Jackson 2009 and Jackson 2015.

618 Jackson 2009, fig. 4.5.

619 Roerich 1949–53, 406–11.

620 Blo gter dbang po, *rGyud sde kun btus thob yig*, p. 165: *rtsa rgyud brtags pa gnyis pa la brten nas slob dpon mtsho skyes zhabs dang / nā ro/ mai tra'i man ngag mnga' bdag mar ston chen por bka' babs pa dgyes mdzad rdo rje lha dgu'i dkyil 'khor du ngag dbang yon tan rgya mtsho'i sgrub dkyil gyi steng nas dbang bzhi rdzogs par thob pa'i brgyud pa ni/ rdo rje 'chang / ye shes kyi mkha' 'gro ma/ byang sems rdo rje snying po/ ārya nā ga rdzu na/ ārya de ba/ tsandra kirti/ ma tanggi pa/ tai lo pradznyā bha dra/ nā ro dznyā na siddhi/ mar po lo tsā ba chos kyi blo gros/ rngog chos sku rdo rje/ rngog zhe sdang rdo rje/ rngog seng ge sgra/ rngog kun dga' rdo rje nas ngag*

621 See ibid., p. 142: *de gsum gas mar pa lo tsā
ba chos kyi dbang phyug /des rngog chos sku
rdo rje/ ba rong gi sba chag gnyis/ gnyis kas
rngog mdo sde'am zhe sdang rdo rje/ de nas
rngog kun dga' rdo rje/ rngog gzi brjid grags
pa/ rngog rin chen bzang po/ rngog chos kyi
rgyal mtshan/ rngog sangs rgyas yon tan/
rngog don grub dpal bzang / rngog byang
chub dpal/ khrus khang lo tsā ba bsod nams
rgya mtsho/ zhwa dmar bzhi pa spyan snga
chos grags/ (p. 143) ye shes dpal bzang po/
snar thang shes rab dpal ldan/ 'bri gung rin
chen phun tshogs/ drung rin chen dpal/ 'bri
gung chos rgyal phun tshogs/ rje btsun bkra
shis phun tshogs/ rig 'dzin chos kyi grags pa/
rje dkon mchog rin chen/ lho dkon mchog
phrin las rnam rgyal/ mkhas grub karma
chags med/ gsang phug padma kun dga'/
chags med mchog sprul phrin las dbang phyug
kun gzigs shes rab grags pa/ pad dbang sprul
sku bstan 'dzin don grub/ theg mchog nges
don bstan 'phel/ nges don gzhan phan bstan
pa rab rgyas/ ngag dbang yon tan rgya mtsho/
des bdag blo gter la'am/ yang na/ rig 'dzin
chos kyi grags pa nas/ rje dkon mchog lhun
grub/ dkon mchog phrin las bzang po/ don
grub chos kyi rgyal po/ si tu chos kyi 'byung
gnas/ rje dbon karma nges legs bstan 'dzin/
tshe dbang kun khyab/ rje dbon mchog sprul
karma rin chen/ khra leb ye shes nyi ma/ ngag
dbang yon tan rgya mtsho/ des so//.*

622 Singer 1993, n.p.

623 See Gö Lotsāwa, *Blue Annals*, in Roerich
1949–53, 450.

624 See also Tanaka and Tamashige 2004, pl. 11,
a Hevajra of the Ngok tradition that portrays
a lineage that continues thirteen generations
after Marpa. I have documented a much later
Ngok and Karma Kagyü lineage in Jackson
2009, fig. 4.9.

625 Essen and Thingo 1989, vol. 2, no. 331.

626 On Drigung lineage thangkas, see Jackson
2015, chaps. 7 and 8; see also Jackson 1996,
343, pl. 64; and Jackson 2002.

627 Jackson 1996, 343, pl. 64.

628 Wrongly identifying the names in inscriptions
is worse than no inscriptions at all.

629 The controversy surrounding this thangka was
described at some length by Brauen 2003.

630 Dr. Brauen kindly sent me black-and-white
photographs of many details of the painting,
including most of the inscriptions.

631 For the complete lineage down to Könchok
Phel, see appendix H.

632 For later continuations of important sets in
the late sixteenth century, see Jackson 1996,
78.

633 In some respects—including the repeated
appearance of Müchen as teacher of both main
figures—the painting's structure resembles
one that portrays the Ngor abbots Kunga
Wangchuk and Gorampa, in the Los Angeles
County Museum of Art (Fig. 13.12).

634 Cf. also the similar gold details of: body
nimbuses of main figures (1560s–1590s) in
Jackson 2010, fig. 8.21 (HAR 457); and head

nimbus of main figure in Essen and Thingo
1989, vol. 2, no. II–229.

635 Cf. Brauen 2003, 74.

636 Cf. Brauen 2003, 75.

637 Cf. Brauen 2003, 88, no. 2.

638 In Jackson 1990 I used internal evidence to
date several earlier (late-fifteenth-century) and
later Ngorpa thangkas. For further references
to internally dated later Ngorpa thangkas,
see Jackson 1996, 87, note 185; and Jackson
2010, chap. 8.

639 See D. Jackson 1996, 77–82.

640 See D. Jackson 2010, chapter 8.

641 That was documented in Jackson 1996, section II, chaps. 3 and 4.

642 See, for instance, Jackson 1996, 283 and
371–74.

643 Jackson 1996, 82, and pl. 1. On that and other
later dated Ngorpa thangkas, see Jackson
1996, 87, note 185.

644 Jackson 1996.

645 Cf. Brauen 2003, 88, no. 2.

646 Barzun and Graff 1970, 155: "In history,
as in life critically considered, *truth rests
not on possibility nor on plausibility but on
Probability.*" By coincidence, a similarly
less stringent burden of proof also applies in
civil suits, at least in countries that inherited
English legal traditions.

647 Ernst 2001, 905.

648 See Bruce-Gardner 1998, 198.

649 Ernst 2001, 902.

650 See Béguin 1995, 21. Some differences in
gold, specifically for the figure wrongly called
"sMra ba'i seng ge" (Lha mchog seng ge).
Perhaps some early (or foreign) painters used
indigo and indigo-yellow instead of azurite
and malachite.

651 See D. Jackson 2010, chapter 2.

Appendixes

652 Kaḥ thog Si tu 1972, 229.5–230.2 (fol.
115a-b).

653 See Khempo Sangyay Tenzin and Gomchen
Oleshey 1975, no. 11.

654 Ibid., no. 14.

655 Ibid., no. 36.

656 Ibid., no. 24.

657 Ibid., no. 18.

658 Ibid., no. 42.

659 Fifth Dalai Lama, *gSan yig*, vol. 3, p. 106b:
*des mdzad pa'i 'khrul grol (ri) gsal byed mun
sel sgron me rnams thob pa las ri'i rtags yod
pa'i dbang lung dang rtags gang yang med
pa'i chos skor rnams kyi bka' ma'i brgyud pa
ni/ chos sku kun bzang yab yum/ longs sku rigs
lnga yab yum/ sprul sku sems dpa' bcu drug/
ston pa dga' rab rdo rje/ slob dpon 'jam dpal
bshes gnyen/ gu ru shrī sidha/ dznyā na su*

*tra/ pan chen bi mā la mi tra/ nyang ban ting
'dzin bzang po/ spas blo gros dbang phyug/
('jam dbyangs mkhyen brtse'i gsan yig na 'di'i
tshab la lce btsun 'dug pa phyag bris nor pa
las gzhan pa'i gnad yod med dpyad)/ snod
ldan rin cen 'bar ba/ ldang ma lhun gyi rgyal
mtshan/ lce btsun seng ge dbang phyug/ ...
yang rgyud lnga'i lung brgyud lugs gcig ni/
lce btsun seng ge dbang phyug nas/ rgyal ba
zhang ston/ bla ma nyi 'bum/ gu ru jo 'ber/
seng ge rgya pa/ grub thob me long rdo rje/
bla ma nam mkha' rdo rje/ rigs 'dzin ku ma
rā dza/ sprul sku klong chen rab 'byams/ drin
cen chos dbang bzang po/ byang sems chos
nyid rang grol/ gu ru shākya bzang po/ gu ru
buddha shrī/ gu ru chos kyi dbang po/ rigs
'dzin legs ldan rje man gong ltar ro//.*

660 Fifth Dalai Lama, *gSan yig*, vol. 3, 103a:
*dbang dang rgyud bcu bdun gyi brgyud pa ni/
chos sku kun tu bzang po/ longs sku zhi khro
rab 'byams/ sprul sku rdo rje 'chang chen/
rdo rje sems dpa'/ gsang bdag phyag na rdo
rje/ rigs 'dzin dga' rab rdo rje/ slob dpon 'jam
dpal bshes gnyen/ mkhas pa shrī sidha/ slob
dpon dznyā na su tra/ pan chen bi ma ia mi
tra/ nyang ban ting 'dzin bzang po/ gnas brtan
ldang ma lhun rgyal/ lce btsun seng ge dbang
phyug/ sprul sku rgyal ba zhang ston bkra shis
rdo rje/ mkhas pa nyi ma 'bum/ chos bdag gu
ru jo 'ber/ 'khrul zhig seng ge rgyab pa/ grub
chen me long rdo rje/ rigs 'dzin ku ma rā dza/
kun mkhyen klong chen rab 'byams/.*

661 Fifth Dalai Lama 1971, vol. 3, 76b: *pen chen
chos kyi shes rab/ don grub legs pa dpal 'bar/
dbu mdzad don grub dpal ba/ rje bstan 'dzin
grags pa/ mkhas mchog mdo sngags bstan
'dzin/ mang thos dam chos bzang po/ rje
'phrin las lhun grub/ drin can gter bdag gling
ba/ des bdag la/o//. See also ibid., vol. 3, 88b:
mtshungs med sna tshogs rang grol/ de sras
kun dga' grags pa/ bla ma kun dga' rdo rje/
rje btsun mdo sngags bstan 'dzin/ rigs 'dzin
'phrin las lhun grub/ chos rgyal gter bdag
gling pa/ des bdag za hor bande la'o//.*

662 This may be the missing fifth Shambhala
king, Chos rgyal Lha yi dbang phyug.

663 See Jackson 1996, 272 and note 631.

664 Kaḥ thog Si tu 1972, 8.6 (4b).

665 In Jackson 1996, pls. 57 and 58, the inscriptions relating to the minor figures were acci-
dentally reversed. In pl. 57, I further mistook
the main figure, Sucandra (Tib. Zla ba bzang
po or Zla bzang), for the fourteenth Kalkin,
whose Tibetan name is Zla ba'i 'od. Cf. Rubin
no. 127 (WT cat. no. 55), which portrays
from another set Rūudracakra, a late Kalkin
(Rigs ldan) of Shambhala. This small painting
portrays a king of Shambhala with sword
and shield, who is identified by an incomplete inscription as the king Rūdracakra. The
thangka shows strong similarities with certain
other Si tu Paṇ chen commissions. Inscription
(on throne): *rgyal po rud....*

666 List drawn from Tibetan Buddhist
Resource Center, sixteen sthaviras, TBRC
Resource ID T1154. http://www.tbrc.
org/?locale=en#!rid=T1154.

667 Tenpa Rabten and Ngawang Jigme 2003, 565.
The dictionary entry begins: *tshe dbang rdo
rje zhes pa ni bris 'bur brkos gsum la rnga'
brnyes pa'i mkhas pa zhig yin/.*

668 See Tshe dbang rdo rje 1999.

669 bsTan pa rab brtan 2007, 226–28.

670 Vitali 1990 asserts that Rangjung Dorje supervised the *mdzad brgya* depiction in Shalu murals, which I discussed in Jackson 1996, 133, note 249. Vitali based himself on and cites Kahthok Situ's account.

671 See Tāranātha, *sTon pa shākya'i dbang po'i mdzad pa brgya pa'i bris yig rje btsun kun snying gis mdzad pa* (rTag brtan phun tshongs gling gi par ma); TBRC no. W22277. Leh: C. Namgyal and Tsewang Taru, 1982–1987 (Block Print). See also Tāranātha, *sTon pa shākya'i dbang po'i mdzad pa brgya pa'i bris yig*, Tā ra nā tha gSung 'bum (dpe bsdur ma); TBRC no. W1PD45495, 8. Pe cin: Krung go'i bod rig pa dpe skrun khang, 2008. dPal brt-segs bod yig dpe rnying zhib 'jug khang nas bsgrigs.

672 See Lauf 1976, 116, pl. 37, "A sTag lung abbot."

673 Pal 1983, 94 (P27, plate 30).

BIBLIOGRAPHY

Ācārya Ngawang Samten: *See* Ngawang Samten, Ācārya.

Akester, Matthew 2012. *The life of Jamyang Khyentsé Wangpo.* New Delhi: Shechen Publications.

Alexander, André. 2005. *The Temples of Lhasa: Tibetan Buddhist Architecture from the 7th to the 21st centuries.* Chicago: Serindia.

Ameshab (A mes zhabs Ngag dbang kun dga' bsod nams, 'Jam mgon). 1975. *'Dzam gling byang phyogs kyi thub pa'i rgyal tshab chen po dpal ldan sa skya pa'i gdung rabs rin po che ji ltar byon pa'i tshul gyi rnam par thar pa ngo mtshar rin po che'i bang mdzod dgos 'dod kun 'byung* [short title: *Sa skya gdung rabs chen mo* (Genealogy of the Sakya 'Khon Family)]. Delhi: Tashi Dorji.

———. 1979. *dPal rdo rje nag po chen po'i zab mo'i chos skor rnams byung ba'i tshul legs par bshad pa bstan srung chos kun gsal ba'i nyin byed.* 2 vols. New Delhi: T. G. Dhongthog Rinpoche.

———. 1980. *Srid pa gsum gyi bla ma dpal sa skya pa chen po sngags 'chang ngag gi dbang po kun dga' rin chen gyi rnam par thar pa ngo mtshar rgya mtsho.* MS, dbu can. 218 fols. Indian ed.. Rajpur: T. G. Dhongthog Rinpoche.

———. 1985. *dPal ldan sa skya pa'i bstan 'dzin ngor rdzong rnam gnyis kyi gsung ngag rin po che'i phyag len gyi rim pa 'ga' zhig las brtsams te so so'i bzhed srol rnams legs par bshad pa lugs gnyis zab don gsal ba'i nyin byed.* Rajpur: Sakya College.

———. 1986, *Sa skya gdung rabs chen mo.* Beijing: Mi rigs dpe skrun khang.

Ameshab, *mGon po chos 'byung.* See Ameshab 1979.

———. 2000. *dPal sa skya pa chen po sngags 'chang thams cad mkhyen pa ngag dbang kun dga' bsod nams kyi gsung 'bum.* [Collected Works]. 29 vols. Kathmandu: rGyal yongs sa chen dpe skrun khang.

Awang Gesang 1999. *Zangzu Zhuangshi Tu'an Yishi. The Art of Tibetan Decoration.* Lhasa: Tibet People's Publishing House.

Bartholomew, Terese Tse, Patricia Berger, and Robert Clark. 2003. *Tibet: Treasures from the Roof of the World.* Santa Ana, CA: Bowers Museum of Cultural Art.

Barzun, Jacques, and Henry F. Graff. 1970. *The Modern Researcher.* Rev. ed. New York: Harcourt, Brace and World.

Batchelor, Stephen. 1987. *The Tibet Guide.* London: Wisdom.

Béguin, Gilles, ed. 1977. *Tibet: Kunst des Buddhismus.* Paris: Réunion des musées nationaux; Munich: Ausstellungsleitung Haus der Kunst München.

———. 1990. *Art ésotérique de l Himalaya. Catalogue de la donation Lionel Fournier.* Paris: Réunion des Musées Nationaux.

———. 1994. *Le Tibet de Jean Mansion: Legs au musée des Arts asiatiques Guimet.* Paris: Éditions Findakly.

———. 1995. *Les peintures du Bouddhisme tibétain.* Paris: Réunion des Musées Nationaux.

Berger, Patricia. 2003. "Diplomatic Gifts." In *Tibet: Treasures from the Roof of the World,* by Terese Tse Bartholomew, Patricia Berger, and Robert Clark. Santa Ana, CA: Bowers Museum of Cultural Art.

Bhikkhu Ñāṇamoli. 2001. *The Life of the Buddha According to the Pali Canon.* Onalaska, WA: BPS Pariyatti Editions.

Binczik, Angelika, and Roland Fischer. 2002. *Verborgene Schätze aus Ladakh: Hidden Treasures from Ladakh.* München: Otter Verlag.

Blo gter dbang po, Ngor dPon slob. 1971. *rGyud sde rin po che kun las btus pa'i thob yig de bzhin gshegs pa thams cad kyi gsang ba ma lus pa gcig tu 'dus pa rdo rje rin po che'i za ma tog.* Vols. 29 and 30 in *rGyud sde rin po che kun las btus pa,* compiled by Blo gter dbang po. 30 vols. Delhi.

Bod ljongs po ta la do dam khru'u [Tibetan Administrative Office of the Potala]. 1996. *Gangs ljongs gnas mchog pho brang po ta la* [The Potala Holy Palace in the Snow Land]. Beijing: Krung go yul skor dpe skrun khang, China Travel and Tourism Press.

Brauen, Martin. 2003. "Forgery, Genuine or Painted Over: On the Impossibility of Dating a Thangka Exactly." In *Dating Tibetan Art: Essays on the Possibilities and Impossibilities of Chronology from the Lempertz Symposium, Cologne,* Contributions to Tibetan Studies 3, ed. I. Kreide-Damani, 73–89. Wiesbaden: Dr. Ludwig Reichert Verlag.

Brent, Peter. 1976. *Genghis Khan. The Rise, Authority and Decline of Mongol Power.* New York: McGraw-Hill.

Bruce-Gardner, Robert. 1998. "Realizations: Reflections on Technique in Early Central Tibetan Painting." In *Sacred Visions, Early Paintings from Central Tibet,* edited by Steven M. Kossak and Jane Casey Singer, 193–205. New York: Metropolitan Museum of Art.

Bryner, Edna. 1956. *Thirteen Tibetan Tankas.* Indian Hills, CO: Falcon's Wing.

bsTan 'dzin padma rgyal mtshan, Fourth Che tshang sPrul sku. 1977. *Nges don bstan pa'i snying po mgon po 'bri gung pa chen po'i gdan rabs chos kyi 'byung tshul gser gyi phreng ba.* Bir: D. Tsondu Senghe.

bsTan pa rab brtan. 2007. *Bod kyi srol rgyun mdzes rtsal las bris 'bur gnyis kyi byung ba mdo tsam brjod pa.* Pe cing: Mi rigs dpe skrun khang.

Burawoy, Robert 1976. *Peinture Lamaique.* Paris: Galerie Robert Burawoy.

Casey, Jane. 2014. "Buddhist Initiation Paintings from the Yuan Court (1271–1368) in the Sino-Himalayan Style." *Asian Art,* June 16. Accessed December 2, 2015. http://www.asianart.com/articles/tsakli-casey/index.html.

Cassinelli, C. W., and Robert B. Ekvall. 1969. *A Tibetan Principality: The Political System of Sa sKya.* Ithaca: Cornell University.

Caumanns, Volker. 2015. *Shākya-mchog-ldan, Mahāpaṇḍita des Klosters gSer-mdog-can. Leben und Werk nach den tibetischen Quellen.* Wiesbaden: Dr. Ludwig Reichert Verlag.

Chan, Victor. 1994. *Tibet Handbook: A Pilgrimage Guide.* Chico, CA: Moon.

Chandra, Lokesh. 1991. *Buddhist Iconography.* Śata-piṭaka Series 342. New Delhi: International Academy of Indian Culture.

Chandra, Lokesh, ed. 1972. *Buddha in Chinese Woodcuts.* Śata-piṭaka Series 98. New Delhi: International Academy of Indian Culture.

Chogay Trichen. 1979. *Gateway to the Temple: Manual of Tibetan Monastic Customs, Art, Building and Celebrations.* Bibliotheca Himalayica, Series III, vol. 12. Kathmandu: Ratna Pustak Bhandar.

Chogyam Trungpa 1975. See Trungpa, Chogyam 1975.

Chos 'phel 2002. *Gangs can ljongs kyi gnas bshad lam yig gsar ma.* 2 vols. Beijing: Mi rigs dpe skrun khang.

Dagyab, L. S. 1977. *Tibetan Religious Art*. 2 vols. Wiesbaden: Otto Harrassowitz.

Das, Sarat Chandra. 2002. *Journey to Lhasa and Central Tibet*. Edited by William Rockhill. Reprint. New Delhi: Paljor. First published 1970.

Debreczeny, Karl 2012. *The Black Hat Eccentric: Artistic Visions of the Tenth Karma*pa. New York: Rubin Museum of Art.

Demo, Ngawang Gelek. 1979. *First Exhibition in the New Tibet House*. Assisted by Gyaltsen Yeshey and Ngawang Phuntshok, edited by N. Ribush and Trisha Donnelly. New Delhi: Tibet House.

De'u dmar dge bshes bsTan 'dzin phun tshogs. *Kun gsal tshon gyi las rim me tog mdangs ster 'ja' 'od 'bum byin*. Photocopy of *dbu med mgo tshem* manuscript, 90 fols. Library of Mr. Tashi Tsering.

———. 1970. "Rab gnas kyi rgyas bshad 'jam mgon dgyes pa'i bzhad gad phun tshogs bkra shis cha brgyad." In *Rab gnas rgyas bshad*, 1–62. Palampur, Himachal Pradesh, India: Sungrab Nyamso Gyunpel Parkhang, Tibetan Craft Community.

Dowman, Keith. 1988. *The Power-Places of Central Tibet, The Pilgrim's Guide*. London: Routledge and Kegan Paul.

dPa' bo gTsug lag phreng ba. *mKhas pa'i dga' ston* (1986 ed.).

dPa' bo gTsug lag phreng ba. *Dam pa'i chos kyi 'khor lo bsgyur ba rnams kyi byung ba gsal bar byed pa mkhas pa'i dga' ston* [History of Buddhism and the Karma Kagyü School]. Beijing: Mi rigs dpe skrun khang, 1985. 2 vols.

Dung dkar Blo bzang 'phrin las. 2002. *Dung dkar tshig mdzod chen mo*. Beijing: Krung go'i bod rig pa dpe skrun khang.

Eberhard, Wolfram 1990. *Times Dictionary of Chinese Symbols: An Essential Guide to the Hidden Symbols in Chinese Art, Customs and Beliefs*. Singapore: Federal Publications.

Ehrhard, Franz-Karl. 2002. *Life and Travels of Lo-chen bSod-nams rgya-mtsho*. Lumbini: Lumbini International Research Institute.

———. 2004. "Spiritual Relationships between Rulers and Preceptors: The Three Journeys of Vanaratna (1384–1468) to Tibet." In *The Relationship Between Religion and State (chos srid zung 'brel) in Traditional Tibet*, edited by Christoph Cüppers, 245–266. Lumbini: Lumbini International Research Institute.

Ernst, Richard R. 2001. "Arts and Sciences. A Personal Perspective if Tibetan Painting." *Chimia* 55, no. 11: 900–914.

———. 2004. "Science and Arts." *EPR Newsletter* 14, nos. 1–2: 15–18.

Essen, Gerd-Wolfgang, and Tsering Tashi Thingo. 1989. *Die Götter des Himalaya: Buddhistische Kunst Tibets. Die Sammlung Gerd-Wolfgang Essen*. 2 vols. Munich: Prestel-Verlag.

Everding, Karl-Heinz. 1993. *Tibet: Lamaistische Klosterkulturen, nomadische Lebensformen und bäuerlicher Alltag auf dem "Dach der Welt."* Köln: DuMont Buchverlag. Also rev. ed. 2001, 2009.

Fermer, Mathias. 2009. "The Life and Works of Gong dkar rDo rje gdan pa Kun dga' rnam rgyal (1432–1496)." Unpublished MA thesis, Department of Indian and Tibetan Studies, University of Hamburg.

Fifth Dalai Lama (Ngag dbang blo bzang rgya mtsho). 1971. *Record of Teachings Received* [*Zab pa dang rgya che ba'i dam pa'i chos kyi thob yig gang ga'i chu rgyun*]. 4 vols. Delhi: Nechung and Lhakhar.

———. 1979. *Zur thams cad mkhyen pa chos dbyings rang grol gyi rnam thar theg mchog bstan pa'i shing rta*. Thimphu: Kunzang Topgyal. 443 pages. [Also xylographic ed., collected works of Fifth Dalai Lama, edited by Zhol, reprint, Sikkim Institute of Tibetology, Gangtok, vol. 9 (*ta*), ff. 1–121.]

———. 1983. *Za hor gyi ban de ngag dbang blo bzang rgya mtsho'i 'di snang 'khrul pa'i rol rtsed rtogs brjod kyi tshul du bkod pa du kū la' gos bzang*. [His autobiography.] Reprint; completed and edited by sDe srid Sangs rgyas rgya mtsho; original edited by 'Bras spungs dGa' ldan pho brang. 3 vols. Dolanji: Tashi Dorje.

———. 1989–91. *Za hor gyi ban de ngag dbang blo bzang rgya mtsho'i 'di snang 'khrul pa'i rol rtsed rtogs brjod kyi tshul du bkod pa du kū la' gos bzang*. [His autobiography.] 3 vols. Beijing: Bod ljongs mi dmangs dpe skrun khang.

Fisher, Robert E. 1997. *Art of Tibet*. London: Thames and Hudson.

Fujita, Hiroki. 1984. *Tibetan Buddhist Art*. Tokyo: Hakusuisha.

Gangs ljongs chol kha gsum du gnas pa'i dpal sa skya'i ring lugs 'dzin pa'i dgon sde dang/ ri khrod/ lha khang (gnas shul) khag gi mtshan byang dkar chag gzig bder bkod pa. Gangs ljongs sa skya pa. Lhasa: gNa' deng lo rgyus rig gnas 'tshol bsdu tshogs chung, 2006.

Gega Lama. 1983. *Principles of Tibetan Art: Illustrations and Explanations of Buddhist Iconography and Iconometry According to the Karma Gardri School*. 2 vols. Translated by Karma Chöchi Nyima (Richard Barron). Darjeeling: Jamyang Singe.

Gendün Rabsal (dGe 'dun rab gsal). *Gong dkar chos sde dgon pa'i lo rgyus rags bsdus rin chen do zhal* [Brief history of Gongkar Chöde Monastery], folios 1a–19, *dbu chen* manuscript.

Glo bo mKhan chen bSod nams lhun grub. *rJe btsun sa skya pa'i yin thang dngos la zhib tu gzigs tshul*. Tibetan ms 44, vol. *ka*, fols. 144a–146a. Tōyō Bunko library, Tokyo.

Gongkar Trinle Namgyal (Gong dkar 'Phrin las rnam rgyal). *Thob yig bum pa bzang po* [Record of Teachings Received]. 244 fols., *dbu med*-manuscript [Also 2008 ed., *Gong dkar bla ma 'phrin las rnam rgyal gyi gsan yig*. Kathmandu: rGyal yongs sa chen dpe skrun khang.]

Gongkar Dorjedenpa Kunga Namgyal (Gong dkar rdo rje gdan pa Kun dga' rnam rgyal) 2005. *rDzong pa kun dga' rnam rgyal gyi gsan yig*. [Record of Teachings Received]. Kathmandu: rGyal yongs sa chen dpe skrun khang.

Gongkar Dorjedenpa Kunga Namgyal (Gong dkar rdo rje gdan pa Kun dga' rnam rgyal), *rJe btsun sa skya pa gong ma rnams la zhu ba'i 'phrin yig* [Petition to the Venerable Sakya Founders]. In *rDzong pa kun dga' rnam rgyal gyi gsan yig*, 444–472. Kathmandu: rGyal yongs sa chen dpe skrun khang, 2005.

Gyatön Changchup Wangyal (rGya ston Byang chub dbang rgyal). 2001. *Chos kyi rje thams cad mkhyen pa rdo rje gdan pa chen po kun dga' rnam rgyal dpal bzang po'i rnam par thar pa ngo mtshar rin po che'i gter mdzod*. Lhasa: Shang kang then ma dpe skrun khang.

Gyurme Dorje. 1999. *Tibet Handbook*. Chicago: Passport.

———. 2004. *Tibet Handbook with Bhutan*. Bath: Footprint Handbooks. Rev. 3rd ed. First published 1996.

Harris, Clare 1999. *In the Image of Tibet*. London: Reaktion Books.

Heller, Amy. 1999. *Tibetan Art: Tracing the Development of Spiritual Ideals and Art in Tibet, 600–2000*. Woodbridge, Suffolk, UK: Antique Collector's Club.

———. 2012. "Fourteen Thangkas of the 'Brug pa bKa' brgyud pa: an 18th century series of thangka linking Tibet and Bhutan in the Zimmerman Family Collection." *Asian Art*. Accessed December 2, 2015. http://www.asianart.com/articles/heller4/.

Henss, Michael. 1997. "The Woven Image: Tibeto-Chinese Textile Thangkas of the Yuan and Early Ming Dynasties." *Orientations*, November, 26–39.

———. 2008. *Buddhist Art in Tibet: New Insights and Ancient Treasures*. Ulm: Fabri Verlag.

———. 2014. *The Cultural Monuments of Tibet*. 2 vols. Munich: Prestel.

Huntington, John C. 1968. "The Styles and Stylistic Sources of Tibetan Painting." PhD dissertation, University of California, Los Angeles.

———. 1980. Review of *Secret Revelation of Tibetan Thangkas: Picture Mediation and Interpretation of Lamaist Cult Paintings* by Detlef-Ingo Lauf. *Journal of the American Oriental Society* 100, no. 3: 326–8.

Huntington, John C., and Dina Bangdel. 2003. *The Circle of Bliss: Buddhist Meditational Art*. Columbus: Columbus Museum of Art; Chicago: Serindia.

Huntington, Susan L., and John C. Huntington. 1990. *Leaves from the Bodhi Tree: The Art of Pāla India (8th–12th centuries) and its International Legacy*. Seattle and London: Dayton Art Institute in association with the University of Washington.

Jackson, David. 1983. "Notes on Two Early Printed Editions of Sa-skya-pa Works." *Tibet Journal* 8.2: 3–24.

———. 1984. *Tibetan Thangka Painting: Methods and Materials*. London: Serindia.[1988 rev. ed., in collaboration with J. Jackson.]

———. 1986. "A Painting of Sa-skya-pa Masters from an Old Ngor-pa Series of Lam 'bras Thangkas." *Berliner Indologische Studien* 2: 181–191.

———. 1987. *The Entrance Gate for the Wise (Section III): Sa-skya Paṇḍita on Indian and Tibetan Traditions of Pramāṇa and Philosophical Debate*. Wiener Studien zur Tibetologie und Buddhismuskunde 17. 2 parts. Vienna: Arbeitskreis für tibetische und buddhistische Studien Universität Wien.

———. 1989. "More on the Old dGa'-ldan and Gong-dkar-ba Xylographic Editions." *Studies in Central and East Asian Religions* 2: 1–18.

———. 1990. "The Identification of Individual Masters in Paintings of Sa-skya-pa Lineages." In T. Skorupski, ed., *Indo-Tibetan Studies*. Buddhica Britannica, Series Continua, 2: 129–144. Tring: The Institute of Buddhist Studies.

———. 1993. "Apropos a Recent Tibetan Art Catalogue." *Wiener Zeitschrift für die Kunde Südasiens*. 37: 109–130.

———. 1996. *A History of Tibetan Painting: The Great Painters and Their Traditions*. Beiträge zur Kultur- und Geistesgeschichte Asiens, no. 15. Vienna: Verlag der Österreichischen Akademie der Wissenschaften.

———. 1997. "Chronological Notes on the Founding Masters of Tibetan Painting Traditions." In *Tibetan Art: Towards a Definition of Style*, edited by Jane Casey Singer and Philip Denwood, 254–261. London: Laurence King.

———. 1998. "Traditions artistiques des premiers Sa-skya-pa: sources écrits et peintures encore existantes." *Annuaire EPHE, Section sciences religieuses* 106 (1997–98), 101–107.

———. 1999a. "Some Karma Kagyupa Paintings in the Rubin Collections." In Marylin M. Rhie and Robert A. F. Thurman, *Worlds of Transformation: Tibetan Art of Wisdom and Compassion*, pp. 75–127.

———. 1999b. "Tibetische Thangkas deuten. Teil 1: Die Hierarchie der Anordnung." *Tibet und Buddhismus* [Hamburg], 50-3: 22–27. "Tibetische Thangkas deuten, Teil 2: Übertragungslinien und Anordnung." *Tibet und Buddhismus*, 50-4: 16–21.

———. 2002. "Lama Yeshe Jamyang of Nyurla, Ladakh: The Last Painter of the 'Bri gung Tradition." *Tibet Journal* 27, 153–176.

———. 2003a. "The Dating of Tibetan Paintings is Perfectly Possible—Though Not Always Perfectly Exact." In *Dating Tibetan Art: Essays on the Possibilities and Impossibilities of Chronology from the Lempertz Symposium, Cologne*, edited by

I. Kreide-Damani, 91–112. Wiesbaden: Dr. Ludwig Reichert Verlag.

———. 2003b. *A Saint in Seattle: The Life of the Tibetan Mystic Dezhung Rinpoche*. Boston: Wisdom.

———. 2005a. "Recent Painting Traditions of Ladakh: Central Tibetan Styles in Far Western Tibet." In *Ladakh: Culture at the Crossroads*, edited by Monisha Ahmed and Clare Harris. *Marg* 57, no. 1 (2005): 104–121.

———. 2005b. "Spuren Târanâthas und seiner Präexistenzen: Malereien aus der Jo nang pa-Schule des tibetischen Buddhismus." In *Die Welt des tibetischen Buddhismus*, edited by S. Knödel et al., Mitteilungen aus dem Museum für Völkerkunde Hamburg, Neue Folge Band 36 (2005): 611–665.

———. 2005c. "Lineages and Structure in Tibetan Buddhist Painting: Principles and Practice of an Ancient Sacred Choreography." *Journal of the International Association of Tibetan Studies*, vol. 1, pp. 1–40.

———. 2007. "Painting Styles in the Rubin Collection: Identifications and Clarifications." In *The Pandita and the Siddha: Tibetan Studies in Honor of E. Gene Smith*, edited by Ramon N. Prats, 98–109. Dharamshala: Amnye Machen Institute.

———. 2008. "'Brug pa bKa' brgyud and Bhutanese Painting: Preliminary Findings on History and Iconography." In *Written Treasures of the Past: Mirror of the Past and Bridge to the Future*, vol. 2, edited by John Ardussi and Sonam Tobgay, 205–231. Thimphu: National Library of Bhutan.

———. 2009. *Patron and Painter: Situ Panchen and the Revival of the Encampment Style*. New York: Rubin Museum of Art.

———. 2010. *The Nepalese Legacy in Tibetan Painting*. New York: Rubin Museum of Art.

———. 2011. *Mirror of the Buddha: Early Portraits from Tibet*. New York: Rubin Museum of Art.

———. 2012. *The Place of Provenance: Regional Styles in Tibetan Painting*. New York: Rubin Museum of Art.

———. 2015. *Painting Traditions of the Drigung Kagyu School*. New York: Rubin Museum of Art.

———. 2015b. "Branch Monasteries of Gongkar Dorjeden and Phenpo Nalendra, Two Sakya Convents in Central Tibet." In Czaja, Olaf and Guntram Hazod eds., 2015, *The Illuminating Mirror: Tibetan Studies in Honour of Per K. Sørensen on the Occasion of his 65th Birthday*. Wiesbaden: Reichert Verlag.

'Jam dpal rdo rje. *Gso byed bdud rtsi'I 'khrul med ngos 'dzin gso rig me long du rnam par shar ba mdzes mtshar mig rgyan*. Śata-piṭaka Series, vol. 82. New Delhi: 1971.

'Jigs med grags pa. *rGyal rtse chos rgyal gyi rnam par thar pa dad pa'i lo thog dngos grub gyi char 'bebs*. Bod ljongs mi dmangs dpe skrun khang, 1987.

Jonang Kunga Drölchok (Kun dga' grol mchog, Jo nang). *dPal ldan bla ma 'jam pa'i dbyangs kyis [sic] rnam par thar pa legs bshad khyad par gsum ldan* [Biography of Lowo Khenchen]. MS, 125 fols.

Jonang Tāranātha (Jo nang Tā ra nā tha). 2008. *Jo nang rje btsun tā ra nā tha'i gsung bum dpe bsdur ma*. [Collected Works]. 45 vols. Pe cin: Krung go'i bod rig pa dpe skrun khang.

Kachen Losang Phüntshok (dKa' chen [bKa' chen] Blo bzang phun tshogs). 1993. *bZo rig pa'i bstan bcos las sangs rgyas byang sems dang yi dam zhi khro'i lha tshogs kyi cha tshad gsal ba'i ri mo don ldan kun gsal me long*. Beijing: Mi rigs dpe skrun khang.

Kaḥ thog Rig 'dzin Tshe dbang nor bu. 1973–82. *Selected Writings*. 4: 437–38. Darjeeling: Kargyud Sungrab Nyamso Khang.

Kaḥ thog Si tu Chos kyi rgya mtsho (Kathok Situ). 1972. *Gangs ljongs dbus gtsang gnes bskor lam yig nor bu zla shel gyi se mo do* [Record of a Pilgrimage to Central Tibet]. Palampur, Himachal Pradesh, India: Sungrab Nyamso Gyunphel Parkhang, Tibetan Craft Community. [Also 2001 ed., Khreng tu'u: Si khron mi rigs dpe skrun khang]

Kapstein, M. 2006. *The Tibetans*. Malden, MA: Blackwell.

Karma rin chen dar rgyas, mkhan po. sKu'i bris 'bur yongs kyi thig tshad bzo bo'i yid bzhin nor bu. In *Ri mo'i thig tshad dang tshon gyi lag len tshad ldan don du gnyer ba rnams la nye bar mkho ba mthong ba don ldan*, pp. 219–260. No place [Bhutan?], 1985

Karma Thinley. 1980. *The History of the Sixteen Karmapas of Tibet*. Boulder: Prajña.

Kent, Richard. 1994. "Depictions of the Guardians of the Law: Lohan Painting in China." In *Latter Days of the Law: Images of Chinese Buddhism*, edited by Marsha Weidner, 183–213. Lawrence, KS: Spencer Museum of Art, University of Kansas.

Khempo Sangyay Tenzin and Gomchen Oleshey. 1975. "The Nyingma Icons: A Collection of Line Drawings of 94 Deities and Divinities of Tibet." *Kailash* 3, no. 4: 319–416.

Khetsun Sangpo (mKhas btsun bzang po). 1973–1979. *Biographical Dictionary of Tibet and Tibetan Buddhism*. 12 vols. Dharamsala: Library of Tibetan Works and Archives.

Khoroche, Peter 2006. *Once the Buddha was a Monkey*. Chicago: University of Chicago Press.

Khreng Hra'o-khrun, et al. 2008. *Bod brgyud nang bstan brnyan ris kun btus*. Kan su'u mi rigs dpe skrun khang.

Klong rdol bla ma Ngag dbang blo bzang. 1973. *bZo dang gso ba skar rtsis rnams las byung ba'i ming gi grangs*. Collected Writings, part 16 (*ma*), 744–792. Śata-piṭaka Series 100. New Delhi: International Academy of Indian Culture. [1963 ed.: Dalama.]

Kong sprul Blo gros mtha' yas. 1970. *Theg pa'i sgo kun las btus pa gsung rab rin po che'i mdzod bslab pa gsum legs par ston pa'i bstan bcos shes bya kun khyab*

[Kongtrul's Encyclopedia of Indo Tibetan Culture]. Śata-piṭaka Series 80. New Delhi: International Academy of Indian Culture.

Kossak, Steven M., and Jane Casey Singer. 1998. *Sacred Visions, Early Paintings from Central Tibet*. New York: Metropolitan Museum of Art.

Kreijger, Hugo E. 2001. *Tibetan Painting: The Jucker Collection*. London: Serindia.

van der Kuijp, Leonard. 1993a. "Apropos of Some Recently Recovered Manuscripts Anent Sa skya Paṇḍita's Tshad ma rigs pa'i gter and Autocommentary." *Berliner Indologische Studien* 7: 149–162.

———. 1993b. "Fourteenth Century Tibetan Cultural History III: The Oeuvre of Bla ma dam pa Bsod nams rgyal mtshan (1312–1375)." *Berliner Indologische Studien* 7: 109–147.

———. 1993c. "Two Mongol Xylographs (*Hor Par Ma*) of the Tibetan Text of Sa Skya Paṇḍita's Work on Buddhist Logic and Epistemology." *Journal of the International Association of Buddhist Studies* 16/2: 279–298.

———. 2001. "On the Fifteenth-Century *Lho rong chos 'byung* by Rta tshag Tshe dbang rgyal and Its Importance for Tibetan Political and Religious History." In *Aspects of Tibetan History*, special issue, edited by Roberto Vitali. *Lungta* 14 (Spring 2001): 57–76.

———. 2004. *The Kālacakra and the Patronage of Tibetan Buddhism by the Mongol Imperial Family.* Central Eurasian Studies Lectures 4. Bloomington: Central Eurasian Studies, Indiana University.

Kunga Gyaltshen Palzangpo. *Theg chen chos kyi rgyal po'i rnam thar rgyas pa.* Kathmandu: 2008. See also Kun dga' rgyal mtshan. *Chos kyi rgyal po'i rnam thar byin rlabs rnam par rol pa.* Bod kyi lo rgyus rnam thar phyogs bsgrigs, set 2, vol. 55 (W1PD153537).

Lauf, Detlef-Ingo. 1976. *Tibetan Sacred Art: The Heritage of Tantra.* Berkeley: Shambhala.

Lee-Kalisch, Jeong-hee, et al. 2006. *Tibet: Klöster öffnen ihre Schatzkammern.* Villa Hügel: Kulturstiftung Ruhr Essen.

Leidy, Denise Patry, and Robert Thurman. 1997. *Mandala: the Architecture of Enlightenment.* New York: Asia Society.

lHag tshing 2004. *dPal kye rdo rje'i lam dus kyi zin bris dang thub bstan rwa smad dgon gyi lo rgyus mkhan chen dpal 'byor ye shes kyi rnam thar bcas.* [Hong Kong?]: Zhang kang gyi ling dpe skrun khang.

Linrothe, Robert. 2004. *Paradise and Plumage: Chinese Connections in Tibetan Arhat Painting.* New York: Rubin Museum of Art.

———. 2006. *Holy Madness: Portraits of Tantric Siddhas.* New York: Rubin Museum of Art.

———. 2012. "Looking East, Facing Up: Paintings in the Karma Gardri Styles in Ladakh and Zangskar." In *The Place of Provenance: Regional Styles in Tibetan Painting*, by David Jackson, 181–211. New York: Rubin Museum of Art.

Lo Bue, Erberto. 1992. "The Princes of Gyantse and their Role as Builders and Patrons of Arts." In *Proceedings of the 5th Seminar of the International Association of Tibetan Studies, Narita 1989*, vol. 2, edited by S. Ihara and Z. Yamaguchi, 559–573.

Lo Bue, Erberto, and Franco Ricca. 1990. *Gyantse Revisited.* Florence: Casa Editrice Le Lettere.

Luczanits, Christian 2001. "Methodological Comments Regarding Recent Research on Tibetan Art." *Wiener Zeitschrift für die Kunde Südasiens*, 45: 125–45

Macdonald, Alexander W., and Anne Vergati Stahl. 1979. *Newar Art: Nepalese Art during the Malla Period.* Warminster: Aris and Phillips.

Mang thos Klu sgrub, *bsTan rtsis.* See Mangthö Ludrup Gyatsho.

Mang thos Klu sgrub rgya mtsho. *bsTan rtsis gsal ba'i nyin byed.* Gangs can rig mdzod, no. 4. Bod ljongs mi dmangs dpe skrun khang, 1987.

Mangthö Ludrup Gyatsho. *Rang gi rnam par thar pa yul sna tshogs kyi bdud rtsi myong ba'i gtam du byas pa zol zog rdzun gyis ma bslad pa sgeg mo'i me long.* Lam 'bras slob bshad rnam thar, vol. *ga.*

Masaki, Akira, and Musashi Tachikawa. 1997. *Chibetto mikkyô no shinpi: nazo no tera 'Konkaru Doruje den' ga kataru: kairaku no sora-chi'e no umi* [*Gong dkar rdo rje gdan*]. Tokyo: Gakushū Kenkyūsha [Gakken Graphic Books Deluxe].

McCausland, Shane. 2015. *The Mongol Century: Visual Cultures of Yuan China, 1271–1368.* London: Reaktion.

Mele, Pietro F. 1975. *Tibet.* Calcutta: Oxford and IBH.

Myang chos 'byung.

See *Myang yul stod smad bar gsum gyi ngo mtshar gtam gyi legs bshad mkhas pa'i 'jug ngogs.* Bod ljongs mi mang dpe skrun khang, 1983.

Nakamura, Hajime, Zuihō Yamaguchi, Yūkei Matsunaga, Kōmei Nara, Tetsuo Yamaori, Akira Miyaji, Naoji Okuyama, and Eiichi Matsumoto. 1996. *Shakuson eden (Tada Tōkan shōrai butsudenzu fukusei).* Tokyo: Gakushū Kenkyūsha.

Nash, Alyce, et al. 1994. *A Tibetan Experience: Paintings from 1300 through 1800.* Naples, FL: Philharmonic Center for the Arts.

Ngag dbang phun tshogs 1994. "Gra nang gra thang dgon gyi byung ba brjod pa rnam dkar dge ba'i zhing sa." *Bod ljongs nang bstan,* no. 15, pp. 47-53, 63.

Ngag dbang legs grub 2011. *Thub dbang gnas brtan bcu drug bcas la phyag mchod gsol ba gdab pa'i cho ga.* Kathmandu: Sa skya rgyal yongs gsung rab slob gnyer khang.

Ngawang Gelek Demo: *See* Demo, Ngawang Gelek.

Ngawang Samten, Ācārya. 1986. *Mañjuśrī: An Exhibition of Rare Thankas.* Sarnath: Central Institute for Higher Tibetan Studies; Leh: Central Institute for Buddhist Studies.

Ngor chen kun dga' bzang po. 1968. *Thob yig rgya mtsho,* in *Sa skya pa'i bka' 'bum,* edited by Bsod nams rgya mtsho. Tokyo: Toyo Bunko.

Ong, Hean-Tatt 1993. *Chinese Animal Symbolisms.* Selangor Darul Ehsan, Malasia: Pelanduk Publications.

Osada, Yukiyasu, et al. 2010. *Mapping the Tibetan World.* Reno, NV: Kotan.

Padma dkar po, 'Brug chen. 1973. *Bris sku'i rnam bshad mthong ba don ldan.* Collected Works 1, 307–317 (*ka cha* 1–6). Darjeeling: Kargyud Sungrab Nyamsokhang,

———. *Li ma brtag pa'i rab byed.* Collected Works 1, 293–306 (*ka cha* 1–7).

———. *Sems dpa' chen po padma dkar po'i rnam thar thugs rje chen po'i zlos gar.* Collected Works 3 (*ga nya*).

Pal, Pratapaditya. 1969. *The Art of Tibet.* New York: Asia Society.

———. 1983. *Art of Tibet: A Catalogue of the Los Angeles County Museum of Art Collection.* Los Angeles: University of California.

———. 1984a. *Tibetan Paintings: A Study of Tibetan Thankas, Eleventh to Nineteenth Centuries.* Basel: Ravi Kumar; Sotheby Publications.

———. 1984b. *Light of Asia: Buddha Shakyamuni in Asian Art.* Los Angeles: Los Angeles County Museum of Art.

———. 1991. *Art of the Himalayas: Treasures from Nepal and Tibet.* New York: Hudson Hills; American Federation of Arts.

———. 2003. *Art from the Himalayas and China.* Asian Art at the Norton Simon Museum 2. New Haven: Yale University.

Pal, Pratapaditya, and Hsien-Chi Tseng. 1969. *Lamaist Art: The Aesthetics of Harmony.* Boston: Museum of Fine Arts.

Parajuli, Punya Prasad. 2014. "Vanaratna and His Activities in Fifteenth-Century Tibet." In *Himalayan Passages: Tibetan and Newar Studies in Honor of Hubert Decleer*, Studies in Indian and Tibetan Buddhism, edited by Andrew Quintman and Benjamin Bogin, 289–300. Somerville, MA: Wisdom.

Pawo Tsuklak Trengwa. See dPa bo gtsug lag phreng ba.

Penny-Dimri, Sandra. 1995. "The Lineage of His Holiness Sakya Trizin Ngawang Kunga." *Tibet Journal* 20.4: 64–92.

Reynolds, Valrae, Amy Heller, and Janet Gyatso. 1986. *The Newark Museum Tibetan Collection. Vol. III: Sculpture and Painting.* Newark: Newark Museum.

Rhie, Marylin M., and Robert A. F. Thurman. 1991. *Wisdom and Compassion: The Sacred Art of Tibet.* New York: Henry N. Abrams.

———. 1999. *Worlds of Transformation: Tibetan Art of Wisdom and Compassion*. New York: Tibet House.

Ricca, Franco, and Erberto Lo Bue. 1993. *The Great Stupa of Gyantse: A Complete Tibetan Pantheon of the Fifteenth Century*. London: Serindia.

Richardson, Hugh. 1998. *High Peaks, Pure Earth: Collected Writings on Tibetan History and Culture*. London: Serindia.

Rig 'dzin rdo rje, et al., eds. 1985. (Bod rang skyong ljongs rig dngos do dam u yon lhan khang, ed.). *Bod kyi thang ka* [Thangkas of Tibet]. Beijing: Rig dngos dpe skrun khang.

Roerich, George N., transl. 1949–53. *The Blue Annals*. 2 vols. Calcutta: Royal Asiatic Society of Bengal.

Rossabi, Morris. 1995. "Mongolia: From Chinghis Khan to Independence." In *Mongolia: The Legacy of Chinghis Khan*, edited by P. Berger and T. Tse Bartholomew, 25–49. San Francisco: Asian Art Museum.

Schaeffer, Kurtis, and Leonard van der Kuijp. 2009. *An Early Tibetan Survey of the Buddhist Literature: the bsTan pa rgyas pa rgyan gyi nyi 'od of Bcom ldan Ral gri*. Harvard Oriental Series, no. 64. Cambridge, MA: Harvard University.

Schoening, Jeffrey D. 1983. "The Sakya Throne Holder Lineage." Unpublished MA thesis, University of Washington, Seattle.

von Schroeder, Ulrich. 2001. *Buddhist Sculptures in Tibet*. 2 vols. Hong Kong: Visual Dharma.

———. 2006. *Empowered Masters: Tibetan Wall Paintings of Mahasiddhas at Gyantse*. Serindia.

———. 2008. *108 Buddhist Statues in Tibet: Evolution of Tibetan Sculptures*. Chicago: Serindia.

sDe srid Sangs rgyas rgya mtsho. 1971. *bsTan bcos bai ḍū rya dkar po las dris lan 'khrul snang g.ya' sel don gyi bzhin ras ston byed*. [*Vaiḍū rya g.ya' sel*]. 2 vols. New Delhi: T. Tsepal Taikhang. [Derge prints ed.: Tau Pon and Sakya Centre, Dehra Dun, 1976.]

———. 1973. *mChod sdong 'dzam gling rgyan gcig rten gtsug lag khang dang bcas pa'i dkar char thar gling rgya mtshor bgrod pa'i gru rdzings byin rlabs kyi bang mdzod*. 2 vols. New Delhi.

———. 1990. *mChod sdong 'dzam gling rgyan gcig rten gtsug lag khang dang bcas pa'i dkar char thar gling rgya mtshor bgrod pa'i gru rdzings byin rlabs kyi bang mdzod*. 1-volume edition. Bod ljongs mi dmangs dpe skrun khang.

Shakabpa, Tsepon W. D. 1967. *Tibet: A Political History*. New York: Potala.

Shakabpa, W. D. (Zhwa sgab pa dBang phyug bDe ldan). 1976. *Bod kyi srid don rgyal rabs* [An Advanced Political History of Tibet]. 2 vols. Delhi: Tsepal Taikhang.

Shankar, Ravi. 1968. *My Music, My Life*. New York: Simon and Schuster.

Shuweng Yang, et al., comp. 1987. *Chos rgyal 'phags pa'i mdzad thang*. Pe cing: Bod ljong mi dmangs dpe skrun khang.

Si tu Paṇ chen Chos kyi 'byung gnas. 1968. *Ta'i si tur 'bod pa karma bstan pa'i nyin byed rang tshul drangs por brjod pa d'i bral shel gyi me long. The Autobiography and Diaries of Si tu Paṇ chen*. Śata-piṭaka Series 77. New Delhi: International Academy of Indian Culture.

Si tu Paṇ chen Chos kyi 'byung gnas, and 'Be lo Tshe dbang kun khyab. 1972. *sGrub brgyud karma kaṃ tshang brgyud par rin po che'i rnam par thar pa rab 'byams nor bu zla ba chu shel gyi phreng ba* [Biographies of the Successive Masters of the Karma Kagyu School]. 2 vols. New Delhi: D. Gyaltsan and Kesang Legshay.

Singer, Jane Casey. 1993. *Tibetan Painted Mandalas*. London: Rossi and Rossi.

———. 1994. "Painting in Central Tibet, ca. 950–1400." *Artibus Asiae* 54, no. 1/2: 87–136.

Singer, Jane Casey, and Philip Denwood, eds. 1997. *Tibetan Art: Towards a Definition of Style*. London: Laurence King.

Smith, E. Gene. 1970. Introduction to *Kongtrül's Encyclopedia of Indo-Tibetan Culture*. Śata-piṭaka Series 80. New Delhi: International Academy of Indian Culture

———. 2001. *Among Tibetan Texts*. Boston: Wisdom.

Snellgrove, David L. 1987. *Indo-Tibetan Buddhism*, 2 vols. Boston: Shambhala.

———. 2013. *Indo-Tibetan Buddhism: Indian Buddhists and Their Tibetan Successors*. Bangkok: Orchid.

Sobisch, Jan. 2008. *Hevajra and Lam 'bras Literature of India and Tibet As Seen Through the Eyes of A-mes-zhabs*. Wiesbaden: Reichert.

Sperling, Elliot. 1982. "The 1413 Embassy to Tsongkhapa and the Arrival of Byams chen Chos rje Shākya ye shes as the Ming Court." *Journal of the Tibet Society* 2: 105–107.

———. 2004. "Karma Rol-pa'i rdo-rje and the Re-Establishment of Karma-pa Political Influence in the 14th Century." In *The Relationship Between Religion and State (chos srid zung 'brel) in Traditional Tibet*, edited by Christoph Cüppers, 229–244. Lumbini: Lumbini International Research Institute.

Stearns, Cyrus. 2001. *Luminous Lives: The Story of the Early Masters of the Lam 'bras Tradition in Tibet*. Boston: Wisdom.

———. 2004. "Sakya (Sa skya)" entry. In *Encyclopedia of Buddhism*, edited by Robert E. Buswell, 752. New York: MacMillan.

———, transl. and ed. 2006. *Taking the Result as the Path: Core Teachings of the Sakya Lamdre Tradition*. Library of Tibetan Classics 1. Boston: Wisdom.

Stoddard, Heather. 1996. "Early Tibetan Paintings: Sources and Styles (Eleventh–Fourteenth

Centuries)." *Archives of Asian Art* 49: 26–50.

———. 2003. "Fourteen Centuries of Tibetan Portraiture." In *Portraits of the Masters: Bronze Sculptures of the Tibetan Buddhist Lineages*, edited by Donald Dinwiddie, 16–61. Chicago: Serindia; London: Oliver Hoare.

———. 2008. *Early Sino-Tibetan Art*. Bangkok: Orchid.

Tada, Tokan, and Shuki Yoshimura. 1958. *Tibetan Pictorial Life of the Buddha*. Tokyo: Tibet Bunka Senyokai.

Tanaka, Kimiaki. 1996. "The Usefulness of Buddhist Iconography in Analyzing Style in Tibetan Art." *Tibet Journal* 21.2: 6–9.

———. 2003. *Art of Thangka from the Hahn Kwang-ho Collection, Vol. 4*. Seoul: Hahn Cultural Foundation.

Tanaka, Kimiaki, and Yoshitomo Tamashige, eds. 2004. *Tamashige Tibet Collection: Gems of Thangka Art*. Tokyo: Watanabe.

Tashi Tsering 2002. *Fading Dreams: Paintings and Sculptures of Pekar (Dus rlabs kyi rmi lam/ pad dkar gyi deng srol bris lder bzo rtsal)*. Dharamshala: Amnye Machen Institute.

Tashi Tsering, ed. 2010. *Bod gzhung zlos gar tshogs pa'i lo rgyus kun bzang zhing gi mchod sprin mig yid rna ba'i dga' ston: btsan byol bod gzhung zlos gar tshogs pa btsugs nas mi lo hril po 50 'khor ba'i dus dran*. Dharamsala: Tibetan Institute of Performing Arts and Tibet writes Dharamsala.

Tenpa Rabten (bsTan pa rab brtan) and Ngawang Jigme (Ngag dbang 'jigs med). 2003. *rGya bod bod rgya'i mdzes rtsal tshig mdzod* [Chinese-Tibetan Tibetan-Chinese Dictionary of Art].

Thekchen Chöje Kunga Tashi (Theg chen chos rje Kun dga' bkra shis). *Theg chen chos kyi rgyal po chen po'i gsan yig ngo bshus* [Record of Teachings Received]. 88 fols., *dbu med*-manuscript.

Tibet House Museum. 1999. *Compassion and Reincarnation in Tibetan Art*. New Delhi: Tibet House.

Tibet House Society. 1969. *Tibetan Art and Handicrafts: Exhibition in Commemoration of Gandhi Centenary, 1969, New Delhi, Rabindra Bhavan*. New Delhi: Tibet House.

Till, Barry, and Paula Swart. 1989. *Art from the Roof of the Word: Tibet*. Victoria, BC: Art Gallery of Greater Victoria.

Toganoo, Shozui M. 1986. *Museum of Fine Arts, Boston. Buddhist Paintings of Tibet and Nepal*. Kyoto: Rinsen.

Trungpa, Chogyam 1975. *Visual Dharma, the Buddhist Art of Tibet*. Berkeley and London: Shambhala.

Tsechang Penba Wangdu (brTse byang sPen pa dbang 'dus). 2005. "Gong dkar rdo rje gdan gyi ldebs bris kyi don snying dang da lta'i gnas babs skor la rags tsam gleng ba." *Bod ljongs zhib 'jug*, no. 94 (2005/2), 105–109.

———. 2010. "Gong dkar sgang stod mkhyen brtse chen mo dge bsnyen rnam par rgyal ba dang mkhyen lugs kyi khyad chos skor rags tsam gleng ba." *Journal of Tibet University* 4 (2010): 112–117.

———. 2012. "A Study of mKhyen brtse chen mo dge bsnyen rnam rgyal, his mural paintings at Gong dkar chos sde and the mKhyen lugs school of Tibetan painting." In *The Arts of Tibetan Painting: Recent Research on Manuscripts, Murals and Thangkas of Tibet, the Himalayas and Mongolia (11th–19th century)*. Proceedings of the Twelfth Seminar of the International Association for Tibetan Studies [IATS], Vancouver, 2010. *Asian Art*. Accessed December 3, 2015. http://www.asianart.com/articles/wangdu/index.html.

Tshewang Dorje (Tshe dbang rdo rje). 1998. "Bod kyi ri mo spyi'i rnam gzhag rags tsam brjod pa dang bye brag rang lugs mkhyen bris zhib tsam gleng ba." *Gangs ljongs rig gnas,* no. 38 (1998/2), 98–105.

Tshewang Rinchen (Tshe dbang rin chen), ed. 2005. *Grub chen brgyad cu'i rnam thar dang zhal thang* [The Lives and Paintings of the Eighty-four Adepts]. Lhasa: Bod ljongs mi dmangs dpe skrun khang.

Tucci, Giuseppe. 1932–41. *Indo-Tibetica*. 4 vols. Rome: Reale Academia d'Italia. [English translation of IV.1: *Gyantse and its Monasteries. Part 1, General Description of the Temples.* Śata-piṭaka Series 351. New Delhi: Aditya Prakashan, 1989.]

———. 1949. *Tibetan Painted Scrolls*. Rome: La Libreria Dello State. 3 vols. [2 vol. reprint: Kyoto: Rinsen, 1980.]

———. 1956. *To Lhasa and Beyond. Diary of the Expedition to Tibet in the Year MCMXLVIII* [1948]. Rome: Instituto Poligrafico dello Stato.

———. 1967. *Tibet, Land of Snows*. London: Elek.

Vira, Raghu, and Lokesh Chandra, eds. 1972. *A New Tibeto-Mongol Pantheon*, 21, part 20. New Delhi: International Academy of Indian Culture.

Vitali, Roberto. 1990. *Early Temples of Central Tibet*. London: Serindia.

Vostrikov, A. 1970. *Tibetan Historical Literature*. Calcutta: Indian Studies Past and Present.

Wang Jia Peng. 2011. *Pictorial Handbook of Tibetan Thangkas in the Palace Museum.* Chinese ed. Beijing: Forbidden City Press.

Weidner, Marsha, ed. 1994. *Latter Days of the Law: Images of Chinese Buddhism, 850–1850.* Lawrence, KS: Spencer Museum of Art, University of Kansas.

Welch, Patricia Bjaaland 2008. *Chinese Art: A Guide to Motifs and Visual Imagery.* Tokyo: Tuttle Publishing.

Williams, C. A. S. 1976. *Outlines of Chinese Symbolism and Art Motives*. 3rd ed. New York: Dover Publications.

Willis, Michael. 1999. *Tibet: Life, Myth, and Art.* New York: Barnes and Noble.

Willson, Martin, and Martin Brauen, eds. 2000. *Deities of Tibetan Buddhism: The Zürich Paintings of the Icons Worthwhile to See.* Boston: Wisdom.

Xiong Wenbin 熊文彬 2012. "A Preliminary Study on Murals Representing Stories from dPag bSam vKhri Shing (Kalpalata) in the Assembly Hall of the Main Temple, Gong dKar Chos sDe, Gong dKar County, TAR." "西藏山南贡嘎寺主殿集会大殿《如意藤》壁画初探," *China Tibetology* (Chinese version), no. 2, 176–187. (with Habib 哈比布 and Owen Wangdu 夏格旺堆)

Xizang yishu [*Bod-ljongs sgyu-rtsal*]. 1991. Shanghai: Renmin Meishu Chubanshe.

Yang Hru'u-wun, et al. 1987. *Chos rgyal 'phags pa'i mdzad thang*. Pe cing: Bod ljongs mi dmangs dpe skrun khang.

Yang Jiaming 2007. [*Appreciating the Art of Tibetan Painting: Analysis of Palpung Monastery's Treasury of Kagyu Sertreng*, in Chinese.] Taibei: Shan yue wenhua.

Ye shes shes rab. 1990. *Rig pa bzo yi 'byung ba thig ris dpe dang bcas pa li khri'i thigs pa.* Chendu: Si khron Mi rigs dPe skrun khang.

Zhong Ziyin 钟子寅 2013, "Lamdre Patriarch Lineage Murals in the Main Hall of Gongkar Chöde Monastery in Shannan of Tibet and Their Significance in Art History." "西藏山南嘎曲德寺大殿道果传承祖师壁画及其艺术史之意义," 法音 (*The Voice of Dharma*), no. 350 (2013), 35–39.

Zhu chen Tshul khrims rin chen. 1973. *gTsug lag khang chos 'byung bkra shis sgo mang rten dang brten pa bcas pa'i ji ltar bskrun pa las brtsam pa'i gleg bam bdud rtsi'i rlabs phreng*. Collected Writings 7, 127–195 (a 64a–98a). New Delhi: N. Lungtok and N. Gyaltsan.

Zhwa lu Ri sbug sprul sku Blo gsal bstan skyong. 1971. *dPal ldan zhwa lu pa'i bstan pa la bka' drin che ba'i skyes bu dam pa rnams kyi rnam thar lo rgyus ngo mtshar dad pa'i 'jug ngogs* [Zhwa lu gdan rabs]. Leh: S. W. Tashigangpa.

Zwalf, Wladimir, ed. 1985. *Buddhism: Art and Faith.* London: British Museum.

Page numbers with an *"f"* refer to a figure; an *"n"* indicates an endnote.

Surchen Chöying Rangdröl, 271
Sureśāna, 201–2, *201f*
Sureśvara, 199–200, *199f*

T

Tachikawa, Musashi, 94, 95
tantric deity, *75f*
tantric guru lineages, Khyentse's mastery of, 105
tantric lama, 244, *245f*
tantric ritual practice, 23, 105–6
Tārā, 291, *292f, 297f*
Tāranātha, 329–30
Tashi Gön, 8
Tashi Gyalpo, 8, 335n30
Tejin, 198–99, *198f*
Tenpa Gyatsho, Uchen: in Lhokha, 285; skylight
    murals painted by, 88; as Tshewang Dorje's
    teacher, 327
Tenpa Rabten, Uchen: on Amdo painting traditions,
    22; *Chinese-Tibetan Tibetan-Chinese
    Dictionary of Art*, 67; on Tshewang Dorje,
    327
thangkas: Chinese, 30, *30f*; Ḍamarupa, *128f*;
    Lamdre lineage thangkas. *See* Lamdre
    lineage thangkas; Phakpa in, 161–62; of
    Shambhala kings. *See* Shambhala king
    thangkas; surviving examples of, 77–80; of
    Virūpa, 140–41, *140f*
thangkas sets, 16th century: Buddha's life
    depictions, 264–69; darkly colored, 251; with
    double arhats, 251–57; with Drukpa Kagyu
    lineage masters, 259–64; with quintuple
    arhats, 257–59
thangkas sets, 17th century: of Buddha [S']
    ākyamuni principal events, 273–75, *274–75f*;
    Fifth Dalai Lama involvement. *See* Dalai
    Lama, Fifth; of Jātaka Stories, 275–79;
    Khyentse style continuation/emulations of,
    271–72
Thekchen Chöje: depictions of, 130–32; early life,
    29; iconography of, 134, 136; images of, 31,
    31f, 32f, 33, *134f, 137f*; information sources
    on, 33; lineage of, 26–27, 28, 29–30, 124,
    133–34, 136; paintings of, *131–32f*; as Sakya
    hierarch, 11, 30; sculptural styles of, 123,
    131f; tradition of, 29; visit to Ming dynasty
    court, 30, 31, 33
Thirteen Tibetan Tankas (Bryner), 276–77
Thousand Buddhas of the Fortunate Eon, 87
Three Great Adepts, 55–58, *56f, 58f*
Three Indian and Two Tibetan Teachers, *117f*
Three Red-Clad Masters, 111, *111f, 113f*, 129–30,
    130f, 148–49f
Three White-Robed Ones, 109–10, *109–10f*
throne backs: Chinese influence in, 130; elegance
    of, 109, 242; Khyentse's use of, 20, 73; parrot
    depictions on, 336n46
Thurman, Robert: *Wisdom and Compassion*, 49;
    Worlds of Transformation, 53–55
Tibet: Buddhist kings of, *297f*, 298; Dharma King
    portrait, 296, *297f*; as gifted to Thekchen
    Chöje, 30; government-in-exile, 296; map of,
    xif; Phakpa as ruler of, 156, 157; public art
    of, 327–28
Tibet, Land of Snows (Tucci), 43
Tibet: A Political History (Shakabpa), 43
The Tibet Guide (Batchelor), 46–47
Tibet Handbook (Gyurme), 55
Tibet House, New Delhi, 44–45
Tibetan Institute of Performing Arts, 296
Tibetan Painted Scrolls (Tucci), 41–42, 329, 330
Tibetan Paintings (Pal), 193
Tibetan Religious Art (Dagyab), 44, 249
Tilopa, *64f, 260f*

To Lhasa and Beyond (Tucci), 42–43
Togön Temür, 19
"Traces of Taranatha and his Previous Lives:
    Paintings from the Jonangpa School of
    Tibetan Buddhism" (Jackson), 58–59
Trakpa Lotrö, 272
transparent head nimbuses, 139
Trulku Dorje, 271
Tsang province: apprenticeship in, ix, 3; Dzong
    tradition of, 27–28; Gyantse as art center
    in, 4, 7, 41; Menthangpa's success in, 14;
    painting style as Khyentse's departure point,
    8, *9f*, 10; painting style of, 44; Tucci on, 41
Tsangpa Gyare, *15f*
Tsangpo Valley, map of, *48f*
Tsechang Penba Wangdu, 22
Tshewang Dorje, 327–28
Tucci, Giuseppe: about, 105; on arhat name order,
    249; on Khyentse murals, 20; *To Lhasa and
    Beyond*, 42–43; *Tibet, Land of Snows*, 43;
    Tibetan Painted Scrolls, 41–42, 329, 330
tutelary deities, 72
Twelve Great Deeds of the Buddha, 64, 83, 85, 329
Twenty-One Tārās, 291, *292f*

U

Ü province: Dzongpa Tradition of, 27–28; Gongkar
    Monastery in, ix; Khyenri tradition in, 22,
    271, 273; Khyentse's birth in, 3; Khyentse's
    career in, 14; Khyentse's murals in, 20; Lama
    Dampa in, 111, 129; Menri style of, 285;
    Menthangpa's birth in, 4; traditions in, 25;
    Tucci's research in, 41–42
unicorns. *See* qilin beasts
Uṣṇīṣavijayā, 36, *37f*

V

Vaiśravaṇa, King: in the Hevajra Chapel, *72f*, 95–
    96, *95f*; in 16th c thangkas, 257, *258f*; in the
    Upper Protector's Chapel, *71f*, 102, *102f*
Vajrabhairava, *71f*, 94
Vajradhara: images of, *34f, 43f, 62f*; lineage of,
    114; in 16th c thangkas, *260f, 263f*; statue of,
    122, 123–24; as teacher, 34–35; with Virūpa
    and Nairātmyā, 315, *315f*
Vajrakīla, *77f*
Vajrāpaṇi, 287, *288f*
Vajrīputra, Arhat: in arhat paintings, 235, *236f*; in
    16th c thangkas, 251, *253f*, 257, 259, *259f*
van der Kuijp, Leonard, 129
Vanaratna, 11, *12f*, 13
Vanavāsin, Arhat, 256, *256f*, 257, 259, *259f*
Vidura, tale of, *69f*, 92–93, *93f*
Vijaya, 203–4, *203f*
Vikrama, 210, *212f*
vīṇās (musical instruments): about, 180–81, *180f*;
    in literature, 179, *179f, 181–82f*; in murals,
    179, *180f*; in thangka paintings, 178–82,
    178f, 183f
Vira, Raghu, 194
Virāya, *128f*
Virūpa: and charnel grounds, *70f*; depictions of,
    139–40; paintings of, *139–42f*, 140–42, 291,
    292f; sculpture of, *140f, 142f*; in thangka
    paintings, 174, *174f*; with Vajradhara, 315,
    315f
Virūpākṣa, King, 242, *244f*, 257, *258f*
Viṣṇugupta, 206, *206f*
Viśvarūpa, 208, *209f*
von Schroeder, Ulrich, 122
vultures, in charnel ground scenes: discussions of,
    57, 93, 97, 100, 231; images of, *57f, 94f, 98f,
    101f, 230f*

W

white goddess, 37, *39f*
White-Clad Founding Masters, 113–15
Wisdom and Compassion (Rhie & Thurman), 49
Worlds of Transformation (Rhie & Thurman),
    53–55, *54f*
wrathful deities: appearance of, 70, 72, 97, *97f*,
    339n185; detail of, *71f*; Fifth Dalai Lama
    commissions for, 272; Khyentse school skill
    in depicting, 69

X

Xanadu, 156–57, 162, *163f*

Y

Yakṣa Vaiśravaṇa and the Eight Horsemen, *71f*
yakṣas, 95–96, 100, 102–3, *102–3f*
Yamāntaka: in the Hevajra Chapel, 96–97, *96f*;
    in the inner sanctum, 294–95, *294f*; with
    lineage, 305–6, *306f*
Yamāri, 96–97, *96–97f, 310f*
Yangpachen murals, 3, 17–20, 21
Yargyap noble family, 24
Yeshe Tendzin: artists predating, 285–90; life as
    an artist, 290–96; life in exile, 296–301,
    296f; with his wife, *296f*; work at Gongkar
    Monastery, *25f*
Yongle Emperor: commissions from, 11; invitation
    from, 8, 335n25; visits to, 30, 31
Yuan Court, Phakpa at, 156–57

Z

Zhong Ziyin, 112
Zhwa lu Lo tsā ba, 122